ANDREW ROBERTS

Napoleon the Great

PENGUIN BOOKS

PENGUIN BOOKS

UK | USA | Canada | Ireland | Australia
India | New Zealand | South Africa

Penguin Books is part of the Penguin Random House group of companies
whose addresses can be found at global.penguinrandomhouse.com.

First published by Allen Lane 2014
Published in Penguin Books 2015

001

Copyright © Andrew Roberts, 2014

The moral right of the author has been asserted

Set in 8.98/12.15 pt Sabon LT Std
Typeset by Jouve (UK), Milton Keynes
Printed in Great Britain by Clays Ltd, St Ives plc

A CIP catalogue record for this book is available from the British Library

ISBN: 978-0-141-03201-6

To my siblings, Ashley Gurdon and Matthew and Eliot Roberts

Contents

PART THREE
Denouement

List of Maps

List of Illustrations

Illustrations in the Text

Colour Plates

Acknowledgements

Having now spent longer researching and writing this book than Napoleon himself spent on St Helena and Elba put together, I've collected a disconcertingly large array of people whom I would like to thank for their unfailing generosity, good nature, time and help. They include President Nicolas Sarkozy for his insights into the state of thinking about Napoleon in France today; David Cameron and Rodney Melville for allowing me to research the Napoleon correspondence at Chequers; Xavier Darcos of the Academie Française and Institut de France for introductions in Paris; Mervyn King for his thoughts on French and British debt-financing of the Napoleonic Wars; Carole Aupoix for showing me a louse such as the ones that spread the typhus that devastated Napoleon's armies in Russia; the late Archduke Otto von Hapsburg for his views on Marie Louise's '*déclassé*' marriage to Napoleon; Lady Mary Berry for showing me the chairs used at the Congress of Vienna; Jayne Wrightsman for showing me her collection of Napoleonic book bindings; Robert Pirie for his encouragement; the late Lady Alexandra Dacre for her memories of the Empress Eugénie; Dušan Frýbort at Austerlitz, for letting me fire his Napoleonic musket; Ms Evan Lattimer for allowing me to see what is purported to be Napoleon's 'tendon'; Charles-Henry and Jean-Pascal Tranié; Jerry and Jane Del Missier for their wonderful hospitality on Lake Geneva; Nicholas Steed for his reports on Napoleon in Malta; the Earl and Countess of Carnarvon for showing me Napoleon's chair from Fontainebleau and desk from the Tuileries; Robin Birley for his great generosity; the Countess of Rosebery for showing me the Emperor's travelling library; Dr Henry Kissinger for his thoughts on the Congress of Vienna; Prof. Charles Esdaile for inviting me to his excellent *Napoleon at the Zenith* conference at Liverpool University in 2007; Deborah Edlmann; Rurik Ingram; my cousins Philip and Sandra Engelen for putting me up in Cape Town on my St Helena journey (which took me a fortnight, largely by Royal Mail ship); Zac Gertler for his hospitality and generosity in Tel Aviv; Caroline Dalmeny for lending me a lock of Napoleon's hair, which has sat on my desk throughout, inspiring me, and Baudouin Prot of BNP

Paribas for allowing me to visit the room in which Napoleon and Jose-phine were married. I would also like to apologize profoundly to Jérôme Tréca and the staff of Fontainebleau Palace for setting off the burglar alarms in Napoleon's throne room no fewer than three times.

A military historian who doesn't visit battlefields is akin to a detective who doesn't bother to visit the scene of the crime. In the course of research-ing this book I have visited fifty-three of Napoleon's sixty battlefields, most of them in the company of the distinguished military historian John Lee. It has been one of the greatest pleasures of writing this book to have walked with John over the ground of Montenotte, Mondovi, Lodi, Mantua, Arcole, Castiglione, Rivoli, Rovereto, Dego, Marengo, Ulm, Austerlitz, Jena, Eylau, Friedland, Abensberg, Landshut, Eggmühl, Ratisbon, Aspern-Essling, Wagram, Maloyaroslavets, Lützen, Bautzen, Dresden, Leipzig, Reichenbach, Brienne, La Rothière, Champaubert, Montmirail, Château-Thierry, Vauchamps, Montereau, Craonne, Lâon, Reims, Arcis-sur-Arbe and St-Dizier. John's advice and insights in our blizzards of emails have been *sans pareil*, his battle-notes from Napoleon's campaigns have proved completely invaluable, and his friendship is a joy. I cannot thank him enough, as well as his wife Celia, who has put up with him coming battlefielding with me so very often.

In the sixty-nine archives, libraries, museums and research institutes that I've visited in fifteen countries during the course of my researches, I've met with nothing but helpfulness and friendliness, and I would in particular like to thank:

France: Sacha Topalovich and Florence Tarneaud at the Archives Nationales, Paris; Y. Bamratta and Laurence Le Bras at the Bibliothèque Nationale de France's Tolbiac and Richelieu sites respectively; Anne Georgeon-Liskenne at the Centre des Archives Diplomatiques, La Courneuve; Claude Ponnou and Thisio Bernard at the Service Histo-rique de la Défense, Vincennes; Sylvie Biet and Danièle Chartier at the Bibliothèque Thiers; Gérard Leyris at the Musée Carnavalet; the British ambassador to Paris, Sir Peter Westmacott, and his butler, Ben Newick, for showing me around Pauline Borghese's house in Paris, now the Brit-ish Embassy; Susanne Wasum-Rainer, the German ambassador to Paris, for showing me around her residence, l'Hôtel de Beauharnais, Joseph-ine's immaculate present to her son Eugène; Léonore Losserand at St-Joseph-des-Carmes; David Demangeot, curator at the former palace of St-Cloud; Aurore Lacoste de Laval at the École Militaire; Christo-pher Palmer, First Secretary at the US Embassy in Paris, and Mrs Robin Smith, the Directrice of the Marshall Center at the Hôtel Talleyrand;

Angelique Duc at the Musée Napoléon de Brienne-le-Château; Fanny de Jubecourt at Les Invalides and the Musée de l'Armée; Dr Thierry Lentz and Prof. Peter Hicks for being so welcoming at the superb Fondation Napoléon; Alain Pougetoux at the Château de Malmaison; Xavier Cayon at the Conseil d'État in the Palais-Royal (formerly the Tribunate); Mme Marianne Lambert at Marshal Lannes' Château de Maisons-Laffitte; M and Mme Benoit D'Abonville; Quentin Aymonier at the Fort de Joux in the Jura; my son Henry and daughter Cassia for accompanying me to Corsica; the staffs of the Palais et Musée de la Légion d'Honneur, Paris; the Musée de la Préfecture de Police, Paris; the Maison d'Éducation de la Légion d'Honneur at St-Denis; the Panthéon, and the Musée Fesch and the Musée National de la Maison Bonaparte in Ajaccio, Corsica.

Russia: Alexander Suhanov and Elvira Chulanova of the State Museum of Borodino for showing me around the battlefield of Borodino; Oleg Aleksandrov of Three Whales Tours for taking me to the battlefield of Maloyaroslavets; Maciej Morawski of City Events for taking me to the battlefields of Eylau and Friedland in the Russian enclave of Kaliningrad; Konstantin Nazarov at the Maloyaroslavets Military History Museum; Alexandr Panchenko of the Bagrationovsk Historical Museum on the Eylau battlefield; Valery Shabanov and Vladimir Ukievich Katz of the Russian State Military Historical Archive in Moscow, and Marina Zboevskaya of the Borodino Panorama Museum in Moscow.

Belarus: Prof. Igor Groutso for showing me the battlefield of the Berezina river, and Rakhovich Natalya Stepanovna of the Borisov Combined Museum.

Israel: Dr Eado Hecht for showing me the battlefields of Kakun, Jaffa and Mount Thabor, and Dr Alon Keblanoff for showing me the siege sites of Acre; Prof. Azar Gat of Tel Aviv University, and Liat Margolit at the Tel Dor Archaeological Museum.

St Helena: Michel Dancoisne-Martineau, the supremely diligent French Honorary Consul and Conservator at Longwood for my hugely enjoyable days there; Aron Legg for showing me Mount Pleasant, Diana's Peak, Prosperous Bay, The Briars, Sandy Bay and Jamestown, and Andrew Wells, the former Chief Secretary of St Helena.

Belgium: Ian Fletcher and Colonel John Hughes-Wilson, who showed me Waterloo; Benoît Histace, President of the Museum of the Battle of Ligny, who took me around the battlefield of Ligny, and Count François and Countess Susanne Cornet d'Elzius, the owners of La Haie Sainte.

Great Britain: Lucy McCann at the Rhodes House Library, Oxford;

Leigh McKiernan at the Special Collections Reading Room of the Bodleian Library, Oxford; Prof. Nick Mayhew of the Heberden Coin Room at the Ashmolean Museum, Oxford; Allen Packwood at the Churchill Archives, Cambridge; Josephine Oxley at Apsley House; Paul Roberts at the British Museum; Katy Canales and Pim Dodd at the National Army Museum; Hilary Burton and John Rochester at the Royal Hospital, Chelsea; Richard Daniels at the London College of Communication; Richard Tennant of the British Commission for Military History, and the staffs of the Royal Navy Museum at Portsmouth, the British Library and the London Library.

Italy: Lario Zerbini at the Rivoli Museum; my daughter Cassia for accompanying me to Elba; Nello Anselmi at the Santuario della Madonna del Monte at Marciana, Elba; Elisabetta Lalatta of the Fondazione Serbelloni at the Palazzo Serbelloni in Milan; Riccardo Bianceli at the Palazzo Ducale in Mantua, and the staffs of the Museo Napoleonico in Rome, the Marengo Museum at Spinetta Marengo, the Villa Reale at Monza, and the Villa di San Martino, Elba.

The Czech Republic: Simona Lipovska of the Cairn of Peace Memorial Museum and Jana Slukova of Slavkov Castle at Austerlitz.

Austria: Helmut Tiller of the Aspern and Essling Museums; Rupert Derbic of the Wagram Museum, and the staffs at Schönbrunn Palace and the Heeresgeschichtliches Museum in Vienna.

Portugal: Mark Crathorne and Luiz Saldanha Lopes for showing me around Forts 40, 41, 42, 95 of the Lines of Torres Vedras; and the staff of the Military Museum of Lisbon.

Germany: The staffs of the Bavarian Army Museum at Ingolstadt, the 1806 Museum at JenaCospeda, and the Torhaus Museum in Markkleeberg on the Leipzig battlefield.

The United States: Jay Barksdale of the Allen Room and Elizabeth Denlinger of the Pforzheimer Room at the New York Public Library; Declan Kiely at the Pierpont Morgan Library; Kathryn James at the Beinecke Library and Steve Ross at the Sterling Memorial Library at Yale; Elaine Engst and Laurent Ferri at the Carl A. Kroch Library's Manuscript Collections at Cornell University; the Merrill family, who so generously funded my visiting professorship at Cornell; Prof. Barry and Dr Marcia Strauss at Cornell for their delightful hospitality and my students there who came up with their own reasons for why Napoleon invaded Russia; Prof. Rafe Blaufarb, Director of the Institute on Napoleon and the French Revolution, for making my stay at Florida State University so enjoyable; Eric Robinson of the New-York Historical

Society Library; Katie McCormick at the Robert Manning Strozier Library at Florida State University Special Collections; Elisabeth Fairman at the Yale Center for British Art; Dr Robert Pickering, Curator of the Gilcrease Museum in Tulsa, Oklahoma, and Dr William J. Lademan, Director of the Wargaming Division at the Marine Corps Warfighting Laboratory.

Sweden: Aviva Cohen-Silber for showing me the Bernadotte Rooms at the Royal Palace in Stockholm.

Switzerland: Paola Gianoli Tuena at the Château Le Coppet on Lake Geneva.

Canada: Bruce McNiven for showing me around the Napoleon galleries at the Montreal Museum of Fine Arts.

I would also like to thank Josh Sutton, Charlie Mitchell, Katie Russell and especially the indefatigable Gilles Vauclair for their historical research, as well as Julie di Filippo for German translations, Beata Widulinska for Polish, Timothy Chapman for Spanish, Eado Hecht for Hebrew, Dr Galina Babkova for Russian, and Annaliese Ellidge, Helena Fosh, Maxine Harfield-Neyrand, Gilles Vauclair and Carole Aupoix for French. Maxine was particularly encouraging and helpful in negotiating through the sometimes arcane byways of five Parisian research institutions.

This book was written while I was filming a BBC TV documentary series about Napoleon, and I would like to thank David Notman-Watt, Simon Shaps, David Barrie, Anna Dangoor, Patrick Duval and Tony Burke for making the whole process so enjoyable and thought-provoking.

Since Napoleon's death has become – needlessly in my view – so controversial, I took expert medical advice about the Emperor's death from Dr Tim Barrie, Prof. Ira Jacobsen of Cornell, Dr Albert Knapp, Dr Robert Krasner, Dr Archana Vats, Dr James Le Fanu, Dr Pamela Yablon, Dr Guy O'Keefe and Dr Michael Crumplin, to whom I extend my thanks. I should also like to thank Dr Frank Reznek for his diagnosis on Napoleon's dental problems on St Helena.

For reading my manuscript and their invaluable suggestions for its improvement, I would like to thank Helena Fosh, Sudhir Hazareesingh, John Lee, Stephen Parker, Jürgen Sacht and Gilles Vauclair.

My agent Georgina Capel of Capel & Land and publishers Stuart Proffitt and Joy de Menil of Penguin have been their usual perfect models of efficiency, professionalism and charm, as were my inspired copy-editors Peter James and Charlotte Ridings. The painstaking work that Stuart and Joy put into this book improved it enormously, and

I really cannot thank them enough for it. I am very grateful also to Richard Duguid, Imogen Scott and Lisa Simmonds of Penguin. Cecilia Mackay researched the illustrations with resourcefulness and flair.

My fabulous wife Susan Gilchrist has examined guillotine blades with me, counted the skulls of massacred monks in the crypt of the church where Josephine was imprisoned, driven with me along the Route Napoléon, and went to the Al-Azhar Mosque in Cairo with me, not just for its inherent architectural and cultural interest, but because it was where the 1798 revolt began and ended. I couldn't have written this book without her constant love and support; she's my Josephine, Marie Louise and Marie Walewska all rolled into one.

This book is dedicated to my siblings Ashley Gurdon and Matthew and Eliot Roberts, for putting up with their know-all big brother for so long and so graciously.

Andrew Roberts
2, rue Augereau, Paris
www.andrew-roberts.net

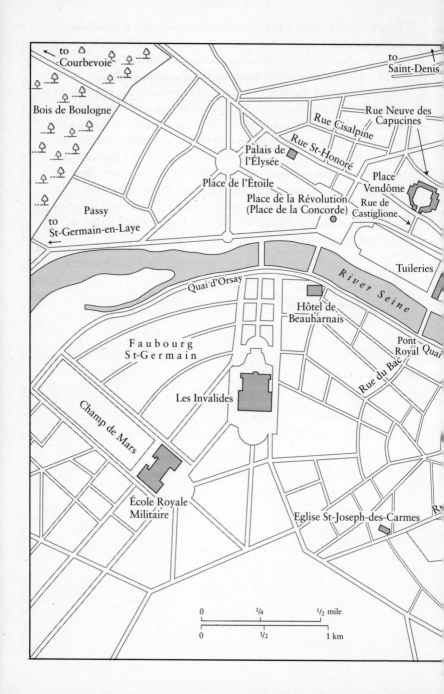

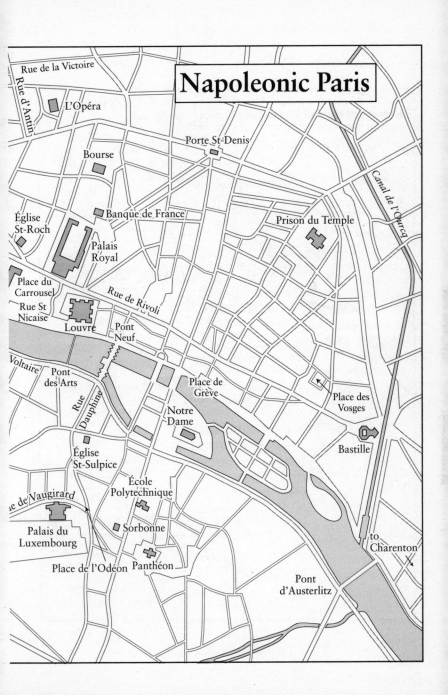

Napoleonic Paris

Rue de la Victoire

Rue d'Antin

L'Opéra

Porte St-Denis

Bourse

Banque de France

Prison du Temple

Canal de l'Ourcq

Église St-Roch

Palais Royal

Place du Carrousel

Rue St Nicaise

Rue de Rivoli

Louvre

Pont Neuf

Voltaire

Pont des Arts

Rue Dauphine

Place de Grève

Place des Vosges

Notre Dame

Bastille

Église St-Sulpice

École Polytechnique

Rue de Vaugirard

Palais du Luxembourg

Sorbonne

Place de l'Odéon

Panthéon

to Charenton

Pont d'Austerlitz

Revolutionary and Napoleonic France

Texel

NETHERLANDS

North Sea

BRITAIN

London

Utrecht
The Hague

Meuse

Walcheren Is.

Flushing
Ostend
Dover
Dunkirk
Calais
Ambleteuse
Boulogne
Pont-de-Briques
Montreuil
Biville

Bruges
Bergen-op-Zoom
Antwerp
Hazebrouck
Brussels
St-Omer
Lille
Courcelles
Étaples
Arras
Douai
Philippeville
Givet

Plymouth
Torbay

English Channel

Cherbourg
Le Havre
Caen
Honfleur
Château Navarre

Rouen
Amiens
Saint-Quentin
Rocroi

Compiègne
Palace of St-Cloud
Soissons
Reims
Thionville
Valmy
Verdun
Metz
Landau
Philippsburg

Brest

Seine

Paris
Versailles
Rambouillet
Malmaison
Fontainebleau

Vincennes
Châtillon
Montmirail

Châlons-sur-Marne
Arcis
Brienne-le-Château

LORRAINE
Strasbourg
Nancy
Lunéville
Kehl
Épinal
Freibourg

ALSACE

Rennes

BRITTANY

Lorient

Quiberon Bay

St-Nazaire
Nantes

Angers
Saumur
Valençay

Orleans
Blois
Tours

Loire

Nemours
Yonne
Briare

Troyes

Chanceaux
Dijon
Auxonne
Besançon
Mulhouse
Basle
Berne

VENDÉE

Les Sables
Île d'Aix
Île d'Oléron
Rochefort

Niort

Nevers

Autun

Chalon-sur-Saône

SWITZ.

Bay of Biscay

Gironde

Pons

Clermont-Ferrand

Roanne

Mâcon

Geneva

Lyons
Chambéry

SEINE

Bordeaux

Dordogne

Garonne

MIDI

Montauban

Tarn

Grenoble
Valence
Donzère

Rhône

Laffrey
Braincon
Gap

Piedmont

Bayonne

Pau

Toulouse

LANGUEDOC

Carcassonne
Limoux

Montpellier
Agde

Narbonne

Perpignan

Nîmes
Beaucaire

PROVENCE
Orange
Avignon

Arles
Aix
La Valette
Ollioules
Marseilles
Toulon

St-Cannat
Antibes
Fréjus
Cannes
Saint-Raphaël
Hyères

Alpes-Maritimes
Nice

SPAIN

Mediterranean Sea

0   50   100   150 miles
0   100   200 km

The immediate families of
Napoleon and Josephine

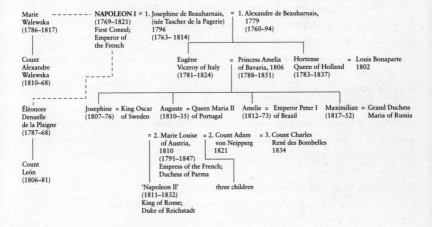

Marie Walewska (1786–1817) – – – – – – NAPOLEON I (1769–1821) First Consul; Emperor of the French = 1. Josephine de Beauharnais, (née Tascher de la Pagerie) 1796 (1763– 1814) = 1. Alexandre de Beauharnais, 1779 (1760–94)

Count Alexandre Walewska (1810–68)

Eugène Viceroy of Italy (1781–1824) = Princess Amelia of Bavaria, 1806 (1788–1851) Hortense Queen of Holland (1783–1837) = Louis Bonaparte 1802

Éléonore Denuelle de la Plaigne (1787–68)

Josephine (1807–76) = King Oscar of Sweden Auguste (1810–35) = Queen Maria II of Portugal Amelie (1812–73) = Emperor Peter I of Brazil Maximilian (1817–52) = Grand Duchess Maria of Russia

Count León (1806–81)

= 2. Marie Louise of Austria, 1810 (1791–1847) Empress of the French; Duchess of Parma = 2. Count Adam von Neipperg 1821 = 3. Count Charles René des Bombelles 1834

'Napoleon II' (1811–1832) King of Rome; Duke of Reichstadt

three children

The Bonaparte family

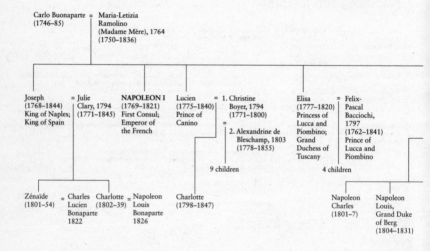

Carlo Buonaparte = Maria-Letizia
(1746–85)   Ramolino
                    (Madame Mère), 1764
                    (1750–1836)

Joseph   = Julie   **NAPOLEON I**   Lucien   = 1. Christine   Elisa   = Felix-
(1768–1844)   Clary, 1794   (1769–1821)   (1775–1840)   Boyer, 1794   (1777–1820)   Pascal
King of Naples; (1771–1845)   First Consul;   Prince of   (1771–1800)   Princess of   Bacciochi,
King of Spain   Emperor of   Canino   Lucca and   1797
                              the French   =   Piombino;   (1762–1841)
                                                              2. Alexandrine de Grand   Prince of
                                                                 Bleschamp, 1803 Duchess of   Lucca and
                                                                 (1778–1855)   Tuscany   Piombino

                                                 9 children   4 children

Zénaïde   = Charles   Charlotte = Napoleon   Charlotte   Napoleon   Napoleon
(1801–54)   Lucien   (1802–39)   Louis   (1798–1847)   Charles   Louis,
               Bonaparte   Bonaparte   (1801–7)   Grand Duke
               1822   1826   of Berg
                                                                                                   (1804–1831)

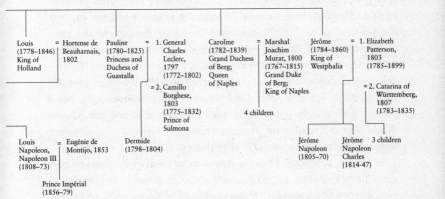

Louis
(1778–1846)
King of
Holland

= Hortense de
Beauharnais,
1802

Pauline
(1780–1825)
Princess and
Duchess of
Guastalla

= 1. General
Charles
Leclerc,
1797
(1772–1802)

= 2. Camillo
Borghese,
1803
(1775–1832)
Prince of
Sulmona

Caroline
(1782–1839)
Grand Duchess
of Berg;
Queen
of Naples

= Marshal
Joachim
Murat, 1800
(1767–1815)
Grand Duke
of Berg;
King of Naples

Jérôme
(1784–1860)
King of
Westphalia

= 1. Elizabeth
Patterson,
1803
(1785–1899)

= 2. Catarina of
Württemberg,
1807
(1783–1835)

4 children

Louis
Napoleon,
Napoleon III
(1808–73)

= Eugénie de
Montijo, 1853

Dermide
(1798–1804)

Jérôme
Napoleon
(1805–70)

Jérôme
Napoleon
Charles
(1814-47)

3 children

Prince Impérial
(1856–79)

Introduction

In October 1944, just as the Netherlands was being liberated from the Nazis, the great Dutch historian Pieter Geyl completed one of the most original books of the many tens of thousands about Napoleon which have appeared over the past 215 years. Its originality lay not in Geyl's own view of Napoleon (though the book certainly made plain what he thought of him) but in its recounting of the views of others, and in the way it traced the different phases of Napoleon's reputation between 1815 and his own time. Because Napoleon was such a gigantic figure in the political as well as the historical landscape throughout the nineteenth century and the early twentieth, both romanticized and vilified to a high degree, the views which Geyl distilled were (unsurprisingly) often diametrically opposed to each other, generally reflecting their authors' own political stances. After Geyl wrote – also unsurprisingly, but I believe misleadingly – the experience of Europe during the Second World War coloured many interpretations of events on the continent during Napoleon's era, and still sometimes casts a shadow over them.

In writing this book, I have tried not to be overly influenced by previous interpretations, but to go back so far as possible to Napoleon's own words and the words of those who knew him personally. Of course, visceral disagreement about him extends there too: almost all the contemporary accounts are heavily slanted according to the situation their authors had occupied during Napoleon's lifetime or afterwards. For those writing immediately after his abdication, the lure of employment or a pension, or merely the right to publish under the Bourbons, wrecked objectivity in dozens of cases. For example, the letters of Claire de Rémusat to her husband, one of Napoleon's courtiers, between 1804 and 1813 were affectionate about the Emperor, but by 1818 her memoirs painted him as a monster 'incapable of generosity' who, moreover, had 'a satanic smile'. What happened in between was that her husband wanted a job as the prefect of a department from the Bourbons. She had burned her contemporaneous notes in 1815, and tried to resuscitate what Chateaubriand called her 'memories of memories'.

Or again: much of our received understanding of Napoleon has been coloured by the highly dubious memoirs written by his former class-mate Louis-Antoine de Bourrienne. Appointed Napoleon's private secretary during the negotiations with Austria in Leoben in 1797, Bour-rienne was then no longer permitted to use the familiar 'tu' with Napoleon, which he said was 'an easy sacrifice' for the honour of becoming head of his *cabinet* (private office), but Napoleon had to sack him twice for corruption and they parted on bad terms. His memoirs have been treated as being generally objective by historians, even though they were actually written by (among others) the fantasist Charles Max-ime de Villemarest. In 1830 a two-volume book totalling eight hundred pages was published by people who knew Napoleon well, including his brother Joseph, which forensically demolished scores of Bourrienne's claims. I have used Bourrienne sceptically, and only to illustrate my accounts of occasions when he was known to have been personally present.

Such contemporary 'sources' which need to be treated with caution are everywhere in the Napoleonic canon. The Comte de Montholon, who was with Napoleon on St Helena, wrote his supposed 'narrative' of his time on the island twenty years later, without contemporaneous notes, and his memoirs were ghosted by the novelist Alexandre Dumas, who also ghosted those of Napoleon's favourite actor Talma. Laure d'Abrantès was banned from Paris by Napoleon in 1813, and by the time her memoirs appeared in the 1830s she was an opium addict who nonetheless claimed to have remembered verbatim long, intimate con-versations with the Emperor. Several of her eighteen volumes of memoirs were ghosted by Balzac and written to stave off creditors. Those of Napoleon's police chief Fouché were actually written by the hack-writer Alphonse de Beauchamp; those of one of Napoleon's favourite mis-tresses, Mademoiselle George, were also drawn up by a ghost-writer, but she found them so boring that she sexed them up, with stories of Napoleon shoving wads of banknotes down her corset.

In the period before copyright laws, people could even publish mem-oirs that were supposedly written by living participants such as Joseph Bonaparte, Marshal Marmont and Napoleon's foreign minister Armand de Caulaincourt without their having any legal recourse. A fraud called Charlotte de Sor published what she claimed were Caulaincourt's memoirs in 1837 on the basis of having briefly met him in 1826 (his real memoirs weren't published until 1934). Although the Napoleonic sections of Talleyrand's memoirs were written by him in the 1820s, they were extensively rewritten in the 1860s by the profoundly anti-Napoleonic Adolphe de Bacourt. Prince Metternich's memoirs were ghosted too, as well as being immensely self-serving; those of Paul Barras, who at one time was Josephine's lover, are a monument to malice, self-pity and would-be revenge against Napoleon. The man Napoleon overthrew in the Brumaire coup, Louis Gohier, promised in the introduction to his memoirs that he was 'an impartial writer' who would 'give full justice to Napoleon', yet they are in fact little more than two volumes of bitter ranting. Neither the minister Lazare Carnot nor Marshal Grouchy wrote their own memoirs either, but had them drawn up from documents they left, some contemporaneous, others not. The diplomat André-François Miot de Melito's so-called memoirs were written by his son-in-law over half a century after the events they describe.

Nonetheless, because so many people wanted to record their impressions of this extraordinary man, there are also plenty of memoirs from people close to Napoleon who kept contemporaneous notes and didn't decry him so that they could find jobs under the incoming regime or exaggerate their intimacy with him in order to make money. The credibility of the Marquis de Caulaincourt's accounts of 1812–14, of Henri Bertrand's diary of events on St Helena and of Cambacérès' memoirs, for example, is greatly enhanced by the fact that they were not written for immediate publication, only emerging in the 1930s, 1950s and 1970s respectively. The memoirs of the little-known Baron Louis de Bausset-Roquefort, who as prefect of Napoleon's palace was closer to him than Bourrienne, were bravely published during the Bourbon period, and equally balanced pictures were drawn by Napoleon's two private secretaries after Bourrienne, namely Claude-François de Méneval and Agathon Fain. Of course they all need to be checked against what we know from other sources, and against each other, but once that is done they tend to present a more coherent and credible portrait of the Emperor than the 'Black Legend' painted by his enemies and their ghost-writers soon after his death.

In threading a way through this labyrinth, the biographer of Napoleon writing in 2014 has one tremendous advantage over those of all earlier generations: since 2004, the Fondation Napoléon in Paris has been superbly editing and publishing Napoleon's 33,000 extant letters, as many as a third of which have not been published before or which were cut or bowdlerized in one way or another in the previous edition that appeared in the 1850s and 1860s. This titanic new edition allows a true re-evaluation of Napoleon, and it has been the bedrock of my book.

Two hundred years after his defeat at the battle of Waterloo, every aspect of Napoleon's life has now been documented, explored and picked over in the most astonishing detail. On Thursday, July 19, 1804, for example, he stopped for a cup of milky coffee at a blacksmith's house near Buigny-St-Maclou in Picardie and distributed some gold coins to its surprised and delighted inhabitants. A fifteen-page treatise has been written about that event alone. Yet the extreme scrutiny and avalanche of facts about him has not led to general agreement about his personality, policies, motives or even his achievements. My book clearly stands in a long tradition of argument about Napoleon, which began, as I recount in Chapter 1, before he was thirty, when the first biography of him was published. In 1817 the Swiss historian Frédéric Lullin de Châteauvieux wrote that 'With cyclonic intensity he swept away the petrified barriers to progress and achieved more for the race than the 800 years of the Habsburgs or the 600 years of Bourbon rule.' In 1818 Madame de Staël posthumously called him a 'Condottiere without manners, without fatherland, without morality, an oriental despot, a new Attila, a warrior who knew only how to corrupt and annihilate'. Johann Wolfgang von Goethe, Germany's greatest literary figure, who met Napoleon in 1808, described him as being 'in a permanent state of enlightenment'. Was he a destroyer or an architect? A liberator or a tyrant? A statesman or an adventurer? 'The argument goes on,' said Geyl in the last sentence of his book. At the end of mine, I hope that the reader will be in no doubt why I have called it *Napoleon the Great*.

PART ONE

Rise

I

Corsica

'The hero of a tragedy, in order to interest us, should be neither wholly guilty nor wholly innocent ... All weakness and all contradictions are unhappily in the heart of man, and present a colouring eminently tragic.'

Napoleon, on François-Just-Marie
Raynouard's play *The Templars*

'The reading of history very soon made me feel that I was capable of achieving as much as the men who are placed in the highest ranks of our annals.'

Napoleon to the Marquis de Caulaincourt

Napoleone di Buonaparte, as he signed himself until manhood, was born in Ajaccio, one of the larger towns on the Mediterranean island of Corsica, just before noon on Tuesday, August 15, 1769. 'She was on her way home from church when she felt labour pains,' he would later say of his mother, Letizia, 'and had only time to get into the house, when I was born, not on a bed, but on a heap of tapestry.'[1] The name his parents chose was unusual but not unknown, appearing in Machiavelli's history of Florence, and, more immediately, being the name of one of his great-uncles.

The Buona Parte family were originally landowners living between Florence and Livorno – a Florentine first took the surname in 1261. While the senior line remained in Italy, Francesco Buonaparte emigrated to Corsica in 1529, where for the next two and a half centuries his descendants generally pursued the gentlemanly callings of the law, academia and the Church.[2] By the time of Napoleon's birth the family occupied that social penumbra encompassing the *haute bourgeoisie* and the very minor nobility.

After he came to power in France, when people attempted to trace his family's descent from the thirteenth-century emperors of Trebizond, Napoleon told them that his dynasty in fact dated back only to the time of his military coup d'état. 'There are genealogists who would date my family from the Flood,' he told the Austrian diplomat Prince Clemens von Metternich, 'and there are people who pretend that I am of plebeian birth. The truth lies between these two. The Bonapartes are a good Corsican family, little known for we have hardly ever left the island, but much better than many of the coxcombs who take it upon themselves to vilify us.'³ On the rare occasions when he discussed his Italian ancestry, he would say he was an heir to the Ancient Romans. 'I am of the race that founds empires,' he once boasted.⁴

The family was far from rich, but it owned enough land for Napoleon's great-uncle Luciano, the archdeacon of Ajaccio, to claim that the Bonapartes never had to buy their wine, bread or olive oil. One can still see the millstone used for grinding flour in the basement of the large, three-storey Casa Bonaparte on the rue Saint-Charles in Ajaccio, where his family had lived since 1682. Napoleon's parents had another home in the countryside, some property in at least three other towns, a flock of sheep and a vineyard and employed a nanny, maid and cook. 'There's no wealth in Corsica,' Napoleon's elder brother Joseph wrote years later, 'and the richer individuals hardly have 20,000 livres of savings; but, because everything is relative, our wealth was one of the most considerable in Ajaccio.' The young Napoleon agreed, adding that 'Luxury is an unwholesome thing in Corsica.'⁵

In 1765, four years before Napoleon's birth, the Scottish lawyer and man of letters James Boswell visited the island and was enchanted with what he found. 'Ajaccio is the prettiest town in Corsica,' he later wrote. 'It hath many very handsome streets, and beautiful gardens, and a palace for the Genoese governor. The inhabitants of this town are the genteelest people in the island, having had a good deal of intercourse with the French.' Three years later these people – some 140,000 in total, most of them peasants – were to experience considerably more intercourse with the French, who numbered around 28 million, than most had ever hoped for or wanted.

The Italian city-state of Genoa had nominally ruled Corsica for over two centuries, but rarely tried to extend her control beyond the coastal towns into the mountainous interior, where the Corsicans were fiercely independent. In 1755 Corsica's charismatic nationalist leader, Pasquale Paoli, proclaimed an independent republic, a notion that became a reality after he won the battle of Pedicoste in 1763. The man the Corsicans nicknamed Il Babbù (Daddy) quickly set about reforming the island's financial, legal and educational systems, built roads, started a printing press and brought something approaching harmony between the island's competing clans of powerful families. The young Napoleon grew up revering Paoli as a lawgiver, reformer and genuinely benevolent dictator.

Genoa had no appetite for the fight that she knew would be required to reassert her authority over Corsica, and reluctantly sold the island to King Louis XV of France for 40 million francs in January 1768. The French foreign minister, the Duc de Choiseul, appointed the Corsican Matteo Buttafuoco to rule the island. Paoli naturally opposed this, so the French sent a force of 30,000 men under the command of the harsh Comte de Vaux with the task of putting down the rebellion and soon replaced Buttafuoco with a Frenchman, the Comte de Marbeuf.

Carlo Bonaparte, Napoleon's father, and his pretty young wife Letizia supported Paoli and were campaigning in the mountains when Letizia became pregnant with Napoleon. Carlo acted as Paoli's private secretary and aide-de-camp, but when Vaux smashed the Corsican forces at the battle of Ponte Nuovo on May 8, 1769, Carlo and the by now heavily pregnant Letizia refused to go into exile with Paoli and 340 other irreconcilables.[6] Instead, at a meeting between Marbeuf and the Corsican gentry, Carlo took an oath of loyalty to Louis XV, as a result of which he was able to retain his positions of responsibility on the island: assessor of the Ajaccio court of justice and superintendent of the island's forestry school. Within two months of Ponte Nuovo, Carlo had dined with the Comte de Vaux, something that was held against him by his former compatriots whose resistance to French rule continued. Hundreds would die over the next two decades in sporadic anti-French guerrilla actions, although major incidents were rare after the mid-1770s.[7] 'He became a good Frenchman,' Joseph Bonaparte wrote of their father, 'seeing the huge advantages his country was taking from its union with France.'[8] Carlo was appointed to represent the Corsican nobility in Paris in 1777, a position that saw him visit Louis XVI at Versailles twice.

It is often alleged that Napoleon, who proclaimed a fierce Corsican nationalism throughout his adolescence, despised his father for switching his loyalties, but there is no proof of this beyond the bitter outpourings of his classmate and private secretary Louis Antoine de Bourrienne, whom he twice had to dismiss for gross peculation. In 1789 Napoleon did write to Paoli denouncing those Corsicans who had changed sides, but he didn't refer to his by-then-deceased father. He chose to call his son Charles, which he would hardly have done if he had imagined his father as a quisling. The Bonapartes were a thrusting, striving, close-knit family of what Napoleon later called *petits gentilshommes*, and understood that no good would have come of being caught on the wrong side of history.

French rule over Corsica turned out to be relatively light-handed. Marbeuf sought to persuade the island's elite of the benefits of French rule, and Carlo was to be one of the prime beneficiaries. If Paoli was Napoleon's early role model for statesmanship, Carlo personified precisely the kind of non-Frenchman whose willingness to collaborate with France was later vital to the smooth running of the Napoleonic Empire.

Carlo was tall, handsome, popular and a fine horseman. He spoke French well, was familiar with the Enlightenment thought of Locke, Montesquieu, Hume, Rousseau and Hobbes, and wrote Voltairean essays sceptical of organized religion for private distribution.[9] Napoleon later described him as 'a spendthrift', and he certainly got through more than the patchy income he earned, building up debts for the family.[10] He was a loving father, but weak, often impecunious and somewhat frivolous. Napoleon inherited little from him beyond his debts, his blue-grey eyes, and the disease that would lead them to their early deaths. 'To my mother', he would say, 'I owe my fortune and all I've done that's worthwhile.'[11]

Maria-Letizia Ramolino, as she had been christened, was an attractive, strong-willed, wholly uneducated woman from a good family – her father was Ajaccio's governor and subsequently Corsica's inspector of roads and bridges. Her marriage to Carlo Buonaparte on June 2, 1764, when he was eighteen, was arranged by their parents. (The burning of Ajaccio's archives during the French Revolution leaves her exact age unclear.) They didn't marry in the cathedral as Carlo regarded himself as a secularized Enlightenment man, although Archdeacon Luciano later altered the church records to record a nuptial Mass there, an early indication of the Bonapartes' willingness to doctor official records.[12] Letizia's dowry was valued at an impressive 175,000 francs, which included 'a kiln and the house adjoining', an apartment, a vineyard and 8 acres of land. This trumped the love that the raffish Carlo is believed to have felt for another woman at the time of his wedding.[13]

Letizia had thirteen children between 1765 and 1786, eight of whom survived infancy, a not untypical ratio for the day; they were eventually to number an emperor, three kings, a queen and two sovereign princesses. Although Napoleon didn't much like it when his mother beat him for being naughty – on one occasion for mimicking his grandmother – corporal punishment was normal practice in those days and he only ever spoke of her with genuine love and admiration. 'My mother was a superb woman, a woman of ability and courage,' he told General Gourgaud, near the end of his life. 'Her tenderness was severe; here was the head of a man on the body of a woman.' This, from Napoleon, was high praise. 'She was a matriarch,' he added. 'She had plenty of brains!'[14] Once he came to power, Napoleon was generous to his mother, buying her the Château de Pont on the Seine and giving her an annual income of 1 million francs, most of which she squirrelled away. When she was teased for her notorious parsimoniousness she replied: 'Who knows, one day I may have to find bread for all these kings I've borne.'[15]

Two children died in infancy before Napoleon was born, and the girl who came immediately after him, Maria-Anna, lived to only five. His elder brother, Giuseppe (who later Frenchified his name as Joseph), was born in January 1768. After Napoleon came Luciano (Lucien) in March 1775, a sister Maria-Anna (Elisa) in January 1777, Louis – significantly, the name of the kings of France – in September 1778, Maria-Paola (Pauline) in October 1780, Maria-Annunziata (Caroline) in March 1782, and Girolamo (Jérôme) in November 1784. Letizia stopped having children at thirty-three when Carlo died at thirty-eight, but Napoleon speculated that if his father had lived longer she would have had twenty.[16]

One of the features that emerges strongly from Napoleon's correspondence is his deep and constant concern for his family. Whether it was his mother's property on Corsica, the education of his brothers or the marriage prospects of his sisters, he was endlessly seeking to protect and promote the Bonaparte clan. 'You are the only man on earth for whom I have a true and constant love', he once wrote to his brother Joseph.[17] His persistent tendency to promote his family would later significantly damage his own interests.

Napoleon's background as a Corsican of Italian extraction later invited endless abuse from detractors. One of his earliest British biographers, William Burdon, said of his Italian ancestry: 'To this may be attributed the dark ferocity of his character, which partakes more of Italian treachery than of French openness and vivacity.'[18] Similarly, in November 1800 the British journalist William Cobbett described Napoleon as 'a low-bred upstart from the contemptible island of Corsica!' When the French senate proposed that Napoleon become emperor in 1804, the Comte Jean-Denis Lanjuinais expostulated: 'What! Will you submit to give your country a master taken from a race of origin so ignominious that the Romans disdained to employ them as slaves?'[19] Because he was Corsican it was assumed that Napoleon would pursue vendettas, but there is no record of the Bonapartes doing so, and Napoleon was notably lenient towards several people who betrayed him, such as his foreign minister Charles-Maurice de Talleyrand and police minister Joseph Fouché.

Napoleon suffered from a hacking cough as a child that might have been a mild bout of undiagnosed tuberculosis; in his post-mortem his left lung showed evidence of it, long-healed.[20] Yet the popular image of a frail introvert hardly squares with his family nickname of 'Rabulione', or troublemaker. Given the paucity of trustworthy sources, much of Napoleon's early childhood must remain conjectural, but there is little doubt that he was a precocious and prodigious reader, drawn at an early age to history and biography. Letizia told a government minister that her son 'had never partaken of the amusements of children his own age, that he carefully avoided them, that he found himself a little room on the third floor of the house in which he stayed by himself and didn't come down very often, even to eat with his family. Up there, he read constantly, especially history books.'[21] Napoleon claimed that he first read Jean-Jacques Rousseau's *La Nouvelle Héloïse*, an 800-page novel of love and redemption, at the age of nine, and said 'It turned my head.'[22]

'I do not doubt the very powerful action of his early readings on the inclination and character of his youth,' his brother Joseph later recalled.[23] He described how, at their primary school, when the students were instructed to sit under either the Roman or the Carthaginian flag, Napoleon insisted that they swap places and utterly refused to join the losing Carthaginians.[24] (Though he was eighteen months younger than Joseph, Napoleon was always stronger-willed.) Later in life, Napoleon urged his junior officers 'to read and re-read the campaigns of Alexander the Great, Hannibal, Julius Caesar, Gustavus Adolfus, Prince Eugene and Frederick the Great. This is the only way to become a great captain.'[25]

Ancient history provided him with an encyclopaedia of military and political tactics and quotations that he would draw on throughout his life. This inspiration was so profound that when posing for paintings he would sometimes put his hand into his waistcoat in imitation of the toga-wearing Romans.

Napoleon's native language was Corsican, an idiomatic dialect not unlike Genoese. He was taught to read and write in Italian at school and was nearly ten before he learned French, which he always spoke with a heavy Corsican accent, with '*ou*' for '*eu*' or '*u*', inviting all manner of teasing at school and in the army. The architect Pierre Fontaine, who decorated and refurbished many of the Napoleonic palaces, thought it 'incredible in a man of his position' that he should speak with such a thick accent.[26] Napoleon was not very proficient in French grammar or spelling, though in the era before standardized spelling this mattered little and he never had any difficulty making himself understood. Throughout his life his handwriting, though strong and decisive, was pretty much a scrawl.

Napoleon's childhood has often been portrayed as a maelstrom of anxieties, but his first nine years in Ajaccio were uncomplicated and happy, surrounded by family, friends and a few domestic servants. In later life he was generous to his illiterate nursemaid, Camilla Illari.[27] It was only when he was sent away to France – 'the continent' as Corsicans called it – to become a French officer and gentleman that complications arose.

As part of his active policy of Gallicization of the island's elite, in 1770 Marbeuf issued an edict declaring that all Corsicans who could prove two centuries of nobility would be allowed to enjoy the extensive privileges of the French *noblesse*. Carlo's father, Joseph, had been officially recognized as noble by the Grand Duke of Tuscany, and subsequently obtained recognition from the archbishop of Pisa as 'a patrician of Florence'.[28] Although titles had little purchase in Corsica, where there was no feudalism, Carlo applied for the right of the Bonapartes to be recognized as one of the island's seventy-eight noble families, and on September 13, 1771 the Corsican Superior Council, having traced the family back to its Florentine roots, declared its official admission into the *noblesse*.[29]

Carlo could now legally sign himself 'de Buonaparte' for the first time and sit in the Corsican assembly. He could also apply for royal bursaries for his sons, whom he was hard put to educate on his income.

The French state was willing to provide for the education of up to six hundred sons of indigent French aristocrats, requiring each scholar to prove that he was noble, that he couldn't pay the fees and that he was able to read and write French. The nine-year-old Napoleon already qualified for two of the three stipulations. For the last he was sent to Autun in Burgundy to begin, in January 1779, a rigorous course of French.

The Comte de Marbeuf personally expedited Carlo's application through the French bureaucracy, a fact that later kindled the rumour that he was Letizia's lover, and possibly Napoleon's biological father – a libel sedulously spread by Bourbon and British writers. Just as Napoleon sought to magnify himself throughout his life, so his enemies found ingenious ways to detract from his myth. In 1797, when the first biographies of the twenty-eight-year-old military hero began to appear, a book entitled *Quelques notices sur les premières années du Buonaparte* was translated from an unknown English author by the Chevalier de Bourgoing. It made the claim that Letizia had 'caught the attention' of Marbeuf, and Sir Andrew Douglas, who had been with Napoleon at Autun, but who had not of course known any other members of the Bonaparte family, testified to its accuracy in a brief introduction.[30]

Napoleon paid little attention to this slur, although he did once point out to the distinguished mathematician and chemist Gaspard Monge that his mother had been in Paoli's stronghold of Corte fighting Marbeuf's forces when he was conceived. As emperor, he went out of his way to show generosity towards Marbeuf's son and when Marbeuf's daughter, Madame de Brunny, was robbed by a band of soldiers during one of his campaigns, he 'treated her with the utmost attention, granted her a piquet of chasseurs of his guard, and sent her away happy and contented' – neither of which he was likely to have done if Mme de Brunny's father had seduced his mother and cuckolded his father.[31] It was also said that Paoli was his biological father, a rumour similarly dismissed.

Napoleon's education in France made him French. Anything else would have been astonishing given his youth, the length of time he spent there and the cultural superiority the country enjoyed over the rest of Europe at that time. His bursary grant (the equivalent of a curate's stipend) was dated December 31, 1778, and he started at the ecclesiastical seminary run by the bishop of Autun the next day. He wasn't to see Corsica again for almost eight years. His name appeared in the school registry as 'M. Neapoleonne de Bonnaparte'. His headmaster, the Abbé Chardon, recalled him as 'a thoughtful and gloomy character. He had no playmate and walked about by himself . . . He had ability and learned quickly . . . If I scolded him, he answered in a cold, almost imperious tone: "Sir, I know it." '[32] It took Chardon only three months to teach this intelligent and determined lad, with a will to learn, to speak and read French, and even to write short passages.

Having mastered the requisite French at Autun, in April 1779, four months shy of his tenth birthday, Napoleon was admitted to the Royal Military School of Brienne-le-Château, near Troyes in the Champagne region. His father left the next day, and as there were no school holidays they were not to see each other again for three years. Napoleon was taught by the Minim order of Franciscan friars as one of fifty royal scholars among 110 pupils. Despite being a military academy, Brienne was administered by the monks, although the martial side of studies were conducted by outside instructors. Conditions were spartan: students had a straw mattress and one blanket each, though they weren't beaten. When his parents did visit, in June 1782, Letizia expressed concern at how thin he had become.

Although Brienne was not considered one of the most socially desirable of the twelve royal military schools founded by Louis XVI in 1776, it provided Napoleon with a fine education. His eight hours of study a day included mathematics, Latin, history, French, German, geography, physics, fortifications, weaponry, fencing, dancing and music (the last three an indication that Brienne was also in part a finishing school for the *noblesse*).[33] Physically tough and intellectually demanding, the school turned out a number of very distinguished generals besides Napoleon, including Louis-Nicolas Davout, Étienne Nansouty, Antoine Phélippeaux and Jean-Joseph d'Hautpoul. Charles Pichegru, the future conqueror of Holland and royalist plotter, was one of the school's instructors.

Napoleon excelled at mathematics. 'To be a good general you must know mathematics,' he later observed, 'it serves to direct your thinking in a thousand circumstances.'[34] He was helped by his prodigious memory. 'A singular thing about me is my memory,' he once boasted. 'As a boy I knew the logarithms of thirty or forty numbers.'[35] Napoleon was given permission to take maths classes earlier than the prescribed age of twelve, and soon mastered geometry, algebra and trigonometry. His weakest subject was German, which he never mastered; another weak subject, surprisingly for someone who so adored ancient history, was

Latin. (He was fortunate not to be examined in Latin until after 1780, by which time it was clear that he would be going into the army or navy and not the Church.) Napoleon also excelled at geography. On the very last page of his school exercise book, following a long list of British imperial possessions, he noted: 'Sainte-Hélène: petite île.'[36]

'History could become for a young man the school of morality and virtue,' read Brienne's school prospectus. The monks subscribed to the Great Man view of history, presenting the heroes of the ancient and modern worlds for the boys' emulation.[37] Napoleon borrowed many biographies and history books from the school library, devouring Plutarch's tales of heroism, patriotism and republican virtue. He also read Caesar, Cicero, Voltaire, Diderot and the Abbé Raynal, as well as Erasmus, Eutropius, Livy, Phaedrus, Sallust, Virgil and the first century BC Cornelius Nepos' *Lives of the Great Captains*, which included chapters on Themistocles, Lysander, Alcibiades and Hannibal. One of his school nicknames – 'the Spartan' – might have been accorded him because of his pronounced admiration for that city-state rather than for any asceticism of character. He could recite in French whole passages from Virgil, and in class he naturally took the side of his hero Caesar against Pompey.[38] The plays he enjoyed as an adult also tended to focus on the ancient heroes, such as Racine's *Alexandre le Grand*, *Andromaque*, *Mithridate* and Corneille's *Cinna*, *Horace* and *Attila*.

A contemporary recalled Napoleon withdrawing to the school library to read Polybius, Plutarch, Arrian ('with great delight') and Quintus Curtius Rufus (for which he had 'little taste').[39] Polybius' *Histories* chronicled the rise of the Roman Republic and offered an eyewitness account of the defeat of Hannibal and the sack of Carthage; Plutarch's *Parallel Lives* included sketches of Napoleon's two greatest heroes, Alexander the Great and Julius Caesar; Arrian wrote the *Anabasis of Alexander*, one of the best sources for Alexander's campaigns; Quintus Curtius Rufus produced only one surviving work, a biography of Alexander. A powerful theme thus emerges from Napoleon's adolescent reading. While his contemporaries played sports outside, he would read everything he could about the most ambitious leaders of the ancient world. For Napoleon, the desire to emulate Alexander the Great and Julius Caesar was not strange. His schooling opened to him the possibility that he might one day stand alongside the giants of the past.

Napoleon was taught to appreciate France's greatest moments under Charlemagne and Louis XIV, but he also learned about her recent defeats in the Seven Years War at the battles of Quebec, Plassey, Minden and Quiberon Bay and 'the prodigious conquests of the English in India'.[40] The intention was to create a generation of young officers who believed implicitly in French greatness, but who were also determined to humiliate Britain, which was at war with France in America for most of Napoleon's time at Brienne. Too often Napoleon's virulent opposition to the British government has been ascribed to blind hatred, or a Corsican spirit of vendetta; it could more accurately be seen as a perfectly rational response to the fact that in the decade of his birth the Treaty of Paris of 1763 had cut France out of the great continental landmasses (and markets) of India and North America, and by the time he was a teenager Britain was busily colonizing Australia too. At the end of his life Napoleon twice asked to live in Britain, and he expressed admiration for the Duke of Marlborough and Oliver Cromwell, but he was brought up to think of Britain as an implacable enemy. When he was studying at Brienne, his only living hero seems to have been the exiled Paoli. Another dead hero was Charles XII of Sweden, who from 1700 to 1706 had destroyed the armies of four states joined in coalition against him, but then marched deep into Russia, only to be catastrophically defeated and forced into exile.

Napoleon was also deeply fond of literature. (He reminisced in later years about how he was attacked by a Cossack in 1814 during the battle of Brienne very close to the tree under which as a schoolboy he had read *Jerusalem Delivered*, Tasso's epic poem about the First Crusade.)[41] He idolized Rousseau, who wrote positively about Corsica, writing a paean to *On the Social Contract* at seventeen and adopting Rousseau's beliefs that the state should have the power of life and death over its citizens, the right to prohibit frivolous luxuries and the duty to censor the theatre and opera.[42] Rousseau's *La Nouvelle Héloïse*, one of the biggest bestsellers of the eighteenth century, which had influenced him so much as a boy, argued that one should follow one's authentic feelings rather than society's norms, an attractive notion for any teenager, particularly a dreamer of ferocious ambition. Rousseau's draft of a liberal constitution for Corsica in 1765 reflected his admiration for Paoli, which was fully reciprocated.

Napoleon read Corneille, Racine and Voltaire with evident pleasure. His favourite poet was Ossian, whose bardic tales of ancient Gaelic conquest thrilled him with accounts of heroism among misty moors and epic battles on stormy seas. He took the Ossian poem *Fingal* on his campaigns, commissioned several Ossianic paintings, and was so impressed with the opera *Ossian* by Jean-François Le Sueur, with its twelve orchestral harps, that he made the composer a chevalier of the Légion d'Honneur at the premiere in 1804. That same year, assuming as most people then did that the Celts and Ancient Gauls had been closely connected, Napoleon founded the Académie Celtique for the study of Gallic history and archaeology, which in 1813 became the Société des Antiquaires de France and today is based at the Louvre. He appears not to have been particularly disconcerted when it was discovered that the epic poem had in fact been written by its self-styled 'discoverer', the literary fraudster James Macpherson.[43]

In 1781, Napoleon received an outstanding school report from the Chevalier de Kéralio, the under-inspector of military schools who, two years later, recommended him for the prestigious École Militaire in Paris with the words, 'Excellent health, docile expression, mild, straightforward, thoughtful. Conduct most satisfactory; has always been distinguished for his application in mathematics ... This boy would make an excellent sailor.'[44] His clear intellectual superiority is unlikely to have helped his popularity with his classmates, who nicknamed him *La Paille-au-Nez* ('straw up the nose'), which rhymed with 'Napoleone' in Corsican.[45] He was teased for not speaking refined French, for having a father who had had to certify to his nobility, for coming from a conquered nation, for having a relatively large head on a thin frame and for being poorer than most of his school contemporaries. 'I was the poorest of my classmates,' he told a courtier in 1811, 'they had pocket-money, I never had any. I was proud, I was careful not to show it ... I didn't know how to smile or play like the others.'[46] When he spoke in later life about his schooldays, he remembered individual teachers he had liked, but few fellow pupils.

Schoolchildren are quick to seize upon and mock marginal differences, and they swiftly spotted that Napoleon's Achilles heel was his inordinate pride in his native land. (The Abbé Chardon also commented on it.) He was an outsider, a foreigner among the scions of a governing class that he believed to be oppressing his countrymen. The teasing had precisely the effect one might expect in a spirited boy, and turned him into a proud Corsican nationalist who never failed to stand up for his motherland. 'His natural reserve,' recalled Bourrienne, 'his disposition to meditate on the subjugation of Corsica, and the impressions which he had received in his youth respecting the misfortunes of his country, and of his family, led him to seek solitude, and rendered his general demeanour somewhat disagreeable.'[47] The first book ever written on Napoleon was by Cuming de Craigmillen, a monk who taught at Brienne, writing under the name 'Mr C. H., one of his schoolfellows'. Published in 1797 in English, the book presented a reserved and anti-social child who, in the words of one reviewer, was 'blunt in his manners, bold, enterprising and even ferocious' – four adjectives that would serve to describe him for the rest of his life.[48]

Much the most famous anecdote of Napoleon's schooldays, of a snowball fight involving the whole school, was probably an invention. In the freezing winter of 1783, Napoleon supposedly organized mass mock-battles around ice-forts that he had designed, in which he commanded the attacking forces on one day and the defending ones the next.[49] This hardly fits with the unpopularity he is supposed to have experienced among his fellow pupils, and the anecdote does not appear in the notes Bourrienne gave his memoirs' ghost-writers and could easily have been a complete invention of theirs. 'This mimic combat was carried on during a period of fifteen days,' the memoirs state, 'and did not cease until, by gravel and small stones having got mixed up with the snow, many of the pupils were rendered *hors de combat*.'[50] Would a school really have let a game that was injuring many of its pupils continue for over two weeks?

On June 15, 1784, Napoleon wrote the first of over 33,000 surviving letters, to his step-uncle Joseph Fesch, Letizia's mother's second husband's son. In it, he argued that his brother Joseph should not become a soldier as 'the great Mover of all human destiny has [not] given him, as to me, a distinct love for the military profession', adding 'He has not the courage to face the perils of action; his health is feeble ... and my brother looks on the military profession from only a garrison point of view.'[51] If Joseph chose to go into the Church, he opined, Marbeuf's kinsman, the bishop of Autun, 'would have given him a fat living and he would have been sure to become a bishop. What an advantage for the family!' As for Joseph joining the infantry, Napoleon asked: 'What is a wretched officer of the infantry? Three-quarters of his time he is a good-for-nothing.' The three-page letter, now at the Pierpont Morgan Library in New York, has a spelling mistake in almost every line – 'Saint Cire' for 'Saint-Cyr', 'arivé' for 'arrivé', 'écrie' for 'écrit', and so on – and is packed with grammatical errors. But his handwriting is clear and legible and he signed the letter 'your humble and obedient servant Napolione di Buonaparte'. In a postscript he wrote 'Destroy this letter,' an early indication of his own concern for careful editing of the historical record.

Napoleon took his final exams at Brienne on September 15, 1784. He passed easily, and late the following month he entered the École Royale Militaire in Paris, on the left bank of the Seine. This was a far more socially elevated institution than Brienne. There were three changes of linen a week, good meals and more than twice as many servants, teachers and staff – including wigmakers – as students. There were also three chapel services a day, starting with 6 a.m. Mass. Although strangely the history of warfare and strategy weren't taught, the syllabus covered much the same subjects as at Brienne, as well as musketry, military drills and horsemanship. It was in fact one of the best riding schools in Europe. (Many of the same buildings survive today, grouped around seventeen courtyards over 29 acres at the opposite end of the Champ de Mars from the Eiffel Tower.) Apart from the Champ de Mars and the École itself, Napoleon saw little of Paris in the twelve months he spent there, although of course he knew a good deal about the city and its monuments, defences, resources and architectural splendours from his reading and his fellow officers.[52]

Napoleon continued to excel intellectually. At Brienne he had decided not to enter the navy, partly because his mother feared he would drown or be burned to death and she didn't like the idea of his sleeping in hammocks, but mainly because his aptitude for mathematics opened the prospect of a career in the far more prestigious artillery. Of the 202 candidates from all of France's military schools in 1784, a total of 136 passed their final exams and only 14 of these were invited to enter the artillery, so Napoleon had been selected for an elite group.[53] He was the first Corsican to attend the École Royale Militaire, where a fellow cadet drew an affectionate caricature of the young hero standing resolutely in defence of Paoli, while an elderly teacher tries to hold him back by pulling on the back of his wig.[54]

Napoleon took classes from the distinguished trio of Louis Monge (brother of the mathematician-chemist Gaspard), the Marquis de Laplace, who later became Napoleon's interior minister, and Louis Domairon, who taught him the value of 'haranguing' troops before battles. (Shorn of its English meaning, which implies a prolonged rant, a French *harangue* could mean an inspiring speech, such as Shakespeare puts in Henry V's mouth or Thucydides in the mouth of Pericles, a skill at which Napoleon was to excel on the battlefield, but not always in public assemblies.) At the École, Napoleon encountered the new thinking in

French artillery practice introduced by Jean-Baptiste de Gribeauval after the Seven Years War. (Defeat had been, as it is so often in history, the mother of reform.) He also studied General Comte Jacques de Guibert's revolutionary *Essai général de tactique* (1770): 'The standing armies, a burden on the people, are inadequate for the achievement of great and decisive results in war, and meanwhile the mass of the people, untrained in arms, degenerates ... The hegemony over Europe will fall to that nation which becomes possessed of manly virtues and creates a national army.'[55] Guibert preached the importance of speed, surprise and mobility in warfare, and of abandoning large supply depots in walled cities in favour of living off the land. Another of Guibert's principles was that high morale – *esprit de corps* – could overcome most problems.

By the time Napoleon had spent five years at Brienne and one at the École Militaire he was thoroughly imbued with the military ethos, which was to stay with him for the rest of his life and was to colour his beliefs and outlook deeply. His acceptance of the revolutionary principles of equality before the law, rational government, meritocracy, efficiency and aggressive nationalism fit in well with this ethos but he had little interest in equality of outcome, human rights, freedom of the press or parliamentarianism, all of which, to his mind, did not. Napoleon's upbringing imbued him with a reverence for social hierarchy, law and order, and a strong belief in reward for merit and courage, but also a dislike of politicians, lawyers, journalists and Britain.

As Claude-François de Méneval, the private secretary who succeeded Bourrienne in 1802, was later to write, Napoleon left school with 'pride, and a sentiment of dignity, a warlike instinct, a genius for form, a love of order and of discipline'.[56] These were all part of the officer's code, and made him into a profound social conservative. As an army officer, Napoleon believed in centralized control within a recognized hierarchical chain of command and the importance of maintaining high morale. Order in matters of administration and education was vital. He had a deep, instinctive distaste for anything which looked like a mutinous *canaille* (mob). None of these feelings was to change much during the French Revolution, or, indeed, for the rest of his life.

On February 24, 1785, Carlo Bonaparte died, probably of stomach cancer but possibly of a perforated ulcer, at Montpellier in southern France, where he had gone to try to improve his health. He was thirty-eight. Napoleon, who was then only fifteen, had seen him twice in the previous six years, and then only briefly. 'The long and cruel death of my

father had remarkably weakened his organs and faculties,' recalled
Joseph, 'to the point that a few days before his death [he was] in a total
delirium.'[57] Napoleon's lifelong distrust of doctors might well have
stemmed from this time, as his father's doctor's advice had been to eat
pears. His father's early death may also in part explain Napoleon's own
drive and boundless energy; he suspected, correctly, that his own life-
span would be short. A month later, Napoleon described his father in a
letter to his great-uncle Luciano as 'an enlightened, zealous and disinterested citizen. And yet Heaven let him die; and in what a place? A
hundred leagues from his native land – in a foreign country, indifferent
to his existence, far from all he held precious.'[58] This letter is interesting
not just for its laudable filial feeling, but for the fact that Napoleon still
considered France 'a foreign country'. After expressing his heartfelt
commiserations, he sent his love to his godmother, cousin and even the
family's maid Minana Saveria, before adding a postscript: 'The French
Queen has given birth to a prince named the Duke of Normandy, on
March 27th, at 7pm.'[59] People then tended not to waste writing paper,
which was expensive, but tacking on such a random message to so
important a letter was bizarre.

Although Joseph was Carlo's eldest son, Napoleon quickly established himself as the new head of the family. 'In his family he began to
exercise the greatest superiority,' recalled Louis, 'not when power and
glory had elevated him, but even from his youth.'[60] He took his final
examinations early, coming forty-second out of fifty-eight candidates –
not so poor a result as it may seem given that he sat the exams after only
one year rather than the normal two or three. He could now dedicate
himself to his military career, and to the serious financial problems
Carlo had left. Napoleon later admitted that these 'influenced my state
of mind and made me grave before my time'.[61]

Carlo had earned 22,500 francs per annum as Ajaccio's assessor. He
had topped up his income by suing his neighbours over property (including at one point his wife's grandfather) while holding down various
minor posts in the local administration. His great scheme for making
his fortune, however, was a nursery of mulberry trees (a *pépinière*), a
project that was to give his second son much anxiety. 'The mulberry
grows well here,' wrote Boswell in his *Account of Corsica*, 'and is not so
much in danger from blights and thunderstorms as in Italy or the south
of France, so that whenever Corsica enjoys tranquillity it may have an
abundance of silk.'[62] In 1782, Carlo Bonaparte obtained the concession

for a mulberry *pépinière* on land previously given to his ancestor Giero-
nimo Bonaparte. Thanks to a royal grant of 137,500 francs, repayable
without interest over ten years, and to considerable investment of his
own money, Carlo was able to plant a large orchard of mulberries.
Three years later, the Corsican parliament revoked his contract on the
grounds that he had not fulfilled his obligations regarding maintenance,
which he strenuously denied. The contract was formally severed on
May 7, 1786, fifteen months after Carlo's death, leaving the Bonapartes
heavily encumbered by the need to repay the grant, as well as by the
regular management of the orchard, for which they continued to be
responsible.

Napoleon took an extended leave from the regiment that he was about
to join in order to resolve the *pépinière* affair, which threatened to bank-
rupt his mother. The bureaucratic miasma persisted for several years, and
was so consuming that the initial rumblings of the French Revolution
were regarded by the family through the prism of whether the political
changes in Paris were more or less likely to relieve the Bonapartes of their
debts, and whether they might perhaps be granted a further agricultural
subsidy by the state to help make the *pépinière* a going concern.[63] Napoleon never seems more provincial than during '*l'affaire de la pépinière*', as
it was known; it threatened his family with bankruptcy and he pursued
the case vigorously. He lobbied everyone he could in Corsica and Paris,
sending many letters in his mother's name as he tried to find a way out of
the problem. Dutifully, he also sent home as much as possible of the
1,100 francs per annum that he earned as a second-lieutenant. Letizia,
'Widow of Buonaparte' as Napoleon described her in their many letters
to France's comptroller-general, came close to having to sell family silver
after borrowing 600 francs from a French officer whom she needed to
reimburse.[64] Archdeacon Luciano saved the Bonapartes from the bailiffs
on that occasion, but the family were chronically short of money until the
archdeacon's death in 1791, when they inherited his estate.

On the first day of September 1785, Napoleon was commissioned into
the Compagnie d'Autume of bombardiers of the 5th Brigade of the 1st
Battalion of the Régiment de La Fère, stationed at Valence, on the left
bank of the Rhône. It was one of the five oldest artillery regiments, and
highly prestigious.[65] At sixteen he was one of the youngest officers, and
the only Corsican to hold an artillery commission in the French army.
Napoleon always recalled his years at Valence as impecunious – his

room had only a bed, table and armchair – and sometimes he had to skip meals in order to afford books, which he continued to read with the same voracious appetite as before. He existed partly on charity; as First Consul he asked one of his interior ministers for news of a café owner who had often treated him to coffee at Valence, and upon hearing that she was still alive said, 'I fear that I did not pay for all the cups of coffee that she served me; here are 50 *louis* [1,000 francs] that you will give to her on my behalf.'[66] He was also slow in picking up restaurant bills. A contemporary recalled: 'Persons who had dined with him at taverns and coffee-houses when it was convenient to him not to pay his reckoning, have assured me that though the youngest and poorest, he always obtained without exacting it a sort of deference or even submission from the rest of the company. Though never parsimonious, he was at that period of his life extremely attentive to the details of expense.'[67] He could not afford to forget the nightmare of the *pépinière*.

The list of books from which Napoleon made detailed notes from 1786 to 1791 is long, and includes histories of the Arabs, Venice, the Indies, England, Turkey, Switzerland and the Sorbonne. He annotated Voltaire's *Essais sur les moeurs*, Machiavelli's *History of Florence*, Mirabeau's *Des lettres de cachet* and Charles Rollin's *Ancient History*; there were books on modern geography, political works such as Jacques Dulaure's anti-aristocracy *Critical History of the Nobility*, and Charles Duclos' gossipy *Secret Memoirs of the Reigns of Louis XIV and Louis XV*.[68] At the same time, he learned verses of Corneille, Racine and Voltaire by heart, perhaps to charm a pretty girl called Caroline de Colombier. 'It will seem very difficult to believe,' he later recalled of the innocence of their relationship as they walked through meadows at dawn, 'but we spent the entire time eating cherries!'[69] Napoleon continued with dancing lessons at Valence, possibly recognizing how important it was for an officer to be socially presentable.* When, in December 1808, his by-then-destitute former dancing master, Dautel, wrote to him to say 'Sire, the one who gave you the first steps in polite society is calling upon your generosity', Napoleon found him a job.[70]

It was at Valence on April 26, 1786 that Napoleon wrote his first surviving essay, about the right of Corsicans to resist the French. He had finished his schooling, so it was written for himself rather than for

---

* It is debatable how good a pupil Napoleon was; in 1807 he asked the Countess Anna Potocka what she thought of his dancing at a ball in Warsaw. 'Sire,' came her diplomatic reply, 'for a great man you dance perfectly' (ed. Stryjenski, *Memoires* p. 125).

publication – an unusual pastime for French army officers of the day. Celebrating Paoli's sixty-first birthday, it argued that laws derived either from the people or from the prince and for the sovereignty of the former, concluding: 'The Corsicans, following all the laws of justice, have been able to shake off the yoke of the Genoese, and may do the same with that of the French. Amen.'[71] It was a curious, indeed treasonous, document for an officer in the French army to write, but Napoleon had idolized Paoli since his schooldays, and from the ages of nine to seventeen he had been largely alone in France, recalling an idealized Corsica.

Napoleon was a writer manqué, penning around sixty essays, novellas, philosophical pieces, histories, treatises, pamphlets and open letters before the age of twenty-six.[72] Taken together they display his intellectual and political development, tracing the way he moved from a committed Corsican nationalist in the 1780s to an avowed anti-Paolist French officer who by 1793 wanted the Corsican revolt to be crushed by Jacobin France. Late in life, Napoleon called Paoli 'a fine character who neither betrayed England nor France but was always for Corsica', and a 'great friend of the family' who had 'urged me to enter into the English service, he then had the power of procuring me a commission . . . but I preferred the French because I spoke the language, was of their religion, understood and liked their manners, and I thought the start of the Revolution as a fine time for an enterprising young man'.[73] He also claimed, with perhaps less truth, that Paoli had paid him the 'great compliment' of saying: 'That young man will be one of Plutarch's ancients.'[74]

In early May 1786, aged sixteen, Napoleon wrote a two-page essay entitled 'On Suicide' which mixed the anguished cry of a romantic nationalist with an exercise in classical oratory. 'Always alone and in the midst of men, I come back to my rooms to dream with myself, and to surrender myself to all the vivacity of my melancholy,' he wrote. 'In which direction are my thoughts turned today? Toward death.'[75] He was then prompted to consider: 'Since I must die, should I not just kill myself?' 'How far from Nature men have strayed!' he exclaimed, echoing a classic Romantic trope. Exhibiting a Hamlet-like combination of arrogance and self-pity, he then mixed in some self-indulgent philosophizing with Rousseauian Corsican nationalism: 'My fellow-countrymen are weighed down with chains, while they kiss with fear the hand that oppresses them! They are no longer those brave Corsicans who a hero animated with his virtues; enemies of tyrants, of luxury, and vile courtesans. You

Frenchmen,' he continued, 'not content with having robbed us of every-thing we held dear, have also corrupted our character. A good patriot ought to die when his fatherland has ceased to exist . . . Life is a burden to me, because I enjoy no pleasure and because everything is painful to me.'[76] Like most tortured young teenagers attracted by romantic hyper-bole Napoleon decided not to kill himself, but the essays give us a glimpse into his evolving sense of self. His essays tended to be written within the classical conventions of the day, filled with exaggerated bom-bast and rhetorical questions, and in them he began to hone the literary style that was later to characterize his proclamations and speeches.

At the age of seventeen, Napoleon's religious views started to coalesce, and they did not change much thereafter. Despite being taught by monks, he was never a true Christian, being unconvinced by the divinity of Jesus. He did believe in some kind of divine power, albeit one that seems to have had very limited interaction with the world beyond its original creation. Later he was sometimes seen to cross himself before battle,[77] and, as we shall see, he certainly also knew the social utility of religion. But in his personal beliefs he was essentially an Enlightenment sceptic. In September 1780, aged eleven, he had been given a public oral examination, during which he was asked to expound upon Christ's four major miracles and was questioned on the New Testament. He later recalled of that test: 'I was scandalised to hear that the most virtuous men of Antiquity would be burned in perpetuity because they did not follow a religion of which they had never heard.'[78] When a priest had offered his services to help him through his father's death, the fifteen-year-old Napoleon had refused. Now, in another unpublished paper, he attacked a Protestant minister from Geneva who had criti-cized Rousseau, and accused Christianity of permitting tyranny because its promises of an afterlife detracted from Man's desire to perfect this life by insisting on a government designed 'to lend assistance to the fee-ble against the strong, and by this means to allow everyone to enjoy a sweet tranquillity, the road to happiness'.[79] Only the Social Contract – that is, agreement between the people and state authority – could secure hap-piness. Alongside that 15,000-word treatise, Napoleon wrote *The Hare, the Hound and the Huntsman*, a short comic fable in verse form echo-ing La Fontaine and featuring a pointer called Caesar who is shot by a huntsman just before he is about to kill a hare. The last couplet goes:

> God helps those who help himself,
> I approve of that idea myself.[80]

Napoleon's next surviving piece of prose is only one page long. Dated Thursday, November 22, 1787 and written from the Hôtel de Cherbourg, on what is today the rue Vauvilliers off the rue Saint-Honoré in Paris, which he was visiting to pursue the *pépinière* affair, it was entitled 'A Meeting at the Palais-Royal'. The private note, written for himself, chronicles his encounter with a prostitute he picked up in that notoriously louche area of central Paris, a neighbourhood of gambling houses, restaurants and *bijouterie* shops:

> I had just come out of the Italian Opera, and was walking at a good pace along the alleys of the Palais-Royal. My spirit, stirred by the feelings of vigour which are natural to it, was indifferent to the cold, but when once my mind became chilled I felt the severity of the weather, and took refuge in the galleries. I was just entering the iron gates when my eyes became fixed on a person of the other sex. The time of night, her figure, and her youth, left me in no doubt what her occupation was. I looked at her; she stopped, not with the impudent air common to her class, but with a manner that was quite in harmony with the charm of her appearance. This struck me. Her timidity encouraged me, and I spoke to her. I spoke to her; I, who, more sensible than any to the horror of her condition, have always felt stained by even a look from such a person. But her pallor, her frail form, her soft voice, left me not a moment in suspense.[81]

He walked with her into the gardens of the Palais-Royal and asked her if there wasn't 'an occupation more suited to your health', to which she replied, 'No, sir; one must live.' 'I was charmed; I saw that she at least gave me an answer, a success which I had never met with before.' He asked her where she was from (Nantes), how she lost her virginity ('An officer ruined me'), whether she was sorry for it ('Yes, very'), how she'd got to Paris, and finally, after a further barrage of questions, whether she would go back with him to her rooms, so that 'we will warm ourselves, and you can satisfy your desire'.[82] He ends by writing: 'I had no intention of becoming over-scrupulous at this stage. I had already tempted her, so that she would not consider running away when pressed by the argument I had prepared for her, and I did not want her to start feigning an honesty that I wished to prove she did not possess.'[83] He was not originally looking for such an encounter, but the fact that he thought it worthy of chronicling suggests that this was probably the occasion on which he lost his virginity. The conversational method of quick-fire questions was pure Napoleon.

A few days later, still in Paris, he began to write a history of Corsica, which he abandoned after only a few lines. Instead he took up writing a rhetorical, declamatory essay entitled 'A Parallel between Love of Glory and Love of Country', which took the form of a letter to an unnamed young lady in which he came down strongly in favour of the former. Love of glory finds its examples in French military history – he mentions Marshals Condé and Turenne – but there is also a great deal about Sparta, Philip of Macedon, Alexander, Charlemagne, Leonidas and 'the first magistrate, the great Paoli'.[84]

In September 1786, after an absence of nearly eight years, Napoleon returned to Corsica and met his three youngest siblings for the first time. It was the first of five trips home between 1786 and 1793, some lasting many months, largely in order to deal with the various problems left by his father's estate. On April 21, 1787 he wrote to the war minister asking for five and a half months' paid leave 'for the recovery of his health'.[85] He was either a good actor or had a pliant doctor, because although he wasn't genuinely ill he enclosed the necessary medical certificates. He would not return for almost a whole year. This long absence from his regiment should be seen in the context of a peacetime army in which two-thirds of infantry officers and three-quarters of cavalry officers left their regiments in winter.[86] Joseph had by then been forced to give up any hopes of going into either the army or the Church in order to help his mother look after the family, but he did take a law degree at the University of Pisa in 1788. All the younger siblings were still at school, with Lucien showings signs of intelligence and ambition.

By late May 1788 Napoleon was stationed at the School of Artillery at Auxonne in eastern France, not far from Dijon. Here, as when he was stationed with his regiment at Valence, he ate only once a day, at 3 p.m., thereby saving enough money from his officer's salary to send some home to his mother; the rest he spent on books. He changed his clothes once every eight days. He was determined to continue his exhaustive autodidactic reading programme and his voluminous notebooks from Auxonne are full of the history, geography, religion and customs of all the most prominent peoples of the ancient world, including the Athenians, Spartans, Persians, Egyptians and Carthaginians. They cover modern artillery improvements and regimental discipline, but also mention Plato's *Republic*, Achilles and (inevitably) Alexander the Great and Julius Caesar.

The School of Artillery was commanded by General Baron Jean-Pierre du Teil, a pioneer in the latest artillery techniques. Napoleon had classes in military theory for up to nine hours a week, as well as advanced mathematics every Tuesday. Artillery was recognized as increasingly important now that advances in metallurgy meant that cannon could be just as effective at half the weight as previously; once big guns became mobile on a battlefield without losing firepower or accuracy, they could be battle-winners. Napoleon's favourites – his 'pretty girls' as he later called them – were the relatively mobile 12-pounders.[87] 'I believe every officer ought to serve in the artillery,' he was to say, 'which is the arm that can produce most of the good generals.'[88] This was not merely self-serving: French artillery commanders of his day were to include the fine generals Jean-Baptiste Éblé, Alexandre-Antoine Sénarmont, Antoine Drouot, Jean de Lariboisière, Auguste de Marmont and Charles-Étienne Ruty.

'There is nothing in the military profession I cannot do for myself,' Napoleon was to boast. 'If there is no-one to make gunpowder, I know how to make it; gun carriages, I know how to construct them; if it is founding a cannon, I know that; or if the details of tactics must be taught, I can teach them.'[89] For all this, he had the Auxonne school to thank. That August saw him in charge of two hundred men testing the feasibility of firing explosive shells from heavy cannon instead of just from mortars. His report was praised for its clarity of expression. His military memoranda from those days were terse and informative, and emphasized the importance of taking the offensive.

A few days after the successful conclusion of the shell-testing project, Napoleon wrote the first paragraph of his 'Dissertation sur l'Autorité Royale', which argued that military rule was a better system of government than tyranny and concluded, unambiguously: 'There are very few kings who would not deserve to be dethroned.'[90] His views were authoritarian but also subversive, and would have got their author into trouble if published under his name, even in the increasingly chaotic political situation in which France found herself in the months preceding the fall of the Bastille. Luckily, just as he was about to send his 'Dissertation' to a publisher, the news arrived that Étienne-Charles de Loménie de Brienne, Louis XVI's finance minister, to whom the essay was dedicated, had been dismissed. Napoleon quickly rescinded publication.

His writing mania extended to drafting the regulations for his officers' mess, which he somehow turned into a 4,500-word document full of literary orotundities such as: 'Night can hold no gloom for he who overlooks nothing that might in any way compromise his rank or his uniform. The penetrating eyes of the eagle and the hundred heads of Argus would barely suffice to fulfil the obligations and duties of his mandate.'[91] In January 1789 he wrote a Romantic melodrama, 'The Earl of Essex: An English Story', not his finest literary endeavour. 'The fingers of the Countess sank into gaping wounds,' begins one paragraph. 'Her fingers dripped with blood. She cried out, hid her face, but looking up again could see nothing. Terrified, trembling, aghast, cut to the very quick by these terrible forebodings, the Countess got into a carriage and arrived at the Tower.'[92] The story includes assassination plots, love, murder, premonitions, and the overthrow of King James II. Continuing in this melodramatic style, in March 1789 Napoleon wrote a two-page short story called 'The Mask of the Prophet', about a handsome and charismatic Arab soldier-prophet, Hakem, who has to wear a silver mask because he has been disfigured by illness. Having fallen out with the local prince, Mahadi, Hakem has his disciples dig lime-filled pits, supposedly for their enemies, but he poisons his own followers, throws their bodies into the pits and finally immolates himself.[93] It is a disturbing tale, full of violent late-teenage angst.

The next month Napoleon was sent 20 miles down the Saône river to Seurre as second-in-command of an operation to put down a riot in which a crowd had killed two grain merchants. 'Let honest men go to their homes,' the nineteen-year-old is reported to have shouted to the crowd, 'I only fire upon the mob.' Although he did his duty efficiently and impressed General du Teil, the political situation was such that before long rioters were attacking public buildings and burning down tax offices in Auxonne itself. It was from this provincial vantage point that Napoleon saw the first harbinger of the great political event that was to transform the history of France and of Europe, and his own life.

The French Revolution, which broke out on July 14, 1789 when a Parisian mob stormed the state prison, the Bastille, was preceded by years of financial crises and turmoil such as the minor uprising Napoleon had been sent to put down. The first stirrings of instability can be dated back to 1783, the last year of the American War of Independence in which France had supported the rebellious colonists against

Britain. Other protests over low wages and food shortages besides those in Seurre were put down violently in April 1789, with twenty-five deaths. 'Napoleon often said that nations had their illnesses just as individuals did, and that their history would be no less interesting to describe than the maladies of the human body,' recorded one of his ministers in later years. 'The French people were wounded in their dearest interests. The nobility and the clergy humiliated them with their pride and privileges. The people suffered under this weight for a long time, but finally wanted to shake off the yoke, and the Revolution began.'[94]

By the time the Estates-General of France was called on May 5, for the first time since 1614, it seemed that the king might be forced to share at least some of his power with the representatives of the Third Estate. But thereafter events moved swiftly and unpredictably. On June 20 the deputies of the Third Estate, who were by then calling themselves the National Assembly, took an oath not to dissolve itself until a new constitution was established. Three days later two companies of royal guards mutinied sooner than put down public unrest. The news that Louis XVI was recruiting foreign mercenaries to suppress what had by then become an insurrection led the radical journalist Camille Desmoulins to call for the storming of the Bastille, which resulted in the deaths of the governor of Paris, its mayor and the secretary of state. On August 26 the National Assembly adopted the Declaration of the Rights of Man, and on October 6 the Palace of Versailles was stormed by the mob.

For a man who was to exhibit such acute political sharpness later in his career, Napoleon completely misread the Revolution's opening stages. 'I repeat what I have said to you,' he wrote to Joseph on July 22, a week after the fall of the Bastille, 'calm will return. In a month, there will no longer be a question of anything. So, if you send me 300 livres [7,500 francs] I will go to Paris to terminate our business.'[95] At the time, Napoleon was more concerned with the *pépinière* saga than with the greatest political eruption in Europe since the Reformation. He returned to writing his history of Corsica, and summoned up the courage to write to his hero Paoli, who was still in exile in London. 'I was born when the country was perishing,' he declared with a flourish. 'Thirty thousand Frenchmen vomited onto our coasts, drowning the thrones of liberty in seas of blood, such was the odious spectacle which first met my eye. The cries of the dying, the groans of the oppressed, the tears of despair surrounded my cradle from my birth.'[96] These were extraordinary sentiments from someone who had taken an oath to serve the King of France when he was commissioned as an officer. With the advent of the Revolution, and the return of Paoli to Corsica in July 1790, Napoleon's divided loyalties could not endure much longer. He was going to have to choose.

2

Revolution

'In whatever time he had appeared he would have played a prominent part, but the epoch when he first entered on his career was particularly fitted to facilitate his elevation.'

Metternich on Napoleon

'At twenty-two many things are allowed which are no longer permitted past thirty.'

Napoleon to Elector Frederick of Württemberg

'Amid the noise of drums, arms, blood, I write you this letter,' Napoleon told Joseph from Auxonne, where rioting had broken out again eight days after the fall of the Bastille.[1] He proudly reported to his brother that General du Teil had asked his advice on the situation. Napoleon arrested thirty-three people and spent the better part of an hour exhorting the rioters to stop.

Despite hating mobs and technically being a nobleman, Napoleon welcomed the Revolution. At least in its early stages it accorded well with the Enlightenment ideals he had ingested from his reading of Rousseau and Voltaire. He embraced its anti-clericalism and did not mind the weakening of a monarchy for which he had no particular respect. Beyond that, it seemed to offer Corsica prospects of greater independence, and far better career opportunities for an ambitious young outsider without money or connections. Napoleon believed that the new social order it promised to usher in would destroy both of these disadvantages and would be built on logic and reason, which the Enlightenment *philosophes* saw as the only true foundations for authority.

The Bonapartes were in the minority among Corsica's gentry in supporting the Revolution, although not quite 'the only persons' on the island to do so, as Napoleon later claimed.[2] What does appear to be true is that he was the only artillery graduate of his year from the École Militaire to support the overthrow of Louis XVI, and one of only a handful of officers from his corps, many of whom fled France in 1789. Although Napoleon faithfully carried out his military duties, putting down food riots in Valence and Auxonne – where some men from his own regiment mutinied and joined the rioters – he was an early adherent of the local branch of the revolutionary Society of the Friends of the Constitution. Back in Ajaccio his fourteen-year-old brother Lucien, whose commitment to radical politics was much more profound and enduring, joined the extremist Jacobin Club.[3]*

On August 8, 1789, when Paris was in uproar and a large part of the French officer corps in disarray, Napoleon was once again granted sick leave to return to Corsica, where he stayed for the next eighteen months, throwing himself energetically into the island's politics. Again, there is no indication that he was genuinely ill. In his *Account of Corsica*, Boswell described how the island was politically split between its cities, its nine provinces and its many ecclesiastical *pieves* (groups of parishes which were 'as much used for civil affairs as for those of the church'). The power of the governor, based in the capital, Corte, was limited. There were traditional rivalries between towns, villages and clans, and strong attachments to the Catholic Church and to the exiled Paoli. Napoleon stepped into this maelstrom with gusto, and over the next four years would be far more concerned with Corsican politics than his career as a French officer.

As soon as he arrived in Ajaccio, Napoleon, supported by Joseph and Lucien, urged Corsicans to adhere to the revolutionary cause, fly the new tricolour flag and wear it as a cockade in their hats, form a revolutionary 'Patriots' club, and organize a regiment of Corsican Volunteers, a National Guard militia that it was hoped would one day match the governor's force. When the governor closed the club and banned the Volunteers, Napoleon's name topped the petition sent in protest to the National Assembly in Paris.[4] In October, he wrote a pamphlet denouncing the French commander in Corsica and criticizing the island's government as insufficiently revolutionary.[5] While Napoleon led the revolutionary party in Ajaccio, Antoine-Christophe Saliceti, a Corsican deputy to the National Assembly, radicalized the larger town of Bastia.

---

* In Paris the Jacobins and the slightly more moderate Girondin Club were on course to see each other as ideological enemies.

When in January 1790 the National Assembly passed a decree at Saliceti's urging making Corsica a department of France, Napoleon supported the move. Paoli denounced it from London as a measure designed to impose the will of Paris. As Saliceti and Napoleon now saw Paris as an ally in the task of revolutionizing Corsica, a major split was likely if Paoli were to return to the island. In the midst of all the politicking – Joseph was elected Ajaccio's mayor in March – Napoleon spent his nights writing his history of Corsica and re-reading Caesar's *Gallic Wars*, committing whole pages of it to memory. As his sick leave came to an end he asked for an extension. With so few officers left in the regiment, his commanding officer couldn't afford to refuse him.

Napoleon spent fifteen months reworking his Corsican history, but he was unable to find a publisher. The parts of it which survive argue that Corsicans personify all the Ancient Roman virtues but are prey to 'an inexplicable fate' that has kept them subjugated. Around this time Napoleon also wrote an exceptionally violent and vindictive short story entitled 'New Corsica', which began as a tale of adventure but then turned into a political rant and ended as a bloodbath. In it, an Englishman meets an old man who relates the atrocities that took place in Corsica after the French invasion of 1768. 'I left my men to fly to the help of my unfortunate father whom I found drowning in his own blood,' he says. 'He had only the strength to tell me: "My son, avenge me. It is the first law of nature. Die like me if you have to, but never recognize the French as your masters."' The old man relates how he found the naked corpse of his raped mother, 'covered in wounds and in the most obscene posture', and reports: 'My wife and three of my brothers had been hung in the same place. Seven of my sons, of whom three were under the age of five, had met the same fate. Our cabin had been burnt; the blood of our goats was mixed with that of my family,' and so on.[6] 'Since that time,' the old man says, 'I have sworn anew on my altar, never to spare another Frenchman.'[7] This disturbing tale, written when Napoleon was twenty years old and a serving army officer, is a Francophobic revenge fantasy. The retribution the old man wreaks is cataclysmic; he kills everyone on board a French ship, up to and including the cabin boy, and then: 'We dragged their bodies to our altar, and there burned them all. This new incense seemed to please the Deity.'[8] When the Revolution began, Napoleon clearly was not immune to the lure of violence.

On June 24, 1790 Napoleon sent his history of Corsica to the Abbé Raynal, an influential Enlightenment thinker whose *Histoire philosophique et politique des établissements et du commerce des Euro-péens dans les deux Indes*, first published anonymously in 1770 and subsequently banned in France, had been a popular success and, despite its length, an influential polemic. The abbé had been forced into exile for several years but he was invited to return in 1787. In his covering letter – dated 'Year 1 of Liberty' – Napoleon wrote: 'Nations slaughter each other for family quarrels, cutting each other's throats in the name of the Ruler of the Universe, knavish and greedy priests working on their imagination by means of their love of the marvellous and their fears.'[9] Equally melodramatically, he told Raynal: 'I eagerly accepted a labour which flattered my love for my country, then abased, unhappy, enslaved.' He added, mimicking Boswell's and Rousseau's hagiography of Corsica's glories: 'I see with pleasure my country, to the shame of the Universe, serve as an asylum for the last remains of Roman liberty, and the heirs of Cato.'[10] The idea that the squabbling Corsicans were the true heirs of Marcus Porcius Cato, paladin of Roman liberty, was more an indication of Napoleon's romantic obsession with the classical world than a useful historical insight. He also sent his manuscript to his old Brienne tutor, Père Dupuy, who suggested a complete rewriting – advice to which few authors take kindly.

On July 12, 1790, the National Assembly passed the Civil Constitution of the Clergy, providing for government control over the Church and abolishing the monastic orders. The demand for priests to take the Constitutional Oath of loyalty to the state split the First Estate between juring (that is, oath-taking) and non-juring priests, and was denounced by Pope Pius VI the following March. Hostility to Christianity in general, and to the Roman Catholic Church in particular, animated many of the revolutionaries. By November 1793, Notre-Dame Cathedral had been re-dedicated to the Cult of Reason, and six months later the Jacobin leader Maximilien Robespierre passed a decree establishing the pantheist Cult of the Supreme Being. As well as tens of thousands of aristocrats being stripped of their possessions and forced into exile to become émigrés abroad, several thousand priests left the country too.

Napoleon supported the Civil Constitution of the Clergy in a pamphlet that was sufficiently inflammatory for him and Joseph only narrowly to avoid a lynching when they happened to walk near a religious procession in Ajaccio soon after its publication. (They were saved by a bandit named Trenta Coste, who was duly rewarded when Napoleon became First Consul.)[11] July 1790 saw the sixty-five-year-old Paoli's return to Corsica after twenty-two years in exile. Napoleon and Joseph were on Ajaccio's reception committee to welcome him. He was immediately and unanimously appointed Lieutenant of Corsica and elected to the presidencies of Corsica's assembly and its recently constituted National Guard.

Paoli saw the Bonaparte boys as the children of a collaborator, and made minimal effort to retain their loyalty, despite Napoleon's patent eagerness for his approbation. One of his first acts was to move the capital from Corte to Bastia, to the irritation of Ajaccio's inhabitants, such as the Bonapartes. According to local legend, Paoli was infuriated by Napoleon's criticism of his troop dispositions when they toured the battlefield of Ponte Nuovo together (though Joseph's memoirs suggest that Napoleon confined his critical remarks to his brother alone).[12] Paoli had been a revered figure in progressive circles in Europe in the later decades of the Enlightenment; the Bonapartes would go to great lengths to accommodate him.

Joseph was elected as one of Ajaccio's deputies to the Corsican assembly on September 15, and later became president of the city's executive government, known as the Directory, but Napoleon failed to be elected either as a deputy or to a senior position in the National Guard. 'This city is full of bad citizens,' he wrote to Charles-André Pozzo di Borgo, a member of the island's government. 'You've no idea of their craziness and meanness.' He proposed that three members of the town council be removed from office. 'This measure is violent, possibly illegal, but essential,' he wrote, ending with a quotation from Montesquieu: 'Laws are like the statues of certain divinities which on some occasions must be veiled.'[13] In this instance, he didn't get his way.

The following month the National Assembly, now effectively the sovereign parliament of France, passed a motion proposed by the Comte de Mirabeau that although Corsica was now a part of France and would be subject to its laws, she would henceforth be governed solely by Corsicans. Huge celebrations greeted the news across the island, *Te Deums* were sung in every church and Napoleon hung a huge banner from the Casa Bonaparte which read: 'Vive la Nation, Vive Paoli, Vive Mirabeau'.[14] To Raynal he trumpeted, with characteristic (if on this occasion pardonable) hyperbole, 'The sea no longer separates us.'[15] Yet Paoli had no place for Napoleon in his new political order. As the Paolists started to fall out with the Paris government, the Bonapartes stayed loyal to the National Assembly – and after September 1792 its successor, the Convention. Their split from the Paolists was gradual, and involved both accelerations and reverses, but by spring 1793 it was complete.

On January 6, 1791 Napoleon was present at the inauguration of the Globo Patriottico, a revolutionary club in Ajaccio that aped the political clubs that the Jacobins and the more moderate Girondins were establishing in Paris. Later that month he published a political pamphlet, 'Letter to M. Buttafuoco', which accused the man who had been appointed to rule the island twenty-three years earlier of being a traitor and supporter of 'the absurd feudal regime'; it accused Paoli of being tricked by Buttafuoco and of being 'surrounded by enthusiasts', a reference to the returned exiles who tended to want a British-style constitution for Corsica, while Napoleon favoured the French revolutionary one. Paoli, who was working well with Buttafuoco at the time, responded aggressively to Napoleon's pamphlet, refusing his offer of the dedication of his history of Corsica. 'History should not be written in youth,' he said, it requires 'maturity and balance'.[16] He added that he couldn't return the manuscript, because he had no time to look for it, and turned down Napoleon's request for documents. Any hopes Napoleon might have had of becoming a successful author were once again stymied, this time by the man he had spent his youth idolizing. When, later on, there were rumours – probably politically inspired, but quite possibly true – that Joseph had pilfered Ajaccio's coffers, Paoli offered no support.[17]

Although his leave had officially ended on October 15, 1790, Napoleon left Corsica for his regiment only on February 1 the following year, taking with him his twelve-year-old brother Louis, whose schooling at Auxonne he was going to pay for. He produced certificates for ill-health and even for the bad weather to his ever-patient commanding officer, who obligingly gave him three months' back-pay. Louis nonetheless had to sleep on the floor in a closet next to Napoleon's bed, with a single table and two chairs as their only furniture. 'Do you know how I managed?' Napoleon later recalled of this period of his life. 'By never entering a café or going into society; by eating dry bread, and brushing my own clothes so that they might last the longer. I lived like a bear, in a little room, with books for my only friends . . . These were the joys and debaucheries of my youth.'[18] He might have been exaggerating slightly, but not much. There was nothing he valued so much as books and a good education.

Between February and August 1791 Napoleon worked on a discourse for the Lyons Academy's essay prize, on the subject: 'What are the Most Important Truths and Feelings for Men to Learn to be Happy?' The Academy and Abbé Raynal offered 1,200 francs – more than Napoleon's annual salary – for the best submission. Napoleon took six months to write his essay. In it he denounced the vanity of ambition, even criticizing Alexander the Great for hubris: 'What is Alexander doing when he rushes from Thebes into Persia and thence into India? He is ever restless, he loses his wits, he believes himself God. What is the end of Cromwell? He governs England. But is he not tormented by all the daggers of the Furies?'[19] He also wrote, surely autobiographically: 'You return to your homeland after an absence of four years: you wander round the sites, the places where you played in those first tender years ... You feel all the fire of love for the homeland.'[20]

Napoleon would later claim that he had withdrawn the essay before it was judged, but that is not in fact true. The Academy's examiners gave it low marks for its excessively inflated style. One judge described it as 'of too little interest, too ill-ordered, too disparate, too rambling, and too badly written to hold the reader's attention'.[21] Years later, Talleyrand obtained the original from the Academy's archives and presented it to Napoleon, who when he had re-read it said: 'I found its author deserved to be whipped. What ridiculous things I said, and how annoyed I would be if they were preserved!'[22] Instead he 'flung it into the fire, and pushed it down with the tongs', fearing that 'It might have exposed me to ridicule.'[23] Although he had comprehensively failed to win the prize, that he even entered a French language essay competition showed considerable confidence.

This formal production was only part of this twenty-two-year-old's literary fecundity. He wrote a 'Dialogue sur l'Amour', in which the figure representing himself is called 'B' and a real-life friend and comrade from the garrison, Alexandre de Mazis, appears under his own name. How close a friend Mazis was might be questioned, since he's depicted as boastful and impatient, compared to the serene, masterful 'B'. The 'Dialogue' argues that love is an incubus both to society and to individual happiness, and that Providence should abolish it in order to make everyone happier. Another composition, 'Reflections on the State of Nature', argued that mankind had lived better before society existed, a concept lifted wholesale from Rousseau.

In June 1791 Napoleon was promoted to lieutenant and transferred to the 4th Regiment of Artillery back at Valence. In the sixty-nine months he'd been with the La Fère Regiment, he had spent no fewer than thirty-five on leave, and he had no intention of changing this pattern now. 'Send me three hundred francs,' he wrote to his uncle Joseph Fesch on arriving; 'that sum will enable me to go to Paris. There, at least, one can cut a figure and surmount obstacles. Everything tells me I shall succeed. Will you prevent me from doing so for the want of 100 crowns?'[24] The urgency and ambition are unmistakable, but either Fesch demurred or Napoleon in the meantime learned that four battalions of National Guards were going to be raised on Corsica, because he then asked for leave to go there instead. His new commanding officer, Colonel Compagnon, understandably refused permission on the grounds that he had been with the regiment for only two months.

In the closing days of June 1791, the royal family attempted to escape from France and were captured in their carriage at Varennes. They were forced to return to near-imprisonment at the Tuileries Palace. On July 10, Emperor Leopold II of Austria issued a request to all the other royal houses of Europe to come to the aid of his brother-in-law Louis XVI. By then Napoleon had become secretary of the Valence branch of the Society of Friends of the Constitution, and at a celebratory banquet on the second anniversary of the fall of the Bastille he proposed a toast 'To the patriots of Auxonne', who were petitioning for the King to be put on trial. 'This country is full of zeal and fire,' he wrote to a friend, adding that although the Revolution could count on only half his regiment's officers, all the lower ranks supported it.[25] 'The southern blood runs through my veins with the rapidity of the Rhône,' he added in a postscript; 'you must therefore pardon me if you experience some difficulty in reading my scrawl.'

Refusing to take his commanding officer's no for an answer, on August 30 Napoleon appealed to General du Teil, who afterwards told his daughter: 'That is a man of great ability; his name will be heard of.'[26] He was given four months' leave to go to Corsica with the understanding that if he were not back with the colours by the time of the regimental parade on January 10, 1792 he would be considered a deserter.

Napoleon found Corsica in turmoil. There had been 130 murders since the Revolution began and no taxes had been collected. His family's money worries, which had taken up so much of his time and effort since his father's death six years earlier, abated somewhat on October 15, 1791 with the death of his great-uncle, Archdeacon Luciano Bonaparte, who left the Bonaparte family his fortune. This money certainly came in useful when, on February 22, 1792, Napoleon stood for election as adjutant, with the rank of lieutenant-colonel, in the 2nd Battalion of the Corsican National Guard. There was a good deal of bribery involved, and one of the three election observers was even kidnapped on the day of the polls and detained in the Casa Bonaparte until the election was safely won. Napoleon's chief opponent, the influential Corsican politician Charles-André Pozzo di Borgo's brother Matteo, was shouted down from the hustings outside the church of San Francesco by Napoleon's armed supporters. Corsican politics was always tough, but these tactics were a serious infringement of accepted practices and Paoli, who supported Matteo Pozzo di Borgo, demanded an official inquiry into what he called 'corruption and intrigue'. He was blocked by Saliceti, who represented the Paris Convention on the island, so the result stood. The January deadline for Napoleon's return to his regiment had meanwhile come and gone. A note in his war ministry file stated simply: 'Has given up his profession and has been replaced on February 6 1792.'[27]

Severe food riots in Paris between January and March 1792 sharpened the political crisis. Then in early February an alliance was announced between Austria and Prussia whose unavowed but hardly secret intention was to topple the revolutionary government in France and restore the monarchy. Although Britain was not part of this first coalition, her hostility to the Revolution was also clear. With war in the air, the revolution in Corsica took a radical turn. On February 28 Saliceti ordered the suppression of the ancient convents and monasteries of Ajaccio, Bastia, Bonifacio and Corte, with the proceeds going into the central government's coffers. Paoli and the vast majority of Corsicans opposed this, and on Easter Sunday fighting broke out in Ajaccio between Napoleon's National Guardsmen and local Catholic citizens who wanted to protect the monastery: one of Napoleon's lieutenants was shot dead at his side. At one point in the four days and nights of confused urban brawling and ill-tempered standoffs between the townspeople and the National Guard, Napoleon tried, unsuccessfully, to capture the town's well-fortified citadel from the French regular troops under the command of Colonel Maillard, who wrote a damning report to the war ministry effectively accusing him of treason. The roads to Ajaccio were filled with peasants carrying empty sacks, eagerly anticipating the pillaging of the town.

Paoli took Maillard's side, ordering Napoleon to leave Ajaccio and report to him at Corte, which he did. Fortunately for Napoleon,

Maillard's report of the messy affair was buried under a mountain of far more pressing war ministry paperwork. France had pre-emptively declared war on Austria and Prussia on April 20 and invaded the Austrian Netherlands (present-day Belgium) eight days later to forestall an expected invasion of France from the north-west, the Austrian and Prussian armies being headquartered in Koblenz. After the Ajaccio imbroglio Napoleon couldn't stay in Corsica, but neither could he return to Valence, where he was officially a deserter. So he left for Paris.

When Napoleon reached the war ministry in the Place Vendôme in Paris he found it in turmoil: the new revolutionary government would go through six war ministers between May and October 1792. It was clear that no-one had had a chance to read Maillard's report, or much cared about what had happened in a provincial backwater like Ajaccio, and no-one seemed to mind that Napoleon's leave had officially expired in January, before his election to the Corsican National Guard. In July 1792 Napoleon was promoted to captain, ante-dated by a year with full pay, but without being assigned a new post. His cheeky demand that he be promoted to lieutenant-colonel in the regular army, on the ground that he was one in the Guard, was marked 'SR' (*sans réponse*) by the ministry.[28]

Napoleon was unimpressed by what he found in Paris. 'The men at the head of the Revolution are a poor lot,' he wrote to Joseph. 'Everyone pursues his own interest, and searches to gain his own ends by dint of all sorts of crimes; people intrigue as basely as ever. All this destroys ambition. One pities those who have the misfortune to play a part in public affairs.'[29] If the part of the honest soldier, detached from the muddy business of politics, sat poorly with the reality of the revolutionary intriguer of Ajaccio, it was nonetheless one that he played well, and strategically. By this time he was a fully-fledged revolutionary, as his support for the overthrow of the monarchy and the nationalization of Corsica's monasteries attested. Politically he veered towards the Jacobin extremists, who moreover seemed to be on the winning side. Although he wasn't personally involved in any of the acts of repression already taking place in Paris as the Revolution moved towards its climax, there is no evidence that he disapproved of them.

Napoleon was in Paris on June 20, 1792 when the mob invaded the Tuileries, captured Louis XVI and Marie Antoinette, and forced the king to wear a red cap of liberty on the palace balcony. Bourrienne had met him at a restaurant on the rue Saint-Honoré, and when they saw a heavily armed crowd marching towards the palace, he claims that Napoleon said, 'Let's follow the rabble.' Taking their place on the riverside terrace, they then watched with (presumably well-disguised) 'surprise and indignation' the historic scenes that followed.[30] Two days later Napoleon described them to Joseph:

> Between seven and eight thousand men armed with pikes, axes, swords, guns, spits, sharpened sticks ... went to the king. The Tuileries gardens were closed and 15,000 National Guards were on guard there. They broke down the gates, entered the palace, pointed the cannon at the king's apartment, threw four doors to the ground, and presented the king with two cockades, one white [the Bourbon colour] and the other tricolour. They made him choose. Choose, they said, whether you reign here or in Coblenz. The king presented himself. He put on a red bonnet. So did the queen and the royal prince. They gave the king a drink. They stayed in the palace for four hours ... All this is unconstitutional and sets a dangerous precedent. It is hard to predict what will happen to the empire in such stormy circumstances.[31]

Bourrienne later reported that Napoleon remarked: 'What madness! How could they allow that rabble to enter? Why do they not sweep away four or five hundred of them with cannon? Then the rest would take themselves off very quickly.' The humiliation of the royal family on that occasion further lowered the monarchy in Napoleon's estimation. He supported the toppling of the king but could not understand why Louis XVI had meekly allowed himself to be humiliated. As it was, the royal couple had less than two months of this hazardous liberty left to them.

Austria and Prussia invaded France ten days later, inviting the well-justified supposition that Louis XVI and his Austrian wife sympathized with the invasion, and were collaborating with France's enemies who now publicly stated their wish to restore them to full authority. Napoleon's contempt for the pusillanimity of the Bourbons was again made clear on August 10, when the mob returned to arrest the king and queen and massacred their Swiss Guards. He had left his hotel in the rue de Mail and gone to watch events from a friend's house on the Place du Carrousel. Seeing the well-dressed young officer on his way there, members of the crowd ordered Napoleon to shout 'Vive la Nation!', which, as he reminisced decades later, 'as you can imagine, I hastened to do!'[32] His friend's house was stuffed with the property of aristocrats who had been forced to sell their belongings at a heavy discount before fleeing

France. '*Che coglione!*' ('What asses!') he exclaimed in Italian when, from an upstairs window, he saw the Swiss Guards refrain from firing on the mob, at what turned out to be the cost of their lives.[33] When he himself moved into the Tuileries seven years later he had the bullet holes from that day effaced from the building.

Napoleon was still in Paris in early September when more than 1,200 people, including 115 priests, were murdered by the mob in the city's prisons in cold blood. Verdun had fallen to the Duke of Brunswick's invading Prussian army on September 3, after which four days of wanton killing of suspected collaborators began. Napoleon later attempted to defend what had happened, saying: 'I think the massacres of September may have produced a powerful effect on the men of the invading army. In one moment they saw a whole population rising up against them.'[34] He claimed that those who had carried them out 'were almost all soldiers, who ... were resolved to leave no enemies behind them'. Of the senior Jacobin revolutionaries he said: 'Whatever people say of them they are not despicable characters. Few men have made their mark on the world as they have done.'[35] Napoleon didn't deny his own Jacobin past when he ruled France, saying, 'At one time every man of spirit was bound to be one', and he gave two of Robespierre's female relatives annual pensions of 7,200 francs and 1,800 francs respectively.[36] He had assessed the situation at first hand and, like his father, aligned himself with what looked like the winning side.

On September 21, 1792 France formally declared itself a Republic and the Assembly announced that Louis XVI would be tried for collaboration with the enemy and crimes against the French people. The day before, the Revolution was saved when Generals François Kellermann and Charles Dumouriez defeated Brunswick's Prussian army at the battle of Valmy in the Champagne-Ardenne region, proving that the citizen army of France could defeat the regular armies of the counter-revolutionary Powers.

By mid-October Napoleon was back in Ajaccio promoting the Jacobin cause, returning to his lieutenant-colonelcy of the Corsican National Guard rather than taking up the captaincy of the 4th Regiment of Artillery in France's regular army. He found the island far more anti-French than it had been when he left, especially after the September Massacres and the declaration of the Republic. Yet he remained, as he put it, 'persuaded that the best thing Corsica could do was to become a province of France'.[37] He moved from being a Corsican nationalist to a French revolutionary not because he finally got over being bullied at school, or because of anything to do with his father, let alone for any of the weird psycho-sexual reasons that have been advanced by historians and biographers in recent years, but simply because the politics of France and of Corsica had profoundly changed and so too had his place within them. Paoli, who preferred alliances with the grander and more politically influential Buttafuoco and Pozzo di Borgo clans than with the Bonapartes, opposed the Republic, the suppression of the monasteries and much of the rest of the revolutionary agenda that the Bonapartes supported. Paoli refused to take Lucien on to his staff, and even tried to prevent Napoleon from returning to his post in the National Guard. It was impossible for Napoleon to remain a Corsican patriot when the man who personified Corsican nationalism rejected him and his family so comprehensively.

In the intricate, intensely personal and fast-moving clan politics of Corsica, the Bonapartes were losing out to the Paolists. Through his reading, education, time in Paris and immersion in French culture, Napoleon had been imbued with French ideas even while he was still a zealous Corsican nationalist. He could see how provincial Corsica's concerns were compared to the universal ideals thrown up by the Revolution, which was threatened by a full-scale invasion from Austria and Prussia. Over the coming months, Napoleon began to think of himself more and more as French, and less and less as Corsican. When, years later, a mayor attempted to compliment him by saying, 'It is surprising, Sire, that though you are not a Frenchman, you love France so well, and have done so much for her,' Napoleon said, 'I felt as if he had struck me a blow! I turned my back on him.'[38]

The alienation between the Bonapartes and the Paolists was accelerated by the decapitation of Louis XVI on January 21, 1793 and the creation of the Committee of Public Safety in Paris. A witness who was present when Napoleon heard the news of Louis' death recalled his privately saying, 'Oh! The wretches! The poor wretches! They will go through anarchy.'[39] Napoleon thought of the king's execution – followed in October by that of Marie Antoinette – as a tactical error. 'Had the French been more moderate and not put Louis to death,' he later opined, 'all Europe would have been revolutionized: the war saved England.'[40] Yet at the time he publicly supported what had been done, and started his letters with the republican address 'Citizen'.[41] On February 1 France declared war on Britain and Holland, shortly after Spain, Portugal and the Kingdom of Piedmont in Italy had declared war on France. Ignoring the verdict of Valmy, the European monarchies were coming together to punish the regicide Republic. In March 1793 the Convention set up the Committee of Public Safety, which by July had become the *de facto* executive government of France. Prominent among its members were the leading Jacobins Robespierre and Louis Saint-Just. On August 23 the French Republic declared a *levée en masse* (mass conscription) in which all able-bodied men between the ages of eighteen and twenty-five were called up to defend the Revolution and *la patrie*, more than doubling the size of the French army from 645,000 to 1.5 million, and uniting the whole nation behind its fortunes.

Although it is likely that war would have broken out eventually anyway, the declaration of war against Britain by the revolutionary regime was a profound mistake; the Tory government of William Pitt the Younger (who had come to power in 1783 at the astonishingly young age of twenty-four) was by then viscerally opposed to regicidal France.* Taking advantage of its insular geography, Britain was to become by far the most consistent of all the opponents of revolutionary and Napoleonic France, with which it was henceforth at peace for only fourteen months of the next twenty-three years. 'Depend upon it,' Pitt was to tell the political philosopher Edmund Burke, whose book *Reflections on the Revolution in France* had as early as 1790 predicted the Reign of Terror and the rise of a dictator, 'we shall go on as we are till the Day of Judgement.'[42] Britain saw an opportunity to use her maritime power to sweep French trade from the world's oceans, neutralize or capture French colonies and cement her position as the world's greatest commercial power after her humiliation in America only a decade earlier. For Pitt and his followers, unyielding opposition to the French Revolution, and later to Napoleonic France, was not only a moral and ideological imperative, it also made perfect geo-political sense in affording Britain the opportunity to replace France as the world's hegemon. To that end, the Pittites in London funded a series of military coalitions against France – numbering no fewer than seven in all – through massive direct government-to-government cash subsidies, what Napoleon would call 'Pitt's gold'.[43]

The month after Louis XVI's execution, Napoleon obtained his first significant command. He was put in charge of the artillery section of an

---

* His father, William Pitt the Elder (1708–78), had been the prime minister who led Britain to victory over France in the Seven Years War.

expedition to 'liberate' three small Sardinian islands from the Kingdom of Piedmont-Sardinia under Paoli's nephew, Pier di Cesari Rocca, whom he privately derided as a 'clothes-horse'.[44] On February 18 he embarked with his Corsican National Guardsmen on the twenty-two-gun corvette *La Fauvette*, part of a small fleet commanded by Admiral Laurent de Truguet, which sailed from Bonifacio. By nightfall on the 23rd, the island of San Stefano had been occupied. It was separated from the other two islands, La Maddelana and Caprera, by only 800 yards. Napoleon placed his cannon so they could fire upon the other islands, and they did so the next day. On board the *Fauvette*, however, the Provençal peasant conscripts who made up the largest part of Rocca's force had noticed that the well-armed and warlike Sardinians thronging the shores showed little sign of wanting to be liberated. They mutinied, and so the entire expedition was aborted by Rocca. A furious Napoleon was forced to spike his own cannon and throw his mortars into the sea.

The first time Napoleon saw military action was therefore an humiliation, but had Paoli furnished the 10,000 men that the Paris Convention had requested for the expedition, rather than only 1,800, it might have succeeded. Napoleon complained to Paoli that his troops had been 'absolutely denuded of all which was necessary for a campaign; they marched without tents, without uniforms, without cloaks and with no artillery train.' He added that it was only 'the hope of success' that had sustained them.[45] It was an inauspicious start for the career of the new Caesar, but it taught him the importance of morale, logistics and leadership more powerfully than any number of academic lectures.

Over the next four months, as Paoli's government grew closer to the British – who were to occupy Corsica with his blessing on July 23, 1794 – and further from the French, Napoleon tried to straddle his two loyalties as long as he could, even when, after one spat, Paoli called Lucien a 'serpent'. With rebels in the deeply Catholic Vendée region of western France – known as Chouans – rising up in support for the Bourbons against the atheist Revolution after the king's execution, government commissioners crisscrossing France to ensure ideological purity – reportedly bringing a portable guillotine with them* – and Paoli fortifying the Ajaccio citadel, Napoleon's options were narrowing.

---

* The first guillotining was of a highwayman in April 1792, but thereafter it quickly came into general practice for political as well as civil executions.

As late as April 18 he wrote a pamphlet entitled 'Address to the Convention' that defended Paoli, but that same month he also composed a 'Petition to the Municipality of Ajaccio' urging the town to take an oath of allegiance to the Republic. When Saliceti had ordered Paoli's arrest for treason an urgent decision was needed. The island rose in revolt for their 'Babbù', Paoli, and burnt Saliceti in effigy, hacking down 'trees of liberty' that had been planted by the republicans. Only Bastia, San Fiorenzo and Calvi, with their French military garrisons, held out for the Republic.

In April 1793, once it became clear that Robespierre's Jacobins had triumphed politically in the Convention, General Dumouriez, the co-victor of Valmy and a Girondin, defected to the Austro-Prussian Coalition. Dumouriez's treachery and other crises led Robespierre to order the wholesale arrest of Girondins, twenty-two of whose heads were cut off in the space of thirty-six minutes on October 31. The Reign of Terror had begun.

Napoleon tried to join Joseph at Bastia on May 3 but was detained by Paolist *montagnards* (mountain men). He was freed soon afterwards by villagers from Bocognano, where the family had had an estate, and allowed to continue on his way. On May 23 the Casa Bonaparte in Ajaccio was ransacked by a Paolist mob, though not burned down as some accounts have suggested (and probably not too badly treated, as the labourers' bill for refurbishing it four years later came to only 131 francs).[46] Corsica's Paoli-dominated parliament now formally outlawed the Bonapartes, though not their thirty cousins on the island. It couldn't resist resurrecting the slur against Letizia, saying the family had been 'born in the mud of despotism, nourished and raised under the eyes and at the expense of a lascivious pasha, the late Marbeuf, of perpetual infamy'.[47]

On May 31 Napoleon and Saliceti, who as commissioner for Corsica represented the Jacobin government in Paris, took part in a failed attempt to recapture Ajaccio. The next day Napoleon wrote a paper, 'Memoir on the Political and Military Position of the Department of Corsica', in which he finally denounced Paoli for having 'hatred and vengeance in his heart'.[48] It was his farewell note to his homeland. On June 11, 1793 the Bonapartes left Calvi on board the *Prosélyte*, landing at Toulon two days later and bringing to an end nearly two and three-quarter centuries of residency on the island.[49] With the collapse of Jacobin power on Corsica, Saliceti was forced to flee to Provence too, and by the end of the month Paoli had recognized Britain's King George III as king of Corsica.*

Napoleon never entirely severed relations with the land of his birth, although he would set foot there only once again, for a few days on his way back from Egypt in 1799. When he ordered the recapture of the island in October 1796, he granted a general amnesty from which he excluded only the most senior Paolists, who had anyhow all gone into exile.[50] In later life he spoke 'with the greatest respect of Paoli', who died in exile in London in 1807, but as he stepped ashore in Provence on June 13, 1793 he knew it was in France that he would have to build his future.[51]

The Bonapartes arrived in Toulon as political refugees with little more than Letizia's life-savings and Napoleon's modest salary as a captain in the 1st Regiment of Artillery to pay for the fatherless family of nine. Otherwise, Napoleon had nothing except his education and his ambition to sustain them. He installed his family at La Valette, a village outside Toulon, and joined his regiment at Nice, armed with yet another certificate explaining his absence, this one signed by Saliceti. Fortunately Colonel Compagnon needed every officer he could get after the king's execution and the mass exodus of aristocrats; only fourteen officers out of eighty in his unit were still serving the Republic.

Napoleon received a commission from General Jean du Teil, the younger brother of his Auxonne commandant, to organize gunpowder convoys to one of France's revolutionary armies, the Army of Italy. In mid-July he was transferred to the Army of the South under General Jean-François Carteaux, a former professional painter who was about to besiege the *fédérés* (anti-Jacobin rebels) in Avignon, which contained an important ammunition depot. Although Napoleon wasn't present at Avignon's capture on July 25, the success there formed the backdrop for what was easily his most important piece of writing to date, the political pamphlet *Le Souper de Beaucaire*. Since January 1792 all his writing had a military or political bent. His purple-prosed rhetoric, which once sounded so false in the context of his own adolescent fantasies, took on a more genuine grandeur when applied to the great events of which he

---

* George III, King of England between 1760 and 1820 and thus for the whole of the Revolutionary and Napoleonic Wars, slipped periodically in and out of lunacy during this period. In 1811 a Regency was formed in which his son the Prince Regent, later King George IV, effectively reigned in his place.

was about to become a prime actor. He stopped taking notes on literary works after 1792, and instead wrote a description of the Easter Sunday incident in Ajaccio, a defence of his actions in the Sardinian expedition and a project for capturing Corsica from the British.

Le Souper de Beaucaire was a fictional account of a supper at an inn at Beaucaire, a village between Avignon and Arles, which Napoleon wrote at the end of July 1793. It took the form of a discussion between an officer in Carteaux's army, two Marseillais merchants and two citizens of Montpellier and of nearby Nîmes. It argued that France was in grave danger, so the Jacobin government in Paris must be supported because the alternative was the victory of European despots and a vengeful French aristocracy. The Napoleon character made some highly optimistic claims for his commander – 'Today there are six thousand men, and before four days are out there will be ten thousand' – claiming that in all the fighting Carteaux has only lost five men killed, and four wounded. Equally, he made dire predictions for the opposing *fédérés* based in Marseilles. Napoleon couldn't resist a self-referential attack on Paoli, saying: 'He plundered and confiscated the belongings of the most well-to-do families because they supported the unity of the Republic, and he declared enemies of the fatherland all those who stayed in our armies.'[52]

The pamphlet showed Napoleon to be a true Jacobin, sarcastically saying of the *fédérés*: 'Every well-known aristocrat is anxious for your success.' The other diners speak only six times, mainly to introduce the soldier's Jacobin rejoinders. Eventually everyone is convinced by the soldier's eloquence and much champagne is drunk until 2 a.m., which 'dissipated all worries and cares'. When Napoleon showed the manuscript to Saliceti, who was now a government commissioner in Provence, and Robespierre's younger brother Augustin, they arranged for it to be published at public expense. It established him as a politically trustworthy soldier in the eyes of the Jacobins.

On August 24 Carteaux retook Marseilles amid mass executions. Four days later Admiral Alexander Hood with 15,000 British, Spanish and Neapolitan troops entered the port of Toulon, France's major naval base on the Mediterranean, at the invitation of the *fédérés* who had risen up there the previous month. With Lyons rising for the royalists too, the Vendée in uproar and Spanish and Piedmontese armies operating inside southern France, while Prussian and Austrian armies were on her eastern borders, recapturing Toulon was of crucial strategic importance. Napoleon was appointed *chef de bataillon* (major) in the

2nd Regiment of Artillery on September 7, and the following week, perhaps at the behest of the Corsican-born Colonel Jean-Baptiste Cervoni, he presented himself at Carteaux's headquarters at Ollioules, just north-west of Toulon.[53]

It so happened that one of Carteaux's *représentants-en-mission* (political commissioners) was none other than Saliceti. Carteaux knew little about artillery and was looking for someone to take over the artillery on the army's right flank after the wounding of its commander, Colonel Dommartin, and in the absence of Dommartin's second-in-command, Major Perrier. Saliceti and his colleague Thomas de Gasparin persuaded Carteaux to appoint Napoleon to the post, despite his only being twenty-four years old. Napoleon suspected that his education at the École Militaire had been a deciding factor in getting him this first major break. He would later say that the artillery was short of 'scientific men, that department was entirely directed by sergeants and corporals. I understood the service.'[54] His youth was overlooked in an army so depleted by mass emigration and the guillotining of the aristocracy, which had previously provided the overwhelming majority of its officers. It also helped, of course, that Carteaux's appointments were overseen by his ally Saliceti.

Carteaux – who Saliceti and Gasparin were privately reporting back to Paris was 'incapable' – had 8,000 men on the hills between Toulon and Ollioules, and another 3,000 under General Jean Lapoype on the La Valette side of the city. Yet he had no plan of attack. By October 9 Saliceti and Gasparin had obtained for Napoleon command of all of the artillery outside Toulon. Since this was clearly going to be an artillery-led operation, the post gave him a central role.* Saliceti and Gasparin were soon reporting to Paris that 'Bonna Parte' was 'the only officer of artillery who knows anything of his duty, and he has too much work'.[55] They were wrong about the second part: for Napoleon there was no such thing as too much work. Later in the three-month siege he was helped by two aides-de-camp, Auguste de Marmont and Andoche Junot. Marmont came from a good family and Napoleon liked him very much, but he loved Junot, a former battalion quartermaster on the Côte d'Or, from the moment that a cannonball landed near them while he

---

* Gasparin's support was remembered by Napoleon on his deathbed. He bequeathed 100,000 francs to his descendants in his will, explaining: 'With his protection, Gasparin shielded me from the persecution of the ignorant general staff commanding the army before the arrival of my friend Dugommier' (ed. Jonge, *Napoleon's Last Will and Testament* p. 78).

was dictating a letter, spraying dust and gravel over them both, and Junot coolly remarked that now he wouldn't need any sand to blot it.[56]

Visiting the site of Napoleon's batteries above Toulon today, it is immediately obvious what he had to do. There is an outer harbour and an inner harbour, and a high promontory to the west called L'Eguillette that dominates both. 'To become master of the harbour,' Napoleon reported to the war minister, Jean-Baptiste Bouchotte, 'one must become master of the Eguillette.'[57] In order to pour heated cannonballs onto the Royal Navy vessels in the inner harbour, it was therefore necessary to capture Fort Mulgrave – built by its commander the 1st Earl of Mulgrave and nicknamed 'Little Gibraltar' because it was so heavily fortified – which dominated the promontory.* Although the fort's importance was obvious to all, it was Napoleon who put in place the plan to capture it. Success would almost instantly unlock the strategic situation, for once the Royal Navy was ejected from the harbour, the city of 28,000 people couldn't be defended by the *fédérés* alone.

Napoleon threw himself into the project of capturing Fort Mulgrave. By cajoling nearby towns he got together fourteen cannon and four mortars as well as stores, tools and ammunition. He sent officers further afield, to Lyons, Briançon and Grenoble, and requested that the Army of Italy furnish him with the cannon not then being used to defend Antibes and Monaco. He established an eighty-man arsenal at Ollioules to make cannon and cannonballs, requisitioned horses from Nice, Valence and Montpellier, and injected a sense of unceasing activity into his men. Constantly imploring, complaining and raging – there wasn't enough gunpowder, the cartridges were the wrong size, trained artillery horses were being requisitioned for other uses, and so on – he sent scores of letters with demands to Bouchotte and even on occasion to the Committee of Public Safety itself, going over the heads of Carteaux and his immediate superiors.

Bemoaning the 'confusion and waste' and the 'evident absurdity' of the current arrangements to his friend Chauvet, the chief *ordonnateur* (quartermaster), Napoleon despaired that 'the provisioning of armies is no more than luck'.[58] In a typical letter to Saliceti and Gasparin he wrote: 'One can remain for twenty-four or if necessary thirty-six hours without eating, but one cannot remain three minutes without gunpowder.'[59] Along with his energy and activity, his letters convey a meticulous attention to detail in everything from the price of rations to the proper

---

* Mulgrave was later to serve as Pitt's foreign secretary in 1805–6.

building of palisades. Overall, however, his message was constant; they only had 600 *milliers* (just over half a ton) of gunpowder, and if they couldn't procure more it would be impossible to start serious operations. On October 22 he wrote to the Committee of Public Safety of the 'extreme pain he felt at the little attention paid to his branch of the service,' adding: 'I have had to struggle against ignorance and the base passions which it engenders.'[60]

The result of all his hectoring, bluster, requisitioning and political string-pulling was that Napoleon put together a strong artillery train in very short order. He commandeered a foundry where shot and mortars were manufactured, and a workshop where muskets were repaired. He got the authorities in Marseilles to supply thousands of sandbags. This took significant powers of leadership – and also the kind of implicit threat that could be made by a Jacobin army officer during Robespierre's Terror. By the end of the siege Napoleon commanded eleven batteries totalling nearly one hundred cannon and mortars.

Napoleon received little support in all this from Carteaux, whom he came to despise, and who Saliceti and Gasparin conspired to have replaced with General François Doppet by November 11. Doppet was impressed with his artillery commander, reporting to Paris: 'I always found him at his post; when he needed rest he lay on the ground wrapped in his cloak: he never left the batteries.'[61] The admiration was not mutual, however, and after an attack on Fort Mulgrave on November 15, during which Doppet sounded the retreat too early, Napoleon returned to the redoubt and swore: 'Our blow at Toulon has missed, because a [expletive deleted in the nineteenth century] has beaten the retreat!'[62]

Napoleon showed considerable personal bravery in the batteries and redoubts of Toulon, at one point picking up a blood-soaked ramrod from an artilleryman who had been killed near him and helping to load and fire the cannon himself. He believed it was this action that gave him scabies. 'I found myself in a very few days suffering under an inveterate itch,' he later said of this 'terrible malady'.[63] The cutaneous irritation stayed with him through the Italian and Egyptian campaigns and was only cured in 1802 when his doctor, Jean-Nicolas Corvisart, applied sulphur baths and by 'putting three blisters on my chest . . . brought on a salutary crisis. Before that I had always been thin and sallow; since then I have always had good health.'[64] Some historians have argued that limited contact with the blood-stained ramrod was unlikely to have been the real cause, but Napoleon would probably have also donned the dead man's gloves, which would have made dermatitis infection far more likely.[65]*

During one assault on an outlying fort protecting Mulgrave, Napoleon was wounded by an English gunner, who 'ran a pike into' his left thigh. He was trying to enter the battery by its embrasure, but fortunately reinforcements came around by the rear, entering at the same moment. Many years later Napoleon showed off to a doctor 'a very deep cicatrix [scar] above the left knee', recalling that 'the surgeons were in doubt whether it might not be ultimately necessary to amputate'.[66] In a book he wrote in exile on St Helena on Julius Caesar's wars, Napoleon contrasted the commanders of the ancient world, who were well protected during battles, with those of the modern, concluding: 'Today the commander-in-chief is forced every day to face the guns, often within range of grapeshot, and all battles within cannon-shot, in order to assess, see and give orders, as the view is not wide enough for generals to be able to keep out of the way of bullets.'[67] One of the accusations made by his detractors was that Napoleon wasn't personally brave. 'Cowardice had of late years been habitual to Bonaparte,' wrote the English writer Helen Williams in 1815, for example.[68] This is absurd; not only do cowards not fight sixty battles, but Napoleon came near death several times between battles too, while reconnoitring close to the enemy. The number of people killed near him and the bullet that hit him at the battle of Ratisbon are further testaments to his great physical bravery. Napoleon's troops appreciated his courage and his ability to magnify their own. When all the gunners trying to establish a battery of cannon within a pistol shot of Fort Mulgrave were killed or wounded, Napoleon christened it 'Hommes Sans Peur' (Men Without Fear) and thereby continued to receive volunteers to man it. Nobody better understood the psychology of the ordinary soldier.

On November 17 the highly competent General Jacques Dugommier took over from Doppet, soon followed by reinforcements that brought the numbers of besiegers up to 37,000. Napoleon got on well with Dugommier. By mid-November he had surrounded Fort Mulgrave

---

* However he contracted this highly communicable, mite-based disease, he wasn't alone – *la Gale* was common to all armies of the day; the French had two nicknames for it, *la Gratelle* (the scratch) and the ironic *la Charmante*. 'Everyone was scratching,' recalled a veteran, and one report to the Committee of Public Health stated that there were no fewer than 400,000 scabetics in the army. Napoleon later set up special hospitals for them during his campaigns (Desclaux, 'A Propos de la "Gale"' p. 868, Brice, *The Riddle* p. 139, Friedman, *Emperor's Itch* p. 32).

with batteries, and on the 23rd he captured its British commander, General Charles O'Hara, who had tried to counter-attack from it in a sortie and spike the French guns of one of them. 'General Dugommier fought with true republican courage,' Napoleon reported of that action. 'We recaptured the battery . . . The guns of the Convention were un-spiked in sufficient time to increase the confusion of their retreat.'[69] It was very rare to be able to repair guns that had had metal spikes hammered into their firing mechanisms, let alone quickly, and it was a sign of the professional pitch to which Napoleon had trained his men.

At one o'clock on the morning of Tuesday, December 17, 1793, Dugommier put Napoleon's plan of attack on Toulon into action. A column under Claude Victor-Perrin (later Marshal Victor) got beyond the first line of defences at Fort Mulgrave, but faltered at the second. At about 3 a.m. Dugommier sent in the next assault of 2,000 men in the teeth of driving rain, high winds and lightning strikes. Led by Napoleon, whose horse was shot from under him, and Captain Jean-Baptiste Muiron, this assault finally took the fort after heavy hand-to-hand fighting. Napoleon then proceeded to pour heated cannonballs onto the Royal Navy vessels across the harbour below. The memory of the explosion of two Spanish gunpowder-ships stayed with him for the rest of his life. Decades later he recalled how 'The whirlwind of flames and smoke from the arsenal resembled the eruption of a volcano, and the thirteen vessels blazing in the roads were like so many displays of fireworks: the masts and forms of the vessels were distinctly traced out by the flames, which lasted many hours and formed an unparalleled spectacle.' He was exaggerating – only two ships caught fire rather than the whole fleet – but the effect was nonetheless dramatic. Dugommier gave a glowing report of Napoleon, whom he called 'this rare officer'.[70]

The Allies evacuated Toulon the next morning, creating pandemonium, especially once General Lapoype took the Faron heights and started bombarding the city from the eastern side too. Soon afterwards Saliceti and Gasparin ordered the execution of some four hundred suspected *fédérés*, though Napoleon took no part in that.[71] Great and deserved benefits flowed to Napoleon from the victory at Toulon. On December 22 he was appointed brigadier-general and inspector of coastal defences from the Rhône to the Var. Saliceti brought him to the attention of the senior politicians Paul Barras and Louis-Stanislas Fréron, but best of all, as he later put it, Toulon 'gave him confidence in himself'.[72] He had shown that he could be trusted with command.

Rarely in military history has there been so high a turnover of generals as in France in the 1790s. It meant that capable young men could advance through the ranks at unprecedented speed. The Terror, emigration, war, political purges, disgrace after defeat, political suspicion and scapegoating, on top of all the normal cases of resignation and retirement, meant that men like Lazare Hoche, who was a corporal in 1789, could be a general by 1793, or Michel Ney, a lieutenant in 1792, could become one by 1796. Napoleon's rise through the ranks was therefore by no means unique given the political and military circumstances of the day.[73] Still, his progress was impressive: he had spent five and a half years as a second-lieutenant, a year as a lieutenant, sixteen months as a captain, only three months as a major and no time at all as a colonel. On December 22, 1793, having been on leave for fifty-eight of his ninety-nine months of service – with and without permission – and after spending less than four years on active duty, Napoleon was made, at twenty-four, a general.

3

Desire

'When the mob gains the day, it ceases to be any longer the mob.
It is then called the nation. If it does not, why, then some are
executed, and they are called the canaille, rebels, thieves and so
forth.'

Napoleon to Dr Barry O'Meara on St Helena

'I win nothing but battles, and Josephine, by her goodness, wins
all hearts.'

Napoleon to his chamberlain,
Baron Louis de Bausset-Roquefort

On February 7, 1794, Napoleon was appointed artillery commander of
the Army of Italy. He played a creditable but unremarkable part in General Pierre Dumberion's five-week campaign against Austria's ally, the
independent kingdom of Piedmont in north-west Italy (which also ruled
Sardinia), in which three small victories were won and he acquainted
himself with the topography of the beautiful but potentially treacherous
mountains and passes of the Ligurian Alps. He fought alongside the
fiery and brilliant General André Masséna, whose campaign that May
to drive the Piedmontese from Ventimiglia and outflank the Austrians
and Piedmontese at the Col di Tenda won him the soubriquet 'the darling child of victory'.

The campaign was over quickly, and by early summer Napoleon was
back in Nice and Antibes, where he began to court Eugénie Désirée
Clary, the pretty sixteen-year-old daughter of a dead royalist textile and
soap millionaire. Désirée's elder sister Julie married Napoleon's brother
Joseph on August 1, 1794, bringing with her a substantial dowry of
400,000 francs, which finally ended the Bonaparte family's money

worries. Napoleon and Désirée's relationship was conducted almost entirely by correspondence and they were engaged the following April. A year earlier the nineteen-year-old Lucien Bonaparte had married Christine Boyer, a charming but illiterate twenty-two-year-old daughter of an innkeeper. He had put his adopted revolutionary name – Brutus – on the wedding certificate, the only one of the Bonapartes to change his name in such a way.

In April 1794 Napoleon submitted a plan to the Committee of Public Safety for the invasion of Italy via Piedmont. It was taken to Paris by Augustin Robespierre, who was attached to the Army of Italy. Fortunately written in Junot's legible handwriting rather than Napoleon's increasingly illegible scrawl, it contained such strategic statements as: 'Attacks must not be disseminated, but concentrated', 'It is [Austria] that must be annihilated; that accomplished, Spain and Italy will fall of themselves' and 'No dispassionate person could think of taking Madrid. The defensive system should be adopted on the Spanish, and the offensive on the Piedmontese frontier.' And eager even then to centralize authority, Napoleon wrote: 'The armies of the Alps and of Italy should be united to obey the same mind.'[1]

Napoleon's hapless *chef de bataillon*, Major Berlier, bore the brunt of his restless impatience, focus on detail and need for everything to be done faster and more efficiently. 'I'm extremely unhappy at the manner in which the loading of the sixteen pieces [of cannon] has been performed,' read one letter. 'You will certainly wish to respond to the following questions ... for which I give you twenty-four hours.' Another: 'I'm surprised that you are so tardy in the execution of orders, it's always necessary to tell you the same thing three times.' No aspect of his command was too small to escape notice. 'Imprison Corporal Carli, the commander of the battery,' he ordered Berlier, 'who absented himself to search for wine in Antibes.'[2]

During the Piedmontese campaign Napoleon received official confirmation of his promotion to brigadier-general, which required him to answer the question 'Noble or not noble?' Very sensibly, given that the Terror was still raging, he answered, technically untruthfully, in the negative.[3] The guillotining of the extremist Hébertist faction on March 5 and of Georges Danton and Camille Desmoulins on April 5, both ordered by Robespierre's Committee of Public Safety, showed the Revolution remorselessly devouring its own children. A contemporary noted 'thousands of women and children sitting on the stones in front of bakers shops', and 'more than half of Paris living upon potatoes. Paper money was without value.'[4] The city was ripe for a reaction against the Jacobins, who had so clearly failed to deliver either food or peace. With the Allies in retreat in 1794 in Spain and Belgium and along the Rhine, a group of conspirators felt confident enough to overthrow the Jacobins and finally end the Reign of Terror.

For six days in mid-July Napoleon took part in a secret mission to Genoa on Augustin Robespierre's behalf to report on its fortifications, conduct a five-hour meeting with the French *chargé d'affaires*, Jean Tilly, and persuade the doge of the need for better Franco-Genoese relations. It drew him closer into the Robespierres' political circle at precisely the worst time, for the 'Thermidorian reaction', led by Barras and Fréron, overthrew Maximilien Robespierre on July 27 (9 Thermidor in the revolutionary calendar). Both brothers and sixty other 'Terrorists' were guillotined the next day. Had Napoleon been in Paris at the time he might well have been scooped up and sent to the guillotine along with them. He had just returned from his brother Joseph's wedding and was at the army camp at Sieg near Nice on August 5 when he heard of the Robespierres' fate. 'I've been somewhat moved by the fate of the younger Robespierre,' he wrote to Tilly, 'whom I liked and believed honest, but had he been my own brother, if he had aspired to tyranny I'd have stabbed him myself.'[5]

Augustin Robespierre's patronage naturally put Napoleon under suspicion. On August 9 he was arrested by an officer and ten men at his lodgings in Nice and taken to the fortress in Nice for a day, before being imprisoned at the Fort-Carré in Antibes, where he was to spend the next ten days. (Both were places he had inspected officially earlier in his career.) Saliceti, from a wholly justifiable sense of self-preservation, did nothing to protect him and indeed ransacked Napoleon's papers looking for evidence of treachery.[6] 'He barely deigned to look at me from the lofty heights of his greatness,' was Napoleon's resentful comment on his fellow Corsican and political comrade of five years.[7]

In 1794, innocence was no defence against the guillotine, and nor was proven heroism fighting on behalf of the Republic, so Napoleon was in genuine danger. The official reason for his arrest was that certain Marseillais believed his positioning of a battery on the landward side of their city had been intended for use against them rather than an invader. Back in January he'd written to Bouchotte, the war minister: 'The batteries which defend Marseilles harbour are in a ridiculous condition. Total ignorance presided over their layout.'[8] The real reason was, of course, political; he had benefited from Augustin Robespierre's patronage and had written a Jacobin tract, *Le Souper de Beaucaire*, which Robespierre had helped him publish. 'Men can be unjust towards me, my dear Junot,' he wrote to his faithful aide-de-camp, 'but it suffices to be innocent; my conscience is the tribunal before which I call my conduct.'[9] (The loyal but impulsive Junot had come up with a Scarlet Pimpernel scheme to spring Napoleon from jail, which the prisoner sensibly and firmly scotched: 'Do nothing. You would only compromise me.'[10])

Napoleon was fortunate that the Thermidoreans didn't pursue their enemies as ruthlessly as the Jacobins had theirs, or indulge in extrajudicial prison murders like the September Massacres. He was released for lack of evidence on August 20. His incarceration had not been physically onerous and he made his prison guard a palace adjutant when he came to power. Once he was freed he returned to planning an expedition against Corsica and harassing poor Major Berlier. He also had time to renew his suit with Désirée Clary – whom he called Eugénie – telling her on September 10, 'the charms of your person and character have won over the heart of your lover'.[11] To increase the charms of her intellect he sent her a list of books he wanted her to read, and promised to follow them with his thoughts on music. He also urged her to improve her memory and 'form her reason'.

Although Napoleon generally saw women as lesser beings, he had clear ideas of how they should be educated in order to make proper companions for men. He asked Désirée about the effect of her reading 'on her soul' and tried to make her think about music intellectually, since it had 'the happiest effects on life'. (Hector Berlioz would later say that Napoleon was a discerning connoisseur of the music of Giovanni Paisiello, whom the Bonapartes had employed in Paris and Rome, composing works almost continuously between 1797 and 1814.) Napoleon's letters to Désirée were not particularly flowery or even romantic, but his interest in her was palpable, and to be the object of his concentrated attention was pleasing to her, even if, despite the new republican informality, he insisted on addressing her as 'vous'.[12]

He seems to have enjoyed her playful chastisement. 'If you could witness, mademoiselle,' he wrote in February 1795, 'the sentiments with which your letter inspired me, you would be convinced of the injustice of your reproaches ... There is no pleasure in which I do not desire to include you, no dream of which you do not furnish half. Be certain then that "the most sensible of women loves the coldest of men" is an iniquitous and ill-judged, unjust phrase which you did not believe in the writing. Your heart disavowed it even as your hand wrote it.'[13] Writing to her, he added, was both his greatest pleasure and 'the most imperative need' of his soul. He subscribed to a clavichord journal on her behalf so that she would receive the latest music from Paris, and was concerned that her teacher was paying insufficient attention to her solfège lessons. He added a long paragraph on singing technique which suggests that he was knowledgeable about (or at least had opinions on) vocal music. By April 11, 1795 he was finally using the familiar 'tu' form, and writing that he was 'yours for life'.[14] Napoleon was in love.

On March 3, 1795 Napoleon set sail from Marseilles with 15 ships, 1,174 guns and 16,900 men to recapture Corsica from Paoli and the British. His expedition was soon scattered by a British squadron of fifteen ships with fewer guns and half the number of men. Two French ships were captured. Napoleon wasn't held responsible for the reverse, but neither did this quintessential landlubber learn the lessons of attempting to put to sea against a similarly sized but far more skilfully deployed force of the Royal Navy. Between 1793 and 1797, the French would lose 125 warships to Britain's 38, including 35 capital vessels (ships-of-the-line) to Britain's 11, most of the latter the result of fire, accidents and storms rather than French attack.[15] The maritime aspect of grand strategy was always one of Napoleon's weaknesses: in all his long list of victories, none was at sea.

Once the expedition was abandoned, Napoleon was technically unemployed and only 139th on the list of generals in terms of seniority. The new commander of the Army of Italy, General Barthélemy Schérer, didn't want to take him because, although an acknowledged expert in artillery, he was thought to be 'too much given to intrigue for promotion'.[16] This was certainly true: Napoleon saw no separation between the military and political spheres any more than his heroes Caesar or Alexander had done. But only eight days after disembarking from the Corsican expedition, he was ordered to take command of the artillery of General Hoche's Army of the West, stationed at Brest, which was then suppressing the royalist uprising in the Vendée.

The government, which was now largely made up of Girondins who had survived the Terror, was conducting a vicious dirty war in western France, where more Frenchmen were killed than in the whole of the Paris Terror. Napoleon knew there was little glory to be had there, even if he were to succeed. Hoche was only a year older than him, so Napoleon's chances of advancement were slim. Having fought against the

British and Piedmontese, he didn't relish the prospect of fighting other Frenchmen, and on May 8 he left for Paris to try to get a better posting, taking his sixteen-year-old brother Louis, for whom he hoped to find a place at the artillery school at Châlons-sur-Marne, and two of his aides-de-camp, Marmont and Junot, with him (Muiron was now his third).[17]

Once installed at the Hôtel de la Liberté in Paris on May 25, Napoleon called on the acting war minister, Captain Aubry, who actually degraded the offer to command of the infantry in the Vendée. 'This appeared to Napoleon as an insult,' recorded his brother Louis, 'he refused, and lived in Paris without employment, enjoying his pay as an unemployed general.'[18] He claimed illness again, and eked out a living on half-pay, nonetheless sending Louis to Châlons. He proceeded to ignore the war ministry's demands that he go to the Vendée, or furnish proof of illness, or retire altogether. These were uncomfortable months for him, but he was philosophical about his lot, telling Joseph in August: 'Me, I'm very little attached to life ... finding myself constantly in the situation in which one finds oneself on the eve of battle, convinced only by the sentiment that when death, which terminates everything, is found amid it, anxiety is folly.' He then made a self-mocking joke which has been drained of all comic charm by being taken seriously by historians: 'Always trusting myself very much to Fate and destiny, if this continues, my friend, I'll end up by not getting out of the way when a carriage approaches.'[19]

Napoleon was in fact determined to enjoy the charms of Paris. 'The memory of the Terror is no more than a nightmare here,' he reported to Joseph. 'Everyone appears determined to make up for what they have suffered; determined, too, because of the uncertain future, not to miss a single pleasure of the present.'[20] He steeled himself to embark on a social life for the first time, although he wasn't comfortable in the company of women. This might in part have been because of his looks; a woman who met him several times that spring called him 'the thinnest and queerest being I ever met ... so thin that he inspired pity'.[21] Another nicknamed him 'Puss-in-Boots'.[22] The socialite Laure d'Abrantès, who knew Napoleon at this time, though probably not as well as she later claimed in her bitchy memoirs, remembered him 'with a shabby round hat drawn over his forehead, and his ill-powdered hair hanging over the collar of his grey greatcoat, without gloves because he used to say they were a useless luxury, with boots ill-made and ill-blackened, with his thinness and his sallow complexion'.[23] Small wonder that Napoleon wasn't comfortable in the fashionable Parisian salons and rather despised those who were: he denounced dandies to Junot (whom Laure d'Abrantès later married) for their modes of dress and adopted lisps, and as Emperor he was convinced that the hostesses of the fashionable *faubourg* salons encouraged opposition to him. His favourite entertainments were intellectual rather than social; he went to public lectures and visited the observatory, the theatre and the opera. 'Tragedy excites the soul,' he later told one of his secretaries, 'lifts the heart, can and ought to create heroes.'[24]

On his way to Paris in May 1795, Napoleon had written to Désirée that he was 'much afflicted at the thought of having to be so far away from you for so long'.[25] He had enough money saved from his salary at this point to consider buying a small chateau at Ragny in Burgundy, listing the potential revenues he could make from various cereal crops there, estimating that the dining room was four times the size of the Casa Bonaparte's, and making the sound republican remark that 'In pulling down three or four towers which give it an aristocratic air, the chateau would be no more than an attractive very large family home.'[26] He told Joseph of his wish to start a family.

'I saw many pretty women of agreeable disposition at Marmont's house in Châtillon,' Napoleon wrote to Désirée in a rather transparent attempt to excite her jealousy on June 2, 'but I never felt even for an instant that any of them could measure up to my dear, good Eugénie.' Two days later he wrote again: 'Adored friend, I have received no more letters from you. How could you go eleven days without writing to me?'[27] Perhaps realizing that Madame Clary had discouraged her daughter from further involvement, thinking that one Bonaparte in the family was quite enough. A week later Napoleon was merely calling her 'Mademoiselle'. By June 14 he acknowledged the situation: 'I know that you will always retain an affection for your friend, but it will be no more than affectionate esteem.'[28] His letters to Joseph make it clear that he still loved Désirée, but in August, calling her 'vous' once more, he wrote: 'Follow your instincts, allow yourself to love what's near to you . . . You know that my destiny lies in the hazard of combat, in glory or in death.'[29] For all their cloying melodrama, his words had the advantage of being true.

Was it self-pity over Désirée as much as fraternal love that compelled Napoleon to dissolve into tears while writing to Joseph on June 24, a letter ostensibly about something as prosaic as his brother's plans to enter the Genoese olive-oil trade? 'Life is like an empty dream which vanishes,' he wrote to Joseph, asking for his portrait. 'We have lived so many years together, so closely united, that our hearts are mingled, and you know better than anyone how entirely mine belongs to you.'[30] By July 12 he was trying to persuade himself that he was over Désirée, railing to Joseph against the effeminacy of men who were interested in women, who 'are mad about them, think only of them, live only by and for them. A woman requires to be but six months in Paris to know what is due to her and the extent of her empire.'[31]

Désirée's rejection of Napoleon contributed to his deep cynicism about women and even about love itself. On St Helena he defined love as 'the occupation of the idle man, the distraction of the warrior, the stumbling block of the sovereign', and told one of his entourage: 'Love does not really exist. It's an artificial sentiment born of society.'[32] Less than three months after the end of his courting of Désirée he was ready to fall in love again, although he seems to have retained a place in his heart for her, even after she had married General Jean-Baptiste Bernadotte, and wound up as queen of Sweden.

'We are so sure of the superiority of our infantry that we laugh at the threats of the English,' Napoleon wrote to Joseph after the British landed a force in Quiberon Bay, near Saint-Nazaire, in late June 1795 to assist the revolt in the Vendée.[33] It was an early example of his overconfidence regarding the British following Toulon (though admittedly justified in this instance, as by October the expedition had comprehensively failed). Besides Toulon, he was to fight the British only twice more, at Acre and in the Waterloo campaign.

By early August he was still lobbying for a post back with the artillery of the Army of Italy, but he also seriously considered taking up an offer to go to Turkey to modernize the Sultan's artillery. According to Lucien's memoirs, during this period of complete flux in his career Napoleon even contemplated joining the East India Company's army, albeit more for its financial than military advantages, saying 'I will return in a few years a rich nabob, bringing some handsome dowries for my three sisters.'[34] Madame Mère, as his mother came to be called, took the suggestion seriously enough to rebuke him for even considering the notion, which she thought him quite capable of taking up 'in a moment of vexation against the Government'. There is also an indication that the Russians were wooing him to help them fight the Turks.

In mid-August 1795 matters came to a head when the war ministry demanded that Napoleon present himself to its medical board to ascertain whether he was in fact sick. He appealed to Barras, Fréron and his other political contacts, one of whom landed him an attachment to the Historical and Topographical Bureau of the war ministry. Despite its title, this was actually the planning staff that co-ordinated French military strategy. So whereas on August 17 Napoleon was writing to Simon Sucy de Clisson, the *ordonnateur* of the Army of Italy at Nice, 'I've been appointed to a generalship in the Army of the Vendée: I won't accept', three days later he was crowing to Joseph: 'I am at this moment attached to the Topographical Department of the Committee of Public Safety for the direction of armies.'[35] The Bureau was under the command of General Henri Clarke, a protégé of the great military administrator Lazare Carnot, known as 'The Organizer of Victory'.

The Topographical Bureau was a small, highly efficient organization within the war ministry that has been described as 'the most sophisticated planning organisation of its day'.[36] Set up by Carnot and reporting directly to the Committee, it took information from the commanders-in-chief, plotted troop movements, prepared detailed operational directives and co-ordinated logistics. Under Clarke, the senior staff included Generals Jean-Girard Lacuée, César-Gabriel Berthier and Pierre-Victor Houdon, all talented and dedicated strategists. Napoleon could hardly have been better placed to learn all the necessary strands of supply, support and logistics that make up strategy (although the word entered the military lexicon only in the early nineteenth century and was not one Napoleon ever used).[37] This period between mid-August and early October 1795 – short, but intellectually intense – was when Napoleon learned the practicalities of strategic warfare, as distinct from the tactical battle-fighting at which he had excelled at Toulon. Napoleon's military success was ultimately down to his own genius and capacity for gruellingly hard work, but France had some exceptionally talented military thinkers and bureaucrats at this time, able to teach him and ultimately to do the detailed work necessary to put his ideas into practice. The Topographical Bureau was also the best place to make his own estimations of which generals were worthwhile and which expendable.

The Bureau didn't decide overall grand strategy; that was done by the politicians on the Committee of Public Safety, which was highly vulnerable to factional struggles. The debate over whether, where and when to cross the Rhine to attack Austria in 1795, for example, had to be fought out there, with the Bureau merely giving advice on each option. In August any plans to fight for – or indeed against – Turkey were quashed by the Committee, which also ordained that Napoleon couldn't leave the country until the end of the war. He still had problems from different bureaucracies within the ministry over whether he was active or retired, and on September 15 he was even struck off the list of serving generals. 'I have fought like a lion for the Republic,' he wrote to his friend the actor François-Joseph Talma, 'and in recompense she leaves me dying of hunger.'[38] (He was soon reinstated.)

The Topographical Bureau's curious office hours – from 1 p.m. to 5 p.m. and 11 p.m. to 3 a.m. – allowed Napoleon plenty of time to write a romantic novella entitled *Clisson et Eugénie*, a swansong for his unrequited love affair with Désirée. Employing the short, terse sentences of the heroic tradition, it was either consciously or unconsciously influenced by Goethe's celebrated novel of 1774, *The Sorrows of Young Werther*, which Napoleon read no fewer than six times during the Egyptian campaign, and probably first when he was eighteen. The most important European *Sturm-und-Drang* novel and the great bestseller of its age, *Werther* deeply affected the Romantic literary movement and Napoleon's own writing. Although the name 'Clisson' was borrowed from one of Napoleon's friends of the time, Sucy de Clisson, the character is pure Napoleon, right down to their identical ages of twenty-six. 'From birth Clisson was strongly attracted to war,' the story opens. 'While others of his age were still listening avidly to fireside tales, he was ardently dreaming of battle.' Clisson joined the revolutionary National Guard and 'Soon he had exceeded the high expectations people had of him: victory was his constant companion.'[39]

Clisson was superior to the frivolous pastimes of his contemporaries such as flirtation, gambling and conversational repartee: 'A man of his fervent imagination, with his blazing heart, his uncompromising intellect and his cool head, was bound to be irritated by the affected conversation of coquettes, the games of seduction, the logic of the tables and the hurling of witty insults.'[40] Such a paragon was only at ease communing Rousseau-like with nature in the forests, where 'he felt at peace with himself, scorning human wickedness and despising folly and cruelty'. When Clisson met the sixteen-year-old Eugénie at a spa, 'she revealed beautifully-arranged pearly white teeth'. After that,

> Their eyes met. Their hearts fused, and not many days were to pass before they realised that their hearts were made to love each other. His love was the most passionate and chaste that had ever moved a man's heart . . .

They felt as if their souls were one. They overcame all obstacles and were joined forever. All that is the most honourable in love, the tenderest feelings, the most exquisite voluptuousness flooded the hearts of the two enraptured lovers.[41]

Clisson and Eugénie marry, have children and live happily together, much admired by the poor for their generous philanthropy. But this idyllic fairy-tale is too good to last. One day a message arrives instructing Clisson that he must leave for Paris within twenty-four hours. 'There he was to be given an important mission, which called for a man of his talents.' Appointed to command an army, Clisson 'was a success at everything; he exceeded the hopes of the people and the army; indeed, he alone was the reason for the army's success.' Seriously wounded in a skirmish, however, Clisson despatches one of his officers, Berville, to inform Eugénie, 'and to keep her company until he had made a full recovery'. For no good reason discernible to the reader, Eugénie promptly sleeps with Berville, which the recuperating Clisson finds out about and understandably wants to avenge. 'But how could he leave the army and his duty? The fatherland needed him here!' The solution was a glorious death in battle, so when 'Beating drums announced the charge on the flanks, and death stalked amongst the ranks,' Clisson writes a suitably emotional letter to Eugénie which he hands to an aide-de-camp, 'and, dutifully placing himself at the head of the fray – at the point where the victory would be decided – and expired, pierced by a thousand blows.'[42] *Finis.*

We should try to view *Clisson et Eugénie* through an eighteenth-century literary prism, rather than as a cheap romance of today. The seventeen-page short story has been described as 'the last manifestation of an incipient Romanticism in a man who would go on to dazzle with his brilliant pragmatism', and Napoleon clearly used the story to fantasize, in this case by making Eugénie despicably adulterous while he remained heroic, faithful and even forgiving of her infidelity at the end.[43] Yet Napoleon can't be excused the melodrama, sentimentality and cliché because his story was tossed off in a furious moment of immature resentment: *Clisson et Eugénie* underwent endless drafting and re-drafting.

In the second half of 1795 France's leaders recognized that she would need a new constitution if she were to put the days of the Jacobin Terror behind her. 'The royalists are stirring,' Napoleon wrote to Joseph on

September 1, 'we shall see how this will end.'[44] Alexis de Tocqueville would write that states are never more vulnerable than when they attempt to reform themselves, and that was certainly true of France in the autumn of 1795.

On August 23 the third constitution since the fall of the Bastille, known as the Constitution of the Year III, establishing a bicameral legislature and a five-man executive government called the Directory, was approved by the Convention. It would come into effect at the end of October. A National Assembly consisting of a Council of Five Hundred and Council of the Elders would replace the Convention, and the Directory would replace the Committee of Public Safety, which had grown to be synonymous with the Terror. This moment of reform provided an opportunity for opponents both of the Revolution and the Republic to strike. As Austria returned to the Rhine in a major counter-attack on September 20, with the French economy still very weak and corruption widespread, the enemies of the Republic coalesced to overthrow the new government in the first week of October, smuggling large quantities of arms and ammunition into Paris.

Although the Terror was over and the Committee of Public Safety would be abolished when the new Directory came into being, the bitterness they had inspired was now directed against their successors. It was in the 'Sections', forty-eight districts of Paris established in 1790 which controlled local assemblies and the local National Guard units, that the insurrection was focused. Although only seven Sections actually rose in revolt, National Guardsmen from others joined in.

The men of the Sections were not all – or even mainly – royalists. The veteran soldier General Mathieu Dumas wrote in his memoirs, 'The most general desire of the population of Paris was to return to the constitution of 1791', and there was little appetite for the civil war that a Bourbon restoration would have entailed.[45] The Sections included middle-class National Guardsmen, royalists, some moderates and liberals, and ordinary Parisians who opposed the government for its corruption and domestic and international failures. The very disparate nature of the rebellion's political make-up made any central co-ordination impossible beyond establishing a date for action, which couldn't be kept secret from the government.

The man whom the Convention had originally relied upon to put down the coming insurrection, General Jacques-François Menou, commander of the Army of the Interior, had attempted to negotiate with the Sections to avoid bloodshed. The leaders of the Convention mistook this for incipient treachery and had him arrested. (He was later acquitted.) With time running out before the anticipated attack, the Thermidorians appointed one of their leaders, the president of the National Assembly, Paul Barras, to command the Army of the Interior, despite his having no military experience since 1783. His instructions were to save the Revolution.

On the evening of Sunday, October 4, Napoleon was at the Feydeau Theatre watching Saurin's play *Beverley* when he heard that the Sections intended to rise the following day.[46] Very early the next morning – 13 Vendémiaire by the revolutionary calendar – Barras appointed him second-in-command of the Army of the Interior, and ordered him to use all means necessary to crush the revolt. Napoleon had impressed the most important decision-makers in his life – among them Kéralio, the du Teil brothers, Saliceti, Doppet, Dugommier, Augustin Robespierre and now Barras, who had heard of him from Saliceti after the victory at Toulon. Having served in the Topographical Bureau, he was known to leading government figures such as Carnot and Jean-Lambert Tallien.[47] (He later recalled with amusement that the politician who had had least qualms about the spilling of blood at Vendémiaire had been the priest and political theorist Abbé Emmanuel Sieyès.) It is astonishing that there were so few other senior officers in Paris to take the job, or at least ones who were willing to fire on civilians in the streets. From Napoleon's reactions to the two Tuileries attacks he had witnessed in 1792, there was no doubt what he would do.

This was Napoleon's first introduction to frontline, high-level national politics, and he found it intoxicating. He ordered Captain Joachim Murat of the 21st Chasseurs à Cheval to gallop to the Sablons military camp two miles away with one hundred cavalrymen, secure the cannon there and bring them into central Paris, and to sabre anyone who tried to prevent him. The Sections had missed a great opportunity as the Sablons cannon were at that point guarded by only fifty men.

Between 6 a.m. and 9 a.m., having assured himself of the loyalty of his officers and men, Napoleon placed two cannon at the entrance of the rue Saint-Nicaise, another facing the church of Saint-Roch at the bottom of the rue Dauphine, two more in the rue Saint-Honoré near the Place Vendôme, and two facing the Pont Royal on the Quai Voltaire. He formed up his infantry behind the cannon, and sent his reserves to the Place du Carrousel to defend the Tuileries where the Convention sat and the government was headquartered. His cavalry was posted in the Place de la Révolution (today's Place de la Concorde).[48] He then spent three hours visiting each of his guns in turn. 'Good and upstanding people must be persuaded by gentle means,' Napoleon would later write. 'The rabble must be moved by terror.'[49]

Napoleon prepared to use grapeshot, the colloquial term for canister or case shot, which consists of hundreds of musket balls packed into a metal case that rips open as soon as it leaves the cannon's muzzle, sending the lead balls flying in a relatively wide arc at an even greater velocity than the 1,760 feet per second of a musket shot. Its maximum range was roughly 600 yards, optimum 250. The use of grapeshot on civilians was hitherto unknown in Paris, and was testament to Napoleon's ruthlessness that he was willing to contemplate it. He was not about to be a *coglione*. 'If you treat the mob with kindness,' he told Joseph later, 'these creatures fancy themselves invulnerable; if you hang a few, they get tired of the game, and become as submissive and humble as they ought to be.'[50]

Napoleon's force consisted of 4,500 troops and about 1,500 'patriots', gendarmes and veterans from Les Invalides. Opposing them was a disparate force of up to 30,000 men from the Sections, nominally under the control of General Dancian, who wasted much of the day trying to conduct negotiations. Only at 4 p.m. did the rebel columns start issuing from side streets to the north of the Tuileries. Napoleon did not open fire immediately, but as soon as the first musket shots were heard from the Sections sometime between 4.15 p.m. and 4.45 p.m. he unleashed a devastating artillery response. He also fired grapeshot at the men of the Sections attempting to cross the bridges over the Seine, who took heavy casualties and quickly fled. In most parts of Paris the attack was all over by 6 p.m., but at the church of Saint-Roch in the rue Saint-Honoré, which became the *de facto* headquarters of the insurrection and where the wounded were brought, snipers carried on firing from rooftops and from behind barricades. The fighting continued for many hours, until Napoleon brought his cannon to within 60 yards of the church and surrender was the only option.[51] Around three hundred insurrectionists were killed that day, against only half a dozen of Napoleon's men. Magnanimously by the standards of the day, the Convention executed only two Section leaders afterwards.* 'The whiff of grapeshot' – as it became known – meant that the Paris mob played no further part in French politics for the next three decades.

---

* By comparison, in 1780 during the Gordon Riots in London, 285 people had been killed, 200 wounded and a further 20 executed.

In 1811 General Jean Sarrazin published a book in London entitled *Confession of General Buonaparté to the Abbé Maury*. As Napoleon had by then had Sarrazin sentenced to death *in absentia* for treachery, it didn't cost him much to claim that on 13 Vendémiaire, 'Far from putting a stop to the blind fury of his soldiers, Buonaparté set them the example of inhumanity. He cut down with his sabre wretched beings, who in their fright had thrown down their arms and implored his mercy.'[52] Sarrazin further claimed that Napoleon's lieutenant, Monvoisin, reproached Napoleon for his cruelty that day and resigned. None of this was true, but it was all part of the 'Black Legend' that came to surround Napoleon from Vendémiaire onwards.

Heavy rainfall on the night of 13 Vendémiaire quickly washed the blood from the streets, but its memory lingered. Even the violently anti-Jacobin *Annual Register*, founded by Edmund Burke, pointed out that 'It was in this conflict that Buonaparte appeared first on the theatre of war, and by his courage and conduct laid the foundation of that confidence in his powers which conducted him so soon thereafter to preferment and to glory.'[53] The urgent political exigencies meant that there was to be no more nonsense from the war ministry about seniority lists, medical boards, desertion and so on. Before the end of Vendémiaire, Napoleon had been promoted to *général de division* by Barras and soon afterwards to commander of the Army of the Interior in recognition of his service in saving the Republic and possibly preventing civil war. It was ironic that he had refused the Vendée post partly because he hadn't wanted to kill Frenchmen, and then gained his most vertiginous promotion by doing just that. But to his mind there was a difference between a legitimate fighting force and a rabble. For a while afterwards Napoleon was sometimes called 'General Vendémiaire', though not to his face. Far from being uneasy about his involvement in the deaths of so many of his compatriots, he ordered the anniversary to be celebrated once he became First Consul, and when a lady asked him how he could have fired so mercilessly on the mob he replied: 'A soldier is only a machine to obey orders.'[54] He did not point out that it was he who had given the orders.

The 'whiff of grapeshot' advanced the Bonaparte family hugely, and overnight. Napoleon would now be paid 48,000 francs per annum, Joseph was given a job in the diplomatic service, Louis advanced through the Châlons artillery school and later became one of Napoleon's burgeoning team of aides-de-camp, while the youngest of the

Bonaparte boys, the eleven-year-old Jérôme, was sent to a better school. 'The family will want for nothing,' Napoleon told Joseph, and that was to be true for the next twenty years. Laure d'Abrantès claimed that she noticed a change after Vendémiaire:

> Muddy boots were out of the question. Bonaparte never went out but in a fine carriage, and he lived in a very respectable house in the rue des Capucines ... His emaciated thinness was converted into a fullness of face, and his complexion, which had been yellow and apparently unhealthy, became clear and comparatively fresh; his features, which were angular and sharp, became round and filled out. As to his smile, it was always agreeable.[55]

No-one would call him 'Puss-in-Boots' anymore.

In the immediate aftermath of Vendémiaire, Napoleon supervised the closing of the opposition Panthéon Club and the expulsion of crypto-royalists from the war ministry, as well as the policing of theatrical productions. In this last role he wrote almost daily to the government about the behaviour of the audiences at four Parisian theatres: the Opéra, Opéra Comique, Feydeau and La République. A typical report reads, 'While patriotic airs were well received in two [of the theatres], and a third was tranquil, the police had to arrest a man (thought to be a Vendéen) who whistled during the penultimate verse of the "Marseillaise" at the Feydeau'.[56]* Another task was to oversee the confiscation of all civilian weaponry, which according to family lore led to his meeting a woman of whom he had possibly heard on the social grapevine but hadn't hitherto met: Vicomtesse Marie-Josèphe-Rose Tascher de la Pagerie, the widow de Beauharnais, whom Napoleon was to dub 'Josephine'.

Josephine's grandfather, a noble called Gaspard Tascher, had left France for Martinique in 1726, hoping to make his fortune with a sugar-cane plantation, although hurricanes, bad luck and his own indolence had prevented him; La Pagerie was the name of an estate the family owned on Saint-Domingue (modern-day Haiti). Josephine's father, Joseph, had served as a page at the court of Louis XVI but returned to his father's estates. Josephine was born in Martinique on June 23, 1763, although in later life she claimed that it was 1767.[57] She arrived in Paris in 1780 aged seventeen, so poorly educated that

---

* The singing of the great revolutionary, anti-monarchical anthem of 1792 was discouraged by Napoleon once he became Emperor, although he reintroduced it in 1815.

her first husband – a cousin to whom she had been engaged at fifteen, the General Vicomte Alexandre de Beauharnais – couldn't hide his contempt for her lack of education. Josephine had blackened stubs for teeth, thought to be the result of chewing Martiniquais cane sugar as a child, but she learned to smile without showing them.[58] 'Had she only possessed teeth,' wrote Laure d'Abrantès, who was to become Madame Mère's lady-in-waiting, 'she would certainly have outvied nearly all the ladies of the Consular Court.'[59]

Although Beauharnais had been an abusive husband – once kidnapping their three-year-old son Eugène from the convent in which Josephine had taken refuge from his beatings – she nonetheless courageously tried to save him from the guillotine after his arrest in 1794. From April 22, 1794 until shortly after her husband's execution on July 22 that year, Josephine was herself imprisoned as a suspected royalist in the crypt underneath the church of Saint-Joseph-des-Carmes in the rue de Vaugirard.* One of her cellmates, an Englishwoman named Grace Elliott, recalled how 'the walls and even the wooden chairs were still stained with the blood and the brains of the priests'.[60] Josephine had to endure truly inhumane conditions: air came only from three deep holes to the underground cells and there were no lavatories; she and her cellmates lived in daily fear of the guillotine; they had one bottle of water a day each, for all uses; and since pregnant women weren't guillotined until after giving birth, the sound of sexual couplings with the warders could be heard in the hallways at night.[61] It is cold down in the Saint-Joseph crypt even in midsummer, and inmates' health broke down fast, indeed it is possible that Josephine survived only because she was too ill to be guillotined. Her husband was executed just four days before Robespierre's fall, and had Robespierre survived any longer Josephine would probably have followed him. There was a paradoxical symmetry in the way that the Thermidor coup released Josephine from one prison and simultaneously put Napoleon into another.

The stench, darkness, cold, degradation and daily fear of violent death for weeks on end makes the Terror well named, and it is likely that for months, possibly even years, afterwards Josephine suffered from a form of what would now be called post-traumatic stress disorder. If she was later sexually self-indulgent, became involved in sleazy

* It can be visited today if you turn up very promptly at 3 p.m. on a Saturday. During the September Massacres of 1792 the mob massacred 115 priests there, and the skulls and bones of 35 of them are on display.

business deals and loved luxury – her dress bills became higher than Marie Antoinette's – and married for stability and financial security rather than for love, it is hard to hold this against her after what she had been through.[62] Josephine has often been seen as a seductive, shallow, extravagant hussy, but she certainly wasn't shallow culturally, having good taste in music and the decorative arts. She was also generous – albeit usually with public money – and one of the most accomplished diplomats of the age, Clemens von Metternich, referred to her 'unique social tact'.[63] She was a skilled harpist – although some said she always played the same tune – and she did something in bed known as 'zigzags'.[64] She couldn't draw, did a bit of tapestry, and played backgammon occasionally, but she received callers all day and enjoyed gossipy lunches with her many girlfriends.

By late 1795 this undeniably sexy femme fatale in her mid-thirties (with an inimitable closed-mouth smile) needed a protector and provider. On leaving prison she had an affair with General Lazare Hoche, who refused to leave his wife for her but whom she would have liked to marry, even up to the day she reluctantly married Napoleon.[65] Another lover was Paul Barras, but that didn't last much longer than the summer of 1795. 'I was long since tired of and bored with her,' recalled Barras in his memoirs, in which he ungallantly described her as a 'cajoling courtesan'.[66] It is a well-known historical phenomenon for a sexually permissive period to follow one of prolonged bloodletting: the 'Roaring Twenties' after the Great War and the licentiousness of Ancient Roman society after the Civil Wars are but two examples. Josephine's decision to take powerful lovers after the Terror was, like so much else in her life, à la mode (though she wasn't as promiscuous as her friend Thérésa Tallien, who was nicknamed 'Government Property' because so many ministers had slept with her). Whatever 'zigzags' were, Josephine had performed them for others besides her first husband, Hoche and Barras; her éducation amoureuse was far more advanced than her near-virginal second husband's.

Josephine took the opportunity of the post-Vendémiaire arms confiscations to send her fourteen-year-old son Eugène de Beauharnais to Napoleon's headquarters to ask whether his father's sword could be retained by the family for sentimental reasons. Napoleon took this for the social opening that it plainly was, and within weeks he had fallen genuinely and deeply in love with her; his infatuation only grew until their marriage five months later. As fellow outsiders, immigrants, islanders and ex-political prisoners, they had a certain amount in common. At first she wasn't attracted to his slightly yellow complexion, lank hair and unkempt look, nor presumably to his scabies, and she certainly wasn't in love with him, but then she herself was beginning to get wrinkles, her looks were fading and she was in debt. (She sensibly didn't admit the extent of her debts until she had Napoleon's ring on her finger.)

Josephine always took a great deal of trouble over her make-up and clothing. She had mirrors placed in the bedrooms of her houses and palaces, was charming and affable – though not intelligent enough to be witty – and knew perfectly what kind of attentions successful men liked. Asked whether Josephine had intelligence, Talleyrand is said to have replied: 'No one ever managed so brilliantly without it.' For his part, Napoleon valued her political connections, her social status as a vicomtesse who was also acceptable to revolutionaries, and the way she compensated for his lack of savoir-faire and social graces. He wasn't good at drawing-room repartee. 'Out of his mouth there never came one well-turned speech to a woman,' recalled the accomplished smooth-talker Metternich, 'although the effort to make one was often expressed on his face and in the sound of his voice.'[67] He spoke to ladies about their dresses or the number of children they had, and whether they nursed them themselves, 'a question which he commonly made in terms seldom used in good society'. While he was gauche around women, she was extremely well-connected in Paris society, with entrées into the influential political salons run by Madames Tallien, Récamier, de Staël and others.

The Revolution had removed responsibility for registering births, deaths and marriages from the clergy, so Napoleon and Josephine married in a civil ceremony at 10 p.m. on Wednesday, March 9, 1796, before a sleepy mayor in the 2nd *arrondissement* on the rue d'Antin. The bride wore a republican tricolour sash over her white muslin wedding dress,[68] and the groom arrived two hours late. The witnesses included Barras, Napoleon's aide-de-camp Jean Lemarois (who was technically a minor), the Talliens, Josephine's son Eugène and his eleven-year-old sister Hortense. In order to minimize the six-year disparity of their ages, Napoleon claimed in the marriage register to have been born in 1768 and she simultaneously shed her customary four years, so they could both be twenty-eight.[69] (Later the *Almanach Impérial* recorded Josephine as having been born on June 24, 1768.[70] Napoleon was always amused by his wife's insistence on lying about her age, joking: 'According to her calculations, Eugène must have been born aged twelve!'[71]) As a wedding gift, Napoleon gave her a gold enamelled medallion engraved with the words 'To Destiny'.[72]

The reason Napoleon had been so late for his own wedding, and why his honeymoon then lasted less than forty-eight hours, was that on March 2 Barras and the other four members of France's new executive government, the Directory, had given him the best wedding present he could ever have hoped for: command of the Army of Italy. Barras later wrote that to persuade his colleagues – the ex-Jacobins Jean-François Reubell and Louis de La Révellière-Lépeaux, and the moderates Lazare Carnot and Étienne-François Le Tourneur – to choose Napoleon for the coming campaign in the Ligurian Alps he told them that, as 'a high-lander' Corsican, he was 'accustomed since birth to scale mountains'.[73] It was hardly a scientific argument – Ajaccio is at sea level – but he also said that Napoleon would lift the Army of Italy out of its lethargy. That was a good deal nearer the mark.

In the nine days between receiving the appointment and leaving for his headquarters in Nice on March 11, Napoleon asked for every book, map and atlas on Italy that the war ministry could provide. He read biographies of commanders who had fought there and had the courage to admit his ignorance when he didn't know something. 'I happened to be at the office of the General Staff in the rue Neuve des Capucines when General Bonaparte came in,' recalled a fellow officer years later:

I can still see the little hat, surmounted by a pickup plume, his coat cut anyhow, and a sword which, in truth, did not seem the sort of weapon to make anyone's fortune. Flinging his hat on a large table in the middle of the room, he went up to an old general named Krieg, a man with a won-derful knowledge of detail and the author of a very good soldiers' manual. He made him take a seat beside him at the table, and began questioning him, pen in hand, about a host of facts connected with the service and discipline. Some of his questions showed such a complete ignorance of the most ordinary things that several of my comrades smiled. I was myself struck by the number of his questions, their order and their rapidity, no less than the way by which the answers were caught up, and often found to resolve into other questions which he deduced in consequence from them. But what struck me still more was the sight of a commander-in-chief perfectly indifferent about showing his subordinates how completely ignorant he was of various points of a business which the youngest of them was supposed to know perfectly, and this raised him a thousand cubits in my opinion.[74]

Napoleon left Paris in a post-chaise on March 11, 1796, along with Junot and his friend Chauvet, the new chief *ordonnateur* of the Army of Italy. In a letter to Josephine of March 14, written from Chanceaux on his journey south, Napoleon dropped the 'u' in his surname. The first time his name had appeared in the state newspaper, the *Moniteur Universel*, had been in 1794 when it was hyphenated as 'Buono-Parte'.* Now he Gallicized it in a conscious move towards emphasizing his French over his Italian and Corsican identities.[75] Another bond with the past had been broken.

He reached Nice in fifteen days. When someone made the rather otiose point that he was very young, at twenty-six, to command an army, Napoleon replied: 'I shall be old when I return.'[76]

---

* For decades thereafter, British and Bourbon propagandists re-inserted the 'u' in order to emphasize Napoleon's foreignness, such as in François-René de Chateaubriand's snappily titled 1814 pamphlet *Of Buonaparte and the Bourbons and the Necessity of Rallying Round our Legitimate Princes for the Happiness of France and that of Europe*, in which he wrote: 'No hope was left of finding among Frenchmen a man bold enough to dare to wear the crown of Louis XVI. A foreigner offered himself, and was accepted' (Chateaubriand, *Of Buonaparte* p. 5). Even after the British royal family changed the name of their dynasty from Saxe-Coburg-Gotha to Windsor in 1917, some British historians still ridiculed Napoleon for dropping the 'u' from his surname.

4

Italy

> 'On 15 May 1796, General Bonaparte made his entry into Milan
> at the head of a youthful army which had just crossed the bridge
> at Lodi and let the world know that after all these centuries,
> Caesar and Alexander had a successor.'
>
> Stendhal, *The Charterhouse of Parma*

> 'A general's most important talent is to know the mind of the
> soldier and gain his confidence, and in both respects the French
> soldier is more difficult to lead than another. He is not a machine
> that must be made to move, he is a reasonable being who needs
> leadership.'
>
> Napoleon to Chaptal

Some would later claim that Napoleon was an unknown quantity when
he arrived at the headquarters of the Army of Italy in Nice on March
26, 1796, and that his divisional commanders all despised him when
they met him for the first time because, as a sneering contemporary put
it, he had 'won his reputation in a street riot and his command in a marriage bed'.[1] He had in fact served as head of artillery of the same force
only two years before, was known to many from his success at Toulon,
and had written no fewer than three detailed reports for the Topographical Bureau on how to win the coming campaign. It was only natural
that there should be some initial resentment at his having been appointed
over the heads of more experienced generals but Napoleon's officers
knew perfectly well who he was.

He was in charge of five divisional commanders. The eldest, Jean
Sérurier, had thirty-four years' service in the French army. He had served
in the Seven Years War and was considering retiring from soldiering

when the Revolution broke out, but had fought well in the years afterwards and had been made a divisional general in December 1794. Pierre
Augereau was a tall, swaggering, somewhat coarse thirty-eight-year-old
former mercenary, clock-seller and dancing-master whose nicknames
were 'child of the people' and 'proud brigand'. He had killed two men
in duels and a cavalry officer in a fight and only escaped torture by the
Lisbon Inquisition through the good offices of his spirited Greek wife.
André Masséna, also thirty-eight, had gone to sea as a cabin boy at thirteen but switched to the army in 1775 and became a sergeant-major
before being discharged just before the Revolution. He became a smug-
gler and fruit trader in Antibes before joining the National Guard in
1791 and rapidly rising up the ranks. His services in the siege of Toulon
won him promotion to divisional general in the Army of Italy, where he
served with distinction in 1795. Amédée Laharpe was a thirty-two-year-
old heavily moustachioed Swiss. Jean-Baptiste Meynier had fought in
the Army of Germany, but in mid-April Napoleon reported to the Directory that he was 'incapable, not fit to command a battalion in a war
as active as this one'.[2] All five men were experienced veterans, whereas
Napoleon hadn't commanded so much as an infantry battalion in his
life. They would be a tough group to impress, let alone inspire. As Masséna later reminisced:

> At first they did not think much of him. His small size and puny face did
> not put him in their favour. The portrait of his wife that he held in his
> hand and showed to everyone, his extreme youth, made them think that
> this posting was the work of another intrigue, but a moment after, he
> donned his general's cap and seemed to grow by two feet. He questioned
> us on the position of our divisions, their equipment, the spirit and active
> number of each corps, gave us the direction that we had to follow,
> announced that, the next day, he would inspect all the corps and that the
> day after that they would march on the enemy to give battle.[3]

Masséna misremembered the last part – they didn't give battle for a
month – but he captured the spirit of activity that Napoleon radiated,
his confidence, his obsessive demand for information, which was to be
a feature throughout his life, and his love of his wife.

In that initial meeting, Napoleon showed his commanders how the
Savona–Carcare road led to three valleys, any one of which could ultimately lead them into the rich plains of Lombardy. Piedmont had opposed
the French Revolution and had been at war with France since 1793.
Napoleon believed that if his army could push the Austrians to the east

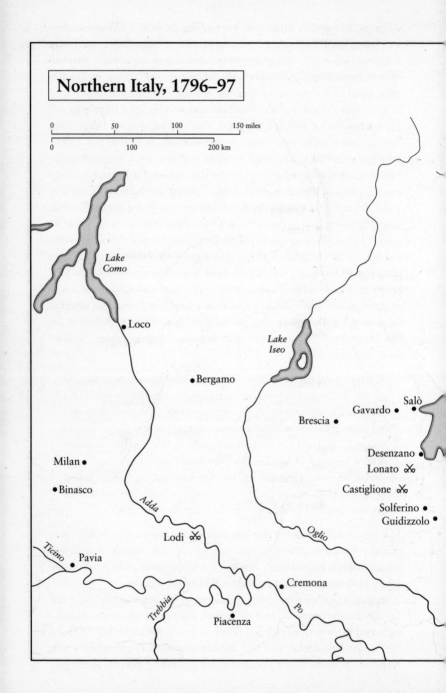

Northern Italy, 1796–97

| 0 | 50 | 100 | 150 miles |
| 0 | 100 | 200 km | |

Lake Como

Loco

Lake Iseo

Bergamo

Salò

Gavardo

Brescia

Desenzano

Milan

Lonato

Binasco

Castiglione

Solferino
Guidizzolo

Adda

Oglio

Lodi

Ticino
Pavia

Cremona

Trebbia

Po

Piacenza

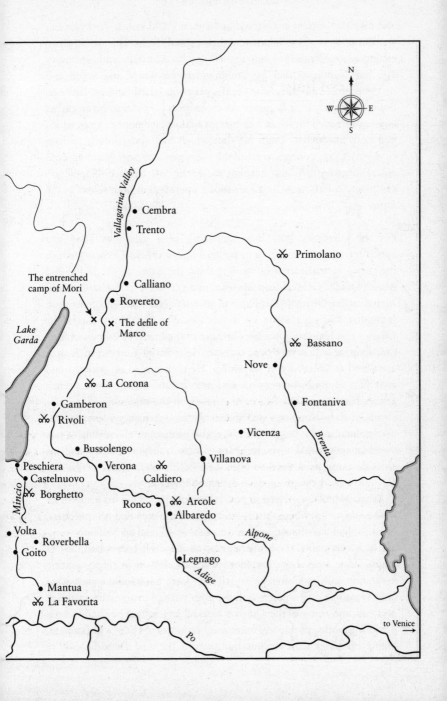

and take the fortress stronghold at Ceva, it could knock the Piedmontese out of the war by threatening their capital, Turin. This would mean pitting 40,000 French troops against 60,000 Austrians and Piedmontese, but Napoleon told his commanders he would use speed and deception to retain the initiative. His plan was based both on Pierre de Bourcet's *Principes de la guerre des montagnes* (1775), and on an earlier strategy intended for use in a campaign against Piedmont of 1745 which had been aborted by Louis XV but which had also concentrated on capturing Ceva. Bourcet wrote of the importance of clear planning, concentration of effort, and keeping the enemy off balance. Napoleon's campaign in Italy was to be a textbook operation in both senses of the term.

For the Directory, Italy was something of a sideshow. They had concentrated their resources in western and southern Germany where the two principal forces of the Republic, the Army of the Rhine and Moselle under General Jean Moreau, and the Army of the Sambre and Meuse under General Jean-Baptiste Jourdan, launched an offensive in June that had seen some initial success. The formidable Archduke Charles von Habsburg, younger brother of the Emperor Francis of Austria, fighting at his very best, defeated Jourdan at Amberg in August 1796 and at Würzburg in September. He then turned on Moreau and beat him at Emmendingen in October, before driving both French armies back across the Rhine. As a result of the sidelining of military efforts in Italy, Napoleon was given only 40,000 francs – less than his own annual salary – to pay for the entire campaign.[4] According to one possibly apocryphal story, in order to help transport himself and his aides-de-camp from Paris to Nice, he sold his silver-hilted sword and had Junot stake the proceeds at the gambling tables.[5]

When Napoleon arrived in Nice, therefore, he found his army in no state to move anywhere. It was freezing and the men had no overcoats. No meat had been issued for three months and bread arrived only irregularly. Mules pulled the artillery, since all the draft-horses had died of malnutrition, and entire battalions were shoeless or in clogs, wearing makeshift uniforms often taken off the dead. Some of the men were only identifiable as soldiers because they carried army-issue cartridge pouches, and many of their muskets lacked bayonets. They hadn't been paid for months, prompting mutterings of mutiny.[6] Fever was rampant, killing no fewer than six hundred men of the 21st Demi-Brigade in twenty days.* Mariana Starke, an English writer in Florence, accurately described the 'wretched state' of the French army before Napoleon's arrival: 'a total want of necessities, and a pestilential fever, the natural consequence of famine ... dejected and enfeebled by sickness, and destitute of horses, cannon, and almost every other sinew of war'.[7]

Napoleon's response to the 'wretched state' of his army was to demote Meynier and give his quartermaster Chauvet a brief to reorganize the commissariat completely, including, as he told the Directory on March 28, to 'threaten the contractors, who have robbed much and who enjoy credit'.[8] He also ordered Citizen Faipoult, France's minister in Genoa, to solicit 'without noise' 3 million francs in loans from the Jewish financiers there and he recalled the cavalry from its winter pastures in the Rhône valley. Within two days of arriving in Nice, Napoleon had disbanded the 3rd Battalion of the 209th Demi-Brigade for mutiny, dismissed its officers and NCOs from the army and distributed the other ranks in groups of five to other battalions. He believed it was essential for everyone to be treated according to the same rules, appreciating, as he put it, that 'If there were a single privilege granted to anyone, no matter whom, not one man would obey the order to march.'[9] On April 8 he reported to the Directory that he had been forced to punish his men for singing anti-revolutionary songs, and he had court-martialled two officers for crying 'Vive le roi!'[10]

Napoleon's divisional commanders were immediately impressed by his capacity for hard work. Subordinates could never say they would attend to something and then let it slide, and the staff who had been stationary in Nice for four years suddenly felt the pulsating effect of Napoleon's energy. In the nine months between his arrival in Nice and the end of 1796 he sent more than eight hundred letters and despatches, covering everything from where drummer-boys should stand in parades to the conditions under which the 'Marseillaise' should be played. Augereau was the first of his generals to be won over, followed by Masséna. 'That little bastard of a general actually frightened me!' Augereau would later tell Masséna.[11]

Napoleon decided to make the best of his reputation as a 'political' soldier. In his Order of the Day of March 29, he told his troops that

---

* A demi-brigade was the forerunner of the infantry regiment; during the French Revolutionary Wars they were rarely at full strength, and generally averaged about 2,400 men in three battalions.

they would 'find in him a comrade, strong in the confidence of the Government, proud of the esteem of patriots, and determined to acquire for the Army of Italy a destiny worthy of it.'[12]* After all, a general with the ear of the Directory might get his troops fed. Napoleon feared the indiscipline that arose when armed men face near-starvation. 'Without bread the soldier tends to an excess of violence', he wrote, 'that makes one blush for being a man.'[13]† Certainly his demands on Paris were constant, and on April 1 he managed to get 5,000 pairs of shoes delivered. An astonishing number of his letters throughout his career refer to providing footwear for his troops. Although he probably never said 'An army marches on its stomach', as legend has it, he was always deeply conscious that it indubitably marched on its feet.[14]

That same Order of the Day of March 29 announced that the forty-three-year-old Alexandre Berthier, a former engineer who had fought in the American War of Independence, was now Napoleon's chief-of-staff, a position he was to retain until 1814. Berthier had fought well in the Argonne campaign in 1792 and in the Vendée over the next three years, and his brother had been in the Topographical Bureau with Napoleon.

Napoleon was the first commander to employ a chief-of-staff in its modern sense, and he couldn't have chosen a more efficient one. With a memory second only to his own, Berthier could keep his head clear after twelve hours of taking dictation; on one occasion in 1809 he was summoned no fewer than seventeen times in a single night.[15] The Archives Nationales, Bibliothèque Nationale and the Archives of the Grande Armée at Vincennes teem with orders in the neat secretarial script and short concise sentences that Berthier used to communicate with his colleagues, conveying Napoleon's wishes in polite but firm terms, invariably starting 'The Emperor requests, general, that on receipt of this order you will . . .'[16] Among Berthier's many qualities was a diplomatic nature

---

* Orders of the Day were usually informational and administrative, read out during the 1 p.m. roll-calls in camp or during rest-halts on marches. These were different from proclamations, which read like speeches and were intended to be inspirational.

† Although the French army didn't resort to flogging as the British army did, it was much freer with the death penalty. When twelve clerks in the victualling department were caught selling the Imperial Guard's rations before the battle of Wagram, they were shot a few hours later (Blaze, *Life in Napoleon's Army*, p. 190). In Spain a man was shot for eating a bunch of grapes (they were thought to cause dysentery), and an indication of violence towards a superior would invite the death penalty. One voltigeur (light infantryman) was even shot during a later campaign in Spain for making a woman's black apron into a cravat.

so finely attuned that he somehow managed to persuade his wife, the Duchess Maria of Bavaria, to share a chateau with his mistress Madame Visconti (and vice versa). He rarely opposed Napoleon's ideas directly except on strict logistical grounds, and built up a team that ensured the commander-in-chief's wishes were quickly put into action. His special ability, amounting to something approaching genius, was to translate the sketchiest of general commands into precise written orders for every demi-brigade. Staff-work was rarely less than superbly efficient. To process Napoleon's rapid-fire orders required a skilled team of clerks, orderlies, adjutants and aides-de-camp, and a very advanced filing system, and he often worked through the night. On one of the few occasions when Napoleon spotted an error in the troop numbers for a demi-brigade, he wrote to correct Berthier, adding: 'I read these position statements with as much relish as a novel.'[17]

On April 2, 1796, Napoleon moved the army's headquarters forward to Albenga on the Gulf of Genoa. On that same day Chauvet died of fever in Genoa. This was 'a real loss to the army', Napoleon reported; 'he was active, enterprising. The army sheds a tear for his memory.'[18] Chauvet was the first of a large number of his friends and lieutenants who were to die on campaign with him, and for whom he felt genuine grief.

The Austrians – who had dominated northern Italy since 1714 – were sending a large army westwards to Piedmont to engage the French, and the Piedmontese were being supplied by the Royal Navy from Corsica. This forced Napoleon to haul everything he needed over the high mountain passes of Liguria. When he reached Albenga on April 5 he told Masséna and Laharpe his plan to cut the enemy off between Carcare, Altare and Montenotte. The Austrian commander, Johann Beaulieu, had much experience and some talent, but he was seventy-one and had been beaten by French armies before. A keen student of past campaigns, Napoleon knew that Beaulieu was cautious, a flaw he planned to exploit. The Austrian alliance with the Piedmontese was weak, and Beaulieu had been warned not to trust too much to it. ('Now that I know about coalitions,' Marshal Foch was to joke during the First World War, 'I respect Napoleon rather less!') Even within the Austrian army, the heterogeneous nature of the sprawling Habsburg Empire meant that its units often didn't speak the same language; the common tongue employed by its officer corps was French. To add to Beaulieu's problems, he had to answer to the unwieldy and bureaucratic Aulic Council in Vienna, which tended to give orders so late that by the time they arrived they had been overtaken by events. By contrast, Napoleon planned to adopt a daring manoeuvre now known in military academies as 'the strategy of the central position': he would remain between the two forces opposing him and would strike first at one and then at the other before they could coalesce. It was a strategy to which he would adhere throughout his career. 'It is contrary to all principle to make corps which have no communication act separately against a central force whose communications are open', was one of his maxims of war.[19]

'I am very busy here,' he wrote to Josephine from Albenga. 'Beaulieu is moving his army. We are face-to-face. I'm a little tired. I'm every day on horseback.'[20]* His daily letters to Josephine continued throughout the campaign, covering hundreds of pages of passionate scrawl. Some were written on the same day as major battles. He would constantly switch from romantic protestations ('I've not passed a day without loving you') to more self-centred considerations ('I've not taken a cup of tea without cursing that glory and that ambition which keep me separated from the soul of my life'), to maudlin reflections on why she hardly ever wrote back. When she did, she called him 'vous', which greatly irritated him. Napoleon's letters were full of coy erotic allusions to his desire to ravish her as soon as she would come out to join him in Italy. 'A kiss on your breast, and then a little lower, then much much lower,' he wrote in one.[21] There is some debate as to whether 'la petite baronne de Kepen' (occasionally 'Keppen') in his letters was a Napoleonic soubriquet for Josephine's sexual parts. Sadly, the etymology of the 'Baronne de Kepen' is lost to history, although it may simply have been the name of one of Josephine's many lap-dogs, so that 'Respectful compliments to the little baroness de Kepen' might have had no sexual overtones.[22] There is not much doubt about the less imaginative 'little black forest', as in: 'I give it a thousand kisses and wait with impatience the moment of being there.'[23] Somewhat unromantically these letters were often signed 'Bonaparte' or 'BP', just like his orders.[24] 'Adieu, woman, torment, joy, hope and soul of my life, whom I love, whom I fear, who inspires in me tender feelings which summon up Nature and emotions as impetuous and volcanic as thunder', is an entirely representative sentence from one of them.

*

* Although he often rode his mount to exhaustion, Napoleon was a fine horseman; he established 'complete mastery' over his horses and on occasion even got them to perform tricks (Balcombe, *To Befriend* pp. 41–2).

'The army is in a terrible state of destitution,' Napoleon reported to the Directory on April 6 from Albenga. 'I have still great obstacles to surmount, but they are surmountable. Distress has led to insubordination, and without discipline, victory is out of the question. I hope all this will be changed in the course of a few days.'[25] The Army of Italy numbered 49,300 men, against some 80,000 Austrians and Piedmontese. Fortunately, by then Berthier had mastered the immediate supply problems. Napoleon had planned to launch his offensive on April 15, but the Austro-Piedmontese forces started theirs five days earlier, coming up the same road Napoleon had intended to go down. Despite this unforeseen move, within forty-eight hours Napoleon had turned the situation around. Once he got his troops back from the town of Savona largely unscathed, he was able to organize a counter-attack. On the evening of April 11, realizing that the Austrian line was overextended, he fixed the enemy in place with an attack at Montenotte, a mountain village 12 miles north-west of Savona in the valley of the River Erro and then sent Masséna around the right flank in the pouring rain at 1 a.m. to envelop them. It was a tough environment in which to fight: a ridge runs down from Montenotte Superiore to a series of peaks between 2,000 and 3,000 feet high and there was (and still is) thick vegetation all around, climbing up exhausting slopes. Many redoubts had been built by the Austrian army, which were now captured by the swift-moving French infantry columns.

When the fighting was over, the Austrians had lost 2,500 men, many of whom were captured. Napoleon had lost 800. Though it was a relatively modest engagement, Montenotte was Napoleon's first victory in the field as commander-in-chief, and was as good for his own morale as for that of his troops. Several of his future battles were to follow the same parameters: an elderly opponent lacking energy; a nationally and linguistically diverse enemy confronting the homogeneous French army; a vulnerable spot which he would latch on to and not let go. The French had moved significantly faster than their enemy, and he had employed a concentration of forces that reversed the numerical odds for just long enough to be decisive.

Another recurring feature was the fast follow-up after victory: the day after Montenotte, Napoleon fought another engagement at Millesimo, a hamlet on the River Bormida, where he managed to prise the retreating Austrian and Piedmontese forces apart. The Austrians wanted to retreat eastwards to protect Milan, and the Piedmontese westwards to protect their capital of Turin. Napoleon was able to exploit their differing strategic imperatives. In order to escape the river valley, both had to fall back to the fortified village of Dego, where on April 14 Napoleon won his third victory in three days. Austro-Piedmontese losses numbered around 5,700 while the French lost 1,500 men, most due to Napoleon's impatience to capture the well-defended castle of Cosseria.

A week later at the battle of Mondovì, a town on the River Ellero, Napoleon vigorously fixed the Piedmontese front while attempting a double-envelopment. It was an ambitious and difficult manoeuvre to pull off but devastating to enemy morale when, as now, it succeeded. The next day the Piedmontese sued for peace. This was fortunate as Napoleon had no heavy siege weaponry with which to besiege Turin. One of the reasons why he maintained such a fluid campaign was that he had no resources for anything else. He complained to Carnot that he had been 'seconded neither by the artillery nor the engineers, as, in spite of your orders, I have not a single one of the officers I asked for'.[26] Conducting (or withstanding) a siege would have been impossible.

On April 26 Napoleon made a stirring proclamation to his army from Cherasco: 'Today you equal by your services the armies of Holland and the Rhine. Devoid of everything, you supplied everything. You have won battles without guns; passed rivers without bridges; accomplished forced marches without shoes; bivouacked without brandy and often without bread ... Today you are amply provided for.'[27] He continued: 'I promise you the conquest of Italy, but on one condition. You must swear to respect the people you deliver, and repress the horrible pillage in which scoundrels, excited by the enemy, have indulged.'[28]

A victorious, hungry army pillages. Napoleon was genuinely concerned by the conduct of his troops and wanted to keep the devastation in check. Four days earlier he had published an Order of the Day blaming 'fearful pillage' on 'perverse men, who join their corps only after the battle, and who commit excesses which dishonour the army and the French name'. He authorized generals to shoot any officers who allowed it, though there are no examples of this actually happening. He wrote privately to the Directory two days after his proclamation: 'I intend to make terrible examples. I shall restore order, or shall cease to command these brigands.'[29] It was the first of many hyperbolic threats of resignation he was to make over the course of this campaign.

Napoleon always differentiated between 'living off the land', which his army had to do by dint of insufficient supply, and 'fearful pillage'.[30] This took some sophistry, but his supple mind was up to the task. Often in the future he would blame Austrian, British and Russian armies for pillaging in a manner that he must have known his army had on many occasions greatly exceeded.* 'We lived upon what the soldiers found,' recalled an officer of the time. 'A soldier never steals anything, he only finds it.' One of Napoleon's most competent commanders, General Maximilien Foy, would later point out that if Napoleon's troops had 'waited for food till the administration of the army caused rations of bread and meat to be distributed, they might have starved'.[31]

'Living off the land' allowed Napoleon a speed of manoeuvre that was to become an essential element of his strategy. 'The strength of the army,' he stated, 'like power in mechanics, is the product of multiplying the mass by the velocity.'[32] He encouraged everything that permitted faster movement, including the use of forced marches which more or less doubled the 15 miles per day a demi-brigade could move. 'No man ever knew how to make an army march better than Napoleon,' recalled one of his officers. 'These marches were frequently very fatiguing; some-times half the soldiers were left behind; but, as they never lacked goodwill, they did arrive, though they arrived later.'[33]

In warm weather the French army didn't sleep in tents at night, because, as a veteran recalled, the armies 'marched so rapidly that they could not have carried with them all the requisite baggage'.[34] The only thing that followed them at pace were the wagons carrying ammunition. Armies moved much faster at the end of the eighteenth century than at the begin-ning due to improved road surfaces – especially after the recommendations of the French engineer Pierre Trésaguet, in his memorandum on scientific road-building of 1775, were taken up. Lighter field guns, more roads, smaller baggage-trains and far fewer camp-followers helped Napoleon's armies to move at what he calculated to be twice the speed of Julius Caesar's.

*

* Wellington's British army was not blameless in this regard. We have relatively few mem-oirs from enlisted men in the Peninsular War, but one by Friedrich Lindau of the King's German Legion makes it clear that they thieved off the local population and would beat up peasants who refused to give them produce and livestock (eds. Bogle and Uffindell, *Waterloo Hero passim, Mars & Clio*, No. 26 pp. 89–90). Napoleon did have a corporal and two soldiers shot who stole sacred vases from a church, which in his own mind was not compar-able to his own removal of much of northern Italy's Renaissance art treasures from churches and palaces. French generals regularly enriched themselves at the expense of the conquered, with some, like Masséna, taking greed to outrageous limits; Napoleon would later make him disgorge millions of francs. It was common practice at that period for commanders to reward themselves handsomely: Wellington returned from his campaigns in India having paid off all his debts and amassed a fortune of £42,000, the equivalent of over 1 million francs, all of it perfectly legally (Weller, *Wellington in India* pp. 257–9).

Armistice negotiations with the Piedmontese at Cherasco began immediately. In one exchange, Napoleon sardonically told a plenipotentiary
who had suggested terms that left him with fewer fortresses than he
desired: 'The Republic, in entrusting to me the command of an army,
has credited me with possessing enough discernment of what that army
requires without having recourse to the advice of my enemy.'[35] One of
the two negotiators, the Savoyard colonel Marquis Henry Costa de
Beauregard, later wrote a memoir in which he described the encounter:
'[He was] always cold, polished and laconic'.[36] At 1 a.m. on April 28 he
took out his watch and said: 'Gentlemen, I give you notice that the general attack is ordered for two o'clock, and if I am not assured that [the
fortress of] Coni will be placed in my hands before the end of the day,
this attack will not be delayed for a moment.'

It might have been a classic Napoleonic bluff, but the Piedmontese
couldn't take the risk. The armistice was signed immediately. Tortona,
Alessandria, Coni and Ceva were handed over to the French, along with
the route to Valence and all the territory between Coni and the Stura,
Tanaro and Po rivers. In a smart ploy, Napoleon insisted on a secret
clause giving him the right to use the bridge over the River Po at Valenza,
knowing the news would be leaked to the Austrians and that Beaulieu
would send troops to cover the bridge. He actually planned to cross the
river near Piacenza, 70 miles further east.

Over bottles of celebratory Asti wine and a pyramid of cakes supplied by the nuns of Cherasco, Napoleon spoke openly of the events
of the previous days, blaming himself for the loss of lives at Cosseria
Castle during the battle of Millesimo, triggered by his 'impatience to
separate the Austrian and Piedmontese armies'. He recounted that he
had been stationed at Dego two years earlier, when he had been in
charge of an artillery column. He had proposed the same invasion strategy then, but it had been rejected by a council of war. Then he added
'Nothing should ever be decided by this means in an army under [my]
command', and said that these councils were only ever resorted to as 'a
cowardly proceeding' intended to distribute blame.[37]

Napoleon told the Piedmontese he had executed a soldier for rape
the previous night, and diplomatically praised them for their strategic
withdrawals on April 17 and 21, saying: 'You twice escaped very dex-
terously out of my claws.' He showed Beauregard the small travelling
case in which he kept all his personal belongings, and said: 'I had a great
deal more of these superfluities when I was a simple artillery officer than
now when I am commander-in-chief.' In their hour-long conversation

while watching the sun rise, Beauregard was impressed with his knowledge of Piedmont's history, artists and scholars. Napoleon likened his movement to 'the combat of the younger Horatius, distancing his three enemies so as to disable them and kill them in succession'. He said he wasn't actually the youngest French general, though he conceded that his age was an asset. 'Youth is almost indispensable in commanding an army,' he told Beauregard, 'so necessary are high spirits, daring, and pride to such a great task.'[38]

The day after the armistice document was signed, Napoleon wrote to Paris, conscious that he had overstepped his authority in concluding a diplomatic agreement with a foreign power – let alone, as a good republican, allowing King Victor Amadeus III of Piedmont-Sardinia to stay on his throne. 'It's an armistice accorded to one wing of an army, giving me time to beat the other,' he wrote. 'My columns are on the march; Beaulieu is flying, but I hope to overtake him.'[39] He hoped to quell any quibbles from Paris with cash, promising to levy what he euphemistically termed a 'contribution' of several million francs on the Duke of Parma and suggesting one of 15 million francs from Genoa. Such 'contributions', once levied right across northern Italy, would allow him to pay the army half its wages in silver, rather than the despised *mandats territoriaux*, paper money that constantly depreciated in value.[40] Saliceti – for whom Napoleon had found a post organizing the Army of Italy, having clearly forgiven him for the incident in Antibes prison – appears to have hit upon the rather obvious recourse of paying the army first, before shipping the balance back to the cash-strapped Directory. Nothing short of military defeat demoralizes a country so totally as hyper-inflation, and the Directory, led by Barras since Vendémiaire, desperately needed the bullion that Napoleon was to send. This largely explains why, though they came to resent and even fear his successes in Italy and Austria, they made only one (feeble) attempt to replace him.

'Leave nothing in Italy which our political situation will permit you to carry away,' Napoleon was instructed, 'and which may be useful to us.'[41] Napoleon embraced this part of his remit enthusiastically. He was determined that Italy – or at least the parts that had opposed him – would be mulcted not merely of cash, but also of its great art. On May 1 he wrote to Citizen Faipoult: 'Send me a list of the pictures, statues, *cabinets* and curiosities at Milan, Parma, Piacenza, Modena and Bologna.'[42] The rulers of those places had every cause to tremble, for many of their finest treasures were destined for the art gallery in Paris known as the Musée Central des Arts from its opening in 1793 until 1803, then as the Musée Napoléon until 1815, and after that as the Musée du Louvre.

The French connoisseurs and curators appointed by Napoleon to choose which objets d'art to remove argued that bringing the greatest examples of Western art together in Paris actually made them far more accessible. 'Formerly it was necessary to climb the Alps and wander over whole provinces in order to gratify this learned and dignified curiosity,' wrote the Briton Rev. William Shephard in 1814, but 'the spoils of Italy are now brought together almost under the same roof, and there thrown open to the whole world'.[43]* As the pro-Bonapartist English writer and translator Anne Plumptre pointed out at the time, much of what the French were removing were objects that Romans such as the consul Lucius Mummius had themselves taken from places like Corinth and Athens.[44]

Napoleon wanted what became his museum – which he refurbished, gilded, filled with sculptures and turned into a 'parade palace' – to boast not only the world's greatest art, but also its greatest collection of historical manuscripts. A committed bibliophile, he would declare that he wanted to 'collect in Paris in a single body the archives of the German Empire, those of the Vatican, of France, and of the United Provinces'. He later instructed Berthier to ask one of his generals in Spain to find out where the archives of Charles V and Philip II were kept, since they 'would so nicely complete this vast European collection'.[45]

Napoleon told the Directory in early May that he intended to cross the River Po, and that it would be a tough operation. He warned them not to listen to 'the soldiers of the clubs, who believe we can swim across broad rivers'.[46] Beaulieu, the commander of the Austrian forces, had retreated into the angle of the Po and Ticino rivers, covering Pavia and Milan with his lines of communication running north of the Po. He had swallowed Napoleon's bait and had been closely watching Valenza. Napoleon made a dash for Piacenza in the dukedom of Parma, bypassing several river defence lines and threatening Milan. This was the first example of what was to become another favoured strategy, the *manoeuvre sur les derrières*, getting behind the enemy. Both the 'dashes' for Vienna in 1805 and 1809 and his strategic movements in Poland in 1806 and 1807 were to mirror this original dash to cross the Po.

---

* This is essentially the argument justifying the Elgin Marbles remaining in the British Museum today, although they were acquired under different circumstances.

Beaulieu was a day's march closer to Piacenza, so Napoleon would need two or preferably three days' advantage to cross the Po safely. He asked the army to move even faster, confident that he had calculated every supply requirement in detail. While Sérurier and Masséna moved to Valenza to deceive Beaulieu, and Augereau added to the confusion by taking up a post midway between Valenza and Piacenza, cutting all cross-river communications, Napoleon rushed forward with Laharpe and General Claude Dallemagne – to whom he had promised a consignment of new shoes, as many of his men were only wearing rags on their feet – and General Charles 'Brave' Kilmaine's cavalry. Technically they would be marching through neutral Parma, but Napoleon knew her duke to be hostile and didn't allow the niceties of international law, such as it existed at the time, to detain him.

By dawn on May 7, the French army were ready to cross the Po where it joins the Trebbia. The intrepid General Jean Lannes scoured the riverbank for miles, gathering every boat and all bridging materials. He found a ferry that could take five hundred men at a time across the 500-yard-wide river, whereupon Augereau (who was 20 miles away), Masséna (35 miles) and Sérurier (70 miles) were all recalled to rejoin Napoleon as soon as possible. Napoleon himself crossed on the 8th and made for Piacenza, whose governor opened the city gates for him after a short but frank explanation of what would happen to his city otherwise. 'One more victory,' Napoleon predicted to Carnot that day, 'and we are masters of Italy.'[47] Horses were forcibly requisitioned so that mules no longer had to pull the artillery, indeed many of the cannon Napoleon used at the coming battle were drawn by the coach-horses of the Piacenza nobility.

After concluding an armistice with the Duke of Parma, whose territory he had so casually invaded, Napoleon sent to Paris twenty paintings, including works by Michelangelo and Correggio, as well as Francesco Petrarch's manuscript of the works of Rome's greatest poet, Virgil.[48] Not content with that, the French also removed flora and fauna: the scientists Gaspard Monge and Claude-Louis Berthollet and the botanist André Thouin were sent to Pavia to take specimens of various plants and animals back to Paris's Jardin des Plantes. Napoleon even found some mercury for Berthollet to use in his experiments.[49]

By May 10, the Austrian army was retreating towards Milan via the town of Lodi, 22 miles south-east of Milan on the right bank of the River Adda. It was there that Napoleon decided to intercept them. Marmont led a hussar regiment and Lannes a battalion of grenadiers and chased the Austrian rearguard through the town. Both were abruptly halted by canister shot from the other end of a 200-yard-long and 10-yard-wide wooden bridge. Napoleon commandeered the first two guns he could find, brought them up to the bridge and directed fire in order to prevent the enemy from destroying the bridge, while sending for more guns and setting up sniper fire from the riverbank and nearby houses. He then went on to direct the battle from the bell-tower of the church directly behind the bridge.*

The Austrian rearguard commander, General Sebottendorf, had three battalions and fourteen guns covering the bridge, with eight battalions and fourteen cavalry squadrons in reserve, about 9,500 men in all. To turn the position might take days, ruining any chance of catching Beaulieu's retreating army. Napoleon decided that the bridge would have to be stormed immediately. He had thirty guns in place by 5 p.m., and sent 2,000 cavalrymen north and south to try to find a ford across the river. Then he formed up Dallemagne's column of 3,500 men in the backstreets of Lodi and gave them an inspirational harangue. ('One must speak to the soul,' he once said of his battlefield speeches, 'it is the only way to electrify the men.'50) He ordered Berthier to double the rate of artillery fire, and at 6 p.m. he sent the 27th and 29th Légère demi-brigades onto the bridge in the teeth of Austrian grapeshot. Colonel Pierre-Louis Dupas' combined companies of carabiniers had actually volunteered to lead the attack, an almost suicidal mission and certainly foreign to any natural instinct for self-preservation. Yet it was this frenzied spirit – known as 'the French fury' – that often gave Napoleon an edge in battle once his harangue had played on regimental pride and whipped up patriotic fervour.

The first soldiers on the bridge were cut down and flung back, but some jumped into the shallow river and continued to fire from under and around the bridge, as Napoleon sent in further waves of men. With great bravery, the bridge was taken and held, despite cavalry and infantry counter-attacks. When a French chasseur regiment appeared on the right bank of the river, having found a ford across it, the Austrians fell back in good order, as was generally their wont. Five days later the Austrians had been forced back to the Adige river and Napoleon was in Milan.†

---

* It was about 15 yards upstream from today's bridge.

† Crossing bridges and seizing bridgeheads in the presence of the enemy was to be a constant feature of Napoleonic campaigns. It would be seen again at Arcole in 1796, in the Danube campaign in 1805, at Jena in 1806, during the Polish campaign of 1807, at Aspern-Essling and Wagram in 1809, at the Berezina in 1812, at Leipzig in 1813, at Montereau in 1814 and at Charleroi in 1815.

The storming of the bridge at Lodi quickly became a central story in the Napoleonic legend, even though Napoleon faced only the Austrian rearguard and both sides lost around nine hundred men. It took tremendous courage to charge down a long, narrow bridge in the face of repeated grapeshot cannonades, and several of the officers who led the attacks that day – Berthier, Lannes and Masséna among them – became Napoleon's greatest commanders.* (Berthier acted as chief-of-staff, artillery captain and column commander that day, but it was the last time he was allowed to lead troops in a tactical capacity, as he was rightly considered too valuable to be risked in battle.) From the battle of Lodi on, Napoleon's men gave him the nickname *le petit caporal*, in that ancient tradition of soldiers affectionately teasing commanders they admire: Julius Caesar's men sang songs about 'the bald adulterer' (according to Suetonius), Wellington was called 'Nosey', Robert E. Lee 'Granny' and so on. 'The little corporal' was a soubriquet that Napoleon liked and encouraged, emphasizing as it did a republican ordinariness of which he was in fact divesting himself. After Lodi, all mutinous rumblings disappeared, and that vital sense of *esprit de corps* took its place and never left for the rest of the campaign.

'I no longer regarded myself as a simple general,' Napoleon later said of his victory, 'but as a man called upon to decide the fate of peoples. It came to me then that I really could become a decisive actor on our national stage. At that point was born the first spark of high ambition.'[51] He repeated this to so many different people on so many different occasions throughout his life that Lodi really can be taken as a watershed moment in his career. Vaunting ambition can be a terrible thing, but if allied to great ability – a protean energy, grand purpose, the gift of oratory, near-perfect recall, superb timing, inspiring leadership – it can bring about extraordinary outcomes.

'I hope soon to send you the keys of Milan and Pavia,' Napoleon told the Directory on May 11, in one of fifteen letters he wrote that day. He told Carnot separately that if he could take the near-impregnable Mantua – where Beaulieu was heading – he thought he could be 'in the heart of Germany' within two *décades* (the republican ten-day

---

* It was not all triumph that day, however. After the battle was won, Napoleon learned that Laharpe had been killed in a skirmish near Piacenza. He wrote to the French ambassador at Berne to ensure that his estate, which had been confiscated by the local authorities during the Revolution, was returned to his six children. The Bernese cantonal government was not about to refuse the demands of the victor of Lodi.

week).[52] He reported that he had lost 150 men against Austria's two to three thousand, even though casualty lists and the counting of corpses had undoubtedly told him the true numbers. The systematic exaggeration of enemy losses and diminution of his own was to be a persistent feature throughout all Napoleon's campaigns, and had of course been a feature of the writings of the classical authors with whom he was so familiar. He even did this in his private letters to Josephine, expecting that she would disseminate the information and that it would be given added credence due to its source. (Writing to Josephine after one battle he put down the number of his wounded as 700 before scribbling it out and inserting 100 instead.[53]) He knew that with no real means of obtaining corroboration, the French people would (at least initially) believe the figures he chose to tell them, not just about the killed and wounded, but also about the numbers of prisoners, cannon and standards captured. He didn't consider himself to be on oath when writing military bulletins.

Napoleon has been criticized for lying in his post-battle reports, but it is absurd to ascribe conventional morality to these reports since disinformation has been an acknowledged weapon of war since the days of Sun-tzu. (Winston Churchill once observed that in wartime, truth is so precious that she needs to be defended by a bodyguard of lies.) Where Napoleon did err, however, was in making the exaggerations so endemic that in the end even genuine victories came to be disbelieved, or at least discounted; the phrase 'to lie like a bulletin' entered the French language. When he could, Napoleon gave the French people hard evidence, sending captured enemy standards to be displayed at the military church of Les Invalides, but throughout his career he displayed an extraordinary ability to present terrible news as merely bad, bad news as unwelcome but acceptable, acceptable news as good, and good news as a triumph.

For two weeks Napoleon had been asking Josephine to join him in Italy. 'I now beg you to leave with Murat,' he had written, asking her to go via Turin,

> thus you would shorten your journey by fifteen days ... My happiness is to see you happy; my joy, to see you gay; my pleasure, to see you pleased. There was never a woman loved with more devotion, passion or tenderness. Never again can I be the complete master of my heart, dictating thereto all its tastes, its inclinations, forming all its desires ... No letter from you; I only get one every four days; instead of which, if you loved me, you would write to me twice a day ... Adieu, Josephine, you are to

me a monster I can't make out ... I love you more every day. Absence cures the small passions; it increases the great ... Think of me, or tell me disdainfully that you do not love me, and then perhaps I shall find in my spirit the means of making myself less pitiable ... That will be a happy day ... the day you pass the Alps. It will be the finest compensation for my sufferings, the happiest reward for my victories.[54]

Josephine had no intention of making the journey. She came up with a particularly cruel excuse – if that is what it was – telling Murat that she thought she was pregnant. This news sent Napoleon into transports of delight and excitement. He wrote to her from his headquarters at Lodi on May 13: 'Would it were possible that I might have the happiness of seeing you with your little belly! ... Soon you will give life to a being who will love you as much as me. Your children and I, we shall always be around you to convince you of our care and love. You will never be cross, will you? No humphs!!! except for fun. Then three or four faces; nothing is prettier, and then a little kiss patches up everything.'[55]

It is possible that Josephine either had a phantom pregnancy or a genuine miscarriage, but there would be no child. There were in fact other distractions preventing her from joining her husband in Italy: she was pursuing an affair with an hussar lieutenant called Hippolyte Charles, a dapper wit and practical joker who was nine years younger than her. 'You will be mad about him,' she wrote to a friend, saying that his face 'is so beautiful! I think that no-one before him has ever known how to tie a cravat.'[56] The financier Antoine Hamelin, who knew Charles fairly well, thought him 'a little shrimp of a man whose only advantage was his good figure', and said he possessed 'the elegance of a wigmaker's boy'.[57] Although this makes him sound like a mere lounge-lizard, it must be acknowledged that Lieutenant Charles did have some courage to cuckold Napoleon Bonaparte in an era when duelling was common.

Even before the Directory had received the news of Napoleon's victory at Lodi, they conceived a plan to try to force him to share the glory of the Italian campaign, not least because the lacklustre performances of Generals Moreau and Jourdan in Germany meant that public adulation was starting to concentrate dangerously around him. Ever since General Dumouriez's treason in 1793, no government had wanted to accord too much power to any one general. When Napoleon requested that reinforcements of 15,000 men be taken from General Kellermann's Army of the Alps, the Directory replied that the men could indeed be sent to

Italy, but Kellermann must go with them and command of the Army of Italy would be split. Replying on May 14, four days after Lodi and the day before he captured Milan, Napoleon told Barras: 'I will resign. Nature has given me a lot of character, along with some talents. I cannot be useful here unless I have your full confidence.' He described Kellermann, the victor of the battle of Valmy, as 'a German for whose tone and principles I have no respect'.[58] At the same time he told Carnot: 'I cannot serve willingly with a man who believes himself the first general of Europe, and furthermore I believe it would be better to have one bad general than to have two good ones. War, like government, is a matter of tact.'[59]

Napoleon showed considerably more tact in his official reply to the Directory: 'Each to his own way of making war. General Kellermann has more experience and will do it better than myself; but both of us doing it together will do it extremely badly.'[60] Coupled with that faux modesty came the arrogance of youth: 'I have conducted the campaign without consulting anyone. I should have accomplished nothing worth the trouble had I been obliged to reconcile my ideas with those of another ... Because I was persuaded of your entire confidence, my moves were as prompt as my thought.'[61] Napoleon was right that the two men would soon have clashed; he would have made an impossible co-commander, let alone subordinate. The campaign so far had proven that a single commander-in-chief had a major advantage over the unwieldy Austrian command structure.* His resignation threat, coming upon the news of the victory at Lodi and capture of Milan, ensured that no more was heard of the scheme. Afterwards, Napoleon knew that if he continued to win battles he would have the whip hand over the Directory, a body to which he continued to pay proper rhetorical obedience but which he was increasingly coming to despise.

Napoleon's letters to the Directory were heavily censored when they were published in the *Moniteur*, excising all the jokes and gossip. Of the weak and unimpressive Duke Hercules III of Modena, for example, Napoleon had written that he was 'as unworthy of his baptismal name as of his descent from the noble house of Este'. He then suggested that the duke's chief negotiator, Seignor Frederic, was his illegitimate brother by a Spanish dancer.[62] Barras later claimed to have been shocked by the

---

* 'Nothing is so important in war as an undivided command,' Napoleon pronounced later in life. 'There should be only one army, acting upon one base, and conducted by one chief' (ed. Chandler, *Military Maxims* p. 213).

'humiliating' and 'sarcastic' remarks in Napoleon's reports, but it is safe to assume that he enjoyed them at the time.

On Sunday, May 15, 1796 Napoleon entered Milan in triumph.* The carabiniers had the honour of entering first, in recognition of their heroism in capturing the bridge at Lodi, and 'were covered with flowers and received with joy' by the populace.[63] Although Napoleon was cheered loudly as he rode through the streets, he understood that conquerors always tended to be welcomed into cities they were about to occupy. While many Italians were delighted that the Austrians had been expelled, they felt little real warmth and plenty of apprehension towards their French replacements. A small but nonetheless significant group, however, was genuinely excited about the effect that French revolutionary ideas might have on Italian politics and society. As a rule, the educated, professional and secularized elites were more likely to regard Napoleon as a liberating force than the Catholic peasantry, who saw the French armies as foreign atheists.

Napoleon was invited to stay at the gorgeous Palazzo Serbelloni in Milan by the Duke of Serbelloni, who had thirty indoor servants and one hundred staff in the kitchens. He needed them, because his guest began to entertain on a lavish scale, receiving writers, editors, aristocrats, scientists, academics, intellectuals, sculptors and opinion-formers, and revelling in Milan's opera, art and architecture. There was a political purpose to all this. 'As a celebrated artist you have a right to the special protection of the Army of Italy,' he wrote to the sculptor Antonio Canova in Rome. 'I have given orders for your board and lodging to be paid at once.'[64] Wishing to appear as an enlightened liberator, rather than just the latest in a long line of conquerors, Napoleon held out the hope of an eventually independent, unified nation-state and thereby kindled the sparks of Italian nationalism. To that end, the day after his arrival in Milan, he declared the creation of a Lombardic Republic. It would be governed by Italian pro-French *giacobini* (Jacobins, or 'patriots') and he encouraged political clubs to mushroom throughout the region (the one in Milan soon included eight hundred lawyers and merchants). He also abolished Austrian governing institutions, reformed Pavia University, held provisional municipal elections, founded a National Guard and conferred with the leading Milanese advocate of Italian unification, Francesco Melzi d'Eril, to whom he handed over as

---

* It was supposedly on this occasion that he remarked to Marmont: 'Fortune is a woman, and the more she does for me, the more I will require of her' (Rose, *Napoleon* I p. 118).

much power as possible. None of this prevented Napoleon and Saliceti from levying a 20-million franc 'contribution' from Lombardy, ironically on the same day he issued an Order of the Day stating that he had 'too lively an interest in the honour of the army to allow any individual to violate the rights of property'.[65]

Italy in 1796 was, as Metternich would later observe, 'merely a geographical expression', a notion far more than a nation, despite her shared culture and slowly developing common language. Lombardy was now a theoretically independent republic, albeit now a French protectorate, but the Veneto was still an Austrian province and Mantua was occupied by the Austrian army. Tuscany, Modena, Lucca and Parma were ruled by Austrian dukes and grand dukes; the Papal States (Bologna, Romagna, Ferrara, Umbria) were owned by the Pope; Naples and Sicily formed a single kingdom (the Two Sicilies) ruled by the Bourbon Ferdinand IV, and the Savoyard monarchy still reigned in Piedmont and Sardinia. Italians such as Melzi who dreamed of a unified state had no alternative but to place their hopes in Napoleon, despite his demands for 'contributions'.

Over the course of the next three years, known as the *triennio*, Italians saw the emergence of the *giacobini* in a series of 'sister-republics' that Napoleon was to set up. He wanted to establish a new Italian political culture based on the French Revolution that would prize meritocracy, nationhood and free-thinking over privilege, city-state localism and Tridentine Catholicism.[66] This was the Directory's political agenda too, although Napoleon increasingly imposed his views with less and less deference to theirs. The *giacobini* were imbued with the principles of the Revolution, and during the *triennio* Napoleon gave them a chance to exercise limited power. Yet much of the old order remained; the Italians, as so often under past occupations, had a way of blunting the zeal of their conquerors. Very often the actual sway of *giacobini* governments never extended much beyond the cities, and rarely for long. French power was too naked, too centralized, too demanding (especially of money and art) and too foreign for most Italians. Yet it is worth noting that but for a few months in Lombardy in the summer of 1796, and later in rural, southern, ultra-Catholic Calabria, there was no mass rebellion against Napoleonic rule in Italy in the way that there was to be in the Tyrol and Spain, because overall the Italians accepted that the French methods of government were better for them than the Austrian ones had been.

Reforms that Napoleon imposed on the newly conquered territories included the abolition of internal tariffs, which helped to stimulate economic development, the ending of noble assemblies and other centres of feudal privilege, financial restructurings aimed at bringing down state debt, ending the restrictive guild system, imposing religious toleration, closing the ghettos and allowing Jews to live anywhere, and sometimes nationalizing Church property. These modernizing measures, which were repeated in most of the territories he conquered over the coming decade, were applauded by middle-class progressives in many lands beyond France, including by people who hated Napoleon. Voltaire's view that European civilization was on a progressive course was fairly universally held in France in Napoleon's time, and underlay his civilizing mission. Where he abolished the Inquisition, obscure feudal practices, anti-Semitic regulations and restraints on trade and industry such as the guilds, Napoleon also brought genuine enlightenment to peoples who, without his armies' victories, would have remained often without rights or equality before the law.

For Napoleon to convince Europe of the essential superiority of the French model of government, he would need active collaboration and not mere submission. He could win the war, but his administrators would have to move in swiftly afterwards to win the peace. As zealous leaders of what they truly considered to be a new form of civilization – although the actual word 'civilization' itself had only entered the French lexicon in the 1760s and was very little used in the Napoleonic era – the French revolutionary elites genuinely believed they were advancing the welfare of Europe under French leadership. They were offering a new design for living whose prerequisite was, of course, unchallenged French military might. Since Louis XIV's time France had called itself the 'Great Nation', and in August 1797 the Army of Italy's newspaper trumpeted the view that 'Every step of the Great Nation is marked by blessings!'[67] Under the Directory, French officers drank such toasts at patriotic banquets as 'To the unity of French republicans; may they follow the Army of Italy's example and, supported by it, regain the energy that is fitting for the leading nation on Earth!'[68] Although this didn't have the brevity essential to the best toasts, it exuded that sense of civilizational superiority necessary to any serious imperial enterprise.

'All men of genius, everyone distinguished in the republic of letters, is French, whatever his nationality,' Napoleon wrote from Milan in May 1796 to the eminent Italian astronomer Barnaba Oriani. 'Men of learning in Milan have not enjoyed proper respect. They hid themselves in their laboratories and thought themselves lucky if ... priests left them alone. All is changed today. Thought in Italy is free. Inquisition,

intolerance, despots have vanished. I invite scholars to meet and propose what must be done to give science and the arts a new flowering.'[69]
Academics were impressed by the abolition of censorship, though of
course this didn't extend to criticism of the French occupation.

Yet, for any of these promises to bear fruit, Napoleon would need to
capture northern Italy altogether. In May 1796 a large Austrian force
was inside Mantua, with little prospect of being dislodged and every
possibility of being relieved. 'Soldiers,' read one of Napoleon's proclamations to his troops soon after entering Milan,

> you have rushed like a torrent from the top of the Apennines. You have
> overthrown and scattered all that opposed your march . . . The Dukes of
> Parma and Modena owe their political existence to your generosity
> alone . . . These great successes have filled the heart of your country with
> joy . . . There your fathers, your mothers, your wives, sisters and
> loved-ones rejoiced in your good fortune, and proudly boasted of belong-
> ing to you.[70]

The praise was fulsome, but any soldier hoping to rest and recuperate
in Milan was immediately disabused:

> An effeminate repose is tedious to you: the days that are lost to glory
> are lost to your happiness. Well then, let us set forth! We still have
> forced marches to make, enemies to subdue, laurels to gather,
> injuries to avenge . . . You will then return to your homes and your coun-
> try. Men will say as they point you out: 'He belonged to the Army of
> Italy.'[71]

On May 23 a revolt against the French occupation in Pavia led by
Catholic priests was put down harshly by Lannes, who simply shot
the town council.[72] A similar incident took place the following day at
Binasco, 10 miles south-west of Milan.[73] The village had been fortified
by armed peasants who launched attacks on the French lines of communication: 'As I was half way to Pavia, we met a thousand peasants at
Binasco and defeated them,' Napoleon reported to Berthier. 'After killing one hundred of them we burned the village, setting a terrible but
efficient example.'[74] The burning of Binasco was similar to the
kind of anti-guerrilla action that was then taking place across the Vendée, where massacres and village-burnings were employed against
Chouans.[75] Napoleon believed that 'bloodletting is among the ingredi-
ents of political medicine', but he also thought that quick and certain

punishments meant that large-scale repression could largely be avoided.[76] He almost never indulged in brutality for its own sake, and could be sensitive to people's suffering. A week after Binasco he told the Directory: 'Although necessary, this spectacle was nevertheless horrible; I was painfully affected by it.'[77] Ten years later Napoleon would write in a postscript of a letter to Junot: 'Remember Binasco; it brought me tranquillity in all of Italy, and spared shedding the blood of thousands. Nothing is more salutary than appropriately severe examples.'[78] 'If you make war,' he would say to General d'Hédouville in December 1799, 'wage it with energy and severity; it is the only means of making it shorter and consequently less deplorable for mankind.'[79]

During the Pavia revolt, which spread over much of Lombardy, five hundred hostages from some of the richest local families were taken to France as 'state prisoners' to ensure good behaviour. In the country around Tortona, Napoleon destroyed all the church bells that had been used to summon the revolt, and had no hesitation in shooting any village priest caught leading peasant bands. Although his earlier anti-clericalism in Corsica was enough to make him resent what he called *la prêtraille* (canting priesthood), it was confirmed now by the way in which parish priests encouraged uprisings. Yet it also instilled in him a respect for the power of the Church as an institution, which he realized that he could not wholly oppose. He promised to protect those priests who did not mix religion and politics.

By late May Napoleon was in torment. Josephine had stopped writing to him, despite his stream of long letters asking 'Are you coming? How is your pregnancy going?' and calling her his *dolce amor* five times in one letter alone.[80] 'I have a presentiment that you have left to come here,' he wrote in one,

> that idea fills me with joy ... As for me, your coming will make me so happy that I shall be quite out of my senses. I am dying with the wish to see how you carry children ... No, sweet love, you will come here, you will be very well; you will give birth to a child as pretty as its mother, which will love you like its father, and, when you are old, when you are a hundred, it will be your consolation and your joy ... come quickly to hear good music and to see beautiful Italy. There is nothing lacking to it except the sight of you.[81]

Josephine wouldn't leave Paris for another month, so fascinated was she by Hippolyte Charles's sky-blue uniform, red morocco boots, tight Hungarian-style breeches and puerile practical jokes.

On June 2, 1796, Napoleon began his siege of the well-provisioned Mantua. His forces were stretched thin, for he had yet to capture Milan's castle, known as the Citadel, and was watching for the return of the Austrians from the Tyrol while simultaneously quelling the revolt in the north. He had been told by the government in Paris to spread the revolution southwards into the Papal States, and to expel the Royal Navy from the papal city of Livorno. He also had to threaten Venice to ensure she would not compromise her neutrality by helping Austria. He called up his siege equipment from Antibes to Milan, hoping to add to it with guns he would capture in Bologna, Ferrara and Modena in a sudden southern sweep against the Papal States in mid-June.

At the battle of Borghetto on May 30, Napoleon crossed the Mincio river and forced Beaulieu to retreat northwards up the Adige valley towards Trento. After he had nearly been captured during the fighting, Napoleon dismissed his bodyguards and appointed a new company of chasseurs to protect him, the forerunner of his Chasseurs à Cheval de la Garde, under the cool and cautious General Jean-Baptiste Bessières. After Borghetto, Emperor Francis relieved the hapless Beaulieu of his command of the Austrian field army – though he stayed in command of Mantua – and appointed Field Marshal General Dagobert von Wurmser, an Alsatian and yet another septuagenarian who had won his reputation in the Seven Years War, which had ended six years before Napoleon was born.

Four fortresses, known as the Quadrilateral, held the key to Austrian power in northern Italy: Mantua, Peschiera, Legnago and Verona. Together they protected the entrance to the Alpine passes to the north and east and the approaches to the Po and Lake Garda. Napoleon generally liked to keep his movements fluid and to avoid sieges, but now he had no choice. He had only 40,400 men with which to besiege Mantua, keep communication routes open and hold the line of the River Adige. Between June 1796 and February 1797 Mantua lay under siege for all but five weeks. Protected on three sides by a wide lake and on the fourth by high thick walls, it presented a formidable challenge to any attacker. The besieged heavily outnumbered the besiegers, and, at least initially, the Austrians fired twice as many cannonballs at the French as the French could fire back. But by early June Napoleon was so well provisioned from the Lombardy plains and by 'contributions' that he could send to the Directory one hundred carriage horses, to 'replace the mediocre horses that draw your coaches'.[82] He also sent them a much-needed 2 million francs in gold.

On June 5 Napoleon met the diplomat André-François Miot de Melito, the French minister to Tuscany. Miot would write of their encounter that Napoleon had an

> extremely spare figure. His powdered hair, oddly cut and falling squarely below the ears, reached down to his shoulders. He was dressed in a straight coat, buttoned up to the chin, and edged with very narrow gold embroidery, and he wore a tricoloured feather in his hat. At first sight he did not strike me as handsome, but his strongly marked features, his quick and piercing eyes, his brusque and animated gestures revealed an ardent spirit, while his wide and thoughtful brow was that of a profound thinker.[83]

Miot noted that when Napoleon gave orders to Murat, Junot and Lannes, 'Everyone maintained towards him an attitude of respect, I may even say one of admiration. I saw none of the marks of familiarity between him and his companions as I had observed in other cases, which was consonant with republican equality. He had already assumed his own place, and set others at a distance.' This was deliberate; even at twenty-seven Napoleon was beginning to use his aides-de-camp, secretaries and domestic staff to regulate his accessibility and enhance his status. To this end he appointed two new aides-de-camp to join Junot, Marmont, Muiron and Murat. These were Joseph Sulkowski, a Polish captain in the revolutionary army, and Géraud Duroc, an artillery officer who had shown his efficiency as General Augustin de Lespinasse's aide-de-camp. Napoleon was years later to describe Duroc as 'the only man who had possessed his intimacy and entire confidence'.[84] Duroc would be one of the very few people outside Napoleon's family to use 'tu' when addressing him.

The Directory had wanted Napoleon to move on Bourbon Naples, but he understood that to march south would be dangerous in light of the threat from the Tyrol, so now, instead of exceeding his orders from Paris as at Cherasco, he defied them. Napoleon ordered Miot to negotiate an armistice with Naples that would require her to withdraw her four cavalry regiments from the Austrian army and her ships from the Royal Navy squadron at Livorno. The alternative was an invasion of Naples by the Army of Italy. Once he was threatened with invasion, the Neapolitan negotiator, Prince de Belmonte-Pignatelli, signed the treaty that was put before him in two hours flat. Napoleon was by then willing to disparage the Directory, asking Pignatelli whether he really thought that he 'was fighting for those scamps of lawyers'.[85] (Although Napoleon liked and admired some individual lawyers, he utterly detested them en masse, and of the five Directors, three were former lawyers and one – Barras – a former judge. Only the mathematician Carnot had no legal background.)

Back in Milan on June 5, Napoleon wrote again to Josephine, who he still thought was pregnant and on her way to see him. The volcanic expressions of love, anger, confusion and self-pity, and the sheer number and length of his letters, suggest that writing them must have been a form of release, an escape from the political and military pressures crowding in upon him at the time. In an age of self-conscious Romantic letter-writing, Napoleon was clearly striving for the greatest possible effect and the boundary between what he was writing to his wife and the fantasy of *Clisson et Eugénie* is all but invisible. 'My soul was all expectant of joy,' reads one letter,

> it is filled with sorrow. The mails keep arriving without bringing anything from you. When you do write, it is only a few words, without any evidence of deep feeling. Your love for me was only a light caprice; you feel that it would have been ridiculous had your heart even deeply engaged ... As for you, my only remaining hope is that the recollection of me will not be odious to you ... My heart has never entertained commonplace feelings ... it has steeled itself against love; you came and inspired a limitless passion, an intoxication which degrades. The thought of you has taken precedence of all else in my soul, the universe besides was nothing; your slightest caprice was to me a sacred mandate; to be able to see you was my supreme happiness. Beautiful you are, gracious; a sweet, a celestial soul expresses itself in heavenly tints through your face ... Cruel!!! How could you have allowed me to imagine in you feelings you never entertained!!! But reproaches are unworthy of me. I have never believed in happiness. Death flutters about me every day ... Is life worth all the fuss and clatter we make about it? Adieu, Josephine ... A thousand daggers stab my heart; do not plunge them in deeper. Adieu my happiness, my life, all that had any real existence for me on this earth.[86]

He had turned to unpublished literary endeavours many times before to seek release from his sadness over Désirée, to recall the loss of his virginity, to express his hatred of France over its 'subjection' of Corsica, to explain his Jacobinism, and so on. But now he actually sent these overwrought letters off to Josephine, who was so bound up in her own love affair that she scarcely bothered to send more than two or three lines once a fortnight – and for a whole month up to June 11 didn't write at all. By then Napoleon seems to have finally guessed that something was amiss, for that day he wrote to her former lover Barras: 'I am in despair that my wife does not come to me; she has some lover who keeps her in Paris. I curse all women but I embrace my good friends with all my heart.'[87]

To Josephine herself he wrote to say that he was almost resigned to the fact that she no longer loved him – if indeed she ever had – but then at the next moment he was so incapable of accepting this somewhat obvious conclusion that he grasped at every other possibility, including the notion that she might be dying (though Murat, currently in Paris, reported that any illness she might have contracted was 'light').

You do not love me anymore. I have only to die ... would it were possible!!! All the serpents of the Furies are in my heart, and already I am only half alive. Oh! You ... my tears flow, there is neither rest nor hope. I respect the will and unchanging law of this destiny; it weighs me down with glory to make me feel my unhappiness all the more bitterly. I will grow accustomed to everything in this new state of affairs; but I cannot accustom myself to no longer respecting it; but no, it is not possible, my Josephine is en route; she loves me, at least a little; so much love promised cannot vanish in two months. I hate Paris, women and the love-making ... That state of affairs is frightful ... and your conduct ... But should I accuse you? No, your conduct is that of your destiny. So kind, so beautiful, so gentle, should you be the perpetrating instrument of my despair? ... Farewell my Josephine; the thought of you was wont to make me happy, but all that is changed now. Embrace for me your charming children. They write me delightful letters. Since I must not love you any longer, I love them all the more. Regardless of destiny and honour, I will love you all my life. I re-read all your letters again last night, even the one written with your blood: what feelings they made me have![88]

At one point he asked her not to wash for three days before they met so he could steep himself in her scent.[89] By June 15 he was frankly telling her, 'I could not tolerate a lover, much less allow you to take one.' He said he recalled a dream 'in which I took off your boots, your dress, and made you enter bodily into my heart'.[90]

Although Napoleon wrote hundreds of pages of emotional rhapsodies to Josephine, endlessly suggesting that he would kill himself if anything were to happen to her, he rarely told her anything about the war that couldn't be gleaned from the public gazettes. Nor did he trust her with his innermost thoughts about people or events. It might have been because he feared that his letters, which took two weeks to reach Paris by special courier, might be captured by the enemy. Perhaps, as the British politician John Wilson Croker suggested in the *Quarterly Review* in 1833, when 238 of Napoleon's letters to Josephine were first published, it was because he thought her 'frivolous, capricious, and giddy – too vain not to be flattered, too indiscreet to be trusted'. Croker was harsh, but not unfair, in denouncing the letters as showing: 'No real confidence, no interchange of mind ... no communication of serious thoughts, no identity of interests.'[91]

Napoleon was capable of compartmentalizing his life, so that one set of concerns never spilled over into another – probably a necessary attribute for any great statesman, but one he possessed to an extraordinary degree. 'Different subjects and different affairs are arranged in my head as in a cupboard,' he once said. 'When I wish to interrupt one train of thought, I shut that drawer and open another. Do I wish to sleep? I simply close all the drawers, and there I am – asleep.'[92] An aide-de-camp wrote of how much his staff 'admired the strength of mind and the facility with which he could take off or fix the whole force of his attention on whatever he pleased'.[93] In the middle of this hurricane in his private life and the growing, gnawing realization that the woman he worshipped was at best lukewarm in her affections towards him, Napoleon was putting the finishing touches to a bold campaign plan that would lead to a string of seven more victories on top of the five already won, the capture of Mantua and the expulsion of Austria from Italy after three centuries of Habsburg rule.

5
Victory

'In order to lead an army you have ceaselessly to attend to it, be ahead of the news, provide for everything.'

Napoleon to Joseph, April 1813

'There is but one step from triumph to downfall. I have seen, in the most significant of circumstances, that some little thing always decides great events.'

Napoleon to Talleyrand, October 1797

Although Napoleon's main enemy was always Austria during the Italian campaign, he was able to use the short moments when the Austrians posed no danger to protect his rear. It has been said that when the French troops arrived in the Papal States in June 1796 they lit their pipes with altar-candles, though the sheer vividness of the image smacks of Francophobic propaganda.[1] What is true is that Pope Pius VI had denounced the French Revolution and supported, but not formally joined, the First Coalition against France. He would soon be made to pay heavily for this insult. The seventy-eight-year-old Pope had already reigned for twenty-one years, and hadn't the military or personal capacity to prevent Napoleon entering Modena on June 18 and Bologna the next day, where he expelled the papal authorities and forced them to come to terms within a week. In late June Napoleon agreed an armistice with the Pope, with a 'contribution' of 15 million francs that was enough to bring round the Directory to the idea of a peace treaty. Saliceti also negotiated the handing over of 'One hundred pictures, vases, busts, or statues, as the French commissioners shall determine', including a bronze bust of Junius Brutus and a marble one of Marcus Brutus, plus five hundred manuscripts from the Vatican library.[2] On August 11

Napoleon's eagle eye spotted the library trying to reduce its commitment and wrote to François Cacault, the French agent in Rome, to say: 'The treaty included five hundred manuscripts, not three hundred.'[3]

On June 21, the twenty-six-year-old Napoleon wrote no fewer than four letters to the Directory in Paris, warning that he had only a 'middling' army with which 'to face all emergencies; to hold the [Austrian] armies in check; to besiege forts, to protect our rear, to overawe Genoa, Venice, Florence, Rome and Naples; we must be in force everywhere.'[4] It was true: the great cities of Italy – he could also have included Milan and Turin – were held in check as much by the awe aroused by his seeming invincibility as by any immediate military force. He was vulnerable to a properly co-ordinated revolt. The Directory offered few reinforcements, still considering the Rhine to be much the more important theatre of operations.

A judicious interplay between threats and insouciance played an important part in Napoleon's Italian statecraft at this time. 'Here, one must burn and shoot in order to establish terror,' he wrote on June 21, 'and there one must pretend not to see because the time has not arrived for action.'[5] He appealed to the pride of those he would conquer but gave them no doubt as to the consequences of resistance. 'The French army loves and respects all peoples, especially the simple and virtuous inhabitants of the mountains,' read a proclamation to the Tyrolese that month. 'But should you ignore your own interests and take up arms, we shall be terrible as the fire from heaven.'[6]

He leaned heavily on Berthier, but was not shy of asserting his own capacities. When he saw Miot de Melito in Bologna on June 22, Napoleon asked the diplomat about the rumour 'that it is to Berthier that I owe my success, that he directs my plans, and that I only execute what he has suggested to me'. Miot, who had known Berthier as a youth in Versailles, denied it, whereupon Napoleon said, with warmth, 'You are right, Berthier is not capable of commanding a battalion!'[7] This was not something he actually believed – he handed command of the Army of Italy to Berthier in 1798 and the Army of the Reserve in 1800 – but it shows how deeply conscious he was of his public image. In a similar vein he would now alter the wording of proclamations to turn the phrase 'Commanders of the French Army' into the singular.

The British, who had been friendly trading partners with the Grand Duchy of Tuscany, were expelled from Livorno on June 27 and £12 million of their merchandise captured; the Milan Citadel fell after a forty-eight-hour bombardment on the 29th. When the British responded on July 11 by seizing the island of Elba off the coast of Italy, a former possession of the Grand Duchy, Napoleon sensibly remarked: 'We shall have no right to complain of a violation of neutrality, of which we ourselves have set the example.'[8] Soon afterwards Napoleon extracted a 'contribution' from the Grand Duke Ferdinand III of Tuscany, Emperor Francis's younger brother, who had given English merchants trading privileges at Livorno. When Napoleon went to Florence on July 1, the streets from the San Fridiano to the Pitti Palace gates were 'filled with the whole population' trying to catch a glimpse of him.[9] Napoleon visited Ferdinand at the Palace there in the Boboli Gardens and saw the gorgeous Pietro da Cortona ceiling paintings commissioned by the Medici, which could not be easily removed to Paris, as well as paintings by Rubens, Raphael, Titian, Van Dyck and Rembrandt, which could. He told the Grand Duke, who received him with all *politesse*, 'Your brother no longer has a foot of land in Lombardy.' It wasn't true: Mantua was still holding out. But although Ferdinand 'was so master of himself as to betray no concern', he knew that its fall would soon be followed by the loss of his throne.[10]

On June 26, Josephine finally left Paris for Milan, in tears. She was accompanied by Joseph Bonaparte (who was nursing a sexually transmitted disease), her *demoiselle-de-compagnie* Louise Compoint, Joseph's brother-in-law Nicolas Clary, the financier Antoine Hamelin (who wanted a job from Napoleon and was sponged off by Josephine), Junot, four servants, a cavalry escort and Josephine's small mongrel Fortuné, which had once bitten Napoleon in bed and later fell in unequal combat to his cook's larger and fiercer dog.[11] With breathtaking gall, Josephine also brought along her boudoir-hussar Hippolyte Charles. Junot seduced Louise on the journey, so Josephine dismissed her when they reached Milan, making an enemy of Junot. Two years later she would come bitterly to regret this.

Napoleon inundated her with long love letters on her journey south, a typical one ending 'Farewell, my love, a kiss on your mouth – another on your heart' and looking forward to the moment when 'I could be in your arms, at your feet, on your breasts.'[12] He wrote from Pistoia in Tuscany to tell her that he had pockets 'full of letters which I have never sent you because they are too foolish, too silly – *bête* is the word'.[13] Considering the nature of the letters he *did* send, these must have been *trop bête* indeed. In a reprise of his earlier emotional masochism he wrote: 'Mock me as you like, stay in Paris, take lovers and let all the world know it, never write to me – Well! I'll only love you ten times more!'[14]

Josephine arrived at the Serbelloni Palace on July 10, and Napoleon joined her there three days later, having marched 300 miles from Milan through the Habsburg, Papal, Venetian and independent cities of Peschiera, Brescia, Tortona, Modena, Bologna, Livorno, Florence, Roverbella, Verona and back to Milan in six weeks, cowed all of central Italy, and seized 'contributions' totalling well over 40 million francs. He was oblivious to Hippolyte Charles – neither Junot, Murat nor Joseph was about to tell him – and Josephine appears to have responded warmly to his attentions, however she might have been feeling emotionally. Hamelin recalled that 'From time to time he would leave his study in order to play with her as if she were a child. He would tease her, cause her to cry out, and overwhelm her with such rough caresses that I would be obliged to go to the window and observe the weather outside.'[15] It was certainly a very tactile relationship; the playwright Carrion de Nisas recorded that 'Madame Bonaparte is neither young nor pretty, but she is extremely modest and engaging. She frequently caresses her husband, who seems devoted to her. Often she weeps, sometimes daily, for very trivial reasons.'[16]

Napoleon had summoned Joseph, for whom Saliceti had obtained the rank of commissary-general in the Army of Italy, in order to have someone near him whom he could trust with delicate confidential negotiations. In that capacity Joseph was to be used by his brother for missions to Livorno, Parma and Rome, and he later went with Miot de Melito to re-establish French control over Corsica. In the course of these expeditions, Joseph discovered a genuine capacity for diplomacy.

Napoleon could stay only two nights: Wurmser was on his way south with 50,000 men and the French needed to capture Mantua from Beaulieu before he could relieve it. 'I propose making a bold stroke,' he told the Directory.[17] Then he informed them of Murat's plan to cross one of the four artificial lakes protecting Mantua at night with men disguised in Austrian uniforms, hoping to open the city gates for long enough for Napoleon's troops to get inside. Napoleon was probably thinking of the Capitoline geese that saved Ancient Rome when he wrote of Murat's 'sudden attack, which, like all of a similar nature, will depend upon luck – a dog or a goose'.[18] In the event an unexpected drop in the level of the Po lowered the water in the lakes enough to stymie the plan.

By late July Napoleon had learned from a paid informer on the Austrian staff that Wurmser was taking his army, which now included excellent veteran units drawn from the Rhine campaign, down both sides of Lake Garda to relieve Mantua, where sickness was starting to wear down Beaulieu's garrison. Napoleon relied a good deal on intelligence in his campaigns, which he insisted on analysing personally rather than getting it through staff officers, so he could decide for himself how much credence to attach to each piece.[19] Methods of gaining intelligence included interrogating deserters and prisoners, sending out cavalry patrols, and even dressing soldiers as farm labourers after having taken the real labourers' wives hostage. Napoleon was conscious of the way that spies and officers on scouting missions could mistake corps for detachments and vice versa and often repeated what they had heard from 'panic-stricken or surprised people' rather than what they had witnessed.[20] His orders for his intelligence officers were: 'To reconnoitre accurately defiles and fords of every description. To provide guides that may be depended upon. To interrogate the priest and the postmaster. To establish rapidly a good understanding with the inhabitants. To send out spies. To intercept public and private letters . . . In short, to be able to answer every question of the general-in-chief when he arrives at the head of the army.'[21]

In this instance the spies were right: Wurmser was moving down the eastern side of Lake Garda with 32,000 men in five columns, while the Croatian-born cavalryman General Peter von Quasdanovich was coming down the western side with 18,000. Napoleon left Sérurier with 10,500 men to maintain the siege of Mantua. This gave him 31,000 men to meet the new threats. He sent 4,400 under General Pierre-François Sauret to Salò to slow down Quasdanovich, ordered Masséna with 15,400 men to the eastern side, deployed General Hyacinthe Despinoy with 4,700 to protect the Peschiera–Verona line, sent Augereau's 5,300 to watch the roads from the east and kept Kilmaine's 1,500 cavalry in reserve. He himself then moved continually between Brescia, Castelnuovo, Desenzano, Roverbella, Castiglione, Goito and Peschiera, taking his mobile headquarters to wherever gave him the best idea of the way the campaign was progressing. This constant activity in the often severe heat led to his losing five horses to exhaustion in quick succession.[22] One of his Polish aides-de-camp, Dezydery Adam Chlapowski, recalled that he 'never used his spurs or knees to make his horse gallop, but always applied his whip'.[23]

On July 29 Quasdanovich drove Sauret out of Salò as expected, although the town changed hands three times. At 3 a.m. the same day, east of Lake Garda, Masséna was attacked at La Corona and Rivoli by large numbers and had to conduct a long fighting retreat down the Adige to Bussolengo by nightfall. The Austrians pushed on boldly and took Rivoli. 'We shall recover tomorrow, or afterwards, what you have lost today,' Napoleon reassured Masséna. 'Nothing is lost while courage remains.'[24] On July 30, however, in an operation known as the 'Surprise of Brescia', the Austrians captured Brescia's garrison and hospitals with only three killed and eleven wounded. The sick included Murat (who had caught venereal disease from a Madame Rugat), Lannes and Kellermann's brilliant cavalryman son, François-Étienne. Josephine, who had gone to Brescia from Milan at Napoleon's request as he had considered the city safely behind the lines, was nearly captured, prompting Napoleon to swear, 'Wurmser shall pay dearly for those tears.'[25]

'We've suffered some setbacks,' Napoleon acknowledged to the Directory, while sending all non-essential equipment to the rear.[26] At noon on July 29 he assumed the enemy were descending from Bassano in strength and ordered a concentration at Villanova, east of Verona. Augereau's division covered 60 miles in fifty-five hours of marching and counter-marching, but by noon the next day Napoleon realized that the main body of the enemy were in fact to his north and west. If he faced Wurmser's main advance and didn't achieve a complete victory he would lose Mantua anyway, so he decided to deal with Quasdanovich first. On July 30 therefore he ordered Sérurier to abandon the siege of Mantua to increase his numbers in the field by adding General Louis Pelletier's brigade to Augereau's force and Dallemagne's to Masséna's.[27] His order to Augereau to retreat to Roverbella read: 'Every moment is precious ... The enemy has broken through our line at three places: he is master of the important points of Corona and Rivoli ... You will see that our communications with Milan and Verona have been cut. Await new orders at Roverbella; I will go there in person.'[28] Augereau lost no time.

Ending the siege of Mantua involved abandoning no fewer than 179 cannon and mortars that couldn't be removed, and dumping their ammunition in the lakes. It pained Napoleon to do this, but he knew that decisive victories in the field, not fortresses, were the key to modern warfare. 'Whatever happens, and however much it costs, we must sleep in Brescia tomorrow,' he told Masséna.[29] That day, the 31st, his constant movements nearly came to grief when he narrowly missed being ambushed by a Croatian unit on the road from Roverbella to Goito.

The terrain between Brescia and Mantua includes 3,000-foot-high mountains and lines of morainic hills through Lonato, Castiglione and

Solferino to Volta, very broken country dropping to a broad, flat plain. On July 31 the French army marched west at 3 a.m. and there was a sharp fight at dawn for the town of Lonato between Sauret and the Austrian General Ott that went on for four hours. Meanwhile, Masséna deployed between Desenzano and Lonato with the 32nd Line Demi-Brigade on his left. Heavily outnumbered, Ott fell back. With Augereau coming up as quickly as he could, Quasdanovich's 18,000 men now faced 30,000 French, so he promptly retreated. That night Napoleon, fearing for his lines of communication, marched with Augereau to Brescia, reaching it by ten o'clock the next morning.

By now Wurmser, who had heard that Napoleon was both marching westwards for Brescia and massing at Roverbella to defend the siege lines at Mantua (which in fact he had abandoned), was thoroughly confused, and he lost the initiative through inaction. The next day General Antoine La Valette, who panicked and fled from Castiglione, was stripped of his command in front of his men of the 18th Légère Demi-Brigade. The enthusiasm of the troops that day helped decide Napoleon to try to crush Quasdanovich. At the second battle of Lonato, on August 3, he sent Despinoy's force from Brescia to turn Quasdanovich's right flank at Gavardo, and a reinforced Sauret to attack his left flank at Salò, with Dallemagne's brigade marching between them as a link. When Sauret's men complained they were hungry, Napoleon told them they could find food in the enemy camp.

Just as General Jean-Joseph Pijon's brigade was being driven from Lonato, with Pijon himself being captured, Napoleon arrived leading elements of Masséna's division. He ordered the 32nd Line into 'columns of platoons' and without pause, and with drummers and musicians playing, sent them into a bayonet charge, supported by the 18th Line. Despite losing both battalion commanders, they hurled the Austrians back towards Desenzano, straight into the path of Napoleon's escort company of cavalry, together with elements of the 15th Dragoons and 4th Légère. Junot received six wounds, but this did not prevent him from accepting the surrender of the entire Austrian brigade. On hearing of the disaster, Quasdanovich retreated right around the north side of the lake to rejoin Wurmser. He would remain out of action for the next ten days. 'I was tranquil,' Napoleon wrote in his post-battle bulletin. 'The brave 32nd Demi-Brigade was there.' The 32nd had those words embroidered in large gold letters on its colours, and their pride spurred them to greater courage. 'It is astonishing what power words have over men,' Napoleon said of the 32nd years later.[30]

Augereau retook Castiglione on August 3, after sixteen hours' hard fighting on the hot, arid plain. For years afterwards, whenever Augereau was criticized by his entourage for disloyalty, Napoleon would say: 'Ah, but let us not forget that he saved us at Castiglione.'[31] By the time the French had regrouped there on August 4, Wurmser had lost any opportunity he might have had to attack Napoleon in the rear. The best he could hope for, as he slowly moved up around Solferino with some 20,000 men, was to buy time for Mantua to prepare for another siege. On the morning of August 4, Napoleon was at Lonato with only 1,200 men when more than 3,000 lost Austrians, who had been cut off from Quasdanovich's command, suddenly blundered into the town. Napoleon calmly informed their *parlementaire* (officer sent to parley) that his 'whole army' was present, and that 'If in eight minutes his division had not laid down its arms, I would not spare a man.'[32] He supported this ruse by issuing orders to Berthier about grenadier and artillery units that Berthier knew were entirely bogus. The Austrians only discovered once they had surrendered and been disarmed that there were no French forces nearby, and that they could have captured Napoleon with ease.

The second battle of Lonato saw the first use by Napoleon of the *bataillon carré* system. Although proposed by Guibert and Bourcet in textbook form in the 1760s and 1770s, it was Napoleon who first put it into practice successfully on the battlefield. Under its diamond-shaped formation of units, if the main body of the enemy was encountered, say, on the right flank, the division on the right became the new advance guard whose job it was to fix the enemy in place. The divisions that had formed the old vanguard and rearguard automatically became the *masse de manoeuvre*, the central strike force capable of supporting the new advance division, with the aim of enveloping the enemy's flanks. The army could therefore turn 90 degrees in either direction with relative ease; the system had the additional advantage of being capable of magnification, as applicable to entire corps as to divisions. The key point was what Bourcet called 'controlled dispersion', and it permitted Napoleon hugely increased flexibility, allowing the battlefront to be constantly adapted according to changing circumstances.[33]

The *bataillon carré* also was employed by Napoleon at the second battle of Castiglione, 20 miles north-west of Mantua, on Friday, August 5. Wurmser was deployed between Solferino on his right flank and a strong redoubt on the Monte Medolano hill on the Mantua–Brescia road on his left, with between 20,000 and 25,000 men. Napoleon had over 30,000 men, Masséna's 10,000 massed in line and column on his left, Augereau's 8,000 drawn up in two lines in front of the town of Castiglione, Kilmaine's cavalry in reserve on the right, Despinoy's 5,000 men returning from Salò, and General Pascal Fiorella's 7,500 men coming from the south, hoping to deliver a decisive blow to the Austrian rear. He planned to draw Wurmser's reserves northwards by feigning to withdraw. Castiglione was a very complicated battle, best understood from atop the magnificent castle of Lonato and the La Rocca bell-tower at Solferino, which command superb views of the whole countryside.

When he heard cannon-fire to the south at 9 a.m. on August 5, Napoleon assumed it signalled Fiorella's arrival, but in fact it was just his 8th Dragoons sacking the Austrian baggage train at Guidizzolo. He launched Masséna and Augereau into the attack, and Marmont was sent with a 12-gun battery towards Monte Medolano. Fighting developed along the whole line, with Augereau taking Solferino and Despinoy arriving in time to help the left-centre, as Wurmser was forced to move infantry away to check Fiorella. Wurmser thus found himself trapped between two armies with a third threatening his rear. He was forced to withdraw, and only narrowly avoided being captured by French light cavalry. Only the exhaustion of the hard-marching French prevented the complete destruction of the Austrian army, which fled across the Mincio.

The Austrians lost 2,000 killed and wounded that day, and 1,000 more were captured along with twenty guns. When Napoleon's officers counted the French dead they found around 1,100 had been killed or wounded or were missing.* 'So there we are,' Napoleon reported to the Directory on August 6, 'in five days another campaign has been completed.'[34] Two days later, as he reoccupied Verona, he added: 'The Austrian army ... has disappeared like a dream and the Italy that it threatened is now quiet.'[35] He resumed the siege of Mantua on August 10. It still held 16,400 Austrian soldiers within its 10-foot-thick walls, although only 12,200 of them were fit for duty.

---

* The word 'missing' covers a multitude of possibilities in the warfare of the day, including dead but impossible to find or identify; hiding; deserted; accidentally or deliberately lost; malingering; captured; concussed; murdered by partisans; wrongly entered in the post-battle roster rolls; temporarily absorbed into a different unit; unconscious and unidentifiable in a field hospital; blown to smithereens or merely absent without leave. Men who were 'missing' therefore often re-entered the combat strengths later on, although of course many didn't.

Napoleon used the three remaining weeks of August to refit his army, and send Sauret and Sérurier, two of his generals who had been wounded and whom he greatly admired, back home. He replaced them with the veteran artilleryman General Claude-Henri de Vaubois and the recently promoted thirty-year-old General Jean-Joseph de Sahuguet, with a minimum of input from Paris. His reputation in France was growing with each victory and the Directory increasingly suspected he could not be contained. 'If there be in France a single pure-minded and honest man capable of suspecting my political intentions,' he told Carnot and Barras, 'I shall at once renounce the happiness of serving my country.'[36] By then he knew there was little danger they could call his bluff. Previously, he had had to negotiate with them over which generals he could promote, as they had a pool of 343 on the active list. The more successful he was on the battlefield, however, and the more the Directory depended on him for their solvency and prestige, the less interference he would face over his choices.

His domestic affairs were distinctly less secure. He tried to track down Josephine on holiday, writing 'My wife has been running around Italy for the last two weeks; I believe she is in Livorno, or in Florence.' He also asked that his 'considerably spirited, but also headstrong' brother Lucien, for whom he had found a war commissary job at Marseilles but who had suddenly gone to Paris without the permission of his commander-in-chief (and brother), be sent to the Army of the North within twenty-four hours of his being found.[37]

In late August Napoleon learned that Wurmser was about to make a second attempt to relieve Mantua. Combing out his lines of communication and receiving some men from the Army of the Alps gave him a total of over 50,000 troops. Since he did not know which of the three possible routes Wurmser would take, he sent Vaubois with 11,000 men up the west side of Lake Garda to block that approach, and Masséna with 13,000 men and Augereau with 9,000 to Rivoli and Verona respectively as his central *masse de manoeuvre*. Kilmaine watched the eastern approaches with 1,200 infantry and most of the cavalry. Napoleon himself stayed with a 3,500 reserve at Legnago while Sahuguet besieged Mantua with 10,000 men and a further 6,000 troops watched for rebellions around Cremona. Once Napoleon had divined Wurmser's route of attack, he would concentrate his force; until then he devoted himself to ensuring that there were plentiful supplies of brandy, flour, fodder, ammunition and army biscuit (hard-tack squares of baked bread).

By September 2 Napoleon knew for certain that Wurmser was coming down the Vallagarina valley of the Adige. He planned to attack once he heard that General Moreau, commanding the Army of Germany, had arrived at Innsbruck, because, if possible, Napoleon's advances should be co-ordinated with what was happening in Germany. However, Archduke Charles defeated General Jourdan at Würzburg on September 3 and Moreau was raiding Munich, deep in southern Bavaria, so neither could be of any help. Napoleon needed to guard against the danger of being forced to fight Archduke Charles's and Wurmser's armies simultaneously, something he simply did not have the manpower to do.

Napoleon advanced to Rovereto, 15 miles south of Trento, where he intercepted Wurmser's advance guard on the 4th. At daybreak he was before the strongly held defile of Marco (just below Rovereto), while another enemy force was across the Adige at the entrenched camp of Mori. Pijon's light infantry gained the heights to the left of Marco and after two hours' stubborn resistance, the Austrian line gave way. Around 750 Frenchmen were killed, wounded or missing. The Austrian General Baron Davidovich lost 3,000 (mostly captured), 25 guns and 7 colours.[38]

With the Austrian army now in full retreat, four more battles were fought up the same valley over the next week. At Calliano poor Austrian picketing meant that the French surprised the Austrians while they were cooking their breakfast and forced them out of their positions. On September 7 at Primolano the French attacked a seemingly impregnable position and carried it by sheer élan. The two sides of the valley come dramatically together in a U-shape with only half a mile between the high cliffs on both sides. The Austrians should have been able to defend the pass easily, but that afternoon columns of French light infantry swarmed up both sides of the mountain, waded through the fast-flowing Brenta up to their waists and simply charged the Austrians, sending them fleeing down to Bassano.

That night Napoleon slept with Augereau's division, wrapped in his cloak under the stars and sharing their rations, as he often did in his early campaigns. The next day he captured 2,000 Austrians and 30 guns at Bassano, along with several ammunition wagons. Only at Cerea on the 11th did Masséna suffer a minor defeat – four hundred French killed and wounded – when he overreached in the pursuit of the enemy. The next day Augereau captured Legnago and twenty-two Austrian guns without loss, releasing five hundred French prisoners-of-war. Then, only three days later, on September 15, at La Favorita outside Mantua, Kilmaine inflicted a defeat on Wurmser that forced the Austrian commander-in-chief into the city.

Napoleon was back in Milan with Josephine on September 19, and remained there nearly a month, sending Marmont to Paris with the best kind of propaganda tool: twenty-two captured Austrian standards for display at Les Invalides. The sheer tempo of the operations ensured that he had always kept the initiative, bowling unstoppably along a narrow valley gorge replete with places where the Austrians should have been able to slow or halt him. This lightning campaign up the valley of the Brenta was the perfect illustration of why *esprit de corps* was so valuable. Napoleon had used his command of Italian to question local people, and employed the *bataillon carré* system to send his army in any direction at a moment's notice. He had split the Austrian army at Rovereto and forced it to march away separately, leaving each part to be defeated in the classic manoeuvre from the central position and keeping up the pressure on Wurmser with regular dawn attacks.

Wurmser had started the campaign with 20,000 men and three days' head start; he ended it when his 14,000 men joined the 16,000 already bottled up in Mantua. By October 10 Mantua was fully under siege again, only this time Wurmser was inside. Four thousand of his men died of wounds, malnutrition and disease in six weeks, and a further 7,000 were hospitalized. With only thirty-eight days of food left, Wurmser had to make sorties for supplies from the countryside, though one cost him nearly 1,000 casualties.

Mantua could not hold out very much longer, but the wider war did not augur well for Napoleon's chances of taking the city. Jourdan had been beaten back across the Rhine by Archduke Charles on September 21, and it was likely that the Austrians would soon make a third attempt to relieve Mantua, this time with a much larger force. Napoleon asked the Directory for 25,000 more reinforcements in case the Papal States and Naples declared war, adding that fortunately 'The Duke of Parma is behaving quite well; he is also useless, in all respects.'[39] On October 2 Napoleon offered peace terms to Emperor Francis, hoping to cajole him to the negotiating table with a mixture of flattery and threat. 'Majesty, Europe wants peace,' he wrote. 'This disastrous war has lasted too long.' He then warned that the Directory had ordered him to close Trieste and other Austrian ports along the Adriatic, adding: 'Until now, I have stayed the execution of this plan in the hope of not increasing the number of innocent victims of this war.'[40] Emperor Francis of Austria – who was also head of the politically separate but Austrian-dominated Holy Roman Empire, a loose conglomeration of semi-independent states that stretched across much of Germany and central Europe – was a proud, ascetic, calculating man, who hated the Revolution that had beheaded his aunt Marie Antoinette and who had briefly commanded the Austrian army in the Flanders campaign of 1794, before handing over to his militarily much more talented brother Archduke Charles. Napoleon received no reply to his peace offer.

Napoleon again threatened to resign on October 8, this time on the basis of general exhaustion. 'I cannot ride a horse anymore,' he wrote, 'only courage remains to me, which is not enough in a post like this.' He also declared that Mantua couldn't be taken before February, and 'Rome is arming, and arousing the fanaticism of the people.' He believed the Vatican's influence to be 'incalculable'.[41] He demanded the right to sign a 'most essential' final treaty with Naples and a 'necessary' alliance with Genoa and Piedmont, warning that the autumn rains had brought illnesses that were filling his hospitals. His central message was 'Above all send troops.' Yet he also wanted Paris to know that 'Whenever your general in Italy is not the centre of everything you run great risks.'

Two days later, and without the Directory's prior agreement, Napoleon signed a comprehensive peace treaty with Naples that permitted the Bourbons to retain their throne unmolested if they agreed not to take part in any activities against the French. If the Austrians were going to invade from the north, Napoleon needed to be safe in the south. He also ensured that his lines of communication ran through the more trustworthy Genoa, rather than Piedmont, whose new king, Charles Emmanuel IV, was an unknown quantity.

Napoleon was conscious of the whispers circulating in Paris, where some were saying that he was driven solely by ambition and might one day overthrow the government. In his letters to the Directory he ridiculed his detractors, saying: 'If two months ago I wished to be Duke of Milan, today I desire to be King of Italy!'[42] Yet they were unconvinced; although Barras and Carnot recognized his undeniable military capacity, all the Directors feared how he might use his growing popularity with the people once the Italian campaign was over. Napoleon's principal preoccupation at the time was the devious unreliability of army contractors, whom he regularly described as swindlers, especially the influential Compagnie Flachat, which was 'nothing but a bunch of fraudsters with no real credit, no money and no morality'. He wished he could have them shot, writing on October 12 to the Directory: 'I never cease having them arrested and tried by courts martial, but they buy the judges; it's a complete fair here, where everything is sold.'[43]

On October 16 Napoleon called upon Wurmser to surrender Mantua. 'The brave should be facing danger, not swamp plague,' he wrote, but he was flatly turned down.[44] The same day, again with the minimum of input from the Directory, he proclaimed the establishment of the Cispadane Republic, formed from Bologna, Ferrara, Modena and Reggio (which involved overthrowing the Duke of Modena who had allowed a convoy of supplies to get into Mantua) with a new 2,800-strong Italian Legion to guard it. The Cispadane Republic (whose name translates as 'By the banks of the Po') abolished feudalism, decreed civil equality, instituted a popularly elected assembly and began the *Risorgimento* (resurgence) unification movement which was eventually – albeit three-quarters of a century later – to create a unified, independent Italy. The writing of its constitution took no fewer than thirty-eight meetings, a testament to Napoleon's patience since he was actively involved. The French were starting to bring about a political unity to a peninsula that hadn't known it for centuries.

In one area, however, French revolutionary institutions never had much hope of prevailing in Italy, and that was in their efforts to reduce the powers of the Roman Catholic Church. Italians opposed Napoleon's religious reforms passionately, and in what is called the *epoca francese* in Italian history, Napoleon's Church reforms were hated as much as the introduction of his administrative culture was admired.[45] His attempted bullying of the Vatican began early. In October 1796 Napoleon warned Pius VI not to oppose the Cispadane Republic, let alone attack the French once the Austrians returned. He ominously informed the Pope that 'to destroy the temporal power of the Pope, the will alone is wanting,' but in peacetime 'everything may be arranged'. He then warned him that if he declared war it would mean 'the ruin and death of the madmen who would oppose the Republican phalanxes'.[46] With the Directory unable to spare the 25,000 troop reinforcements he needed so desperately after Jourdan and Moreau's defeats in Germany – barely 3,000 arrived for the coming campaign – Napoleon had to buy time. As he told Cacault in Rome: 'The game really is for us to throw the ball from one to the other, so as to deceive that old fox.'[47]

In early November the Austrians were ready for their third attempt to relieve Mantua, using a strategic plan that could have been thought up only by a committee, in this case the Aulic Council in Vienna. The Hungarian veteran General József Alvinczi and his 28,000 men were to drive the French back from Rivoli to Mantua, while General Giovanni di Provera was to advance with 9,000 men from Brenta to Legnago as a diversion, and 10,000 men at Bassano would try to prevent Napoleon from concentrating his forces. To have 19,000 men essentially taking part in diversionary attacks, with only 28,000 in the main force, showed that the Council had not learned the lessons of the previous six months. Napoleon later said that the sixty-one-year-old Alvinczi, who had fought in Bavaria, Holland and Turkey in his long career, was the best general he had fought thus far, which was why he never said anything either positive or negative about him in his bulletins (by contrast he praised Beaulieu, Wurmser and Archduke Charles whom he didn't rate). He also showed great respect to General Provera in his proclamations and Orders of the Day because he thought him the worst of the lot and hoped he wouldn't be dismissed.

Napoleon now had 41,400 men. He positioned them as far back as possible to give him maximum warning of where and when the Austrians were coming. In addition he had 2,700 men garrisoning Brescia, Peschiera and Verona, and the 40th Demi-Brigade of 2,500 men were en route from France. Alvinczi crossed the Piave on November 2. He instructed Quasdanovich and Provera to make their way to Vicenza, Quasdanovich via Bassano, and Provera via Treviso. The Austrian advance had begun.

Much to his chagrin, Masséna had to obey Napoleon's orders to fall back on Vicenza without a fight. He had followed Augereau in coming to appreciate Napoleon as a leader and soldier, but he was also jealous of his own reputation as one of France's best generals and proud of his nickname 'the darling child of victory'. He didn't like being ordered to retreat, even before larger forces. On November 5 Napoleon brought Augereau up to Montebello and, seeing the Austrian vanguards crossing the Brenta river well in front of their columns, decided to attack them the next day. Meanwhile Masséna hit Provera's column at Fontaniva, driving them back onto some islands in the river but not completely across it.

On November 6, Augereau attacked Quasdanovich's force as it emerged from Bassano, but despite hard fighting he failed to push it back over the Brenta. The village of Nove changed hands several times over the course of the day and Napoleon, now outnumbered by 28,000 to 19,500, had to withdraw. There are several ways to ascribe victory: number of casualties, retention of the battlefield, stymying of the enemy's plans among them. Whichever way the battle of Bassano is viewed it was Napoleon's first defeat, albeit not a serious one.

Falling back to Vicenza, Napoleon received news of Vaubois' defeat at Davidovich's hands over five days of skirmishes in the villages of Cembra and Calliano. Over 40 per cent of his force had been killed or were wounded or missing. Augereau was immediately ordered back to the Adige, south of Verona, Masséna to Verona itself, and General Barthélemy Joubert – a lawyer's son who had run away from home at fifteen to join the artillery – was told to send a brigade from Mantua to Rivoli to help Vaubois rally there. Napoleon then harangued Vaubois' men: 'Soldiers of the 39th and 85th Infantry, you are no longer fit to belong to the French Army. You have shown neither discipline nor courage; you have allowed the enemy to dislodge you from a position where a handful of brave men could have stopped an army. The chief-of-staff will cause to be inscribed upon your flags: "These men are no longer of the Army of Italy".'[48] With his acute sense for what would energize and what demoralize a unit, Napoleon correctly gauged that this public shaming would ensure that both demi-brigades would fight harder and with more determination over the next few days than ever before.

Austrian inactivity after the victory at Bassano allowed Napoleon to regroup. By the 12th he held Verona with 2,500 men and the banks of the Adige river with 6,000, while the disgraced Vaubois contained Davidovich at Rivoli and Kilmaine continued besieging Mantua. This left Masséna with 13,000 men on the right flank and Augereau with 5,000 on the left to attack Alvinczi at Caldiero, a village 10 miles east of Verona. With rain pouring straight into their faces, they showed none of the usual dash of the Army of Italy. The wind blew gunpowder away, their shoes slipped in the mud and their attacks throughout the morning gained only a little ground on the right, which they had to concede once Austrian reinforcements arrived at 3 p.m. About 1,000 were killed or wounded on both sides. Although he naturally claimed it as a victory, it was telling that when Napoleon had medals struck to commemorate Montenotte, Millesimo and Castiglione that year, he didn't order one for Caldiero.

On November 13 both armies rested. Napoleon used the time to write a despairing letter to the Directory from Verona, effectively blaming them for his predicament:

> Perhaps we are on the verge of losing Italy. None of the relief I was waiting for has arrived ... I am doing my duty, the army is doing its duty. My soul is in tatters, but my conscience is at peace ... The weather continues to be bad; the entire army is excessively tired and without boots ... The wounded are the elite of the army; all our superior officers, all our best generals are *hors de combat*. Everyone who comes to me is so inept and doesn't even have a soldier's confidence! ... We have been abandoned to the depths of Italy ... Perhaps my hour ... has come. I no longer dare expose myself as my death would discourage the troops.[49]

It was true that Sérurier and Sauret were wounded, and Lannes, Murat and young Kellermann were ill in hospital, but he had plenty of other fine generals serving under him. He certainly ended on a note so upbeat as to belie everything else he had written: 'In a few days, we will try one last effort. If Fortune smiles upon us, Mantua will be taken, and with it, Italy.'

Napoleon had devised a bold plan: to get behind Alvinczi at Villanova and force him to fight for his line of retreat in country so flooded with rice fields that his larger numbers would count for little. Eschewing the easier crossing of the Adige at Albaredo, where Austrian cavalry could give the alarm, he chose to cross at Ronco, where a pontoon bridge had been built for the previous campaign; it had been dismantled but was stored safely nearby. On the night of November 14, Masséna left Verona by the west to fool Austrian spies in the city, but then turned south-east to join Augereau on the road there.

The causeways in that part of Italy were (and still are) remarkable, with very steep sides and standing well above the marshes, so the French approach and the building of the pontoon bridge went entirely unnoticed by the Austrian pickets. The 51st Line crossed in boats to secure the bridgehead at daybreak and the bridge was finished by seven o'clock the next morning. Where the road forked on the other side of the river, Augereau went off to the right alongside a dyke to the town of Arcole, intending to cross over the Alpone stream and march north towards Villanova, to attack Alvinczi's artillery park. Meanwhile, Masséna went to the left towards Porcile to try to turn Alvinczi's left flank from behind. Augereau advanced with General Louis-André Bon's 5th Légère into the gloom, but soon found himself under fire all along the road running alongside the Alpone stream from two battalions of Croats and two guns protecting Alvinczi's left-rear. Arcole was strongly held – loop-holed and barricaded – and repulsed the first attack, as well as a second from the 4th Line directed by Augereau himself. Attackers had to slide down the steep banks to seek shelter from the fire. Meanwhile Masséna met another Croat battalion and an Austrian regiment under Provera halfway to Porcile and drove them back, thus securing the left of the bridgehead. Fighting in the Lombardy plains was different from the mountains, and afforded the Austrian cavalry more opportunity, but here the swift streams and networks of dykes worked in favour of a young commander with a feeling for tactical detail but far fewer cavalry.

Although Alvinczi was quickly informed of the French move, he assumed because of the marshlands that it was merely a light force effecting a diversion. When his patrols found Verona quiet, he sent them to see what was happening to his left, where Provera's 3,000 troops had been beaten by Masséna. Another 3,000 had marched swiftly to Arcole, arriving just after noon. They placed two howitzers to bring the cause-way under a plunging fire, where Lannes, having only just rejoined the army from hospital in Milan, was wounded again.

Napoleon arrived at the bridge at Arcole just as Augereau's attempt to capture it had been beaten off. He ordered another attack, which stalled under heavy fire. Augereau then seized a flag and walked out fifteen paces in front of his skirmishers, saying, 'Grenadiers, come and seek your colour.' At that point Napoleon, surrounded by his aides-de-camp and bodyguard, grasped another flag and led the charge himself, haranguing the troops about their heroism at Lodi. For all his statements to the Directory two days earlier about not exposing himself to danger, he certainly did at Arcole. Yet it failed – the men displayed 'extraordinary cowardice' according to Sulkowski – and they didn't rush the body-strewn bridge, although his aide-de-camp Colonel Muir-on and others were killed on it at Napoleon's side. During an Austrian counter-attack, Napoleon had to be bundled back into the marshy ground behind the bridge and was saved only by a charge of grenadiers. He was a brave man, but there was only so much anyone could do in the face of concentrated fire being directed by a stalwart Austrian resist-ance, which would continue for two more days. Visiting the bridge today, one can see how Napoleon could have been pushed down into the large drainage ditch just adjacent to it, which for all the indignity probably have saved his life.

Once it became clear that the bridge would not be taken, Napoleon ordered Masséna and Augereau to return south of the Adige, leaving campfires burning at Arcole to suggest that the French were still there. He needed to be ready to move against Davidovich if Vaubois retreated any further at Rivoli. From the church tower of the small village of Ronco, the French could see Alvinczi marching back to Villanova and deploying east of the Alpone. The bridge at Arcole wouldn't be captured for another two days, by Augereau and Masséna, who returned there on the 17th, and Napoleon wasn't present when it fell. Although French losses were significant – 1,200 were killed, including 8 generals, and 2,300 were wounded, against Austria's 600 killed and 1,600 wounded – Arcole was ultimately a French victory, as they emerged with 4,000 captured Austrians and 11 cannon. 'It took good luck to defeat Alvinczi,' Napoleon later admitted.[50]

As winter closed in and the fighting season ended with Mantua still under siege, the Austrians would make a fourth attempt to relieve the city. The campaign had cost Austria nearly 18,000 casualties, and the French over 19,000. The French were now short of everything – officers, shoes, medicine and pay. Some were so hungry that there was a mutiny in the 33rd Line, where three companies had to be imprisoned and two ringleaders shot. As soon as the fighting ceased Napoleon dismissed Vaubois and promoted Joubert to command the division covering Rivoli.

Napoleon's report to Carnot of November 19 was far more optimistic than his previous one. 'The destinies of Italy are beginning to become clear,' he wrote. 'I hope, before ten days are up, to be writing to you from headquarters based in Mantua. Never has a battlefield been more fought over than that of Arcole. I have almost no generals left; their devotion and courage know no equal.' He ended by saying that he intended to march on 'obstinate' Rome as soon as Mantua capitulated.[51] When in late November the Directory sent General Henri Clarke, Napoleon's former boss at the Topographical Bureau, to Vienna to explore the possibilities of peace, Napoleon persuaded him that, as Mantua was about to fall, he shouldn't sacrifice the Cispadane Republic in the negotiations.[52] 'He is a spy whom the Directory have set upon me,' Napoleon supposedly told Miot, 'he is a man of no talent – only conceited.'[53] This was hardly Napoleon's considered view, because he was to raise the highly competent Clarke, whom he later made the Duc de Feltre, to be his private secretary, then war minister and, by 1812, one of the most powerful men in France. 'Send me 30,000 men and I will march on Trieste,' Napoleon told the Directory, 'carry the war into the Emperor's lands, revolutionize Hungary, and go to Vienna. You will then have a right to expect millions, and a good peace.'[54]

'I arrive at Milan,' Napoleon told Josephine on 27 November, who was still holidaying with Hippolyte Charles in Genoa, 'I rush to your apartment; I have left everything to see you, to press you in my arms ... You were not there: you run from town to town after the fêtes; you leave as I am about to arrive; you do not concern yourself about your dear Napoleon anymore ... The whole world is only too happy if it can please you, and your husband alone is very, very unhappy. Bonaparte.'[55] The next day he wrote again, saying: 'When I require of you a love equal to mine I do wrong; how should one weigh lace in the scales against gold?'[56] Yet Josephine was good at allaying Napoleon's suspicions. Antoine Lavalette, a relative by marriage who had taken the late Muiron's place as one of Napoleon's eight aides-de-camp, recalled how in Milan: 'Madame Bonaparte used to take her husband upon her lap after breakfast, and hold him fast for a few minutes.'[57] Apart from anything else, it was an indication of how light he was in those days. An equally charming vignette from this period can be glimpsed in Napoleon's letter to Jérôme de Lalande, the director of the Paris Observatory, to whom he mused: 'To spend the night between a pretty woman and a fine sky, and spend the day recording observations and making calculations, seems to me to be happiness on earth.'[58]

Less happy was the letter sent by Battaglia, the chief officer of neutral Venice, who had written in December to complain of the behaviour of French troops on Venetian soil. Napoleon indignantly denied that any women had been raped by French troops, asking, 'Does the Republic of Venice really want to declare itself so openly against us?'[59] Battaglia immediately backed down and Napoleon's reply two days later was calmer, promising 'to punish in exemplary fashion any soldiers who stray from the regulations of severe discipline'.

Recognizing that after the fall of Livorno they could no longer defend Corsica from the French, the British under the brilliant thirty-eight-year-old Commodore Horatio Nelson had conducted a model evacuation of the island in October. Paoli and his supporters left with them. Napoleon sent Miot de Melito and Saliceti to organize the French departments that would be set up there once the British left. The same day he wrote to Battaglia, he also wrote to Joseph, who went with Melito, to say that he wanted the Casa Bonaparte to be made 'clean and habitable. It needs to be put back to how it was', that is, before it was ransacked by the

Paolists four years before.[60] His years fighting the French bureaucracy over the *pépinière* would not be entirely wasted.

Between September and December 1796, nearly 9,000 people died of disease and starvation in Mantua. Of the 18,500 soldiers garrisoned inside the city only 9,800 were now fit for duty. The last rations were due to run out on January 17. The next Austrian attack must therefore come soon, and Napoleon's main concern was to get his army ready for it. He sent forty letters to Berthier from Milan over the course of eighteen days in December, and begged the Directory for more reinforcements. 'The enemy is withdrawing his troops from the Rhine to send them to Italy. Do the same, help us,' he wrote on the 28th. 'We are only asking for more men.'[61] In the same letter he said he had captured an Austrian spy who had carried a letter for Emperor Francis in a cylinder in his stomach. 'If they have diarrhoea,' Napoleon added helpfully, 'they make sure to take the little cylinder, soak it in liqueur and swallow it again. The cylinder is dipped in Spanish wax mixed with vinegar.'

There was no aspect of Napoleon's soldiers' lives and welfare that didn't concern him. When he discovered that some of Joubert's men weren't presenting themselves to their quartermasters on pay-day, he wanted to be told why, suspecting a swindle of some kind. 'The more I delve, in my leisure moments, into the incurable sores of the administration of the Army of Italy,' he wrote to the Directory on January 6, 1797, 'the more I'm convinced of the necessity of applying a prompt and fool-proof remedy.' Claiming that 'the principal actresses of Italy are all being kept by French army contractors', and that 'luxury and embezzlement are at their height', he repeated his request 'to have any administrator of the army shot'.[62] (The Directory were too sensible, or keen on self-preservation, to give a general the arbitrary power of life and death over other Frenchmen.) Napoleon did not hesitate to use the powers he did hold ruthlessly when he could. On January 7 he ordered General Jean-Baptiste Rusca to have the chiefs of a rebellion in Modena shot, and the house of its leader, the Duke of Modena's confessor, destroyed. A pyramid was erected on the rubble with a sign reading: 'The punishment of a raving priest who abused his ministry and preached revolt and murder.'[63]*

---

* Napoleon had an active imagination when it came to devising unusual punishments. Believing that it was 'abominable women' camp-followers who were responsible for 'exciting the soldiers to pillage', in mid-April 1797 he ordered every woman still with Bernadotte's division within twenty-four hours of the publication of the order to 'be smeared with soot and exposed for two hours in the market-place' (ed. Bingham, *Selection* I p. 151).

Napoleon received news the same day that Alvinczi was on the move south, this time with 47,000 troops. Once again the Austrians split their forces: Alvinczi's main force of 28,000 (which included Quasdanovich) marched down the east side of Lake Garda in six columns, using all available roads and tracks, thus avoiding having to face the French on the plain, while Provera's 15,000 advanced across the plain from the east, heading for Verona. Over 4,000 were posted to the west of Lake Garda. Alvinczi ordered Wurmser to break out of Mantua and head to the south-east to join them. Napoleon immediately left Milan and made multiple visits to Bologna, Verona and his headquarters at Roverbella, trying to divine Alvinczi's intentions. He had 37,000 men in the field and 8,500 under Sérurier in the Mantuan siege lines.

On January 12 Joubert reported an attack at La Corona, well to the north of Rivoli, which misfired in the very deep fresh snow. 'General Brune has had seven bullets through his clothing without his being touched at all,' Napoleon told Josephine, 'he deals in luck.'[64] He assumed the campaign would be decided in the foothills of the Italian Alps along the Adige river, but he needed far more information before launching his counter-attack. While he waited, he ordered Masséna to garrison Verona and pull 7,000 men back over the Adige; General Gabriel Rey was to concentrate two brigades at Castelnuovo. Lannes was to leave his Italian soldiers in the south and march his 2,000 French troops back to Badia to prevent any Austrian move southwards, while Augereau defended Ronco.

The next day, as Napoleon prepared to move up and crush Provera, he learned at 10 p.m. that Joubert was facing a major offensive and pulling back to Rivoli in good order, leaving his campfires burning behind him. Realizing that Provera's advance was thus a feint and that the main attack would be coming via Rivoli, Napoleon rode there fast from Verona, issuing a completely new set of orders. Now Joubert was to hold Rivoli at all costs; Sérurier was to put the siege lines on high alert, but also to send cavalry, artillery and six hundred infantry to Rivoli at once; Masséna was to march the 18th, 32nd and 75th demi-brigades to take up position on Joubert's left; Augereau was to detain Provera on the Adige but send some cavalry and artillery to Rivoli. Everyone was told that a decisive battle was in the immediate offing. With General Gabriel Rey's two brigades, Napoleon expected to concentrate 18,000 infantry, 4,000 cavalry and 60 guns at Rivoli by noon on January 14, leaving 16,000 on the Adige and 8,000 at Mantua.

The old maxim 'March separately, fight together' could not have been better followed. Alvinczi had failed to bring any more forces to Rivoli than the 28,000 and 90 guns with which he had started out.

Napoleon arrived at 2 a.m. on Saturday, January 14 1797 at the plateau above the gorges of Rivoli, which would be the key deciding place – the *point d'appui* or *Schwerpunkt* – of the battle. It was a clear, very cold, brightly moonlit night and he interpreted the number and positions of the campfires as meaning that the Marquis de Lusignan, an energetic, Spanish-born Austrian general, was too far off to engage until mid-morning. He knew the area intimately, having ridden across it often over the previous four months. If he could retain the Osteria gorge and the slope containing the chapel of San Marco on the eastern side of the battlefield, he believed he could hold off the main attack relatively easily. He needed to let Masséna's division rest and to buy time for Rey to arrive, so he decided on a spoiling attack to concentrate Alvinczi's attention. Joubert was ordered to march back onto the Rivoli plateau and send one brigade to Osteria before attacking in the centre, covered by all the French guns on the plateau. Meanwhile Masséna was told to send one brigade to hold Lusignan off for as long as possible.

At 4 a.m., three hours before dawn, General Honoré Vial's brigade of the 4th, 17th and 22nd Légère drove the Austrians back on San Giovanni and Gamberon, capturing the San Marco chapel. At daybreak, Joubert attacked at Caprino and San Giovanni but his line was very thin and was checked by greatly superior numbers. The Austrians counter-attacked at 9 a.m., routing Vial's brigade, whereupon Napoleon immediately sent one of Masséna's brigades to rescue the centre, thereby recovering the village of Trambassore. This fighting in the centre continued non-stop for a marathon ten hours.

By 11 a.m. Lusignan had arrived with 5,000 men. He had driven off Masséna's detached brigade, and penetrated deep into the French left-rear near Affi, preventing any reinforcements from arriving. Napoleon was only just holding his centre, was under huge pressure on his right flank and Lusignan had turned his left. He had only one brigade in reserve and Rey was still an hour away. When the news arrived that Lusignan had got behind him, staff officers looked anxiously at the preternaturally calm Napoleon, who simply remarked: 'We have them now.'[65] Deciding the Austrians in the centre were a spent force and that Lusignan was still too far off to affect the battle, Napoleon concentrated on Quasdanovich in the east as the main threat. He thinned out Joubert's line and sent every man he could spare to San Marco. When the dense Austrian columns, covered by artillery, assailed the gorge and reached the plateau, they were struck by French artillery firing canister shot into their close ranks from all sides, then bayonet-charged by an infantry column, and then attacked by all the French cavalry available. As they recoiled into the gorge, a lucky shot hit an ammunition wagon – all the more devastating in the narrow space – whereupon Quasdanovich ordered the attack aborted.

Napoleon immediately shifted his own attack to the centre, where the Austrians had next to no artillery or cavalry. Having gained the plateau at great cost, all three Austrian columns were driven off it. Lusignan was checked on his arrival on the battlefield, just as Rey suddenly appeared to his rear. He barely escaped with some 2,000 men. By 2 p.m. the Austrians were in full retreat, and the pursuit was abandoned only when news came from Augereau that Provera had crossed the Adige and was heading for Mantua, whereupon Masséna was sent off to help Augereau prevent its relief.

Napoleon lost 2,200 men at the battle of Rivoli and 1,000 more were captured, but the Austrian toll was far higher: 4,000 killed and wounded and 8,000 captured, along with 8 guns and 11 standards. It was an impressive feat, though not quite the 6,000 killed and wounded, 60 guns and 24 standards – 'embroidered by the hand of the Empress' – that Napoleon claimed when he wrote home, nor, for that matter, had he faced 45,000 Austrians.[66] But Alvinczi's retreat gradually turned into a rout as a further 11,000 prisoners were taken over the following days.

At noon on January 15, Provera reached La Favorita with his relief column of 4,700 men, many of them half-trained recruits. At first light the next day, Wurmser attempted to sally out of Mantua, but he was stopped short. By the time Napoleon arrived, Provera was caught between Masséna and Augereau at La Favorita, a village outside Mantua. He fought bravely, but surrendered before a massacre ensued and his entire force was captured. In Mantua the food had finally run out. Wurmser had managed to eke it out for a fortnight longer than expected in the vain hope that Alvinczi might miraculously appear, but on Thursday, February 2, 1797 he surrendered the city and its emaciated garrison. Some 16,300 Austrians had died in Mantua over the course of the previous eight months, and many more civilians, who had been reduced to eating rats and dogs. The French captured 325 Austrian guns and retook the 179 they had abandoned back in August. Wurmser and five hundred of his staff were allowed to march out with the honours of war and return to Austria, on condition that they would not fight against France until there was a prisoner exchange. The rest went into captivity in France, where they were put to work in agriculture and building projects. The news of the fall of Mantua caused a sensation in Paris, where it was announced to the sound of trumpets by, as a contemporary recalled, 'the public officer, who proclaimed the glory of French arms in the midst of an immense multitude'.[67]

Napoleon wasn't present to witness his triumph. He went on to Verona and then Bologna to punish the Papal States for threatening to rise in Austria's support despite the armistice they had signed the previous June. Shamelessly usurping the Directory's powers, on January 22 he asked the French envoy to Rome, Cacault, 'to leave Rome within six hours of receiving this letter' in order to pressurize the Vatican. The same day he wrote to the papal negotiator, Cardinal Alessandro Mattei, to say that Austrian and Neapolitan influence over Rome's foreign policy must cease. But he softened his tone in closing and asked him to 'assure His Holiness that he can remain in Rome without the least uneasiness' on account of his being 'the first minister of religion'.[68] Napoleon feared, as he told the Directory, that 'If the Pope and all the cardinals were to fly from Rome I should never be able to obtain what I demanded.' He also knew that storming the Vatican would earn him the ire, even the lifetime enmity, of Europe's devout Catholics. 'If I went to Rome I should lose Milan,' he told Miot.[69]

Napoleon issued a proclamation on February 1 stating that all priests and monks who failed to 'conduct themselves according to the principles of the New Testament' would be dealt with 'more severely than other citizens', hoping to blunt their opposition to French rule in Italy.[70] Ludicrously, but undeniably bravely, the troops of the Papal States nevertheless tried to put up a fight. At Castel Bolognese on February 3, General Claude Victor-Perrin (known as Victor) easily overpowered the soldiers he encountered, and a week later he captured the papal garrison of Ancona without loss. By February 17 the Pope was suing for peace. He sent Mattei to Napoleon's headquarters at Tolentino to sign a treaty under which he ceded Romagna, Bologna, Avignon and Ferrara to France, closed all ports to the British, and promised to pay a 'contribution' of 30 million francs and one hundred works of art. 'We will have everything that is beautiful in Italy,' Napoleon told the Directory, 'with the exception of a small number of objects in Turin and Naples.'[71]

On February 18, 1797 the Army of Italy launched a news-sheet entitled *Journal de Bonaparte et des Hommes Vertueux*, whose masthead proclaimed 'Hannibal slept at Capua, but Bonaparte doesn't sleep at Mantua'.[72] Napoleon was highly conscious of the power of propaganda, and he now made a conscious effort to influence public opinion, which was already heavily in his favour. He began his new career as a press proprietor and journalist by dictating such sentences as 'Bonaparte flies like lightning and strikes like a thunderbolt.' Within ten days the *Journal* was obliquely criticizing the Directory, which it would not have done without Napoleon's permission. Later in the year he also set up two army news-sheets, the *Courrier de l'Armée d'Italie*, edited by the ex-Jacobin Marc-Antoine Jullien, and the less substantial *La France Vue de l'Armée d'Italie*, edited by Michel Regnaud de Saint-Jean d'Angély, excerpted regularly in the Parisian papers. With the Rhine front much closer to France, Napoleon did not want the Italian campaign to be sidelined in the public imagination, and he thought his men would appreciate news from Paris. D'Angély was a former parliamentarian and lawyer who ran Army of Italy hospitals and was to become one of Napoleon's senior lieutenants. Jullien's appointment was a sign of Napoleon's readiness to ignore past political stances if the individual in question was talented and showed a willingness to bury the past. In a polity as fluid as France's, this was not so much tolerance as common sense. Napoleon had, after all, been a Jacobin himself only three years before.

In Paris the *Moniteur* reported the celebration of Napoleon's victories with dances, cantatas, public banquets and processions. These were arranged by his growing cadre of supporters who, the Directors privately noted, did not always support them too. Quite apart from politics, Napoleon made good copy; the conservative paper *Nouvelles Politiques* mentioned the Army of Italy sixty-six times in six months.[73] Overall, Napoleon's exploits were mentioned far more often than those of any other French general, to the increasing chagrin of the high commands of the Army of the Rhine and Moselle and the Army of the Sambre and Meuse, which resented being eclipsed by the Army of Italy.

Seventeen ninety-six was the first year when prints and engravings of Napoleon began to be produced and marketed, with titles such as

'General Bonaparte á Lodi', 'Bonaparte Arrivant á Milan' and so on. Some added an 'e' to his Christian name and 'u' to his surname, others read 'Bounaparte'.[74] The scores, perhaps even hundreds, of different representations of him by 1798 prove that the cult of personality had already begun. Artists felt no need to have set eyes on him before they drew him, so in some prints we find him depicted as a middle-aged man with grey hair, more in keeping with what one expected of a victorious general.[75]

It was after Montenotte that Napoleon first ordered a medal be struck to commemorate his victory, and these too became potent propaganda tools. Other generals did not do this, and he didn't ask permission from the Directory. The best of the bronze medals were designed by the skilled engraver and former erotic novelist Vivant Denon, who later became director of the Louvre. The Montenotte medal, for example, was just over 1½ inches in diameter, depicting a bust of Napoleon on the obverse side with his coat embroidered with oak leaves and acorns, and a figure representing the 'Genius of War' on the reverse.[76] In all, 141 different official medals were struck by 1815 commemorating battles, treaties, coronations, river crossings, his marriage and entries into foreign capitals, and were distributed widely to the crowds at official events and celebrations. Some commemorated comparatively mundane events such as the creation of the Paris School of Medicine, the opening of the Ourcq Canal and the establishment of a mining school in the Mont Blanc department. A medal was even struck when Napoleon remained inactive at Osterode throughout March 1807, showing the notoriously cautious (but successful) Roman general Fabius Maximus 'Cunctator' on its reverse.

On Friday, March 10, 1797, Napoleon set off on the northern campaign that he had promised the Directory; a risky expedition of only 40,000 men through the Tyrol to Klagenfurt and eventually to Leoben in Styria, from where, atop the Semmering hills, his advance guard could discern the spires of Vienna. Jourdan and Moreau's armies – both twice the size – had been driven out of Germany by Archduke Charles; France now hoped Napoleon's more modest forces would compel the Austrians to make peace by threatening the capital itself. Napoleon had originally intended to work in tandem with the Army of the Rhine in a pincer movement, and became increasingly concerned when he learned that neither Jourdan nor Moreau had managed to re-cross the Rhine after their defeats that autumn. To encourage his men he denounced

Charles's brother, the Emperor Francis, in one of his proclamations as 'the paid servant of the merchants of London' and claimed that the British, 'strangers to the ills of war, smile with pleasure at the woes of the Continent'.[77] This line of attack in Napoleon's propaganda war against Austria came because the British government was about to furnish Austria with a £1.62 million loan, the equivalent of more than 40 million francs.[78] Although the British made no attempt to land troops on the continent at this time, they were consistently generous in subsidizing whichever of France's enemies were willing to take the field against her.

On March 16 Napoleon crossed the Tagliamento river, inflicting a small defeat on Archduke Charles at Valvassone, which General Jean-Baptiste Bernadotte the next day turned into a bigger one when he captured a sizeable detachment of Austrians who had become separated from the main body. At the Tagliamento Napoleon introduced the *ordre mixte* – a compromise between attacking in line and attacking in column first developed by Guibert to cope with the vagaries of a terrain which didn't permit regular deployments. This was a technique he would use again a few days later while crossing the Isonzo into Austria; on both these occasions he intervened personally to put into operation a formation that combined the firepower of a battalion in line with the attack weight of two battalions in column.[79]

'Banish your uneasiness,' he told the people of the Habsburg province of Gorizia in north-east Italy, 'we are good and humane.'[80] He was unimpressed by his new opponent, whose reputation as a strategist he found unjustified even though Charles had won battles in Holland in 1793 and had defeated Jourdan and Moreau in 1796. 'Up to now Archduke Charles has manoeuvred worse than Beaulieu and Wurmser,' Napoleon told the Directory, 'he makes mistakes at every turn, and extremely stupid ones at that.'[81] Without a major battle being fought between Napoleon and Archduke Charles, the Austrians – who were also now facing a reinvigorated assault through Germany by Moreau – decided not to take the risk of losing their capital to Napoleon, and accepted his offer of an armistice at Leoben on April 2, a little over one hundred miles south-west of Vienna.

Since the campaign had begun a year earlier, Napoleon had crossed the Apennines and the Alps, defeated a Sardinian army and no fewer than six Austrian armies, and killed, wounded or captured 120,000 Austrian soldiers. All this he had done before his twenty-eighth birthday. Eighteen months earlier he had been an unknown, moody soldier writing essays on suicide; now he was famous across Europe, having defeated mighty Austria, wrung peace treaties from the Pope and the kings of Piedmont and Naples, abolished the medieval dukedom of Modena, and defeated in every conceivable set of military circumstances most of Austria's most celebrated generals – Beaulieu, Wurmser, Provera, Quasdanovich, Alvinczi, Davidovich – and outwitted the Archduke Charles.

Napoleon had fought against Austrian forces that were invariably superior in number, but which he had often outnumbered on the field of battle thanks to his repeated strategy of the central position. A profound study of the history and geography of Italy before he ever set foot there had proved extremely helpful, as had his willingness to experiment with others' ideas, most notably the *bataillon carré* and the *ordre mixte*, and his minute calculations of logistics, for which his prodigious memory was invaluable. Because he kept his divisions within one day's march of each other, he was able to concentrate them for battle and, once joined, he showed great calmness under pressure.

The fact that the Army of Italy was in a position to fight at all, considering the privations from which it was suffering when Napoleon took over its command, was another testament to his energy and organizational abilities. His leadership qualities – acting with harshness when he thought it deserved, but bestowing high praise on other occasions – produced the *esprit de corps* so necessary to victory. 'In war,' he was to say in 1808, 'moral factors account for three-quarters of the whole; relative material strength accounts for only one-quarter.'[82] His personal courage further bonded him to his men. Of course he was hugely helped by the fact that the Austrians kept sending septuagenarian commanders against him who continually split their forces and moved at around half the speed of the French. That would not continue for ever.

Napoleon was also fortunate in his lieutenants, especially the superb Joubert, Masséna and Augereau, with excellent contributions also from Lannes (at Lodi and Arcole), Marmont (at Castiglione), Victor (at La Favorita) and Sérurier (at Mantua) as well as from Brune, Murat and Junot. Napoleon deserves credit for identifying these able commanders, regardless of their age and background, and for sacking those like Meynier and Vaubois who were unable to rise to the level of events. It was no coincidence that when he came to power, former Army of Italy commanders found themselves promoted well. With the 'immense multitude' of Paris celebrating twelve victories in as many months, and northern and central Italy now firmly within the orbit of the French Republic, if anyone could be said to be 'the darling child of victory', it was Napoleon.

It was in the early Italian campaigns that Napoleon's military philosophy and habits first became visible. He believed above all in the maintenance of strong *esprit de corps*. Although this combination of spirit and pride is by its nature intangible, he knew an army that had it could achieve wonders. 'Remember it takes ten campaigns to create *esprit de corps*,' he was to tell Joseph in 1807, 'which can be destroyed in an instant.'[83] He had formulated a number of ways to raise and maintain morale, some taken from his reading of ancient history, others specific to his own leadership style and developed on campaign. One was to foster a soldier's strong sense of identification with his regiment. In March 1797, Napoleon approved the right of one, the 57th, to stitch onto its colours the words '*Le Terrible 57ème demi-brigade que rien n'arrête*' (The Terrible 57th demi-brigade which nothing can stop), in recognition of its courage at the battles of Rivoli and La Favorita. It joined other heroic regiments known by their soubriquets such as 'Les Braves' (18th Line), 'Les Incomparables' (9th Légère) and 'Un Contre Dix' (One Against Ten) (84th Line) and showed how well Napoleon understood the psychology of the ordinary soldier and the power of regimental pride. Plays, songs, operatic arias, proclamations, festivals, ceremonies, symbols, standards, medals: Napoleon instinctively understood what soldiers wanted, and he gave it to them. And at least until the battle of Aspern-Essling in 1809 he gave them what they wanted most of all: victory.

On campaign Napoleon demonstrated an approachability that endeared him to his men. They were permitted to put their cases forward for being awarded medals, promotions and even pensions, after which, once he had checked the veracity of their claims with their commanding officer, the matter was quickly settled. He personally read petitions from the ranks, and granted as many as he could. Baron Louis de Bausset-Roquefort, who served him on many campaigns, recalled that Napoleon 'heard, interrogated, and decided at once; if it was a refusal, the reasons were explained in a manner which softened the disappointment'.[84] Such accessibility to the commander-in-chief is impossible to conceive in the British army of the Duke of Wellington or in the Austrian army of Archduke Charles, but in republican France it was an invaluable means of keeping in touch with the needs and concerns of his men.

Soldiers who shouted good-naturedly from the ranks would often be rewarded with a quip: when, during the Italian campaign, one called out a request for a new uniform, pointing to his ragged coat, Napoleon replied: 'Oh no, that would never do. It will hinder your wounds from being seen.'[85] As Napoleon told Brune in March 1800: 'You know what words can do to soldiers.'[86] He would later on occasion take off his own cross of the Légion d'Honneur to give to a soldier whose bravery he'd witnessed. (When Roustam, his Mamluk bodyguard, attempted to sew Napoleon's cross onto his uniform, Napoleon stopped him – 'Leave it; I do it on purpose.'[87])

Napoleon genuinely enjoyed spending time with his soldiers; he squeezed their earlobes, joked with them and singled out old *grognards* (literally 'grumblers', but also translatable as 'veterans'), reminiscing about past battles and peppering them with questions. When campaign marches halted for lunch, Napoleon and Berthier would invite the aides-de-camp and orderlies to eat with them, which Bausset recalled as 'truly a fête for every one of us'. He also ensured that wine from his dinner table was always given to his sentries. Small things, perhaps, but they were appreciated and helped breed devotion. His constant references to the ancient world had the intended effect of giving ordinary soldiers a sense that their lives – and, should it come to that, their deaths in battle – mattered, that they were an integral part of a larger whole that would resonate through French history. There are few things in the art of leadership harder to achieve than this, and no more powerful impetus to action. Napoleon taught ordinary people that they could make history, and convinced his followers they were taking part in an adventure, a pageant, an experiment, an epic whose splendour would draw the attention of posterity for centuries to come.

During military reviews, which could last up to five hours, Napoleon cross-examined his soldiers about their food, uniforms, shoes, general health, amusements and regularity of pay, and he expected to be told the truth. 'Conceal from me none of your wants,' he told the 17th Demi-Brigade, 'suppress no complaints you have to make of your superiors. I am here to do justice to all, and the weaker party is especially entitled to my protection.'[88] The notion that *le petit caporal* was on their side against *les gros bonnets* ('big-hats') was generally held throughout the army.

Proper care of the wounded was a particular concern, in part because he needed them to return to the ranks as quickly as possible, but also because he knew how important prompt medical treatment was for morale. 'If he happened to meet with convoys of wounded,' recalled an aide-de-camp, 'he stopped them, informed himself of their condition, of their sufferings, of the actions in which they had been wounded, and never quitted them without consoling them by his words or making them partakers in his bounty.'[89] By contrast he regularly upbraided doctors, most of whom he regarded as quacks.

Napoleon learned many essential leadership lessons from Julius Caesar, especially his practice of admonishing troops he considered to have fallen below expectations, as at Rivoli in November 1796. In his book *Caesar's Wars*, which he wrote in exile on St Helena, he recounts the story of a mutiny in Rome: Caesar had laconically agreed to his soldiers' demands to be demobilized, but then he addressed them with ill-concealed contempt as 'citizens' rather than 'soldiers' or 'comrades'. The impact was swift and telling. 'Finally,' he concludes, 'the result of this moving scene was to win the continuation of their services.'[90] Far more often, of course, he lavished praise: 'Your three battalions could be as six in my eyes,' he called to the 44th Line in the Eylau campaign. 'And we shall prove it!' they shouted back.[91]

Napoleon's addresses to his troops were posted up in camp on billboards and widely read. He enjoyed firing off series of statistics, telling the troops how many victories they had won in what length of time and how many fortresses, generals, cannon, flags and prisoners they had captured. Some of these proclamations might sound vainglorious, but they were written for the often uneducated soldiers. Napoleon flattered his troops with references to the ancient world – though only a tiny minority would have been conversant with the Classics – and when with a special flourish he compared them to eagles, or told them how much their families and neighbours would honour them, he captivated the minds of his men, often for life.

Napoleon's rhetorical inspiration came mostly from the ancient world, but Shakespeare's St Crispin Day's speech from *Henry V* can also be detected in such lines as 'Your countrymen will say as they point you out, "He belonged to the Army of Italy." '[92] The avalanche of praise he generally lavished on his troops was in sharp contrast to the acerbic tone he adopted towards generals, ambassadors, councillors, ministers and indeed his own family in private correspondence. 'Severe to the officers,' was his stated mantra, 'kindly to the men.'[93]

Efficient staff-work helped Napoleon to 'recognize' old soldiers from the ranks, but he also had a phenomenal memory. 'I introduced three deputies of the Valais to him,' recalled an interior minister, 'he asked one of them about his two little girls. This deputy told me that he had only seen Napoleon once before, at the foot of the Alps, as he was on his way to Marengo. "Problems with the artillery forced him to stop for a moment in front of my house," added the deputy, "he petted my two children, mounted his horse, and since then I had not seen him again."[94] The encounter had taken place ten years earlier.

6

Peace

'*Winning is not enough if one doesn't take advantage of success.*'

Napoleon to Joseph, November 1808

'*In my opinion the French do not care for liberty and equality, they have but one sentiment, that of honour ... The soldier demands glory, distinction, rewards.*'

Napoleon to the Conseil d'État, April 1802

'Everything leads me to believe that the time for peace is now upon us and we must make it when we have the chance to dictate the conditions, provided they are reasonable,' Napoleon wrote to Paris on April 8, 1797.[1] The negotiations with what he called 'this insolent and arrogant court' began on April 15, with the Austrian plenipotentiary the Marquis de Gallo pedantically demanding that the pavilion where they were to take place be officially declared neutral ground. Napoleon happily conceded the point, explaining to the Directory that 'this neutral ground is surrounded on all sides by the French army, and is in the middle of our tents'.[2] When Gallo offered to recognize the existence of the French Republic, Napoleon told him that it 'did not require or desire recognition. It is already as the sun on the horizon in Europe: too bad for those who do not wish to see it and derive the benefit of it.' Gallo persevered, clearly thinking he was making a concession when he said that Austria would recognize it 'on condition that the Republic preserved the same etiquette as did the King of France'. This allowed Napoleon to make the irreproachably republican remark that since the French 'were completely indifferent to everything concerning etiquette, it wouldn't matter to us to adopt the article'.[3]

Napoleon believed his hand would be considerably strengthened if only Generals Moreau and Hoche would cross the Rhine. 'Ever since history has commenced to chronicle military operations,' he told the Directory on April 16, 'a river has never been considered a serious obstacle. If Moreau wishes to cross the Rhine, he will cross it . . . The armies of the Rhine can have no blood in their veins.'[4] If French troops were on Austrian soil, he said forcefully, 'we should now be in a position to dictate peace in an imperious manner'. In fact Hoche did cross on April 18, the very day the preliminaries were signed, followed by Moreau two days later. They then discovered to their great chagrin that they would have to halt their armies while their rival negotiated the peace.

Napoleon adopted an equally imperious manner in dealing with a threat that seemed to be arising from the ancient city-state of Venice, which was keen to guard its independence but hadn't the armies to ensure it. On April 9 he wrote to Doge Ludovico Manin demanding that Venice choose between war and peace. 'Do you suppose,' he said, 'that because I'm in the heart of Germany I'm powerless to cause the first nation in the universe to be respected?'[5] Although the French did have some legitimate complaints against Venice – which leaned towards Austria, was arming rapidly and had opened fire on a French frigate in the Adriatic – Napoleon was undoubtedly bullying the state when a few days later he sent Junot to demand a reply within twenty-four hours to his letter. Matters got far worse on April 17 when Verona, part of the Venetian Republic that clearly hadn't learned the lessons of Pavia, Binasco and Modena, staged an uprising in which between three and four hundred Frenchmen, many of them wounded soldiers in hospital in the city, were massacred.

'I will take general measures for all the Venetian mainland,' Napoleon promised the Directory, 'and I will issue such extreme punishments that they won't forget.'[6] Bourrienne later recorded that, on hearing of the insurrection, Napoleon said, 'Be tranquil, those rascals will pay for it; their republic has had its day.'[7] At 2 a.m. on Wednesday, April 19, 1797 – although it carried the official date of the previous day – Napoleon signed the Preliminaries of Leoben. That it was he rather than a plenipotentiary from Paris who negotiated and signed the document was a significant indication of how the balance of power with the Directory had tipped in his favour. This was not the final comprehensive peace treaty between France and Austria, which wasn't to be signed until October at Campo Formio, but Napoleon would negotiate that too. Under the terms of Leoben, Austria ceded the duchies of Milan and

Modena as well as the Austrian Netherlands to France. Austria agreed to recognize 'the constitutional limits' of France – which the French considered to extend to the Rhine – while France recognized the integrity of the rest of Francis's empire. Secret clauses forced Austria to renounce all her Italian possessions west of the Oglio river to the Cispadane Republic, but in compensation she would receive all the mainland territories of Venice east of the Oglio, as well as Dalmatia and Istria, while Venetian lands west of the Oglio would also go to France. Napoleon was simply assuming that he would be in a position to dispose of Venetian territory before the treaty was ratified.

Outwardly it looked as though Austria had done well, since the left bank of the Rhine was to be agreed at a future date and the territorial integrity of Austria itself was respected. Defending his negotiations, Napoleon told the Directory that Bologna, Ferrara and Romagna 'will always remain in our power', because they were ruled over by France's sister-republic based in Milan. Less persuasive was his argument that 'By ceding Venice to Austria the Emperor will be ... obliged to be friendly towards us.' In the same letter he told the Directory bluntly that they had got everything wrong from the very start of the Italian campaign: 'If I had persisted in marching on Turin, I should never have crossed the Po; if I had persisted in marching on Rome, I should have lost Milan; if I had persisted in marching on Vienna, I should perhaps have lost the Republic. The real plan for destroying the Emperor was the one I adopted.' Napoleon's next remarks must have sounded implausibly disingenuous: 'As for myself ... I have always considered myself as nothing in the operations I have directed, and I pushed on to Vienna after having acquired more glory than is necessary to be happy.'[8] Asking for permission to return home, he promised: 'My civil career shall resemble my military career by its simplicity.' He was surely imagining himself as the ancient hero Lucius Quinctius Cincinnatus, who returned to his farm and plough after saving the Roman Republic, and since these were semi-public reports, the non-secret paragraphs of which were published in the *Moniteur*, it is likely that he wrote these lines as much for public consumption as for the enlightenment of 'those scamps of lawyers' in the Directory, who nonetheless approved the terms of Leoben by four to one, with only Jean-François Reubell – who thought the terms too harsh on Austria – opposing.

In the course of the negotiations, the Duke of Modena tried to bribe Napoleon with 4 million francs not to depose him. According to the not altogether reliable Bourrienne the Austrian negotiators, Gallo and General Count von Merveldt, even offered him a German principality, to which Napoleon replied: 'I thank the Emperor, but if greatness is to be mine, it shall come from France.'[9] At the time, Austria seemed to be content with the Leoben terms. Gallo's only complaint was trivial, that he 'wished it to be transcribed onto parchment and that the seals should be bigger', which Napoleon duly accommodated.[10]

On April 20 the Venetians played directly into Napoleon's hands by opening fire on and killing a French sea captain called Laugier after he had illegally moored his vessel near the powder-magazine on the Venetian Lido. This gave Napoleon the justification he needed for what he was going to do anyway: demand that Venice expel the British ambassador and pro-Bourbon French émigrés, hand over all British goods, pay a 20-million franc 'contribution' and arrest Laugier's 'assassins' (who included a noble-born Venetian admiral). Napoleon ignored the doge's promise of reparations for the Verona massacre, saying his envoys were 'dripping with French blood'. Instead, he demanded the evacuation of Venice's mainland territories, which he needed to have under his control before the secret Leoben clauses could come into effect. Meanwhile he encouraged revolts in Brescia and Bergamo, and on May 3 he declared war. The Verona massacre was punished by the payment of 170,000 *sequins* (around 1.7 million francs) from the city, and the confiscation of everything in its municipal pawnshop valued at more than 50 francs. There were garrottings and transportations to French Guiana in South America, where the revolutionary government had taken to sending its undesirables. Church plate was expropriated, as were pictures, collections of plants and even 'seashells belonging to the city and private individuals'.[11]

Only ten days into his war with Venice, Napoleon inspired a coup d'état in the city. Using the secretary of the French legation, Joseph Villetard, to undermine the oligarchy there with threats of French retribution, the doge and senate – whose forefathers had once held the mighty Ottoman Empire at bay – meekly abolished themselves after 1,200 years as an independent state. They too tried to bribe Napoleon, this time with 7 million francs. He replied 'French blood has been treacherously shed; if you could offer me the treasures of Peru – if you could cover your whole dominion with gold – the atonement would be insufficient: the lion of St Mark must lick the dust.'[12] On May 16, 5,000 French troops under General Louis Baraguey d'Hilliers entered

Venice as 'liberators' and the four bronze horses that may once have graced Trajan's Arch in Rome were removed from the portico of the Basilica di San Marco and taken to the Louvre, where they remained until they were returned in 1815.

The treaty with the new pro-French puppet Venetian government stated that it should furnish three battleships and two frigates to the French navy, pay a 'contribution' of 15 million francs, provide twenty paintings and five hundred manuscripts, and hand over the mainland territories that France wanted to divide between the Cispadane Republic and Austria. In return, France offered professions of 'eternal friendship'. All of this was done without the Directory's involvement. At the start of the 1796 campaign, Napoleon had not been allowed to sign the armistice with Piedmont without the permission of Saliceti, who (though sympathetic to Napoleon) was nominally a commissioner of the Directory. Since then he had signed four major peace agreements on his own authority – with Rome, Naples, Austria and now Venice.

He was about to sign a fifth. On May 23 street fighting had broken out in Genoa between pro-French *giacobini* democrats and the forces of the Genovese doge and senate. The authorities prevailed, and documents were discovered revealing Saliceti and Faipoult's part in fomenting the botched uprising. Napoleon was furious with the Genoese democrats for rising too early, but he used the excuse of the deaths of some Frenchmen to send his aide-de-camp Lavalette to cajole the Genovese government. Like their Venetian counterparts, they soon capitulated and Napoleon personally drew up a constitution for a new Ligurian Republic – again without any input from the Directory.* This was based on the French constitution of 1795 and introduced a bicameral legislature of 150 and 300 members respectively, religious liberty, civic equality and measures of local self-government, principles which reflected neither the strict Jacobinism of his earlier days, nor (as some contemporaries suggested) a Corsican spirit of vendetta against Genoa. Indeed, after the democrats had destroyed the statue of Genoa's great hero, Andrea Doria, Napoleon admonished them, writing that Doria had been 'a great sailor and a great statesman. Aristocracy was liberty in his day. The whole of Europe envies your city the honour of having produced

---

* Napoleon couldn't ignore the Directory entirely. When in June Pius VI had an apoplectic attack, he asked for 'a positive instruction regarding the course I must take if the Pope dies. Should I allow a new Pope to be instated?'(CG1 no. 1725 p. 1030). Pius recovered and lived another two years.

that celebrated man. You will, I doubt not, take pains to rear his statue again: I pray you to let me bear a part of the expense which that will entail.'[13]

Napoleon's main residence in the spring of 1797 was the palazzo of Mombello outside Milan, where he summoned Miot de Melito for discussions. Miot noted the grandeur of Napoleon's daily life there. Not only did Napoleon bring his family to live with him – Madame Mère, Joseph, Louis, Pauline and his uncle Joseph Fesch in the first wave, with more to come – but he also introduced a quasi-courtly etiquette. Italian nobility appeared at his table instead of his aides-de-camp, dining took place in public as it had at Versailles under the Bourbons, and Napoleon betrayed a very un-republican taste for flunkeys. These were paid for out of a fortune that he himself stated amounted at that time to 300,000 francs. Bourrienne claimed it was more than 3 million francs – equivalent to the entire monthly pay of the Army of Italy. In either case, it suggests that it was not just his generals who had mulcted Italy.[14]

Miot claimed in his memoirs (largely written by his son-in-law General Fleischmann) that on June 1, 1797 Napoleon took him for a walk in the garden of Mombello, and said: 'Do you believe that I triumph in Italy in order to aggrandize the pack of lawyers who form the Directory, for the likes of Carnot and Barras? What an idea! . . . I wish to undermine the Republican party, but only for my own profit . . . As for me, my dear Miot, I have tasted authority and I will not give it up.' He is further reported to have said of the French: 'Give them baubles – that suffices them; they will be amused and let themselves be led, so long as the end to which they are going is skilfully hidden from them.'[15] Yet this whole cynical speech – which many historians have taken at face value – fails to ring true. Would so subtle a statesman as Napoleon simply have blurted out the extent of his (at that time treacherous) ambitions to undermine French republicanism to a public functionary like Miot de Melito, whose loyalty could not be known and who supposedly recalled the conversation perfectly decades later?[16]

It was at this time, with many of them under his eye at Mombello, that Napoleon began his persistent interference in the love-lives of his siblings. On May 5, 1797 the twenty-year-old Elisa married the Corsican noble Captain Felice Baciocchi, who thereafter found swift promotion in the army and ultimately became a senator and Prince of Lucca, sensibly ignoring her several infidelities. The next month, on June 14, under Napoleon's similar encouragement and prompting, the seventeen-year-old Pauline married the twenty-five-year-old General Charles Leclerc, whom Napoleon had served with at Toulon and who had also fought at Castiglione and Rivoli. Napoleon knew that Pauline was in love with someone else at the time, whom their mother Letizia thought unsuitable, but he supported the nuptials regardless. He also encouraged the cavalryman Murat to court his other sister, Caroline, and they married in January 1800.

In Paris, the Directory was in a precarious position. With inflation out of control – shoes cost forty times more by 1797 than they had in 1790 – and paper money, *assignats*, trading at 1 per cent of its face value, politics were in a febrile state.[17] Discontent with the government was evident on May 26, when the Marquis de Barthélemy, a constitutional royalist, became a Director after royalist gains in elections. The Directory now consisted of Barras and Carnot, the lawyers Reubell and Louis de La Révellière-Lépeaux, and Barthélemy, the first four of whom were regicides, although Carnot was now tacking strongly towards the more liberal, non-royalist moderates. Napoleon had not taken such a prominent part in saving the Republic at Vendémiaire only to see it replaced by royalists, so he sent Lavalette to Paris to observe political developments there. Lavalette found plots for the return of the Bourbons, one of which involved General Charles Pichegru, a former military instructor at Brienne and the conqueror of Holland, but also conspiracies on the extreme left, the uncovering of one of which led to the guillotining in late May of the journalist and agitator François-Noël Babeuf, whose ideas were essentially communist (although neither the term nor the concept had yet been invented).

Napoleon was particularly sensitive to opposition to his own actions in the National Assembly. When a moderate ex-Girondin deputy called Joseph Dumolard made a speech complaining that Venice had been unfairly treated, that the Assembly had been kept in ignorance of Napoleon's treaties and that 'France' (by which he meant Napoleon) had violated international law with her interference in the domestic affairs of sovereign states, Napoleon reacted explosively. 'Ignorant and garrulous lawyers have asked why we occupied Venice,' he told the Directory, 'but I warn you, and I speak in the name of eighty thousand men, that the time when cowardly lawyers and wretched babblers guillotined soldiers is past; and if you oblige them, the troops of Italy will march on Clichy, and woe to you!'[18] Clichy was the name both of the royalist club in the rue de Clichy and of the Parisian gate through which an army might march into the city.

Napoleon used his Bastille Day proclamation to the army to warn the domestic opposition that 'The Royalists, as soon as they show themselves, will cease to exist.' He promised 'Implacable war to the enemies of the Republic and of the constitution!'[19] Five days later he held big celebrations in Milan, which aimed to convey the message to France that the Army of Italy were more trustworthy as republicans than the *messieurs* ('gentlemen') of the Army of the Rhine. Such was the mutual dislike between the two forces that when Bernadotte's division came from Germany to Italy in early 1797, fights broke out between the officers, and when Napoleon gave Bernadotte the honour of taking the standards captured at Rivoli back to Paris, some suggested it had been a ploy to remove him from Italy. Napoleon's relations with the ambitious and independent Bernadotte had always been strained, and were to become far more so the following year when Bernadotte married Napoleon's ex-fiancée, Désirée Clary.

On July 7, 1797, Napoleon published the constitution of the new Cisalpine ('on this side of the Alps') Republic. Comprising Milan (its capital), Como, Bergamo, Cremona, Lodi, Pavia, Varese, Lecco and Reggio, it represented a greater step towards the creation of an Italian national identity and consciousness than had the Cispadane Republic, as the large numbers of Italians who volunteered for its military units indicated.[20] Napoleon appreciated that a large, unified, pro-French Italian state covering the Lombardy plain and beyond would provide protection against Austrian revanchism, and offer him the opportunity to strike once more against Styria, Carinthia and Vienna should the need arise. Its constitution, based on that of France, was drawn up by four committees under his direction, but because the first elections of the Cispadane Republic had seen many priests voted into office, this time Napoleon appointed its five Directors and all 180 of its legislators himself, with the Duke of Serbelloni as its first president.

By mid-July the situation in Paris had become dangerous. When the republican General Hoche was appointed war minister in the hope of cowing opposition to the government, he was accused by members of the Assembly of violating the constitution as he was not yet thirty, the minimum age for government office – except for Directors, who had to be forty – and he was forced to resign after only five days in the post. Napoleon, who was then twenty-seven, took note. 'I see that the Clichy Club means to trample over my corpse to the destruction of the republic,' he histrionically told the Directory on July 15 after Dumolard went so far as to table a motion critical of him in the Assembly.[21] The separation of powers under the Constitution of the Year III of August 1795 had meant that while the Directory could not dissolve the Assembly, the Assembly could not force policy on the Directors. There being no court of higher appeal, politics in Paris had reached a deadlock.

On July 17, Charles-Maurice de Talleyrand became foreign minister for the first of his four terms in the post. Clever, lazy, subtle, well travelled, club footed, a voluptuary and bishop of Autun (a bishopric he never visited) before he was excommunicated in 1791, Talleyrand could trace his ancestry back (at least to his own satisfaction) to the ninth-century sovereign counts of Angoulême and Périgord. He had contributed to the Declaration of the Rights of Man and the Civil Constitution of the Clergy and had been forced into exile, which he spent in England and the United States between 1792 and 1796. Insofar as he had a guiding principle it was a *soi-disant* affection for the English constitution, though he would never have imperilled his own career or comforts for one moment in order to promote that or any other. For many years Napoleon held a seemingly unbounded admiration for him, writing to him often and confidentially and calling him 'the King of European conversation', although by the end of his life he had seen through him completely, saying, 'He rarely gives advice, but can make others talk ... I never knew anyone so entirely indifferent to right and wrong.'[22] Talleyrand betrayed Napoleon in due course, as he did everyone else, and Napoleon took it very personally. The likelihood that he would die peacefully in his bed was proof for Napoleon later in life 'that there can be no God who metes out punishment'.[23]

Yet this bitterness was all in the future. In July 1797 the first thing Talleyrand did on becoming foreign minister was to write to Napoleon asking oleaginously for his friendship – 'The mere name of Bonaparte is an aid which ought to smooth away all my difficulties' – eliciting a letter of equally embarrassing effusiveness in return.[24] 'Alexander triumphed perhaps only to enthuse the Athenians,' replied Napoleon. 'Other captains are the elite of society, you for example. I've studied the Revolution too much not to know what it owes you. The sacrifices that you made for it deserve recompense ... You would not have to wait for it were I in power.'[25] Amid the mutual flattery was the promise of what might come from a political alliance.

By late July, Napoleon had decided that he would support a Barras-led purge of the French government and legislature, ridding it of the royalists and moderates whom he thought were endangering the Republic. On the 27th he sent the strongly republican (indeed, neo-Jacobin) Augereau to Paris. He warned Lavalette of Augereau's ambition – 'Do not put yourself in his power: he has sown disorder in the Army; he is a factious man' – but recognized that he was the right man to have in Paris at this time.[26] He told the Directory that Augereau was 'called by private affairs' to Paris, but the truth was altogether more dramatic.[27] With Pichegru taking the presidency of the lower house, the Five Hundred, and another crypto-royalist, the Marquis de Barbé-Marbois, becoming president of the upper house, the Elders, and with Moreau hardly bothering to celebrate Bastille Day in his Army of the Rhine, Barras now needed Napoleon's political support, his military muscle and his money. Lavalette is believed to have taken up to 3 million francs – the equivalent of Napoleon's entire net worth if Bourrienne is to be believed – to Paris to buy influence prior to the coup which was now intended.[28]

The Fructidor coup took place in the early hours of September 4, 1797 (18 Fructidor in the republican calendar) and was a complete success. Augereau occupied the important strategic points in Paris, despite a law against troops approaching the capital without the Assembly's permission. He placed soldiers around the Tuileries where the legislature sat, and arrested eighty-six deputies and several editors, whom he sent to the Temple prison. Many of these, including Barthélemy, Pichegru and Barbé-Marbois, were subsequently deported 4,400 miles away to the penal colony of Guiana. Carnot escaped the net, and managed to make it to Germany. Unsurprisingly, Dumolard was imprisoned too, though on the Île d'Oléron off the Atlantic coast of France rather than in South America. The rump of the legislative chambers then annulled the forthcoming elections in forty-nine pro-royalist departments and passed laws against named priests and unpardoned émigrés who had returned to France. The reliable republicans Philippe Merlin de Douai and François de Neufchâteau joined the Directory in place of the purged Carnot and Barthélemy, and the re-radicalized body took extra powers to close newspapers and political clubs (such as the Clichy). It was now as powerful as the old Committee of Public Safety had been in the days of the Terror. The Army of Italy had saved the Directory, at least for the moment; in Miot's view, Napoleon's adherence to the Fructidor purge 'secured its triumph'.[29] The Directory purged the officer corps too, sacking thirty-eight suspected crypto-royalist generals, including Napoleon's former rival General Kellermann, commander of the Army of the Alps.

Bourrienne recorded that Napoleon was 'intoxicated with joy' when he heard of the outcome.[30] Although Carnot was one of the coup's most prominent victims, he seems not to have held Fructidor against Napoleon personally. When he published his defence, from exile in 1799, he claimed that it had been he rather than Barras who had proposed Napoleon for the Italian command in 1796 and that by 1797 Barras had become an enemy of Napoleon, making 'gross and calumnious sarcasms on a person who must be dear to Bonaparte' (that is, Josephine).[31] He claimed that for Barras, Reubell and La Révellière, 'Bonaparte was ever odious to them, and they never lost sight of their determination to destroy him' and said they had privately made 'exclamations against the preliminaries of Leoben'.[32] Napoleon clearly believed this, because when he seized power he recalled Carnot to the war ministry.

Napoleon himself had no wish to be seen intriguing and spent the day of the coup negotiating peace in Italy at Passeriano. But as soon as Lavalette – who had been with Barras on the night of 17 Fructidor – got back a few days later he was made to spend four hours recounting the events to Napoleon, describing in detail the 'hesitations, fits of passion, and almost every gesture of the principal actors'.[33] Carnot's protégé Henri Clarke was recalled to Paris, leaving Napoleon the sole plenipotentiary for the Campo Formio peace negotiations.

Napoleon was regularly vexed by his discussions with the Austrian plenipotentiary, Count Ludwig von Cobenzl. 'It would appear difficult to understand the stupidity and bad faith of the Court of Vienna,' he told Talleyrand on September 12, calling the negotiations 'just a joke'. After Fructidor he had no more interference from the Directory over issues such as Venice joining the Cisalpine Republic (which he opposed) and compensation for the Austrians in Germany for territorial losses in Italy (which he supported).[34] The Austrians saw that there was no immediate hope of a Bourbon restoration, and so no further point in stalling negotiations. Demanding on September 26 that the Directory ratify his peace treaty with Piedmont, which stipulated that the kingdom send 10,000 men to serve alongside the French army, Napoleon predicted that in six months' time King Charles Emmanuel IV of Piedmont would be dethroned. As he told Talleyrand, 'When a giant embraces a pygmy and folding him in his arms, stifles him, he cannot be accused of having committed a crime.'[35]*

Napoleon's letters from this period refer constantly to his supposed ill-health – 'I can hardly get on horseback; I require two years'

---

* In fact King Charles Emmanuel stayed on his throne until his abdication in favour of his brother in 1802.

repose' – and are replete once again with threats of resignation for not being properly appreciated by the government, especially after the 'factious' Augereau was given command of the Army of the Rhine after Hoche's death from consumption on September 17. He also continually complained about the difficulty of negotiating with Cobenzl.* In the course of a frank discussion over the future of the Ionian Isles, Napoleon smashed on the floor either a beautiful piece of antique china (the Austrian version) or a cheap tea set (the Bonapartist version), or possibly Cobenzl's 'prized porcelain teacups that had been given him by sovereigns such as Catherine the Great' (Napoleon's own version twenty years after the event).[36] His negotiating technique often involved such histrionics, usually put on for show. Whatever was broken, Cobenzl remained calm, merely reporting back to Vienna: 'He behaved like a fool.'[37] One of Napoleon's private secretaries recorded how Napoleon's anger worked:

> When excited by any violent passion his face assumed a ... terrible expression ... his eyes flashed fire; his nostrils dilated, swollen with the inner storm ... He seemed to be able to control at will these explosions, which, by the way, as time went on, became less and less frequent. His head remained cool ... When in good humour, or when anxious to please, his expression was sweet and caressing, and his face was lighted up by a most beautiful smile.[38]

In a long and exasperated letter to Talleyrand on October 7, recounting to him yet again Cobenzl's obstinacy, Napoleon openly wondered whether fighting for Italy had ultimately been worth it, calling it 'an enervated, superstitious, *pantalon* and cowardly nation' that was incapable of greatness and certainly 'not worthy of having forty thousand Frenchmen die for it'.[39]† He added that he had had no aid from the Italians from the start of his campaign, and that the Cisalpine Republic had only a couple of thousand men under arms. 'This is history,' he wrote; 'the remainder, which is all very fine in proclamations, printed discourses, etc., is so much romance.' Napoleon's letters to Talleyrand

---

* If Austria turned out to prefer a return to war, the army would have to be ready, so Napoleon was also writing letters such as that to Citizen Haller, its financial administrator in Paris, saying: 'Please go to the place where they make buttons, and tell me what the situation is; the entire army is still naked because the buttons haven't been made.' The postscript to the letter merely states: 'Money, money, money!'(CG1 no. 2146 p. 1243).

† A reference to Pantalone, the *commedia dell'arte* character who was mercenary and greedy.

resemble streams of consciousness, so close had their epistolary relationship become in only a matter of weeks. 'I write to you as I think,' he told his new ally and confidant, 'which is the greatest mark of esteem I can give you.'[40]

On the morning of October 13, 1797, Bourrienne entered Napoleon's bedroom at daybreak to tell him that the mountains were covered in snow, whereupon Napoleon – at least according to Bourrienne – leaped up from his bed, crying: 'What! In the middle of October! What a country this is! Well, we must make peace.' He had immediately calculated that the roads would soon be so impassable that the Army of the Rhine couldn't reinforce him.[41] At midnight on Tuesday, October 17, at the hamlet of Campo Formio halfway between Napoleon's headquarters at Passariano and Cobenzl's at Udine, he and Cobenzl signed the treaty. Under its terms, Austria ceded Belgium (the Austrian Netherlands) and the west bank of the Rhine to France; France took the Ionian Isles from Venice; Austria took Istria, Friuli, Dalmatia, Venice itself, the Adige river and the lower Po; Austria recognized the Ligurian and Cisalpine republics, the latter of which would now merge with the Cispadane Republic; France and Austria formed a 'most favoured nation' customs union; and the Duke of Modena lost his Italian lands but was compensated by Austria with the Duchy of Breisgau, east of the Rhine. A conference was summoned at Rastatt in November to decide the future of the Holy Roman Empire and to work out compensation for the expropriation of the Rhineland princes; and to establish a pro-French independent Lemanic Republic around Geneva (which sits on Lake Léman) as well as a Helvetian Republic in Switzerland.

'I have no doubt there will be lively criticism of the treaty I've just signed,' Napoleon wrote to Talleyrand the next day, but he argued that the only way to get a better deal was by going to war again and conquering 'two or three more provinces from Austria. Was that possible? Yes. Probable? No.'[42] He sent Berthier and Monge to Paris with the treaty to expound its merits. They did such a good job, and so enthusiastic was the public enthusiasm for peace, that the Directory ratified it swiftly despite several of its members privately regretting the lack of republican solidarity shown to Venice. (It is said that when asked about the Venetian clauses, Napoleon explained: 'I was playing *vingt-et-un*, and stopped at twenty.'[43]) On the same day that he signed the Campo Formio treaty, bringing five years of war with Austria to an end, he also wrote to the interior minister of the Cisalpine Republic setting up a competition for a composition honouring the late General Hoche, open to all Italian musicians.[44]

While commending Campo Formio to Talleyrand, Napoleon mused on the next set of priorities for France. 'Our Government must destroy the Anglican monarchy, or expect itself to be destroyed by the corruption of these intriguing and enterprising islanders. The present moment offers us a fine opportunity. Let's concentrate all our activity upon the naval side and destroy England. That done, Europe is at our feet.'[45] Talleyrand was active on Napoleon's behalf, and only nine days later the Directory appointed him to command a new force, the Army of England. Napoleon immediately set to work. He suggested getting Hoche's maps of England off his heirs, had new surveys made of all the ports between Dunkirk and Le Havre, and ordered the construction of a large number of troop-carrying gunboats.[46] On November 13 he sent an artillery expert, Colonel Antoine Andréossy, to Paris 'in order to cast guns in the same calibre as the English cannon so that, once in the country, we may be able to use their cannonballs'.[47]

Napoleon also made sure that the heroes of the Army of Italy were recognized, sending a list of the bravest one hundred soldiers of the campaign, who were to be awarded the coveted golden sabres of honour. They included Lieutenant Joubert of the 85th Line, who had captured 1,500 Austrians with thirty men at Rivoli, Drum-Major Sicaud of the 39th Line, who single-handedly took forty prisoners at Calliano, Colonel Dupas of the 27th Légère for being 'one of the first on the bridge at Lodi', and Grenadier Cabrol of the 32nd Line, who had scaled Lodi's walls under enemy fire and opened the town gates.[48] He also sent a flag to Paris enumerating what he claimed to be the number of prisoners taken during the campaign (150,000), standards captured (170), guns (600), ships-of-the-line (9), peace treaties signed, cities 'liberated' and artists whose masterpieces he had sent to Paris, including Michelangelo, Titian, Veronese, Correggio, Raphael and Leonardo da Vinci.[49]

Leaving the Army of Italy in the hands of his brother-in-law Charles Leclerc, Napoleon went to the Congress of Rastatt in November, passing through Turin, Chambéry, Geneva, Berne and Basle, where he was lauded by the crowds. One night in Berne, recalled Bourrienne, they passed through a double line of carriages which were 'well lit up, and filled with beautiful women, all of whom raised the cry: "Vive Bonaparte! Vive the Pacificator!"'[50] He entered Rastatt in a carriage drawn

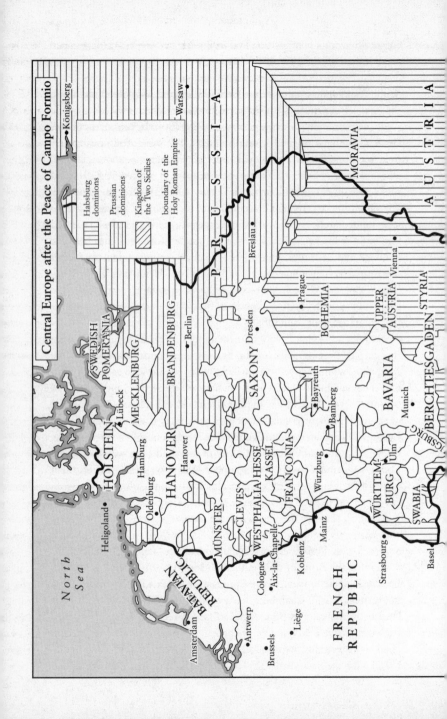

Central Europe after the Peace of Campo Formio

Habsburg dominions
Prussian dominions
Kingdom of the Two Sicilies
boundary of the Holy Roman Empire

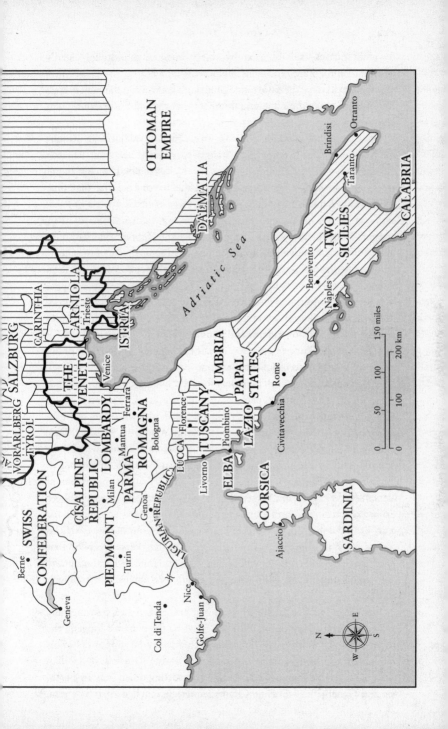

by eight horses and escorted by thirty hussars, a protocol usually adopted by reigning monarchs. Napoleon understood the power that spectacle held over the public imagination, and wanted the new French Republic to make the same visual impact that the old European monarchies enjoyed.

The Treaty of Campo Formio was officially ratified at Rastatt on November 30. It compelled Austria to give up her chief Rhenish strongholds – Mainz, Philippsburg and Kehl – evacuate Ulm and Ingolstadt, and withdraw her forces beyond the River Lech. At that time there were 16 million Germans who didn't live in either Austria or Prussia, and Napoleon wanted France to make a vigorous bid for their support since the glory days of the Holy Roman Empire that had once united them were now long gone. (In one of his coarser turns of phrase, he described the Holy Roman Empire as 'an old whore who has been violated by everyone for a long time'.[51]) Napoleon wanted to compensate the German princes who were going to lose lands to France under the treaty, posing as the protector of the medium-sized German states against the designs of Austria and Prussia. As he had presciently put it in a letter to the Directory on May 27: 'If the concept of Germany didn't exist, we would need to invent it for our own purposes.'[52]

The negotiations, which Napoleon opened but which continued until April 1799, gave him the perfect opportunity for a calculated act of diplomatic rudeness, when the King of Sweden – who had territory in Germany – had the gall to send Baron Axel von Fersen, Marie Antoinette's former lover, as his delegate. 'He came to see me with all the complacency of a courtesan of the Oeil-de-Boeuf,' Napoleon quipped to Talleyrand, referring to a room in Louis XIV's private apartments at Versailles.[53] He told von Fersen that he was 'essentially disagreeable to every French citizen', and that he was 'only known by your affection for a government justly proscribed in France, and for your useless exertions for its re-establishment'.[54] Napoleon recalled that Fersen 'replied that his Majesty would consider what I had said, and then he left. I naturally conducted him to the door with the usual ceremonies.'[55] Fersen was recalled.

Napoleon left Rastatt for Paris on December 2, 1797, pausing only to be the guest of honour at a dinner given by the masonic lodge in the town of Nancy on the way. (Freemasons tended to be supporters of his modernization programme, especially in Italy.) Dressed in civilian clothes, in an undistinguished carriage and accompanied only by Berthier and General Jean-Étienne Championnet, he reached Paris at 5 p.m.

on the 5th. 'It was in the general's plans to pass unnoticed,' recorded a contemporary, 'at this moment at least, and he quietly played his game.'[56] Too young to become a Director, Napoleon deliberately decided to adopt a low profile in Paris so as not to antagonize the Directory, despite the sensation that his presence in the capital caused as soon as it became known. Josephine's daughter Hortense recalled 'keeping back a crowd made up of all classes of people, impatient and eager to catch sight of the conqueror of Italy'.[57] The rue Chantereine on which Napoleon and Josephine had rented a house at number 6 (the name meant 'singing frogs', because there was once a marsh nearby) was changed in his honour to the rue de la Victoire.* Napoleon bought the house soon afterwards for 52,400 francs.† The extent of Josephine's almost psychotic extravagance may be discerned in the fact that she had spent 300,000 francs decorating it with Pompeian frescoes, mirrors, cupids, pink roses, white swans and so on, when it was still only rented.[58]

Years later, Napoleon recalled that this Parisian period of his life was fraught with peril, not least because soldiers would shout 'He ought to be king! We must make him king!' in the street. He feared this might get him poisoned, as many people thought (wrongly) had happened to Hoche.[59] For this reason, as a supporter recorded, 'he avoided taking part in politics, appeared rarely in public, and admitted to his intimacy only a small number of generals, scientists and diplomats'.[60] He thought the people would not remember his victories for long, saying: 'The Parisians retain no impression.'[61]

At 11 a.m. on December 6 Napoleon met Talleyrand at the foreign ministry at the Hôtel Galifet on the rue du Bac. They sized each other up over a long conversation, and liked what they saw. That evening Napoleon dined privately with the Directory; he was received warmly (if disingenuously) by Barras and La Révellière, amicably enough by Reubell but coldly by the others.[62] The whole government threw a huge official welcoming ceremony for him at the Luxembourg Palace at midnight on Sunday, December 10, where the great court was roofed over with flags and a specially constructed amphitheatre featured statues representing Liberty, Equality and Peace. Napoleon adopted a diffident demeanour throughout. A Briton living in Paris at the time noted that 'As he passed through the crowded streets, he leaned back in his

---

* Redeveloped extensively in 1865, this house, now number 60, is a bank; unusually for Napoleonic sites it is not worth a detour.
† A general was paid roughly 5,000 francs per annum in this period.

carriage . . . I saw him decline placing himself in the chair of State which had been prepared, and seemed as if he wished to escape from the general bursts of applause.'[63] Another contemporary observed: 'The cheers of the crowd contrasted with the cold praises of the Directory.'

Placing oneself in the limelight while seeming modestly to edge away from it is one of the most skilful of all political moves, and Napoleon had mastered it perfectly. 'All the most elegant and distinguished people then in Paris were there,' recalled another observer, including the Directory and both chambers of the legislature and their wives. When Napoleon entered, another witness observed, 'everyone stood up, uncovered [that is, took off their hats]; the windows were full of young and beautiful women. But, notwithstanding this splendour, an icy coldness characterized the ceremony. Everyone seemed to be present only for the purpose of beholding a sight, and curiosity rather than joy seemed to influence the assembly.'[64]

Talleyrand introduced Napoleon with a very flattering speech, to which Napoleon replied by commending the Campo Formio treaty and praising his soldiers' zeal in fighting 'for the glorious Constitution of the Year Three'. Then he proclaimed his belief that 'When the happiness of the French shall be secured on the best practical laws then Europe shall be free.'[65] Barras, who like the other Directors wore a toga on official occasions, then made an adulatory speech. 'Nature had exhausted all her powers in the creation of a Bonaparte,' he said, comparing him to Socrates, Pompey and Caesar. He then said of Britain, which had by now completely swept the French navy from the world's oceans: 'Go and capture that gigantic corsair who infests the seas. Go and chain up that gigantic freebooter who oppresses the oceans. Go and chastise in London outrages left too long unpunished.'[66] After his speech, Barras and all the other Directors embraced Napoleon. Bourrienne concluded, with pardonable cynicism, 'Each acted to the best of his ability his part in this sentimental comedy.'[67]

Napoleon was much happier on Christmas Day, when he was elected a member of the Institut de France, then (as now) the foremost intellectual society in France, in place of the exiled Carnot. With the help of Laplace, Berthollet and Monge he won the support of 305 members out of 312, with the next two candidates gaining only 166 and 123 votes respectively. Thereafter he often wore the dark-blue uniform of the Institut with its embroidered olive green and golden branches, attended science lectures there, and signed himself as 'Member of the Institut, General-in-Chief of the Army of England' in that order. Writing to

1. The energetic and determined General Bonaparte, commander-in-chief of the Army of Italy, at the age of twenty-seven.

2. (*above*) The substantial Casa Bonaparte in central Ajaccio in the mid-nineteenth century, now one storey higher than when Napoleon was born there on a pile of tapestry in 1769.

3. (*left*) A caricature by a fellow pupil at the military academy of Brienne showing the sixteen-year-old Napoleon resolutely marching to defend the Corsican nationalist leader Pasquale Paoli, as one of his teachers tries to restrain him by holding onto his wig. 'Buonaparte runs,' it says underneath, 'flies to help P from his enemies.'

4. (*above*) The long narrow bridge
at Lodi which French troops
captured on May 10, 1796,
throwing open the road to Milan.
It was Napoleon's first significant
victory and greatly increased his
belief in his own military capacity.
The painter, Louis-François
Lejeune, fought in many battles
of the Napoleonic Wars.

5. (*left*) Antoine-Jean Gros'
highly stylized propaganda portrait
of Napoleon carrying the flag on
the bridge at the battle of Arcole
on November 15, 1796, which he
only did momentarily before being
bundled into a ditch.

6. (*top*) The battle of the Pyramids on July 21, 1798 saw the Mamluks' power break against the well-disciplined French squares. 'Soldiers! From the top of those pyramids, forty centuries are contemplating you.' Napoleon took Cairo the following day.

7. (*below*) Napoleon showed genuine courage in March 1799 when tending to the French army's plague victims in the hospital on the sea front at Jaffa.

8. Napoleon seized power in the chaotic Brumaire coup of 9–10 November, 1799. He was manhandled by members of the Council of 500 in the Orangery at the palace of St Cloud before being rescued by grenadiers, who then cleared the hall at bayonet-point.

9. (*above left*) Napoleon's younger brother Lucien, a key figure in the Brumaire coup. Napoleon opposed his marriage and they became alienated, though Lucien finally came back to support Napoleon before Waterloo.

10. (*above right*) Napoleon was close for most of his life to his intelligent but weak elder brother Joseph, whom he made first King of Naples and then King of Spain, but who was politically more of a burden to him than a benefit.

11. (*top left*) Napoleon's shrewd mother, Madame Mère. When asked why she was so thrifty, despite the huge income Napoleon gave her, she replied, 'One day I may have to find bread for all these kings I have borne.'

12. (*top right*) Napoleon's younger sister Elisa, whom he made Princess of Lucca and Piombino, and Grand Duchess of Tuscany.

13. (*above left*) Napoleon's younger brother Louis, whom he made King of Holland before dethroning him for putting Dutch interests before those of the French empire.

14. (*above right*) Pushed together by Napoleon and Josephine, Hortense, Josephine's daughter, married Louis. Their union was unhappy, though it produced the future Emperor Napoleon III.

Napoleon's alluring younger sister Pauline (15. *above left*) was the closest to him of all his siblings, and showed him genuine love and loyalty – unlike their sister Caroline (16. *above right*) who, despite being created Queen of Naples, betrayed Napoleon to try to save her throne and that of her husband, Marshal Joachim Murat.

17. (*left*) Napoleon's impulsive youngest brother Jérôme, who married an American heiress without Napoleon's permission, was forced to divorce and then to marry Princess Catarina of Württemberg (*seated*). He briefly became King of Westphalia.

18. (*top left*) Josephine de Beauharnais, whom Napoleon married in March 1796, before he left for the front forty-eight hours later. Despite mutual infidelity and eventual divorce, he always thought of her as his lucky star. On their wedding day he gave her a gold enamelled medallion engraved 'To Destiny'.

19. (*top right*) Napoleon was very fond of Josephine's good-natured son Eugène de Beauharnais, whom he appointed Viceroy of Italy and to senior commands on several campaigns.

20. (*above*) Josephine's *nécessaire*, its centerpiece a portrait of Napoleon.

thank Armand-Gaston Camus, the Institut's president, the next day, Napoleon said: 'The true conquests, the only ones that cause no regret, are those made over ignorance.'[68] It was not only the French people he was hoping to impress when he displayed these intellectual credentials: 'I well knew that there was not a drummer in the army but would respect me the more for believing me to be not a mere soldier,' he said.[69]

His proposers and supporters at the Institut undoubtedly thought it a boon to have the foremost general of the day as a member, but Napoleon was a bona fide intellectual, and not just an intellectual among generals. He had read and annotated many of the most profound books of the Western canon; was a connoisseur, critic and even amateur theorist of dramatic tragedy and music; championed science and socialized with astronomers; enjoyed conducting long theological discussions with bishops and cardinals; and he went nowhere without his large, well-thumbed travelling library. He was to impress Goethe with his views on the motives of Werther's suicide and Berlioz with his knowledge of music. Later he would inaugurate the Institut d'Égypte and staff it with the greatest French *savants* of the day. Napoleon was admired by many of the leading European intellectuals and creative figures of the nineteenth century, including Goethe, Byron, Beethoven (at least initially), Carlyle and Hegel; he established the University of France on the soundest footing of its history.[70] He deserved his embroidered coat.

Napoleon showed considerable tact when, having been offered a major role by the Directory in the no-longer-popular anniversary celebrations of Louis XVI's execution on January 21, he modestly attended in his Institut rather than his military uniform, sitting in the third row rather than next to the Directors.

Napoleon's gaucheness with women was on display at a reception thrown by Talleyrand in his honour on January 3, 1798, at which the celebrated intellectual Madame Germaine de Staël, as Josephine's daughter Hortense later remembered, 'kept following the General about all the time, boring him to a point where he could not, and perhaps did not, sufficiently attempt to hide his annoyance'.[71] The daughter of the stupendously rich banker and Louis XVI's finance minister Jacques Necker, and a leading Parisian *salonnière* in her own right, Madame de Staël hero-worshipped Napoleon at the time, refusing to leave a dinner before Lavalette after the Fructidor purge, simply because he was Napoleon's aide-de-camp. At Talleyrand's fête she asked Napoleon: 'Whom do you consider the best kind of woman?' clearly expecting a compliment of some kind to her own famed intelligence and writing ability, whereupon Napoleon answered: 'She who has had the most children.'[72] As a throwaway remark to a near-stalker it did the trick (and since France's low birth-rate was to become a problem over the next century it might even be considered prescient), but it reveals much about his fundamental attitude to women.

Turning his thoughts to the invasion of Britain, Napoleon had arranged to meet Wolfe Tone, the leader of the rebel United Irishmen in December to elicit help. When Tone had told him he wasn't a military man and couldn't be of much use, Napoleon had interrupted him: 'But you're brave.' Tone modestly agreed that he was indeed. '*Eh bien*,' said Napoleon, according to Tone's later account, 'that will suffice.'[73] Napoleon visited Boulogne, Dunkirk, Calais, Ostend, Brussels and Douai over two weeks in February to evaluate the chances of a successful invasion, interviewing sailors, pilots, smugglers and fishermen, sometimes until midnight. 'It's too hazardous,' he concluded. 'I will not attempt it.'[74] His report to the Directory on February 23, 1798 was unequivocal:

> Whatever efforts we make, we shall not for some years gain naval supremacy. To invade England without that supremacy is the most daring and difficult task ever undertaken ... If, having regard to the present organization of our navy, it seems impossible to gain the necessary promptness of execution, then we must really give up the expedition against England – be satisfied with keeping up the pretence of it – and concentrate all our attention and resources on the Rhine, in order to try to deprive England of Hanover ... or else undertake an eastern expedition which would menace her trade with the Indies. And if none of these three operations is practicable, I see nothing else for it but to conclude peace.[75]

The Directory were by no means ready to conclude peace, and chose the last of Napoleon's three alternatives; on March 5 they gave him carte blanche to prepare for and command a full-scale invasion of Egypt in the hope of dealing a blow to British influence in and trading routes through the eastern Mediterranean. It was in the Directors' interests for Napoleon to go to Egypt. He might conquer it for France or – just as welcome – return after a defeat with his reputation satisfyingly tarnished. As the pro-Bonapartist British peer Lord Holland put it, they sent him there 'partly to get rid of him, partly to gratify him, and partly to dazzle and delight that portion of Parisian society who ... had considerable influence on public opinion'.[76] For Napoleon it represented an opportunity to follow in the footsteps of both his greatest heroes,

Alexander the Great and Julius Caesar, and he did not rule out the possibility of using Egypt as a stepping-stone to India. 'Europe is but a
molehill,' a delighted Napoleon told his private secretary, 'all the great
reputations have come from Asia.'[77]

Later that month a mini scandal emerged that threatened to drag Napoleon into a vortex of financial corruption and political embarrassment
which could have prevented him from ever having a chance to make his
reputation on the banks of the Nile. Alongside large-scale army contractors such as the Compagnie Flachat and Compagnie Dijon that accepted
deferred, long-term payments from the Treasury for supplying the
army's immediate needs were smaller firms that were regularly accused
of short-changing the taxpayer through invoice-manipulation, sub-
standard equipment, rotting provisions and even direct horse-thieving
from peasants. One such group of war-profiteers was the Compagnie
Bodin, run by the notorious Louis Bodin, among whose investors,
Napoleon discovered to his horror from his brother Joseph, were Barras, Hippolyte Charles (who had by then left the army to become a
full-time contractor) and Josephine.[78] Although Charles had left Italy in
August 1796, his relationship with Josephine had remained close.

It was one thing for Barras, Talleyrand and others to make their fortunes through loans, currency speculation and insider-trading, since
their murky dealings were virtually taken for granted by the public, but
if it emerged that Napoleon's own wife was also profiting from corrupt
army provisioning, one of his strongest appeals to the populace – his
integrity – would vanish overnight. Furthermore, his own private war
against the Compagnie Flachat in Milan, in the course of which he had
chased one of its directors into exile, would now seem like the grossest
hypocrisy rather than what it genuinely had been, a burning desire to
get the best deal for the Army of Italy.

Napoleon and Joseph subjected Josephine to a tough interrogation
on March 17 that left her shaken, angry and vengeful, but as untruthful
as ever. They demanded to know exactly what she knew about Bodin,
whether she had got him supply contracts, whether Hippolyte Charles
lived at the same address as Bodin at 100 Faubourg Saint-Honoré and
whether the rumour that she went there almost daily was true.[79] Josephine's panicked letter to Charles immediately afterwards suggests not
only that she had denied everything, but that she still loved Charles,
hated the Bonaparte brothers, had possibly seen the Bodin speculations
as a way out of her marriage as well as of her debts, and that she now

desperately wanted to cover her tracks. 'I replied that I knew nothing about what he was saying to me,' she told her lover. 'If he wished a divorce he had only to say; he had no need to use such means, and I was the most unfortunate of women and the most unhappy. Yes, my Hippolyte, they have my complete hatred; you alone have my tenderness and my love . . . Hippolyte, I shall kill myself – yes, I wish to end a life that henceforth would be only a burden if it could not be devoted to you.'[80]

She then told him to get Bodin to deny all knowledge of her involvement and say that he hadn't used her to get Army of Italy contracts; to instruct the doorman at the Faubourg Saint-Honoré to deny all knowledge of Bodin, and to tell Bodin not to use the letters of introduction which she had given him for his business trip to Italy. She signed off with 'a thousand kisses, as burning as is my heart, and as amorous'.[81] A subsequent letter to Charles concludes: 'You alone can make me happy. Tell me that you love me, and only me. I shall be the happiest of women. Send me, by means of Blondin [a servant], 50,000 livres [1.25 million francs] from the notes in your possession . . . *Toute à toi*.'[82]

As he contemplated a new campaign in Egypt, Napoleon thus had every reason to wish to escape Paris, a place he had come to equate with corruption, disloyalty, heartache, secret malice and the potential for deep embarrassment. He always had a certain idea of himself as a noble knight, like Clisson from his own short story, and the behaviour of both the Directory and Josephine threatened the ideal. It was time to double the stakes once again.

7

Egypt

'*This year the pilgrimage to Mecca was not observed.*'
Anonymous Islamic historian on 1798

'*If I had stayed in the East, I would have founded an empire, like Alexander.*'
Napoleon to General Gourgaud on St Helena

Although the idea of invading Egypt has been variously ascribed to Talleyrand, Barras, Monge (albeit only by himself), the encyclopaedist and traveller Constantin de Volney and several others, in fact French military planners had been considering it since the 1760s, and in 1782 Emperor Francis's uncle, Joseph II of Austria, had suggested to his brother-in-law Louis XVI that France annex Egypt as part of a wider plan to partition the Ottoman Empire.[1] The Ottoman Turks had conquered Egypt in 1517 and still officially ruled it, but *de facto* control had been long wrested from them by the Mamluks, a military caste originally from Georgia in the Caucasus. Their twenty-four beys (warlord princes) were unpopular among ordinary Egyptians for the high taxes they imposed, and were considered foreigners. After the Revolution, the idea of invading Egypt had appealed both to French radical idealists for its promise of extending liberty to a people oppressed by foreign tyrants, and to more calculating strategists such as Carnot and Talleyrand, who wanted to counter British influence in the eastern Mediterranean. Napoleon was of the latter group, telling the Directory in August 1797: 'To destroy England thoroughly, the time is coming when we must seize Egypt.'[2] Talleyrand suggested that he would go to Constantinople personally to persuade Sultan Selim III not actively to oppose the expedition. It was the first occasion, but by no means the last or most serious, when he was to mislead Napoleon.

Between his secret appointment to command the Army of Egypt on March 5, 1798 and the date set for the expedition to set sail, May 19, there were fewer than eleven weeks for Napoleon to organize and equip the entire enterprise, yet somehow he also managed to attend eight lectures on science at the Institut. As part of a misinformation campaign he spoke openly in the salons about the holiday he hoped to take in Germany with Josephine, Monge, Berthier and Marmont. To further the ruse, he was officially reconfirmed as commander of the Army of England, based at Brest.

Napoleon described Egypt as 'the geographical key to the world'.[3] His strategic aim was to damage British trade in the region and replace it with French; at very least he hoped to stretch the Royal Navy by forcing it to protect the mouths of the Mediterranean and Red Sea and trade routes to India and America simultaneously.[4] The Royal Navy, which had lost Corsica as a base in 1796, would be further constrained if the French fleet could operate from the near-impregnable harbour of Malta. 'Why should we not seize the island of Malta?' he had written to Talleyrand in September 1797. 'It would further threaten British naval superiority.' He told the Directory that 'This little island is worth any price to us.'[5] The three reasons he gave the Directory for the expedition were to establish a permanent French colony in Egypt, to open up Asian markets to French produce and to establish a base for a force of 60,000 men which could then attack British possessions in the Orient. His ultimate ambition – or fantasy – may be gauged by his demand for English maps of Bengal and the Ganges from the war ministry, and his request to be accompanied by Citizen Piveron, the former envoy to Britain's greatest enemy in India, Tipu Sahib, 'the Tiger of Mysore'. Yet the Directory deflated these dreams; Napoleon was authorized only to invade Egypt and was told to raise the funds himself. He was expected to be back in France in six months.

As it transpired he had relatively little difficulty in raising the 8 million francs the expedition would cost, through 'contributions' extorted by Berthier in Rome, Joubert in Holland and Brune in Switzerland. Napoleon chose his senior officers carefully. On March 28 General Louis Desaix, a nobleman who had shown great promise fighting in Germany, brought another noble, General Louis-Nicolas Davout, to the rue de la Victoire to meet Napoleon for the first time. The twenty-eight-year-old Burgundian didn't make a very good first impression, but Desaix's assurances that Davout was a highly capable officer won him a place on the expedition. Although Napoleon was impressed with Davout's performance in Egypt, they never became personally close, to Napoleon's great disadvantage since Davout was later one of the few of his marshals to shine in independent command. Napoleon predictably took Berthier as his chief-of-staff, his brother Louis as an aide-de-camp after he had graduated from the Châlons artillery school, his handsome stepson Eugène (nicknamed 'Cupid') as another, the divisional generals Jean-Baptiste Kléber (a stentorian figure, a whole head taller than the rest of his soldiers and a veteran of the Army of the Rhine), Desaix, Bon, Jacques-François de Menou, Jean-Louis Reynier and fourteen other generals, including Bessières and Marmont, many of whom had fought under him in Italy.

The cavalry was to be under the command of the Haitian-born General Davy de la Pailleterie, known as Thomas-Alexandre Dumas, whose father was a French nobleman and whose mother was of Afro-Caribbean descent, hence the nickname 'Schwarzer Teufel' (black devil) which the Austrians had given him when he prevented them from re-crossing the Adige in January 1797.* Napoleon further chose General Elzéar de Dommartin to command the artillery, and the one-legged Louis Caffarelli du Falga the engineers. Lannes was to be quartermaster-general, a surprisingly desk-bound job for one of the most dashing cavalry commanders of the era. The chief doctor was René-Nicolas Desgenettes, who wrote a history of the campaign from a medical point of view four years later, which he dedicated to Napoleon. It was a formidable officer corps, abounding with talent and promise.

Napoleon also took 125 books of history, geography, philosophy and Greek mythology in a specially constructed library, including Captain Cook's three-volume *Voyages*, Montesquieu's *The Spirit of the Laws*, Goethe's *Sorrows of Young Werther* and books by Livy, Thucydides, Plutarch, Tacitus and, of course, Julius Caesar. He also brought biographies of Turenne, Condé, Saxe, Marlborough, Eugène of Savoy, Charles XII of Sweden and Bertrand du Guesclin, the notable French commander in the Hundred Years War. Poetry and drama had their place too, in the works of Ossian, Tasso, Ariosto, Homer, Virgil, Racine and Molière.[6] With the Bible guiding him about the faith of the Druze and Armenians, the Koran about Muslims, and the Vedas about the Hindus, he would be well supplied with suitable quotations for his

---

* He was the father of Alexandre Dumas, the author of *The Count of Monte Cristo*.

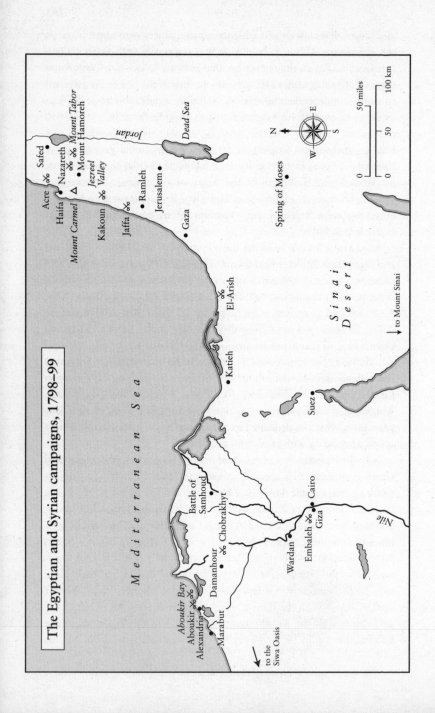

The Egyptian and Syrian campaigns, 1798–99

Mediterranean Sea

Marabut
Alexandria
Aboukir
Aboukir Bay
Damanhour
Chobrakhyt
Battle of Samhoud
Wardan
Embaleh
Giza
Cairo
Nile
Suez
Katieh
El-Arish
Sinai Desert
→ to Mount Sinai

Gaza
Jaffa
Kakoun
Ramleh
Jerusalem
Mount Carmel
Haifa
Acre
Safed
Nazareth
Jezreel Valley
Mount Tabor
Mount Hamoreh
Jordan
Dead Sea
Spring of Moses

→ to the Siwa Oasis

N
W   E
S

0   50   100 km
0   50 miles

proclamations to the local populations virtually wherever this campaign
was finally to take him. He also included Herodotus for his – largely
fantastical – description of Egypt. (Years later he would state that he
believed 'Man was formed by the heat of the sun acting upon mud.
Herodotus tells us that the slime of the Nile changed into rats, and that
they could be seen in the process of formation.'[7])

Napoleon knew that Alexander the Great had taken learned men and
philosophers along on his campaigns in Egypt, Persia and India. As
befitted a member of the Institut, he intended his expedition to be a cultural and scientific event and not merely a war of conquest. To that end
he took 167 geographers, botanists, chemists, antiquaries, engineers,
historians, printers, astronomers, zoologists, painters, musicians, sculptors, architects, Orientalists, mathematicians, economists, journalists,
civil engineers and balloonists – the so-called *savants*, most of whom
were members of the Commission des Sciences et des Arts – whose work
he hoped would give the enterprise a significance beyond the military.[8]
He failed in his hopes to persuade a professional poet to accompany
him, but he did enlist the fifty-one-year-old novelist, artist and polymath
Vivant Denon, who made more than two hundred sketches during his
travels. Under their leaders Monge and Berthollet, the *savants* included
some of the most distinguished men of the day: the mathematician and
physicist Joseph Fourier (author of Fourier's Law concerning heat con-
duction), the zoologist Étienne Saint-Hilaire and the mineralogist Déodat
de Dolomieu (after whom dolomite was named). The *savants* were not
told where they were going, merely that the Republic needed their talents and that their academic posts would be protected and stipends
increased. '*Savants* and intellectuals are like coquettes,' Napoleon was
later to tell Joseph; 'one may see them and talk with them, but don't
make one your wife or your minister.'[9]

'Soldiers of the Army of the Mediterranean!' Napoleon proclaimed
from Toulon on May 10, 1798:

> You are now a wing of the Army of England. You have campaigned in the
> mountains, in the plains and before fortresses, but you have yet to take
> part in a naval campaign. The Roman legions that you have sometimes
> rivalled, but have yet to equal, fought Carthage on this very sea ... Vic-
> tory never forsook them ... Europe is watching you. You have a great
> destiny to fulfil, battles to fight, dangers and hardships to overcome. You
> hold in your hands the future prosperity of France, the good of mankind

and your own glory. The ideal of Liberty that has made the Republic the arbiter of Europe will also make it the arbiter of distant oceans, of far-away countries.[10]

In the same speech, Napoleon promised his men 6 *arpents* (5 acres) of land each, although he didn't stipulate precisely where they would be. Denon later recalled that when the soldiers saw the barren sand-dunes of Egypt from the boats before they landed, the men joked to each other: 'There are the six *arpents* they promised you!'[11]

Napoleon prepared for the first French military action in the Middle East since the Crusades with his usual mastery of minutiae. In addition to all the military equipment necessary for his army, he collected astronomical telescopes, ballooning equipment, chemical apparatus, and a printing press with Latin, Arabic and Syriac type.[12] 'You know how much we will need good wine,' he wrote to Monge, telling him to buy 4,800 bottles, most of it his favoured red burgundy, but also to find 'a good Italian singer'.[13] (In all, the expedition took 800,000 pints of wine to Egypt.) Napoleon's prestige was by now sufficient to overcome most supply difficulties. François Bernoyer, whom he appointed to clothe the army, set about hiring tailors and saddlers and recorded that 'When I told them that Bonaparte was leading the expedition, all obstacles disappeared.'[14]

Napoleon's armada left Toulon for Alexandria in fine weather on Saturday, May 19, 1798 and was joined by fleets from Marseilles, Corsica, Genoa and Civitavecchia. It was the largest fleet ever to sail the Mediterranean. There were 280 ships in all, including 13 ships-of-the-line of between 74 and 118 guns (the latter, Vice-Admiral François Brueys' flagship *L'Orient*, was the biggest warship afloat). Napoleon had assembled 38,000 soldiers, 13,000 sailors and marines and 3,000 merchant seamen. His army was somewhat top-heavy as it included 2,200 officers, a ratio of seventeen to one against the more usual twenty-five to one – an indication of how many ambitious young men wanted to see action under him. 'Have a good bed prepared for me,' Napoleon – a bad sailor – told Brueys before setting sail, 'as if for a man who will be ill for the entire duration of the voyage.'[15]

This gigantic armada was fortunate to make it across the Mediterranean without being set upon by Nelson, who was looking for him with thirteen ships-of-the-line. Nelson's fleet had been scattered towards Sardinia by a gale the evening before Napoleon set sail, and on the night of

June 22 the two fleets crossed paths only 20 miles from each other in fog near Crete. Nelson made an educated guess that Napoleon was heading for Egypt but reached Alexandria on June 29 and left on the 30th, the day before the French arrived.[16] To evade Nelson on three occasions was extraordinary; the fourth time they would not be so lucky.

Napoleon asked his *savants* to give lectures for his officers on deck during the voyage; in one Junot snored so loudly that Napoleon had him woken up and excused. He later discovered from his librarian that his senior officers were mostly reading novels. (They had started out gambling, until 'everyone's money soon found itself in a few pockets, never to come out again'.) He pronounced that novels were 'for ladies' maids' and ordered the librarian, 'Only give them history books. Men should read nothing else.'[17] He was apparently overlooking the forty novels, including English ones in French translation, he himself had brought out.

On June 10 the fleet reached Malta, which commanded the entrance to the eastern Mediterranean. Napoleon sent Junot to order the Grand Master of the Knights of St John, Ferdinand von Hompesch zu Bolheim, to open Valletta harbour and surrender. When two days later he did, Caffarelli told Napoleon how fortunate they had been, because otherwise 'the army would never have got in'.[18] Malta had survived sieges before – notably in 1565, when the Turks had fired 130,000 cannonballs at Valletta over four months – and would do so again over the course of thirty months during the Second World War, but in 1798 the Knights were in schism – the pro-French knights refused to fight and their Maltese subjects were in revolt.

In his six days at Malta Napoleon expelled all but fourteen of the Knights and replaced the island's medieval administration with a governing council; dissolved the monasteries; introduced street lighting and paving; freed all political prisoners; installed fountains and reformed the hospitals, postal service and university, which was now to teach science as well as the humanities.[19] He sent Monge and Berthollet to plunder the treasury, mint, churches and artworks (though they missed the silver gates of the Church of St John, which had cleverly been painted black). On June 18 he wrote fourteen despatches covering the island's future military, naval, administrative, judicial, taxation, rental and policing arrangements. In them he abolished slavery, liveries, feudalism, titles of nobility and the arms of the Order of the Knights. He allowed the Jews to build a hitherto banned synagogue and even denoted how much each professor in the university should be paid, ordering that the librarian there should also lecture on geography for his 1,000 francs per annum. 'We now possess', he boasted to the Directory, 'the strongest place in Europe, and it will cost a good deal to dislodge us.'[20] He left the island under the direction of his political ally Michel Regnaud de Saint-Jean d'Angély, who as well as being an editor of the *Journal de Paris* during the Revolution had been the maritime provost of the French harbour of Rochefort.

While sailing to Egypt from Malta, Napoleon wrote General Orders about how the army was to behave once ashore. Public treasures and the houses and offices of the revenue collectors were to be sealed up; Mamluks were to be arrested and their horses and camels requisitioned; all towns and villages would be disarmed. 'Every soldier who shall enter into the houses of the inhabitants to steal horses or camels shall be punished,'[21] he instructed. He was particularly careful to give no cause for a jihad. 'Do not contradict them,' he ordered his men with regard to Muslims. 'Deal with them as we dealt with the Jews and with the Italians. Respect their muftis and imams as you respected rabbis and bishops . . . The Roman legions protected all religions . . . The people here treat their wives differently from us, but in all countries the man who commits rape is a monster.'[22] He added that the first town they would enter had been founded by Alexander the Great, something that meant much more to him than to them.

On Sunday, July 1 the fleet arrived off Alexandria and Napoleon landed on the beach 8 miles away at Marabut at 11 p.m. He captured Alexandria the next morning by storm, Menou's men going over the walls with ease. 'We began by making an assault upon a place [Alexandria] without any defence,' General Pierre Boyer, the army's adjutant-general, wrote to his friend General Kilmaine back in France, 'and garrisoned by about five hundred Janissaries [elite Mamluk soldiers], of whom scarcely a man knew how to level a musket . . . We lost, notwithstanding, 150 men, whom we might have preserved by only summoning the town [to surrender] but it was thought necessary to begin by striking terror into the enemy.'[23] Napoleon had the dead buried beneath the granite Pompey's Pillar, and inscribed their names on its sides.*

---

* It was hardly an ideal totem; Pompey had been murdered on stepping ashore in Egypt in 48 BC. Of the 150 men mentioned by Boyer, only 40 were killed; the rest were wounded.

Napoleon stayed in Alexandria for a week, overseeing the disembarkation of his army, disarming the local population (except imams, muftis and sheikhs), making contact with the French merchants in Egypt, capturing nearby Rosetta, setting up a *lazaretto* (plague hospital) and writing an anti-Mamluk letter to the Turkish pasha in Cairo – 'You know that France is the only ally the Sultan has in Europe' – as well as producing proclamations on the printing press. One, dated 'of the month of Muharrem, the Year of the Hegira 1213', stated of the Mamluks:

> The hour of their chastisement has come. For too long this rabble of slaves, purchased in Caucasus and in Georgia, has tyrannized over the fairest part of the world, but God, on whom everything depends, has decreed that their Empire shall be no more! ... People of Egypt! I am come to restore your rights, to punish usurpers. I reverence ... God, his prophet Muhammed, and the Koran! ... Have we not destroyed the Pope, who made men wage war on the Muslims? Have we not destroyed the Knights of Malta, because those fools believed it to be God's will to fight against Muslims?[24]

Napoleon was not afraid to invoke the deity – even to appear to take the side of the Muslims against the Pope – if it would serve his purpose and win over the population. Probably referring to the 1536 Franco-Ottoman alliance between François I and Sultan Suleiman the Magnificent, he then rhetorically asked: 'Have we not for centuries been the friends of the Grand Signor (may God accomplish his desires!) and the enemy of his enemies?' His reading had served him well and in his proclamation he echoed the rhythm and style of the Koran.

Leaving the fleet harboured in Aboukir Bay with orders that it be moored close enough to the land to be protected from attack, Napoleon set off for Cairo at 5 p.m. on July 7 and marched through the moonlit night. It was the first desert crossing by a modern Western army. They reached the first stop on the 150-mile road to Cairo, the town of Damanhour, at eight o'clock the next morning. Thereafter his men marched during the day, which they loathed to do because of the heat, the racking thirst, the flies, mosquitoes, snakes and scorpions, the swirling sandstorms and hostile Mamluks and Bedouin Arab tribesmen riding on their flanks ready to kill stragglers. Many of the wells and cisterns along the way had been poisoned or filled with stones. Berthier recalled that water sold for the same weight as gold on that march. One particular problem was trachoma (granular conjunctivitis or 'Egyptian' ophthalmia) whereby the scorching sunshine caused a roughening of the inside of the eyelids, which left at least two hundred men blinded.[25] The young artillery staff lieutenant Jean-Pierre Doguereau never forgot how hard it was to move cannon in the soft sand, where they could sink up to their axles. 'Well, general, are you going to take us to India like this?' shouted a soldier at Napoleon, only to receive the reply: 'No, I wouldn't undertake that with soldiers such as you!'[26]

Morale suffered badly in the desert. 'It would be difficult to describe the disgust, the discontent, the melancholy, the despair of that army, on its first arrival in Egypt,' wrote the contemporary historian Antoine-Vincent Arnault. Napoleon even saw two dragoons rush out of the ranks and drown themselves in the Nile.[27] Captain Henri Bertrand, a talented engineer who became a colonel during this campaign, saw generals as distinguished as Murat and Lannes 'throw their laced hats in the sand, and trample on them'.[28] The soldiers' major gripe was that in the entire seventeen-day march from Alexandria to Cairo there was no bread and 'nor a drop of wine' and, as Boyer told Kilmaine, 'We were reduced to living on melons, gourds, poultry, buffalo meat and Nile water.'[29]

At 8 a.m. on July 13, Mamluks attacked Napoleon's camp at Chobrakhyt (also known as Chebreis) on the riverbank. Murad Bey, a tall, scarred Circassian who had co-ruled Egypt for years with Ibrahim Bey, attacked with around 4,000 men. Napoleon formed battalion squares, with cavalry and baggage inside, which the Mamluks merely circled on horseback. They looked magnificent in colourful costumes, medieval armour and riding fine horses, but Boyer was unimpressed with the way they 'straggled round and round our army, like so many cattle; sometimes galloping, and sometimes pacing in groups of ten, fifty, one hundred etc. After some time, they made several attempts, in a style equally ridiculous and curious, to break in upon us.'[30] Napoleon's aide-de-camp Sulkowski used the same word, saying 'against a disciplined army it was only ridiculous'.[31] Armed with javelins, axes (which they sometimes threw), scimitars, bows and arrows and antiquated firearms, the Mamluks were no match for trained volleys of musketry. When he had lost around three hundred men, Murad rode off. It was a useful encounter for Napoleon, giving him a chance to practise tactics he later put to good use. He told the Directory about 'a new kind of warfare, requiring much patience compared with the usual French impetuosity', one that relied on steadiness in defence.[32] The encounter did nothing to dent Mamluk hubris. 'Let the Franks come,' said one bey, possibly Murad himself, 'we will crush them beneath our horses' hooves.'[33] (Another version was: 'I will ride through them and sever their heads from their bodies like watermelons.'[34])

On July 19, while they were at Wardan on the way to Cairo, Junot confirmed what Napoleon might have already have suspected: that Josephine had been having an affair with Hippolyte Charles. (Although Joseph Bonaparte had long known it, he seems not to have told his brother at the time of their fraught interview with her.) Junot now showed Napoleon evidence in the form of a letter – we don't know who it was from, and no post had been received since landing – and added that his cuckolding was the talk of Paris.[35] It is a mystery why Junot chose that particular time and place to confront Napoleon. Charles had played a joke on him, gluing his sword into its scabbard, but that had been months earlier.

'I have a great, great deal of domestic sorrow as now the veil has been completely lifted,' Napoleon wrote to Joseph six days later. 'Only you remain there for me on this earth. Your friendship is very precious to me: I have only to lose it and see you betray me for me to become a misanthrope . . . it is my sad condition to have all these feelings for the same person in one heart alone. You understand me!'[36] This letter – which recalls parts of Clisson's final letter to Eugénie – was intercepted by the Royal Navy on its way to France. Part of it was published, but not enough to make it clear to what Napoleon was alluding.[37]

Bourrienne states that Napoleon intended to divorce Josephine when he returned to France. Napoleon wrote again to Joseph to say, 'Please try to arrange a country dwelling for me when I arrive, either near Paris or in Burgundy, I intend to confine myself there for the winter. I am so tired of human nature! I need solitude and isolation, grandeur has harmed me; my feelings have dried up.'[38] No letters from Napoleon to Josephine survive from the Egyptian campaign, which some historians have taken to mean they were lost or destroyed, but a much more likely explanation is that he simply didn't write any. The next surviving letter is dated May 11, 1800, by which point he called her, more sedately, '*ma bonne amie*'.[39]

To Napoleon's understandable embarrassment, the British government published annual books of intercepted correspondence, covering 1798, 1799 and 1800. In order to underline what the editors gleefully

called the 'miseries and disappointments' of his army, they reprinted letters from, among many others, Napoleon himself, Louis Bonaparte,
Tallien, Bourrienne, Desgenettes, Menou, Boyer, Dumas, Brueys and
Lasalle. (The last, perhaps the most dashing hussar in the army, wrote
to his mother complaining that his hair was falling out due to 'my total
want of powder and pomatum'.[40]) Writing to their friends, families and
mistresses, they were honest and, except for Napoleon, uniformly
wanted to come home as soon as possible from a country that several
described as 'pestilential'. The collection included letters from Napoleon
to Joseph complaining about Josephine's profligacy – though that was
hardly a state secret – and from Eugène to Josephine 'expressing his
hopes that his dear Mamma is not as wicked as she is represented!'
Rear-Admiral Jean-Baptiste Perrée, commander of the Nile flotilla,
wrote to a friend: 'The beys have left us some pretty Armenian and
Georgian wenches, whom we have confiscated to the profit of the
nation.'[41]

On July 21 Murad Bey appeared again, this time with 6,000 Mamluks
and 54,000 Arab irregulars, many of them mounted, at the town of
Embaleh on the left bank of the Nile.[42] The Great Pyramid of Cheops at
Giza, the tallest building in the world until the twentieth century, was
clearly visible nearly 9 miles away, and Napoleon referred to it in his
pre-battle Order of the Day: 'Soldiers! You came to this country to save the
inhabitants from barbarism, to bring civilization to the Orient and sub-
tract this beautiful part of the world from the domination of England.
From the top of those pyramids, forty centuries are contemplating you.'[43]*
Napoleon often said thereafter that 'of all the objects that had impressed
him in his life, the pyramids of Egypt and the size of the giant Frion
[the tallest man in France] were those that had most astonished him'.[44]
The reference to England, which had no plans whatever to interfere in
Egypt's affairs or in any way benefited from Egypt, was entirely hyper-
bolic, but it presumably went down well with the troops.

Napoleon formed his 20,000 men into five division-sized squares
with artillery at each corner and the baggage, cavalry and *savants* inside.
The men had quenched their thirst in watermelon fields, and were ready.
They knew that if they pointed their bayonets at the Mamluk horses'
heads, in the words of one officer, 'the horse rears up, unseating his

---

* In fact forty-four centuries separated 1798 from the construction of the Great Pyramid
of Cheops.

rider'.[45] The Mamluks attacked Desaix's and Reynier's divisions first, which, according to Boyer, 'received them with steadiness, and at the distance of only ten paces opened a running fire upon them ... Then they fell upon Bon's division, which received them in the same manner. In short, after a number of unavailing efforts, they made off.'[46] The battle of the Pyramids was over in two hours. Dommartin's aide-de-camp Jean-Pierre Doguereau kept a journal of the campaign, in which he recalled that many of the Mamluks 'threw themselves into the Nile; firing at the thousands of heads appearing above the water continued for a long while; all their cannon were captured by us. The enemy losses were considerable.'[47]

Many of the three hundred French casualties were due to friendly fire between the squares rather than to the Mamluks, who lost twenty guns, four hundred camels and all their equipment and baggage. Because the Mamluks traditionally went into battle carrying their life savings, a single corpse could make a soldier's fortune. After the battle, the victorious French measured out gold coins by the hatful. 'Our brave men were amply compensated for the trouble they had experienced,' was how Berthier put it in his report to the war ministry, printed in Le Moniteur. Napoleon won the soubriquet 'Sultan Kebir' (Lord of Fire) from the Egyptians as Murad fled to Upper Egypt, where Desaix was despatched in pursuit. After one of Desaix's victories there, the corpses of drowned Mamluks were fished out of the Nile to be picked over.

The day after the battle Napoleon entered Cairo, a city of 600,000 inhabitants, the same size as Paris and easily the largest in Africa. He set up headquarters in the house of Elfey Bey in Ezbekyeh Square and immediately started issuing orders for reforms. Each of Cairo's sixteen districts was to receive its own *diwan* (council) made up of local dignitaries who would then send a representative to a Grand Diwan, under the presidency of the pro-French Sheikh al-Sharqawi. Napoleon accorded the *diwans* some powers over justice and administration, hoping they might eventually 'accustom the Egyptian notables to the ideas of assembly and government'. His meetings with the Grand Diwan appear to have been jolly: one Muslim historian records that Napoleon was 'cheerful and sociable with the gathered people and used to joke with them'.[48] By direct decree Napoleon established a postal system, street lighting and cleaning, a coach service between Cairo and Alexandria, a mint and a rational tax system with lower impositions on the Egyptian *fallaheen* (peasantry) than the Mamluks' extortionary demands. He also abolished feudalism, replacing it with rule by the *diwans*, set up a new French trading company, built modern plague hospitals and produced Egypt's first printed books (in three languages). None of these reforms were undertaken on orders from the Directory, who were unable to get messages through; they were entirely on Napoleon's initiative.

When he invaded Egypt, Alexander the Great visited the Temple of Amon at Siwa in 332 BC to consult the great oracle there. Napoleon considered it 'a great stroke of policy' and said, 'It enabled him to conquer Egypt.'[49] As Egypt had been Muslim since the seventh century, Napoleon felt it would be wise to embrace Islam as much as possible, although he never went so far as the general he called 'that fool Menou', who married an Egyptian, converted to Islam and took on the middle name Abdallah. (Marmont asked him whether he 'intended, in the customs of the country', to practise polygamy as well; Menou indicated not.[50]) Asked two decades later whether he had ever truly embraced Islam, Napoleon laughingly replied: 'Fighting is a soldier's religion; I never changed that. The other is the affair of women and priests. As for me, I always adopt the religion of the country I am in.'[51]

Napoleon respected Islam, regarding the Koran as 'not just religious; it is civil and political. The Bible only preaches morals.'[52] He was also impressed by the way that the Muslims 'tore more souls away from false gods, toppled more idols, pulled down more pagan temples in fifteen years than the followers of Moses and Christ had in fifteen centuries'.[53]* He had no objection to polygamy, saying that Egyptian men were *gourmands en amour*, and, when permitted, 'will prefer having wives of various colours'.[54]† His flattery of the *ulama* (clergy), his discussions of the Koran, and his holding out the possibility of his conversion to Islam – as well as his attempts to impress the sheikhs with French science – were all intended to establish a collaborationist body of Egyptians, with mixed results. As it turned out, no amount of complying with Islamic ceremonies, salutations and usages prevented Selim III from declaring jihad against the French in Egypt, meaning that any attacks upon them were thenceforth blessed.

Napoleon used to joke regularly about how close he had come to embracing Islam. On Elba he 'described humorously' to a British

---

* He was referring to Muslim iconoclasm after the conquest of Mecca in 630.
† He once proposed to a French bishop that polygamy be permitted in the French West Indies, 'but Monseigneur would hear none of it' (ed. Kerry, *The First Napoleon* p. 99).

MP his theological discussions with the imams and how he procured, 'after many meetings and grave discussions at Cairo, a dispensation from being circumcised and a permission to drink wine, under the condition of their doing a good deed after each draught'.[55] He said that after being excused adult circumcision – or being 'cut about' as he put it – he agreed to pay for the building of a mosque (a cheap price under the circumstances).[56] This story grew in the telling, and historians have subjected anecdotes like these to intense analysis and found them exaggerated, concluding that Napoleon was a compulsive liar. But who hasn't embroidered the details of a good story to improve its effect?

Of course a good deal of real lying was going on too, in the propaganda sheets that Napoleon set up in Egypt, echoing those of the Italian campaign. *Le Publiciste* reported that the Copts sang hymns in honour of 'the new Alexander'.[57] The *Courrier de l'Egypte*, published for the troops, claimed that he 'was close to being talked of as a successor to Mohammed'.[58] One Order of the Day featured a verbatim report of a conversation between Napoleon and three imams, one called Mohammed, which took place after he had climbed the Great Pyramid and seen the Sphinx (whose nose was *not* shot off by French artillery, as one myth alleged). Even the briefest extract shows it to have been beyond satire:

BONAPARTE: Honour to Allah! Who was the *calif* who opened this pyramid and disturbed the ashes of the dead?

MOHAMMED: They think it was the Commander of the Faithful, Mahmoud ... Others say it was the renowned [ninth-century ruler of Baghdad] Haroun al-Raschid in quest of treasure; but he found only mummies.

BONAPARTE: Bread stolen by the wicked fills the mouth with gravel.

MOHAMMED (*inclining*): That is the observation of wisdom.

BONAPARTE: Glory to Allah! There is no other God but God; Mohammed is his prophet, and I am one of his friends ...

SULIMAN: Salutations also to you, invincible general, favourite of Mohammed!

BONAPARTE: Mufti, I thank you. The Koran delights my mind ... I love the prophet, and intend to visit and honour his tomb in the Sacred City. But my mission is first to exterminate the Mamluks.

IBRAHIM: May the angels of victory sweep the dust from your path and cover you with their wings ... O most valiant amongst the sons of Jesus, Allah has caused you to be followed by the exterminating angel, in order to deliver the land of Egypt.[59]

There was a good deal more in this vein, in the course of which Napoleon referred to 'the Great Sultan our ally whom God surround with glory'. This might have surprised Selim, who was at that moment raising two armies to expel the French from Egypt. He then quoted the Prophet Mohammed – 'who passed through all the heavens in a night' – from memory, and came out with such lines as 'Evil, thrice evil, to those who search for perishable riches, who covet gold and silver, which resemble dross.'[60]

Napoleon enjoyed all this mummery, and possibly the imams did too, but it was a serious attempt to elicit support from the Egyptians. When one of them, Suliman, said that he had treated the Pope 'with clemency and kindness', Napoleon retorted that His Holiness had been wrong to condemn Muslims to eternal hellfire. His reading of the Koran had led him to believe that 'the will of Mohammed' was for Egyptians to join the French in annihilating the Mamluks, and that the Prophet favoured 'trade with the Franks', supported their efforts to reach Bramah (that is, India), wanted the French to have depots in Egyptian ports, and apparently also wanted Egyptians to 'drive out the islanders of Albion, accursed among the sons of Jesus'. For this, Napoleon promised, 'the friendship of the Franks will be your reward until you ascend to the seventh heaven and sit beside black-eyed *houris*, always young and always maidens'.[61]

The three most important Arab witnesses of the French occupation were the historians Abd al-Rahman al-Jabartī, Hasan al-Attar and Niqula Turk. Al-Jabartī felt that the invasion was God's punishment on Egypt for ignoring Islamic principles. He saw the French as the new Crusaders, but made no secret of his admiration for French weaponry, military tactics, medical advances, scientific achievements and interest in Egyptian history, geography and culture. He enjoyed his interaction with the *savants* and was impressed by Napoleon's lack of ostentation and the way that on his journey to Suez he took engineers and Muslim merchants with him instead of cooks and a harem. Yet still he saw him as a rapacious, untrustworthy, atheistic beast, and was delighted when jihad was declared against the infidels.[62]

The Revolution's principle of equality offended against much of the Koran, yet al-Jabartī appreciated how well the French treated local workers in their building projects, and he followed their chemical and electrical experiments with interest. He was unimpressed that French soldiers failed to haggle successfully in the souks, thinking it a way of ingratiating themselves with the populace, and was disgusted by the way the French *dhimmis* (infidel) allowed 'the lowliest Copts, Syrian and Orthodox Christians, and Jews' to ride horses and carry swords, in transgression of Islamic law.[63]

Al-Jabartī's friend Hasan al-Attar, by contrast, was so fearful of being seen as a collaborator that he refused the *savants*' invitations to visit their library and laboratories. Niqula Turk described Napoleon as 'short, thin and pale; his right arm was longer than his left, a wise man and a fortunate person'.[64] (There is no indication he was correct about the relative length of Napoleon's arms.) Turk added that many Muslims assumed that Napoleon was the Mahdi (Guided One) who was expected to redeem Islam, and many more would have done so had he appeared in Middle Eastern rather than Western clothing. It was a surprising oversight. Napoleon wore a turban and baggy trousers only once, when it provoked laughter among his staff. Years later he told a courtier's wife that since the hitherto Protestant Henri IV thought it was worth converting to Catholicism for the sake of ruling France, 'Do you not think the Empire of the East, and perhaps the subjection of the whole of Asia, were not worth a turban and loose trousers?', adding that the army 'would undoubtedly have lent itself to this joke'.[65]

Napoleon was impressed with the healthy climate and fertile countryside in the regions adjoining the Nile, but contemptuous of its 'stupid, miserable and dull-witted' people. He described Cairenes to the Directory, only one day after arriving there, as 'the most evil population in the world', without explaining why. Ignorance reigned in the rural areas: 'They would rather have a button off our soldiers than a six-franc *écu*. In the villages they don't even have any idea what scissors are.'[66] He was shocked that the country had no watermills and only one windmill, and that otherwise grain was milled between stones turned by cattle. The army hated Egypt because, as he later put it, unlike in Italy there was 'no wine, no forks, and no countesses to make love to'.[67] (He meant no local wine; in December he ordered Marmont to sell 64,000 pints of the wine he had brought from France, writing: 'Take care to sell only the wine that looks as if it might be going off.'[68])

When Napoleon reached Cairo he sent orders to Admiral Brueys to sail the fleet to Corfu, where it would be better protected and able to threaten Constantinople. But by the time his messenger reached Aboukir Bay, there was no fleet: it had been sunk on August 1 after an exceptionally daring attack by Admiral Nelson. Brueys himself had been killed when *L'Orient* exploded at 10 p.m. Two ships-of-the-line were destroyed, including *L'Orient*, and nine were captured; only four ships under Rear-Admiral Pierre de Villeneuve escaped. After spending two weeks at Aboukir convalescing from a wound to his forehead, Nelson sailed to Naples, leaving the Egyptian coast under close watch. 'If, in this disastrous event, he made mistakes,' Napoleon later wrote generously of Brueys, 'he expiated them by a glorious death.'[69]

'I feel your pain deeply,' he wrote in a heartfelt letter to Brueys' widow. 'The moment that separates us from the object we love is terrible; it isolates us from the earth; the body feels convulsions of agony. The faculties of the soul are changed; it only communicates with the universe through a nightmare that distorts everything.'[70] This was only a month after he had been informed of Josephine's adultery, and one has to imagine that he had her in mind. To the Directory he wrote more clinically, characteristically distorting the figures, that there had been an 'inconsiderable' number killed and eight hundred wounded in the battle, whereas in fact the numbers were 2,000 and 1,100 respectively (against 218 British killed and 678 wounded).[71]

'It seems you like this country,' Napoleon told his staff at breakfast on August 15, the morning after he heard the news, 'that's very lucky, for now we have no fleet to carry us back to Europe.'[72] In addition to cutting him off from France, with all the problems that implied, the Aboukir Bay catastrophe left Napoleon with a pressing cash-flow problem, since the Maltese 'contribution', estimated at 60 million francs, had gone down with *L'Orient*. But he refused to accept what he called 'this reverse' as evidence that Fortune had forsaken him. 'She has not abandoned us yet, far from it,' he told the Directory, 'she has served us during this entire operation beyond anything she has ever done.'[73] He even told Kléber the disaster might be beneficial, as the British were now forcing him to consider marching on to India: 'They will perhaps oblige us to do greater things than we proposed to perform.'[74]

While Napoleon did what he could to woo the local populace, he made it clear that he would brook no disobedience. On August 1, in one of eight letters sent that day to Berthier, he insisted that exemplary punishments be meted out to the rebellious town of Damanhour, including beheading the five most influential inhabitants, at least one of whom must be a lawyer. But harshness was generally tempered with encouragement. When he discovered that the imams of Cairo, Rosetta and elsewhere were not intending to celebrate the Prophet's birthday that year, pleading lack of funds and the unstable political situation – but really indicating to the faithful that, in Denon's phrase, the French were 'opposed to one of the most sacred acts of their religion' – Napoleon insisted that France would pay for everything, despite his shortage of funds.[75] The celebrations started on August 20 and lasted three days, with coloured lanterns on poles, processions to mosques, music, poetry-chanting, sideshows featuring bears and monkeys, magicians who made live snakes disappear, and illuminated representations of the Prophet's tomb in Medina. Even the former erotic novelist Denon was shocked by the lewdness of the dances performed by some of the male dancers. On the Prophet's birthday itself, French artillery fired salutes and a regimental band joined the throngs, as the French officers were presented to a cleric, Sayyid Khalil al-Bakri, whom Napoleon decided to declare the most senior of Mohammed's descendants. At a feast of one hundred clerics at which the French were allowed to drink wine, Napoleon was declared a son-in-law of the Prophet with the name 'Ali-Bonaparte'. The Egyptians were humouring him and he them; as one French officer recalled: 'The soldiers were politic in their expressions; when they returned to their quarters they laughed at the comedy.'[76]

On the last day of the celebrations, Napoleon inaugurated the Institut d'Égypte, with Monge as its president, and himself vice-president. Its headquarters in Qassim Bey's former palace on the outskirts of Cairo were large enough to house the Institut's library, laboratories, nine workshops, an antiquarian collection and menagerie; the hall where the mathematics seminars were held was the former harem. Nicolas Conté, the chief balloonist, was put in charge of the workshops, which among much else produced spare parts for windmills, clocks and the printing press. After Desaix's conquests in Upper Egypt, various stones and treasures were taken to Cairo, Rosetta and Alexandria intended for the Louvre, as soon as ships arrived that could transport them.

The Institut was divided into four sections – mathematics, physics, political economy and the arts – and met every five days. At its opening session Napoleon suggested very practical subjects as topics for its consideration, such as how the army's baking could be improved; was there any substitute for hops in the brewing of beer; could Nile water be made drinkable; were watermills or windmills better for Cairo; could Egypt produce gunpowder; and what was the state of Egyptian law and education? He also wanted the *savants* – who had their own newspaper,

La Décade Égyptienne – to teach Egyptians the benefits of wheelbar-
rows and handsaws. Yet not all the *savants'* activities and deliberations
were connected to commerce and colonization: there were few practical
applications for the studies they undertook of Egyptian flora and fauna,
ancient sites, geology and mirages.

Napoleon tried to use Enlightenment science and reason to win over
the Egyptians and even suggested the construction of an astronomical
observatory.[77] The French made full use of their printing press, medical
instruments, telescopes, clocks, electricity, balloons and other modern
wonders to try to awe them, which al-Jabartī readily admitted did
'baffle the mind', but none of it appears to have advanced their cause
politically. (When Berthollet demonstrated a chemical experiment at the
Institut, a sheikh asked whether it could enable him to be in Morocco
and Egypt at the same time. Berthollet replied with a Gallic shrug, which
led the sheikh to conclude: 'Ah well, he isn't such a sorcerer after all.'[78])

On the day he opened the Institut, Napoleon wrote to Talleyrand –
whom he believed to have honoured his commitment to go to
Constantinople – to say that Egypt would soon be sending rice to Turkey and protecting the pilgrims' route to Mecca.* That same day he sent
a senior staff officer, Colonel Joseph Beauvoison, to the Holy Land to
try to open negotiations with Ahmed Jezzar, the pasha of Acre (discour-
agingly nicknamed 'The Butcher'), an enemy of the Mamluks and a
rebel against the Turks. Jezzar specialized in maiming and disfiguring
people, but also in devising horrific tortures such as having his victims'
feet shod with horseshoes, walling up Christians alive and stripping
corrupt officials naked before having them hacked to death.[79] He killed
seven of his own wives, but his hobby was cutting flower shapes out of
paper and giving them to visitors as presents. Now that Ibrahim Bey
had been forced out of Egypt into Gaza, Napoleon hoped he and Jezzar
might destroy him together. Jezzar refused to see Napoleon's envoy
Beauvoison and instead made peace with the Ottomans. (Beauvoison
was fortunate; Jezzar sometimes beheaded unwelcome messengers.)

Napoleon had intended to return to France once the conquest of Egypt
was secure, but on September 8 he wrote to the Directory (like all his

---

* That day he also wrote to Berthier to ask that Sergeant Latreille of the 75th Line receive
double pay for two months for meritorious service, as well as eleven other letters (CG2 no.
2798 p. 265). Between landing in Egypt in July 1798 and leaving it thirteen months later,
Napoleon sent 2,196 surviving letters and despatches.

correspondence, this letter had to run the gauntlet of the Royal Navy in the Mediterranean): 'I can't possibly return to Paris in October, as I promised, but the delay will last only a few months. All is going on well here; the country is subdued, and is becoming accustomed to us. The rest must be the work of time.'[80] Yet again he was misleading the Directory: the country was certainly not 'becoming accustomed' to French rule. Much of his correspondence refers to the beheadings, hostage-taking and village-burning that the French had to employ to secure its presence.* Napoleon was content with the army's clothing and payment, however, and in a letter to Barras all he could think of asking for was a troupe of actors to entertain his soldiers.[81]

On October 20 Napoleon learned that a Turkish army was gathering in Syria to attack him. He needed to move against it but that night minarets across Cairo rang out with a call for a general uprising against French rule, and by the next morning much of the city was in open revolt. General Dominique Dupuy, the city's governor, was lanced to death in the street and Sulkowski was killed with fifteen of Napoleon's personal bodyguard, whose bodies were subsequently fed to dogs.[82] (Of Napoleon's eight aides-de-camp who went to Egypt, four died and two were wounded, including Eugène at the siege of Acre.) Several boats were sunk on the Nile during the uprising, and overall about three hundred Frenchmen were killed, not the fifty-three that Napoleon later claimed to the Directory.[83] The rebels took over the Gama-el-Azhar Grand Mosque, one of the largest in the city, as their headquarters. A rumour spread that it was Napoleon himself who had been killed rather than Dupuy, which inflamed the rebellion almost as much as the *ulama* had, so (as Bourrienne recalled), 'Bonaparte immediately mounted his horse and, accompanied by only thirty guides, advanced on all threatened points, restored confidence, and, with great presence of mind, adopted measures of defence.'[84]

Napoleon's most important objective was to retain the Cairo citadel, which then as now commands the city with its high elevation and 10-foot-thick walls. Once secured, the height allowed Dommartin to use his 8-pounder guns to shell enemy positions over thirty-six hours; he did not hesitate to put fifteen cannonballs into the Grand Mosque,

---

* Village-burning was a standard method of controlling potentially hostile areas in Asia; the British army in India routinely 'restored tranquillity', as an historian of Wellington's campaigns there put it, 'usually by the wanton torching of villages and stealing of livestock' (Davies, *Wellington's Wars* p. 25).

which was later stormed by infantry and desecrated. Over 2,500 rebels died and more were executed in the citadel afterwards. Years later, Pierre-Narcisse Guérin painted Napoleon forgiving the rebels, which he did not do until a long time afterwards.[85] At the time he ordered that all rebels captured under arms should be beheaded and their corpses thrown into the Nile, where they would float past and terrorize the rest of the population; their heads were put in sacks, loaded on mules and dumped in piles in Ezbekyeh Square in central Cairo.[86] 'I cannot describe the horror,' recalled an eyewitness, 'but I must confess that it had the effect for a considerable time of securing tranquillity.'[87] Napoleon wrote to Reynier on October 27: 'Every night we cut off thirty heads', and Lavalette described how the Egyptian police chief 'never went out but accompanied by the hangman. The smallest infraction of the laws was punished by blows on the soles of the feet', a technique known as the *bastinado*, which was especially painful because of the large number of nerve-endings, small bones and tendons there and was even meted out to women.[88] These brutal measures ensured that, unlike the zealots, ordinary Cairenes did not rise up en masse against the French, who could not have resisted 600,000 people. Once the revolt was over, on November 11, Napoleon abolished the *bastinado* for interrogations. 'The barbarous custom of having men beaten who are suspected of having important secrets to reveal must be abolished,' he ordered Berthier. 'Torture produces nothing worthwhile. The poor wretches say anything that comes into their mind that the interrogator wishes to hear.'[89]

By November 30 Cairo had sufficiently returned to normality to allow Napoleon to open the Tivoli pleasure gardens, where he noticed an 'exceedingly pretty and lively young woman' called Pauline Fourès, the twenty-year-old wife of a lieutenant in the 22nd Chasseurs, Jean-Noël Fourès.[90] If the beautiful round face and long blonde hair described by her contemporaries are indeed accurate, Lieutenant Fourès was unwise to have brought his wife out on campaign. It was six months since Napoleon had discovered Josephine's infidelity and within days of his first spotting Pauline they were having an affair. Their dalliance was to take on the aspect of a comic opera when Napoleon sent Lieutenant Fourès off with allegedly important despatches for Paris, generally a three-month round-trip, only for his ship to be intercepted by the frigate HMS *Lion* the very next day. Instead of being interned by the British, Fourès was sent back to Alexandria, as was sometimes the custom with military minnows. He therefore reappeared in Cairo ten weeks before he was expected, to find his wife installed in the grounds of Napoleon's Elfey Bey palace and nicknamed 'Cleopatra'.[91]

According to one version of the story, Fourès threw a carafe of water on her dress in the subsequent row, but another has him horsewhipping her, drawing blood.[92] Whichever it was, they divorced and she thereafter became Napoleon's *maîtresse-en-titre* in Cairo, acting as hostess at his dinners and sharing his carriage as they drove around the city and its environs. (The deeply chagrined Eugène was excused from duty on those occasions.) The affair deflected charges of cuckoldry from Napoleon, which for a French general then was a far more serious accusation than adultery. When Napoleon left Egypt he passed Pauline on to Junot, who, when injured in a duel and invalided back to France, passed her on to Kléber. She later made a fortune in the Brazilian timber business, wore men's clothing and smoked a pipe, before coming back to Paris with her pet parrots and monkeys and living to be ninety.[93]

Napoleon's decision to embark on what was called his Syrian campaign – though he never set foot in present-day Syria and stayed entirely within the bounds of modern Gaza, Israel and the West Bank – was presaged by his threat to Jezzar on November 19: 'If you continue to offer refuge to Ibrahim Bey on the borders of Egypt, I will look on that as a mark of hostility and go to Acre.'[94] Jezzar responded in early December by occupying the Ottoman provinces of Gaza, Ramleh and Jaffa and taking up position at El-Arish, only 22 miles from Napoleon's Egyptian fort at Katieh on the edge of the Sinai desert, declaring that he was going to liberate Egypt from the French.

Napoleon visited Suez in late December, both to inspect fortifications and to trace the route of Ramses II's canal connecting the Nile to the Red Sea, following it for 40 miles until it disappeared into the desert sands. (Little could he have guessed that his own nephew would be involved in building its successor in 1869.) He also announced his wish to visit Mount Sinai 'through respect for Moses and the Jewish nation, whose cosmology retraces the earliest ages'.[95] Berthier, Caffarelli, Dommartin, Rear-Admiral Honoré Ganteaume (whose survival of the battle of the Nile was, according to Napoleon, its sole commiseration), the chief *ordonnateur* Jean-Pierre Daure, Monge and four other *savants* came with him, as well as his guides.[96] 'We travelled fast,' recalled Doguereau, 'the commander-in-chief left Cairo at the gallop, and we urged our horses on at full speed so that they arrived out of breath.'[97]

It was on this sightseeing trip from Suez into Sinai (he never reached

Mount Sinai itself) on December 28 that Napoleon appears to have come as close to death as he ever did in any of his battles, after taking advantage of the low tide to cross a section of the Red Sea.* 'We reached the far shore without difficulty,' stated Doguereau, and the party visited the so-called Spring of Moses and other antiquarian sites, but having lunched and watered the horses at the Nabah wells, they got lost as night fell and wandered through the low-lying marshy sea-shore as the tide rose:

> Soon we were bogged down up to the bellies of our mounts, who were struggling and having great difficulty in pulling themselves free ... After a thousand problems and having left many horses trapped in the bog, we reached another arm of the sea ... It was nine at night and the tide had already risen three feet. We were in a terrible situation, when it was announced that a ford had been found. General Bonaparte was among the first to cross; guides were situated at various places to direct the rest ... We were only too happy not to have shared the fate of Pharaoh's soldiers.[98]

* Even today, the north-eastern shore has many salt-water marshes with areas of dry land in between; the tidal flow in this area is ferocious. One can be crossing a stretch of what looks like an ordinary beach when suddenly the tide comes in and covers it rapidly.

8

Acre

'The frontiers of states are either large rivers, or chains of mountains, or deserts. Of all these obstacles to the march of an army, the most difficult to overcome is the desert.'

Napoleon's Military Maxim No. 1

'The decision that Caesar took to have a hand cut off all the soldiers was completely atrocious. He was clement towards his own in civil war, but cruel and often ferocious towards the Gauls.'

Napoleon, *Caesar's Wars*

Once Desaix had routed Murad Bey at the battle of Samhoud in January 1799, captured his flotilla on the Nile and ended the threat from Upper Egypt, Napoleon's rule extended over almost the whole country. He could now unleash his attack on Jezzar. He told the Directory on the day he left Cairo that he hoped to deny the Royal Navy the use of Levantine ports such as Acre, Haifa and Jaffa, raise the Lebanese and Syrian Christians in revolt against the Turks, and decide later whether to march on Constantinople or India.[1] 'We have plenty of enemies to vanquish in this expedition,' he wrote, 'the desert, the local inhabitants, the Arabs, Mamluks, Russians, Turks, English.'[2] The mention of Russians was no mere Napoleonic hyperbole; Tsar Paul I hated everything the French Revolution stood for and considered himself the protector of the Knights of Malta (indeed he had engineered his own election as Grand Master in succession to von Hompesch). On Christmas Eve 1798 he made common cause with Russia's traditional enemy, Turkey, and also with Britain, and made plans to send a Russian army deep into western Europe. But for the moment Napoleon had no inkling of that.

Historians have long taken Napoleon at his word that he planned to go further than Acre, to Constantinople perhaps or even India, but since he took only 13,000 men with him, one-third of his entire force in Egypt, this seems very unlikely. Even if Acre had fallen, and the Druze, Christians and Jews had all joined him, the logistics and demographics would not have permitted an invasion of either Turkey or India, even by a general as ambitious and resourceful as Napoleon. He later claimed that with the help of the Indian Mahratta princes he would have expelled the British from India, marching to the Indus with a long halt on the Euphrates in daily 15-mile marches through deserts, with his sick, ammunition and food carried by dromedaries, his men fed by a pound each of rice, flour and coffee per day. Yet there are more than 2,500 miles between Acre and Delhi, and the march would have required crossing the whole width of modern-day Syria, Iraq, Iran and Pakistan as well as part of northern India, far further than his journey from Paris to Moscow. The logistics would have been impossible; these plans were only ever pipe-dreams prompted by the conquests of Alexander the Great.

In February 1799 Napoleon's immediate objective was to pre-empt the Sultan's proposed eastern land invasion of Egypt, supported by Jezzar, before returning to deal with the amphibious Ottoman invasion of northern Egypt he had long expected that summer – the two fortunately not co-ordinated. It was his old strategy of the central position writ very large. On January 25, 1799 he did write to Britain's foremost enemy in India, Tipu Sahib, announcing his imminent 'arrival on the shores of the Red Sea with a numerous and invincible army, animated with the desire of delivering you from the iron yoke of England'.[3] A British cruiser intercepted the letter, and Tipu was killed in the capture of his capital, Seringapatam, by the young and highly impressive British Lieutenant-General Sir Arthur Wellesley that May. Napoleon's intention was probably simply to spread disinformation, as he knew his letters were falling into enemy hands.

Leaving Desaix in Upper Egypt, Marmont in Alexandria and General Charles Dugua in Cairo, Napoleon invaded the Holy Land with Regnier in the vanguard, three infantry divisions under Kléber, Bon and Lannes, and Murat leading the cavalry. As the troops marched out of Cairo they sang the stirring 1794 revolutionary anthem 'Le Chant du Départ', which thereafter became a Bonapartist anthem. At a council of war the only general openly to oppose the invasion was General Joseph Lagrange, who pointed out that Acre was 300 miles away through hostile desert and past several well-defended cities which, if captured, would require garrisoning by detachments from the relatively small force that Napoleon proposed to take. He suggested that it would be better to await an attack inside Egypt, forcing the enemy to cross the Sinai instead of taking the battle onto their terrain.[4] Yet with the amphibious assault expected in June, Napoleon felt he didn't have the luxury of time; he needed to cross the desert, defeat Jezzar and then re-cross it before it became impassable in the summer.

Napoleon left Cairo on Sunday, February 10, 1799 and reached Katieh at 3 p.m. on the 13th. Just before leaving, he wrote a long letter to the Directory. One sentence was in code, which once deciphered read: 'If, in the course of March . . . France is at war with the kings, I will return to France.'[5] On March 12 the War of the Second Coalition began, with France eventually pitted against the monarchs of Russia, Britain, Austria, Turkey, Portugal and Naples, and the Pope.

To cross the then unmapped Sinai Napoleon would have to overcome problems of food, water, heat and hostile Bedouin tribesmen. His use of a dromedary camel corps, fast-firing drill by alternating ranks, and *pieux* (hooked stakes for swiftly erected palisades) were to be retained by French colonial armies up to the Great War.[6] 'We have crossed seventy leagues [over 170 miles] of desert which is exceedingly fatiguing,' he wrote to Desaix on the journey; 'we had brackish water and often none at all. We ate dogs, donkeys and camels.'[7] Later they also ate monkeys.

In the past five millennia there have been an estimated five hundred military engagements fought in the area between the Jordan river and the Mediterranean. The western coastal route that Napoleon took – eschewing the mountain and Jordan valley routes – was the same that Alexander the Great had taken in the opposite direction. Of course Napoleon appreciated the historical aspects of his campaign, later reminiscing, 'I constantly read Genesis when visiting the places it describes and was amazed beyond measure that they were still exactly as Moses had described them.'[8]

The fort of El-Arish, 170 miles from Cairo, was defended by about 2,000 men of the Turkish vanguard and their Arab allies. By February 17 Napoleon and the main body of his army had arrived there and constructed trenches and batteries. There were 'violent murmurs among the soldiers', who were exhausted and thirsty and who insulted the *savants*, unfairly blaming them for the entire expedition, but they quietened at the prospect of action.[9] By the 19th a bombardment of the walls had created breaches large enough to send troops through. Napoleon demanded the surrender of the fort, which was accepted by Ibrahim Nizam, the co-commandant, as well as by El-Hadji Mohammed, commander of the Maghrebians, and El-Hadji Kadir, Aga of the Arnautes.* These men and their senior *agas* (officers) swore on the Koran 'that neither they nor their troops will ever serve in Jezzar's army and they will not return to Syria for a year, counting from this day'.[10] Napoleon therefore agreed to allow them to keep their weapons and go back home, although he broke his agreement with the Mamluk contingent by disarming them. Before the second half of the twentieth century, and especially in the Middle East, the rules of war were simple, harsh and essentially unchanging; to give one's word and then break it was generally recognized as a capital offence.

On February 25, Napoleon chased the Mamluks out of Gaza City, capturing large amounts of ammunition, six cannon and 200,000 rations of biscuit. 'The lemon trees, the olive groves, the ruggedness of the terrain look exactly like the countryside of the Languedoc,' he told Desaix, 'it is like being near Béziers.'[11] On March 1 he learned from the Capuchin monks at Ramleh that the El-Arish garrison had passed through on its way to Jaffa 10 miles away, 'saying they did not intend to abide by the articles of capitulation, which we had been the first to break when we disarmed them'.[12] The monks estimated the Jaffa force at 12,000 strong and 'many cannons and much ammunition had arrived from Constantinople'. Napoleon therefore concentrated his force at Ramleh before moving on, laying siege to Jaffa from noon on March 3. 'Bonaparte approached, with a few others, to within a hundred yards,' recalled Doguereau of Jaffa's city walls. 'As we turned back, we were observed. One of the cannonballs fired at us by the enemy fell very close to the commanding general, who was showered with earth.'[13] On March 6 the defenders made a sortie, which allowed Doguereau to notice how heterogeneous the Ottoman army was: 'There were Maghrebians, Albanians, Kurds, Anatolians, Caramaneniens, Damascenes, Alepese and Negroes from Takrour [Senegal],' he wrote. 'They were hurled back.'[14]

At dawn on the next day, Napoleon wrote the governor of Jaffa a polite letter calling on him to surrender, saying that his 'heart is moved by the evil that will fall upon the whole city if it subjects itself to this assault'. The governor stupidly replied by displaying the head of

---

* The Maghrebians came from Algeria, Morocco, Tunisia, Mauretania and Libya; the Arnautes from as far afield as Albania.

Napoleon's messenger on the walls, so Napoleon ordered the walls to be breached and by 5 p.m. thousands of thirsty and angry Frenchmen were inside. 'The sights were terrible,' wrote one *savant*, 'the sound of shots, shrieks of women and fathers, piles of bodies, a daughter being raped on the cadaver of her mother, the smell of blood, the groans of the wounded, the shouts of victors quarrelling about loot.' The French finally rested, 'sated by blood and gold, on top of a heap of dead'.[15]

Reporting to the Directory, Napoleon admitted that 'twenty-four hours was handed over to pillage and all the horrors of war, which never appeared to me so hideous'.[16] He added, wholly prematurely, that as a result of the victories of El-Arish, Gaza and Jaffa, 'The Republican army is master of Palestine.' Sixty Frenchmen had been killed and 150 wounded at Jaffa; the numbers of enemy soldiers and civilians killed are unknown.*

Napoleon's treatment of the prisoners captured at Jaffa, of whom some, though not all, were men who had given their word at El-Arish and then broken it, was extremely harsh. On March 9 and 10, thousands of them were taken to the beach about a mile south of Jaffa by men of Bon's division and massacred in cold blood.† 'You . . . will order the adjutant to lead all the artillerymen who were taken in arms and other Turks to the water's edge,' Napoleon wrote unambiguously to Berthier, 'and have them shot, taking precautions that none escape.'[17] In his own account Berthier stated his belief that these men had forfeited their lives when Jaffa refused to surrender, regardless of what had happened at El-Arish, and he didn't differentiate between the deaths taken in battle or in cold blood.[18] Louis-André Peyrusse, a senior quartermaster, described to his mother what happened next:

> About three thousand men deposited their arms and were led right away
> to the camp by order of the general-in-chief. They split up the Egyptians,
> Mahgrebians and the Turks. The Mahgrebians were all led the next day
> to the seaside and two battalions started to shoot them. They had no
> other recourse to save themselves but to throw themselves in the sea.

* Cities that refused to surrender when given the chance were considered to deserve sacking; the British subjected Badajoz to three days of looting and mass rape in 1812 so severe that Wellington finally regained control over his men only by erecting a gallows in the main square (it wasn't used). He no more approved of rape and pillage than did Napoleon.
† Using aerial photos taken by the German army in 1917 it is possible to identify the beach where the massacre took place just south of Old Jaffa, which is today under a car park; the rocks to which the victims swam are now part of the beach's breakwater.

They could shoot them there and in a moment the sea was dyed with blood and covered with corpses. A few had the chance to save themselves on rocks; they sent soldiers in boats to finish them off. We left a detachment on the seaside and our perfidy attracted a few of them who were mercilessly massacred ... We were recommended not to use powder and we had the ferocity to kill them with bayonets ... This example will teach our enemies not to trust the French, and sooner or later the blood of these three thousand victims will revisit us.[19]

He was right; when El-Aft on the banks of the Nile was abandoned by the French in May 1801, the Turks beheaded every Frenchman unable to flee, and when the British present remonstrated, they 'answered by indignant exclamations of "Jaffa! Jaffa!"'[20] Captain Krettley, another eyewitness to the Jaffa massacre, saw how although 'the first batch of prisoners were shot, the rest were charged by the cavalry ... they were forced into the sea, where they attempted to swim, trying to reach the rocks a few hundred yards offshore ... but they were not saved in the end, since these poor unfortunates were overwhelmed by the waves'.[21]

Contemporary French sources – there are no Turkish ones for obvious reasons – differ very greatly over the numbers killed, but generally give a number between 2,200 and 3,500; higher figures exist but tend to come from politically motivated anti-Bonapartist sources.[22] As only 2,000 or so gave their word at El-Arish, Napoleon certainly executed some in the polyglot Turkish army who had not been present there, but who had been promised clemency by Eugène when they held out in an inn after Jaffa's walls had been breached and the rest of the city captured. (This may be what Peyrusse had in mind when he said the massacre would teach them not to trust the French.) There was, of course, a racial element to this; Napoleon would not have executed European prisoners-of-war.

Napoleon himself gave the number killed at fewer than 2,000, saying: 'They were devils too dangerous to be released a second time so that I had no choice but to kill them.'[23] On another occasion he admitted to 3,000 and told a British MP: 'Well, I had a right ... They killed my messenger, cut off his head, and put it on a pike ... there were not provisions enough for French and Turks – one of them must go to the wall. I did not hesitate.'[24] The food argument is unconvincing; some 400,000 rations of biscuit and 200,000 pounds of rice were captured in Jaffa. He might well have thought himself too short of men to detach a battalion to escort so many prisoners across the Sinai back to Egypt, however.[25] As his remarks on the September Massacres in Paris and his actions in Binasco, Verona and Cairo demonstrated, Napoleon approved of uncompromising – indeed lethal – measures if he felt the situation demanded them. He was particularly interested in ensuring that the eight hundred trained Turkish artillerymen weren't able to fight against him again. (Had he taken up the Sultan's job offer of 1795, many of these same men would have been his pupils.) Having accepted their word once, he couldn't have been expected to do so again. And in a war against the seventy-nine-year-old Jezzar, fabled for his spectacular cruelty, who that year had had four hundred Christians sewn into sacks and thrown into the sea, he might have felt the need to be seen as equally ruthless.[26]

On March 9, during the massacres, Napoleon wrote to Jezzar, saying that he had been 'harsh towards those who had violated the rules of war', adding: 'In a few days I shall march upon Acre. But why should I shorten the life of an old man I do not know?'[27] Luckily for that messenger, Jezzar chose to ignore this threat. The same day, Napoleon also made a proclamation to the sheikhs, *ulama* and commandant of Jerusalem, telling them of the terrible punishments awaiting his enemies, but further declaring: 'God is clement and merciful! . . . It is not my intention to wage war against the people; I am a friend of the Muslim.'[28]*

In an all-too-rare example of poetic justice in history, the French caught the plague off Jaffa's inhabitants whom they had raped and pillaged.† With a mortality rate of 92 per cent for sufferers, the appearance of its buboes on the body was akin to a death sentence.[29] Captain Charles François, a veteran of Kléber's division, noted in his journal that after the sack of Jaffa 'soldiers who had the plague were right away covered with buboes in the groin, in the armpits and on the neck. In less than twenty-four hours the body became black as well as the teeth and a burning fever killed anyone who was affected by this terrible disease.'[30] Of all the various types of plague infecting the Middle East at the time,

---

* Napoleon never set foot in Jerusalem, although that didn't deter the Israeli tourist board's poster campaign on the Paris Métro in 1996 stating: 'Napoleon enjoyed many a siesta in Jerusalem; why don't you?'

† When the plague had appeared in Alexandria in January, Napoleon had invented another of his unusual punishments. Surgeon Boyer, who had refused to attend to its victims, was forced to walk the streets dressed as a woman and wearing a placard stating: 'Unworthy to be a French citizen: he fears death.'

this, *la peste*, was one of the worst, and Napoleon ordered the Armenian Monastery hospital on the seafront of Old Jaffa – where it still is today – to be turned into a quarantine station. On March 11 Napoleon visited it along with Desgenettes, and there according to Jean-Pierre Daure, an officer in the pay commissariat, he 'picked up and carried a plague victim who was lying across a doorway. This action scared us a lot because the sick man's clothes were covered with foam and disgusting evacuations of abscessed buboes.'[31]

Napoleon spoke to the sick, comforted them and raised their morale; the incident was immortalized in 1804 in Antoine-Jean Gros' painting *Bonaparte Visiting the Plague House at Jaffa*. Napoleon said, 'As general-in-chief he found it a necessary part of his duty to endeavour to give them confidence and reanimate them, by visiting frequently, himself, the plague hospital, and talking to, and cheering, the different patients in it. He said he caught the disorder himself, but recovered again quickly.'[32] (There is no corroborating evidence for this claim.) Napoleon believed *la peste* to be susceptible to willpower, telling someone years later that 'Those who kept up their spirits, and did not give way to the idea that they must die ... generally recovered; but those who desponded almost invariably fell a sacrifice to the disorder.'[33]

Napoleon left Jaffa for Acre on March 14, the day before the British commodore Sir Sidney Smith and the French royalist military engineer and Brienne contemporary Antoine de Phélippeaux arrived off the port with two Royal Navy frigates, HMS *Theseus* and HMS *Tigre*. The Anglo-Russo-Turkish alliance had little common purpose except a desire to turn back French conquest, but that was enough for the Royal Navy to try to prevent Acre from falling to Napoleon. The city had been captured in 1104 by the crusading King Baldwin I of Jerusalem, who built walls 8 feet thick. The intervening centuries had left its defences much weakened, but the walls were still there, if not so high, and there was a deep moat. Defending the port were about 4,000 Afghans, Albanians and Moors, Jezzar's efficient Jewish chief-of-staff, Haim Farhi – who had lost a nose, ear and eye to his master over the years – and now Commodore Smith with two hundred Royal Navy seamen and marines, and the talented Phélippeaux. They added sloping glacis defences, reinforcing the bases of the walls at an angle, and constructed ramps to get cannon up onto the walls (which had been impossible at Jaffa as the walls were too weak). Some of these defences can still be seen today, along with some naval cannon positioned by Smith.

On March 15 Napoleon, Lannes and Kléber easily thrust aside an attack by Arab cavalry from Nablus in a skirmish at Kakoun, suffering only forty casualties. Three days later, Napoleon was forced to watch in horror from the cliffs above Haifa as his flotilla of nine vessels under Commodore Pierre-Jean Standelet, carrying his entire siege artillery and equipment, rounded the Mount Carmel promontory straight into the clutches of *Tigre* and *Theseus*. Six ships were captured and only three escaped to Toulon. Most of Napoleon's heaviest weaponry was then taken into Acre and turned against him. In an equally unmistakable signal that the course of events was turning, Jezzar reverted to form and beheaded the messenger sent with peace terms.[34]

Napoleon began his assault on Acre at noon on March 19, surrounding the town with fortifications and trenches at a distance of 300 yards. He hoped that the light artillery he had, and sheer French élan once a breach was made, might still capture the city. Although his headquarters were on the Turon hillside 1,500 yards from Acre – coincidentally the place Richard the Lionheart had chosen for the same job in 1191 – some of his siege lines had to go through a mosquito-infested swamp, which soon caused malaria outbreaks. The French set to work digging trenches and making the fascines, *gabions* and *saucissons* needed for fortifications.

'At first the place looked indefensible,' considered Doguereau, 'and unlikely to hold out for eight days. It was thought that we only had to present ourselves before Acre, when the memory of the fate of Jaffa, which we had taken so easily, would terrify the Pasha.'[35] With the benefit of hindsight, Doguereau concluded that Napoleon ought to have gone back to Egypt at that point, as Jezzar was in no position to threaten Egypt after the loss of El-Arish, Gaza, Jaffa and, on March 18, Haifa, which Napoleon could have garrisoned before withdrawing. But he had not yet defeated the Turkish army that was massing at Damascus, which had been the primary purpose of his invasion.

Napoleon launched no fewer than nine major and three minor attacks on Acre over the next nine weeks. At the same time, he had to send off forces to defend himself from Turks, Arabs and Mamluks, who fortunately came piecemeal rather than in co-ordinated assaults. At one point he ran so low on ammunition that he had to pay soldiers to pick up cannonballs fired from the city and from Royal Navy vessels; they received between a half-franc and a franc each, depending on the calibre. The French weren't the only ones being incentivized; one of the explanations for the large number of Turkish sorties (twenty-six) was that Jezzar was paying a high bounty for French heads.[36] (Of the four skeletons found on the battlefield in 1991, two had been decapitated.) On March 28 a cannonball buried itself three paces from Napoleon, between his two aides-de-camp, Eugène and Antoine Merlin, the son of the new Director, Philippe Merlin de Douai. Part of a tower fell down during a bombardment, but the subsequent attack failed because the ladders were too short, which understandably demoralized the men. One Turkish sortie was repelled only after several hours' fighting. Sappers started to dig under a different tower, but they were foiled by counter-mining.

Meanwhile, Napoleon sent Murat off to capture Safed and Junot to take Nazareth to foil any relief attempts from Damascus. When on April 8 Junot defeated a raiding party of Turks in a skirmish near the village of Loubia with no losses, Napoleon described it as 'a renowned combat that did credit to French sangfroid'.[37] A far more serious engagement, indeed one that justified the entire Syrian campaign, was fought six days later.

The battle of Mount Tabor is a misnomer, since it was actually fought on nearby Mount Hamoreh, although Kléber had marched around Tabor, which was 8 miles away. Kléber's intentions had been very bold, to attack the far larger Turkish and Mamluk army of some 25,000 that had been massing at Damascus with his 2,500 men at night at the springs where the Turks were watering their horses and camels (a long process, as a thirsty camel can drink about 40 litres). However, when the sun rose at 6 a.m. on April 16, Kléber's force had not yet crossed the central Jezreel valley and was in full view of the Turks, who attacked across the plain. He had plenty of time to form two large squares, which despite being quickly surrounded stayed in formation as they trudged up the gently inclining slope of Mount Hamoreh, where the enemy could use their cavalry to less effect. By noon, at which point he had been fighting in the heat for six hours taking losses, and getting low on water and ammunition, Kléber successfully effected the dangerous and difficult manoeuvre of merging the two squares into one.

He had earlier warned Napoleon that he was in contact with a large body of the enemy, so Napoleon took over Bon's division and marched to Nazareth in an effort to help him. By the time he got there on the 16th, Kléber was already engaged, so Napoleon drove his men in a circling manoeuvre from the west on to Mount Hamoreh. Ignoring one of the most basic rules of warfare, Pasha Abdullah of Damascus had failed to post scouts to watch for just such an attempt to relieve Kléber. Marching south-east from Nazareth, Napoleon could see from the smoke and dust where Kléber – outnumbered ten to one – was fighting. He appeared at about noon on the battlefield directly behind the Turks. His route climbed the watershed of the ridge, so there was no line of sight that even Turks on horseback could have used to spot him. Although the Vale of Jezreel looks flat from afar, there are undulations and natural curves in the ground of between 30 and 60 feet. Looking across the vale from the (untouched) battlefield today, it is easy to see how these contours hid Napoleon's force as it rounded Mount Hamoreh and took the Turks completely by surprise in their rear, a dream combination for any general and one that Napoleon exploited to the full. Although they fled before really significant losses could be inflicted, the Ottoman army was completely scattered and their hopes of reconquering Egypt wrecked.

After the battle, Napoleon slept at the convent in nearby Nazareth, where he was shown the supposed bedchamber of the Virgin Mary. When the prior also pointed out a broken black marble pillar and told his staff, 'in the gravest manner possible', that it had been split by the Angel Gabriel when he 'came to announce to the Virgin her glorious and holy destination', some of the officers burst out laughing, but as one of them recorded, 'General Bonaparte, looking severely at us, made us resume our gravity.'[38] The next day Napoleon revisited the Tabor battlefield, a common practice of his, before returning to Acre for more attacks and counter-attacks throughout late April.

On April 27 the army lost one of its most popular commanders when gangrene set into a wound in Caffarelli's right arm, which had been hit by a cannonball some days earlier. 'Our universal regrets accompany General Caffarelli to the grave,' Napoleon wrote in his Order of the Day. 'The Army is losing one of its bravest leaders, Egypt one of its legislators, France one of its best citizens, and science an illustrious scholar.' Those wounded at Acre included Duroc, Eugène, Lannes and four brigadiers, and on May 10 Bon was mortally wounded under its walls. The officer corps was thus at the forefront of the action, a key aspect of their service that won them their soldiers' affection and respect. In one bombardment from Acre, Berthier's aide-de-camp was killed standing near Napoleon, and Napoleon was himself knocked over by 'the effect of the commotion of the air' as a cannonball passed close by.[39] With paper for cartridges no longer available, one Order of the Day required all unused paper to be handed in to the quartermasters.

On May 4 a surprise night attack was attempted, but failed. Three days later, with the sails of a Turkish naval relief force seen on the horizon, Napoleon sent Lannes to try to storm the city. The enterprising general managed to get a tricolour onto the north-east tower but no further, and was subsequently expelled. By now Napoleon was describing Acre to Berthier as a mere 'grain of sand', an indication that he was considering abandoning the siege. He was also convinced that Sir Sidney Smith was 'a kind of lunatic', because the British commodore had challenged Napoleon to single combat under the walls of the city. (Napoleon replied that he didn't see Smith as his equal, and 'would not come forth to a duel unless the English could fetch Marlborough from his grave'.)[40] Smith also devised the forging of an 'intercepted' letter from Napoleon to the Directory bemoaning his army's perilous situation. Copies were distributed around the French army by deserters, and it was said that when one was handed to Napoleon he 'tore it up in a great rage' and forbade anyone to discuss it. This *ruse de guerre* certainly fooled the Turks, whose ambassador in London sent a copy to the Foreign Office under the impression that it was genuine.[41]

Easily Smith's finest piece of psychological warfare, however, was neither disinformation nor misinformation, but simply supplying Napoleon with true information. Under a flag of truce, he sent over several editions of recent British and European newspapers, from which Napoleon was able to piece together the series of disasters that had recently overtaken French arms. Napoleon had been actively trying to obtain newspapers since January; now he could read of Jourdan's defeats in Germany at the battles of Ostrach and Stockach in March and Schérer's at the battle of Magnano in Italy in April – only Genoa was left to France in Italy. Napoleon's brainchild, the Cisalpine Republic, had collapsed and there were renewed risings in the Vendée. The newspapers made him realize, as he explained later, that 'it was impossible to expect reinforcements from France in its then state, without which nothing further could be done'.[42]

On May 10, a brigade attacked Acre at dawn – climbing over the decomposing remains of their comrades from earlier attacks, but not deliberately using them as scaling ladders as alleged by British propagandists. As an eyewitness recalled, 'some got into the town, but, assailed by a hail of bullets and finding new entrenchments there, they were compelled to retire to the breach'. There they fought for two hours, cut down by the crossfire.[43] It was to be the last assault; the next day Napoleon decided to raise the siege and return to Egypt. 'The season is too far advanced,' he told the Directory; 'the end I had in view has been accomplished. My presence is required in Egypt . . . Having reduced Acre to a heap of stones, I shall re-cross the desert.'[44]

The proclamation he made to his troops was just as disingenuous as his claim to have reduced Acre to rubble: 'A few days more, and you would have captured the Pasha in the very middle of his palace, but at this season the capture of Acre would not be worth the loss of some days.'[45] (On re-reading his Acre proclamation years later, Napoleon ruefully admitted: '*C'est un peu charlatan!*'[46]) He also told the Directory that he had heard reports that sixty people were dying of the plague in Acre every day, implying that it might be better not to capture it anyhow. In fact Jezzar didn't lose anyone to the plague throughout the siege.[47] It was however true that he needed to re-cross the desert before the heat made it impassable.

Napoleon had indeed accomplished 'the end I had in view' at the battle of Mount Tabor; the only reason to take Acre had been to pursue his dream of attacking India via Aleppo and setting up a French Empire in Asia stretching to the Ganges, or possibly to capture Constantinople. Yet, as we have seen, these were romantic fantasies rather than achievable ends, especially once the Syrian Christians made it clear they were going to stay loyal to Jezzar (not least because Smith cleverly collected all Napoleon's proclamations to the Muslims and gave them to the Syrian and Lebanese Christians). 'But for Acre the whole population would have declared for me,' Napoleon lamented years later.[48] 'My intention was to take the turban at Aleppo,' which he believed would have won him 200,000 Muslim adherents.

On May 20, 1799 the French army quietly left their siege lines, moving off between 8 and 11 p.m. to avoid attacks from *Theseus* and *Tigre* as they marched some miles along the beach.[49] They were forced to spike twenty-three cannon they couldn't remove, burying some and throwing others into the sea.* 'General Bonaparte remained on the hillock throughout the withdrawal,' recalled Doguereau, only leaving with the rearguard.[50] Napoleon had suffered the first significant reverse of his career (since Bassano and Caldiero could hardly count as such), and he had to abandon any dream of becoming another Alexander in Asia. He later summed up his glorious aspirations, claiming: 'I would found a

---

* A few were found in 1982 and can today be seen at the Tel Dor Archaeological Museum, including a cannon with the crest of Charles IV of Spain cast in 1793 and a mortar with Selim III's calligraphic monogram that was captured at Jaffa.

religion, I saw myself marching to Asia, mounted on an elephant, a turban on my head, and in my hand a new Koran that I would have composed to suit my needs.'[51] There was undoubtedly an element of self-mockery as well as fantasy in his portrayal of his ambitions. It seems hardly likely that he would actually have converted, though he clearly thought about it. Later, he would tell Lucien, 'I missed my destiny at Acre.'[52]

Whether because he was angry at this, or to deter Jezzar from following him closely, Napoleon employed scorched-earth tactics on the way back to Egypt, laying waste to the Holy Land. Similar tactics were later to be used against Masséna by Wellington in his retreat to Lisbon in 1810, and of course by the Russians in 1812. He had to leave fifteen badly wounded men behind in the hospital at Mount Carmel in the care of the monks; all of them were massacred when the Turks arrived, and the monks were driven from the monastery they had occupied for centuries.[53] On the retreat to Jaffa, harried in the rear by Arab tribesmen from Lebanon and Nablus, Napoleon ordered some of his cavalry to dismount so that their horses could be used for the sick and wounded. An equerry asked him which one he wanted reserved for himself, upon which Napoleon hit him with his riding crop, shouting: 'Didn't you hear the order? Everyone on foot!'[54] It made for good theatre (unless you were the equerry). Lavalette said it was the first time he had ever seen him strike a man.

Arriving at Jaffa at 2 p.m. on May 24, Napoleon was confronted with an agonizing dilemma. With a gruelling desert crossing ahead, he would have to decide what to do with those plague victims who could not make the journey back to Cairo, since the nature of their illness meant they couldn't be put on ships. 'Nothing could have been more horrible than the sights brought before our eyes in the port of Jaffa throughout our stay there,' recalled Doguereau. 'The dead and dying were everywhere, begging passers-by for treatment or, fearful of being abandoned, praying to be taken on board ship ... There were plague victims in every corner, lying in tents and on the cobblestones, and the hospitals were filled with them. We left many of them behind when we left. I was assured that steps had been taken to prevent them falling alive into the hands of the Turks.'[55] The 'steps' taken were laudanum (opium) overdoses, administered in food by a Turkish apothecary after Desgenettes protested that euthanasia contravened his Hippocratic Oath. From the French eyewitness accounts there seem to have been around fifty men who died in this way.[56] Napoleon himself put the number killed at around fifteen, but he defended his actions passionately: 'Nor would any man under similar circumstances, who had the free use of his senses, have hesitated to prefer dying easily a few hours sooner, than expire under the tortures of those barbarians.'[57] To the Bourbon and British accusations that he was wantonly cruel to his men, which began as soon as the Syrian campaign was over, he replied:

> Do you think that if I had been capable of secretly poisoning my soldiers, or of such barbarities as have been ascribed to me, of driving my carriage over the mutilated and bleeding bodies of the wounded, that my troops would have fought under me with the enthusiasm and affection they uniformly displayed? No, no; I should have been shot long ago; even my wounded would have tried to pull a trigger to despatch me.[58]

While the Jaffa mercy-killings were twisted by propagandists to blacken Napoleon's reputation, there seems no reason not to accept his aide-de-camp Andréossy's conclusion that 'those few who were killed were past recovery, and that he did it out of humanity'.[59]

The march through the desert back to Cairo, featuring terrible thirst in the scorching heat – Napoleon reported 47°C temperatures – was a desperately low point, with incidents of amputee officers being thrown off their stretchers though they had paid men to carry them. An eyewitness noted how such utter demoralization was 'destroying all generous sentiments'.[60] Although they didn't know it, the water table is fairly close to the surface along the coastal route they marched, and if they had only dug a few yards down they would have found water along almost its entirety. 'Bonaparte rode his dromedary, which forced our horses to adopt a tiring pace,' recalled Doguereau.[61] This was because, as Napoleon reported to the Directory, 'eleven leagues [29 miles] had to be covered per day to get to the wells where there was a little hot, sulphurous salty water, which was drunk with more eagerness than a good bottle of champagne in a restaurant'.[62] According to a letter intercepted and published by the British, another soldier recounted: 'Discontent is general . . . Soldiers have been seen to kill themselves in presence of the general-in-chief, exclaiming "This is your work!" '[63]

Napoleon re-entered Cairo on June 14, having sent orders ahead that celebrations were to be organized for his victorious troops' parade, featuring captured standards and prisoners-of-war. 'Although we put on all that we had of finery,' recalled Doguereau of the event, 'yet we presented a miserable appearance; we lacked everything . . . most of us were without hats or boots.'[64] The leading sheikhs came to Cairo to welcome Napoleon, and 'expressed the utmost satisfaction on his return', though with how much sincerity might be doubted.[65] Napoleon lost around 4,000 men in the Syrian expedition, far more than the 500 killed and 1,000 wounded he reported to Paris.[66] A week after returning to Cairo, he ordered Ganteaume to go to Alexandria to prepare the Venetian-built frigates *Carrère* and *Muiron* (named after his former aide-de-camp) for a long, top-secret voyage.

'We are masters of all the desert,' Napoleon told the Directory on June 28, 'and we have disconcerted enemy projects for this year.'[67] The former wasn't much of a boast and the latter wasn't true, since an Ottoman fleet was on its way. On July 15, just as he was coming out of the Great Pyramid with Monge, Berthollet and Duroc, Napoleon was told of the arrival of the Turks off Aboukir.[68] He wrote to the Grand Diwan saying that among the invasion force was a Russian contingent, 'who abhor those who believe in the unity of God, because, according to their lies, they believe that there are three', which was a clever way of trying to use the Russians' Orthodox faith against them and to appeal to Muslim beliefs.[69] He sent Marmont, whom he assumed would soon be besieged in Alexandria, a list of tips, such as 'only sleep in the day', 'sound the reveille well before dawn', 'make sure no officer undresses at night', and to keep a large number of dogs tied up outside the city walls to warn against stealth attacks.[70]

Napoleon gathered together every available man from Cairo to march to Alexandria, which he reached on the night of July 23. At night many of the soldiers slept under the stars, wrapped in their cloaks. On approaching Alexandria, they learned that the small French garrison in the fort at Aboukir had been overwhelmed and beheaded in front of the Turkish commander, Mustafa Pasha. 'This news had a very bad effect,' recorded Doguereau; 'the French do not like this cruel way of making war.'[71] Hypocritical as that may sound after Jaffa, it meant that few prisoners were taken two days later, when Napoleon's 8,000 men inflicted a devastating defeat on the 7,000-strong Turkish, Mamluk and Bedouin forces under Mustafa Pasha at the battle of Aboukir. 'We were obliged to kill them all to a man,' wrote Lavalette, 'but they sold their lives dearly.'[72] Many of the Turks were simply driven into the sea by Lannes, Murat and Kléber. 'If it had been a European army,' said Doguereau, 'we should have taken three thousand prisoners; here there were three thousand corpses.'[73] In fact there were probably closer to five thousand. It was a stark confession of complete indifference to the fate of non-white, non-Christian enemies.[74]

With the second Turkish invasion force destroyed and Egypt safe, Napoleon decided to return as soon as possible to a vulnerable France facing a new Coalition led by Britain, Russia and Austria. Long accused afterwards of deserting his men, in fact he was marching to the sound of the guns, for it was absurd to have France's best general stuck in a strategic sideshow in the Orient when France itself was under threat of invasion. He left Egypt without warning Kléber or Menou – indeed he even ordered Kléber to meet him at Rosetta as a diversion while he headed for the sea. Trying to sweeten the pill of being ordered to assume command, in a very long letter of instructions Napoleon promised Kléber that he would 'take particular care' to send him a company of actors, which he said was 'very important for the army, and also to start changing the customs of this country'.[75] When Kléber discovered that Napoleon – whom he took to calling 'that Corsican runt' – had left Egypt, the plain-speaking Alsatian told his staff: 'That bugger has deserted us with his breeches full of shit. When we get back to Europe we'll rub his face in it.'[76] That pleasure was denied him, for in June 1800 a twenty-four-year-old student named Soliman stabbed him to death. (Soliman was executed with a pike driven into his rectum up to his breast.)[77]

Far from showing cowardice, it took a good deal of courage for Napoleon to cross the Mediterranean when it was virtually a British lake. He sailed on August 23 from Beydah, 9 miles from Alexandria, with most of his senior staff, including Berthier, Lannes, Murat, Andréossy, Marmont, Ganteaume and Merlin, as well as the *savants* Monge, Denon and Berthollet. Napoleon also took with him a young – between fifteen and nineteen, accounts differ – Georgian-born, Mamluk-dressed slave boy called Roustam Raza, who had been a present from Sheikh El-Bekri in Cairo. Roustam became Napoleon's bodyguard, sleeping on a mattress outside his door every night for the next fifteen years, armed with a dagger.[78] 'Don't fear anything,' Napoleon told Roustam, who had been sold into slavery at eleven and was scared of sailing. 'We'll soon be in Paris, and we'll find a lot of beautiful women and a lot of money. You'll see, we'll be very happy, happier than in Egypt!'[79] He ordered Desaix, who was still chasing Murad Bey, and Junot, who was too far away from the embarkation point, to stay behind, writing to Junot of the 'tender friendship that I devote to you', using 'tu' throughout.[80]

Napoleon told the army he had been recalled to France by the government, which was true.[81] 'It's painful to me to leave soldiers to whom I am so much attached,' he said, 'but it shall not be for long.'[82] He boarded the *Muiron* on August 22 and, accompanied by the *Carrère*, set sail at eight o'clock the next morning with a north-easterly wind that blew for two days and, with his customary good fortune, took him away from where British cruisers might have been. The two slow-moving Venetian-built frigates followed a circuitous route to France down the African coast to the Gulf of Carthage, and then northwards towards Sardinia. 'During the whole of this tedious coasting, we had not descried a single sail,' recalled Denon. 'Bonaparte, as an unconcerned passenger, buried himself with geometry and chemistry, or unbent his mind by sharing in our mirth.'[83] On the journey, as well as learning from the *savants*, Napoleon 'would tell us ghost stories, in which he was very clever ... He never mentioned the Directory but with a severity that savoured of contempt.'[84] Bourrienne read him history books late into the night, even when Napoleon was feeling seasick. 'When he asked me for the life of Cromwell,' Denon recalled, 'I believed that I would not go to bed.'[85] Oliver Cromwell, the conservative revolutionary general who effected a coup d'état against a government he despised, was about to become more of a role-model for Napoleon than Denon could have guessed.

Denon recorded that Corsica was 'the first sight of a friendly shore'. Coming into Ajaccio on September 30 'the batteries saluted on both sides; the whole population rushed to the boats and surrounded our frigates'. Lavalette recalled that the sight of Ajaccio left Napoleon 'deeply affected', a phrase generally used at that period to denote tears.[86] Napoleon's time there was spent dining with old partisans and retainers, picking up some ready cash from Joseph Fesch and 'reading in the public papers the melancholy story of our disasters' in Italy and Germany.[87] One can still see the room he occupied on that occasion in the Casa Bonaparte; it was the last time he set foot in his childhood home.

On October 6 Napoleon and his entourage left Ajaccio for Hyères. When, two days later, the sails of some English ships were spotted at 6 p.m., Ganteaume wanted to turn back to Corsica. Giving his first and last navigational order of the journey, Napoleon told him to head for the port of Fréjus on the Côte d'Azur, not far from Cannes. At noon on Wednesday, October 9, 1799 he stepped ashore in France at an inlet at nearby Saint-Raphaël. That same evening he was on his way to Paris. It had been a remarkable journey, and after 1803 Napoleon kept a scale-model of the *Muiron* on his desk; later he ordered that the ship herself 'be kept as a monument and placed somewhere where she will be preserved for a few hundred years ... I would feel very superstitious if anything bad happened to this frigate.'[88] (She was scrapped in 1850.)

The Egyptian adventure was over for Napoleon after nearly a year and five months, though not for the French army he had left behind. They would remain until Menou was forced to capitulate to the British two years later. In 1802 he, his army and the remaining *savants* were allowed to return to France. Napoleon admitted to the loss of 5,344 men in his expedition, which was a considerable underestimation since by the time of the surrender in August 1801, around 9,000 soldiers and 4,500 sailors had died, and relatively little fighting had taken place after he left, even in the final siege of Alexandria.[89] Nonetheless, he had captured the country as ordered, fought off two Turkish invasions and returned to help France in her hour of peril. Kléber wrote a devastating report to the Directory denouncing Napoleon's conduct of the campaign from its inception, describing the dysentery and ophthalmia and the army's dearth of weapons, powder, ammunition and clothing. But although this document was captured by the Royal Navy it wasn't published in time to damage Napoleon politically – yet another example of the luck that he was starting to mistake for Fate.

The greatest long-term achievements of Napoleon's Egyptian campaign were not military or strategic, but intellectual, cultural and artistic. The first volume of Vivant Denon's vast and magisterial *Description de l'Égypte* was published in 1809, its title page proclaiming that it was 'published by the order of His Majesty Emperor Napoleon the Great'. Its preface recalled that Egypt had been invaded by Alexander and the Caesars, whose missions there had been the models for Napoleon's. For the rest of Napoleon's life, and indeed after it, further volumes of this truly extraordinary work appeared, finally numbering twenty-one and constituting a monument in the history of scholarship and publishing. The *savants* had missed nothing. From Cairo, Thebes, Luxor, Karnak, Aswan and all the other sites of Ancient Egyptian temples, there were immensely detailed scale drawings (20 inches by 27) in both colour and black and white of obelisks, sphinxes, hieroglyphics, cartouches, pyramids and sexually aroused pharaohs, as well as mummified birds, cats, snakes and dogs. (According to volume twelve, King Ozymandias didn't have a 'wrinkl'd lip and sneer of cold command' as Shelley suggests, but

DESCRIPTION
DE L'ÉGYPTE,

OU

RECUEIL

DES OBSERVATIONS ET DES RECHERCHES

QUI ONT ÉTÉ FAITES EN ÉGYPTE

PENDANT L'EXPÉDITION DE L'ARMÉE FRANÇAISE,

PUBLIÉ

PAR LES ORDRES DE SA MAJESTÉ L'EMPEREUR

NAPOLÉON LE GRAND.

———

ANTIQUITÉS, PLANCHES.

TOME PREMIER.

A PARIS,

DE L'IMPRIMERIE IMPÉRIALE.

M. DCCC. IX.

a rather engaging smile.) Off-duty soldiers were occasionally shown lounging around in the foreground of prints, but for scale rather than propaganda.

As well as Ancient Egyptology, the volumes contained exceptionally detailed maps of the Nile, modern cities and towns, prints of minarets and landscapes, sketches of irrigation courses, and drawings of monasteries and temples, different types of columns, views of shipping, souks, tombs, mosques, canals, fortresses, palaces and citadels. There were encyclopaedic architectural blueprints with longitudinal and lateral plans of elevation, accurate down to the last centimetre. Although not politically triumphalist, the multiple volumes of the *Description de l'Égypte* represent an apogee of French, indeed Napoleonic, civilization, and had a profound effect on the artistic, architectural, aesthetic and design sensibilities of Europe.

Additionally, having narrowly escaped being bitten by a 'horned serpent' in a Theban grotto, Citizen Ripaud, the librarian of the Institut de l'Égypte, wrote a 104-page report for the Commission of Arts on the existing state of the antiquities from the Nile cataracts to Cairo.[90] The *savants'* greatest discovery was the Rosetta Stone, a *stele* in three languages found at El-Rashid in the Delta. They made copies and translated the Greek portion before starting to work on the hieroglyphics.[91] Under the peace agreement covering the French withdrawal in 1801, the Stone was handed over to the British and sent to the British Museum, where it still safely resides. Tragically, the Institut near Tahrir Square in Cairo was burned down during the Arab Spring uprising on December 17, 2011, and almost all its 192,000 books, journals and other manuscripts – including the only handwritten manuscript of Denon's *Description de l'Égypte* – were destroyed.

9

Brumaire

'I returned to France at a fortunate moment, when the existing government was so bad it could not continue. I became its chief; everything else followed of course – there's my story in a few words.'

Napoleon on St Helena

'The men who have changed the world never succeeded by winning over the powerful, but always by stirring the masses. The first method is a resort to intrigue and only brings limited results. The latter is the course of genius and changes the face of the world.'

Napoleon on St Helena

Napoleon made his way to Paris from Saint-Raphaël via Aix (where he had his luggage stolen), Avignon, Valence, Lyons and Nevers, arriving in the capital on the morning of Wednesday, October 16, 1799. He enjoyed 'a triumphal march' along the route, and was given a hero's welcome everywhere as France's saviour.[1] When he arrived in Lyons a play entitled The Hero's Return was staged in his honour in front of large crowds who thronged the streets. They cheered so loudly that the lines were drowned out, which was probably just as well as they had been written overnight and were unrehearsed. The seventeen-year-old future cavalry officer Jean-Baptiste de Marbot recalled: 'People were dancing in the open spaces and the air rang with cries of "Hurrah for Bonaparte! He will save the country!"'[2] He marvelled at Napoleon and his senior colleagues, especially 'their martial air, their faces bronzed by the eastern sun, their strange costumes, and their Turkish sabres, slung by cords'.[3]

Before he could determine what to do politically, Napoleon needed to decide what he wanted matrimonially. Although he didn't know it, Josephine had made an attempt at ending her affair with Hippolyte Charles in February 1799. 'You can be assured, after this interview, which will be the last, that you will no longer be tormented by my letters or by my presence,' she had written to him. 'The honest woman who has been deceived retires and says nothing.'⁴ In fact she continued writing to him about various sleazy business dealings they had had over Army of Italy contracts as late as October, and she tried (unsuccessfully) to find a job for a friend of his even after that. It was Charles who finally rejected the bereft Josephine romantically, whereupon the dapper boulevardier-hussar strolled off the pages of history. When Napoleon came to absolute power very shortly afterwards, he made no attempt to pursue or punish him.

It had been sixteen months since he had learned of Josephine's infidelity, so much of his anger was spent, and he had retaliated comprehensively with Pauline Fourès. A divorce might damage him politically, especially with devout Catholics, and Josephine was helpful to him politically with her royalist and social connections, as well as in smoothing over the sensibilities of those rebuffed by his brusqueness. Although her overspending was pathological, the bills her tradesmen sent were negotiable, and they were often happy to settle for fifty centimes in the franc, which still gave them sizeable profits.

Napoleon went first to rue de la Victoire, perhaps in itself an indication that he was going to forgive her, and when on October 18 Josephine arrived from Malmaison – a lovely chateau 7 miles west of Paris bought for 325,000 (borrowed) francs while Napoleon was in Egypt – having taken the wrong road to intercept him, they had a full-scale domestic scene. There was shouting, weeping and pleading on knees outside locked doors. Bags were packed, Hortense and the wounded Eugène were recruited by their mother to appeal to Napoleon's step-fatherly sensibilities (which were strong and genuine), and finally there was a dramatic reconciliation. When Lucien arrived to see his brother the next morning he was shown into the bedroom where the couple were sitting up in bed.⁵ It is hard not to suspect that Napoleon stage-managed at least part of the titanic row to ensure total domination over her for the rest of their marriage: afterwards she was faithful to him, though he certainly wasn't to her.

Other theories as to why he stayed with her have been that he was 'softened by her tears', was sensually aroused and didn't care, believed her denials (the least likely), was too concerned with politics to have time for domestic strife, wanted a child, and that he did love her despite everything. Whichever was the true explanation, or combination of them, he forgave Josephine totally, and never made allusion to her infidelity again, either to her or to anyone else. Thereafter, they slipped into comfortable domestic happiness, until dynastic considerations emerged a full decade later. She seems now genuinely to have fallen in love with him, although she always called him 'Bonaparte'. The story of Napoleon and Josephine is thus certainly not the romantic Romeo-and-Juliet love story of legend, but something subtler, more interesting and, in its way, no less admirable.

Between his arrival in Paris and his reconciliation with Josephine, Napoleon had met Louis Gohier, a lawyer-politician who had joined the Directory in June and on the basis of its three-month revolving presidency was at its head. On October 17 he was fêted at a public meeting at which he wore an Egyptian round hat, an olive green coat and a Turkish scimitar attached by silk cords. In reply to Gohier's eulogy, Napoleon said he would only draw his sword in defence of the Republic and its government.[6] The Directory privately had to decide whether to arrest Napoleon for desertion (he had left his army in Egypt without orders) and quarantine-breaking, or to congratulate him for winning the battles of the Pyramids, Mount Tabor and Aboukir, conquering Egypt, opening up the East and establishing a vast new French colony, as his propagandists were putting out. If the Directors ever seriously considered a suggestion from Bernadotte that he be court-martialled, they quickly dropped it after hearing their own guard break out into spontaneous cheers of 'Vive Bonaparte!' once he was recognized outside their council chamber.[7]

Over the following days, the rue de la Victoire was besieged by crowds of spectators and well-wishers. General Paul Thiébault, who had fought at Rivoli, was in the Palais-Royal when he heard that Napoleon had returned:

The general commotion in Paris left no doubt as to the truth of the news. The regimental bands belonging to the garrison of the city were already promenading the streets as a sign of public cheerfulness, swarms of people and soldiers following them. At night illuminations were hastily got up in every quarter, and in all the theatres the return was announced by shouts of 'Vive la République! Vive Bonaparte!' It was not the return of a general; it was the return of a leader in the garb of a general . . . Only the ghost of a government remained in France. Breached by all parties, the Directory was at the mercy of the first assault.[8]

Yet that assault still needed to be planned. To plot to overthrow the Constitution of the Year III – which Napoleon had solemnly sworn to uphold – constituted treason, punishable by the guillotine. Moreover there were so many plots to overthrow the Directory swirling around Paris that Napoleon might not be the first to mount one. That June, only the day after the legislature had replaced Jean-Baptiste Treilhard with the ex-Jacobin Gohier, there had been a mini-coup, the so-called *journée parlementaire* (parliamentary day), when General Joubert, with Barras' and Sieyès' support, had used force to replace La Révellière and Douai as Directors with Pierre-Roger Ducos and the ex-Jacobin General Jean-François Moulin. With the exceptions of Barras, Carnot and Sieyès, none of the thirteen men who held the post of Director between 1795 and 1799 were particularly impressive politicians.

Among those visiting Napoleon over the following days were almost all the key conspirators of the coming coup. First through the door was Talleyrand, who had been forced to resign as foreign minister in July when he was caught repeatedly and insistently demanding $250,000 in 'gratification' from the three impeccably honourable American envoys to Paris (one of whom was the future Supreme Court justice John Marshall) before he would deign to negotiate with them over loan repayments.[9] Talleyrand worried that Napoleon would hold his non-appearance in Constantinople against him, but was instantly forgiven. Another early visitor was Pierre-Louis Roederer, a malleable but highly intelligent politician who had been elected to the Estates-General in 1789 and had survived every subsequent regime; he was to become one of Napoleon's closest advisors. Michel Regnaud de Saint-Jean d'Angély, the former editor whom Napoleon had left to administer Malta, turned up, as did Antoine Boulay de la Meurthe, a key supporter from the lower house of the legislature, the Council of the Five Hundred. Other co-conspirators during those October days included Vice-Admiral Eustache Bruix of the Brest squadron, the 'well-bred and gentlemanlike' bureaucrat Hugues-Bernard Maret, and a senior police official, the former Jacobin Pierre-François Réal.[10]

These men were all to hold key positions in Napoleon's government after the coup; several became members of the Conseil d'État and almost all peers of France. Another crucial figure in the coup was Lucien Bonaparte, who had been elected to the Five Hundred in June 1798 aged twenty-three and was shortly to become its president, allowing the plotters their opportunity to clothe their coup with a spurious constitutionalism. 'Tall, ill-shaped, having limbs like those of a field-spider, and a small head,' Laure d'Abrantès described Lucien, 'very near-sighted, which made him half shut his eyes and stoop his head.'[11] As one had to be thirty to qualify for election, his birth certificate was doctored to meet the requirement.[12]

'Brumaire' means 'season of mists and fog', and it is appropriately hard to piece together the mechanics of what took place next because Napoleon deliberately committed nothing to paper; only two letters of his survive for the twenty-three days between his arrival in Paris on October 16 and the 18 Brumaire when the coup was launched, neither of them compromising.[13] For a man who wrote an average of fifteen letters a day, this time everything was to be done by word of mouth. He had already once in his life had his correspondence ransacked for evidence with which to guillotine him, and he wasn't going to allow it to happen again. In his public appearances he went back to wearing his uniform of the Institut de France rather than that of a general.

The coup wasn't Napoleon's brainchild, but that of the Abbé Sieyès, who had replaced Reubell as a Director in May 1799 but who soon concluded that the government of which he was a leading member was simply too incompetent and corrupt to deal with the issues facing France. His co-conspirators, including fellow Director and crony Ducos, the police chief Joseph Fouché and the justice minister Jean-Jacques-Régis de Cambacérès, had far more political weight than Napoleon's friends (except Talleyrand), and Sieyès regarded Napoleon as merely the 'sword', or muscle, necessary to see the enterprise through. Sieyès was one of those who personally detested Napoleon, a feeling that was entirely mutual. Sieyès had privately suggested that he be shot for deserting his post in Egypt, while Napoleon had said that Sieyès should lose his Directorship for having sold himself to Prussia (of which there's no proof).[14] When his first choice of 'sword', General Joubert, had been shot through the heart at the battle of Novi, north of Genoa (coincidentally on Napoleon's birthday), Sieyès had little choice but to turn to Napoleon: of the other leading generals Jourdan supported the constitution, Schérer had been discredited by defeat, Jacques Macdonald (the son of a Jacobite Highlander) and Moreau seem to have refused the offer, and Pichegru was by then fighting for the enemy. As on Vendémiaire, the key role fell to Napoleon almost by process of elimination.

It was Talleyrand who finally persuaded a reluctant Sieyès to choose

Napoleon on the basis of his irreproachable republican record, and the lack of alternatives.[15] To Napoleon he is credited with saying, 'You want the power and Sieyès wants the constitution, therefore join forces.'[16] Napoleon's popularity with Parisians was obviously a factor in Sieyès' decision; at a visit to the Celestins theatre at this time Napoleon sat at the back of the box and placed Duroc at the front, but 'the call for Bonaparte grew so violent and so unanimous' that they were forced to swap places, as Napoleon presumably expected would happen.[17]

Napoleon and Sieyès only met for the first time on the afternoon of October 23. 'I was in charge of negotiating the political conditions of an agreement,' recalled Roederer. 'I was forwarding to one and the other their respective views of the constitution to be established, and the position that each would take.'[18] Napoleon wanted to keep his options open and was entertaining other offers, though none from a group as politically well-connected. There may have been as many as ten active plots to overthrow the Directory being secretly discussed in these months.

None of the myriad failures of the Directory over the previous four years could credibly be laid at the door of the absent Napoleon. Defeats abroad had stripped France of the territories he had won in 1796–7 and had cut her off from German and Italian markets. While Russia, Britain, Portugal, Turkey and Austria had joined the War of the Second Coalition against her, there was also a so-called 'Quasi-War' with America over the repayments of debts that the United States argued she owed the French Crown and not the French state. There had already been no fewer than four French war ministers in eight months that year, and with army pay so deeply in arrears, desertion, brigandage and highway robbery were rampant in the countryside. Royalist revolts in Provence and the Vendée had reignited. A Royal Navy blockade had wrecked overseas trade and the paper currency was next to worthless. The taxation of land, doors and windows, the seizure of suspected pro-Bourbon hostages, and the Jourdan Law of 1798 that turned the earlier emergency *levées en masse* into something approaching universal military conscription, were all deeply unpopular. Corruption over government contracts was even more rife than usual, and was correctly assumed to involve Directors such as Barras. Freedom of the press and association were heavily restricted. The 1798 and 1799 elections for one-third of the legislature had seen widespread fraud, and, crucially, the middle-class buyers of the *biens nationaux* (nationalized property) feared for the security of their acquisitions.

Few blights undermine a society more comprehensively than hyper-inflation, and great political prizes would go to anyone who could defeat it. (The deputies of the legislature paid themselves in an inflation-proof way, by index-linking their salaries to the value of 30,000 kg of wheat.) The Directory had abolished the Law of the Maximum, which kept prices down on staples such as bread, flour, milk and meat, so the bad 1798 harvest had led to a pound of bread reaching above 3 *sols* for the first time in two years, leading to hoarding, riots and genuine distress. Perhaps worst of all, people couldn't see how anything could improve, because revisions of the constitution had to be ratified three times by both chambers at three-year intervals and then by a special assembly at the end of the nine-year process.[19] This was unlikely to happen in a legislature as fluid and unstable as that of late 1799, which included covert royalists, Feuillant constitutionalists (moderates), former Girondins, neo-Jacobin 'patriots', but precious few supporters of the Directory. By contrast, the constitutions that Napoleon had recently imposed on the Cisalpine, Venetian, Ligurian, Lemanic, Helvetian and Roman republics, along with his administrative reforms of Malta and Egypt, made him look like a zealous, efficient republican who believed in strong executives and central control, solutions that might also work well for metropolitan France.

France was not quite a failed state in the autumn of 1799, indeed in some areas the Directory had reason to be optimistic. Some economic reforms were being undertaken, Russia had left the Second Coalition, the situation in the Vendée was improving, British forces had been expelled from Holland, and Masséna had won some victories in Switzerland that meant that France was no longer in imminent danger of invasion.[20] Yet none of this was enough to dispel the overall impression among Frenchmen that the Directory had failed and, as Napoleon put it at the time, 'the pear was ripe'.[21] Nor was there a place for Napoleon within the existing political structure, as the minimum age for Directors was still forty, whereas Napoleon was thirty, and Gohier hadn't seemed keen to alter the constitution for him.

Napoleon has been accused of killing French democracy at Brumaire, and so he did, but even the Westminster parliament was hardly a paragon of Jeffersonian ideals, containing many seats that only had a few score electors and remaining firmly in the grip of an aristocratic oligarchy until well into the second half of the nineteenth century. Although the coup has been depicted as destroying French liberty too, since the Thermidor coup that overthrew Robespierre and brought the Directory into being in July 1794 there had been the coup attempt of Vendémiaire in 1795, the purge of Fructidor in 1797 and the Prairial parliamentary day of June 1799. For all its undoubted unconstitutionality, the Brumaire coup was hardly a new departure in French politics. Napoleon had sworn to uphold the constitution and much of his popularity had been based on the belief that he was a true republican. But 'When the house is crumbling, is it the time to busy oneself in the garden?' Napoleon asked Marmont rhetorically. 'A change here is indispensable.'[22]

At breakfast at the rue de la Victoire on October 26 Napoleon openly criticized the Directory to Thiébault, contrasting their soldiers' *esprit* on the Italian campaign with the government's lethargy. 'A nation is always what you have the wit to make it,' he said. 'The triumph of faction, parties, divisions, is the fault of those in authority only . . . No people are bad under a good government, just as no troops are bad under good generals . . . These men are bringing France down to the level of their own blundering. They are degrading her, and she is beginning to repudiate them.' Forthright opinions like those had cost lives earlier in the Revolution, but Napoleon felt secure enough to talk sedition to a comrade he was hoping to win over, ending with one of his most regular condemnations: 'Well, what can generals expect from this government of lawyers?'[23]

'There's no-one more pusillanimous than me when I make a military plan,' Napoleon told Roederer on the 27th. 'I exaggerate all the possible dangers and all the possible harms in the circumstances. I get in a very tiresome agitation. This doesn't prevent me looking very serene in front of those surrounding me. I'm like a woman who's giving birth. And when I'm resolved, everything is forgotten except what can make it succeed.'[24] Napoleon applied the same obsessive attention to the planning of the Brumaire coup. His precise actions are impossible to know because of the total dearth of contemporary written evidence, but once it was launched everyone seems to have known where to be and what to do.

Days before the coup the Directory, probably suspecting what was afoot, offered Napoleon his pick of foreign commands, which he refused on health grounds. They also secretly accused him through the press of embezzlement in Italy, which he vigorously denied.[25] The story is told from this period of Napoleon plotting at Talleyrand's house when loud noises were heard in the street below. Fearing they were about to be arrested, the conspirators blew out the candles, rushed to the balcony and were hugely relieved to see the commotion had been caused by a carriage accident involving gamblers returning from the Palais-Royal.[26]

The gamble they were embarked upon was aided greatly on October 29 when a new law suspended the payment of pre-assigned monies to government contractors until their accounts were audited. The contractor Jean-Pierre Collot, a protégé of Cambacérès who was bankrolling the conspiracy, now felt he had less to lose.[27]

The moment that decided Napoleon to cross his Rubicon came the next day, when he dined with Barras at the Luxembourg Palace, where the whole Directory lived and worked. After dinner Barras proposed that General Gabriel d'Hédouville, whom Napoleon thought 'excessively mediocre', should become president of France to 'save' the Republic. Although he'd fought at Valmy, d'Hédouville had recently been forced to flee Saint-Domingue (modern-day Haiti) by the black nationalist leader Toussaint L'Ouverture's revolution, and certainly wasn't presidential material. 'As for you, General,' Barras told Napoleon, 'your intention is to return to the army; and I, sick, unpopular, worn out, I am good for nothing except to return to private life.'[28] In one of Napoleon's recollections of that occasion he merely stared at Barras without replying, but in another, 'I answered with a manner calculated to convince him that I was not his dupe. He looked down and muttered a few remarks that at once decided me. From his apartment in the Luxembourg, I went down to that of Sieyès ... I told him I had made up my mind to act with him.'[29]

Barras, realizing his terrible error, visited the rue de la Victoire at 8 a.m. the next morning to try to make amends, but Napoleon replied that he 'was tired, indisposed, that he could not get used to the humidity of the atmosphere in the capital, coming from the dry climate of the sands of Arabia', and ended the interview 'with similar platitudes'.[30] Napoleon met Sieyès secretly at Lucien's house on November 1 to co-ordinate the details of the coup which by then Talleyrand and Fouché had also joined.

Joseph Fouché was no ordinary police chief. An Oratorian intending to join the Church until he was twenty-three, he became a regicide Jacobin in 1793. More interested in power than ideology, he kept up many contacts among the royalists, and he protected priests, especially Oratorians, despite being a leader of the anti-clerical party. 'Everyone knows this personage', wrote Napoleon's future aide-de-camp Comte Philippe

Ségur, 'his medium stature, his tow-coloured hair, lank and scanty, his active leanness, his long, mobile face with the physiognomy of an excited ferret; one remembers his piercing keen gaze, shifty nevertheless, his little bloodshot eyes, his brief and jerky manner of speech which was in harmony with his restless, uneasy attitude.'[31]

Fouché recruited spies from, among many others, pedlars, butchers, hairdressers, locksmiths, wigmakers, perfumers, bartenders, Louis XVI's former valet, an ex-Jacobin known as 'Wooden-Leg Collin', the Baroness Lauterbourg, and the madame of the brothel at No. 133 Palais-Royal.[32] 'One day he'll look into my bed,' Napoleon joked of him, 'then next into my wallet.'[33] It was welcome news for Napoleon that Fouché was supporting the coup, since he was never found on the losing side (although he also had contingency plans to arrest the 'rebels' should the attempt fail.[34]) Napoleon's attitude towards Fouché both during the coup and thereafter was that 'Fouché, and Fouché alone, is able to conduct the ministry of police. We cannot create such men; we must take as we find.'[35]

On November 6 both chambers of the legislature threw a subscription banquet of seven hundred covers in honour of Napoleon and General Moreau in the church of St-Sulpice – renamed the Temple of Victory in the Revolution – whose cavernous dimensions resemble a cathedral and whose towers were so high that they were used by the government for semaphore. With its black walls and acoustics designed to turn words into echoing incantations, it was perhaps the last place to choose for such a vast dinner on a cold November night, though the place has an undeniable majesty. Most of political France was there, but not Bernadotte, who (so Barras claimed) refused to put his name to the subscription 'until Bonaparte has satisfactorily explained the reasons which have caused him to forsake his army', adding: 'I do not care to dine in the company of a plague-carrier.'[36] It was said that Napoleon 'ate nothing but eggs' at the dinner, for fear of being poisoned by the Directory, and left early.[37] In his speech he concentrated on the importance of unity between Frenchmen, a safe enough theme to which he would return repeatedly in the coming weeks and months.

Otherwise, of all the many people who asked to throw dinners in his honour after he returned from Egypt, almost the only invitation Napoleon accepted was from Cambacérès, whom he said he 'esteemed greatly'.[38] A fat, flamboyant, homosexual gastronome and epicurean, Cambacérès came from a distinguished Montpellier legal family. He had voted for the execution of Louis XVI, but only should the Austrians invade. He was one of the few lawyers Napoleon liked, and was to become with Duroc his closest and most trusted advisor. 'He had great conversational powers,' recalled Laure d'Abrantès, 'and his narratives acquired novelty and grace from the turn of his language ... He bore ... the character of the ablest civilian in the country.'[39] She also added that he was 'extraordinarily ugly ... long nose, long chin, and yellow skin'. Cambacérès sought influence rather than power and never the limelight, and he was later allowed to express private opposition to what Napoleon did because his loyalty was unquestionable. (Napoleon wasn't a bigot; besides his closeness to Cambacérès he made the openly homosexual Joseph Fiévée prefect of the Nièvre department, where he and his lifelong partner deeply shocked the locals.)

Cambacérès' judgement of both men and measures was exemplary. 'The only two people who could calm Bonaparte's rages were Cambacérès and Josephine,' recalled a minister. 'The former made sure never to rush or contradict this impetuous character. That would have been to push him to ever-greater fury; but he let him get on with his rage; he gave him time to dictate the most iniquitous edicts, and waited with wisdom and patience for the moment when this fit of anger had finally blown over to make some observations to him.'[40] For all the 'grace' of his narratives, Cambacérès also had a broader side to his humour. After news of one of Napoleon's victories arrived during a dinner and Josephine announced to the table that they had 'vaincu' (vanquished), Cambacérès pretended that she had meant 'vingt culs' (twenty bottoms) and quipped: 'Now we must choose!' Later in his reign Napoleon tried to persuade Cambacérès to stop taking so many drugs, but conceded that 'these are the habits of a confirmed bachelor (vieux garçon)' and didn't insist.[41] So great was Napoleon's trust in Cambacérès that he allowed him to run France during his absences on campaigns, a confidence returned by Cambacérès' daily reports to him on every conceivable subject.

Two separate stages of the coup were planned. On Day One, which was originally intended to be Thursday, November 7 (16 Brumaire), 1799, Napoleon would attend a specially called session of the upper house, the Elders, where it sat at the Tuileries, to inform them that because of British-backed plots and neo-Jacobin threats, the Republic was in danger, so they must authorize that the next day's meeting of both the Elders

and the lower house, the Five Hundred, should be held 7 miles west of
Paris in the former Bourbon palace of Saint-Cloud. Primed by Sieyès,
the Elders would appoint Napoleon as commander of all the troops in
the 17th military district (i.e. Paris). That same day Sieyès and Ducos
would resign from the Directory, and Barras, Gohier and Moulin would
be prevailed upon to resign also by a judicious mixture of threats and
bribery, leaving a power vacuum. Then, on Day Two, Napoleon would
go to Saint-Cloud and persuade the legislature that in view of the
national emergency, the Constitution of the Year III must be repealed
and a new one established replacing the Directory with a three-man
executive government called – with fittingly Roman overtones – the
Consulate, comprising Sieyès, Ducos and himself, with elections to be
held thereafter for new representative assemblies that Sieyès had been
formulating. Sieyès believed he had the Elders under control. If the Five
Hundred baulked at abolishing themselves, their newly elected president, Lucien, would dissolve the body.

The flaws in the plan were glaring. A two-day coup might lose the
conspirators the all-important initiative, yet without the move to
Saint-Cloud it was feared that the deputies on the Left would be able to
raise the Parisian *faubourgs* and Sections in defence of the Constitution
of the Year III, and fighting in central Paris could wreck the chances of
success. The second problem was to keep the coup secret to prevent
Barras, Gohier and Moulin from taking counter-measures, while still
bribing successfully enough of the Elders to assure a positive vote on the
motion to move the session to Saint-Cloud.

The first thing to go wrong was that the whole coup had to be put
back forty-eight hours when some key Elders – 'these imbeciles' as
Napoleon called them – started baulking at the whole prospect at the
last moment and needed to be reassured.[42] 'I'm leaving them some time
to convince them that I can do without them,' Napoleon said optimisti-
cally, employing the two days usefully in persuading Jourdan not to
stymie the coup even if he couldn't support it. When the officer corps
of the Paris garrison asked to be presented to Napoleon, he told them
to attend on him at 6 a.m. on November 9, the new Day One.

On the night of the 7th he dined with Bernadotte and his family at
the rue Cisalpine, along with Jourdan and Moreau, trying to put the
three generals' minds at rest about the coming events. Bernadotte, who
had married Napoleon's former fiancée (and Joseph's sister-in-law)
Désirée Clary while Napoleon was in Egypt, was deeply sceptical, and

watched the coup from the sidelines, telling Napoleon: 'You'll be guillotined,' to which Napoleon 'coldly' replied, 'We'll see.'[43] Moreau, by
contrast, agreed to help by arresting the Directors at the Luxembourg
Palace on Day One, whereas Jourdan stuck to his policy merely not to
hinder the coup. (His republicanism meant that he was never truly reconciled to Napoleon, and was later the only one of the twenty-six
marshals of the Empire not to be ennobled by him.)[44]

On November 8, the day before the coup, Napoleon revealed the plot
to Colonel Horace Sébastiani, who had been wounded at Dego and had
fought at Arcole; he promised that the 9th Dragoon regiment would
be at Napoleon's disposal the next morning. Napoleon dined that
night with Cambacérès at the ministry of justice and was reported to
be extremely relaxed, singing a favourite revolutionary song, the
'Pont-Neuf', that his entourage said he only sang when 'his spirit was
tranquil and heart satisfied'.[45] Of course he might well have been putting
on a show for his fellow conspirators and been secretly nerve-wracked,
as he had implied in his letter to Roederer comparing himself to 'a
woman giving birth'.

At 6 a.m. on the cold and grey morning of November 9 (18 Brumaire),
1799, sixty officers of the 17th District and adjutants of the National
Guard assembled in the courtyard of the house at rue de la Victoire.
Dressed in civilian clothes, Napoleon 'explained to them in a forcible
manner the desperate situation of the Republic, and asked of them a
testimony of devotion to his person, with an oath of allegiance to the
two chambers'.[46] It was a smart move to suggest that he was in fact
protecting the chambers even while he was in the very process of abolishing them.

Meanwhile, at the Tuileries, Sieyès' influence ensured that all the
necessary decrees were passed by the Elders by 8 a.m., including the one
appointing Napoleon commander of the 17th District and the National
Guard, although technically that appointment lay with the war minister,
who reported to the Directory, rather than with the Elders.[47] A second
decree stated that the Elders had changed the venue of their session
from the Tuileries to Saint-Cloud 'to restore domestic peace', and
ordered Parisians to 'be calm', stating that 'in a short time, the presence
of the Legislative Body will be returned to you'.[48] Those members of the
Elders likely to oppose the decree simply weren't given proper notice of
the extraordinary (and extraordinarily early) meeting, one of the oldest

tricks in politics. Failing to spot what was going on, Gohier gullibly countersigned the Saint-Cloud decree.

On receiving the news of his appointment by the Elders, Napoleon changed into his general's uniform and rode to the Tuileries, arriving at 10 a.m., where he found Sébastiani and his dragoons. The new war minister, the neo-Jacobin Edmond Dubois de Crancé, had specifically forbidden any troop movements in the capital without his personal order 'under pain of death', but this was simply ignored. Napoleon was received with great ceremony in the Elders' chamber and delivered another speech calling for national unity, which was well received. 'You are the wisdom of the nation,' he flattered them, 'it's up to you to indicate the measures in these circumstances that can save our country. I come here, surrounded by all the generals, to promise you all their support. I name General Lefebvre as my lieutenant. I will faithfully carry out the mission you have entrusted to me. No attempt should be made to look in the past for examples of what is happening: nothing in history resembles the end of the 18th century.'[49] Hard-headed and brave, François-Joseph Lefebvre was a miller's son who had been a sergeant at the outbreak of the Revolution and had fought in Belgium and Germany; reassuringly, he seemed to personify the republican virtues.

As Napoleon rode past the Place de la Révolution that evening, where Louis XVI, Marie Antoinette, Danton, Babeuf, the Robespierre brothers and so many others had been guillotined, he is said to have remarked to his co-conspirators: 'Tomorrow we'll either sleep at the Luxembourg, or we'll finish up here.'[50]

On Day Two, November 10 (19 Brumaire), Napoleon was up at 4 a.m. and rode out to Saint-Cloud. Meanwhile, over at the Luxembourg Palace, Gohier was woken by a message from Josephine taken personally by Eugène, inviting him and his wife to breakfast at 8 a.m., where they would have been put under house-arrest had they accepted. Dubois de Crancé had accused Napoleon of plotting a coup, but Gohier refused to believe the rumours as he had spoken to his police minister asking the news, and Fouché had replied: 'New? Nothing, in truth.'[51] Gohier was not so naive as to be convinced and sent his wife, a friend of Josephine's, to the breakfast in his stead. Lavalette recorded that Josephine had to 'work upon Madame Gohier's alarm to obtain her husband's submission'.[52]

Moreau arrived at the Luxembourg later that morning and subverted the palace guard; he arrested Barras, Gohier and Moulin and demanded their resignations as Directors. Barras was persuaded by Talleyrand and

Bruix, who offered him a deal whereby he kept his large estate and all the proceeds from his many years of peculation at the top of government.[53] Gohier and Moulin held out for over twenty-four hours, but signed the next day.* Talleyrand was characteristically profiting from the situation. When Napoleon years later asked him how he had made his fortune, he insouciantly replied 'Nothing simpler; I bought *rentes* [government securities] on the 17th Brumaire and sold them on the 19th.'[54]

At Saint-Cloud Napoleon addressed the Elders, but it was an unimpressive oratorical performance which reads better than it apparently sounded:

> You are on a volcano. The Republic no longer has a government; the Directory has been dissolved, the factions are agitating; the time to make a decision has arrived. You have summoned me and my companions-in-arms to aid your wisdom, but time is precious. We must decide. I know that we speak of Caesar, of Cromwell, as if the present time could be compared to past times. No, I want only the safety of the Republic, and to support the decisions that you are going to take.[55]

He referred to his grenadiers, 'whose caps I see at the doors of this chamber', and called on them to tell the Elders 'Have I ever deceived you? Have I ever betrayed my promises, when, in the camps, in the midst of privations, I promised you victory and plenty, and when, at your head, I led you from success to success? Tell them now: was it for my interests or for those of the Republic?' Of course he got a cheer from the troops, but then a member of the Elders named Linglet stood up, and said loudly: 'General, we applaud what you say; therefore swear obedience with us to the Constitution of Year III, that is the only thing now that can maintain the Republic.' These words produced 'a great silence': Napoleon had been caught in a trap. He collected himself for a moment, and said: 'The Constitution of Year III you have no more: you violated it on 18 Fructidor, when the government made an attempt on the independence of the legislature.' He then reminded them of the Prairial coup, arguing that since the constitution had been 'violated, we need a new pact, new guarantees', failing to point out that one of the senior instigators of Fructidor had been himself.[56]

Receiving a reasonably respectful audience from the Elders, and

---

* Moulin rejoined the army and served under Napoleon; Gohier retired to his estate, and later became Napoleon's ambassador to Holland.

bolstered by his comrades outside, Napoleon then walked the hundred yards or so up the slight incline to where the Five Hundred were meeting in the palace Orangery. There he received a very different reception. The interval between Day One and Day Two had given the opposition time to organize to try to block the provisional Consulate that Napoleon and Lucien were about to propose. The Five Hundred included many more neo-Jacobins than the Elders and was twice the size; it was always going to be far harder to convince. At the very start of their session, which had also begun at noon, its members had taken a roll-call pledge of loyalty to the Constitution of the Year III.[57] Lucien, Boulay and all the Bonapartists were forced to pledge their allegiance in their alphabetical turn, to catcalls from the neo-Jacobins at their hypocrisy. These pledges allowed deputies to make short speeches about the glories of the constitution that were listened to by their guards.

When Napoleon arrived with fellow officers and other troops, the younger deputies of the Left professed themselves outraged at seeing men in uniform at the door of a democratic chamber. Napoleon entered on his own and had to stride half-way into the room to reach the rostrum, in the course of which deputies started to shout at him. An eyewitness, the neo-Jacobin Jean-Adrien Bigonnet, heard Napoleon shouting back: 'I want no more factionalism, this must finish; I want no more of it!'[58] Bigonnet recalled: 'I confess that the tone of authority coming from a leader of the armed forces in the presence of the disposers of legitimate power made me indignant ... This feeling of danger was apparent on almost every face.' Napoleon has been described as 'pale, emotional, hesitating' and as soon as he looked like he might be in physical danger, Lefebvre and four tall grenadiers armed with swords – one was over six-foot even without his bearskin – stepped into the room to surround him, which only infuriated the deputies more.[59]

'Down with the tyrant!' the deputies started to yell, 'Cromwell!', 'Tyrant!', 'Down with the dictator!', '*Hors la loi!*' (Outlaw!)[60] These cries had dangerous overtones for the conspirators because during the Terror – which had only ended five years earlier – the outlawing of someone had often been a precursor to their execution, and the cry '*À bas le dictateur!*' had last been heard when Robespierre was stepping up onto the scaffold. Lucien tried to establish order, banging his presidential gavel and shouting for silence, but by then several of the deputies had come down from their seats into the main body of the Orangery and had started to push, shake, boo, jostle and slap Napoleon, some grabbing him by his high brocaded collar, so that Lefebvre and the grenadiers had to place themselves between him and the outraged deputies.[61]

Lavalette had been sent to the Orangery chamber earlier in the day to report to Napoleon everything that was happening there, and he recalled how Napoleon 'was so pressed between the deputies, his staff, and the grenadiers ... that I thought for a moment he would be smothered. He could neither advance nor go back.'[62] Eventually Napoleon was hustled out of the Orangery, with Grenadier Thomé's sleeve getting torn in the scuffle. 'He managed to get down to the courtyard,' recalled Lavalette, 'mounted his horse at the foot of the staircase, and sent an order for Lucien to come out to him. At this point the windows of the chamber were flung open and members of the Five Hundred pointed at him still shouting "Down with the dictator!" and "Outlaw!"'[63] Another eyewitness, the deputy Théophile Berlier, related how 'After his retreat, followed by a great commotion to which was added several shouts of "Outlaw", his brother Lucien, appearing at the tribune to justify him, couldn't be heard; such that, stung, and having taken off the uniform of his post, he left the room.'[64] Some deputies tried physically to hold Lucien down in the president's chair in order to keep the continued session technically lawful while they put the motion to outlaw Napoleon, but grenadiers managed to get him out of the Orangery too.[65]

Talleyrand's secretary, Montrond, later told Roederer of Napoleon's 'sudden pallor' when he heard the motion that the Five Hundred were voting on.[66] Yet this testimony is doubtful, as Talleyrand and Montrond only observed the events at a distance, from the palace's pavilion.[67] Collot was there too, with 10,000 francs in cash on him in case things went wrong. Sieyès – who was closer to events, although he had a carriage and six horses at the ready too – kept his head, and argued that anyone declaring Napoleon an outlaw was himself by definition an outlaw, which was just the kind of rationale used during the Terror about defenders of aristocrats, but which, for all its lack of logic, encouraged the conspirators.[68]

Napoleon has been accused of dithering for as long as half an hour after his expulsion from the Orangery. Lavalette believed this to have been the most dangerous moment of all, for if 'a general of some reputation had put himself at the head of the troops of the interior' – Augereau, say, or Jourdan, or Bernadotte – 'it would be difficult to guess what might have happened'.[69] Did Napoleon lose his nerve on 19 Brumaire, as some have alleged, accusing him of cowardice, and even of fainting and having to be carried out by his bodyguards?[70] The manhandling must have been off-putting, but hardly much compared to being stabbed in the thigh by a pike or seeing one's aide-de-camp killed by a cannon-ball. 'I'd rather talk to soldiers than to lawyers,' he said of the Five Hundred the next day. 'I am not accustomed to assemblies; it may come in time.'[71]

Napoleon had been taken aback by the ferocity of the deputies' response, but claims of his losing his composure and handing every-thing over to Lucien are exaggerated. Although Lavalette reported that he found Napoleon 'walking with much agitation in an apartment which had no other furniture than two armchairs', saying to Sieyès: 'Now you see what they are doing!' and 'beating the ground with his whip' exclaiming 'This must have an end!', this all relates to the period before he spoke to the Elders on Day Two, not after he spoke to the Five Hundred, and is therefore evidence of his frustration and impatience rather than any lack of nerve.[72] For the period after his escape/expulsion from the Orangery, the conspirators had a contingency plan, which they put into operation once Lucien had also got out. The half-hour was spent waiting for Lucien to emerge, collecting the conspirators, spread-ing the word of Napoleon's manhandling by the deputies, and planning how to persuade the Corps Legislatif guards to support the coup.

It was during this dangerous hiatus that Augereau, who was a mem-ber of the Five Hundred but who had not committed himself either way, came out to Napoleon at the Gallery of Mars to say, somewhat unhelp-fully, 'You're in pretty deep water now,' to which Napoleon replied: 'So what, it was much worse at Arcole.'[73] In Napoleon's later recollection he even threatened Augereau, saying, 'Believe me, keep quiet if you don't want to be a victim. In half an hour you'll see how things turn out.'[74] Whichever response is more accurate, both imply that Napoleon knew he had botched the start of the second phase of the coup, and was in a scrape, but also that he was hardly suffering a catastrophic haemor-rhage of courage.[75] Moreover, both responses imply that he had a plan to reverse the situation.

The next stage was to win over the four-hundred-strong Corps Legis-latif guard under Captain Jean-Marie Ponsard. This was achieved not by Napoleon alone but instead by a piece of pure theatre that one suspects might have been stage-managed, possibly even practised beforehand. It bears an uncanny resemblance to a remark Napoleon had made to the French consul in Genoa, Tilly, just before his arrest in 1794, when he wrote of Augustin Robespierre, 'Had he been my own brother, if he'd aspired to tyranny I'd have stabbed him myself.'[76] Now, five years later, Lucien made precisely the same point when he leaped onto a horse to harangue the guards about how the majority of the Five Hundred were being terrorized by a minority of fanatics in the pay of English gold. He then drew his sword, held its point against Napoleon's breast, and cried: 'I swear that I will stab my own brother to the heart if he ever attempts anything against the liberty of Frenchmen.'[77] It was a promise as disingenuous as it was histrionic, but it worked. (It was also the last time that any of Napoleon's brothers proved anything other than a complete liability to him until the battle of Waterloo itself.)

'Captain,' Napoleon told Ponsard, at least according to one much later account, 'take your company and go right away to disperse this assembly of sedition. They are not the representatives of the nation anymore, but some scoundrels who caused all its misfortunes.' Ponsard asked what to do in case of resistance. 'Use force,' Napoleon replied, 'even the bayonet.' 'That will suffice, *mon général*.'[78] With General Charles Leclerc (who was married to Napoleon's sister Pauline) and Murat (who was engaged to Napoleon's other sister Caroline), Bessières, Major Guillaume Dujardin of the 8th Line and other officers, including Lefebvre and Marmont, denouncing the lawyer-politicians who had supposedly been bought by English gold, Ponsard's soldiers simply cleared out the Orangery, ignoring the deputies' cries of 'Vive la République!' and appeals to the law and the constitution.[79]

'Only half an hour had passed,' Berlier recalled, 'when one of the main doors of the room opening with a great noise, we saw the army, led by Murat, penetrating, bayonets fixed, into the room to evacuate it.' When they entered, the deputies Joseph Blin, Louis Talot and Bigonnet – one source also cites Jourdan – implored them to disobey their officers, but they didn't.[80] Fearing arrest, many deputies then fled, according to legend some of them jumping out of the Orangery's ground floor windows. Lavalette recorded them 'doffing their Roman toga and square cap costumes, the easier to flee incognito'.[81] The grenadiers seem to have viewed their vital role in overthrowing the constitution with perfect equanimity. They put the orders of the officers under whom many of them had served on campaign – and whom all had heard of in the barrack-room as heroes back from Egypt – before those of their elected representatives. When it came down to a choice between obeying these giants of their profession or the politicians baying for their arrest in the Orangery, there was simply no contest. It helped that a former war minister, General Pierre de Beurnonville, was present and supportive: by the end of the month Napoleon had sent him a pair of pistols inscribed 'Day of St-Cloud, 19th Brumaire Year VIII'. Similar presents were also given to Lefebvre and Bessières.[82]

At the end of Day Two and late into the night, Lucien assembled as many deputies in the Orangery as he could find who supported the coup, whose numbers vary according to the sources but seem to have been around fifty, so only 10 per cent of the lower chamber.[83] 'The Directory is no more', they decreed, 'because of the excesses and crimes to which they were constantly inclined.'[84] They appointed Sieyès, Ducos and Napoleon – in that order – as provisional Consuls, pointing out that the first two were former Directors, which offered a sense of constitutional continuity, however spurious. Lucien's rump of the Five Hundred also adjourned both chambers for four months – but as it turned out, for ever – and ordered the expulsion from the legislature of sixty-one mostly neo-Jacobin opponents of the new regime, although only twenty people were exiled.[85] An interim commission of fifty members, twenty-five from each chamber, would draw up a new constitution, which everyone assumed Sieyès had already written.

Was a dagger ever actually pulled on Napoleon in the Orangery, as the supporters of the coup alleged? In the large number of conflicting and highly politically motivated accounts of what happened, it is impossible to say for certain, but it is extremely unlikely, partly because no blood – Napoleon's or anyone else's – was shed that day. Many people carried small knives for everyday use from quill-sharpening to oyster-shucking rather than for self-defence, and the Five Hundred's uniform of a long blue velvet toga-like cape made them easy to conceal. Lucien and Marmont of course told the troops at the time that Napoleon had been attacked with a dagger, and Lavalette named the Corsican anti-Bonapartist deputy Barthélemy Aréna as wielding one, but no-one else seems to have seen it. (Aréna wrote a letter to *Le Journal des Républicains* on 23 Brumaire pointing out that he was at the opposite end of the room, but he fled the country just in case.)[86] An early, anti-Napoleonic four-volume account of the coup, published in 1814, states that when the shouts were of 'Cromwell' and 'Tyrant', 'Fifty deputies moved in around him, pushed him, spoke to him, seemed to push him back; one amongst them pulled a dagger innocently scratching the hand of the grenadier closest to the general, dropped his weapon and lost himself in the crowd.'[87] How one can innocently scratch someone with a dagger under those circumstances wasn't explained, and Grenadier Thomé seems only to have been lightly scratched when his sleeve was torn or ripped, rather than cut.[88]

The first time a dagger was mentioned in the *Moniteur* was on 23 Brumaire, by which time the Bonapartists were fully in charge of the government propaganda machine. No other papers reported one, but the supposed dagger attack nonetheless became an important part of the justification for the clearing of the chamber, and a staple of the prints and engravings that started to appear shortly afterwards. Within a year a print had been published in London entitled *Bonaparte at the Corps Legislatif*, for example, showing Napoleon bravely withstanding a murderous assault from furious, dagger-wielding deputies. 'General Bonaparte,' read his Order of the Day of November 11, 'expresses his particular satisfaction to those brave grenadiers who covered themselves with glory in saving the life of their general when on the point of falling beneath the blows of representatives armed with daggers.'[89] A hero was made of Thomé, who was granted a 600-franc pension for life, given a 2,000 écu diamond ring and a kiss from Josephine at a luncheon three days later.*

The real question perhaps ought to be: why *wasn't* even so much as a penknife pulled in defence of the constitution, if not at Saint-Cloud then at least back in Paris? If either the Directory or the Five Hundred had had any popular support at all there would have been barricades in Paris that night and in other major French cities once the news reached them, but in fact not one was raised nor a shot fired in their defence. The working-class *arrondissements* such as the Faubourg Saint-Antoine had no love for the Directory, and failed to rise. Instead the price of 3 per cent consols on the Stock Exchange rose from Fr. 11.4 the day before the coup to Fr. 20 a week later.[90] Far from Paris there was some localized opposition: the Pas-de-Calais, Jura and Pyrénées Orientales authorities voiced disquiet, but no-one was in a mood for a civil war against the Consulate and Napoleon, and it very soon sputtered out.

The key point about Brumaire, however, is not that the Directory was abolished, since it was clearly failing and likely to fall, but that both houses of the legislature were effectively abolished too, along with the Constitution of Year III. The legislature had not been deeply infected with the Directory's unpopularity; the neo-Jacobins were no great threat, and the nation was in no immediate danger. Yet Sieyès and

---

* The son of the deputy Auguste-Louis Petiet later claimed that Thomé had merely caught his sleeve on a comrade's weapon (Lentz, *18-Brumaire* p. 329, Sciout, *Le Directoire* IV p. 652 n. 1).

Napoleon succeeded in closing down both the Elders and the Five Hundred without any significant popular reaction. After a decade of Revolution, many Frenchmen were desperate for leadership and recognized that the parliamentary process inhibited that, as did a constitution that was next to impossible to amend. They were thus willing to see representative government temporarily suspended in order for Napoleon and his co-conspirators to cut the Gordian knot. Certainly public opinion in Paris was indifferent to whether Napoleon had used force to gain power or not. Army officers prize order, discipline and efficiency, each of which Napoleon considered by then to be more important than liberty, equality and fraternity, and at that moment the French people agreed with him. He was able to present France with a narrative of national success, whereas, as he himself put it, 'These Directors know how to do nothing for the imagination of the nation.'[91] Although his victories were part of Napoleon's attraction, so too were the peace treaties he had delivered to a nation now exhausted by war.

Brumaire was not described as a coup d'état at the time, though of course it was one and the term was very much in the political vernacular (it had been used to describe the Thermidor purge). To contemporaries these were simply *les journées* (the days). For all the melodramatic aspect of the events – Lucien pointing his sword at Napoleon's chest, Thomé getting a diamond ring for a dagger attack which probably never happened, and so on – the neo-Jacobins had proved tougher than expected, and if the Guard of the Corps Legislatif had showed any loyalty to the Five Hundred the conspirators would have faced great danger. The day after the Brumaire coup, in fulfilment of his own prophecy, Napoleon and Josephine did indeed sleep at the Luxembourg Palace, moving into Gohier's apartment on the ground floor, to the right of the main palace on the rue de Vaugirard, only a hundred yards from the prison of Saint-Joseph-des-Carmes where Josephine had come so close to death five years earlier.

PART TWO

Mastery

10

Consul

'If he lasts a year, he'll go far.'

Talleyrand on Napoleon's consulship

'The masses ... should be directed without their being aware of it.'

Napoleon to Fouché, September 1804

At ten o'clock on the dark and rainy morning of Monday, November 11, 1799, Napoleon arrived at the Luxembourg Palace in civilian dress escorted by six dragoons to start the business of the provisional Consulate* in the same room where the Directory had met.[1] Having pulled off a coup the previous day, he was intent on conducting a second as soon as was practicable against his chief co-conspirator. Sieyès had already written two constitutions for France, in 1791 and 1793, and Napoleon did not believe the Revolution would be safeguarded by his third, which was packed with checks and balances to centralized power. He later wrote of Sieyès, 'He was not a man of action: knowing little of men's natures, he did not know how to make them act. His studies having always led him down the path of metaphysics.'[2]

At the first meeting of the three consuls, Ducos said to Napoleon: 'There's no point having a vote for the presidency: it's yours by right.'[3] When Sieyès grimaced, Napoleon proposed a compromise: it would rotate every twenty-four hours, starting alphabetically by surname (that is, with him). He then took the large chair at the centre of the table where the president of the Directory had sat, and that was his chair thereafter. 'Come on,' he chivvied them. 'Swear the oath, we're in a

---

* It was not officially the Consulate until ratified by plebiscite.

hurry.'⁴ As the dynamo of the Consulate, it hardly mattered who formally presided over what was, after all, only a three-man meeting; it was Napoleon who tended to come up with most of the ideas discussed and who also then drove them forward.

The day after the coup the city was already placarded with Napoleon's version of events – 'twenty assassins threw themselves upon me and aimed at my chest' – and his call for national unity. The narrative mentioned neither Sieyès nor Ducos. 'Conservative, protective and liberal ideas have been restored to their rightful place by the dispersal of the agitators,' the posters stated, appealing to Frenchmen who had lost patience with the Directory and didn't think a government run by a successful general could be any worse.⁵

Although Napoleon's propagandists had been up all night printing the posters and plastering them around Paris, Sieyès and his supporters weren't so energetic. When Boulay de la Meurthe, the chairman of an inner committee of seven from the interim commission of fifty that had been appointed to draw up the new constitution, arrived at Sieyès' apartment to receive the new document, all Sieyès had to show him was a bundle of notes. So Boulay and Sieyès sat down to fashion a first draft, which was later worked on by the constitutional expert and ex-Girondin Pierre Daunou.⁶ Roederer soon afterwards warned Napoleon that Sieyès planned to propose that a 'Grand Elector' oversee the work of the other two consuls, one responsible for foreign affairs and the other domestic. In a complex system of separation of powers, 'notables' would control the Senate, and only they could dismiss the Grand Elector.⁷ Sieyès clearly saw himself as this philosopher-king, with Napoleon as his consul for war and Ducos for the interior. This was very different from how Napoleon viewed the situation.⁸

Over the next five weeks, before 'the Constitution of the Year VIII' was read out in public places around Paris to the sound of drumbeats and trumpet fanfares, there followed intense discussion in various unofficial committees and sub-committees formed by the Brumairians, during which Napoleon's faction, led by Lucien and Boulay, brought over Daunou, who thought authority needed to be more concentrated, and comprehensively outmanoeuvred Sieyès and his smaller group of supporters. Cambacérès' timely defection to Napoleon's side helped greatly. Boulay finally made it clear to the interim committee that it was their 'mission' to give Napoleon decisive powers for ten years as First Consul, without any Grand Elector to watch over him but with a Conseil d'État to advise him, which would have the sole authority to initiate legislation.[9] Article 41 of the new constitution stated: 'The First Consul promulgates laws; he names and dismisses at his pleasure members of the Conseil d'État, ministers and ambassadors and other chief foreign agents, officers of the army and navy, the members of local administrations and government commissioners attached to the courts.'[10] He also had treaty-making powers, would live at the Tuileries and would receive 500,000 francs per annum, fifty times an ambassador's salary. It was thus very clear, right from the beginning, where true power lay; the second and third consuls would also live at the Tuileries but they would draw only 150,000 francs per annum for their roles as constitutional figleafs.

The Consulate issued a spate of decrees aimed at making the new regime popular and, in its own phrase, 'completing the Revolution'. Versailles was turned over to wounded soldiers; a vicious anti-émigré law was repealed, with Napoleon going personally to the Temple prison to set hostages free; the police were ordered not to harass returning émigrés or to make them take out forced 'loans'; and the anniversary of the storming of the Bastille and 1 Vendémiaire (the republican New Year's Day) were made public holidays. Pensions would be awarded to the war-wounded as well as to soldiers' widows and orphans and non-juring priests were no longer deported for refusing to take the Constitutional Oath. A full ten days of mourning was ordained for George Washington, who died in December, despite the fact that France and America were still fighting the Quasi-War; in the public eulogies to 'the American Cincinnatus', analogies were drawn between Washington and Napoleon.[11] Nor did Napoleon forget his parting promise to Kléber, ordering the new interior minister, the mathematician and astronomer the Marquis de Laplace, to send 'a troupe of comedians' out to Egypt on the first available boat.[12] 'A newly born government must dazzle and astonish,' he told Bourrienne at this time. 'When it ceases to do that it fails.'[13]

The appointment of a distinguished scientist like Laplace to such a high-profile post made it clear that, just because Napoleon was a soldier and Brumaire had been a military coup, this was emphatically not a military dictatorship. Talleyrand returned as foreign minister and only one soldier joined the government, the new minister of war Alexandre Berthier.[14] 'If I die within three or four years of fever in my bed,' Napoleon told Roederer the following year, 'I will say to the nation to watch out against military government. I will tell it to appoint a civil magistrate.'[15] Fouché predictably became minister of police and Martin Gaudin, a former high official in the treasury who had served every regime since Louis XVI, was appointed finance minister. Gaudin quickly set about reforming the fiendishly complex French tax code and lowering rates. Financial management moved from local authorities to the finance ministry and the whole public accounting system was eventually centralized.[16] Napoleon quickly established a central system for the payment of the army, hitherto done through the departments, a classic example of how he was able to slice through bureaucracy and implement a much-needed reform without delay.

At the final meeting of the constitutional commission on December 13, Napoleon invited Sieyès to propose the names of the three consuls to be presented to the nation as part of the new Constitution of the Year VIII in a plebiscite in February. Having by then accepted a reputed 350,000 francs in cash, an estate outside Versailles and a house in Paris (funded by the state), Sieyès duly proposed Napoleon as First Consul, Cambacérès as Second and the infinitely flexible lawyer and former deputy Charles-François Lebrun, who had supported every party except the Jacobins in his time, as Third. Sieyès was merely allocated the presidency of the Senate and Ducos (who took 100,000 francs for giving up his provisional consulship) its vice-presidency. Napoleon's second coup had taken a little longer than the first, but it was just as bloodless and successful. Although a formal plebiscite, scheduled for February, would be required to confer legal legitimacy on the Consulate, Napoleon himself never doubted that he had the moral right to rule France. As he was to write of Julius Caesar, 'In such a state of affairs these deliberative assemblies could no longer govern; the person of Caesar was therefore the guarantee of the supremacy of Rome in the universe, and of the security of citizens of all parties. His authority was therefore legitimate.'[17] His attitude to the government of France in 1799 was identical.

'Frenchmen!' Napoleon proclaimed on December 15, 'A Constitution is presented to you. It ends the uncertainties . . . [in] the internal and military situation of the Republic . . . The Constitution is founded on the true principles of representative government, on the sacred rights of property, equality and liberty . . . Citizens, the Revolution is established on the principles which began it. It is finished.'[18]

The placing of property rights before those of equality and liberty was indicative of how Napoleon intended to defend the interests of tradesmen, employers, strivers and the owners of the *biens nationaux* – the kind of people who struggled to run small businesses like a mulberry orchard. These were France's backbone; he understood their concerns and needs. Article 94 of the ninety-five-article constitution (less than a quarter the length of the previous one) stated categorically that the property and lands of the monarchy, Church and aristocracy which had been taken and sold during the Revolution would never be returned to their original owners. These were promises Napoleon reiterated in 1802 and 1804, but he did not promise further redistribution. When he spoke of equality, he meant equality before the law and not of economic situation. His strongest natural supporter, the army, did well out of the coup, with better pay and conditions, pensions and the promise of land (though no-one seems to have been given six *arpents*). The law suspending payments to contractors was repealed and they were quickly paid in full.

Late December saw the formal installation of what would become the institutions of Napoleonic rule. On the 22nd the Conseil d'État was inaugurated in its own rooms at the Luxembourg. Consisting largely of apolitical technocrats appointed by the First Consul and very much under his personal control, the Conseil was the main deliberative body of the new government of France, advising the First Consul and helping him to draft laws. Only six of the fifty members were soldiers. So long as they were respectful, members of the Conseil were invited to be as outspoken as they felt was necessary, and Napoleon encouraged debate between them. Under the new constitution the Conseil was both the final court of appeal in administrative law cases and the body responsible for the examination of the wording of bills before they went before the legislature, functions it still retains today. Ministers were *ex officio* members of the Conseil; they attended meetings when the agenda covered their areas of responsibility.

At 8 a.m. on December 25 (Christmas Day was not officially recognized again until 1802) the Constitution of the Year VIII came into force. A speech by Boulay served as a preface to its printed version, which argued that the vast majority of French citizens wanted a republic that was neither 'the despotism of the Ancien Régime nor the tyranny of 1793'.[19] The new constitution, he stated, could be summed up in the dictum: 'Confidence comes from below, power from above.'[20] Under it, the First Consul would hold political and administrative power for ten years and the other two consuls would advise him for that period. A sixty-man Senate, whose members served 'inviolable and for life' and whose numbers would increase by two every year to a maximum of eighty, would choose the consuls, the deputies to the three-hundred-strong Legislative Body and the hundred-man Tribunate from national lists which were produced as the result of four rounds of elections. Most importantly, proclamations made by the majority of the Senate, called *sénatus-consultes*, had the full force of law, although initially they were intended to be passed solely for the purpose of altering the constitution.

The Tribunate would discuss the draft laws that the First Consul and the Conseil had formulated, but couldn't veto; the Legislative Body could vote on the laws, but not discuss them. The Tribunate could discuss legislation that the Consulate sent to it, and tell the Legislative Body what it thought; the Legislative Body would sit for no longer than four months a year to consider their views. Only the Senate could amend the constitution, but none of the three chambers had powers to initiate or amend legislation. By these means, Napoleon ensured the separation of fairly feeble powers among them, keeping the lion's share for himself.

Citizens could vote on the initial selection of Legislative Body deputies, though the final selection would be made by the Senate. All adult male voters in a community would thus choose 10 per cent of their number as 'Notabilities of the Commune', who would then choose 10 per cent of their number as the 'Notabilities of the Departments', who would then choose the five or six thousand 'Notabilities of the Nation' from whom the four hundred members of the Legislative Body and Tribunate would be appointed. As it turned out, there was a good deal of continuity with the earlier chambers. Out 60 senators, 38 had sat in a national assembly before, as had 69 of the 100 tribunes and 240 of the 300 deputies.[21] Their experience was useful as Napoleon went about consolidating, adapting and, in his own description, 'finalizing' the Revolution.[22] The sheer complexity of the constitution, especially the triple-voting system of election to the legislature, suited Napoleon perfectly as it gave him ample opportunity to winnow out opposition.[23]

There was plenty more in the new constitution to calm the nation: authorities could enter a Frenchman's home without invitation only in the case of fire or flood; citizens could be held for no more than ten days without trial; 'harshness used in arrests' would be a crime.[24] On January 1, 1800 (a date with no particular significance in the revolutionary calendar as it was 11 Nivôse Year VIII) the Legislative Body and Tribunate met for the first time.

Just because the freedom of the legislature was circumscribed did not mean that the Napoleonic regime didn't listen. Petitioners always got a hearing, and debates within the departments at the *conseils de préfecture* and *conseils généraux* tended to be reasonably open, though they had little effect on government policy.[25] The regime heard people's complaints well enough; it just didn't provide them with any means of amplifying criticism and there was little possibility of concerted political opposition.

In his first week as First Consul, Napoleon wrote two letters proposing peace to Emperor Francis of Austria and to Britain's King George III. 'I venture to declare that the fate of all civilized nations is concerned in the termination of a war which kindles a conflagration over the whole world,' he told the latter.[26] When the British foreign secretary, Lord Grenville, responded by saying that Napoleon should restore the Bourbons, Napoleon replied that if the same principle were applied to Britain it would result in the restoration of the Stuarts. He made sure that *milord* Grenville's letter received wide publicity in France, and it consolidated support behind the Consulate.[27] The Russians having dropped out of the Second Coalition after their defeat at Masséna's hands at the Second Battle of Zurich in late September 1799, the Austrians entered peace negotiations which went on for months, but without success. By the time the new campaigning season began in the spring they would be ready to try to capture Genoa and invade south-east France.

'I want you all to rally around the mass of the people,' Napoleon wrote of the French political class to a former deputy of the Five Hundred, François Beyts, who had been one of the sixty-one people proscribed during Brumaire. 'The simple title of French citizen is worth far more than that of Royalist, Chouan, Jacobin, Feuillant, or any of those thousand-and-one denominations which have sprung, during these past ten years, from the spirit of faction, and which are hurling the nation into an abyss from which the time has at last come to rescue it, once and for all.'[28] This worked for Beyts, who was appointed prefect of the Loir-et-Cher department the following March. But not all were seduced and Napoleon responded harshly to those who questioned his policy of national unification. When the mayor of Lille expressed reservations about welcoming a former Jacobin general to his city, Napoleon retorted: 'Do not dare to say anything of the kind; do you not see that now we are all equally serving France? I would have you know, sir, that between 17 and 18 Brumaire I have erected a wall of brass which no glance may penetrate, and against which all recollections must be dashed to pieces!'[29] It was the first time since the Revolution that an incoming regime had not comprehensively purged its predecessor, and although opposition figures were indeed removed from the Legislative Body three years later, Frenchmen were no longer guillotined for their political views.

Napoleon's brass-wall policy allowed him to rally a very wide spectrum of opinion to his government, spanning every faction except the neo-Jacobins. Despite having been a Jacobin himself, or perhaps because of it, he recognized that while plenty of ex-Jacobins might rally to his cause, the neo-Jacobin movement itself would always be ideologically opposed to him. The process of national unification regardless of previous political stances was called *ralliement* – literally, winning over – and although some joined the Napoleonic regime out of self-interest, many did it out of genuine patriotism, once they saw how Napoleon was regenerating France.[30] A second, related policy, called *amalgame* – consolidation – sought to encourage active enthusiasm for the regime, as distinct from mere support.[31]

These policies allowed Napoleon to recruit a very talented group of public officials to his government, led by Cambacérès (a regicide), and including the future minister of justice Louis-Mathieu Molé (a royalist whose father had been guillotined), Jean-Étienne Portalis (an anti-Directory moderate) who dealt with religious affairs, and his equally efficient son Joseph-Marie, the scientist and future interior minister Jean Chaptal (a Girondin), the military administrator General Jean-Gérard Lacuée (a moderate), the councillor of state Antoine Thibaudeau (another regicide), Étienne-Denis Pasquier (a moderate whose father had been guillotined) at the prefecture of police, and the treasury minister Nicolas-François Mollien (who had been in Louis XVI's finance ministry). 'The art of appointing men', Napoleon told Mollien, 'is not nearly so difficult as the art of allowing those appointed to attain their full worth.'[32] Despite having overthrown him at Fructidor, Napoleon recognized Carnot's great abilities and appointed him minister of war on April 2, 1800, sending Berthier to command the Army of the Reserve.[33]

Within a week of Brumaire, as a result of the new sense of stability, efficiency and sheer competence, the franc–dollar and franc–pound exchange rates had doubled. By the end of January 1800 100-franc government bonds that had been languishing at 12 francs had soared to 60 francs. Two years later, partly by forcing the tax-collecting authorities to make deposits in advance of estimated yields, the finance minister

Martin Gaudin had balanced the budget for the first time since the American War of Independence.[34]

On taking power, Napoleon had made it clear that the new Constitution of the Year VIII would be legitimized by a nationwide plebiscite of all French citizens, taking place over several days at the end of January and beginning of February 1800. All adult males could vote by signing a register, which was kept open for three days. In order to make certain of a positive outcome Napoleon replaced Laplace as interior minister with his brother Lucien in December. On February 7 Lucien formally announced the results of the plebiscite, asserting that 3,011,007 Frenchmen had voted in favour of the Constitution of the Year VIII and only 1,562 against.[35] It was of course ludicrous to claim that 99.95 per cent of Frenchmen had voted yes, even on the low turnout of 25 per cent – which can in part be blamed on the weather and lack of transportation for a rural population – not least because the Midi and Vendée were still rife with royalism.[36] In Toulon, for example, it was claimed that 830 people had voted in favour and one Jacobin cobbler against.

There are over four hundred bundles of votes in the Archives Nationales which show clear proof of the systematic falsification of the results by Lucien in his own handwriting. On February 4 he ordered the interior ministry to stop counting the votes as he wanted to announce the total three days later. So for the south-west region, the government simply calculated what they thought the result might be from the twenty-five departments that had already been counted, including Corsica.[37] By simply adding an additional 8,000 yes votes to twenty-four departments' totals and 16,000 to that of the Yonne, Lucien extrapolated an extra 200,000 yes votes in the south-west alone. In the south-east he added about 7,000 votes per department and in the north-east between 7,000 and 8,000. He often didn't even bother to falsify using unusual numbers, but simply added round ones, with the goal of getting the yes vote to over 3 million. In total he added around 900,000 yes votes between February 4 and 7.[38] The military vote of 556,021 in favour and precisely nil against was simply invented. Although there were 34,500 naval votes cast, often only a ship's officers would vote but the whole ship's complement would be added on. The true result was probably around 1.55 million yes against several thousand no.[39] Napoleon had therefore won some kind of democratic legitimacy, but by far less than he claimed and indeed less than a plebiscite that Robespierre had won in 1793.[40] Even the figures that Lucien falsified had themselves already been manipulated by local officials, who knew that an important part of their job was to please whoever was in power in Paris. Officials went unscrutinized, voting was open rather than by secret ballot and so liable to intimidation, and half the electorate was illiterate but nevertheless had the right to vote, so the mayors filled in their ballot papers for them.

Lucien's fiddling of the figures provides a perfect insight into one of the most characteristic aspects of the Napoleonic story. Napoleon was always going to win by a huge landslide, yet the Bonapartists simply couldn't resist exaggerating even those numbers, thereby allowing the opposition – neo-Jacobins, royalists, liberals, moderates and others – to argue in their salons and underground cells that the whole process was a fraud. So often, when it came to manipulating battle casualties, or inserting documents into archives, or inventing speeches to the Army of Italy, or changing ages on birth certificates, or painting Napoleon on a rearing horse crossing the Alps, Napoleon and his propagandists simply went one unnecessary step too far, and as a result invited ridicule and criticism of what were genuinely extraordinary achievements.

Of all the Consulate's policies, the one to smash rural brigandage was among the most popular. 'The art of policing is in punishing infrequently and severely,' Napoleon believed, but in his war against the brigands who were terrorizing vast areas of France, he tended to punish both frequently and severely.[41] Brigands could be royalist rebels (especially in western and southern France), groups of deserters or draft-dodgers, outlaws, highwaymen, simple ruffians or a combination of all these. The Ancien Régime, the Committee of Public Safety and the Directory had all fought against endemic lawlessness in the countryside, but the Consulate fought to win with every means at its disposal. Napoleon interned and deported suspected brigands, and used the death penalty against convicted ones, who were often called such unedifying names as 'The Dragon', 'Beat-to-Death' and 'The Little Butcher of Christians', and who raided isolated farmhouses as well as hijacking coaches and robbing travellers.

Although the *gendarmerie* or paramilitary police had been inaugurated in April 1798 with a force of 10,575 men, Napoleon reorganized it, increased its numbers to 16,500, paid it well and on time, improved its morale and stamped out most of the corruption within its ranks.[42] Patrols were increased and were mounted on horseback when before they had been on foot; special tribunals and military commissions guillotined suspects on circumstantial evidence without the right to a defence lawyer; and huge mobile columns were sent out which meted out summary justice. In November 1799, some 40 per cent of France was under martial law, but within three years it was safe to travel around France again, and trade could be resumed. Not even his Italian victories brought Napoleon more popularity.[43]

In March 1800 the Consulate replaced more than 3,000 elected judges, public prosecutors and court presidents with its own appointees. Political opinions don't seem to have been the deciding factor so much as practical expertise, as well as Napoleon's keenness to sack elderly, corrupt or incompetent lawyers. It took seven months for the system to run smoothly again due to the backlogs, but thereafter the delivery of justice was improved.[44]

In his bid to end some of the more symbolic aspects of the Revolution once he had declared it to be over, Napoleon ordered that the red bonnets that had been put on church steeples and public buildings during the Revolution be taken down. *Monsieur* and *Madame* replaced *citoyen* and *citoyenne*, Christmas and Easter returned, and finally, on January 1, 1806, the revolutionary calendar was abolished. Napoleon had always been alive to the power of nomenclature and so he renamed the Place de la Révolution (formerly the Place Louis XV) as the Place de la Concorde, and demolished the giant female statue of Liberty there. 'Concord,' he later wrote, 'that is what renders France invincible.'[45] Other examples of his passion for renaming included rechristening his invention the Cisalpine Republic as the Italian Republic, the Army of England as the Grande Armée (in 1805), and the Place de l'Indivisibilité – the old Place Royale – as the Place des Vosges. Over the Consular period, Napoleon's written style subtly altered, with revolutionary clichés such as *inaltérable* and *incorruptible* being replaced by the more incisive *grand, sévère* and *sage*.[46]

Napoleon next went about persuading the émigrés – aristocrats, property-owners, royalists and priests who had fled during the Revolution – to return to France, on the understanding that they must not expect to get their property back. He eventually restored their voting and citizenship rights.[47] In October 1800 he removed 48,000 émigrés' names from the list of 100,000 proscribed during the Revolution, and in April 1802 all but 1,000 irreconcilable royalists were removed altogether. Although much of the Ancien Régime nobility stayed aloof, several prominent members agreed to serve Napoleon, including men

such as the Comte de Ségur, the Duc de Luynes, the Comte de Narbonne, the Duc de Broglie, Talleyrand and Molé. Other supporters were
from non-émigré families who had been on the brink of ennoblement in
1789, such as Marmont, Rémusat, Berthier and Roederer. By May 1803,
some 90 per cent of all émigrés had returned to France, reversing the
huge drain of talent that had so weakened the country.[48] Of the 281 prefects appointed by Napoleon between 1800 and 1814, as many as
110 (39 per cent) had been Ancien Régime nobles.[49]

As well as appealing to royalists abroad, Napoleon appealed to them
in the Vendée, offering a general amnesty to any Chouans who laid
down their weapons. He told them that the 'unjust laws' and 'arbitrary
acts' of the Directory had 'offended personal security and freedom of
conscience' and offered a 'complete and total amnesty' for all past
events, in return for which the insurgents were asked to hand in their
weapons by February 18, 1800.[50] The priest Étienne-Alexandre Bernier
accepted these terms, although the Chouan leaders Comte Louis de
Frotté, Georges Cadoudal and Comte Louis de Bourmont fought on.
(Bernier became bishop of Orleans, part of what Napoleon called his
'sacred gendarmerie' of loyal bishops.) Napoleon instructed General
d'Hédouville to deal with the rebels robustly: 'If you make war, employ
severity and activity; it is the only means by which you make it shorter,
and consequently less deplorable for humanity.'[51]

By early 1801 Napoleon had succeeded in decapitating the leadership of the Chouan rebellion, literally as well as metaphorically in some
cases. He was criticized for deceit, but guerrilla campaigns have always
invited different rules of engagement. Frotté was executed on February
18, Cadoudal came to breakfast with Napoleon on March 5 but later
went into English exile, and Bourmont eventually changed sides
altogether and fought for France. The Chouans had been fighting
against the Republic in twelve western departments ever since 1793 and
once numbered 30,000 armed rebels, but by the end of 1800 the Vendée
was quiet. The Chouan activities would henceforth be largely confined
to plotting against Napoleon's own life.

On January 17, 1800, Napoleon closed no fewer than sixty of France's
seventy-three newspapers, saying that he wouldn't 'allow the papers to
say or do anything contrary to my interests'.[52] The decree, which wasn't
subjected to parliamentary scrutiny, stated that some 'of the newspapers
which are printed in the departments of the Seine are instruments in the
hands of the enemies of the Republic', and that therefore 'during the

course of the war' only thirteen newspapers could publish, except those 'devoted to the sciences, arts, literature, commerce and advertisements'.[53] It further warned that any newspaper that included articles 'disrespectful' of the social order, of the sovereignty of the people, of the glory of the armies or of friendly governments 'will be suppressed immediately'. Napoleon also blocked the circulation of foreign newspapers within France.[54] He believed that any attempt to foster national unity would be impossible if the royalist and Jacobin newspapers were permitted to foment discontent.

The word 'newspaper' overly dignifies several of the scandal sheets that were alleging, among many other things, that Napoleon was sleeping with his own sister Pauline, but the decree was undoubtedly a powerful blow against free speech in France. 'Controlled by the government, a free press may become a strong ally,' Napoleon said years later, apparently unaware of the contradiction in terms. 'To leave it to its own devices is to sleep beside a powder keg.'[55] On another occasion he declared: 'The printing press is an arsenal; it cannot be private property.'[56] He had learned the power of stage-managed proclamations in Italy and Egypt and was not now prepared to cede control over communications at home. France had no tradition of press freedom before the Revolution. Freedom of speech was declared to be a universal right in 1789, and the number of officially sanctioned journals ballooned from four to over three hundred, but the government started closing journals as early as 1792, and periodic purging on political grounds had brought the number down to seventy-three by 1799.[57] Freedom of the press didn't exist in Prussia, Russia or Austria at the time, and even in 1819 the British government passed the notorious Six Acts, which tightened the definition of sedition, and by which three editors were arraigned. That was in peacetime, whereas France in January 1800 was at war with five countries, each of which had vowed to overthrow its government. Objectionable by modern standards, Napoleon's move was little other than standard practice for his time and circumstances.

After the decree, most journalists stayed in the profession and merely sang a more Bonapartist tune, writing for papers such as the Bertin brothers' *Journal des Débats*, Amélie Suard's *Publiciste* and the *Journal de Paris*. Royalist writers started praising Napoleon, not least for his tough law-and-order stances which they had long advocated. The numbers of papers shrank, but overall readership remained much the same.[58] Napoleon also co-opted a large number of former royalist journalists into his regime, an indication of his growing conservatism. Pierre-Louis

Roederer was appointed to the Conseil, Louis Fontanes to the chancellorship of the Imperial University set up in 1808, Charles de Lacretelle to the Académie Française.

The *Moniteur Universel*, founded in 1789, became in the words of Comte Molé, 'nothing but the docile instrument and depository of all [Napoleon's] desires'.[59] It was a private concern but government officials wrote articles for it and the provincial press relied on it as the government's news-sheet.[60] Its 'Interior' column was written by the interior ministry, and Napoleon's office wrote the 'Paris' column, often from his direct dictation, especially its criticisms of Britain. 'Miscellany' was written by other officials, including some in the police ministry. Though it was a state propaganda news-sheet, full of lies and exaggerations, it was rarely dull, with contributions about poetry, literature, theatre and the Institut de France. Napoleon took a deep personal interest in the strategic dissemination of news. 'Spread the following reports in an official manner,' he once instructed Fouché. 'They are, however, true. Spread them first in the salons, and then put them in the papers.'[61] Overall, as he told his interior minister in 1812, 'My intention is that everything is printed, absolutely everything except obscene material and anything that might disturb the tranquillity of the State. Censorship should pay no attention to anything else.'[62]

Ten days after announcing the results of the plebiscite in February 1800, the Consulate passed a law (by 71 to 25 in the Tribunate and 217 to 68 in the Legislative Body) placing the administration of all eighty-three departments or regions of France, which had been created in 1790 in an effort to devolve power, under prefects who were appointed by the minister of the interior. An essential element of local democracy established by the Revolution was thus completely abolished at a stroke, and brought about a massive concentration of power into Napoleon's hands. Each department now had a centrally appointed prefect, with sub-prefects to look after the *arrondissements* and mayors for *communes*, who were also centrally appointed if they had more than 5,000 inhabitants in their charge. To the original eighty-three departments of 1790, the Consulate added twenty more in 1800, as well as between two and six *arrondissements* within each department. The *département–arrondissement–commune* system is still in place today.

Local self-government, in which after 1790 about one Frenchmen in thirty was a local official of some kind, was thus replaced by one in which initiative and control were vested ultimately in the First Consul.

There were local elected councils, but these functioned in a purely advisory capacity and sat for only two weeks a year. The *juges de paix* (magistrates), who had formerly been elected, were now named by the prefects. Although sub-prefects came from the department itself, the prefects – who lasted on average 4.3 years in office – almost always came from outside, to ensure that their ultimate loyalty was to Napoleon.[63] But despite its authoritarianism, the prefectorial system turned out to be far more efficient than its ungainly predecessor.[64] As First Consul Napoleon made all public officials salaried servants of the state, ensured they were properly trained, and abolished promotion through corruption and nepotism, replacing it with rewards for talent and merit. He insisted that his prefects provide him with systematic statistical data, ordering them to make extensive annual tours of their departments to glean first-hand information.[65] He would later describe them as *empereurs au petit pied* (mini-emperors). Boniface de Castellane-Novejean, prefect of the Basses-Pyrénées, summed up the prefect's task as to 'make sure that the taxes are paid, that the conscription is enacted, and that law and order is preserved'. In fact he also had to impound horses for the cavalry, billet troops, guard prisoners-of-war, stimulate economic development, deliver political support for the government at plebiscites and elections, fight brigands and represent the views of the department, especially its elites, to the government.[66] Only in areas in which Napoleon wasn't interested, such as the relief of the poor and primary education, was much power left with the departments.[67]

With renewed fighting against Austria and her allies – though not now Russia – looming as soon as weather permitted, Napoleon needed to replenish the near-empty Treasury. He instructed Gaudin to borrow at least 12 million francs from the fifteen or so richest bankers in Paris. The best they would offer was 3 million francs, helpfully suggesting that a national lottery be established to raise the rest. Unimpressed, on January 27, 1800 Napoleon simply arrested Gabriel Ouvrard, the most powerful banker in France and the owner of the vast navy supply contract from which he was rumoured to have made a profit of 8 million francs over the previous four years.[68] (It cannot have helped Ouvrard that he had refused to help finance the Brumaire coup.) Ouvrard's experience helped loosen the purse-strings of other bankers, but Napoleon wanted to place France's finances on a far surer footing. He could not continue, in effect, to need bankers' and contractors' permission before he could mobilize the army.

On February 13, Gaudin opened the doors of the Banque de France, with the First Consul as its first shareholder. Not wanting to solicit the instinctively cautious and unco-operative Parisian banking establishment for its creation, he had turned to a Rouen manufacturer, Jean-Barthélémy le Couteulx de Canteleu, and a Swiss banker, Jean Perregaux, for initial funding and guidance. They were two of the six regents who initially governed the bank. To encourage people to subscribe to the Banque de France's start-up capital of 30 million francs, in share blocks of 1,000 francs, Napoleon decreed that it had the protection of the Consulate and ensured that his entourage, including Joseph, Hortense, Bourrienne, Clarke, Duroc and Murat all joined the subscription list.[69] The bank would theoretically be independent of the government, indeed the *Moniteur* had to state before its official launch that it 'had been wrongly compared to the Bank of England, as none of its capital went to the Government', but in time this policy was quietly dropped, and the bank did indeed help finance Napoleon's wars.

In April 1803 the bank was granted the exclusive right to issue paper money in Paris for fifteen years, notes which in 1808 became French legal tender, supported by the state rather than just the bank's collateral. In time the confidence that Napoleon's support gave the bank in the financial world allowed it to double the amount of cash in circulation, discount private notes and loans, open regional branches, increase revenues and the shareholder base, lend more, and in short create a classic virtuous business circle. It was also given important government business, such as managing all state annuities and pensions. Napoleon kept a tight control over so important an institution; in April 1806 he replaced the regents with a governor and two deputy governors appointed by himself. He never quite escaped the situation whereby the Treasury had to borrow from other banks, but it did alleviate the need to arrest their owners.

On February 19, 1800, Napoleon left the Luxembourg Palace and took up residence at the Tuileries. He was the first ruler to live there since Louis XVI had been taken away to the Temple prison in August 1792, an event he had witnessed as a young officer. Although Cambacérès had the right to live in the Tuileries on becoming Second Consul he shrewdly decided not to, noting that he would only have to leave it soon – that is, once Napoleon had won the plebiscite and wanted the palace to himself.

When the Bonapartes moved in, Napoleon took Louis XVI's first-floor rooms overlooking the gardens laid out by Catherine de Médici, and Josephine took Marie Antoinette's suite on the ground floor. 'I can feel the Queen's ghost, asking what I am doing in her bed,' she is credited with having told a chamberlain. Napoleon appears to have had no such scruples, allegedly picking Josephine up and carrying her into their bedroom with the words 'Come on, little Creole, get into the bed of your masters.'[70] They put the Tuileries to good use, throwing dinners for two hundred people every ten days. Bronzes and tapestries were brought out of storage from Versailles, and a drawing room was decorated in yellow and lilac silk. From this period can be dated Josephine's central role in the creation of what became the Empire style, which influenced furniture, fashion, interior decoration and design. She also championed the revival of etiquette after a decade of revolution.

Soon after his arrival at the Tuileries, Napoleon collected twenty-two statues of his heroes for the grand gallery, starting, inevitably, with Alexander and Julius Caesar but also featuring Hannibal, Scipio, Cicero, Cato, Frederick the Great, George Washington, Mirabeau and the revolutionary general the Marquis de Dampierre. The Duke of Marlborough, renowned for his victory at the battle of Bleinheim, was included, as was General Dugommier, whose presence alongside such genuine military giants as Gustavus Adolphus and Marshal Saxe must have been based on his perspicacity in spotting Napoleon's worth at Toulon. Joubert was there too, since he was now safely dead. Surrounded by these heroes, about half of whom were in togas, had its effect: it was in Jean-Auguste Ingres' painting of him as First Consul that Napoleon is first seen with his hand tucked inside his waistcoat.[71]

When the well-born Englishwoman Mary Berry was shown around the Bonapartes' living quarters by Josephine's Swiss tailor, Sandos, she recorded that 'Republican simplicity might well be excused for being startled at such magnificence. I have formerly seen Versailles, and I have seen the Petit Trianon, but I never saw anything surpassing the magnificence of this.' She described the salon as being 'hung and furnished with blue-lilac lustring embroidered in the honeysuckle [pattern] with *maron*, in the best taste possible'. The second salon, 'furnished with yellow satin and brown and *sang-de-boeuf* fringes', was even more magnificent, she enthused, especially as 'the glasses [that is, mirrors] were all *drapés* and not framed'; she went on to describe in loving detail the Sèvres vases, porphyry tables, ormolu mounts, chandeliers, chairs, 'exquisite tapestry', candelabra and so on. She was astounded to enter the Bonapartes' bedchamber, with its blue silk upholstery with white and gold fringes, and find that 'they actually both sleep in one bed'.[72]

It was characteristic of Napoleon that he wanted value for money in all this. Concerned that the upholsterers were cheating him he asked a minister how much the ivory handle at the end of a bell-rope should cost. The minister had no idea, whereupon Napoleon cut it off, called for a valet, told him to dress in ordinary clothes and inquire the price in several shops and order a dozen. When he discovered they were one-third cheaper than billed he simply struck one-third off the charges made by all the tradesmen.[73]

'It was part of the First Consul's policy', recalled Laure d'Abrantès, 'to make Paris the centre of pleasure it had been before the Revolution.'[74] This was in part to revive the luxury trades – dressmakers, carriage-makers, silversmiths, etc. – at which the French had traditionally excelled; but Napoleon also felt that a revived social life would reflect the solidity of the new regime. A significant part of the pre-revolutionary French economy, especially in areas like Lyons, the centre of the European silk industry, had been dependent on luxury goods, and Napoleon was determined to revive it. As First Consul he habitually wore a red, gold-embroidered taffeta coat known as the *habit rouge*, which Josephine and the prominent silk mercer M. Levacher had persuaded him to adopt. 'I will not deny that I have some repugnance to equip myself in this fantastic costume,' he told d'Abrantès, 'but for that reason my resolution will be better appreciated.'[75] It attracted the attention of illustrators, one of whom entitled his drawing *Buonaparte Premier Consul de la République Française dans son grand costume*.[76] The Consular Guard was also given new uniforms: shoes replaced clogs; grenadiers wore bearskins and royal-blue uniforms with white facings and red epaulettes.[77]

With exquisitely bad timing, the very day after Napoleon moved into the Tuileries, Louis XVI's younger brother, the Comte de Provence, who had styled himself King Louis XVIII after the death of his nephew in 1795, wrote to Napoleon from exile at the Jelgava Palace in Courland (present-day Latvia) with a request to be allowed to return to France. Louis suggested that Napoleon could take any post in the kingdom if he would only restore him to the French throne. Napoleon took more than six months to reply. 'Thank you for the honest things you wrote in it,' he finally wrote, in terms more sympathetic than one might have expected of a former Jacobin, but his message was clear and unflinching: 'You must not wish for your return to France; you would have to march over a hundred thousand corpses. Sacrifice your interest to the peace and happiness of France. History will recognize it. I am not insensitive to the misfortunes of your family . . . I will gladly contribute to the sweetness and tranquillity of your retirement.'[78] Napoleon informed Roederer and Maret of Louis' letter: 'The letter is very beautiful, very beautiful indeed!' he wrote. 'But I have my answer in consequence, and it is also very fine.'[79] When Josephine teasingly told Napoleon that her royalist friends promised if he restored the Bourbons they would erect a statue in the Place du Carrousel in which he would be represented as a genius placing the crown upon the king's head, Napoleon joked: 'Yes, and my body will be under the pedestal!'[80] But the Bourbons would not so easily accept a life of exile. The finality of Napoleon's reply to Louis meant that from the autumn of 1800 onwards they started plotting against his life.

In less than fifteen weeks Napoleon had effectively ended the French Revolution, seen off the Abbé Sieyès, given France a new constitution, established her finances on a sound footing, muzzled the opposition press, started to end both rural brigandage and the long-running war in the Vendée, set up a Senate, Tribunate, Legislative Body and Conseil d'État, appointed a talented government regardless of past political affiliations, rebuffed the Bourbons, made spurned peace offers to Britain and Austria, won a plebiscite by a landslide (even accounting for the fraud), reorganized French local government and inaugurated the Banque de France.

'Today I'm a sort of mannequin figure that's lost its liberty and happiness,' Napoleon wrote to Moreau, the commander-in-chief of the Army of the Rhine, on March 16 as France prepared to re-engage Austrian forces. 'Grandeur is all very well, but only in retrospect and in the imagination. I envy your happy lot; you are going to accomplish grand things with your gallant men. I would willingly exchange my consular purple for the epaulette of a brigadier under your orders . . . I strongly hope that the circumstances may allow me to come and give you a helping hand.'[81] Three weeks later circumstances would allow just that, when the Austrian General Michael von Melas defeated General Nicolas Soult at the battle of Cadibona, pushing him back towards Savona and forcing Masséna into Genoa, which was subsequently besieged. It was time to return to the battlefield.

11

Marengo

'We are struggling against ice, snow, storms and avalanches. The
St Bernard Pass, astonished to see so many persons crossing it,
throws obstacles in our way.'
Napoleon to the Second and Third Consuls, May 18, 1800

'Caesar was right to cite his good fortune and to appear to
believe in it. That is a means of acting on the imagination of
others without offending anyone's self-love.'
Napoleon, *Caesar's Wars*

Napoleon began to prepare for a renewed outbreak of fighting against
Austria from the moment he became First Consul, sending Berthier,
soon to be his chief-of-staff again, twenty-eight memoranda on the subject over the next six weeks. On January 7, 1800 he ordered the covert
formation of a 30,000-strong Army of the Reserve based at Dijon.
Many of its soldiers were veterans who knew the hardships of war,
others were brought in from demi-brigades on garrison duty in the
provinces. Some were transferred from the Vendée, but there was also a
large number of conscripts who would learn how to load and fire their
muskets only after the campaign had begun. The 'canteen' system,
whereby groups of eight veterans and eight recruits would march, eat
and bivouac together under the command of a corporal, allowed the
recruits to learn soldiering fast.

'You will keep thoroughly secret the formation of the said army,'
Napoleon ordered Berthier on January 25, 'even among your office
staff, from whom you will ask nothing beyond the absolutely necessary
information.'[1] The thoroughness of this secrecy may be inferred from
the fact that even General Moreau assumed the force being assembled

really was a reserve, rather than an army that Napoleon was going to lead over the Italian Alps to attack the exposed right flank of the septuagenarian Austrian General Michael von Melas. (Napoleon was being kept abreast of Austrian movements by French detachments in Italy, particularly those stationed in Genoa.) Despite his age von Melas was a formidable opponent, a senior lieutenant of the great Russian commander Marshal Alexander Suvorov, who never lost a battle but who had died in St Petersburg on May 18.

Napoleon would have to choose by which pass to cross the Alps into northern Italy. He would have preferred the easternmost ones – Splügen or St Gothard – so that he could carry out his favoured *manoeuvre sur le derrière*, but the speed of the Austrians' westward advance through northern Italy towards southern France forced him to choose between the 8,100-foot Great St Bernard or the 7,100-foot Little St Bernard. The Little St Bernard was too far west, so Napoleon sent only one division there and decided on the Great St Bernard for the main body of the army. He also sent one division under General Adrien Moncey over the St Gothard Pass.

He was counting on an element of surprise: no one had taken an army over the Alps since Charlemagne, and before him Hannibal. Although Napoleon wouldn't be travelling with elephants, he did have Gribeauval 8-pounder and 4-pounder cannon, whose barrels weighed over a quarter of a ton, to heave over the mountain range. Snow was still thick on the ground in early May, when the advance began, so Marmont devised sledges for the barrels made out of hollowed-out tree-trunks, which one hundred men at a time hauled up the Alps and then down again, to drumbeats. (Since the Italian side is much steeper than the French, they found it harder going down than up.) Money and supplies were sent ahead to the monasteries and hostelries along the route, and local guides were hired and sworn to secrecy. Napoleon, Berthier and, after April 2, Carnot – who had been appointed minister of war when Napoleon despatched Berthier to the Army of the Reserve – together organized every facet of an operation that was to become one of the wonders of military history. 'An army can pass always, and at all seasons,' Napoleon told a sceptical General Dumas, 'wherever two men can set their feet'.[2]

On March 17 Napoleon held a consuls' meeting, which he did most days at this time, a Conseil d'État, which he did every couple of days, and then a military strategy session with his chief cartographer, General Bacler de l'Albe, kneeling on huge large-scale maps of Piedmont spread out on the floor and covered in red and black wax-tipped pins to show the positions of the armies. (Sometimes, when crawling around the floor together on the maps, Napoleon and de l'Albe would bump heads.) In the strategy meeting he allegedly asked Bourrienne where he thought the decisive battle would be fought. 'How the devil should I know?' answered his Brienne-educated private secretary. 'Why, look here, you fool,' said Napoleon, pointing to the plains of the River Scrivia at San Giuliano Vecchio, explaining how he thought Melas would manoeuvre once the French had crossed the Alps.[3] It was precisely there that the battle of Marengo was fought three months later.

On April 19 the 24,000 men under the Austrian General Karl von Ott laid siege to Masséna's 12,000 men inside Genoa. There was little food to be had in the city, which the Royal Navy was blockading. Lieutenant Marbot recalled that over the following weeks they had to live on a 'bread' that was 'a horrible compound of bad flour, sawdust, starch, hair powder, oatmeal, linseed, rancid nuts, and other nasty substances, to which a modicum of solidity was given by a little cocoa'.[4] General Thiébault likened it to peat mixed with oil. Grass, nettles and leaves were boiled with salt, all the dogs and cats were eaten, and 'rats fetched a high price'. Civilians and soldiers started to die in their thousands of starvation and the diseases associated with malnutrition. Whenever more than four Genoans were gathered together, French troops had orders to fire on them for fear they might surrender the port.

Napoleon was itching to act, writing to Berthier on April 25, 'The day when, either because of events in Italy or because of those on the Rhine, you think my presence will be necessary I will leave an hour after receiving your letter.'[5] In order to calm speculation and deal with the wider logistical problems of the coming campaign, Napoleon stayed at Malmaison and in Paris, reviewing his worst-equipped troops in full view of the populace (and Austrian spies) and going to the opera on the night of Monday, May 5. The whole balance of the war seemed to be tipped towards the German theatre, where Moreau had far larger forces and was doing well, crossing the Rhine on April 25 to Napoleon's effusive and almost deferential private congratulations. To those unversed in the realities of power-politics, it might even have seemed that Napoleon was the Grand Elector and Moreau his consul for war.

Then Napoleon struck. Leaving Paris at 2 a.m. only a few hours after the end of the opera, he was in Dijon the next morning, and by 3 a.m. on May 9 he was in Geneva. Once there he made himself conspicuous at parades and reviews, and gave out that he was going to Basle, despite the fact that the vanguard of General François Watrin's division was already starting to ascend the Great St Bernard Pass, soon followed by the forces under Lannes, Victor and General Philibert Duhesme. Napoleon kept Bessières' Consular Guard and Murat's cavalry back with him.[6] (Duhesme, who owned a vineyard, sent Napoleon some wine, receiving the reply: 'We'll drink it in honour of the first victory you win.'[7])

It had been a hard winter and the track – there was no road over the St Bernard until 1905 – was icy and banked high with snow, yet Napoleon was extremely lucky with the weather, which was much worse both before the army started crossing the Alps on May 14 and after it had finished eleven days later (half the time it took Hannibal). Only one cannon out of forty was lost to avalanche. 'Since Charlemagne, it has never seen such a large army,' Napoleon told Talleyrand on the 18th, 'it wanted above all to block the passage of our large campaign equipment, but finally, half our artillery is in Aosta.'[8] Napoleon didn't lead his army over the Alps, but he followed it once the most important logistical issues – food, ammunition and mules – had been dealt with.[9] He kept a constant pressure on the *ordonnateurs*, with warnings such as 'We risk dying in the valley of Aosta, where there is only hay and wine.'[10] He himself crossed the most difficult part, at Saint-Pierre, on May 20, by which time Watrin and Lannes were 40 miles inside Piedmont.

In all 51,400 men crossed the Alps, with 10,000 horses and 750 mules. They went by single file in some places, and had to start at dawn every day to reduce the risk of avalanches once the sun had risen.[11] When they reached the formidable Fort Bard at the entrance to the Aosta valley, which commands a narrow gorge high above the Dora Baltea river, four hundred Hungarians under Captain Joseph Bernkopf held out for twelve days, blocking the advance of almost all of Napoleon's heavy traffic – the guns, thirty-six caissons and one hundred other vehicles – which therefore fell far behind, severely disrupting the campaign. Some wagons managed to get past at night, with dung and straw strewn in the path of the covered wheels to deaden the noise, but it was not until the walls of the fort were breached in several places and it fell on June 2, at the cost of half of Bernkopf's forces, that the rest were able to follow. The delay at Fort Bard meant that Napoleon went forward desperately short of artillery and ammunition, and had to scour Lombardy and Tuscany to requisition whatever he could.

Managing expectations was a vital part of Napoleon's statecraft, and he knew better than to allow his countrymen's to be stoked up after his

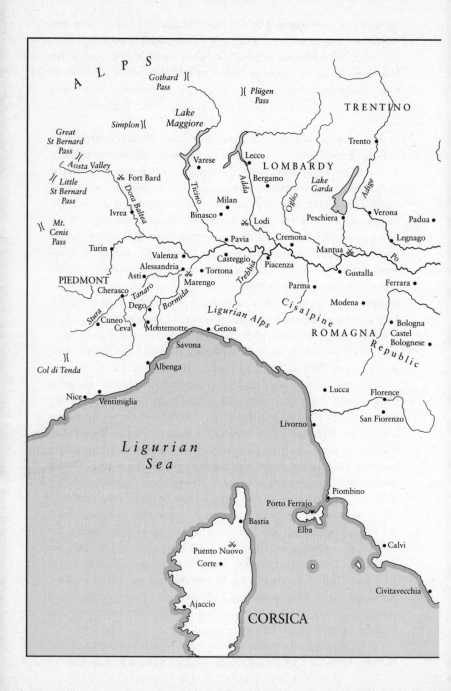

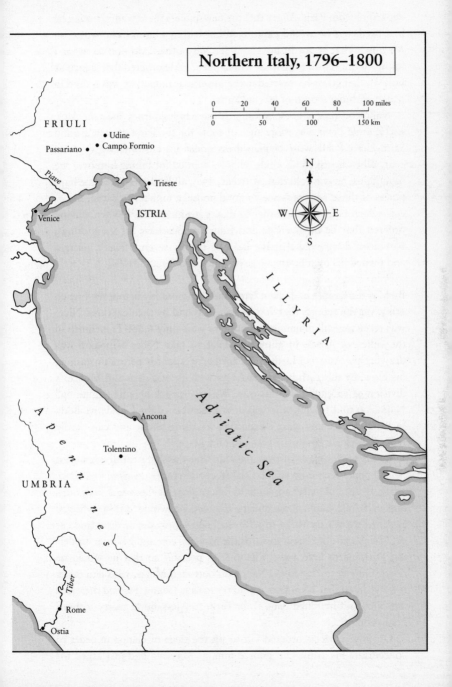

Northern Italy, 1796–1800

| 0 | 20 | 40 | 60 | 80 | 100 miles |
| 0 | | 50 | | 100 | 150 km |

FRIULI

• Udine

Passariano • • Campo Formio

Piave

• Trieste

• Venice

ISTRIA

N

W — E

S

ILLYRIA

Adriatic Sea

• Ancona

Apennines

• Tolentino

UMBRIA

Tiber

• Rome

Ostia

departure from Paris. Angry that the newspapers there were claiming he had predicted he would capture Milan within a month, he wrote on May 19, 'That is not in my character. Very often I do *not* say what I know: but never do I say what will happen.'[12] He ordered that 'a jocular note' to that effect be inserted in the *Moniteur*. In fact, he was indeed in Milan within a month of leaving Paris.

Napoleon rode a horse for almost the whole journey over the Alps, and a mule (as it was more sure of foot) for the iciest stretch around Saint-Pierre.[13] He wore civilian dress under his customary grey overcoat. When he asked his guide what he wanted for taking him over the mountains, he was told that, at twenty-two, all he desired was 'the happiness of those who possessed a good house, a number of cattle, sheep, etc.' which he needed in order to marry his girlfriend.[14] When, having ordered that he be given 60,000 francs to purchase all those things, Napoleon discovered that the lad was twenty-seven, already married and owned his own house, he gave him 1,200 francs instead.[15]

By May 22 Lannes had taken Ivrea and Piedmont lay before the French army, yet the reports that von Melas (who had by then captured Nice) was receiving still maintained that there were only 6,000 Frenchmen in the valley of Aosta. In allowing Melas to take Nice, Napoleon was drawing the Austrian further and further westwards before unleashing his blow. By the 24th he was at Aosta with 33,000 men and Moncey's division of 12,500 was on its way. 'We have struck here like lightning,' Napoleon told Joseph, who was now a member of the Legislative Body in Paris, 'the enemy wasn't expecting anything like it and can hardly believe it. Great events are going to take place.'[16]

It was at this stage of the campaign that the sheer ruthlessness that helped make Napoleon so formidable a commander revealed itself once again. Instead of marching south to relieve starving Genoa, as his troops and even his senior commanders assumed he would do, he wheeled eastwards towards Milan to seize the huge supply depot there and cut off Melas's line of retreat towards the Mincio river and Mantua. Ordering Masséna to hold out for as long as possible so that he would tie down Ott's besieging force, Napoleon outfoxed Melas, who had taken it for granted that Napoleon would try to save Genoa. He had therefore left Nice and marched back from Turin to Alessandria to try to head Napoleon off.

On June 2 Melas ordered Ott to lift the siege of Genoa in order to concentrate his army. Ott ignored him, as Masséna had just asked for terms of surrender. At 6.30 p.m. that same day Napoleon entered Milan by the Verceil Gate in the pouring rain and installed himself at the arch-ducal palace, staying up until 2 a.m. dictating letters, receiving Francesco Melzi d'Eril, who had run the Cisalpine Republic, setting up a new city government and releasing political prisoners interned by the Austrians, who had used Milan as their regional headquarters. He also read Mel-as's captured despatches from Vienna, which told him the enemy's strengths, dispositions and state of morale. Moncey joined Napoleon in Milan with his division, but with few guns and little ammunition. Mean-while Lannes entered Pavia, and although the thirty guns he captured there had been spiked, he managed to get five working again. To Napo-leon's amusement a letter was intercepted from Melas to his mistress in Pavia telling her not to worry, as a French army could not possibly appear in Lombardy.[17] On both May 11 and 16 Napoleon wrote to Josephine, asking her about 'the little cousin' and sending her news of her son Eugène. On the 29th he wrote again, saying: 'I hope to be in the arms of my Josephine in ten days, who is always good when she doesn't cry and isn't coquettish.'[18]

Genoa surrendered on June 4, by which time around 30,000 of its 160,000 inhabitants had died of starvation and of diseases associated with malnutrition, as had 4,000 French soldiers. Another 4,000 soldiers who were fit enough to march out were allowed to return to France with the honours of war, and a further 4,000 sick and wounded were transported to France in Royal Navy ships under Admiral Lord Keith, who had blockaded the port but saw the advantage of evacuating so many French away from the theatre of war.[19] Masséna's health was broken, not least because he had insisted on only eating what his troops did. He never wholly forgave Napoleon for not rescuing him. Equally, Napoleon – who was never besieged in the whole of his career – criticized Masséna for not having held out for ten days longer, recalling when in exile on St Helena, 'A few old men and some women might have died of hunger, but then he would not have surrendered Genoa. If one thinks always of humanity – only of humanity – one should give up going to war. I don't know how war is to be conducted on the rosewater plan.'[20] He even castigated Masséna in his memoirs, contrasting his actions with those of the Gauls under Vercingetorix when besieged by Caesar at Alesia. If Masséna had indeed managed to hold out another ten days, Ott might not have arrived in time at the battlefield of Marengo.

Napoleon was playing for far larger stakes than one city; he wanted to kill or capture every Austrian west of Milan.[21] It was Genoa's resistance that allowed him to get behind Melas, who then had to abandon his plans of taking Toulon in conjunction with Admiral Keith and somehow get back east to re-establish his severed lines of communication. Piacenza and Valenza were now the last major crossing-points over the Po that were not in French hands, so Melas despatched several columns towards both cities.

In Milan, Napoleon questioned spies such as the double (or possibly triple) agent Francesco Toli as to Austrian dispositions. On June 4 he attended La Scala, where he received a huge ovation, and that night he slept with its star singer, the beautiful twenty-seven-year-old Giuseppina Grassini, with whom Berthier found him breakfasting the next morning.[22] 'I don't invite you to come here,' Napoleon told Josephine coolly in his next letter. 'I shall be on my way back in a month. I hope that I shall find you very well.'[23] Later on that day, presumably after Signorina Grassini had left, two hundred Catholic priests arrived at the palace to discuss theology. Napoleon asked them to allow him to 'acquaint you with the sentiments which animate me towards the Catholic, Apostolic and Roman religion'.[24] He made no reference to the view he had expressed to the Cairo *diwan* less than a year before, that 'There is no other God but God; Mohammed is his prophet,' but instead explained that Catholicism 'is particularly favourable to republican institutions. I am myself a philosopher, and I know that, in no matter what society, no man is considered just and virtuous who does not know whence he came and whither he is going. Simple reason cannot guide him in this matter; without religion one walks continually in darkness.'[25] Faith, for Napoleon, was an evolving concept, even a strategic one. When he said he adopted the faith of wherever he was fighting at the time he was quite serious, and in northern Italy that meant Roman Catholicism.

Melas had three routes to safety: via Piacenza and along the southern bank of the Po, towards Genoa and evacuation by sea courtesy of the Royal Navy, or crossing the Ticino river at Pavia. Returning to the field on June 9, Napoleon attempted to block all three, but in doing so he had to violate his own first principle of warfare: concentration of force. That day Lannes defeated Ott between Montebello and Casteggio, forcing the Austrians to withdraw westwards over the Scrivia to Alessandria, where he joined Melas. 'Without exaggerating,' Napoleon told State Councillor Claude Petiet the next day, 'the enemy had 1,500 killed, one can imagine twice as many wounded.' Of course he was exaggerating, as usual; 659 had been killed and 1,445 wounded.[26]

Over the next three days, Napoleon waited at Stradella to see what Melas intended. The night of June 11 he spent talking with Desaix, who had arrived from Egypt just in time for the coming clash, albeit without his men, having taken advantage of a brief armistice with the British signed by Sir Sidney Smith but not ratified by the British government. The previous month Napoleon had written to Desaix that theirs was 'a friendship that my heart, which today is very old and knows men too profoundly, has for no other'.[27] He immediately gave Desaix a corps made up of Monnier's and Boudet's divisions.

At 10 a.m. on the 13th Napoleon rode to San Giuliano Vecchio. Before him were the fields adjoining the village of Marengo, about 2½ miles east of Alessandria near the confluence of the Tanaro and Bormida rivers. Three roads converge at Marengo, beyond which a bridge crosses the Bormida for Alessandria; a double bend in the Bormida created a natural bridgehead position. The villages of Castel Ceriolo, Marengo and Spinetta line the Bormida, and 4 miles to the east is San Giuliano. The ground between the Bormida and Marengo was broken by vineyards, cottages, farms and some marshland, but beyond it the plain was so broad and flat that the military historian Colonel Henri de Jomini, who, years later, was attached to Napoleon's staff, described it as one of the few places in that part of Italy where masses of cavalry could charge at full speed. (The fields are much more cultivated today, but in 1800 the taller crops could still obscure vision.) In the pouring rain of June 13, the small numbers of French cavalry (generally put at 3,600) failed properly to scout the 140-square-mile plain and merely accompanied the infantry marching towards Tortona. It was to prove a costly error.

An hour after arriving at San Giuliano, Napoleon was informed that Melas was preparing to march to Genoa. It looked as if he had entirely abandoned the plain and was covering his retreat by holding Marengo. Napoleon left Lapoype's division north of the Po with the task of seizing the crossing-point at Valenza, and allowed Desaix to take Boudet's division and march for Novi, to head off Melas. Victor, commanding a corps in the vanguard, was ordered to take Marengo: at 5 p.m. General Gaspard Gardanne engaged some 3,000 Austrians there. As General Achille de Dampierre closed in from the south, Gardanne charged into the village. A heavy downpour of rain slowed the action for a while, filling up the streams and rivers before the French took the village, two guns and about a hundred prisoners. Though the Austrians halted the French pursuit by 7 p.m. with vigorous cannonading from the other

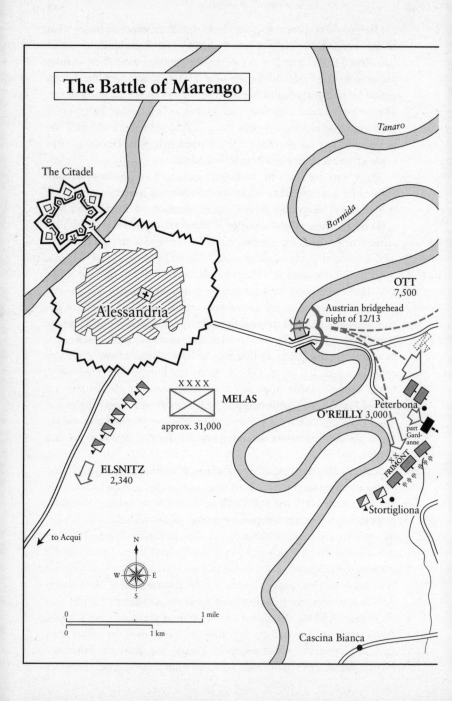

The Battle of Marengo

The Citadel

Tanaro

Bormida

Alessandria

OTT
7,500

Austrian bridgehead
night of 12/13

XXXX
MELAS
approx. 31,000

O'REILLY 3,000

Peterbona

part
Gard-
anne

ELSNITZ
2,340

FRIMONT

Stortigliona

to Acqui

N
W E
S

0   1 mile
0   1 km

Cascina Bianca

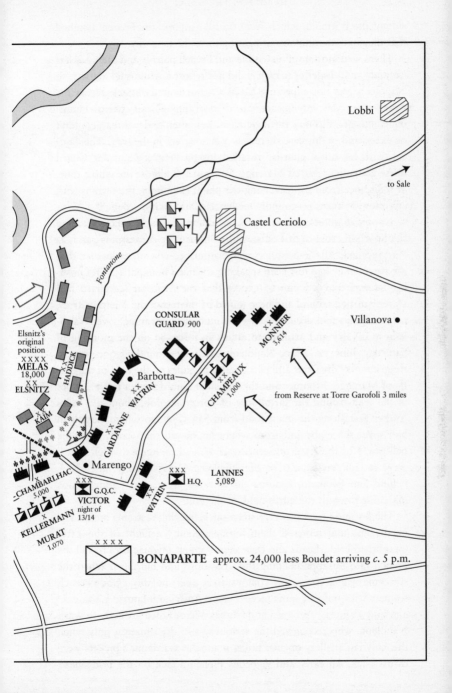

Lobbi

to Sale

Castel Ceriolo

Fontanone

Villanova •

CONSULAR
GUARD 900

MONNIER
3,614

Elsnitz's
original
position
XXXX
MELAS
18,000
XX
ELSNITZ

HADDICK

Barbotta

CHAMPEAUX
1,000

from Reserve at Torre Garofoli 3 miles

KAIM

GARDANNE WATRIN

CHAMBARLHAC
5,000

Marengo

LANNES
5,089

XXX
H.Q.

XXX
VICTOR
night of
13/14

G.Q.C.

WATRIN

KELLERMANN

MURAT
1,070

XXXX
BONAPARTE approx. 24,000 less Boudet arriving c. 5 p.m.

side of the Bormida, which went on till 10 p.m., the French assumed that they had no intention of fighting there the next day.

There were no campfires visible and French patrols and their *piquets* (infantry) and *vedettes* (cavalry) did not report any unusual activity, so Napoleon was not expecting Melas's major counter-attack across the river the next day. Intelligence was often scrappy. Cavalry patrols counting troops at a distance through telescopes, often under threat, couldn't be exact, and in this case there was a major river in the way. 'The Consul, with his horse guards,' recalled Joseph Petit, a Consular Guard horse-grenadier, 'skirted Marengo. We saw him almost the whole time, at a distance from us, traversing the plain, examining the terrain with attention, by turns profoundly meditating, and giving orders.'[28]

Napoleon questioned deserters, including an émigré officer wearing the Bourbon cross of St Louis, 'with considerable earnestness', and, as Petit recalled, 'All the prisoners were astonished when they learned that the person they had just been speaking with was Bonaparte.'[29] Yet nothing he was told led him to expect that the Austrian rearguard had secretly turned around and been joined by the rest of the Austrian army, or that Melas had decided to use his numerical advantage over Napoleon in cavalry and artillery to attack in force. So on the morning of Saturday, June 14, 1800, Napoleon had only around 15,000 men in three infantry divisions and two cavalry brigades on the field of the battle of Marengo. Monnier and the Consular Guard were a full 7½ miles in the rear around the farmhouse of Torre Garofoli, about 2½ miles further east along the main road from San Giuliano where Napoleon had spent the night and from where he viewed the terrain from the bell-tower of the sixteenth-century church of St Agnes (which is still there today). Victor was in Marengo, but Desaix was 5 miles back behind San Giuliano, heading off towards Novi, and Lapoype was marching towards the north bank of the Po.[30]

The Bormida river has very steep sides, but the Austrians built floating bridges and tethered them into place on the night of the 13th, established bridgeheads and then slept without bivouac fires to lull the French into misapprehending their positions and numbers. When the sun came up at 4.30 a.m. on what was to be a very hot day, 15,000 French soldiers with only 15 guns faced 23,900 Austrian infantry, 5,200 cavalry and 92 guns.[31] Yet even at daybreak Victor failed properly to warn Napoleon, who recognized the seriousness of the situation only when the Austrian artillery opened fire at 9 a.m., as Gardanne's pickets were thrust back. An early and vigorous French attack on the bridgehead might have halted the Austrian debouchment, but by 9 a.m. that was impossible. If the Austrians had simply surged forward as each unit crossed the bridge, instead of wasting an hour forming up in order to move off together, they might well have overwhelmed Victor. A major defeat at Marengo could have toppled the Consulate, as Sieyès and others were already plotting in Paris.

Murat ordered the cavalry brigade of François-Étienne Kellermann (the son of the victor of Valmy) forward from San Giuliano, as Berthier, who had a fine view from a small hill at Cascina di Buzana, ordered Victor to offer stubborn resistance and sent word to Napoleon to bring up the troops from Torre Garofoli as quickly as possible. By 9.30 a.m. Gardanne was under heavy artillery fire, which on that hard and flat plain involved much ricocheting, but as the French fought this battle in line their losses were minimized. The firefight raged for two hours, the French firing steadily by platoon volley, but Gardanne's six battalions were pounded by the Austrian guns and had to fall back slowly to the Fontanone brook, whose steep sides can be seen today outside the Marengo museum. Dampierre's small force on the Austrian right, well hidden in ditches and ravines, wasn't overwhelmed until 7 p.m. when he surrendered, having fired off all his ammunition and finding himself surrounded by hussars.

By 10 a.m. on June 14 Napoleon had ordered Lannes towards Cascina La Barbotta to shore up Victor's right. Singing the 'Marseillaise', the 6th Légère and 22nd Line launched attacks that pushed the Austrians back over the Fontanone, swollen from the rains of the previous night. 'The Austrians fought like lions,' Victor later acknowledged. The French refused to abandon the Fontanone line when the Austrians counter-attacked; soldiers urinated on muskets that had become too hot to handle from the constant firing. By noon the French line was being pounded by forty guns and incessant musketry, and was running low on ammunition. 'Bonaparte advanced in front,' recalled Petit, 'and exhorted to courage and firmness all the corps he met with; it was visible that his presence reanimated them.'[32]

At this point the Austrian Archduke Joseph, Archduke Charles's younger brother, crossed the Fontanone with his infantry – the sides were too steep for cavalry or artillery. The French failed to dislodge him and his men started building a trestle bridge, covered by artillery firing canister shot which flayed the French brigade sent to stop them. By 2 p.m. Marengo had fallen: the Austrians had brought eighty guns into play, the Fontanone was being crossed everywhere and Gardanne's

division was broken, fleeing the field, though not before it had bought
Napoleon 3½ hours' respite with which to organize his counter-attack.
Only Kellermann's cavalry brigade, carefully retiring squadron by squadron, intimidated the Austrians from releasing their numerically superior
cavalry force. As the Austrians deployed into line of battle beyond
Marengo, Victor was forced to retreat almost to San Giuliano before he
could re-form his ranks, which he did across the plain in squares, suffering severe losses from a battery of fifteen guns that the Austrians brought
well forward. By this point the Austrians were taunting the French, twirl-
ing the bearskins of dead French grenadiers around on their sabres.[33]

Meanwhile, Lannes was thrown on to the defensive by Ott's infantry
advance, his right bent back and short of ammunition. With no artillery,
almost surrounded, and pounded by enemy guns, he ordered a retreat
over the plain at less than a mile per hour, retiring by echelon in a disciplined but expensive movement in front of the Austrian guns. Napoleon,
who now had only Monnier's division and the Consular Guard in
reserve, had sent desperate word to Desaix at 11 a.m. to return with
Boudet's division as quickly as possible. 'I had thought to attack the
enemy, instead it is he who has attacked me,' went his message; 'in the
name of God, come back if you still can!' Luckily for Napoleon's consulship, Desaix had been severely delayed by the swollen Scrivia. He
sent a messenger back at 1 p.m. telling Napoleon to expect him at about
5 p.m. He and Boudet had to halt the division, turn it around and march
it back 5 miles in the searing heat to the sound of guns, but they managed it in the nick of time. Napoleon's similar message recalling Lapoype
from much further afield didn't reach him until 6 p.m., by which time it
was too late.

When Napoleon and Monnier arrived at the battlefield, at 2 p.m., the
situation could hardly have been more serious, with the French slowly
retreating in the centre, broken on the left and seriously menaced on the
right.[34] Napoleon knew he had to defend the Tortona road but couldn't
do so frontally, so he deployed his reserves off to the right. Lannes could
be relied upon to hold the line there, which if necessary could be used as
an alternative line of retreat. Ott was the foremost problem: he was
only held back by six hundred men. In order to help disengage Lannes,
Monnier sent General Claude Carra Saint-Cyr and seven hundred men
of the 19th Légère into a thinly held Castel Ceriolo while the 70th Line
moved to take Ott in the rear and the 72nd Line was held in reserve. Ott
was initially driven back into the Bormida marshes, but he retook the
village after an hour-long firefight with Saint-Cyr.

This was therefore emphatically not the time for Melas, who had had two horses shot from under him and had suffered a slight contusion to his forearm, to quit the battlefield, return to Alessandria, announce a victory to Vienna and give orders for his deputy to take over, capture San Giuliano and send cavalry to pursue the routed French. Yet, astonishingly, that is what he did.

At 3 p.m., as more Austrian cavalry rode out onto the plain to threaten Lannes' flank, Napoleon decided to commit nine hundred infantry of the Consular Guard, who were deployed between La Poggi and Villanova in column, singing '*On va leur percer le flanc*' (We'll pierce their flank). The 96th Line later said they had saved the day by handing over some of their ammunition as they marched up. When one of Ott's dragoon regiments charged them they formed a square, and beat them off aided by their skirmishers and four regimental guns. The Guard were then attacked by infantry, with whom they traded volleys for forty minutes at ranges from 50 to 100 yards; 260 of them were killed that day, and roughly the same number wounded. They beat off three cavalry charges, but, as the Austrian infantry fixed bayonets and charged home, they were forced to make a fighting retreat in square back towards Li Poggi. This sacrifice by the Guard nonetheless bought the time Monnier needed to complete his manoeuvres, which, in turn, bought time for the whole army to reorganize. Napoleon later spoke of the 'fortress of granite' that had been his Consular Guard that day, and awarded twenty-four decorations to their infantry, eighteen to their cavalry and eight to their artillery.

By 4 p.m. both the Consular Guard and Monnier's division were in controlled retreat as the Austrians closed in on San Giuliano. The French moved backwards in good order, one battalion at a time, fighting as they went. It was an utter test of discipline not to succumb to the temptation to break ranks under those circumstances, and it paid off. The day continued very hot, with no water, little artillery support, and sustained attacks from the Austrian cavalry, but some units retreated steadily from 9.30 a.m. to about 4 p.m. over 5 miles, never breaking ranks.

Napoleon calmly called out encouragement and exuded leadership 'with his accustomed sangfroid', in the words of one of his guards, ensuring that his infantry, cavalry and paltry artillery each supported one another.[35] 'The Consul seemed to brave death,' recalled Petit, 'and to be near it, for the bullets were seen more than once to drive up the ground between his horse's legs.'[36] He had now completely used up his reserves, had barely 6,000 infantry across a 5-mile front, with 1,000 cavalry and only 6 usable guns, and his army was exhausted, desperately thirsty, low on ammunition and one-third *hors de combat*, but he behaved as if victory were certain.[37] He even managed to be light-hearted; noticing that the horse Marbot was riding was slightly wounded in the leg, he 'took me by the ear and said, laughing, "You expect me to lend you my horses for you to treat them in this way?"'[38]

With a dense mass of Austrian infantry preparing to advance, Napoleon ordered Berthier to organize a safe retreat while he went to the Villa Gholina to scout for Desaix from the roof. Seeing the dust rising from Desaix's column, he rode over to speed them up and then quickly countermanded his retreat order to Berthier. When the army saw Desaix arrive, riding a little ahead of his men who were on foot, their morale was reignited. Once Boudet reached San Giuliano, and Lannes, Monnier and Watrin got their men into something like a line of battle, the Austrians halted their columns and started to deploy into line for what they assumed would be a final triumphant assault. 'We have gone back far enough today,' Napoleon harangued his men. 'Soldiers, remember it is my custom to bivouac on the field of battle!'[39]

With the six still-usable guns on the field joined by five from the reserve and eight from Boudet, Marmont now had a respectable battery to deploy on a slight elevation. Boudet deployed his 4,850 infantry in the *ordre mixte* onto the main road, partly hidden by hedges and vineyards. Napoleon rode along the line encouraging the men; he now had 11,000 infantry and 1,200 cavalry for his long-awaited counter-attack.

When the Austrians came forward at 5 p.m., the front of their centre regiments were ripped apart by canister fire from Marmont's battery. As at Rivoli, a lucky shot hit an ammunition wagon that exploded and caused chaos. The Austrians recoiled sharply and the shock effect was serious, especially once Boudet's division advanced upon them. Aggressive Austrian charges soon threw Boudet on the defensive, but just as nearly 6,000 Austrian infantry fired a musket volley and then charged with their bayonets, Kellermann unleashed his cavalry, which had moved up concealed by vines in the trees. As a result, the Austrians' muskets were unloaded when four hundred men of the 2nd and 20th Cavalry regiments crashed into the left flank of the central column of Hungarian grenadiers. The 2nd Cavalry sabred three battalions, taking 2,000 prisoners and sending 4,000 men fleeing. Immediately afterwards, Kellermann turned the 200 men who had been at the rear of the last charge and attacked some 2,000 Austrian cavalry that were standing inactive, routing them as well.

The French army then advanced across the whole front. It was at this triumphant moment that Desaix was struck in the chest and killed. 'Why am I not allowed to weep?' a grief-stricken Napoleon said on being told the news, but he had to concentrate on directing the next assault.[40] Kellermann's next attacks sent Austrian cavalry charging back into their own infantry, completely disorganizing them and giving Lannes, Monnier and the Consular Guard the chance to complete the victory by moving forward on all fronts. 'The fate of a battle is the result of a single instant – a thought,' Napoleon was later to say about Marengo. 'The decisive moment comes, a moral spark is lit, and the smallest reserve accomplishes victory.'[41] Austrian troops who had fought bravely all day simply cracked under the shock and strain of seeing victory snatched from them, and fled back to Alessandria in disorder.

The exhausted French indeed slept that night on the battlefield. In total, 963 Austrians were killed, 5,518 wounded and 2,921 captured; 13 guns indeed were seized and a further 20 dumped in the Bormida. Just over 1,000 Frenchmen were killed, 3,600 wounded and 900 captured or missing, but the numbers mask what was a crushing strategic victory for Napoleon.[42] According to the terms of the armistice that Melas signed soon afterwards, Napoleon would be given the whole of Piedmont, Genoa, most of Lombardy, 12 fortresses, 1,500 guns and massive ammunition magazines. When the news of Marengo reached Paris, government bonds that had been standing at 11 francs six months earlier, and 29 just before the battle, shot up to 35 francs.[43] After the battle, Napoleon gave orders to Masséna on July 22 to 'plunder and burn the first village which revolts in Piedmont', and to Brune on November 4: 'All foreigners, but especially Italians, need to be dealt with severely from time to time.'[44] But now that the Austrians had been expelled for the second time, northern Italy was swiftly pacified with a minimum of repression, and was to remain quiescent for the next fourteen years. Marengo confirmed Napoleon in his position as First Consul, and added to the myth of his invincibility.

Napoleon had worked his three arms of infantry, artillery and cavalry together perfectly at Marengo, but it was still a very lucky victory, won largely by the shock value of Desaix's arrival on the field at precisely the right psychological moment, and Kellermann's superbly timed cavalry charges. The French reconquered a plain in one hour that it had taken the Austrians eight to occupy. The conscript French troops, guided by the veterans, had acquitted themselves very well.

'After a great battle,' wrote Captain Blaze, 'there is plenty of food for
the crows and the bulletin-writers.'[45] Napoleon had made three major
errors: in going onto the plain in the first place, in not anticipating
Melas's attack and in sending Desaix so far away. But he had won, and
for political reasons it was imperative that Marengo be seen as his
triumph, or at least one shared with the dead Desaix. The post-battle
bulletin was thus pure propaganda, implying that the Austrians had
fallen into his trap. 'The battle appeared to be lost,' it stated somewhat
fancifully. 'The enemy was allowed to advance within musket range of
the village of San Giuliano, where General Desaix's division was drawn
up in the line of battle.'[46] Napoleon also invented some last words for
Desaix: 'Go tell the First Consul that I die with the regret of having not
done enough to live in posterity.' (In fact he had died instantaneously.)
Berthier's official history of the battle had to go through three revisions
before Napoleon approved it. By January 1815 Napoleon was unchari-
tably claiming that Marengo had been won before Desaix arrived.[47] The
view of Desaix's aide-de-camp Anne-Jean-Marie-René Savary was that
'If General Desaix had delayed an hour in arriving, we'd have been
driven into the Po.'[48]

The day after the battle, Napoleon wrote to the other consuls that he
was 'in the deepest pain over the death of the man I loved and respected
the most'.[49] He took Savary and Desaix's other aide-de-camp, Jean
Rapp, onto his staff as a sign of respect, and he allowed the 9th Légère,
which Desaix had been leading when he was killed, to sew the word
'Incomparable' in gold onto their standard.[50] He had Desaix's corpse
embalmed, and a medal struck in his honour, as well as one commemorating Marengo.* All that he said to Kellermann after the battle was, 'You
made a pretty good charge,' which infuriated him, especially as he had
gushed to Bessières, 'The Guard cavalry covered itself with glory today.'[51]
(Kellermann is supposed to have replied in anger, 'I'm glad you are satisfied,
general, for it has placed the crown on your head', but it is doubtful that he
really did.[52]) Privately, Napoleon admitted to Bourrienne that Kellermann
had 'made a lucky charge. He did it just at the right moment. We are much
indebted to him. You see what trifling circumstances decide these affairs.'
Kellermann was given his own division within a month, and later in his
career Napoleon turned a blind eye to his outrageous looting. Perhaps the

---

* A further medal was struck to celebrate the opening of the Quai Desaix in Paris later that
year, and yet another when Desaix's body was moved to a tomb in the Great St Bernard
Hospice in 1805 (Crowdy, *The Incomparable* pp. 94–7; Petit, *Marengo* p. 47).

best summing up of the battle was Napoleon's terse statement to Brune and Dumas: 'You see, there were two battles on the same day; I lost the first; I gained the second.'[53]

On June 16 Napoleon offered Emperor Francis peace once again, on the same basis as Campo Formio, writing: 'I exhort Your Majesty to listen to the cry of humanity.' In his Order of the Day he claimed the Austrians had recognized 'that we are only fighting each other so that the English can sell their sugar and coffee at a higher price'.[54] The next day 'the Liberator of Italy' was back in Milan again, enjoying the charms of Giuseppina Grassini, whom he invited to sing in Paris at the Quatorze Juillet celebrations and at Desaix's obsequies. 'Berthier informs me that he is counting on sending either Mrs Billington or Madame Grassini,' he wrote somewhat disingenuously to Lucien on June 21, 'who are the two most famous virtuosi in Italy. Have a fine piece composed in Italian. The voices of these actresses should be known to Italian composers.'[55] Grassini complained that Napoleon's 'caresses were on the furtive side', and often left her unsatisfied, and in this she wasn't alone. He never took time over his lovemaking, once reporting to an aide, 'The matter was over in three minutes.'[56]

For all his military genius, intellectual capacity, administrative ability and plain hard work, one should not underestimate the part that sheer good luck played in Napoleon's career. In May 1800 there was a gap in the weather for crossing the Alps, and in June the rains slowed Desaix's march away from Marengo enough so that he could return to the battle-field in time to save his commander-in-chief. In 1792 Colonel Maillard's report on the events in Ajaccio was swamped under war ministry paper-work on the outbreak of war; in 1793 the pike-thrust at Toulon didn't go septic; in 1797 Quasdonovich's ammunition wagon received a direct hit at Rivoli, as Melas's did at Marengo; in 1799 the *Muiron* had perfect winds on leaving Alexandria; the same year Sieyès' other choices for the Brumaire coup were unavailable, and Kléber's report on the Egyptian campaign didn't arrive in Paris before the coup, during which Thomé's sleeve was torn enough to anger his comrades. Napoleon recognized this, and spoke more than once of 'the goddess Fortune'. Later in his career he would believe that the goddess was spurning him, but for now he was persuaded that she was on his side.

12

Lawgiver

'I must give the people their full rights in religion. Philosophers will laugh, but the nation will bless me.'

Napoleon to Chaptal

'My true glory is not to have won forty battles . . . What nothing will destroy, what will live for ever, is my Civil Code.'

Napoleon on St Helena

Napoleon had no intention of resting on his laurels after Marengo. With his political capital rising, he decided on a gamble which, if it paid off, would significantly deepen his domestic support. 'The boldest operation that Bonaparte carried out during the first years of his reign', wrote Jean Chaptal, 'was to re-establish worship upon its old foundations.'[1] Napoleon wanted to ensure that no independent Church would provide a focus of opposition to his rule, and the simplest solution was to co-opt the Pope.

Anti-clericalism had been a driving force during the French Revolution, which had stripped the Catholic Church of its wealth, expelled and in many cases murdered its priests, and desecrated its altars. Yet Napoleon sensed that many among his natural supporters – conservative, rural, hard-working skilled labourers, artisans and smallholders – had not abjured the faith of their fathers and yearned for a settlement between the Roman Catholic Church and the Consulate they were growing to admire. Any settlement, however, would have to ensure that those who had acquired *biens nationaux* previously owned by the Church (known as *acquéreurs*) should be allowed to retain their property, and there could be no return to the old days when the peasantry were forced to pay tithes to the clergy.

Napoleon had for some time respected the Pope's ability to organize uprisings in Italy, telling the Directory in October 1796 that 'it was a great mistake to quarrel with that Power'.[2] In his post-coital meeting with the Milanese priesthood on 5 June, 1800, he had promised 'to remove all obstacles in the way of a complete reconciliation between France and the head of the Church'. Pius VI had died the previous August, aged eighty-one. The new Pope, Pius VII, was at heart a simple and holy monk whose views on social questions were not thought to be overtly hostile to the French Revolution.[3] Napoleon knew that any negotiations would be delicate and occasionally hard fought, but the prize was great: the adherence of Catholic France to the Napoleonic cause. A papal agreement would remove one of the central grievances of the remaining rebels in the Vendée and might improve relations with Catholics in Belgium, Switzerland, Italy and the Rhineland too.

The population of France was about 28 million, only one-fifth of whom dwelt in urban areas of over 2,000 people; most of the rest lived in 36,000 rural communes of a few hundred residents.[4] Napoleon appreciated how invaluable it would be if the person who played an important social role as the centre of information in those communities, who was often the most educated person and who read out government decrees, was also on the national payroll. 'The clergy is a power that is never quiet,' Napoleon once said. 'You cannot be under obligations to it, wherefore you must be its master.'[5] His treaty with the Papacy has been accurately described as attempting 'to enlist the parish clergy as Napoleon's "moral prefects"'.[6]

As we have seen, Napoleon himself was at best sceptical about Christianity.[7] 'Did Jesus ever exist,' he asked his secretary on St Helena, Gaspard Gourgaud, 'or did he not? I think that no contemporary historian has ever mentioned him.'[8] (He was clearly unfamiliar with Josephus' *Antiquities of the Jews* which does indeed mention Jesus.) He nonetheless enjoyed theological discussions and told his last doctor, Antommarchi, 'Wishing to be an atheist does not make you one.'[9] 'Although Bonaparte was not devout,' Chaptal reported, mirroring these ambiguities, 'he did believe in the existence of God and in the immortality of the soul. He always spoke about religion with respect.'[10] When the Sermon on the Mount was read to him on St Helena, he told Bertrand: 'Jesus should have performed his miracles not in remote parts of Syria but in a city like Rome, in front of the whole population.'[11] On another occasion he said, 'Were I obliged to have a religion, I would worship the sun – the source of all life – the real god of the earth.'[12] On yet another he said: 'I like the Muslim religion best; it has fewer incredible things in it than ours.'[13] On that score he dictated a note logistically disproving the biblical claim that Moses could have quenched 2 million Israelites' thirst by striking a rock.[14] A major problem with Christianity, as he told Bertrand, was that it 'does not excite courage' because 'It takes too much care to go to heaven.'[15]

Despite his own attitudes to the substance of the Christian faith, he was in no doubt about its social utility. 'In religion,' Napoleon told Roederer, one of the few state councillors allowed into the secret of the negotiations, 'I do not see the mystery of the Incarnation, but the mystery of the social order. It associates with Heaven an idea of equality that keeps rich men from being massacred by the poor ... Society is impossible without inequality; inequality intolerable without a code of morality, and a code of morality unacceptable without religion.'[16] He had already shown in Egypt how flexible he was in using religion for political ends; as he once remarked to Roederer: 'If I ruled a people of Jews, I would rebuild the Temple of Solomon!'[17] This essentially pragmatic view of religion was common among Enlightenment thinkers and writers. Edward Gibbon famously wrote in the *Decline and Fall of the Roman Empire* that 'The various modes of worship which prevailed in the Roman world were all considered by the people as equally true; by the philosopher as equally false; and by the magistrate as equally useful.'[18] 'The idea of God is very useful,' Napoleon said, 'to maintain good order, to keep men in the path of virtue and to keep them from crime.'[19] 'To robbers and galley slaves, physical restrictions are imposed,' he said to Dr Barry O'Meara on St Helena, 'to enlightened people, moral ones.'[20]

In June 1800, as soon as he returned to Paris from Milan, Napoleon opened negotiations with the Vatican secretary of state, Cardinal Hercules Consalvi, offering to restore full public worship in France if all French bishops resigned their sees and allowed Napoleon to select new ones who would then be 'nominated' by the Pope.[21] (Since 1790 French bishops had been split between the Orthodox, who recognized only the authority of the Pope, and the Constitutionalists, who had taken an oath of obedience to the government.) The negotiations, conducted by Joseph Bonaparte and the former Vendéen leader Étienne-Alexandre Bernier on the French side, and Consalvi, the papal legate Cardinal Giovanni Caprara and the Pope's theological advisor Charles Caselli on the Vatican's, were conducted in secret, without informing even the Conseil d'État. A total of 1,279 documents were sent back and forth over the course of a year, and there were no fewer than ten draft agreements. 'One should render unto God that which is God's,' Napoleon was later to say, 'but the Pope is not God.'[22] Cardinal Consalvi visited the Tuileries in April 1802 and Napoleon had the rooms perfumed before his arrival. When the chemist Fourcroy commented on the smell, Napoleon teased him: 'It's a saintly odour which is going to purify your old sins.'[23]

As the negotiations reached their climax in early July 1801, Napoleon wrote to Talleyrand: 'I had a second blister on my arm yesterday. It is a fitting moment to come to terms with the priests when one is laid up ill.'[24] Although the Concordat was officially signed in July, it wasn't ratified and published until nine months later, once Napoleon had tried to calm the deep opposition to it in the army and legislature. 'The Government of the Republic acknowledges that the Catholic, Apostolic and Roman religion is the religion of the great majority of French citizens,' the Concordat began. 'His Holiness, in like manner, acknowledges that this same religion has derived, and is likely to derive, the greatest splendour from the establishment of the Catholic worship in France, and from its being openly professed by the consuls of the Republic.'[25] In the course of the next seventeen articles it stated that the Catholic faith 'shall be freely exercised in France ... conformable to the regulations ... which the Government shall judge necessary for the public tranquillity'.

There were to be new dioceses and parishes. Ten archbishops (each on a 15,000-franc annual salary) and fifty bishops (10,000 francs each) would be appointed by Napoleon and the Pope together; bishops would swear to do nothing to 'disturb the public tranquillity' and would communicate all information about those who did to the government; all divine services would include a prayer for the Republic and the consuls; although the bishops would appoint the parish priests, they couldn't appoint anyone unacceptable to the government. The Concordat cemented the land transfers of the Revolution; all former Church property belonged to the *acquéreurs* 'for ever'.

Napoleon made a number of concessions, none too onerous. The ten-day week was suppressed and Sunday was restored as the day of rest; the Gregorian calendar eventually returned in January 1806; children were to be given saints' or classical rather than wholly secular or revolutionary names; salaries were paid to all clergy; orders of nuns and of missionaries were reintroduced in a minor way, and primary education was restored to the clergy's remit.[26] Meanwhile, the Church would sing *Te Deums* for Napoleon's victories, read his proclamations from its pulpits and depict conscription as a patriotic duty. On all the major points of contention, Napoleon got what he wanted. With the end of the schism, no fewer than 10,000 Constitutional priests returned to the bosom of the Roman Church and one of the deepest wounds of the Revolution was healed.[27] Any trust Pius might have had in Napoleon's good faith was however undermined on April 8, 1802, when, without prior consultation, a whole new raft of restrictions and regulations, known as the Organic Articles, was appended to the Concordat, which protected the rights of France's 700,000 Protestants and 55,000 Jews.*

Although it was generally welcomed in France, especially in conservative, rural France, the Concordat was deeply unpopular in the army, the Conseil and the Tribunate – where there were still plenty of former revolutionaries and ex-Jacobins. It was formally proclaimed with huge pomp at a *Te Deum* Mass at Notre-Dame on Easter Sunday, April 18, 1802, when the tenor bells rang out for the first time in a decade and Napoleon was received by the recently nominated archbishop of Paris, Jean-Baptiste de Belloy-Morangle. Senior state officials were ordered to arrive with suitable grandeur, but it was noticed that some of their coaches were actually hackney-carriages with their numbers painted over.[28] Generals scraped their spurs and sabres on the floor of the cathedral, refused to give up seats to the clergy and talked during the ceremony, making plain the anger of the very anti-clerical army over the Concordat. Augereau requested permission to be absent, which Napoleon refused. Moreau simply ignored the order and smoked a cigar ostentatiously on the Tuileries terrace. When General Antoine-Guillaume Delmas was heard to remark, '*Quelle capucinade* [what banal moralizing], the only thing missing are the one hundred thousand men who died to get rid of all this!' Napoleon exiled him 50 miles from Paris.[29]

The Concordat won Napoleon the soubriquet 'Restorer of Religion' from the clergy, though few clerics went as far as the archbishop of Besançon, who described him as 'like God himself'.[30] Within a month the Tribunate had approved it by seventy-eight votes to seven. In the hamlets and small towns across France it had its intended effect. 'Children listen with more docility to the voice of their parents, youth is more submissive to the authority of the magistrate, and the conscription is now effected in places where its very name used to arouse

---

* From 1804 Protestant ministers were also paid by the state. Religious toleration was not by any means universal across Europe at the time; in Britain, for example, Catholics were banned from entering the House of Commons until 1829, as were Jews until 1858.

resistance,' Napoleon told the legislature in 1803, illustrating that he primarily saw religious reconciliation in terms of propaganda and public discipline.[31] The Concordat remained the basis for relations between France and the Papacy for a century. A recent study of Rouen during the Consulate concluded that Napoleon's most popular measures to have been the Concordat, the defeat of brigandage and the guaranteeing of the land-ownership rights of the *acquéreurs*, in that order.[32]

After the Concordat was finally adopted by the Legislative Body, Lucien gave a reception for his brother during which Napoleon sought out the Catholic philosopher and writer François-Réne de Chateaubriand, author of the successful new book *Génie du christianisme*, an emotional celebration of Catholicism. 'Rank after rank opened up,' Chateaubriand recalled in his memoirs,

> each person hoping the Consul would stop at him ... I was then left standing by myself, for the crowd drew back and soon gathered together to form a circle around the two of us. Bonaparte addressed me with simplicity, without paying me any compliments, without any idle questions, without any preamble, he spoke to me straight away about Egypt and the Arabs, as if I had always been a close friend of his and we were simply continuing a conversation we had already begun.[33]

It was beguiling, and Chateaubriand accepted a diplomatic post to the Vatican soon afterwards. Later his admiration faded: in 1804 he resigned from the diplomatic service and in July 1807 he likened Napoleon to Nero, for which he was banished from Paris.

At the end of January 1801, Napoleon inaugurated an ambitious project of legal reform whose consequences would outlast even the Concordat. The Ancien Régime had no fewer than 366 local codes in force, and southern France observed a fundamentally different set of legal principles, based on Roman law, rather than customary law as in the north.[34] Napoleon instinctively understood that if France was to function efficiently in the modern world, she needed a standardized system of law and justice, uniform weights and measures, a fully functioning internal market and a centralized education system, one that would allow talented adolescents from all backgrounds to enter careers according to merit rather than birth.

His first and most important task was to unify France's forty-two legal codes into a single system. For this monumental undertaking Napoleon had an invaluable ally in Cambacérès, who had been the secretary of the committee which had been given the task of overhauling the civil law code back in 1792 and was the author of the *Projet de Code Civil* (1796). 'If the whole Code were to be mislaid,' Napoleon once quipped, 'it could be found in Cambacérès' head.'[35] To assist the Second Consul in revisiting this long-overdue reform, a commission was formed of the country's most distinguished jurists and politicians, including Lebrun, François Tronchet, Félix Bigot de Préameneu and Jean-Étienne Portalis. Napoleon chaired no fewer than 55 of its 107 plenary sessions, frequently intervening on matters of particular interest such as divorce, adoption and the rights of foreigners.[36] Napoleon's constant refrain on questions of 'the general interest' and civil justice were: 'Is this fair? Is this useful?'[37] Some meetings started at noon and went on long into the night. Napoleon involved himself intimately in the entire lengthy and elaborate process of getting the new laws onto the statute books, from the initial debates in the Conseil, the drafting process, the critiques and attempted amendments of various interested parties, through the special committees, the subsequent assaults by special interest groups and lobbyists, and then the parliamentary legislative procedures. Nor was ratification a foregone conclusion: in December 1801 the preliminary bill was rejected in the Legislative Body by 142 votes to 139 and fared similarly in the Tribunate. If Napoleon hadn't shown his resolute personal support, it could never have become law. Although Cambacérès did the groundwork, it deserved to be called the Code Napoléon because it was the product of the rationalizing universalism of the Enlightenment that Napoleon embraced.

Essentially a compromise between Roman and common law, the Code Napoléon consisted of a reasoned and harmonious body of laws that were to be the same across all territories administered by France, for the first time since the Emperor Justinian. The rights and duties of the government and its citizens were codified in 2,281 articles covering 493 pages in prose so clear that Stendhal said he made it his daily reading.[38] The new code helped cement national unity, not least because it was based on the principles of freedom of person and contract. It confirmed the end of ancient class privileges, and (with the exception of primary education) of ecclesiastical control over any aspect of French civil society.[39] Above all, it offered stability after the chaos of the Revolution.

The Code Napoléon simplified the 14,000 decrees and laws that had been passed by the various revolutionary governments since 1789, and the 42 different regional codes that were in force, into a single unified body of law applicable to all citizens, laying down general principles and offering wide parameters for judges to work within. ('One should not overburden oneself with over-detailed laws,' Napoleon told the Conseil. 'Law must do nothing but impose a general principle. It would be vain if one were to try to foresee every possible situation; experience would prove that much has been omitted.'[40]) It guaranteed the equality of all Frenchmen in the eyes of the law, freedom of person from arbitrary arrest, the sanctity of legal contracts freely entered into, and allowed no recognition of privileges of birth. Reflecting the Organic Articles, it established total religious toleration (including for atheists), separating Church and state. It allowed all adult men to engage in any occupation and to own property. Laws had to be duly promulgated and officially published, and could not apply retrospectively. Judges were of course required to interpret the law in individual cases but were not allowed to make pronouncements on principles, so that specific cases could not set precedents, as under Anglo-Saxon common law. Fearing the disintegration of the family as the basic social institution, the framers of the Code gave the paterfamilias almost total power, including over the property of his wife. Under Article 148 the father's permission was required for the marriage of sons up to the age of twenty-five and daughters to twenty-one, and the marriage age was raised to fifteen for women, eighteen for men. Fathers also had the right to have their children imprisoned for disobedience for a month in the case of under-sixteens, and for six months for those between sixteen and twenty-one.

The major criticisms levelled at the Code over the past two centuries have been that it was socially conservative, too supportive of the middle classes, of the individual and of the paterfamilias, that it made wives too dependent on their husbands, and that its inheritance provisions were damaging for an agrarian economy. It was certainly true that the Code was deeply sexist by twenty-first century standards, with a strong patriarchal bias. Article 213 of the Civil Code stated: 'A husband owes protection to his wife, a wife obedience to her husband.'[41] Grounds for divorce were restricted to adultery (and then only if the husband introduced a permanent mistress into the family household), conviction of a serious crime, and grave insults or cruelty, but it could also be obtained by mutual agreement so long as the grounds were kept private.[42] A wife could be imprisoned for two years for adultery, while a man would only be fined. A husband would not be prosecuted if he murdered his wife caught *in flagrante*. The Code protected married and single men from having to support an illegitimate child, or even being identified as the father.[43] It also prevented women from making legal contracts, taking part in lawsuits, serving as a witness in court or to births, deaths or marriages. Wives could not sell produce in markets without their husbands' permission, and were forbidden to give, sell or mortgage property without their husbands' written consent.[44] Unmarried women could not be legal guardians or witness wills. In all this, the Code reflects Napoleon's profound sexism: 'Women should not be looked upon as equals of men,' he said. 'They are, in fact, only machines for making babies.'[45]

The Code also dealt a death blow to primogeniture. Property of up to 25 per cent of the total could be bequeathed away from the family, but the rest had to be divided equally among all sons on the death of their father, with no inheritance rights allowed for illegitimate children.[46]* It displayed a powerful bias towards employers too, whose word was accepted in all points of law.[47] On December 1, 1802 a law was passed requiring every worker to keep a *livret* (passbook), which had to be handed over to the employer at the start of the period of employment and signed by them at the end, without which the worker was unemployable and liable to six months' imprisonment.[48]† Napoleon didn't invent the tough anti-strike and anti-union legislation in the Code, which had been in place since the Le Chapelier Law of 1791 and wasn't repealed until 1884. He did put it into effect, however. Building workers who went on strike in 1806 were arrested in their beds.[49]‡

The Civil Code, which became law in 1804, was only one of several legal reforms promulgated by Napoleon, though undoubtedly the most important. By 1810 it had been joined by the Code of Civil Procedure, the Commercial Code, the Code on Criminal Procedure and the Penal Code. (In the last of these the provisions were extremely tough, but didn't display the viciousness of Britain's penal code of the time, under which children could be transported to Australia and adults hanged for the theft of goods worth more than a shilling.) It was this body of law together that came to be known as the Code Napoléon. The Code was extended to almost all parts of the French Empire in March 1804. It

---

* Despite this, Napoleon put down his own family's relative wealth in Ajaccio to the fact that their property hadn't been sub-divided for more than a century.

† Labour laws were tough on workers throughout Europe at this time; on New Year's Day 1812, the bishop of Durham, interpreting his ecclesiastical powers widely, ordered the British army forcibly to break up miners' strikes in northern England.

‡ Nonetheless, the labour-shortages caused by constant war meant that wages rose by a quarter in real terms during the fifteen years of his rule.

was imposed on those parts of Spain that were under martial law in 1808 and on Holland after its annexation in 1810. 'The Romans gave their laws to their allies,' Napoleon told his brother Louis, 'why should France not have its laws adopted in Holland?'[50] In some places, such as Naples, it only ever received lip-service. In others, however, it was so popular that it was retained even after Napoleon's fall.[51] It survived in the Prussian Rhineland until 1900, and Belgium, Luxembourg, Mauritius and Monaco, as well as France, still operate it today. Aspects of it remain in a quarter of the world's legal systems as far removed from the mother country as Japan, Egypt, Quebec and Louisiana.[52]

Although the Code Napoléon standardized the laws, it would take equally radical reforms to standardize the other aspects of French life that Napoleon wished to rationalize. In the Corbières region of the Languedoc, for example – whose 129 parishes spoke Occitan rather than French, except for three southern villages that spoke Catalan – the administrative, judicial, policing and taxation duties were undertaken by authorities in four cities, namely Carcassonne, Narbonne, Limoux and Perpignan, yet there was no consistency as to which city administered which commune. There were no fewer than ten different volumes for which the term *setier* (usually about 85 litres) could be used, and fifty different terms to measure area, one of which – the *sétérée* – differed depending on whether it applied to lowland or highland areas.[53] Napoleon didn't personally admire the metric system that Laplace invented, saying, 'I can understand the twelfth part of an inch, but not the thousandth part of a metre,' but he nonetheless forced it through after 1801 in the interests of commercial consistency.[54] He also established a standardized coinage: copper coins of two, three and five centimes; silver coins of one-quarter, one-half and three-quarters of a franc, and of one, two and five francs, and gold coins of ten, twenty and forty francs. The silver one-franc piece was to weigh five grams, and quickly became western Europe's standard unit of currency. Its value and metallic composition remained constant until 1926.

Out of the population of 28 million, 6 million were completely ignorant of the French tongue and another 6 million could only just about make themselves understood in it. Flemish was spoken in the north-east, German in Lorraine, Breton in Brittany, and Basque, Catalan, Italian, Celtic and Languedoc patois elsewhere.[55] Although Napoleon didn't have particularly good French himself he knew from personal experience how important it was to speak the language in order to get on.[56]

His educational reforms made French the only permitted language of instruction, as it became for all official documents.

Napoleon was conservative about primary education, putting it back, as we have seen, in the hands of the clergy, but in secondary education, which began at age eleven, he was revolutionary. In May 1802 he passed a law setting up forty-five *lycées* (state secondary schools) whose aim was to produce future soldiers, administrators and technicians. The *lycée* was his answer to the question of how to create a patriotic, loyal generation of future leaders.[57] All eligible French children were now taught Greek, Latin, rhetoric, logic, ethics, mathematics and physics, and also some of the other sciences and modern languages. Here religion was kept to a minimum: he did not want a secondary system dominated by the Church as that of the Ancien Régime had been. Discipline was strict, school uniforms of blue jackets and trousers with round hats were worn until fourteen, and pupils were grouped into companies with one sergeant and four corporals commanded by the best student, who was called the sergeant-major.

Lycées offered 6,400 full-fees scholarships for what were called 'national students', but were also open to others who passed exams to enter, and to those whose parents paid fees.[58] Students followed a mandatory programme of courses, instead of the old system where they could choose. The departmental prefects and presidents of the criminal and appeal courts oversaw the administration of these new schools, and there was a professional inspectorate.[59] By 1813 French secondary schools were the best in Europe and some of Napoleon's original *lycées*, such as Condorcet, Charlemagne, Louis-le-Grand and Henri IV, are still among the best schools in France two centuries later. The concept was exported far beyond France; it served as a model in Spain and Holland, which accepted French educational ideas even as they denounced French occupation.[60]

In an unscripted speech to the Conseil in 1806, which he made only because his education minister, Antoine Fourcroy, hadn't brought his report to the meeting, Napoleon was almost poetic about how education was

> the most important of all the institutions, since everything depends upon it, the present and the future. It is essential that the morals and political ideas of the generation which is now growing up should no longer be dependent on the news of the day or the circumstances of the moment ... Men already differ enough in their inclinations, their characters and everything that

education does not give and cannot reform ... Let us have a body of doctrine that doesn't vary and a body of teachers that doesn't die.[61]

Napoleon planned to institute *lycées* throughout France. Overall, his educational reforms were, like his architectural plans for Paris, admirable, but cut off long before they could reach fruition. On March 17, 1808 Napoleon took his reorganization a stage further when he promulgated a decree calling for the creation of the Imperial University, which would oversee all education in France. All teachers were to be members of one of its five faculties (Theology, Law, Medicine, Literature, and Maths & Physics). He designed a military-style hierarchical structure, with a strong-willed chancellor in Louis Fontanes, the president of the Legislative Body between 1804 and 1810, and below him a Council of Thirty who controlled all French secondary schools and the universities.[62] The Sorbonne had been closed by the Revolution, but in 1808 Napoleon resuscitated it.

Napoleon's profound sexism emerged in his education provisions as elsewhere. 'Public education almost always makes bad women flighty, coquettish and unstable,' he told the Conseil in March 1806. 'Being educated together, which is so good for men, especially for teaching them to help each other and preparing them by comradeship for the battle of life, is a school of corruption for women. Men are made for the full glare of life. Women are made for the seclusion of family life and to live at home.'[63] As with the Code Napoléon, the lack of girls' formal education needs to be seen here too in the context of his time; at the beginning of the nineteenth century there were very few girls' schools in England or America, and none run by the state.

The greatest reforms of the Consulate were carried out between July 1800 and May 1803, when Napoleon was in Paris in regular conclave with his Conseil d'État, which was mainly made up of moderate republicans and former royalists, although there were occasions when some councillors had to sit next to others who had sent their fathers or brothers to the guillotine.[64] 'We have done with the romance of the Revolution,' he told an early meeting of his Conseil État, 'we must now commence its history.' Napoleon gave the Conseil direction, purpose and the general lines of policy, which have been accurately summed up as 'a love of authority, realism, contempt for privilege and abstract rights, scrupulous attention to detail and respect for an orderly social hierarchy'.[65] He was the youngest member of the Conseil and, as Chaptal recalled,

> He was not at all embarrassed by the little knowledge he had about the details of general administration. He asked many questions, asked for the definition and meaning of the most common words; he provoked discussion and kept it going until his opinion was formed. In one debate this man, who is so often portrayed as a raging egomaniac, admitted to the aged and respected jurist François Tronchet 'Sometimes in these discussions I have said things which a quarter of an hour later I have found were all wrong. I have no wish to pass for being worth more than I really am.'[66]

The Conseil discussed an extraordinary range of issues. On the single day of June 17, 1802, to take an example at random, its agenda covered the examination of surgeons; the organization of chemists; the appointment of sub-prefects to important *arrondissements*; the state of the harvest; Maltese refugees; a draft law concerning the National Guard; responsibility for roadworks; the government of the commissariat; pawnbroking; larger communes' accounts; gamekeepers; the chambers of commerce; the law allowing émigrés right of return to specific regions; electoral law; bridge-building in the Ardèche; merging two Corsican departments into one; and demarcating those on the left bank of the Rhine.[67]

Some Conseil meetings lasted eight to ten hours, and Chaptal recalled that it was always Napoleon 'who expended the most in terms of words and mental strain. After these meetings, he would convene others on different matters, and never was his mind seen to flag.'[68] When members were tired during all-night sessions he would say: 'Come, sirs, we haven't earned our salaries yet!'[69] (After they ended, sometimes at 5 a.m., he would take a bath, in the belief that 'One hour in the bath is worth four hours of sleep to me.'[70]) Other than on the battlefield itself, it was here that Napoleon was at his most impressive. His councillors bear uniform witness – whether they later supported or abandoned him, whether they were writing contemporaneously or long after his fall – to his deliberative powers, his dynamism, the speed with which he grasped a subject, and the tenacity never to let it go until he had mastered its essentials and taken the necessary decision. 'Still young and rather untutored in the different areas of administration,' recalled one of them of the early days of the Consulate, 'he brought to the discussions a clarity, a precision, a strength of reason and range of views that astonished us. A tireless worker with inexhaustible resources, he linked and co-ordinated the facts and opinions scattered throughout a large administration system with unparalleled wisdom.'[71] He quickly taught himself to ask short questions that demanded direct answers. Thus Conseil member Emmanuel Crétet, the minister of public works, would be asked 'Where are we with the Arc de Triomphe?' and 'Will I walk on the Jena bridge on my return?'[72]

The Conseil was split into sections to cover various areas of government – army, navy, finance, justice, home affairs, police and provinces. 'The long horseshoe-shaped table with its array of men of such varied origins and opinions,' Comte Molé recalled, 'was simply transformed when the organizing genius appeared on a dais at the end of the horseshoe.'[73] Another remembered how 'His seat – a mahogany chair with green morocco seat and arms – was little more than an office chair, and was raised one step above the floor.'[74] It took a battering, as during the discussions Napoleon would display some of the classic signs of nervous energy:

> In the middle of a debate, we would see him with a knife or scraper in his hand, carving at the arms of his chair and gouging out deep cuts. We were constantly busy bringing replacement parts for this chair that we were sure he would be cutting to pieces again tomorrow. To vary the pleasures of this kind, he would seize a quill pen and cover each sheet of paper in front of him with wide bars of ink. Once they were well blackened, he crumpled them up in his hands and threw them to the ground.[75]

Ambitious men preferred to take junior positions as *auditeurs* in the Conseil to grander ones elsewhere in the civil service, because it was a good place to catch Napoleon's eye. They formulated the proposed laws that the Conseil had agreed upon. As he grew older, if he wanted a particular *auditeur* to report to the Conseil he would use a lorgnette to search the window ledges on which they sat. Many people rightly saw a place in the Conseil as being a faster route to promotion that a seat in the Senate.

Sometimes Napoleon would announce in advance that he was going to attend a session, at others the councillors didn't know he was coming until they heard the drumroll on the Tuileries staircase. He would take his seat, ask searching questions, fall into reveries, go off on monologues. 'Do you know why I allow so much discussion at the Conseil?'

he once boasted to Roederer. 'It is because I am the strongest debater in the whole Conseil. I let myself be attacked, because I know how to defend myself.'[76] A proposed decree would be read out, then the specialist committee's report on it, and then Napoleon urged acknowledged experts on the subject to speak. The tone was matter-of-fact, and attempts at oratorical grandstanding tended only to inspire derision.

Napoleon made little effort to conceal his role-model as a lawgiver, civil engineer and nation-builder. 'He reformed the calendar,' he wrote of Julius Caesar, 'he worked on the wording of the civil, criminal and penal codes. He set up projects to beautify Rome with many fine buildings. He worked on compiling a general map of the Empire and statistics for the provinces; he charged Varro with setting up an extensive public library; he announced the project to drain the Pontine marshes.'[77] Although it is too early to say whether the institutions Napoleon put in place will last as long as Caesar's, he clearly put down what he called 'some masses of granite as anchors in the soul of France'.

13

Plots

'What a pity the man wasn't lazy.'

Talleyrand on Napoleon

'After great revolutions all sorts of events are to be expected, before things calm down.'

Napoleon to Jourdan, January 1800

'I shall blow into Paris unexpectedly,' Napoleon wrote to Lucien from Lyons on June 29, 1800. 'I want no triumphal arches or any such *colifichets* [fripperies]. I have too good an opinion of myself to care about such nonsense. The only real triumph is the satisfaction of the people.'[1] Napoleon arrived at the Tuileries at 2 a.m. on July 2, and on the 14th, by now a firm date in the republican calendar, huge parades were organized on the Champ de Mars (where the Eiffel Tower stands today) featuring captured standards, as well as ceremonies at Les Invalides, the Place de la Concorde and the Place Vendôme. He told his fellow consuls he didn't want a re-enactment of a chariot race, which 'might have been very good in Greece, where one fought on chariots, but that doesn't mean much *chez nous*'.[2] The Consular Guard had arrived only that morning, so they paraded in their tattered and bloodstained uniforms. Lucie de La Tour du Pin was surprised to find the crowd quiet and shocked at the sight of the wounded; she concluded that above all they wanted an early peace.[3] Although peace terms were being negotiated with Austria from as early as July, they wouldn't be signed until Moreau inflicted a crushing defeat on Archduke Johann at Hohenlinden on December 3, capturing 8,000 prisoners, 50 guns and 85 ammunition and baggage wagons. The Austrians fought on listlessly until Christmas Day, when the Archduke Charles agreed an armistice at Steyr, only

90 miles from Vienna. 'You surpassed yourself again in this campaign,' Napoleon wrote to Moreau. 'These wretched Austrians are very obstinate. They were relying upon the ice and snow; they weren't yet acquainted with you. I salute you affectionately.'[4]

The end of the Quasi-War with America came on October 3, with a treaty negotiated by Joseph and signed at Mortefontaine, his chateau on the Loire. This meant that France no longer had to face the threat of a nascent American navy co-operating with the British Royal Navy. 'The First Consul was grave,' wrote the American envoy William Van Murray after its ratification, 'rather thoughtful, occasionally severe – not inflated nor egotistical – very exact in all his motions which show at once an impatient heart and a methodical head ... of a most skillful fencing master ... He speaks with a frankness so much above fear that you think he has no reserve.'[5] Four days later, France and Spain agreed to the secret Convention of San Ildefonso, which provided that when France made peace with Austria, Habsburg-owned Tuscany would be ceded to the Bourbon heir of the Duke of Parma, King Charles IV of Spain's son-in-law Don Louis; in return Spain would cede Louisiana (then a vast territory covering land in thirteen modern-day US states from the Gulf of Mexico to the Canadian border) to France.* Under one of the provisions of San Ildefonso, France promised not to sell Louisiana to a third power.

Meanwhile, the prospect of Malta, which had been subjected to a two-year blockade by the Royal Navy, falling to Britain led Napoleon formally to give the island to Paul I of Russia, in the Tsar's capacity as the new grand master of the Knights of St John. Although this didn't carry any weight with the British once they captured the island on September 5, it served to improve Franco-Russian relations, and the Tsar offered to recognize the Rhine and the Alpes-Maritimes as France's natural borders. By the end of the year he had inaugurated the League of Armed Neutrality, by which Prussia, Sweden and Denmark joined Russia in opposing Britain's harsh and deeply unpopular maritime trade laws, particularly its unlimited searches of neutral shipping for French contraband. So friendly were Napoleon's relations with Paul by early 1801 that plans were even drawn up for Masséna to enter Astrakhan with 35,000 men, join up with 35,000 Russians and 50,000 Cossacks, and then cross the Caspian Sea to take Kandahar, from where they

---

* France had ceded Louisiana to Spain in the Treaty of Fontainebleau (1762).

would invade India.[6] It was another of Napoleon's far-fetched Oriental schemes, though not so fantastical as a march from Aleppo.

Just after 8 p.m. on Wednesday, December 24, 1800, Napoleon and Josephine took separate carriages to the Opéra to listen to Haydn's oratorio *The Creation*. At the corner of Place du Carrousel and rue Saint-Niçaise, gunpowder had been placed in a water-barrel on a seed-merchant's cart, drawn by a small dray horse, by Joseph Picot de Limoelan, a Chouan who had arrived from London just over a month earlier.* The fuse was lit by a former naval officer, Robinault de Saint-Régant, an accomplice of the Chouan leader Georges Cadoudal, who gave the horse's reins to a young girl to hold as he made off. A combination of the fuse being slightly too long and the speed with which Napoleon's coachman César was driving, swerving past the cart in the street, saved Napoleon's life.[7] 'Napoleon escaped by a singular chance,' recorded his aide-de-camp Jean Rapp, who was in the following coach with Josephine at the time. 'A grenadier of the escort had unwittingly driven one of the assassins away from standing in the middle of the rue Niçaise with the flat of his sabre and the cart was turned round from its intended position.'[8] Josephine's carriage was far enough behind for all its occupants to survive the massive explosion too, although Hortense was lightly cut on her wrist by the flying glass of the carriage windows. The *machine infernale*, as it was dubbed, killed five people (including the young girl holding the horse) and injured twenty-six.[9] It could have been far more, since no fewer than forty-six houses were damaged.

Both carriages came to a halt, and through the scene of carnage Rapp got out of Josephine's carriage to check on Napoleon. When Josephine was told that her husband was unharmed, and indeed insisted on continuing to the Opéra, she bravely followed and found 'Napoleon was seated in his box, calm and composed, and looking at the audience through his opera-glass.' 'Josephine, those rascals wanted to blow me up,' he said as she entered the box, and he asked for the oratorio's programme.[10] Napoleon's performance was as masterly as anything they were likely to see on stage that night. When the audience learned what had happened, they cheered his escape.

Ever since Napoleon had replied to the would-be Louis XVIII explaining the impossibility of a Bourbon restoration there had been plots of

* Since demolished, the rue Saint-Niçaise started where today's rue de l'Échelle meets the rue de Rivoli.

differing degrees of seriousness against his life. On September 4, seventeen men had been arrested and accused of a *projet d'assassination*.[11] Then on October 11 a conspiracy was uncovered to stab Napoleon as he left the Opéra. One of the plotters, Joseph-Antoine Aréna, was the brother of the Corsican deputy who had allegedly brandished the knife during Brumaire.[12] 'I didn't run any real danger,' Napoleon told the Tribunate when it congratulated him on his escape. 'The seven or eight wretches, in spite of their desire, were unable to commit the crimes they meditated.'[13] On October 24 a dozen more people were arrested for a plot which involved throwing *oeufs rouges* (hand grenades) into Napoleon's carriage on his way to Malmaison.[14] The pyrotechnician Alexandre Chevalier escaped the net, as did another plotter, Thomas Desforges, who had been a friend of Josephine's before her marriage.

Two weeks after that, on November 7, the royalist Chevalier was finally arrested and a multi-firing gun was seized, along with plans for fireworks to frighten Napoleon's horses and for iron spikes to be laid across the street to prevent the Consular Guard from coming to the rescue. A week later yet another plot, involving the blocking of a street down which Napoleon was to pass, was discovered by a hardworking Fouché. In an official report he listed no fewer than ten separate conspiracies against Napoleon's life since he had come to power, including by accomplices of Chevalier who were still at large.[15] Police reports began to indicate that the public assumed Napoleon would indeed be assassinated sooner or later.

Of all these plots, the *machine infernale* came closest to success. Some excellent forensic work by Fouché's detectives reassembled the horseshoes, harness and cart, and a grain merchant identified the man to whom he had sold it.* As the net tightened, Limoelan escaped, perhaps to become a priest in America.[16] Although everything pointed to the Chouan royalists, the incident was too good an opportunity for Napoleon to waste politically and he told the Conseil that he wanted to act against 'the Terrorists' – that is, the Jacobins who had supported the Terror and opposed Brumaire. Six years after his imprisonment in 1794 for his Jacobin loyalties Napoleon now believed them to be enemies of the state even more dangerous than the Chouan assassins, because of their ideology, familiarity with power and superior organization. 'With one company of grenadiers I could send the whole Faubourg

---

* The bomb's firing mechanism is on display in the Musée de la Préfecture de Police in the rue de Carmes in Paris.

Saint-Germain flying,' he said at this time of the royalist salons found there, 'but the Jacobins are made of sterner stuff, they are not beaten so easily.'[17] When Fouché ventured to blame British-backed royalists such as Cadoudal, Napoleon demurred, referring to the September Massacres of 1792: 'They are men of September [*Septembriseurs*], wretches stained with blood, ever conspiring in solid phalanx against every successive government. We must find a means of prompt redress,' and adding that 'France will be tranquil about the existence of its Government only when it's freed from these scroundrels.'[18] So, emotionally at least, Napoleon left behind his revolutionary past.

On New Year's Day 1801, Louis Dubois, who was then a member of the central police bureau but the following month was appointed prefect of police, read a report to the Conseil about the various assassination plots, including one to infiltrate assassins into the Guard Grenadiers, another where a man called Metgen was going to try to stab Napoleon at the Comédie-Française during Racine's *Britannicus* (which Napoleon hadn't attended that particular night) and a third from a M. Gombault-Lachaise who had invented a machine containing 'Greek Fire' explosives that he was to have launched at Napoleon during Desaix's obsequies, before he found that heavy decorations were in the way.[19] 'Chouannerie and the émigrés are skin diseases,' Napoleon said at that meeting. 'Terrorism is an internal malady.'*

On January 8, 130 Jacobins were arrested and deported – mainly to Guiana – by means of a *sénatus-consulte* passed three days earlier. (Although the *sénatus-consulte* was originally intended to be used only to alter the constitution, Napoleon found it increasingly useful as a way of bypassing the Legislative Body and Tribunate.) Guiana was nicknamed 'the dry guillotine' because its climate was almost as lethal as a death sentence. There was no public outcry. Even though they were innocent of plotting the *machine infernale*, many had been involved in judicial murders, especially those who had been in decision-making roles during the Terror. When Théophile Berlier sought to argue with Napoleon over the fates of two Jacobins called Destrem and Talon, the First Consul replied frankly that he was deporting them not because he thought they were behind the *machine infernale*, but 'for their conduct during the Revolution'. Berlier countered that without the bomb going off the question of transporting Destrem and Talon would never have

---

* Napoleon wrote to Jourdan on January 13 saying 'England seems to be very much involved in all this' (CG3 no. 5913, p. 513).

arisen, upon which Napoleon merely laughed and said: 'Aha, Monsieur Lawyer, you won't allow that you are beaten!'[20]*

Unusually, unless there was another agenda lost to us, Fouché's list of deportees was idiosyncratic and slapdash; one Jacobin had been a judge in Guadaloupe for five years, another had been dead for six months, and several others had made their peace with the new regime and were even working for it. It was the last of the mass roundups that had characterized the previous twelve years of French politics. 'From that time the spirit of the capital changed as if by the waving of a wand,' Napoleon later reminisced.[21] Simultaneously with his wholly political purge of the Jacobins, the real Chouan plotters were also rounded up, and nine, including Chevalier, were guillotined on January 30–31, although the Comte de Bourmont was merely imprisoned (and escaped in 1804, later fighting for Napoleon in Portugal). When, in December 1804, evidence was produced that there had been yet another assassination plot similar to Cadoudal's, Napoleon merely exiled one of its members, Jean de La Rochefoucauld-Dubreuil.[22]

Before the *machine infernale*, Napoleon had attempted to introduce draconian security laws that extended the use of extraordinary military tribunals into civilian life. The Conseil d'État thought them over-authoritarian and they had to be withdrawn on the protests of liberal and moderate legislators in the Tribunate, including Pierre Daunou, the poet Marie-Joseph Chénier (who had written the lyrics to 'Le Chant du Départ') and the writer Benjamin Constant.[23] After the explosion they were quickly passed. Napoleon had taken an aggressive stance towards the Tribunate almost as soon as he had invented it, denouncing Constant, Daunou and Chénier as 'Metaphysicians whom it were well to duck in water ... You must not think that I will let myself be attacked like Louis XVI. I will not allow it.'[24] In a bid to foil future plots, he never let it be publicly known where he meant to go until five minutes before his departure.[25]

On February 9, 1801, the Peace of Lunéville, negotiated by Joseph and Talleyrand and an eventually exhausted Count Ludwig von Cobenzl, finally ended the nine-year war between Austria and France. The treaty was loosely based on Campo Formio, securing French gains in Belgium, Italy and the Rhineland, but stripping Austria of much of the territorial compensations she had received in northern Italy in that treaty four years earlier, to which Francis would have done well to adhere. The Franco-Russian rapprochement, and the fact that Moreau was within

---

* Destrem died on the Île d'Oléron in 1803; Talon was back in government by 1809.

striking distance of Vienna, gave Cobenzl little room for diplomatic manoeuvre. Austria lost Tuscany to France, which under the terms already agreed between France and Spain at the Convention of San Ildefonso then became the Kingdom of Etruria and was bestowed upon Don Louis, the 'astonishingly stupid' (according to Laure d'Abrantès) twenty-eight-year-old great-grandson of Louis XV who had married the Infanta María Luisa of Spain. 'Rome will be tranquil,' Napoleon said of the new king. 'This one won't cross the Rubicon.'[26]

Etruria was only nominally independent, of course; despite having Bourbons at its head it paid heavily to maintain its French garrison.[27]* Napoleon's creation of a kingdom rather than a sister-republic was rightly seen in France as a step towards conditioning the French people for a monarchy at home, but when King Louis I of Etruria visited Paris in January 1802 and Napoleon took him to the Comédie-Française to watch *Oedipus*, the audience heartily cheered Philoctetes' line from Act II scene 4: 'I have made sovereigns, but have refused to become one.'[28] Napoleon still needed to tread with caution.

The Lunéville peace was greeted with huge relief in France, especially when it was announced that most of the conscripts who were going to be called up from the class-year 1802 would not now be needed, and that soldiers who had served in four campaigns – up to one-eighth of the army – could be demobilized.[29] In his message to the Senate of February 13, Napoleon declared that he would 'fight only to secure the peace and happiness of the world', although he could not resist threatening to 'avenge' the 'insults' suffered from a boundlessly ambitious Britain, which he always called England.[30] Yet Britain too was tired of continual conflict, and almost ready to sheathe the sword after nearly a decade of war.

On February 17, Napoleon attended Talleyrand's fête to celebrate the Peace of Lunéville held at the foreign ministry, the Hôtel Galifet in the rue du Bac, which extended southwards from the Pont Royal through the Faubourg Saint-Germain and contained a long gallery with a theatre attached. Among those present was the American consul-general Victor du Pont.† 'It was the most magnificent thing of the kind I ever saw,' du

---

* Because the departing Grand Duke of Tuscany had stripped his Florentine palace bare before the new king and queen arrived, the Infanta noted in the third person that 'This was the first time that the daughter of the King of Spain, accustomed to be served on gold and silver, saw herself obliged to eat off porcelain' (Etruria, *Memoirs* p. 309).

† Son of the economist Pierre du Pont de Nemours who had left France after two imprisonments to set up a successful commercial enterprise in the United States (today's chemical giant DuPont).

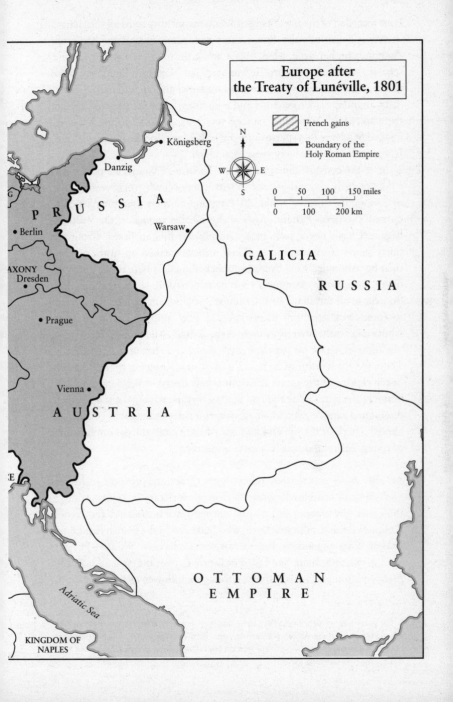

Europe after
the Treaty of Lunéville, 1801

///// French gains

—— Boundary of the
Holy Roman Empire

N
W · E
S

0   50   100   150 miles
0   100   200 km

Königsberg

Danzig

PRUSSIA

• Berlin

Warsaw •

GALICIA

RUSSIA

AXONY
Dresden •

• Prague

Vienna •

AUSTRIA

OTTOMAN
EMPIRE

Adriatic Sea

KINGDOM OF
NAPLES

Pont recorded of the fête.* Giuseppina Grassini 'displayed all the charms of a most delicious voice. She is a very handsome woman and had more diamonds on her neck, head, breast and arms than I remember to have seen on any woman before.' It was said that Napoleon had given these to her in Italy when she became his mistress, although diamonds were 'very abundant since generals and commissaries of the government get them so cheap'. Napoleon 'seemed very much pleased during her singing and Madame Bonaparte quite out of humour; for she is very jealous'. Josephine, too, wore 'very large' diamonds.

After the concert, the actors of the Théâtre de Vaudeville performed a light comedy about the peace 'in which almost every verse was a praise of Bonaparte' and of what du Pont inaccurately but prophetically termed 'the royal Family'. After a short ballet sequence, the waltzing began. 'I have never seen such a display of human flesh,' wrote the thirty-four-year-old diplomat. 'Their arms are naked up to the armpit, their breasts entirely uncovered and their shoulders bare below the middle of their backs.' Moreover their petticoats were short, thin and few, 'to expose all the shape of their limbs'.[31] Napoleon walked from room to room with four tall handsome aides-de-camp in hussar uniform whose cap-feathers were 'as high as the ceiling'. Meanwhile Talleyrand, 'dandling along on his lame feet, kept close, to do honours of the fête'.[32] These were celebrations he could well afford. Knowing that under one of the clauses of the treaty Austrian bonds issued in Belgium would be honoured at par, Talleyrand had made a fortune buying them up at their discounted rates.[33] Even in an age where insider-dealing was considered almost a perk of the job and had few of the moral or legal implications of today, Talleyrand was in a class of his own.

An even more momentous peace treaty came into prospect in March 1801, when Lord Hawkesbury, the foreign secretary in Henry Addington's new government in London, opened discussions with the French diplomat Louis-Guillaume Otto, who had been in the British capital for several years organizing prisoner-of-war exchanges. William Pitt the Younger's government had fallen in February over the issue of Catholic Emancipation and Hawkesbury, although a follower of Pitt, cautiously

---

* The party management might have been improved, however. With 1,200 people arriving at an average of three people per carriage, and each carriage having ninety seconds to unload its passengers from 9 p.m. onwards, du Pont noticed some people still arriving at six o'clock the next morning.

began to explore the possibility of an accommodation with France, which had been anathema to the Pitt ministry. At the same time, a British expeditionary force landed at Aboukir in Egypt on March 8. With generals Friant, Belliard, Lanusse and Menou still unable to evacuate their troops because the Royal Navy was off Toulon blockading Admiral Ganteaume, who was supposed to go to pick them up, Napoleon faced a seriously deteriorating position in Egypt.

The assassination of Tsar Paul I on March 23 came as a blow to Napoleon, who is said to have cried out in rage at the news. He suspected British spies were behind the murder, although the actual perpetrators were a group of Russian nobles and the Hanoverian General Levin von Bennigsen.[34] Paul was mentally unstable, although not certifiably insane like George III of Britain, Christian VII of Denmark and Maria 'the Mad' of Portugal, who all occupied European thrones at the time, albeit with regencies exercising actual control. Paul's policies supporting the middle classes had been seen as threatening the Russian nobility. His twenty-three-year-old son and heir Alexander, who was in the palace at the time of the assassination, may have had an intimation that the nobles were going to demand his father's abdication (which they did indeed secure, before they stabbed, strangled and kicked the Tsar to death). Alexander was crowned tsar later that year. Although he theoretically had absolute power, he knew that he had to work with the nobility if he were to escape his father's fate.

Alexander I was a riddle. Reared in the Enlightenment atmosphere of his grandmother Catherine the Great's court, and taught Rousseauian principles at a young age by his Swiss tutor Frédéric de La Harpe, he was nonetheless capable of telling his justice minister, 'You always want to instruct me, but I am the autocratic emperor, and I will this and nothing else!' He has been described as combining a theoretical love of mankind with a practical contempt for men. Well-meaning, impressionable and egotistical, he was so good at playing a part that Napoleon later dubbed him 'the Talma of the North', and on another occasion 'a shifty Byzantine'. He claimed that he would happily abolish serfdom if only civilization were more advanced, but never genuinely came close to doing so, any more than he ever carried through the codification of Russian law that he promised in 1801 or ratified the liberal constitution he had asked his advisor Count Mikhail Speranski to draw up a few years later. Although La Harpe had initially enthused Alexander about Napoleon's reforms as First Consul, when the tutor returned from Paris he was so disillusioned that he wrote a book, *Reflexions on the True Nature of the First Consulship for Life*, that described Napoleon as 'the most famous tyrant the world has produced', which had a great effect on the young tsar. Since Alexander ultimately did more than any other individual to bring about Napoleon's downfall, his emergence on to the European scene with his father's assassination was a seminal moment.

Napoleon rightly feared that Alexander and the Russian nobility, which tended to be pro-British because they profited from the Baltic trade with them, would now make Russia leave Tsar Paul's League of Armed Neutrality. The League was badly weakened on April 2 when Nelson attacked Copenhagen and captured twelve Danish ships and destroyed another three. When, years later, Napoleon met a Royal Navy officer called Lieutenant Payne who had fought at the battle of Copenhagen, he said: 'You had warm work there for the time it lasted.'[35] It was true; the Danes put up a strong fight and remained thereafter loyally in Napoleon's camp. Napoleon ordered the *Moniteur* to state ominously in its report of the Tsar's assassination and the attack on Copenhagen: 'History will unveil the connection which may exist between these two events.'[36] (It hasn't.) To the courier carrying his message of friendship to Tsar Alexander, Napoleon said: 'Go, sir, gallop, and don't forget that the world was made in six days.'[37]

On April 14, Hawkesbury proposed that the French should evacuate Egypt in return for the British evacuation of Minorca, thus leaving Britain with Malta, Tobago, Martinique, Trinidad, Ceylon and the Dutch Guianan sugar colonies of Essequibo, Demerara and Berbice as the price of peace. Napoleon refused, demanding instead that Britain give up all of those wartime gains as well as the territory taken from the late Tipu Sahib in India. The mutual outrageousness of both proposals implies that both sides knew these to be merely opening gambits with months of haggling ahead, and so it turned out. On April 24 Napoleon sent Duroc to see the King of Prussia in Berlin and the new Tsar in St Petersburg and 'speak as if we are sure of being able to hold Egypt' – a clear sign that they weren't. Duroc was told to say that if the British expedition there 'should succeed, it will be a great misfortune for Europe'.[38] Time seemed to be on Britain's side, however, as Paul's assassination led to the collapse of the League of Armed Neutrality in May and June when first Sweden, then Denmark and finally Russia herself signed peace treaties with London.

Napoleon spent May attempting to cajole admirals Bruix, Ganteaume, Villeneuve, Rosily and Linois to relieve the army in Egypt. They used news of missing Spanish ships, vessels going aground, epidemics and anything else that occurred to them to avoid sailing across the Mediterranean on what they feared might be a suicide mission against the Royal Navy. (Napoleon's understanding of naval affairs was dismal. He never truly grasped that the British ability to fire broadsides far more often per minute made the sheer numbers of ships in any engagement largely irrelevant, and that blockading France at sea strengthened rather than weakened British fighting ability.) Frustrated by the slow pace of negotiations, the British began besieging Alexandria, intending to expel the French from Egypt altogether.

On August 5 Hawkesbury told Otto that he might allow Malta to become independent. This – denying the use of the strategically vital island to the Royal Navy – was the concession Napoleon had been seeking. When he learned that Menou had capitulated to British forces on September 2 after a two-week siege, he ordered Otto to offer a French withdrawal from Egypt, Naples and the Papal States in exchange for peace, before the news reached the British Government.* Not knowing that the French had been defeated in Alexandria, Hawkesbury agreed.

On October 1, 1801 Otto signed the fifteen articles of an accord, and celebrations broke out in both France and Britain. 'The public were so impatient to express their feelings on the occasion of the news of the preliminaries of peace being signed', reported *The Times*, 'that almost all the public streets were illuminated last night.'[39] Otto's portrait was exhibited in shop windows and his praises sung by balladeers. When Napoleon's aide-de-camp General Jacques de Lauriston arrived in London with the official ratification a few days later, the crowd detached the horses from his coach and pulled it themselves from Oxford Street to St James's Street, and then from Downing Street to the Admiralty and through St James's Park, while celebrations carried on throughout the night despite a thunderstorm and torrential rain.[40] All this was deeply unwelcome to Hawkesbury, who believed it would only strengthen Napoleon's negotiating position prior to the ratification of the full treaty.[41]†

---

* Napoleon absolved Menou from any personal responsibility for the Egyptian disaster, but he was never given a battlefield command again.

† Napoleon's correspondence on September 30, 1801, the day before the preliminary treaty was signed, perfectly represents his compartmentalized mind. He sent off eleven letters: three to Chaptal (one appointing a prefect to the Liamone department), one to Fouché ordering the incarceration in the Ham prison of anyone caught exporting wheat, one each to François Barbé-Marbois the treasury minister and André Abrial the justice minister, three to Talleyrand and two to Berthier demanding that beds be found for the men of the 23rd

Under Article 2 of the preliminary treaty, Britain restored to France, Spain and Holland nearly all the territories she had captured since 1793, encompassing the Cape of Good Hope, Dutch Guiana, Tobago, Martinique, St Lucia, Minorca and Pondicherry, retaining only Trinidad and Ceylon (present-day Sri Lanka). Article 4 stipulated that Britain would return Malta to the Knights of St John within a month, who would then be protected by a third power to be decided by the final treaty (it was eventually six powers); Article 5 returned Egypt to the Ottoman Empire; Article 7 required France to evacuate Naples and the Papal States and Britain to evacuate Elba and 'all the ports and islands which she may occupy in the Mediterranean or in the Adriatic Seas'. Other, unremarkable articles, covered the Ionian Islands, prisoner exchanges and fishing rights in Newfoundland.[42]

Napoleon had been able to extract great concessions due to the British desire for peace, which, because of the disruption of trade with Europe from nine years of war, amounted almost to desperation. The treaty was a massive diplomatic coup, since Egypt was being evacuated anyway after Menou's defeat, as the British discovered on October 2, the very day after its signature. The whole of France's overseas empire was returned to her for the cost of parts of Italy that Napoleon was under pressure from Russia – which retained interests in the Mediterranean and had an army in Switzerland as recently as 1800 – to give up in any case, and which he could easily recapture if necessary. Territorially, all Britain had gained after nearly a decade of war and £290 million – which more than doubled her National Debt – were Trinidad and Ceylon, neither of which had belonged to France anyway.[43] By contrast, French troops were on the Rhine, in Holland and in north-west Italy, and France had hegemony over Switzerland and influence over her ally Spain – none of which the treaty mentioned.

Despite all that, London continued to celebrate. 'The Peace is an event which had excited a tumult of joy such as I never before saw equalled,' a friend wrote to the diarist Henry Crabb Robinson.

The Funds were falling and the expectation of an invasion very general . . .
The demonstrations of joy have risen almost to madness. Illuminations have been general throughout the kingdom . . . It is said that 'Long live

---

Division garrisoning Bastia, who were still sleeping on straw (CG3 nos. 6525–35 pp. 795–8).

Buonaparte!' was repeatedly cried in the streets . . . Indeed it is curious to observe the change of style in the Government papers. The 'Corsican adventurer', 'the atheistical adventurer', is now 'the august hero', 'the restorer of public order', etc, etc, in fact everything that is great and good. It reminds one of the transformation in a pantomime, where a devil is suddenly converted into an angel.[44]

Napoleon signed a treaty of friendship with Bavaria in August 1801, then a peace treaty with Russia on October 8, 1801, by which 6,000 Russian prisoners were returned home with their arms and uniforms. The next day a peace treaty was also concluded with Turkey, by which each country's ports were opened to the other. Thus within the space of a year, Napoleon had made peace with Austria, Naples, Turkey, Russia, Britain and the émigrés. Prussia would follow in the early summer of the following year. On October 14 the sixty-three-year-old Lord Cornwallis, the British general who had surrendered to Washington at Yorktown in 1781, was welcomed to Calais with a salute of cannon and a guard of honour and conducted first to Paris, where there were celebrations and public illuminations,* and then to Amiens to conduct the detailed negotiations of the treaty with Joseph and Talleyrand.[45] (Amiens was chosen for its good omens; Henry VIII and François I had signed a peace treaty there in 1527.)

On November 20, 1801, Napoleon appointed the first functionaries for the Tuileries: chamberlains, chancellors, almoners, equerries, footmen and even *tranchants* (carvers), whose job it was to cut his meat for him.[46] Miot de Melito noted that instead of high cavalry boots, sabres and cockades there were now knee-breeches, silk stockings, silver-buckled shoes, dress swords and hats carried under the arm.[47] These liveried flunkeys and courtiers were instructed in etiquette by Marie Antoinette's former first lady of the bedchamber, who explained who might approach the First Consul, when and under what circumstances.[48] Within six months the Marquis de Lucchesini, the Prussian ambassador to Paris, was reporting that 'Everything around the First Consul and his wife is resuming the general character and etiquette of Versailles.'[49] Small wonder that men

---

* Napoleon was worried that paintings and statues in the Louvre were being disturbed during the celebrations 'to make space for foreigners to be able to see out of the windows'. When visitors asked for stoves to be installed to warm the museum he sensibly rejected the idea as far too dangerous (CG3 no. 6624 p. 836).

like Moreau wondered why France had gone to the bother of decapitating Louis XVI.

A week after Cornwallis arrived in France, Otto informed Hawkesbury that now that the Atlantic Ocean was safe to cross, France was going to send an expedition of 12,000 men from Rochefort and Brest 'to re-establish order on Saint-Domingue' (present-day Haiti).[50] In the early 1790s the produce of this former slave colony of 8,000 plantations was greater than all of Europe's other Caribbean and American colonies combined, providing 40 per cent of Europe's consumption of sugar and 60 per cent of its coffee, and accounting for 40 per cent of all of France's overseas trade.[51] By 1801, however, because of the slave revolt led over the course of the previous six years by Toussaint l'Ouverture, sugar exports were a mere 13 per cent of their 1789 total and cotton 15 per cent.[52] The effects on French trade, and thus on the prosperity of ports such as Bordeaux, Nantes and Le Havre, had been devastating, and merchants were calling loudly for the reintroduction of direct French control – and that meant slavery too. The Jacobins who had abolished slavery and the slave trade in 1794 were either dead, in disgrace or in prison. Napoleon was keen to return to the days when Saint-Domingue produced 180 million francs per annum for the French treasury, gave employment to 1,640 ships and thousands of seamen, and kept the French Atlantic ports thriving. He hoped it might even provide a strategic springboard for a new French empire in the western hemisphere, especially now that France had exchanged Tuscany for Louisiana.

Although Napoleon wrote proclamations to the Saint-Dominguans about how all men were free and equal in the sight of God, and to l'Ouverture – significantly for the first time using the royal 'we' – of 'these brave blacks whose courage we like and whom we would be most regretful of punishing for rebellion', this was only for show.[53] Napoleon had bought slaves when in Egypt, and he now ordered his brother-in-law, the twenty-nine-year-old General Charles Leclerc (married to his sister Pauline), whose expedition of 20,000 men arrived on the island on January 29, 1802 and was soon reinforced by 8,000 more the next month, to reintroduce slavery as soon as he safely could.[54] As Napoleon warned the local population, anyone daring to 'separate himself from the Captain-General [Leclerc] shall be considered a traitor to his country, and the wrath of the Republic shall consume him as the fire burns up your withered sugar-canes'.[55] He ordered Leclerc to follow a three-stage plan: first, to promise the blacks anything and everything while he occupied the key strategic positions on the island, secondly, to arrest and deport all potential opponents, and only then to embark on the reintroduction of slavery.[56]

The charismatic and ruthless Toussaint l'Ouverture, a black freeman who had himself owned slaves, had imposed a constitution on Saint-Domingue in May 1801 that made him dictator for life, ostensibly in the name of the French revolutionary principles of liberty and equality. He had also created an army of 20,000 former slaves and taken over the whole island, expelling the Spanish from the eastern half (the present-day Dominican Republic).[57] He was not about to fall for Leclerc's fine words, and fighting broke out before Leclerc could implement the first stage of Napoleon's plan. While Leclerc's armada of fifty-four ships was on its way, l'Ouverture had put down an internal uprising, executing the ringleader (his own nephew) and 2,000 rebels. His plan to defeat the French was to destroy any resources they might find on the coast and then to retreat into the mountainous jungle interior to conduct guerrilla warfare.

Leclerc had failed to take into account the horrific ravages that malaria and yellow fever would wreak on his army. Once a shortage of supplies and the outbreak of those diseases struck he faced impossible odds. His only reinforcements were a few Polish and Swiss conscripts.[58] (Two Swiss brigades mutinied at Toulon the moment they learned where they were headed.) The war swiftly turned into a bloody campaign of racial extermination, for which the absent Napoleon must take a large share of the responsibility. Although there is no evidence to support the modern accusation that, as one historian recently put it, 'Bonaparte hated black people', he undoubtedly shared the widespread Western assumption of the day that whites were superior to all non-whites, and he expected Leclerc to prevail easily with such a large, well-armed force against native fighters, just as he had at the battles of the Pyramids and Aboukir.[59] 'If I were black,' Napoleon said, 'I would be for the blacks; being white, I am for the whites.'[60] At Jaffa, as we have seen, he had executed several thousand non-European prisoners-of-war. Now he was harsh on miscegenation, ordering that 'White women [in Saint-Domingue] who have prostituted themselves to blacks, no matter what their rank, will be sent to Europe.'[61]

On May 20, 1802, Napoleon passed a law reintroducing the slave trade (though technically not slavery itself) to all French colonies according to the rules pertaining in 1789.[62] Britain – which punished the murder of a slave in Barbados in 1802 with a fine of £11 4 shillings, and retained slavery until 1834 – sent a large watching force to Trinidad in case either the slave revolt or Napoleonic imperialism spread there. In America President Thomas Jefferson, who also owned slaves, declared American neutrality, watching equally nervously.[63]

The fighting on Saint-Domingue was brutal. Plantations were torched, massacres and torture were common, towns were razed; there were mass drownings; corkscrews were used to draw out the eyes of French prisoners, and the French even constructed a makeshift gas chamber (*étouffier*) on board a ship in which volcanic sulphur was used to asphyxiate four hundred prisoners, before the ship was scuttled.[64] Toussaint l'Ouverture finally surrendered on May 1 on terms whereby the freedom of Saint-Domingue's blacks was officially guaranteed, black officers were accepted into the French army, and l'Ouverture himself and his staff were allowed to retire to one of his several plantations.[65] However, on June 7, on his own initiative, Leclerc suddenly reneged on the deal, kidnapped l'Ouverture and sent him to prison in France. The guerrilla war continued, and on October 7 Leclerc wrote to Napoleon: 'We must destroy all the mountain negroes, men and women, only keep children under twelve years old, destroy half the ones of the plains, and so not leave in the colony one coloured man who wears the epaulette.'[66] Napoleon did not respond directly to this, but certainly did not forbid it.

On November 27 Napoleon wrote to Leclerc about Pauline, who had bravely gone out on the expedition, saying he was 'highly satisfied with the conduct of Paulette. She ought not to fear death, as she would die with glory in dying with the army and being useful to her husband. Everything passes rapidly on earth, with the exception of the mark we leave on history.'[67] At the time he wrote, Leclerc himself was nearly four weeks dead from yellow fever. 'Come back soon,' Napoleon wrote to Pauline on learning of Leclerc's death, 'here you will find consolation for your misfortunes in the love of your family. I embrace you.' Pauline – whom Laure d'Abrantès described as 'a less-than-desolate widow' – returned with the body on January 1, 1803, and by the end of August she was remarried, to the handsome and rich Don Camillo Filippo Ludovico Borghese, Prince of Sulmona and of Rossano, Duke and Prince of Guastalla, whom she privately thought 'an imbecile' and to whom she was soon wildly unfaithful.[68]*

---

* The plaster-cast of one of Pauline's breasts taken by Canova in 1804 can be seen today in the Museo Napoleonica in Rome. She was beautiful, although Laure d'Abrantès claimed she had over-large ears.

The extermination on Saint-Domingue continued unabated after Leclerc's death, as l'Ouverture's lieutenants and successors continued the struggle against his exceptionally cruel second-in-command, the Vicomte de Rochambeau, who, despite receiving large numbers of reinforcements, managed to sail only 8,000 men back to France in May 1803. Twenty generals, 30,000 Frenchmen and possibly as many as 350,000 Saint-Dominguans (of both races) had died.[69] Toussaint l'Ouverture, 'the Black Spartacus', died of pneumonia on April 7, 1803 in a large cold cell that can be visited today in the Fort de Joux in the Jura mountains.[70]

'The Saint-Domingue business was a great piece of folly on my part,' Napoleon later admitted. 'It was the greatest error that in all my government I ever committed. I ought to have treated with the black leaders, as I would have done the authorities in a province.'[71] One lesson he did learn was that blacks could make excellent soldiers, and in November 1809 he set up a unit called the Black Pioneers, made up of men from Egypt and the Caribbean under a black battalion commander, Joseph 'Hercules' Domingue, to whom he gave a special award of 3,000 francs. By 1812 Napoleon didn't believe any colonies could be held in perpetuity, predicting that they would all eventually 'follow the example of the United States. You grow tired of waiting for orders from five thousand miles away; tired of obeying a government which seems foreign to you because it's remote, and because of necessity it subordinates you to its own local interest, which it cannot sacrifice to yours.'[72] The defeat in Saint-Domingue ended for ever Napoleon's dreams of a French empire in the West.

14

Amiens

'The French people need to support me with my flaws, if they find in me some advantages. My flaw is being unable to bear insults.'

Napoleon to Roederer, 1800

'Ambassadors are essentially spies with titles.'

Napoleon to Eugène, 1805

At 9 p.m. on Monday, January 4, 1802, Napoleon's brother Louis was married to Josephine's daughter Hortense by the mayor of Paris' 1st *arrondissement*. It was only one of a large number of marriages arranged by Napoleon, whose involvement in the nuptial lives of others was almost uniformly disastrous – certainly so in this case, as very soon Louis, who was in love with someone else at the time, could hardly bear to share a room with Hortense, and vice versa. Napoleon treated Hortense as his own daughter. Everyone liked her except the man Napoleon selected to marry her. (She later described her schooldays as the only happy time of her life; there can be no sadder statement.) Josephine was also to blame for the match, which tied her family closer to her husband's at the cost of her own daughter's happiness.

Although Joseph had shown himself a skilful negotiator over the Concordat and ending the Quasi-War, and Napoleon was pleased with his youngest brother Jérôme, who had entered the French navy, his siblings were now becoming a mixed blessing to him in public life. Lucien, in particular, was hard to control. Napoleon was reportedly furious in November 1800 that Lucien, as interior minister, had permitted the publication of Louis de Fontanes' pamphlet *Parallèle entre César, Cromwell, Monk et Bonaparte* which, although predictably sycophantic in its conclusion, Napoleon rightly feared would draw attention to the fact that none had come to power constitutionally. 'There can be no comparison between me and Cromwell,' he later stated. 'I was three times elected by my people; and besides, in France my army has never made war on Frenchmen, but only on foreigners.'[1] (The *fédérés* of Toulon, people of the Vendée and the Paris Sections might have taken issue with that last remark.) Fontanes was one of Napoleon's chief propagandists, so it is doubtful the publication came as a complete surprise; he may in fact have been feigning anger because the public reaction to the pamphlet, which effectively hinted by historical analogy that Napoleon should become an absolute ruler, was immediately hostile. Printing was halted and Lucien was sent off to Spain as ambassador soon afterwards. After Lucien's first wife, Christine Boyer, died in May 1800, he married, again for love, the widow Alexandrine Jouberthon, by whom he was to have ten children. Napoleon disapproved of his second marriage because he would have preferred a more advantageous match for the family, upon which Lucien broke with his brother and retired to live in Rome.[2]

Reviving the old royal practice by which generals and senior dignitaries had to ask the head of state's permission to marry, Napoleon attempted to marry his generals into Ancien Régime families. The marriages that Napoleon opposed, such as Lucien's and Jérôme's (to his first wife), tended to be happier than the ones that he and Josephine matchmade. Even when the marriages he had organized were successful, he did little to help them; when Murat asked permission to leave Italy to see his wife, Napoleon's sister Caroline, and their new-born baby, Napoleon refused on the ground that 'A soldier must remain faithful to his wife, but only wish to see her again when it's judged that there is nothing left to do.'[3] Napoleon's difficult relations with some members of his family were undoubtedly self-inflicted.

At midnight on January 8, 1802, Napoleon left with Josephine for Lyons, where he was going to be offered the chief magistracy (that is, presidency) of the new Italian Republic, which would be made up of the Cisalpine Republic and those provinces of Italy taken from Austria by the Treaty of Lunéville. The next day Cambacérès, who was left in charge in Paris, wrote the first of what were to total 1,397 letters detailing everything of interest going on in France, allowing Napoleon to keep in close touch with events wherever he was in Europe. In an early letter, Napoleon learned that Les Halles central food market was well procured, the mayor of Brussels had apologized for condoning smuggling, General Belliard wanted a particular paragraph inserted in the *Moniteur*, the navy minister reported good winds at Flushing, a Senate commission had met to discuss constitutional reform, and Junot had received a report about the secret seditious activity of a tribune.[4] In many respects these letters were the precursors of the reports that the ministry of police would send Napoleon daily between 1804 and 1814.

The Consultation of Lyons lasted for two weeks and was marked by many parties, parades, receptions and factory visits, but the key moment came on January 25 when Napoleon, after reviewing the troops that had returned from Egypt in the Place Bellecour, was elected chief magistrate of the Italian Republic at a meeting in the Jesuit College (today the Lycée Ampère). A Committee of Thirty, headed by Francesco Melzi d'Eril, proposed Napoleon's name to the 450 Italian delegates present, with the gavel banged down immediately after the question was put just in case anyone had the temerity to demur.[5] Melzi had organized the delegates into sections according to whether they had come from the Austrian, Piedmontese, Venetian or Papal areas, thereby deliberately maximizing disunity and minimizing the chances of opposition. Though it was humiliating that the new Italian Republic should be founded in France, where Talleyrand could better keep an eye on the delegates, this was the first time that the word 'Italy' had appeared on the political map of Europe since the collapse of Rome in the fifth century AD. Napoleon wrote a constitution that was a far cry from the universal suffrage favoured by the Revolution, with elective power resting firmly in the hands of landowners, clergy, professionals, academics and merchants voting in electoral colleges for the legislative bodies.

Back in Paris on March 18, while Napoleon examined medals of Alexander the Great and Julius Caesar at the Louvre and handled the sword of Henri IV at the Bibliothèque Nationale, Cambacérès carried out a constitutional coup, purging the Legislative Body and the Tribunate through a *sénatus-consulte*.[6] 'One cannot work with an institution so productive of disorder,' Napoleon had said of the Tribunate in a discussion in the Conseil shortly before leaving for Lyons. Those considered *idéologues* and 'zealous republicans' were therefore now excluded from it, including Chénier, Daunou, Benjamin Constant, the ex-Girondin Maximin Isnard and the political economist Charles Ganilh.[7] Much of the liberal opposition to Napoleon was made up of Enlightenment thinkers and disciples of the late Marquis de Cordorcet, such as the philosopher Pierre Cabanis, Antoine Destutt de Tracy (who coined the term 'ideology'), the history professor and editor Dominique Garat, the Constitutionalist bishop Henri Grégoire, the author Pierre-Louis Guinguené, and the lawyer-politician Comte Jean-Denis Lanjuinais, men who always played by the rules and didn't plot assassinations.[8] Although Napoleon took occasional action against them – he suppressed the Institut de France's moral and political science section, exiling Constant and de Staël, for instance – he left the ones whom he called *honnêtes gens* (honest men) pretty much alone (except when he could persuade them to serve him, as Jean de Bry did as prefect of the Doubs department).[9] Napoleon even had Cabanis buried in the Panthéon and Chateaubriand elected to the Institut, making it clear that he didn't see the people he pejoratively termed *idéologues* as a serious political threat.

On Thursday, March 25, 1802, after nearly six months of negotiations, the Anglo-French peace treaty, to which France's allies Spain and Holland were also signatories, was finally signed in the *hôtel de ville* at Amiens. Discussions had ranged over the Falkland Islands, whaling, Barbary pirates, salutes to flags on the high seas, and so on, and had been characterized by mutual suspicion of bad faith, not least when the British came up with the idea of having a Bourbon appointed grand master of the Knights of St John of Malta.[10] Nonetheless, there was great public rejoicing in France, and colour engravings were made of angels and female representations of France crowning busts of the 'pacificator' Napoleon with laurel leaves, above poems stating: 'The whole world reveres / the Hero of France / He is the God of War / He is the Angel of Peace.'[11] This impression was further underlined on June 26 when Napoleon signed another treaty, with Turkey, that opened up the Dardanelles to French trade.

The provisions of Amiens were substantially similar to the preliminary treaty, with Britain promising to leave Malta and declare it a free port within three months of ratification, returning the island to the Knights of St John, and to cede its control over Pondicherry, and France regaining her colonies for the price of evacuating Naples, Taranto and those parts of the Papal States such as Ancona that were not in the Italian Republic. Yet Amiens was almost as important for what it left unsaid as for what it actually stipulated. There was no mention of commerce, and although the treaty provided for 'an adequate compensation' for the exiled Prince Willem V of Orange-Nassau for the loss of his Dutch estates and revenues when Holland had become the Batavian Republic in 1795, there was no mention of the futures of Holland, Switzerland or Piedmont, or any recognition of the Italian, Ligurian or Helvetian republics. There had been a Franco-Dutch convention in August 1801 which stipulated that French troops would leave Holland when the general peace was signed, and the Peace of Lunéville guaranteed Swiss independence, so the British didn't feel the need to address either in the treaty itself.

The lack of a commercial treaty attached to the political one meant that the powerful British merchant class soon came to oppose a peace that gave them no privileged access to the markets of France, Holland, Spain, Switzerland, Genoa and (later) Etruria. This has been regarded as a deliberately hostile act by Napoleon, and contrary to the 'spirit' of Amiens, but no state is required to enter into a commercial treaty she knows would work to her disadvantage.[12] Napoleon wanted to levy tariffs on British imports, and the fact that he didn't intend to return to the conditions of the badly skewed 1786 Anglo-French trade treaty delighted French merchants in places like Rouen, who could continue to operate behind the French protective tariff – which made British goods more expensive – but also with newly opened seas free of the Royal Navy. France now saw a flourishing of her maritime economy, with raw cotton supplies flooding in from abroad. The prisoner-of-war exchanges were popular in France, since by then there were nearly 70,000 French prisoners-of-war in Britain, almost all sailors captured in the dozens of minor naval engagements Britain had won since 1793, many of whom had been kept for years in extremely bad conditions on crowded and insanitary prison hulks moored off the south coast and in the Thames estuary.[13]*

When Joseph returned to Paris from Amiens, Napoleon ushered him to the front of the state box at the Opéra to receive the cheers of the audience. France had kept all her 'natural' frontiers up to the Rhine and the Alps, retained hegemony over western Europe, and had all her colonies restored to her. Yet in a sense Joseph and Talleyrand had been too successful: because Britain gained so little, her commitment to the peace was correspondingly weak. Britain was obliged to return Malta to the Knights of St John after the election of a new grand master overseen by the Pope within three months of the treaty's ratification; the neutrality

---

* General Sir Charles Napier, who had been a prisoner-of-war of France, denounced 'the idea of shutting up honourable soldiers ... in the hulks of ships for years, a punishment far beyond that inflicted on the most infamous felons ... [which] was disgraceful to the government of those days, and forms a strong contrast to the honourable treatment which the English prisoners received in France, by order of the Emperor Napoleon' (Blaze, *Life in Napoleon's Army* p. 66).

and independence of the island were then to be guaranteed by France, Britain, Russia, Austria, Spain and Prussia, with no French or British to be admitted into the Order, which was now based in St Petersburg as the former grand master had been the assassinated Tsar Paul. But although the Pope appointed an Italian nobleman, Giovanni Battista Tommasi, as grand master in March 1803, the British refused to recognize his rights and exiled him to Sicily. France evacuated all of the possessions stipulated in the treaty even before the three-month time limit, but Britain prevaricated over Pondicherry and Malta, partly because she (wrongly) feared that France and Russia were preparing to dismember the Ottoman Empire.[14] Pondicherry stayed in British hands until 1816.

On the conclusion of the Peace of Amiens, around 5,000 Britons descended on Paris. Some were curious, some wanted to see the Louvre collections, some wanted to use that excuse to visit the fleshpots of the Palais-Royal (which did a roaring trade), some wanted to renew old friendships and almost all of them wanted to meet or at least catch a glimpse of the First Consul. Napoleon was delighted to oblige, and ordered his ministers to throw dinners for distinguished foreigners at least once every ten days.[15] The Irish MP John Leslie Foster attended one of Napoleon's levées at the Tuileries, and described him as:

> delicately and gracefully made; his hair a dark brown crop, thin and lank; his complexion smooth, pale and sallow; his eyes grey, but very animated; his eyebrows light brown, thin and projecting. All his features, particularly his mouth and nose, fine, sharp, defined, and expressive beyond description ... He speaks deliberately, but very fluently, with particular emphasis, and in a rather low tone of voice. While he speaks, his features are still more expressive than his words. Expressive of what? ... A pleasing melancholy, which, whenever he speaks, relaxes into the most agreeable and gracious smile you can conceive ... He has more unaffected dignity than I could conceive in man.[16]

Similarly, a former captive of the French called Sinclair wrote of 'the grace and fascination of his smile', and a Captain Usher said he had 'dignified manners'.[17] Charm is a notoriously hard phenomenon to describe, yet when he so chose, Napoleon was clearly suffused with it. He certainly went out of his way to show Anglophilia at this time, displaying busts on either side of a chimney-piece at the Tuileries of the Whig leader Charles James Fox and Admiral Nelson.[18] The Francophile

Whig politician Fox one might have expected, but to honour the man who sank his fleet at Aboukir Bay only four years earlier was truly extraordinary. (We can be certain that Nelson wasn't displaying a bust of Napoleon on *his* mantelshelf.)

For some British Radicals and Whigs, admiration for Napoleon hardly abated even up to Waterloo. The future prime minister Lord Melbourne wrote odes to Napoleon at university, Keats had a snuffbox with his portrait on it, Byron ordered an exact replica of his coach in which to travel the continent, and William Cobbett's *Weekly Political Register* and Daniel Lovell's *Statesman* praised him in extravagant terms. His reforms appealed to British liberals, who thought their own country was itself mired in an *ancien régime*. Fox himself visited Paris with three members of his family for a very friendly series of meetings with Napoleon in September 1802; other Britons presented to him included another future prime minister the Earl of Aberdeen, the Irish conspirator Thomas Emmet, the classical scholar the Rev. G. H. Glasse, Lord and Lady Holland, Lord Henry Petty (later the 3rd Marquess of Lansdowne), Sir Spencer Smith, and scores more prominent people. So many British visitors rushed to Paris that James Gillray drew a caricature entitled *The First Kiss this Ten Years!* showing a thin French officer embracing a buxom representation of Britannia.[19] Nor was it just one way; commenting on the 'astonishing' number of French people arriving at Dover, the naturalist James Smithson remarked that the two countries seemed likely 'completely to exchange their inhabitants'.[20]

Napoleon took this opportunity to infiltrate spies to make plans of Irish harbours, but they were soon unmasked and repatriated. When years later a Briton put to him the theory that the British government had not thought Napoleon sincere in his desire for peace because of this, he laughed and said: 'Oh! That was not necessary, for every harbour in England and Ireland was known.'[21] Of course the usefulness of the operation wasn't the point: the fact that it was embarked upon at all was understandably taken as an indication of hostile intent. Naturally, British intelligence used the peace to spy on French harbours too.

Although the ten-year term of the Consulate was not due to expire until 1810, in May 1802 a Senate motion to extend it for a second ten-year term passed by sixty to one, only the ex-Girondin Comte Lanjuinais voting against. This led to seemingly spontaneous but in fact well-orchestrated calls for a new Constitution of the Year X, under which Napoleon would become First Consul for life. 'You judge that I owe the people another sacrifice,' he disingenuously told the Senate. 'I will give it if the people's voice orders what your vote now authorizes.'[22] Like Julius Caesar refusing the Roman diadem twice, he wanted it to look as if he were being dragged reluctantly to lifelong power. It was a complete reversal of the principles of the Revolution, yet the French people supported it. The plebiscite's question was: 'Shall Napoleon Bonaparte be consul for life?' and the result, which was fixed even more completely and unnecessarily than that of February 1800, was 3,653,600 in favour to 8,272 against.[23] It was the first plebiscite in French history where turnout was, supposedly, over half of those eligible to vote, although double-voting for the 'yes' camp was not questioned in some areas; once again the large proportion of the country that was illiterate had no way of telling how their mayor had cast their ballots.[24]

Napoleon was duly declared First Consul for life on August 2, with the power to appoint his successor. 'His manner was neither affected nor assuming,' recorded the pro-Bonapartist British peer Lord Holland, who was present when the Senate deputation conferred the honour on him, 'but certainly wanted that ease and attraction which the early habits of good company are supposed exclusively to confer.'[25] Joseph was nominated as Napoleon's successor, but on October 10, 1802 Louis and Hortense had a son, Napoléon-Louis-Charles, who was later spoken of as a possible heir (although, with typical viciousness, Louis cast doubts on his own son's paternity). With Josephine nearing forty, Napoleon had given up expecting an heir from her. 'I love you as on the first day,' he wrote to her as she once again took the spa waters at Plombières in June, which were supposed to help with infertility, 'because you are good and above all amiable.'[26] He had written to her about taking care of her 'little cousin' on her previous visit, but it was all a far cry from the way he loved her 'on the first day'.[27]

The bad 1801 harvest had led to worrying food-price increases by the following spring, and on May 16, 1802 Napoleon told Chaptal: 'My intention is to take all possible measures to prevent bread prices going up in the city. It is necessary to have directors of the soup kitchens come to you and for you to give them 12,000 francs per month, more if necessary, so that they double and treble their distribution ... Divulge absolutely nothing about such a delicate matter.'[28] By such means, and with the help of a better harvest in 1802, Napoleon staved off a danger of which he was always highly conscious. He started to build and stock strategically placed granaries to minimize the risk. As well as bread,

Napoleon provided circuses: there were fêtes to celebrate his birthday – he was thirty-three in August 1802 – the uncovering of the plots against him, his becoming Life Consul and the anniversary of the Brumaire coup. At the same time the celebration of the fall of the Bastille and the execution of Louis XVI were carefully and gradually downgraded as the First Consul came closer to declaring himself a monarch.

In early July, as soon as the British had evacuated Elba, Napoleon ordered Berthier, who had returned to the post of war minister, to secure the island as a department of France (and not of the Italian Republic), disarm the inhabitants of Portoferraio, take a dozen prominent hostages for good behaviour and send the children of twelve of the best families to school in France as a way of Gallicizing them.[29] (It had worked for him, after all.) Elba was officially annexed in August, after Berthier had given 3,000 francs each to the three deputies from the island.[30] None of this contravened the Peace of Amiens, and was fully anticipated by Britain.

When the Constitution of Year X, France's fifth since the Revolution, became law in early August, Napoleon – now using only his Christian name in his message to the Senate, as monarchs did – announced that all adult males of each district could vote for the members of the electoral colleges for their *arrondissements* and departments from among the six hundred people who paid the most taxes (*plus imposés*), who would then hold their offices for life.[31] Thereafter the electoral colleges would nominate two candidates for both the Legislative Body and the Tribunate, from whom Napoleon would choose one each. He was carefully building up a cadre of political supporters who owed their positions to him. Many of the Legislative Body's powers went to the Senate, which also had the power to dissolve it and the Tribunate. The number of tribunes was also halved to fifty and could now debate only in secret session, where, as Napoleon said, 'they could jabber as they liked'.[32] Even the Conseil d'État had its powers circumscribed and handed to a privy council within it. The new constitution therefore had the appearance of political involvement, but genuine power rested completely with Napoleon. In the fervour of approbation won by Napoleon's victories, reforms, Concordat and peace treaties it wasn't surprising that those initially elected to the electoral colleges were often his most vocal supporters.

On September 5 Napoleon ordered Brigadier Horace Sébastiani, the officer who had been so supportive of him during the Brumaire coup, to go on a four-month tour of Tripoli, Alexandria, Cairo, Jaffa, Acre and

Jerusalem, to promote French interests in a region that could be forgiven for feeling that it had seen quite enough of the tricolour.[33] His report when he returned was to be explosive. Later that same week Napoleon invited King Charles Emmanuel of Piedmont to return to his throne, effectively as a French puppet. Safe in his second kingdom of Sardinia, the king refused, so Napoleon formally annexed Piedmont on the 21st and turned it into six new French departments. This disappointed the leaders of the Italian Republic, who had wanted Elba and Piedmont to join Italy, but it gave France direct access over the western Alpine passes such as the two St Bernards, which led to the rich Lombard plain that produced rice, grain and raw silk, the last of which was needed for Lyons' luxury clothes and furniture industries.[34]

The outcry in London, where Napoleon was seen as violating the spirit, albeit not the letter, of Amiens, helped to derail the implementation of the treaty and made it even less likely that the British would evacuate Malta or Pondicherry. British hawks were further enraged when Napoleon acted in another region that was also unmentioned at Amiens, but that had long been within the French sphere of influence, and where had Britain never had any national interests. On September 23 Napoleon wrote to Talleyrand saying that since he needed the border at Franche-Comté to be secure, there had to be either 'a Swiss Government solidly organized and friendly to France' or 'no Switzerland'.[35] Remembering his need to cross the Alps two years before, he required the ceding of the Valais region so that he could build a military road across the Simplon Pass, which some of the thirteen cantons that had governed confederated Switzerland for three centuries – though by no means all – refused to give him.

Swiss politics were complicated by rifts between the aristocratic and the populist cantons and between the German-speaking, Italian-speaking and French-speaking ones. On September 30, 1802, Napoleon's Act of Mediation reorganized Switzerland into nineteen cantons, with a very weak central government and an army of only 15,200 men (fewer than the 16,000 it had to provide to Napoleon under a recent Franco-Swiss defence pact). 'There are no people more impudent or more demanding than the Swiss,' he was later to say. 'Their country is about as big as a man's hand, and they have the most extraordinary pretensions.'[36]

The Act of Mediation violated the Treaty of Lunéville, especially when Napoleon sent General Michel Ney into Switzerland with 40,000 men to see it enforced on October 15, but Austria gave him a free hand, the Russians and Prussians failed to protest, and those Swiss who weren't already in favour swiftly acquiesced. 'The possession of Valais is one of the matters closest to my heart,' Napoleon told one of his Swiss supporters, the republican philosopher Philipp Stapfer, one that 'the whole of Europe would not make him give up'.[37] Despite the silence of Amiens on Switzerland, Britain now halted the return of Pondicherry to France and the Cape of Good Hope to Holland, and her troops remained in Alexandria (which she had promised to evacuate under Article 8) and Malta.

Napoleon was impressed by the activity of Ney in the Swiss affair. The son of a cooper from the Saar who had married one of Marie Antoinette's chambermaids, Ney was born in the same year as Napoleon and joined the hussars in 1787.[38] He was to gain the reputation of being almost insanely brave. Having served with distinction in the Army of the Sambre-et-Meuse, he did not encounter Napoleon until May 1801, when he was invited to Paris to meet the consuls. In October 1802 he was ordered by Talleyrand to go to Switzerland with a small army to support the pro-French elements there, which he did with speed and success, occupying Zurich without bloodshed, closing the anti-French Diet of Schwytz, releasing pro-French sympathizers from prison, putting down an insurrection that had been led by the government of Berne, overseeing the installation of a pro-French successor governor and extracting 625,000 francs to pay for the operation, which was all achieved in two months.[39]

The official report of Napoleon's meeting with Swiss cantonal deputies at Saint-Cloud on December 12 stated: 'It is recognized by Europe that Italy and Holland, as well as Switzerland, are at the disposition of France.' The trouble was, Britain recognized nothing of the sort. Two months earlier, the Bourbon Duke Ferdinand of Parma had died. The duchy was annexed by France, as had been agreed at Lunéville, and Napoleon sent the French official Médéric Moreau de Saint-Méry to impose French law there. This was not an unwarranted annexation, but the new British ambassador to Paris, Lord Whitworth, chose to take it as such and demanded compensation, as also for the annexation of Piedmont and the invasion of Switzerland, hinting that as Prussia and Russia had not yet agreed to guarantee Maltese independence, that island might be a suitable exchange. As things turned out, it wouldn't have been a bad compromise for Napoleon to have made.

The Peace of Amiens gave Napoleon a breathing space to pursue plans to stimulate economic growth through state intervention and protectionism, a policy originally pioneered by Louis XIV's finance minister,

Jean-Baptiste Colbert. Napoleon had read Adam Smith's *Wealth of Nations* in translation in 1802, but considered Britain's Industrial Revolution too advanced for France to be able to compete against her in open markets. Instead he put his faith in government subsidies in strategic industries, technical training schools, prizes for inventions, visits to British factories (that is, industrial espionage), technology fairs, the improvement of the Jacquard silk-weaving process, an industrial exhibition in Paris (at which the cotton-spinning business of Richard Lenoir took 400,000 francs' worth of orders) and the setting up of twenty-two chambers of commerce across France in December 1802.[40] Yet by the end of his reign, France had reached only the level of industrialization that Britain had enjoyed in 1780, an indictment of revolutionary, Directory and Napoleonic economic policy and the Colbertism they all followed.[41] 'I never saw him reject a proposition that was aimed at encouraging or supporting industry,' recalled Chaptal. But for all Napoleon's efforts, and especially once war broke out again, French industrialization was only ever on a small scale compared to that of the powerhouse across the Channel.[42] (In 1815 there were still only 452 mines employing 43,395 workers in the whole of France, 41 ironworks with 1,202 workers, 1,219 forges with 7,120 workers, and 98 sugar refineries with 585; Marseilles, centre of the French soap-making industry, employed a thousand workers in seventy-three workshops.[43])

The Colbertian use of tariffs furthermore skewed trade so that high customs barriers in Italy meant that raw silk from Piedmont which used to go to Lombardy was instead sent to Lyons; Dutch producers had to pay duties on goods sold in France, but not vice versa, and so on.[44] It was economic imperialism in action, which could hardly fail to stoke resentment in France's satellite states. Napoleon had managed greatly to increase confidence in France's finances and in her ability to honour her government's bonds, but even so they never managed to match Britain's in this period. At his best, he was forced to borrow at higher rates than Britain at its worst.[*]

After the *machine infernale* explosion, Otto, the French envoy in London, had sent Talleyrand copies of British newspapers, journals and gazettes which implicitly, and on occasion explicitly, expressed the hope

---

[*] After the Peace of Amiens, the 5 per cent French consolidated bonds were quoted at 48 to 53 francs, while the 3 per cent British consols had a spread of between 66 and 79 francs, despite the lower rate of return they promised (Lefebvre, *Napoleon* p. 132).

that the next attempt would succeed.[45] French newspapers published by émigrés in London particularly infuriated Napoleon, such as *Paris Pendant l'Année* and *L'Ambigu*, both edited by Jean-Gabriel Peltier, which used classical and poetical allusions to call for his assassination. He even went so far as to undertake a prosecution of Peltier in the British courts.[46] State Councillor Joseph Pelet de la Lozère recorded that the English press drove Napoleon 'into a fury that resembled the lion in the fable, stung to madness by a swarm of gnats'.[47]* Eventually, in August 1802 he banned all British newspapers from France. The Bourbon family had close connections with the émigré press, as the British government knew from intercepting, copying, decoding and resealing letters sent through the Post Office (just as Lavalette's *bureau noir* was doing in Paris).[48]

Hawkesbury told Otto repeatedly that Britain could do nothing to curtail 'the liberty of the press as secured by the constitution of this country', but Otto pointed out that under the 1793 Alien Act there were provisions for the deportation of seditious foreign writers such as Peltier.[49] Talleyrand added that far from being immutable, the British constitution was unwritten and even habeas corpus had been suspended at various moments during the Revolutionary Wars. It has been alleged that Napoleon was too authoritarian to understand the concept of freedom of the press; in fact the question was not simply one of freedom or repression, since there were 'ministerial' papers which were owned by members of the government, and the prime minister's own brother, Hiley Addington, even wrote articles for them. He also knew that London had been the place of publication of equally vicious *libelles* against Louis XV and Louis XVI written by disaffected Frenchmen.[50]

The diatribes of Peltier, Jacques Régnier, Nicolas Dutheil and other writers published in England led to bad blood, and Napoleon could never quite accept that the British government were as powerless and uninvolved as they claimed to be. He inserted no fewer than five articles in his own hand in the *Moniteur* on this issue and also produced ideas for political cartoons that he ordered to be drawn up and distributed.[51] After the *machine infernale* episode he thought it reasonable to expect that a now supposedly friendly power would help restrict incitements to terrorism.

---

* The *Annual Register* described Josephine as 'wanton almost from birth for at the age of thirteen she was debauched by her mother's two servants, a black and a mulatto, by whom she proved pregnant'. According to this publication, founded by Edmund Burke, Josephine apparently gave birth to a mixed-race son while married to Beauharnais, and Napoleon 'was determined to marry the Pope to his mother' (*Annual Register 1809* p. 342).

Napoleon was unlucky that his time in power coincided with the flourishing of the first fully professional British political caricaturists – James Gillray, Thomas Rowlandson and George Cruikshank – still among its greatest exponents, who all fastened on him as their victim. Gillray fought in the Duke of York's Flanders campaign and never saw Napoleon, but virtually single-handedly created the image of him as physically small – 'Little Boney'. Yet even the British caricaturists never reached the level of pure loathing achieved by the Russian Ivan Terebenev or the Prussian Johann Gottfried Schadow, let alone the Bavarian Johann Michael Voltz, whose caricature *The Triumph of the Year 1813* depicted Napoleon's head entirely composed of corpses.[52] Of course there were also pro-Napoleon engravings on sale in London for as much as 2s 6d in 1801, a reminder that he had his British admirers.[53] Yet overall, British Francophobia easily matched French Anglophobia. The market for highly abusive prints of Napoleon was much larger than for positive images of him, and the standard work on English anti-Napoleonic caricature and satire covers two full volumes, even without the illustrations.[54] Meanwhile, as one contemporary noted, the sheer number of British biographies of Napoleon published in the years after 1797 meant that they had 'to out-Herod each other in the representations they give alike of the hateful and malignant cast of his features, and of the deformity and depravity of his moral character'.[55] As well as newspapers, caricatures, books and even nursery rhymes, Napoleon was the regular butt of British ballads, songs and poems. In an age when absolutely everything was regarded as a fit subject for an ode – one was entitled 'On a Drunken Old Woman Who was Accidentally Drowned on a Ferry Crossing' – Napoleon's supposed crimes excited an avalanche of poetry, none of it memorable.[56]

There was a good deal of hypocrisy in Napoleon's objections, since the *Moniteur* roundly abused the British government, likening it to Barbary pirates and Milton's Satan virtually on a monthly basis from August 1802 to March 1803.[57] It even claimed that the Chouan terrorist Georges Cadoudal would have been awarded the Order of the Garter if the *machine infernale* had succeeded.[58] Napoleon's attempts to have Cadoudal deported from Britain to Canada at this time came to nothing, but in a gesture of support for the British monarchy he nonetheless expelled any Stuarts taking refuge in France, even though the last Jacobite rebellion had taken place fifty-eight years before.[59]

Under pressure from France, the British attorney-general, Spencer Perceval, finally decided that Peltier – a strange man who charged people a shilling each to watch him behead geese and ducks in his garden on a miniature guillotine made of walnut – could be tried for criminal libel, and the case was heard at the Court of King's Bench on February 21, 1803. He was found guilty by the unanimous vote of the jury after just one minute's deliberation, but as war resumed shortly afterwards he was never imprisoned, and went on violently lampooning Napoleon.[60] When Peltier later published an anti-Napoleonic work by the French Gothic-Romantic vampire-novelist Charles Nodier, who had not taken the rather obvious precaution of emigrating first, the author was imprisoned for several months in the Sainte-Pélagie prison.[61]

That Napoleon suspected that the Amiens peace might be short lived is clear from his orders to General Mathieu Decaen, whom he sent to India with four men-of-war and 1,800 sailors in March 1803 to 'communicate with the peoples or princes who are most impatient under the yoke of the English [that is, East India] Company'. He also wanted Decaen to report on the strength of the British forts in India and the chances of maintaining a French army there, taking into account the fact that the French would 'not be masters of the sea' and so he could 'expect little significant help'.[62] Napoleon told Decaen that, if war should break out before September 1804, he would be 'in a position to acquire that great glory which hands down the memory of men beyond the lapse of centuries'. He was treading the thin dividing line between the grand and the grandiose – but his instructions to Decaen show that he didn't expect the treaty to break down as early as it did.

By September 1802, Napoleon was reverting to his habitual Anglophobia; that month he wrote to the interior ministry to complain that during his three-hour visit to the Louvre, he had seen a Gobelins tapestry of the 1346 siege of Calais by the English. 'Such subjects should not be available for public viewing in Paris.'[63] On December 28 he wrote to Talleyrand from Saint-Cloud, 'We do not seem to be at peace, but only in truce ... the fault lies entirely with the British Government.'[64] The problems facing the Amiens peace – the Sébastiani and Decaen expeditions, Cadoudal's continued residence in London, the émigré press, compensation for the King of Sardinia and Prince Willem V of Orange, Swiss independence, the non-evacuations of Holland, Alexandria, Pondicherry, the Cape of Good Hope and, especially, Malta, and France's tariff regime – all of those might have been resolved given trust and goodwill, but there wasn't any on either side. With his customary good sense – at least when he was sane – George III described the peace as 'experimental', which is all the British government ever considered it to be, and for Britain it soon became apparent that the experiment had failed.[65]

On January 30, 1803 Sébastiani's report of his Levantine tour, which claimed that Egypt could be retaken with an expedition of fewer than 10,000 men, was published across eight pages of the *Moniteur*. It was a deliberate provocation and Britain's fears of a Franco-Russian dismemberment of the Ottoman Empire were naturally rekindled. 'As no one imagined that Bonaparte did anything without a motive,' recorded State Councillor Pelet, 'the inference was obvious.'[66] Napoleon refused to discuss the report with Ambassador Whitworth, or even to give a clarifying statement. Yet the fact that the report was published at all showed it was meant as a diplomatic tool rather than a serious plan of action: if Napoleon had truly been contemplating a return to Egypt he would hardly have trumpeted the fact in the *Moniteur*. He did not want a return to war in 1803, but he was not willing to lessen France's position in order to prevent it. 'Every day weakens the deep impression of their late defeats and lessens the prestige we have gained by our victories,' he told a councillor of state at this time. 'All the advantage of delay is on their side.'[67]

On February 9 the British announced a halt to all further withdrawals until France had provided a 'satisfactory explanation' for its recent actions over Etruria, Switzerland and the Levant. Nine days later Napoleon complained to Whitworth about both Malta and Alexandria and about the lack of progress in quelling press attacks on him. 'Let us unite rather than fighting over this,' he concluded, encompassing all the issues threatening peace, 'and together we will decide the future of the world.' Whitworth took this as mere rhetoric, but as Napoleon's later proposal of the same tenor to Tsar Alexander at Tilsit was to show, he may well have been perfectly serious. Whitworth didn't consider it even worth engaging with, however, and responded by raising the question of Parma, Piedmont and Switzerland, which Napoleon dismissed as mere 'bagatelles'. Napoleon was denounced in Britain after the resumption of war for being cavalier about these small countries, but when seen in the context he intended – that of a partnership whereby the world's future could be decided between Britain dominating a vast overseas empire and France dominating Europe – the remark made perfect sense.[68] In other respects, he must have used forceful language on that occasion (perhaps calculatedly so), as Whitworth reported to Addington: 'I thought I was listening to a captain of dragoons and not to the head of the greatest State in Europe.'[69]

On February 20, Napoleon told the Paris legislature that due to 'the abdication of the sovereign and the wishes of the people, the necessity of things have placed Piedmont in the power of France'.[70] Similarly, he said, Swiss sovereignty had been violated to 'open up a triple and easy access to Italy'. More ominously he referred to the British troops still occupying Malta and Alexandria, and said that France's half-million troops were 'ready to defend and avenge'.[71] The next day the British handed over Cape Town to the Dutch East India Company, but no blandishments or threats would persuade them to honour their commitments over Malta and Alexandria.

On February 25 the Diet of the Holy Roman Empire passed the Final Declaration of the Imperial Deputation (*Reichsdeputationshauptschluss*), which put the Lunéville peace terms into effect in Germany. To compensate German states and princes for France's gain of the west bank of the Rhine, it was necessary for Austria and the other large German states to 'mediatize', or rationalize, the over two hundred states of Germany into forty, largely by secularizing ecclesiastical territories and connecting the 'free' and 'imperial' cities to their more substantial neighbours. This was to be the largest transfer of statehood and property in Germany before 1945, with nearly 2.4 million people and 12.7 million guilden per annum of revenue going to new rulers. It came as a result of months of bartering between Talleyrand and the rulers who would benefit from this wholesale takeover of the smaller, hitherto self-governing entities. Those that survived tended to receive far more territory to the east of the Rhine than they had had to give up to France to its west. Baden received seven times more, for example, Prussia nearly five times, Hanover gained the bishopric of Osnabrück despite losing no territory to France, and Austria made large gains too. Württemberg lost 30,000 citizens but gained 120,000, and between 1803 and 1810 it doubled its territory at the expense of seventy-eight other political entities and the Swabian imperial knights.[72] Prussia lost 140,000 but gained 600,000. The map of Germany was hugely simplified, in return for the extinction after centuries of hundreds of tiny states such as the hereditary county of Winneburg-Bilstein that belonged to Prince Klemens von Metternich's father.

Mindful of his hero Frederick the Great of Prussia, who had built up his Fürstenbund (Princes' League) as a check to Austria, Napoleon now sought to present France to these newly expanded German states as a check to the power of both the Hohenzollerns and Habsburgs, and he promoted marriage alliances with Bavaria, Baden and Württemberg to complement strategic alliances that he had already concluded with those three powers by the time of the outbreak of further European hostilities in 1805.[73] By July 1804 he had spotted the sixteen-year-old Princess Augusta of Bavaria as wifely material for Eugène; in April 1806 Stéphanie de Beauharnais, a cousin of Josephine's by marriage, married Prince Karl of Baden; and in August 1807 the twenty-two-year-old Jérôme married Princess Catharina of Württemberg.

On March 8, 1803 George III delivered a King's Speech asking parliament for war supplies and mobilizing Britain's militia, blaming the French for making major military preparations in French and Dutch ports, even though a despatch from Whitworth afterwards made it clear that the French weren't doing anything of the sort. Like the publication of Sébastiani's report, the speech was a threat rather than a declaration of war. 'England is not asleep,' he wrote to Charles IV of Spain on the 11th, 'she is always on the watch, and will not rest until she has seized all the colonies and all the commerce of the world. France can alone prevent this.' Napoleon wrote this despite the fact that Britain had already disgorged Martinique, Tobago, St Lucia and Minorca under the terms of Amiens.[74]

Spotting Whitworth at his levée at the Tuileries on Sunday, March 13, Napoleon, according to the ambassador's account, 'accosted me evidently under very considerable agitation. He began by asking me if I had any news from England,' to which Whitworth said he had received letters from Hawkesbury two days before.[75]

> NAPOLEON: 'So you are determined to go to war.'
> WHITWORTH: 'No, First Consul, we are too sensible of the advantages of peace.'
> NAPOLEON: 'We have already been at war for fifteen years.'
> WHITWORTH: (after a pause) 'That is already too long.'
> NAPOLEON: 'But you wish me to fight fifteen years more, and you force me to do it.'
> WHITWORTH: 'That was very far from His Majesty's intentions.'

Napoleon then walked over to talk to the Russian and Spanish ambassadors, Count Markov and the Chevalier d'Azara. 'The English want war,' Napoleon said, 'but if they are the first to draw the sword, I will be the last to return it to the scabbard. They don't respect treaties. From now on they must be covered with black crêpe.'[76] Whitworth reported that Napoleon then returned to him, 'to my great annoyance, and resumed the conversation, if such it can be called, by saying something personally civil to me'. He then returned to the point at issue:

> NAPOLEON: 'Why the armaments? What are these precautionary measures aimed against? I don't have a single ship-of-the-line [being built] in French ports, but if you are arming, I must also; if you want to fight, I will fight too. You might perhaps kill France, but you won't intimidate her.'
> WHITWORTH: 'No one wishes to do either. We want to live on good terms with her.'
> NAPOLEON: 'Then one must respect treaties! They will be responsible for this to all of Europe.'[77]

Whitworth added that Napoleon was 'too agitated to make it advisable to prolong the conversation: I therefore made no answer, and he retired to his apartment repeating the last phrase'.[78] This exchange was heard by as many as two hundred people, all of whom, according to Whitworth, felt 'the extreme impropriety of his conduct, and the total want of dignity as well as of decency on the occasion'.

Yet was what Napoleon said truly so appalling? A warmonger would not have been 'agitated' in the way Napoleon was, but only someone sincerely worried that peace was about to break down, perhaps through a misunderstanding about maritime armaments. Napoleon has been accused of being threatening and abusive to Whitworth at this levée, but, although one cannot know the tone of voice or gestures used, the words employed do not themselves imply it. (Certainly the later accusation that Whitworth was in fear of being struck by Napoleon is not borne out by any eyewitnesses, and was not made by Whitworth himself; it can safely be ascribed to British propaganda.[79]) By the time they met again on April 4, the phlegmatic Whitworth reported, 'I had every reason to be satisfied with his manner towards me.'[80]

With the Saint-Domingue expedition still underway, Decaen sailing towards India and the economic reconstruction of France proceeding, Napoleon did not want war in the spring or summer of 1803. France had 42 ships-of-the-line, of which only 13 were ready for active service, against the Royal Navy's 120. He knew, however, that they should be prepared. 'What's the best way, in the current position and in the case of a maritime war,' he asked his navy minister, Admiral Denis Decrès, on March 13, 'of doing the most harm to English commerce?'[81] Sending

Brigadier Colbert to Tsar Alexander two days later, Napoleon accurately summed up his stance as being 'very busy mapping canals, establishing factories, and dealing with matters of public education'; nonetheless, 'If war with England be spoken about, you will say that the French nation desires nothing more than to measure swords with her, seeing the amount of antipathy which exists.'[82] As usual he attended at the same time to other matters, telling the police chief of Rouen the next month to order two kept women, called Lise and Gille, to move 60 miles from Rouen and to forbid prostitutes (*filles publiques*) from appearing in the principal boxes of the theatre there.[83]

On April 23, Britain demanded the retention of Malta for another seven years, the ceding of the lightly populated Mediterranean island of Lampedusa, 70 miles from Tunisia, as a naval base, the evacuation of Holland by France, and for compensation to be paid to the Sardinians for Piedmont. 'Show yourself cold, haughty, and even somewhat proud,' Napoleon instructed Talleyrand on May 10 when telling him how to deal with Whitworth. 'If the Note contains the word "ultimatum", make him understand that the word means war ... If the note does not contain this word, make him insert it, remarking that we must really know where we are, and that we are weary of this state of uncertainty ... that once the ultimatum is given, everything is broken.'[84] In fact Whitworth merely asked for his passports, the traditional ambassadorial request prior to a declaration of war. 'It's difficult to conceive how a great, powerful, and sensitive nation can undertake to declare a war which will necessitate such terrible misfortunes,' Napoleon told him as the ambassador left Paris, 'the cause of which will be so small since it's merely a miserable rock.'[85] At Brooks's Club in London on May 6, the 9th Earl of Thanet wagered the 5th Baronet Sir Watkin Williams-Wynn, the former Lord Mayor of London Harvey Combe MP and Humphrey Howarth MP 50 guineas each 'that hostilities do not commence between France and England within a month from this date' – a bet he comprehensively lost.[86]

Napoleon summoned the seven members of the foreign affairs section of the Conseil d'État to discuss the British demands on May 11; of these seven, only Joseph and Talleyrand wanted France to continue negotiations. The next day Whitworth left Paris, and on the 16th General Andréossy, the French envoy to London, embarked at Dover just as Britain issued letters of marque and reprisal authorizing the seizure of all French ships in British ports and waters.[87] 'It is manifest Buonaparte still is very anxious for peace,' wrote William Pitt's confidant and mentor the Earl of Malmesbury the next day, 'rather dreads war and at this very hour I have a misgiving he will end by agreeing to all our proposals, and that for the present war will be evaded – postponed but not lost altogether.'[88] After the collapse of Amiens Whitworth told Malmesbury that 'the effects of war will soon be so severely felt in France as to produce great disgust and disaffection; that it will shake Buonaparte's power; that the army is not so much attached to him as it was. If he trusts an army to Moreau, he will risk its acting against him.'[89] In those predictions at least, Whitworth got absolutely everything wrong.

To avoid the (in fact non-existent) danger of Napoleon accepting her demands, Britain formally declared war on May 18, 1803. Napoleon responded by interning all male Britons of military age who were still on French soil, many of whom were subsequently exchanged but some of whom stayed under house arrest for the next decade.[90] His message to the Senate of May 20 was pure propaganda, arguing that in Britain the Peace of Amiens 'was the object of bitter censure; it was represented as fatal to England, because it was not shameful for France ... vain reckoning of hatred!'[91] Two days later he ordered Decrès to construct a prototype of a flat-bottomed boat which could carry one cannon and one hundred men across the English Channel, and to contact Cambacérès, Lebrun and Talleyrand to find individuals who would privately sponsor the building of these transports, which would be named after them.[92] The collapse of Amiens was meanwhile commemorated by one of Denon's bronze medals, depicting a leopard – the traditional if somewhat laudatory beast signifying Britain – tearing up a treaty in its teeth.

At the Treaty of San Ildefonso, Napoleon had promised Spain not to sell Louisiana to a third party, a commitment he now decided to ignore. On the same day that Whitworth called for his passports in Paris, across the Atlantic President Thomas Jefferson signed the Louisiana Purchase, doubling the size of the United States at the stroke of his pen. The Americans paid France 80 million francs for 875,000 square miles of territory that today comprises all or some of thirteen states from the Gulf of Mexico across the Midwest right up to the Canadian border, at a cost of less than four cents an acre.[93] 'Irresolution and deliberation are no longer in season,' Napoleon wrote to Talleyrand. 'I renounce Louisiana. It is not only New Orleans that I cede; it is the whole colony, without reserve; I know the price of what I abandon ... I renounce it with the greatest regret: to attempt obstinately to retain it would be folly.'[94]

After the Saint-Domingue debacle and the collapse of Amiens, Napoleon concluded he must realize his largest and (for the immediate future) entirely useless asset, one that might eventually have drawn France into conflict with the United States. Instead, by helping the United States to continental greatness, and enriching the French treasury in the process, Napoleon was able to prophesy: 'I have just given to England a maritime rival that sooner or later will humble her pride.'[95] Within a decade, the United States was at war with Britain rather than with France, and the War of 1812 was to draw off British forces that were still fighting in February 1815, and which might otherwise have been present at Waterloo.

The negotiations were carried out by the treasury minister François Barbé-Marbois, partly because he had lived in America, was married to an American and knew Jefferson, but also partly because Napoleon suspected that if Talleyrand led them – he had initially opposed the deal – he would inevitably demand bribes from the Americans.[96] Joseph and Lucien pleaded with Napoleon not to sell, and even threatened to oppose the sale publicly. Lucien recorded Napoleon half rising from his bathtub and telling his brothers that no opposition would be brooked, and certainly no discussions in the legislature. He then fell back into the tub with a splash that drenched Joseph.[97] In rage over their opposition he also broke a snuffbox featuring Josephine's portrait.

When Robert Livingston, one of the American plenipotentiaries, asked the French negotiators precisely where the Purchase territories extended north-westwards, since very few Europeans, let alone cartographers, had ever set foot there, he was told that they included whatever France had bought off Spain in 1800, but beyond that they simply didn't know. 'If an obscurity did not already exist,' Napoleon advised, 'it would perhaps be a good policy to put one there.'[98] The deal was done after nearly three weeks of tough haggling in Paris with Livingston and his fellow negotiator James Monroe, all conducted against the backdrop of the deteriorating situation over Amiens, and was concluded only days before the resumption of war. The financing was arranged via the Anglo-Dutch merchant banks Barings Brothers and Hopes, which in effect bought Louisiana from France and sold it on to the United States for $11.25 million of 6 per cent American bonds, meaning that the American government did not have to provide the capital immediately.[99] As a result, Barings were paying Napoleon 2 million francs a month even when Britain was at war with France. When the prime minister, Henry Addington, asked the bank to cease the remittances Barings agreed, but Hopes, based on the continent, continued to pay and were backed by Barings – so Napoleon got his money and Barings and Hopes made nearly $3 million from the deal.

'We have lived long,' said Livingston when the deal was concluded, 'but this is the noblest work of our whole lives. The treaty which we have just signed has not been obtained by art or dictated by force; equally advantageous to the two contracting parties, it will change vast solitudes into flourishing districts. From this day the United States take their place among the powers of first rank.'[100]

15
Coronation

'We must show the Bourbons that the blows that they strike at others will rebound on their own heads.'

Napoleon on the Duc d'Enghien

'We are here to guide public opinion, not to discuss it.'

Napoleon to the Conseil d'État, 1804

After the declaration of war on May 18, events moved swiftly. France invaded George III's ancestral electorate of Hanover at the end of the month, and Napoleon ordered General Édouard Mortier, whose mother was English and who had been educated at the English College at Douai, to cut down timber from its forests to build the flat-bottomed boats needed for the invasion of Britain.[1] The Royal Navy blockaded the mouths of the Elbe and Weser rivers in Germany in retaliation; Nelson closed off Toulon in July; and by September Britain had recaptured St Lucia, Tobago, Berbice, Demerara and Essequibo. Napoleon meanwhile sent the outstanding soldier (and failed artist) General Laurent de Gouvion Saint-Cyr, whose aloofness led to his being nicknamed 'The Owl' by his men, to re-garrison Taranto, Brindisi and Otranto, in Italy, in violation of a Franco-Neapolitan treaty signed in 1801, and despite a vigorous Russian protest.

In June Napoleon ordered the construction of five large invasion camps at Brest, Boulogne, Montreuil, Bruges and Utrecht. The Bruges camp was later transferred to Ambleteuse, near Boulogne, and soon the main camp there stretched along 9 miles of the coast, complete with kitchen gardens. 'I am housed in the middle of the camp and on the edge of the ocean,' Napoleon told Cambacérès from his headquarters at Pont-de-Briques on November 5, 'where at a glance it is easy to measure the distance that separates us from England.'[2]

Support camps for cavalry and the reserve were set up at Saint-Omer, Compiègne, Arras, Étaples, Vimereaux, Paris and Amiens. The Army of England absorbed the men from the Army of the West in the Vendée and was renamed the Army of the Ocean Coasts. By January 1804 it numbered 70,000 men, and by March 120,000.[3] Napoleon later claimed that he only ever meant to scare Britain, lull Austria and train his army, and had no real intention of actually invading. This was nonsense. Captain Édouard Desbrière's five-volume work, *Projets et tentatives de débarquement aux îles Britanniques* (published in 1900–1902), reviewed Napoleon's invasion plans and outlined in no fewer than 2,636 pages precisely where each demi-brigade was intended to land, and, despite the misprints of 'Frey-Harock' for Grays-Thurrock and 'Green-hill' for Greenhithe, makes it clear that Napoleon was not bluffing.[4] He had books and articles published about successful invasions of England from Julius Caesar onwards, began to refer to Britain as Carthage, put the Bayeaux Tapestry on display in the Louvre and instructed Denon to strike a 'Descent on England' medal – depicting a near-naked Napoleon wrestling successfully with a merman – which states on the reverse: 'Struck in London 1804'.[5]

The huge amount of work done on the canals which would enable him to maintain internal communications between Nantes, Holland, Antwerp, Cherbourg, Brest and Rochefort, and the expansion of the docks at Flushing to allow the entire Dutch navy to go to sea at twenty-four hours' notice, all point to the deadly seriousness of his intentions.[6] So too do the mountains of detailed correspondence with his admirals and generals. In 1803 and 1804, Napoleon wrote to Berthier 553 times and to Admiral Decrès 236 times.[7] When General Nicolas Jean-de-Dieu Soult, who was in charge at Saint-Omer (77 letters) reported that it was impossible to embark the entire force in twenty-four hours, Napoleon expostulated, 'Impossible, sir! I am not acquainted with the word; it is not in the French language, erase it from your dictionary.'[8]

On December 23, 1803, Berthier drew up a list of the forces composing what he and Napoleon privately called in their correspondence *l'armée d'expédition d'Angleterre*. It consisted of 79,000 infantry, 17,600 cavalrymen with 15,000 horses, 4,700 artillerymen, 4,600 carters and 7,800 civilians, an unnumbered amount of caïques (each of which was to carry 20 men, 2,000 cartridges, 200 biscuits, 10 bottles of eau-de-vie and a haunch of mutton) and large numbers of semi-armed fishing boats.[9] State Councillor Pelet put the size of the flotilla at 250 sloops with three guns each, 650 gunboats and pinnaces with one each, many 6-gun praams, and 750 transports with artillery.[10] At its height the flotilla numbered over 1,831 craft of all descriptions, and 167,000 men.[11]

The flat bottoms of many of the boats, whose maximum draft was 6 feet fully loaded, meant that they could be run up on a beach, but although most were ready by the spring of 1804 they tended to ship water and sailed very badly unless the wind was dead astern, and south-eastern winds are rare in the English Channel.[12] The pinnaces also needed to be rowed if they were not going dead ahead, which over 22 miles of sea would have been exhausting for the troops. Although a night attack was intended, a full eight hours of darkness came only in the autumn and winter, when the weather was too bad to risk a crossing in flat-bottomed boats.[13] The Channel made up for its narrowness by its notorious unpredictability; there were sound logistical reasons why England hadn't been successfully invaded since the fifteenth century (when she had been by land from Wales). By the early nineteenth she had the largest, best-trained and best-led navy in the world.

Napoleon was undeterred. On July 30, 1804 he told General Brune, we 'only await a favourable wind in order to plant the imperial eagle on the Tower of London. Time and fate alone know what will happen.'[14] On his tours of inspection of the camps, which could take up to twenty-five days, he checked everything from the fortifications to sanitary arrangements, but particularly enjoyed talking to the men. 'He would mix with them freely,' recalled an aide-de-camp, 'entering into every little detail of their comfort and bestowing with discrimination his praise, his favours, and any well-merited advancement, thus provoking their utmost enthusiasm.'[15] On July 22 he wrote to the naval ministry to complain that, due to non-payment of expenses, workers in the Channel ports were having to sell their silver sleeve-buttons. 'They must absolutely not be the ones to suffer,' he insisted, 'no matter how things stand the workers must be paid.'[16] They must also drink. Writing about the houses to be requisitioned in the Boulogne area for the billeting and provisioning of the invasion force, he told Decrès, 'Make sure there are cellars for wine.' He then added that the invasion of Britain would require 300,000 pints of brandy.[17]

Napoleon began negotiations with the leaders of the United Irishmen in Paris in August, hoping that 20,000 Irish rebels would support the French army if he landed in Ireland.[18] He wanted them to join the corps of 117 guide-interpreters he would need in England. He designed a uniform for them of 'dragoon-green coats with red lining, scarlet facings, white buttons', right down to the colour of their spurs, and decided that they would have two drummers.[19] This mania for micro-management extended to ordering that a marble bust of the seventeenth-century naval hero Jean Bart be placed in the town hall of his birthplace, Dunkirk, to encourage pride in French maritime exploits.

As always, Napoleon required more than warfare and politics for his mental nourishment. On October 1 he thanked the American physicist Sir Benjamin Thomson, who was living in Paris, for his dissertation on heat conservation, and commented:

> The rough surface of unpolished bodies is mountainous compared to the extreme attenuation of calorific molecules; their total surface area is much greater than that of the same body when polished, and from the area of the surface used for measuring the number of issues or accesses of calories, it follows that this number must be greater, and therefore, temperature changes should be faster for an unpolished body than for a body that is polished. These are the ideas that I formulated, and that were confirmed by your paper. It is through many experiments made with precision, in order to arrive at the truth ... that we advance gradually and arrive at simple theories, useful to all states of life.[20]

That last sentence alone confirms Napoleon as a product of the Enlightenment.

His sexual life too was very active at this time. It seems likely that Napoleon had a mistress in the Boulogne region, as he wrote to an unidentified 'Madame F' while stationed there in early November, promising that the next time they met, 'I will again be the gate-keeper, if you like; but this time I will absolutely not let the care of accompanying you on the voyage to the island of Kythira fall to any others.' Kythira was the home of Aphrodite, the goddess of love, and none of the other recipients of his letters at the time were designated by an initial alone. He was also sleeping with Chaptal's mistress, Marie-Thérèse Bourgoin, an actress at the Comédie-Française, to Chaptal's intense chagrin.

Did Josephine know? In November 1804 he replied to what he called a 'sad' letter from her: 'The good, the tender Josephine cannot be erased from my heart except by Josephine herself, by her becoming despondent, tetchy, troublesome. My life is made up of many sorrows; a sweet agreeable home, free from all strain, can alone make me endure them.'[21] In January, however, he was writing 'a thousand kind things to the little cousin', as well as telling her that Eugène was 'wooing all the women in Boulogne and is none the better for it'.[22]

All the leading French admirals – Ganteaume, Eustache Bruix, Laurent Truguet, Pierre de Villeneuve, as well as Decrès – opposed the English expedition as far as they reasonably could, chastened by the two Channel squadrons of over thirty British ships-of-the-line on permanent station. The most capable officer for its overall command, Louis Latouche Tréville, had been ill since returning from Saint-Domingue, and died in August 1804; his replacement, Bruix, died of tuberculosis in March 1805. Napoleon and his senior advisors recognized that it would be impossible to send large numbers of men over on a single tide, and a surprise crossing in fog was also deemed too dangerous. Louis XIV had prepared for an invasion of Britain in 1692, plans had been made by Louis XVI in 1779 and Napoleon himself had looked into the possibilities in 1797–8. The best strategy that could be devised on any of these occasions was the ruse of luring the Royal Navy away from the English south coast for long enough to cross the Channel. Yet the idea that the Admiralty Board in London could be induced to leave the narrows of the Channel under-guarded for even one tide was always utterly fanciful.

Napoleon wrote to Ganteaume on November 23, 1803 about the flotilla of 300 armed longboats (*chaloupes cannonières*), 500 gunboats (*bateaux cannoniers*) and 500 barges he hoped soon to have ready. 'Do you think it will take us to the shores of Albion? It can carry 100,000 men. Eight hours of night in our favour would decide the fate of the universe.'[23] The next day he asked Chaptal to have several songs written 'for the invasion of England', one to the tune of 'Le Chant du Départ'.[24] In mid-December he directed that brigadiers could take four servants to England but colonels would have to make do with two.* 'Everything is beautiful here and comforting to see,' he wrote to Joseph. 'I really like this beautiful, good Normandy. It's the real France.'[25] A year later, on November 12, 1804, he wrote to Augereau from Boulogne, 'I have been here for the last ten days, and I have reason to hope that I shall arrive at the goal for which Europe awaits. We have six centuries of insults to avenge.'[26] Four days later he told Cambacérès that

---

* He continued, as always, to immerse himself in the minutiae of public administration, ordering Gaudin to dismiss the postmistress at Angers 'for violating the confidentiality of correspondence' (something he had an entire government department busily doing for himself) (CG4 no. 8520 p. 547).

he could distinguish 'the houses and the movement' on the English coast from the cliffs at Ambleteuse, after which he described the Channel as 'a ditch which will be crossed when we have the audacity to try'.[27]

On January 24, 1804 Napoleon ordered the double-agent Mehée de la Touche to leak to Francis Drake, the British envoy at Munich, the information that 'the preparations at Boulogne are false demonstrations which, however costly, are less than would appear at first glance; that the launches are so constructed that they can be turned into merchant vessels, etc, etc; that the First Consul is too crafty and considers his position too firmly established today to attempt a doubtful operation where a mass of troops would be compromised'.[28] That month Napoleon even tried to draw the Pope into supporting the operation, writing to him of the 'intolerable . . . oppression' of Irish Catholics. There was no response from Rome.[29]

Napoleon spoke openly and frequently about his invasion plans while in exile on Elba a decade later, saying that all he had needed were superior numbers in the Channel for three or four days to protect the flotilla. 'As he should march immediately to London, he should prefer landing on the coast of Kent,' he later recalled of himself, 'but this must depend upon wind and weather.'[30] He claimed that he would place himself in the admirals' and pilots' hands over where to land his 100,000 men, with artillery and cavalry following on soon afterwards. He believed he could have 'arrived in London in three days', just at the moment that Nelson would have returned from the West Indies from chasing another French fleet, too late to save his country.[31]

Yet even if Napoleon had succeeded in getting ashore in Britain, Nelson's return would have cut him off from resupply and reinforcement, and 100,000 men was not a large enough force with which to conquer 17 million waiting Britons, many of them under (admittedly makeshift) arms. Britain had undertaken intense preparations to repel an invasion from 1803 onwards: southern towns were garrisoned, fire beacons prepared; provisions stockpiled in depots located at places such as Fulham, Brentford and Staines, and every landing place was itemized from Cornwall to Scotland. Seventy-three small 'Martello' beacon towers were built along the south coast between 1805 and 1808, defensive breastworks were dug around south London, and some 600,000 men (between 11 and 14 per cent of the adult male population) were enlisted in the British army and Royal Navy by the end of 1804, with a further 85,000 in the militia.[32]

*

In the early hours of August 23, 1803, a Royal Navy intelligence officer, Captain John Wesley Wright, secretly landed Georges Cadoudal, a Dr Querelle and a small number of other Chouans at Biville in Normandy.* Wright had fought alongside the Chouans in the 1790s and been imprisoned and had subsequently escaped from the Temple prison; he had spied on the French disguised as an Arab during the Syrian campaign and had run a number of similar clandestine operations.[33]

Fouché and Napoleon – who insisted on seeing all the raw secret service intelligence, so as not to be dependent on others for its interpretation – discovered the presence of Querelle and an accomplice named Troche. 'Either I'm very wrong,' Napoleon said of Querelle, 'or this one knows something.'[34] When a plotter named Danouville was captured at one of Wright's landing-places he hanged himself in his cell, which as one of Napoleon's aides-de-camp, Philippe de Ségur, commented, 'confirmed the gravity of the plot without throwing any light upon it'.[35]

Wright next landed General Charles Pichegru, the former Brienne instructor, French Revolutionary War hero and Jacobin-turned-royalist, along with seven co-conspirators at Biville on January 16, 1804, and returned to Walmer Castle in Kent, where British naval intelligence was based.[36] Wright was acting under the orders of Admiral Lord Keith, commander-in-chief of the North Sea Fleet, who reported to Admiral Earl St Vincent, the First Sea Lord. St Vincent's own orders from Lord Hawkesbury were that it was 'of the utmost importance that Captain Wright should be involved in the fullest latitude'. Other documents, including one from Keith specifying that Wright 'is employed on a secret and delicate service', connect the British government intimately with the Cadoudal conspiracy, at the highest levels of both.[37] Further evidence of direct British government involvement in the 1804 plot to murder Napoleon lies in several letters, the first written on June 22, 1803, from a Mr Walter Spencer to Lord Castlereagh, a senior British cabinet minister, asking for the repayment of £150 for himself and £1,000 for Michelle de Bonneuil, a royalist plotter with several identities who is known to have met Louis XVIII's brother the Comte d'Artois (the future King Charles X) in Edinburgh during the Amiens peace. Spencer said the money had been advanced 'relative to a political intrigue planned by Lord Castlereagh to abduct Bonaparte in 1803', which was

---

* The French security services, led by Fouché and Savary, estimated the number of would-be assassins of Napoleon in the capital at this time at around forty, though they may have overestimated as far fewer were ever identified (Ségur, *Memoirs* p. 97).

co-ordinated by Mr Liston, the British envoy to The Hague.[38] (Plots to 'abduct' Napoleon at this time were transparent covers for his assassination.) Although there is nothing directly incriminating from the government side in the exchange – as might be expected – George Holford, a member of parliament who was Castlereagh's closest friend in politics, wrote to Spencer saying that if he would 'take the trouble of calling in Downing Street his Lordship will see him upon it'. This would hardly have been the case if Spencer had been a crank.

On January 28 Pichegru met General Moreau, who seems to have equivocated over the plot, and who crucially failed to warn the authorities, thereby making himself complicit. He was waiting to see what developed; the nation might well have turned to him, as the victor of Hohenlinden, in the event of Napoleon's 'abduction'. By then he had already told General Thiébault that he believed Napoleon 'the most ambitious soldier who ever lived', whose rule meant 'the end of all our labours, all these hopes, all that glory'.[39]

The arrest of a British secret agent called Courson on January 29 helped Fouché piece together the outlines of the plot. A French intelligence officer by the name of Captain Rosey also managed to persuade Spencer Smith, the British envoy to Stuttgart and Sir Sidney Smith's brother, that he, Rosey, was the aide-de-camp of a dissident French general, a ploy which yielded information once Smith had taken him into his confidence.[40] Fouché informed Napoleon, thanks to his spy network in London, that Pichegru had dined with a British minister in Kensington three days before leaving for France, and that the conspirators were connected to Moreau. Napoleon was genuinely astonished. 'Moreau!' he cried. 'What! Moreau in such a plot!' He ordered the general's arrest as soon as he was certain that Pichegru was indeed in France. 'Nothing can equal the profound stupidity of this whole plot,' Napoleon wrote to Moreau's friend and former chief-of-staff General Jean-Joseph Dessolle, who was commanding in Hanover, 'unless it is its wickedness. The human heart is an abyss that is impossible to predict; the most piercing looks cannot gauge it.'[41]

Quickly thereafter guards were increased on the gates of Paris and ordered to look out for the tall and burly Cadoudal; the Tuileries and Malmaison were put on high alert and the passwords changed; Dr Querelle was captured and taken to the Abbaye prison in the capital.[42] Threatened with the guillotine, he gave away Cadoudal's safe-house (*maison de confiance*) as the Cloche d'Or tavern. Meanwhile Savary, who commanded a separate secret police unit from Fouché as

Napoleon didn't like placing too much power in Fouché's hands, went to Biville to try to intercept Wright. Cadoudal's servant Louis Picot was arrested at the Cloche d'Or on February 8. He broke when he was subjected to thumbscrews and gave the police Cadoudal's safe-house in Chaillot, near Passy, but Cadoudal wasn't there either. Cadoudal's lieutenant, Bouvet de Lozier, who was, tried to strangle himself, but on being 'restored to life and misery' he confirmed that Pichegru and Moreau were indeed implicated in the plot.[43]

At 8 a.m. on February 15, Moreau was arrested on the bridge at Charenton and taken to the Temple prison.[44] The next day Napoleon ordered the arrests of generals Jean-Jacques Liébert and Joseph Souham, on the basis of their closeness to Moreau (both were exonerated and reinstated). On the 19th he told Soult that the police had seized fifteen horses and uniforms which were to be used in an attack on him on the road between Paris and Malmaison, but added phlegmatically: 'You must not attach more importance to the affairs of Paris than they deserve.'[45] To Melzi he wrote: 'I was never in any danger, since the police had their eye on all machinations.'[46]

Pichegru fought three gendarmes with his fists when they came to arrest him in bed in the rue Chabanais in the 2nd *arrondissement* on the night of February 26.[47] 'The struggle was severe,' recalled Ségur, 'and was only ended by violent pressure on the most tender part of his body, causing him to become unconscious.'[48] The next day, Napoleon received his first indication that the Duc d'Enghien might in some way be implicated.

The handsome, thirty-one-year-old Louis de Bourbon Condé, Duc d'Enghien, was a direct descendant of Louis XIII and grandson of the Prince de Condé who had commanded the émigré army at Valmy. When one of the plotters attested that everyone had stood up when a leader had entered the room, Fouché decided that d'Enghien was the only Bourbon prince who matched the man's physical description and had been close enough to France to have attended the meeting. It was a tragic error, based on circumstantial evidence.

Until as late as March 12, Napoleon believed that Charles François Dumouriez, the French general who had defected to the Austrians in 1793, had met d'Enghien at his house at Ettenheim, only 10 miles across the French border in Baden. 'What,' Ségur reports Napoleon saying to the police chief Réal,

> you did not tell me that the duc d'Enghien was only four leagues [that is, 12 miles] from my frontier! Am I a dog to be killed in the street? Are my

murderers sacred beings? Why was I not warned that they are assembling at Ettenheim? My very person is attacked. It is time that I should give back blow for blow. The head of the most guilty amongst them must atone for this.[49]

Fouché – who told Napoleon 'the air is full of daggers' – convinced himself that d'Enghien was behind the plot, as did Talleyrand on the same flimsy evidence.[50]

Cadoudal was finally captured at 7 p.m. on March 9, in the Place de l'Odéon, but not before he had killed one gendarme in a carriage chase and wounded another. Napoleon told Davout two hours later that the news of the capture 'has made the people touchingly happy'.[51] Cadoudal openly admitted that he had come to Paris to kill Napoleon, but didn't mention d'Enghien.

The next day Napoleon held a meeting at the Tuileries attended by Talleyrand, Fouché, Cambacérès, Lebrun and Regnier, at which they agreed to kidnap d'Enghien. Napoleon's much later claim that it had been Talleyrand who persuaded them to adopt this course of action was supported by Cambacérès in his 1828 memoirs.[52]* Napoleon told Berthier of his decision, and chose his master of horse General Armand de Caulaincourt to oversee the operation from Offenburg, and his own commander of the *grenadiers à cheval* of the Consular Guard, General Michel Ordener – 'a man who knew only how to obey', according to Cambacérès – to carry it out. 'This is getting beyond a joke,' Napoleon told Savary on March 12, 'coming from Ettenheim to Paris to organize an assassination, and to believe oneself safe because one is behind the Rhine! I would be too stupid if I were to allow it.'[53] Napoleon then went to Malmaison and stayed there until the morning of the 20th.

At 5 a.m. on Thursday, March 15, 1804, Ordener and a detachment of dragoons kidnapped the Duc d'Enghien at his house in Ettenheim and took him, his dog, his papers and 2.3 million francs that had been in his safe to the fortress at Strasbourg.[54] There was no sign of Dumouriez, whose name (it soon emerged) had only come up due to a misunderstanding. Meanwhile Caulaincourt went to Carlsruhe to present a note from Talleyrand to the Duke of Baden explaining the violation of Baden's sovereignty. On the morning of March 18 Napoleon told Josephine

---

* Talleyrand had form for escapades of this kind; in late 1797 he had proposed to the French ambassador in Berlin that Louis XVIII be abducted from Blankenburg and taken to France (Mansel, *Louis XVIII* p. 81).

what had happened. She strongly disapproved and begged him not to have d'Enghien executed – as much to protect Napoleon's own reputation as out of her latent royalist sympathies or pity for d'Enghien.[55] She was told she didn't understand politics and was ignored.*

The next morning Napoleon was informed by a courier from Alsace that d'Enghien's papers revealed no evidence of complicity in the Cadoudal conspiracy, but did show that the duke had offered to serve in the British army, was receiving large amounts of money from London, was paying British gold to other émigrés, and was hoping to follow the Austrians into France should they invade.[56] He had also corresponded with William Wickham at the Aliens Office (that is, the British secret service) in London and with Spencer Smith in Stuttgart.[57] 'There are few months in which I don't receive from the Left Bank some requests from our former comrades-in-arms,' d'Enghien had written in one letter, 'officers and soldiers alike, employed or not, who are only waiting for a gathering point and an order to arrive and bring me some of their friends.'[58] In September 1803 he had promised to start a Legitimist (that is, royalist anti-revolutionary) coup in Alsace should Napoleon be assassinated, writing, 'I am waiting, hoping, but don't know anything.' So although he was not specifically aware of the Cadoudal–Pichegru plot, he was clearly holding himself in readiness. It hardly constituted strong enough grounds to have him executed, however, except as a ruthless message to Louis XVIII to call off any further plots.

'There is nothing inviolate about the blood of the Legitimists,' Napoleon said at this time.[59] On the afternoon of March 18, 1804 he ordered Murat, as governor of Paris, to set up a court martial. Murat said, or at least later claimed he had said, that he wanted no part in what would effectively be a judicial execution.[60] The entire incident is full of claims, counter-claims, finger-pointing and excuses, as everyone attempted to escape responsibility for what happened next. Talleyrand blamed Savary and vice versa, Caulaincourt claimed that he had had no idea that d'Enghien would be executed. Only Napoleon, upon whom the ultimate responsibility must of course rest, argued afterwards that it had been the correct course of action, pleading the right of self-defence and saying of the Bourbons, 'My blood, after all, was not made of mud: it was time to show that it was the equal of theirs.'[61] On Elba he justified

---

* Tourists who in 1814 were shown the very patch of carpet at Fontainebleau on which she had pleaded on her knees, clasping Napoleon's legs in tears while begging for the duke's life, were misled; they were both at Malmaison at the time (ed. North, *Napoleon on Elba* p. 30).

his actions 'on the score of [d'Enghien] having been engaged in a treasonable conspiracy, and having made two journeys to Strasbourg in disguise'.[62]

Napoleon returned to the Tuileries on the morning of Tuesday, March 20. He had an argument with Murat and threatened to send him back to his estates in Quercy, after which Murat finally agreed to call the court martial. Napoleon went then to Malmaison, where Talleyrand joined him in the afternoon for a walk in the park.[63] Joseph arrived shortly afterwards and then at 3 p.m. a courier reported that d'Enghien was on his way to Le Donjon, the forbidding, 150-foot-high keep at Vincennes Castle, the tallest in Europe, in which Mirabeau, Diderot, the Marquis de Sade and Mata Hari were all imprisoned at different times. He arrived there at 5.30 p.m., and Napoleon sent Savary to Murat with a message to ensure that 'the business' was finished that same night. Napoleon personally drew up the list of eleven questions for the police chief Réal to ask d'Enghien – 'Have you borne arms against your country?', 'Are you in the pay of England?', 'Did you offer your services to England to fight against General Mortier in Hanover?', 'Have you offered to raise a legion of deserters from the Republic's army?' and so on – which the duke answered honestly, making no attempt not to incriminate himself.[64] The president of the court martial was General Pierre-Augustin Hulin, the man who had captured the Bastille in 1789 and was now the commander of the Consular Guard grenadiers. He later protested that he too had thought d'Enghien would be reprieved.

There was the briefest excuse of a trial, held at 2 a.m. on Wednesday, March 21, during which d'Enghien told Hulin and five colonels that he lived at Ettenheim for his love of sport. He also 'frankly declared that he was ready to make war with France in concert with England, but he protested that he had never had any relations with Pichegru, and was glad of it'.[65] The law of 25 Brumaire, Year III, Title 5, Section 1, Article 7 provided that 'émigrés who have borne arms against France shall be arrested, whether in France or in any hostile or conquered country, and judged within twenty-four hours'. D'Enghien had admitted to being in the pay of England and of bearing arms against France, both of which were capital offences for Frenchmen. If he hadn't admitted it, the vast amount of money in his safe would anyway have condemned him.

D'Enghien was thereafter, in Ségur's words, 'hurriedly led to the castle moat, where he was shot, and buried in a grave that had already been dug'.[66] His last words were 'I must die then at the hands of Frenchmen!', which was rather a statement of the obvious but excusable under the circumstances.[67] His dog was later owned by Gustav IV of Sweden, and wore a collar declaring: 'I belong [sic] to the unhappy Duc d'Enghien'.[68]

That evening a reception was held at Malmaison to celebrate the proclamation of the Civil Code, which neatly underlines the two sides of Napoleon as both ruthless dictator and inspired lawgiver. When d'Enghien's execution became public, a shocked Europe almost universally recalled the Corsican penchant for vendettas, and Pelet recorded that Parisians worried that Napoleon had 'fallen into the evil ways' of Robespierre.[69] Liberals across Europe started to perceive Napoleon differently: this was the moment when René de Chateaubriand and Benjamin Constant turned against him. In reply to a Russian protest over the execution, Napoleon ordered his ambassador to St Petersburg, General d'Hédouville, to call for his passports, which he did on June 7, inaugurating a period of very bad Franco-Russian relations that was eventually to erupt into war.[70] The cynical remark made about d'Enghien's execution – 'It was worse than a crime; it was a blunder' – has often been wrongly attributed to Talleyrand, but whether it was Fouché who said it or Boulay de la Meurthe, it was true. Everyone could see that, except the First Consul.

Napoleon was back in Paris on March 23, where he tacitly acknowledged the unpopularity of his actions. He 'flung himself' into his armchair at the Conseil d'État 'with his brows knitted' and said, 'The population of Paris ... is a collection of blockheads [un ramas de badauds] who believe the most absurd reports.' He then added that public opinion 'has caprices which we ought to learn to despise'.[71] Echoing (presumably unconsciously) Queen Elizabeth I, he went on, 'I don't investigate the hearts of men to discover their secret sorrows.' He spoke of the Duke of Baden's minimal reaction, Louis XIV's expulsion of the Stuarts after the Treaty of Utrecht, Russian agents, and his anger with the Journal de Paris for publishing details of d'Enghien's 'conspiracy' too early. 'Napoleon frequently interrupted himself while running on in this way,' noted Pelet, 'for he evidently felt the need to make out a justification, but was puzzled what to say, and hence the vagueness of his expressions, and their want of coherence.'[72] After he had stopped speaking no one else followed, and Pelet thought that 'this silence was abundantly significant'. Napoleon left the room and the meeting was over.

After Mass that Sunday, Ségur noticed that the groups which formed around Napoleon 'listened to him with watchful curiosity, in a dejected and embarrassed attitude, and for the most part in a silence of evident disapproval'. As a result, 'His haughty and severe demeanour, though at first inclined to expand, became more and more sombre and reserved.'[73] D'Enghien might not have had a funeral, but it seems he had a wake.

On the morning of April 6, Charles Pichegru was found dead in his cell. According to the *Moniteur*, he was reading Seneca's account of the suicide of Cato, and the page was left open at the quotation: 'He who conspires should not fear death.'[74] The official explanation was that he had strangled himself 'by means of a stick which he had twisted into his silk necktie'.[75] Napoleon has been regularly blamed for ordering the murder so soon after d'Enghien's, and it was even alleged that he sent four Mamluks to do the deed, who were themselves shot the next day.[76] Talleyrand, who could always be relied upon for a quip, said of Pichegru's demise: 'It was very sudden and very opportune.'[77] Yet there is no evidence, even circumstantial, that Napoleon was involved; indeed his supporters argued that after the d'Enghien debacle he particularly wanted the opportunity to have Pichegru's guilt demonstrated in open court and then punished equally publicly, so he had nothing to gain from having Pichegru murdered.

The following month Napoleon had the satisfaction of hearing that Captain Wright had been captured after a two-hour fight when his brig was becalmed off Port-Navalo in Brittany. Recognized by a French officer who had served in Syria, Wright was sent back to the Temple prison from which he had escaped years six years earlier. On October 27, 1805, eighteen months after Pichegru's death, Wright's corpse was found in his cell with his throat cut. Sir Sidney Smith, who investigated the death ten years later, alleged that he had been murdered, but the authorities again stated it had been suicide. Napoleon claimed in 1815 that he hadn't heard of Captain Wright until Lord Ebrington mentioned him the previous year on Elba, and said he had been of too inferior rank for him to have 'attached importance to his death'.[78] In fact Napoleon had written to Admiral Federico Gravina, the Spanish ambassador, expressing satisfaction at Wright's capture, observing: 'It's for posterity to stamp the seal of infamy upon Lord Hawkesbury and those men who are base enough to adopt murder and crime as a method of war.'[79] That does not mean he was lying – he sent tens of thousands of letters in the intervening years and might have just forgotten. Yet the argument that someone was of too 'inferior a rank' to warrant his attention is unconvincing. Only the month before Wright's death Napoleon had written to his religious affairs minister ordering him to 'Convey my dissatisfaction to M. Robert, the priest of Bourges, who gave a very bad sermon on 15 August.'[80]

The deaths of d'Enghien, Pichegru and Wright have been presented as conclusive proof that Napoleon was a vengeful ruler, but this is too much of a construction to put on what happened. D'Enghien's judicial murder was an utterly ruthless, if misjudged, act of self-defence, and the other two are unproven as murders, let alone murders ordered by Napoleon. Prisoners about to be condemned to death (in Pichegru's case) or imprisoned for the duration of a long war (in Wright's) become depressed, though the circumstances in both cases point elsewhere.* The most likely explanation is that an overzealous underling such as Fouché or Savary was doing what he thought Napoleon wanted, rather in the manner of Henry II's knights who murdered Thomas à Becket. The trials of Cadoudal, Moreau and the other plotters were set for June.

Shortly after the failure of the Cadoudal plot, Napoleon said to the Conseil: 'They seek to destroy the Revolution by attacking my person. I will defend it, for I am the Revolution.'[81] He clearly believed it, and to some extent it was true, yet it was precisely at this moment that he took his most visible turn away from the republicanism that the Revolution had proclaimed. A few days after the Duc d'Enghien's death, the Senate had adopted a message of congratulation to Napoleon that suggested, in Fouché's wording, that 'other institutions' might be needed to destroy the hopes of any future plotters.[82] 'Great man,' it urged him sycophantically, 'finish your work; make it as immortal as your own glory.'[83] The only way to make his work 'immortal' was to create an 'other institution' that would secure his legacy and guarantee the stability of the state in the event that a future assassin should succeed. It was felt that the uncertainty of succession would serve to fuel plots.

On March 28 Napoleon told the Conseil that 'the subject deserved the greatest attention, that for his part he wanted nothing; he was perfectly content with his lot, but that it was his duty to consider also the lot of France, and what the future was likely to produce'. He had revised his former estimation of the legitimacy of monarchs. 'The hereditary principle could alone prevent a counter-revolution', he added in similar vein.[84] Afterwards, petitions started arriving from the departments begging Napoleon to take the crown. Newspapers began running articles praising monarchical institutions, and officially inspired pamphlets such

---

* The theory that Napoleon had Wright killed in revenge for the defeat at Trafalgar is negated by the fact that Wright died on October 27 and Napoleon first learned about the battle on November 18.

as Jean Chas's *Réflexions sur l'hérédité du pouvoir souverain* were published suggesting that the best way to foil the conspirators would be to found a Napoleonic dynasty.[85]

By late March this carefully arranged campaign had become so successful that the Conseil d'État debated the best title for Napoleon to take. 'No one proposed to say King!' noted Pelet. Instead 'consul', 'prince' and 'emperor' were discussed. The first two sounded too modest, but Pelet believed the Conseil thought 'that of Emperor too ambitious'.[86] Ségur, whose father the Comte de Ségur was present at the meeting and later became the imperial grand master of ceremonies, stated that twenty-seven of the twenty-eight state councillors approved of Napoleon taking an hereditary title of some kind. When the committee chairmen reported, they all recommended that the title 'of Emperor is the only one worthy of him and of France'.[87] Napoleon told the actor Talma, who happened to be present, 'At this moment we are talking as if we are having a conversation, well, we are making history!'[88]

By the time Napoleon was ready to declare himself emperor, many of the great republican generals who might have objected were gone: Hoche, Kléber and Joubert were dead; Dumouriez was in exile; Pichegru and Moreau were about to go on trial for treachery. Only Jourdan, Augereau, Bernadotte and Brune remained and they were about to be placated with marshals' batons. The explanation Napoleon gave Soult – 'An end should be put to the hopes of the Bourbons' – was of course not the whole reason; he also wanted to be able to address Francis of Austria and Alexander of Russia as equals, and perhaps also Augustus, Hadrian and Constantine.[89] France was *de facto* an empire by 1804, and it was only acknowledging that fact that Napoleon declared himself an emperor *de jure*, just as Queen Victoria would become for the British Empire in 1877. Astonishingly few Frenchmen opposed the return to an hereditary monarchy only eleven years after the execution of Louis XVI, and those who did were promised the opportunity to vote against it in a plebiscite.

On May 10, 1804, William Pitt the Younger returned to the British premiership, replacing the shaky Addington government and committed to building a third coalition against France, on which he was willing to spend £2.5 million and to which he hoped to recruit Russia and Austria.[90] Eight days later Napoleon was officially proclaimed emperor in a fifteen-minute ceremony at Saint-Cloud, in which Joseph was appointed Grand Elector and Louis became Constable of France. He henceforth took the somewhat convoluted and seemingly contradictory style 'Napoleon, through the grace of God and the Constitution of the Republic, Emperor of the French'.[91] At dinner that evening he drily mused over the way his family were squabbling over the spoils: 'Really, to listen to my sisters, you'd think that I'd mismanaged the inheritance of our father, the late king.'[92]

Should Napoleon die without an heir it was resolved that Joseph and then Louis would inherit the crown, with Lucien and Jérôme cut out of the line of succession due to the marriages of which their brother disapproved. Napoleon was furious that while Jérôme, who was serving in the French navy, had been on shore leave in America in December 1803 and had married the beautiful Baltimore heiress Elizabeth Patterson rather than holding himself back for a European dynastic union. Napoleon did everything in his power thereafter to end the marriage, including importuning the Pope to have it annulled and ordering French officials to 'say publicly that I do not recognize a marriage that a young man of nineteen has contracted against the laws of his country'.[93] All of his brothers except Louis had married for love, as he himself had, which was of no use to France.

'Sole instrument of my destiny, I owe nothing to my brothers,' he told the French ambassador to America, Louis Pichon, on April 20, insisting that he find a way of annulling Jérôme's marriage. He later told Cambacérès, 'there was no more of a marriage than between two lovers united in a garden, upon the altar of love, in presence of the moon and stars'.[94] The Pope disagreed, and declared the marriage indissoluble, yet Napoleon continued to refer to Elizabeth as Jérôme's 'mistress' and 'the woman with whom he lives' and in April 1805 he even threatened to have Jérôme arrested.[95] The following month Jérôme buckled, rejoined the navy and disowned his pregnant wife. Elizabeth fled to London and gave birth to a son before returning to America, where she was taken in by her father's family. (In due course, her grandson became attorney-general.)

Napoleon severely reprimanded Pauline for her infidelities in Rome. 'Do not count on me to help,' he warned her, 'if at your age you let yourself be governed by bad advice.'[96] Of her husband, Prince Camillo Borghese, he added: 'If you quarrel with him it will be your fault, and France will be closed to you.'[97] He ordered their uncle Cardinal Fesch to tell the vain but undeniably sexy twenty-three-year-old, 'on my behalf, that she is no longer pretty, that she will be much less so in a few years, and ... she should not indulge in those bad manners which the *bon ton* reproves'. Despite these warnings her relations with her husband deteriorated further and she never forgave him for the death by fever of her six-year-old son Dermide Leclerc that August.[98]

The day after he was proclaimed emperor, Napoleon appointed four honorary and fourteen active 'Marshals of the Empire'. The fourteen active marshals were Alexandre Berthier, Joachim Murat, Adrien Moncey, Jean-Baptiste Jourdan, André Masséna, Pierre Augereau, Jean-Baptiste Bernadotte, Nicolas Soult, Guillame Brune, Jean Lannes, Édouard Mortier, Michel Ney, Louis-Nicolas Davout and Jean-Baptiste Bessières.* Between 1807 and 1815 a further eight were created. The marshalate wasn't a military rank but an honorific one intended to recognize and reward something that Napoleon later called 'the sacred fire', and of course to incentivize the rest of the high command.[99] The title came with a silver and velvet baton studded with gold eagles in a box of red Moroccan leather and indicated that Napoleon considered these men to be the fourteen best military commanders in the French army.† Not everyone was impressed: when his staff congratulated Masséna, he merely snorted, 'There are fourteen of us!' Masséna was lucky to get his baton at all, having voted against the Life Consulate and criticized the coming Moreau trial, but his military capacity was undeniable.[100] Davout was appointed despite not having yet commanded a division in combat, though he did have a command in the Consular Guard; he probably wouldn't have been elevated in the first creation if his brother-in-law, General Leclerc, had lived.[101] Marmont felt chagrin that he wasn't one of the original eighteen, and Junot wasn't considered of marshal – or even sometimes martial – calibre.

Napoleon ensured a seven–seven balance between the Armies of the Rhine and Italy, which was roughly retained in the later elevations of Victor, Marmont and Suchet from the Army of Italy, and Macdonald, Oudinot, Saint-Cyr and Grouchy from the Army of the Rhine. Mortier and Soult came from the Army of Sambre-et-Meuse, and although Napoleon didn't know them well they were clearly good fighting soldiers, and Soult had the capacity for independent command. There was an attempt at political balance too; Brune conciliated the Jacobins, Jourdan and Moncey had led important republican armies. Bernadotte

---

* The honorary marshals were François Christophe de Kellermann, Dominique-Catherine de Pérignon, Jean Sérurier and François-Joseph Lefebvre.

† One of the batons can be seen today in the Bernadotte Gallery of the Royal Palace at Stockholm.

was Joseph's brother-in-law, but also a dissident whom Napoleon thought it best to tie firmly to his regime.

The saying went that every soldier carried a marshal's baton in his knapsack, and the working-class origins of many of the marshals served as a powerful reminder of this. Ten of them had risen from the ranks, and they included the son of a cooper (Ney), tanner (Saint-Cyr), bailiff (Victor), brewer (Oudinot), wealthy peasant (Mortier), miller (Lefebvre), innkeeper (Murat), household servant (Augereau) and storekeeper (Masséna).[102] Only Prince Józef Poniatowski and the Marquis de Grouchy (who won their batons in 1813 and 1815 respectively) were aristocrats, although Pérignon, Macdonald, Marmont, Berthier and Davout were scions of the Ancien Régime *noblesse*.[103] Sérurier used to boast that his father held 'a royal appointment', but it turned out he was mole-catcher at the royal stud at Lâon.[104] Whatever their social origin, Napoleon addressed all the marshals as '*Mon cousin*' in correspondence, as he did Cambacérès and some of the senior imperial dignitaries.*

The marshals were awarded titles, such as the Prince de Ponte Corvo (Bernadotte), the Prince de Neufchâtel (Berthier), the Duc d'Istrie (Bessières) and the Prince d'Eckmühl (Davout). As well as titles and batons, Napoleon gave *dotations* (land presents) to his marshals, some of which were huge. Of the twenty-six eventual marshals, twenty-four received *dotations* – only the crypto-republicans Brune and Jourdan received none, although Brune became a count.[105] Napoleon's favouritism was evident in the very unequal distribution of the *dotations* over the years. The top four marshals – Berthier with 1 million francs, Masséna 933,000 francs, Davout 817,000 francs and Ney 729,000 francs – received over half the total of 6 million francs. The next four – Soult, Bessières, Lannes and Bernadotte – got between 200,000 and 300,000 francs each. All the rest received less than 200,000 francs, with Saint-Cyr, whom Napoleon respected as a soldier but couldn't warm to as a man, getting only 30,211 francs.[106]

As well as founding the marshalate, on May 18, 1804 Napoleon

---

* Lower down the ranks, Napoleon tended to appoint roughly one-third of the officers himself and left his colonels to choose the rest. He often behaved like the middle-class, conservative army officer that he essentially was when it came to promotions. Young men from good families who'd graduated from the military academies tended to do better than those who had been educated 'at the drumhead', who found it hard to rise to major and colonel unless they were particularly talented. This tendency wasn't too noticeable at a time when high casualties meant that commissions were constantly falling vacant, but Napoleon's social bias is apparent in retrospect. Even so, Napoleon's army was far more open to talent than the Bourbon army had been, or any other European army of the day.

formally constituted the Imperial Guard, an amalgamation of the Consular Guard and the unit that guarded the Legislative Body. It consisted of staff, infantry, cavalry and artillery components, with battalions of sappers and marines attached. It was later split into the Old Guard of long-standing veterans, the Middle Guard of soldiers who had fought in the 1807–09 campaigns and the Young Guard who were the cream of each year's conscript intake. A burgeoning elite corps that numbered 8,000 men in 1804 but 100,000 by 1812, the Imperial Guard was conscious of its superiority to regular Line regiments, and was often used by Napoleon as a strategic reserve, only to be flung into battle at the critical moment, if at all. Their morale was generally considered the highest in the army, though they incurred resentment from the rest of the Grande Armée, which correctly believed that Napoleon treated them with favouritism, scoffing that their nickname, 'the Immortals', derived from the way that the Emperor protected them.

The great Moreau–Cadoudal conspiracy trial of June 1804 was nearly botched by the authorities. The evidence against Moreau, who was still widely regarded as France's greatest popular hero after Napoleon, was largely based on hearsay and circumstantial evidence, as he never wrote down anything compromising. He spoke movingly to the special tribunal of civilian judges and admitted that the conspirators 'proposed to me (as is very well known) to put myself at the head of a popular commotion, similar to that of 18th Brumaire', but he claimed to have rejected them because, although he was adequate to command armies, he 'had no wish to command the republic itself'.[107] The tribunal, arraigned under emergency legislation, witnessed scenes of genuine popular sympathy for Moreau, and much to Napoleon's fury it handed down the lightest possible sentence of two years' imprisonment, which Napoleon subsequently revised to exile in the United States. When Madame Moreau visited Napoleon to plead for a remission of the sentence, he expostulated: 'The judges have left me nothing to remit!'[108] Moreau's former lieutenant in Germany, General Claude Lecourbe, who had publicly shaken hands with him during the trial, attended the Tuileries shortly afterwards, whereupon Napoleon exclaimed: 'How dare you sully my palace with your presence?'[109]

Although twenty-one people were acquitted, four others besides Moreau were sentenced to prison terms, while Cadoudal and nineteen others – including one of the aristocratic Polignac brothers – were sentenced to death.[110] Two weeks later, after Moreau had left for Philadelphia, Napoleon commuted some of the death sentences, including those of

Bouvet de Lozier, Polignac and another aristocrat, the Marquis Rivière. The rest, including Picot, were guillotined in the Place de Grève on June 25 in the only mass guillotining to take place in Napoleon's reign.[111] Murat was furious that Armand de Polignac's sentence had been commuted, he thought on class grounds, but it also might have helped that he had been at Brienne with Napoleon. 'We have achieved more than we intended,' Cadoudal remarked on the way to the scaffold. 'We came to give France a king; we have given her an emperor.'[112] He insisted on being executed first, so that his co-conspirators wouldn't believe a rumour that he had accepted a pardon timed to arrive after their deaths.

On June 12, 1804 the new Imperial Council (essentially the old Conseil d'État) met at Saint-Cloud to decide what form Napoleon's coronation should take. Reims (where coronations of French kings had traditionally taken place), the Champs de Mars (turned down because of the likelihood of inclement weather) and Aix-la-Chapelle (for its connections with Charlemagne) were briefly considered before Notre-Dame was decided upon. The date of December 2 was a compromise between Napoleon, who had wanted November 9, the fifth anniversary of the Brumaire coup, and the Pope, who had wanted Christmas Day, when Charlemagne had been crowned in AD 800.[113] The Council then discussed heraldic insignia and the official badge of the Empire, with Crétet's special committee unanimously recommending the cockerel, emblem of Ancient Gaul, but if that was not accepted the eagle, lion, elephant, Aegis of Minerva, oak tree and ear of corn also had their supporters. Lebrun even suggested commandeering the Bourbons' fleur-de-lis.[114] Miot rightly denounced the fleur-de-lis as 'an imbecility' and instead proposed an enthroned Napoleon as the badge.

'The cock belongs to the farmyard,' said Napoleon, 'it is far too feeble a creature.' The Comte de Ségur supported the lion as it supposedly vanquished leopards, and Jean Laumond supported the elephant, a royal beast that according to (incorrect) popular belief couldn't bend its knee. Cambacérès came up with the bee, as they have a powerful chief (albeit a queen), and General Lacuée added that it could both sting and make honey. Denon suggested the eagle, but the problem with that was that Austria, Prussia, the United States and Poland were already represented by eagles. No vote was taken, but Napoleon chose the lion, and they moved on to the question of inscriptions on the new coinage, rather strangely agreeing to keep the words 'French Republic' on it, which remained the case until 1809. Shortly after the meeting broke up

Napoleon changed his mind from the lion to an eagle with spread wings, on the basis that it 'affirms imperial dignity and recalls Charlemagne'.[115] It also recalled Ancient Rome.

Not content with having just one symbol, Napoleon also chose the bee as a personal and family emblem, which then found its way as a decorative motif onto carpets, curtains, clothes, thrones, coats of arms, batons, books and many other items of imperial paraphernalia. The symbol of immortality and regeneration, hundreds of small gold-and-garnet bees (or possibly cicada, or even mis-drawn eagles) had been found in 1653 when the tomb was opened of the fifth-century King Childeric I of France, father of Clovis, in Tournai.[116] By thus appropriating Childeric's bees, Napoleon was consciously connecting the house of Bonaparte with the ancient Merovingian dynasty that created the sovereignty of France itself.

The result of the plebiscite on the establishment of the hereditary Empire was announced on August 7.[117] When the interior minister, Portalis, showed Napoleon the yes votes of the armed services – 120,032 for the army and 16,224 for the navy – he simply took out his pen and rounded the former up to 400,000 and the latter to 50,000, with nil no votes recorded.[118] Even so in the final result – 3,572,329 in favour to 2,579 against – there were 80,000 fewer yes votes than in the plebiscite held over the Life Consulate.[119] Although there is evidence that certain officers were cashiered for voting no, they tended to be allowed back later, and one, General Solignac, reached the post of divisional commander after he personally begged the Emperor four years later 'to be allowed the honour of going to Spain to share the honours and dangers of the army'.[120]

On July 14, 1804 the remains of the great French marshals Vauban and Turenne were transferred to Les Invalides. Napoleon chose the occasion to make the inaugural awards of a new French order, the Légion d'Honneur, to reward meritorious service to France regardless of social origin. The first medals were five-pointed crosses in plain white enamel hanging from a red ribbon, but they had financial stipends attached according to one's ranking in the organization. The fifteen cohorts of the order comprised grand officers, commanders, officers and legionaries, and each received 200,000 francs to distribute annually to worthy recipients.

Some on the Left complained that the reintroduction of honours fundamentally violated the revolutionary concept of social equality.

21. Napoleon as First Consul by Antoine-Jean Gros, pointing to the peace treaties he signed in 1801 and 1802. The flamboyant red velvet jacket was intended to encourage the luxury clothing industry of Lyons.

22. (*top*) A propaganda caricature of Napoleon protecting the crucified Jesus from the Devil. His Concordat with Pope Pius VII, restoring the Catholic religion in France in 1802, was among his most popular reforms.

23. (*above left*) The uniform of the Institut de France, to which Napoleon was elected in 1797, which he wore regularly. He was proud of being an intellectual as well as a soldier.

24. (*above right*) Jean-Jacques Régis de Cambacérès effectively deputized for Napoleon as ruler of France when he was away on campaign. A lawyer, regicide and politician from the time of the Revolution, he devised much of what became the Code Napoléon. Napoleon didn't mind that he was homosexual.

25. (*top left*) Napoleon's closest friend, General Louis Desaix, would have been made a marshal of the empire had he not been shot in the forehead at Marengo in June 1800.

26. (*top right*) Marshal Jean Lannes was one of the few people who could always talk to Napoleon candidly, but he lost his leg at the battle of Aspern-Essling in April 1809 and died in agony some days afterwards.

27. (*above left*) Marshal Jean-Baptiste Bessières, a confidant of Napoleon's until he was killed by a cannonball to the chest while reconnoitring enemy positions in May 1813.

28. (*above right*) Later in May 1813, General Gérard Duroc, Napoleon's grand marshal of the palace and the only person outside the family to use the familiar 'tu', was disembowelled by a cannonball at the battle of Reichenbach.

29. (*top*) A French caricature of William Pitt the Younger on the back of King George III hiding behind a hillock and observing the powerful French invasion fleet, which threatened Britain from 1803 until it was largely sunk by Admiral Horatio Nelson at the battle of Trafalgar in October 1805.

30. (*inset*) A medal hubristically designed to celebrate the successful invasion of Britain in 1804, with the inscription '*Frappé à Londres*' (Struck in London).

31. (*above*) On Quatorze Juillet 1804, Napoleon distributed the first medals of the Légion d'Honneur. Unlike the decorations of the Ancien Régime, or of an honour in any other European country, it was open to all ranks of French society.

32. (*top*) Napoleon placed the imperial crown over his own head at his coronation in Notre-Dame on December 2, 1804; as previously arranged, Pius VII merely looked on. It was the supreme moment of the self-made man.

33. (*above*) General Jean Rapp bringing captured enemy standards to Napoleon during his greatest victory, the battle of Austerlitz, on December 2, 1805.

34. (*top left*) The meticulous Alexandre Berthier, Napoleon's chief-of-staff in every campaign except the last, was one of the essential elements of his success.

35. (*top right*) André Masséna was known as 'the Darling Child of Victory' until he was stopped outside Lisbon by the formidable defences of the Lines of Torres Vedras. Napoleon persistently undersupported him during the campaigns in the Peninsula and shot him in the eye in a hunting accident in September 1808.

36. (*above left*) Michel Ney, 'the Bravest of the Brave', was the last Frenchman out of Russia in 1812. Three years later he promised Louis XVIII that he would bring Napoleon to Paris 'in an iron cage'. Instead, he became battlefield commander at the battle of Waterloo.

37. (*above right*) Nicolas Soult was perfectly competent in the Peninsular War, but no match for the Duke of Wellington there, and proved to be an inadequate chief-of-staff in the Waterloo campaign.

38. (*top left*) Louis-Nicolas Davout, 'the Iron Marshal', never lost a battle, and at Auerstädt in 1806 he defeated an enemy three times his number. He was the best of all the marshals in independent command, but lacked rapport with Napoleon.

39. (*top right*) Nicholas Oudinot, the son of a brewer, sustained more wounds – 34 – than any other Napoleonic senior commander, the first in December 1793 and the last at Arcis in March 1814, when a spent cannonball was deflected by his Légion d'Honneur.

40. (*above left*) Pierre Augereau was a tall, swaggering former mercenary, clock-seller and dancing-master who killed two men in duels and a cavalry officer in a fight. He commanded an infantry attack in a blizzard at Eylau.

41. (*above right*) Joachim Murat was the greatest cavalry officer of his age, whose outlandish costumes made him conspicuous on the battlefield. Despite marrying Napoleon's sister Caroline and being made King of Naples, Murat was the first marshal to betray him.

42. (*top*) The Battle of Jena in 1806 saw the catastrophic defeat of one of the Prussian armies. The French cannon on the extreme right are firing at Prussian positions on the Landgrafenberg plateau above the town of Jena.

43. (*above left*) Gebhard Leberecht von Blücher, 'Marshal Forwards', who was often defeated by Napoleon but who arrived decisively at the battle of Waterloo.

44. (*above right*) King Frederick William III of Prussia, whom Napoleon disdained and sidelined at Tilsit, but who put his country on the path of reform and regeneration.

Moreau had sneered at a previous attempt by Napoleon to reintrodeuce honours, awarding his cook 'the order of the saucepan'. In the army, however, the Légion was an instant success. It's impossible to say how many acts of valour were undertaken at least in part in the hope of being awarded 'the cross', as it was universally known. Napoleon chose 'Honneur et Patrie' as its motto, the words embroidered on all French standards.[121] Soldiers prized the medals, promotions, pensions and recognition that came directly from Napoleon far above the previous revolutionary concepts of self-sacrifice for the common good that the Jacobins had tried to inculcate into the army of the 'Republic of Virtue' in the 1790s.[122]

The inclusion of civilians in the Légion was deliberate; the rest of society could also attain honour if it copied the military virtues, especially those of loyalty and obedience. Napoleon became grand master but he turned down General Matthieu Dumas, who had helped create the order, as its grand chancellor, 'in order to do away with very notion of preference for the military'. Instead the naturalist, senator and vice-president of the Institut, Bernard Lacépède, was chosen to run it.[123] Out of the 38,000 people who received the *rubans rouges* (red ribbons) under Napoleon, 34,000 (or 89 per cent) were soldiers or sailors, but *savants* like Laplace, Monge, Berthollet and Chaptal got them too, as did prefects and several of the jurists who had helped write the Code. Napoleon also set up the Maison d'Éducation de la Légion d'Honneur at Saint-Denis, an excellent boarding school providing free education for the daughters of recipients of the medal who had been killed on active service, which still exists today, as does a Légion *lycée* in Saint-Germain-en-Laye.

At one of the Conseil meetings in May 1802, when the foundation of the Légion was under discussion, the lawyer Théophile Berlier sneered at the whole concept, to which Napoleon replied:

You tell me that class distinctions are baubles used by monarchs, I defy you to show me a republic, ancient or modern, in which distinctions have not existed. You call these medals and ribbons baubles; well, it is with such baubles that men are led. I would not say this in public, but in an assembly of wise statesmen it should be said. I don't think that the French love liberty and equality: the French are not changed by ten years of revolution: they are what the Gauls were, fierce and fickle. They have one feeling: honour. We must nourish that feeling. The people clamour for distinction. See how the crowd is awed by the medals and orders worn by foreign diplomats. We must recreate these distinctions. There has been too much tearing down; we must rebuild. A government exists, yes and power, but the nation itself – what is it? Scattered grains of sand.[124]

In order to alter that, Napoleon said, 'We must plant a few masses of granite as anchors in the soil of France.' All too often his phrase 'it is with such baubles that men are led' has been quoted wildly out of context to imply that he was being cynical, whereas fuller quotation shows that he was in fact commending the 'baubles' as the physical manifestations of honour. At that meeting, ten of the twenty-four councillors present voted against the institution of the Légion, because of the way it reintroduced class distinctions; nine of them subsequently accepted either the cross or the title of count.[125] (Berlier himself took both.)

A magnificent ceremony was held at the Boulogne camp on Thursday, August 16, 1804, at which Napoleon distributed the first crosses of the Légion d'Honneur to the army. The medals were presented resting on the armour of Bertrand du Guesclin, a military commander during the Hundred Years War, and alongside the helmet of the sixteenth-century personification of French chivalry, the Chevalier de Bayard. Announced by the guns of Boulogne, Antwerp and Cherbourg, 2,000 members were decorated by Napoleon in front of 60,000 soldiers and 20,000 spectators. More than a thousand drummers played the 'Aux Champs' martial air, with cannon-fire reverberating in time to the music. One of the spectators recorded that two hundred standards taken from France's enemies, 'tattered by cannonballs and stained with blood, formed a canopy appropriate to the occasion'.[126] The next month Napoleon used the phrase 'my people' for the first time, in a letter to the Pope.[127] He also started calling Josephine 'Madame and dear wife' in the way Henri IV had used to address Marie de Médici.[128]

On October 2, Sir Sidney Smith made an ineffective attack on the Boulogne flotilla, worrying Napoleon about the effect of fireships in the harbour. As ever he was also thinking about other things, great and small, and he ordered Fouché four days later to lift the ban on Piedmontese theatregoers from whistling at dancers' performances they didn't like.[129] Three days after Smith's abortive attack the Royal Navy had much more success when four frigates attacked the Spanish bullion fleet without a declaration of war, sinking one vessel and capturing the other three, with £900,000 worth of Spanish silver dollars and gold ingots on board. It was a blatant act of piracy, but Britain suspected that

Spain – which had been allied to France since the Treaty of San Ilde-fonso – was planning to declare war as soon as the treasure had been safely unloaded at Cadiz.

Napoleon's dexterity in governance is well illustrated by the twenty-two letters he wrote on a single day in October 1804. These covered, among much else, the re-establishment of the Jesuits in Spain ('I will never toler-ate this happening in France'), the number of Britons in Paris ('Have all those found there been sent away?'), a letter to his naval minister Decrès asking, 'What exactly is the purpose of leaving admirals in Paris?', the desirability of uniting forty Parisian convents for female education, the introduction of British-style hunting laws, and a denunciation of the legal profession ('this heap of chatterboxes and revolution-fomenters who are inspired only by crime and corruption').[130] His constant harry-ing of Decrès was interspersed with occasional flashes of charm. 'I'm sorry you are angry with me,' he wrote to him in December, saying of his own rages that 'finally, when the anger has passed, nothing remains, so I hope you will not harbour any grudge against me'.[131]

Displaying the same disregard for international law as the Royal Navy had recently, on the night of October 24 the French kidnapped the British diplomat Sir George Rumbold at his country house near Ham-burg, a free Hanseatic League city under Prussian protection, and took him to the Temple prison. He was involved, like Francis Drake in Munich and Spencer Smith in Stuttgart, in supporting émigré plots; he was released after forty-eight hours and returned to Britain. The King of Prussia complained in a measured way about the French violation of Hamburg's sovereignty. Napoleon's view was that an ambassador was supposed to be 'a minister of reconciliation, his duty is always a sacred one, based on morality', but the British government had used Rumbold as 'an instrument of war, who has the right to do anything'. He ordered Talleyrand to ask of the British: 'Does it take the sovereigns of Europe to be no more than a lot of Indian nabobs?'[132]

Preparations for the coronation were under way. 'There's tardiness in making the costumes,' Cambacérès warned Napoleon. 'However, mine's already done.'[133] The Pope left Rome for Paris on November 2, though he made it known that he had wept over d'Enghien, 'that great and innocent victim'.[134] On the 25th Napoleon met him between Nemours and Fontainebleau and they entered Paris together three days later. Napoleon ordered his officials to treat the pontiff as though he had

200,000 troops at his back, just about his greatest compliment.[135] To ensure the Pope's officiation at the coronation he had promised to marry Josephine according to the rites of the Church, rather than continue to rely on the state ceremony they had held in 1796, so on the night of December 1 Cardinal Fesch performed the religious nuptials at the Tuileries in the presence of Talleyrand, Berthier and Duroc.[136] Josephine sent the wedding certificate to Eugène for safe-keeping, in case Napoleon ever denied it had happened.

The latent hostilities between the Bonaparte and Beauharnais families were brought to the fore by the coronation. Joseph argued against Josephine being crowned because it would mean that Hortense and Louis' children would be the grandchildren of an empress whereas his were only the grandchildren of a bourgeois.[137] All three of Napoleon's sisters resisted carrying Josephine's train, Lucien refused to attend the ceremony at all, and Madame Mère supported him and decided to stay with him in Rome, despite Napoleon having given her a large house in Paris.[138] 'There are thousands of people in France who have given greater service to the State than them,' an infuriated Napoleon said to Roederer of his own brothers, 'yourself among them.'[139] By contrast, he adored Eugène and Hortense. 'I love those children, because they're always in a rush to please me.'[140] Eugène's wounding in Egypt raised him high in the Emperor's estimation: 'If there's a cannon-shot it's Eugène who sees what's happening; if there's a ditch to cross, it's him who gives me a hand.' Of his siblings' sniping, Napoleon shrugged: 'They say my wife is false and that the over-zealousness of her children is studied. Well, I want them to treat me as an old uncle; this makes a sweetness of my life; I'm becoming old . . . I want some rest.'[141] He was thirty-five, but the point stands, as did his support for Josephine: 'My wife's a good woman who doesn't harm them. She satisfies herself . . . with having diamonds, nice dresses and the misfortunes of her ageing. I have never loved her blindly. If I make her empress, it's an act of justice. I am above all a fair man.'[142] He insisted when she took the waters at Aix in July that a canopy be placed over her in church services and she was given a throne on the right of the altar.[143] Her visits to towns were henceforth to be accompanied by cannon-fire salutes.

Napoleon was almost as generous to his sisters as he was to his brothers: Elisa was the first to get a principality, that of Lucca, though it didn't stop her from complaining. Pauline, who wasn't politically ambitious, became the ruling Duchess of Guastalla and Caroline the Grand Duchess of Berg in March 1806. None seemed grateful. At least Madame Mère, who would probably have made a better ruler than any of her daughters but had no appetite for power, thanked Napoleon when he gave her the Château de Pont near Brienne in June 1805 – 'You have there some of the most beautiful countryside in France,' he told her – along with 160,000 francs for its renovation and upkeep.[144] Over the years she built up a fortune estimated at 40 million francs.[145] At the same time that he was heaping titles and riches upon his family, Napoleon continued to worry more mundanely about the quality of bread his men were receiving, complaining to Berthier that poor grain was being bought by the army and ordering 'instead of white beans, use yellow beans continually'.[146]

Napoleon and Josephine's coronation at Notre-Dame on Sunday, December 2, 1804 was a magnificent spectacle, despite the somewhat last-minute organization. It was snowing when the first guests started to arrive at 6 a.m., and they entered under a wooden and stucco neo-Gothic awning designed to mask the destructive iconoclasm wrought during the Revolution. This had been blown about by a storm four nights before, breaking its fastenings and timber supports, and the final hammer strokes died away only as the pontifical procession approached at 10.30 a.m.[147] Representatives from the legislature, Court of Cassation (in flame-coloured togas), departments, Légion d'Honneur, Procurator-General, war commissariat, colonies, chambers of commerce, the National Guard, the Institut de France, ministries, the Agricultural Society and many other institutions – especially the army, from brigadiers upwards – handed their invitations to the ninety-two ticket collectors. Once inside they wandered around over the stands, chatting and hindering the workmen and generally creating disorder. At 7 a.m. 460 musicians and choristers began to congregate in the transepts, including the entire orchestras of the imperial chapel, the Conservatoire, the Feydeau theatre, the Opéra and the Grenadiers and Chasseurs of the Guard.* One of the chief organizers of the ceremony, Louis Fontanes, finally had to instruct soldiers to order everyone to sit down.[148]

At 9 a.m. most of the Diplomatic Corps arrived, although the coronation came too soon after d'Enghien's death for the ambassadors of Russia and Sweden to attend. Over at the Tuileries, fifty-seven cartloads of Seine river sand had been spread over the muddy patches of the courtyard, the workmen being paid the unheard-of rate of 4 francs each for the night's work. That morning, the new chamberlain, Théodore de

---

* The coronation cost 194,436 francs, nearly four times the original budget.

Thiard, had walked into Napoleon's dressing room to find him 'already wearing his white velvet trousers, sprinkled in golden bees, his lace Henri IV-like ruff, and over the top his chasseurs à cheval uniform'.[149] 'Had it not been a solemn moment,' Thiard recorded, he 'would have burst out laughing at the incongruity of the sight.' Napoleon took off his military uniform before leaving for Notre-Dame.

At 10 a.m. artillery salvoes announced the departure of Napoleon and Josephine from the Tuileries. 'The Coronation carriage is very grand,' wrote a courtier, 'with glass and without panels ... When their Majesties entered, they mistook the side, and placed themselves in the front; but in an instant perceiving their error, they threw themselves, laughing, into the back.'[150] The procession was so large that it had to stop at several points along the route as bottlenecks were negotiated. Murat, as governor of Paris, was at its head, then came his staff, four squadrons of carabiniers, then cuirassiers, horse chasseurs of the Guard, and a squadron of Mamluks in the brightest uniforms of all. Afterwards there came the heralds-at-arms on horseback, wearing violet velvet tabards embroidered with eagles and carrying staves adorned with bees.

Napoleon and Josephine's coach was drawn by eight white horses with white plumes and was driven by the coachman César in a long green coat with gold lace. Napoleon wore a purple velvet tabard embroidered with gold and precious stones; Josephine – 'her face so well made up that she looked like five-and-twenty' – wore a white robe and satin mantle embroidered with gold and silver. She had diamonds in her coronet, earrings, necklace and belt. Nothing was contemporary except the grenadiers' uniforms lining the route, otherwise everything was part classical, part Gothic and wholly extravagant. The sheer number of soldiers – some accounts estimate 80,000 – tended to block the crowds' view, which, along with the freezing temperatures, meant that they cheered but stayed calm.[151]

The procession arrived at the archbishop's palace adjacent to the cathedral at 11 a.m., and Napoleon dressed for the ceremony as the congregation shivered in the pews. He wore a long satin, gold-embroidered gown that reached his ankles, over which he had an ermine-lined crimson velvet mantle with a golden bee motif bordered with olive, laurel and oak leaves, which weighed more than 80 pounds, so it took Joseph, Louis, Lebrun and Cambacérès to lift it on to him.[152] 'If only Daddy [Babbù] could see us now,' Napoleon said to Joseph in Italian as they admired each other in their finery.[153] At 11.45 a.m. Napoleon and

Josephine emerged in their ceremonial costumes, ready for the Cardinal du Belloy, archbishop of Paris, to greet them at the entrance to the cathedral and sprinkle them with holy water.[154]

'The length of the ceremony seemed to weary him,' noted Laure d'Abrantès, who, as a lady-in-waiting, was only ten paces away from Napoleon, 'and I saw him several times check a yawn. Nevertheless, he did everything he was required to do with propriety. When the Pope anointed him with the triple unction on his head and both hands, I fancied from the direction of his eyes that he was thinking of wiping off the oil rather than anything else.'[155] Although the ceremony was based on those of the Bourbons, Napoleon broke with tradition in not making confession or taking communion.

Napoleon had two crowns during the coronation: the first was a golden laurel-wreath one that he entered the cathedral wearing which was meant to evoke the Roman Empire and which he wore throughout; the second was a replica of Charlemagne's crown, which had to be specially made because the traditional French coronation crown had been destroyed during the Revolution and the Austrians wouldn't lend him Charlemagne's. Although he lifted the Charlemagne replica over his own head, as previously rehearsed with the Pope, he didn't actually place it on top because he was already wearing the laurels. He did however crown Josephine, who knelt before him.[156] Laure d'Abrantès noted how Josephine's tears rained onto her hands joined in prayer.[157] Napoleon took great care fitting her small crown behind her diamond diadem, and patting it gently until it was safely in place. When the Pope had blessed them both, embraced Napoleon and intoned '*Vivat Imperator in aeternam*', and the Mass had finished, Napoleon pronounced his coronation oath:

> I swear to maintain the integrity of the territory of the Republic: to respect and to cause to be respected the laws of the Concordat and of freedom of worship, of political and civil liberty, of the irreversibility of the sale of the *biens nationaux*; to raise no taxes except by virtue of the law; to maintain the institution of the Légion d'Honneur; to govern only in view of the interest, the wellbeing and the glory of the French people.[158]

Napoleon's crowning of himself was the ultimate triumph of the self-made man, and in one way a defining moment of the Enlightenment. It was also fundamentally honest: he had indeed got there through his own efforts. It is possible that he later regretted doing it, however, because of the vaulting egoism it suggested. When the great classical painter Jacques-Louis David, who was commissioned to commemorate the coronation, wrote to Napoleon's senior courtier Pierre Daru in August 1806 about the 'great moment' that had 'astonished spectators' (his sketch of the self-crowning is reproduced as Plate 31), he was instead ordered to paint the moment when Napoleon crowned Josephine.[159] His formal painting, *Sacre de L'Empereur Napoléon Ier et Couronnement de l'Impératrice Joséphine*, which was exhibited at the Louvre to huge crowds in February 1808, wasn't intended to be historically accurate: Madame Mère was included, and Hortense and Napoleon's three sisters were depicted standing well away from Josephine's train, which in fact they had been prevailed upon to carry at the moment of Josephine's coronation.[160] Cardinal Caprara didn't like the look of his bald head in the painting, and demanded of Talleyrand that he force David to depict him in a wig, but at that David baulked.[161] The Bolivian dictator Manuel Malgarejo was later laughed at for his ignorance in contrasting the relative merits of Bonaparte and Napoleon, whom he thought were two separate people, but on some level he was right. The Emperor Napoleon felt the need to stand on ceremony in a way that General Bonaparte rarely had.

The Bourbons sneered, of course. A commentator likened Napoleon's tabard to that of the king of diamonds in a pack of playing cards. 'It was an invention worthy of a painting master in a young ladies' academy,' sneered another.[162] Yet the occasion was intended for the soldiers and spectators rather than for Ancien Régime sophisticates, who were anyway going to hate it whatever form it took. The people of Paris enjoyed it, not least because that evening there were massive firework displays, cash distributions and public fountains flowing with wine.[163] Although Madame Mère hadn't attended the coronation, when she was congratulated on her son's elevation to the imperial purple her reply was replete with her natural fatalism and great common sense. '*Pourvu que ça dure*,' she said. 'Let's hope that it lasts.'[164]

16

Austerlitz

'There is a moment in combat when the slightest manoeuvre is decisive and gives superiority; it is the drop of water that starts the overflow.'

Napoleon on Caesar at the battle of Munda

'For myself, I have but one requirement, that of success.'

Napoleon to Decrès, August 1805

A few days after the coronation the army's colonels descended on Paris to receive eagle standards from the Emperor in a ceremony on the Champ de Mars. 'Soldiers!' he told them, 'here are your colours! These eagles will always be your rallying point . . . Do you swear to lay down your lives in their defence?' 'We swear!' they ceremoniously replied in unison.[1] Cast out of six pieces of bronze welded together and then gilded, the eagles each measured 8 inches from eartip to talons, 9½ inches between wingtips, and weighed 3½ pounds.* They were mounted on a blue oaken staff with the regimental colours and the role of eagle-bearer was much prized, although with the customary irreverence of soldiers the standards were soon nicknamed 'cuckoos'.[2] In the 55th bulletin of the Grande Armée in 1807, Napoleon stated: 'The loss of an eagle is an affront to regimental honour for which neither victory nor the glory acquired on a hundred battlefields can make amends.'[3]

Training continued at the camps along the Channel coasts in readiness for the invasion of Britain. 'We manoeuvre by division three times a week, and twice a month with three divisions united,' Marmont reported

---

* Six of them can be seen today in the Royal Hospital, Chelsea in London; several more are in the Musée de l'Armée at Les Invalides.

to Napoleon from the Utrecht camp. 'The troops have become very highly trained.'[4] Napoleon ordered him to

> pay great attention to the soldiers, and see about them in detail. The first time you arrive at the camp, line up the battalions, and spend eight hours at a stretch seeing the soldiers one by one; receive their complaints, inspect their weapons, and make sure they lack nothing. There are many advantages to making these reviews of seven to eight hours; the soldier becomes accustomed to being armed and on duty, it proves to him that the leader is paying attention to and taking complete care of him; which is a great confidence-inspiring motivation for the soldier.[5]

In December 1804 William Pitt signed an alliance with Sweden; once Britain had also signed the Treaty of St Petersburg with Russia in April 1805 the core of the Third Coalition was in place. Britain was to pay Russia £1.25 million in golden guineas for every 100,000 men she fielded against France. Austria and Portugal joined the coalition later.[6] Napoleon used his full capacity for diplomatic threat to try to prevent others gathering round. As early as January 2, he wrote to Maria Carolina, the queen consort of the joint kingdom of Naples and Sicily, who was Marie Antoinette's sister and Emperor Francis's aunt. He warned her plainly: 'I have in my hands several letters written by Your Majesty which leave no doubt with regard to your secret intentions' of joining the nascent coalition. 'You have already lost your kingdom once, and twice you have been the cause of a war which threatened the total destruction of your paternal house,' he wrote, alluding to Naples' support for the two earlier coalitions against France. 'Do you therefore wish to be the cause of a third?' Napoleon prophesied that should war break out again because of her, 'You and your offspring' – she and her husband, King Ferdinand IV, had an extraordinary eighteen children in all – 'will cease to reign, and your errant children will go begging through the different countries of Europe.'[7] He demanded that she dismiss her prime minister (and lover) the Englishman Sir John Acton, and also expel the British ambassador, recall the Neapolitan ambassador from St Petersburg and dissolve the militia. Although she did none of these things, the Kingdom of the Two Sicilies* did sign a treaty of strict neutrality with France on September 22, 1805.

Napoleon took no holiday after his coronation; even on Christmas

---

* The name given to the joint kingdom of Naples and Sicily since 1443.

Day he was ordering that an Englishman named Gold should not have been arrested for duelling with a Verdun casino-owner, as 'a prisoner-of-war on parole may fight duels'.[8] Later in January he wrote to the Sultan of Turkey adopting the informal 'tu' throughout, as befitting of fellow sovereigns: 'Descendant of the great Ottomans, emperor of one of the greatest kingdoms in the world,' he asked, 'have you ceased to reign? How comes it that you permit the Russians to dictate to you?'[9] (There had been problems with Russophile governors of Turkish-owned Moldavia and Wallachia.) He warned that the Russian army in Corfu would, with Greek support, 'one day attack your capital ... Your dynasty will descend into the night of oblivion ... Arouse yourself, Selim!' Shah Fat'h Ali of Persia also received a letter written in the flowery language Napoleon had adopted in addressing Eastern potentates since the Egyptian campaign: 'Fame, which broadcasts everything, has informed you of who I am and what I have done; how I have raised France above all nations of the West, and in what a startling manner I have displayed the interest I feel in the kings of the East.' After mentioning some great shahs of the past, Napoleon wrote of Britain: 'Like them, you will distrust the counsels of a nation of shopkeepers [*nation de marchands*], who in India traffic the lives and crowns of sovereigns; and you will oppose the valour of your people to the incursions of the Russians.'[10]* If Pitt was going to buy allies in an attempt to stave off an invasion of Britain, Napoleon was hoping to flatter them at least into neutrality. In April 1805 Napoleon wrote to the King of Prussia, saying he had little hope of staying at peace with Russia, and laying all the blame on the Tsar: 'The character of the Emperor Alexander is too fickle and too weak for us reasonably to be able to expect anything good for general peace.'[11]

Pitt had set the precedent for subsidizing France's enemies as early as 1793 when he had started hiring troops from the German princes to fight in the Low Countries, but he was often deeply disappointed with his investments, as when the Prussians seemed happier to fight the Poles than the French in 1795, or Austria took the Veneto at Campo Formio in 1797 in return for Belgium (and peace). Overall, however, the subsidy policy was seen by successive British governments as well worth the cost. Napoleon naturally characterized it as Britain being willing to

---

* The phrase 'nation of shopkeepers' was first used by Adam Smith to describe Britain in his book *The Wealth of Nations*, published in 1776 and translated into French in 1802.

fight to the last drop of her allies' blood. 'Please have caricatures drawn,' Napoleon ordered Fouché in May 1805, of 'an Englishman, purse in hand, asking different Powers to take his money, etc.'[12] In 1794, payments to allies amounted to 14 per cent of British government revenue; twenty years later, with Wellington's army actually inside France, it was still 14 per cent, although the British economy had grown so considerably in the intervening period that this now represented £10 million, a vast sum. The heir to the French Revolution's debts, Napoleon was fighting against a government fuelled by the Industrial Revolution's profits, which it was willing to share round in support of its cause. Although the grand total of £65,830,228 paid to France's enemies between 1793 and 1815 was astronomical, it was markedly less than the cost of maintaining, and then fielding, a huge standing army.

On February 1, 1805, Baron Louis de Bausset-Roquefort was appointed Prefect of the Palace. This involved personally attending on Napoleon along with Grand Marshal Duroc, Napoleon's closest friend. As one who knew him well at the end of his life put it, 'unless Napoleon's ambition, to which every other consideration was sacrificed, interfered, he was possessed of much sensibility and feeling, and was capable of strong attachment'.[13] True friendship at the apex of power is notoriously difficult to maintain, and as time went on and death in battle claimed his four closest friends, there were fewer and fewer people who were close enough to Napoleon to tell him what he did not want to hear. Bausset, though a courtier rather than a friend, spent more time near Napoleon than almost anyone else outside his family, and served him loyally until April 1814, accompanying him on almost all his tours and campaigns. If anyone can be said to have known him intimately, it was Bausset, whose memoirs were published six years after Napoleon's death, when pro-Bonapartist books were severely discouraged. Moreover, Bausset was politically a royalist, and hadn't been mentioned in Napoleon's will, unlike scores of others. But even so he had nothing but admiration. 'Genius and power were expressed on his large high forehead,' wrote Bausset. 'The fire which flashed from his eyes expressed all his thoughts and feelings. But when the serenity of his temper was not disturbed, the most pleasing smile lit up his noble countenance, and gave way to an indefinable charm, which I never beheld in any other person. At these times it was impossible to see him without loving him.' Napoleon's charisma didn't lessen for Bausset over the decade that he lived with and worked for him, serving his food, running his household and allowing him to cheat him at chess. He reported that Napoleon's 'deportment and manners were always the same; they were inherent and unstudied. He was the only man in the world of whom it may be said without adulation, that the nearer you viewed him the greater he appeared.'[14]

Napoleon accepted the crown of the newly created kingdom of Italy in a grand ceremony in the throne room at the Tuileries on Sunday, March 17, 1805. Having been chief magistrate of the Italian Republic, it was only logical for him to become king of Italy once he had been made emperor of France. Writing to the Emperor Francis he blamed his decision on the British and Russians, arguing that while they continued to occupy Malta and Corfu, 'the separation of the crowns of France and Italy is illusory'.[15] Two days later he appointed his sister Elisa and her husband, Felice Baciocchi, as rulers of Lucca and Piombino.[16]*

On his way to Milan to be crowned king of Italy, Napoleon spent six days in Lyons, where he slept with the wife of a rich financier, Françoise-Marie de Pellapra (née LeRoy), despite the fact that Josephine was accompanying him on the journey.[17]† The coronation in Milan's magnificent Duomo on May 26 was celebrated in the presence of Cardinal Caprara, seven other cardinals and an estimated 30,000 people. 'The church was very beautiful,' Napoleon reported to Cambacérès. 'The ceremony was as good as the one in Paris, with the difference that the weather was superb. When taking the Iron Crown and putting it on my head, I added these words: "God gives it to me; woe betide any who touches it." I hope that will be a prophecy.'[18] The Iron Crown of Lombardy, a heavy oval band of gold containing metal supposedly from one of the nails of the True Cross, had been worn by every Holy Roman

---

* 'Eh bien, mon prince, so Genoa and Lucca are now no more than private estates of the Bonaparte family', is the opening line of War and Peace, although the speaker, Anna Pavlovna Scherer, was wrong about Genoa, which was a department of the Empire.
† The claim by Pellapra's daughter Émilie, Princess de Chimay, that she was the result can be dismissed, as she was born that November (Pellapra, Daughter of Napoleon passim). Pellapra was a minor distraction from his other mistress, Adèle Duchâtel, the wife of State Councillor Charles-Jacques Duchâtel. Adèle received 6,000 francs from the Emperor on December 22, 1804 and a further 19,000 francs on January 10, 1805 (Branda, Le prix de la gloire p. 57). Yet she was unimpressed by his sexual performance and said so. 'The Empress said you were useless,' she said, laughing at (or possibly with) him. 'That it was like pissing about' (Tulard, Dictionnaire amoureux p. 218). Astonishingly for a man so proud in other areas of life, Napoleon doesn't seem to have minded. She wasn't his only expense at the time; Mlle Grassini also received 15,000 francs in July 1805. He very likely took one of his new subjects to bed at this time too, because in early June his expense accounts record 24,000 francs being given to 'a beautiful Genoese' (Branda, Le prix de la gloire p. 57).

Emperor since Frederick Barbarossa in 1155. Napoleon's use of it was thus a further sabre-rattle against the present incumbent, Francis of Austria.

Napoleon visited Marengo on the fifth anniversary of the battle, wearing a uniform that Bausset recalled as 'threadbare, and in some places torn. He held in his hand a large old gold-laced hat pierced with holes.'[19] It was the uniform he had worn at the battle, and whether the holes were bullet-holes or not it is a reminder of Napoleon's genius for public relations. He spent the next month in Brescia, Verona, Mantua, Bologna, Modena, Piacenza, Geneva and Turin, before returning to the palace of Fontainebleau – a former Bourbon hunting lodge that Napoleon enjoyed visiting – on the night of July 11, only eighty-five hours after leaving Turin 330 miles away. It turned out to be the last time that Napoleon set foot in Italy. He appointed as viceroy his twenty-three-year-old stepson Eugène, whose good-natured reasonableness made him quite popular among ordinary Italians.[20] Over three days that June Napoleon sent Eugène no fewer than sixteen letters on the art of ruling – 'Know how to listen, and be sure that silence often produces the same effect as does knowledge', 'Do not blush to ask questions', 'In every other position than that of Viceroy of Italy, glory in being French, but here you must make little of it' – even though the actual day-to-day running of the country continued to be undertaken by Melzi, the former vice-president of the Italian Republic, whom Napoleon had refused to allow to retire despite endless complaints about his gout.[21] Melzi had no difficulty in finding talented Italians to run the government, believers in the modern French administrative ways. Joseph and Louis felt chagrin at Eugène's elevation, of course, even though either could have become king of Italy if they had been willing to renounce their rights to the throne of France.[22]

'My continental system has been decided,' Napoleon told Talleyrand in June 1805. 'I don't want to cross the Rhine or the Adige; I want to live in peace, but I will not tolerate any bad quarrel.'[23] Although Napoleon did not have territorial aspirations beyond Italy and the Rhine, he did expect France to remain the greatest of the European Powers and the arbiter of events beyond her borders, and was quite prepared to take on any country or group of them that wished to 'quarrel'.

In the early summer it seemed that he might at last be able to gain the upper hand against the nation which was so determinedly challenging his vision for Europe. On March 30, taking advantage of a storm that blew Nelson's blockading fleet off-station at Toulon, Admiral Villeneuve had escaped and sailed through the Straits of Gibraltar, rendezvoused with a Spanish fleet from Cadiz and headed off for Martinique, which he reached on May 14. Once Nelson realized that Villeneuve was not sailing to Egypt, he crossed the Atlantic in pursuit, reaching the West Indies on June 4. The next part of Napoleon's master-plan for the invasion of Britain was in place. 'It is necessary for us to be masters of the sea for six hours only,' Napoleon wrote to Decrès on June 9, 'and England will have ceased to exist. There is not a fisherman, not a miserable journalist, not a woman at her toilette, who does not know that it is impossible to prevent a light squadron appearing before Boulogne.'[24] In fact the Royal Navy had every intention of preventing a squadron of any size from appearing at Boulogne or any of the invasion ports. Yet with Villeneuve now re-crossing the Atlantic and hoping to break the blockade at Brest, Napoleon was convinced by mid-July that the long-awaited invasion might at last take place. 'Embark everything, for circumstances may present themselves at any moment,' he ordered Berthier on the 20th, 'so that in twenty-four hours the whole expedition may start ... My intention is to land at four different points, at a short distance from each other ... Inform the four marshals [Ney, Davout, Soult and Lannes] there isn't an instant to be lost.'[25] He also gave orders that letters from Italy should no longer be disinfected with vinegar for a day before being sent on: 'If plague was going to come from Italy, it would be through travellers and troop movements. This is simply bothersome.'[26]

On July 23, after losing two ships in the fog-bound battle of Cape Finisterre against Rear-Admiral Sir Robert Calder's smaller fleet, Villeneuve obeyed Napoleon's orders to sail to Ferrol near Corunna in northern Spain, thereby losing the crucial time advantage he had won on his transatlantic journey. On Elba, Napoleon criticized Calder for not attacking on the second day of the action, so allowing Villeneuve to escape. His British interlocutor pointed out that Calder was to the leeward, and therefore couldn't attack, which Napoleon dismissed as 'only an excuse, advanced from national pride, for the Admiral ran away during the night of the 23rd'.[27] In failing to appreciate the difference between leeward and windward, Napoleon once again demonstrated his huge nautical lacuna.

Under constant harrying from Napoleon – 'Europe is in suspense waiting for the great event that is being prepared' – Villeneuve put to sea from Ferrol with thirty-three ships-of-the-line on August 10, hoping to join Ganteaume at Brest with twenty-one ships, which, when added to Captain Zacharie Allemand's squadron at Rochefort, would give the Combined Fleet no fewer than fifty-nine ships-of-the-line.[28] Yet the next day, fearful that the Royal Navy was tracking his movement, instead of sailing north to the Channel Villeneuve sailed south to Cadiz, where he anchored on August 20 and was soon afterwards blockaded by Nelson, who had raced back across the Atlantic and instinctively found him.

Unbeknown to Napoleon, Austria had secretly joined the Third Coalition on August 9, angered by the Italian coronation, the Genoan annexation and the alliances that Napoleon had concluded with Bavaria, Württemberg and Baden. Although Napoleon privately told Talleyrand on August 3 'there is no sense in a war', he was ready for one if it broke out.[29] Within the space of a few days in early August he ordered Saint-Cyr to be ready to invade Naples from northern Italy if necessary, gave Masséna the command in Italy and sent Savary to Frankfurt to secure the best maps of Germany available and to try to spy on the Aulic Council in Vienna.[30]

Tuesday, August 13 was a very busy day for Napoleon. At 4 a.m. the news of the battle of Cape Finisterre was brought to him at Pont-de-Briques. The intendant-general of the imperial household, Pierre Daru, was summoned and later reported that the Emperor 'looked perfectly wild, that his hat was thrust down to his eyes, and his whole aspect was terrible'. Convinced that Villeneuve would be blockaded at Ferrol – even though he was in fact sailing away from it by then – Napoleon cried: 'What a navy! What an admiral! What useless sacrifices!'[31] With separate news that the Austrians seemed to be mobilizing, it was clear that the invasion of Britain would have to be postponed. 'Anyone would have to be completely mad to make war on me,' he wrote to Cambacérès. 'Certainly there isn't a finer army in Europe than the one I have today.'[32] Yet once it became clear later in the day that Austria was indeed mobilizing, he was adamant. 'My mind is made up,' he wrote to Talleyrand. 'I want to attack Austria, and to be in Vienna before November to face the Russians, should they present themselves.' In the same letter he ordered Talleyrand to try to frighten 'this skeleton Francis, placed on the throne by the merit of his ancestors', into not fighting, because 'I want to be left in peace to carry out the war with England.'[33] He instructed him to say to the Austrian ambassador to Paris, who was a cousin of the foreign minister Ludwig von Cobenzl, 'So, M. de Cobenzl,

you want war then! In that case you shall have it, and it is not the
Emperor who will have started it.'[34] Not knowing whether Talleyrand
would succeed in cowing Austria, Napoleon continued to urge
Villeneuve – whom he described to Decrès as 'a poor creature, who sees
double, and who has more perception than courage' – to sail north,
writing: 'If you can appear here for three days, or even twenty-four
hours, you'll have achieved your mission . . . In order to help the invasion
of that power which has oppressed France for six centuries, we could all
die without regretting life.'[35]

Although Napoleon still did not want to abandon his plans to invade
Britain, he appreciated that it would be unwise to try to fight simultaneously on two fronts. He now needed a detailed plan to crush Austria.
He had Daru sit down to take dictation. 'Without any transition,' Daru
later told Ségur,

> without any apparent meditation, and in his brief, concise and imperious
> tones, he dictated to [me] without a moment's hesitation the whole plan
> of the campaign of Ulm as far as Vienna. The Army of the Coast, ranged
> in a line of more than two hundred leagues [600 miles] long fronting the
> ocean, was, at the first signal, to break up and march to the Danube in
> several columns. The order of the various marches, their durations; the
> spots where the various columns should converge or re-unite; surprises;
> attacks in full force; divers movements; mistakes of the enemy; all had
> been foreseen during this hurried dictation.[36]

Daru was left in admiration at 'the clear and prompt determination of
Napoleon to give up such enormous preparations without hesitation'.[37]

Berthier's detailed filing system (which could fit into one coach) was one
of the edifices upon which the coming campaign was based; the other
was Napoleon's adoption of the corps system – essentially a hugely
enlarged version of the division system with which he had fought in
Italy and the Middle East. The time spent in encampment at Boulogne
and on continual manoeuvres between 1803 and 1805 allowed Napoleon to divide his army into units of 20,000 to 30,000 men, sometimes
up to 40,000, and to train them intensely. Each corps was effectively a
mini-army, with its own infantry, cavalry, artillery, staff, intelligence,
engineering, transport, victualling, pay, medical and commissary sections, intended to work in close connection with other corps. Moving
within about one day's march of each other, they allowed Napoleon to
swap around the rearguard, vanguard or reserve at a moment's notice,

depending on the movements of the enemy. So, in either attack or retreat, the whole army could pivot on its axis without confusion. Corps could also march far enough apart from each other not to cause victualling problems in the countryside.

Each corps needed to be large enough to fix an entire enemy army into position on the battlefield, while the others could descend to reinforce and relieve it within twenty-four hours, or, more usefully, outflank or possibly even envelop the enemy. Individual corps commanders – who tended to be marshals – would be given a place to go to and a date to arrive there by and would be expected to do the rest themselves. Having never commanded a company, battalion, regiment, brigade, division or corps of infantry or cavalry in battle, and trusting to his marshals' experience and competence, Napoleon was generally content to leave logistics and battle-field tactics to them, so long as they delivered what he required.[38] Corps needed to be capable of making significant inroads into an enemy force on the offensive too.[39]

It was an inspired system, originally the brainchild of Guibert and Marshal de Saxe.[40] Napoleon employed it in almost all his coming victories – most notably at Ulm, Jena, Friedland, Lützen, Bautzen and Dresden – not wishing to relive the perils of Marengo where his forces had been too widely spread. His defeats – particularly at Aspern-Essling, Leipzig and Waterloo – would come when he failed to employ the corps system properly.

'During the Revolutionary wars the plan was to stretch out, to send columns to the right and left,' Napoleon said years later, 'which did no good. To tell you the truth, the thing that made me gain so many battles was that the evening before a fight, instead of giving orders to extend our lines, I tried to *converge* all our forces on the point I wanted to attack. I massed them there.'[41] Napoleon pioneered an operational level of warfare that lies between strategy and tactics. His corps became the standard unit adopted by every European army by 1812, and which lasted until 1945. It was his unique contribution to the art of war, and its first use in 1805 can be regarded as heralding the birth of modern warfare.

'Austria appears to want war,' Napoleon wrote to his ally Elector Maximilian-Joseph of Bavaria on August 25. 'I cannot account for such erratic behaviour; however, she will have it, and sooner than she expects.'[42] The next day he received confirmation from Louis-Guillaume Otto, then France's envoy at Munich, that the Austrians were about to cross the River Inn and invade Bavaria. In expectation of this, some French units of what was now officially renamed the Grande Armée had already left Boulogne between August 23 and 25.[43] Napoleon called it his 'pirouette', and finally said to his staff of his plan to invade Britain: 'Well, if we must give that up, we will at any rate hear the midnight mass in Vienna.'[44] The Boulogne camp wasn't physically dismantled until 1813.

In order to keep Prussia out of the Coalition, he told Talleyrand to offer Hanover, 'but it must be understood that this is an offer I shall not make again in a fortnight'.[45] The Prussians declared their neutrality, but still insisted on the independence of Switzerland and Holland. Even while preparing for war – sending three letters to Berthier on August 31, two each to Bessières, Cambacérès and Gaudin, and one each to Decrès, Eugène, Fouché and Barbé-Marbois – Napoleon was decreeing that 'Horse-racing shall be established in those departments of the Empire the most remarkable for the horses they breed: prizes shall be awarded for the fleetest horses.'[46] Of course there was a military application to this but it is illustrative of the cornucopia of his thinking even, or perhaps particularly, in a crisis. In the same month he also declared that dancing near churches shouldn't be forbidden, for 'Dancing isn't evil ... If everything the bishops said was to be believed, then balls, plays, fashions would be forbidden and the Empire turned into one great convent.'[47]

By September 1, when Napoleon left Pont-de-Briques for Paris to ask the Senate to raise a fresh levy of 80,000 men, he told Cambacérès, 'there is not a single man in Boulogne beyond those necessary for the protection of the port'.[48] He imposed a total news blackout about troop movements, telling Fouché to ban all newspapers 'from mentioning the army, as if it no longer exists'.[49] He also came up with an idea for tracking enemy mobilization, ordering Berthier to get a German-speaker 'to follow the progress of the Austrian regiments, and file the information in the compartments of a specially made box ... The name or number of each regiment is to be entered on a playing-card, and the cards are to be changed from one compartment to another according to the movements of the regiments.'[50]

The following day the Austrian General Karl Mack von Leiberich crossed the Bavarian border and quickly captured the fortified city of Ulm, expecting to be reinforced soon afterwards by the Russians under General Mikhail Kutuzov, bringing the Coalition forces up to a total of 200,000 men in that theatre. Yet Ulm was dangerously far forward for

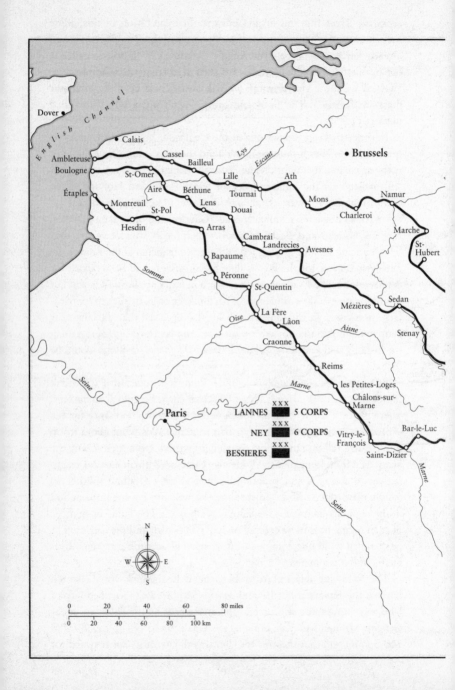

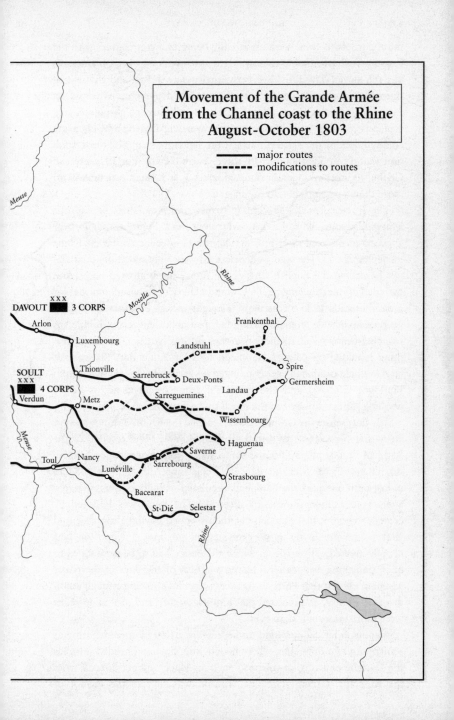

Movement of the Grande Armée
from the Channel coast to the Rhine
August–October 1803

———— major routes
- - - - - modifications to routes

Meuse

Meuse

Moselle

Rhine

Rhine

DAVOUT ☓☓☓ 3 CORPS
Arlon
Luxembourg
Landstuhl
Frankenthal
Thionville
Sarrebruck
Spire
SOULT
☓☓☓ 4 CORPS
Verdun
Metz
Deux-Ponts
Germersheim
Sarreguemines
Landau
Wissembourg
Haguenau
Toul
Nancy
Saverne
Lunéville
Sarrebourg
Strasbourg
Bacearat
St-Dié
Selestat

the Austrians to come without already being in direct contact with the Russians, who for some reason – bad staff-work has been blamed, as has the eleven-day difference between Russia's Julian and the rest of Europe's Gregorian calendar – were very late deploying.[51] Meanwhile, Archduke Charles prepared to attack in Italy, where Napoleon had replaced Jourdan with Masséna. After warning Eugène and his army commanders of the Austrian attack on September 10, Napoleon took time that day to instruct the fifty-three-year-old Pierre Forfait, prefect of Genoa, to stop taking his young mistress – 'a Roman girl who is no more than a prostitute' – to the theatre.[52]

The seven corps of the Grande Armée under marshals Bernadotte, Murat, Davout, Ney, Lannes, Marmont and Soult, totalling over 170,000 men, raced eastwards at astonishing speed, crossing the Rhine on September 25. The men were delighted to be fighting on dry land and not hazarding the English Channel in flimsy flat-bottomed boats, and marched off merrily, singing 'Le Chant du Départ'. (It wasn't unusual for a demi-brigade to know as many as eighty songs by heart; as well as keeping up morale on marches and before attacks, musicians doubled as stretcher-bearers and medical orderlies during battles.) 'Finally every-thing is taking on colour,' Napoleon told Otto that day.[53] It was the largest single campaign ever conducted by French troops. Arriving from Boulogne, Holland and elsewhere, the front stretched across nearly 200 miles, from Koblenz in the north to Freiburg in the south.

The day before the Grande Armée reached the Rhine, a rumour swept Paris that Napoleon had seized all the gold and silver reserves of the Bank of France to pay for the campaign and that consequently there wasn't enough to cover the notes in circulation. (Although no gold had in fact been removed, the Bank had circulated 75 million francs in paper against 30 million francs in collateral.) The Bank was besieged by crowds, whom it first paid slowly, then stopped paying altogether, and later paid very slowly at 90 centimes in the franc.[54] Napoleon was acutely aware of the crisis, in which the police had to be summoned to quell panicking crowds who feared a return of the days of the paper *assignat*. He felt that Parisian bankers were not showing enough confi-dence in France, and realized that a quick victory and profitable peace were more important than ever.

Napoleon left Saint-Cloud on September 24 and joined the army at Strasbourg two days later, where he left Josephine and headed towards the Danube east of Ulm to try to encircle Mack and cut him off from the Russians. General Georges Mouton was sent to the Elector of

Württemberg to demand passage for Ney's corps of 30,000 men, which could hardly be refused, and when the Elector asked that Württemberg be promoted to a kingdom Napoleon laughed: 'Well, that suits me very well; let him be a king, if that's all he wants!'[55]

The corps system allowed Napoleon to turn his entire army 90 degrees to the right once over the Rhine. The manoeuvre was described by Ségur as 'the greatest change of front ever known' and meant that by October 6 the Grande Armée was in a line facing south, all the way from Ulm up to Ingolstadt on the Danube.[56] This agile placing of a very large army across Mack's line of retreat before he even knew what was happening, at the loss of no troops, stands as one of Napoleon's most impressive military achievements. 'There is no further premise to negotiate with the Austrians,' he told Bernadotte at this time, 'except with cannon-fire.'[57] He was buoyed by the fact that contingents from Baden, Bavaria and Württemberg had all now joined with the Grande Armée.

Years after the campaign, Napoleon's toymaker made a miniature carriage that was harnessed to four mice, in order to amuse some children with whom the Emperor was staying. When it wouldn't move, Napoleon told them 'to pinch the tails of the two leaders, and when they started the others would follow'.[58] All through late September and early October, he pinched the tails of Bernadotte and Marmont, pushing them on to Stuttgart and beyond, with Bernadotte marching through the Prussian territories of Ansbach and Bayreuth, to Berlin's private fury but without any public response. 'I am at the court of Württemberg, and although waging war, am listening to some very good music,' Napoleon told his interior minister, Champagny, from Ludwigsburg on October 4, commenting on Mozart's 'extremely fine' *Don Juan*. 'The German singing, however, did seem somewhat baroque.'[59] To Josephine he added that the weather was superb and the pretty Electress 'seems very nice', despite being the daughter of George III.[60]

On the evening of October 6 Napoleon pushed on to Donauwörth, in the words of Ségur, 'in his impatience to see the Danube for the first time'.[61] The word 'impatience' recurs often in Ségur's narrative, and might almost be considered the most constant of all Napoleon's military, indeed personal, traits. Of those closest to him on this campaign – Berthier, Mortier, Duroc, Caulaincourt, Rapp and Ségur – all mention his great impatience throughout, even when his plans were ahead of schedule.

Napoleon wrote the first of thirty-seven bulletins while still at Bamberg, prophesying from there the 'total destruction' of the enemy.[62] 'Colonel Maupetit, at the head of the 9th Dragoons, charged into the village of Wertingen,' he wrote in a report of a fight in which Murat and Lannes defeated an Austrian force on October 8; 'being mortally wounded, his last words were: "Let the Emperor be informed that the 9th Dragoons have showed themselves worthy of their reputation, and that they charged and conquered, exclaiming 'Vive l'Empereur!' "'[63] Napoleon's bulletins were exciting to read, even as fiction. He used them to inform the army of the meetings he had held, how cities were decorated, and even of the 'extraordinary beauty' of Madame de Montgelas, wife of the Bavarian prime minister.[64]

On October 9 the French were victorious at a minor engagement at Günzburg, and then again at Haslach-Jungingen on the 11th. By 11 p.m. the next evening, after Bernadotte had captured Munich, and an hour before Napoleon left for Brugau on the River Iller, he was already telling Josephine, 'The enemy is beaten, he has lost his head, and everything proclaims the happiest of my campaigns, the shortest, the most brilliant ever waged.'[65] It was hubristic to say so, of course, but his words eventually proved true. To encourage Mack not to retreat from his exposed position, French intelligence planted 'deserters' to be captured who would tell the Austrians that the French army was ready to mutiny and return to France, and even that there were rumours of a coup in Paris.

His envelopment of Ulm almost complete, on October 13 Napoleon ordered Ney to re-cross the Danube and take the heights of Elchingen, the last major obstacle before Ulm: from Elchingen Abbey there is a magnificent view across the floodplain all the way to Ulm cathedral, 6 miles away. Ney took it the next day. If one scans the slopes of Elchingen, up which the voltigeurs, carabiniers and grenadiers charged to take the abbey, one appreciates the importance of the high morale and *esprit de corps* that Napoleon did so much to instil in his men. In the course of the fighting a grenadier of the former Army of Egypt lay wounded on his back in the pelting rain crying 'Forwards!', so Napoleon, who recognized him, took off his own cloak and threw it over him, saying: 'Try to bring this back to me, and in exchange I will give you the decoration and the pension that you have so well deserved.'[66] In the fighting that day Napoleon came to within a pistol-shot of Austrian dragoons.

That night an aide-de-camp made Napoleon an omelette, but couldn't find any wine or dry clothing, upon which the Emperor remarked good-humouredly that he had never before gone without his Chambertin, 'even in the midst of the Egyptian desert'.[67] 'The day was dreadful,' he wrote of the capture of Elchingen, 'the troops were up to their knees in mud.'[68] But he now had Ulm completely surrounded.

On October 16 Ségur found Napoleon in a farmhouse in the hamlet of Haslach near Ulm, 'dozing by the side of a stove, while a young drummer was dozing also on the other side'. Sometimes Napoleon's naps would last only ten minutes, but they would leave him re-energized for hours. Ségur recalled the incongruity of seeing how 'the Emperor and the drummer slept side by side, surrounded by a circle of generals and high dignitaries, who were standing while waiting for orders'.[69] The next day Mack opened negotiations with a promise to surrender if he hadn't been relieved by the Russians within twenty-one days. Napoleon, who was starting to run low on provisions and didn't want to lose momentum, gave him a maximum of six.[70] When Murat defeated a relief effort by Field Marshal Werneck and captured 15,000 men at Trochtelfingen on October 18, the news hit Mack like a blow to the solar plexus and he 'was obliged to support himself against a wall of the apartment'. Napoleon wrote to Josephine from Elchingen the next day to say that 'Eight days of constantly being soaked to the skin and having cold feet have made me a little unwell, but I have not gone out all day today and that has rested me.'[71] In one bulletin he boasted of not having removed his boots for over a week.[72]

Mack surrendered Ulm at 3 p.m. on October 20, together with around 20,000 infantry, 3,300 cavalry, 59 field guns, 300 ammunition wagons, 3,000 horses, 17 generals and 40 standards.[73] When a French officer who did not recognize him asked who he was, the Austrian commander replied: 'You see before you the unfortunate Mack!'[74] The soubriquet stuck. 'I have carried out all my plans; I have destroyed the Austrian army simply by marches,' Napoleon told Josephine, before inaccurately claiming, 'I have made 60,000 prisoners, taken 120 artillery pieces, over ninety flags, and over thirty generals.'[75] In his 7th bulletin he wrote 'not more than 20,000 men escaped of that army of 100,000 men', another wild exaggeration even taking into account all the engagements since Günzburg.[76]

The surrender took place on the Michelsberg plateau outside Ulm. From the Aussichtsturm tower just outside the Old Town one can see the (now partly afforested) place where the Austrian army filed out of the city and laid down their muskets and bayonets, prior to going off into captivity to work on French farms and Parisian building projects. When an Austrian officer, remarking on Napoleon's mud-spattered uniform, said how fatiguing the campaign in such wet weather must have been, Napoleon said: 'Your master wanted to remind me that I am a soldier. I hope he will own that the imperial purple has not caused me to forget my first trade.'[77] Speaking to the captured Austrian generals, he added: 'It's unfortunate that people as brave as you, whose names are honourably quoted everywhere you fought, should be the victims of the stupidity of a cabinet which only dreams of insane projects, and which does not blush to compromise the dignity of the State.'[78] He tried to persuade them that the war had been entirely unnecessary, merely the result of Britain bribing Vienna to protect London from capture. In one Order of the Day, Napoleon described the Russians and Austrians as mere *'mignons'* of the British (meaning 'plaything' or 'lapdog', although the word also had the slight sexual connotation of a catamite).

Rapp recalled that Napoleon 'was overjoyed at his success' – as he had every reason to be, since the campaign had been flawless and almost bloodless.[79] 'The Emperor has invented a new method of making war,' Napoleon quoted his men saying in one bulletin; 'he makes use only of our legs and our bayonets.'[80]

With almost poetic timing – though Napoleon wasn't to learn of it for another four weeks – the Coalition wreaked its revenge on France the very next day. Off Cape Trafalgar, 50 miles west of Cadiz, Villeneuve's Franco-Spanish fleet of thirty-three ships-of-the-line were destroyed by Admiral Nelson's twenty-seven ships-of-the-line, with a total of twenty-two French and Spanish ships lost to not one British.* Displaying what later became known as 'the Nelson touch' of inspired leadership, the British admiral split his fleet into two squadrons that attacked at a ninety degree angle to the Combined Fleet's line and thereby cut the enemy into three groups of ships, before destroying two of them piecemeal. With the Grande Armée on the Danube it was entirely unnecessary for Villeneuve to have given battle – even if he had won, Britain couldn't now have been invaded until the following year at the earliest – yet Napoleon's persistent orders to engage had led directly to the disaster.† The battle led to British naval dominance for over a century. As the philosopher Bertrand de Jouvenel put it, 'Napoleon was master in Europe, but he was also a prisoner there.'[81] The only slight compensation for

---

* The British lost 1,666 men in the battle, against 13,781 French and Spanish.
† Villeneuve was captured at Trafalgar, but was allowed to return to France, and committed suicide in Rennes in April 1806.

Napoleon was Nelson's death in the battle. 'What Nelson had he did not acquire,' Napoleon was to say on St Helena. 'It was a gift from Nature.'[82] The victory at Trafalgar allowed Britain to step up its economic war against France, and in May 1806 the government passed an Order-in-Council – effectively a decree – which imposed a blockade of the entire European coast from Brest to the Elbe.

Instead of now abandoning his invasion dreams entirely, Napoleon continued to spend huge amounts of money, time and energy trying to rebuild a fleet that he believed could threaten Britain again through sheer numbers. He never understood that a fleet which spent seven-eighths of its time in port simply could not gain the seamanship necessary to take on the Royal Navy at the height of its operational capacity. While a conscript in the Grand Armée could be – indeed very often was – trained in drill and musketry while on the march to the front, sailors couldn't be taught on land how to deal with top-hamper lost in a gale, or to fire off more than one broadside in a rolling sea against an opponent who had been trained to fire two or even three in the same length of time.[83] Napoleon's mastery of land warfare was perfectly balanced by British mastery at sea, as the events of the autumn of 1805 were to demonstrate.

There was now nothing to hold up the Grande Armée before it reached Vienna. Yet the campaign was far from over, as Napoleon had to stop Kutuzov's 100,000-strong westward-moving Russian army from combining with the 90,000-strong Austrian army under Archduke Charles, which was then in Italy. Napoleon's hope that Charles could be prevented from protecting Vienna was realized when Masséna managed to hold the Austrians to a draw in the hard-fought battle of Caldiero over three days in late October.

'I'm on the grand march,' Napoleon told Josephine from Haag am Hausruck on November 3. 'The weather is very cold; the country covered by a foot of snow . . . Happily there is no lack of wood; here we are always in the midst of forests.'[84] He couldn't know it, but that same day Prussia signed the Treaty of Potsdam with Austria and Russia, promising armed 'mediation' against France on receipt of a British subsidy. Rarely has a treaty, which was ratified on November 15, been more swiftly overtaken by events. Frederick William III of Prussia was willing to put pressure on France when her lines of communication were extended, but he was too timid to strike, and failed to extract Hanover from Britain as the price for his 'mediation'.

Napoleon marched on towards Vienna. The supply dislocations

encountered led to vocal complaints from the ranks, and even from officers as senior as General Pierre Macon, but he spurred the army forward
and on November 7 gave 'most stringent orders' against pillaging, with
hundreds being punished at Braunau and elsewhere, deprived of their
spoils and even flogged by their comrades (which was very unusual in
the French army).[85] 'We are now in wine country!' he was able to tell the
army from Melk on November 10, though they were allowed to drink
only what had been requisitioned by the quartermasters.[86] The bulletin
ended with a now-customary tirade against the English, 'the authors of
the misfortunes of Europe'.[87]

At 11 a.m. on November 13, the key Tabor bridge over the Danube
was taken by little more than bluster by the French, who spread the
entirely false news that peace had been signed and Vienna declared an
open city. Austrian artillery and infantry under Field Marshal Prince
von Auersperg were ready to fight, and charges were primed to blow up
the bridge, but Murat and other officers screened the advance of two
battalions of Oudinot's grenadiers, who 'threw the combustible matters
into the river, sprinkled water on the powder, and cut the fuses'; one tale
is told of a grenadier grabbing a lit match off an Austrian soldier.[88] Once
the truth had been discovered it was too late, and Murat peremptorily
ordered the Austrians to vacate the area. It was thus a *ruse de guerre*
that delivered Vienna into French hands, although the Austrian high
command had not planned to resist much beyond blowing up the
bridges. When Napoleon heard the news he was 'beside himself with
delight' and quickly pushed on to occupy the Habsburg palace of
Schönbrunn, staying there that same night and entering Vienna in pomp
with his army the next day as Francis and his court retreated eastwards
towards the oncoming Russians.[89] The triumph was only marred when
Murat allowed an Austrian army to escape capture at Hollabrünn on
November 15.

Eager to press on fast for the decisive victory he required, Napoleon
left Schönbrunn on the 16th 'in a fit of anger' with Murat.[90] He was no
happier with Bernadotte, of whom he wrote to Joseph: 'He made me
lose one day and on one day depends the fate of the world; I would not
have let one man escape.'[91] He was at Znaim on the 17th when he learned
about Trafalgar. The censorship he ordered was so complete that most
Frenchmen heard about the disaster for the first time only in 1814.[92]

The need to garrison captured towns and protect his supply lines
meant that Napoleon was reduced to 78,000 men in the field by late
November, as he marched a further 200 miles eastwards to make

contact with the enemy. With the Prussians adopting a threatening posture to the north, archdukes Johann and Charles marching from the south and Kutuzov still ahead of him to the east in Moravia, the Grande Armée was starting to seem very exposed. It had been marching solidly for three months and was by now hungry and weary. Captain Jean-Roch Coignet of the Imperial Guard estimated that he had covered 700 miles in six weeks. In one of the clauses of the subsequent peace treaty Napoleon demanded shoe-leather as part of the war reparations.

Napoleon was 'surprised and delighted' by the surrender of Brünn (present-day Brno) on November 20, which was full of arms and provisions and where he made his next base.[93] The following day he stopped 10 miles east of the town, on 'a small mound by the side of the road' called the Santon, not far from the village of Austerlitz (present-day Slavkov), and gave orders that the lower section should be dug out towards the enemy's side so as to increase its escarpment.[94] He then rode over the ground, carefully noting its two large lakes and its exposed areas, and 'stopping several times over its more elevated points', principally the plateau known as the Pratzen heights, before declaring to his staff: 'Gentleman, examine this ground carefully. It's going to be a battlefield, and you will have a part to play upon it!'[95] Thiébault's version goes: 'Take a good look at those heights; you will be fighting here in less than two months.'[96] On that same reconnaissance, which took him in addition to the villages of Girzikowitz, Puntowitz, Kobelnitz, Sokolnitz, Tellnitz and Mönitz, Napoleon told his entourage: 'If I wished to stop the enemy from passing, it is here that I should post myself; but I should only have an ordinary battle. If, on the other hand, I refuse my right, withdrawing it towards Brno, [even] if there were three hundred thousand of them, they would be caught *in flagrante delicto* and hopelessly lost.'[97] From the start, therefore, Napoleon was planning a battle of annihilation.

The Russians and Austrians had developed a plan to try to trap Napoleon between them. The main field army, accompanied by the two emperors, was to march west from Olmütz with a force totalling 86,000 men, while Archduke Ferdinand would strike south from Prague into Napoleon's open rear. Napoleon stayed at Brno until November 28, allowing the army some rest. 'Each day increased the peril of our isolated and distant position,' recalled Ségur, and Napoleon decided to use that fact to his advantage.[98] In his meetings at Brno with two Austrian envoys on November 27, Count Johann von Stadion and General Giulay, he feigned concern over his position and general weakness, and

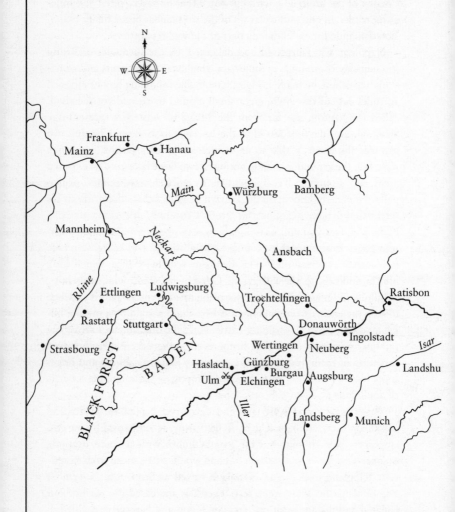

From Ulm to Austerlitz

N
W · E
S

Frankfurt · · Hanau
Mainz ·

Main · Würzburg · Bamberg

Mannheim · *Neckar*

· Ansbach

Rhine Ludwigsburg
Ettlingen · · Trochtelfingen · Ratisbon

Rastatt · Stuttgart · Donauwörth
Strasbourg · Wertingen · Ingolstadt
BADEN Günzburg · Neuberg *Isar*
Haslach · Burgau · · Landshu
Ulm ✗✗ Elchingen Augsburg
BLACK FOREST *Iller*

Landsberg · Munich

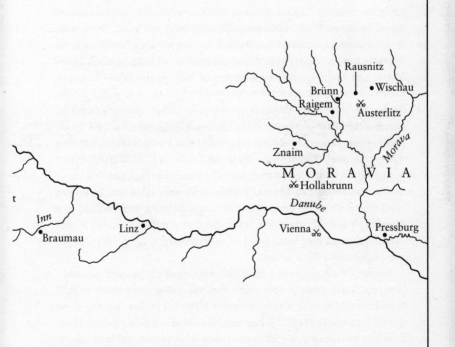

gave orders for units to retreat in front of the Austrians, hoping to instil over-confidence in the enemy. 'The Russians believed the French did not dare fight a battle,' wrote General Thiébault of this stratagem.

> The French had evacuated all the points they threatened, fled from Wischau, Rausnitz and Austerlitz at night; had retreated eight miles without halting; had concentrated instead of trying to threaten the Russian flanks. These signs of hesitation and apprehension, this appearance of backing down, seemed to them a final proof that our nerve was shaken and for themselves a sure presage of victory.[99]

Napoleon was tougher towards Frederick William's envoy, Count Christian von Haugwitz, the next day, rejecting any concept of 'mediation', before leaving at noon for a post-house and coaching inn at Posorsitz, the Stara Posta.

Learning from a deserter that the Coalition forces were definitely on the offensive, and from Savary's intelligence service that they were not going to wait for 14,000 Russian reinforcements, Napoleon concentrated his forces. With Marmont at Graz, Mortier in Vienna, Bernadotte in the rear watching Bohemia, Davout moving towards Pressburg (now Bratislava, in Slovakia), watching so-far-quiescent Hungary, and Lannes, Murat and Soult spread out in front of him on the Brno–Wischau–Austerlitz axis, Napoleon needed to bring all his corps together for the battle. He met Tsar Alexander's arrogant young aide-de-camp, the twenty-seven-year-old Prince Peter Petrovich Dolgoruky, on the Olmütz road outside Posorsitz on November 28. 'I had a conversation with this whippersnapper,' Napoleon told Elector Frederick II of Württemberg a week later, 'in which he spoke to me as he would have spoken to a boyar that he was sending to Siberia.'[100] Dolgoruky demanded that Napoleon hand over Italy to the King of Sardinia, and Belgium and Holland to a Prussian or British prince. He was answered suitably drily, but Napoleon didn't send him away until he was allowed to spot what looked like preparations for a retreat.[101]

A sentry from the 17th Légère had overheard the prince's demands. 'Do you know, these people think they are going to swallow us up!' Napoleon told him, to which the sentry replied, 'Let them just try it; we should soon choke them!'[102] That put Napoleon in a better mood. These brief but obviously heartfelt interactions with private soldiers, inconceivable for most Allied generals, were an integral part of Napoleon's impact on his men. That night, after giving orders urgently recalling

Bernadotte and Davout, on the receipt of which the latter moved 70 miles in just forty-eight hours, Napoleon slept at the Stara Posta (the Old Post Station at Posorsitz).

Napoleon's original plan was for Soult, Lannes and Murat to fight a holding action to lure forward the 69,500 Austro-Russian infantry, 16,565 cavalry and 247 guns, and for Davout and Bernadotte to arrive once the enemy were fully engaged and their weak points had become apparent. Although Napoleon had only 50,000 infantry and 15,000 cavalry with him in total, he had 282 guns and managed to concentrate more men at Austerlitz than the Allies – who were ill-served by their intelligence departments – even knew he possessed. In order further to lull the enemy into thinking that he was about to retreat, Soult was ordered to abandon the Pratzen heights with what looked like undue haste. Despite their name, the heights are more undulations than cliff-like slopes and the folds of the ground were capable of hiding relatively large bodies of troops quite close to its plateaued summit. Some parts of them were deceptively steep, and must have seemed more so when marching uphill under fire.

The days of November 29–30 were both spent in reviews and reconnaissance, entrenching the Santon hillock on the north end of the battlefield with earthworks that can still be seen today, and awaiting the arrival of Davout and Bernadotte. 'Bivouacking for the last four days among my grenadiers,' Napoleon wrote to Talleyrand at 4 p.m. on the 30th, 'I've only been able to write on my knees, thus I have been unable to write anything to Paris; besides that I'm very well.'[103]

The Allies also recognized the importance of the Pratzen heights; their plan, drawn up by the Austrian chief-of-staff General Franz von Weyrother, was for General Friedrich von Buxhöwden to oversee the attack of three (out of five) columns from the heights onto the French right in the south. These would then turn north and roll up the French line as the whole army closed in. In the event, this concentrated far too many men on broken ground in the south of the battlefield, where they could be checked by smaller French forces, while leaving the centre wide open for Napoleon's counter-attack.[104] Tsar Alexander approved these plans, although his battlefield commander, Kutuzov, disagreed with them. By contrast, French strategy derived solely from one presiding authority.

Thomas Bugeaud of the Imperial Guard wrote to his sister on November 30 and told how within two miles of the enemy 'The Emperor

came there himself and slept in his carriage in the middle of our camp . . .
He was always walking through all the camps, and talking to the soldiers or their officers. We gathered round him. I heard much of his talk;
it was very simple and always turned upon military duty.' Napoleon
promised them he would keep his distance so long as victory followed,
'but if by mischance you hesitate a moment, you will see me fly into
your ranks to restore order'.[105]

On December 1 Napoleon learned that Bernadotte was at Brno and
would arrive the next day, so battle could now be joined. After giving
his generals orders at 6 p.m., he dictated some ideas about the establishment of the Saint-Denis boarding school for the daughters of members
of the Légion d'Honneur.[106] Later, at 8.30 p.m., he dictated the general
dispositions of the army for the forthcoming battle, the last thing that
survives on paper from him until his post-battle bulletin. Later that
night, after an alfresco dinner of potatoes and fried onions, he walked
from campfire to campfire with Berthier, talking to the men. 'There was
no moon, and the darkness of the night was increased by a thick fog
which made progress difficult,' recalled one of those present, so torches
were made of pine and straw and carried by the Chasseurs à Cheval of
the Guard. As they approached the troops' bivouacs, 'In an instant, as if by
enchantment, we could see along our whole line all our bivouac fires lighted
up by thousands of torches in the hands of the soldiers.'[107] Louis-François
Lejeune of Berthier's staff, who later became one of the greatest of all
Napoleonic battlefield painters, added 'Only those who know the difficulty
of securing a little straw to sleep on in camp can appreciate the sacrifice
made by the men in burning all their beds to light their general home.'[108]
The cheers that greeted Napoleon, thought Marbot, were all the louder
because of the good omen that the following day would be the first anniversary of his coronation. The many torches held aloft by the troops were
mistaken by the Austrians for the burning of the French camp before a
retreat, in a classic example of cognitive dissonance, whereby pieces of evidence are forced into a predetermined set of assumptions.

Thiébault recalled some of the banter that night. At one point Napoleon promised that if the battle went badly he would expose himself to
wherever the danger was greatest, whereupon a soldier from the 28th
Line called out, 'We promise you'll only have to fight with your eyes
tomorrow!' When he asked the 46th and 57th demi-brigades if their
supply of cartridges was adequate, a soldier replied, 'No, but the Russians taught us in the Grisons [a canton of Switzerland] that only
bayonets were needed for them. We'll show you tomorrow!'[109] Thiébault

added that the men also 'danced a *farandole** and shouted "Vive l'Empereur!"'[110]

At 4 a.m. on Monday, December 2, 1805, the French troops were moved into their initial positions on the battlefield of Austerlitz, largely unobserved because the lower ground was shrouded in a thick mist that continued to confuse the Allied high command about Napoleon's intentions through the early hours of the battle. 'Our divisions were silently assembling in the bright and bitterly cold night,' recalled Thiébault. 'In order to mislead the enemy, they made up the fires which they were leaving.'[111]

Napoleon had been reconnoitring since long before daybreak, and at 6 a.m. he called marshals Murat, Bernadotte, Bessières, Berthier, Lannes and Soult, as well as several divisional commanders including General Nicolas Oudinot, to his field headquarters on a small hillock on the centre-left of the battlefield called the Zuran (now Žuráň in the Czech Republic), which was later to give him a superb view towards what was to become the centre of the battle at the Pratzen heights, but from where he couldn't see the villages of Sokolnitz and Tellnitz where much of the early fighting took place. The conference continued till 7.30 a.m., when Napoleon was certain that everyone understood precisely what was required of them.

Napoleon's plan was to keep his right flank weak to draw the enemy into an attack in the south, yet to have it well protected by Davout's approaching corps, while the left flank in the north was held by Lannes' infantry and Murat's cavalry reserve at the Santon, on which he placed eighteen cannon. General Claude Legrand's 3rd Division of Soult's corps would hold up the Austrian attack in the centre, while Bernadotte's corps – which was moved from the Santon to re-form between Girzikowitz and Puntowitz – would support the main attack of the day. That would be Soult's assault on the Pratzen, led by Saint-Hilaire's and Vandamme's divisions, which would begin as soon as the Allies' troops had started to vacate it to attack the French in the south.

'You engage,' Napoleon said of his tactical art, 'and then you wait and see.'[112] So he kept the Imperial Guard, Murat's cavalry reserve and Oudinot's grenadiers in reserve to use either as an emergency force on the southern flank or to trap the enemy once the Pratzen heights were captured. In the Bavarian State Archives is a sketch he drew outlining how the battle had been fought, which shows how remarkably closely

---

* A Niçois chain community dance not unlike a jig or gavotte.

it progressed to his original concept. Although Napoleon continually changed his battle-plans according to circumstances, on some occasions engagements did go according to plan, and Austerlitz was one such.

Shortly after 7 a.m., even before the conference ended and Soult's men were formed up, fighting had started around Tellnitz when Legrand was attacked by the Austrians as expected. At 7.30 a.m. Soult's troops were formed up at Puntowitz to deceive the Allies into thinking they were moving on the right flank, whereas in fact they were going to storm the Pratzen heights and smash through the centre of the battle-field. By 8 a.m. the Russians (who did most of the fighting that day) were moving south off the Pratzen heights towards the French right flank, weakening the Allied centre. By 8.30 a.m. the Allies had captured Tellnitz and Sokolnitz, but at 8.45 a.m. Sokolnitz fell back into French hands following a counter-attack by Davout, who personally commanded a brigade there. Entering the village, the thirty-five-year-old marshal, who was fighting his first large-scale battle, received an urgent appeal from the defenders at Tellnitz and sent off his brother-in-law, General Louis Friant, with the 108th Line to charge into the smoke-covered village to recapture it from the Russians. At one point Friant's superb 2nd Division was down to 3,200 effectives, only half its proper size; but although it was stretched thin it didn't break. As often happened in the era of gun-powder, there were some severe 'friendly-fire' incidents, as when the 108th Line and 26th Légère fired on one another outside Sokolnitz and stopped only when they caught sight of each other's eagles.

Legrand now defended Sokolnitz with two demi-brigades, one of which, the Tirailleurs Corses, was a Corsican unit nicknamed 'The Emperor's Cousins'. He was up against twelve battalions of Russian infantry advancing towards the walled pheasantry just outside the vil-lage, which was defended by only four French battalions. During the struggle, the 26th Légère was flung into Sokolnitz and put five Russian battalions to flight, just as Friant's 48th Demi-Brigade turned back another 4,700 Russians. By 9.30 a.m., however, the Russians had stormed Sokolnitz castle in a general assault; out of the twelve most senior French commanders in Sokolnitz, eleven were killed or wounded. As was often the case, it was the last, fresh, formed-up body of troops to be sent in who swung the battle, justifying Napoleon's policy of always holding back reserves. By 10.30 a.m. Davout's 10,000 men had neutralized 36,000 of the enemy, as he fed his infantry and artillery slowly into the battle and held back his cavalry. Davout bought Napo-leon the all-important time he needed to dominate in the centre, and furthermore allowed him to reverse the odds there, bringing up 35,000 troops against 17,000 Austro-Russians at the decisive point of the battlefield, the Pratzen heights.

At 9 a.m. Napoleon was waiting impatiently at the Zuran for two of the four enemy columns to leave the Pratzen heights. 'How long will your troops take to crown the plateau?' he asked Soult, who said twenty minutes should be enough. 'Very well, we will wait another quarter of an hour.' Once that time had elapsed Napoleon concluded: 'Let us finish this war with a thunderclap!'[113] The attack was to start with Saint-Hilaire's division, which was hidden in the undulations and lingering mists of the Goldbach valley. By 10 a.m. the sun had risen and burned off the mist, and thenceforth 'the sun of Austerlitz' became an iconic image of Napoleonic genius, and luck. Soult harangued the 10th Légère, gave them treble brandy rations and sent them up the slope. The French adopted the *ordre mixte* combination of line and column to attack, with a line of skirmishers in front, who charged straight into the fourth Russian column that was moving off the heights. Seeing the danger, Kutuzov sent Kollowrath's Austrians to plug the gaps between the Russian columns. In the fierce struggle that ensued, very few prisoners were taken and virtually no wounded were left alive.

Saint-Hilaire took Pratzen village and much of the high ground of the plateau amid heavy fighting. Colonel Pierre Pouzet's advice that he mount a fresh attack under terribly adverse conditions in order to prevent the enemy from counting their dwindling numbers seems to have won the day there, with troops returning to pick up weapons they had previously flung down in retreat. By 11.30 a.m. Saint-Hilaire had reached the plateau, and Soult poured in many more men than the Russians, as soon as they became available. The 57th Line ('Les Terribles') again distinguished itself.

Kutuzov was left watching in dismay as 24,000 French engaged the 12,000 Allied forces still on the heights; he reversed the direction of the last of the south-bound columns, but it was too late. Watching from the Zuran, and also receiving reports from streams of aides-de-camp, Napoleon could see the dense columns moving up the slopes of the Pratzen and at 11.30 a.m. gave Bernadotte the order to advance. Bernadotte asked for cavalry to accompany him, only to receive the curt reply: 'I have none to spare.' One can hardly expect politeness on a battlefield, and it was no more than the truth, but if there was such a thing as the opposite of a favourite at Napoleon's court, Bernadotte filled that role.

At 11 a.m. Vandamme's division had stormed Tsar Alexander's

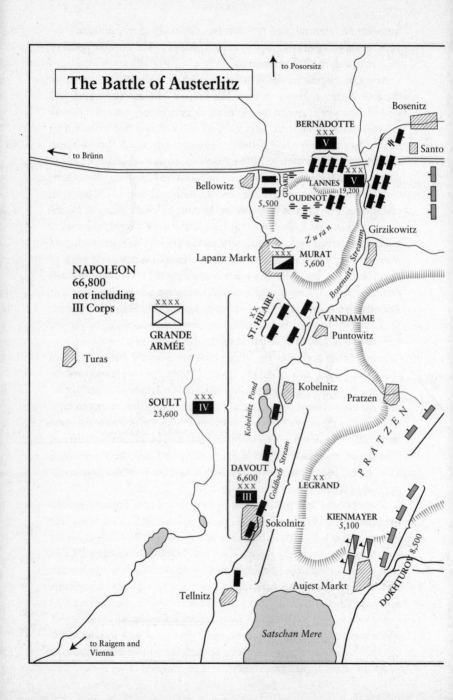

The Battle of Austerlitz

to Posorsitz

to Brünn

Bosenitz

Santo

BERNADOTTE
XXX
V

LANNES
XXX
V
19,200

Bellowitz

GUARD
5,500

OUDINOT

Zuran

Girzikowitz

Bosenitz Stream

Lapanz Markt

MURAT
XXX
5,600

**NAPOLEON
66,800
not including
III Corps**

XXXX
GRANDE
ARMÉE

ST. HILAIRE
XX

VANDAMME
XX

Puntowitz

Turas

Kobelnitz

Pratzen

SOULT
23,600
XXX
IV

Kobelnitz Pond

Goldbach Stream

DAVOUT
6,600
XXX
III

LEGRAND
XX

P R A T Z E N

KIENMAYER
5,100

Sokolnitz

DOKHTUROV
8,500

Tellnitz

Aujest Markt

Satschan Mere

to Raigern and
Vienna

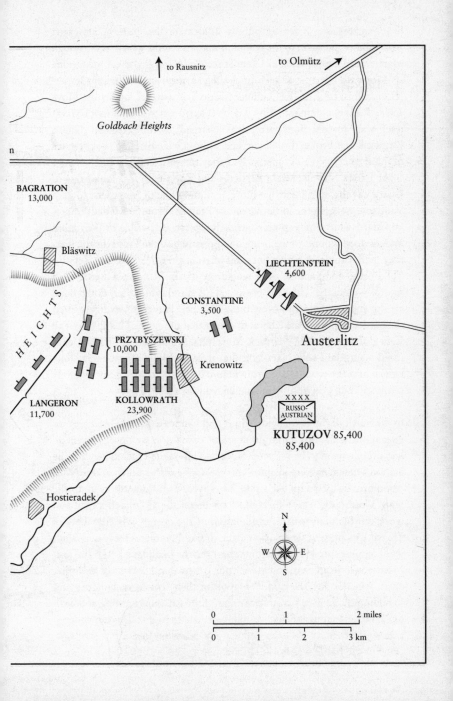

to Rausnitz

to Olmütz

Goldbach Heights

n

BAGRATION
13,000

Bläswitz

LIECHTENSTEIN
4,600

H E I G H T S

CONSTANTINE
3,500

Austerlitz

PRZYBYSZEWSKI
10,000

Krenowitz

LANGERON
11,700

KOLLOWRATH
23,900

XXXX
RUSSO-
AUSTRIAN

KUTUZOV 85,400
85,400

Hostieradek

N

W   E

S

0   1   2 miles

0   1   2   3 km

headquarters, the Stare Vinohrady hillock on the Pratzen, attacking with wild enthusiasm to the sound of massed bands, which 'was enough to galvanize a paralytic', as Coignet recalled. Grand Duke Constantine sent forward the 30,000 men (including cavalry) of the Russian Imperial Guard to take on Vandamme, whose line wavered under the blow. The 4th Line, commanded by Major Bigarré but whose honorary colonel was Joseph Bonaparte, was charged by the Russian Guard Cuirassiers; it broke, turned and fled, although its men had the presence of mind to cry 'Vive l'Empereur!' as they ran past Napoleon.[114]

At 1 p.m. Napoleon sent Bessières and Rapp with five squadrons of Guard cavalry, and later two more, including one of Mamluks, to help Vandamme regain the initiative on the Pratzen from the Russian Imperial Guard. Marbot was present when Rapp arrived, with a broken sabre and a sword wound to the head, and presented to the Emperor the flags they had captured along with his prisoner, Prince Nikolai Repnin-Volkonsky, commander of a squadron of the Russian Guard. 'One mortally wounded chasseur presented his standard and fell down dead on the spot,' recalled an eyewitness.[115] When François Gérard painted the battle, Napoleon asked him to depict that moment of Rapp's arrival. Less glorious was the Mamluk Mustapha, who although he had captured a standard told Napoleon that if he had killed the Grand Duke Constantine he would have brought him his head, to which the Emperor retorted: 'Will you hold your tongue, you savage?'[116]

In the north of the battlefield, Murat and Lannes engaged General Peter Bagration, who took large numbers of casualties. By noon Napoleon had every reason to be satisfied. Soult had taken the Pratzen heights, the Santon's defences were keeping the line stable in the north and Davout stood firm in the south. At 1 p.m. he moved his headquarters up to the Stare Vinohrady, where he could look down the Goldbach valley and work out his plan for the annihilation of the enemy. His chamberlain Thiard was present when Soult came to find Napoleon there and Soult was complimented on the brilliant part that he had played. 'For the rest, Monsieur le Maréchal, it was on your Corps that I was most counting on to win the day,' he said.[117] Napoleon then sent Saint-Hilaire's and Vandamme's divisions around the rear of the Russians fighting at Sokolnitz, and, despite still being outnumbered three to one, Davout ordered a general offensive between Tellnitz and Sokolnitz. By 2 p.m. the outcome of the battle was not in doubt.

With the Pratzen heights now occupied by Bernadotte, Napoleon was able to order Oudinot, Soult and the Imperial Guard south to envelop Buxhöwden, as Davout's cavalry attacked towards the southern village of Aujest Markt (now plain Újezd, a suburb of Brno). Napoleon then left the Pratzen heights at speed for the tower of the Chapel of St Anthony which overlooked the whole lake region, in order to command the last stage of the battle. Buxhöwden's Russian force was split in two and fled east of the frozen lakes and across them, whereupon Napoleon had his gunners open fire on the ice. This incident led to the myth that thousands of Russians drowned as the ice cracked, though recent excavations of the reclaimed land at Lake Satschan turned up only a dozen corpses and a couple of guns.[118] Overall, however, the Allied forces suffered terribly as they fled the field closely pursued by French cavalry and fired upon by artillery that had been brought up to the heights. (Austrian cavalrymen wore no backs to their breastplates, which made them lighter to carry in attack but left them highly vulnerable to sword and lance thrusts and to canister shot in retreat.) Although a Russian regiment and two Austrian battalions that had shut themselves up in Sokolnitz castle were massacred, large-scale surrender was allowed in the pheasantry and far beyond, as the French bands struck up 'La Victoire est à Nous'.

At 10 p.m. Napoleon returned to the Stara Posta. 'As may be imagined,' recalled Marbot, 'he was radiant, but frequently expressed regret' that his brother Joseph's regiment should have lost its eagle to that of Alexander's brother, the Grand Duke Constantine.[119] The next day Napoleon berated those soldiers for losing their eagle to the Russian Guard cavalry. Even though he wasn't a member of the regiment, a spectator to this monumental dressing-down recalled, 'I must own that my flesh crawled. I broke into a cold sweat, and at times my eyes were coursing with tears. I do not doubt the regiment would have performed miracles if it had been led into action at the very next instant.'[120]

'Soldiers of the Grande Armée,' Napoleon wrote to his victorious army on the night of Austerlitz, with his customary rhetoric:

> Even at this hour, before this great day shall pass away and be lost in the ocean of eternity, your emperor must address you, and say how satisfied he is with the conduct of all those who have had the good fortune to fight in this memorable battle. Soldiers! You are the finest warriors in the

world. The recollection of this day, and of your deeds, will be eternal! Thousands of ages hereafter, as long as the events of the universe continue to be related, will it be told that a Russian army of 76,000 men, hired by the gold of England, was annihilated by you on the plains of Olmütz.[121]

He added that they had captured 140 cannon and 10,000 prisoners and 'left 26,000 men dead on the field'. The next day he revised the number of cannon down to 120 but trebled the prisoners-of-war taken, along with twenty generals. Reliable modern sources put the Austrian and Russian losses at 16,000 killed and wounded, including 9 generals and 293 officers, and 20,000 captured, as well as 186 guns, 400 ammunition wagons and 45 standards.[122] The French losses came to 8,279, of whom only 1,288 were killed. Of the wounded 2,476 needed long-term care, although Saint-Hilaire's division had suffered 23 per cent casualties, and Vandamme's 17 per cent.

With large numbers of Russians still unengaged, Archduke Charles on his way from Italy and the Prussians threatening to declare war against France, the Allies could theoretically have fought on, but the Austrians' nerve was broken at Austerlitz and so too was Alexander's. He retreated into Hungary. Prince Johann of Liechtenstein arrived at the Stara Posta soon afterwards to discuss terms. 'Never, perhaps,' noted General Dumas, 'was so important an affair treated of in any palace of the European sovereigns as in this miserable dwelling.'[123] Napoleon explained his victory to Joseph, saying the enemy 'was caught *in flagrante delicto* while manoeuvring' (he was clearly fond of the phrase). He was almost equally succinct in his letter to Josephine: 'I have beaten the Russian and Austrian army commanded by the two emperors. I am a little tired. I have bivouacked eight days in the open air, with the nights rather cool . . . The Russian army is not merely beaten; it is destroyed.'[124] A masterful plan, an appreciation of terrain, superb timing, a steady nerve, the discipline and training instilled at Boulogne, the corps system, exploitation of a momentary numerical advantage at the decisive point, tremendous *esprit de corps*, fine performances on the day by Friant, Davout, Vandamme, Soult and Saint-Hilaire, and a divided and occasionally incompetent enemy – Büxhowden was drunk during the battle – had given Napoleon the greatest victory of his career.*

---

* Napoleon's battles, especially the celebrated ones, were widely discussed and analysed in detail across Europe, and throughout the nineteenth century formed part of the continent's collective memory and cultural heritage. In 1807 the Tsar's brother, the Grand Duke Constantine, told one of Davout's staff that Austerlitz had been won by Friant's 48th Demi-Brigade.

17
Jena

'*Prussia was hatched from a cannonball.*'

Attributed to Napoleon

'*When I receive the monthly reports on the state of my armies
and my navy, which fill twenty thick volumes . . . I take greater
pleasure reading them than a young lady does in reading a
novel.*'

Napoleon to Joseph, August 1806

On the morning after Austerlitz, having changed his shirt for the first
time in eight days, Napoleon rode around the battlefield. On the shore
of Lake Satschan he saw a Lithuanian sergeant who had been shot in
the thigh, lying on a block of floating ice. 'His blood stained the ice
bright red,' recalled Marbot, 'a horrible sight.'[1] The soldier called out to
Napoleon, who sent two officers to swim over. Afterwards he rewarded
them with rum, asking them how they had enjoyed their bath.[2] (The
sergeant later joined the Guard lancers.)

The next day, Napoleon granted Emperor Francis's request for an
interview, and at 2 p.m. the two men met for the first time by a fire at
the foot of the windmill known in Czech as the Spaleny Mlýn or Burnt
Mill, 10 miles south-west of Austerlitz on the road to Hungary. They
embraced cordially and spoke for 90 minutes. 'He wanted to conclude
peace immediately,' Napoleon told Talleyrand afterwards, 'he appealed
to my finer feelings.'[3] On getting back on his horse, Napoleon told his
staff: 'Gentlemen, we return to Paris; peace is made.'[4] He then galloped
back to Austerlitz village to visit the wounded Rapp. 'A strange sight for
the philosopher to reflect on!' recalled one of those present. 'An Emperor
of Germany come to humble himself by suing for peace to the son of a

small Corsican family, not long ago a sub-lieutenant of artillery, whose talents, good fortune and the courage of the French soldier had raised to the summit of power and made the arbiter of the destinies of Europe.'[5] Napoleon refused to commit his thoughts about Francis to paper when writing to Talleyrand – 'I'll tell you orally what I think of him.' Years later he would say that Francis was 'so moral that he never made love to anyone but his wife' (of whom he had four).[6] He was less charitable in his assessment of Tsar Alexander of Russia, who had not sued for peace. In a letter to Josephine he wrote 'He has shown neither talent nor bravery.'[7]

Talleyrand advised Napoleon to take the opportunity to turn Austria into an ally and 'a sufficient and necessary rampart against the barbarians', meaning the Russians.[8] Napoleon rejected this, believing that while Italy remained French, Austria would always be bellicose and resentful. As a friend of General Thiébault's said of him that year: 'He can subdue, but he cannot reconcile.'[9]

Soon after the battle, Napoleon decreed that the widow of every soldier killed at Austerlitz would receive an annual pension of 200 francs for life, with the widows of generals receiving 6,000 francs. He also undertook to find employment for the sons of every fallen soldier, and allowed them to add 'Napoleon' to their baptismal names. He could afford this, and much else besides, thanks to the return of financial confidence that swept the country as government bonds leaped from 45 to 66 per cent of their face value on the news of the victory.[10] He nonetheless didn't forgive the bankers who had shown insufficient confidence in him during the early part of the campaign. State Councillor Joseph Pelet de la Lozère noted 'the bitterness with which he invariably expressed himself when speaking of the bankers' and what he called 'the bankers' faction'.[11]

On December 15 Count von Haugwitz was presented with the Franco-Prussian Treaty of Schönbrunn, which promised that Hanover, the ancestral territory of the British monarchs, would go to Prussia in exchange for the much smaller Ansbach, Neuchâtel and Cleves. It was such an attractive offer that Haugwitz signed it immediately on his own authority. Prussia therefore ended her commitments to Britain under the Treaty of Potsdam, which she had made only the month before, and Napoleon drove an effective wedge between her and her former ally. Schönbrunn also committed Prussia to close her ports to British shipping. 'France is all-powerful and Napoleon is the man of the century,' Haugwitz wrote in the summer of 1806, having forced the resignation of his rival Karl von Hardenberg as Prussia's foreign minister in March.

'What have we to fear if united with him?'[12] Yet Hardenberg was kept on in secret government service by King Frederick William and his fiercely anti-Napoleonic wife, the beautiful and independent-minded Queen Louise, daughter of the Duke of Mecklenburg, not least in order to keep diplomatic channels open to Russia.

Napoleon was irritated by the way that French papers such as the *Journal de Paris* were writing loosely about the blessings of peace. 'It is not peace that is important but the conditions of peace,' he told Joseph, 'and it's too complicated for the comprehension of a Paris citizen. I am not accustomed to shape my policy after the discourses of Paris loungers.'[13] Unusually superstitious, he told Talleyrand that he wanted to wait until the new year before signing the treaty with Austria, 'for I have a few prejudices, and I should like peace to date from the renewal of the Gregorian calendar, which presages, I hope, as much happiness for my reign as the old one'.[14] Not receiving the letter in time, Talleyrand signed the Treaty of Pressburg in the ancient capital of Hungary on December 27, 1805, so ending the War of the Third Coalition.

The treaty confirmed Napoleon's sister Elisa in the principalities of Lucca and Piombino; transferred what Austria had previously received from Venice (mainly Istria and Dalmatia) to the Kingdom of Italy; passed the Tyrol, Franconia and Vorarlberg to Bavaria, which was recognized as a new kingdom; and incorporated five Danubian cities, a county, a landgravate and a prefecture into Württemberg, which also became a kingdom. Baden became a grand duchy with yet more Austrian territory. Francis was forced to recognize Napoleon as king of Italy, pay 40 million francs in reparations, and promise that there would be 'peace and friendship' between him and Napoleon 'for ever'.[15] The Austrian Emperor had lost over 2.5 million subjects and one-sixth of his revenues overnight, as well as lands that the Habsburgs had held for centuries, making the likelihood of eternal friendship very unlikely.[16] Meanwhile, Napoleon recognized the 'independence' of Switzerland and Holland, guaranteed the integrity of the rest of the Austrian Empire and promised to separate the crowns of France and Italy after his death – none of which meant or cost him anything.[17]

When Vivant Denon presented Napoleon with a series of gold medals commemorating Austerlitz, one of which showed the French eagle holding the British lion in its talons, Napoleon threw it 'with violence to the end of the chamber', saying: 'Vile flatterer! How dare you say the French eagle stifles the English lion? I cannot launch upon the sea a single petty fishing boat but she's captured by the English. In reality it's the lion that stifles the French eagle. Cast the medal into the foundry, and never bring me another!'[18] He told Denon to melt down the other Austerlitz medals, too, and come up with a far less grandiose design, which Denon did (it had Francis and Frederick William's heads on the reverse). There was a modicum of modesty still left in Napoleon in 1805; he also turned down Kellermann's proposal for a permanent monument to his glory and had David destroy an over-flattering gilt model of him.

The Treaty of Pressburg made no mention of Naples, which had joined the Third Coalition despite Napoleon's very clear warnings to Queen Maria Carolina in January, and despite the treaty of neutrality it had signed thereafter. The Bourbons had welcomed a Russo-British landing of 19,000 troops in Naples on November 20, though the troops had left again on receipt of the news of Austerlitz. Maria Carolina was quoted as calling Napoleon 'That ferocious beast . . . that Corsican bastard, that *parvenu*, that dog!'[19] So on December 27 Napoleon simply announced: 'The dynasty of Naples has ceased to reign; its existence is incompatible with the peace of Europe and the honour of my crown.' Maria Carolina's disingenuous declarations that the Allied landings had been a surprise were rebuffed. 'I will finally punish that whore,' Napoleon supposedly told Talleyrand, demonstrating a capacity for invective quite as colourful as the queen's.[20]

Although Masséna – marching down from Milan – quickly conquered most of Naples, hanging the bandit leader Michele Pezza (known as Brother Devil) in November 1806, the Bourbons escaped to Sicily and a dirty war developed in the mountains of Calabria, where peasant guerrillas fought against the French for years in a conflict characterized by vicious reprisals, especially after Napoleon appointed General Charles Manhès military governor there in 1810. The guerrilla war sapped French energy, manpower and morale, while devastating Calabria and its population. Although the British helped on occasion – landing a small force which won the battle of Maida in July 1806 – their main contribution was in guarding the Straits of Messina. 'Had Sicily been closer and had I been with the vanguard,' Napoleon told Joseph that month, 'I would do it; my experience of war would mean that with 9,000 men I would defeat 30,000 English troops.'[21] Here was another indication of his disastrous underestimation of the British, whom he was not personally to face across a battlefield until Waterloo.

In order to cement France's alliance with Bavaria, Napoleon asked its newly minted monarch, King Maximilian I (who had ruled Bavaria

under the title Elector Maximilian-Joseph IV of the Palatinate since 1799),
that Princess Augusta, his eldest daughter, should marry Eugène, despite
the fact that she was engaged to Prince Karl Ludwig of Baden and Eugène
was in love with someone else. He sent Eugène a cup with her picture on
it, assuring him that she was 'much better' looking in real life.[22] They married on January 14, 1806, and it turned out to be a far more successful
marriage than some of the others that Napoleon insisted upon in order to
lend his court respectability, such as the disastrous marriages he imposed
on Rapp and Talleyrand. 'Make sure you do not give us a girl,' Napoleon
only half joked to Augusta when she became pregnant, suggesting she
'drink a little bit of undiluted wine every day' as a way of avoiding that
unfortunate outcome.[23] When, in March 1807, Augusta gave birth to a
daughter, whom Napoleon ordered to be called Josephine, he wrote to
Eugène to congratulate him: 'All that now remains for you to do is to
make sure that next year you have a boy.'[24] (They had another girl.)

Napoleon had other plans for the nineteen-year-old Karl Ludwig of
Baden, and on April 8, 1806 he was married to Josephine's cousin, Stéphanie de Beauharnais, although they lived separately until he became
Grand Duke in June 1811, whereupon they had five children over the
course of seven years. And when he finally divorced his pretty American
wife, Elizabeth Patterson of Baltimore, Jérôme wedded Princess Catarina
of Württemberg in August 1807. Napoleon had therefore married members of his family into the ruling houses of all three of the key buffer
states between the Rhine and the Danube in the course of only nineteen
months, a move intended to legitimize his dynasty as well as to create
strategically important political and military alliances.

A report from the Grande Armée's receiver-general in January 1806
showed just how profitable the victory at Austerlitz had been for
France.[25] Some 18 million francs had been collected from Swabia as
well as the 40 million francs demanded from Austria by the Pressburg
treaty. British merchandise was seized and sold across all the newly conquered territories. In all, revenue amounted to about 75 million francs,
which, after deducting costs and French debts to the German states, left
France nearly 50 million francs in profit.[26] Although Napoleon constantly told his brothers that paying the army was the primary duty of
government, troops were typically paid at the end of campaigns, as a
disincentive to desertion and because those killed and captured needn't
be paid at all.[27] 'War must pay for war,' Napoleon was to write to both
Joseph and Soult on July 14, 1810. He used three methods in a bid to

achieve this end: straightforward seizure of cash and property from enemies (known as 'ordinary contributions'); payments from enemy treasuries agreed in peace treaties ('extraordinary contributions'), and the billeting and maintenance of French troops at foreign or allies' expense. France would train, equip and clothe her armies, after that they were expected to be largely self-financing.[28]

Ordinary and extraordinary contributions produced 35 million francs in the War of the Third Coalition, 253 million francs in the War of the Fourth Coalition, 90 million francs of requisitions in kind from Prussia in 1807, 79 million francs from Austria in 1809, a huge 350 million francs from Spain between 1808 and 1813, 308 million francs from Italy, 10 million francs in goods seized from Holland in 1810 and a special 'contribution' from Hamburg of 10 million francs the same year.[29] The savings made by the use of allied military contingents (253 million francs) and by despatching French troops to be billeted on satellite states (129 million francs), as well as a total of 807 million francs in 'ordinary contributions' and 607 million francs in 'extraordinary contributions' over more than a decade brought in a total of nearly 1.8 billion francs. Yet still it wasn't enough, because between the breakdown of Amiens and 1814 no less than 3 billion francs was required to finance Napoleon's campaigns.[30] To make up the difference, he needed to raise over 1.2 billion francs, of which 80 million came from taxation (including in 1806, now secure on his throne, deeply unpopular Ancien Régime *droits réunis* taxes on tobacco, alcohol and salt), 137 million in customs duties and 232 million in sales of national and communal property (*biens nationaux*), as well as by taking loans from the Bank of France. Officers of the state (including Napoleon himself) donated a further 59 million francs.[31] 'We must take care not to overload our donkey,' Napoleon told his Conseil.

So the war did not pay for the war, but only for 60 per cent of it, with the remaining 40 per cent being picked up by the French people in various other ways. Yet these did not include the imposition of direct taxes on Napoleon's strongest supporters – French tradesmen, merchants, professionals and the peasantry – except for the discretionary taxes on drinkers and smokers. Nor did it involve any direct taxes on middle- and upper-class incomes, even though Britain levied income tax at 10 per cent on all incomes over £200 per annum, an unheard-of imposition at the time. By the time of Napoleon's first abdication in 1814, French public debt was down to only 60 million francs when income from taxes and other levies were bringing in between 430 million francs and 500 million francs per annum.[32] It was an impressive feat to finance fifteen years of warfare without imposing any income taxes, especially considering that the Ancien Régime had been destroyed in part as a result of its far smaller outlays helping the American Revolution. 'When I have overthrown England, I will take off 200 million francs of taxes,' Napoleon promised the Conseil in May 1806.[33] It was never to happen, but that is no reason to doubt he would have done it.

In January 1806 Napoleon made his first really significant error of statesmanship, when he offered his brother Joseph the throne of Naples, saying: 'It will become, like Italy, Switzerland, Holland and the three kingdoms of Germany, my federal states, or, truly, the French Empire.'[34] Joseph was crowned king on March 30, and Louis became king of Holland in June. This reversion to the pre-revolutionary system of governance struck at the meritocratic system for which Napoleon had initially stood, installed largely inadequate brothers in key positions and stoked up problems for the future. In December 1805 Napoleon was writing to Joseph of Jérôme: 'My very positive intention is to let him go to prison for debt if his allowance isn't enough ... It's inconceivable what this young man costs me for causing nothing but inconvenience, and being useless to my system.'[35] Yet within two years he had made the utterly unchanged Jérôme king of Westphalia. There were plenty of local pro-French reformers whom he could have installed in power – Melzi in Italy, Rutger Jan Schimmelpenninck in Holland, Karl Dalberg in Germany, Prince Poniatowski in Poland, for example, even Crown Prince Ferdinand in Spain – who would have done a far better job than most Frenchmen, let alone squabbling, vain, disloyal and often incompetent members of the Bonaparte family.

Although Napoleon wrote scores of rude and exasperated letters admonishing Joseph over his manner of ruling – 'You must be a king and talk like a king' – nonetheless his love for his elder brother was profound and genuine.[36] When Joseph complained that he was no longer the brother he once knew, Napoleon wrote to him from his hunting chateau at Rambouillet in August 1806, telling him he was upset that he felt that way, for – adopting Joseph's grammar of writing about Napoleon in the third person – 'It's normal that he should not have, at forty, the same feelings towards you he had when he was twelve. But he has more real and much stronger feelings for you. His friendship bears the hallmarks of his soul.'[37]

Holland had astonished the world in its heyday, defying Imperial

Spain, moving its Stadtholder, William of Orange, to become king of England, founding a global empire, buying Manhattan, inventing capitalism and glorying in the golden age of Grotius, Spinoza, Rembrandt and Vermeer. Yet by the late eighteenth century, Britain had taken over most of Holland's colonies, often without a fight, her shipping and overseas trading systems were all but destroyed, her cities were declining in population (in sharp contrast to the rest of Europe), and in manufacturing only gin production was doing well.[38] By appointing Louis king (which the Dutch didn't oppose) Napoleon administered the coup de grâce to Holland's sovereignty. In many ways Louis was a good monarch, continuing the unification of the country from federated provinces, a process that had already started under her blind veteran Grand Pensionary Schimmelpenninck, who was beginning to reverse the long national decline. Local government reforms stripped the departments and local elites of influence in 1807; the ancient guilds were abolished in 1808; the justice system was rationalized in 1809. Louis moved his court from The Hague, via Utrecht, to Amsterdam, where the city council vacated its town hall so that it could become the royal palace.[39]

'From the moment I set foot on Dutch soil I became Dutch,' Louis told the legislature, which explained in a sentence the problem Napoleon was to have with him over the next four increasingly unhappy years.[40] Napoleon inundated Louis with immensely rude letters throughout his reign, complaining that he was too 'good-natured' to be the kind of tough, uncompromising monarch that he needed. A typical letter would read:

> If you continue to govern by whingeing, if you allow yourself to be bullied you will ... be even less use to me than the Grand Duke of Baden is ... You tire me needlessly ... Your ideas are narrow and you have little interest in the common cause ... Don't come and plead poverty anymore; I know the Dutch well ... Only women cry and complain; men take action ... If you are not more energetic, you will end up in a situation that will make you regret your weakness ... More energy, more energy![41]

The only surprise is that Louis stayed on his throne for as long as he did. He received little support from his wife Hortense, who although she carried out her regal duties conscientiously, and was relatively popular with the Dutch, cordially hated Louis and was soon to start conducting an affair with Talleyrand's illegitimate son, the dashing Comte Charles de Flahaut, by whom she had a son in 1811, the Duc de Morny.

Napoleon was to spend an inordinate amount of time complaining about his brothers, and would even joke of one, 'It's really unfortunate he's not illegitimate', but he kept them on long after their failures were clear.[42] One immediate problem was that the Pope refused to recognize Joseph as king of Naples, which together with his designation of Jérôme's wedding as against canon law began an entirely unnecessary quarrel between Napoleon and Pius VII that was to lead to the seizure of papal lands in June 1809 and Napoleon's excommunication. Napoleon felt he could trust his siblings more than others outside his family – although that was not borne out by events – and he wished to ape the dynastic aggrandizement of the Habsburgs, Romanovs and Hanoverians. 'My brothers have done me a great deal of harm,' Napoleon admitted years later in a characteristic bout of honest self-evaluation, but by then it was far too late.[43]

More defensibly, Napoleon began doling out titles and lands to the leaders of his Empire in 1806. Murat became the ruling Grand Duke of Berg (roughly the Ruhr valley) in April, Talleyrand became Prince of Benevento in Italy (a former papal principality south-east of Naples), Bernadotte was made Prince of Ponte Corvo (an entirely artificial principality created out of another former papal possession in south Lazio near Naples), Fouché was given the hereditary dukedom of Otranto, and Berthier became Prince of Neuchâtel on the condition that he got married.[44] Napoleon wrote to Murat asking him to organize Berg so well as to 'make the neighbouring states envious and want to be part of the same dominion'.[45] After his coronation he had created Grand Dignitaries of the Empire for Eugène (arch-chancellor) Murat (grand admiral, despite being a cavalryman), Lebrun (arch-treasurer), Cambacérès (grand chancellor), Talleyrand (grand chamberlain) and Fesch (grand almoner), while Duroc became grand marshal of the palace. Several of these jobs came with very large budgets; the grand chamberlain received nearly 2 million francs in 1806, the master of the horse (Caulaincourt) 3.1 million francs and the grand almoner 206,000 francs, among many others.[46] Although there was undoubtedly a Ruritanian feel to some of these titles, and they were duly sniggered at by Bourbon snobs and propagandists, they all came with lands and incomes that were real enough.*

Marshals and ministers weren't the only ones to be rewarded in 1806; on March 24 he gave his seventeen-year-old mistress, the 'dark-eyed

---

* In 1799 Admiral Nelson had accepted the Sicilian dukedom of Brontë and its £3,000 per annum from Ferdinand IV of Naples.

brunette beauty' Éléonore Denuelle de la Plaigne, 10,000 francs from the imperial treasury.[47] Her husband was in prison for fraud when Caroline Murat, whose *lectrice* (reader) she was, introduced her to Napoleon in yet another bid to undermine Josephine. The de la Plaignes divorced that April. Keen to establish that he wasn't impotent, Napoleon impregnated Éléonore, who on December 13 gave birth to his illegitimate child, Comte Léon (who was rather unsubtly given the last four letters of his father's name). The experiment reassured Napoleon that he could found a dynasty if he were to divorce Josephine. It also solved Éléonore's financial problems, especially once Napoleon found her an army lieutenant to marry and gave her a large dowry.

On January 23, 1806, the forty-six-year-old William Pitt the Younger died of a peptic ulcer of the stomach, a disease that would today be cured with a short course of acid-inhibiting pills. In William Grenville's so-called Ministry of All the Talents, which followed from February 1806 to March 1807, Charles James Fox, who had long been sympathetic to the French Revolution and to Napoleon, became Britain's foreign secretary. Napoleon had made peace overtures to Tsar Alexander when he sent Prince Repnin back to St Petersburg after Austerlitz; now he entertained them from Fox, who on February 20 wrote from Downing Street 'in my capacity as an honest man' to warn Talleyrand of an assassination attempt that was to be made against Napoleon from plotters in the 16th *arrondissement* at Passy, and even going so far as to name them.[48] He added that George III 'would share the same emotions' about this 'detestable assignment'. This act of decency initiated full-scale peace negotiations lasting throughout the summer, largely conducted by lords Yarmouth and Lauderdale on the British side and by Champagny and Clarke on the French, which even reached the stage of bases for a proposed treaty.

Negotiations were conducted in secret as neither side wanted to admit to their having taken place if they failed, but there are no fewer than 148 separate documents in the French foreign ministry archives relating to the period between February and September 1806.[49] These protracted negotiations – which covered Malta, Hanover, the Hanse Towns, Albania, the Balearic Islands, Sicily, the Cape of Good Hope, Surinam and Pondicherry – had effectively stalled by August 9 when Fox fell ill, but it was the fifty-seven-year-old foreign secretary's death on September 13 that doomed them completely.[50] 'I know full well that England is but a corner of the world of which Paris is the centre,' Napoleon wrote to Talleyrand as the talks broke down, 'and that it would be to England's advantage to have a foothold there, even in times of war.'[51] He therefore preferred to have no relations at all with Britain than ones that were not leading to peace, and once Grenville's government was replaced in March 1807 by that of the 3rd Duke of Portland, who re-dedicated himself to Pitt's bellicose policy against France, any hope of that was inconceivable.

Much of the first nine months of 1806 was spent by Napoleon in his Conseil, covering a characteristically wide range of matters. March saw him complaining about his 300,000-franc upholsterer's bill for his throne and six armchairs, which he was refusing to pay, as well as insisting that priests charge no more than 6 francs for conducting the funerals of the poor: 'We ought not to deprive the poor merely because they are poor of that which consoles their poverty,' Napoleon said. 'Religion is a kind of vaccination, which, by satisfying our natural love for the marvellous, keeps us out of the hands of charlatans and conjurors. The priests are better than the Cagliostros, the Kants, and all the visionaries of Germany.'[52]*

Napoleon came up with a way of taxing the butter and egg markets in March 1806, by announcing that all the proceeds would go to the hospitals of Paris, which the municipal authorities would then defund by a corresponding amount.[53] He approved a duty on newspapers, saying that when it came to the press 'the celebrated maxim of *laissez-faire* is a dangerous one if taken too literally, and must be moderately and cautiously applied'.[54] A few days later, stating that the words 'wholesale', 'retail', 'pint' and 'pot' could with perfect propriety be inserted into the new Excise Act, he told the Conseil that the bill was, after all, 'anything but an epic poem'.[55] On March 11 he told the Conseil that his bedtime reading was 'the old chronicles of the third, fourth, fifth and sixth centuries', which taught him that the ancient Gauls weren't barbarians, and that 'governments had devolved too much power over education to the clergy'.[56]

Civil administration didn't occupy Napoleon's mind completely that month; he also had time to complain to General Jean Dejean, the director of war administration, that the 3rd Légère still hadn't received the

---

* Joseph Balsamo, aka Count Alessandro di Cagliostro (1743–95), had been a famous occultist and fraud, unmasked during his lifetime, so it was strange for Napoleon to dismiss the great rationalist and one of the founders of German idealism, Immanuel Kant, alongside such a notorious mountebank.

thousand uniforms and bandoliers that they'd been promised eight days before.[57] The Conseil also discussed the colour of the Grande Armée's uniforms, because indigo dye was expensive and came via Britain. 'It would be no small economy to dress the troops in white,' Napoleon said, 'though it may be said, truly enough, that they have succeeded pretty well in blue. I don't think, however, that their strength lies in the colour of their coats, as that of Samson did in the length of his hair.'[58] Other considerations against having white uniforms were how filthy they would get and how much they would show blood.

Although Napoleon worked phenomenally hard, he believed 'Work should be a way to relax.'[59] He thought that if one got up early enough, as he told Eugène on April 14, 'One can get a lot of work done in little time. I lead the same life you do; but I have an old wife who doesn't need me around to have fun, and I'm also busier; however I allow myself more time for relaxation and amusement than you . . . I have spent the last two days with Marshal Bessières; we played like 15-year-old children.' As he had written fourteen letters that day, six of them to Eugène himself, Napoleon probably hadn't played precisely like a fifteen-year-old, but the fact that he thought he was relaxing was probably therapeutic in itself.

Some of the letters Napoleon sent to Eugène in April were absurdly nannying: 'It's important that the Italian nobility learns to ride,' he ordered.[60] More practical was the advice he gave Joseph about how to avoid being assassinated in Naples. 'Your valets, your cooks, the guards that sleep in your apartment, the people who wake you up in the night to bring you despatches, have to be French,' he wrote.

> Nobody must ever come in during the night, except for your aide-de-camp who must sleep in a room preceding yours. Your door must be locked from the inside and you should unlock it only if you have recognized your aide-de-camp's voice: he should only knock on your door after having locked the one of the room he sleeps in to make sure nobody has followed him and that he is alone. These precautions are important; they're not a nuisance and as a result they generate confidence, apart from the fact that they can save your life.[61]

On May 30, 1806 Napoleon passed a 'Decree on Jews and Usury' that accused the Jews of 'unjust greed' and lacking 'the sentiments of civic morality', gave a year's relief from debt repayment in Alsace and called a Grand Sanhedrin in order to reduce 'the shameful expedient' of lending money (something his own Bank of France did on a daily basis, of course).[62] This was the first sign of hostility towards a people to whom Napoleon had hitherto shown amity and respect; henceforth he seems to have been uncharacteristically unsure of himself when it came to policy towards the Jews. Although he didn't meet many Jews during his childhood or at school, and none of his friends were Jewish, during the Italian campaign he had opened up the ghettos of Venice, Verona, Padua, Livorno, Ancona and Rome, and ended the practice of forcing Jews to wear the Star of David.[63] He had stopped Jews being sold as slaves in Malta and allowed them to build a synagogue there, as well as sanctioning their religious and social structures in his Holy Land campaign. He had even written a proclamation for a Jewish homeland in Palestine on April 20, 1799, which was rendered redundant after his defeat at Acre (but was nonetheless published in the *Moniteur*).[64] He extended civil equality for the Jews beyond the borders of France in all his campaigns.* Yet on his return to Paris after Austerlitz, Napoleon was petitioned by Salzburg businessmen and bankers to restrict Jewish lending to Alsatian farmers. Alsatian Jews made up nearly half of France's Jewish population of 55,000, and they were blamed for 'excessive' usury in that curious inversion whereby people who borrow money under free contracts in an open market blame those who lend it to them.[65] The Conseil investigated the issue further, and was severely split over it. Napoleon told his councillors that he did not want to 'sully my glory in the eyes of posterity' by allowing the anti-Semitic Alsatian laws to stand, so they were repealed clause by clause over the following months.[66]

When the Grand Sanhedrin met it put many of Napoleon's worries to rest, and exposed his ignorance of Judaism, which he seemed to believe promoted polygamy. The Jewish elders answered the questions he posed brilliantly, pointing out that exogamous marriage was as unpopular with Jews as it was with Christians, that interest rates reflected the risks of non-repayment, and that French Jews were patriotic supporters of his Empire.[67] Napoleon thereafter proclaimed Judaism one of France's three official religions, saying 'I want all people living in France to be equal citizens and benefit from our laws.'[68] One reason for his toleration of the Jews, at least relative to the restrictions that prevailed in Austria, Prussia, Russia and especially the Papal States, might

---

* Even in religiously tolerant Britain, Lionel de Rothschild had to be elected to the House of Commons three times before he could take his seat for the City of London constituency as the first practising Jewish MP in 1858.

have been self-interest. As he later said, 'I thought that this would bring to France many riches because the Jews are numerous and they could come in large numbers to our country where they would enjoy more privileges than any other nation.'[69]

Yet, despite all this, when Napoleon thought the interests of the Jews conflicted with those of his natural constituency of French landlords, tradesmen and the better-off peasantry, he supported the latter with little regard for natural justice. On March 17, 1808 he passed 'The Infamous Decree' which imposed further restrictions on the Jews, making debts harder to collect, conscription harder to avoid and the purchase of new trading licences compulsory.[70] Although Napoleon lifted many of these within a few months in many departments, they lasted until 1811 in Alsace.[71] In Germany Jews became full citizens under Napoleon's edict forming Westphalia in 1807, with special taxes on them abolished. Similarly, in 1811 the five hundred Jewish families of the Frankfurt ghetto were made full citizens, as were all Jews except moneylenders in Baden. In Hamburg, Lübeck and Bremen the entry of Napoleon's troops brought civil rights for the Jews, however much the local rulers and populace hated it.[72]

There were only about 170,000 Jews in Napoleon's extended Empire, one-third within the old frontiers of France, but there was also a good deal of anti-Semitism, as exhibited in particular by Fesch, Molé, Regnier and Marshal Kellermann. Anti-Semitism was rife in the army, where there was only one Jewish general, Henri Rottembourg, and where the flocks of carrion crows that often followed the baggage-trains were nicknamed 'the Jews'.[73] Napoleon himself has been quoted making anti-Semitic remarks, telling one of his secretaries that the biblical Jews were 'a vile people, cowardly and cruel'.[74] In the January 1806 Conseil meeting to consider the Usury Decree he called Jews 'a debased, degraded nation . . . a state within a state . . . not citizens', 'a plague of caterpillars and grasshoppers [who] ravage all France!', adding 'I cannot regard as Frenchmen those Jews who suck the blood of true Frenchmen.' He also spoke of 'rapacious and pitiless moneylenders', despite the fact that the Conseil's *auditeurs* confirmed that the Alsatian debts and mortgages were 'engagements voluntarily entered into', and that the law of contract had 'sanctity'. Repulsive though such remarks are to all civilized people today, these were pretty standard views for an upper-middle-class French army officer in the early nineteenth century. It seems that, although Napoleon was personally prejudiced against Jews to much the same degree as the rest of his class and background, he saw advantages

The Confederation
of the Rhine, 1807

SWEDEN

DENMARK

Copenhagen

*Baltic
Sea*

*North
Sea*

Stralsund

Swedish
Pomerania

HOLLAND

Lübeck

Rostock

Hamburg

Mecklenburg

Oldenburg

Bremen

Lüneburg

Amsterdam

Arenberg

Weser

Hanover

Elbe

PRUSSIA

The Hague

Utrecht

Berlin

Cleves

Brunswick

Blankenburg

Westphalia

Oder

Düsseldorf

Berg

Hesse

Saxony

Cottbus

Elster

Rhine

Maas

Leipzig

Nassau

Erfurt

Weimar

Dresden

Koblenz

Frankfurt

THURINGIA

Moselle

Mainz

Würzburg

Main

FRENCH
EMPIRE

Bayreuth

Karlsruhe

Ansbach

Nuremberg

AUSTRIA

Carlsruhe

Ratisbon

Rastatt

Baden

Stuttgart

Donauwörth

Danube

Strasbourg

Württemberg

Offenburg

Ulm

Bavaria

Ettenheim

Inn

Munich

SWABIA

Braunau

Haag am Hausruck

Franche-Comté

Rhine

Basle

Lake
Constance

Liechtenstein

Leoben

SWITZERLAND

Tyrol

Carinthia

Lake
Geneva

Valais

Lech

Graz

Gorizia

ITALY

| 0 | 50 | 100 | 150 miles |

| 0 | 100 | 200 km |

for France in making them less unwelcome there than they were elsewhere in Europe. Napoleon therefore hardly deserves his present
reputation in Jewry as a righteous Gentile.

His continuing lack of sympathy with the essence of the religion of
most of his subjects, together with the failure for once of his normally
well-tuned ear for propaganda, led on August 15 – his birthday and the
Festival of the Assumption – to the introduction into the French religious calendar of a new saint's day: St Napoleon's. This was a step too
far, even for the normally quiescent Gallican Church. The idea flopped
among Catholics, who understandably found it blasphemous. Napoleon had asked Cardinal Caprara to canonize a new saint for his
birthday, and the cardinal had found a Roman martyr called Neopolis
who was alleged to have been martyred for refusing to pledge allegiance
to the Emperor Maximilian, but who was in fact a complete invention
by the Vatican.[75]

The Holy Roman Empire had a logic to it in the Middle Ages, when it
brought together hundreds of tiny German and central European states
in a loose agglomeration for mutual trade and security, but after the
legal foundations of the modern nation-state had been laid by the Treaty
of Westphalia in 1648, and once the Imperial Rescript had rationalized
Germany in 1803 (and especially once Austerlitz had neutralized Austrian
power across much of Germany), it was entirely stripped of its raison
d'être. On July 12, 1806 Napoleon made it yet more irrelevant when he
proclaimed himself Protector of a new German entity, the Confederation
of the Rhine (Rheinbund), comprising the sixteen client states allied to
France, from which Austria and Prussia were notably excluded. By the
end of 1806 the kingdoms of Bavaria, Saxony and Württemberg, the
principalities of Regensburg, Hohenzollern-Sigmaringen, Hohenzo-
llern-Hechingen, Isenburg-Birstein, Leyen, Liechtenstein and Salm,
the grand duchies of Baden, Berg, Hesse-Darmstadt and Würzburg
and the duchies of Arenberg, Nassau, Saxe-Coburg, Saxe-Gotha,
Saxe-Hildburghausen, Saxe-Meiningen and Saxe-Weimar had all joined
the Confederation. In 1807 the Kingdom of Westphalia also joined,
along with nine principalities and three duchies. Karl Dalberg, archbishop of Mainz, former arch-chancellor of the Holy Roman Empire
and a great admirer of Napoleon's, was appointed Prince Primate of the
Confederation.

The foundation of the Rhine Confederation had profound implications
for Europe. The most immediate was that its members' simultaneous

withdrawal from the Holy Roman Empire meant that the Empire, established by Charlemagne's coronation in AD 800, was formally abolished by Francis on August 6, 1806. (Goethe noted that day that the people staying in the same inn as him were far more interested in the quarrel between their coachman and the innkeeper than in its demise.) With the Holy Roman Empire no more, Francis II became merely Francis I of Austria, which he had already proclaimed an empire in August 1804, making him the only *Doppelkaiser* (double emperor) in history.[76]

Under the terms of the founding of the Rhine Confederation, Napoleon now had an extra 63,000 German troops at his disposal, a number that was soon increased; indeed the term 'French army' becomes something of a misnomer from 1806 until the Confederation's collapse in 1813. Another consequence was that Frederick William III of Prussia had to give up any further hope of playing a significant leadership role beyond the borders of his own state, unless he was prepared to take part in a fourth coalition against France. Meanwhile, the Confederation fostered a nascent sense of German nationalism, and dreams that one day Germany could be an independent state ruled by Germans. There is no more powerful example of history's law of unintended consequences than that Napoleon should have contributed to the creation of the country that was, half a century after his death, to destroy the French Empire of his own nephew, Napoleon III.

'Your Majesty has been placed in the singular position of being simultaneously allied with both Russia and France,' Karl von Hardenberg, the former Prussian foreign minister, wrote to Frederick William in June 1806. 'This situation cannot last.'[77] Frederick William's decision to go to war with France, taken in early July but not put into effect until October, stemmed from his fear that time wasn't on Prussia's side. Although Prussia had been the first state to recognize Napoleon as emperor, had expelled the Bourbons from her territory and had signed the Treaty of Schönbrunn the previous December, by October 1806 she was at war.[78] Frederick William dreamed of regional hegemony free of both France and Austria, and harboured growing fears of French encroachment in northern Germany.[79] In late June and early July 1806 Hardenberg's successor, von Haugwitz, who had earlier lauded the French alliance, wrote three memoranda that concluded that Napoleon was looking for a *casus belli* against Prussia, and was trying to detach Hesse from the Prussian orbit. He recommended that Prussia build up an anti-French alliance comprising Saxony, Hesse and Russia,

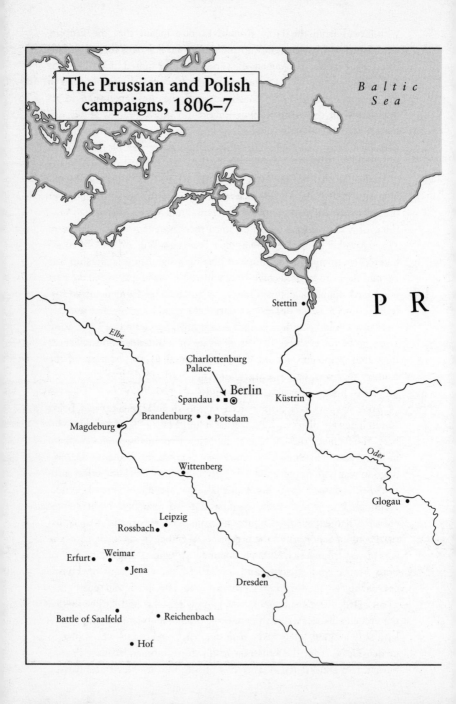

The Prussian and Polish campaigns, 1806–7

Baltic Sea

Elbe

Stettin •

P R

Charlottenburg
Palace
Spandau • ■ ◉ Berlin
Brandenburg • • Potsdam   Küstrin •
Magdeburg •

Oder

Wittenberg •

Leipzig •
Rossbach •

Glogau •

Erfurt • Weimar •
• Jena

Dresden •

Battle of Saalfeld •   • Reichenbach

• Hof

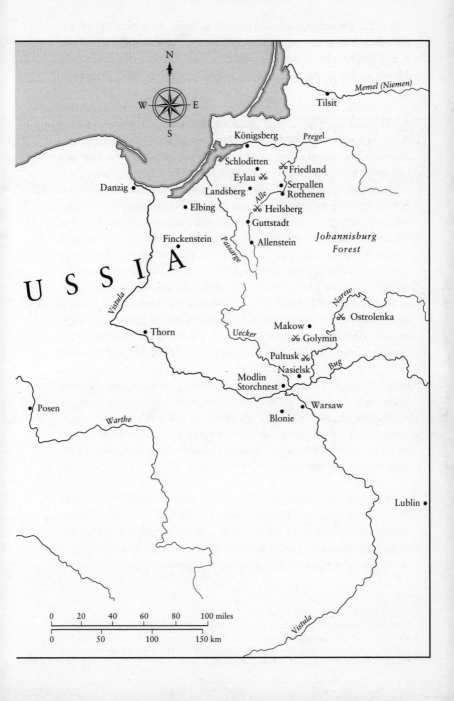

and forgo the annexation of Hanover in order to secure British war subsidies. His stance was supported by the influential General Ernst von Rüchel, who nonetheless admitted to the king that war with France within a year of Austerlitz would be a *Hazardspiel* (dangerous game).[80]

Meanwhile in Paris, the Tsar's envoy Peter Yakovlevich Ubri agreed to the wording of an 'eternal peace and friendship' treaty with France on 20 July, which required only the Tsar's ratification in St Petersburg to undercut any Prussian hopes of a fourth coalition. Yet the Tsar was infuriated by reports that General Sébastiani, the French ambassador in Constantinople, was encouraging Turkey to attack Russia, so he waited before choosing between France and Prussia. The extent to which Sébastiani was acting on Napoleon or Talleyrand's orders is unknown, but in the absence of a peace treaty after Austerlitz it made sense for France to follow that diplomatic path in Constantinople.* Napoleon didn't want a war with either Prussia or Russia, however, let alone both simultaneously. On August 2 he ordered Talleyrand to tell the French ambassador in Berlin, Antoine Laforest, 'that I desire, at no matter what price, to remain on good terms with Prussia, and, if necessary, allow Laforest to remain under the conviction that I really will not make peace with England on account of Hanover'.[81] The same day he ordered Murat in Berg in the Ruhr valley not to take any action that might be construed as hostile towards Prussia. 'Your role is to be conciliatory, very conciliatory with the Prussians, and not to do anything to upset them,' he wrote. 'Faced with a power like Prussia, one can't take it slowly enough.'[82] A scratched-out sentence on the original notes for that letter to Murat reads: 'Everything you do will only end one way, with the pillaging of your states.'

Early August 1806 saw Napoleon meet the new Austrian ambassador to Paris, Count Clemens von Metternich, for the first time. The Emperor wore a hat indoors at Saint-Cloud, which Metternich noted was 'improper in any case, for the audience was not a public one, [and] struck me as a misplaced pretension, showing the parvenu'.[83] Since Metternich

---

* As usual Napoleon was intensely active in micro-managing his Empire at the same time as following the international situation. 'Yesterday, apparently, a coachman caused an accident that killed a little child,' he wrote to Fouché on July 16. 'Have him arrested, whomever he may belong to, and severely punished' (CG6 no. 12507 p. 616).

was to become one of Napoleon's implacable foes, his generally positive first impressions – headwear excepted – are of interest:

> What at first struck me most was the remarkable perspicuity and grand simplicity of his mind and its processes. Conversation with him always had a charm for me, difficult to define. Seizing the essential point of subjects, stripping them of useless accessories, developing his thought and never ceasing to elaborate it till he had made it perfectly clear and conclusive, always finding the fitting word for the thing, or inventing one where the image of language had not created it, his conversation was ever full of interest. Yet he did not fail to listen to the remarks and objections addressed to him. He accepted them, questioned or opposed them, without losing the tone or overstepping the bounds of a business conversation; and I have never felt the least difficulty in saying to him what I believed to be the truth, even when it was not likely to please him.[84]

At this stage of their relationship at least, Metternich did not see Napoleon as the raging egotist that he portrayed him as in his memoirs.

On August 25, Prussians were outraged at the trial of the Württemberg-born publisher-bookseller Johann Palm, who sold nationalist German and anti-Napoleonic publications and who was living in neutral Nuremberg when he was arrested. Palm refused to divulge the name of the author of one of his pamphlets, *Germany's Profound Degradation* – thought to be the German nationalist Philipp Yelin – so he was shot in Braunau the next day.* 'It's no ordinary crime to spread libels in places occupied by the French armies in order to excite the inhabitants against them,' Napoleon told Berthier, but Palm quickly attained the status of martyr.[85]

On the same day that Palm was indicted, Frederick William – influenced by Queen Louise and a war party in Berlin that included two of his brothers, a nephew of Frederick the Great and von Hardenberg – sent Napoleon an ultimatum ordering him to withdraw all French troops west of the Rhine by October 8. Stupidly he had not concluded preparations with Russia, Britain or Austria before doing this.[86] Young Prussian officers then went so far as to sharpen their sabres on the front steps of the French embassy in Berlin.[87]

---

* When the Scottish poet Thomas Campbell proposed a toast to Napoleon at a literary dinner he was greeted with catcalls. 'But, gentlemen,' he cried out in his defence, 'he once shot a publisher!'

By the beginning of September Napoleon recognized that as Tsar Alexander had not ratified Ubri's treaty, Russia was likely to be fighting alongside Prussia in any coming war. On the 5th, he ordered Soult, Ney and Augereau to concentrate on the Prussian frontier, estimating that if he got his army beyond Kronach in eight days it would take only ten days to march to Berlin, and he might be able to knock Prussia out before Russia could come to her aid. He called up 50,000 conscripts, mobilized 30,000 men of the Reserve and sent spies to reconnoitre the roads from Bamberg to the Prussian capital.

If he were to move 200,000 men in six corps plus the Reserve Cavalry and Imperial Guard hundreds of miles into enemy territory, Napoleon would need accurate intelligence of its terrain, especially its rivers, resources, ovens, mills and magazines. The topographical engineers who made his maps were ordered to include every piece of information imaginable, especially 'the length, width and nature of the roads ... streams must be traced and measured carefully with bridges, fords and the depth and width of the water ... The number of houses and inhabitants of towns and villages should be indicated ... the heights of hills and mountains should be given.'[88]

At the same time, the enemy should be fed misinformation. 'You must send on sixty horses from my stables tomorrow,' Napoleon told Caulaincourt on September 10. 'Do this with as much mystery as possible. Try and make people believe that I am going to hunt at Compiègne.' He added that he wanted his campaign tent 'to be sturdy and not theatrical [*tente d'opéra*]. You will add some thick rugs.'[89] The same day he ordered Louis to form up 30,000 men at Utrecht 'on the pretext of preparing for war with England'. At 11 p.m. on September 18, while the Imperial Guard was moved in post-chaises from Paris to Mainz, Napoleon dictated to his war minister Henri Clarke his 'General Dispositions for the Reunion of the Grande Armée', the founding document of the campaign. It stated precisely which troops needed to be in which positions under which marshals by which dates between October 2 and 4. On September 20 alone he wrote thirty-six letters, his record for 1806.*

*

---

* One of them was an order to send the King of Sardinia's coachman, whom he suspected of being a spy, to the Fenestrelle prison. The next day he wrote to Denon about the Louvre's short opening hours, complaining, 'The public had to wait. Nothing can be more contrary to my intentions' (CG6 no. 13047 p. 900). He wrote 2,679 letters altogether in 1806.

Napoleon left Saint-Cloud with Josephine at 4.30 a.m. on September 25; he wasn't to return to Paris for ten months.[90] Four days later, when he was at Mainz, a report arrived from Berthier which, when added to the reports of two spies, completely changed his view of the strategic situation. Instead of the Prussians taking up advanced positions, as Berthier had feared, it was now clear that they were still around Eisenach, Meiningen and Hildburghausen, which would allow the French to cross the mountains and the Saale river and deploy without being intercepted. He therefore entirely altered his plan of operations, which, since Murat and Berthier were also issuing instructions, led to some confusion for a short time. 'It is my intention to concentrate all my forces on my right,' Napoleon told Louis, 'leaving the space between the Rhine and Bamberg entirely open, so as to be able to unite about 200,000 men on the same field of battle.'[91] A tremendous amount of marching would be needed; Augereau's 7th Corps marched 25, then 20 and then 24 miles on three consecutive days, and two demi-brigades attained an extraordinary average of 24 miles a day for nine consecutive days, the last three over mountainous country.[92]

Davout soon occupied Kronach, which Napoleon was astonished the Prussians had not defended. 'These gentlemen care little about positions,' he told Rapp, 'they are reserving themselves for grand strokes; we will give them what they want.'[93] Napoleon's overall plan, to capture Berlin while carefully protecting his lines of communication, was in place by the time he left Josephine in Mainz and reached Würzburg by October 2. The army was ready to attack by the 7th. A week later Josephine wrote to Berthier from Mainz, asking him to take 'especially good care of the Emperor, making sure he doesn't expose himself [to danger] too much. You are one of his oldest friends and it is that attachment I depend upon.'[94]

Napoleon was at Bamberg by the 7th, waiting to see what the enemy intended, expecting either a retreat towards Magdeburg or an advance via Fulda. The Prussian declaration of war arrived the same day, along with a twenty-page manifesto so predictable that Napoleon didn't even read through to the end, sneering that it was just cribbed from British newspapers. 'He threw it away contemptuously,' recalled Rapp, and said of Frederick William, 'Does he think himself in Champagne?' – a reference to the Prussian victories of 1792. 'Really, I pity Prussia. I feel for William. He is not aware what rhapsodies he is made to write. This is too ridiculous.'[95] Napoleon's private reply, sent on October 12 as his army advanced into Thuringia read:

Your Majesty will be defeated, you will compromise your repose and the existence of your subjects without the shadow of a pretext. Prussia is today intact, and can treat with me in a manner suitable to her dignity; in a month's time she will be in a very different position. You are still in a position to save your subjects from the ravages and misfortunes of war. It has barely started, you could stop it, and Europe would be grateful to you.[96]

This letter has been denounced as 'a breath-taking blend of arrogance, aggression, sarcasm and false solicitude'.[97] It can also be read as giving Frederick William one (very) last opportunity for a dignified exit, and extremely accurately estimating Prussia's chances in the coming war (indeed the prediction of disaster 'within a month' was an underestimate, since the battles of Jena and Auerstädt took place within two weeks). The true arrogance and aggression came from the Prussian princes, generals and ministers who had sent the ultimatum.

Although Prussia had a potentially very large army of 225,000 troops, 90,000 of them were tied up garrisoning fortresses. No immediate help could be expected from Russia or Britain, and although some of her commanders had fought under Frederick the Great, none had seen a battlefield in a decade. Her commander-in-chief, the Duke of Brunswick, was a septuagenarian and her other senior commander, General Joachim von Möllendorf, an octogenarian. Moreover, Brunswick and the general in charge of the left wing of the Prussian army, Prince Friedrich von Hohenlohe, had rival strategies and hated each other, so councils of war could take up to three ill-tempered days to reach a conclusion. Napoleon didn't hold a single council of war throughout the entire campaign.[98]

Some of the Prussians' more bizarre movements in the campaign, born of committee-generalship, were hard to comprehend even from their own perspective. On the night of October 9, Napoleon concluded from reports that the enemy was moving eastward from Erfurt to concentrate at Gera. In fact they were not doing that, although perhaps they should have been as it would have covered Berlin and Dresden better than their actual manoeuvre of crossing the Saale river.[99] Napoleon made a mistaken assumption, but once he had discovered it the next day he moved with extraordinary rapidity to correct the error and take advantage of the new situation.

The French advance into Prussian-occupied Saxony was screened by only six light cavalry regiments under Murat. Behind them came Bernadotte's corps in the lead, Lannes and Augereau on the left, Soult and

Ney on the right, the Imperial Guard in the centre and Davout and the main body of the cavalry in reserve. At the battle of Saalfeld on October 10, Lannes defeated the Prussian and Saxon vanguard under Prince Louis Ferdinand, Frederick William's nephew, who was killed leading a desperate charge against the French centre, cut down by Quartermaster Guindet of the 10th Hussars. This defeat, in which 1,700 Prussians were killed, wounded or captured at the cost of 172 French, had a bad effect on Prussian morale. The Grande Armée then formed up, its soldiers with their backs to Berlin and the Oder, cutting the Prussians off from their lines of communication, supply and withdrawal.[100] By the following morning it was deployed on the Saxon plain, ready for the next phase of the campaign. Moving quickly, Lasalle captured Hohenlohe's supply train in Gera at 8 p.m., forcing the Prussians to march away via Jena. When Napoleon heard this from Murat at 1 a.m. on October 12 he thought hard for two hours, and then started sending out a blizzard of orders that had the effect of wheeling the whole army westwards towards the Prussian army behind the River Saale.[101]

Murat's cavalry and spies confirmed on October 12 that the main Prussian army was now at Erfurt, whereupon Murat fanned out his cavalry to the north, and Davout seized the river crossing at Naumburg, ending any hopes Brunswick might have had of adopting a forward defence. The Prussians therefore began another major retreat to the north-east, demoralized and psychologically on the back foot even before any major engagement had taken place. On the 13th Lannes threw his vanguard into the town of Jena, expelled the Prussian outposts there and immediately sent troops to seize the Landgrafenberg plateau above the town, guided by a Prussophobe Saxon parish priest.

By now Napoleon had correctly deduced that the Prussians were retreating on Magdeburg, and that Lannes was therefore isolated and in danger of being hit by a powerful counter-attack from some 30,000 Prussians he had reported in the vicinity. He ordered the whole Grande Armée to concentrate on Jena the next day. Davout and Bernadotte were ordered to move via Naumburg and Dornburg to turn the enemy left at Jena. Davout couldn't have known that the main Prussian army was in fact heading towards him, and perhaps over-confidently didn't warn Berthier of the large numbers of enemy troops he was already encountering. Bernadotte and the Reserve Cavalry moved more slowly towards Jena, out of fatigue.

On the afternoon of October 13, as Napoleon rode through Jena, he was spotted by the philosopher Georg Wilhelm Friedrich Hegel from

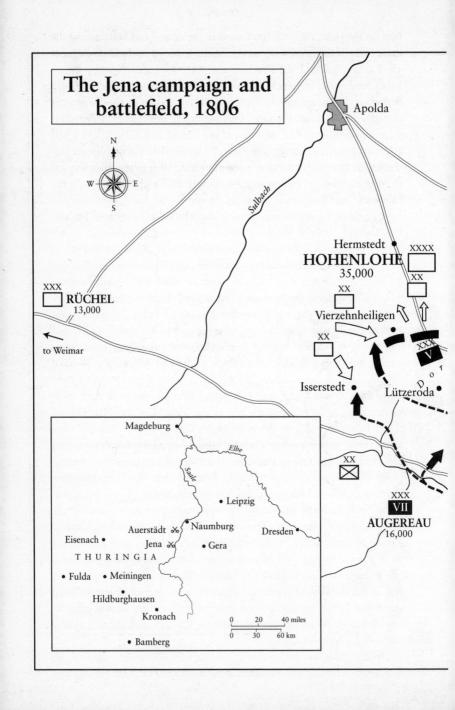

The Jena campaign and battlefield, 1806

N
W · E
S

Apolda

Sulbach

Hermstedt •
HOHENLOHE
35,000

XXXX

XX

XX

XXX
RÜCHEL
13,000

Vierzehnheiligen •

XX

← to Weimar

XX

XXX
V

Isserstedt •

Lützeroda
D
o
r

XX

XXX
VII
AUGEREAU
16,000

Magdeburg •

Elbe

Saale

• Leipzig

Auerstädt ⚔ Naumburg

Eisenach •

Jena ⚔
• Gera

Dresden •

THURINGIA

• Fulda • Meiningen

Hildburghausen •

Kronach •

| 0 | 20 | 40 miles |
| 0 | 30 | 60 km |

• Bamberg

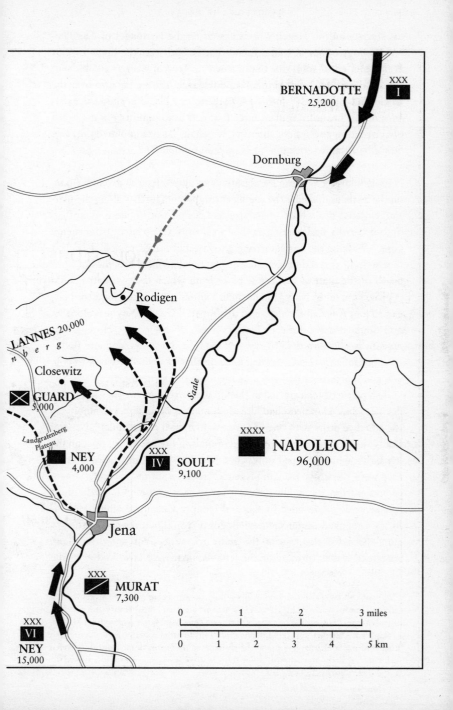

BERNADOTTE
25,200
XXX
I

Dornburg

Rodigen

LANNES 20,000
nberg

Closewitz

GUARD
5,000

Landgrafenberg Plateau

NEY
4,000

XXX
IV **SOULT**
9,100

Saale

XXXX
NAPOLEON
96,000

Jena

XXX
MURAT
7,300

XXX
VI
NEY
15,000

0   1   2   3 miles

0   1   2   3   4   5 km

his study window. Hegel, who was writing the last pages of *The Phenomenology of Spirit*, told a friend that he had seen 'the Emperor, this *Weltseele* [world-soul] ride out of town . . . Truly it is a remarkable sensation to see such an individual on horseback, raising his arm over the world and ruling it.'[102] In his *Phenomenology* Hegel posited the existence of the 'beautiful soul', a force that acts autonomously in disregard of convention and others' interests, which, it has been pointed out, was 'not a bad characterisation' of Napoleon himself.[103]

Napoleon arrived on the Landgrafenberg above Jena at around 4 p.m. on the 13th, and, seeing the enemy encampments further along the plateau, ordered the whole of Lannes' corps and the Imperial Guard up onto it, a risky undertaking as they were only 1,200 yards from enemy guns.* Walking the Landgrafenberg today, it becomes immediately clear that so long as it didn't come under sustained artillery fire, the flat open heath of the plateau was a fine place from which the two corps could deploy. That night Napoleon brought Lannes' artillery up onto the plateau to join Augereau's corps and the Imperial Guard. Ney was close by, and Soult and the Reserve Cavalry were on their way. Hoping that Davout would turn the Prussian left the next day, Napoleon and Berthier sent him a carelessly worded message that 'If Bernadotte is with you, you can march together' towards the town of Dornburg.[104]

The battle of Jena started in thick fog at 6.30 a.m. on Tuesday, October 14, 1806. Napoleon had already been up since 1 a.m. reconnoitring the advance posts with one of Lannes' divisional commanders, General Louis Suchet. There they were fired upon by a French sentry-post on the left flank, which stopped only when Roustam and Duroc shouted that they were French.[105] Back in his tent, Napoleon started issuing a stream of orders from 3 a.m. His plan was for Lannes to use both his divisions (the second commanded by General Honoré Gazan) to attack Hohenlohe's vanguard under General Bogislav von Tauentzien, in order to gain space for the rest of the army to manoeuvre onto the plain. Augereau was to form up on the Jena–Weimar road (also known as the

---

* A Napoleonstein (Napoleon stone) up on the Landgrafenberg above Jena cites the distances to various places that played a major part in Napoleon's life. Thus it states that Jena is 700km from Paris, 2,838km from Cairo, 707km from Marengo, 1,657km from Madrid, 429km from Austerlitz, 1,683km from Borodino, 503km from Waterloo and no fewer than 7,626km from St Helena. It is a powerful reminder of the energy of the man who covered such distances in the horse-drawn, sailing-ship era in the seventeen years that separated the first of those journeys from the last.

Cospeda ravine), and move up on Lannes' left while Ney came in on his right. Soult would guard the right flank, and the Imperial Guard and cavalry would be held in reserve to exploit weaknesses as they developed in the enemy's line.

Napoleon harangued Lannes' corps in person at 6 a.m., before sending them off towards Tauentzien. The military historian Colonel Baron Henri de Jomini, whose 1804 book on strategy had caught Napoleon's attention and whom he appointed as official historian on his staff, was impressed how he understood 'that it is necessary never to inspire too much contempt for the enemy, because where you should find an obstinate resistance, the morale of the soldier might be shaken by it'. So when he addressed Lannes' men he praised the Prussian cavalry, but promised that 'it could do nothing against the bayonets of his Egyptians!', by which he meant Lannes' veterans who had fought in the battle of the Pyramids.[106]

Suchet advanced on the village of Closewitz in columns ready to deploy into line once they had reached the plateau, but in the fog they veered off to the left and struck the enemy between Closewitz and the village of Lützeroda. As the fog slowly lifted, stubborn fighting developed for nearly two hours, disordering the French and using up a great deal of ammunition as masses of enemy cavalry formed up on the Dornburg, the highest point on the battlefield. Nonetheless, Lannes, a consummate drill-master, passed his second line through to the front and fought to clear the plateau, beating off a counter-attack from Lützeroda and turning to face the village of Vierzehnheiligen in the process. Beyond Vierzehnheiligen, the ground on the battlefield suddenly becomes very flat, ideal for cavalry. Both Vierzehnheiligen and the Dornberg were captured and then lost in the course of the fighting, as Hohenlohe sent in units piecemeal against the French, rather than co-ordinating a massive counter-attack. Napoleon joined Lannes at this stage of the battle, massing a twenty-five-gun battery once the fog had cleared by about 7.30 a.m., and directing the 40th Line to attack Vierzehnheiligen.

With the arrival of Soult, Saint-Hilaire drove the Prussians from Closewitz, and once his artillery and cavalry had caught up he began to move on to the village of Rödigen. He was held up by fierce Prussian resistance, but by 10.15 a.m. was able to resume his advance through Hermstedt to turn the enemy's left flank. Because Augereau had packed an entire division into the Cospeda ravine he didn't emerge onto the plateau until 9.30 a.m., but once there he engaged the enemy east of Isserstedt. Meanwhile, Ney had reached the plateau with about

4,000 men and had seen a gap opening up on Lannes' left. So on his own initiative he moved behind Lannes and came into the line on his left, just as Lannes was being driven out of Vierzehnheiligen. Ney's attack recovered the village and got the French onto the south end of the Dornberg. The sheer weight of Prussian artillery fire checked their advance, but Ney's infantry clung to the burning village. A cavalry attack forced Ney to shelter in an infantry square. At that point Napoleon made another appeal to Lannes, whose corps stormed the Dornberg and joined Ney at 10.30 a.m., just as Hohenlohe sent 5,000 infantry, with some 3,500 cavalry and 500 gunners in support, in perfect parade-ground order, to trade thunderous volleys with the defenders of Vierzehnheiligen. Crucially, Hohenlohe's troops did not storm the village.

By 11 a.m. Augereau had taken Isserstedt and linked up with Ney, and at noon Soult had arrived on the right flank. With Ney's two divisions on Lannes' left, and the cavalry under generals Dominique Klein, Jean-Joseph d'Hautpoul and Étienne Nansouty arriving, Napoleon judged the moment right for a major assault. On his order, the French army surged forward in thick skirmish lines followed by battalion columns. The Prussians fell back doggedly for an hour, but their losses rose and in the face of Murat's repeated cavalry charges Tauentzien's regiments finally broke and ran. By 2.30 p.m. Hohenlohe's army was fleeing the battlefield in total disorder, with only a few battalion squares retreating under the command of their officers. Murat, riding-whip in hand, followed by dragoons, cuirassiers and the light cavalry of all three corps, engaged in a relentless pursuit over 6 miles, slaughtering many and capturing several thousand Saxons on the way. He stopped only when he reached Weimar at 6 p.m. The deep pursuit of the Prussian forces after Jena was a textbook operation – literally so, as it is still taught in military academies today – of how to maximize victories.

It was only once victory had been won that Napoleon realized he had not been fighting the main enemy army under the Duke of Brunswick at all, but just its rearguard under Hohenlohe. For Davout, 13 miles away at Auerstädt, that same day defeated Frederick William and Brunswick, the former escaping only after many hours in the saddle, and the latter dying of his wounds shortly after the battle. With 30,000 men and 46 guns, Davout had performed a double envelopment on the 52,000 Prussians with their 163 guns, losing 7,000 French soldiers killed and wounded in that bloody engagement, but inflicting almost twice as many casualties on the Prussians.[107] It was one of the most remarkable victories of the Napoleonic Wars, and, as at Austerlitz,

Davout had radically altered the odds in Napoleon's favour. When Napoleon was told by Colonel Falcon, Davout's aide-de-camp, that he had not defeated the main Prussian army but only Hohenlohe's detachment, he didn't believe it, telling Falcon: 'Your marshal must be seeing double.'[108] Napoleon was effusive once he had realized the truth, however. 'Tell the marshal that he, his generals and his troops have acquired everlasting claims on my gratitude,' he told Falcon, giving Davout's corps the honour of leading the triumphal entry into Berlin on October 25.[109] Even so, Auerstädt was never sewn onto flags as a battle honour, because that would have contrasted Napoleon's fine victory over Hohenlohe with Davout's stunning one over Brunswick.

Bernadotte, by contrast, had not managed to arrive on either battlefield, something for which Napoleon and Davout never truly forgave him. 'I ought to have had Bernadotte shot,' Napoleon said on St Helena, and at the time he seems to have briefly considered court-martialling him.[110] Napoleon wrote him a sharp letter on October 23 – 'Your Corps was not on the battlefield, and that could have been fatal for me.' Bernadotte had taken Berthier's orders at face value and marched his men to Dornburg. He didn't cross paths with Napoleon between October 9 and December 8, by which point the Emperor had written to praise him for capturing Lübeck from Blücher, so the stories of a fiery personal interview are myths.[111] It was rare for Berthier to give garbled orders, but Bernadotte's absence from both battlefields was indicative of what could happen if he did. Nonetheless, Bernadotte knew that he was once more the butt of Napoleon's ire, and his own longstanding private dislike and envy of Napoleon only made the situation worse.

'My love, I've executed some fine manoeuvres against the Prussians,' Napoleon boasted to Josephine from Jena at three o'clock on the morning after the battle. 'I won a great victory yesterday. The enemy numbered 150,000; I have taken 20,000 prisoners, 100 artillery pieces, and flags. I saw the King of Prussia and got near to him, but failed to capture him, so also to the Queen. I have been in bivouac for two days. I am wonderfully well.'[112] The numbers were exaggerated as usual, and Frederick William had been at Auerstädt rather than Jena so he couldn't have seen him or the queen, but Napoleon had indeed captured eighty-three guns and Davout fifty-three, and after his near-flawlessly executed battle there was no doubt that Napoleon was 'wonderfully well'.

18

Blockades

*'The Emperor Napoleon was often known to take off his cross
of the Légion d'Honneur and place it with his own hands on the
bosom of a brave man. Louis XIV would have first inquired if
this brave man was noble. Napoleon asked if the noble was
brave.'*

Captain Elzéar Blaze of the Imperial Guard

*'The first qualification of a soldier is fortitude under fatigue and
privation. Courage is only the second. Hardship, poverty and
want are the best school for a soldier.'*

Napoleon's Military Maxim No. 58

'I've never seen men so completely beaten,' Napoleon said of the Prussians after Jena.[1] Yet Frederick William didn't surrender. Instead he withdrew north-eastwards to continue fighting, knowing that the Russian army was on its way. Although negotiations were opened after the battle between the Marquis Girolamo di Lucchesini, the Prussian ambassador to Paris, and Duroc, nothing came of them. Napoleon rightly suspected Lucchesini to have been a prime supporter of the war.[2] 'I think it would be difficult to give a greater proof of the imbecility of this pantaloon,' he wrote to Talleyrand.[3]

Meanwhile the Grande Armée continued its relentless drive through Prussia, never allowing the Prussians a chance to stop and regroup. Spandau capitulated to Suchet on October 25, Stettin to Lasalle on the 29th and the heavily fortified Magdeburg to Ney on November 11, which secured the whole western half of Prussia. On November 7 General Gerhard von Blücher, who had fought bravely at Auerstädt, was forced to surrender his whole force at Lübeck when he completely ran out of ammunition.

The fall of Berlin came so quickly that shopkeepers didn't have time to take down the numerous satirical caricatures of Napoleon from their windows.[4] As in Venice, the Emperor had the city's Quadriga and winged Victory chariot removed from the Brandenburg Gate and taken back to Paris, while prisoners from the Prussian Guard were marched past the same French embassy on whose steps they had so hubristically sharpened their swords the previous month.[5] Napoleon visited the battlefield of Rossbach (now Braunsbedra), the scene of France's humiliation by Frederick the Great in 1757, and ordered the column erected there to be sent to Paris too.[6] 'I am wonderfully well,' he repeated to Josephine from Wittenberg on October 23, 'fatigue agrees with me.'[7] His habit of signing off so very many letters to Josephine with the words 'I'm well' (Je me porte bien), turned out later to become a dangerous one.[8]

Sheltering in a hunting lodge in a surprise storm that day, a young widow told him of being married to the chef de bataillon of the 2nd Légère who had died at the battle of Aboukir, leaving her with their son. On being shown proof of the child's legitimacy, Napoleon gave her a pension of 1,200 francs per annum, to revert to the boy on her death.[9] The next day at Potsdam he was shown Frederick the Great's sword, belt, sash and all his decorations at his palace of Sanssouci, which he sent to Les Invalides, as further 'revenge for the disasters of Rossbach'.[10] (He kept the king's alarm clock by his bed for the rest of his life, but didn't take Frederick's flute, which can still be seen at Sanssouci.) 'I would rather have these than twenty million,' said Napoleon of his booty, and, gazing on Frederick's tomb with his staff, he modestly added: 'Hats off, gentlemen. If this man were alive I would not be standing here now.'[11]

While at Potsdam, Napoleon nearly took an altogether more serious revenge when it was discovered that Prince Franz Ludwig von Hatzfeld, who was on a Prussian delegation from Berlin, had been writing in code to Hohenlohe reporting on the size and state of the French army there. Even though Berthier, Duroc, Caulaincourt and Rapp tried to appease Napoleon's anger, the Emperor wanted to arraign Hatzfeld as a spy in front of a military tribunal and have him shot. Shades of d'Enghien must have weighed heavily with Caulaincourt, and Berthier actually left the room when Napoleon 'lost all patience' with his advisors.[12] Recognizing that he had overreacted, Napoleon arranged a touching scene whereby Hatzfeld's pregnant wife threw herself in tears at his feet begging for her husband's life. The Emperor then magnanimously tossed the intercepted coded letter into the fire, destroying the evidence.[13]

On the same day that Davout entered Berlin and Suchet took

Spandau, Napoleon was writing to Fouché about the expense of the stage scenery for Pierre Gardel's ballet *The Return of Ulysses*, and asking for a detailed report 'to make sure there is nothing bad in it; you understand in what sense' (Penelope had suitors when Ulysses was abroad).[14] Yet somewhat hypocritically Napoleon was perfectly willing to make exactly the same insinuations against Queen Louise that he feared being made about himself, stating in a bulletin: 'There was found in the apartment that the Queen occupied at Potsdam the portrait of the Emperor of Russia which that prince had presented to her.'[15]

The accusations that Frederick William had succumbed to petticoat government were unrelenting. 'The notes, reports and State papers were scented with musk,' read the campaign's 19th bulletin from the Charlottenburg Palace on October 27, 'and were found mixed with scarves and other objects on the dressing table of the Queen.'[16] In case anyone missed the point, it stated how these 'historical documents ... demonstrate, if it needs demonstration, how unfortunate princes are when they allow women to have influence on political affairs'. Even the devoted Bausset thought that Napoleon wrote 'with anger and without courtesy' about Queen Louise, and when Josephine complained of the queen's treatment in his bulletins, Napoleon admitted: 'It's true that beyond all I hate manipulative women. I am used to good, gentle and compassionate women ... but that is maybe because they remind me of you.'[17]

'Soldiers,' Napoleon proclaimed from Potsdam on October 26, 'the Russians boast of coming to us. We will march to meet them, and thus spare them half the journey. They shall find another Austerlitz in the heart of Prussia.'[18] This was not what the army wished to hear. Now that the Prussian capital had fallen they wanted to return home.

Napoleon entered Berlin on the 27th in a grand procession at the head of 20,000 grenadiers and cuirassiers in their full-dress uniform. 'The Emperor moved proudly along in his plain dress with his small hat and his one-*sou* cockade,' recalled Captain Coignet. 'His staff was in full uniform and it was a curious sight to see the worst dressed man the master of such a splendid army.'[19] In 1840, writing to the future Empress Eugénie, Stendhal recalled how Napoleon 'rode twenty paces ahead of his soldiers; the silent crowd was but two paces from his horse; he could have been shot down by a rifle from any window'.[20] He settled in Frederick William's vast rococo Charlottenburg Palace in Berlin, which became his headquarters. Napoleon's treasury expenses record some 23,300 francs being given to a lady at this time who is described merely as 'a Berliner'.[21] On October 30, Napoleon offered peace on the basis of Prussia renouncing all its territories west of the Elbe, which Frederick William was prepared to do, but when he then added that the kingdom must also serve as his operational base for the coming struggle with Russia, the king ignored the advice of the majority of his council and continued the war, retreating to Königsberg (present-day Kaliningrad) up on the Baltic coast.[22]

France provided Napoleon with around 80,000 French conscripts a year, and many of the 1806 intake were now on their way to Prussia. These together with the 80,000 men he already had in the field – not including the garrisons in captured Prussian cities – and various detachments from the Confederation of the Rhine, meant that by November 1806 Napoleon could cross the Vistula into what had recently been Poland, and he could do so in force before winter closed down the campaign. Poland had been a European nation since 966, a kingdom since 1205 and part of a commonwealth with Lithuania after the Union of Lublin of 1569. It had been steadily erased from the map when it was partitioned in 1772, 1793 and 1795 between Russia, Prussia and Austria, but although it no longer existed as a country there was nothing the three partitioning powers could do to damage Poles' sense of nationhood. This Napoleon continually encouraged, allowing the Poles to believe that one day he would restore their nation. Perhaps he would have done so eventually, but he had no plans for it in the short-term. Since 1797, when the French revolutionary army created 'Polish Legions', some 25,000 to 30,000 Poles had served in the two Italian campaigns, Germany and Saint-Domingue. Napoleon's apparent sympathy with their cause encouraged many more Poles than that to rally to him, and some of Napoleon's finest troops were Polish – including the first lancer units in the Grande Armée, who proved so effective that by 1812 he had converted nine regiments of dragoons into lancer regiments.

Horses were collected from all over France and Germany for the coming campaign, and the Army of Italy was stripped of cavalry in favour of the Grande Armée. Napoleon requisitioned uniforms, food, saddles, shoes, and so on from Prussia, but the state of Polish roads meant there were constant supply shortages. His abiding concern with how his soldiers were shod led him to write twenty-three letters about boots and shoes in November and December alone, including one to General François Bourcier, commandant of the cavalry depot in Potsdam, ordering that Prussian cavalrymen be made to give up their boots in exchange for French shoes, explaining: 'They won't be needing their boots again, and needs must . . .'[23]

On November 2 Napoleon ordered Davout to push east to Posen (now Poznań, in Poland), with Beaumont's dragoons, followed by Augereau.[24] Once there they set up a base and built bakeries before the corps under Lannes, Soult, Bessières, Ney and Bernadotte followed, with approximately 66,000 infantry and 14,400 cavalry in total. Napoleon took the territory between the Oder and the Vistula primarily to deny it to the Russians, but he also hoped to prevent the Prussians from staging a resurgence and to persuade the Austrians to remain neutral. He himself remained in Berlin. On the 4th he learned that 68,000 Russian soldiers were marching west from Grodno with the aim of joining the 20,000 Prussians under the command of General Anton von Lestocq.* 'If I let the Russians advance I should lose the support and the resources of Poland,' he said. 'They might decide Austria, which only hesitated because they were so far off; they would carry with them the whole Prussian nation.'[25] Murat, Davout, Lannes and Augereau therefore marched on towards the Vistula to establish bridgeheads before repairing to their winter cantonments on the western side of the river. Marching eastwards a thousand miles from Paris into a freezing winter through some of Europe's worst-provisioned, poorest countryside against two enemy nations, with a third possibly hostile one to the south, was always going to be a considerable risk, though no worse a one than the Austerlitz campaign had been.

Almost all the fighting in the next part of the campaign took place inside East Prussia, formerly Polish territory, in what is today the 5,830 square mile Russian enclave of Kaliningrad. Much of it is a flat, boggy plain with many rivers, lakes and forests. In winter temperatures drop to –30°C and there is daylight only between 7.30 a.m. and 4.30 p.m. The roads were often only tracks unmarked on maps; even the main road from Warsaw to Posen was unpaved and lacked side ditches. Heavy rain turned the entire countryside into seas of mud, with cannon moving at 1¼ mph. Napoleon joked that he had discovered a fifth element to add to water, fire, air and earth: mud! He sent his survey department forward to map and sketch the countryside, note the name of each village, its population and even soil type, all recorded beside the

---

* Of the half of Russia's 50 million population who were serfs, the Tsar levied a man-tax of 5 per cent, so his armies never had a manpower problem (Summerville, *Napoleon's Polish Gamble* p. 19). The Russian peasants were conscripted for twenty-five years, with no leave. Often illiterate, ill-fed, ill-lodged, ill-cared for and virtually unpaid, they nonetheless made excellent soldiers (Lieven, *Russia Against Napoleon passim*).

officer's signature so that he could summon him to learn more details later.

Even as he prepared to confront the Russians again, Napoleon's thoughts turned to Britain, which he saw as an equally serious threat to France's long-term interests. On Friday, November 21, 1806, he signed into law the Berlin Decrees. These were designed to force Great Britain to the negotiating table, but instead were to lead – once he tried to impose them by force on Portugal, Spain and Russia – to his own downfall. The 'Continental System' created by the Berlin Decrees (and their successors the Milan and Fontainebleau Decrees of 1807 and 1810) was what Napoleon called 'a retaliation' against the British Order-in-Council of May 16, 1806, which had imposed a blockade of the European coast from Brest to the Elbe.[26] 'That England does not admit at all the law of nations followed universally by all civilized people,' the Berlin Decrees began, means her adversaries have 'a natural right to oppose the enemy with the same arms he uses.' Therefore the articles, drafted and redrafted by Talleyrand, who supported the policy, were uncompromising:

1. The British Isles are in a state of blockade.
2. All trade and all correspondence with the British Isles is forbidden.
3. Every British subject, of whatever state or condition he may be . . . will be made a prisoner of war.
4. All warehouses, all merchandise, all property, of whatever nature it might be, belonging to a subject of England will be declared a valid prize . . .
7. No ship coming directly from England or the English colonies, or having been there since the publication of the present decree, will be received in any port.[27]

Since one-third of Britain's direct exports and three-quarters of her re-exports went to continental Europe, Napoleon intended the decrees to put huge political pressure on the British government to restart the peace negotiations broken off in August.[28] Writing to Louis on December 3, he explained: 'I will conquer the sea through the power of the land.'[29] Later he stated: 'It's the only means of striking a blow to England and obliging her to make peace.'[30] It was true; since the destruction of the French fleet at Trafalgar there was no direct way to damage Britain other than commercially.

Although Napoleon believed that the Berlin Decrees would be

popular with French businessmen, who he hoped would pick up the trade that previously went to Britain, he was soon disabused by the reports from his own chambers of commerce. As early as December that of Bordeaux reported a dangerous downturn of business. International trade simply wasn't the zero-sum game that, with his crude Colbertism, Napoleon assumed it to be. By March 1807 he had to authorize special industrial loans from the reserve funds to offset the crises that were resulting.[31]

Although the most ardent articles in the influential British Whiggish journal the *Edinburgh Review* (apart from those attacking Wordsworth's poetry) called for peace in order to allow trade to resume, the British government managed to ride out domestic criticism. By contrast, the Continental System damaged precisely those people who had done well from Napoleon's regime and had hitherto been his strongest supporters: the middle classes, tradesmen, merchants and better-off peasantry, the acquirers of *biens nationaux* property he had always sought to help. 'Shopkeepers of all countries were complaining about the state of affairs,' recalled the treasury minister Mollien, but Napoleon was in no mood to listen, let alone compromise.[32]

On January 7, 1807 Britain retaliated with further Orders-in-Council, 'subjecting to seizure all neutral vessels trading from one hostile port in Europe to another ... interdicting the coastal trade of the enemy to neutrals'.[33] Then, in November, still more Orders stated that France and all its tributary states were under a state of blockade and that all neutral vessels intending to go to or from France had to sail to Britain first, pay duties there and obtain clearance. All American trade with France was therefore blocked unless the United States' ships bought a licence in a British port for a substantial fee. Along with the British practice of 'impressing' (i.e. kidnapping) thousands of Americans for service in the Royal Navy, the November 1807 Orders-in-Council were the primary cause of the War of 1812 between Britain and the United States.

One major problem with the Continental System was that it could not be imposed universally. In 1807, for example, because Hamburg and the Hanseatic towns such as Lübeck, Lüneburg, Rostock, Stralsund and Bremen couldn't manufacture the 200,000 pairs of shoes, 50,000 greatcoats, 37,000 vests and so on that the Grande Armée required, their governors were forced to buy them from British manufacturers under special licences allowing them through the blockade. Many of Napoleon's soldiers in the coming battles of the Polish campaign wore uniforms made in Halifax and Leeds, and British ministers boasted in the House of Commons that Napoleon couldn't even provide the insignia stitched onto his officers' uniforms except by resort to British manufacturers.[34]

In some parts of the Empire, the Continental System caused genuine distress as it unbalanced, dislocated and occasionally wrecked entire industries. There were serious disturbances in the Grand Duchy of Berg, and two demi-brigades had to be sent to Mainz to confiscate all English and colonial goods. Comestibles destined for larders across Europe were publicly burned, and the parts of Germany closest to France suffered more than Britain.[35] Napoleon's protectionist decrees led to huge bonfires of confiscated British produce on the beaches of Dieppe and Honfleur.

Another problem was that there was widespread undermining of the System, even by the imperial family. Louis turned a blind eye to smuggling in Holland, Murat failed to impose the System fully when he became king of Naples, and Josephine herself bought smuggled goods on the black market.[36] Even the ultra-loyal Rapp allowed contraband into Danzig when he became governor in 1807, and refused to burn merchandise.[37] 'No prohibited merchandise whatever may enter without my order,' an infuriated Napoleon told his finance minister, Gaudin, 'and I should be expressly derelict to permit any abuse which touches my House so closely. Where there is a law, everybody should obey it.'[38] He dismissed Bourrienne in 1810 – who as governor of Hamburg had been taking bribes from merchants to relax the System's prohibitive measures – and dethroned Louis the same year to set an example, but abuses continued virtually unabated.

Although Napoleon was not so naive as to believe that smuggling could be stamped out altogether, he went to great lengths to suppress it, posting three hundred customs officers along the Elbe in 1806, for example. Yet the British made even greater efforts to facilitate smuggling, setting up a huge operation on the North Sea island of Heligoland.[39] By 1811 there were 840 vessels plying their often night-time trade between Malta and southern Mediterranean ports. Once landed, coffee and sugar were smuggled across borders despite the penalty of ten years' penal servitude and branding, and after 1808 the death penalty on occasion for repeat offenders.[40] (Britain had imposed the death penalty for smuggling in 1736, which was regularly enforced.)

The blockaded French navy could not hope to police the European coastline, and Lisbon, Trieste, Athens, Scandinavia, the Balearics, Gibraltar, Livorno, the Ionian Islands and St Petersburg all provided points at which, at different times and in differing amounts, British goods could enter the continent overtly or covertly. When French customs officials did capture contraband a proportion of it was often returnable for a bribe, and in due course it became possible to take out insurance against seizures at Lloyd's of London. Meanwhile, French imperial customs revenues collapsed from 51 million francs in 1806 to 11.5 million in 1809, when Napoleon allowed the export of grain to the British at high price when their harvest was weak – some 74 per cent of all British imported wheat came from France that year – in order to deplete British bullion reserves.[41]* The Continental System failed to work because merchants continued to accept British bills-of-exchange, so London continued to see net capital inflows.[42] Much to Napoleon's frustration, the British currency depreciated against European currencies by 15 per cent between 1808 and 1810, making British exports cheaper. The Continental System also forced British merchants to become more flexible and to diversify, investing in Asia, Africa, the Near East and Latin America much more than before, so exports that had been running at an average of £25.4 million per annum between 1800 and 1809 rose to £35 million between 1810 and 1819. By contrast, imports fell significantly, so Britain's balance of trade was positive, which it hadn't been since 1780.[43]

Napoleon hoped, by preventing continental consumers from buying British produce, to stimulate European production, especially French, and to encourage producers to explore alternatives. When it was discovered in 1810 that sugar beet and indigo could be produced in France, he told his secretary that it was like discovering America a second time.[44] An experimental school was set up in Saint-Denis to teach sugar-making and in March 1808 Napoleon asked Berthollet to research whether 'it is possible to make good sugar from turnips'.[45] He could not persuade people to drink Swiss tea, however, let alone chicory rather than coffee, and his plans to manufacture cotton out of thistles in 1810 also came to nothing.[46]

Had Britain merely been 'a nation of shopkeepers', the economic downturn in the fiscal years 1810 and 1811 that has been attributed to the Continental System might well have stirred up political problems for the government, but the Cabinet was largely made up of upper-class former colleagues of William Pitt – indeed the Duke of Portland's government

---

* One small area where the Continental System did succeed was in denying the Royal Navy the north German timber it most liked to use, and forcing it to secure lesser woods from Africa and teak from the Malabar coast in south-west India, which the Admiralty disliked because, not being so fibrous, they splintered and thus caused higher casualties in battle (Albion, Forests and Sea Power passim, TLS 9/6/27 p. 399).

of 1807–9 abjured the labels 'Whig' and 'Tory' altogether and simply called itself 'the friends of Mr Pitt' – who put their support for the war against Napoleon above all commercial considerations. Spencer Perceval, who followed Portland as prime minister in October 1809, was quite unhinged on the subject. He told his brother-in-law Thomas Walpole that Napoleon could be identified in the Book of Revelation as 'the woman who rides upon the beast, who is drunk with the blood of the saints, the mother of harlots'.[47] When Napoleon was stopped at Acre in 1799, Perceval wrote an anonymous pamphlet, catchily entitled *Observations Intended to Point out the Application of a Prophecy in the Eleventh Chapter of the Book of David to the French Power*, which sought to argue that the Bible had foretold the fall of Napoleon. (Perceval's detailed calculations from the scriptures also convinced him that the world was going to end in the year 1926.)[48] With Britain's politicians possessed by beliefs so resistant to reason, it is hard to see how Napoleon could ever have persuaded Britain to make peace after the death of Fox. When in 1812 Perceval was assassinated by someone even more deranged than him, his place as prime minister was taken by another disciple of Pitt, Lord Liverpool (formerly the foreign secretary Lord Hawkesbury), who was just as committed to the destruction of Napoleon and who would serve until 1827.

At 3 a.m. on November 25, 1806 Napoleon left Berlin for a tour of the Polish front, inviting Josephine, who was in Mainz, to come east to stay with him,[49] a suggestion he was later to regret. He entered the Polish city of Posen on the night of the 27th to a tremendous reception from the inhabitants, whose hopes for nationhood he had excited but avoided making any commitment to gratify. 'I ought not to have crossed the Vistula,' he later said in one of his many acknowledgements of blunders. 'It was the taking of Magdeburg that induced me to enter Poland. I did wrong. It led to terrible wars. But the idea of the re-establishment of Poland was a noble one.'[50] To the town fathers begging for the restitution of their kingdom he chose his words carefully: 'Speeches and empty wishes are not enough ... What force has overthrown only force can restore ... what has been destroyed for lack of unity only unity can re-establish.'[51] It sounded positive and martial, but fell well short of a promise to re-establish Poland as a nation-state.

The next day Count Levin von Bennigsen, the Hanoverian-born commander of the Russian army, retreated from Warsaw and stopped 40 miles to the north near Pultusk. Murat entered Warsaw that evening, installing himself as governor. Napoleon was not about to be coerced by the Poles' enthusiastic welcome into alienating for ever the three countries which had partitioned and extinguished Poland for their own immense territorial gain in 1795. 'I am old in my knowledge of men,' he told Murat on December 2. 'My greatness does not rest on the help of a few thousand Poles . . . It is not for me to take the first step.' As for General Prince Józef Poniatowski, the pro-French nephew of Poland's last king, Napoleon said: 'He is more frivolous and lightweight than most Poles, and that is saying a good deal.'[52] Napoleon wanted Murat to convey to the Poles 'that I am not begging for a throne for a member of my family; I have no shortage of thrones to give them.'[53]

The Grande Armée hated life on the Vistula, and saw only 'want and bad weather' ahead.[54] One of the army's jokes was that the entire Polish language could be reduced to five words – '*Chleba? Nie ma. Woda? Zaraz!*', 'Bread? There is none. Water? Immediately!' – so when an infantryman in a column near Nasielsk shouted out to Napoleon: 'Papa, *Chleba?*', he immediately called back '*Nie ma*', whereupon the whole column roared with laughter.[55] During a storm before the army went into its winter quarters (cantonments), another soldier shouted: 'Have you bumped your head, leading us without bread on roads like this?' To which Napoleon replied: 'Four more days of patience, and I won't ask you for anything more. Then you'll be cantoned.' The soldier shouted back: 'Well, it's not too much, but remember it, because after that we'll canton ourselves!'[56] The *grognards* had genuine grievances – on occasion they were reduced to drinking horses' blood from saucepans while on the march – but Savary recalled of this period of the campaign how: 'He loved the soldiers who took the liberty of talking to him, and always laughed with them.'[57]

To a letter from Josephine saying that she wasn't jealous of him spending his evenings with Polish women, Napoleon replied on December 5:

> I have long since perceived that choleric people always maintain they are not choleric; those who are afraid declare repeatedly that they are not afraid; you, then, are convicted of jealousy; I'm enchanted! Anyway, you're wrong to think that in the wastes of Poland I think of beautiful women. There was a ball last night given by the provincial aristocracy, with quite pretty and rich women, but badly dressed, even though they tried to emulate Parisian fashion.[58]

The following week he pulled off a significant coup when the Elector Frederick Augustus of Saxony, whose forces had fought alongside the

Prussians at Jena and Auerstädt, left his alliance with Frederick William III and joined the Confederation of the Rhine. Napoleon arrived in Warsaw to an ecstatic welcome on December 19. He immediately set up a provisional government of Polish nobles, albeit with little more than consultative powers. He assumed that the Russians would not retreat much further and were ready to fight, so he ordered all his corps over the Vistula. Hoping to make for the gap between the German-born Russian generals Bennigsen and Buxhöwden, he told the corps commanders to expect a major offensive soon. When Davout's corps reached the village of Czarnowo on the Bug river on December 23, Napoleon reconnoitred the area and launched a night attack, which was successful in putting to flight 15,000 overextended Russians under Count Alexander Ostermann-Tolstoy,* at the end of which the waterways north of Warsaw were in French hands.[59]

On Christmas Day 1806, Napoleon tried to destroy Bennigsen's army while it was retreating to the north-east by sending Lannes to Pultusk to cut off his line of retreat, while Davout, Soult and Murat marched north, Augereau went north-east from the Necker (in Polish the Wkra river) and Ney and Bernadotte south-east from the Vistula. The weather ruined his chances, cutting movement down to 7 miles a day. 'The ground over which we passed was a clayey soil,' recalled Rapp, 'intersected with marshes: the roads were excessively bad: cavalry, infantry and artillery stuck in the bogs, and it cost them the utmost difficulty to extricate themselves.'[60] When battle was joined at Pultusk the next day, 'Many of our officers stuck in the mud and remained there during the whole of the battle. They served as marks for the enemy to shoot at.'

Bennigsen fought a successful rearguard action during a snowstorm at Pultusk with 35,000 men against Lannes' 26,000-strong corps, and withdrew the next day.[61] On the same day at Golymin, Prince Andrei Galitzin fought until dark before neatly extricating his force from one of Napoleon's traps (Murat, Augereau and Davout were to descend on him from three sides) – when they met at Tilsit in July Napoleon congratulated Galitzin on his escape.[62] He visited the Golymin battlefield the next day, and the soldier-painter Lejeune recorded how 'the Emperor and Prince Berthier stopped a few minutes to hear us sing airs from the latest operas of Paris'.[63]

Having withdrawn successfully, the Russians went into winter

* Count Alexander Ivanovich Ostermann-Tolstoy was a cousin of the author of *War and Peace*.

quarters around Bialystok, and on December 28 Napoleon suspended hostilities and cantoned the army along the Vistula, returning to Warsaw on New Year's Day. He had little choice considering the bad weather, terrible state of the roads and the fact that due to fever, injury, hunger and exhaustion, 40 per cent of his army was absent at any one time, much of it looking for food in land that could barely support its own population in peacetime, let alone two huge armies at war.[64] Orders were given to build hospitals, workshops, bakeries and supply depots, as bridgeheads and fortified camps went up so that the Grande Armée wouldn't have to force a passage over the river in the spring.

'Never was the French army so miserable,' noted Baron Pierre Percy, its surgeon-in-chief.

> The soldier, always marching, bivouacking each night, spending days in mud up to his ankles, doesn't have one ounce of bread, not a drop of brandy, doesn't have the time to dry his clothes, and he falls from exhaustion and hunger. We found some who had expired on the side of ditches; a glass of wine or brandy would have saved them. His Majesty's heart must be torn by all this, but he marches to his goal and fills up the great destinies he prepares for Europe; if he failed or only got mediocre results the army would be demoralized and cry out.[65]

It was estimated that one hundred soldiers had committed suicide by Christmas.[66]

Napoleon had long placed great emphasis on the treatment, evacuation and care of the wounded, writing around six hundred detailed letters on the subject since the start of the Italian campaign ten years earlier. He often wrote to his senior doctors, Percy and Dominique Larrey, praising the 'courage, zeal, devotion and, above all, patience and resignation' of the army's *service de santé*.[67] He was constantly quizzing surgeons about diseases, and asking them how French medicine differed from that of other countries.[68] 'Here you are, you great charlatan,' Napoleon would tease his own doctor, Jean-Nicolas Corvisart. 'Did you kill a lot of people today?'[69] He liked and trusted Corvisart, who cured his sciatica and kept him generally healthy until a series of minor but irritating diseases starting afflicting him from the Russian campaign onwards. On other occasions Napoleon could be coruscating about doctors, writing to Jean-Gérard Lacuée in January 1812: 'The inexperience of the surgeons does more harm to the army than the guns of the enemy.'[70]

Napoleon only put suggestions for an ambulance service into

practice in 1813, when lack of resources prevented it from taking proper effect.[71] Yet he did increase the numbers of medical officers serving in the French army, from 1,085 in 1802 to 5,112 a decade later, and the number of battlefield surgeons from 515 to 2,058.[72] These few doctors had to deal with truly vast numbers of patients in the Polish campaign; between October 1806 and October 1808, French military hospitals treated 421,000 soldiers. Even when the fighting was fiercest in that period, less than a quarter of these were actually wounded in battle; the rest were ill, mostly from fever.[73]

On January 1, 1807, on his way back from Pultusk to Warsaw, Napoleon changed horses in a post-house at Błonie and there met the beautiful blonde, white-skinned twenty-year-old Polish Countess Marie Colonna-Walewska, who he soon discovered was married to an aristocratic landowner a full fifty-two years older than her.[74] He arranged to meet her again at a ball, after which she quickly became the mistress to whom he became the most attached. One of the other ladies present at the ball, the gossipy diarist Countess Anna Potocka, 'saw him squeeze her hand' at the end of a dance, which she assumed equated to a rendezvous. She added that Marie had a 'delicious figure but no brains'.[75]

Napoleon quickly rescinded his invitation to Josephine to join him in Warsaw. 'It's too great a stretch of country to cover between Mainz and Warsaw,' he told her two days after meeting Marie. 'I've many things to settle here. I think you should return to Paris, where you are needed . . . I'm well, the weather's bad. I love you with all my heart.'[76] To her subsequent pleas to be allowed to join him, he replied: 'I'm more vexed about this than you are; I would have loved to share these long winter nights with you, but one has to yield to circumstances.'[77]*

Napoleon visited Rapp in Warsaw, who had been wounded for the ninth time at the battle of Golymin, this time in his left arm. 'Well, Rapp,' he said, 'you are wounded again, and in your unlucky arm too.'

---

* During the first three months of 1807, Napoleon wrote 1,715 letters, and over 3,000 in that calendar year, even more than in 1806. Half went to military figures, principally Clarke as governor-general of Prussia and the naval minister Decrès, and the rest were on diplomatic (more than two hundred to Talleyrand), administrative, family or personal matters. The subject of shoes and boots generated sixty-three letters, and sometimes caused confusion. 'I got sent shoes when I asked for bread,' Napoleon complained to Duroc in February. 'What did I need nineteen barrels of shoes for, following the army around? This is madness' (CG7 no. 14341 p. 207).

Rapp told him it was small wonder, as 'we are always in the midst of battles'. 'We shall perhaps have done fighting when we are eighty years old,' Napoleon replied.[78] This indication that he expected to live far longer than his father is supported by a letter to Dalberg at this time, in which he wrote: 'One is only two-thirds of the way through life at sixty.'[79]

Although Napoleon was quite content to let the Russians hibernate through the winter, Ney was desperately short of supplies, so entirely contrary to orders he suddenly struck north on January 10, hoping to capture the major supply depot of Königsberg by surprise. It was the kind of adventurous insubordination that he knew Napoleon would condone if he were successful. He reached Heilsberg (now Lidzbark Warmiński, in Poland) a week later, where he stumbled on Lestocq's Prussian Corps, thereby uncovering the fact that Bennigsen had begun his own surprise attack, and was moving quietly through the 500-square-mile Johannisburg Forest, north-east of Warsaw.

Prisoners captured by Ney and later Bernadotte allowed Napoleon to piece together a major enemy offensive moving towards the Vistula. He immediately spotted the opportunity for a devastating counter-attack. With so much of his army to the south, Napoleon saw a way of operating on Bennigsen's flank and maybe also on his rear, since the further west the Russians moved, the easier it would be for the French to cut them off. He therefore decided on an attack from Warsaw one hundred miles north to Allenstein on the Alle river. Marshal Lefebvre, who had been taken off the inactive list in 1805, was given a corps with which to besiege Danzig, and was retained at Thorn. Augereau was moved across the Vistula. Bernadotte was ordered to put a screen along the Passarge river and to be ready to make a fighting retreat through Elbing if necessary. Meanwhile, Napoleon pivoted on Thorn, swinging the entire army from south to north. Davout was guarding the eastern flank until replaced by Lannes, whereupon his corps pushed forward towards Ostrolenka and Makow. By January 19 Napoleon's advance guard met Bennigsen's moving towards Danzig. The weather was still dire. 'Never has a campaign been tougher,' wrote the artillery General Alexandre de Sénarmont. His cannon were up to their axles and his gunners up to their knees in mud.[80] Soon after the ground hardened in the frost, and several feet of snow further slowed the army.

On January 27 the Grande Armée was still moving north by forced marches, while Ney and Bernadotte were ordered to continue their retreat westwards, thereby drawing Bennigsen further into Napoleon's trap. 'My health has never been better,' he boasted to Joseph, 'and in consequence I have become more *galant* than before.'[81] He was by now vigorously pursuing his affair, using the 'tu' form to address Marie which he otherwise reserved solely for Josephine and the Shah of Persia: 'Oh! come to me! Come to me!' he wrote to her, 'all your desires will be fulfilled. Your homeland will be dear to me if you take pity of my poor heart. A few days later, sending her a brooch, he wrote

> Please accept this bouquet; may it become a secret link that ties us together through the crowds that surround us. When all eyes are on us, we will have a secret code. When my hand touches my heart, you will know that you fill it entirely, and in response, you will put your hand on your bouquet! Love me, my sweet Marie, and may your hand never leave your bouquet![82]

He was generous to her too, giving her 50,000 francs in three tranches up to October 1809.[83]*

On January 31, the day after Napoleon left Warsaw for the front, Cossacks in the Russian General Bagration's advance guard captured an aide-de-camp carrying a message from Napoleon to Bernadotte, the aide having failed to destroy his uncoded despatches in time. (Napoleon ordered his aides-de-camp to keep messages sewn into the heels of their boots; 'An aide-de-camp may lose his trousers on his way,' he once quipped, 'but never his despatches or his sabre.'[84]) The message ordered Bernadotte to rejoin the left of the Grande Armée by a secret night march. It included the dispositions of the whole Grande Armée and made clear his intention to cut off the entire Russian army by attacking up from the south. Bennigsen calmly ordered an immediate retreat to the Alle.[85] Unaware that his plan had been compromised, Napoleon continued striking north, along terrible roads in atrocious weather. For a commander for whom speed was always the essential element, Poland's winters were exceptionally frustrating. On February 2 Napoleon learned that instead of advancing to the Vistula, Bennigsen was now retreating towards the Alle, back to safety. He moved as fast as possible to Bergfried in an effort to fix him in position before he escaped.

---

* Napoleon took twenty-one or possibly twenty-two mistresses that we know of over the course of two decades. In total he bestowed the enormous sum of 480,000 francs on them between December 1804 and August 1813, with large amounts in his secret mistresses' account book registered only as 'given to His Majesty'.

He only had five infantry divisions, Murat's Cavalry Reserve and part of the Imperial Guard with him. The next day Bennigsen crossed the Alle, leaving only a rearguard to hold off the French. Napoleon called off the assault, and by the following day the Russians had gone. 'I'm in pursuit of the Russian army,' he told Cambacérès, 'and am going to force it back beyond the Niemen.'[86]*

When Murat caught up with the Russian rearguard at the bridge over a tributary of the River Frisching at Hoff on February 6, General Jean-Joseph d'Hautpoul charged his cuirassiers straight at the Russian cannon, taking the position. Half an hour later in front of the whole division Napoleon embraced the enormous, loud and salty-tongued veteran, who true to form turned to his troops afterwards and bellowed: 'The Emperor is pleased with you, and I am so pleased with you that I kiss all your arses!'[87] Murat took 1,400 casualties at Hof. His adversary, the Scots-Lithuanian-born General Michael Barclay de Tolly, lost 2,000 Russians, but Bennigsen had successfully extricated himself again.[88] The only way for Bennigsen to protect Königsberg 20 miles to the north – where he could not allow himself to be trapped – was to give battle at Eylau (present-day Bagrationovsk), then an East Prussian town of 1,500 inhabitants 130 miles from the Russian border. He had around 58,000 men with him but was expecting Lestocq to arrive shortly with 5,500 more. Napoleon had 48,000, but Ney 12 miles to the west and Davout 10 miles to the south-east were on their way with nearly 30,000. The Russians had a huge advantage in artillery, however, with 336 guns to Napoleon's 200.

The main road from Landsberg to Königsberg passes for some 9 miles between a plain and a forest until it emerges onto an undulating plain about 1½ miles from Eylau, which ends in a slight elevation. From this point Napoleon had a clear view over the broad valley leading to the pronounced ridge on which the Russian army was deployed. On his left foreground was Lake Tenknitten, on his right Lake Waschkeiten. For a thousand yards between them is a small rise, more marked at the road crossing after which the road then drops down for the last half mile into Eylau across a minor decline. A church and its cemetery stand on a small hillock to the right of what was in 1807 a town of solid houses on an important crossroads. There were several frozen lakes and marshes and

---

* It was not all haste, however. One night during the campaign, Napoleon had time to play cards with Berthier, Duroc and others, giving his Mamluk bodyguard Roustam 500 francs of his winnings (ed. Cottin, *Souvenirs de Roustam* pp. 140–41).

birch woods dotted about. The high point of the plain was the village of Serpallen, where the snow was three feet deep in places.

Bennigsen's army deployed for battle on the late morning of Saturday, February 7, 1807. At 2 p.m. Murat's cavalry and the head of Soult's infantry reached the woods before the village of Grünhofschen. Augereau came up next and deployed towards Tenknitten. Soult sent the 18th and 46th Line into battle against the Russian vanguard unsupported; the former crossed the end of the frozen Tenknitten lake under heavy artillery fire, veered to its right and, much shaken, were attacked by bayonet. Then the St Petersburg Dragoons, looking for revenge after their defeat at Hoff, crossed the frozen lake and attacked their left rear, catching both battalions out of square and breaking them, where the 18th Line lost its eagle.* French dragoons arrived in time to counter-charge and save them from complete destruction, but there was much carnage. The 46th Line were able to retire in good order. When Soult deployed his artillery between Schwehen and Grünhofschen, the Russian vanguard began to fall back towards the main body of the army.

Napoleon now held all the plateau ground up to the valley, but his losses had been severe; three weeks later there was still a mound of corpses visible there. He had not intended to storm Eylau that evening, preferring to wait for Ney and Davout to arrive, but various accidents and misunderstandings summed up in that useful phrase 'the fog of war' forced him to do so. Soult's explanation was probably best, that some of the Reserve Cavalry had followed the Russians into Eylau, and that his 24th Line had gone in after them, whereupon general fighting for the church and cemetery had begun which naturally sucked in more men as it progressed. Whatever the reason, the battle was now a two-day affair, with 115,000 men contesting an area only five miles square.

The church and cemetery were stormed by Saint-Hilaire's division, during which Barclay de Tolly, one of the best generals of the Russian army, was severely wounded by grapeshot, which left him *hors de combat* for fifteen months. Bagration would have evacuated Eylau but Bennigsen ordered it recaptured at all costs, so he led three columns in on foot against French infantry and artillery firing canister shot. By 6 p.m. the Russians had retaken most of the town, though not the church and cemetery. Bennigsen then changed his mind, and at 6.30 p.m.

---

* As the Russians didn't capture it, there is speculation that it might be at the bottom of the lake. Thereafter Napoleon restricted eagles to first battalions only, and light cavalry was not allowed to carry them into battle at all (CG6 no. 13006 p. 879).

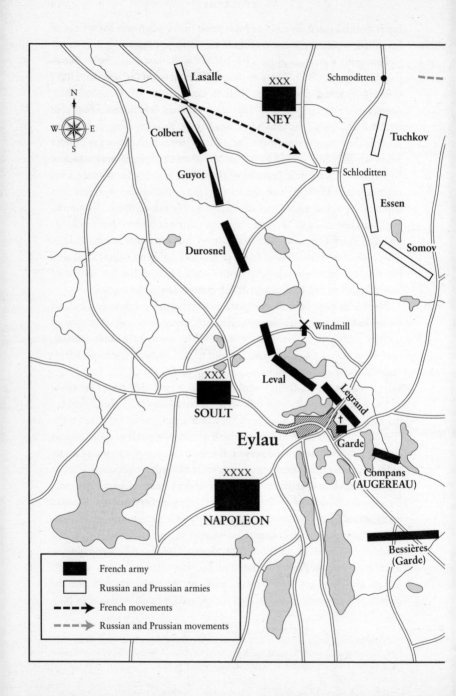

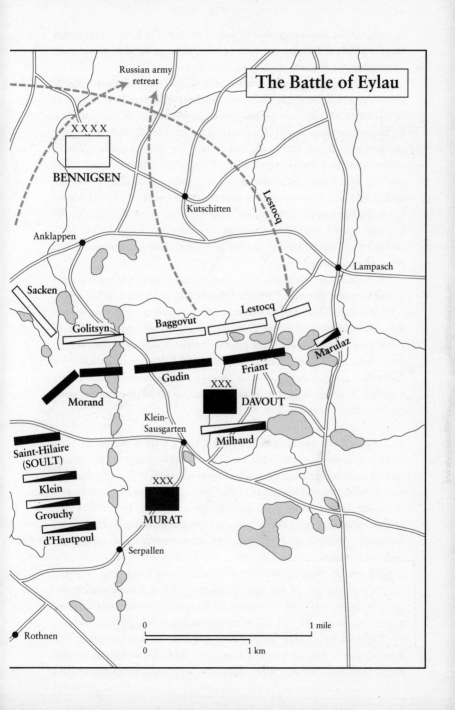

The Battle of Eylau

Russian army retreat

Lestocq

X X X X
BENNIGSEN

Kutschitten

Anklappen

Lampasch

Sacken

Lestocq

Golitsyn

Baggovut

Marulaz

Gudin

Friant

Morand

XXX
DAVOUT

Klein-
Sausgarten

Milhaud

Saint-Hilaire
(SOULT)

Klein

XXX

Grouchy

MURAT

d'Hautpoul

Serpallen

Rothnen

0   1 mile

0   1 km

he ordered the Russian troops to pull back from the town to the slight elevation that contemporary writers referred to as 'heights' to the east, whereupon the French reoccupied the town.

As night fell, Legrand's division moved just beyond Eylau; Saint-Hilaire camped out in the open near Rothenen; Milhaud's cavalry was at Zehsen; Grouchy was behind Eylau; Augereau was in a second line between Storchnest and Tenknitten, and the Imperial Guard slept on the elevated area where Bagration had started the day. As snow fell both armies huddled around bivouac fires. Because the supply wagons could not stay apace with the army on forced marches, a number of soldiers hadn't had bread for three days, and some ate the flesh of dead horses from the battlefield. One soldier complained to Captain Blaze of the Imperial Guard that he had nothing to smoke but hay.[89] In Marbot's words, the French army had 'for days been living on nothing but potatoes and melted snow'.[90]

An hour before nightfall, Napoleon visited Eylau. 'The streets were full of corpses,' Captain François-Frédéric Billon recalled, 'what a horrible spectacle. Tears welled in the Emperor's eyes; nobody would have believed possible such an emotion from this great man of war, however I saw them myself, these tears ... The Emperor was doing his best to prevent his horse stepping on human remains. Being unsuccessful ... it's then that I saw him crying.'[91] On a freezing night with snow falling after midnight, Napoleon slept in a chair in the ransacked post-house below the Ziegelhof without taking off his boots.

At 8 a.m. on the morning of Sunday February 8 the Russians began a furious cannonade upon Eylau, their sheer numbers making up for any lack of accuracy. The French artillery reply did great damage to the Russian formations exposed against the snow. With freezing winds and recurrent snow flurries, visibility was to be a major factor that day, dropping down to ten yards at times, so that the Russians on the heights sometimes couldn't see Eylau and very often commanders couldn't see their own troops.

At 9.30 a.m. Napoleon ordered Soult to move north-west of Eylau on the extreme left of his line. Davout's corps was approaching the town from the other direction, and the Emperor wanted to divert Bennigsen's attention. By 10 a.m., however, Soult was being forced back by the Russians into Eylau itself. 'Three hundred cannon on either side pouring out a hail of grapeshot at close quarters wreaking terrible havoc,' recalled Lejeune. When Davout's corps arrived on Napoleon's right they were held up by ferocious attacks from Ostermann-Tolstoy's cavalry against Friant's advance-guard. With the left under Soult weak, and Davout deploying painfully slowly, Napoleon needed a major diversion on the right. He instructed Augereau to attack the Russian left with his 9,000 men and try to link up with Davout. Augereau was very ill before the battle and so cold he had a scarf wrapped around his head with his marshal's hat jammed on top; he had to be supported in his saddle by an aide-de-camp. As he advanced he got lost in the blizzard and marched straight into a Russian battery firing grapeshot at point-blank range, its direction only discernible by the flashes from the barrels. (Walking along Augereau's approach at Eylau, with its multiple slopes and folds in the ground, it's easy to see how brigades could have become completely disorientated in the snowstorm.) Five thousand soldiers and officers were killed or wounded in fifteen minutes, and Augereau himself was wounded.[92] Saint-Hilaire's division, which had stayed on course to try to relieve Davout, was also flung back. By 11.15 a.m. the situation was serious. Napoleon watched from Eylau church despite its being fired at by Russian artillery. His left was effectively wrecked, his right had been badly mauled, and reinforcements were delayed. He found himself in personal danger too, when a column of Russian infantry managed to get into Eylau during the battle and came close to the church before it was checked and destroyed.

At 11.30 a.m., once it was clear that Augereau had failed, Napoleon sprung one of the great audacious moves of his military career. As the blizzard abated, he flung almost the whole of Murat's Cavalry Reserve into the greatest cavalry charge of the Napoleonic Wars. Pointing to a Russian cavalry attack developing on Augereau's smashed corps, he said to Murat either 'Are you going to let those fellows eat us up?' or 'Take all your available cavalry and crush that column' (or possibly both).[93] Murat, who was wearing a green Polish cape and green velvet bonnet for the occasion, and carried only a riding whip, then led 7,300 dragoons, 1,900 cuirassiers and 1,500 Imperial Guard cavalry into a headlong attack. 'Heads up, by God!' cried Colonel Louis Lepic of the Guard grenadiers-à-cheval. 'Those are bullets, not turds!' The Russian cavalry was hurled back against its own infantry; Russian gunners were sabred alongside their guns; Serpallen was recaptured, and Murat only stopped when he reached Anklappen. (Lepic refused to surrender during a Russian counter-attack and was later rewarded by Napoleon with 50,000 francs for his bravery, which he shared out to his men.)

Murat's charge checked the Russian centre and regained the initiative for Napoleon. It came at the high cost of up to 2,000 casualties, including d'Hautpoul, who was hit by grapeshot and died some days after the battle. Meanwhile, Ney made his way agonizingly slowly through the blizzard across the terrible roads to the battlefield. By 3.30 p.m. Davout had managed to get behind Bennigsen, and was almost at Anklappen. Napoleon was about to snap shut his trap, encircling the Russian army, when Lestocq suddenly appeared and launched an attack on Friant's division. He evicted the French from Anklappen with only half an hour of daylight left, thus saving Bennigsen's left flank. At 7 p.m. Ney finally arrived but he was too late to deliver the devastating blow for which Napoleon had been hoping. The fighting slowly wound down as darkness descended and both sides succumbed to total exhaustion. At midnight Bennigsen, now very short of ammunition and realizing that Ney had arrived, ordered a retreat, leaving the field to the French.

'When two armies have dealt each other enormous wounds all day long,' Napoleon commented, 'the field has been won by the side which, armoured in constancy, refuses to quit.'[94] Yet the field was all that Napoleon did win at Eylau. Because he hadn't known whether he faced the Russian rearguard or Bennigsen's whole army, his attacks had been disjointed and costly, and the street-fight in Eylau had been an unnecessary accident. Ney was only called in at 8 a.m. on the 8th, far too late, because Murat had erroneously reported a Russian retreat that morning. Augereau's attack in the snowstorm had been so disastrous that his corps had to be split up and distributed to other marshals as he convalesced, something for which he never truly forgave Napoleon. Murat's cavalry charge had been splendid and worthwhile, but a desperate remedy, as the presence of Napoleon's own bodyguard in it eloquently attested. The Guard infantry also took serious losses at Eylau, having been exposed to enemy artillery fire to conceal Napoleon's numerical weaknesses.[95]

It had been a truly horrific two days. 'Not a lot of prisoners but a lot of corpses,' recalled Roustam of Eylau, who nearly died of exposure there. 'The wounded on the battlefield were hidden under the snow, you could only see their heads.'[96] Napoleon attempted to minimize his losses as usual, claiming only 1,900 killed and 5,700 wounded, but more reliable sources list 23 generals, 924 other officers and about 21,000 other ranks killed and wounded. Eleven days after the battle Lestocq buried around 10,000 corpses, over half of whom were French.[97] Similarly the Russians lost 18,000 killed and wounded; 3,000 prisoners were captured and 24 guns. The Prussians suffered around 800 casualties.

Bennigsen's orderly retreat is illustrated by the fact that he lost less than 1 per cent of his guns, but – demonstrating that it wasn't just Napoleon who 'lied like a bulletin' – he claimed to the Tsar to have suffered only 6,000 casualties. To Duroc Napoleon admitted 'although the losses on both sides were very heavy, yet my distance from my base renders mine more serious to me'.[98]

As the Revolutionary and Napoleonic Wars progressed, the casualty rates in battles increased exponentially: at Fleurus they were 6% of the total number of men engaged, at Austerlitz 15%, at Eylau 26%, at Borodino 31% and at Waterloo 45%. This was partly because with ever-larger armies being raised, battles tended to last longer – Eylau was Napoleon's first two-day engagement since Arcole; Eggmühl, Aspern-Essling and Wagram in 1809, Dresden in 1813 were also two and Leipzig in 1813 went on for three – but mainly because of the huge increase in the numbers of cannon present. At Austerlitz the ratio was two guns per thousand men, but by Eylau this had leapt to nearly 4, and at Borodino there were 4.5. Eylau therefore represented a new kind of battle of the Napoleonic Wars, best summed up by Ney at its close: 'What a massacre! And without any result!'[99]

19
Tilsit

'My love, we had a great battle yesterday,' Napoleon reported to Josephine from Eylau at 3 a.m. on the night of the battle, February 10. 'Victory rested with me, but I have lost many men; the enemy's loss, which is still more considerable, does not console me.'[1] That evening he wrote again, 'in order that you may not be uneasy', now claiming that he had taken 12,000 prisoners at the loss of 1,600 killed and between three and four thousand wounded. One of the dead, his aide-de-camp General Claude Corbineau, had been Josephine's master of horse. 'I was singularly attached to that officer, who had so much merit,' he wrote, 'his death caused me pain.'

The Grande Armée had been battered so badly that it could not follow up the victory, as it had after Jena. Soult's aide-de-camp Colonel Alfred de Saint-Chamans recalled after the battle, 'The Emperor was passing in front of the troops; in the middle of cries of "Vive l'Empereur!" I heard many soldiers cry "Vive la paix!", others "Vive la paix et la France!", others even shouted "Pain et paix!" [Bread and peace!]'[2] It was the first time he had seen the morale of the army 'a bit shaken', which he put down to 'the butchery of Eylau'. The day after the battle, Napoleon announced in a bulletin that an eagle had been lost, and said, 'The Emperor will give that battalion another standard after it has taken one from the enemy.'[3] The reason the unit wasn't named was that in fact five eagles had been lost.[*]

Napoleon was still at Eylau on February 14, writing to Josephine: 'This country is strewn with dead and wounded. It is not the prettiest side of war; one suffers, and the soul is crushed to see so many victims.'[4] He soon became concerned that officers' letters back to Paris were dwelling too much on the losses. 'They know as much about what happens in an army as people walking in the gardens of the Tuileries know about what happens in a cabinet,' he told Fouché. Then he heartlessly added: 'And what are two thousand men killed in a great battle? Every single battle of Louis XIV and Louis XV claimed many more lives.' This was demonstrably untrue; Blenheim, Malplaquet, Fontenoy and Rossbach claimed more, but by no means every battle of the Wars of Spanish and Austrian Successions or the Seven Years War. Napoleon as usual was dissembling about the number killed at Eylau, which was closer to 6,000, with around 15,000 more wounded.[5]

After Eylau there was one significant clash at Ostrolenka on February 16, and another between Bernadotte and Lestocq in late February, but otherwise both armies went into their winter cantonments – the French along the Passarge river, the Russians along the Alle – until the campaigning season could start again in mid-May. This didn't mean that Napoleon rested, of course. Pierre Daru was intendant-general of the imperial household on campaign and in his correspondence from March 1807 are scores of letters concerning the army's shortages of cash, horses, ovens, mutton, beef, uniforms, shirt fabric, caps, sheets, flour, biscuit, bread and, especially, shoes and eau-de-vie.[6] Daru did his best, boasting to Napoleon on March 26 that the army had 231,293 pairs of shoes, for example, but the soldiers were suffering. Daru requisitioned 5,000 horses from eight German cities in December, of which 3,647 were delivered by the end of the month.[7] Napoleon was kept informed of how much rye, wheat, hay, meat, straw, oats and bread had been requisitioned from which provinces by which date, figures presented to him in neat lists; similarly he was told how many men were in his 105 hospitals in Germany and Poland. (On July 1, for example, there were 30,863 French, 747 French allies, 260 Prussians and 2,590 Russians.[8]) The army needed its time of rest and recuperation after the desperate rigours of the campaign.

When Joseph tried to equate the travails of the Army of Naples

---

[*] Those of the 10th Légère and the 18th, 24th, 44th and 51st Line.

fighting the Calabrian rebels to those of the Grande Armée, Napoleon would have none of it:

> Staff officers, colonels and officers did not undress for two months and some not for four (I myself went fifteen days without removing my boots). We were surrounded by snow and mud, without bread, wine, brandy, potatoes and meat. We went on long marches and counter-marches without anything to relieve the harshness, fighting with bayonets, often under fire, having to evacuate the wounded on open sledges over distances of fifty leagues [130 miles]. It is therefore in bad taste to compare us to the Army of Naples, doing battle in the beautiful Neapolitan countryside, where there is wine, bread, oil, cloth, bed-linen, a social life and even women. Having destroyed the Prussian monarchy, we are fighting against the rest of the Prussians, against the Russians, the Cossacks, the [Volgan] Kalmyks and those people of the North that once invaded the Roman Empire.[9]

With Russia and Prussia still at war with him, Napoleon also used the time to call up a Bavarian division of 10,000 men, raise a levy of 6,000 Poles, bring in reinforcements from France, Italy and Holland, and conscript the 1808 recruits more than a year early. Eylau had struck at his myth of invincibility, a blot that needed to be expunged if the Austrians were to remain neutral – especially when in late February Frederick William rejected much more lenient peace terms than Duroc had offered the Marquis di Lucchesini, the Prussian ambassador to Paris, after Jena.

An aggressive campaign could not be fought in the spring until the rich and well-fortified port of Danzig (present-day Gdańsk) had fallen, as otherwise the Russians could launch an attack in Napoleon's rear with the help of the Royal Navy. After Victor had been kidnapped in Stettin on January 20, 1807 by twenty-five Prussian soldiers disguised as peasants, the grizzled fifty-two-year-old Marshal Lefebvre was given the task of besieging Danzig. When he succeeded in taking it on May 24, so securing the French left flank, Napoleon sent him a box of chocolates. The marshal was unimpressed until he opened it, when he found it stuffed with 300,000 francs in banknotes. A year later the proud republican Lefebvre, who had been Napoleon's deputy on 18 Brumaire, became the Duke of Danzig.

As he rebuilt his army and prepared for the campaign, Napoleon's imperial micro-management continued. On the same day that he heard that Danzig had fallen – upon which news he ordered Clarke to have salutes fired and *Te Deums* sung in Paris – he asked Lacépède, the chancellor of the Légion d'Honneur, to 'write a letter to Corporal Bernaudat of the 13th Line enjoining him not to drink more than is good for him. The decoration has been given to him because he is brave; it must not be withdrawn from him just because he likes a bit of wine. Tell him not to get into situations that could debase the decoration he wears.'[10] In April 1807, perhaps the quietest month of his entire reign, Napoleon still wrote 443 letters. Staying at Finckenstein Castle with its many fireplaces – 'as I often get up at night, I love to see an open fire' – he involved himself in a dispute between the head stage-hand of the Paris Opéra, Boutron, and his deputy, Gromaire, over who had been responsible for dropping the singer Mlle Aubry from a mechanical cloud above the stage, breaking her arm. 'I always support the underdog,' Napoleon told Fouché, taking Gromaire's side from over a thousand miles away.[11]

On April 26 the Convention of Bartenstein confirmed that Russia and Prussia would continue the war, that of the Fourth Coalition, and invited Britain, Sweden, Austria and Denmark to join. The first two responded positively, Britain joining in June and sending money as its contribution, while maintaining the naval stranglehold on French trade. Sweden – which had not made peace with Napoleon after the end of the Third Coalition at Austerlitz – sent a small body of troops. Napoleon never forgave King Gustav IV, whom he called 'a lunatic who should be king of the Petites-Maison [a Paris lunatic asylum] rather than of a brave Scandinavian country'.[12]

By late May, Napoleon was ready: Danzig was his, the sick had been sent away from the front, there were enough provisions for eight months. He had 123,000 infantry, 30,000 cavalry and 5,000 artillerymen in the field. He set the date of June 10 for his major offensive, but, as in January, Bennigsen moved first, attacking Ney at Guttstadt on June 5. 'I am very happy to see the enemy wished to avoid our coming to him,' Napoleon quipped as he left Finckenstein the next day in an open carriage due to the extreme heat.[13] That day he put all his corps in motion, as keen as ever for a decisive battle that might end the campaign. Davout, who had already moved two divisions up from Allenstein to threaten the Russian left, deliberately allowed a messenger to be captured carrying the false news that he had 40,000 men in place to fall on the Russian rear, when his whole corps really numbered 28,891.

Bennigsen ordered a withdrawal the next day. Meanwhile Soult crossed the River Passarge in strength and pressed back the Russian right.

On June 8 Napoleon interviewed prisoners-of-war from Bagration's rearguard, who told him that Bennigsen was marching on Guttstadt. It seemed that he might offer battle there, but instead he retreated to the well-fortified camp of Heilsberg. Napoleon advanced with Murat and Ney in the lead, followed by Lannes and the Imperial Guard, with Mortier a day's march behind them. Davout was off to the right and Soult on the left; the corps system was working well. Bagration covered Bennigsen's retreat, destroying bridges and villages behind him as his men marched along the long, dusty roads in the searing heat. Believing that Bennigsen might be heading to Königsberg, on June 9 Napoleon decided to attack what he thought was only the enemy rearguard. In fact it was the entire Russian army of 53,000 men and 150 guns.

The town of Heilsberg, in a hollow on the left bank of the Alle, was an entrenched operational base used by the Russian army. Several bridges led to a suburb on the right bank. The Russians had built four great redoubts to protect against river crossings, interspersed with *flèches* (arrowhead-shaped earthworks) where they fought from the early morning of June 10. Napoleon arrived at 3 p.m., furious at the costly way Murat and Soult had conducted the battle, with three more eagles lost. At one stage the fighting swirled so close to Napoleon that Oudinot asked him to leave the area, saying his grenadiers would take him away if he refused. 'At 10 o'clock the Emperor passed through us,' recalled the young aide-de-camp Lieutenant Aymar-Olivier de Gonneville, 'and was saluted by acclamations to which he seemed to pay no attention, appearing gloomy and out of spirits. We learnt later that he had no intention of attacking the Russians so seriously as had been done, and especially had desired not to engage his cavalry. [Murat] had been reprimanded for this, and followed the Emperor with a tolerably sheepish air.'[14] The fighting didn't end until 11 p.m., after which there were disgusting scenes of camp-followers of both sides despoiling the dead and wounded. Dawn rose over a truly desolate battlefield – over 10,000 Frenchmen and as many as 6,000 Russians had been wounded – and as the sun reached its height both armies recoiled from the stench of death.

Although large amounts of stores and provisions were captured in Heilsberg, Napoleon had set his sights on the far larger provisions of Königsberg. For the Russians to reach Königsberg they needed to re-cross the Alle. Napoleon knew there was a bridge at the small market

town of Friedland (present-day Pravdinsk), so he sent Lannes to reconnoitre there, while he split the rest of his army between Murat with
60,000 men – his own cavalry, plus Soult's and Davout's corps – who
were sent off to capture Königsberg, while he himself took 80,000 men
back to Eylau.

On June 13 Lannes' advance guard reported a large Russian concentration at Friedland, a mid-sized town nestling in the U-bend of the
river, which in accordance with corps doctrine he engaged and then
managed to hold in place for a full nine hours as reinforcements arrived.
At 3.30 p.m., 3,000 cavalry of the Russian advance guard crossed the
Alle and threw the French out of the town. Bennigsen seems to have
assumed he could cross the Alle the next day, crush Lannes and then
re-cross before Napoleon could arrive from Eylau, which was 15 miles
west of Friedland. It was never wise to underestimate Napoleon's speed,
especially when he was marching over ground baked hard by the summer sun.

The Alle river curves around Friedland, enveloping the town to the
south and the east while a lake called the Millstream flanks it to the
north. The Alle is deep and fast flowing, its banks over 30 feet high. In
front of the town was a broad fertile plain nearly 2 miles wide waist-deep
in wheat and rye, abutted by a dense forest, known as Sortlack Wood.
The Millstream, which also has steep banks, divides the plain. The belfry of Friedland's church offers a superb panoramic view of the entire
battlefield, and Bennigsen, his staff and his British liaison officer Colonel John Hely-Hutchinson wisely climbed it. But they failed to spot
that the three pontoon bridges Bennigsen had put across the river to
augment the stone one in the town were too far behind his left flank,
and that if the bridges were destroyed or congested, Friedland, in the
bend of what is almost an ox-bow lake, would become a gigantic
death-trap.

Between two and three o'clock on the morning of Sunday, June 14 –
the anniversary of the battle of Marengo – Oudinot arrived on the plain
before the village of Posthenen. A soldier's soldier, impetuous and formidable, beloved by his men, he survived a total of thirty-four wounds
in his career, losing several teeth in the 1805 campaign and about to lose
part of an ear.[15] The only child of nine to survive into adulthood, he had
ten children himself, collected clay pipes, was an amateur painter and
spent evenings with Davout on this campaign snuffing out candles with
pistol-shots. Oudinot now sent his men into the Sortlack Wood, and
heavy skirmishing fire and cannonades developed along the front. When

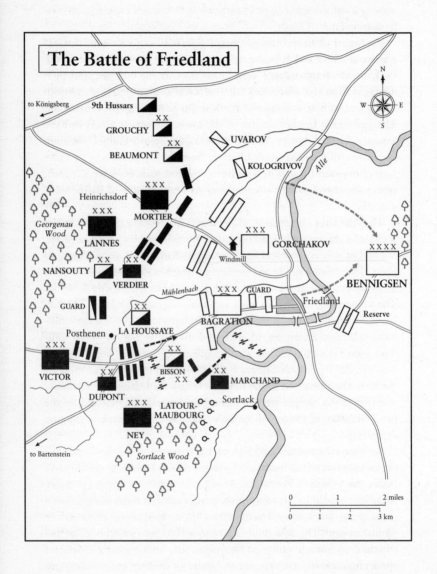

The Battle of Friedland

to Königsberg

9th Hussars

GROUCHY

BEAUMONT

UVAROV

KOLOGRIVOV

Alle

Heinrichsdorf

MORTIER

Georgenau
Wood

LANNES

GORCHAKOV

Windmill

NANSOUTY

VERDIER

Mühlenbach

GUARD

BENNIGSEN

GUARD

Friedland

LA HOUSSAYE

BAGRATION

Reserve

Posthenen

VICTOR

BISSON

DUPONT

MARCHAND

Sortlack

LATOUR-
MAUBOURG

NEY

Sortlack Wood

to Bartenstein

0		1		2 miles
0	1	2		3 km

the talented aristocratic cavalry leader General Emmanuel de Grouchy
arrived with a division of French dragoons, Lannes, who had by then
been joined by the Saxon Light Horse, had enough men to face down
some 46,000 Russians until Napoleon arrived.

Bennigsen sent large bodies of men across the Alle into Friedland,
and ordered them to begin fanning out towards Heinrichsdorf, where
they could threaten the French rear. Nansouty's cuirassiers were directed
by Lannes towards Heinrichsdorf and drove the leading Russians back.
Grouchy then moved up quickly from Posthenen, charged in from the
flank and got in among the Russian guns, sabring the unprotected
gunners. The by-then-disordered French cavalry were themselves
counter-charged, but by 7 a.m. Grouchy had stabilized the French line
to the east of Heinrichsdorf.

In the desultory fighting that followed, the wily, agile Gascon Marshal Lannes was in his element. Covered by an unusually thick line of
skirmishers in the tall crops, he continually moved small units of infantry and cavalry up and down and inside and outside the woods,
exaggerating the size of his force, for he still only had 9,000 infantry
and 8,000 cavalry to hold off the six Russian divisions that had crossed
the Alle. Fortunately, just as Bennigsen deployed his forces and attacked,
Mortier's corps arrived on the field and drove into Heinrichsdorf just in
time to deny it to the Russian infantry. Leaving three battalions of
Oudinot's grenadiers in the village, Dupas deployed to its right. Mortier's Polish division then came onto the field and General Henri
Dombrowski's three Polish regiments moved into position, supporting
the artillery at Posthenen. In terrific fighting in Sortlack Wood, Oudinot's division effectively sacrificed itself to hold off the Russian infantry.
By 10 a.m. Lannes had been joined by General Jean-Antoine Verdier's
division, bringing his total up to 40,000 men.

Bennigsen realized that the absent Napoleon – who was galloping to
Friedland as fast as he could – was feeding more and more men onto the
battlefield against him, and he changed his expectations for the outcome. He now merely hoped to hold his line until the end of the day so
that he could effect another escape. Yet nightfall in midsummer falls
very late at that latitude and at noon, having galloped on his Arab horse
from Eylau with his bodyguard straining to keep up, Napoleon appeared
on the battlefield. Oudinot, riding a wounded horse, his uniform torn by
bullet holes, made his way over and begged the Emperor: 'Give me reinforcements and I shall throw the Russians into the river!' From the hill
behind Posthenen, Napoleon immediately spotted Bennigsen's gross

tactical error. The split of the plain caused by the Millstream lake meant that Bennigsen's left was vulnerable to being pushed up against the river.

While Napoleon and Oudinot awaited reinforcement, Napoleon allowed a lull in the battle, certain that Bennigsen couldn't repair the damage even if he had seen it. The men on both sides welcomed the chance to find shade and water. Many were delirious with thirst as they had spent hours ripping saltpetre cartridges off with their teeth on a stifling, cloudless midsummer day that reached 30°C in the shade. Napoleon sat on a simple wooden chair and ate a lunch of black bread within range of the Russian guns. When his attendants begged him to withdraw, he said: 'They will dine less comfortably than I will lunch.'[16] To those who worried that it was getting late to attack, and that the assault should be postponed to the next day he replied: 'We won't catch the enemy making a mistake like this twice.'[17] The soldier-diplomat Jacques de Norvins watched Napoleon walking up and down hitting tall weeds with his riding crop and saying to Berthier: 'Marengo day, victory day!'[18] Napoleon was always highly attuned to the propaganda possibilities of anniversaries, as well as being superstitious.

At 2 p.m. he issued orders for the resumption of hostilities at 5 p.m. Ney was to attack towards Sortlack; Lannes would continue holding the centre, and Oudinot's grenadiers would lean to the left to draw attention to themselves and away from Ney; Mortier would take and hold Heinrichsdorf, with Victor and the Imperial Guard staying in reserve behind the centre. Over on the church belfry, Bennigsen and his staff watched, as Hely-Hutchinson recorded, as 'the horizon seemed to be bound by a deep girdle of glittering steel'.[19] Too late, Bennigsen began issuing orders for a retreat, which he had to cancel immediately as withdrawal was by now too dangerous to attempt in the face of an oncoming enemy.

At 5 p.m. three salvoes of twenty guns signalled the start of the Grande Armée's attack. Ney's 10,000 infantry surged through Sortlack Wood and completely cleared it by 6 p.m. His columns then marched against the Russian left. General Jean-Gabriel Marchand's division drove into Sortlack village and pushed many of its defenders bodily into the river. He then moved westwards along the river, sealing off the Friedland peninsula, bottling the Russians up inside. The French artillery could hardly miss them. Napoleon then sent Victor's corps up the Eylau road towards Friedland itself from the south-west.

When Ney's exhausted corps began to fall back, Sénarmont divided his thirty guns into two batteries of fifteen each, with 300 rounds per cannon and 220 per howitzer. Sounding 'Action Front' on his bugles, his teams galloped forward, unlimbered and fired first at 600 yards, then at 300, then at 150, and finally, with nothing but canister-shot, at 60. The Russian Ismailovsky Guards and the Pavlovsky Grenadiers tried to attack the batteries, but some 4,000 men fell to their fire in about twenty-five minutes. An entire cavalry charge was destroyed with two volleys of canister. The Russian left was utterly destroyed, and trapped against the Alle river. Sénarmont's action became famous in military textbooks as an 'artillery charge', although his gunners suffered 50 per cent casualties. Ney's regenerated corps, led by the 59th Line, battled through the streets of Friedland from the west, securing the town by 8 p.m. The Russians were pressed back towards the bridges, which caught fire, and many soldiers were drowned trying to cross the Alle.

At that point, Lannes' and Mortier's divisions poured out onto the plains and the Russian units to the right of Friedland were simply pushed into the river. Many Russians fought to the end with bayonets, although twenty-two cavalry squadrons escaped along the left bank of the Alle. Heat, exhaustion, nightfall and the pillaging of the town for food have all been advanced as explanations for why there was no Jena-style pursuit of the Russians after Friedland. It is also possible that Napoleon felt a wholesale massacre might have made it harder for Alexander to come to terms, and by then he very much wanted peace. 'Their soldiers in general are good,' he told Cambacérès, something he had hitherto not recognized, and which he would have done well to remember five years later.[20]

For sheer concentration of effort, Friedland was Napoleon's most impressive victory after Austerlitz and Ulm. At the cost of 11,500 killed, wounded and missing, he had utterly routed the Russians, whose losses have been estimated at around 20,000 – or 43 per cent of their total – though only around twenty guns.[21] Percy's hundred surgeons had to work through the night, and a general later recalled 'meadows covered with limbs severed from their bodies, those frightful places of mutilation and dissection which the army called ambulances'.[22]

The day after the battle Lestocq evacuated Königsberg and Napoleon issued a classic bulletin:

Soldiers! on 5 June we were attacked in our cantonments by the Russian army, which misconstrued the causes of our inactivity. It perceived, too late, that our repose was that of the lion; now it does penance for its mistake ... From the shores of the Vistula, we have reached those of the Niemen with the rapidity of the eagle. At Austerlitz you celebrated the anniversary of the coronation; you have this year worthily celebrated that of the battle of Marengo, which put an end to the War of the Second Coalition. Frenchmen, you have been worthy of yourselves, and of me; you will return to France covered with laurels, after having acquired a peace which guarantees its own durability. It is time for our country to live in repose, sheltered from the malign influence of England. My rewards will prove to you my gratitude and the greatness of the love I bear you.[23]

On June 19 Tsar Alexander sent Prince Dmitry Lobanov-Rostovsky to seek an armistice, as the Russians re-crossed the Niemen and burned the bridge of the last Prussian town at Tilsit (present-day Sovetsk), where Napoleon arrived at 2 p.m. The Prussians, unable to continue the war without Russian help, would now simply have to follow in the Tsar's diplomatic wake. A month's armistice was agreed in two days' negotiation, and on the third evening Napoleon invited Lobanov-Rostovsky to dinner, drank a toast to the Tsar's health and suggested that the Vistula was the natural boundary between the two empires, thus implying that he would not demand any Russian territory if an all-embracing peace could be reached. On that basis, arrangements were swiftly made for Napoleon and Alexander to meet. In order to provide neutral ground a pavilion was erected by General Jean-Ambroise Baston de Lariboisière, commander of the Guard artillery, on a raft in the middle of the Niemen river securely tethered to both banks at Piktupönen (now Piktupėnai in Lithuania), the official ceasefire line near Tilsit.[24] 'Few sights will be more interesting,' wrote Napoleon in his 85th campaign bulletin. Large crowds of soldiers did indeed turn up on both banks to watch the meeting.[25] Its purpose, Napoleon repeated, was nothing less than to 'give repose to the existing generation'. After eight months on campaign, he was keen to make peace, return to Paris and continue to oversee his far reaching reforms of so many aspects of French life.

The interview between the emperors on Thursday, June 25, 1807 was remarkable for much more than its bizarre location; it was one of the great summit meetings of history. Though genuine friendship is impossible at the apex of power, Napoleon made every effort to charm the twenty-nine-year-old absolute ruler of Russia, and establish a warm personal relationship with him as well as an effective working one. The peace treaties that the negotiations produced – signed with Russia on July 7 and Prussia two days later – effectively divided Europe into zones of French and Russian influence.

Napoleon arrived on the raft first, and when Alexander came aboard, dressed in the dark-green uniform of the Preobrazhensky Guards, the two men embraced. The Tsar's first words were 'I will be your second against England.'[26] (A less regal version has it, 'I hate the English as much as you do.') Alexander had not shown the same antipathy to the English gold he had been readily accepting for years, but, whatever the phrase he used, Napoleon immediately appreciated that a wide-ranging agreement would be possible – indeed, as he put it later, 'Those words changed everything.'[27] They then entered the pavilion's sumptuous salon and spoke alone for two hours. 'I've just met the Emperor Alexander,' Napoleon reported to Josephine. 'I'm very well satisfied with him; he is a very handsome and good young emperor; he has more intelligence than one thinks.'[28]

Although the door of the raft's pavilion (which Napoleon pronounced 'beautiful') was surmounted by representations of the eagles of Russia and France and large painted monograms of 'N' for Napoleon and 'A' for Alexander, there was no 'FW' for Frederick William of Prussia, who was present at Tilsit but made to feel very much the junior monarch. On the first day he wasn't invited onto the raft at all but had to wait on the riverbank wrapped in a Russian greatcoat while the fate of his kingdom was decided by two men who had no instinctive affection for it.[29] He was allowed onto the raft on the second day, June 26, so that Alexander could introduce him to Napoleon, whereupon it became clear to him that the coming Franco-Russian alliance was going to be bought at the grievous expense of Prussia. When, at the end of the second meeting on the raft, Alexander entered the town of Tilsit at 5 p.m. he received a 100-gun salute, was welcomed by Napoleon in person and was put up in the best mansion in the town. When Frederick William arrived there was no salute, no welcome, and he was billeted at the house of the local miller.[30] His position was not helped by the fact that both Napoleon and Alexander found him a pedantic, narrow-minded bore of limited conversation.[31] 'He kept me half an hour talking to me of my uniform and buttons,' Napoleon reminisced, 'so that at last I said: "You must ask my tailor."'[32] Night after night thereafter, the three men would dine early, say goodnight, and then Alexander would return to

Napoleon's apartments to talk long into the small hours without Frederick William knowing.

Although there was a good deal of reviewing of each other's guards and exchanging of orders and decorations – Napoleon gave a Russian grenadier the Légion d'Honneur at Alexander's request – and mutually flattering toasts at grand banquets, it was the late-night conversations about philosophy, politics and strategy that shaped Napoleon's relationship with the Tsar. In letters to his sister, Alexander wrote of these talks sometimes lasting four hours at a stretch. They discussed the Continental System, the European economy, the future of the Ottoman Empire and how to bring Britain to the negotiating table. 'When I was at Tilsit I used to chat [*je bavardai*],' Napoleon recalled, 'call the Turks barbarians, and say that they ought to be turned out of Europe, but I never intended to do so, for . . . it was not in the interest of France that Constantinople should be in the hands of either Austria or Russia.'[33] In one of their more surreal discussions, on the best form of government, the autocrat Alexander argued for an elective monarchy, whereas Napoleon – whose crown was at least confirmed by a plebiscite – argued for autocracy. 'For who is fit to be elected?' Napoleon asked. 'A Caesar, an Alexander only comes along once a century, so that the election must be a matter of chance, and the succession is surely worth more than a throw of dice.'[34]

Alexander was under pressure to make peace from his mother, the Dowager Empress Maria Feodorovna, who felt that enough Russian blood had been shed for the Hohenzollerns, and from his brother Constantine, who frankly admired Napoleon. The deal he struck at Tilsit hardly reflected the scale of his defeat; Prussia paid almost the entire price and Russia lost no territory except the Ionian Isles (including Corfu, which Napoleon called 'the key to the Adriatic').[35] Napoleon guaranteed that those German states such as Oldenburg which were ruled by the Tsar's close family would not be forced into the Confederation of the Rhine. Alexander agreed to evacuate Moldavia and Wallachia, recently taken from the Turks (they had never been Russian), and he was given a free hand to invade Finland, which belonged to Sweden. The only significant concession that Alexander had to make at Tilsit was to promise to join the Continental System, which Napoleon hoped would greatly increase the pressure on Britain to make peace. Meanwhile, Alexander invited Napoleon to St Petersburg. 'I'm aware he's terrified of cold,' he told the French ambassador, 'but despite this I won't spare him the journey. I'll order his quarters warmed to Egyptian heat.'[36] He also ordered that anti-Napoleonic literature be burned in Russia, where his new ally was now to be referred to in print only as 'Napoleon' and never as 'Bonaparte'.[37]

By complete contrast with the extreme leniency shown to Russia, Prussia was subjected to drastic penalties. 'Where I erred most fatally was at Tilsit,' Napoleon said later. 'I ought to have dethroned the King of Prussia. I hesitated for a moment. I was sure that Alexander would not have opposed it, provided I had not taken the King's dominions for myself.'[38] Alexander took the eastern Białystok region of Poland from Prussia – hardly the action of an ally – but the other heavy lashes were all dealt by Napoleon. Out of Prussian provinces acquired during the Second and Third Partitions of Poland he carved the Duchy of Warsaw, which Poles hoped would be the first stage on the path to the re-creation of their own kingdom, though it had no diplomatic representation abroad and its Duke was a German, Frederick Augustus of Saxony, with a toothless parliament. Prussian lands west of the Elbe formed a new kingdom of Westphalia, Cottbus went to Saxony, and a huge war indemnity of 120 million francs was imposed. To pay it off, Frederick William had to sell land and raise the overall tax burden from 10 per cent of national wealth to 30 per cent. Prussia was forced to join the Continental System and was not permitted to impose tolls on various waterways such as the Netze river and the Bromberg Canal (now the Noteć river and the Bydgoszcz Canal, both entirely in Poland).[39] Joseph was to be recognized as king of Naples, Louis as king of Holland and Napoleon as Protector of the Confederation of the Rhine, and French garrisons remained in the Vistula, Elbe and Oder fortresses. Prussia was reduced to a population of 4.5 million (half its pre-war number) and two-thirds of its territory, and was allowed an army of only 42,000 men; in almost all territories between the Rhine and the Elbe 'all actual or eventual rights' of the Kingdom of Prussia 'shall be obliterated for perpetuity'. The King of Saxony would even have the right to use Prussian roads to send troops to the Duchy of Warsaw. By imposing these humiliations on the great-nephew of Frederick the Great, Napoleon guaranteed that Prussia would feel perpetual resentment, but he calculated that Austrian revanchism over Pressburg and Prussian over Tilsit could be held in check by his new friendship with Russia.

As he began to approach the zenith of his power, Napoleon's strategy was to ensure that, although he could always count on British hostility, there would be no moment when all three continental powers of Russia, Austria and Prussia would be ranged against him at the same time. He thus needed to play each off against the others, and as much as possible against Britain too. He used Prussia's desire for Hanover, Russia's inability to fight on after Friedland, a marriage alliance with Austria, the differences between Russia and Austria over the Ottoman Empire and the fear of Polish resurgence that all three powers felt to avoid having to fight the four powers simultaneously.[40] That he achieved this for a decade after the collapse of the Peace of Amiens, despite clearly being the European hegemon that each power most feared, was a tribute to his statesmanship. The effective dividing of Europe into French and Russian spheres of influence was the defining moment of this strategy.

One evening towards the end of his life, while he was in exile on St Helena, the conversation turned to when Napoleon had been most happy in his life. Members of his entourage suggested different moments. 'Yes, I was happy when I became First Consul, happy at the time of my marriage, and happy at the birth of the King of Rome,' he agreed, referring to the future birth of his son. 'But then I did not feel perfectly confident of the security of my position. Perhaps I was happiest at Tilsit. I had just surmounted many vicissitudes, many anxieties, at Eylau for instance; and I found myself victorious, dictating laws, having emperors and kings pay me court.'[41] It was a wise moment to have chosen.

When Queen Louise of Prussia arrived at Tilsit on July 6, only three days before the Franco-Prussian treaty was signed, she had a two-hour meeting with Napoleon in which she begged for the return of Magdeburg on the west bank of the Elbe. She was an extremely attractive woman, so much so that in 1795 Johann Gottfried Schadow's statue of her and her sister Frederike was determined to be too erotic for public display.[42] (Napoleon merely remarked that she was 'as handsome as could be expected at thirty-five'.[43]) Reporting their meeting to Berthier, he wrote, 'The beautiful queen of Prussia really cries,' after which he added, 'She believes I came all the way here for her nice eyes.'[44] He was fully aware of the strategic importance of Magdeburg from his studies of Gustavus Adolphus's campaigns, and it was never likely that he would do anything so frivolous as concede a vital military stronghold because he succumbed to a lachrymose queen.* He later likened Lou-

---

* Napoleon was deeply loathed by Maria Carolina of Naples, Maria Feodorovna of Russia, Louise of Prussia and Madame de Staël, who sensed his deeply misogynist attitude

ise's entreaties over Magdeburg to Chimène begging 'in the tragic style' for Count Rodrigue's head in Corneille's play *Le Cid*, '"Sire! Justice! Justice! Magdeburg!" At last to make her stop I begged her to sit down, knowing that nothing is so likely to cut short a tragic scene, for when one is seated its continuance turns into comedy.'[45] He claimed that during the whole of dinner one night all she talked of was Magdeburg, and that after her husband and Alexander had withdrawn, she kept on pressing. Napoleon offered her a rose. 'Yes,' she said, 'but with Magdeburg!' 'Eh! Madam,' he replied, 'it is I who is offering the rose to you, not you to me.'[46]

Magdeburg instead went to Westphalia, a new 1,100-square-mile kingdom carved out of the territories of Brunswick and Hesse-kassel, as well as Prussian territory west of the Elbe, to which were later added parts of Hanover. To this strategically important new entity, however, Napoleon sent as monarch a boy who had achieved nothing in his twenty-two years beyond taking unauthorized leave in America, making an ill-advised marriage which had been only semi-legally annulled, and then serving perfectly competently (but no more) in charge of Bavarians and Württembergers in the recent campaign.[47] Jérôme didn't have a good enough curriculum vitae for a crown, but Napoleon continued to feel that he could depend upon his family more than anyone else – despite the clear indications to the contrary from Lucien's exile, Jérôme's marriage, Joseph's weakness in Naples, Pauline's insubordinate infidelities and Louis' blind eye to British smuggling in Holland.

Napoleon wanted Westphalia to be a model for the rest of Germany, encouraging other German states to join the Confederation, or at least to stay out of the Prussian and Austrian orbit. 'It is essential that your people enjoy a liberty, an equality, a well-being unknown to the people of Germany,' he wrote to Jérôme on November 15, sending him a constitution for the new kingdom and predicting that no-one would want to return to Prussian rule once they had 'tasted the benefits of a wise and liberal administration'. He ordered Jérôme to 'follow it faithfully . . . The benefits of the Code Napoléon, public trials, the establishment of juries, will be, above all, the defining characteristic of your rule . . . I count more on their effects . . . than the greatest military victories.' Then, ironically given to whom he was writing, he extolled the virtues

---

regarding women and power. 'One finds it hard not to be indignant when one sees what this tart [*catin*] is capable of!' he had written of Madame de Staël that April, 'and ugly to boot!' (CG7 no. 15337 p. 650).

of meritocracy: 'The population of Germany anxiously awaits the moment when those who are not of noble birth but who are talented, have an equal right to be considered for jobs; for the abolition of all serfdom as well as intermediaries between the people and their sovereign.' This letter wasn't written for publication, but it nevertheless represents Napoleon's finest ideals. 'The people of Germany, as those of France, Italy and Spain, want equality and liberal values,' he wrote. 'I have become convinced that the burden of privileges was contrary to general opinion. Be a constitutional king.'[48]

As he did with Joseph, Louis and Eugène, Napoleon constantly criticized Jérôme, even admonishing him on one occasion for having too good a sense of humour: 'Your letter was too witty. You don't need wit during times of war. You need to be precise, display backbone and simplicity.'[49] Although none of his brothers made competent rulers, Napoleon's endless carping didn't help. 'He has it in him to become a man of quality,' he told Joseph of Jérôme. 'However, he would be surprised to hear this, as all my letters to him are full of reproach . . . I purposefully put him in a position of isolated leadership.'[50] Napoleon knew how demanding he was being of his family, but his approach failed every time.

'By the time you read this letter,' Napoleon wrote to Josephine on July 7, 'peace with Prussia and Russia will have been concluded, and Jérôme recognized as King of Westphalia, with three million in population. This piece of news is for you alone.'[51] The last sentence indicates how much Napoleon usually regarded his letters to Josephine and others as a sophisticated propaganda tool. The day before he had written 'the little Baron de Kepen has some hope of receiving a visit', which implies that he was telling the truth when he wrote: 'I very much wish to see you, when destiny decides the time is right. It's possible that could be soon.'[52] Marie would be left behind in Poland.

He returned to Saint-Cloud at 7 a.m. on July 27 after a 100-hour night-and-day carriage ride, moving so fast that his escort had no time to remove the barrier in front of a triumphal arch that had been specially built for him (he simply ordered his coachman to swerve round it).[53] He had been away from France for 306 days, the longest absence of his career. 'We saw Napoleon return from the depths of Poland without stopping,' recalled Chaptal, 'convene the Conseil when he arrived and show the same presence of mind, the same continuity and the same strength of ideas as if he had spent the night in his bedroom.'[54] Sending

Marie Walewska his portrait and some books, he wrote from Saint-Cloud: 'My gentle and dear Marie, you who love your country so much, will understand the joy I feel at being back in France, after nearly a year away. This joy would be complete had you been here too, but I carry you in my heart.'[55] He didn't contact her again for eighteen months.

20

Iberia

'There is no country in Europe in the affairs of which foreigners
can interfere with so little advantage as in those of Spain.'
The Duke of Wellington to Lord Castlereagh, 1820

'That unfortunate war destroyed me; it divided my forces,
multiplied my obligations, undermined morale ... All the circumstances of my disasters are bound up in that fatal knot.'
Napoleon on the Peninsular War

Napoleon was conscious of the need for a new social hierarchy in
France, one based on service to the state rather than accident of birth,
and on his return to Paris in the summer of 1807 he set about putting it
in place. 'It was at Tilsit that the main titles of a new nobility were
launched,' recalled Anatole de Montesquiou, the son of Napoleon's
grand chamberlain, who served as an artillery officer under Davout.
'For a long time, all the European cabinets were reproaching the
Emperor for the lack of titles around him. According to them, it gave
France a revolutionary appearance.'[1] The Légion d'Honneur had gone
some way towards inaugurating a new system of privilege based on
merit, but couldn't provide the basis for an entire social system. In May
1802 Napoleon had complained that his new order would remain as
'grains of sand' unless it could be anchored by 'some masses of granite'.[2]
As an army officer, his mind naturally gravitated towards a hierarchical
structure of ranks and titles, but he also wanted to avoid the damning
flaws of the Ancien Régime – those of heredity and legal privileges. As
ever he looked to the ancient world for guidance. 'A prince gains nothing from the displacement of the aristocracy,' he wrote later in *Caesar's*

Wars, 'on the contrary he puts everything back in order by letting it subsist in its natural state, by restoring the old houses under the new principles.[3]

In March 1808 the ranks of count, baron and chevalier of the Empire were created. By introducing nobility based on merit – one in which 20 per cent came from the working classes and 58 per cent from the middle classes – Napoleon harnessed the revolutionary Frenchman's ambition to serve his country.[4] He did not see the reintroduction of nobility as contradicting the spirit of the Revolution. 'The French people fought for only one thing: equality in the eyes of the law,' he told Cambacérès. 'Now, my nobility, as they style it, is in reality no nobility at all, because it is without prerogatives or hereditary succession . . . its hereditary succession depends on the will of the sovereign in confirming the title on the son or nephew of the deceased holder.'[5] Unlike anywhere else in Europe, a French family's noble status simply lapsed if the next generation hadn't done enough to deserve its passing on.[6] Napoleon's new titles were therefore analogous to the British concept of the life peerage, which wasn't instituted until 1958.

What has been described as Napoleon's 're-hierarchization' of French life involved a complete reordering of the social system.[7] At the top were high-ranking army officers, ministers, councillors of state, prefects, presidents of the electoral colleges, senior judges, the mayors of the larger cities, and a few academics, professionals and artists. Below them came the more than 30,000 members of the Légion d'Honneur. Further down were around 100,000 sub-prefects, mayors of lesser cities, officials of the educational, judicial and administrative arms of the state, members of the electoral colleges, chambers of commerce, prefects' councils and other office-holders and notables.[8] These were Napoleon's true 'masses of granite'. Lying deep within the French Revolution were the seeds of its own destruction because the concepts of liberty, equality and fraternity are mutually exclusive. A society can be formed around two of them, but never all three. Liberty and equality, if they are strictly observed, will obliterate fraternity; equality and fraternity must extinguish liberty; and fraternity and liberty can only come at the expense of equality. If extreme equality of outcome is the ultimate goal, as it was for the Jacobins, it will crush liberty and fraternity. With his creation of a new nobility Napoleon dispensed with that concept of equality, and instead enshrined in the French polity the concept of equality before the law in which he believed wholeheartedly.

Under the Ancien Régime the *noblesse* had numbered anywhere between 80,000 and 400,000 people; under Napoleon the figures were much more exact and limited. In 1808 he created 744 nobles, in 1809 502, in 1810 1,085, in 1811 428, in 1812 131, in 1813 318, and in 1814 55. So whereas seven in 10,000 Frenchmen had been noble in 1789, by 1814 it was only one in every 10,000.[9] Of the 3,263 nobles Napoleon created, 59 per cent were military, 22 per cent *fonctionnaires* and 17 per cent *notables*.[10] Several doctors, scientists, writers and artists were ennobled too.* No fewer than 123 of Napoleon's 131 prefects were ennobled, and the Paris appeal court boasted four counts, three barons and eleven chevaliers. In 1811 all but three ambassadors were titled. The system also allowed Napoleon to perpetuate the names of military victories, with principalities and dukedoms bearing such names as Castiglione, Auerstädt, Rivoli and Eckmühl.†

Separate from the new nobility, though often overlapping with it, he also introduced *donations* in 1806, whereby loyal subjects, the *donataires*, received lands and property confiscated from defeated enemies in the conquered territories. With them often came endowments, generally from Italy, Germany and, later, Poland. By 1815 there were 6,000 recipients of such land gifts, totalling 30 million francs.

The creation of the imperial aristocracy coincided with a hardening of Napoleon's attitude towards internal dissent. On August 9, 1807 he told an extraordinary meeting of the Conseil d'État that he wanted the Tribunate, 'whose name and object seemed foreign to a monarchical government', to be abolished. This was duly done by a *sénatus-consulte* ten days later.[11] A minority of the Tribunate had spoken and voted against the Concordat, the Légion d'Honneur, various sections of the Civil Code and the proclamation of the Empire. Even though it was precisely in order to hear different voices that the Tribunate had been created, Napoleon increasingly took an army officer's view of these expressions of dissent in the legislative ranks; indeed it is remarkable that such a body had survived under him for as long as eight years.

---

* The first British poet to be ennobled was Alfred Tennyson in 1884; the first artist was Frederic Leighton, the day before his death in 1896.

† For all his genuine belief in meritocracy (except where his own family was concerned) Napoleon was not without snobbishness, telling Molé in 1813: '"There are families which it is impossible to ennoble. How many colonels are brothers of ladies' maids?" Molé replied that a member of Napoleon's Conseil had a brother who was a Parisian street-sweeper' (ed. Noailles, *Count Molé* p. 197). Napoleon did make Lefebvre Duke of Danzig – see p. 447 – despite the fact that his wife was a former regimental washerwoman. On being announced as the Duchess of Danzig at a reception, she winked at the footman and said: 'Eh, boy, what do you think of that?!' (Haythornthwaite, *Final Verdict* p. 231).

Savary explained in his memoirs that Napoleon never minded people disagreeing with him, so long as they did it in a loyal spirit and in private: 'He never resented anyone who frankly showed opposition to his opinion; he liked his opinions to be discussed.'[12] While he liked discussing his views with Cambacérès and the Conseil, he was less enthusiastic about tribunes such as Constant, Daunou and Chénier doing so. 'Keep an eye on Benjamin Constant,' he told Cambacérès about the notorious philanderer, 'if he meddles with anything I'll send him to Brunswick to be with his wife.'[13] At the same time that the *sénatus-consulte* abolished the Tribunate, Napoleon raised the lower age limit for all members of the legislature to forty. He himself was still only thirty-eight.

Once back in Paris, Napoleon could concentrate on improving French finances, a task that was greatly helped by his recent victories. In September 1807, Daru drew up a detailed list of the cash and supplies that twenty-two Prussian cities would have to pay as part of the Tilsit settlement, which totalled 72,474,570 francs and 7 centimes in cash, and 30,994,491 francs and 53 centimes in supplies. Once other regions were included, the total came to over 153 million francs.[14] This, as well as the declaration of peace, saw a huge surge in confidence in Napoleon's government on the Paris Bourse: 5 per cent government stock, which had been trading at 17.37 in February 1800, rose to 93.00 on August 27, 1807, and thereafter stabilized in the mid-80s.[15]

This period back from what he called the Polish War was not all work for Napoleon. On October 4, 1807 he is recorded as having given 30,000 francs to the Comtesse de Barral, Pauline's mistress of the robes and the wife of one of Jérôme's notoriously adulterous chamberlains in Westphalia.[16] He also displayed his controlling nature when in September 1807 he ordered the arrest of Mr Kuhn, the American consul in Genoa, for wearing the Order of Malta awarded him by the British. In the same month he demanded to know which Bordeaux aristocrats had boycotted Senator Lamartillière's ball and why. He even assumed the role of amateur sleuth in a murder mystery, instructing Fouché to reopen a poisoning case from May 1805 concerning 'a certain Jean-Guillaume Pascal, from Montpellier. This scoundrel is said to have murdered his wife.' Napoleon ordered M. Pascal's brother-in-law be interviewed by police and a post-mortem conducted on the couple's dog, which he suspected might also have been poisoned.[17]

After such a long absence on campaign he was able to enjoy domestic life for the first time in nearly a year. While Napoleon was in Egypt,

Josephine had borrowed money to buy the lovely Malmaison, a chateau 7 miles west of Paris, and she and Napoleon had split their time between there and the Tuileries. Featuring an aviary, a botanical hothouse for exotic plants, a summer pavilion, a tower, a 'temple of love', vineyard and fields adjoining the Seine, the Malmaison estate grew to three hundred acres of gardens, woods and fields, and a magnificent collection of statuary.* Josephine also kept there a menagerie of kangaroos, emus, flying squirrels, gazelles, ostriches, llamas and a cockatoo that had only one word ('Bonaparte') which it repeated incessantly. She would occasionally invite a female orang-utan dressed in a white chemise to eat turnips among her guests at table.[18] Napoleon brought back gazelles from Egypt, to which he would occasionally give snuff.† 'They were very fond of tobacco,' recalled his private secretary, 'and would empty the snuffbox in a minute, without appearing any the worse for it.'[19] Although Napoleon kept a carbine in his study at Malmaison, with which he would sometimes shoot at birds through an open window, Josephine persuaded him not to open fire on her swans.[20] (He would probably have missed; his valet Grégoire recalled that he 'didn't hold his gun properly on his shoulder, and as he asked for it to be tightly loaded, his arm was always black after he'd fired a shot'.[21] He once took seven shots to kill a cornered stag.)

At its height, Napoleon's imperial household covered thirty-nine palaces,‡ almost amounting to a state within a state, even though he never visited several of them.[22] Taking Louis XIV as his model, he reintroduced public Masses, meals and levées, musical galas and many of the other trappings of the Sun King.[23] He was certain that such outward

---

* After Josephine took the aristocrat Lucie de La Tour du Pin around Malmaison, claiming how all the pictures and sculptures had been presents from foreign courts, du Pin noted: 'The good woman was an inveterate liar. Even when the plain truth would have been more striking than an invention, she preferred to invent' (Moorehead, *Dancing to the Precipice* p. 286).

† A chamberlain recalled of Napoleon's own snuff-taking that 'he lost more than he took. It was rather a fancy, a kind of amusement, than a real want. His snuff boxes were very plain, of an oval shape, made of black shell, lined with gold, all exactly alike, and differing only in the beautiful antique silver medals which were set in the lid.' (Bausset, *Private Memoirs* p. 428) Despite his snuff habit, Napoleon believed smoking to be 'good for nothing but to enliven idlers' (Constant, *Memoirs* II p. 11).

‡ These included the Tuileries, Fontainebleau, Saint-Cloud, Compiègne, the Grand Trianon and Petit Trianon at Versailles, Rambouillet (for hunting), Meudon, the Château de Marracq outside Bayonne, the Deutschhaus near Mainz, Laeken Palace near Brussels, the Palais Royal in Milan, the Pitti Palace in Florence, the Palazzo Durazzo in Genoa, the Castello Stupinigi in Turin and the Monte-Cavallo in Rome.

displays of splendour inspired feelings of awe in the populace – 'We must speak to the eyes,' he said – as well as encouraging the French luxury-goods industry.[24] The palaces had an annual budget of 25 million francs, comprising the sixth largest outlay in the whole of French public expenditure. In all he amassed a total of 54,514 precious stones in his personal treasury, which he saw as indistinguishable from that of France (although that wasn't uncommon: the British Civil List only started in 1760).*

When he toured France, his entourage drove in sixty coaches in a deliberate attempt to impress, not unlike today's American presidential motorcades that can number forty-five vehicles, a similarly visible metaphor for the power of the office. In private, however, he retained the modesty of the *petit noblesse* army officer that was always his true persona. 'When he received on his throne,' recalled Chaptal, 'he displayed himself with great luxury. His orders were made of beautiful diamonds, as was the hilt of his sword, the cord and button of his hat and his buckles. These clothes ill became him, he seemed embarrassed, and he took them off as soon as he could.'[25] His daily wear was either the blue undress uniform of a colonel of grenadiers of his Imperial Guard or the green uniform of its Chasseurs à Cheval, and when it was discovered that no cloth could be procured of the right shade of green on St Helena, he simply turned his coat inside out.

The contrast between Napoleon's personal lack of adornment away from official occasions and the gorgeousness of the costumes of those around him was noted by many, as it was intended to be; indeed Denon instructed the painter François Gérard to 'Take care to emphasize the full splendour of the uniforms of the officers surrounding the Emperor, as this contrasts with the simplicity he displays and so immediately marks him out in their midst.'[26] Captain Blaze also noticed that 'His small hat and green chasseur's frock distinguish him amid the crowd of princes and generals with embroidery on every seam.'[27] As well as the Légion d'Honneur, Napoleon wore his medal of the Iron Crown of Italy, but none of the many other decorations to which he was entitled, an array which might have drawn a sniper's attention in battle (a consideration Nelson might

---

* Despite his excessive spending, Napoleon was always on the lookout for economies, as we saw in his cutting of the upholsterer's bills, p. 401. '155 cups of coffee were being drunk here per day,' he once told a minister at the Tuileries, 'each cup cost me 20 centimes, which came to 56,575 francs per year. I stopped the coffee and granted 7 francs and 6 centimes in compensation. I will pay 21,575 francs and will save 35,000 francs' (Chaptal, *Souvenirs* p. 335).

have done well to consider). In 1811 a list was made of all Napoleon's clothes, which included only nine coats (to last three years), two dressing-gowns, twenty-four pairs of silk stockings, twenty-four pairs of shoes and four hats. 'Nothing is to be spent except after the approbation of His Majesty,' it noted, and when the chamberlain Comte Charles de Rémusat did spend too much on Napoleon's wardrobe he was dismissed.[28]

Everything in the organization of Napoleon's palaces revolved around work. Dinner was at 6 p.m. but he very often missed it, instead eating whenever work permitted; dozens of chickens were put on spits throughout the day so that one would always be ready for him (hardly in conformity with his wishes for economy). He ate food as it was brought to him, in no particular order. He was no gastronome, and was perfectly happy eating macaroni. 'Napoleon preferred the most simple dishes,' recalled one of his chamberlains, 'he drank no wine but Chambertin, and that rarely undiluted'.[29] Even the Chambertin wasn't always of the best vintages; when asked for his opinion, Augereau judged, 'I've known better.'[30] Napoleon brandy is ill named as he never drank any spirits, habitually taking one cup of coffee after breakfast and another after dinner. There is no known example of his ever being drunk. Napoleon recognized that he was no gourmand. 'If you want to dine well, dine with Cambacérès,' he told General Thiébault during the consulate, 'if you want to dine badly, dine with Lebrun; if you want to dine quickly, dine with me.'[31] He would generally spend less than ten minutes at table, except for family suppers on Sunday nights when he might stay for a maximum of half an hour.[32] 'We all obeyed the Emperor's signal of rising from table,' recorded a fellow diner, 'his manner of performing this ceremony being brusque and startling. He would push the chair suddenly away, and rise as if he had received an electric shock.'[33] Napoleon once said that although a number of people, especially Josephine, had told him he ought to stay longer at table, he considered the amount of time he spent there to be 'already a corruption of power'.[34]

At home as on campaign, he slept only when he needed to, regardless of the time of day. 'If he slept,' his finance minister Comte Molé recalled, 'it was only because he recognized the need for sleep and because it renewed the energies he would require later.'[35] He needed seven hours' sleep in twenty-four, but he slept, as one secretary recalled, 'in several short naps, broken at will during the night as in the day'.[36] Since his bedroom was close to his study in all his palaces, he could be at work in his dressing-gown at any time of the day or night, with his secretaries on rotations to take dictation. 'He used to get up,' recalled another secretary, 'after an hour's sleep, as wide awake and as clear in the head as if he had slept quietly the whole night.'[37]

Napoleon was excellent at prioritization, dealing immediately with urgent matters, placing important but not urgent papers in a stack to be dealt with afterwards and throwing anything he considered unimportant onto the floor. Whereas Louis XVIII had a stamp made up for his signature, Napoleon always read letters through before signing them personally, not least because his speed of dictation meant that secretaries could sometimes take words down incorrectly. 'The ideas go on fastest,' Napoleon said in explaining his need for secretaries, 'and then goodbye to the letters and the lines! I can only dictate now. It's very convenient to dictate. It's just as if one were holding a conversation.'[38] He virtually never sat down at his desk except to write to his wives and mistresses (who received the only letters he didn't dictate) and to sign documents. His three private secretaries – Bourrienne, who held the post from 1797 to 1802, Claude-François de Méneval (1802–13) and Agathon Fain (1813–15) – all developed their own shorthand to keep up with his torrent of words at their small desks while he sat on a green taffeta sofa in his study at the Tuileries near a folding screen that shielded him from the fire, an arrangement that was replicated in all his palaces. If they were still working at 1 a.m., Napoleon would sometimes take his secretary out incognito to the rue Saint-Honoré, where they would drink cups of hot chocolate.[39] (On one occasion he complained to the prefect of police the next morning that the lamps at the palace gates had gone out: 'He could not imagine how I had found it out.'[40])

Each of his secretaries and ministers had his own story of Napoleon's prodigious memory and dictating capacity. His interior minister Jean Chaptal's tale of when he wanted to establish a military academy at Fontainebleau might be taken as entirely typical. Napoleon sat Chaptal down and dictated 517 articles to him, entirely without notes. Chaptal spent all night drawing them up, after which Napoleon 'told me it was good but incomplete'.[41] He once told Méneval that after he had left Brienne he started to work sixteen hours a day and never stopped.[42]

Everything around Napoleon happened at a tremendous pace. Molé recalled him going from a Mass to a levée at Saint-Cloud in the summer of 1806, 'walking fast, with an escort of foreign princes and . . . grand French dignitaries, who were out of breath in their efforts to keep up with him'.[43] He hated wasting a minute of the day, and was constantly performing several tasks simultaneously. He loved taking long hot baths which, unusually for early nineteenth-century Europeans, he did most days, but during those one or two hours he would have newspapers or political writings read to him, as he also did when his valet shaved him, and sometimes during breakfast. He was almost masochistic in listening to the British newspapers, which his secretaries hated translating for him: he insisted on hearing everything written about himself, however abusive.[44] On long journeys in their carriage, Josephine read novels to him, chosen from the précis of newly published ones that he had the historical novelist the Comtesse de Genlis draw up for him every week.[45]

Although he worked them inordinately hard, Napoleon was considerate to his staff, who almost universally admired him. He was indeed a hero to his valets, aides-de-camp and orderlies, and far more of his personal servants volunteered to go into exile with him than the British could allow, a remarkable tribute to his talent as an employer. Mademoiselle Avrillon, who worked for Josephine, remembered him as being 'extremely polite' and 'very indulgent when small errors were committed'. His chamberlain, the Comte de Bausset, wrote: 'I can categorically say that few men were more level in their character and gentle in their behaviour.' Agathon Fain thought 'Napoleon was a loyal friend and the best of masters', not least because 'he would spoil everybody'.[46] An alcoholic coachman was kept on the payroll years after he should have been sacked, because he had driven a wagon at Marengo.

'I had expected to find him brusque, and of uncertain temper,' recalled Méneval, 'instead of which I found him patient, indulgent, easy to please, by no means exacting, merry with a merriness which was often noisy and mocking, and sometimes of a charming bonhomie.'[47] The one secretary who wrote critically of Napoleon was Bourrienne, whose gross corruption had led to his demotion in 1802. Napoleon had later given him another job, as governor of Hamburg, which Bourrienne also abused for personal gain, and he went on to repay his master's kindness with years of libels.

Insofar as there was ever an average evening in the life of Napoleon, it featured many of the pleasures of normal French bourgeois family life. As Méneval recalled:

> He dined with his family, and after dinner would look in on his *cabinet* [office] and then, unless kept there by some work, would return to the drawing room to play chess. As a general rule he liked to talk in a familiar way. He was fond of discussions, but didn't impose his opinions, and

made no pretension of superiority, either of intelligence or of rank. When only ladies were present he liked to criticize their dresses, or tell them tragic or satirical stories – ghost stories for the most part. When bedtime came, Madame Bonaparte followed him to his room.[48]

He danced at the little balls given at Malmaison on Sunday nights, praised his stepchildren for their playlets and 'found a charm in this patriarchal life'.[49] He hunted stags and wild boar, but more for the exercise than the pleasure of the chase, and occasionally cheated at board and card games – though he usually repaid the money he won in that way. He simply could not bear not winning.

By early 1808 Prussia had been subdued and there was a grand understanding with Russia. Napoleon could now turn his mind to the means by which he might force Britain to the negotiating table. After Trafalgar it was clear that he could not revive plans to invade, but the British were still actively encouraging smuggling across Europe in an attempt to wreck the Continental System, blockading French ports and showing no signs of wanting to end the war. So Napoleon looked southwards in his hopes to damage British trade, which he had always thought was the key to bringing the 'nation of shopkeepers' to heel. Ever since November 1800, when he had written to Joseph, 'The greatest damage we could inflict upon English commerce would be to seize upon Portugal', Napoleon had seen Britain's oldest ally as her Achilles heel.[50]* While he was galloping through Dresden on July 19, 1807 he had demanded that Portugal close her ports to British shipping by September, arrest all Britons in Lisbon and confiscate all British goods. Portugal had been defaulting on the indemnity she had agreed to pay when she sued for peace in 1801. She let British ships into her ports to buy wine, her largest export, and had large colonies and a substantial fleet, but an army of only 20,000 men. The country was ruled by the lazy, obese and slow-witted but absolute Prince João, whose Spanish wife Carlota had attempted to overthrow him in 1805.[51]

After the French had invaded Etruria on August 29, 1807 to try to suppress its chronic smuggling of British goods, the Spanish premier,

* First signed in 1376, the Anglo-Portuguese alliance is the oldest in the world and was reaffirmed in 1386, 1643, 1654, 1660, 1661, 1703 and 1815, by a secret declaration in 1899, then again in 1904 and 1914, and was cited by Britain during the Falklands War of 1982.

Don Manuel de Godoy y Álvarez de Faria, knew he would need to co-operate with Napoleon in order to get suitable compensation for the Infanta María Luisa, Queen of Etruria and daughter of Charles IV of Spain, whose husband King Louis I had died of epilepsy in May 1803. Napoleon didn't like or trust Godoy; when in 1801 Godoy had asked Lucien for a picture of Napoleon, he had retorted: 'I shall never send my portrait to a man who keeps his predecessor in a dungeon [Godoy had imprisoned the previous prime minister, the Count of Aranda, after a Spanish defeat at the hands of the French in 1792] and who adopts the customs of the Inquisition. I may make use of him, but I owe him nothing but contempt.'[52] He was highly suspicious when Godoy mobilized the Spanish army on the same day as the battle of Jena, only to demobilize quickly on hearing of its outcome. Godoy decided that it would be wise to allow French troops through Spain to attack Portugal.

'Above all Portugal must be wrested from the influence of England,' Napoleon wrote to King Charles IV on September 7, 1807, 'so as to oblige this latter Power to sue for peace.'[53] On October 27 Godoy's representative signed the Treaty of Fontainebleau, which contained secret clauses planning for the partition of Portugal into three, the north going to Infanta María Luisa as compensation for Etruria, the centre coming under Franco-Spanish military occupation, and the south becoming the personal fiefdom of the handsome, wily, vulgar and ostentatious Godoy himself, who would become prince of the Algarves. He already carried the self-aggrandizing title the Prince of the Peace, a reference to the Treaty of Basle he had negotiated in 1795 with France.[54] (He preferred either title to the popular nickname 'The Sausage-Maker', attached to him because he came from Estremadura, the centre of Spanish pig-breeding.) The treaty guaranteed Charles IV's domains and would allow him the title 'Emperor of the Two Americas'.[55]

Napoleon ratified the treaty on October 29, by which time French troops were already deep inside the Iberian peninsula. On October 18 Junot had crossed the Bidasoa river into Spain en route to Portugal. He met no resistance even at Lisbon, and on November 29 the Portuguese royal family escaped to Rio de Janeiro in good time on Royal Navy warships, booed at the docks by the crowds for their desertion.[56] Napoleon ordered Junot to ensure that his engineers sketched Spanish roads along the way. 'Let me see the distances of the villages, the nature of the country, and its resources,' he wrote, indicating that even then he was contemplating invading his ally.[57]

Spanish politics were so rotten, and the Spanish Bourbons so deca-
dent and pathetic, that their throne seemed ripe for the taking. Charles
IV and his domineering wife, María Luisa of Parma, hated their eldest
son and heir, the twenty-four-year-old Ferdinand, Prince of the Asturias
(later Ferdinand VII), a feeling that was entirely reciprocated. Although
he had both a wife and a mistress living in his house, Godoy was also
the lover of the queen. The king was so compliant that when Godoy had
intercepted a letter from Napoleon to Charles warning him of Godoy's
cuckolding some years earlier, he merely passed it on. Godoy's power in
Spain was such that he was appointed an admiral without once having
been to sea. Ferdinand, who was just as weak and pusillanimous as his
father, loathed Godoy, a sentiment that was mutual. Godoy was in fact
hated throughout Spain for the sorry state to which he had brought
the country by 1808, and in particular for the loss of her colonies to
Britain, the catastrophe at Trafalgar (where Spain lost eleven ships-of-the-
line), the weak economy, corruption, famines, the sale of clerical land,
the abolition of bull-fighting and even for the yellow fever outbreak in
the south.[58]

A tantalizing prospect presented itself in October 1807, when Ferdinand wrote to Napoleon – or rather to 'that hero who effaces all those
who preceded him', as the prince sycophantically put it – asking to
marry into the Bonaparte family.[59] His father had had him arrested for
treason (under false pretences) that month, only to release him with ill
grace, and he probably wanted to outmanoeuvre his parents as well as
to protect the throne from a French invasion. It would have been the
ideal solution, saving Napoleon from what he was later to call 'the
Spanish ulcer', but the best candidate, his eldest niece, Lucien's daughter
Charlotte, was only twelve. During her brief sojourn at Napoleon's
court she had written several letters to her parents in Rome complaining of its immorality and begging to be allowed to go home, to which
Napoleon, who had intercepted the letters, acceded.[60]*

Once Junot had occupied Lisbon he formally deposed the absent
Braganza dynasty and confiscated their property, imposed a 'contribution' of 100 million francs and promulgated a constitution which
included religious toleration, equality before the law and the freedom of

* Two years later, Lucien was captured by the Royal Navy trying to flee to America, and
spent several years in comfortable exile in Worcestershire writing unflattering poetry about
'Charlemagne' – that is, his brother.

Bay of Biscay

Ferrol
Corunna
ASTURIAS
B

Cape Finisterre
GALICIA

LEON

Burgos

Benavente
Medina del Rioseco
OLD CASTILE
Valladolid

Atlantic
Ocean

Almeida
GUADALAJARA

Salamanca
Sierra de Guadarrama
Somosierra

Fuentes d'Oñoro
San Ildefonso
Madrid

Battle of
Bussaco

Aranjuez
Talavera
Toledo
NEW

Roliça
Santarém
Lines of
Torres Vedras
Vimeiro

EXTREMADURA
SPAIN

Cintra
Lisbon

PORTUGAL

Bailén

Cordoba

ANDALUSIA

Cadiz

Cape Trafalgar
Gibraltar

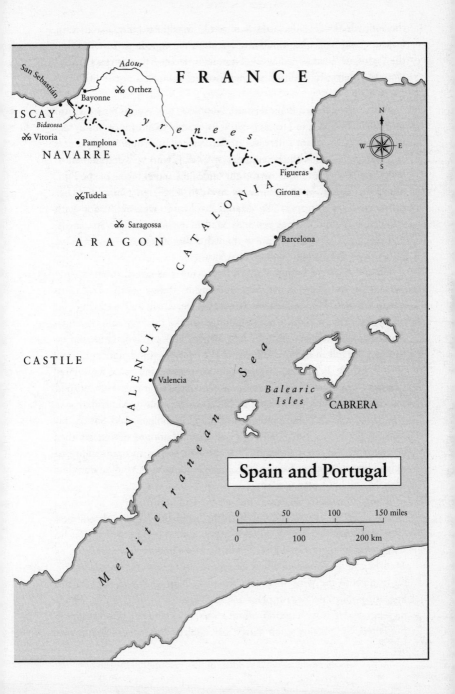

Spain and Portugal

the individual.[61] He declared that roads would be built, canals dug, industry and agriculture improved and public education fostered, but the Portuguese remained wary. Napoleon decreed that Junot's troops were to receive, in addition to their normal rations, a bottle of Portuguese wine a day.[62]

With Portugal seemingly secured, Napoleon sent troops under Murat into northern Spain in January 1808, ostensibly to aid Junot but in fact to take over the great fortresses of San Sebastián, Pamplona, Figueras and Barcelona, all with the support of Godoy, who was determined to become a sovereign in his own right under the secret terms of the Fontainebleau treaty. Spain was being invaded in all but name, with her prime minister's support. By March 13 Murat was in Burgos with 100,000 men, and moving towards Madrid itself. To lull the Spaniards, Napoleon gave orders to 'spread the word that it is part of my plan . . . to lay siege to Gibraltar and go to Africa'.[63]*

On the night of March 17, 1808 Godoy was overthrown by 'the Tumult of Aranjuez', a popular uprising 25 miles south of Madrid where the royal family had their winter palace, which had been whipped up by the rumour that he was planning to take the king and queen to America via Andalusia. A mob burst into his house to lynch him, but he successfully hid in a rolled-up carpet (or possibly some matting) in his attic.[64] Prince Ferdinand supported the revolt, and two days later Charles IV abdicated. The previous day he had reluctantly been pushed into dismissing Godoy, leading to huge celebrations in Madrid. 'I was well prepared for some changes in Spain,' Napoleon told Savary on hearing the news, 'but I believe I see that affairs are taking another course from the one I expected.'[65] Napoleon, seeing an opportunity to extend his influence, refused to recognize Ferdinand as king, saying that Charles had been his loyal ally.

When, desperate for food and water after thirty hours in hiding, Godoy tried to surrender himself to the authorities, the mob grabbed him, nearly blinded him in one eye and wounded him in the hip, but he was nevertheless arrested alive.[66] His finance minister was murdered in Madrid and the mob sacked the houses of his family and friends before moving on to the wine shops. At the time, Napoleon was seen by the Spanish public and British press as the instigator of the Tumult, which he was not. He was, however, about to try to exploit the opportunity it presented by playing each party off against the other. Spain was

---

* Gibraltar had been ceded to Britain by the 1713 Treaty of Utrecht.

strategically and economically far too important to be allowed to remain in the hands of Ferdinand, whom Napoleon suspected of being the pawn of reactionary aristocratic and Church elements (which he was) and in secret alliance with the British (which – for the moment – he wasn't).

Napoleon could ill afford to have a chaotic state on his southern border, especially one that had hitherto been providing him with a steady 5 million francs a month and even after Trafalgar possessed a large navy that he would need if he were ever to resuscitate his dream of invading Britain. Power abhors a vacuum, and the Bourbons – who had ruled Spain only since 1700, when they were installed by Louis XIV – had effectively created one. As 18 Brumaire had demonstrated, Napoleon was perfectly willing and capable to carry out a coup if he deemed it advantageous.

Now, after Tilsit, the Grande Armée had no continental commitments beyond garrison duty and some anti-guerrilla activity in Calabria. '[I] did not invade Spain in order to put one of [my] own family on the throne,' Napoleon was to claim in 1814, 'but to revolutionize her; to make her a kingdom of laws, to abolish the Inquisition, feudal rights, and the inordinate privileges of certain classes.'[67] He hoped that the modernization formula that seemed to have gone down so well in Italy, Belgium, Holland and the western parts of the Rhine Confederation might also reconcile Spaniards to his rule. There was a good deal of *post facto* rationalization in all of this of course, but he did genuinely expect his reforms to be popular with some classes in Spain, and to an extent they were. Denying that he wanted her vast Latin American treasures, he said that all he needed was 60 million francs a year to Frenchify Spain (*pour la francifier*).[68] Despite these aspirations, however, this was to be a dynastic war, unlike any of his previous ones, and in that sense it represented a break from the Revolutionary Wars of the past.

On March 21 Charles IV withdrew his abdication on the perfectly reasonable grounds that it had been made under compulsion.[69] Two days later, Murat occupied Madrid with 50,000 men of Moncey's and Dupont's corps. Initially all seemed quiet, even after Ferdinand had arrived in Madrid to wild scenes of welcome the next day. Ferdinand was under the impression that Napoleon wanted only Godoy's removal from office, and on April 10 he left Madrid bound for a conference with Napoleon near the Spanish border at Bayonne, where his parents were also headed separately. On his way to Bayonne ordinary Spaniards took off their jackets and placed them under the wheels of his carriage in order to 'preserve the marks of a journey which occasioned the happiest moment of their lives', assuming – as did Ferdinand himself – that Napoleon would recognize him as the rightful king of Spain.[70]

Napoleon arrived in Bayonne on April 15, 1808 and installed himself at the nearby Château de Marracq, where he was to remain for over three months with a detachment of the Imperial Guard bivouacked on the lawn. On the battlefield he always sought to take advantage of his opponents by striking at the hinge point where their forces were weakest: now he would do the same in his negotiations with the Bourbons. Charles and María Luisa's hatred for their son Ferdinand, and his for them, was much greater than any feelings any of them had for him. He was perfectly willing to intrude on that highly dysfunctional family's private grief, and as he had 50,000 men stationed in Madrid neither side could reign without his support. This enabled him to engineer a truly remarkable construct.

Under the terms of a series of agreements at Bayonne, Ferdinand would cede the crown of Spain back to his father Charles IV, on condition that Charles should then immediately cede it in turn to Napoleon, who would then pass it to his own brother Joseph.[71] Meanwhile, Godoy was spirited out of Spain by Murat, to the delight of María Luisa who could now be with him, and it seemed that yet another country had fallen into the lap of the Bonaparte family. 'Unless I am mistaken,' Napoleon told Talleyrand on April 25, 'this tragedy is in Act Five; the denouement will soon play out.'[72]

He was wrong: only the second act was about to begin. On May 2, with rumours leaking from Bayonne and by this stage expecting the worst, the people of Madrid (*madrileños*) rose in revolt against Murat's occupation, killing about 150 of his men in the insurrection known as El Dos de Mayo.[73] As in Pavia, Cairo and Calabria, the French brutally suppressed the uprising. They were not, however, facing a united national uprising in Spain. In some regions, such as Aragon, there was very little opposition to French rule; in others such as Navarre, there was a great deal. The Cortes in Cadiz found it just as difficult as Joseph would do to raise taxes or impose conscription.[74] Spain was of such a size that in the provinces that did rebel, regional insurgent governments (*juntas*) could be set up around the country and France had to fight a war against both the regular Spanish army and local guerrilla bands.

The French started by besieging Girona, Valencia, Saragossa and other strategically important cities – indeed there were more sieges undertaken in the Peninsular War than in all other theatres of the Napoleonic Wars put together.[75] Thus even while Calabria was still not pacified, Napoleon undertook the occupation of another, far bigger territory in which much the same factors were in play: bad communications, fanatical Catholic priests, a hardened, primitive peasantry, a Legitimist Bourbon monarchy with a far better claim to the people's loyalty than the Bonaparte candidate, and every prospect of easy resupply by the Royal Navy. Spain had been easily defeated by France in 1794–5 and Napoleon assumed that in the absence of any Spanish general and army of any distinction, it would happen again. Despite the experience of Calabria, he had not learned how effective a guerrilla insurgency can sometimes be against even the most powerful and well-disciplined army. It didn't help that Napoleon interfered with his generals' fighting of the war in Spain after he left, moving units from places where they had become familiar with the terrain, and sending orders to officers that arrived only after they had been made irrelevant by events.

'Grapeshot and the bayonet cleared the streets,' Murat reported to Napoleon from Madrid.[76] After the insurrection was over, Murat had groups of peasant insurgents shot by firing squad, in scenes later immortalized by Francisco Goya which can today be seen at the Prado. Years later, Napoleon's secretary inserted into his memoirs an entirely forged letter, purportedly written by Napoleon to Murat from Bayonne on March 29, 1808, urging caution and moderation.[77] Generations of historians fell for this Bonapartist fraud before the truth was discovered, despite Napoleon not having arrived in Bayonne until April 15. A letter that Napoleon genuinely did write to Murat, however, on the Dos de Mayo, read: 'I will give you the kingdom of Naples or of Portugal. Give me your answer immediately as this must happen in a day.'[78] (Luckily for him, Murat chose Naples, as within three months a British army had arrived in Portugal.)

Although the Dos de Mayo revolt certainly had patriotic, anti-French, anti-atheist and pro-Ferdinand aspects to it, there were also issues of class, land ownership, military desertion, smuggling, regionalism, anti-conscription lawlessness, anti-clericalism, food shortages and a collapse in trade that made the coming war vastly more complex than the simple narrative of a struggle between grasping French invaders and heroic Spanish resisters, though there were undoubtedly elements of that.[79] A few of the militarized bands fighting the French – such as those of Juan Martín Díez in Guadalajara and Francisco Espoz y Mina in Navarre – were well organized, but many were little more than bandit gangs of the kind Napoleon had suppressed in France as First Consul, and that any government would have had to act against. As in any guerrilla insurgency, some of the partisans were motivated by patriotism, others by revenge for what were undeniably atrocities, others by opportunism, and several bandit groups preyed on their fellow Spaniards. The Imperial Guard's Captain Blaze found many villages in which the local people simply didn't differentiate between the French army and Spanish brigands.[80]

When the news of the Dos de Mayo arrived from Madrid, Napoleon decided to expedite the very outcome that the rioters had most hoped to avoid. On May 6, after an hour-long ceremony in which everybody – even the poor old gouty and rheumatic Charles IV – was kept standing, Ferdinand VII signed the Treaty of Bayonne, abdicating in favour of his father.* Charles, keen that his hated son shouldn't succeed him, two days later handed over all his rights to Napoleon and requested asylum in France.[81] Writing to persuade Joseph to accept the throne, Napoleon said: 'Spain is not Naples; it has eleven million people, a revenue of more than 150 million francs, without counting the immense colonial revenues and the possession of "all the Americas". It is a crown that installs you in Madrid three days from France, which covers one of her borders. Naples is at the end of the world.'[82] Later he would repent at leisure, saying 'I committed a great mistake in putting that fool of a Joseph on the Spanish throne.'[83] When Joseph was crowned in Madrid in July, Murat took over his Neapolitan crown, and Louis and Hortense's eldest surviving son, the three-year-old Prince Napoléon-Louis, filled Murat's place as Grand Duke of Berg.

To keep him under Napoleon's control should the Spanish people reject the Bayonne arrangements, Ferdinand stayed at Talleyrand's country estate at Valençay, which he allowed his supporters to characterize as a kidnapping and imprisonment.† When the dashing

---

* At Brooks's Club in St James's Street in London, on July 5 Humphrey Howarth MP wagered the 4th Earl of Cholmondeley 100 guineas to 25 'that Joseph Buonaparte is not at this period exercising sovereign authority in Madrid or its neighbourhood' (Brooks's Club Betting Book). The French were indeed in control there, although Joseph didn't arrive until July 20.

† Talleyrand did well out of the arrangement, as Ferdinand laid down carpets costing 200,000 francs, bought a hydraulic engine to supply the chateau with water and even paid for the vegetables he took from the kitchen garden (Kolli, *Memoirs* p. 3).

twenty-eight-year-old colonel of his Guard, Don José de Palafox, suggested that he try to escape, Ferdinand said he preferred to remain there doing his embroidery and cutting out paper patterns.[84] (When he did return to Spain, in the spring of 1814, he cancelled all of Napoleon's liberal reforms and even reintroduced the Inquisition.) 'The King of Prussia is a hero compared to the Prince of the Asturias,' Napoleon told Talleyrand; 'he is indifferent to everything; very materialistic, eats four times a day and hasn't got a single idea in his head.'[85] Napoleon asked Talleyrand to make sure that Ferdinand enjoyed Valençay. 'If the Prince of the Asturias became attached to a pretty woman there will be no harm,' he wrote, 'especially if she can be depended upon.'[86] So affected was Ferdinand by what is today known as Stockholm Syndrome that he wrote to Napoleon in November 1808 to congratulate him on a French victory over the Spanish army at the battle of Tudela, and once again tried to solicit marriage with a Bonaparte. His father Charles IV travelled first to Marseilles and then went to live quietly in Rome for the rest of his life. Although Napoleon agreed to pay the Bourbons a pension of 10 million francs per annum, he ensured that it was all refunded by Spain, and as early as July 1808 was writing to Mollien: 'There is no rush in paying the King of Spain's pension – he is not short of cash.'[87]

For all the criticism that was to fall upon Napoleon for his Spanish heist, it is often forgotten that during the same year Tsar Alexander simply took Finland from Sweden in a short but equally illegitimate war. 'I sold Finland for Spain,' as Napoleon said, but he got the worst of the deal.[88] He hadn't needed to make explicit threats against anyone or even really to fight at all for the Spanish throne to fall into his hands, but his error was to believe, as he told Talleyrand in May, that 'The Spaniards are like other peoples and not a race apart; they will be happy to accept the imperial institutions.' Instead, they dubbed Joseph 'El Rey Intruso' (the intruder king), and even before he entered Madrid there were full-scale insurrections in Biscay, Catalonia, Navarre, Valencia, Andalusia, Estremadura, Galicia, León, the Asturias and part of both Castiles, and many Iberian ports were handed over to the Royal Navy. Napoleon's impatience had got the better of him. As Savary later admitted: 'We rushed the outcome of the affair, and we didn't show enough consideration for national self-esteem.'[89]

On June 2 Napoleon brought together as many Spanish grandees at Bayonne as he could muster in order to ratify the first written constitution of the Spanish-speaking world.[90] This abolished privileges and the Inquisition, preserved the national parliament (Cortes) with three estates and established Catholicism as the country's sole religion. It certainly appealed to those pro-French collaborators, largely from the liberal, enlightened, middle and professional classes, known as the *josefinos* or *afrancesados* (Francophiles), but they made up only a small minority of the population of what was then very much still a rural, illiterate, economically backward, ultra-Catholic and reactionary country. (Seats on Spanish town councils had been hereditary until 1804 and the Inquisition was still in operation.)

'I seized by the hair the chance Fortune gave me to regenerate Spain,' Napoleon later told one of his secretaries.[91] Perhaps one of the reasons he expected the Spanish to co-operate with his regime was that his own father had been just such a pro-French collaborator; if so he ought to have recalled his own youthful hatred of the French occupying Corsica, and to have seen Spain as Corsica writ large. Even Napoleon's chamberlain and admirer Bausset had to admit that the constitution was received 'with a silent and equivocal indifference' in French-occupied Spain but with 'bitter contempt' everywhere else.[92]

On May 25 the fortified medieval city of Saragossa, the capital of Aragon, rose in revolt under the command of Colonel Palafox, who had escaped from France dressed as a peasant. He had only 220 men and the Spanish equivalent of £20 6s 8d in the treasury, but nonetheless he declared war on the French Empire.[93] Although on June 8 at Tudela General Charles Lefebvre-Desnouettes had flung aside a force commanded by Palafox's elder brother, the Marquis of Lazán, by the time he tried to storm Saragossa a week later with 6,000 men he was rebuffed with 700 casualties; the first siege of the city of 60,000 people began. When Lefebvre-Desnouettes demanded Palafox's surrender with two words, '*La capitulation*', Palafox replied with three: '*Guerra al cuchillo*' (War by knife).[94]

Although one of Napoleon's primary reasons for invading Spain had been to try to secure the Spanish navy so that the dream of invading Britain could be resuscitated, on June 14 Admiral Villeneuve's successor, Admiral François de Rosily-Mesros, was forced to surrender to the Spanish army that small part of the French fleet – six ships – moored at Cadiz that had not been sunk or captured at Trafalgar.* Napoleon suffered another blow on June 25 when he heard that Archduke Charles

---

* Yet even that didn't end Napoleon's naval plans, and very many of the letters he wrote to Decrès in 1808 covered different aspects of ship-building, the types of trees needed, their

had ordered a 150,000-man levy to be raised in Austria. He had Champagny warn Vienna that his army was still 300,000 strong, but it had no effect. A month later he told Jérôme: 'Austria is arming; she is denying it; she is therefore arming against us ... If Austria is arming, we should too ... There's no grudge between Austria and me, I ask nothing from her, and the only reason I'm arming is because she is.'[95]

Napoleon assumed that even if Joseph wasn't welcomed as a saviour-reformer in Spain, he could always defeat the Spanish army in the field, and indeed on July 14 Bessières did defeat Captain-General Don Gregorio de la Cuesta and the Spanish Army of Galicia at the battle of Medina del Rioseco. Yet only eight days later a catastrophe befell French arms when General Pierre Dupont surrendered his entire corps of 18,000 men, 36 guns and all his colours to General Francisco Castaños's Army of Andalusia after being defeated at the battle of Bailén. When the Royal Navy, which had not been party to the surrender terms, refused to repatriate Dupont's army back to France as promised by Castaños, his troops were despatched to the Balearic isle of Cabrera, where more than half were starved to death, though Dupont and his senior officers were allowed home.[96]

The news of Bailén reverberated around Europe; it was France's worst defeat on land since 1793. Napoleon was of course completely livid. He court-martialled Dupont, imprisoned him in the Fort de Joux for two years and stripped him of his peerage (he had been a count of the empire), later saying, 'Out of all the generals who served in Spain, we ought to have selected a certain number and sent them to the scaffold. Dupont made us lose the Peninsula in order to secure his plunder.'[97] While it was true that Dupont's army was loaded down after sacking Córdoba, few French generals could have escaped the trap Castaños had set for him. Nonetheless Napoleon insisted that Cécile, the wife of General Armand de Marescot who had signed the capitulation, be dismissed as one of Josephine's ladies-in-waiting, 'no matter how innocent she may be'. At a Tuileries reception he grabbed the wrist of General Legendre, who had also signed it, demanding, 'Why didn't this hand wither?'[98]

'He seemed to do everything very well at the head of a division,' Napoleon wrote to Clarke of Dupont, 'he has done horribly as a chief.'[99] It was a problem that was to recur so frequently with Napoleon's

---

felling and transportation, the storage of timber, and so on. In July 1810 he wrote to Decrès of his plans to have a 110-ship navy by the end of 1812 (ed. Bingham, *Selection* III p. 50).

subordinates that Napoleon himself has been blamed for it, accused of being so controlling as to stifle initiative. On occasion he reproached himself for the fact that most of his lieutenants, even marshals, seemed to perform at their best only when he was present. Yet besides being ordered into Andalusia, Dupont had not been inundated with orders. 'In war, men are nothing, but one man is everything,' Napoleon wrote to Joseph on August 30.[100] Long interpreted as an egotistical expression of heartlessness towards his own troops, this was in fact written in reference to Dupont, in a letter full of self-criticism: 'Up to now we had to look for examples of this only in the history of our enemies; unfortunately today we find it in our own midst.' Far from being a paean to his own genius, it was in fact a recognition that a bad leader could bring disaster.

'You should not think it anything extraordinary to conquer a kingdom,' Napoleon had written to Joseph before he heard the news of Bailén. 'Philip V and Henri IV were obliged to conquer theirs. Be gay, and do not allow yourself to be affected, and do not doubt that things will finish better and more quickly than you think.'[101] Joseph scuttled out of his capital only eleven days after he arrived, fleeing 135 miles north to Burgos. The sieges of Girona and Saragossa were raised on August 14 and 16; Bessières withdrew from the Portuguese border, and large numbers of troops began to be diverted to Spain from the rest of the Empire. 'The army is perfectly organized to tackle the insurgents,' Napoleon told Joseph on August 16, 'but it needs a head.'[102] Of course that should have been him, but back in June he had arranged to meet Tsar Alexander for another conference in September, so even a letter from Joseph asking for permission to abdicate, which sent Napoleon into another fury, didn't persuade him to go to Spain. He would not appear there for another three months, during which time the situation steadily worsened.

While Joseph huddled in Burgos, Napoleon, who had left Bayonne on the night of July 22, visited Pau, Toulouse (where he visited the Canal du Midi), Montauban, Bordeaux (where he received the news of Bailén on August 2), Pons, Rochefort (where he visited the prefecture, dockyards, arsenal and hospital), Niort, Fontenay (where he visited the new town of Napoléon-Vendée which he had ordered to be built three years earlier), Nantes (where he attended a ball at the Rouge Chapeau Circus with Josephine, who had come to join him), Saumur, Tours, Saint-Cloud (where he went hunting and had a heated 75-minute discussion with Prince Clemens von Metternich about Austrian rearmament), Versailles (where he watched the ballet *Vénus et Adonis*) and the Tuileries (where he met the Persian ambassador). At the supposedly model town of Napoléon-Vendée he was so furious that the houses had only been built from mud and straw that he took out his sword and drove it into one of the walls up to the hilt, before sacking the builder responsible. In Toulouse he asked to see the man who had built a bridge over the Midi canal. In the course of questioning the engineer-in-chief who presented himself, Napoleon realized that although he was hoping to take the credit, he couldn't have built the bridge, so he told the prefect, M. Trouvé, to produce the real bridge-builder, to whom he said, 'I'm happy that I came myself, otherwise I'd not have known that you were the author of such a fine work, and would have deprived you of the reward to which you're entitled.' With a poetic justice found all too rarely in history, he then gave the bridge-builder the engineer-in-chief's job.

On September 7, Napoleon received more bad news, this time of Junot's surrender to the British in Portugal, having lost the battles of Roliça and Vimeiro to Sir Arthur Wellesley commanding a small British expeditionary force of only 13,000 men.* Under the very lenient terms of the Convention of Cintra signed on August 30 – for which Wellesley was later court-martialled, though afterwards acquitted – Junot's army, with its arms and even its booty, was returned to France by the Royal Navy, but nothing could disguise the fact that France had lost Portugal. Napoleon has been criticized for not taking Wellington (as he became in August 1809) more seriously at this juncture, but seen in the context of Britain's earlier failed amphibious excursions – against Holland in 1799, Naples in 1805, northern Germany in 1805–6, Stralsund, Alexandria and South America in 1807 and Sweden in 1808 – his attitude was understandable. Over the next five years Wellington enormously helped the Spanish and Portuguese regular and guerrilla forces to expel the French from Iberia at the cost of fewer than 10,000 British lives. When it became clear that Wellington was indeed likely to be a formidable opponent, in August 1810 Napoleon inserted a paragraph in the *Moniteur* describing him as a mere 'sepoy general', that is a soldier who had only commanded Indian troops. He was perhaps unaware that the Indian soldiers fighting for the British included some superb fighting men.[103]

---

* Going over the details of the battle of Vimeiro with Thiébault five months afterwards, Thiébault was impressed by the way that Napoleon 'laid his finger on most of the weak points in our disposition, and I was amazed to find that he really remembered the contents of my report better than I did myself' (ed. Butler, *Baron Thiébault* II p. 238).

From Saint-Cloud on September 18 Napoleon issued another classic proclamation, promising peace once 'the leopard' (that is, England) was defeated, Gibraltar captured and Bailén avenged. 'Soldiers, I have need of you,' he declared.

> The hideous presence of the leopard defiles Spain and Portugal; at your approach let him fly away in terror. Let us carry our triumphant eagles to the Pillars of Hercules [that is, Gibraltar], there also we have insults to avenge. Soldiers, you have surpassed the renown of modern armies, have you yet equalled the glories of the armies of Rome, who in the same campaign triumphed on the Rhine, the Euphrates, in Illyria, and on the Tagus? A long peace and durable prosperity will be the prize of your labours.[104]

Such a victory ought to be all the easier because, as he told Joseph of his new subjects, 'The Spanish people are despicable and cowardly, and remind me of Arabs I have known.'[105]

Napoleon had used his time in Paris productively, ensuring that the legislature passed a measure calling up 160,000 recruits from the classes of 1806 to 1809. He visited a panorama depicting Tilsit in the Boulevard des Capucines on the 21st, and the next day left for Erfurt, 400 miles away, a distance he covered in five days.

The conference at Erfurt took place against a background of noticeably cooler Franco-Russian relations. It was, as he put it to Savary, 'the moment to judge the solidity of my work at Tilsit'.[106] Napoleon had been writing warm letters to Alexander throughout the year – 'In these few lines I've expressed my entire soul to your Majesty ... our work at Tilsit will determine the destiny of the world' – but with the crisis of the Friedland defeat abated and Finland ingested into his Empire, Alexander was growing lukewarm about an alliance that was costing him a good deal domestically because of the deeply unpopular Continental System.[107] Earlier that month he had written to his mother, the Dowager Empress Maria Feodorovna, saying 'Our interest obliged me' to conclude an alliance with Napoleon, but 'We will see his fall with calmness, if such is the will of God ... the wisest policy is to await the right moment to take measures.'[108] Going to Erfurt was necessary, he told her, because 'it would save Austria and conserve its strength for the true moment when it can be used for the general good. This moment may be near, but it has not sounded; to accelerate it would be to ruin everything, to lose everything.' Meanwhile, Russia 'must be able to breathe freely for a while and, during this precious time, augment our means and our forces ... It is only in the most profound silence that we must work, and not in publicizing our armaments and our preparations, nor in declaring loudly against the one whom we are defying.'[109] In these private letters Alexander still called him 'Bonaparte' or sometimes 'the Corsican'.[110] While ordering his foreign minister, Count Nikolai Rumiantsev, to stay close to France, Alexander was preparing, diplomatically and militarily, for 'the right moment to take measures'.

The pretty Thuringian town of Erfurt was chosen for the conference because it was a French enclave in the middle of the Confederation of the Rhine, a principality that had been a personal fiefdom of Napoleon's since Tilsit. Napoleon met Alexander on the road 5 miles outside the town on Wednesday, September 28; they descended from their carriages and 'cordially embraced'.[111] Alexander wore the grand cross of the Légion d'Honneur, Napoleon the Russian order of St Andrew. At Tilsit Alexander had given Napoleon the malachite furniture now in the Emperor's Salon at the Grand Trianon at Versailles, so at Erfurt Napoleon gave Alexander one of only two sets of the Sèvres porcelain Egyptian service which featured scenes from Denon's *Voyage dans la Basse et la Haute Égypte*. It has rightly been described as one of the most lavish gifts ever given by one sovereign to another.[112]* Napoleon placed Alexander at his right hand at meals, they visited each other's apartments, led each other down to the entrance halls on receiving and saying farewell each time, and dined together almost every day. They even took it in turns to give the grand marshal the night-watch passwords every evening.

One can still see where the Tsar lodged in the Angerplatz, and where Napoleon stayed in what is now the state chancellery, as well as where they met in the classically baroque 1715 Kaisersaal. Napoleon took a large entourage, including Berthier, Duroc, Maret, Champagny (the foreign minister), Rémusat, Savary, Caulaincourt, Daru, Lauriston, Méneval, Fain, his doctor Yvan, four equerries and eight pages.[113] He had dismissed Talleyrand as foreign minister in August 1807 because the kings of Bavaria and Württemberg had complained about how much he was demanding in bribes.[114] He nevertheless retained him as Vice-Grand Elector, with access to the palaces and his person. Napoleon enjoyed Talleyrand's company – 'You are aware of the esteem and attachment I entertain for that minister,' he told Rapp – so he was therefore prepared to overlook, and perhaps did not fully realize, that this

---

* The other set was made for Josephine, but in 1818 Louis XVIII presented it to Wellington, and it can be seen today at Apsley House in London.

access allowed Talleyrand to sell secrets whenever he chose. He took him to Erfurt for his experience and advice. Since Talleyrand had encouraged Napoleon to execute the Duc d'Enghien, drew up the Berlin Decrees instituting the Continental System and supported the invasion of Spain, it is a wonder that he still took his advice, but he did. It was a serious error to bring him now, because Talleyrand hadn't forgiven Napoleon for his dismissal, and (in return for cash) he leaked French plans to both the Russians and the Austrians, while advising Napoleon to withdraw from Germany.[115] 'Sire,' Talleyrand said to Alexander at the first of several secret meetings at Erfurt, 'what have you come to do here? It is for you to save Europe, and the only way of doing this will be for you to resist Napoleon. The French are a civilised people; their sovereign is not.'[116]

Alexander brought twenty-six senior officials in his entourage. There were also four kings present – those of Bavaria, Saxony, Westphalia and Württemberg – as well as the Prince Primate of the Confederation, Karl Dalberg, two grand dukes and twenty other princes, whose order of precedence was established by the date that they acceded to the Rhine Confederation. (Bausset rightly identified this as a clever move by Napoleon to give the Confederation more prestige.[117]) The overt friendliness – and the balls, concerts, reviews, receptions, banquets, plays, hunting trips and fireworks – did not mean that the negotiations were easy. Most of the important discussions were conducted tête-à-tête between the two emperors. 'Your Emperor Alexander is as stubborn as a mule,' Napoleon told Caulaincourt. 'He plays deaf when things are said that he is reluctant to hear.'[118] Napoleon teased Caulaincourt about being pro-Russian (hence the 'your') but it was true that the Tsar didn't want to listen to Napoleon's evidence of Russian customs inspectors surreptitiously allowing British produce into St Petersburg and elsewhere. At one point during the negotiations, Napoleon threw his hat on the ground and started kicking it. 'You're hot-tempered while I'm stubborn,' said an unruffled Alexander. 'But by anger no one can get anywhere with me. Let's talk, discuss things, otherwise I will leave.'[119]

Russia's adherence to the Continental System had damaged her economy, preventing her from selling wheat, timber, tallow and hemp to Britain. The mere existence of the Duchy of Warsaw left her concerned about the re-emergence of a kingdom of Poland. For his part, Napoleon looked unfavourably on Russian schemes against Turkey, not wanting a Russian warm-water fleet in the Mediterranean. Much of the talk at Erfurt was speculative. Napoleon approved in theory of Alexander's desire for territorial gain against Turkey in Moldovia and Wallachia – for which France would be compensated – while Alexander in theory promised to 'make common cause' with Napoleon in the event of a French war against Austria, even though another Austrian defeat would tilt the European balance of power yet further towards France.

It seems that one matter Napoleon might have discussed was the possibility of divorcing Josephine, because only eight days after Alexander returned to St Petersburg the Dowager Empress announced the marriage of her daughter, Alexander's sister the Grand Duchess Catherine Pavlovna, to Prince George of Holstein-Oldenburg, the younger brother of the heir to the Duchy of Oldenburg, a Baltic coastal duchy not part of the Rhine Confederation. By a special *ukaz* (decree) of Tsar Paul I, Alexander's sisters could marry only with the permission of their mother, so Alexander could genuinely claim that he did not have the final say despite being 'the Autocrat of All the Russias'. With Alexander's other unmarried sister Anna only thirteen, both Romanov girls seemed to have been saved from what Maria Feodorovna may have seen as the threatened ravages of the Corsican minotaur.

Napoleon took advantage of being in Erfurt to meet his greatest living literary hero, who lived only 15 miles away in Weimar. On October 2, 1808, Goethe lunched with Napoleon at Erfurt, with Talleyrand, Daru, Savary and Berthier in attendance. As he entered the room, the Emperor exclaimed, '*Voilà un homme!*' (Here's a man!), or possibly '*Vous êtes un homme!*' (You're a man!).[120] The two men discussed *Werther*, Voltaire's play *Mahomet*, which Goethe had translated, and drama in general.* Napoleon complained that Voltaire should not have 'made such an unfavourable portrait of the world-conqueror' Julius Caesar in his play *La Mort de César*.[121] Goethe later reported that Napoleon 'made observations at a high intellectual level, as a man who has studied the tragical scene with the attention of a criminal judge'. Napoleon told him he felt that French theatre had strayed too far from nature and truth. 'What have we now to do with Fate?' he asked, referring to plays in which prearranged destiny formed the determining agency. 'Politics is fate.'[122] When Soult arrived, Napoleon spent a few moments addressing Polish

---

* Napoleon's well-thumbed copy of Goethe's epistolary and loosely autobiographical novel *The Sorrows of Young Werther*, complete with the imperial coat of arms embossed in gold on the front and back, can today be seen in the Pierpont Morgan Library in New York. It has been read so often that the pages are barely attached to the binding. That edition was published in Paris in 1804, which suggests that Napoleon read the book regularly even after becoming emperor.

affairs, allowing Goethe to look at tapestries and portraits, before returning to discussing Goethe's personal life and family – '*Gleich gegen Gleich*' (on equal terms), as Goethe later put it.

They met again at a ball in Weimar four days later, where the Emperor told the author that tragedy 'should be the training ground of kings and peoples, and is the highest achievement of the poet'.[123] (He wrote to Josephine that Alexander 'danced a lot, but not me: forty years are forty years'.[124]) Napoleon suggested that Goethe write another play on Caesar's assassination, portraying it as a blunder. He went on to denounce Tacitus' prejudices, obscurantism and 'detestable style', and also the way that Shakespeare mixed comedy with tragedy, 'the terrible with the burlesque', and expressed his surprise that such a 'great spirit' as Goethe could admire such undefined genres.[125] Napoleon did not give his opinions didactically, but regularly ended by asking, 'What do you think, Herr Goethe?'[126] He unsuccessfully pressed Goethe to move to Paris, where he said he would find a broader view of the world and an abundance of material for poetic treatment, and he conferred the Légion d'Honneur on him before they parted. Goethe was to describe his time discussing literature and poetry with Napoleon as one of the most gratifying experiences of his life.[127]

The Emperor and Tsar spent eighteen days in each other's company at Erfurt. They watched plays almost every night, sitting together on thrones set apart from the rest of the audience; reviewed each other's regiments (Napoleon was keen that Alexander see as much of the Grande Armée going through its manoeuvres as possible); spoke long into the night; shared the same carriages on visits; shot stag and roebuck together (killing fifty-seven) and toured the battlefield of Jena, lunching where Napoleon had bivouacked the night before the battle. When Alexander noticed that he had left his sword at his palace, Napoleon took off his own and presented it to him 'with all possible grace', and the Tsar said, 'I accept it as a mark of your friendship: Your Majesty is well assured that I shall never draw it against you!'[128] Watching the first scene of *Oedipus* on October 3, when the actor playing Philoctetes said to the hero's friend and confidant Dimas, 'A great man's friendship is a gift of the gods!', Alexander turned to Napoleon 'and presented to him his hand, with all the grace possible'. The wildly applauding audience saw Napoleon bow in reply, 'with an air of refusing to take to himself so embarrassing a compliment'.[129] A few nights later they spoke for three hours alone together after dinner. 'I'm happy with Alexander;

I think he is with me,' Napoleon told Josephine on October 11. 'Were he a woman, I think I'd take him as my lover [*amoureuse*]. I'll be with you shortly; stay well, and may I find you plump and fresh [*grasse et fraîche*].'[130]

The Erfurt talks reinforced the agreement reached at Tilsit to divide Europe between France and Russia, but despite the many hours of intimate discussions Napoleon and Alexander came to few concrete arrangements. Although they couldn't agree on dismembering Turkey, by a secret article of the Erfurt Convention signed on October 12 Napoleon recognized Finland, Moldavia and Wallachia as part of the Russian Empire and agreed that France would join Russia if Austria opposed these arrangements by force. Alexander agreed to recognize Joseph as king of Spain, and promised to come to Napoleon's aid should Austria attack France, although crucially the precise extent of any help wasn't discussed in detail. That day, Napoleon wrote to George III to offer Britain peace once more in familiar terms – 'We are gathered here to beg your Majesty to listen to the voice of humanity' – a plea that was again ignored by the British government.[131] The two emperors embraced and took their leave on October 14, near the spot on the Erfurt–Weimar road where they had met. They were never to see each other again.

Napoleon's writ now ran from the Channel ports to the Elbe, in central Germany up to the Oder–Neisse line, in southern Germany to the River Inn and beyond. In Italy he controlled everywhere but the Papal States and Calabria. Denmark was his ally, Holland was ruled by his brother. The glaring exception to his control of western Europe was Spain, where no fewer than half a million of his troops were to serve over the next six years, including significant numbers of Dutch, Germans, Italians and Poles. 'This war could be over in one fell swoop with a clever manoeuvre,' Napoleon told Joseph on October 13 of the fighting in Spain, 'but I must be there for that.'[132] By November 5 he was at the Basque city of Vitoria in northern Spain, indignant as ever with the war commissariat, sending a series of letters to General Dejean, the war administration minister, complaining, 'Your reports to me are nothing but paper ... Yet again, my army is naked as it's about to start campaigning ... It's like throwing money into the water', and 'I'm being told fairy tales ... Those at the head of your department are stupid or thieves. Never has one been so badly served and betrayed', and so on.[133] He absolutely refused to pay local contractors for sixty-eight mules that had been supplied to the artillery, because they were three and four years old and 'I gave the order only to buy mules that are five years old.'[134]

It is estimated that there were only 35,000–50,000 guerrillas operating in Spain. Even in regions they controlled completely there was not much co-operation between bands; when the French had been forced out of an area, many of the guerrilla fighters simply returned to their villages.[135] But even once Napoleon had recaptured Madrid at the end of the year and attempted to establish control from the centre outwards, the large distances and poor roads made it hard for the French to impose their will.[136]

Lines of communication were constantly harried by the guerrillas in a countryside that was perfect for ambushes, until it got to the point where it took two hundred men to escort a single despatch. In 1811 Masséna would need 70,000 men merely to maintain safe communications between Madrid and France.[137] All told, the Spanish and Portuguese guerrillas killed more Frenchmen than the British, Portuguese and Spanish regular armies combined, and also ensured that *josefino* civilians caught collaborating with the French, supplying them with information or food, faced summary execution.[138] (As before, Britain stepped in quickly to help finance the opposition to Napoleon, giving various local *juntas* in Spain and Portugal an average of £2.65 million each year between 1808 and 1814.[139]) Once the French started responding to guerrilla terror tactics – which included mutilation (especially of the genitals), blinding, castration, crucifixions, nailing to doors, sawing in half, decapitation, burying alive, skinning alive, and so on – with almost equally vicious measures, the fighting in Spain swiftly took on a character that was a far cry from the warfare of élan, *esprit de corps* and gorgeous uniforms that had characterized Napoleon's earlier campaigns, which for all their carnage had been generally free of deliberate torture and sadism.[140] When Spanish *banditti* – men not in regular army uniform – were captured, they were hanged. There was no logic to killing a uniformed regular soldier in battle and not hanging a bandit when captured.

'I'm pretty well,' Napoleon reported to Josephine on November 5 as he assumed command of the army on the Ebro, resolving to march on Madrid, 'and I hope that all this will soon be ended.'[141] If the war in Spain could have been won in the manner of his earlier campaigns, by defeating the enemy's regular army and occupying his capital, it is safe to assume that Napoleon would have soon been victorious. He quickly appreciated that this was not going to happen, telling General Dumas, who had complained about being left in the rear of Soult's army at

Burgos, 'General, in such a theatre of war there is no rear nor van ... you will have employment enough here.'[142]

At 3 a.m. on November 30, Napoleon was 5 miles from the pass at Somosierra, which protected the route to Madrid. Clad in a 'superb fur' given to him by Tsar Alexander, he was warming himself by a campfire and, 'seeing himself on the point of engaging in an important affair, was unable to sleep'. At the battle later that day, his 11,000 men ground down and pushed back the smaller Spanish regular forces of 7,800 before Napoleon unleashed two charges of Polish lancers and one of the Guard chasseurs, which took the pass and sixteen guns. After the battle, Napoleon ordered the whole Imperial Guard to present arms to the much reduced Polish squadron as it rode past.[143]

Reaching Madrid on December 2, Napoleon recognized that the best-defended place there was the Retiro Palace, which Murat had fortified. Some shells were exchanged, and on the morning of the 3rd Bausset, who spoke Spanish and thus translated for the Emperor, recorded that Napoleon walked outside the walls 'without taking much notice of the projectiles which were discharged from the highest points of Madrid'.[144] The city capitulated at 6 a.m. on the 4th but Napoleon stayed at Chamartin, his headquarters in a small country house just outside Madrid, going into the capital only once, incognito, to inspect Joseph's Royal Palace, which he was astonished to see the Spanish had respected, including David's portrait of him crossing the Alps and the 'precious wines' in the royal cellar. He pardoned the Marquis de Saint-Simon, a French émigré who had been captured while firing on French troops from Madrid's Fuencarral gate, after his daughter pleaded for his life.[145]

Napoleon stayed at Chamartin until December 22, when he heard news that a British expeditionary force under General Sir John Moore had returned to Salamanca, 110 miles west of Madrid. Bausset recorded that he 'experienced a lively joy at finding that he could at last meet these enemies on *terra firma*'.[146] Moore began to retreat towards Corunna on December 23, and to pursue him Napoleon had to cross the Sierra de Guadarrama mountain range in gales and blizzards. Together with the Alpine crossing and the Eylau campaign this convinced him that his men were hardy enough for any climatic conditions, a disastrous conclusion for his decision-making in the future. Up in the mountains, Napoleon fell off his horse, but was unhurt.[147] For most of the crossing he went on foot at the head of one of the columns, through weather that froze Bausset's brandy-sozzled servant to death on the mountainside.[148] 'We passed the mountains of Guadarrama in a frightful hurricane,' recalled Gonneville, 'the snow was driven by whirlwinds and fell with extreme violence, enveloping and covering us with a thick coating that made its way through our cloaks ... There was incredible difficulty in taking the artillery over.'[149] They managed it, however, with Napoleon continually pressing them on, even though on occasion the *grognards* swore at him to his face. 'My love,' he wrote to Josephine from Benavente on the last day of 1808, 'I've been in pursuit of the English for some days; but they keep on flying in panic.'[150] The English were not in fact panicking, merely pragmatically withdrawing before his far larger force.

Although Napoleon was looking forward to catching up with Moore and throwing the British off the peninsula, his spies in Vienna were warning him that Austria was rearming fast, indeed might be mobilizing. Years later Wellington would claim that Napoleon left Spain because 'he was not sure of victory' against Moore, but that is quite wrong.[151] 'I am pursuing the English, sword to their kidneys,' Napoleon wrote on January 3, 1809.[152] Yet the next day the dire news from Austria compelled him to hand over the pursuit to Soult, so that he could return to Benavente and then Valladolid to assume better communications with France.[153] From Valladolid he sent his Polish aide-de-camp Adam Chlapowski to Darmstadt, Frankfurt, Cassel and Dresden to warn the German princes that they needed 'to ready their forces immediately for war', and another aide-de-camp, the son of the Comte de Marbeuf, his family's benefactor from Corsica, to Stuttgart and Munich with the same message.[154]

At Valladolid, Napoleon suppressed the Dominican monastery when the corpse of a French officer was found in its well.[155] He summoned all forty monks and furiously 'expressed himself somewhat militarily, and plainly used a very strong word', in Bausset's prim reminiscence of the event. The diplomat Théodore d'Hédouville, who was translating, passed over the expletive, upon which Napoleon 'ordered him to deliver the villainous word in question with firmness, and the same tone'.[156] In the middle of January, when he became certain of the need to return to Paris, he asked Joseph to put some apartments aside for him in the Royal Palace for the time when he could come back to Madrid.[157] He never did.

The 'Spanish ulcer' forced Napoleon to station 300,000 men in the Iberian peninsula in the winter of 1808; the number rose to 370,000 for the spring offensive of 1810 and to 406,000 in 1811, before falling to

290,000 in 1812 and to 224,000 in 1813. Except at the very beginning, these were troops he simply could not afford to spare.[158] Too often he sent untested conscript battalions, led by elderly or wounded veterans or inexperienced National Guard officers, and conscripts were grouped together rather than being fed into established regiments to make up losses.[159] He constantly raided units fighting in Spain to fill spaces in artillery, garrison, gendarme, transport, Imperial Guard and engineering units elsewhere, so that four-battalion brigades that ought to have had 3,360 men in them actually had only around 2,500. While he didn't take many men away from Spain for the 1812 campaign in Russia, he severely cut back the number of recruits who were sent there, and no army can fight without reinforcements, especially considering the regular wastage experienced in Iberia, where one-fifth of the army was on the sick list at any one time.[160] Overall, France suffered around a quarter of a million casualties in Spain and Portugal.[161] 'I embarked pretty badly on this affair, I admit it,' Napoleon acknowledged years later, 'the immorality showed too obviously, the injustice was too cynical, and the whole of it remains very ugly.'[162]

21
Wagram

'Artillery should always be placed in the most advantageous positions, and as far as possible in the front of the line of cavalry and infantry, without compromising the safety of the guns.'

Napoleon's Military Maxim No. 54

'To cannon, all men are equal.'

Napoleon to General Bertrand, April 1819

'The Court of Vienna is behaving very badly,' Napoleon wrote to Joseph from Valladolid on January 15, 1809, 'it may have cause to repent. Don't be uneasy. I have enough troops, even without touching my army in Spain, to get to Vienna in a month ... In fact, my mere presence in Paris will reduce Austria to her usual irrelevance.'[1] He did not know at that stage that Austria had already received a large British subsidy to persuade her to fight what would become the War of the Fifth Coalition. Archduke Charles had been putting all able-bodied men between eighteen and forty-five into uniform in the new Landwehr militia, some of whose units were indistinguishable from the regular army. He had used the period since Austerlitz to impose deep-seated reforms on the Austrian army, streamlining command structures, improving service conditions, simplifying drill movements, introducing the *Bataillonsmasse* method of protecting infantry against cavalry through making squares more solid, abolishing regimental guns to provide a larger artillery reserve, modifying skirmishing tactics, raising nine Jäger regiments (one-third rifle-armed) – and, above all, adopting the corps system. The archduke had co-written a book on military strategy in 1806, *Grundsätze der Kriegkunst für die Generale* (The Art of War for Generals), and meant to put his ideas to the test.

When in April 1807 Talleyrand had suggested to Napoleon that Austria should be encouraged to love (*aimer*) France and her successes, Napoleon had replied, '*Aimer*: I don't really know what this means when applied to politics.'[2] It was true; his view of international affairs was largely self-interested, based on the assumption that states were in continual competition. Napoleon understood that Austria wanted revenge for the humiliations of Mantua, Marengo, Campo Formio, Lunéville, Ulm, Austerlitz and Pressburg, but he felt she would be foolish to go to war with only Britain and Sicily as allies, especially when Britain offered no troops. By contrast, Napoleon led a coalition that included Italy, Belgium, Switzerland, Naples, Holland, Bavaria, Württemberg, Saxony and Westphalia. 'Prussia is destroyed,' said Metternich, the Austrian ambassador in Paris, summing up the prevailing situation, 'Russia is an ally of France, France the master of Germany.'[3] Despite it being an inopportune time for Austria to declare war, they did, in yet another attempt to win back their position in Italy and Germany. It was precisely because there was no long period of peace after 1805 that the European Powers were able to wear France down, and much of the credit for that must go to Austrian persistence.

Once he was certain of his intelligence, Napoleon made a lightning dash from Valladolid to Paris. Galloping with Savary, Duroc, Roustam, an aide-de-camp and a small detachment of chasseurs, he covered the 70 miles to Burgos in four hours, much of it through guerrilla country. Thiébault saw him riding past his carriage 'simultaneously lashing the horse of his aide-de-camp and digging the spurs into his own'.[4] He left at 7 a.m. on January 17 and was back in Paris by 8 a.m. on the 23rd, having covered more than 600 miles in six days, an extraordinary feat. 'While all the cabinets of the Allied powers believed he was engaged in operations in the north of Spain,' recorded General Dumas, 'he had returned to the centre of the empire, was organising another great army ... surprising by this incredible activity those who expected to surprise him.'[5] Napoleon later contrasted the campaigning in Spain and Austria, describing the Austrians to Davout as 'a nation so good, so reasonable, so cold, so tolerant, so far removed from all excesses that there is not an example of a single Frenchman having been assassinated during the war in Germany', whereas the Spanish were fanatics.[6]

As soon as he was in Paris, Napoleon ordered the legislature, a now emasculated body that sat for a total of only four months in 1809 and 1810, to call up the 1810 conscription class a year early, allowing him to mobilize 230,000 troops, the largest army he had ever commanded.

In addition to keeping him extremely well informed about Austrian intentions and actions – Francis had taken the decision to go to war on December 23 and confirmed it in February – Napoleon's spy network had also warned him of a dangerous rapprochement between Talleyrand and Fouché, who had long been sworn enemies but who were now plotting to put Murat on the French throne if Napoleon was killed in Spain. Lavalette's interceptions of letters between Fouché's and Talleyrand's friends, supported by information that Eugène passed on, told Napoleon all he needed to know. On the afternoon of Saturday, January 28 he summoned Cambacérès, Lebrun, Decrès, Fouché and Talleyrand to his office at the Tuileries to deliver a diatribe against the last two that continued either for half an hour (according to Pasquier, who heard about it from Madame de Rémusat, who was told by Talleyrand) or two hours (according to Mollien, who wasn't present but knew everyone involved).

Napoleon complained that Fouché and Talleyrand had criticized the Spanish campaign in the salons, despite the fact that it was going relatively well – Soult had forced the British off the peninsula from Corunna, killing Sir John Moore on January 16. They had also conspired against Joseph's succession to the throne by promoting Murat, which meant they had broken their oath of allegiance to him. 'Why,' Napoleon concluded, addressing Talleyrand, 'you are nothing but a shit in silk stockings.'[7] Talleyrand remained perfectly calm, listening 'with apparent insensibility', and confined himself to telling a friend later on, 'What a pity that such a great man should be so ill bred.'[8] Two days after the interview Napoleon dismissed Talleyrand as Vice-Grand Elector, but allowed him to retain his other titles and rank and, inexplicably, didn't exile him. Fouché kept his ministry as well. Soon afterwards, Metternich paid a 'Monsieur X' between 300,000 and 400,000 francs for detailed information about the French order of battle; Talleyrand is considered the prime suspect.[9]

Metternich remained in Paris until the last possible moment before requesting his passports, perhaps in order to continue gathering secret intelligence from 'Monsieur X'. As usual, Napoleon gave his enemy dire warnings of the consequences of going to war. When he saw Metternich just prior to the rupture of diplomatic relations on March 23, he asked:

Were you bitten by a tarantula? What's threatening you? Who do you resent? You still want to set fire to the world? Why? When I had my army in Germany, you didn't find your existence threatened, but now it's in

Spain you find it compromised! There's some strange reasoning. What will result? I'm going to arm because you are arming; because finally I have something to fear, and it pays to be cautious.[10]

Metternich protested in suave diplomatic language but Napoleon cut in: 'Where do your concerns come from? If it's you, monsieur, who have communicated them to your Court, speak, I'll give all the explanations you need to reassure it . . . Monsieur, I was always duped in all my transactions with your Court; we have to talk straight.'[11] As with the Wars of the Third and Fourth Coalitions, Napoleon did not want or need this conflict, and was vocal in his desire to avoid it. Yet he once again wasn't willing to make any compromises to prevent it, since he was confident he would win. On March 9 alone he sent twenty-nine letters preparing for the coming clash.*

Archduke Charles's plan was to lead eight corps into Bavaria, while simultaneously sending one into Poland and two into Italy. He hoped for a declaration of war from Prussia and significant revolts against Napoleon's rule across Germany, but when it became clear that neither would be forthcoming he switched his main effort south of the Danube, to cover Vienna and liaise with his forces in Italy. This led to extreme disorder in the army as units crossed and re-crossed the region, and the loss of precious time. When Saragossa finally fell on February 20, after an heroic resistance, Joseph was re-established in Madrid two days later, and Napoleon could concentrate fully on the threat to his ally Bavaria.

By March 30 Napoleon had set out his entire strategy for Berthier, whom he put in command of the Army of Germany until he could arrive in person, knowing he could not give either Davout or Masséna command over the other, since both were proud, successful, senior marshals who thought themselves equals. A huge *bataillon carré* was to be put in place, to lure the Austrians into a gigantic trap when they launched their offensive, which was expected some time after April 15. In the vanguard, along the Isar river, was Lefebvre's Bavarian corps of three divisions under Prince Louis of Bavaria, Prince Carl-Philipp Wrede and Count Bernard Deroy, with General Jean-Baptiste Drouet (later Comte d'Erlon) its chief-of-staff. Lefebvre would be joined by Lannes' corps

---

* He was as diligent a correspondent as ever in 1809, writing 3,250 letters during the course of the year, including one to Fouché pointing out a discrepancy in his ministerial accounts of 1 franc and 45 centimes.

once that great fighter had returned from Spain. On the left between Bayreuth and Nuremberg was Davout's large corps of three infantry divisions plus one new reserve and one new German division, the 2nd Heavy Cavalry Division and a light cavalry brigade, some 55,000 men and 60 guns in all. On the right was Oudinot's corps of infantry and light cavalry at Pfaffenhoffen. Masséna's corps formed the rearguard around Augsburg. The Cavalry Reserve under Bessières, consisting of two light and two heavy divisions, and the Imperial Guard and Vandamme's Württembergers were formed up at Strasbourg. In total, the Army of Germany numbered 160,000 men and 286 guns, the corps within relatively short marching distances of each other, with Ratisbon (present-day Regensburg) as the central pivot of their deployment. Should the Austrians attack before April 15, Napoleon ordered Berthier to concentrate instead between Augsburg and Donauwörth.

In reply to Napoleon's request for aid against Austria under the terms of the Erfurt Convention, Tsar Alexander sent 70,000 men under Prince Golitsyn, but they managed to cross the border into Austrian Galicia (now parts of southern Poland and western Ukraine) near Lemberg (now Lviv in Ukraine) only on May 22 and thereafter avoided all contact with the enemy; they suffered just two casualties throughout the entire campaign.[12] The Austrians therefore had to divert the minimum resources to the east, and were able to concentrate almost everything against Napoleon, to his deep ire.

Austria formally declared war on France and Bavaria on April 3, and Archduke Charles (though he was personally opposed to the declaration, thinking that war came too early) issued a martial proclamation to the Austrian people on the 6th.* Four days later, 127,000 Austrians crossed the River Inn and entered Bavaria, but instead of showing the speed Archduke Charles had hoped for, they were slowed down by bad weather to 6 miles a day and reached the Isar only on the 15th, the same day that Austria also invaded the Duchy of Warsaw. The opening moves of the French campaign were badly bungled by Berthier, who misunderstood Napoleon's orders and panicked when the Austrians attacked five days earlier than expected. On April 14 he sent Davout's corps to concentrate on Ratisbon rather than Augsburg and he dispersed the army

---

* That day Napoleon ordered his sister Elisa – whom he had made Grand Duchess of Tuscany the previous month – to ban gambling in Florence, as in the rest of his Empire, because 'it causes the ruin of families and sets a bad example' (CG9 no. 20738 p. 443). He made an exception for Paris, because 'it cannot be prevented, and because it is turned to account by the police'.

along the River Lech, 52,300 troops to the north of it and 68,700 south, many of whom were out of marching range of each other, while a concentrated mass of Austrians descended on Landshut. Calm returned to the Donauwörth headquarters only when Napoleon – having been warned by telegraph on April 12 that the Austrians had crossed the Inn – arrived five days later.* 'Soldiers!' he proclaimed. 'I arrive in the midst of you with the rapidity of the eagle.'[13]

'Berthier had lost his head when I reached the seat of war,' Napoleon later recalled.[14] It was true, but as soon as he arrived in Donauwörth and discovered how badly dispersed his forces were he recognized the Austrian attack on Landshut to be both a threat and an opportunity: his corps could now converge on Archduke Charles from several directions at once. Masséna and Oudinot were ordered to advance on Landshut to threaten enemy lines of communication; Vandamme and Lefebvre were sent to Abensberg; Davout was ordered to rejoin the main army, which involved a tough 80-mile march, leaving a garrison of the 65th Line under his cousin, Colonel Baron Louis Coutard, to hold the bridge at Ratisbon. So important were these orders that Napoleon sent four aides-de-camp with each, rather than the usual three. Masséna was ordered to push forward quickly to Pfaffenhoffen and attack the enemy's flank, while making sure that Augsburg was kept as an impregnable base of operations.

By April 18 the Austrians found themselves not pursuing a retreating enemy, as they had imagined they would be, but instead facing a resurgent one. Napoleon was on the road to Ingolstadt with Lannes at his side, encouraging his German troops as he passed them. A colonel of the Austrian general staff was captured during the day and brought before Napoleon for questioning. When he refused to answer, the Emperor said, 'Don't worry, sir, I know everything anyway,' and he then quickly and accurately described the locations of all the Austrian corps and even the regiments facing him. 'With whom have I the honour of speaking?' asked the impressed Austrian. 'At this,' recalled Chlapowski, 'the Emperor inclined himself forward, touched his hat and replied "Monsieur Bonaparte".'[15] (The colonel must have been spectacularly unobservant, because, as Chlapowski noted, throughout the interview

* The Chappe telegraph system, named after its brother inventors, used movable beams with 196 different combinations, representing single letters or whole phrases, and could send messages relatively accurately at speeds of up to 250 miles a day. Napoleon extended the system enormously from its original use within France, sending it deep into Germany and Italy (eds. Olsen and van Creveld, *Evolution of Operational Art* p. 17).

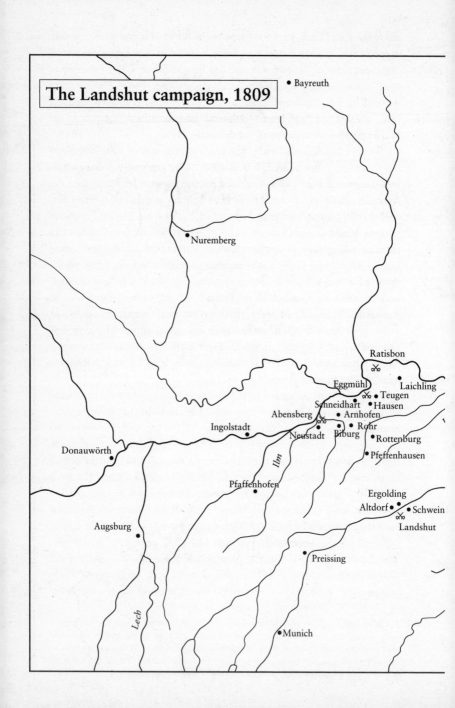

The Landshut campaign, 1809

Bayreuth

Nuremberg

Ratisbon

Eggmühl • Laichling
• Teugen
Schneidhart • Hausen
Abensberg • Arnhofen
Ingolstadt Neustadt Biburg • Rohr
• Rottenburg
• Pfeffenhausen

Donauwörth

Pfaffenhofen

Ergolding
Altdorf • • Schwein
Landshut

Augsburg

Preissing

Ilm

Lech

• Munich

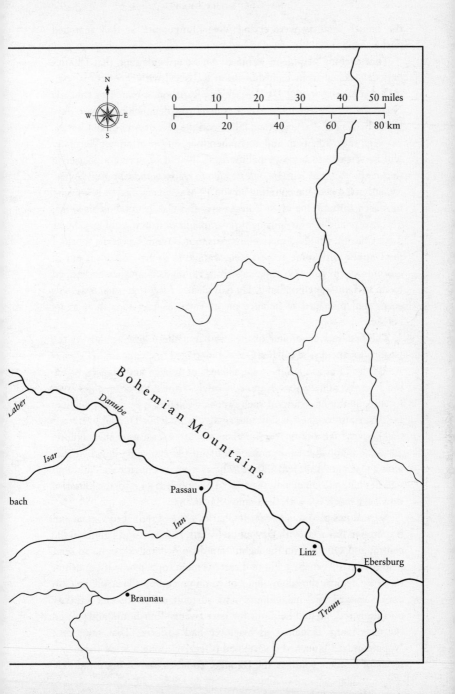

the French infantry were crying 'Vive l'Empereur!' as they marched past.)

That evening Napoleon wrote to Masséna explaining that Charles 'has debouched from Landshut upon Ratisbon with three corps, estimated at 80,000 strong. Davout, leaving Ratisbon, is marching towards Neustadt ... the enemy is lost if your corps, debouching before daybreak by way of Pfaffenhoffen, falls upon the rear of Archduke Charles. Between the 18th, 19th and 20th, therefore, all the affairs of Germany will be settled.' In his own handwriting, Napoleon wrote a postscript that read: '*Activité, activité, vitesse! Je me recommande à vous.*' (Activity, activity, speed! I'm counting on you.)[16] Masséna replied by promising to march through the night if necessary, and was as good as his word; his bravery and tenacity during this campaign were extraordinary. Archduke Charles, who had received reports that Davout had come south of the Danube with some 30,000 men, wanted to destroy his corps in isolation from the rest of Napoleon's army, rather as Bennigsen had hoped to do to Lannes at Friedland. He had clearly forgotten what Davout's corps had managed to achieve on its own at Auerstädt three years before.

The first real encounter of the campaign the following day set the pattern for the rest of it when Davout managed to escape destruction at Archduke Charles's hands in the villages of Teugen and Hausen below the Danube and to join Napoleon safely. Under lowering skies, two forces, equally uncertain of each other, collided in hilly country, where the Austrians fought in a slow and rigid fashion while Davout's veterans manoeuvred with skill. The Austrians withdrew east after their failure, allowing Napoleon to organize a pursuit. On the same day, Lefebvre won a clash at Arnhofen, and Montbrun won at Schneidhart. Although Charles had 93,000 men in the field to Napoleon's 89,000, the initiative now very much lay with the Franco-Bavarians.

Napoleon's plan was to cut off Charles's line of retreat to Vienna and trap him in Bavaria. With Davout on his left, Lefebvre and Lannes in the centre, and Oudinot on the right, Napoleon ordered Masséna to send help towards Abensberg but to direct his main force towards Landshut, to strike against the enemy lines of communication. On April 20 Colonel Coutard hid his colours and surrendered Ratisbon. Heavily outnumbered, he had held out for over twenty-four hours and caused twice as many casualties as his force had suffered. That same day, Napoleon had launched a sustained offensive along a wide front in a series of hamlets south of the Danube, 20 miles east of Ingolstadt. He

had been up at 3 a.m., sending orders to Lefebvre, Masséna and Vandamme, and by 6.30 he, Lannes and Bessières were riding for Abensberg.
On a hillside later called the Napoleonshöhe* outside the town, Napoleon delivered this stirring declaration to the officers of the Bavarian
corps, translated for him by Crown Prince Ludwig of Bavaria and published as an Order of the Day:

> Bavarian soldiers! I do not come to you as a French emperor, but as Pro-
> tector of your country and the Confederation of the Rhine. Today you
> will fight alone against the Austrians. No French serve in your front
> ranks; I am entirely confident in your bravery. For two hundred years,
> Bavarian flags, protected by France, have resisted Austria. We are going to
> Vienna, where we will know how to punish Austria for the harm she has
> so often done to your country. Austria wants to partition your country
> and disband your units and distribute you among their regiments. Bavar-
> ians! This war is the last you will fight against your enemies; attack them
> with the bayonet and annihilate them![17]

He then launched attacks along two axes, one south-eastwards from
Abensberg and Peissing towards Rohr and Rottenburg, and a second
one south-eastwards from Biburg to Pfeffenhausen. The well-placed
and equally numerous Austrians fought well for most of the day, but
once Napoleon knew that his left under Lannes was making progress he
rode forward from the Napoleonshöhe to oversee it.

After the battle, the *chef d'escadron* of the 2nd Chasseurs à Cheval
presented Napoleon with two captured Austrian flags, the first of the
campaign, with blood pouring from his face from a sabre slash. Napoleon asked his name, which was the splendid one of Dieudonné Lion. 'I
will remember you and you will be grateful,' Napoleon told him, 'you
are well marked.' Months later, when Berthier suggested a man to fill a
vacancy in the Guard chasseurs, Napoleon demurred, saying he wanted
to give the promotion to Lion.

Napoleon believed he was pursuing the main body of the enemy
towards Landshut, whereas in fact Archduke Charles was heading for
Ratisbon. Two large Austrian columns under Baron Johann von Hiller
converged on Landshut, creating a vast traffic jam near the two bridges.
The French artillery under General Jacques de Lauriston (who, like
many of Napoleon's senior commanders, had been taken from Spain)
was deployed on the ridge between Altdorf and Ergolding and poured

---

* Today it can be found around the back of the McDonald's restaurant car park.

fire into the crowded town. (Standing on the bridge at Landshut today one can see in how few places the Austrians could have organized counter-fire.) Once the Austrians were over the bridge they tried to burn it, but the flames were doused by a persistent rain. At 12.30 p.m. Napoleon turned to his aide-de-camp General Georges Mouton and said: 'Put yourself at the head of that column, and carry the town.'[18]

It must have seemed like a death sentence at the time, but Mouton led his grenadiers in a charge, covered by heavy musket fire from the island banks. His sappers smashed the town gates with axes, and men of the 13th Légère joined the attack, as did three battalions and two squadrons of Bavarians and some Württembergers, so that by 1 p.m. Landshut had fallen. Archduke Charles lost nearly 5,000 men, 11 guns and all his baggage-train, amounting to 226 wagons.[19] Napoleon later gave Mouton a magnificent painting of the action at the bridge, and made an uncharacteristically weak pun about his 'sheep' (mouton) being a lion. 'This keepsake from Napoleon was worth more than the highest eulogies,' said another aide-de-camp of the picture, and by the end of the campaign Mouton had been made the Comte de Lobau.[20]*

Just as in 1806, Napoleon discovered only after the battle that Davout, the 'Iron Marshal', had been facing the main body of the enemy, this time at Laichling, where he had managed to hold off Archduke Charles. Davout sent Napoleon four messages from 7 a.m. to 5 p.m. on April 21, telling him that Charles was bringing up his reserves for a major counter-attack. From 2 a.m. on the 22nd Napoleon exploded into activity, ordering Lannes, Vandamme and Saint-Sulpice with 20,000 infantry and 5,500 cavalry to go north as soon as possible. Oudinot and the rest of the Bavarians were already under orders to join Davout, so within an hour Napoleon had 50,000 infantry, 14,000 cavalry and 114 guns closing in on Archduke Charles.

On the 22nd, Napoleon fought Charles at the battle of Eggmühl, the culmination of the Landshut Manoeuvre, where the corps system once again brought victory. Davout's corps had fixed the 54,000 Austrians and 120 guns, but Charles delayed his attack until General Johann

---

* It wasn't just his aides-de-camp who were rewarded. After the successful storming of Landshut Napoleon asked the colonel of the 13th Légère who had been the bravest man in the demi-brigade. The colonel hesitated, possibly thinking it invidious to pick any particular man, so Napoleon asked the officers, who also fell silent. Finally an elderly captain replied that it had been the drum-major. 'You have been designated the bravest in a brave regiment,' Napoleon told the drum-major, to cheers from the men, and he made him a chevalier in the Légion d'Honneur on the spot (ed. Haythornthwaite, Final Verdict p. 220).

Kollowrath's corps had arrived from Ratisbon 15 miles to the north, giving Napoleon time to rush Lannes and Masséna 25 miles up from Landshut to relieve Davout. When Charles saw Bavarian and Württemberger cavalry arriving on the field, forcing one of his divisions back onto the heights behind the town, he called off the whole assault. Napoleon arrived on the battlefield with Lannes' and Masséna's corps soon after 2 p.m. and fell on the enemy's left. Victory was won with Austrian losses of over 4,100 and 39 guns to Napoleon's 3,000 men. He made Davout the Prince d'Eckmühl shortly afterwards.

'With the army I generally travelled in a carriage during the day with a good, thick pelisse on, because night is the time when a commander-in-chief should work,' Napoleon said years later. 'If he fatigues himself uselessly during the day, he will be too tired to work in the evening ... If I had slept the night before Eggmühl I could never have executed that superb manoeuvre, the finest I ever made ... I multiplied myself by my activity. I woke up Lannes by kicking him repeatedly; he was so sound asleep.'[21] Napoleon was more fond of Lannes than of any other marshal – after the death of Desaix, Lannes and Duroc were his closest friends – and accepted teasing from him that he wouldn't from others. Lannes went so far as to say 'that he was to be pitied for having such an unhappy passion for this harlot [*cette catin*]', that is, Napoleon. As Chaptal recalled: 'The Emperor laughed at these jokes because he knew that he would always find the marshal there for him when he needed him.'[22]

The French victory at Eggmühl forced the Austrians to fall back to Ratisbon in some disorder hoping to escape across the Danube. Reaching Ratisbon on April 23, Napoleon ruled out a siege as taking too long, and instead insisted on storming the town by escalade – ladders placed twenty paces apart against the wall – which was achieved at the third attempt. The strong 30-foot-wide stone bridge was Charles's only line of escape. It was – and is – one of the great bridges over the Danube, with six big stone pillars, and it would have been hard to destroy by cannon-fire. Charles was about to cross it to safety, but lost a further 5,000 men and 8 guns doing so. Near where the railway line is today Napoleon was hit in the right ankle by a spent bullet, which caused a contusion. He sat on a drum as the wound was dressed by Yvan, and a hole was cut in his boot so that it wouldn't hurt too much when he was riding.[23] So as not to demoralize the troops, the instant his wound was dressed he 'rode down the front of the whole line, amid loud cheers'.[24]

Later in the battle he said, 'Doesn't it seem as though the bullets are reconnoitring us?'[25] On May 6 he reassured Josephine, 'The bullet which touched me did not wound me. It barely shaved my Achilles tendon.'[26]

After the battle of Ratisbon, a *grognard* asked Napoleon for the cross of the Légion d'Honneur, claiming that he had given him a watermelon at Jaffa when it 'was so terribly hot'. Napoleon refused him on such a paltry pretext, at which the veteran added indignantly, 'Well, don't you reckon seven wounds received at the bridge of Arcole, at Lodi and Castiglione, at the Pyramids, at Acre, Austerlitz, Friedland; eleven campaigns in Italy, Egypt, Austria, Prussia, Poland . . .' at which a laughing emperor cut him short and made him a chevalier of the Légion with a 1,200-franc pension, fastening the cross on his breast there and then. 'It was by familiarities of this kind that the Emperor made the soldiers adore him,' noted Marbot, 'but it was a means available only to a commander whom frequent victories had made illustrious: any other general would have injured his reputation by it.'[27]

Victories were rarely more frequent than over the four consecutive days of Abensberg, Landshut, Eggmühl and Ratisbon. On the 24th the army rested, and the Emperor interviewed some of his officers. Captain Blaze recorded Napoleon's conversation with a colonel who had clearly mastered his regimental rolls:

'How many men present under arms?'
'Sire, eighty-four.'
'How many conscripts of this year?'
'Twenty-two.'
'How many soldiers who have served four years?'
'Sixty-five.'
'How many wounded yesterday?'
'Eighteen.'
'And killed?'
'Ten.'
'With the bayonet?'
'Yes, Sire.'
'Good.'[28]

It was considered bravest of all to fight with the bayonet, and after an action on May 3 Napoleon was delighted that the bravest soldier in the 26th Légère actually bore the name Carabinier-Corporal Bayonnette, whom he made a chevalier of the Légion with a pension.[29]

When Napoleon reached the gates of Vienna on May 10, 1809, his Polish aide-de-camp Adam Chlapowski

> saw a sight that I would not have believed had I not seen it with my own eyes and heard it with my own ears. Even then I found it hard to believe. The city walls were not crowded, but there were still a good many well-to-do inhabitants on the ramparts. The Emperor rode right up to the glacis, so only a ditch ten yards wide separated him from these people. When they recognized him, from the last time he had been there, in 1805, they all took off their hats, which I suppose could be expected, and then began cheering, which seemed unnecessary and less fitting to me ... When I expressed my surprise to some French officers, they assured me that they had seen and heard exactly the same thing at the Brandenburg Gate in Berlin in 1806.[30]

Napoleon spent half an hour riding around the defences of Vienna 'and from time to time raised his hat in response to the cheering, just as if he were riding around Paris'. He had an escort of only twenty-five men riding with him. Turning towards Schönbrunn Palace outside the city, where he was staying as he had in 1805, he told Chlapowski: 'A bed will already be made up for you there. You've spent so many nights on horseback, it's time you had a rest courtesy of the Emperor Francis.'[31]

After a very brief bombardment, Vienna surrendered to Napoleon at 2 a.m. on May 13, by which time the Archduke Charles – having destroyed all the bridges – was on the right bank of the Danube, which had a very different, far wilder watercourse than today's calm and heavily canalized river. 'The princes of this House have abandoned their capital,' Napoleon declared in a proclamation that day, 'not like soldiers of honour who cede to the circumstances and setbacks of the war, but like the perjured who are pursued by their own remorse.'[32] Yet while he didn't mind rebuking the Habsburgs, he didn't want to alienate the Viennese, who had promised to police the city themselves. 'All stragglers who under the pretext of fatigue have left their units to maraud,' he ordered on the 14th, 'shall be rounded up, tried by summary provost courts, and executed within the hour.'[33] Each column had a tribunal set up to punish pillaging.

Napoleon's men spent three days constructing a bridge of boats downstream from Vienna which he could cross to attack the Austrian army. At 5 p.m. on May 18, General Gabriel Molitor's infantry division started to traverse the Danube by boat. They made it only to the two-mile-wide Lobau Island, from which they began to build more substantial bridges onto the opposite bank. Napoleon has been criticized subsequently for not having built sufficiently strong bridges, but there were few specialist engineers in his army, it was a fast-flowing river, and the Austrians kept floating trees and other detritus downstream – on one occasion an entire dismantled watermill – to damage them.

Once again, as at Austerlitz and in Poland, Napoleon was at the end of a very long supply line, deep inside enemy territory, fighting an opponent who hadn't sued for peace when his capital had fallen. An Austrian army under Archduke Johann von Habsburg – Emperor Francis and Archduke Charles's younger brother – was now coming back from Italy, after having been defeated by Eugène at the battle of the Piave river on May 8. The Tyrol was in revolt against Bavaria under its charismatic leader Andreas Hofer. There was discontent among Germans who resented French hegemony, and Archduke Charles's strategy seemed to be designed to deny Napoleon a decisive battle. Yet on the late afternoon of the 19th a bridge 825 yards long, built on eighty-six boats and nine rafts, spanned the Danube, and by noon the next day the army was crossing over to Lobau Island in force. Another bridge, 100 yards long resting on fifteen captured pontoons and three trestles, stretched to the opposite bank. It looked decidedly rickety, but Napoleon decided to risk a crossing.

The villages of Aspern and Essling lie 3 miles apart on the north-eastern side of the Danube 2 miles east of Vienna. At midnight on May 20, Masséna climbed the church tower at Aspern and, seeing relatively few campfires, informed Napoleon that the Austrians were retreating, whereas in fact they were forming up to attack. It was the same mistake that Murat had made on the morning of Eylau. Napoleon crossed at dawn on Sunday, May 21, and, showing characteristic foresight, immediately ordered that the defences of the bridgehead be improved. Unfortunately, Masséna had failed to fortify Aspern properly, probably considering it unnecessary if Archduke Charles was withdrawing. By 8 a.m. it became very clear that he wasn't.

In 1809, Aspern consisted of 106 two-storey houses with walled gardens running east–west along two roads with a handful of traverse streets, a church and cemetery with a chest-high wall (the church houses today's museum), a solid vicarage and a large garden on a slight rise at its western end. An earth bank lined the road to Essling – and still does – which in turn had fifty-six houses in two groups on either side of the village square, and a large granary with 3-foot-thick stone walls. Napoleon intended to use these two villages and the road between them as bastions, while developing his attack across the Marchfeld plain beyond. The plain was so flat that it had been used by the Austrian army as a parade-ground.

The Danube had risen 3 feet overnight and by 10 a.m. the northern-most boat-bridge had been smashed by a laden barge. The French repaired it in time for General Jean d'Espagne's heavy cavalry to get across, walking over by dismounted squadrons. Napoleon, just east of Aspern, considered retreating when he learned about the damage to the bridge, since one of the cardinal laws of war is never to fight with a river to one's back, but his generals (except the silent Berthier) assured him they could hold the ground. At 1 p.m. he heard that a large Austrian army was on its way across the Marchfeld, something he might have been aware of earlier had his light cavalry's intelligence gathering not been disrupted by Austrian skirmishers. The numbers involved were daunting: some 37,000 Austrians attacked on Sunday May 21 and the next day 85,000 with 292 guns. Some 30,000 Frenchmen had crossed on Sunday and 20,000 more on Monday, but they had only 58 guns.[34] If Davout's corps had managed to get across the Danube, those unprom-ising ratios would have been more even, but the state of the bridges now precluded that.

The first clashes came between 1 and 2 p.m. at Aspern, where 5,000 French defenders had to fend off vastly more attackers. French artillery punished the attacking columns and a battalion of the 67th Line stood up behind the cemetery walls and delivered a crushing volley. But the Austrians came on relentlessly, and savage fighting developed in the village streets. Dense clouds of smoke from gunfire added to the grimness of the struggle. After 3 p.m. a ninety-gun Austrian battery fur-ther blasted the village, sweeping away the outer barricades.

Napoleon followed the battle's progress sitting on a drum in a little hollow near where the Aspern Tileworks is today, about halfway between the two villages. He ordered Bessières to use four divisions to secure the centre – a role similar to that of Murat at Eylau – which was achieved in four major cavalry charges. As the charges went forward, Napoleon massed his artillery to help defend Aspern by punishing Aus-trian cavalry that came too close. By 4.30 p.m. an Austrian attack of three columns after a major bombardment forced the defenders out of the church and cemetery. An hour later Legrand's division was ordered in, and the 26th Légère and 18th Line recaptured Aspern, but half an hour later Archduke Charles himself accompanied a six-battalion attack, with thirteen more in support, crying: 'For the Fatherland! Forward courageously!' (It was said he carried a flag himself, but he later denied this.) The church and cemetery were stormed as the village caught fire and the French pulled out.

Despite several further bridge collapses, General Claude Carra Saint-Cyr of Masséna's 4th Corps – no relation to Gouvion Saint-Cyr – managed to get his division across the Danube and rush to Aspern, retaking the southern edge of the village. The fighting went on until 9 p.m. Some 8,000 Austrian and 7,000 French spent the night there, as the bridge was repaired yet again by 10 p.m. Fourteen Guard battalions, Lannes' corps and enough guns to give Napoleon a total of 152 now managed to cross the Danube, but still not Davout's corps. The Austrians had attacked the village of Essling and its near-impregnable granary (where one can still see the bullet holes in the wooden door) at 4.40 p.m. Lannes personally supervised the defences – cutting loopholes, sighting batteries, barricading streets, crenellating walls – until the fighting there ceased at 11 p.m.

The second day began at 3.30 a.m. when Masséna's 18th and 4th Line crashed into Aspern and charged in column up the two main streets, supported by the 26th Légère and 46th Line, and the Baden Jägers. Most of the village was regained by 4 a.m., though not the church. Fighting carried on at sunrise, and at 7 a.m. Masséna reported to Napoleon that he had the whole village back after seeing it change hands four times, although by 11 a.m. the Austrians had regained most of it again. At Essling, the Young Guard pushed into the village just in time to stop it falling.

Between 6 and 7 a.m. Napoleon was ready to launch a major three-divisional attack in close battalion columns. Lannes went in on the right with Saint-Hilaire's division, Oudinot was in the centre and General Jean Tharreau on the left. Behind them were General Antoine de Lasalle's light cavalry and Nansouty's heavy cavalry. Though covered by an early-morning fog, the massed Austrian artillery punished them terribly. Immense courage was shown. At one point Saint-Hilaire had the 105th Line bayonet-charge a regiment of Austrian cuirassiers, forcing them back onto the reserve grenadiers behind them. By 9 a.m. the French were low on ammunition, since wagons couldn't cross the bridge, and the attack stalled after Saint-Hilaire – who had been promised a marshal's baton – lost his foot to a cannonball (he died fifteen days later when the wound went gangrenous).

With the bridge down again and Charles bringing up a huge battery in the centre, making further French attacks there impossible, Napoleon began considering the complexities of a full-scale retreat over the makeshift bridges, sending word to Lannes to wind down the attack. Lannes got his battalions into two lines of squares and they fell back with remarkable discipline, as if on parade. In the course of the withdrawal, Oudinot's entire staff was killed or wounded, and he himself picked up yet another wound. Napoleon had to refuse the suicidal request of General Dorsenne, who had had no fewer than three horses shot from under him, to attack the enemy guns with the Old Guard.

By 3 p.m. Austrian grenadiers had taken most of Essling except the granary, which was held by General Jean Boudet. When Napoleon personally ordered the Old Guard to the left of Essling to check an advance by Archduke Charles, the soldiers insisted that he retire to safety before they attacked. It was just as well, as one in four men were killed or wounded in the ensuing fight. Masséna led three battalions of the Young Guard on foot into Aspern at 11 a.m., but by 1 p.m. the Austrians were again in control. An hour later both sides were utterly exhausted after eleven hours of almost non-stop fighting. By 3.30 p.m. Archduke Charles had concentrated a grand battery of between 150 and 200 guns – the largest in the history of warfare up to that moment – in the centre, silencing one battery of Lannes' artillery after another. Then they turned on any exposed French formations; in all the Austrian artillery fired 44,000 rounds during the two days of battle. Among their many victims was Lannes himself. Sitting cross-legged on the bank of a ditch, he had both knees smashed by a ricocheting 3-pound cannonball. The thirty-year-old was taken back to the French camp of Kaiserebersdorf, beyond the Danube, where the head surgeon, Larrey, amputated his left leg and fought to keep the right one. In the days before anaesthetics, the pain of these operations is unimaginable, but all the witnesses of Lannes' wounding agree that his courage was exemplary.

At about 4 p.m., with the bridges just about passable again, Napoleon ordered his army to fall back over the Danube to Lobau Island. He commandeered twenty-four guns and all the available ammunition to cover the bridgehead. First the wounded, then the artillery, then the Guard infantry (except the tirailleurs or light infantry skirmishers still engaged at Essling), then the heavy cavalry, then the infantry, then the light cavalry and finally the rearguard infantry divisions went back over the Danube; some voltigeurs did not make it to the island until long after nightfall, making the journey by boat. Archduke Charles felt that his army was too exhausted to disturb the French retreat, although several Austrian generals heatedly disagreed, so the Austrians remained on the other side of the river. At 7 p.m. Napoleon held one of his very infrequent conferences of war. Berthier, Davout and Masséna all wanted to retreat far back beyond the Danube, but Napoleon persuaded them that Lobau had to be the base for future operations and that if he evacuated the island he would have to abandon Vienna.

Napoleon had been defeated for the first time since Acre ten years before, and for only the fourth time in his career so far. (The relatively minor Bassano and Caldiero battles had both taken place in November 1796.) His total losses were estimated at between 20,000 and 23,000 killed and wounded and 3,000 captured, but only 3 guns had been lost, testament to the discipline of the retreat. Austrian losses were similar, with 19,000 killed and wounded, though only 700 captured.[35] Napoleon's bulletin the next day, which admitted only to 4,100 killed and wounded, referred to the battle of Aspern-Essling as 'a new memorial to the glory and inflexible firmness of the French army' – which was as close as he could come to an admission of defeat. Later he would claim that when Lannes regained consciousness he had said: 'Within an hour you will have lost him who dies with the glory and conviction of having been and being your best friend', a grammatical construction unlikely to have leaped to the mind of a man who had just had one leg amputated and might have been about to lose the other.[36]

As the Austrians were claiming to have won the battle of Aspern, Napoleon made Masséna the Prince of Essling, although Masséna hadn't set foot there during the battle. In Paris, the prefecture of police was ordered to put up posters asking Parisians to light up their front rooms to celebrate the victory.[37] Yet on the morning of May 23 the bridge linking Lobau with the northern bank was dismantled, and the island was turned into a fortress. That evening, exhausted French soldiers sat down to a dinner of horseflesh, which Marbot recalled was 'cooked in cuirasses and seasoned with gunpowder' instead of pepper. Provisions and ammunition were taken to Lobau by boat, the wounded were sent to Vienna, field hospitals were set up and new, stronger bridges were built and protected by stakes driven into the riverbed.

Gangrene set into Lannes' leg and it took him nine days to die. Napoleon visited him twice daily, and arrived to see him moments after he had expired.[38] His valet Louis Constant found the Emperor shortly afterwards in his quarters, 'seated immobile, mute, and staring into space, in front of his hastily prepared meal. Napoleon's eyes were inundated with tears; they multiplied and fell silently into his soup.'[39] Napoleon's anguish is confirmed by the accounts of Ségur, Las Cases, Pelet, Marbot, Lejeune and Savary.* Both Constant and Napoleon's pharmacist, Cadet de Gassicourt, claimed that Lannes had berated the Emperor for his ambition, but Marbot, Savary and Pelet vehemently denied it.[40] Today Lannes lies in *caverne* XXII of the Panthéon, in a coffin draped with the tricolour, under nine flags hanging from walls covered with the names of his battles. 'The loss of the Duke of Montebello, who died this morning, has grieved me much,' Napoleon wrote to Josephine on May 31. 'So everything ends!!! Adieu, my love; if you can do anything toward consoling the Marshal's poor widow, do it.'[41]

'I was right not to count on allies like those,' Napoleon told Savary of the Russians in early June,

> what could be worse if I hadn't made peace with Russia? And what advantage do I get from their alliance, if they aren't capable of ensuring peace in Germany? It is more likely that they would have been against me if a remnant of human respect hadn't prevented them from betraying right away the sworn faith; let's not be abused: they all have a rendezvous on my grave, but they don't dare to gather there ... It's not an alliance I have here; I've been duped.[42]

By the time Napoleon returned to Schönbrunn Palace on June 5 the goodwill of Tilsit, more or less maintained at Erfurt, had been seriously damaged.

It was not all anger at that time, however, especially once Marie Walewska arrived.† One evening at Schönbrunn, Napoleon asked for a cold chicken as a late supper; when it was brought he asked: 'Since when has a chicken been born with one leg and one wing? I see that I am expected to live off the scraps left me by my servants.' He then pinched Roustam's ear, teasing him for having eaten the other half.[43] Rapp records the Emperor as being 'pretty generally in good humour' at this time, despite the loss of Lannes, though he was understandably infuriated by a police report from Paris containing the latest rumour,

---

* Although Las Cases was not personally present he had plenty of opportunity to discuss it with Napoleon on St Helena.

† That month 12,000 francs left his special account for mistresses, for 'the Viennese adventures', and a further 17,367 francs that September, when he was back at the palace with Marie after Wagram (Branda, *Le prix de la gloire* p. 57).

that he had gone mad. 'It is the *faubourg* St Germain which invents these fine stories,' he said, settling on his habitual bugbear of the aristocratic and intellectual salons of that district; 'they will provoke me at last to send the whole tribe of them to the flea-bitten countryside.'[44] The problem, as he told Caulaincourt, was that 'Society in the salons is always in a state of hostility against the government. Everything is criticized and nothing praised.'[45]

After Aspern-Essling Archduke Charles massed his forces along the Danube north of Vienna. Although the Austrians invaded Saxony on June 9, five days later Eugène won a significant victory over Archduke Johann at the battle of Raab in Hungary, which delighted Napoleon both because it denied Archduke Charles much-needed reinforcements and because Eugène's Army of Italy could now join him. He was also impressed with the fight that Prince Poniatowski's Poles were putting up against the Austrians in Silesia, in conspicuous contrast to the Russians, who were reluctant to engage at all.

By early July the Grande Armée's engineers had built such strong bridges to Lobau Island that Napoleon could boast, 'The Danube no longer exists; it's been abolished.'[46] With flexible pontoons capable of being swung into operation from Lobau to the north bank, he was now ready, six weeks after Aspern-Essling, to exact revenge. Wearing a sergeant's greatcoat he personally reconnoitred the best places to cross, going to within musket-range of the Austrian pickets on the other bank. Instead of due north, as he had previously, he decided this time he would head east towards the town of Gross-Enzersdorf. On the evening of July 4, 1809 the crossings began.

Napoleon had now amassed 130,800 infantry, 23,300 cavalry and no fewer than 544 guns manned by 10,000 artillerymen, three times his force at Aspern-Essling. Captain Blaze recalled that 'all the languages of Europe were spoken' on Lobau Island – 'Italian, Polish, Arab, Portuguese, Spanish, and every kind of German'. Through intense planning and preparation, Napoleon got this enormous polyglot force – roughly the same number as attacked Normandy on D-Day – across one of Europe's largest rivers into enemy territory on a single night, with all its horses, cannon, wagons, supplies and ammunition, and without losing a single man.[47] It was an astonishing logistical achievement. As soon as his men reached the far bank they crossed over the Marchfeld to face Archduke Charles's army numbering 113,800 infantry, 14,600 cavalry and 414 guns. The battle they were about to fight was the largest in European history up to that point.

Like Arcole, Eylau, Eggmühl and Aspern-Essling, the battle of Wagram was fought over two days. By 8 a.m. on Wednesday, July 5, Gross-Enzersdorf had fallen to the French and by 9 a.m. Oudinot, Davout and Masséna had all crossed the river. (Masséna rode in a carriage having been injured in a fall from his horse on Lobau.) Napoleon set up his head-quarters on the knoll at Raasdorf, the only pimple of ground for miles around on the otherwise totally flat Marchfeld. Archduke Charles lined his troops behind the fast-flowing Russbach, a stream about 25 to 30 feet across, hoping that his brother Archduke Johann would arrive in time from Pressburg, some 30 miles away to the south-east.

Napoleon placed Davout's corps and two dragoon divisions on the right flank, with Oudinot in the centre and Masséna and the light cavalry on the left. Bernadotte's corps of 14,000 Saxons were in close support, and a second great line was formed by the Army of Italy under Eugène and Macdonald, Marmont's corps and the Imperial Guard. Bessières' Reserve Cavalry made up a third. The Portuguese Legion secured the bridgehead from Lobau, and ammunition and supply wagons continued to pour across in prodigious numbers. Napoleon's plan was for Davout to turn the enemy's left flank while Oudinot and Bernadotte pinned down the Austrians frontally and Masséna protected the connection to the island. At the right moment the Army of Italy would then break through the centre. Archduke Johann's appearance behind Davout on the right flank could have compromised Napoleon's plan seriously, so both sides were constantly on the lookout for him.

At 2 p.m. the French army advanced under a hot sun across the waist-high cornfields of the Marchfeld, fanning out over the 16-mile-wide battlefield as they went. At 3.30 p.m. Bernadotte quickly took Raasdorf without firing a shot and by 5 p.m. was deployed before Aderklaa, a vital village on the battlefield, the seizure of which could nearly cut the Austrian army in two. Napoleon assaulted the whole Austrian line from Markgrafneusiedl to Deutsch-Wagram, ordering Oudinot, rather ambiguously, to 'push forward a little, and give us some music before night'.[48] Oudinot sent his troops wading across the Russbach, their muskets and ammunition pouches carried above their heads. At 7 p.m. his 7,300 troops attacked Baumersdorf, a thirty-house hamlet on the river defended by 1,500 Austrians, taking heavy casualties. Napoleon's evening attacks on July 5 came too late in the day, were too unspecific in their objectives and were unco-ordinated. Although the Russbach was little more than a stream, it disordered infantry and was impassable to cavalry and artillery except by its very few bridges. The attack did pin down the Austrians,

The Battle of Wagram

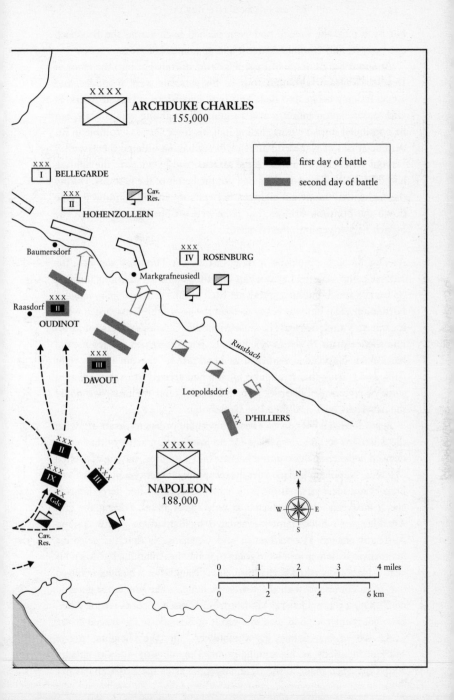

ARCHDUKE CHARLES
155,000

first day of battle

second day of battle

I BELLEGARDE

II HOHENZOLLERN

Cav. Res.

Baumersdorf

IV ROSENBURG

Markgrafneusiedl

Raasdorf

II

OUDINOT

III

DAVOUT

Russbach

Leopoldsdorf

D'HILLIERS

II

IX

Gde

Cav. Res.

NAPOLEON
188,000

N
W E
S

| 0 | 1 | 2 | 3 | 4 miles |

| 0 | | 2 | | 4 | | 6 km |

but by 9 p.m. the French had been pushed back across the Russbach everywhere, and Oudinot had lost a large number of men.

At about 8 p.m. some of Eugène's Army of Italy got into the town of Deutsch-Wagram, although four of his generals were wounded and 2,000 Italians broke and fled. At 9 p.m. Bernadotte attacked Aderklaa with 9,000 Saxon infantry and 14 guns. The fighting was chaotic, but he continued until 11 p.m., losing half his force; he was voluble in his denunciations of Napoleon afterwards for having ordered the assault.[49] Davout wisely called a halt to the attacks, and by 11 p.m. the fighting had died down. The Austrians had got the better of the first day. During the night, they launched eighteen fire-rafts down the Danube to take down the pontoon bridges, but they were stopped by the stakes the French had driven into the riverbed.

As Davout was preparing a dawn attack on Thursday the 6th, his aide-de-camp Colonel Lejeune ran into thousands of Austrians forming up for the attack but he couldn't get back in time to warn the marshal.[50] Fortunately, Davout was ready to meet the assault on Grosshofen when it came at 4 a.m., not least because Archduke Charles's orders for absolute silence prior to the attack had not got through to the regimental bandsmen. Napoleon, disturbed at breakfast by the din on his right flank and fearing that Archduke Johann had arrived from the east, sent some heavy cavalry reserves to help Davout. Over the next two hours the Austrians took and then lost Grosshofen.

Bernadotte fell back from Aderklaa without orders to do so, allowing the Austrians to take the village for no losses, as an artillery duel commenced between the two grand batteries. At 7.30 a.m., having consulted Masséna, Napoleon had to order the recapture of Aderklaa by Saint-Cyr's French and Hessian division, which was successful after fierce fighting and a musketry duel conducted at only eighty paces. During the day, Aderklaa – so nonchalantly evacuated by Bernadotte – saw 44,000 Austrians engage 35,000 French and Germans. 'Is that the scientific manoeuvre by which you were going to make the Archduke lay down his arms?' Napoleon asked Bernadotte sarcastically, after which he removed him from command with the words: 'A bungler like you is no good to me.'[51] By 9.45 a.m. General Molitor from Masséna's corps retook Aderklaa, but many men had died as a result of Bernadotte's unforced error.

At 10 a.m., using a watchtower on the heights above Markgrafneusiedl as his aiming-point, Davout sent 10,000 cavalry across the open plain to the right, sweeping aside the Austrian cavalry and providing room for Friant's and Morand's infantry divisions to advance, forcing the Austrians to extend the line in order to prevent their flank being turned.* If Archduke Johann had arrived at this point it could have been disastrous for Napoleon, but he had allowed his men a lunch stop on the way and told his brother he couldn't arrive before 5 p.m., so Charles now had to commit his reserves. When Johann's scouts finally arrived they advised him that the battle was lost and there was no point in his coming out onto the field at all, so he didn't. Anyone other than the Emperor's brother would have faced a court martial for this decision.

Markgrafsneusiedl was now the key to the Austrian position. An escarpment turns north-east there and the slopes are gentle. The village is just below. Fierce house-to-house and hand-to-hand fighting took place between the stone houses, the windmill, the monastery and old moated church, but unco-ordinated Austrian counter-attacks failed to retake what was soon a burning village. Astonishingly, Napoleon – who had spent sixty of the previous seventy-two hours in the saddle – took one of his ten-minute naps at about this point of the battle, a measure of his sangfroid as much as of his exhaustion. When he woke and saw that Markgrafneusiedl was still in Davout's hands, he pronounced the battle won.[52] Napoleon's ability to sleep on a battlefield with 700 cannon firing is all the more remarkable considering that on or near the Raasdorf knoll that served as his headquarters no fewer than twenty-six staff officers were killed or wounded that day. Both the men commanding the two regiments composing the Guard Chasseurs à Cheval lost a leg: Major Pierre Daumesnil, who was riddled with wounds and was admired by the whole army, lost his left leg, while his friend Major Hercules Corbineau, brother of Napoleon's aide-de-camp who had died at Eylau, lost his right. (When Corbineau went to Napoleon years later to discuss the deposit he needed to put down before he could become a tax inspector in the Seine department, the Emperor is credited with saying that he would take his leg in lieu of any need for a down-payment.) After a howitzer shell caused Napoleon's horse to shy, Oudinot exclaimed, 'Sire, they are firing on the headquarters.' 'Monsieur,' the Emperor replied, 'in war all accidents are possible.'[53] And when a staff officer had his helmet knocked off by a cannonball, Napoleon joked: 'It's a good job you're not any taller!'[54]

When shortly before 11 a.m. Archduke Charles sent 14,000 men marching along the Danube towards the Lobau bridgehead, hoping to

---

* The tower which is there today was built after the battle.

cut off Napoleon's line of retreat and get behind the French lines, Masséna's corps undertook one of the most ambitious manoeuvres of the campaign, marching 5 miles right across the battlefield, directly in front of two Austrian corps.[55] Napoleon then ordered Bessières to launch a cavalry attack at the junction between Kollowrath's corps and the Austrian grenadier reserves. He watched as 4,000 heavy cavalrymen rode past him crying 'Vive l'Empereur!', to which he replied, '*Ne sabrez pas: pointez, pointez*' (Don't slash, use the points of your swords, use the points).[56] Bessières' horse was shot from under him and Bessières himself was hit by a cannonball and taken from the field. Napoleon urged those who knew not to draw attention to what had happened as he feared it would affect morale. Once Bessières recovered he teased him that that his absence cost him 20,000 prisoners.[57] His charge was the last decisive use of cavalry on a Napoleonic battlefield, just as the battle as a whole was the start of the dominance of artillery. Cavalry would no longer be the pivotal arm in warfare, though it was to take several decades before this was fully appreciated.

The French lost huge numbers of horses at Wagram, but Bessières' charge bought time for the deployment of Lauriston's massive Grand Battery of 112 guns. These included sixty 12-pounders of the Imperial Guard artillery – Napoleon's 'cherished daughters' – in the centre of the battlefield. He pounded the Austrian positions with 15,000 rounds, which bounced often on the flat hard ground and set the cornfields alight, burning many of the wounded to death. The battlefield resounded with a gigantic percussive din.

When the Austrians fell back, the Grand Battery pushed forward. Napoleon asked for twenty volunteers from each company of the Old Guard infantry to run forward to help manoeuvre and service these guns, and he got them. At about 1 p.m., as Davout advanced along the Russbach, Napoleon ordered Macdonald to make an attack that would pin down the Austrian reserve formations and stop them from moving against Davout. Macdonald had hoped to be raised to the marshalate when it was first created in 1804, but his republican politics – he still wore his old uniform with its tricolour sash – and his friendship with Moreau had precluded that. As Eugène's immensely competent second-in-command, he had done very well in Italy, and at Wagram he performed superbly. His 8,000 men now formed a gigantic, hollow, open-backed square 900 yards wide and 600 yards deep, which he marched towards the Austrian line, with cavalry covering its open back. It was the last time such a formation was used in the Napoleonic Wars because it was so hard to control; the front battalions could fire but not those behind them, and it naturally drew much artillery fire. Nonetheless, there was far too much Austrian cavalry near by not to have the men in square. The formation also made it look as though Macdonald had far more men than he really did.

Although it took heavy casualties, Macdonald's square – supported by the light cavalry of the Army of Italy on the right and heavy cavalry on the left, and with covering fire from the Grand Battery – bought the time necessary for Masséna and Davout to outflank the Austrian right and left respectively. Seeing that Macdonald needed further support, Napoleon released Wrede's 5,500-strong Bavarian Division and some of the Young Guard. (Lightly wounded in this attack, Wrede melodramatically cried out, 'Tell the Emperor I die for him!' only to receive the robust reply from Macdonald: 'You'll live; tell him yourself.'[58])

At 2 p.m. Archduke Charles decided on a phased withdrawal. The Grenadiers and Reserve Cavalry covered each other as the villages of Stadlau, Kagran, Leopoldsdau and Strebersdorf continued to be contested. There was no sign of panic. It was at this late stage of the battle that the brilliant French cavalry general Antoine de Lasalle – who had distinguished himself at Austerlitz, Eylau and Stettin, saved Davout's life in Egypt, broken seven swords in the 1800 campaign and saved Murat's life at Heilsberg – was shot dead at the head of his men. 'Any trooper who is not dead by thirty is a coward,' he had once said of the hussars, 'and I don't anticipate exceeding that length of time.'[59] He was thirty-three.

Some of the French units had spent forty hours in almost continuous action, and most were simply too exhausted to pursue the enemy. As he shared some soup, bread and chicken with a voltigeur at around 7 p.m., Napoleon recognized that he could not follow up his victory on the field. Although the name of Wagram is to be found in marble alongside Austerlitz and Arcole at the foot of Napoleon's tomb at Les Invalides, in fact it was something of a pyrrhic victory. No fewer than 30,000 men of the Grande Armée were killed or wounded at Wagram and 4,000 captured, and it lost many of its horses, eleven guns, three eagles and nine colours. The Austrian losses, at 23,000 killed and wounded and 18,000 captured, were substantial, but they lost only nine guns and one colour owing to their disciplined withdrawal back towards Znaim. 'The whole French army got drunk the night after the battle of Wagram,' Captain Blaze recalled. 'The vintage was good, the quantity abundant, the soldiers drank immoderately.'[60] After two such days, they deserved it.

*

'No rancour,' Napoleon said to Macdonald afterwards, in recognition of their past political differences; 'from today we'll be friends, and I will send you, as proof, your marshal's baton that you won so gloriously yesterday.'[61] It was one of only two battlefield batons Napoleon ever bestowed, the other being Poniatowski's during the battle of Leipzig. Despite his disapproval of Oudinot's high losses on the first day, and his criticisms of Marmont's tardiness in crossing the Danube, they too received batons a week later. Marmont was only thirty-four, bringing the average age of the active-duty marshalate down to forty-three. These three post-Wagram creations were described by the soldiers at the time as 'One for friendship, one for France, and one for the army', as Marmont had been with Napoleon since Toulon, Macdonald was a fine soldier and Oudinot was beloved by his men.[62]

'My enemies are defeated, thrashed, in full rout,' Napoleon wrote to Josephine at 2 a.m. on the night after the battle; 'they were very numerous; I have crushed them. My health is good today.'[63] Three hours later he told her that he had captured one hundred guns – an absurd exaggeration – and complained of sunburn. A further, inconclusive battle was fought by Marmont against Archduke Charles at Znaim on July 10–11, and Napoleon accepted the Archduke's offer of an armistice the next day. He wasn't to see a battlefield again for another three years.

Francis I refused the armistice agreed between Napoleon and Archduke Charles six days after Wagram. Some 40,000 British troops had just landed on Walcheren Island in Holland, carried in 35 ships-of-the-line and 200 other vessels, and he wished to see how Britain's attack developed before he sued for peace. The expedition was a disaster: it was immediately struck down by a malarial-dysentery infection that disabled half the men and killed over 10 per cent of them (as against only 106 lost in battle). 'Fever and inundation will render an account of the English,' Napoleon wrote to his war minister Henri Clarke with remarkable foresight as early as August 9. 'As long as they remain on the island of Walcheren there is nothing to fear . . . Allow them to lash their buttocks in the marshes and pursue the shadow of a prey.'[64] With 11,000 sick soldiers, the expedition limped home just before Christmas. Fouché had acted quickly, raising a large army to protect Antwerp should the British land there too, but Napoleon was only mildly impressed: 'You might take it into your head to raise an army against me!' he shot back.[65] Even before that, in September, Francis acknowledged that the Walcheren expedition could not save him, and Austria began negotiations to end the War of the Fifth Coalition.

22

Zenith

'Everyone knows that the ties of family count for very little in
political calculations, and are nullified after twenty years. Philip
V waged war against his grandfather.'
Napoleon to Tsar Alexander, July 1808

'Ought princesses to fall in love? They are political chattels.'
Napoleon on St Helena

'There must be a superior power which dominates all the other powers,'
Napoleon baldly stated, 'with enough authority to force them to live in
harmony with one another – and France is best placed for that purpose.'[1] When he came to power, France's population (then the largest in
Western Europe), agricultural production, scientific advances, opera,
furniture, painting, design, theatre and literature, together with the
ubiquity of its language and the size and beauty of Paris, all combined
to make it the leading as well as the predominant nation in Europe.

In his belief in rational progress and in the possibility of benificent
dictatorship, Napoleon was the last of the Enlightened absolutists who
had emerged so frequently in Europe since the late seventeenth century;
his own reverence for its most famous exemplar, Frederick the Great,
underscored this identification. He believed, as many Frenchmen did,
that modern ideas of governance could be spread across Europe through
the agency of the Grande Armée.[2] 'You have nothing but special laws,'
he told an Italian delegation at Lyons in 1805, 'henceforth you must
have general laws. Your people have only local habits; it is necessary
that they should take on national habits.'[3] For many German and Italian public officials, Napoleon's Empire, in the words of the British
historian H. A. L. Fisher, 'shattered the obdurate crust of habit and

substituted wide ideals of efficient combination for narrow, slovenly, lethargic provincialism'.[4] By 1810 he was moving towards a progressive unitary Empire with uniform laws based on the Napoleonic Code, enlightened secularism and religious toleration, equality before the law, and uniform weights, measures and currency.[5] Yet the French administrative model was almost never simply imposed on conquered territories so much as adapted subtly according to prevailing local circumstances. If the Code was likely to create resistance and impede 'contributions' and recruitment, then its implementation was delayed.[6] In Bavaria and Baden, for example, administrators totally overhauled all the state structures in the Napoleonic manner, whereas in less Francophile Mecklenburg and Saxony next to no reforms were made.[7]

Napoleon's political support from inside the annexed territories came from many constituencies: urban elites who didn't want to return to the rule of their local Legitimists, administrative reformers who valued efficiency, religious minorities such as Protestants and Jews whose rights were protected by law, liberals who believed in concepts such as secular education and the liberating power of divorce, Poles and other nationalities who hoped for national self-determination, businessmen (at least until the Continental System started to bite), admirers of the simplicity of the Code Napoléon, opponents of the way the guilds had worked to restrain trade, middle-class reformers, in France those who wanted legal protection for their purchases of hitherto ecclesiastical or princely confiscated property, and – especially in Germany – peasants who no longer had to pay feudal dues.[8] Yet although Napoleon wanted all traces of feudal entitlements, entailments and privileges abolished, some parts of the Empire, such as Westphalia, Poland, Spain, Illyria (the western Balkans) and Calabria, were so backward that they remained feudal in all but name.[9] If his system was to work smoothly, what it most needed was time.

Of course some Legitimist governments had attempted to modernize before Napoleon, but they had tended to encounter resistance from Church hierarchies, privileged orders, entrenched guilds, obstructive judiciaries, penny-pinching *parlements*, reactionary nobilities and a suspicious peasantry.[10] Because the Napoleonic state had so much more capacity than any of its predecessors, Napoleon could slice through these Gordian knots and deliver what has been described as a 'systematic reorganisation of the administrative, bureaucratic and financial institutions' of the wider Empire.[11] The result was a hierarchical and uniform administration controlled from Paris in which, in the words of an admiring contemporary, 'the executive chain descends without interruption from the minister to the administered and transmits the law and the government's orders to the furthest ramification of the social order'.[12] It was the fulfilment of the dream of the eighteenth-century enlightened despots.

To large numbers of people across Europe Napoleon seemed to represent the ideas of progress, meritocracy and a rational future. When Count Maximilian von Montgelas, effectively the prime minister of Bavaria, secularized the monasteries, introduced compulsory education and vaccination, instituted examinations for the civil service, abolished internal tolls and extended civil rights to Jews and Protestants there between 1806 and 1817, he did so because it conformed to what he called the *Zeitgeist* (spirit of the age).[13] Why should an Italian, Dutch, Belgian or German lawyer, doctor, architect or businessman prefer to be ruled by some inbred princeling than by Napoleon, a member of the Institut de France who believed in opening careers to the talents? Of course practically they often had little choice but to serve the French in the short term, but for many the advent of French military victory gave them an opportunity to adopt modern practices from a revolutionary system shorn of the guillotine and the Terror. Nor were they required to like Napoleon or the French to appreciate that their ways were more efficient. In Italy, for example, the system of tax collection instituted by Napoleon lasted for a century after his fall.[14] It is a myth, however, that Napoleon was a believer in pan-Europeanism; in 1812 he propagated the idea that he was the defender of European Christian civilization, holding back the barbarian Asiatic hordes of Russia, and made much of the idea of European unity when constructing his legacy, but his Empire was always primarily a French construct, not a European one.

One of the many areas in which Napoleon's commitment to the Continental System damaged him was in his relations with the Papacy. Pius VII refused to join his European blockade against British trade and produce. Taken together with Pius' refusal to grant Jérôme a divorce or to recognize Joseph as king of Naples, this seemed to Napoleon to suggest that he had an enemy in the Vatican. In February 1808 he sent General Sextius Miollis down the west coast of Italy to occupy the Papal States, including the Castel Sant'Angelo, the papal fortress on the Tiber. French cannon could soon be seen pointing directly at St Peter's. The

Pope nonetheless refused to declare war on Britain, and was unmoved when Napoleon pointed out that it was an heretical power. Once it became clear that the Pope would not bow to his will over the expulsion of British goods and merchants from the Papal States, on June 10, 1809 Napoleon annexed them to the French Empire, and in retaliation Pius immediately excommunicated the Emperor of the French.

Back in July 1807 Napoleon had scoffed at the notion of papal punishment to Talleyrand. 'It only remains for them to shut me up in a monastery, and to have me whipped like Louis le Débonnaire.'[15] (Charlemagne's son Louis I had whipped himself for having red-hot stilettos poked into the eyeballs of his nephew, Prince Bernard.) Excommunication was no laughing matter, however, since in Poland, Italy and France there were millions of pious Catholics who now had to rethink their loyalty to an infidel emperor. This was especially problematic at a time when he was hoping to win the allegiance of the ultra-Catholic Spaniards, whose priests were to use Napoleon's new heretical status as a potent propaganda tool against the French occupiers.

Franco-Vatican relations had continued to deteriorate over the next thirteen months, and on the night before the battle of Wagram, on July 5, 1809, under orders from Napoleon, Savary took the extraordinary step of having General Étienne Radet arrest the Pope in the Vatican, giving him half an hour to pack his bags before escorting him to the bishop's palace in the small Italian Riviera port of Savona. This allowed Pope Pius to make one of the wriest remarks of the nineteenth century. 'Assuredly, my son,' he told Radet, 'those orders will not bring divine orders upon you.'[16] Napoleon meanwhile told his brother-in-law Prince Camillo Borghese, who was governor-general of the Alpine region which included Savona, that 'The guard of the Pope should have all the appearance of a guard of honour.'[17]*

Pius behaved with great dignity, but it was a sorry tale of strong-arm tactics with absolutely no advantage for Napoleon. The only material change was that British goods now had to be smuggled into Livorno rather than landing openly on the docks as hitherto. While pious

---

* In May 1812, when it was recognized that Royal Navy cruisers could get close enough to Savona to rescue the pontiff, he was taken to Fontainebleau Palace, where he lived in some luxury until his release in 1814. One can still see the rooms he occupied there. 'The Pope must not travel in papal dress,' Napoleon told Borghese with his typical eye for public opinion, 'but only in clerical garments so that nowhere en route ... can he be recognized.' (CN12 no. 8710 p. 417)

Catholics privately fumed at the treatment meted out to the Vicar of Christ, Napoleon found an historical precedent for his action, declaring that Rome had always been part of Charlemagne's Empire. He added that now it would be an 'imperial free city', 'the second city of the Empire', and France would donate 2 million francs per annum to cover Church expenses.[18] Canova also had no difficulty persuading him to spend 200,000 francs per annum preserving Roman antiquities. 'The Pope is a good man,' Napoleon told Fouché on August 6, 'but ignorant and fanatical.'[19] Those adjectives alas better describe Napoleon's behaviour towards the pontiff.

On July 27–28, 1809 Joseph, Jourdan and Victor were soundly defeated at the hands of Wellington and the Spanish Captain-General Cuesta at the battle of Talavera. Napoleon was particularly incensed by the way Jourdan misled him in his report, claiming that Wellington had lost 10,000 men – that is, one-third of his army – and possession of the battlefield. When Napoleon discovered that the number was really 4,600 and that the French had been 'repulsed all day long', he described Jourdan's lies as 'a straightforward crime', and was furious that they might well have influenced his strategy in Spain. 'He may say what he likes in the Madrid newspapers,' he wrote, thus acknowledging the endemic untruthfulness of press accounts, 'but he has no right to disguise the truth from the Government.'[20] Napoleon tended to believe the accounts in the British papers over those of his own generals, telling Clarke: 'You must also tell General Sénarmont that he has not sent a correct account of his artillery; that the English captured more guns than he admits.'[21] (It wasn't six as Sénarmont reported, but seventeen.) 'As long as they will attack good troops like the English, in good positions without making sure they can be carried,' he continued, 'my men will be led to death to no purpose.'[22]

Napoleon celebrated his fortieth birthday on August 15, 1809 by making Masséna, Davout and Berthier princes, each title coming with a large *dotation*. That night, after a grand parade, a review of the Guard at Enzersdorf and a gala dinner, he and Berthier slipped incognito into Vienna, an enemy capital under occupation where he might have been recognized, to watch the firework display in his honour.[23] He nonetheless worked as hard as ever during the day, writing from Schönbrunn to Cambacérès about a message to the Senate, his ambassador to Moscow, General Caulaincourt, about rumoured British attempts to buy muskets in Russia, the war minister General Clarke about Spain, and ordering the intendant-general of the Army of Germany, Pierre Daru, to give 300 francs to every child whose father had died at Austerlitz. Further letters that day went to Murat about setting up duchies in Sicily once their enemies were 'purged' from there and to Berthier about building boats that could transport 6,600 men across the Danube.[24]

By September Francis was obliged to start negotiations. 'Your master and I are like two bulls,' Napoleon told the Austrian negotiator, Colonel Count Ferdinand Bubna, 'who wish to mate with Germany and Italy.'[25] To Murat's aide-de-camp (and Hortense's lover) Colonel Charles de Flahaut, he went on to say: 'I need Germany and I need Italy; for Italy means Spain, and Spain is a prolongation of France.'[26] This virtually guaranteed the eternal enmity of Austria, which had been the predominant power in both Italy and Germany for generations before the French Revolution. 'I am not afraid of him,' Napoleon said privately of Francis, 'I despise him too much. He is not a knave; on the contrary, he is a simple soul like Louis XVI, but he is always under the influence of the last person to whom he has spoken. One can never trust him.'[27] As for the coming negotiations: 'What matters it to them if they give up a few provinces; they are so dishonest that they will seize them again whenever they get the chance?' The experiences of 1796–7, 1800–01, 1805 and 1809 certainly suggested that that was true. 'Here's the second time I've been to the battlefield of Austerlitz,' Napoleon said, dining with his generals at Brno on September 17. 'Will I have to come here a third time?' 'Sire,' they replied, 'according to what we're seeing every day, nobody would dare bet against it.'[28]

The Treaty of Schönbrunn was signed on October 14 by Champagny and Liechtenstein and ratified the next day by Napoleon and soon afterwards by Francis. Given that Francis had launched the war after several warnings, he could hardly complain of its harsh terms. Confining her armed forces to 150,000 men, and almost cutting her off from the sea by annexing the Illyrian provinces (she retained Fiume), Napoleon effectively reduced Austria to a second-rate power. She ceded Istria and Carinthia to France, and Salzburg, Berchtesgaden and parts of Upper Austria to Bavaria; was made to join the Continental System, and had to recognize all of Napoleon's changes in Iberia and Italy. Austrian Galicia was split, the western four-fifths going to the Duchy of Warsaw and one-fifth (mainly eastern Galicia) to Russia. Despite the fact that 400,000 people had been added to the Russian Empire, this nevertheless raised new fears in St Petersburg that Napoleon intended to recreate the Kingdom of Poland.[29] In total, Austria had to give up 3½ million of her population and to pay large indemnities. Francis also had to promise 'peace and friendship … in perpetuity', a similar phrase to the one he had assented to only four years earlier, which he did with the same degree of sincerity.[30]

On the day the treaty was signed, Napoleon ordered Eugène to help the Bavarians crush a pro-Austrian rebellion that had broken out in the Tyrol in April.[31] On October 17 Eugène took 56,000 Bavarian and French troops into the region to crush the resistance movement led by the charismatic former-innkeeper Andreas Hofer, who was betrayed and captured in the village of St Martin in the South Tyrol in late January. (The soldiers who seized him tore at his beard till his cheeks bled, wanting souvenirs of their formidable enemy.)[32] Eugène pleaded for clemency, but on February 11, 1810 Napoleon replied that with the negotiations over his approaching marriage in full swing he didn't want matters complicated by an official Austrian request for Hofer to be spared, so a military tribunal needed to be convened and he would have to be shot within twenty-four hours.[33]

The Treaty of Schönbrunn has been criticized as a Carthaginian peace, which ultimately worked against Napoleon's interests because it forced the Austrians to go to war against him yet again, but that happened only after he had been catastrophically defeated by Russia in 1812. At the time it seemed that a new kind of Franco-Austrian relationship was necessary to prevent these constant wars of revenge. Metternich, who was appointed foreign minister on October 8, had already concluded that Austria's only alternative after her fourth successive defeat in twelve years was to join France as her junior partner. He spoke of 'adapting to the triumphant French system'.[34] This could be achieved at a stroke, of course, if Napoleon were to divorce Josephine and marry Francis's daughter, the Archduchess Marie Louise, who would be eighteen that December. Tentative preliminary soundings were taken. By 1809, Napoleon hadn't given up the idea of marrying a Romanov princess, but neither an Austrian nor a Russian bride was possible while he was still married to Josephine.

Two developments, one two years previously and one very recent, may have concentrated Napoleon's mind on the prospect of the succession and have renewed his desire for a child of his own to continue his dynasty.[35] In the early hours of May 5, 1807, Louis and Hortense's four-year-old son Napoléon-Louis-Charles, the Crown Prince of Holland, whom Napoleon might have been considering as his ultimate heir, had died at The Hague of a croup-like illness. Hortense fell into a deep depression that could not have been much helped by letters such as Napoleon's of June 16 that read, 'I am touched by your suffering, but I wish that you were more courageous. To live is to suffer, and a human being who is worthy of honour must always struggle for mastery of self.' He ended three sentences later, writing of Friedland: 'I had a great victory on 14 June. I am well, and I love you very much.'[36] The child's death ended any lingering attachment Hortense might have had to Louis, and she later had a child by the Comte de Flahaut.[37] 'I could wish to be near you, to make you moderate and sensible in your grief,' Napoleon wrote to Josephine of her grandson's death. 'You have had the good fortune not to lose any children, but such loss is one of the conditions and pains attached to our human misery. Might I only learn that you have been reasonable and are well! Would you add to my sorrow?'[38] Although Napoleon himself might not have immediately spotted the way in which the infant's death would increase the pressure on his own marriage, the far more emotionally intelligent, now forty-five-year-old Josephine did. Part of the reason why she could not be 'sensible in her grief' was that she was grieving not just for her daughter and grandson but for her own marriage, realizing that Napoleon might now wish to produce his own heir. Napoleon knew himself to be capable of this, because he had already had an illegitimate son, Count Léon, by his former mistress Éléonore de la Plaigne, and in the late summer of 1809 Marie Walewska also became pregnant by him.

Then, at 9 a.m. on Thursday, October 12, as Napoleon was about to interview some released French prisoners-of-war not far from the horseshoe-shaped double staircase at the back of Schönbrunn Palace, Friedrich Staps, the eighteen-year-old son of a Lutheran pastor from Erfurt, attempted to assassinate him while pretending to hand him a petition. He would have succeeded had Rapp not seized him a few paces away, whereupon Rapp, Berthier and two gendarmes found a large carving knife on him. 'I was struck with the expression of his eyes when he looked at me,' Rapp recalled, 'his decided manner roused my suspicions.'[39] Napoleon interviewed Staps soon afterwards, in the company of Bernadotte, Berthier, Savary and Duroc, with the Alsatian-born Rapp interpreting. The Emperor hoped that the young student was insane and thus might be pardoned, but Corvisart pronounced him healthy and rational, albeit a political fanatic. When asked by Napoleon what he would do if he were freed, he replied, 'I would try to kill you again.' He was shot at 7 a.m. on the 17th, crying 'Long live Germany!' to the firing squad, and 'Death to the tyrant!'[40] It had been impressed upon Napoleon in a very direct, personal manner that a new and uncompromising spirit of German nationalism was now alive in the lands that only three years before had been slumbering in the centuries-old embrace of the Holy Roman Empire.* 'I've always had a dread of madmen,' Napoleon told his secretary, recalling an evening when he'd been accosted at the theatre by an escapee from the Bicêtre lunatic asylum. 'I am in love with the Empress!' the man had cried. 'You seem to have chosen an extraordinary confidant,' Napoleon replied.[41]†

Napoleon's ruthlessness came out starkly in his next move. The close, comfortable, companionable marriage that he and Josephine had built up since his return from Egypt – in which she complained about his affairs but stayed faithful to him – was now a block to his political and dynastic ambitions and what he conceived to be the best interests of France, and so it had to end. His close proximity to men killed on many battlefields, lucky survival of the *machine infernale*, injury at Ratisbon, and the recently failed assassination attempt, now helped to concentrate his advisors' minds. He left Schönbrunn on October 16 and arrived back at Fontainebleau at 9 a.m. on the 26th. (Pauline and one of her ladies-in-waiting, the plump and pretty twenty-five-year-old Piedmontese reader Baroness Christine de Mathis, came to visit that evening and Napoleon embarked on an affair with Christine almost immediately, which was to last until the night before his wedding. He would later say of her, 'she accepted presents'.[42]) He ordered that the connecting door between his and Josephine's bedrooms be walled up; there was nothing metaphysical or ambiguous about this message of rejection. 'All tenderness on the Emperor's part, all consideration for my mother had vanished,' wrote Hortense of this painful time, 'he became unjust and vexatious in his attitude . . . I wished that the divorce had already been pronounced.'[43] The family left for the Tuileries on November 15 and by the 27th Bausset, who watched closely as the marriage entered its

---

* One evening after Wagram, Napoleon and Rapp, who would tease him in a way few others were permitted, were playing *vingt-et-un* (pontoon or blackjack) for gold twenty-franc coins minted since 1803 and called napoleons, when the Emperor attempted a pun. 'Rapp, are not the Germans very fond of these little napoleons?' he asked. 'Yes, Sire,' Rapp replied. 'They like them much better than the big one.' 'That, I suppose,' laughed the Emperor, 'is what you call German frankness' (Rapp, *Memoirs* p. 26).

† Napoleon not only dreaded madmen, but inspired them: at the time of his burial in Paris in December 1840 there were no fewer than fourteen patients at Bicêtre who believed they were him.

pathological final stage, had noticed 'a great alteration in the features of the Empress, and a silent constraint in Napoleon'.[44]

Had his Empire been an ancient, established one it might have survived the accession of a brother or nephew, but Napoleon's Empire was not yet five years old, and he came to the conclusion that for the Bonaparte dynasty to survive he needed a son. After thirteen years of trying, the forty-six-year-old Josephine clearly wasn't going to produce one. Napoleon knew all about the bloody power struggles that had followed the deaths of Alexander the Great and Julius Caesar, who died without obvious heirs. His current heir was Joseph, whose wife Julie Clary had not borne him any sons, and who was manifestly failing in Spain. As early as July 1806 the Duc de Lévis, an émigré who had returned after 18 Brumaire, had warned the Emperor, 'Atlas carried the world, but after him came chaos.'[45]

On November 30 Napoleon told Josephine he wanted to annul their marriage. 'You have children,' he said, 'I have none. You must feel the necessity that lies upon me of strengthening my dynasty.'[46] She wept, said she couldn't live without him, implored him to reconsider. 'I have seen her weep for hours together,' Rapp recalled of this period; 'she spoke of her attachment for Bonaparte, for so she used to call him in our presence. She regretted the close of her splendid career: this was very natural.'[47] She wore a large white hat at dinner that night to hide the fact that she had been crying but Bausset found her 'the image of grief and of despair'.[48] Dining alone together, neither Napoleon nor Josephine ate much and the only words that passed were Napoleon asking Bausset about the weather. At one point during dinner, Napoleon recalled, 'she gave a scream and fainted', and had to be carried away by her lady-in-waiting.[49] On another occasion, or perhaps the same one but differently remembered, Bausset heard 'violent cries from the Empress Josephine issue from the Emperor's chamber', and Bausset entered to find her lying on the carpet 'uttering piercing cries and complaints' saying she would 'never survive' a divorce. Napoleon asked Bausset and a secretary to take her to her bedroom up the private staircase, which they managed to do although Bausset nearly tripped over his dress-sword as he was doing so.

Eugène's arrival on December 5 helped calm his mother, and the Bonapartes and Beauharnais were soon able to get down to discussing specifics. In order to qualify for the Church ceremony that Napoleon needed for his next wedding, his religious marriage to Josephine on the eve of his coronation had to be declared invalid, even though it had been performed by a prince of the Church, Cardinal Fesch. So Napoleon argued that it had been clandestine, with insufficient witnesses, and that he had been acting under Josephine's compulsion.[50] Josephine agreed to go along with this absurdity, but no fewer than thirteen out of France's twenty-seven cardinals refused to attend Napoleon's next wedding. (When Napoleon banned them from wearing their scarlet robes of office, the dissenters became known as 'the black cardinals'.) In nullifying the marriage, the government law officers took as their precedents the divorces of Louis XII and Henri IV.[51]

At the meeting on December 7 at which Josephine had to declare before the grand officers of the Empire that she consented to the divorce, her niece's husband, the minister Antoine Lavalette, recorded: 'She displayed so much courage and firmness of mind that all the spectators were deeply moved. The next day she left the Tuileries, never to return more.'[52] When she got into her carriage with her lady-in-waiting, 'not one single person remained to show her a grateful face'. Such is the cruelty of courts. She was hardly exiled from Paris, however, as she kept the Élysée Palace as part of her settlement. Napoleon gave her Malmaison and the fourteenth-century Château Navarre in Normandy, which had cost him 900,000 francs, and she maintained her rank of empress, all honours and prerogatives, while her debts of 2 million francs were paid off and she enjoyed 3 million francs per annum in income for life.[53] As Frederick the Great said of Maria Theresa at the time of the first partition of Poland: 'She wept, but she took.'

The financial aspects worked well for both of them: Josephine was given a vast income, and it is a fortunate man who has his divorce settlement paid by the state. Ironically, although it was to get an imperial heir that Napoleon divorced Josephine, it would turn out to be her grandson, rather than any offspring of Napoleon, who would become the next emperor of France and her direct descendants who today sit on the thrones of Belgium, Denmark, Sweden, Norway and Luxembourg. His sit on none.

Even before breaking the news to Josephine, Napoleon had written to Caulaincourt, the French ambassador to Russia, on November 22, to ask him privately to sound out the Tsar over the prospect of his marrying his sister, the Grand Duchess Anna Pavlovna: 'I do not make a formal request, I solicit an expression of your opinion.'[54] So began a dual courtship with the Russians and the Austrians. Napoleon made it clear in mid-December that his preference was for Anna and he didn't care about the religious considerations involved – to a man who had flirted with Islam and embraced excommunication, the fact that she was Russian Orthodox was not an insurmountable problem. There was an alternative princess available in Saxony, but she would not have brought the geopolitical benefits of a marriage to Tsar Alexander's sister or Emperor Francis's daughter. The age gap – Anna wouldn't be fifteen until January – would probably have meant that she would have stayed in St Petersburg for a few years before moving to Paris.

On December 16 Napoleon's marriage to Josephine was dissolved by a four-sentence *sénatus-consulte*, and immediately afterwards he ordered Caulaincourt to propose to Anna on his behalf, asking for a response in two days. The Russians took thirty-eight. 'I tell you frankly,' Alexander told Caulaincourt, 'my sister could not do better.'[55] He wasn't being frank: the Tsar did not want a *mésalliance* between the Romanovs and a Corsican upstart any more than did his mother. Equally, he couldn't afford to offend Napoleon while France was so much in the ascendant and Russia had no allies. He wanted at very least a signed agreement with France on the future of Poland as the price for his assent, and to that end Caulaincourt and the Russian foreign minister Rumiantsev drafted a convention on December 28, the first article of which was a 'Reciprocal engagement never to permit the re-establishment of Poland', and the second suppressed the word 'Poland' and 'Poles' in all public acts, while Article 5 forbade any further territorial extension of the Duchy of Warsaw.[56] When the Tsar implied he could remove his mother's objection to the marriage, Caulaincourt signed. The Tsar of All the Russias was therefore perfectly willing to sacrifice his teenage sister to the man his family saw as a forty-year-old Corsican parvenu in order to keep Poland partitioned. What Napoleon's brave Polish lancers would have made of all this is impossible to say. On January 10 Caulaincourt received orders from Napoleon to obtain a definite reply to the proposal within ten days of receipt, at a time when couriers took nearly three weeks to get from Paris to St Petersburg.[57]

By February 6 Napoleon no longer thought it worth tying his hands over Poland for Anna, and he ordered Champagny not to ratify the signed treaty, calling it 'ridiculous and absurd'. Disavowing Caulaincourt's actions, he stated, 'I cannot say that the kingdom of Poland will never be re-established because that would mean that if one day the Lithuanians or any others would re-establish it, I would be forced to send some troops to oppose it. This is contrary to my dignity. My goal is to tranquillize Russia.'[58] He proposed an alternative convention promising not to help any other Power re-establish Poland, but the Tsar considered that insufficient.[59] The result was that Napoleon felt snubbed, and started to look to Vienna for his future bride, and Alexander, for his part, realized that Napoleon could not be trusted over Poland.[60] He also soon suspected that a dual courtship had been taking place and was offended over that too, or at least pretended to be.[61]

'I don't know what is required after all this,' Napoleon wrote to Alexander on the last day of 1809, hoping to keep the friendship alive. 'I can't destroy chimeras and fight against clouds.'[62] By early February 1810 Alexander was pushing ahead with thoroughgoing reforms of the Russian army.[63] In January he had appointed the modernizer General Barclay de Tolly as minister for war, and plans for defending Russia's western border along the line of the Dvina and Berezina rivers were drawn up. That year also saw a nationalist propaganda movement start in Russia, and criticism of France was once more allowed in the press. Francophobic literary and philological clubs were also permitted.[64] When Marie Walewska gave birth to Napoleon's son on May 4 1810, the baby was given the name Alexandre. It didn't help.

Years later, Napoleon recalled briefly considering taking a Parisian wife. He said he had made a list of five or six women, but at a vote at the Tuileries five councillors had supported the Austrian alliance, two the Saxon, with Fouché and Cambacérès still holding out for Anna. Napoleon suspected that the last two opposed the Austrian marriage only because they had voted for the execution of Marie Louise's great-aunt, Marie Antoinette. Cambacérès denied it, saying that he knew Napoleon would end up going to war with whichever country wasn't chosen, and 'I dread a march to St Petersburg more than a march to Vienna.'[65]

The initial auguries for Napoleon's marriage to Marie Louise were not good: as a child she had played with 'a ferocious effigy' of him in her nursery, and at fourteen and eighteen she had been forced to leave her home to escape his armies. 'I pity the poor princess he chooses,' she wrote before she had any inkling it would be her. Once she realized it would be, she wrote: 'I resign my fate into the hands of Divine Providence', asking a friend to 'Pray that it may never happen.'[66] Napoleon was much happier with the situation. 'When I heard Marie Louise was fair I was very glad,' he recalled.[67] She was better than just fair; Lavalette described her as 'tall, well made, and in excellent health. She appeared adorned with all the grace and beauty that usually accompany youth', and also had an 'air of kindness, and, unlike the rest of her family, her smile was amiable and sweet'.[68] The first of Napoleon's 318 surviving letters to Marie Louise was his marriage proposal from Rambouillet on February 23, 1810, written by a secretary:

Ma cousine, The brilliant qualities that distinguish your person have inspired us with the desire to serve and honour you by approaching the Emperor, your father, with the request that he shall entrust to us the happiness of Your Imperial Highness. May we hope that the feelings which prompt us to take this step will be acceptable to you? May we flatter ourselves with the belief that you will not be guided solely by the duty of obeying your parents? Should the feelings of your Imperial Highness be partial to us, we would cultivate them so carefully and strive so constantly to please you in every way that we flatter ourselves with the hope of succeeding some day in winning your regard; such is the aim that we would fain encompass, and in respect of which we beg your Highness to favour us.[69]

It was a gracious proposal to an eighteen-year-old from a forty-year-old man. Two days later he addressed her as '*Ma Soeur*' in his own (execrable) handwriting, before settling into 'Madame' until they were married, and thence '*ma chère Louise*', '*Ma bonne Louise*' and other variations.

The nuptials between the continent's oldest and newest monarchies involved a complex process, whereby Marie Louise married Napoleon by proxy in the Capuchin Chapel of the Hofburg Palace in Vienna on March 11, Archduke Charles standing in for her at the ceremony and Berthier for Napoleon. When the aristocratic Archbishop Ferdinand de Rohan, who held the ancient honorific title First Almoner of France, wrote an absurdly oleaginous letter congratulating him on his coming marriage, the Emperor told Duroc that he must 'pay 12,000 francs to the First Almoner *out of the theatrical fund*'.[70]

Napoleon choreographed his first meeting with his bride minutely for Tuesday, March 27, 1810, after the proxy marriage but before the civil one. They were going to meet 3 miles from Soissons in a tent, he was going to bow to her, but as she was bowing before him in response he was going to raise her up. Instead it rained and anyway he was too impatient so he and Murat drove past the tent to intercept Marie Louise's carriage, which they did in front of the church at Courcelles. 'Madam,' he told her rather less imposingly as he got into her coach, 'it gives me great pleasure to meet you.'[71] He then took her in his coach to his palace at Compiègne, where they arrived at 9.30 p.m. and defied protocol by dining together, with close family, including Caroline (who as Queen of Naples had usurped the position of Marie Louise's other great-aunt, Queen Maria Carolina).[72]

During the dinner in the François I Gallery at the palace, Napoleon asked the ever-useful Cardinal Fesch in Marie Louise's presence whether they were legally already married, and was assured that they were because of the proxy ceremony in Vienna. Napoleon was supposed to be staying in the nearby Hôtel de la Chancellerie while she slept at the palace that night, to observe propriety, but Bausset thought that, judging by the breakfast Napoleon had caused to be served at the Empress's bedside at noon the next day, 'we think it probable that he did not sleep at the Hôtel de la Chancellerie', any more than he was to sleep in the Italian pavilion at Saint-Cloud on the night of their civil marriage.[73]

Recalling that first night he made love to Marie Louise, Napoleon later told a confidant: 'She liked it so much that she asked me to do it again.'[74] Despite her trepidation it started out as a happy marriage; they spent every night under the same roof from July 1810 until September 1811 and Napoleon dropped Marie Walewska, whom he had installed in Paris, when he remarried. Indeed it is not clear that Napoleon was ever unfaithful to Marie Louise, at least until after she had been unfaithful to him. 'Neither of his wives had ever anything to complain of from Napoleon's personal manners,' Metternich wrote, recalling how Marie Louise had once told him, 'I have no fear of Napoleon, but I begin to think that he is afraid of me.'[75] She was not the love of his life, however. 'I think,' he said years later, 'although I loved Marie Louise very sincerely, that I loved Josephine better. That was natural; we had risen together; and she was a true wife, the wife I had chosen. She was full of grace, graceful even in the way she prepared herself for bed; graceful in undressing herself ... I should never have parted from her if she had borne me a son; but, *ma foi* ...'[76] Napoleon was eventually to come to regret his second marriage, blaming it for his downfall. 'Assuredly but for my marriage with Marie I never should have made war on Russia,' he said, 'but I felt certain of the support of Austria, and I was wrong, for Austria is the natural enemy of France.'[77]

After their civil wedding in the Grand Gallery at Saint-Cloud on Sunday April 1, 1810, at which the Austrian ambassador, Prince Karl von Schwarzenberg, wore a field marshal's uniform that made him look 'white as a miller' and which Madame Mère attended, they went to the

Tuileries the next day for a religious wedding and public celebrations.[78] At a silver-gilt altar erected in the Salon d'Apollon at the Louvre, a square room usually used to exhibit paintings, Cardinal Fesch gave the nuptial blessing. Paris celebrated with fireworks, 3,000 legs of mutton and 1,000 sausages given to the poor, dances in the Champs-Élysées, a prisoner amnesty, horsemanship displays, concerts, parades and a hot-air balloon flying on the Champ de Mars. No one understood the importance of 'bread and circuses' as well as the modern Caesar, and the 6,000 veterans who married on the same day as him received 600 francs each.[79] Marie Louise didn't represent a very significant cost-saving for Napoleon, even vis-à-vis Josephine, who had cost him an average of 899,795 francs each year, since his new wife cost him (or at least the French treasury) 772,434 francs per annum.[80]

Marie Louise had 1,500 people presented to her on her wedding day. 'I felt ill all the time because of the diamond crown,' she told a friend afterwards; 'it was so heavy that I could scarcely bear it.' The template used was Marie Antoinette's wedding to Louis XVI in 1770 – about as unromantic a precedent as can be imagined but the one that best fitted Napoleon's view of what royal nuptials should be like. The day after his wedding, Napoleon wrote to Tsar Alexander of 'the feeling of perfect esteem and tender friendship with which I am, Monsieur *mon frère*, Your Majesty's good brother'.[81] Brother he might be according to the official courtesies of the day, but they were not going to be brothers-in-law. Only two days after Napoleon wrote those words Alexander predicted to his Polish confidant and former foreign minister, Prince Adam Czartoryski, that there would be a crisis in Franco-Russian relations 'nine months from now'.[82] The Tsar stayed in touch with Czartoryski, asking him how loyal the Duchy of Warsaw truly was towards Napoleon. The Electorate of Bavaria, Grand Duchy of Württemberg and region of Westphalia had been turned into kingdoms by Napoleon as recently as 1807, and Alexander feared the Duchy of Warsaw might be next.

Three months after Napoleon's wedding, on July 1, Schwarzenberg threw a celebratory ball at his embassy in the rue de Mont Blanc. A candle set alight a muslin curtain and then the whole building, killing four people of the six hundred present, including Schwarzenberg's sister-in-law who could be identified afterwards only by the rings she had been wearing. 'I wasn't frightened but if the Emperor had not forced me to leave the room, I would have burned because I hadn't the slightest idea of the danger,' Marie Louise told Pauline a week later. After taking his wife to safety, Napoleon returned to oversee the rescue operation, and was so unimpressed with the response times that he completely overhauled Paris's fire-engine system, creating the *sapeurs-pompiers*.[83] His superstition about the incident led him to believe that either he or Schwarzenberg lay under a curse.

It was fitting that Napoleon's wedding should have taken place at the Louvre, because the visual arts were vital to the perception of his Empire, both by contemporaries and by succeeding generations. 'My intention is to turn the arts towards subjects which could tend to perpetuate the remembrance of what has been accomplished these last fifteen years,' he told Daru, and his lavish patronage bore extraordinary fruit.[84] If Napoleon is to be criticized, as he sometimes is, for the paucity of great literature during his reign, then logically he must also deserve praise for the great art produced in the Empire period, which he did so much to encourage. Of course he used culture for political propaganda, as had Louis XIV, the French revolutionaries and indeed the Emperor Augustus and the many other Roman emperors Napoleon admired.[85] But any period that can boast painters as talented as Jacques-Louis David – who once said of Napoleon, 'In the shadow of my hero I will glide into posterity' – François Gérard, Théodore Géricault, Anne-Louis Girodet (who in 1812 was commissioned to paint no fewer than thirty-six identical full-length portraits of Napoleon; he managed twenty-six before the first abdication), Antoine-Jean Gros, Jean Urbain Guérin, Jean-Auguste Ingres, Pierre-Paul Prud'hon, Carle Vernet and his son Horace, and Élisabeth Vigée-Lebrun, as well as the miniaturists Augustin and Isabey, must be entitled to the overused soubriquet 'golden age'.[86] (In Spain, even Goya worked in King Joseph's court for a time.) Napoleon had a 60,000-franc annual budget to encourage painting, and he regularly overspent it. At the Salon of 1810 alone he bought twenty paintings for 47,000 francs for the Louvre.[87]

Napoleon's image and deeds were immortalized in paintings, prints, tapestries, medals, porcelain, objets d'art and sculpture as a way both of legitimizing his rule and, in one art historian's phrase, of 'inscribing himself permanently on the French memory'.[88] He would sit for a painter and a sculptor simultaneously, so long as they came at lunch-time and didn't talk. In the age before photography no one expected precise verisimilitude in art. Nobody thought Napoleon actually crossed the Alps on a constantly rearing stallion, as in David's painting, for example; rather it was intended as a magnificent allegorical comment on the glory of the achievement. In the bottom left-hand corner the graffiti on the Alpine rocks read 'Hannibal', 'Karolus Magnus' (that is, Charlemagne) and 'Bonaparte'.

Opponents dismissed Napoleonic art as mere propaganda, but many discerning non-French connoisseurs appreciated, collected and even commissioned it. The 10th Duke of Hamilton commissioned David to paint *Napoleon in his Study at the Tuileries* in 1811, for example; the Prince Regent bought Isabey's *The Review at the Tuileries*. The 2nd Marquis of Lansdowne bought a good deal of Napoleonic art, while Sir John Soane collected Napoleonic book-bindings and John Bowes hung portraits of Napoleon's marshals on the staircase at Barnard Castle.[89]

On occasion Napoleon displayed modesty; he refused to have himself depicted as a demi-god and when in April 1811, just prior to its public exhibition, he viewed Antonio Canova's marble statue of him as 'Mars the Peacemaker', for which he had given a record five sittings, he immediately ordered it into storage, hidden behind a wooden and canvas screen for the rest of his reign.[90] He feared people might laugh at its near-nudity and compare his physique when Canova had started the statue in 1803 with his much stouter self eight years later. (Today it can be seen in the stairwell of Apsley House in London, where the Duke of Wellington's guests used to hang their umbrellas on it.)

The patronage of Napoleon, and much more actively that of Josephine, launched an entire neo-classical artistic style, which came to comprise houses, furniture, clocks, dining rooms, tableware, textiles, wallpaper, bedrooms, painted decorations, chandeliers, mirrors, lighting and gardening. The lavish decor of the Ancien Régime had already made a mild reappearance in the Directory, but it really took the Napoleonic Empire to define the style.[91] Napoleon's fascination with Ancient Greece and Rome meant that classical architecture would always be favoured, and his Egyptian expedition inspired architects like Percier, Fontaine and Berthault and many interior decorators to experiment with Egyptian themes too.[92]

Many of the glories of the Empire style can still be seen today, and reinforce the idea that under Napoleon French architecture and decorative arts led the world. They include, taken at random: the ballroom and library at Compiègne, the façade of the Château Margaux near Bordeaux, Maison Prelle's textiles, the Grand Salon of the Hôtel de Beauharnais and the ground floor of the Hôtel Bourrienne (by Étienne Leconte) in Paris, the staircase of the Élysée Palace, Jacob-Desmalter's *secrétaires*, Canova's statue of Madame Mère at Chatsworth, Josephine's boudoir at Saint-Cloud, Martin Biennais' silver mustard pots, Pius VII's bed and Josephine's bidet at Fontainebleau, Blaise Deharme's varnished metal tea-tables, the Emperor's salon in the Grand Trianon at Versailles (where Napoleon had apartments rather than in the chateau of Versailles itself, because of its Ancien Régime overtones), Antoine-Denis Chaudet's bronzes, Auguste Famin's bathroom decorations at Rambouillet (which admittedly Napoleon didn't much like), Pierre Bellangé's armchairs, Darte Frères' swan-shaped cups, Joseph Revel's clocks, Percier's library ceiling and Berthault's Temple of Love at Malmaison, Sallandrouze's carpets from Aubusson, Joseph Thouvenin's book-bindings, the Lancelot firm's two-candle lampshades, Josephine's champagne flutes from the Montcenis factory at Le Creusot, Joseph Dufours' wallpaper, the Gobelins factory's tapestries and Marie-Joseph Genu's silver sauceboats.[93] Such an astonishing explosion of artistic creation during the Consulate and First Empire cannot be entirely detached from Napoleon, who was for over a decade the greatest art patron in Europe. Of course many of these craftsmen would have found employment anywhere in Europe – and many flourished before 1799 and after 1815 – but the sublime Empire style is unlikely to have developed as it did without the encouragement, and inspiration, of the Emperor and his wife.

On April 16, 1810 Napoleon appointed André Masséna to command the new Army of Portugal, against the marshal's own pleadings. Masséna had been suffering from respiratory problems ever since his fall from his horse on Lobau, and was nearly blinded when Napoleon shot him in a hunting accident in September 1808. ('Being wounded during a shoot is such a stroke of bad luck after all the dangers you've escaped' was all the apology he got.[94]) But when he and Masséna met face to face, Napoleon managed to persuade him to take on the Portuguese command, not least because he promised him control over strategy and assured him that 'You will lack nothing in supplies.'[95] Yet he was only given three corps, totalling fewer than 70,000 men, to recapture Portugal from Wellington, despite the fact that when Napoleon had contemplated undertaking the campaign himself he had earmarked over 100,000. By May 29, Napoleon's mania for micro-management had got the better of him, and he started sending Masséna detailed orders about where to march and when, through the medium of Masséna's hated enemy Berthier.

Masséna's wholly justified complaints by late July – that his troops hadn't been paid for six months, that thousands of rations had to be abandoned for lack of wagons, that one-third of the artillery had to be left behind in Spain for lack of mules, that the promised reinforcements hadn't arrived, and so on – fell on Berthier's unsympathetic ears. Nonetheless, in less than a month Masséna had pursued Wellington to within 20 miles of Lisbon, where he came up against the formidable defensive Lines of Torres Vedras and was forced to halt. With heavy guns and large-scale reinforcement, Masséna might have found the weakest place of the Lines to storm, but he did not have them. Napoleon assumed that Masséna's much larger force would easily overcome Wellington's 25,000 men, entirely failing to take into account the additional 25,000 Portuguese serving with Wellington. Having never seen the Lines himself he underestimated their defensive capacity, until it was explained to him on November 24 by General Maximilien Foy.

To visit the Lines today, especially in those places where they are being expertly restored to their 1810 condition, one appreciates the almost insurmountable problem that Masséna faced. Seven thousand Portuguese labourers had constructed no fewer than three lines across the 29-mile Lisbon peninsula, including 165 fortified redoubts, defended by 628 guns.[96] The Royal Navy established a telegraph system for rapid communication along each of them and the flanks were covered by gunboats anchored in the River Tagus and the sea.

Napoleon might deride Wellington as a mere 'sepoy general' in the *Moniteur*, but in private he was impressed with Wellington's ruthless scorched-earth policy on the retreat to Torres Vedras, telling Chaptal: 'In Europe only Wellington and I are capable of carrying out these measures. But there is this difference between him and me, which is that France . . . would blame me, while England will approve of him.'[97] It was true; Wellington has not generally been criticized for the scorched-earth tactics he employed in Portugal, while Napoleon has been castigated for using much the same methods in the Holy Land, Prussia and later Russia. By January 1811, reinforced only by Drouet and 6,000 men, Masséna's army at Santarém outside the Lines was starving, deserting and marauding. Masséna stayed until the retreat could not be put off any longer, and on the night of March 5, erecting scarecrows stuffed with straw to resemble sentries, he left Santarém. 'He is used up,' Napoleon said of Masséna, 'he isn't fit to command four men and a corporal!'[98]

*

In May 1810 the heir to the sixty-one-year-old King Charles XIII of Sweden died.* The Swedes alighted upon the idea of offering the future throne to Bernadotte, who had been kind to Swedish prisoners-of-war during the Eylau campaign. They clearly didn't mind that their future monarch was a former rabid republican who had had 'Death to Kings' tattooed on his chest, and assumed that after their defeat by Russia and the loss of Finland, having a French marshal on their throne – especially one related to Napoleon by marriage – would bring them a useful alliance.

Yet, as we have seen, Napoleon and Bernadotte were not at all on good terms, as the Swedes assumed they were. 'The vanity of that man is excessive,' Napoleon had written to Fouché from Vienna the previous September. 'I've ordered the War Minister to recall him. His talent is very mediocre. I've no kind of faith in him. He lends a willing ear to all the intriguers who inundate this great capital ... He almost made me lose the battle of Jena; he behaved feebly at Wagram; he wasn't at Eylau, although he might have been, and he didn't do all he might have done at Austerlitz.'[99] It was all true, and he might have added plenty more slights going back beyond Brumaire – Bernadotte had married Désirée, after all. Yet when the Swedes, who could have been invaluable in any future war against Russia, asked Napoleon's permission to offer Bernadotte the (eventual) crown, he agreed, albeit hesitantly enough to irritate Bernadotte, who was still smarting over the sarcastic words directed at him during the battle of Wagram.

Tsar Alexander chose to regard Bernadotte's move to Sweden, like the spurning of Anna Pavlovna, as an insult and a provocation. Only in the army was the apparent meritocracy of the elevation admired. 'The example of Bernadotte turned all heads,' recalled Captain Blaze; 'we all fancied that we had a sceptre in the sheath of our sword. A soldier had become a king; each of us thought we might do the same.'[100]

On June 3, 1810, Napoleon dismissed Fouché for conducting unauthorized secret peace negotiations with Britain. 'I'm aware of all the services which you have rendered me,' he wrote, 'and I believe in your attachment and your zeal; however it is impossible for me to allow you to keep your portfolio. The post of minister of police requires an absolute

* Charles had been on the throne only since March 1809, when the Swedish aristocracy had deposed his nephew King Gustav IV, yet another European monarch who suffered from imbecilism.

and entire confidence, and that can no longer exist because you have compromised my tranquillity and that of the State.'[101] Employing the banker Gabriel Ouvrard (who used invisible ink in his correspondence with Fouché), the British banker Sir Francis Baring and other intermediaries, Fouché had indulged in detailed peace negotiations with the British foreign secretary, Lord Wellesley, Wellington's elder brother, without Napoleon's knowledge.[102]

Napoleon was understandably furious when he discovered that Wellesley had been led to believe that Fouché was acting on his behalf, which would have meant 'a total change in all my political relations', as well as 'a stain upon my character'. Napoleon was hoping to force Britain to sue for peace through the pressure of the Continental System, but this unauthorized démarche could only have sent a mixed message to London. Fouché's intrigues, Napoleon complained, meant that 'I am obliged to keep up a constant supervision, which fatigues me.'[103] He sent Fouché to Rome as governor, and appointed his rival Savary as police minister.[104] Ouvrard was sent to the debtors' prison of Sainte-Pélagie, where he stayed for three years playing charades and whist in conditions of some luxury.[105]

By July 1810 Napoleon appreciated that the Continental System was not working as he had hoped, but rather than scrap it altogether he decided to modify it, introducing 'Le Nouveau Système', which permitted the selling of special licences that allowed certain individuals and companies to trade with Britain in a number of named products. The sale of these was open to abuse – Bourrienne skimmed off a vast fortune selling them in Hamburg, for example – and rife with accusations of favouritism. Non-French manufacturers within the Empire were rightly convinced that the granting of licences tended to be skewed towards the French, and they deeply resented it. Between 1810 and 1813, Bordeaux received 181 general licences and 607 one-off permits to trade with America, for example, against Hamburg's 68 and 5 respectively.[106] Even the treasury minister Mollien suspected that Napoleon 'wanted to take a part of the monopoly of [trade with] England through a system of licences, at the expense of the Continent'.[107] By April 1812 Napoleon was writing to Berthier to say that 'as there is no customs service in Corsica, there are no objections to sugar and coffee going in, without permitting it however, but by turning a blind eye'.[108]

Bureaucracy plagued the licensing system as further decrees were promulgated over the years. In the area between Antwerp on the

Channel and Lorient on the Bay of Biscay for example, one-sixth of all exports had to be of wine, with the rest composed of brandies, seeds (except grass) and non-prohibited French merchandise. The area of the Charente Inférieure could export grains, but half of exports there too had to be wines and brandies. Ships from ports between Ostia (near Rome) and Agde (near the Spanish border) could go to nine named ports in the Levant and Spain, but no others. Further circulars in July 1810 authorized prefects to refuse licences to non-French vessels.[109] Different types of licences costing different amounts authorized different companies from different departments to trade in different prescribed commodities with different foreign ports. The rules were constantly changing, seemingly capriciously, with endless clauses and sub-clauses covering every likely combination and permutation. Napoleon oversaw all this with his customary attention to minutiae. 'Who authorized the admission of the *Conciliateur* which arrived on Genoa on July 11th with a cargo of ebony?' he asked the excise chief in Paris on August 14.

The Russians considered Le Nouveau Système to be an outrage against them, since they were still banned from trading with Britain, whereas French manufacturers seemed to be evading the blockade. A sign of how far Alexander had come from the friendliness he had shown Napoleon at Tilsit, and even the good nature of Erfurt, may be judged from the visit in July 1810 of Frederick William's aide-de-camp, Baron Friedrich von Wrangel, who announced the death of Queen Louise from damaged lungs and a heart polyp. 'I swear to you to avenge her death,' a clearly upset Alexander told Wrangel, absurdly blaming Napoleon's behaviour towards the queen at Tilsit for her demise, 'and her murderer is to pay for it.'[110] He added that he was rearming fast, not in order to help Napoleon invade India, as one unfounded rumour went, or even to prosecute the wars he was currently fighting against both Turkey and Persia, but to fight France. 'By 1814,' he said, 'I can, according to my most exact calculations, enter the lists with a well-equipped army of 400,000. With 200,000 I will cross the Oder, while another 200,000 will cross the Vistula.'[111] He added that he expected Austria and Prussia to rise up at that point, and follow his lead.

While Napoleon expected family obligations to keep Austria in France's political orbit, they didn't prevent him from dethroning his own brother Louis on July 3, 1810, for putting his Dutch subjects' interests over those of the French Empire, especially with regard to conscription and the Continental System. 'In spite of all his faults I cannot forget that I brought him up as a son,' Napoleon wrote to Marie Louise.[112] 'When I was a lieutenant of artillery,' he told Savary, 'I raised him on my pay; I was sharing what bread I had with him, and this is what he does to me!'[113] Holland was annexed and run as a series of imperial departments, while Louis went into exile in various Austrian spa towns, where he had hot baths in grape-skins and wrote anti-Napoleonic tracts under his cadet title, the Comte de Saint-Leu.

Napoleon was not naive about his worsening relations with Alexander. In early August he wrote to the King of Saxony, asking him secretly to strengthen his armaments and in particular to reinforce the Polish fortress of Modlin against a possible Russian attack. 'My relations are very good,' he said of Alexander, 'but one must be prepared.'[114] With Russia seemingly coming to terms with Turkey, Napoleon told Caulaincourt to warn Alexander that although he was content for Russia to take Moldavia and Wallachia and the left bank of the Danube, 'Russia would violate her agreements with me should she keep anything on the right bank, and if she interfered with the Serbians', because 'a single place kept by Russia on the right bank of the Danube would destroy the independence of Turkey, and would entirely change the state of affairs.'[115] Napoleon asked for intelligence on Russian troop movements, and by mid-October he was starting to strengthen his forces in Danzig and northern Germany, while the Russians fortified the Dvina and Berezina rivers. The number of flashpoints between the two superpowers was multiplying dangerously.

The year 1810 had been a mixed one for Napoleon; although his Empire had reached the zenith of its power and territorial extent, he had made mistakes that boded ill for its future. Most of these errors had been unforced, and many of his problems, we can now see, were self-inflicted. He need not have quarrelled publicly with the Pope, certainly not to the point of arresting him. Impatience to make a dynastic alliance had offended Alexander and made him suspicious over Poland, even though Napoleon had no intention of restoring that kingdom. The Austrian marriage was never going to be enough to assuage the harsh peace of Schönbrunn. Masséna should have been supported properly, or not sent to Portugal at all; better still, Napoleon should have gone there himself to fight Wellington. It was an error of judgement to let an untrustworthy, resentful Bernadotte go to so strategically important a place as Sweden, and another to have left Fouché's *prima facie* act of treason go essentially unpunished. Similarly, Napoleon should have seen the Continental

System's new licensing regime for the hypocrisy that it was in the eyes of the Empire, his allies and especially the Russians. Although Alexander was rearming and planning a war of revenge, the Grande Armée in its present state would be more than capable of taking care of a border war against Russia in Germany, especially with Austria tied into the marriage alliance. None of his opponents could threaten the existence of the largest European empire since Ancient Rome, larger even that Charlemagne's. Only Napoleon himself could do that.

PART THREE

Denouement

23

Russia

'A Frenchman is brave but long privations and bad climate would wear him down and discourage him. Our climate, our winter, will fight on our side.'

Tsar Alexander to Caulaincourt, early 1811

'One must never ask of Fortune more than she can grant.'

Napoleon on St Helena

Napoleon toured his Empire for many weeks of the year, and always at breakneck speed. In the autumn of 1811, he visited forty cities in twenty-two days, despite losing two and half days stuck on board the warship *Charlemagne* at Flushing due to a gale and another day at Givet when the Meuse flooded its banks. He was much more interested in gleaning information than in listening to laudatory speeches from local worthies. On one occasion when a mayor had taken great pains to commit a speech to memory, Napoleon had 'scarcely given him time to present the keys before the coachman was impetuously ordered to drive on, and the mayor left to harangue the air'. The mayor was perhaps consoled by seeing an account of the presentation of the keys and his entire speech reproduced in the next day's *Moniteur*. '"No harangue, gentlemen!" is frequently the discouraging apostrophe with which Bonaparte cuts short these trembling deputations,' recalled the civil servant Theodor von Faber.[1] The questions Napoleon asked mayors were testimony to his omnivorous appetite for information. One might have expected inquiries about population, deaths, revenues, forestry, tolls, municipal rates, conscription and civil and criminal lawsuits, and Napoleon certainly asked them, but he also wanted to know 'How many sentences passed by you are annulled by the Court of Cassation?' and 'Have you found means to provide suitable lodgings for rectors?'[2]

'There is proof', Napoleon wrote to Tsar Alexander on November 4, 1810, 'that the colonial produce at the last Leipzig Fair was brought from Russia in seven hundred wagons . . . and that 1,200 merchant vessels, under Swedish, Portuguese, Spanish and American colours, which the English escorted with twenty warships, have partly landed their cargoes in Russia.'[3] The letter went on to ask him to confiscate 'all the goods introduced by the English'. In December Napoleon ordered Champagny to give Alexander Kurakin, the Russian ambassador to Paris, and simultaneously Caulaincourt to give the Tsar, a direct warning that should Russia open her ports to ships carrying English merchandise in direct contravention of the Tilsit treaty, then war would become inevitable.[4]

It was largely in order to combat smuggling across the German north-west littoral that Napoleon annexed the Hanseatic Towns such as Hamburg, Bremen and Lübeck on December 19 1810. After Rome, Hanover and Holland, it was Napoleon's fourth annexation in the past twelve months, and like them it arose directly as a result of his obsession with his protectionist economic war against Britain. Yet taking over the direct rule of these major cities made no geographical or commercial sense without also acquiring the 2,000-square-mile Duchy of Oldenburg on the left bank of the Weser, whose regent-ruler, Duke Peter, was the father-in-law of Alexander's sister, the Grand Duchess Catherine Pavlovna. Despite repeated warnings from Napoleon it continued to trade relatively openly with Britain, to the point that it has been likened to an enormous warehouse for smuggled goods.[5] Although the duchy's independence had been guaranteed by Tilsit, Napoleon decided to close this loophole and annexed Oldenburg on the same day as the Hanseatic Towns. A month later he offered Duke Peter the small principality of Erfurt in compensation for the duchy, which was six times larger, and this left Alexander even more affronted.[6]

Franco-Russian tensions had long pre-dated Napoleon; Louis XVI had supported the Ottomans against Russian expansionism, and had made common cause with Gustav III of Sweden in the Baltic.[7] Successive tsars and empresses had looked westwards since Peter the Great visited every major European court (except Versailles) on his travels at the end of the seventeenth century, and St Petersburg was a testament to this westward outlook. Alexander had brought Russia up to the

45. Imperial grandeur: Napoleon in his Coronation robes by Jacques-Louis David.

46. (*top*) Murat's massive cavalry charge of over 10,000 men at Eylau in February 1807, the largest of the Napoleonic Wars.

47. (*above*) The battle of Friedland in June 1807, one of Napoleon's most brilliant victories, forced Russia to sue for peace.

48. (*above*) The Franco-Russian and Prussian peace negotiations in July 1807 began when Napoleon welcomed Tsar Alexander I to a pavilion on a specially designed raft tethered to the middle of the River Niemen near Tilsit. Alexander's first words were, 'I will be your second against England.'

49. (*left*) Tsar Alexander and Napoleon befriended each other at Tilsit, but by late 1810 the Tsar was chafing at the treaty he had signed there. Soon afterwards he began plotting Napoleon's downfall.

50. (*top left*) Desirée Clary was Napoleon's first love; he proposed to her but was refused. She later married Marshal Bernadotte and became Queen of Sweden.

51. (*top right*) Pauline Fourès was the twenty-year-old wife of a cavalry lieutenant when Napoleon took her as his mistress in Cairo after discovering Josephine's infidelity with the hussar Hippolyte Charles.

52. (*above left*) Giuseppina Grassini was a twenty-seven-year-old opera singer when Napoleon began a long affair with her in Milan in 1800.

53. (*above right*) Marguerite Weimer's stage name was 'Mademoiselle George' when she became Napoleon's mistress in 1802 at the age of fifteen.

54. (*top left*) The Polish Countess Marie Colonna-Walewska was twenty and married to a 72-year-old Polish landowner when Napoleon met her on New Year's Day 1807. She was to become the favourite of his twenty-two mistresses, and came to visit him on Elba in 1814 and at Fontainebleau the following year.

55. (*centre*) Napoleon's illegitimate son Count Alexandre Walewski, who became foreign minister and president of the National Assembly under Napoleon III.

56. (*top right*) In 1806 Napoleon took a seventeen-year-old mistress, the 'dark-eyed brunette beauty' Éléonore Denuelle de la Plaigne, by whom he had an illegitimate son, Count Léon, who looked so like the Emperor that in later life people stared at him in the street.

57. (*above left*) The actress Anne Hippolyte Boutet Salvetat took the stage name 'Mademoiselle Mars'. In 1815 she greeted him with violets, the symbol of his springtime return to Paris.

58. (*above right*) Albine de Montholon was Napoleon's last mistress, on St Helena, and possibly had a daughter by him whom she named Joséphine-Napoléone.

59. (*above left*) A tall porcelain vase made by Sèvres which belonged to Napoleon's mother and features David's famous portrait of Napoleon crossing the Great St Bernard Pass in 1800.

60. (*top right*) The Imperial Throne from the Legislative Body, 1805.

61. (*above right*) Golden spice cellars in the form of a ship, called *nefs*, indicated the presence of a sovereign. This one was made by Henry Auguste for Napoleon's coronation in 1804, with the lid featuring his personal emblem of bees. Other symbols represented were of Fame, Justice and Prudence, the rivers Seine and Marne, Egypt (palm trees), France (cockerels), Victory (laurel leaves), the crown of Charlemagne and the twelve *arrondissements* of Paris.

62. (*top*) The Vendôme Column, built between 1803 and 1810, carried a statue of Napoleon on its apex and praised 'Napoleon the Great' at its base. It was pulled down in the Communard uprising in 1870.

63. (*above*) The Palais Brongniart exemplifies Napoleon's love of classical architecture and for nearly two hundred years housed the Paris Bourse.

Grande hazaña! Con muertos!

64. (*top left*) Claude-François Méneval was Napoleon's devoted secretary from 1803 to 1813.

65. (*top right*) Baron Agathon Fain took over from Méneval and was equally admiring of his master. Both Méneval and Fain provide intimate portraits of the Emperor at work.

66. Francisco Goya's depictions of 'The Disasters of War' in the Peninsular campaign, where guerilla warfare was invented and which saw horrific brutality on both sides.

Danube with the annexations of Moldavia and Wallachia, and looked covetously towards Turkey's Balkan possessions. The Russians under Alexander's grandmother, Catherine the Great – herself a German princess who had long seen France as a potential antagonist – had partitioned Poland three times between 1772 and 1795, and Alexander's father, Paul I, had become Grand Master of the Knights of Malta and sent the great General Suvorov into Lombardy and Switzerland. Russia's ambitions to be a major European power were therefore very long-standing, and were always likely to cause tensions with whichever was the hegemonic European power of the day. For much of the eighteenth century, and certainly by Napoleon's time, that was France.

Even before Napoleon's annexation of Oldenburg, Alexander had been making plans for another war against France.[8] His war minister Barclay de Tolly, his military advisor General Ernst von Phull, a French émigré Comte d'Allonville and a former adjutant to the Tsar, Count Ludwig von Wolzogen, were all sending him detailed schemes from October 1810 onwards that covered every offensive and defensive contingency. In early December, Barclay planned for a defensive battle on both sides of the Pripet Marshes, in modern-day southern Belarus and northern Ukraine, after a quick pre-emptive Russian attack had destroyed Napoleon's bases in Poland.[9] From being (Napoleon hoped) an enthusiastic friend at Tilsit, and a more reluctant ally at Erfurt, Alexander was now looking more and more like a future enemy.

Tilsit's constraints on trade had meant that the Russian treasury had been running unsustainably large deficits, of 126 million rubles in 1808, 157 million in 1809 and 77 million in 1810. Her national debt increased thirteen-fold, with dire consequences for the value of her currency. In 1808 the volume of Russia's Baltic exports had dropped to one-third of their 1806 level.[10] On December 19, the same day that Napoleon annexed the Hanseatic Towns and Oldenburg, Tsar Alexander retaliated by publishing a *ukaz* (decree) which stated that from the end of the year Russian trade would be opened to neutral countries (such as America, though not including Britain) and that certain French Empire luxury goods would be banned, while others – such as wine – would be subjected to heavy import duties.[11] Cambacérès believed that the *ukaz* had 'destroyed our commercial relationship with Russia and . . . revealed the true intentions of Alexander'.[12] It did state that all goods manufactured in England would be burned, but added that so too would certain silks and cloths manufactured in France and the Rhine Confederation. On hearing the news, Napoleon said: 'I would sooner receive a blow on the

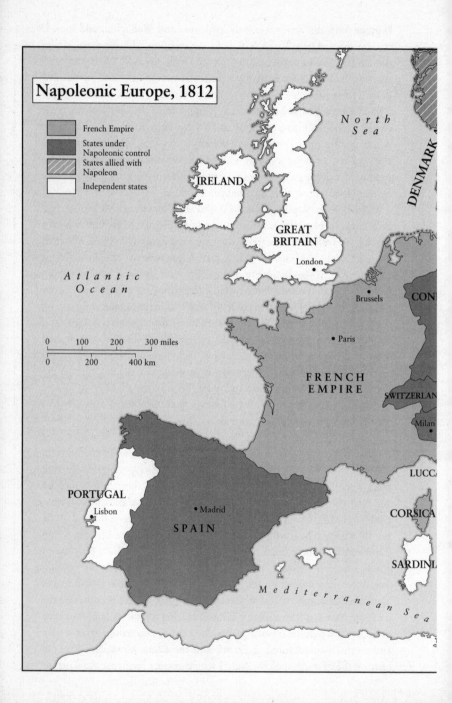

Napoleonic Europe, 1812

French Empire

States under
Napoleonic control

States allied with
Napoleon

Independent states

*North
Sea*

IRELAND

GREAT
BRITAIN

London

*Atlantic
Ocean*

Brussels

Paris

DENMARK

CON

0   100   200   300 miles

0   200   400 km

FRENCH
EMPIRE

SWITZERLAN

Milan

LUCC

PORTUGAL

Lisbon

Madrid

SPAIN

CORSICA

SARDINL

Mediterranean Sea

cheek than see the produce of the industry and labour of my subjects burnt.'[13] It wasn't long before British ships flew the Stars and Stripes so that they could evade the *ukaz* regulations, with the covert complicity of Russian customs officials.[14]

The year 1811 saw the start of a continental economic crisis that lasted two years and that also engulfed Britain, which was beset by bad harvests, mass unemployment, wage cuts, Luddism and food shortages.[15] Mulhouse in eastern France saw two-thirds of its workforce of 60,000 unemployed, and over 20,000 were unemployed in Lyons.[16] Napoleon needed to stimulate growth, but his Colbertian economic views, which rejected the idea of competition and free exchange as positive phenomena, sent him back to attempting to enforce ever more strictly the Continental System, even if it might eventually mean fighting Russia again. Napoleon feared that if Russia were allowed to leave the System other countries might follow, but in 1811 none was likely to try.

By 1812 Napoleon believed that the Continental System was working, and cited the bankruptcies of various London banks and commercial enterprises to support this. As his private secretary Baron Fain put it: 'A little more effort and the blockade would have subdued British pride.'[17] Napoleon assumed that Britain couldn't simultaneously afford, in Fain's list, 'the occupation of India, the war against America, the establishments in the Mediterranean, defending Ireland and its own coasts, the garrisoning of the huge navy, and at the same time the stubborn war ... against us in the Peninsula'.[18] In fact such was the credit-worthiness of the British government and the underlying strength of the British economy that all those commitments could just about be sustained simultaneously, but Napoleon was certain that to break British commerce it was necessary for the Continental System to encompass all Europe. Having brought Prussia and Austria into the System in 1807 and 1809 he was not about to allow the Russians to break it, even though Russian trade was never an important factor in the British economy – certainly not as important a factor as British trade was for Russia's. By then some 19 per cent of Britain's exports went to the Iberian peninsula, another reason why Napoleon should have gone back there rather than putting pressure on Russia.[19]

Napoleon was not wrong in assuming that Britain was suffering very seriously as a result of his Continental System throughout 1811 and the first half of 1812, which have been described as 'years of grave danger for the British state'.[20] Trade declined rapidly, government 3 per cent consols fell from 70 in 1810 to 56 in 1812, the bad harvests of 1811 and 1812 led to food shortages and inflation, and war expenditure increased budget deficits from £16 million in 1810 to £27 million in 1812. Some 17 per cent of Liverpool's population was unemployed during the winter of 1811/12, and the militia had to be deployed against potential rioters and Luddites across the Midlands and North of England, with ringleaders sentenced to transportation to Australia, or even in some cases death.[21] The worst moment for the British economy in fact came with the outbreak in June 1812 of the war against America over trade and impressment issues.[22] Yet Spencer Perceval stuck rigidly to his programme of funding the Peninsular War, while meeting all Britain's other commitments as listed by Fain. The immense pressure on Britain only lifted in late 1812 and early 1813 as a result of Napoleon's campaign in Russia; had he not undertaken it, there is no way of knowing how long Britain could have held out against the Continental System.

The *ukaz* directly contravened the Tilsit and Erfurt agreements and was a clear *casus belli*, threatening Napoleon's imperial system at a time when he was capable of raising an army of over 600,000 men. Yet even if Napoleon had defeated Russia in 1812, it is doubtful that he could have enforced the Continental System. Would he have then annexed the rest of the south Baltic coastline, and installed French customs officials at St Petersburg? He probably assumed that a defeated Alexander would administer the System for him again, as he had between 1807 and 1810, but it is doubtful that this crucial aspect of his plan was properly thought through. There are certainly no letters in his vast correspondence that even refer to how he intended to enforce his ban on British trade after the war.

On Christmas Day 1810, Alexander wrote to Prince Adam Czartoryski about 'the restoration of Poland', baldly stating: 'It is not improbable that Russia will be the Power to bring about that event ... This has always been my favourite idea; circumstances have twice compelled me to postpone its realisation, but it has nonetheless remained in my mind. There has never been a more propitious moment for realising it than the present.'[23] He asked Czartoryski to canvass opinion among Poles as to whether they would accept nationhood 'from whatever quarter it might come, and would they join any Power, without distinction, that would espouse their interests sincerely and with attachment?' Asking for absolute secrecy, he wanted to know 'Who is the officer who has the greatest influence upon opinion in the army?', freely admitting that his offer of 'a regeneration of Poland ... is based not on a hope of counterbalancing the genius of Napoleon, but solely on the diminution of his forces through the secession of the Duchy of Warsaw, and the general exasperation of the whole of Germany against him'. He attached a table showing that the Russians, Poles, Prussians and Danes together could amount to 230,000 men, against Napoleon's forces in Germany of 155,000. (Since Alexander included a figure of only 60,000 French, and the Danes were loyal allies of France, the table made little sense.) Alexander concluded by warning Czartoryski that 'Such a moment presents itself only once; any other combination will only bring about a war to the death between Russia and France, with your country as the battlefield. The support on which the Poles can rely is limited to the person of Napoleon, who cannot live for ever.'[24] Czartoryski replied sensibly, questioning the Tsar's figures and pointing out that 'the French and Poles are brothers in arms ... the Russians are her bitter enemies', and that there were 20,000 Poles fighting in Spain, who would be open to 'the vengeance of Napoleon' if they suddenly swapped sides.[25]

This correspondence had the effect of turning Alexander against an offensive war from the spring of 1811, although Napoleon was still worried about a surprise attack well into the spring of 1812. Had he known that Alexander was seeking secret military conventions with Austria and Prussia at this time he would have been even more concerned. In September 1810, Alexander had approved Barclay's increases in army recruitment and introduction of deep-seated military and social reforms.[26] Russia adopted the corps and divisional system; the War College was abolished and all military authority was brought into the war ministry; orders were given for military production factories to stay open on Church holidays; a law entitled The Regulation for the Administration of a Large Active Army was passed, providing for – among many other things – the better collection and distribution of food; the powers of army commanders were codified and regulated; and a more efficient staff structure was introduced.[27] Alexander himself took charge of an extensive fortification programme of Russia's western frontier, which, because her most recent wars had been fought in the north against Sweden and in the south against Turkey, was relatively under-protected. These fortifications, and the relocation of troops from Siberia, Finland and the Danube to the Polish border, were considered a provocation by Napoleon, who, according to Méneval, came to the conclusion by early 1811 that Russia intended 'to make common cause with England'.[28] In the first week of January 1811, Alexander wrote to his sister Catherine: 'It seems like blood must flow again, but at least I have done all that is humanly possible to avoid it.'[29] His actions and correspondence over the previous year clearly belied him.

A huge military concentration was beginning, on both sides. On January 10, 1811 Napoleon reorganized the Grande Armée into four corps. The first two, under Davout and Oudinot, were stationed on the Elbe, a third under Ney occupied Mainz, Düsseldorf and Danzig – the last of which, by January 1812, was turned into a major garrison city containing enough stores to sustain 400,000 men and 50,000 horses. By April 1811 a million rations had been amassed in Stettin and Küstrin (present-day Szczecin and Kostrzyn) alone.[30] Napoleon managed everything, from the significant – 'If I were to have war with Russia,' he told Clarke on February 3, 'I reckon that I should require two hundred thousand muskets and bayonets for the Polish insurgents' – down to a complaint a few days later that twenty-nine out of one hundred conscripts on a march to Rome had deserted at Breglio (now Breil-sur-Roya, on the French side of the border).[31]

Napoleon didn't actively want war with Russia, any more than he had wanted it with Austria in 1805 or 1809, but he was not about to avoid it through concessions that he feared might compromise his empire. Writing to Alexander in late February 1812, in a letter he gave the Tsar's aide-de-camp, Colonel Alexander Chernyshev, who was attached to the Russian embassy in Paris, he enumerated in friendly, temperate language all his various grievances, saying that he had never intended to revive the Kingdom of Poland, and insisting that their differences over issues such as Oldenburg and the *ukaz* could be resolved without conflict.[32] Chernyshev, who unbeknown to Napoleon was Russia's extremely successful spymaster in Paris, took eighteen days to get the letter to Alexander and another twenty-one days to have the necessary discussions and return.[33] By the time Chernyshev got back to Paris, Poniatowski had heard of Czartoryski's soundings among the Polish nobility and Napoleon had put his forces in Germany and Poland on full alert for a Russian attack expected between mid-March and early May.

'I cannot disguise from myself that Your Majesty no longer has any friendship for me,' Napoleon had written to Alexander.

You raise all kinds of difficulties on the subject of Oldenburg, when I do not refuse an equivalent for that country, which has always been a hotbed of English smugglers ... Allow me to say frankly to Your Majesty that you forget the benefits you have derived from this alliance, and yet what has happened since Tilsit? By the treaty of Tilsit you should have restored Moldavia and Wallachia to Turkey; yet, instead of restoring those provinces, you have united them to your empire. Moldavia and Wallachia form one-third of Turkey-in-Europe; it is an immense addition which in resting the vast empire of Your Majesty on the Danube, deprives Turkey of all force.[34]

Napoleon went on to argue that if he had wanted to re-establish Poland, he could have done it after the battle of Friedland, but he deliberately hadn't done so.

Having ordered a fresh military levy of serfs on March 1, Alexander replied: 'Neither my feeling nor my politics have changed, and I only desire the maintenance and consolidation of our alliance. Am I not rather allowed to suppose that it is your Majesty who has changed towards me?'[35] He mentioned Oldenburg, and ended, somewhat hyperbolically: 'If war must begin, I will know to fight and sell my life dearly.'[36]

On March 19, 1811, almost a year after her first encounter with Napoleon, Marie Louise felt birth-pangs, and as Bausset recalled, 'all the court, all the great functionaries of the State assembled at the Tuileries, and waited with the greatest impatience'.[37] None more so than Napoleon, who, Lavalette remembered, was 'much agitated, and went continually from the salons to the bedchamber and back again'.[38] He took Corvisart's advice to hire the obstetrician Antoine Dubois, whom he paid the vast sum of 100,000 francs, but advised, 'Pretend you're not delivering the Empress but a bourgeois from the rue Saint-Denis.'[39]

Napoléon-François-Joseph-Charles was born at 8 a.m. on Wednesday, March 20, 1811. It was a difficult, even traumatic birth. 'I'm not naturally soft-hearted,' admitted Napoleon years later, 'yet I was much moved when I saw how she suffered.' It required instruments which meant that the baby emerged with 'a little scratching about the head' and needing 'much rubbing' on delivery.[40] 'The redness of his face showed how painful and laborious his entry into the world must have been,' wrote Bausset. Despite everything he had done for an heir, Napoleon instructed the doctors that if it came to a choice the Empress's life must be saved rather than the baby's.[41] The infant was proclaimed 'King of Rome', a title of the Holy Roman Empire, and was nicknamed 'L'Aiglon' (the Eaglet) by Bonapartist propagandists.

The baby's second name was a tribute to his grandfather, the Emperor of Austria, and the fourth was further indication that Napoleon had loved his father, even if he hadn't much admired him. Because it had been announced that the birth of a daughter would be signalled by a salute of twenty-one guns and that of a son by a hundred and one, there was huge celebration in Paris on the twenty-second boom of the cannon, which was so widespread that the prefecture of police had to stop all traffic in the city centre even days later.[42] 'My son is big and healthy,' Napoleon wrote to Josephine, with whom he had stayed affectionately in touch. 'I hope that he will grow up well. He has my chest, my mouth, and my eyes. I trust that he will fulfil his destiny.'[43] Napoleon was a doting father. 'The Emperor would give the child a little claret by dipping his finger in the glass and making him suck it,' recalled Laure d'Abrantès. 'Sometimes he would daub the young prince's face with gravy. The child would laugh heartily.'[44] Many royals were stern and unloving towards their children at that time – the Spanish Bourbons and British Hanoverians almost made a practice of hating their children – but Napoleon adored his son. He was inordinately proud of the boy's bloodline, pointing out that through his mother's brother-in-law he was related to the Romanovs, through his mother to the Habsburgs, through his uncle's wife to the Hanoverians and through his mother's great-aunt to the Bourbons. 'My family is allied to the families of all the sovereigns of Europe,' he said.[45] The fact that all four families currently longed for his overthrow in no way lessened his satisfaction.

In early April 1811 Napoleon sent a letter to the King of Württemberg, asking him to join the kings of Saxony, Bavaria and Westphalia in providing men to protect Danzig from the Royal Navy. In it he mused with a certain poetic resignation on the tendency of talk of war to lead ineluctably to a confrontation, and suggested that the Tsar might be forced into war whether he wanted one or not.

> If Alexander desires war, public opinion is in uniformity with his intentions; if he does not wish for war ... he will be carried away by it next year and thus war will take place in spite of him, in spite of me, in spite of the interests of France and those of Russia. I have seen this happen so often that my experience of the past unveils the future. All this is an operatic scene, the shifting of which is in the hands of the English ... If I do not wish for war, and if I am far from desiring to be the Don Quixote of Poland, I have the right to insist upon Russia remaining faithful to the alliance.[46]

He also feared the effect of Russia and Turkey coming to terms, something he ought to have calculated far earlier, and taken steps to prevent.

Another consideration should have figured much more prominently in his calculations: Spain. In early May 1811 Masséna was defeated by Wellington at the battle of Fuentes de Oñoro, after which the French were forced out of Portugal altogether, never to return. Napoleon replaced Masséna with Marmont – who did even worse against Wellington – and never employed 'the darling child of victory' in any significant capacity again. Yet Masséna had never been adequately supplied or reinforced, so his failure had been largely Napoleon's fault. However, the situation in Spain in mid-1811 was not desperate; the guerrilla war still raged, but the Spanish regular army posed no serious danger. Wellington was far from Madrid on the Spanish–Portuguese border and most of the Spanish fortresses (except Cadiz) were in French hands. If Napoleon had not ordered a concentration on Valencia or had provided more reinforcements, or had taken command himself, the situation would have improved enormously, and perhaps even been reversed.[47]

Because of disease, desertion, guerrilla and British action, the Russian campaign and virtually no reinforcements, Napoleon had only 290,000 troops in the Iberian peninsula in 1812, and by mid-1813 the figure had fallen to a mere 224,000. As the annual intake of 80,000 French recruits was only just enough to cover the 50,000 per annum attrition rate in Spain and the need for garrison forces in central Europe, Napoleon simply did not have enough Frenchmen to conduct a major campaign in Russia.[48] Had he cauterized the 'Spanish ulcer' by restoring Ferdinand and withdrawing to the Pyrenees in 1810 or 1811 he would have saved himself much trauma later on.

On April 17, 1811 Champagny, who opposed the coming war, was replaced as foreign minister by Hugues-Bernard Maret, later Duc de Bassano, a bureaucrat who has been described as docile, even servile, and who certainly wouldn't cause any difficulties.[49] Napoleon's Russian plans were more or less vocally criticized by Cambacérès, Daru, Duroc, Lacuée and Lauriston, as well as by Caulaincourt and Champagny.[50] Perhaps they did not all warn quite so presciently or loudly as they later claimed, but nonetheless they all counselled to some degree against a confrontation with Russia. Part of the problem was that many of those to whom in earlier years Napoleon might have had to listen were now unavailable: Moreau and Lucien were in exile in America and Britain respectively; Talleyrand, Masséna and Fouché were in disgrace; Desaix and Lannes were dead. Furthermore, Napoleon had been proved right against the advice of others too often in the past for him to feel that the nay-sayers were right, even when there were a number of them. Almost all the French diplomatic service opposed the war, but Napoleon didn't heed them either.[51] He had no intention of going deep into the Russian interior, so a war did not seem at the time like any great gamble. Besides, he had succeeded through audacity before.

Caulaincourt – who had been replaced by Lauriston as ambassador to St Petersburg in mid-May and brought back to Paris so that Napoleon could call on his inside knowledge of Russia during the coming crisis – spent five hours one day in June 1811 trying to persuade the Emperor not to go to war. He told him of Alexander's admiration for the Spanish guerrillas' refusal to make peace despite losing their capital, of Alexander's remarks about the severity of the Russian winter, and of his boast 'I shall not be the first to draw my sword, but I shall be the last to sheathe it.'[52] He said that Alexander and Russia had fundamentally changed since Tilsit, but Napoleon replied, 'One good battle will see the end of all your friend Alexander's fine resolutions – and of his sandcastles as well!'[53] Napoleon crowed similarly to Maret on June 21: 'Russia appears to be frightened since I picked up the gauntlet, but nothing is yet decided. The object of Russia seems to be to obtain, as an indemnity for the Duchy of Oldenburg, the cession of two districts of Poland, which I will not consent to, by honour and because they would altogether destroy the Duchy [of Warsaw].'[54]

By 'honour' Napoleon meant his prestige, but he obviously didn't realize that he would be risking honour, prestige and his throne itself over two Polish districts and the so far non-existent integrity of the Duchy of Warsaw. Still expecting a campaign of the Austerlitz–Friedland–Wagram kind, Napoleon believed that a sharp, focused re-run of his 1807 campaign – albeit on a larger scale – would not entail great risk. Yet three emergency levies in 1812 raised no fewer than 400,000 new recruits for Russia, out of 1.1 million new recruits in the period 1805–13. Napoleon failed to take into account the fact that he would be fighting a very different Russian army from earlier ones, though one with the same doggedness that had aroused his admiration at Pultusk and Golymin. Over half of the Russian officer corps were seasoned veterans and one-third had fought in six or more battles. Russia had changed, but Napoleon had not noticed. So while not actively seeking war, Napoleon was more than willing to 'pick up the gauntlet' that was thrown down by Alexander's *ukaz*.

Another good reason not to embark on another war came in July 1811 when it became clear that the harvest had failed across northern France in Normandy, and in much of the Midi, leading to what Napoleon privately described as famine.[55] Subsidizing the baking industry to prevent civil unrest turned into what the minister concerned, Pasquier, called 'an immense burden for the government'. By September 15 a 4-pound loaf had nearly doubled in price to 14 sous and Napoleon was 'most reluctant' to see that figure exceeded.[56] He chaired a Food Committee which met frequently, investigating price controls while, in Pasquier's words, 'Anxiety began to give way to terror' in the countryside. With violence breaking out in corn-markets, gangs of starving beggars roaming the Norman countryside and flour-mills being pillaged and even destroyed, Napoleon at one point ordered the gates of Paris closed to prevent the export of bread. He also distributed 4.3 million dried-pea and barley soups.[57] Troops were sent into Caen and other towns to quell bread riots, and rioters (including women) were executed. In the end a combination of price controls of grain and bread, charitable efforts by the *notables* of departments as co-ordinated by prefects, soup-kitchens, the sequestration of food stocks and harsh punishments for rioters helped alleviate the problem.[58]

Although Lauriston and Rumiantsev continued negotiating over compensation for the Oldenburg annexation and the amelioration of the *ukaz* during the summer of 1811, preparations for war continued on both sides of the Polish border. On August 15 Napoleon confronted Ambassador Kurakin at his birthday reception at the Tuileries. He had a long history of addressing ambassadors in very forthright language – including Cardinal Consalvi over the Concordat, Whitworth over Amiens, Metternich on the eve of the 1809 war, and so on – but full and frank discussions are partly what ambassadors are for. In a half-hour rebuke, the Emperor now told Kurakin that Russia's support for Oldenburg, her Polish and (supposedly) English intrigues, her breaking of the Continental System and her military preparations meant that war seemed likely, yet she would be left alone and friendless like Austria had been in 1809. All this could be avoided if there were a new Franco-Russian alliance. Kurakin said he had no powers to negotiate such a thing. 'No powers?' Napoleon exclaimed. 'Then you must write at once to the Tsar and request them.'[59]

The next day Napoleon and Maret went through the laborious process of looking into all the issues of the Oldenburg compensation, recognition of Poland, Turkish partition plans and the Continental System, reviewing all the papers on those subjects going back to Tilsit. These convinced him that the Russians had not been negotiating in good faith, and that evening he told the Conseil d'État that although a campaign against Russia in 1811 was impossible for climatic reasons, once Prussian and Austrian co-operation was assured, Russia would be punished in 1812.[60] Russia's hopes for military conventions with Prussia and Austria were dashed by those countries for fear of Napoleon's reprisals, although both gave Alexander secret oral assurances that their support to the French would be minimal, rather as the Russian attack on Austria in 1809 had been. Metternich's word for it was 'nominal'.

The seriousness of Napoleon's intentions can be ascertained by his renewed focus on the condition of the army's shoes. A report in the Archives Nationales from Davout to Napoleon on November 29 stated: 'In the 1805 campaign many men stayed behind for lack of shoes; now he is accumulating six pairs for each soldier.'[61] Soon afterwards, Napoleon ordered his director of war administration, Lacuée, to supply provisions for 400,000 men for a fifty-day campaign, requiring 20 million rations of bread and rice, 6,000 wagons to carry enough flour for 200,000 people for two months, and 2 million bushels of oats to feed horses for fifty days.[62] The weekly reports in the war ministry archives are testament to the huge operation taking place in early 1812. On February 14, 1812, to take an example almost at random, French troops were heading eastwards to over twenty German cities from all over the western part of the Empire.[63] Further indication of Napoleon's thinking can be seen in his order in December 1811 to his librarian, Barbier, to collect all the books he could find on Lithuania and Russia. These included several accounts, including Voltaire's, of Charles XII of Sweden's catastrophic invasion of Russia in 1709 and the annihilation of his army at the battle of Poltava, but also a five-hundred-page description of Russia's resources and geography and two recent works on the Russian army.[64]*

---

* As ever, Napoleon was also busy on other fronts. 'I have just seen the porcelain service sent to the Empress as a new year's gift,' he wrote to Champagny on December 31. 'It is very ugly. See that it be prettier another year' (ed. Bingham, *Selection* III p. 132).

In early January 1812 the Tsar, who still had six months to avert war if he cared to, wrote to his sister Catherine: 'All this devilish political business is going from bad to worse, and that infernal creature who is the curse of the human race becomes every day more abominable.'[65] Alexander was receiving reports from Chernyshev's spy codenamed 'Michel', who worked in the transport department of the war administration ministry in Paris until his arrest and execution with three accomplices in late February 1812. These reports revealed to Alexander the vast extent of France's war preparations and troop movements, and even Napoleon's order of battle.[66]

On January 20, in another short-sighted act, France annexed Swedish Pomerania in order to enforce the Continental System along the Baltic coast. Cambacérès recalled that Napoleon had shown 'little tact' with Bernadotte, who after all had become a royal prince and deserved a new degree of respect. The annexation threw Sweden into the hands of the Russians, with whom she had been at war as recently as September 1809.[67] Instead of establishing a useful ally in the north, capable of drawing Russian troops away from his own, Napoleon had ensured that Bernadotte would sign a treaty of friendship with Russia, which he did at Åbo (now Turku, in Finland) on April 10, 1812.

In February Austria agreed to furnish Napoleon with 30,000 men under Prince von Schwarzenberg for the invasion, but as Metternich told the British Foreign Office, 'It is necessary that not only the French Government but the greater part of Europe should be deceived as to my principles and intentions.'[68] At the time, Metternich had no discernible principles, and his intention was simply to see how the invasion of Russia would go. A week later Prussia promised 20,000 men, whereupon fully a quarter of the Prussian officer corps resigned their commissions in protest, many of them, such as the strategist Carl von Clausewitz, actually joining the Russians.[69] Napoleon used to say, 'It's better to have an open enemy than a doubtful ally,' but he did not act according to that belief in 1812.[70] With Davout reporting on the huge size of the Russian army, he believed he needed as many foreign contingents as possible, and he needed them to be well armed.[71] 'I have ordered the light horse to be armed with carbines,' he had written to Davout on January 6. 'I would also like the Polish to have them; I learned that they only have six per company, which is ridiculous, given they have to deal with the Cossacks, who are armed from head to foot.'[72]

On February 24 Napoleon wrote to Alexander saying that he had 'decided to talk with Colonel Chernyshev about the unfortunate events that have occurred over the last fifteen months. It only depends on Your Majesty to end it all.'[73] The Tsar rebuffed this further open-ended effort at peace. On the same day Eugène started marching 27,400 men of the Army of Italy to Poland. According to Fain, Napoleon briefly considered dismembering Prussia at this time, and so 'secure, from the first cannon-shot, an indemnity against all the unfavourable risks of a Russian campaign'.[74] With the Russians having gathered more than 200,000 men between St Petersburg and the Duchy of Warsaw, however, he had to face what he considered to be a serious Russian threat and could not afford to cause chaos in his rear.*

Although Napoleon hoped for another swift victory, he gave his enemies far more time to organize in 1811–12 than in any of his earlier campaigns. From the moment that the first mobilization orders went out to Rhine Confederation contingents in early 1811, the Russians had well over a year to prepare, time that they used extremely well. In all his other campaigns Napoleon's opponents had been lucky if they had a matter of weeks to get ready for his onslaught. Although the plan to concentrate forces upon Drissa (now Verkhnyadzvinsk in Belarus) that General von Phull drew up in the spring of 1812 wasn't adopted, the Russian high command was constantly thinking through alternative strategies, and certainly out-thinking Napoleon's by then transparent strategy of a quick decisive battle fought on the border.

Although Napoleon called it the 'Second Polish Campaign', he privately told his staff, 'We don't have to listen to inconsiderate zeal for the Polish cause. France before anything else: those are my politics. The Poles aren't the subject of this fight; they mustn't be an obstacle to peace, but they might be a tool of war for us, and, on the eve of such a great crisis I will not leave them without advice or guidance.'[75] He appointed the Abbé de Pradt as French ambassador to Warsaw. 'The campaign began without any provisioning, which was Napoleon's method,' Pradt later wrote in his (violently anti-Napoleon) memoirs. 'Some admiring imbeciles believe it was the secret of his success.'[76] Though untrue – there was plenty of provisioning at the start of the campaign – it was a fair criticism later on, partly due to the negligence

---

* Along with hundreds of orders concerning every aspect of his armies' move east down to whether they had enough cooking pots and brandy flasks, Napoleon also sent the Comte de Montesquiou-Fezensac a 'list of young people and young ladies who have been invited to balls' in Paris, pointing out that 'All the young ladies whose aunts or mothers have been invited can come. It would be unseemly to invite young ladies whose mothers have not been asked' (CN23 no. 18482 p. 208).

and incompetence of Pradt himself as Poland was the major supply depot for the campaign. Napoleon's other possible appointee for Pradt's post had been Talleyrand. That either man was even considered was a sign of how his usual good judgement of people had begun to slip badly and his lacuna over Talleyrand continued.

It took Napoleon dangerously long to realize that Alexander was about to pull off significant diplomatic coups in both the north and south, allowing him to concentrate his forces against the coming invasion. As late as March 30, 1812 he told Berthier, 'I assume the Russians will avoid making any movement, they cannot be unaware that Prussia, Austria and probably Sweden are with me; that with hostilities starting again with Turkey, the Turks will make new efforts, that the Sultan himself is going to join the army, and that all this makes it unlikely they will defy me easily.'[77] In fact Napoleon had lost the north flank through his inability to treat Bernadotte and Sweden with respect and indulgence, and in late May 1812 he also lost the south flank, despite sending General Andreossy to Constantinople to tell Sultan Mahmud II 'If one hundred thousand Turks, their Sultan at their head, went through the Danube, I promise in exchange not only Moldavia and Wallachia, but also the Crimea.'[78] Alexander matched Napoleon's offer over the Danubian provinces and signed the Treaty of Bucharest with Turkey on May 29, which meant that the Russian Army of the Danube could begin to threaten Napoleon's southern flank.

'The Turks will pay dearly for this mistake!' Napoleon said on hearing news of the treaty. 'It is so stupid that I couldn't foresee it.'[79] But the stupidity in this instance was in fact his – he had counted too complacently on Ottoman support. In turning back Napoleon at Acre in 1799, and by allowing Russia to redeploy her Balkan forces against him in 1812, the supposed 'sick man of Europe' was in fact instrumental in two of Napoleon's major reverses. 'If I'm ever accused of having provoked this war,' Napoleon told Fain in August, 'please consider, to absolve me, how little my cause was linked with the Turks, and how harassed I was by Sweden!'[80]

By March 15 all the Grande Armée's corps had reached the Elbe. That same day Napoleon ordered Louis Otto, the French ambassador in Vienna, to buy 2 million bottles of Hungarian wine at 10 sous each, to be delivered to Warsaw.[81] To strengthen the invasion force, Belgian National Guard units replaced French troops in garrisons along the Atlantic coast, Princess Pauline Borghese's bodyguard were called up, cannon were stripped from the navy and the hospitals scoured for malingerers. Reserve units were disbanded and reassembled to maximize the numbers that could go to Russia; the 10th Cohort of the Paris National Guard, for example, was soon almost entirely comprised of men with flat feet.[82]

On April 8, a week after the Grande Armée had reached the Oder, Alexander issued an ultimatum ordering Napoleon immediately to evacuate his troops from Prussia, Swedish Pomerania and the Duchy of Warsaw and to reduce the Danzig garrison. This was to be a preliminary to a new settlement of the frontiers of Europe, under which Russia would be allowed to trade with neutrals but would negotiate compensation for Oldenburg and reduce Russian duties on French goods.[83] These terms would clearly be unacceptable to Napoleon, and in any case sounded more like a propaganda bulletin than genuine bases for negotiation. On April 21 Alexander left St Petersburg for his army base at Vilnius. On the 17th Napoleon had made a peace offer to the British foreign secretary, Lord Castlereagh, saying that he would withdraw from the Iberian peninsula if the British did too, and that Sicily could stay Bourbon if Murat was recognized as king of Naples and Joseph as king of Spain. 'If this fourth attempt should be unsuccessful,' he concluded of his various peace offers since the breakdown of Amiens, 'as those that have preceded it, France will at least have the consolation of thinking that the blood that could flow again will fall entirely on England.'[84] It was cheekily opportunistic – especially the absurd provision regarding Joseph and Murat – and Castlereagh, as befitting a true disciple of Pitt, treated it with predictable contempt.

On April 25 Napoleon sent his aide-de-camp General Comte Louis de Narbonne-Lara (who was probably the illegitimate son of Louis XV) with more realistic counter-proposals to the Tsar's ultimatum that didn't involve evacuations from allies' territory. 'These will prove to Your Majesty my desire to avoid war and my steadfastness in the sentiments of Tilsit and Erfurt,' Napoleon wrote. 'However, Your Majesty will allow me to assure you that, if fate makes war between us inevitable, it would not change the sentiments that Your Majesty has inspired in me and which are safe from any alteration and vicissitude.'[85] Historians have tended to view cynically Napoleon's repeated attempts to stay personally friendly with a head of state of a country he was about to ravage, yet it was part of his belief in the almost ethereal brotherhood of emperors that this should be possible. Their time at Tilsit together had clearly meant much more to him than it had to Alexander. Speaking to

Pasquier in May before he left for the front, Napoleon described the coming campaign against Russia as 'The greatest and most difficult enterprise I've ever attempted. But what has been begun must be carried through.'[86]

At 6 a.m. on Saturday, May 9, Napoleon left Saint-Cloud with Marie Louise and the baby King of Rome to make his way to the front. The day before he had imposed wheat taxes and swingeing food-price controls. 'In this way he hoped to ensure that they would remain contented during his absence,' Pasquier concluded, but it was only a short-term solution.[87] As always he moved fast: the imperial family passed the Rhine on the 13th, the Elbe on the 29th and the Vistula on June 6, travelling 530 miles in seven days and averaging over 75 miles a day in a horse-drawn carriage over unmetalled, rutted roads. There was nonetheless time for meetings in Dresden with the kings of Württemberg, Prussia, Saxony and Bavaria, the first of whom had refused to send a contingent to Spain in 1810, but would against Russia; the last was still angry that Napoleon had never reimbursed him for the expenses of the war of 1805, but nonetheless sent a contingent too. Marie Louise saw her father there for the first time since her wedding; and Napoleon for the first time since they had met at the windmill near Austerlitz. Francis also met his grandson. The King of Rome was attended by his governess Madame de Montesquiou, whose official title, 'Governess to the Imperial Children', indicates that Napoleon and Marie Louise hoped for more. Indeed, Napoleon later said he would have liked another son for the Kingdom of Italy and a third to be safe.

Metternich much later claimed that when they met in Dresden Napoleon had told him his Russian strategy. 'Victory will go to the most patient,' the Emperor supposedly said, according to Metternich's unreliable and immensely self-serving memoirs. 'I shall open the campaign by crossing the Niemen, and it will be concluded at Smolensk and Minsk. There I shall stop and fortify those two points. At Vilnius, where the main headquarters will spend next winter, I shall busy myself with organizing Lithuania ... Perhaps I myself shall spend the most inclement months of the winter in Paris.'[88] On being asked what would happen if Alexander didn't sue for peace, Napoleon allegedly replied: 'In that case I shall advance next year to the centre of the empire, and I shall be patient in 1813 as I have been in 1812!' Whether Napoleon genuinely vouchsafed such secrets to a man he must have suspected didn't want him to be victorious in Russia, and had excellent connections with the Russians, might be doubted.

Leaving Marie Louise with her parents in Dresden when he departed at dawn on May 29, Napoleon wrote later that morning that he would be back within two months. 'All my promises to you shall be kept,' he said, 'thus our absence from each other will be but a short one.'[89] It was to be nearly seven months before he saw her again. Going eastwards via Bautzen, Reichenbach, Hainau, Glogau, Posen, Thorn, Danzig and Königsberg, he reached the banks of the Niemen by June 23. He deliberately didn't go to Warsaw, where, if he had proclaimed the Kingdom of Poland, he could have raised, one Russian general estimated, 200,000 men and turned the ethnically Polish provinces of Lithuania, Volhynia and Podolia against the Tsar.[90] Instead he preferred not to antagonize his Prussian and Austrian allies.

At 1 a.m. on the night of June 4, Colonel Maleszewski, one of Napoleon's staff officers, heard the Emperor pacing up and down his room in Thorn, singing the verse from 'Le Chant du Départ' that includes the line '*Tremblez, ennemis de la France*.'[91] On that day alone, Napoleon had written letters to Davout complaining of the marauding of Württemberger troops in Poland, to Clarke about raising a company of Elban sappers, to Marie Louise to say that he had been twelve hours in the saddle since 2 a.m., to Cambacérès that the frontier was quiet, to Eugène ordering 30,000 bushels of barley, and no fewer than twenty-four letters to Berthier about everything from a paymaster who should be punished for incompetence to a fever hospital that needed to be relocated.[92] Preparing for the attack on Russia caused Napoleon to write nearly five hundred letters to Berthier between the beginning of January 1812 and the crossing of the Niemen, and another 631 to Davout, Clarke, Lacuée and Maret between them.

On June 7 staying in Danzig with Rapp – to whom he was far more likely to speak about his strategic thinking than to Metternich – Napoleon said his plans were limited to crossing the Niemen, defeating Alexander and taking Russian Poland, which he would unite to the Duchy of Warsaw, turn into a Polish kingdom, arm extensively and leave with 50,000 cavalry as a buffer state against Russia.[93] Two days later he expanded further to Fain and others:

> While we finish with the north, I hope that Soult will maintain himself in
> Andalusia and that Marmont will contain Wellington on the Portuguese

border. Europe will breathe only when these affairs with Russia and Spain are over. Only then can we reckon on a true peace; reviving Poland will consolidate it; Austria will take care of more of the Danube and less of Italy. Finally, exhausted England will resign herself to share the world's trade with continental vessels. My son is young, you have to prepare him for a quiet reign.[94]

These war aims – even for peace with Britain, against whom America had declared war on June 1 – were limited and possibly even achievable, and certainly far from the lunatic hubris with which Napoleon is generally credited on the eve of his invasion of Russia. There was no word of marching to Moscow, for example (any more than there had been in his supposed heart-to-heart with Metternich). Against the French Empire's 42.3 million inhabitants, and a further 40 million living in the 'Grand Empire' of satellite states, Russia's population in 1812 was about 46 million.[95] Napoleon had fought against the Russians twice before and had defeated them on both occasions. His army of over 600,000 men was over twice the size of the Russian army in the field at the time. On June 20 he specified only twelve days' marching rations for the Imperial Guard, implying that he was hoping for a short campaign – certainly not one that would take him over 800 miles from the Niemen to Moscow.

On June 22 Napoleon issued his second bulletin of the campaign:

> Soldiers! The Second Polish War has commenced. The first ended at Friedland and Tilsit. At Tilsit, Russia swore an eternal alliance with France, and war with England. Today she violates her oaths ... Does she believe us degenerate? Are we no longer the soldiers of Austerlitz? She places us between dishonour and war; the choice cannot be in doubt ... Let us cross the Niemen! ... The peace which we shall conclude shall put an end to the baneful influence which Russia has for fifty years exercised over the affairs of Europe.[96]

Not since his hero Julius Caesar crossed the Rubicon in 49 BC had the traversing of a river held a heavier portent than when Napoleon's vast army started crossing the Niemen into Russia before dawn on Wednesday, June 24 1812. Since Lauriston had been sent away from Alexander's headquarters without reply to Napoleon's last-minute peace offer a few days before, there was no need for a formal declaration of war, any more than there had been at the outbreak of the War of Austrian Succession or the Seven Years War.

While Napoleon was reconnoitring the river on the day of the crossing, his horse shied at a hare and threw him onto the sandy riverbank,
leaving him with a bruised hip.[97] 'This is a bad omen, a Roman would
recoil!' someone exclaimed, although it is not known whether it was
Napoleon himself or one of his staff who said it – but with his penchant
for ancient history (and the understandable reluctance of anyone else to
make that obvious point) it may well have been the Emperor himself.[98]
Napoleon had ordered the artillery commander-turned-engineer General Jean-Baptiste Éblé to throw three pontoon bridges over the river
near a village called Ponemun (now Panemunė, near Kaunas in Lithuania), and he spent the rest of the day in his tent and in a nearby house,
in Ségur's words, 'listlessly reclining in the midst of a breathless atmosphere and a suffocating heat, vainly courting repose'.[99]

The sheer size of Napoleon's army is hard to compute. He had over
1 million men under arms in 1812; once he subtracted garrisons,
reserves, eighty-eight National Guard battalions, soldiers in the
156 depots back in France, various coastal artillery batteries and
twenty-four line battalions stationed around the Empire, as well as the
men in Spain, he was left with 450,000 in the first line with which to
invade Russia and 165,000 mobilized in the second. A reasonably
accurate total might therefore be 615,000, which was larger than the
entire population of Paris at the time.[100] It was certainly the largest invasion force in the history of mankind to that time, and very much a
multi-national one. Poles made up the largest single foreign contingent,
but it also comprised Austrians, Prussians, Westphalians, Württembergers, Saxons, Bavarians, Swiss, Dutch, Illyrians, Dalmatians, Neapolitans,
Croats, Romans, Piedmontese, Florentines, Hessians, Badeners, Spaniards and Portuguese. Much has been made of the breadth of the seven
coalitions that Britain brought together against France during the
Napoleonic Wars, which is indeed impressive and significant, but the
broadest coalition of all was this one that fought for France against
Russia.[101] Some 48 per cent of Napoleon's infantry were French
and 52 per cent foreign, whereas the cavalry was 64 per cent French and
36 per cent foreign.[102] Even the Imperial Guard had Portuguese and Hessian cavalry units in it, and a squadron of Mamluks were attached to
the Chasseurs à Cheval of the Old Guard. The problem with relying so
heavily on foreigners was that many felt, as the Württemberger Jakob
Walter's journal admitted, 'total indifference as to the outcome of the
campaign', treating French and Russians alike and certainly feeling no
personal loyalty to Napoleon.[103] No amount of haranguing would

convert a Prussian, for example, to an ardent adherence to the French cause.

The numbers of men involved and the distances over which they were spread forced Napoleon to adopt a different army formation from the six or seven corps he had previously used. The first line was organized into three army groups. The central one under Napoleon's personal command had 180,000, mostly French, soldiers. It included Murat with two corps of reserve cavalry, the Imperial Guard, Davout's and Ney's corps and Berthier's general staff, which itself now numbered nearly 4,000. On his right was Eugène's 4th Corps of 46,000 men with Junot as his chief-of-staff, and the 3rd Reserve Cavalry Corps, with Poniatowski's 5th Corps even further to the south. On Napoleon's left was Oudinot's corps, guarding the northern flank. In total the Grande Armée had over 1,200 guns.[104]

Napoleon invaded Russia with around 250,000 horses – 30,000 for the artillery, 80,000 for the cavalry and the rest pulled 25,000 vehicles of every kind – yet the supply of forage for so many horses was entirely beyond any system Napoleon or anyone else could have put into effect.[105] He delayed the invasion until forage would be plentiful, but nonetheless the heat and their diet of wet grass and unripe rye killed 10,000 horses in the first week of the campaign alone.[106] As horses required 20 pounds of forage per day, he had a maximum of three weeks before supplies would start to become inadequate. There were twenty-six transport battalions, eighteen of which consisted of six hundred heavy wagons drawn by six horses each, capable of transporting nearly 6,500 pounds, but the wagons were quickly found to be too heavy for Russian roads once they turned to mud, as ought to have been remembered from the First Polish Campaign.[107] The men had four days' food supply on their backs and a further twenty in the wagons following the army – enough for the very short campaign Napoleon envisaged, but if he had not comprehensively defeated the main Russian army within a month of crossing the Niemen, he would need either to withdraw or to stop and resupply. The critical moment of the campaign should therefore fall in the third week of July, if not earlier.

But the army that was crossing the Niemen was no longer the highly mobile entity of Napoleon's earlier campaigns, designed to catch and swiftly envelop the enemy. Napoleon's headquarters alone required 50 wagons pulled by 650 horses.[108] Murat took along a famous Parisian chef, and many officers packed their evening dress and brought their private carriages.[109] Many of the phenomena of Napoleonic warfare that had been characteristic of his earlier campaigns – elderly opponents lacking energy, a nationally and linguistically diverse enemy against the homogeneous French, a vulnerable spot onto which Napoleon could latch and not let go, a capacity for significantly faster movement than the enemy, and to concentrate forces to achieve numerical advantage for just long enough to be decisive – were not present or were simply impossible in the vast reaches of European Russia. The Russian generals tended to be much younger than the generals Napoleon had faced in Italy – averaging forty-six years old against the French generals' forty-three – and the Russian army was more homogeneous than Napoleon's. This was to be a campaign utterly unlike any he had fought before, indeed unlike any in history.

24

Trapped

'He didn't want to conquer Russia, not even to re-establish
Poland; he had only renounced the Russian alliance with regret.
But conquering a capital, signing a peace on his terms and her-
metically sealing the ports of Russia to British commerce, that
was his goal.'

Champagny's memoirs

'Rule one on page one of the book of war, is: "Do not march on
Moscow."'

Field Marshal Viscount Montgomery,
House of Lords, May 1962

Napoleon crossed the River Niemen at 5 a.m. on June 24, 1812, and
then stationed himself on a hillock nearby as his soldiers marched past
crying, 'Vive l'Empereur!'[1] He hummed the children's song '*Malbrough
s'en va-t'en guerre*' to himself. ('Marlborough is going to war, / who
knows when he'll be back?')[2] He wore a Polish uniform that day, and
equally symbolically rode a horse named Friedland. That afternoon he
went on to cross the Viliya river and entered Kovno. It took five days for
the whole army to make it across the river.

Although Russia had 650,000 men under arms in 1812, they were
spread out widely across her Empire – in Moldavia, the Caucasus, central Asia, the Crimea, Siberia, Finland and elsewhere – with only around
250,000 men and guns, organized in three armies, facing Napoleon in
the west. Barclay de Tolly's First Army of the West, of 129,000 men, was
widely deployed either side of Vilnius; Bagration's Second Army of the
West, of 48,000 was 100 miles to the south of Vilnius at Volkovysk; and
General Alexander Tormasov's Third Army of the West, of 43,000 was

coming from much further south, freed from Danubian service by the Russo-Turkish peace. Napoleon wanted to keep these three forces separate and to defeat them piecemeal. He sent Eugène and Jérôme out on wide enveloping movements in the hope of surrounding Bagration's Second Army before it could join Barclay's First Army. Why he chose to give this vital task to his stepson and brother rather than to senior, experienced soldiers such as Davout, Murat or Macdonald is unclear. Jérôme had commanded the 9th Corps during the 1806–07 campaign (the army's German contingent) but had not particularly distinguished himself. 'The heat is overpowering,' Napoleon wrote to Marie Louise from the convent at Kovno where he had set up his headquarters, adding: 'You can present the University with a collection of books and engravings. This will please it vastly and will cost you nothing. I have plenty of them.'[3]

Opinion in the Russian high command was split between the aristocratic generals who supported Bagration's counter-offensive strategy and the 'foreigners' (often Baltic Germans) who supported Barclay de Tolly's strategy of withdrawal, essentially that of Bennigsen in 1807 except across a far wider area. By the time Napoleon crossed the Niemen the latter had won, partly because the sheer size of the Grande Armée made a counter-offensive unthinkable. Having a smaller army would therefore paradoxically have helped Napoleon by tempting the Russians into the early battle he logistically needed to fight, and would also have allowed him (because of its lesser supply needs) more time to fight it. Had Alexander appointed the Russian-born Bagration as war minister and commander of the First Army of the West instead of Barclay – an appointment that would have been popular in the Russian officer corps – Napoleon might have destroyed the Russian army at, or even before, Vilnius. Instead he picked the less flamboyant, more incisive Barclay and stuck by Barclay's plan to lure the Grande Armée deep into Russian territory, stretching its supply lines away from the huge military depots in Mainz, Danzig, Königsberg and elsewhere.

Napoleon entered Vilnius, the capital of Polish Lithuania, on June 28 and turned it into a massive supply centre, the Russians having removed or burned all theirs before they left. He told Marie Louise that he had chosen for his headquarters 'a rather fine mansion where the Emperor Alexander was living a few days ago, very far from thinking at the time that I was so soon to enter here'.[4] Half an hour before Napoleon made his entry into the city, he ordered a Polish artillery officer on his staff, Count Roman Soltyk, to fetch Jan Śniadecki, the renowned

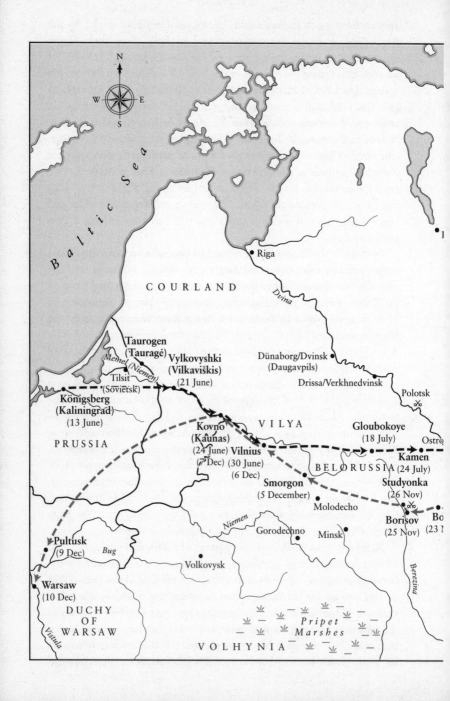

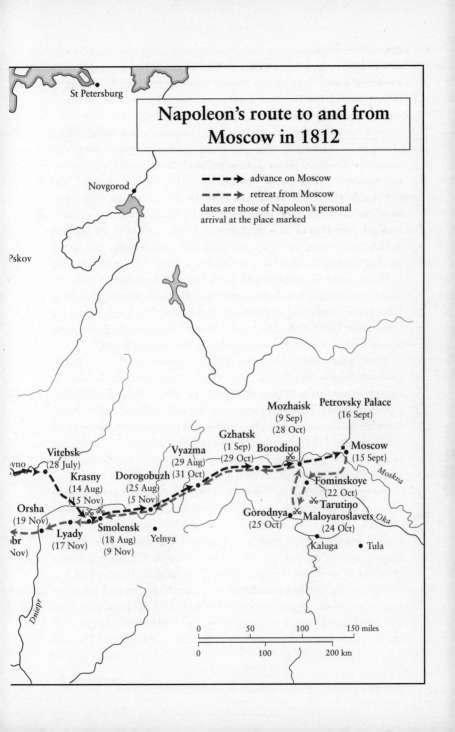

Napoleon's route to and from
Moscow in 1812

- - - ▶ advance on Moscow
- - - ▶ retreat from Moscow

dates are those of Napoleon's personal
arrival at the place marked

St Petersburg

Novgorod

Pskov

Mozhaisk
(9 Sep)
(28 Oct)

Petrovsky Palace
(16 Sept)

Gzhatsk
(1 Sep)

Borodino

Moscow
(15 Sept)

Vyazma
(29 Aug)
(29 Oct)

Moskva

Vitebsk
(28 July)

Dorogobuzh (31 Oct)
(25 Aug)
(5 Nov)

Fominskoye
(22 Oct)

Krasny
(14 Aug)
(15 Nov)

vno

Tarutino

Orsha
(19 Nov)

Gorodnya
(25 Oct)

Maloyaroslavets
(24 Oct)

Oka

Lyady
(17 Nov)

Smolensk
(18 Aug)
(9 Nov)

Yelnya

Kaluga

Tula

br
Nov)

Dniepr

| 0 | | 50 | | 100 | | 150 miles |

| 0 | | 100 | | 200 km |

astronomer, mathematician and physicist, and rector of Vilnius University, to talk to him there. When Śniadecki insisted on putting on silk stockings before leaving his house, Sołtyk expostulated: 'Rector, it doesn't matter. The Emperor attaches no importance to exterior things which only impress the common people . . . Let's be off.'[5]

'Our entry into the city was triumphal,' wrote another Polish officer. 'The streets . . . were full of people, all the windows were garnished with ladies who displayed the wildest enthusiasm.'[6] Napoleon showed characteristic sensitivity to public opinion by having himself preceded and followed by Polish units in the procession. He set up a provisional government for the Lithuanian Poles there, and Lithuania was ceremonially reunited with Poland in a ceremony at Vilnius cathedral. At Grodno French troops were met by processions with icons, candles and choirs blessing them for the 'liberation' from Russian rule.* A *Te Deum* was sung in Minsk, where General Grouchy handed around the collection plate, but once the rural population heard that the French troops were requisitioning food, as they always did on campaign, they herded their livestock into the forests. 'The Frenchman came to remove our fetters,' said the Polish peasants in western Russia that summer, 'but he took our boots too.'[7]

'I love your nation,' Napoleon told the representatives of the Polish nation at Vilnius. 'For the last sixteen years I have seen your soldiers at my side in the battles in Italy and Spain.' He offered Poland 'my esteem and protection'. With Schwarzenberg protecting his southern flank, however, he needed to add: 'I've guaranteed to Austria the integrity of her states, and I cannot authorize anything that will tend to trouble her in the peaceful possession of what remains to her of her Polish provinces.'[8] He was having to perform a delicate balancing act.

He stayed ten days in Vilnius to allow much of the army to rest, regroup and allow that part of the right wing of the army that was under the untried and untested Jérôme – comprising two of Davout's divisions, Schwarzenberg's Austrians, Poniatowski's Poles and Reynier's Saxons, 80,000 men in all – to advance towards the lower Berezina river and try to pincer Bagration's army. The vanguards moved on and on June 29 the broiling heat broke in a great hailstorm and deluge of rain, after which Sergeant Jean-Roch Coignet of the Imperial Guard noted that 'in the cavalry camp nearby, the ground was covered with horses which had died of cold', including three of his own.[9] The rain

---

* Lithuania had been part of the Polish-Lithuanian Commonwealth since 1569, before the Russians annexed it in the three partitions between 1772 and 1795.

also made the ground boggy and roads muddy, causing supply problems and slowing down the vanguards in pursuit of the Russians. In some marshes and swamps men waded up to their chins.[10]

Berthier wrote to Jérôme from Vilnius on June 26, the 29th and the 30th encouraging him to keep in close proximity to Bagration and to capture Minsk.[11] 'If Jérôme pushes strongly ahead,' Napoleon told Fain, 'Bagration is deeply compromised.'[12] With Jérôme moving in from the west and Davout from the north, Bagration ought to have been crushed between them at Bobruisk, but Jérôme's bad generalship, as well as Bagration's skill at withdrawal, meant that the Russian Second Army escaped. By July 13 it was clear that Jérôme had failed. 'If it had been more rapid and better concerted between the Corps of the army,' General Dumas, the intendant-general, later opined, 'the object would have been obtained and the success of the campaign decided at the very opening.'[13] When Napoleon learned of the failure he appointed Davout to command Jérôme's army. His outraged youngest brother resigned his command and flounced back to Westphalia only three weeks into the campaign.[14]

'The weather is very rainy,' Napoleon wrote to Marie Louise from Vilnius on July 1, 'the storms in this country are terrible.'[15] Although we don't have her letters to him, the Empress wrote one every other day that month. 'God grant I may soon meet the Emperor,' she told her father at this time, 'for this separation weighs much too heavily upon me.'[16] As well as mentioning his state of health – almost always positively – Napoleon asked after his son in every letter he wrote, begging for news about 'whether he is beginning to talk, whether he is walking' and so on.

On July 1, Napoleon received Alexander's aide-de-camp, General Alexander Balashov, who told him somewhat belatedly that Napoleon could still withdraw from Russia and avoid war. He wrote Alexander a very long letter reminding the Tsar of his anti-British remarks at Tilsit, and pointing out that at Erfurt he had accommodated Alexander's needs with regard to Moldavia, Wallachia and the Danube. Since 1810, he said, the Tsar had 'rearmed on a large scale, declined the path of negotiations' and demanded modifications to the European settlement. He recalled 'the personal esteem which you have sometimes shown to me' but said that the ultimatum of April 8 to withdraw from Germany had been designed 'clearly to place me between war and dishonour'.[17] Even though 'for eighteen months you have refused to explain anything',

Napoleon wrote, 'My ear will always be open to peace negotiations ... you will always find in me the same feelings and true friendship.' He blamed the Tsar's bad advisors and Kurakin's arrogance for the war, using a phrase he had employed in writing to the Pope, the Emperor of Austria and others in the past: 'I pity the wickedness of those who gave Your Majesty such bad advice.' Napoleon then argued that if he had not had to fight Austria in 1809, 'the Spanish business would have been ended in 1811, and probably peace would have been brokered with England at that time.' In conclusion, Napoleon offered:

> a truce on the most liberal grounds, such as not considering men in hospital as prisoners – so that neither side has to hurry evacuations, which involves heavy losses – such as the return every two weeks of prisoners made by either side, using a rank-for-rank exchange system, and all the other stipulations that the custom of war between civilized nations has allowed: Your Majesty will find me ready for anything.[18]

He ended by repeating that, notwithstanding the war between them, 'the private feelings that I bear for you are not in the least affected by these events ... [I remain] full of affection and esteem for your fine and great qualities and desirous of proving it to you.'*

Alexander took up none of Napoleon's proposals. The Russians were retreating steadily before the Grande Armée – the first clash to cost either side more than a thousand casualties didn't come for four weeks – but that didn't mean they were offering no resistance. Recognizing that this war was going to be as much about logistics as battles, they systematically destroyed anything that couldn't be removed. Crops, windmills, bridges, livestock, depots, fodder, shelter, grain – everything that could be of any use whatever to the oncoming French was either taken away or burned, for many miles on both sides of the road. Napoleon had done the same thing on his retreat from Acre, and had admired Wellington's skilful execution of a similar scorched-earth policy while withdrawing to the Lines of Torres Vedras, for, as Chaptal recorded: 'It was on traits like these that he judged the skill of generals.'[19]

Because eastern Poland and Byelorussia were grindingly poor and sparsely populated regions where malnutrition was common even in

---

* After writing such an extraordinary, open-hearted letter, Napoleon was probably joking when he asked Balashov which was the best road to Moscow. 'Sire,' came the superb retort, 'one can take whichever one wants. Charles XII went by way of Poltava.' (Foord, *Napoleon's Russian Campaign* p. 75, Mowat, *Diplomacy of Napoleon* p. 256)

peacetime – unlike the lush and fertile grounds of northern Italy and Austria – there would always have been a serious supply problem when its backward agrarian economy was suddenly called upon to feed hundreds of thousands of extra mouths. Yet with entire villages set ablaze by the retreating Russians, the situation quickly became dire. Worse, there were squadrons of light Russian cavalry operating deep behind French lines, including a famously daring one led by Alexander Chernyshev, which threatened Napoleon's lengthening lines of communication.[20]

No sooner was the violently wet weather of late June over than the baking sun returned; fresh water was in short supply and recruits fainted from exhaustion. The heat threw up a choking dust so thick that drummers had to be stationed at the head of battalions so that the men marching behind wouldn't get lost. By July 5, because of bottlenecks of wagons on the pontoon bridges across rivers, the Grande Armée was facing severe food shortages. 'Difficulties over food remain,' noted the Comte de Lobau's aide-de-camp Boniface de Castellane, 'soldiers are without food and horses without oats.'[21] When Mortier told Napoleon that several members of the Young Guard had actually died of hunger, the Emperor said: 'It's impossible! Where are their twenty days' rations? Soldiers well commanded never die of hunger!'[22] Their commander was brought, and stated, 'either from weakness or uncertainty', that in fact the men had died from intoxication, upon which Napoleon concluded that 'One great victory would make amends for all!'[23]

An average of 1,000 horses were to die for every day of the 175 days that the Grande Armée spent in Russia. Ségur recalled that the more than 10,000 horses that died from dehydration and heat exhaustion, when unripe rye had been their only fodder, 'sent forth a stench impossible to breathe'.[24] Caulaincourt, Napoleon's master of horse, was devastated. 'The rapidity of the forced marches, the shortage of harness and spare parts, the dearth of provisions, the want of care, all helped to kill the horses,' he recorded.

> The men, lacking everything to supply their own needs, were little inclined to pay heed to their horses, and watched them perish without regret, for their death meant the breakdown of the service on which the men were employed, and thus the end of their personal privations. There you have the secret and cause of our earlier disasters and of our final reverse.[25]

As early as July 8 Napoleon had to write to Clarke in Paris to say that it wasn't necessary to increase cavalry recruitment 'since we are losing so many horses in this country that we will have great difficulty, with all the resources of France and Germany, in keeping the current number of men in the regiments mounted'.[26]

That same day Napoleon learned that the main Russian force, the First Army of the West, was at Drissa, a powerful fortress that was badly situated strategically. Filled with hope, he sent his advance guard there, but by the time they arrived there on the 17th they found it abandoned. On July 16 he was told that although Davout had captured Minsk, Bagration had managed to slip away again. Just before he left Vilnius, Napoleon dined with General de Jomini; they spoke of how close Moscow was – it was actually 500 miles away – and Jomini asked if he intended to march there. Napoleon burst out laughing, saying:

> I much prefer to get there in two years' time ... If M. Barclay thinks that I want to run after him all the way to the Volga, he is very much mistaken. We shall follow him as far as Smolensk and the Dvina, where a good battle will allow us to go into cantonments. I shall return here, to Vilnius, with my headquarters to spend the winter. I shall send for an opera company and actors from the Théâtre-Français. Then, next May, we shall finish the job, if we do not make peace during the winter. That is better, I think, than running to Moscow. What do you say, Monsieur Tactician?[27]

Jomini agreed.

By then Napoleon was facing a devastating new threat for which no army of the day was prepared. Typhus fever is a disease of dirt; its causative organism, *Rickettsia prowazekii*, lies midway between the relatively large bacteria that cause syphilis and tuberculosis and the microscopic smallpox and measles viruses. Carried by lice which infest unwashed bodies in the seams of dirty clothing, the organism is not transferred by the louse's bite but through its excrement and corpse.[28] It had been endemic in Poland and western Russia for years.

Heat, lack of water for washing, troops packed together in large numbers at night, the hovels in which they sheltered, scratching irritable areas, not changing clothes: all were ideal conditions for spreading typhus. In the first week of the campaign alone, 6,000 men fell ill with it every day. By the third week of July over 80,000 men had either died or were sick, at least 50,000 of them from typhus. Within a month of the start of the invasion, Napoleon had lost one-fifth of the men in his central army group.[29] Larrey, the Grande Armée's surgeon-general, was a fine doctor, but typhus had not yet been medically linked to lice, which were thought of as an unpleasant pest but no killer, and he was at a loss to know how to respond. Dysentery and enteric fever were dealt with in hospitals in Danzig, Königsberg and Thorn, but typhus was different. Napoleon supported vaccination, especially for smallpox – he had had his son vaccinated at two months – but there was none to be had against typhus. Recent research on the DNA taken from the teeth of 2,000 corpses in a mass grave in Vilnius shows that they almost all carried the *typhus exanthematicus* pathogen, known as 'war plague'. Ironically, Napoleon insisted that hospitalized men be made to bathe, but it wasn't known that healthy men needed to as well.[30] Even the Emperor caught lice on the retreat from Moscow, when it was too cold to remove any of his clothes for days on end.[31] The way to defeat them was to boil undergarments and iron outer garments with a hot iron, neither of which could be done in the sub-zero temperatures that first arrived on November 4.[32]

Typhus (which is quite different from typhoid fever, dysentery and the other 'diseases of the poor') had been a growing problem in France itself as the Revolutionary and Napoleonic Wars progressed, with outbreaks prevalent in villages situated along the major roads. In the Seine-et-Marne, outbreaks were almost uninterrupted after 1806, as well as in the eastern Parisian communes where the troops arrived back from the Rhine. Mortality was heavy in 1810–12 and, when asked to explain this, the medical officers of Melun and Nemours agreed that the principal cause was 'continual war'.[33] Typhus returned when the Allied armies invaded France in 1814 and 1815. The most eminent physicians of the day assumed that it could break out spontaneously given 'great hardship, colds, lack of the necessaries of life, and the consequent consumption of spoiled foodstuffs'.[34] Even twenty years after the end of the wars, J. R. L. de Kerckhove, a former chief of French hospitals in 1812, understood the cause of typhus incorrectly, writing: 'The typhus that had so decimated the French army had its origin in privation, fatigue and the polluted air that one breathes in places overflowing with the sick and the exhausted. Then it spread by contagion.'[35] The connection between lice and typhus was not made until 1911. De Kerckhove got the symptoms absolutely right, however:

> The infection manifested itself through general malaise, accompanied most often by a state of languor; a weak, slow or irregular pulse; an alteration in facial traits; a difficulty executing movements . . . extreme fatigue, difficulty standing, lack of appetite; vertigo, ringing in the ear, nausea, headaches

were very frequent; sometimes he suffered from vomiting; sometimes the
tongue was covered in a white or yellow mucus.

After about four days a fever developed which 'was evident firstly in
shaking followed by an irregular feeling of heat . . . the fever developed
and became continual, the skin was dry . . . congestions of the brain and
sometimes the lung'.[36] In most cases, death followed. Up to 140,000 of
Napoleon's soldiers died of disease in 1812, the majority of them from
typhus but a significant number from dysentery and related illnesses.

Napoleon could not allow disease to derail the entire invasion, and
pressed on eastwards in the hope of keeping the Russian First and
Second Armies of the West separate. He himself was, in the estimation
of the ordnance officer attached to his staff, Captain Gaspard Gourgaud, 'in excellent health' during the campaign, spending hours a day
on horseback with no serious illnesses reported.[37] The speed of the
Grande Armée's advance and the rawness of the young recruits meant
that many could not keep up. 'Stragglers are committing awful horrors,'
wrote Castellane, 'they are sacking and pillaging: mobile columns are
organized.'[38] On July 10 Napoleon ordered Berthier to send a column of
gendarmes to Vorovno 'to arrest the pillagers of the 33rd, who are committing horrible devastation in that country'.[39] By mid-July troops were
also deserting in bands.

On July 18 Napoleon arrived at Gloubokoïe, where he stayed for
four days in the Carmelite convent, attending Mass, setting up a
hospital, inspecting the Guard and hearing reports about the severe
problems the army was facing as a result of the constant marching.
'Hundreds killed themselves,' recalled Lieutenant Karl von Suckow, a
Mecklenburger serving with the Württemberg Guard, 'feeling no longer
able to endure such hardship. Every day one heard isolated shots ring
out in the woods near the road.'[40] Medicine had become almost unob-
tainable, except with cash. The Bavarian General von Scheler reported
to his king that even as early as crossing the Vistula 'all regular food
supply and orderly distribution ceased, and from there as far as Moscow not a pound of meat or bread, not a glass of brandy was taken
through legal distribution or regular requisition'.[41] It was an exaggeration, but a pardonable one.

There is evidence to suggest that Napoleon was being misled about
both food supplies and the number of healthy soldiers in his army. Units
that Napoleon was told had food for ten days had actually run out of it
altogether, and General Dumas recalled that Davout's brother-in-law,

General Louis Friant, the commander of two Guard grenadier demi-brigades, 'wanted me to produce a report on the 33rd Line to say it amounted to 3,200 men, whilst I knew that in reality no more than 2,500 men, at most, were left. Friant, who was under Murat's orders, said Napoleon would be angry with his chief. He preferred to introduce an error, and Colonel Pouchelon provided the mendacious report required.'[42] That single deception, therefore, involved three senior officers (and possibly Murat too), or at least required them to be compliant. Somehow the culture of the army had changed, so that Napoleon, who used to be so close to his men, was now regularly lied to by his senior commanders. He continued his personal inspections, but the sheer size of the Grande Armée and the breadth of its advance meant that he relied far more on his commanders than in any previous campaign. Another of his bodyguards also recalled in his memoirs that during the retreat in December Napoleon asked Bessières about the condition of the Guard. 'Very comfortable, Sire,' came the reply. 'The spit is turning at a number of fires; there are chicken and legs of mutton, etc.' The bodyguard stated: 'If the marshal had looked with both eyes he would have found that these poor devils had little to eat. Most of them had heavy colds, all were very weary, and their number had greatly decreased.'[43]

When on July 19 Napoleon heard from Murat's aide-de-camp Major Marie-Joseph Rossetti that the Russians had abandoned Drissa, 'he could not contain himself for joy'.[44] Writing to Maret from Gloubokoïé, he said: 'The enemy has evacuated its fortified camp at Drissa and burnt all its bridges and a huge quantity of stores, sacrificing work and provisions that were the focus of their work over many months.'[45]* According to Rossetti's journal, the Emperor, 'striding quickly up and down', said to Berthier: 'You see, the Russians don't know how to make either war or peace. They are a degenerate nation. They give up their palladium without firing a shot! Come along, one more real effort on our part and

---

* As ever Napoleon was also thinking about what was happening in France. 'I must remind you that I had the intention of buying all parts of the islands of Hyères,' he told Clarke on July 21, referring to a small group of islands in the south of France, 'and doing something to populate them' (CG12 no. 31281 p. 899). He was also fearful that a large granary in Paris would not be built in the time he had allowed for it. 'The Arc de Triomphe, the Pont d'Iéna, the Temple of Glory, the abattoirs can be delayed by two or three years without inconvenience,' he told his minister for trade and commerce, 'instead it is of the utmost importance that this enormous warehouse be finished.' (CG12 no. 31255 p. 885)

my brother [that is, the Tsar] will repent of having taken the advice of my enemies.'[46] He quizzed Rossetti closely about the morale of the cavalry and the condition of the horses, getting favourable responses and making Rossetti a colonel on the spot. Yet in fact Murat was asking far too much of the cavalry, wrecking the horses' constitutions with the constant work he demanded from them. 'Always at the forefront of the skirmishers,' Caulaincourt complained, 'he succeeded in ruining the cavalry, ending by causing the loss of the army, and brought France and the Emperor to the brink of an abyss.'[47]

On July 23 Barclay arrived at Vitebsk, 200 miles east of Vilnius, ready to make a stand if Bagration joined him. But that same day, in the first major engagement of the campaign, Davout blocked Bagration's drive northward at the battle of Saltanovka (also called Mogilev), albeit at a loss of 4,100 killed, wounded and missing. Bagration was forced to head towards Smolensk instead. Two days later, Murat's advance guard skirmished with Barclay's rearguard under Count Ostermann-Tolstoy at Ostrovno, west of Vitebsk. Napoleon hoped that a major battle might be joined. As ever, he wildly exaggerated the facts in his bulletin (his tenth), claiming that Murat had fought against '15,000 cavalry and 60,000 infantry' (in fact the Russians had totalled 14,000) and that they had suffered 7,000 killed, wounded and captured against the true total of 2,500. He put the French losses as 200 killed, 900 wounded and 50 captured, whereas the best modern estimates are 3,000 killed and wounded and 300 captured.[48]

Napoleon had high hopes that the Russians might fight rather than surrender the city of Vitebsk, writing to Eugène on the 26th: 'If the enemy wants to fight, then that's very fortunate for us.'[49] That same day, Jomini's question about the possibility of marching on Moscow seems to have entered his strategic thinking as a serious possibility for the first time. On July 22 he had told General Reynier that the enemy would not dare attack Warsaw 'at a time when Petersburg and Moscow are menaced so closely'. Four days later he wrote to Maret: 'I am inclined to think that the regular divisions will want to take Moscow.'[50] His plans to stop at Vitebsk or Smolensk if the enemy didn't give battle were now morphing into something altogether grander and more ambitious. He was allowing himself to be drawn into Barclay de Tolly's trap.

At dawn on July 28, Murat sent word that the Russians had disappeared from Vitebsk and that he was in pursuit. They had taken everything with them, leaving nothing that gave any indication of which direction they had gone. 'There appeared more order in their defeat than in our victory!' noted Ségur.[51] At a meeting with Murat, Eugène and Berthier, Napoleon had to face the fact that the decisive victory they so wanted 'had just escaped our grasp, as it had at Vilnius'.[52] Victory seemed tantalizingly close, and always just over the next hill or on the other side of the next lake, plain or forest – as, of course, the Russians intended. During the sixteen days he spent in Vitebsk, Napoleon very seriously considered ending the year's campaigning there, to resume in 1813. He was now on the borders of Old Russia, where the Dvina and Dnieper rivers formed a natural defensive line. He could establish ammunition magazines and hospitals, reorganize Lithuania politically – the Lithuanians had already raised five infantry and four cavalry regiments for him – and build up the numbers for his central force, one-third of whom had by then died or were sick from typhus and dysentery. From Vitebsk he could threaten St Petersburg if need be.[53] Murat's chief-of-staff, General Auguste Belliard, told Napoleon frankly that the cavalry was exhausted and 'stood in absolute need of rest' since it could no longer gallop when the charge was sounded. Furthermore, there weren't enough horseshoe-nails, smiths or even metal suitable for making nails. 'Here I stop!' Ségur recalled Napoleon saying on entering Vitebsk on the 28th. 'Here I must look around me; rally, refresh my army and reorganise Poland. The campaign of 1812 is finished; that of 1813 will do the rest.'[54]

Napoleon certainly had a fine line of defence at Vitebsk; his left flank was fixed at Riga on the Baltic, and ran through Dünaborg, Polotsk, fortified Vitebsk with its wooded heights at the centre, then down the Berezina and through the impassable Pripet Marshes, with the fortress town of Bobruisk on his right, 400 miles south-east of Riga. Courland could support Macdonald's corps for food and supplies, Samogitia would do the same for Oudinot's, the Klubokoë plains for Napoleon himself, and Schwarzenberg could stop in the fertile southern provinces. There were huge supply depots at Vilnius, Kovno, Danzig and Minsk to see the army through the winter. That he truly considered this option is evident from the fact that he ordered twenty-nine large ovens to be built at Vitebsk, capable of baking 29,000 pounds of bread, and had houses pulled down to improve the appearance of the palace square where he stayed. Yet it was hard thinking of winter quartering when, as Napoleon wrote to Marie Louise, 'We are having unbearable heat, 27 degrees.

This is as hot as in the Midi.'[55] Ségur blamed Murat for persuading Napoleon to push on, despite the Emperor supposedly saying, '1813 will see us in Moscow, 1814 at Petersburg. The Russian war is a war of three years.'[56]

Napoleon chose to continue chasing Barclay for several perfectly rational military reasons. He had advanced 190 miles in a month and suffered fewer than 10,000 battle casualties; July was absurdly early in the campaigning calendar to order a halt for the year; audacity had always served him well up till then and he would cede the initiative if he stopped at Vitebsk so early in the year; the Tsar had called up the 80,000-strong militia in Moscow on July 24 as well as 400,000 serfs, so it made sense to attack before they were trained and deployed; and the only two occasions when he had ever been forced to fight defensively, at Marengo and Aspern-Essling, he had not initially fared well. Murat also pointed out that Russian morale must have been devastated by the constant retreats. How much more of Russia could the Tsar see ravaged before he sued for peace? He couldn't know that Alexander had declared in St Petersburg that he would never make peace, saying: 'I would sooner let my beard grow to my waist and eat potatoes in Siberia.'[57]

The French learned that Barclay's army was only 85 miles away at Smolensk, where it was joined by Bagration's on August 1. Napoleon assumed that the Russians would not surrender one of the greatest cities of Old Russia without a major battle. He therefore decided not to stop in Vitebsk after all, but kept the option open of returning there after fighting the Russians at Smolensk. He was advised by Duroc, Caulaincourt, Daru and Narbonne to remain at Vitebsk, and he also heard similar views from Poniatowski, Berthier and Lefebvre-Desnouettes, with Murat putting the opposing opinion, before deciding on his own course.[58] Ségur recalled that the Emperor would occasionally address people with such half-sentences as 'Well! What shall we do? Shall we stay where we are, or advance?', but 'He did not wait for their reply but still kept wandering about, as if he were looking for something or someone to end his indecision.'[59] Clues to his thinking can be gleaned from phrases such as that of August 7 to Marie Louise: 'Here we are only one hundred leagues from Moscow.'[60] (In fact Vitebsk is 124 leagues – 322 miles – away.)

The decision to press on to Smolensk was not taken lightly. 'Did they take him for a madman?' Ségur recorded Napoleon saying to Daru and Berthier around the 11th.

Did they imagine he made war from inclination? Had they not heard him say that the wars of Spain and Russia were two ulcers which ate into the vitals of France and that she could not bear them both at once? He was anxious for peace but in order to treat for it, two persons were necessary and he was only one.[61]

Napoleon also pointed out that the Russians would be able to march over frozen rivers in the winter, and at Smolensk he could win either a great fortress or a decisive battle. 'Blood has not yet been spilled, and Russia is too powerful to yield without fighting. Alexander can only negotiate after a great battle,' he said.[62] This conversation lasted a full eight hours and during it Berthier burst into tears, telling Napoleon that the Continental System and the restoration of Poland weren't good enough reasons for over-extending French lines of communication. Duroc's friendship with Napoleon was almost ended by the decision.

Napoleon stuck nevertheless to his conviction 'that boldness was the only prudential course'.[63] He reasoned that the Austrians and Prussians might rethink their alliances with him if he stagnated, that the only way to shorten the lines of communication was to secure a quick victory and return, and that 'a stationary and prolonged defence isn't in the French nature'. He also feared that British military aid to Russia was about to start taking effect. He concluded, as recorded by Fain, 'Why stop here for eight months when twenty days might suffice for us to reach our goal? . . . We have to strike promptly, otherwise everything will be compromised . . . In war, chance is half of everything. If we were always waiting for a favourable gathering of circumstances, we'd never finish anything. In summary, my campaign plan is a battle, and all my politics is success.'[64]*

On August 11 Napoleon gave orders to move on Smolensk, leaving Vitebsk himself at 2 a.m. on the 13th. 'His Majesty rides much less

* That same week Napoleon's secretary Méneval wrote to his librarian Barbier, 'The Emperor would like to have some amusing books. If there were some good new novels, or older ones that he does not know, or memoirs that make agreeable reading, please be so kind as to send them to us, since we have moments of leisure here that are difficult to fill' (CN24 no. 19052 p. 128). One book Napoleon claimed to be too busy to read was Laplace's *The Analytical Theory of Probabilities*. 'I received your treatise for the calculation of probabilities with pleasure,' he wrote to the chancellor of the Senate. 'There'll be a time when I'll read it with interest but today I must confine myself to showing you the satisfaction I feel whenever I see you produce new books that develop and expand this first among sciences. They contribute to the enlightenment of the nation. The advancement and perfection of mathematics are intimately connected with the prosperity of the State.' (CG12 no. 31388 p. 949)

quickly these days,' noted Castellane, who was deputed to accompany him,

> he has put on a good deal of weight, and rides a horse with more diffi-
> culty than before. The grand equerry [Caulaincourt] has to give him a
> hand in mounting. When the Emperor travels, he goes most of the jour-
> ney by carriage. It is very tiring for the officers who have to follow,
> because His Majesty is rested by the time he has to mount ... When His
> Majesty is on the move, one cannot expect a moment's rest in twenty-four
> hours. When [General Jean-Baptiste] Éblé spoke to the Emperor about
> the lack of horses, His Majesty replied: 'We shall find some fine carriage
> horses in Moscow.'[65]

When Napoleon was moving at top speed, water had to be poured on the wheels of his carriage to prevent them overheating.

The situation on both Napoleon's flanks looked promising in mid-August, with Macdonald protecting his north successfully, Schwarzenberg in the south dealing a serious blow to Tormasov's Third Army of the West at Gorodeczna on the 12th (for which Napoleon asked Francis to promote him to field marshal), and Oudinot and Saint-Cyr holding off General Peter Wittgenstein's Army of Finland at Polotsk four days later. Napoleon was therefore able to launch the 'Smolensk Manoeuvre', a huge operation intended to pin the Russian army north of the Dnieper while swiftly moving most of the Grande Armée to the south bank, thanks to impressive bridge-building from Éblé's engineers. Yet this rush for Smolensk was frustrated by the heroic sacrificial rearguard action of General Neverovski's 27th Division at Krasnoi on the 14th, a fighting withdrawal that bought time for the First and Second Armies to reach Smolensk and defend it.

At 6 a.m. on the 16th Murat's cavalry drove in the Russian outposts on the approaches to Smolensk. 'At last I have them!' Napoleon said, as he and Berthier reconnoitred the position at 1 p.m., coming to within 200 yards – some sources say closer – of the city walls.[66] At the battle of Smolensk on August 17, Napoleon hoped to turn the Russians' left flank, cut them off from Moscow and drive them back to the Lower Dvina. But a stout defence of the city, protected by its strong wall and deep ravines, gave Barclay the opportunity to retreat eastwards after suffering losses of around 6,000, while Ney's and Poniatowski's corps lost over 8,500. Under Lobau's shelling Smolensk caught fire, which Napoleon watched with his staff from his headquarters. Ségur states that 'The Emperor contemplated in silence this awful spectacle', but Caulaincourt recalled Napoleon saying, 'Isn't that a fine sight, my Master of Horse?' 'Horrible, Sire!' 'Bah!' Napoleon replied. 'Gentlemen, remember the words of a Roman emperor: a dead enemy always smells sweet!'[67]*

French troops entered the smouldering city at dawn on August 18, stepping over rubble and corpses to find it deserted. When he heard that the Russians sang a *Te Deum* in St Petersburg to celebrate their supposed victory, Napoleon said wryly: 'They lie to God as well as to men.'[68] He inspected the battlefield and Ségur said 'The pain felt by the Emperor might be judged by the contraction of his features and his irritation.' At the gates of the citadel near the Dnieper he held a very rare council of war, with Murat, Berthier, Ney, Davout, Caulaincourt (and possibly also Mortier, Duroc and Lobau), who were seated on some mats that had been found. 'The scoundrels!' he said. 'Fancy abandoning such a position! Come on, we must march on Moscow.'[69] This led to 'a lively discussion' which lasted over an hour. Rossetti, Murat's aide-de-camp, heard that everyone but Davout had been in favour of stopping at Smolensk, 'but that Davout, with his usual tenacity, had maintained that it was only at Moscow that we could sign a peace treaty'.[70] This was also thought to be Murat's view, and it was certainly a line that Napoleon was to repeat often thereafter. Years later he would admit 'I should have put my soldiers into barracks at Smolensk for the winter.'

Napoleon's hopes for a close pursuit of the Russians were dashed the very next day when they successfully withdrew yet again after dealing Ney a heavy blow at the battle of Valutina-Gora (also known as Lubino, just east of Smolensk), where the talented divisional commander General Gudin was killed when a cannonball skimmed along the ground and broke both his legs. After the battle medical shortages were so bad that surgeons tore up their own shirts to dress wounds, and then used hay and afterwards paper taken from documents in Smolensk's archives. Yet those wounded in this part of the campaign were the lucky ones; statistically they had a far better survival rate than the healthy men who marched on eastwards.

Ney's hopes to pincer the Russians at Valutina had been wrecked by Junot's failure to advance his troops in time, to Napoleon's understandable

---

* It was Vespasian.

fury. 'Junot has lost for ever his marshal's baton,' he said, after which he gave the command of the Westphalians to Rapp. 'This affair will, perhaps, hinder me from going to Moscow.' When Rapp said the army didn't know that Moscow was now the ultimate destination, Napoleon replied: 'The glass is full; I must drink it off.'[71] Junot, who hadn't won a victory since the Acre campaign, should have been disgraced after the loss of Portugal at the Convention of Cintra but Napoleon kept him on for friendship's sake.*

The day after Valutina, 'well aware that it is more especially amidst such destruction that men think of immortality', Napoleon distributed no fewer than eighty-seven decorations and promotions among Gudin's 7th Légère and 12th, 21st and 127th Line.[72] Gudin's division was surrounded by 'the corpses of their companions and of the Russians, amidst the stumps of broken trees, on ground trampled by the feet of the combatants, furrowed with balls, strewn with the fragments of weapons, tattered uniforms, overturned carriages and scattered limbs'.[73] By then disease, starvation, desertion and death in battle had brought Napoleon's central army down to 124,000 infantry and 32,000 cavalry, with 40,000 left to protect his supply routes.[74]

Despite the fact that Barclay had escaped yet again, this time towards Dorogobuzh – or perhaps because of it, since the policy of withdrawal was so unpopular in the Russian army – on August 20 the Tsar replaced him as commander-in-chief with the sixty-seven-year-old Field Marshal Prince Mikhail Kutuzov, who had been defeated at Austerlitz. Napoleon was delighted, assuming that 'He has been summoned to command the army on condition that he fights.'[75] In fact, for the first two weeks after his appointment Kutuzov continued to fall back towards Moscow, carefully reconnoitring for the place to take his stand. He chose a village 65 miles to the west of Moscow, just south-west of the River Moskva, called Borodino. Despite his supply difficulties, Napoleon decided, on August 24, to press on after him.

He left Smolensk at 1 p.m. the next day, arriving at Dorogobuzh at 5 p.m. 'Peace is in front of us,' he told his staff, genuinely believing that

---

* Junot's judgement might have been affected by the syphilis that was to drive him insane. At a ball at Ragusa the following year, he arrived stark naked except for his epaulettes, gloves, dancing shoes, orders and decorations (D'Abrantès, *At the Court* p. 21). He died in July 1813 as a result of gangrene setting into injuries sustained when jumping from a second-floor window under the impression that he could fly. (The surprise was that he could fit through, as he had taken to eating three hundred oysters a day.) (Strathearn, *Napoleon in Egypt* p. 422)

Kutuzov couldn't surrender the holy city of Moscow, the venerable previous capital of the Empire, without a major battle, and that afterwards the Tsar would have to sue for peace.[76] Napoleon marched on Moscow to force the Russians to give battle, and his mind was already turning to the terms of surrender he could impose. He told Decrès that under any peace terms that were concluded he would try to secure trees in the Dorogobuzh area for ships' masts.[77] Murat's aide-de-camp Charles de Flahaut wrote from Vyazma to his mother of his own certainty of 'a victory which will finish the war'. While soldiers are not on oath when writing to their mothers from the front line, his assumption that the Tsar 'will certainly now ask for peace' was widespread in the high command.[78]

'The heat was excessive; I never experienced worse in Spain,' wrote Captain Girod de l'Ain, General Joseph Dessaix's aide-de-camp after it hadn't rained for a month. 'This heat and dust make us extremely thirsty and water was scarce . . . I saw men lying on their bellies to drink horses' urine in the gutter!'[79] He also noticed that Napoleon's orders were being disobeyed for the first time. Having ordered that a private carriage, which he saw as an unnecessary luxury, should be burned, the Emperor 'had barely gone a hundred yards before people hastened to put out the flames and the carriage joined the column, bowling along as before'.

On August 26 Napoleon wrote to Maret to say that he had heard that 'the enemy is resolved to wait for us in Vyazma. We will be there in a few days, and then we will be halfway between Smolensk and Moscow, and, I believe, forty leagues from Moscow. If the enemy is beaten there, and nothing can secure this great capital, then I will be there on the 5th of September.'[80] Yet the Russians weren't in Vyazma either. The Grande Armée entered the city on the 29th, and found it empty of its 15,000 inhabitants. When told that a local priest had died of shock at his approach, Napoleon had him buried with full military honours. The priest may have been overcome by the official declaration by the Holy Synod of the Russian Orthodox Church that Napoleon was in fact the Anti-Christ from the Book of Revelation.[81]

On September 2 Napoleon received Marmont's report of his defeat at the hands of Wellington at the battle of Salamanca on July 22. 'It's impossible to read anything more unimpressive,' Napoleon told Clarke; 'there's more noise and clatter in it than in a clock, and not a word to explain the real state of affairs.' He could read between the lines well enough to work out, however, that Marmont had left the well-protected

Salamanca and given Wellington battle without waiting for Joseph's reinforcements. 'At the proper time you must let Marshal Marmont know how indignant I am with his inexplicable conduct,' the Emperor told his war minister.[82] Napoleon could nevertheless later take solace from the fact that Wellington had been forced out of Madrid by converging French forces in October and made to retreat back to Portugal. Joseph was back in his palace by November 2.

The food shortages brought with them other dangers besides those simply of hunger. When men went foraging too far from the main body of the army, they were sometimes captured by Russian irregulars, commanded by regular officers, operating well away from the main roads. This happened to Ségur's brother Octave. By September 3 Napoleon told Berthier that Ney was 'losing more men than if we gave battle' because of the practice of sending out small foraging parties, and that 'the number of prisoners being taken by the enemy is increasing by several hundred every day'. This needed to stop, through better co-ordination and protection.[83] Napoleon was indignant about the incompetence and negligence he saw everywhere, especially in the treatment of the sick and wounded. 'In the twenty years that I have commanded French armies,' he wrote to Lacuée that day,

> I've never seen military administration to be so useless . . . the people who've been sent here have neither capability nor knowledge. The inexperience of the surgeons is doing worse harm to the army than enemy batteries. The four organizing officers accompanying the Quartermaster-General have no experience. The health committee is extremely culpable to have sent such ignorant surgeons . . . The organization of nursing companies has, like all the war operations administration, entirely failed. Once we give them guns and military uniforms, they no longer want to serve in the hospitals.[84]

The simple fact that Napoleon had missed was also the most obvious one: its vast size made Russia impossible to invade much beyond Vilnius in a single campaign. His military administration was incapable of dealing with the enormous strain that he was putting on it. Each day, in his desperation for a decisive battle, he had fallen further into Barclay's trap.

On September 5 Napoleon took the Shevardino Redoubt on the south-western edge of the Borodino battlefield, too distant from the main Russian position to be properly defended. Some 6,000 Russians were killed, wounded or captured to 4,000 Frenchmen. He then braced his army for the clash that he had been longing for ever since crossing the Niemen ten weeks earlier. In the intervening time 110,000 men had fallen victim to typhus, though not all had died, and many others had been picked off or fallen away.[85] The army Napoleon could deploy for the great battle was therefore down to 103,000 men and 587 guns, against Kutuzov's 120,800 men and 640 guns. The Russians had used the previous three days to dig formidable redoubts and arrowhead-shaped defensive earthworks called *flèches*, deepen ravines and clear artillery fields of fire on the battlefield. Several of the redoubts and *flèches*, rebuilt to their 1812 dimensions, can be seen there today.

The day before the battle, Baron de Bausset arrived at headquarters with François Gérard's portrait of the King of Rome strapped to the roof of his carriage. Napoleon received the painting, wrote Fain, 'with an emotion that he could hardly contain', and set it up on a chair outside his tent so that his men could admire their future Emperor.[86] 'Gentlemen,' he told officers arriving for a briefing, 'if my son were fifteen, believe me he would be here in place of that painting.'[87] The next day he said, 'Take it away; keep it safe; he's too young to see a battlefield.' (He was indeed only eighteen months old. The painting was lost in the retreat, but Gérard had made copies.)

Bausset found Napoleon 'quite well … not in the slightest degree inconvenienced by the fatigues of so rapid and complicated an invasion', which contradicts those historians who have variously diagnosed the Emperor with cystitis, fever, influenza, an irregular pulse, difficulty in breathing, a bad cold and inflammation of the bladder that day.[88] He told Marie Louise that he was 'very tired' the day before the battle but the day after it (as in so many of his letters) he pronounced his health to be 'very good'. On the day of the battle itself he rose at 3 a.m. after a broken night's sleep, and stayed up until past 9 p.m. Count Soltyk attested to his having a bad cold during the battle, but Ségur wrote of Napoleon being afflicted by 'a burning fever and above all by a fatal return of that painful malady which every violent movement and high emotion excited in him'. (This might have been a reference to a return of the haemorrhoids which had been cured with leeches more than five years before.[89]) During the battle he stayed fairly sedentary at the Shevardino Redoubt and Lejeune afterwards recalled, 'Every time I returned from one of my numerous missions, I found him sitting there in the same position, following all the moves through his pocket telescope, and issuing his orders with imperturbable calm.'[90]

Reconnoitring the edge of the battlefield the day before, Napoleon,

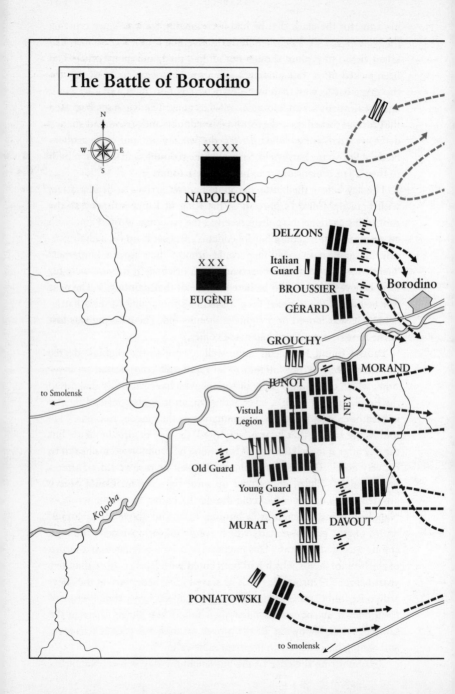

The Battle of Borodino

N

W — E

S

XXXX

NAPOLEON

XXX

EUGÈNE

DELZONS

Italian
Guard

BROUSSIER

GÉRARD

Borodino

GROUCHY

MORAND

JUNOT

NEY

Vistula
Legion

to Smolensk

Old Guard

Young Guard

MURAT

DAVOUT

Kolocha

PONIATOWSKI

to Smolensk

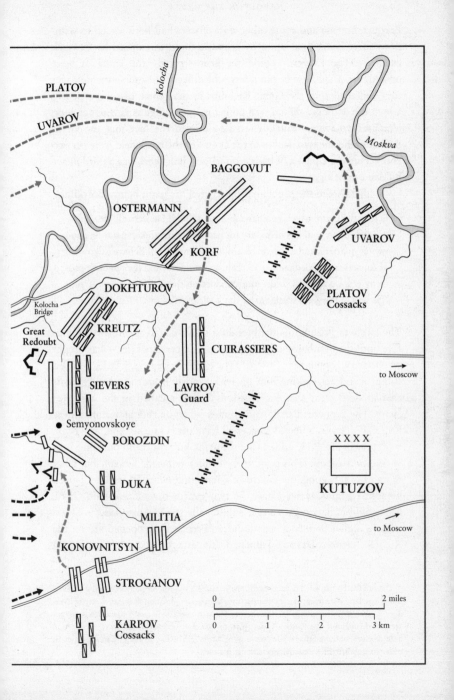

Berthier, Eugène and some other staff officers had been forced to withdraw after being fired upon by grapeshot and threatened by Cossack cavalry.[91] The Emperor could see how strongly the Russians were posted, yet when he sent out a series of officers to observe the defences they failed to spot the Great Redoubt in the centre of the battlefield which the Moscow militia had built for eighteen guns (a number soon increased to twenty-four). They also missed the fact that the Great Redoubt and the two *flèches* in the centre of the battlefield were on two entirely separate pieces of high ground, and that there was a third *flèche* hidden out of sight.

'Soldiers,' read the proclamation written the night before Borodino,

> here is the battle which you have so long desired! Henceforth the victory depends upon you; it is necessary for us. It will give you abundance, good winter quarters, and a speedy return to our homeland! Behave as you did at Austerlitz, at Friedland, at Vitebsk, at Smolensk, and the remotest posterity will quote with pride your conduct on this day. Let it say of you: 'He was at the great battle under the walls of Moscow.'[92]

The battle of Borodino – the bloodiest single day in the history of warfare until the first battle of the Marne over a century later – was fought on Monday, September 7, 1812.* 'The emperor slept very little,' recalled Rapp, who kept waking him up with reports from the advance posts that made it clear that the Russians hadn't escaped in the night yet again. The Emperor drank some punch when he rose at 3.a.m., telling Rapp: 'Fortune is a liberal mistress; I have often said so, and now begin to experience it.'[93] He added that the army knew it could only find provisions in Moscow. 'This poor army is much reduced,' he said, 'but what remains of it is good; my Guard besides is untouched.'[94] He later parted his tent curtains, walked past the two guards outside and said, 'It's a little cold but here comes a nice sun; it's the sun of Austerlitz.'[95]

At 6 a.m. a battery of one hundred French guns opened fire on the Russian centre. Davout launched his attack at 6.30, committing

---

* Overall the French fired 60,000 cannonballs and 1.4 million musket balls that day. Even if the Russians were firing at a lesser rate, and there is no indication that they were, an average of over three cannonballs and seventy-seven musket balls were therefore fired per second throughout the battle (Cate, *War of the Two Emperors* p. 235). A Russian aide-de-camp observed that while crossing the battlefield he had to keep his mouth open in order to stabilize the percussive pressure on his ears.

22,000 superb infantry in three divisions under generals Louis Friant, Jean Compans and Joseph Dessaix deployed in brigade columns, with seventy guns in close support. Ney's three divisions of 10,000 men followed them in, and 7,500 Westphalians were in reserve. This truly savage fight took all morning, during which Davout had a horse shot from under him and was himself wounded. The Russian soldiers showed their customary reluctance to cede ground in battle. By the end some 40,000 French infantry and 11,000 cavalry had to be committed to the struggle to take the *flèches*. Only when two of them had been captured by close-quarter bayonet fighting did the French discover the third, which then started pouring fire into the unprotected rear of the other two; that too had to be captured at great expense. The *flèches* were taken and retaken seven times – just the kind of attritional combat at which the Russians excelled and Napoleon, so far from home, needed to avoid.

By 7.30 a.m. Eugène had captured the village of Borodino by bayonet charge, but then he went too far, crossing the bridge over the Kalatscha river and charging on towards Gorki. His men were mauled as they retreated to Borodino, which they nonetheless managed to retain for the rest of the battle. At 10 a.m. Poniatowski took the village of Utitsa, and the Great Redoubt was captured by an infantry brigade under General Morand, but as it wasn't properly supported he was soon ejected with heavy losses. Also at 10 a.m., with the Bagration *flèches* finally in French hands, Bagration himself was mortally wounded in a counter-attack when his left leg was smashed by a shell splinter. When the 120-house village of Semyonovskoe was captured by Davout in the late morning, Napoleon was able to move up artillery to fire into the Russian left flank. Noon saw the crisis of the battle as several marshals – there were seven present, and two future ones – begged Napoleon to unleash the Imperial Guard to smash through the Russian line while it was still extended. Rapp, who was wounded four times in the battle, also implored Napoleon to do this.

Napoleon refused – there was a limit even to his audacity 1,800 miles from Paris without any other reserves – and so the opportunity, if such it was, was lost. Ségur recalled General Belliard being sent by Ney, Davout and Murat to ask for the Young Guard to be committed against the half-opened flank of the Russian left when Napoleon 'hesitated and ordered the general to go and look again'.[96] Bessières arrived at this point and said that the Russians were merely falling back in good order to a second position. Belliard was told by Napoleon that before he would commit his reserves he wanted 'to see more clearly upon his chessboard', a metaphor he used several times.

Ségur thought there might have been a political motive behind the decision: due to the polyglot nature of 'an army of foreigners who had no other bond of union except victory', Napoleon 'had judged it indispensable to preserve a select and devoted body'.[97] He couldn't commit the Guard with the Russian General Platov threatening his left flank and rear; and if he had sent them down the Old Post Road on the southern flank of the battlefield at noon, when Poniatowski had not captured one side of the road, it might have been severely damaged by the Russian artillery. Later in the battle, when Daru, Dumas and Berthier again urged him to commit the Guard, Napoleon replied: 'And if there should be another battle tomorrow, with what is my army to fight?' For all the wording of his pre-battle proclamation, he was still 65 miles from Moscow. Ordering the Young Guard to take their position on the battlefield that morning, Napoleon had been keen to emphasize to Mortier that he must not act without direct orders: 'Do what I ask and nothing more.'[98]

Kutuzov lost little time in tightening his line, and the cannon in the Great Redoubt continued, in the words of Armand de Caulaincourt, to 'belch forth a veritable hell' against the French centre, holding up any other major advance elsewhere.[99] At 3 p.m. Eugène attacked the Redoubt with three infantry columns, and a cavalry charge managed to get into it from its rear, though at the cost of the lives of both Montbrun and Auguste de Caulaincourt, the grand equerry's brother. 'You have heard the news,' Napoleon said to Caulaincourt when Auguste's death was reported at headquarters, 'do you wish to retire?'[100] Caulaincourt made no reply. He merely raised his hat in acknowledgement, with only the tears in his eyes signifying that he had heard it.[101]

By 4 p.m. the Grande Armée had taken the field of battle. When Eugène, Murat and Ney repeated their request to release the Guard, this time its cavalry, Napoleon again refused.[102] 'I do not wish to see it destroyed,' he told Rapp. 'I am sure to gain the battle without it taking a part.'[103] By 5 p.m. Murat was still arguing for the Guard's deployment but Bessières was now against it, pointing out that 'Europe was between him and France'. At this point Berthier also changed his mind, adding that by then it was too late anyhow.[104] Having withdrawn half a mile by 5 p.m., the Russians stopped and prepared to defend their positions, which an exhausted Grande Armée was ready to shell but unwilling to attack.

Napoleon ordered the commander of the Guard artillery, General Jean Sorbier, to fire at the new Russian positions, saying: 'Since they want it, let them have it!'[105]

Under the cover of darkness, Kutuzov withdrew that night, having lost an immense number of casualties – probably around 43,000, though so dogged was the Russian resistance that only 1,000 men and 20 guns were captured.[106] ('I made several thousand prisoners and captured 60 guns,' Napoleon nonetheless told Marie Louise.[107]) The combined losses are the equivalent of a fully laden jumbo jet crashing into an area of 6 square miles every five minutes for the whole ten hours of the battle, killing or wounding everyone on board. Kutuzov promptly wrote to the Tsar claiming a glorious victory, and another *Te Deum* was sung at St Petersburg. Napoleon dined with Berthier and Davout in his tent behind the Shevardino Redoubt at seven o'clock that evening. 'I observed that, contrary to custom, he was much flushed,' recorded Bausset, 'his hair was disordered, and he appeared fatigued. His heart was grieved at having lost so many brave generals and soldiers.'[108] He was presumably also lamenting the fact that although he had retained the battlefield, opened the road to Moscow and lost far fewer men than the Russians – 6,600 killed and 21,400 wounded – he had failed to gain the decisive victory he so badly needed, partly through the unimaginative manoeuvring of his frontal assaults and partly because of his refusal to risk his reserves. In that sense, both he and Kutuzov lost Borodino. 'I am reproached for not getting myself killed at Waterloo,' Napoleon later said on St Helena. 'I think I ought rather to have died at the battle of the Moskwa.'[109]

Napoleon was clearly sensitive to the idea that he ought to have committed the Guard at noon. At 9 p.m. he summoned generals Dumas and Daru to his tent to inquire about care of the wounded. He then fell asleep for twenty minutes, woke suddenly and continued talking: 'People will be surprised that I did not commit my reserves to obtain greater results,' he said, 'but I had to keep them for striking a decisive blow in the great battle the enemy will fight in front of Moscow. The success of the day was assured, and I had to consider the success of the campaign as a whole.'[110] Soon afterwards he completely lost his voice, and had to give all further orders in writing, which his secretaries found hard to decipher. Fain recalled that Napoleon 'piled up the pages during this mute work and banged on the table when he needed each order to be transcribed'.[111]

Larrey amputated two hundred limbs that day. After the battle the

2nd Light Horse Lancers of the Guard, known as the Dutch Red Lancers, spent the night in woods that had been captured by Poniatowski's infantry, where the ground around the trees was so heavily littered with corpses that they were forced to carry scores out of the way before they could clear a space for their tents.[112] 'In order to get some water it was necessary to travel far from the field of battle,' wrote the veteran Major Louis Joseph Vionnet of the Middle Guard in his memoirs. 'Any water to be found on the field was so soaked with blood that even the horses refused to drink it.'[113] When the next day Napoleon arrived to thank and reward the remains of the 61st Demi-Brigade for capturing the Grand Redoubt, he asked its colonel why its third battalion wasn't on parade. 'Sire,' came the reply, 'it is in the redoubt.'[114]

25

Retreat

'More battles are lost by loss of hope than loss of blood.'
                            Attributed to Napoleon

'Retreats always cost more men and matériel than the bloodiest engagements.'
                        Napoleon's Military Maxim No. 6

On the afternoon following Borodino, Napoleon visited the battlefield. 'Whole lines of Russian regiments, lying on the ground wet with their blood, showed that they preferred death to retiring a single step,' recalled Bausset. 'Napoleon collected all possible information on these sorrowful places, he even observed the numbers on the buttons of their uniforms in order ... to ascertain the nature and positions of the Corps put in motion by the enemy, but what he was chiefly anxious about was the care of the wounded.'[1] When his horse trod on a dying Russian, Napoleon reacted by 'lavishing the attentions of humanity on this unfortunate creature', and when one of the staff officers pointed out that he was 'only a Russian' Napoleon snapped back, 'After a victory there are no enemies, only men.'[2]

The Emperor hoped that his taking Moscow might ease the pressure on Macdonald's and Schwarzenberg's forces to the north and south, telling the latter on September 10: 'Now the enemy has been struck at his heart, he is concentrating only on the heart and not thinking about the extremities.'[3] Murat began to pursue the retreating Russians, occupying Mozhaisk and capturing 10,000 of their wounded. The next day the main French force resumed its advance after two days' rest, by which time it was clear that the Russians were not going to fight another major battle in front of Moscow. 'Napoleon is a torrent,' Kutuzov said in deciding to surrender the city, 'but Moscow is the sponge that will soak him up.'[4] The Russian army marched straight through Moscow on the morning of the 14th; when it became clear that it was being abandoned, virtually the entire population of the city evacuated their homes in a mass exodus, hiding or destroying anything of use to the invader that they couldn't carry away with them. Of its 250,000 inhabitants, only around 15,000 stayed on, many of them non-Russians, although looters did come in from the surrounding countryside.[5] On September 13, the president of Moscow University and a delegation of French Muscovites had visited Napoleon's headquarters to tell him that the city was deserted and no deputation of notables would therefore be coming to offer the traditional gifts of bread and salt and to surrender its keys.[6] Instead an enterprising old peasant sidled up to offer the Emperor a guided tour of the city's major places of interest – an opportunity that was politely refused.[7]

When the soldiers saw the city laid out before them from the Salvation Hills they shouted 'Moscow! Moscow!' and marched forward with renewed vigour. 'Moscow had an oriental, or, rather, an enchanted appearance,' recalled Captain Heinrich von Brandt of the Vistula Legion, 'with its five hundred domes either gilded or painted in the gaudiest colours and standing out here and there above a veritable sea of houses.'[8] Napoleon more prosaically said: 'There, at last, is that famous city; it's about time!'[9] Murat arranged a truce with the Russian rearguard and occupied the city. For supply and security reasons, and in the hope that the Grande Armée would not sack it wholesale, only the Imperial Guard and Italian Royal Guard were billeted inside the city; all others remained in the fields outside, though men swiftly made their way through the suburbs for pillage.

Napoleon entered Moscow on the morning of Tuesday the 15th, installed himself in the Kremlin (once it had been checked for mines), and went to bed early.* 'The city is as big as Paris,' Napoleon wrote to Marie Louise, 'provided with everything.'[10] Ségur recalled how 'Napoleon's earlier hopes revived at the sight of the palace', but at dusk that evening fires broke out simultaneously across the city which could not be contained because of a strong north-easterly equinoctal wind and the fact that the city's governor, Fyodor Rostopchin, had removed or

---

* The innumerable clocks were still ticking in the palace, but the Russians did put acid in some of the wine in the cellar, which 'dreadfully burned' the mouth of the Comte de Turenne's valet (Merridale, *Red Fortress* p. 212, Bausset, *Private Memoirs* p. 328).

destroyed all the city's fire-engines and sunk the city's fleet of fire-boats before leaving.[11] 'I am setting fire to my mansion', he wrote to the French on a sign on his own estate at Voronovo outside Moscow, 'rather than let it be sullied by your presence.'[12] (Although he later was fêted for having ordered the burning of Moscow, some of it initiated by criminals he had released from the city's jails for the purpose, towards the end of his life Rostopchin denied that he had done so, to the bemusement of his friends and family.[13]) That night the fires were so bright that it was possible to read in the Kremlin without the aid of lamps.

No sooner had the French entered Moscow and begun to ransack it, therefore, than they had to try to save it from being razed by its own inhabitants. With no knowledge of its geography and no fire-fighting equipment, they were unequal to the task. They shot around four hundred arsonists, but 6,500 of the 9,000 major buildings in the city were either burned down or ruined.[14] Many of his soldiers, Napoleon remembered, died while 'endeavouring to pillage in the midst of the flames'.[15] When they cleaned up the city after the French had left, Muscovites found the charred remains of nearly 12,000 humans and over 12,500 horses.[16]

Napoleon was fast asleep on his iron camp bed beneath the chandeliers of the Kremlin when he was woken at 4 a.m. on September 16 and told about the fires. 'What a tremendous spectacle!' he exclaimed, watching them from a window whose panes were already hot to the touch. 'It is their own work! So many palaces! What extraordinary resolution! What men! These are indeed Scythians!'[17] (Typically, he reached back to ancient times for an analogy, here to the famously ruthless Persian tribe mentioned by Herodotus who left their Iranian homeland to fight on the Central Eurasian steppes.) He was fortunate not to fall victim to the fires himself, as incompetent guards allowed an artillery convoy – including gunpowder wagons – to draw up under his bedroom window in the Kremlin. If one of the burning brands that were flying around had landed there, Ségur noted, 'The flower of the army and the Emperor would have been destroyed.'[18] After spending much of the day organizing his soldiers into units of firefighters, pulling down houses in the path of the blaze and interviewing two arsonists, at 5.30 p.m. Napoleon bowed to the exhortations of Berthier, Murat and Eugène to leave the city when flames reached the Kremlin arsenal. As Ségur recalled, 'We already breathed nothing but smoke and ashes.'[19] The two-hour journey to the imperial palace of Petrovsky, 6 miles outside the city, was dangerous and at times had to be made on foot because of the horses' terror of the flames. As front entrances of the Kremlin were by then blocked by the fire and debris, Napoleon escaped through a secret postern gate in the rocks above the river.[20] 'With long detours,' recalled the veteran General Fantin des Odoards, 'he was out of danger.'[21] One of the household comptrollers, Guillaume Peyrusse, who was also evacuated, told his brother: 'We were boiling in our carriages . . . the horses didn't want to go forward. I had the sharpest worries for the treasure.'[22] It survived and was soon augmented when an on-site forge was built to melt down 11,700lbs of gold and 648lbs of silver, much of it taken from palaces and churches.[23]

Discussing the Russian campaign two years later, Napoleon admitted 'that when [I] got to Moscow, [I] considered the business as done'.[24] He claimed he could have stayed in the well-stocked city throughout the winter had it not been for the burning of Moscow, 'an event on which I could not calculate, as there is not, I believe, a precedent for it in the history of the world. But by God, one has to admit that showed a hell of a strength of character.'[25] Although the part of the city that survived the fire was large enough for winter cantonments, and some supplies were found there in private cellars, it was not remotely capable of wintering an army of over 100,000 men for half a year. There was not enough fodder for the horses, campfires had to be built of mahogany furniture and gilded window-frames, and the army was soon subsisting off rotten horseflesh.[26] In retrospect it would have been better for the French had the whole city been razed to the ground, as that would have forced an immediate retreat.

The central striking force of the Grande Armée had shrunk to less than half its original size in the eighty-two days between crossing the Niemen and entering Moscow. According to the figures Napoleon was given at the time, he had lost 92,390 men by the end of the battle of Borodino.[27] Yet he did not act like a man whose options were limited. During the two days he spent at the beautiful Petrovsky Palace he considered almost immediately retreating to the Lower Dvina in a circular movement, while sending out Eugène's corps to make it appear as if he were marching on to St Petersburg.[28] He told Fain that he believed he could be between Riga and Smolensk by mid-October. Yet although he started looking at maps and drawing up orders, only Eugène supported the idea. Other senior officers reacted with 'repugnance', arguing that the army needed rest, and to go north would 'look for the winter, as if it wasn't coming soon enough!' They urged Napoleon to ask Alexander for peace.[29] Army surgeons needed more time to treat the wounded and they argued that Moscow still had resources to offer under the ashes.[30] Napoleon told his advisors: 'Don't believe that the ones who burnt Moscow are people to make peace a few days later; if the parties who are guilty of this determination dominate today in Alexander's cabinet, all the hopes with which I see you flatter yourselves are in vain.'[31]

Another plan, to march on Alexander's court nearly four hundred miles away in St Petersburg itself, was proposed, but Berthier and Bessières quickly convinced Napoleon on logistical grounds 'that he had neither time, provisions, roads, nor a single requisite for so extensive an expedition'.[32] Instead they discussed marching south nearly 100 miles to Kaluga and Tula, the granary and arsenal of Russia respectively, or retreating to Smolensk. Napoleon eventually chose what turned out to be the worst possible option: to return to the Kremlin, which had survived the fire, on September 18 to wait to see whether Alexander would agree to end the war. 'I ought not to have stayed in Moscow more than two weeks at the utmost,' Napoleon said later, 'but I was deceived from day to day.'[33] This was untrue. Alexander didn't deceive Napoleon into thinking he was interested in peace; he simply refused to reply either positively or negatively. Nor was Napoleon self-deceived; the burning of Moscow confirmed him in his belief that there was no hope of peace, even though he would probably have accepted as little as Russia's return to the Continental System as the price.[34] The reason he stayed in Moscow for so long was that he thought he had plenty of time before he needed to get his army back to winter quarters in Smolensk, and he preferred to live off the enemy's resources.

On September 18, Napoleon distributed 50,000 plundered rubles to Muscovites who had lost their houses and he visited an orphanage, dispelling the widespread rumour that he was going to eat its inhabitants.[35] 'Moscow was a very beautiful city,' he wrote to Maret, using the past tense. 'It will take Russia two hundred years to recover from the loss which she has sustained.'[36] He wrote to Alexander on the 20th, as autumnal rains finally quenched the fires, which in some places had burned for six days. (The letter was delivered by the brother of the Russian minister to Cassel, the most senior Russian to be captured in Moscow, which shows how thorough the nobility's evacuation of the city had been.) 'If Your Majesty still preserves for me some remnant of your former feelings, you will take this letter in good part,' he began.

The beautiful and superb city of Moscow no longer exists; Rostopchin had it burnt ... The administration, the magistrates and the civil guards should have remained. This is what was done twice at Vienna, at Berlin and at Madrid ... I have waged war on Your Majesty without animosity. A letter from you before or after the last battle would have halted my march, and I should have even liked to have sacrificed the advantage of entering Moscow.[37]

On receipt of this letter, the Tsar promptly sent for Lord Cathcart, the British ambassador, and told him that twenty such catastrophes as had happened to Moscow would not induce him to abandon the struggle.[38] The list of cities Napoleon gave in that letter – and it could have been longer – demonstrates that he knew from experience that capturing the enemy's capital didn't lead to his surrender, and Moscow wasn't even Russia's government capital. It was the destruction of the enemy's main army at Marengo, Austerlitz and Friedland that had secured his victory, and Napoleon had failed to achieve that at Borodino.

While waiting for Alexander's reply, the Emperor made life in Moscow as easy as possible for his troops by organizing entertainments for them, although there were some practices at which he drew the line. 'Despite repeated warnings,' read one order, 'soldiers are continuing to relieve themselves in the courtyard, even under the windows of the Emperor himself; orders are now issued that each unit will set punishment parties to dig latrines and ... buckets will be placed in the corners of the barracks and these will be emptied twice a day.'[39] Napoleon used his time at the Kremlin to rationalize the units of the army and take into account their losses, review them and receive detailed reports on their state, which told him he still had over 100,000 effectives after reinforcement. Meanwhile, cannonballs collected from the field of Borodino started arriving by the cartload.[40] He liked to cultivate the appearance of constant industry: one of his ushers, Angel, later revealed that he had been ordered to put two candles in Napoleon's window every evening, 'so that the troops exclaim "See, the Emperor doesn't sleep by day or at night. He works continuously!"'[41]

When Napoleon discovered the plight of Madame Aurore Bursay's troupe of fourteen French actors and actresses, who had been robbed by both Russian and French troops, he came to her assistance and asked her to put on eleven plays, mostly comedies and ballets, in the Posniakov Theatre.[42] He didn't go himself, but he did listen to Signor Tarquinio, a famous Muscovite singer. He drew up new regulations for the Comédie-Française, and decided that he wanted the gigantic golden cross from the Ivan the Great bell tower to be placed on the dome of Les

Invalides.[43] (Once they got it down, it turned out to be made only of gilded wood, and it would be thrown into the Berezina on the retreat by General Michel Claparède's Polish division.[44])

One way in which Napoleon could have caused severe problems for the Russian governing class would have been by freeing the serfs from their lifetime of bondage to their aristocratic landowners. Emelian Pugachev's violent serf revolt in the mid-1770s had in some respects presaged the French Revolution, and the Russian elite were terrified that Napoleon might reach back to its ideas.[45] He certainly ordered the papers covering Pugachev's revolt to be brought to him from the Kremlin archives and asked Eugène for information about a peasant uprising in Velikiye Luki, and to 'let me know what kind of decree and proclamation can be made to excite the revolt of the peasants in Russia and rally them'.[46] Yet despite abolishing feudalism in all the lands he conquered, he did not emancipate the Russian serfs, whom he thought of as ignorant and uncivilized.[47] It certainly wouldn't have helped bring Alexander to the negotiating table.

In the first week of October, Napoleon sent his former ambassador to Russia, Jacques de Lauriston, to Kutuzov, who had entrenched himself at Tarutino behind the River Nara, 45 miles south-west of Moscow. According to Ségur, Napoleon's parting words to his envoy were: 'I want peace, I must have peace, I absolutely will have peace – only save my honour!'[48] Kutuzov refused to offer Lauriston safe passage to St Petersburg, saying his message could be taken by Prince Sergei Volkonsky instead. Once again, there was no reply. By this stage Murat was losing forty to fifty men a day to Cossack raiders on the outskirts of Moscow, and Kutuzov's army had grown to 88,300 regular troops, 13,000 regular Don Cossacks and another 15,000 irregular Cossack and Bashkir cavalry, with 622 guns. By contrast, Napoleon received only 15,000 reinforcements during the thirty-five days he spent in Moscow, while 10,000 died of wounds or disease there.

The fine weather in Moscow, which Napoleon told Marie Louise was 'as warm as in Paris' on October 6, made it seem less important that the men had thrown away their winter clothing on the boiling march from the Niemen, although it worried him that he couldn't buy the shoes, boots and horses they would soon need.[49] In a second letter to Marie Louise that day he asked her to persuade her father to reinforce Schwarzenberg's corps, 'so that it may be a credit to him'.[50] He could not know that Metternich had given secret undertakings to the Tsar that Austria would do nothing of the kind, and at about this time

Schwarzenberg started to behave suspiciously independently, avoiding any engagement with the Russians that he could. 'Right now,' Napoleon told Fain in mid-September, acknowledging his other diplomatic failings of that year, 'Bernadotte should have been in St Petersburg and the Turks in the Crimea.'[51]

Napoleon had collected all available almanacs and charts on the Russian winter, which had told him that sub-zero temperatures weren't to be expected until November. 'No information was neglected about that subject, no calculation, and all probabilities were reassuring,' recalled Fain; 'it's usually only in December and January that the Russian winter is very rigorous. During November the thermometer doesn't go much below six degrees.'[52] Observations made of the previous twenty years' winters confirmed that the Moskva river didn't freeze until mid-November, and Napoleon believed this gave him plenty of time to return to Smolensk. It had taken his army less than three weeks to get from Smolensk to Moscow, including the three days at Borodino.[53]

Voltaire's *History of Charles XII*, which Napoleon read while in Moscow, described the Russian winter as so cold that birds froze in mid-air, falling from the skies as if shot.[54] The Emperor also read the three-volume *Military History of Charles XII* by the king's chamberlain, Gustavus Adlerfeld, published in 1741, which concludes with the disaster of Poltava.[55] Adlerfeld attributed the King of Sweden's defeat to stubborn Russian resistance and the 'very piercing' cold of the winter. 'In one of these marches two thousand men fell down dead with the cold,' reads a passage in the third volume, and in another Swedish troopers 'were reduced to warm themselves with the skins of beasts as well they could; they often wanted even bread; they were obliged to sink almost all their cannon in morasses and rivers, for want of horses to draw them. This army, once so flourishing, was ... ready to die with hunger.'[56] Adlerfeld wrote of how the nights were 'extremely cold ... many died of the excessive rigour of the cold, and a great number lost the use of their limbs, as their feet and hands.' From this if nothing else, Napoleon would have keenly understood the severity of the Russian winter. When the army did finally leave Moscow on October 18 he told his staff: 'Hurry up, we need to be in winter quarters in twenty days.'[57] The first major snowfall took place seventeen days later, so he was only three days out. Only military considerations, rather than any insouciance over the weather, forced him to take a different, far longer route to Smolensk than the one originally intended.

The first flurries of snow fell on the 13th. By then the forage situation for the horses had become critical, with teams leaving Moscow at dawn and rarely returning before nightfall, their horses exhausted.[58] With no reply from Alexander and winter clearly now approaching, on October 13 Napoleon finally gave the order for an evacuation of the city five days later. This decision was reinforced by Lauriston's return on the 17th with Kutuzov's refusal of an armistice. As the Grande Armée, now comprising around 107,000 men, thousands of civilians, 3,000 Russian prisoners, 550 cannon and over 40,000 vehicles loaded with the fruits of over a month's looting – which people chose to carry in favour of edible provisions – began to evacuate Moscow on the 18th, Kutuzov mounted an impressive surprise attack at Tarutino (also known as Vinkovo), in which Murat lost 2,000 killed and wounded and 1,500 men and 36 guns were captured.[59]

Napoleon himself left Moscow in bright sunshine around noon on October 19, 1812, taking the southern road towards Kaluga – which he nicknamed 'Caligula', just as he called Glogau 'Gourgaud' – 110 miles to the south-west.[60] He retained the option of going to Tula, where he hoped to destroy Russia's arms factories, and reach the fertile Ukraine while drawing in reinforcements from Smolensk, or moving back up to Smolensk and Lithuania if need be. Either way it permitted him to present the retreat from Moscow merely as a strategic withdrawal, the next stage in the campaign to punish Alexander. But his weakened, lumbering army was too slow for the kind of operation he now needed to pull off, and the mud produced by heavy rainfall on the night of October 21 only slowed it down further. Kutuzov didn't learn of the evacuation for two days, though as the Grande Armée was limping along in a column that extended for 60 miles this was of little consequence. He sent General Dokhturov's 6th Corps to block Napoleon's route at Maloyaroslavets. Dokhturov arrived on the 23rd and the next day ran straight into Eugène's advance guard commanded by General Alexis Delzons.

Napoleon's order to Mortier to blow up the Kremlin has been denounced as an act of Corsican revenge, but it was actually a means to keep his options open. He told General de Lariboisière, 'It is possible that I will return to Moscow', and calculated that he would find it easier to recapture without its formidable defences.[61] Mortier laid 180 tons of explosives in the vaults under the Kremlim and Napoleon heard the explosion at 1.30 a.m. on the 20th from 25 miles away. He boasted in a bulletin that 'The Kremlin, ancient citadel, coeval with the rise of the [Romanov] monarchy, this palace of the tsars, has ceased to exist, but in fact although the arsenal, one of the towers and the Nikolsky Gate were destroyed, and the Ivan bell tower damaged, the rest of the Kremlin survived.[62] Napoleon also urged Mortier to take all the wounded from Moscow, drawing from classical precedent to say: 'The Romans gave civic crowns to those who saved citizens; the Duc de Treviso will be worthy of this as long as he saves soldiers ... he must make them ride on his horses and those of his men; this is what the Emperor did at Acre.'[63] Mortier carried off all the wounded who could be moved, though 4,000 had to be left behind in the Foundlings Hospital. Just before he left, Napoleon had ten Russian prisoners-of-war shot as arsonists.[64] It was hardly Jaffa, but it was an inexplicable act of cruelty and unlikely to help the chances of the French wounded he was compelled to abandon.

The battle of Maloyaroslavets, the third largest of the campaign, fought high above the River Luzha on October 24, had consequences far in excess of its immediate result. The French ultimately captured and held the town and Kutuzov withdrew down the Kaluga road, but the extremely bitter fighting – in which the town changed hands nine times over the course of the day – convinced Napoleon, who arrived only at the very end, that the Russians would contest the southern route bitterly. ('It's not enough to kill a Russian,' went the admiring saying in the Grande Armée, 'you have to push him over too.') Although the Emperor described Maloyaroslavets as a victory in his bulletin, the cartographer Captain Eugène Labaume, who was a bitter critic, recalled the men saying: 'Two such "victories" and Napoleon would have no army left.'[65] Maloyaroslavets burned down during the battle – only the stone monastery remains today, complete with bullet holes in its gate – but from the positions of the piles of calcinated corpses the Emperor could tell how obstinately the Russians had fought.

At 11 p.m. Bessières arrived at Napoleon's quarters in a weaver's hut near the bridge at Gorodnya, a village some 60 miles south-west of Moscow, telling the Emperor that he believed that Kutuzov's position further down the road was 'unassailable'. When Napoleon went out at 4 a.m. the next morning to try to see for himself – one can't see beyond the town from the hillside on the other side of the ravine – he was almost captured by a large body of Tatar *uhlans* (light cavalry), who got to within forty yards of him yelling, '*Houra! Houra!*' (Plunder! Plunder!) before two hundred Guard cavalry dispersed them.[66] He later laughed about this close escape to Murat, but thereafter he wore a phial of poison around his neck in case of capture. 'Things are getting serious,' he told Caulaincourt an hour before daybreak on the 25th. 'I beat the Russians every time, and yet never reach an end.'[67] (That wasn't quite true; Murat's defeat at Tarutino had been a significant reverse, although Napoleon himself hadn't been present.)

Fain said that Napoleon was 'shaken' by the sheer number of wounded at Maloyaroslavets, and moved by their fate; eight generals including Delzons had been killed or wounded.[68] Continuing down the Kaluga road would almost certainly lead to another costly battle, whereas a withdrawal northwards towards the supply depots of the Moscow–Smolensk road along which they had come the previous month would avoid that necessity. There was a third possible route, through Medyn and Yelnya, where a fresh division of reinforcements from France awaited them. (Of Yelnya, Napoleon was to write on November 6: 'The region is said to be beautiful and to have ample supplies.'[69]) Had they taken that route, though the maps gave no clues to the state of its roads, they might have reached Smolensk before the first major snowfall. Was the fact that the Grande Armée now had a huge tail of wagons, carts, prisoners, camp-followers and booty a factor in Napoleon's thinking? The record is mute. What did influence his thinking was that 90,000 men under Kutuzov would have been shadowing his left flank all the way to Yelnya, and an army stretched out 60 miles along the road would have been vulnerable at several points. Moving blind across country, a quartermaster's nightmare, seemed riskier than returning via the Mozhaisk route, where he at least knew that there were food depots. However, it would take far longer, effectively tracing a dog-leg of several hundred miles due north just as winter was closing in.

Napoleon didn't usually convene councils of war – he hadn't called a single one during the entire campaign against Russia and Prussia in 1806–7 – but he did now. On the night of Sunday, October 25 the weaver's hut at Gorodnya, whose sole room was divided into the Emperor's bedroom and study by a single canvas sheet, played host to a *galère* of marshals and generals whose advice Napoleon sought before making his crucial decision. 'This mean habitation of a humble workman', wrote one of his aides-de camp later, 'contained within it an emperor, two kings and three generals.'[70] Napoleon said that the expensive victory at Maloyaroslavets had not compensated for Murat's outright defeat at Tarutino; he wanted to strike south towards Kaluga, towards the main bulk of the Russian army which was straddling that road. Murat, smarting from the drubbing he had sustained, agreed, and urged an immediate attack towards Kaluga. Davout supported the other, at that point undefended, southern route via Medyn and through the unspoiled fertile fields of north Ukraine and the Dnieper, before regaining the main highway at Smolensk, if it went well, several days march ahead of Kutuzov. The 'Iron Marshal' feared that following Kutuzov down the Kaluga road would draw the Grande Armée ever deeper into Russia without achieving a decisive battle before the snows fell in earnest, whereas turning the whole army around to get onto the Mozhaisk–Smolensk road would create delays, congestion and supply problems.

'Smolensk was the goal,' recorded Ségur. 'Should they march thither by Kaluga, Medyn or Mozhaisk? Napoleon was seated at a table, his head supported by his hands, which concealed his features, as well as the anguish which they no doubt expressed.'[71] Most of those present thought that because part of the army was already stationed at Borovsk, on the way to Mozhaisk, along with a large number of guns that had not been present at Maloyaroslavets, the Borovsk–Mozhaisk–Smolensk route was the best one. They pointed out 'how exhausting this change of direction [to follow Kutuzov] would prove to cavalry and artillery already in a state of exhaustion, and that it would lose us any lead we might have over the Russians'. If Kutuzov 'would not stand and fight in an excellent position such as at Maloyaroslavets' he was hardly likely to join battle 60 miles further away, they argued. Of this opinion were Eugène, Berthier, Caulaincourt and Bessières. Murat furiously criticized Davout's plan to head for Medyn because it would present the army's flank to the enemy; this prompted an ill-tempered exchange of views between the two marshals, who had long been at odds with each other. 'Well, gentlemen,' said Napoleon as he concluded the conference that night. 'I will decide.'[72]

He chose the northern route back to Smolensk. His only recorded explanation for perhaps the single most fateful decision of his reign is to be found in what he told Berthier to write to Junot about the Russians, 'We marched on the 26th to attack them, but they were in retreat; [Davout] went in pursuit of them, but the cold and the necessity of offloading the wounded who were with the army made the Emperor decide to go to Mozhaisk and from there to Vyazma.'[73] Yet this made no sense; if the enemy was retreating it would have been the ideal time to attack him. It was likely to be much colder to the north, and the needs of the wounded had never decided strategy before. When, years later, Gourgaud tried to blame Murat and Bessières for the route the army took, Napoleon corrected him: 'No; I was the master, and mine was the fault.'[74] Like a Shakespearian tragic hero, he chose the fatal path despite others being available. Ségur later described Maloyaroslavets as 'This fatal field which put a halt to the conquest of the world, where twenty victories were thrown to the wind, and where our great empire began to crumble to the ground.' The Russians were plainer yet no less accurate, erecting a small commemorative plaque on the battlefield stating simply: 'End of offensive. Start of ruin and rout of the enemy.'

As soon as Kutuzov understood Napoleon was retreating, he turned his army around and adopted a 'parallel mark' strategy to harry him out of Russia, marching alongside the French army and attacking when he saw weakness, but refusing Napoleon the opportunity of a decisive counter-attack. Napoleon had retreated from Acre and Aspern-Essling, but neither of those situations even approximated what he now faced, especially once the thermometer plunged to −4°C in late October. In his memoirs, *The Crime of 1812*, Labaume recalled the continual sound of the rearguard blowing up their own ammunition wagons, 'which reverberated from afar like the roar of thunder'. The horses that could pull them had died, sometimes as a result of eating tainted straw from thatch torn off cottage roofs. On reaching Uvaroskoye, close to Gorodnya, Labaume found 'numerous corpses of soldiers and peasants, as well as infants with their throats cut, and young girls murdered having been ravished'.[75] As Labaume was in the same army as the perpetrators, there was no reason for him to have invented these outrages, which began once discipline evaporated.

Men who had kept bread since Moscow now 'crept off to eat it in secret'.[76] On October 29–30 the army tramped – it no longer marched – past the Borodino battlefield, which was full of 'bones gnawed by famished dogs and birds of prey'. A French soldier was found who had had both his legs broken and for two months had been living off herbs, roots and a few bits of bread he had found on corpses, sleeping at nights inside the bellies of eviscerated horses. Although Napoleon ordered that any survivors be carried on carts, some were unceremoniously pushed off shortly afterwards.[77] By late October even generals were eating nothing but horseflesh.[78] On November 3 a Russian attempt to encircle Davout was repelled at Vyazma, when Ney, Eugène and Poniatowski (who was wounded) turned back to aid him. The abnormally large number of French prisoners taken there – 3,000 – indicates how close the Grande Armée was to demoralization.

The first heavy snowfall came on November 4, as the French retreated in disorder from Vyazma. 'Many, suffering far more from the extreme cold than from hunger, abandoned their accoutrements,' Labaume recalled, 'and lay down beside a large fire they had lighted, but when the time came for departing these poor wretches had not the strength to get up, and preferred to fall into the hands of the enemy rather than to continue the march.'[79] That took courage in itself, as the rumours about what the peasantry and Cossacks were doing to captured Frenchmen easily equalled those of what the Turks, Calabrians and Spanish had done, and included skinning them alive. (Peasants would buy prisoners off the Cossacks at two rubles a head.) The luckiest were merely stripped of their clothing and left naked in the snow, but torture was commonplace (hence the high rate of suicide on the retreat).[80] Even surrendering successfully en masse to the Russian regular army was akin to a death sentence: of one column of 3,400 French prisoners-of-war only 400 survived; in another only 16 out of 800. When fifty French soldiers were captured by peasants and buried alive in a pit, 'a drummer boy bravely led the devoted party and leapt into the grave'.[81] There were occasional tales of altruism: Labaume recorded a French soldier sharing his food with a starving Russian woman whom he had found in a cemetery just after she had given birth, for example. But overall the retreat now became reminiscent of Hieronymus Bosch's depiction of Hades.[82]

Ney took command of the rearguard on November 5, as the snowfalls obliterated landmarks and iced-up roads. Little thought had been given to fitting ice-resistant horseshoes except by the Poles and some Guard regiments, which led to many horses slipping and falling. By the second week of November, 'The army utterly lost its morale and its military organization. Soldiers no longer obeyed their officers; officers paid no regard to their generals; shattered regiments marched as best they could. Searching for food, they dispersed over the plain, burning and sacking everything in their way ... Tormented by hunger, they rushed on every horse as soon as it fell, and like famished wolves fought for the pieces.'[83] Meanwhile toes, fingers, noses, ears and sexual organs were lost to frostbite.[84] 'The soldiers fall,' Castellane recalled of the Italian Royal Guard, 'a little blood comes to their lips, and all is over. When they see this sign of an approaching death, their comrades often give them a push, throw them on the ground, and take their clothes before they are quite dead.'[85]

At Dorogobuzh on November 6 Napoleon received the extraordinary news in a letter from Cambacérès of a coup d'état that General Claude-François de Malet had attempted in Paris two weeks earlier. Malet had forged a document stating that Napoleon had died under the walls of Moscow as well as a *sénatus-consulte* that appointed General

Moreau as interim president.[86] With fewer than twenty co-conspirators, Malet had taken control of 1,200 National Guardsmen at 3 a.m. on October 23. The police minister, Savary, was arrested and taken to La Force prison, and the prefect of police, Pasquier, was chased from his prefecture.[87] The governor of Paris, General Hulin, was shot in the jaw, where the bullet remained lodged and gave rise to his nickname, 'Bouffe-la-balle' (Bullet-eater).[88] François Frochot, the prefect of the Seine and a member of the Conseil, accepted Malet's story and did nothing to oppose him, for which he was later dismissed.

Cambacérès seems to have kept his head admirably, doubling the sentries protecting Marie Louise and the King of Rome at Saint-Cloud and ordering Marshal Moncey, who commanded the gendarmerie, to rush in troops from nearby departments, release Savary and reinstate Pasquier.[89] 'By 9 a.m. it was all over,' recalled Lavalette, 'and the happy inhabitants of Paris, when they awoke, learned of the singular event, and made some tolerably good jokes upon it.'[90] Napoleon didn't find any of it remotely funny. He was infuriated that no one besides Cambacérès seemed to have given any thought to Marie Louise or his son as being the legitimate rulers of France in the event of his demise. 'Napoleon II,' the Emperor cried to Fain, 'nobody thought about him!'[91] At his brief court martial, before being shot with a dozen others on October 29, Malet, a former political prisoner and devout republican, replied to a question by saying: 'Who were my accomplices? Had I been successful, all of you would have been my accomplices!'[92] Napoleon feared that this was true. The Malet conspiracy reminded him how much the dynasty he had so recently inaugurated depended upon him alone.

With the thermometer dropping to −30°C on November 7, and blizzards seemingly continuous, the retreat slowed to a crawl. Some 5,000 horses died in a matter of days. Men's breath turned to icicles when it left their mouths, their lips stuck together and their nostrils froze up. In an echo of the desert ophthalmia of the Egyptian campaign, men were afflicted with snow-blindness. Comradeship collapsed; men were charged a gold louis to sit by a fire, and declined to share any food or water; they ate the horses' forage, and drove wagons over men who had slipped in front of them.[93] General Comte Louis de Langeron, a French émigré who commanded one of the Russian divisions, saw 'a dead man, his teeth deep in the haunch of a horse which was still quivering'.[94] On November 8 Eugène warned Berthier that 'These three days of suffering so depressed the soldiers' spirits that I believe they are very unlikely to make any more effort. A lot of men died from cold or hunger and others, desperate, want to be captured by the enemy.'[95] There were several well-documented instances of cannibalism; Kutuzov's British liaison officer Sir Robert Wilson saw that when groups of French were captured around a campfire, 'many in these groups were employed in peeling off with their fingers and making a repast of the charred flesh of their comrades' remains'.[96]

With the Russian army of the German-born General Peter Wittgenstein coming from the north and that of Admiral Paul Chichagov from the south, both heading for the Berezina river, there was now a possibility that the entire army might be captured. Napoleon reached Smolensk at noon on November 9. He was still nearly 160 miles east of Borisov, where there was a bridge over the Berezina. Between him and the bridge was Kutuzov, who was taking up a blocking position at Krasnoi, ready to give battle. Two days earlier Napoleon had urgently written a coded message to Marshal Victor, ordering him to march south from his position near Vitebsk without delay:

> This movement is one of the most important. In a few days your rear could be inundated with Cossacks; the army and the Emperor will be in Smolensk tomorrow, but very tired by a non-stop march of 120 leagues. Take the offensive, the salvation of armies depends on it; every day of delay is a calamity. The cavalry of the army is on foot, the cold has made all the horses die. March, that is the order of the Emperor and of necessity.[97]

The cool and tenacious Victor would arrive just in time.

Napoleon's force was down to fewer than 60,000 men – though no one was keeping records any more – and much of the artillery had been spiked and ditched along the route for lack of horses to pull it. For more than three miles around the River Vop nothing could be seen but ammunition wagons, cannon, carriages, candelabras, antique bronzes, paintings and porcelain. One wag described it as 'half artillery-park, half auctioneer's storeroom'. Meanwhile, as another soldier recalled, wolfhounds 'bayed as if they had gone mad, and in their fury often fought with the soldiers for the dead horses strewn along the road. The ravens ... attracted by the stench of the dead bodies, came wheeling in black clouds above us.'[98]

Most of the provisions in Smolensk were eaten on the first day, although it took five days for the whole army to get there, so when Ney's rearguard arrived it found nothing. Larrey had a thermometer attached to his coat that recorded –16°F (–26°C), and noted that the extreme cold turned even the lightest of wounds gangrenous.[99] Over five days between November 14 and November 18, Napoleon fought the desperate battle of Krasnoi as Eugène's, Davout's and Ney's severely depleted corps tried to smash through Kutuzov's army to reach the Berezina. Some 13,000 of his men were killed and over 26,000 captured, including 7 generals.[100] A total of 112 guns had been spiked at Smolensk, and another 123 were now captured at Krasnoi, leaving Napoleon virtually without artillery as well as cavalry.[101] He was nonetheless superbly calm throughout the battle as he struggled to keep the road to Borisov open for as long as possible. Kutuzov, though outnumbering the French by nearly two to one, failed to deliver the coup de grâce he could have achieved by deploying Tormasov at the right moment. The Russians suffered grievously too: at Tarutino Kutuzov had had 105,000 men; by the end of the battle of Krasnoi he was down to 60,000. He was nonetheless still capable of continuing his parallel-mark strategy.

'It is impossible to express the grief of Napoleon, on learning the desperate situation of one of the bravest of his brave marshals,' Bausset recalled of the period when Napoleon believed that Ney's entire corps had been annihilated on the way back from Krasnoi. 'I heard him several times during the day make use of terms that showed the extreme agitation of his mind.'[102] Ney eventually caught up with the main army at Orsha, almost midway between Smolensk and Borisov, on November 21, albeit with only 800 survivors of a corps which had crossed the Niemen with him in June 40,000 strong. 'Those who have returned,' Ney announced, 'have their balls attached with iron wire.'[103] On hearing that Ney had survived, Napoleon said: 'I have more than four hundred million [francs] in the cellars of the Tuileries, and would gladly have given the whole for the ransom of my faithful companion-in-arms.'[104]*

'A great many of you have deserted your colours and proceed alone, thus betraying your duty, the honour and safety of the Army,' Napoleon proclaimed from Orsha on November 19. 'Offenders will be put under arrest and punished summarily.' For once his words had little effect. That same day he burned the notes he had been making for his autobiography, about which nothing more is known. On November 21 the first units of the armed rabble formerly dignified with the name 'Grande Armée' reached the 300-foot-wide Berezina, its banks deep set with marshes, to find the western side occupied by the Russians under Chichagov, who had captured the Borisov bridge, the only one along

---

* He had nothing like that amount in the Tuileries, of course.

that stretch of the river, and had burned it. The French right flank was threatened by Wittgenstein, who was marching down the east bank of the river. Kutuzov was following from behind. In all, some 144,000 Russians were moving in on around 40,000 French effectives (once reinforced by Victor and Oudinot) and several thousand stragglers and camp-followers. Langeron recalled that his Russian troops 'were smashing the unfortunate stragglers' heads with their musket butts, calling them "Moscow arsonists"'.[105]

What happened next, in this most dangerous part of the retreat from Moscow, was to become another integral part of the Napoleonic epic. Although Napoleon had ordered Éblé to destroy his *pontonniers*' six carts of bridging tools to lighten the baggage-train, he had fortunately been disobeyed. Oudinot suggested crossing the Berezina at the village of Studzianka – which means 'very very cold' in Byelorussian – and Napoleon agreed to try. Working alongside his four hundred mainly Dutch engineers in the freezing waters of the swollen river, which was 'thick with large ice-floes' sometimes 6 feet across, Éblé built two pontoon bridges across the river there, 8 miles north of Borisov.[106] One was for cavalry, guns and baggage, and the second, 180 yards upstream, for infantry.

Oudinot drew Chichagov away to the south in a decoying action, and Victor held off Wittgenstein's 30,000 men to the north-east in what is called the battle of the Berezina, while Ney, Eugène and Davout got through Bobr to Studzianka.[107] A sign of the desperation of the situation was that the army burned its eagles in the woods near Bobr on November 24, to prevent them becoming trophies.[108] 'The weather is very cold,' Napoleon wrote to Marie Louise the same day. 'My health is very good. Kiss the little King for me and never doubt the sentiments of your faithful husband.'[109]

The Dutch engineers began to build the bridges at 5 p.m. the next day, dismantling the wooden village and driving stakes into the 7- or 8-foot-deep riverbed. What Saint-Cyr in his memoirs accurately described as 'the miraculous crossing of the Berezina' had begun, in temperatures that plunged to −33°C.[110] François Pils, Oudinot's batman, recalled that because the operation had to be kept secret from Chichagov's patrols on the opposite bank, 'The bridge-builders had been warned not to talk and the troops of all arms were told to keep out of sight. As all the preparatory work and the building of the trestles was done behind a hillock, which formed part of the river bank, the enemy lookout posts were unable to see what our workmen were doing.'[111]

Napoleon arrived at 3 a.m. on Thursday, November 26. By then what was described as 'fragile scaffolding' was in evidence.[112] He wore a fur-lined coat and a green velvet cap trimmed with fur which came over his eyes and spent the day by the riverside encouraging the *pontonniers* and handing them wine, ensuring that they were relieved every fifteen minutes and warmed beside fires, and organizing another deception operation further upriver. 'He'll get us out of here,' Fain recalled the men saying, with 'their eyes fixed on their Emperor'.[113] When Oudinot arrived shortly after 7 a.m., Napoleon took him and Berthier down to the river's edge. 'Well,' he said to Oudinot, 'you shall be my locksmith to open this passage.'[114] From 8 a.m., with the opposite bank now protected by a skeleton force that had crossed unopposed on rafts, the *pontonniers* were ready to place twenty-three trestles of between 3 and 9 feet in height in the freezing water at equal distances across the river. 'The men went into the water up to their shoulders,' recalled an observer, 'displaying superb courage. Some dropped dead and disappeared with the current.'[115]

At about 9.30 a.m. the Emperor returned to Berthier's quarters and was served with a cutlet, which he ate standing up. When his maître d'hôtel presented him with a salt-cellar, consisting of a screw of paper containing old greying salt, Napoleon jested: 'You're well equipped; all you lack is white salt.'[116] To find any humour at all at a moment like that suggests nerves of steel – or indeed Ney's balls of wire. But the ravages were unsurprisingly taking a toll on him. One Swiss officer, Captain Louis Bégos in Oudinot's corps, thought Napoleon looked 'tired and anxious', and another, Captain Rey, 'was struck by the Emperor's worried expression'.[117] He said to Éblé, 'It's taking a long time, general. A very long time.' 'Sire,' Éblé replied, 'you can see that my men are up to their necks in water, and the ice is delaying their work. I have no food or brandy to warm them with.' 'That will do,' replied the Emperor, looking at the ground.[118] A few moments later he started complaining again, seeming to have forgotten what Éblé had said.

Just before 11 a.m. the first bridge was in place and Napoleon ordered the 1st Battalion of General Joseph Albert's 1st Demi-Brigade of the 6th Division over. 'My star returns!' he cried as they crossed safely.[119] He was also delighted that 'I've fooled the admiral!' – meaning Chichagov – which indeed he had.[120] The rest of Oudinot's corps crossed in the afternoon. The bridges had no guardrails, were almost at the water line, sagged unsteadily and frequently had to be repaired by the freezing *pontonniers*. The cavalry bridge was quickly covered in manure, and dead horses and debris had to be thrown off it into the river to stop blockages, while the stragglers and camp-followers were held back until the soldiers had crossed.[121] That night Ney and his men couldn't cross, as three trestles had given way under the weight; they would have to be repaired twice before he could finally make it to the other side.[122]

According to Jakob Walter's diary, Napoleon was audibly sworn at by the troops crossing the river. Walter's unit came to

> a place where Napoleon ordered his pack horses to be unharnessed and where he ate. He watched his army pass by in the most wretched condition. What he may have felt in his heart is impossible to surmise. His outward appearance seemed indifferent and unconcerned over the wretchedness of his soldiers ... and, although the French and Allies shouted into his ears many oaths and curses about his own guilty person, he was still able to listen to them unmoved.[123]

This was a new experience for Napoleon, who was more used to hearing 'Vive l'Empereur!', or at worst, good-natured chaffing. With an army in which there were so many non-French, who didn't have the same motivation, the murmurs turned to outright dissent. The Swiss, Westphalians, Badeners and Hesse-Darmstadters resented having to fight in what they saw as a French war, but nonetheless distinguished themselves at the Berezina, with the Swiss and Westphalians winning most of the crosses of the Légion d'Honneur in the battles that raged on both sides of the river. (The four Swiss regiments were awarded a total of thirty-four.)[124]

Napoleon crossed the rickety trestle bridge at noon on November 27, sleeping that night in a village hut at Zaniwski. 'I have just traversed the Berezina,' he wrote to Maret in Vilnius, 'but the ice floating down that river makes the bridges very precarious ... The cold is intense, and the army very tired. I shall not lose a moment in getting to Vilnius in order to recuperate a little.'[125] In all it is thought that more than 50,000 soldiers and re-formed stragglers crossed the Berezina, over Éblé's unstable but ultimately effective trestle bridges. On November 28, as Wittgenstein's men began to approach, Victor destroyed the bridges: around 15,000 stragglers and 8,000 camp-followers and civilians who hadn't crossed the night before were left to the Russians' mercy. 'On the bridge I saw an unfortunate woman sitting,' recalled the émigré Comte de Rochechouart, 'her legs dangled outside the bridge and were caught in the ice. For twenty-four hours she had been clasping a frozen child to her breast. She begged me to save this child, unaware that she was holding out a corpse to me!'[126] A Cossack eventually 'put an end to her appalling agony' by blowing her brains out. Abandoned on the east bank of the river were over 10,000 vehicles, including berline, calèche and phaeton carriages that had survived Napoleon's repeated injunctions that they should be burned. Langeron saw 'sacred goblets from the churches of Moscow, the gilded cross from the church of St John [Ivan] the Great, collections of engravings, many books from the superb libraries of Counts Buturlin and Razumovsky, silver dishes, even porcelain'.[127] Ten years later a Prussian officer visiting the scene found that 'melancholy relics lay ... in heaps, mingled with the bones of human beings and animals, skulls, tin fittings, bandoliers, bridles, scraps of the bearskins of the Guard'.[128]

General Miloradovich reached Borisov on November 29 and Kutuzov on the 30th. At Studzianka there is a memorial stone that states that this is the place where Kutuzov 'completed the defeat of Napoleon's troops'. This is quite untrue, indeed Admiral Chichagov never lived down the shame of not having done so. Napoleon had listened to Oudinot's advice and changed his plans accordingly, showing his customary flexibility on the field. He acted quickly, used deception to effect a brilliant feint which drew the Russians south, and his whole army had crossed on two makeshift wooden trestle bridges in two days. It had been a miracle of deliverance, although so expensive that one of the common expressions for a disaster in French became *une bérézina*. 'Food, food, food,' he wrote to Maret from the west bank of the river on the morning of the 29th, 'without it there are no horrors that this undisciplined mass won't commit at Vilnius. Perhaps the army will not rally before the Niemen. There must be no foreign agents in Vilnius. The army does not look good now.'[129]

On December 3, having reached Molodechno (present-day Maladzyechna), 45 miles north-west of Minsk, Napoleon issued the most famous of all his bulletins, his 29th of the 1812 campaign. Entirely blaming the weather – 'so cruel a season' – for the disaster, he wrote that, with temperatures unexpectedly down to -27°C, 'the cavalry, artillery and baggage horses perished every night, not only by hundreds, but by thousands ... It was necessary to abandon and destroy a good part of our cannon, ammunition and provisions. The Army, so fine on the 6th, was very different on the 14th, almost without cavalry, without artillery and without transport.' Napoleon gave the Russians no credit for their victory, writing merely that 'The enemy, who saw upon the roads traces of that frightful calamity which had overtaken the French Army, endeavoured to take advantage of it.' He wrote off the Cossacks as 'This contemptible cavalry, which only makes noise and is not capable of penetrating a company of voltigeurs,' but admitted that General Louis Partouneaux's entire division, part of Victor's corps, had been captured near Borisov.

Napoleon acknowledged that the losses were such that 'it was necessary to collect the officers who still had a horse remaining, in order to
form four companies of 150 men each. The generals performed the functions of captains, and the colonels of subalterns.'[130] For the French people,
so used to having to read between the lines for the truth, this bulletin –
which was three times the normal length – came as a profound shock
when it was published in Paris on December 16. Napoleon hadn't entirely
broken with his habit of exaggerating success and minimizing failure: he
was now getting his account of the disaster out before worse rumours
arrived in his capital, and attempting to create the narrative of a defeat at
the hands of Nature. All the figures he gave were wildly inaccurate,
although no-one would compute accurate ones until long afterwards.

It was the final sentence – 'The health of His Majesty has never been
better' – that caused most outrage in France. It has been described as 'a
remarkably brutal expression of imperial self-centredness', whereas it
was in reality little more than the result of habit.[131] He had used the
phrase 'My health is good' thirty times in his letters to Marie Louise
before he reached Moscow, and twelve more during his stay there and
during the retreat, so it was almost a tic. He would employ it twenty-two
times in five months the following year too.[132] More importantly, in the
wake of the Malet conspiracy, any rumours that his health might be less
than excellent had to be comprehensively quashed.

On December 5, at the small town of Smorgoniye where, Bausset
recalled, there was a 'veterinary academy for the instruction of Russian
dancing bears', Napoleon informed Eugène, Berthier, Lefebvre, Mortier,
Davout and Bessières that he 'must return to Paris at the earliest possible moment if I am to overawe Europe and tell her to choose between
war and peace'.[133] He told them he would be leaving at ten o'clock that
night, taking Caulaincourt, Duroc, Lobau, Fain and Constant with him.

He chose Murat to assume command of the army. The flamboyant
marshal tried to hold the line of the Vistula after Napoleon left as
reserves, new drafts and transferred units flowed towards Poland. Yet
his task proved impossible in the face of the Russian advance. The Prussian General Johann Yorck von Wartenburg suddenly declared his
troops' neutrality under the terms of the Convention of Tauroggen, a
non-aggression pact he concluded with the Russians on December
30 and negotiated in part by Carl von Clausewitz.[134] Murat had to
abandon first Poland, and then the line of the Oder. After secret talks
with the Austrians, he suddenly left for Naples to try to save his throne,
handing command of the Grande Armée over to Eugène. With Lefebvre,

Mortier and Victor back in France, Oudinot and Saint-Cyr recovering from wounds and Ney now *hors de combat* from fatigue and nervous exhaustion, it was Eugène, Davout and Poniatowski who saved what remained of the Grande Armée. Together these three reorganized the corps, resupplied them and created the kernel of a new fighting force. Although the *Moniteur* stated that Murat was ill, a furious Napoleon told Eugène: 'It would take very little for me to have him arrested by way of an example ... He is a brave man on the field of battle, but he is totally devoid of intelligence and moral courage.'[135]

'The French are like women,' Napoleon told Caulaincourt on the journey home. 'You mustn't stay away from them for too long.'[136] He was all too aware of the effect that reports of his defeat would have in Vienna and Berlin, and was right to get back to Paris as quickly as possible.[137] The remnants of the Grande Armée were only a day or two days' march from Vilnius and relative safety.[138] Although, as with the Egyptian campaign, many denounced his desertion – Labaume said the troops used 'all the most vigorous epithets our language can supply, for never had men been more basely betrayed' – Napoleon needed to be in Paris to deal with the political and diplomatic repercussions of the disaster.[139] Castellane, who had lost a total of seventeen horses in the campaign, denied that the army felt outrage. 'I saw nothing of the sort,' he said. 'Notwithstanding our disasters, our confidence in him was intact. We feared only that he might be made prisoner on the road.' He added that the army understood Napoleon's motives, 'knowing well that his return alone could stop a revolt in Germany, and that his presence was necessary for the reorganization of an army which could be in a condition to come to our rescue.'[140] After the Berezina crossing there were no clashes with the Russians until mid-February 1813. 'When they know that I am in Paris,' Napoleon said of the Austrians and Prussians, 'and see me at the head of the nation and of 1,200,000 troops which I shall organize, they will look twice before they make war.'[141]

Travelling under the alias of Count Gérard de Reyneval, ostensibly as part of Caulaincourt's retinue, Napoleon covered the 1,300 miles over the winter roads from Smorgoniye to Paris in thirteen days, going via Vilnius, Warsaw, Dresden and Mainz (where he bought some sugar-plums for his son). In Warsaw he told the Abbé de Pradt, apropos the campaign, 'There is but a step from the sublime to the ridiculous.'[142] He was to repeat the line – which was to become one of his most famous – to Caulaincourt on the journey home. He met the King of Saxony in Leipzig (who exchanged

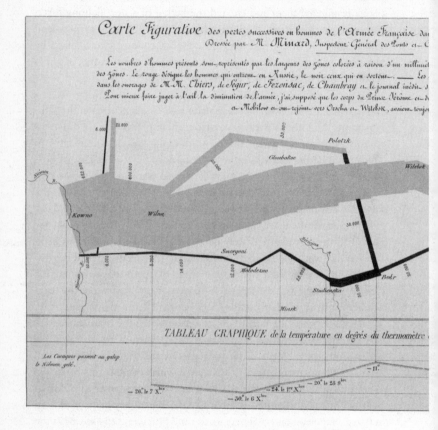

The celebrated diagram of French losses in Russia published in 1869 by Charles-Joseph Minard, Inspector-General of Roads and Bridges 1830–36. Lighter shading indicates the number of men entering Russia, black indicates those leaving. Minard assumed that the forces of Prince Jérôme and of Marshal Davout which were despatched to Minsk and Mogilev, and which re-joined in the vicinity of Orsha and Vitebsk, continued to march with the army. The parallel diagram below shows the temperature in Fahrenheit on the retreat.

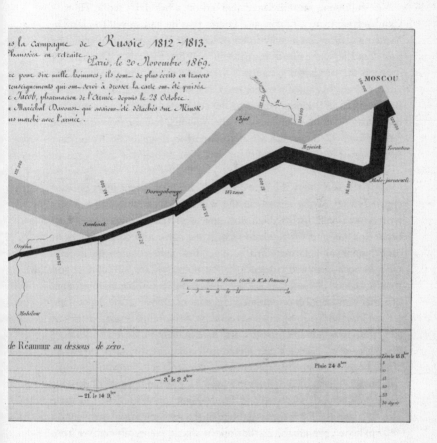

s la Campagne de *Russie* 1812 - 1813.

Aranuées en retraite. Paris, le 20 Novembre 1869.

re pour dix mille hommes ; ils sont— de plus écrits en travers
rreuseignements qui ont—servi à dresser la carte ont—été puisée
e Jacob, pharmacien de l'Armée depuis le 28 Octobre.
a Maréchal Davoust qui avaient—été détachés sur Minsk
us marché avec l'armée.

MOSCOU

Chjat

Mojaïsk

Tarantino

Malo-jarossewli

Dorogobouge

Wizma

Smolensk

Orszha

Mohilow

Lieues communes de France (Carte de Mr de Fezensac)

de Réaumur au dessous de zéro.

Pluie 24 8.bre

Zéro le 18 8.bre

— 9.° le 9 9.bre

— 21. le 14 9.bre

his sleigh for a carriage) and sent his good wishes to Goethe when he passed through Erfurt. As the clock sounded a quarter to midnight on Friday, December 18, he descended from his carriage at the Tuileries.

The following morning he embarked on a full day's work. He told Cambacérès, Savary, Clarke and Decrès that he had stayed too long in Moscow waiting for a reply to his peace offer. 'I made a great error,' he said, 'but I have the means to repair it.'[143] When a courtier who had not been on the campaign assumed 'a very doleful air' and remarked 'We have, indeed, sustained a severe loss!' Napoleon replied, 'Yes, Madame Barilli is dead.'[144] His reference to the celebrated opera singer mocked his courtier's obtuse statement of the obvious, but the horrors of the retreat from Moscow had affected Napoleon deeply – no fewer than forty-four of his household servants had died during it.

Once it reached safety the Grande Armée was meticulous in its bureaucracy. Typical of the records in the war ministry archives is a neatly written 150-page list of the 1,800 men who served in the 88th Line between 1806 and 1813, which records the name and serial number of each, his date and place of birth, both parents' names, canton and department of both birth and residence, height, shape of face, size of nose and mouth, colour of eyes, hair and eyebrows, distinguishing features, date of either conscription or volunteering, date of arrival at the depot, profession, number of company and battalion, promotion history, details of all actions, wounds and honours, and date of demobilization or death.[145] For entire demi-brigades that served in Russia, the list states over page after page 'presumed captured by the enemy', 'prisoner-of-war', 'wounded', 'died', 'died of fever in hospital', 'dead in hospital of nervous fever', 'fell behind', 'deserted', 'certified absent' or 'unknown'. On some rare occasion the list records that one of the very few survivors went on 'reform leave', presumably in the hope he would eventually recover from what we would now call post-traumatic stress disorder.[146]

Napoleon had lost some 524,000 men, around 100,000 to 120,000 of whom had been captured. Many of those captured died over the coming years, and virtually none returned to France before Waterloo, although about 20,000 non-French volunteered to fight in the new Russian army that would soon be raised against Napoleon. Macdonald's corps of 32,300 on the northern flank may have emerged largely unscathed, but half of them were Prussians who would soon be ranged against France, and Schwarzenberg's 34,000 Austrians were now not to be trusted either. A further 15,000 survivors of the Berezina crossing had been lost on the retreat between there and Vilnius.* Ney was the last man to re-cross the Niemen on December 14, by which point he had barely four hundred infantry and six hundred cavalry with him, along with a grand total of nine cannon.[147] (Although none died, four marshals were wounded during the campaign.) Stragglers returned in small numbers over the next few weeks, though a number of them were quietly murdered by Prussian villagers as they made their way westwards. The entire central force of the Grande Armée was now fewer than 25,000 men, of whom only about 10,000 were capable of combat.[148] Even if one considers the French contingent of Macdonald's corps and the 60,000 reinforcements coming from France, the army that Napoleon would have in Poland and Germany at the turn of the year was pitifully small, and greatly lacking in artillery and cavalry.[149] Many units were at just 5 per cent of their strength: Davout's corps of 66,000 was down to 2,200; of the 47,864 original effectives of Oudinot's corps, only 4,653 remained; the Imperial Guard of 51,000 was left with a little over 2,000; of the 27,397 Italians who crossed the Alps, fewer than a thousand returned (and of the 350 members of the Italian Royal Guard, all but eight perished). Of the Dutch Grenadier Guard, only thirty-six survived out of five hundred.[150] And out of the four hundred brave Dutch *pontonniers* who saved the army at the Berezina, only fifty ever saw Holland again.

In late December 1812, Tsar Alexander dined with the Lithuanian novelist and noblewoman Sophie de Tisenhaus in Vilnius, which had been evacuated earlier that month by Murat. He spoke of Napoleon's 'light-grey eyes, which gaze at you so piercingly that you cannot withstand them', and later: 'What a career he has ruined! Having gained so much glory, he could bestow peace on Europe, and he has not done so. The spell is broken.'[151] She noted that he repeated the last phrase several times.

---

* A crude but fairly effective estimation of Napoleon's troops who were killed, wounded or captured in combat in 1812 can be made by simply adding up the casualties in each engagement and deducting them from the overall loss of 524,000. Adding together the Grande Armée's losses in the forty-six battles, clashes, skirmishes, sieges and ambushes between the first engagement on July 9 and the last on November 26, there were 186,500 killed and wounded. Rounded up to 200,000 to take into account the lesser actions for which there are no accurate figures, this means that Russian regular military action in significant confrontations accounted for just under 40 per cent of the overall losses that Napoleon's army suffered in Russia. Disease, exposure, starvation, partisan action, suicide and all of the myriad other ways in which death sought out soldiers in that campaign accounted for the other 60 per cent, with as many men losing their lives when advancing on Moscow as retreating from it (Muir, *Tactics and Experience of Battle* p. 9, Smith, *Data Book* pp. 379–408).

26

Resilience

'Posterity would never have seen the measure of your spirit if it had not seen it in misfortune.'

Molé to Napoleon, March 1813

'He could sympathize with family troubles; he was indifferent to political calamities.'

Metternich on Napoleon, July 1813

'On seeing what he created twenty days after his arrival in Paris,' Marshal Saint-Cyr wrote in his memoirs, 'we must agree that his brusque departure from Poland was wise.'[1] Napoleon embarked upon a maelstrom of activity, recognizing that it could not be long before the Russians coalesced with the Prussians, and possibly with his father-in-law Emperor Francis of Austria too, first to expel France from Poland and Germany and then to try to overthrow him. In attempting to repair the Russian disaster Napoleon showed, in the view of Count Molé, who was shortly to be appointed minister of justice, 'a furious activity which perhaps surpassed everything he had revealed hitherto'.[2] Hortense, who hurried to the Tuileries, found her former stepfather preoccupied but resolute. 'He seemed to me wearied, worried, but not disheartened,' she wrote. 'I had often seen him lose his temper about some trifle such as a door opened when it should have been shut or vice versa, a room too brightly or too dimly lighted. But in times of difficulty or misfortune he was completely master of his nerves.' She sought to give him some comfort, saying 'Surely, our enemies have suffered huge losses too?' To which he replied, 'No doubt, but that does not console me.'[3]

In less than seventeen weeks between returning to Paris in mid-December 1812 and setting off on campaign the following April,

Napoleon incorporated the 84,000 infantry and 9,000 gunners of the National Guard into the regular army; called up 100,000 conscripts from the 1809–12 year groups and 150,000 from 1813 and 1814; formed thirty new infantry regiments consisting of dozens of new demi-brigades; ordered 150,000 muskets from arms factories; combed through the depots and garrisons for extra men; moved 16,000 marines from the navy to the army as well as veteran naval gunners to the artillery; demanded that the Empire's 12,000 cantons each provide one man and one horse; ransacked the line army in Spain to rebuild the Imperial Guard; bought and requisitioned horses wherever they could be obtained; ordered the allies to rebuild their armies; and created Corps of Observation on the Elbe, on the Rhine and in Italy.[4] The recruits called up were of course described in the *Moniteur* as 'magnificent men' but some were as young as fifteen and Molé noted at a review at the Carrousel that 'their extreme youth and poor physique roused a deep pity among the crowds around them'.[5] These young recruits were nicknamed 'Marie Louises', partly because the Empress had signed the orders for their conscription in Napoleon's absence, and partly because of their innocent smooth-cheeked youth. The *grognards* referred to the newly recruited cavalrymen as 'chickens mounted on colts'. Since the new French recruits had no time to train they were far less manoeuvrable in battle; one of the reasons for the unimaginative frontal assaults of the next two years was the need to keep undertrained masses moving together.

If Napoleon's imperial rule had been tyrannical, one would have expected those parts of Europe that had endured it for the longest to be the first to rise up once he had been comprehensively humiliated, yet that was not what happened. East Prussia and Silesia, which hadn't been occupied by the French, revolted in 1813, but the parts of Prussia that had been occupied since 1806, such as Berlin and Brandenburg, did not.[6] Similarly Holland, Switzerland, Italy and much of the rest of Germany either didn't rise against him at all or waited for their governments to declare against him, or sat passively until the Allied armies arrived. In France itself, apart from some bread riots in Brittany and minor trouble in the Vendée and Midi, no risings materialized – in 1813, 1814 or indeed 1815. Although much of France was heartily sick of war, and there was substantial local opposition to conscription, especially during harvest-time, the French did not want to oust their Emperor while he was fighting France's enemies. Only those openly denouncing Napoleon were liable to arrest, and even this mild crackdown was carried out in a classically French eighteenth-century manner. When the royalist Charles de Rivière 'proclaimed his hopes a little too spitefully and prematurely', he was sent to La Force prison, but was later released when a friend won his freedom in a game of billiards against Savary.[7] Some ambitious army officers even wanted the war to continue. 'One thing disturbed us,' wrote Captain Blaze of the Imperial Guard. 'If, we said, Napoleon should stop short in so glorious a career, if he should unfortunately take it into his head to make peace, farewell to all our hopes. Luckily, our fears were not realized, for he cut out more work for us than we were able to perform.'[8]

Although they rarely draw much attention, Russian losses in 1812 were also enormous. Around 150,000 Russian soldiers had been killed and 300,000 wounded or frostbitten over the course of the campaign, and very many more civilians. Russia's field army was down to 100,000 weary men and much of the area from Poland to Moscow had been devastated, depriving the Russian treasury of hundreds of millions of rubles in taxes, though Alexander remained utterly committed to destroying Napoleon. In early 1813 four Russian divisions crossed the Vistula and invaded Pomerania, forcing the French to evacuate Lübeck and Stralsund, though they left garrisons in Danzig, Stettin and other Prussian fortresses. On January 7 Sweden, which had hitherto been neutral under the terms of the 1812 Treaty of Åbo but was now under Bernadotte's influence, declared war against France. Bernadotte told Napoleon that he was not acting against France but for Sweden, and that Napoleon's seizure of Swedish Pomerania was the cause of the rupture – adding, however disingenuously, that he would always bear for his old commander the sentiments of a former comrade in arms.[9] Apart from his natural inclination as a Frenchman not to shed French blood, Bernadotte recognized that doing so would mean for ever giving up his hopes, which had been stoked by Alexander, of one day becoming king of France.

'My army has suffered losses,' Napoleon told the Senate on December 20, 'due to the premature rigour of the season.'[10] Using Yorck's defection to whip up patriotic indignation, he set as his target to raise 150,000 men and ordered prefects to stage meetings in support of his recruiting drive. 'Everything is in motion here,' he told Berthier on January 9.[11] It needed to be. The Russian army advanced 250 miles between Christmas Day 1812 and January 14 when they reached Marienwerder in Prussia (now Kwidzyn, in Poland), despite having to recapture

Königsberg and other French strongholds in the depths of a northern winter.[12] Eugène had no choice but to withdraw back to Berlin.

Napoleon was surprisingly open about the depth of his setback in Russia. 'He is the first to speak about the misfortunes and he even brings them up,' wrote Fain.[13] Yet if the Emperor was willing to acknowledge his misfortune, he did not always do so truthfully. 'There was not an affair in which the Russians captured either a gun or an eagle; they took no other prisoners but skirmishers,' he told Jérôme on January 18. 'My Guard was never engaged, and did not lose a single man in action, and it could not therefore have lost any eagles as the Russians declare.'[14] The Guard lost no eagles because it had burned them at Bobr, but it suffered badly at the battle of Krasnoi, as Napoleon well knew. As for the Russians not capturing a single gun, something he also told Frederick VI of Denmark, Tsar Alexander conceived a scheme to build a massive column out of the 1,131 French cannon captured in the 1812 campaign. It never came to fruition, but scores of Napoleonic cannon can still be seen in the Kremlin today.[15]

In an effort to minimize domestic discontent, Napoleon concluded a new Concordat with the Pope at Fontainebleau in late January. 'Perhaps we will achieve the much desired aim of ending the differences between State and Church,' he had written on December 29. It seemed ambitious, but within a month a wide-ranging and comprehensive document had been signed covering most areas of disagreement.[16] 'His Holiness will exercise the Pontificate in both France and Italy,' it began, 'the Holy See's ambassadors abroad will have the same privileges as diplomats ... the domains of the Holy Father which are not alienated will not be subject to tax, those alienated will be compensated up to 2 million francs of income ... the Pope will give canonical institution to the Emperor's archdioceses within six months' – that is, he would recognize Napoleon's appointments as archbishops. Napoleon was also given permission to appoint ten new bishops.[17] It was a good outcome for Napoleon, which the Pope immediately regretted and tried to renege upon. 'Would you believe,' Napoleon told Marshal Kellermann, 'that the Pope, after having signed this Concordat freely and of his own accord, wrote to me eight days afterwards ... and earnestly entreated me to consider the whole affair null and void? I replied that as he was infallible he could not be mistaken, and that his conscience was too quickly alarmed.'[18]

On February 7 Napoleon held a great parade at the Tuileries and a meeting of the Conseil d'État afterwards to set up a regency for periods when he would be away on campaign. The Malet conspiracy had rattled him and he wanted to protect himself against any renewed effort to take advantage of his absence. He was also keen to ensure that in the event of his death his son would be accepted even in infancy as his successor. (He had come a long way since his youthful fulminations against monarchs.) Under the nineteen-clause *sénatus-consulte* drawn up by Cambacérès, in the event of Napoleon's death power would reside with Marie Louise, who would be advised by a Regency Council until the King of Rome came of age. Napoleon wanted Cambacérès to be the effective ruler of France, but with Marie Louise to 'give the Government the authority of her name'.[19] The meeting to establish the regency was attended by Cambacérès, Regnier, Gaudin, Maret, Molé, Lacépède, d'Angely, Moncey, Ney, the interior minister the Comte de Montalivet and the once-again forgiven Talleyrand. Napoleon, in Molé's words, 'though apparently calm and confident as to the campaign he was about to open, mentioned the vicissitudes of war and the fickleness of fortune in words which gave the lie to his imperturbable expression'.[20] Ordering Cambacérès only to 'show to the Empress what it is good for her to know', Napoleon told him not to send her the daily police reports as 'It's pointless to speak to her of things which could worry her or sully her mind.'[21]

By February 13 Napoleon had received the deeply ominous news that Austria was mobilizing a field army of at least 100,000 men. Shortly afterwards, Metternich offered to 'mediate' a European peace settlement – hardly the stance expected of an ally. A long talk with Molé in the billiards room of the Tuileries after dinner that evening laid bare Napoleon's thinking on several issues. He spoke highly of Marie Louise, saying he saw something of her ancestress, Anne of Austria, in her. 'She knows quite well that so-and-so voted for the death of Louis XVI, and also knows everyone's birth and record,' he said, yet she never showed bias towards the old nobility or against the regicides. He then spoke of the Jacobins who were 'fairly numerous in Paris and particularly formidable', but 'As long as I am alive that scum will not move, because they found out all about me on 13th Vendémiaire and know that I'm always ready to stamp on them if I have any trouble.'[22] He knew his foreign and domestic enemies would be 'much more venturesome since the Russian disaster. I must have one more campaign and get the better of these wretched Russians: we must drive them back to their frontiers and make them give up the idea of leaving them again.'[23] He went on to complain about his marshals: 'There's not one who can command the others and none of them knows anything but how to obey me.'[24]

Napoleon told Molé that he had hopes for Eugène, despite the fact that he was 'only a mediocrity'. He complained that Murat cried 'fat tears on the paper' when he wrote to his children and said he had suffered from 'despondency' during the retreat from Moscow, whereas:

> In my own case it's taken me years to cultivate self-control to prevent my emotions from betraying themselves. Only a short time ago I was the conqueror of the world, commanding the largest and finest army of modern times. That's all gone now! To think I kept all my composure, I might even say preserved my unvarying high spirits ... Yet don't think that my heart is less sensitive than those of other men. I'm a very kind man but since my earliest youth I have devoted myself to silencing that chord within me that never yields a sound now. If anyone told me when I was about to begin a battle that my mistress whom I loved to distraction was breathing her last, it would leave me cold. Yet my grief would be just as great as if I'd given way to it ... and after the battle I should mourn my mistress if I had the time. Without all this self-control, do you think I could have done all I've done?[25]

So rigid a control of one's emotions might seem distasteful to the modern temperament, but at the time it was considered a classical virtue. It undoubtedly helped Napoleon deal with his extraordinary reversals of fortune.

This self-control was in evidence when he spoke to the opening of the Legislative Body and Senate on February 14. A spectator recalled that he mounted the steps of the throne to cheers from the deputies, 'though their faces betrayed infinitely more anxiety than his'.[26] In his first full presentation to his deputies since his return from what he called the Russian 'desert', he explained the defeat by saying, 'The excessive and premature harshness of the winter caused my army to suffer an awful calamity.' He then announced an end to his 'difficulties' with the Pope, said that the Bonaparte dynasty would for ever reign in Spain and proclaimed that the French Empire had a positive trade balance of 126 million francs, 'even with the seas closed'.[27] (Three days later Montalivet published statistics that backed up everything the Emperor had claimed, as dictatorships so often do.) 'Since the rupture which followed the treaty of Amiens, I have proposed peace [with Britain] on four occasions,' he said, in this instance truthfully, after which he added: 'I will never make any peace but one that is honourable and suitable to the grandeur of my empire.'[28] The phrase 'perfidious Albion' had been employed occasionally ever since the Crusades (and had appeared in an

'Ode on the Death of Lannes') but it was in 1813, on Napoleon's orders, that it came into general use.[29]

The 1812 campaign had been disastrous for French finances. Until 1811 the franc had maintained its value against sterling, indeed it had slightly gained on it. The 1810 budget had seen a small surplus of 9.3 million francs, and bond yields were at a manageable 6 per cent. But after the infamous 29th bulletin, bonds – reflecting the lack of confidence in Napoleon's future – shot up from 6 per cent to 10 per cent, and the budget deficit for 1812 of 37.5 million francs could be serviced only through new taxes and new sales of state property, which fetched a fraction of earlier sell-offs because their title was so insecure. When the public sale of 370 million francs' worth of state-owned land raised only 50 million francs, sales taxes had to be increased by 11.5 per cent and land taxes by 22.6 per cent.[30] Napoleon meanwhile made some personal economies, telling his chief steward that he wanted 'fewer cooks, fewer plates, dishes, etc. On the battlefield, tables, even mine, shall be served with soup, a boiled dish, a roast, vegetables, no pudding.'[31] Officers were no longer going to be able to choose between wine and beer, but would drink whatever they were given. On an interior ministry proposal to spend 10 per cent of a prefect's salary on his funeral if he died in office, Napoleon scrawled: 'Refused. Why look for occasions to spend more?'[32] The Army of Catalonia would no longer be sent wine, brandy, oats and salted meats when there was plenty locally. 'All the deals that are being made by General Dumas are madness,' Napoleon wrote of the intendant-general's plans for provisioning the Oder fortresses. 'He apparently believes that money is nothing more than mud.'[33] All state building projects had been suspended before the Russian campaign, and were never resumed. The years 1813 and 1814, when there was no sign that an end to mass mobilization and high military spending was in sight, produced still higher deficits.

Although in early January 1813 Frederick William III offered to have General Yorck court-martialled for concluding the non-aggression pact with the Russians at Tauroggen, he was merely biding time. Prussia had undergone a modernizing revolution since Tilsit, which meant that Napoleon now faced a very different enemy from the one he had crushed at Jena nearly seven years before. The country had reformed, with defeat as the spur and the Napoleonic administrative–military model as its template. Barons vom Stein and von Hardenberg and generals von Gneisenau and von Scharnhorst demanded a 'revolution in the good sense' which, by destroying 'obsolete prejudices', would revive Prussia's 'dormant strengths'. There had been major financial and administrative reforms, including the abolition of many internal tariffs, restrictive monopolies and practices, the hereditary bondage of the peasantry and restrictions on occupation, movement and land ownership. A free market in labour was created, taxation was harmonized, ministers were made directly responsible and the property, marriage and travel restrictions on Jews were lifted.[34]

In the military sphere Prussia purged the high command (out of the 183 generals en poste in 1806, only eight still remained by 1812), opened the officer corps to non-nobles, introduced competitive examination in the cadet schools, abolished flogging, and mobilized her adult male population in the Landwehr (militia) and Landsturm (reserve). By 1813 she had put more than 10 per cent of her total population into uniform, more than any other Power, and over the next two years of almost constant fighting she lost the fewest through desertion.[35] With a hugely improved general staff, Prussia was able to boast fine commanders in the coming campaigns, such as generals von Bülow, von Blücher, von Tauentzien and von Boyen.[36] Napoleon was forced to admit that the Prussians had come on a great deal since the early campaigns; as he rather crudely put it: 'These animals have learnt something.'[37] It was hardly a consolation that they had learned much of it from him, just as Archduke Charles's military reforms since Austerlitz had copied many Napoleonic practices and several of Barclay de Tolly's reforms in Russia since Friedland had also echoed them. The wholesale adoption by all European armies of the corps system by 1812, making the Allies' armies far more flexible in manoeuvre, was a tribute to the French, but also a threat to them.

On February 28, 1813 Frederick William signed the Treaty of Kalisch (now Kalisz, in Poland) with Alexander, whereby the Tsar promised to restore Prussia to her pre-Tilsit borders and provide 150,000 troops if Prussia would send 80,000 to fight Napoleon. No sooner had the treaty been signed than the British began shipping arms, equipment and uniforms into the Baltic ports for use by both armies. Eugène was forced to abandon Berlin while leaving behind garrisons in Magdeburg, Torgau and Wittenberg. Because it was already besieging the French in Stettin, Küstrin, Spandau, Glogau, Thorn and Danzig, the Russian field army was down to 46,000 infantry and 10,000 Cossacks, although they were about to be joined by 61,000 Prussians. The Allied plan was to move on Dresden in order to detach Saxony from Napoleon, while sending

Cossack units pouring across the north German plain to try to stir up rebellion in the Hanseatic Towns and the Rhine Confederation.

'At the least insult from a Prussian town or village burn it down,' Napoleon commanded Eugène on March 3, 'even Berlin.'[38] Fortunately burning the Prussian capital was no longer possible, since the Russians entered it that same day. 'Nothing is less military than the course you have pursued,' Napoleon raged to Eugène on hearing the news. 'An experienced general would have established a camp in front of Küstrin.'[39] He further complained that as he wasn't getting daily reports from Eugène's chief-of-staff, 'I only learn what's happening from the English press.' He was even angrier with Jérôme, who complained about the high taxes that Westphalians had to pay to provision fortresses like Magdeburg. 'These means are authorized by a state of war; they have constantly been employed since the world was the world,' Napoleon raged in a characteristically blistering response. 'You will see how much the 300,000 men cost that I have in Spain, all the troops which I have raised this year, and the 100,000 cavalry I am equipping . . . You always argue . . . All your arguments are nonsense . . . Of what use is your intelligence since you take such a wrong view? Why gratify your vanity by vexing those who defend you?'[40] Before sending off a force to defend Magdeburg on March 4, Napoleon went through a familiar checklist with its commander: 'Make absolutely certain that each man has a pair of shoes on his feet and two pairs in his knapsack; that his pay is up to date, and, if it isn't, have the arrears paid. Make sure that each soldier has forty cartridges in his ammunition pouch.'[41]

Writing to Montalivet, Napoleon said he was about to go to Bremen, Münster, Osnabrück and Hamburg, but in his new spirit of thrift his lodgings and guards of honour in those cities 'must cost the country nothing'.[42] It was a ruse, however, to deceive the enemy about his movement. It was just as well he didn't go to Hamburg, however, as on March 18 Cossacks arrived and sparked a Hanseatic revolt just as the Allies hoped. Mecklenburg was the first state to defect from the Confederation of the Rhine. By late March the situation was so bad that Napoleon told Lauriston, now the commander of the Observation Corps of the Elbe, that he no longer dared to write to Eugène about his plans for the defence of Magdeburg and Spandau as he didn't have a cipher code and 'the Cossacks might intercept my letter.'[43] To make things even worse, Sweden then agreed to contribute 30,000 men to the Sixth Coalition if Britain would subsidize her with £1 million, and in early April General Pierre Durutte's small garrison was forced to evacuate Dresden.

It was at this time that Napoleon spoke to Molé about the prospect of France returning to her 'old', pre-war borders of 1791. 'I owe everything to my glory,' he said.

> If I sacrifice it I cease to be. It is from my glory that I hold all my rights . . . If I brought this nation, which is so anxious for peace and tired of war, a peace on terms which would make me blush personally, it would lose all confidence in me; you would see my prestige destroyed and my ascendancy lost.[44]

He compared the Russian disaster to a storm which shakes a tree to its roots but 'leaves it still more firmly fixed in the soil from which it has failed to tear it'. Dubious arboreal analogies aside, he wanted to discuss the French nation: 'It fears me more than it likes me and would at first regard the news of my death as a relief. But, believe me, that is much better than if it had liked me without fearing me.'[45] (The contrast between being loved and feared of course echoes Machiavelli's *The Prince*, a book with which he was very familiar.) Napoleon went on to say that he would beat the Russians as 'they have no infantry' and that the borders of the Empire would be fixed on the Oder as 'The defection of Prussia will enable me to seek compensation.' He also thought Austria would not declare war, because 'The best act of my political career was my marriage.'[46] In those last three points at least he was clearly trying to boost Molé's morale without any real consideration of the facts of the situation.

It was a measure of Napoleon's resilience and resourcefulness – and of the confidence that he still commanded – that having returned from Russia with only 10,000 effectives from his central invading force, he was able within four months to field an army of 151,000 men for the Elbe campaign, with many more to come.[47] He left Saint-Cloud at 4 a.m. on April 15 to take the field, with the kings of Denmark, Württemberg, Bavaria and Saxony and the grand dukes of Baden and Würzburg as allies, albeit some of them reluctant ones. 'Write to Papa François once a week,' he told Marie Louise three days later, 'send him military particulars and tell him of my affection for his person.'[48] With Wellington on the offensive in Spain, Murat negotiating with Austria over Naples, Bernadotte about to land with a Swedish army, fears of rebellion in western Germany and an Austria that was rearming quickly and at best only offering 'mediation', Napoleon knew he needed an early and decisive victory in the field. 'I will travel to Mainz,' he had told Jérôme in March, 'and if the Russians advance, I will make plans accordingly;

but we very much need to win before May.'[49] The Allies grouping around Leipzig – commanded by Wittgenstein after Kutuzov's death from illness in April – had massed 100,000 men; 30,000 of them were well-horsed cavalry, and they were being heavily reinforced. As a result of the equinocide in Russia the previous year, the rapidly reconstituted Grande Armée, by contrast, had only 8,540 cavalry.

Napoleon reached Erfurt on April 25 and assumed command of the army. He was shocked to find how inexperienced some of his officers were. Taking captains from the 123rd and 134th Line to make them *chefs de bataillon* in the 37th Légère, he complained to his war minister General Henri Clarke: 'It's absurd to have captains who have never fought a war ... You take young people just out of college who have not even been to Saint-Cyr [Military Academy], with the result that they know nothing, and you put them in new regiments!'[50] Yet this was the material Clarke had to work with after the loss of over half a million men in Russia.

Within three days of his arrival Napoleon had led the Grand Armée of 121,000 men back across the Elbe and into Saxony. His aim was to recover north Germany and relieve Danzig and the other besieged cities, to release 50,000 veterans, and hopefully sweep back to the line of the Vistula. Adopting the *bataillon carré* formation, he aimed for the enemy army at Leipzig with Lauriston's corps in the van followed by Macdonald's and Reynier's corps on the left flank, Ney's and General Henri Bertrand's on the right and Marmont's as the rearguard. On his left Eugène had a further 58,000 men. Poniatowski rejoined the army in May, but Napoleon sent Davout off to be governor of Hamburg, a dangerous underuse of his best marshal.

On May 1, while out reconnoitring enemy positions, Bessières was killed when a cannonball ricocheted off a wall and hit him full in the chest. 'The death of this exalted man affected him much,' Bausset recorded. Bessières had served in every campaign of Napoleon's career since 1796. 'My trust in you', Napoleon had once written to him, 'is as great as my appreciation of your military talents, your courage and your love of order and discipline.'[51] (To calm her, he asked Cambacérès to 'Make the Empress understand that the Duc d'Istrie [Bessières] was a long way away from me when he was killed.'[52]) He now wrote to Bessières' widow saying: 'The loss for you and your children is no doubt immense, but mine is even more so. The Duc d'Istrie died the most beautiful death and suffered not. He leaves behind a flawless reputation: this is the finest inheritance he could bestow upon his children.'[53] She might justifiably have taken issue with him as to whose loss was the greater, but his letter was heartfelt nonetheless, and accompanied by a generous pension.

Napoleon now faced a force totalling 96,000 men.[54] On Sunday May 2, when he was watching Lauriston's advance, he heard that Wittgenstein had launched a surprise attack on Ney near the village of Lützen at ten o'clock that morning. Listening intently to the cannonading, he ordered Ney to hold his position while he twisted the army round, sending Bertrand to attack the enemy's left and Macdonald its right in a textbook corps manoeuvre, with Lauriston forming the new reserve.[55] 'We have no cavalry,' Napoleon said; 'that's all right. It will be an Egyptian battle; everywhere the French infantry will have to suffice, and I don't fear abandoning myself to the innate worth of our young conscripts.'[56] Many of these conscripts had received their muskets for the first time when they reached Erfurt only days before the battle, and some only the day before the battle itself.[57] Yet the 'Marie Louises' performed well at Lützen.

At 2.30 p.m. Napoleon appeared on the battlefield at the head of the Guard cavalry, riding to the village of Kaja. He formulated his plan rapidly. Ney would continue to hold the centre while Macdonald came in on the left, Marmont secured Ney's right, and Bonnet would try to get round the enemy's rear from the Weissenfels–Lützen road. The Guard infantry of 14,100 would assemble out of view as a reserve and then deploy between Lützen and Kaja. Seeing some of the younger soldiers of Ney's corps making for the rear, and even a few dropping their muskets, Napoleon formed the Guard cavalry as a stop-line, and harangued and cajoled them until they returned to their ranks. Overall, however, Ney told Napoleon that he thought the young recruits fought better than his veterans, who tended to calculate probabilities and so take fewer risks. The *Moniteur* subsequently stated: 'Our young soldiers are not afraid of danger. During this great action, they have revealed the absolute nobility of French blood.'[58]

The four villages of Gross-Gorschen, Kaja, Rahna and Kleingorschen formed the centre of the battle. The Tsar – who along with Frederick William was present, although Wittgenstein as Allied commander-in-chief took all the important military decisions – sent in Russian horse artillery, and Ricard's division was fought to a standstill as each village changed hands several times. Ney was wounded on the front line and all the senior officers of Souham's division were either killed or wounded

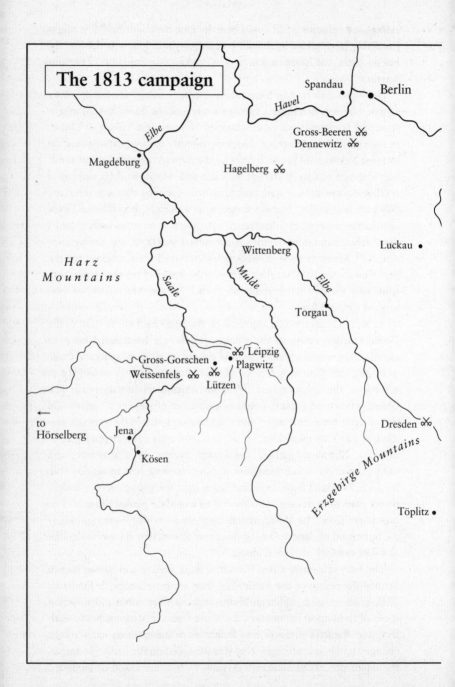

The 1813 campaign

Spandau
Berlin
Havel
Gross-Beeren ✖
Dennewitz ✖
Elbe
Hagelberg ✖
Magdeburg
Luckau
Harz Mountains
Wittenberg
Mulde
Saale
Elbe
Torgau
Gross-Gorschen ✖ Leipzig
Plagwitz
Weissenfels ✖ ✖
Lützen
Dresden ✖
← to Hörselberg
Jena
Kösen
Erzgebirge Mountains
Töplitz

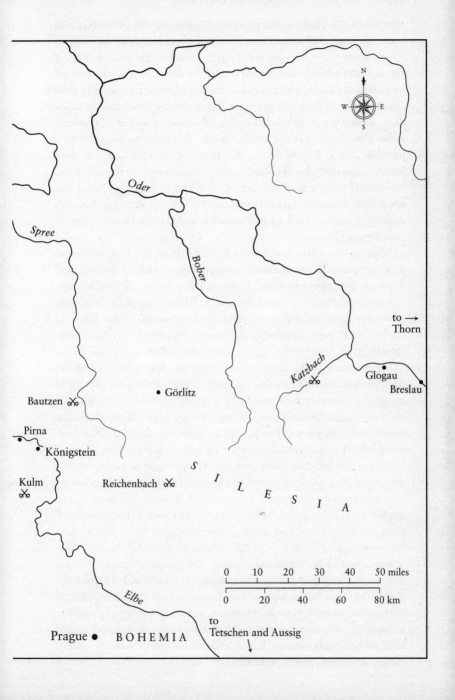

N
W   E
S

Oder

Spree

Bober

to →
Thorn

Katzbach

Glogau

Breslau

Bautzen ⚔

• Görlitz

Pirna
• Königstein

Kulm
⚔

Reichenbach ⚔

S   I   L   E   S   I   A

0	10	20	30	40	50 miles
0	20	40	60	80 km

Elbe

Prague •   B O H E M I A

to
Tetschen and Aussig
↓

except Souham himself. Wittgenstein was running out of reserves and could see more and more French arriving every hour, but he chose to renew the attack on Kaja. By about 6 p.m. Napoleon decided the moment for the final assault was fast approaching. Drouot brought forward 58 guns of the Guard artillery to join the Grand Battery, so that 198 guns could now pound the enemy centre. Remembering his mistake at Borodino when he had failed to employ the Guard decisively, Napoleon ordered Mortier to lead the Young Guard – 9,800 men in four columns – into the attack, backed by six battalions of the Old Guard in four squares. Two divisions of Guard cavalry, comprising 3,335 men, were in line behind them, and to the roar of 'Vive l'Empereur!' they swept forward from Rahna to Gross-Gorschen. At the same moment, Bonnet's division launched itself from Starsiedel, and Morand's continued to attack from the west.

With all the Allied reserves totally committed, the Russian Guard massed behind Gross-Gorschen to encourage retreating Russian and Prussian formations to rally. As night fell – lit by the five burning villages – the French renewed the attack, further unsettling the enemy. After the battle the Allies withdrew in good order, having failed to exploit their huge superiority in cavalry. Napoleon was victorious, though at a heavy cost: 2,700 had been killed and as many as 16,900 wounded. The Russians and Prussians lost a similar number (though they admitted to only 11,000). Napoleon had no cavalry to conduct a pursuit, which was to be a major problem throughout the 1813 campaign. He did, however, begin the recovery of Saxony and the west bank of the Elbe. 'My eagles are again victorious,' he told Caulaincourt after the battle, adding ominously, 'but my star is setting.'[59]

'I'm very tired,' Napoleon wrote to Marie Louise at eleven o'clock that night. 'I've gained a complete victory over the Russian and Prussian armies under Emperor Alexander and the King of Prussia. I lost 10,000 men, killed and wounded. My troops covered themselves with glory and proved their love in a way that went to my heart. Kiss my son. I'm in very good health.'[60] To her father he wrote that Marie Louise 'continues to please me in the extreme. She is now my prime minister and acquits herself of this role to my great satisfaction; I did not want Your Majesty to be unaware of this, knowing how much it will please his paternal heart.'[61] Napoleon's appeal to Francis's paternal pride was a clear effort to prevent him siding with his enemies. Russia and Prussia he could just about manage, but should Austria join them his chances of victory would be severely reduced.

'Soldiers! I am satisfied with you; you have fulfilled my expectations!' Napoleon exclaimed in his post-battle proclamation, after which he took a dig at Alexander with a mention of 'parricidal plots' and the Russian practice of serfdom: 'We will drive back these Tartars into their frightful regions, which they ought never to have left. Let them remain in their frozen deserts, the abode of slavery, of barbarism, and of corruption, where man is debased to equality with the brute.'[62]

As the Allies retreated across the Elbe in two great columns – one mainly Prussian, one mainly Russian – the French could follow only at infantry pace. The Prussians naturally wanted to retire north to protect Berlin, while the Russians wanted to move eastwards to protect their lines of communication through Poland. Wittgenstein, still looking for opportunities to attack the French in the flank and rightly suspecting that Napoleon wanted to recapture Berlin, massed his army close to Bautzen, only 8 miles from the Austrian border, from where he could cover both Berlin and Dresden.

Napoleon entered Dresden on May 8 and stayed there for ten days. He received a Young Guard division and four battalions of the Old Guard, incorporated the Saxon army into a corps of the Grande Armée, sent Eugène back to Italy in case of Austrian encroachment, and secured three separate lines of communication back to France. 'I have reason to be happy with Austria's intentions,' he told Clarke, 'I do not suspect her provisions; however my intention is to be in a position not to have to depend on her.'[63] It was a sensible policy. He was however angry with the Dresden city delegation who welcomed him, telling them that he knew they had aided the Allies during their occupation. 'Fragments of garlands are still clinging to your houses, and your streets are still littered with the mush of the flowers your maidens strewed before the monarchs' feet,' he said. 'Still, I am willing to overlook all that.'[64]

Napoleon then did one of those dumbfounding things of which he was so often capable. He wrote to his former intelligence chief Fouché and instructed him to come to Dresden in secret, as quickly as possible, in order to run Prussia once it was captured. 'No one must know of this in Paris,' he told him. 'It must seem as if you are about to leave to go on campaign ... Only the Empress-Regent knows of your departure. I'm very glad to have the opportunity to call upon you for new duties and to have new proof of your attachment.'[65] Fouché felt no attachment to Napoleon since his abrupt sacking following his secret peace talks with Britain, as the events of the following year were to illustrate. The military situation meant that he never took over Prussia, but as with Talleyrand, Napoleon had either lost his antennae for who opposed and who supported him, or was so confident in his powers that he didn't care. The circle of loyal advisors he could count on was shrinking.

The news that Austria was arming, and seemed ever more bellicose, worried Napoleon. He wrote to Marie Louise constantly to ask her to intercede with her father, saying on May 14 for example: 'People are trying to mislead Papa François. Metternik [*sic*] is a mere intriguer.'[66] He wrote to Francis himself three days later, calling him 'Brother and dearly beloved father-in-law'. 'No one desires peace more ardently than me,' he began. 'I agree to the opening of negotiations for a general peace and the summoning of a Congress', but 'Like all warm-blooded Frenchmen, I would rather die sword in hand than yield, if an attempt be made to force conditions on me.'[67] At the same time, he sent Caulaincourt to the Tsar asking for peace, telling him: 'My intention is to build him a golden bridge ... you must try to tie up a direct negotiation on this basis.' Even now he believed he could rekindle their friendship. 'Once we have come to speak to each other,' he said, 'we will always finish by finding an agreement.'[68] But when Caulaincourt arrived at Allied headquarters, the Tsar would see him only in the presence of the King of Prussia and the Austrian and British ambassadors.

Napoleon left Dresden at 2 p.m. on May 18 to attack the Allied main army at the fortified town of Bautzen on the River Spree. One would hardly have surmised this from the letter he wrote Marie Louise the next day: 'The valley of Montmorency is very beautiful in this season, yet I fancy the time when it's pleasantest is the beginning of June when the cherries are ripe.'[69] That day he ordered Eugène in Italy to 'Busy yourself with the organization of your six regiments right away. To begin with, you will dress them in jackets, trousers and shakos ...' In another letter he elaborated on how Eugène's six-year-old daughter, Josephine of Leuchtenberg, would receive the revenues of the Duchy of Galliera, which Napoleon had especially created for her in the Emilia-Romagna region of Italy.[70]

The Allied armies, some 97,000 strong, had fallen back to the low hills overlooking Bautzen, a naturally strong position quickly improved with field fortifications. All reports indicated that they would stand their ground there, which is exactly what Napoleon wanted them to do. He had 64,000 men in Bertrand's, Marmont's and Macdonald's corps facing the enemy directly, supported by Oudinot's corps and the

Imperial Guard: 90,000 in all. The Allies had built eleven strong redoubts in the hills as well as some in the town, and had three fortified villages in their second line of defence. But their northern flank was dangerously open, and that was where Napoleon intended to send Ney's and Lauriston's corps. In all he would engage some 167,000 men by the end of the battle. When his officers told him that some of the Prussian regiments they would be facing had fought under Frederick the Great, he made the obvious point: 'That's true, but Frederick isn't around any more.'[71]

The battle of Bautzen opened on Thursday, May 20, 1813 with Oudinot vigorously attacking the Allied left. Napoleon waited for Ney's enlarged wing of the Grande Armée of some 57,000 men to march up and into position before decisively turning the open Allied right flank and driving it into the Erzgebirge mountains. The plan worked well on the first day, as the Tsar mistakenly committed most of the Allied reserves to the left, just as Napoleon hoped. The next day, Napoleon was confident that Ney and Lauriston would join the battle and complete the victory. Oudinot again vigorously assaulted the Allied left; Macdonald and Marmont joined the attack in the centre and then Napoleon committed the Imperial Guard when he thought the moment right. But Ney arrived late after a confusing order led him to halt for an hour, allowing the Allies to spot the danger and march away to safety. The level of ferocity of the fighting is reflected in the casualties: 21,200 Frenchmen were killed or wounded whereas the Allies, enjoying the benefit of strong defences, lost half that. Once again the lack of cavalry meant Napoleon was unable to exploit his tactical victory in any meaningful way.

'I had a battle today,' Napoleon told Marie Louise. 'I took possession of Bautzen. I dispersed the Russian and Prussian armies . . . It was a fine battle. I am rather unwell, I got soaked two or three times during the day. I kiss you and ask you to kiss my son for me. My health is good. I lost no one of any importance. I put my losses at 3,000 men, killed or wounded.'[72] The proximity of the phrase 'My health is good' so soon after 'I am rather unwell' implies that the sign-off was by then just a reflex.

Only hours after writing that he hadn't lost anyone of any importance, his closest friend, Géraud Duroc, the Duc de Frioul, was disembowelled by a cannonball in front of him on a hill overlooking Nieder-Markersdorf at the battle of Reichenbach (now Dzierżoniów, in Poland) on May 22. 'Duroc, there is another life,' Napoleon was represented in the *Moniteur* as having told him. 'There you will await my coming.' Duroc is supposed to have answered: 'Yes, Sire, when you have fulfilled all the hopes of our Fatherland', and so on, before saying: 'Ah, Sire, leave me; the sight of me is painful to you!'[73] A year later Napoleon spoke about what had really happened, admitting that 'when his bowels were falling out before my eyes, he repeatedly cried to me to have him put out of his misery. I told him: "I feel pity for you, my friend, but there is no remedy but to suffer till the end." '[74]

The loss of such a friend, who could read Napoleon's moods and could distinguish between his real and feigned anger, was at once personally traumatic and politically devastating, especially in that spring of 1813 when Napoleon badly needed wise and disinterested counsel. 'I was very sad all day yesterday over the death of the Duke of Frioul,' Napoleon wrote to Marie Louise the next day. 'He was a friend of twenty years' standing. Never did I have any occasion to complain of him, he was never anything but a comfort to me. He is an irreparable loss, the greatest I could suffer in the Army.'[75] (He remembered Duroc's daughter in his will.) 'The death of the Duc de Frioul pained me,' he wrote a few weeks later to his son's governess, Madame de Montesquiou. 'This was the only time in twenty years that he did not guess what would please me.'[76] The list of friends and close comrades Napoleon had lost in battle was by now long and doleful: Muiron at Arcole, Brueys at the Nile, Caffarelli at Acre, Desaix at Marengo, Claude Corbineau at Eylau, Lannes at Aspern-Essling, Lasalle at Wagram, Bessières the day before Lützen and now his closest friend Duroc at Reichenbach. Nor was it to end there.

The victories at Lützen and Bautzen gave Napoleon control of Saxony and most of Silesia, but his losses were high enough to force him to accept a temporary ceasefire on June 4. The Armistice of Pleischwitz (now Blizanowice, in Poland) was originally intended to last until July 20. 'Two considerations have caused me to make this decision,' Napoleon told Clarke, 'my lack of cavalry, which prevents me from striking strong blows, and the hostile attitude of Austria.'[77] It was not in Napoleon's nature to agree to armistices, which went totally against his concept of war as a fast-moving surge of aggression in which he always kept the initiative. (Indeed the codename that the Bourbons' intelligence service gave him was 'The Torrent'.) He later acknowledged that the Allies used the time bought by Pleischwitz more profitably than he did, almost doubling their forces and strengthening their defences in Brandenburg and Silesia. Britain also used the time to organize the Treaty of

Reichenbach, which funded Russia and Prussia with a massive £7 million, the largest subsidy of the war.[78] Yet Caulaincourt, who took over Duroc's roles as advisor and grand marshal of the palace, was in favour of the armistice, as was Berthier; only Soult thought it a mistake.

At the time Napoleon desperately needed to train, reorganize and reinforce his army, especially his cavalry, fortify the Elbe crossings, and replenish ammunition and food stocks. 'A soldier's health must take precedence over economic calculations or any other consideration,' he told Daru when trying to buy 2 million pounds of rice. 'Rice is the best way to protect oneself from diarrhoea and dysentery.'[79] He worked throughout the truce at his normal frenetic pace – on June 13 he caught sunstroke having been in the saddle all afternoon. The other reason he needed time was to persuade Austria not to declare war on him. During the armistice, Metternich sent Count Stadion to the Allies and Count Bubna to Napoleon to discuss a French withdrawal from Germany, Poland and the Adriatic. Metternich had demanded an international congress at Prague to discuss peace, but Napoleon feared that was merely a pretext for Austria joining the Allies. A French evacuation of Holland, Spain and Italy was also to be tabled there.

Napoleon was outraged that he should have to give up Illyria to Austria without a fight. 'If I can, I will wait until September to attack with heavy strikes,' he wrote. 'I therefore want to be in a position to beat my enemies, as far as is possible, so that when she sees me capable of doing so, Austria will . . . face up to her deceptive and ridiculous pretensions.'[80] Yet he also had to acknowledge to Fain: 'If the Allies don't want peace in good faith, then this armistice could be very deadly to us.'[81] He wasn't always glum, however; when he was told that Marie Louise had received the homosexual Cambacérès while in bed, he told her: 'I beg that under no circumstance will you receive, no matter who, when in bed. That is permitted only to persons over thirty years of age.'[82]

Some of Napoleon's marshals wanted to retreat to the Rhine if the armistice collapsed, but he himself pointed out that this would mean abandoning for ever the garrisons in the fortresses on the Oder, Vistula and Elbe, as well as his Danish, Polish, Saxon and Westphalian allies. 'Good God!' he said. 'Where's your prudence? Ten lost battles could hardly reduce me to the position you want to place me in right away!' When his marshals reminded him of the long lines of communication to Dresden he said: 'Certainly, you don't have to risk your lines of operation lightly; I know it; it's the rule of common-sense and the ABC of the job . . . But when great interests are unravelled, there are moments in which one must sacrifice to the victory and not fear to burn one's boats! . . . If the art of war was only the art of not risking anything, glory would be prey to mediocrities. We need a full triumph!'[83]

Napoleon intended to use Dresden's geography to his advantage. 'Dresden is the pivot from which I want to manoeuvre in order to face all the attacks,' he told Fain.

> From Berlin to Prague, the enemy is developing on a circumference of which I occupy the centre; the shortest communications get longer for him on the contours that they have to follow; and for me some marches suffice to take me wherever my presence and my reserves need to be. But in the places where I will not be, my lieutenants must know to wait for me without committing anything to chance . . . Will the Allies be able to keep up such a spread of operations for long? And myself, shouldn't I reasonably hope to surprise them sooner or later in any false movement?[84]

The reasoning was sound, though it relied completely on the clarity of his own judgement and manoeuvring on internal lines.

To those in the French high command who argued that the Russians might try to put light cavalry beyond the Elbe and even the Rhine, Napoleon retorted: 'I'm expecting it, I've provided for it. Independently of the strong garrisons of Mainz, Wesel, Erfurt and Würzburg, Augereau is gathering a Corps of Observation on the Main.' 'Only one victory,' he added, 'will force the Allies to make peace.'[85] Napoleon's victories early in his career had quickly led to peace by negotiation; his central mistake now was to assume that peace would still be found in that way. He now faced an enemy with as firm a resolve as his own, and a newfound determination to force him to yield. 'You bore me continually about the necessity of peace,' he wrote on June 13 to Savary, who had told him again how much Parisians yearned for it. 'No one is more interested in concluding peace than me, but I will not make a dishonourable peace or one that would see us at war again in six months. Don't reply to this; these matters do not concern you, don't get mixed up in them.'[86]

On June 19 Talma, his former mistress from ten years previously Marguerite Weimer (whose stage name was Mademoiselle George) and fifteen other actors arrived in Dresden. There's no indication that Napoleon had specifically asked for Mademoiselle George to come, but he appeared to be grateful for the distraction of theatre. 'A remarkable change took place in Napoleon's taste,' remarked his chamberlain, Bausset, 'who until this time had always preferred tragedy.'[87] Now he chose only comedies to be performed and plays that drew closely observed 'delineations of manner and characters'. Perhaps he had seen quite enough genuine tragedy by then.

The following week Napoleon wrote to Marie Louise: 'Metternich arrived in Dresden this afternoon. We shall see what he has to say and what Papa François wants. He is still adding to his army in Bohemia; I'm strengthening mine in Italy.'[88]

What precisely happened during the eight-hour – some accounts say nine-and-a-half-hour – meeting in the Chinese Room of the Marcolini Palace in Dresden on June 26, 1813 is still a matter of speculation, since only Napoleon and Metternich were present and they gave contradictory accounts. Yet taking the most unreliable narrative, Metternich's memoirs written decades later, and comparing it with the other available sources – Metternich's own short official report to Francis of that same day, a letter Metternich wrote to his wife Eleonore two days later, Napoleon's contemporaneous report to Caulaincourt, Maret's report to Fain published in 1824 and some remarks Napoleon made to the Comte de Montholon six weeks before he died – it is possible to arrive at a fair understanding of what transpired in the climactic encounter that would do so much to determine the fate of Europe.[89]

Napoleon began the meeting shortly after 11 a.m. hoping to browbeat Metternich, the most imperturbable statesman in Europe, into dropping Austria's plans for mediation. He thought he could persuade him to return to the French camp. Metternich, by contrast, was determined to arrive at a negotiated peace agreement covering all the outstanding territorial issues over Germany, Holland, Italy and Belgium. The vast discrepancy in their respective positions partly explains the length of the meeting. As the diplomat who had negotiated Napoleon's marriage, in Vienna Metternich was considered pro-French. He had (at least publicly) shown dismay when the Grande Armée was shattered in Russia. Was he vague as to the precise terms of the peace, as Napoleon later charged? Or was he deliberately employing delaying tactics to allow his country to rearm? Was he demanding more than he thought Napoleon could ever give in the hope of making him look unreasonable? Or did he really want peace but thought it could be assured only on the basis of massive French withdrawals across Europe? Given Metternich's mercurial inconsistency, he was probably driven by an ever-changing *mélange* of several of these motives and others. He certainly thought that Dresden was the moment when he, rather than Napoleon, could decide the fate of the continent. 'I am making all of Europe revolve around the axis that I alone determined months ago,' he boasted to his wife, 'at a time when all around me thought my ideas were insignificant follies or hollow fantasies.'[90]

There are several contradictions in the various reports of the meeting. Napoleon admitted he threw his hat on the ground at one stage: Metternich told his wife that Napoleon threw it 'four times . . . into the corner of the room, swearing like the Devil'.[91] Fain said that Napoleon agreed to participate in the Congress of Prague at the end of the meeting; Metternich said it was four days later, as he was stepping into his carriage to leave Dresden. Metternich claimed to have warned Napoleon, 'Sire, you are lost!', and Napoleon accused him of being in the pay of the English.[92] This last remark was a stupid one; on his deathbed Napoleon admitted it had been a disastrous faux pas, turning Metternich into 'an irreconcilable enemy'.[93] Although Napoleon tried to make amends almost immediately, pretending it had been a joke, and although the two men seem to have ended the meeting on civil terms, Metternich emerged convinced – or so he claimed – that Napoleon was incorrigibly committed to war.

'Experience is lost on you,' Metternich has Napoleon tell him. 'Three times I have replaced the Emperor Francis on his throne. I have promised always to live in peace with him; I have married his daughter. At the time I said to myself you are perpetrating a folly; but it was done, and today I repent of it!'[94] Napoleon digressed on the strength and strategy of the Austrian forces and boasted that he knew their dispositions down to 'the very drummers in your army'. Going into his study, they spent over an hour going over his daily list from Narbonne's spies, regiment by regiment, to prove how good his intelligence network was.

When Metternich brought up the 'youthful' nature of the French army, Napoleon is alleged to have snapped, 'You are no soldier, and you do not know what goes on in the mind of a soldier. I was brought up in the field, and a man such as I am does not concern himself much about the lives of a million men.'[95] In his memoirs Metternich wrote, 'I do not dare to make use of the much worse expressions employed by Napoleon.' Napoleon has been heavily criticized for this line about the million lives, which has been taken as *prima facie* evidence that he cared nothing for his soldiers, yet the context was critical – he was desperately trying to convince Metternich that he was perfectly willing to return to war unless he received decent peace terms. It was bluster, not the heartless cynicism it has been represented as being. If indeed he ever said it at all.

The terms Metternich demanded for peace went far beyond the

restitution of Illyria to Austria. He seems to have asked Napoleon for the independence of half of Italy and the whole of Spain, a return to Prussia of almost all the lands taken from her at Tilsit, including Danzig, the return of the Pope to Rome, the revocation of Napoleon's protectorate of the German Confederation, the evacuation of French troops from Poland and Prussia, the independence of the Hanseatic ports and the abolition of the Duchy of Warsaw. At one point Napoleon shouted from the map room adjoining his study, so loudly that the entourage heard, that he did not mind giving up Illyria but the rest of the demands were impossible.[96]

Napoleon had told his court several times that the French people would overthrow him if he signed a 'dishonourable' peace sending France back to her pre-war borders, which is effectively what Metternich was demanding. His police reports were currently indicating that the French people wanted peace far more than *la Gloire*, but he knew that national glory was indeed one of the vital four pillars – along with national property rights, low taxation and centralized authority – that bolstered his rule. Metternich might have been sincere in his desire for peace (though the words 'Metternich' and 'sincerity' tend to sit uncomfortably together at the best of times) but he clearly asked far too much as a price for it.

'I had a long and wearisome talk with Metternich,' Napoleon told Marie Louise the next day. 'I hope peace will be negotiated in a few days' time. I want peace, but it must be an honourable one.'[97] That same day, Austria secretly signed a second Treaty of Reichenbach, with Prussia and Russia, in which she promised to go to war with France if Napoleon rejected peace terms at Prague. This, of course, had the effect of increasing the terms that Prussia and the by then irreconcilable Russia would demand.

Napoleon met Metternich again on June 30, this time for a four-hour conference at which they extended the armistice to August 10 and Napoleon accepted Austrian mediation at the Prague Congress, set to start on July 29. 'Metternich,' Napoleon told his wife afterwards, 'strikes me as an intriguer and as directing Papa François very badly.'[98] Although Napoleon denounced it as 'unnatural' for Emperor Francis to make war on his son-in-law, he himself had demanded that Charles IV of Spain make war against his son-in-law, the King of Portugal, in 1800, so he was not on very sure ground.

Napoleon's position at the coming Congress was severely weakened when the news arrived on July 2 of Wellington's crushing victory over

Joseph and his chief-of-staff Marshal Jourdan at the battle of Vitoria in northern Spain on June 21, which cost Joseph 8,000 men and virtually the entire Spanish royal art collection. (It can today be seen at Apsley House in London. Jourdan's red velvet marshal's baton studded with golden bees is today on display outside the Waterloo Gallery at Windsor Castle.) Napoleon said the defeat at Vitoria was 'because Joseph slept too long', which is absurd.[99] At the time, he wrote to Marie Louise to say that Joseph 'is no soldier, and knows nothing about anything', though that begs the question why he gave his brother overall command of an army of 47,300 men against the greatest British soldier since Marlborough.[100] The trust and affection between the brothers had almost completely broken down over the disasters in Spain, for which each blamed the other. Five days later Napoleon told Marie Louise that if Joseph took up residence at his lovely Château de Mortefontaine in the Oise, with its islets, orangery, aviary, two parks and some of the finest landscaped gardens in Europe, then 'it must be incognito and you must ignore him; I will not have him interfere with government or set up intrigues in Paris.' He ordered Soult to take command of Joseph's shattered army, with the very competent generals Honoré Reille, Bertrand Clauzel, Jean-Baptiste d'Erlon and Honoré Gazan as his principal lieutenants, hoping to protect Pamplona and San Sebastián.

On July 12 the Russian, Prussian and Swedish general staffs met at Trachenberg (now Żmigród, in Poland) to co-ordinate strategy in the event that the Prague Congress should fail. It was one of those rare occasions when leaders showed they had learned the lessons of history. Appreciating that Napoleon had often outflanked enemy armies and then punished the centre, they accepted the Austrian General Joseph Radetzky's strategy to divide their forces into three armies that would advance into Saxony, not offering battle to Napoleon himself, but instead withdrawing before him and concentrating on the inferior forces of his lieutenants. If one of the Allied armies was attacked by Napoleon, the other two would attack his flank or rear. The idea was to force Napoleon to choose between three options: going on the defensive, leaving open his lines of communication or dividing his forces.[101] The Trachenberg strategy was explicitly tailored to counteract Napoleon's military genius and it would be used to tremendous effect.

The Congress of Prague finally met on July 29. Caulaincourt and Narbonne represented France. 'Russia is entitled to an advantageous peace,' Napoleon told Fain at this time:

she would have bought it by the devastation of her provinces, by the loss of her capital and by two years of war. Austria, on the contrary, doesn't deserve anything. In the current situation, I have no objection to a peace that might be glorious to Russia; but I feel a true repugnance to seeing Austria, as a price for the crime she committed by violating our alliance, collect the fruits and honours of the pacification of Europe.[102]

He did not wish to reward Francis and Metternich for what he saw as their scheming perfidy. After receiving intelligence reports from his spies, he warned his marshals on August 4 that 'Nothing is happening at the Congress of Prague. They will arrive at no result, and the Allies intend to denounce the armistice on the 10th.'[103]

On August 7 Metternich demanded that the Duchy of Warsaw be repartitioned, that Hamburg (which Davout had captured before the armistice) be liberated, that Danzig and Lübeck become free cities, that Prussia be reconstructed with a border on the Elbe and that Illyria, including Trieste, be ceded to Austria.[104] Despite the fact that it would have meant forswearing the last seven years, leaving allies in the lurch and rendering the sacrifice of hundreds of thousands of lives in vain, almost every other statesman of the day would have agreed to these terms. But the Emperor of France, the heir to Caesar and Alexander, simply could not bring himself to accept what he saw as a humiliating peace.

27

Leipzig

'Fear and uncertainty accelerate the fall of empires: they are a thousand times more fatal than the dangers and losses of an ill-fated war.'
Napoleon, statement in the *Moniteur*, December 1804

'When two armies are in order of battle, and one has to retire over a bridge while the other has the circumference of the circle open, all the advantages are in favour of the latter.'
Napoleon's Military Maxim No. 25

'There's not an ounce of doubt that the enemy will call off the armistice on the 10th and that hostilities will recommence on the 16th or 17th,' Napoleon warned Davout from Dresden on August 8, 1813. He predicted that Austria would then send 120,000 men against him, 30,000 against Bavaria and 50,000 against Eugène in Italy.[1] Nonetheless, he concluded: 'Whatever increase in forces this gives to the Allies, I feel able to face up to them.' His birthday celebrations were therefore brought forward five days, to August 10; they were to be the last formally held while he ruled France. The Saxon cavalry colonel Baron Ernst von Odeleben recalled in his memoirs the two-hour review of 40,000 soldiers, a *Te Deum* sung at Dresden cathedral accompanied by the roar of artillery salutes, the Imperial Guard banqueting with the Saxon Royal Guard under the linden trees by the Elbe, bands playing martial airs, every soldier receiving double pay and double meat rations, and the King of Saxony giving thousands of bottles of wine to the troops. As for Napoleon, 'the *vivats* resounded as he passed along the ranks at a full gallop, attended by his brilliant suite.' Few would have predicted that the French and Saxon artillerymen who 'caroused together' would within weeks be firing on each other. At 8 p.m. Napoleon visited the King of Saxony's palace for a birthday banquet, after which their soldiers jointly cheered and discharged fireworks from either side of the bridge. 'An azure sky gave a charming effect to the multitude of rockets,' remembered Odeleben, 'which crossed each other in their flight over the dark roofs of the city, illuminating the air far and wide ... After a pause the cipher of Napoleon appeared in the air, above the palace.'[2] Later on, as the crowds dispersed, the 'doleful cries' of a fisherman could be heard from the shore; he had approached too close to the rockets and had been mortally wounded. 'Was this an omen,' Odeleben wondered, 'of the dreadful career of the hero of the fête?'

By mid-August 1813 Napoleon had assembled 45,000 cavalry, spread over four corps and twelve divisions.[3] It was far more than he had had at the start of the armistice, but still not enough to counter the forces massing against him. The Allies denounced the armistice at noon on the 11th, within twenty-four hours of Napoleon's estimate, and stated that hostilities would resume at midnight on the 17th.* Austria declared war on France on the 12th. The deftness with which Metternich had drawn Austria out of her alliance, then into neutrality, then into supposedly objective mediation, and then, the day after the end of the armistice, into the Sixth Coalition has been described as 'a masterpiece of diplomacy'.[4] Napoleon saw only duplicity. 'The Congress of Prague never seriously took place,' he told the King of Württemberg. 'It was a means for Austria to choose to declare herself.'[5] He wrote to Ney and Marmont saying he would take up a position between Görlitz and Bautzen and see what the Austrians and Russians would do. 'It seems to me that no good will come of the current campaign unless there is first a big battle,' he concluded in what was by now a familiar refrain.[6]

The strategic situation was serious but not disastrous. As he had stated, Napoleon had the advantage of internal lines within Saxony, although he was surrounded by large enemy armies on three sides. Schwarzenberg's Army of Bohemia now consisted of 230,000 Austrians, Russians and Prussians, who were coming up from northern Bohemia; Blücher was

---

* Even at this moment of crisis, Napoleon ensured that the actors of the Théâtre-Français got back to Paris before hostilities recommenced (Bausset, *Private Memoirs* p. 395). He gave Mademoiselle George 20,000 francs on August 12, which might have been just for her singing (Branda, *Le prix de la gloire* p. 57).

leading the Army of Silesia, comprising 85,000 Prussians and Russians, westwards from Upper Silesia, and Bernadotte headed a Northern Army of 110,000 Prussians, Russians and Swedes moving southwards from Brandenburg: 425,000 men in total, with more on the way. Facing them, Napoleon had 351,000 men spread between Hamburg and the upper Oder.[7] Although he had a further 93,000 men garrisoning German and Polish towns and 56,000 training in French army depots, they were not readily available. He would need to keep his army concentrated centrally and defeat each enemy force separately, as he had done so often in the past. Yet instead he made the serious error of splitting his army – contradicting two of his own most important military maxims: 'Keep your forces concentrated' and 'Do not squander them in little packets.'[8]

Napoleon took 250,000 men to fight Schwarzenberg, while sending Oudinot (against the marshal's protestations) northwards to try to capture Berlin with 66,000 men, and General Jean-Baptiste Girard to defend Magdeburg 80 miles to the west of Oudinot with 9,000 men. He also ordered Davout to leave 10,000 men behind to defend Hamburg and to support Oudinot with a further 25,000. As in the attack on Moscow, Napoleon rejected the strategy that had served him so well in the past – that of concentrating solely on the enemy's main force and annihilating it – and instead allowed secondary political objects to intervene, such as his desire to take Berlin and punish Prussia. Nor did he place Davout under Oudinot's command or vice versa, with the result that there was no unity of command in the northern theatre.

Even had Oudinot succeeded in capturing Berlin it would not have guaranteed victory in 1813 any more than it had in 1806; had Schwarzenberg been comprehensively defeated by the combined French forces, Bernadotte could not have defended Berlin in any case. Although Napoleon knew the campaign was going to be decided in Saxony or northern Bohemia, he failed to give Oudinot more than a skeleton force to protect the Elbe from Bernadotte and defend his rear.[9] Leaving Davout to counter non-existent threats from north-west Germany was also a shocking waste of the marshal who had best proved his ability in independent command.

On August 15, his forty-fourth birthday, Napoleon left Dresden for Silesia, where he hoped to strike Blücher, who had captured Breslau (now Wrocław, in Poland). On the way he was joined at Bautzen by Murat, who was rewarded for his unexpected re-adherence to Napoleon's cause with his old position in overall charge of the cavalry. That day Napoleon told Oudinot that Girard's division at Magdeburg was

8,000 to 9,000 strong, which was true. The very next day he assured Macdonald it numbered 12,000.[10]

'It is he who wanted war,' Napoleon wrote to Marie Louise in reference to her father, 'through ambition and unbounded greed. Events will decide the matter.'[11] From then on he referred to Emperor Francis only as 'ton père' or 'Papa François', as when writing on August 17, 'Deceived by Metternich, your father has sided with my enemies.'[12] As regent of France and a good wife, Marie Louise was loyal to her husband and adopted country, rather than to her father and her fatherland.

Putting their Trachenberg strategy into effect as agreed, the Allies fell back in front of Napoleon's force while seeking out those of his principal lieutenants. Blücher was thus ready to take on Ney between the Bober river and the Katzbach on August 16, but he pulled back when Napoleon moved up with large elements of his main field army. Oudinot, whose advance on Berlin was slowed by torrential rain that all but halted his artillery, was pounced upon by Bülow's Prussians and Count Stedingk's Swedish corps in three separate actions from August 21 to 23 at Gross-Beeren, and defeated. He withdrew to Wittenberg rather than, as Napoleon would have preferred, Luckau. 'It's truly difficult to have fewer brains than the Duke of Reggio,' Napoleon said to Berthier, after which he despatched Ney to take over Oudinot's command.[13]

By August 20 Napoleon was in Bohemia, hoping to impede Schwarzenberg's movement towards Prague. 'I drove out General Neipperg,' he reported to Marie Louise that day. 'The Russians and Prussians have entered Bohemia.'[14] (Only a year later, the dashing one-eyed Austrian General Adam von Neipperg would exact a horribly personal revenge.) Hearing of a major attack on Dresden by the Army of Bohemia, Napoleon turned his army around on the 22nd and dashed back there, leaving Macdonald to watch Blücher. As he did so he wrote to Saint-Cyr: 'If the enemy has effectively carried out a big movement towards Dresden, I consider this to be very happy news, and that will even force me within a few days to have a great battle, which will decide things for good.'[15] The same day he also wrote to his grand chamberlain, the Comte de Montesquiou, expressing his dissatisfaction with his birthday festivities in Paris. 'I was much displeased to learn that matters were so badly managed on the 15th of August that the Empress was detained for a considerable time listening to bad music,' he wrote, 'and that consequently the public were kept waiting two hours for the fireworks.'[16]

*

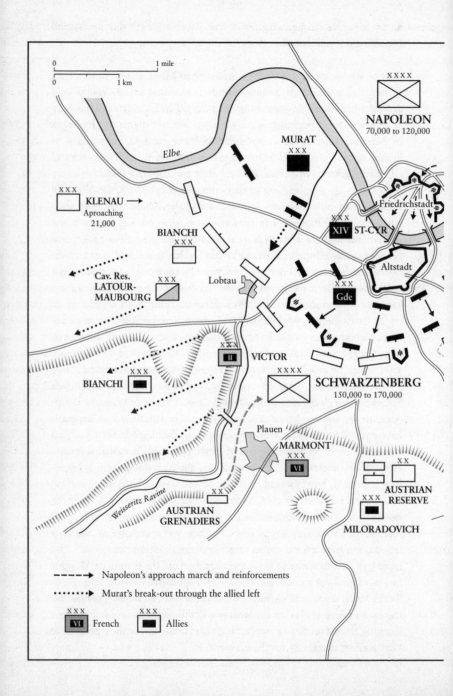

0 _____ 1 mile
0 _____ 1 km

XXXX
NAPOLEON
70,000 to 120,000

Elbe

MURAT
XXX

XXX
KLENAU →
Aproaching
21,000

Friedrichstadt

XXX
XIV ST-CYR

BIANCHI
XXX

Altstadt

Cav. Res.
LATOUR-
MAUBOURG
XXX

Lobtau

XXX
Gde

XXX
II VICTOR

XXX
BIANCHI

XXXX
SCHWARZENBERG
150,000 to 170,000

Plauen

MARMONT
XXX
VI

XX
AUSTRIAN
RESERVE

XX
AUSTRIAN
GRENADIERS

Weisseritz Ravine

XXX
MILORADOVICH

- - - → Napoleon's approach march and reinforcements

•••••••▶ Murat's break-out through the allied left

XXX
VI French

XXX
Allies

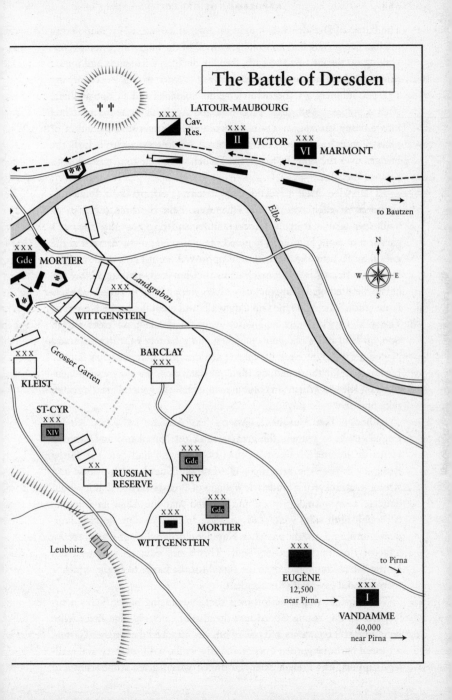

The Battle of Dresden

LATOUR-MAUBOURG

XXX Cav. Res.

XXX II VICTOR

XXX VI MARMONT

to Bautzen

Elbe

N
W — E
S

XXX Gde MORTIER

Landgraben

XXX WITTGENSTEIN

XXX BARCLAY

Grosser Garten

XXX KLEIST

ST-CYR
XXX XIV

XX RUSSIAN RESERVE

XXX Gde NEY

XXX Gde MORTIER

XXX WITTGENSTEIN

Leubnitz

XXX EUGÈNE 12,500 near Pirna →

to Pirna →

XXX I VANDAMME 40,000 near Pirna →

The battle of Dresden was fought on August 26–27, 1813. Napoleon's intelligence service had accurately warned of the huge Allied forces converging on the city. By the 19th, Barclay de Tolly's Russians had joined Schwarzenberg to form a vast army 237,770 strong – comprising 172,000 infantry, 43,500 cavalry, 7,200 Cossacks and 15,000 artillery, with a colossal 698 guns. This enlarged Army of Bohemia marched into Saxony on August 21 in five columns. Wittgenstein's column of 28,000 men headed for Dresden. Since Napoleon controlled all the bridges over the Elbe, however, the French were able to march on both sides of the river.

At Dresden itself the Old City defences, effectively a semicircle anchored at each end on the Elbe, were held by three divisions of Saint-Cyr's corps, roughly 19,000 infantry and 5,300 cavalry. The city's garrison of eight battalions manned the walls. Napoleon arrived at the gallop at 10 a.m. on the 26th and approved Saint-Cyr's deployments. Despite suffering from stomach pains that induced vomiting before the battle, he fired off his instructions. Guns were placed in each of the five large redoubts outside the Old City walls and eight inside the New City. The Old City's streets and gates were barricaded, all trees within 600 yards of the walls were cut down and a battery of thirty guns was placed on the right bank of the river to fire into Wittgenstein's flank.[17] Fortunately for those making these preparations, the slowness of General von Klenau's Austrian column meant that the general attack had to take place the next day.

Although Tsar Alexander, General Jean Moreau (who had left his English exile to witness the great assault on Napoleon) and General Henri de Jomini (Ney's Swiss chief-of-staff who had defected to the Russians during the armistice) all thought Napoleon's position too strong to attack, King Frederick William of Prussia argued that it would damage army morale not to, and insisted that the Allies gave battle. Although both sides were ready to fight from 9.30 a.m. nothing happened until mid-afternoon, when Napoleon ordered Saint-Cyr to retake a factory just outside the city walls. This minor advance was mistaken by the Allied commanders as the signal for the battle to begin, which it therefore did essentially by accident.

Wittgenstein was in action by 4 p.m., advancing under heavy artillery fire as the Young Guard met the Russian attack. Five Jäger (elite light infantry) regiments and one of hussars attacked the Grosser Garten, a formal baroque garden outside the city walls, with infantry and artillery support. The French defended the Grosser Garten stubbornly, and managed to bring up a battery through the Prinz Anton Gardens to hit the enemy in the flank. Two Russian attack columns were meanwhile caught by murderous artillery fire from beyond the Elbe. By the end of the day each side held about half of the Grosser Garten. (A fine view of the battlefield can be seen today from the 300-foot dome of the Frauen-kirche.) Marshal Ney led a charge at Redoubt No. 5 composed of Young Guard units and men of Saint-Cyr's corps, which forced the Austrians to feed in reserves, but even these couldn't prevent an entire Hessian battalion from being surrounded and forced to surrender. When the first day's fighting ended at nightfall, the Allies had lost 4,000 killed and wounded, twice as many as the French.

Napoleon was reinforced by Victor's corps during the night. They went up to Friedrichstadt as Marmont moved to the centre, and the Old Guard crossed the Elbe to form a central reserve. Using the corps system effectively, Napoleon now had massed 155,000 men for the next day's fighting. It poured with rain all night and there was a thick fog on the morning of August 27. As it cleared, Napoleon spotted that the Allied army was divided by the deep Weisseritz ravine, which cut off its left wing under Count Ignaz Gyulai from its right and centre.[18] He decided on a major attack at 7 a.m. with almost all his cavalry and two corps of infantry. Murat, wearing a gold-embroidered cloak over his shoulders and a plume in his headdress, had sixty-eight squadrons and thirty guns of the 1st Cavalry Corps ready for the attack on Gyulai's corps, along with thirty-six battalions and sixty-eight guns of Victor's corps.

By 10 a.m. the Austrians were under huge pressure despite the fact that Klenau had finally rejoined the Army of Bohemia. Victor's corps and General Étienne de Bordessoule's heavy cavalry succeeded in turning their flank. At 11 a.m. Murat ordered a general assault, charging forward with the cry 'Vive l'Empereur!' Around Lobtau the Austrian infantry stood at bay, with good artillery support, streets barricaded and houses loopholed for muskets. Their skirmishers were driven back and through the patchy fog they saw the massive attack columns of Murat's infantry advancing. Under heavy artillery fire, the French made for the gaps between the villages and got past them, before turning to attack them from the rear. Although the Austrians made counter-attacks, their line of retreat was relentlessly compromised.

In the centre, the Austrians and Prussians were ready from 4 a.m., expecting to renew the fight. Marmont's task was to fix them in place while the French wings defeated the enemy. By 8 a.m. Saint-Cyr was attacking the Prussian 12th Brigade on the Strehlen heights, forcing them back to Leubnitz, where they were joined by the Russian 5th Division. This stubborn fighting was mainly done by bayonet as the heavy rain soaked the muskets' firing-pans despite their protective frizzens.

By 10 a.m. Napoleon had massed a large battery on the Strehlen heights, from where it dominated the centre of the battlefield. As Saint-Cyr paused to reorganize, he was counter-attacked by Austrian infantry. He tried to push on but the sheer weight of Allied artillery fire pinned him back. Napoleon was by his side at noon and ordered him to keep up the pressure, while the Young Guard was pitched into Leubnitz to try to wrest the village from the Silesian infantry. At 1 p.m. Napoleon was opposite the Allied centre-right, in the middle of a formidable artillery exchange where he personally directed some horse artillery that largely silenced many of the Austrian guns. During this firefight Moreau had both legs smashed by a cannonball. By the early afternoon the Prussian cavalry was beginning to move away to the right. Saint-Cyr's pressure was slowly tipping the balance.

On Napoleon's left flank, Ney began his attack at 7.30 a.m. As the Prussians had already been driven out of the Gross-garten, he used the garden to mask part of his advance. Napoleon arrived at 11 a.m. and encouraged the enthusiastic attack of the tirailleurs (skirmishers), although they were occasionally checked by Prussian and Russian cavalry. Despite Barclay de Tolly having no fewer than sixty-five squadrons of Russian and twenty of Prussian cavalry to hand, he didn't commit them. In the pouring rain this was a fight of bayonet and sabre, punctuated by blasts of artillery. Schwarzenberg contemplated a major counter-attack, only to find all his units already too heavily engaged, just as Napoleon had intended.

By 2 p.m. Napoleon was back in the centre forming a battery of thirty-two 12-pounders near Rachnitz to smash the Allied centre. At 5.30 p.m. Schwarzenberg received the news that Vandamme had crossed the Elbe at Pirna and was marching on his rear. He now had no alternative but to give up the fight altogether. (Vandamme was a reckless swashbuckler of whom Napoleon said that every army needed one, but that if there were two he would have to shoot one of them.[19]) By 6 p.m. the French had halted in the position occupied by the Allies that morning. Although both sides had lost around 10,000 men, Murat's victory on the right flank had led to the capture of 13,000 Austrians, and the French captured 40 guns.[20] When he was told that Schwarzenberg had been killed in the battle, Napoleon had exclaimed, 'Schwarzenberg has purged the curse!' He hoped his death would finally lift the shadow of the fire at his marriage celebrations in 1810. As he explained later: 'I was delighted; not that I wished the death of the poor man, but because it took a weight off my heart.'[21] Only later did he find out to his profound chagrin that the dead general was not Schwarzenberg but Moreau. 'That rascal Bonaparte is always lucky,' Moreau wrote to his wife just before he expired from his wounds on September 2. 'Excuse my scrawl. I love and embrace you with all my heart.'[22] It was brave of the renegade general to apologize for his handwriting while dying, but he was wrong about Napoleon's extraordinary run of good luck.

'I've just gained a great victory at Dresden over the Austrian, Russian and Prussian armies under the three sovereigns in person,' Napoleon wrote to Marie Louise. 'I am riding off in pursuit.'[23] The next day he corrected himself, saying 'Papa François had the good sense not to come along.' He then said Alexander and Frederick William 'fought very well and retired in all haste'. Napoleon was harder on the Austrians. 'The troops of Papa François have never been so bad,' he told his Austrian-born wife. 'They put up a wretched fight everywhere. I have taken 25,000 prisoners, thirty colours and a great many guns.'[24] In fact it had been the other way around; the Allied sovereigns and generals had failed their men strategically and tactically in their positioning and lack of co-ordination, and it was only the stubborn, brave troops who had saved the two-day battle from becoming a rout.

Riding over the battlefield in the driving rain worsened Napoleon's cold, and he was struck with vomiting and diarrhoea after the battle. 'You must go back and change,' an old *grognard* called out to him from the ranks, after which the Emperor finally went back to Dresden for a hot bath.[25] At 7 p.m. he told Cambacérès, 'I am so tired and so preoccupied that I cannot write at length; [Maret] will do so for me. Things are going very well here.'[26] He couldn't afford to be ill for long. 'In my position,' he had written in a general note to his senior commanders only a week earlier, 'any plan where I am not myself in the centre is inadmissible. Any plan which removes me to a distance establishes a regular war in which the superiority of the enemy cavalry, in numbers, and even in generals, would completely ruin me.'[27] Here was an open recognition that his marshals couldn't be expected to pull off the coups necessary to win battles against forces 70 per cent larger than theirs – indeed that most of them to his mind were barely capable of independent command.

This judgement was largely confirmed when on August 26 – the first day of the battle of Dresden – in Prussian Silesia on the Katzbach river (present-day Kaczawa) Marshal Macdonald, with 67,000 men of the French army and the Rhine Confederation, was crushed by Blücher's Army of Silesia.[28] On St Helena Napoleon would confirm his opinion: 'Macdonald and others like him were good when they knew where they were and under my orders; further away it was a different matter.'[29] The very next day General Girard's corps was effectively destroyed at Hagelberg on the 27th by the Prussian Landwehr, which had only recently exchanged its pikes for muskets, and some Cossacks. Girard's stricken and much depleted force made it back to Magdeburg only with the greatest difficulty. On August 29 General Jacques Puthod's 17th Division of 3,000 men was trapped up against the flooded River Bober at Plagwitz, fired off all their ammunition and had to surrender en masse. They lost three eagles, one of which was found in the river after the battle.[30]

Hoping to hold up Schwarzenberg's retreat into Bohemia, Napoleon ordered Vandamme to leave Peterswalde (now Piotraszewo, in Poland) with his force of 37,000 men and to 'penetrate into Bohemia and throw back the Prince of Württemberg'. The goal was to cut the enemy lines of communication with Tetschen, Aussig and Töplitz (now Děčín, Ústi and Teplice, in the Czech Republic). But Barclay, the Prussian General Kleist and Constantine together had twice Vandamme's numbers and although his troops fought valiantly and exacted a heavy toll he was forced to surrender on the 30th near the hamlet of Kulm (now Chlumec, in the Czech Republic) with 10,000 of his men. Napoleon had sent Murat, Saint-Cyr and Marmont to attack the Austrian rearguard at Töplitz as Vandamme bravely held up its vanguard, but they couldn't save him. Napoleon himself was ill and unable to leave his bedroom; even on the afternoon of the 29th he could only get as far as Pirna.[31] When Jean-Baptiste Corbineau arrived the next day with the disastrous news Napoleon could only say: 'That's war: very high in the morning and very low in the evening: from triumph to failure is only one step.'[32]

By the end of August all the advantage Napoleon had gained from his victory at Dresden had been thrown away by his lieutenants. Yet there was more bad news to come. Having sent Ney off to resume the attack on Berlin to recover the situation after Oudinot's defeat by Bernadotte, on September 6 Ney and Oudinot together were defeated by General von Bülow at the battle of Dennewitz in Brandenburg. Bavaria then declared her neutrality, which made other German states consider their position, especially once the Allies proclaimed the abolition of the Confederation of the Rhine at the end of the month.

Napoleon spent most of September in Dresden, occasionally dashing out to engage any Allied forces that came too close, but incapable of making any large, campaign-winning strokes because of the Allies' determination to avoid giving him battle, while continuing to concentrate on his subordinates. These were frustrating weeks for him, and his impatience and distemper would occasionally show. When General Samuel-François l'Héritier de Chézelles' 2,000 men of the 5th Cavalry Corps were attacked by 600 Cossacks between Dresden and Torgau, he wrote to Berthier that Chézelles' men should have fought them more aggressively even if they 'had neither sabres nor pistols, and were armed only with broomsticks'.[33]

This kind of fighting was bad for morale, and on September 27 an entire Saxon battalion deserted to Bernadotte, under whom they had fought at Wagram. In Paris Marie Louise asked for a *sénatus-consulte* for a levy of 280,000 conscripts, no fewer than 160,000 of them an advance on the 1815 class year, the 1814 year having already been called up. Yet there was already widespread opposition to further conscription over large areas of France.

General Thiébault, a divisional commander in the campaign, accurately summed up the situation in the autumn of 1813:

> The arena of this gigantic struggle had increased in an alarming fashion. It was no longer the kind of ground of which advantage could be taken by some clever, secret, sudden manoeuvre, such as could be executed in a few hours, or at most in one or two days. Napoleon . . . could not turn the enemy's flank as at Marengo or Jena, or even wreck an army, as at Wagram, by destroying one of its wings. Bernadotte to the north with 160,000 men, Blücher to the east with 160,000, Schwarzenberg to the south with 190,000, while presenting a threatening front, kept at such a distance as to leave no opening for one of those unforeseen and rapid movements which, deciding a campaign or a war by a single battle, had made Napoleon's reputation. The man was annihilated by the presence of space. Again, Napoleon had never till then had more than one opposing army to deal with at one time; now he had three, and he could not attack one without exposing his flank to the others.[34]

By early October Allied forces were moving across the French lines of communication at will, and there were several days when Napoleon could neither send nor receive letters. The situation worsened significantly on October 6 when Bavaria declared war against France. 'Bavaria will not march seriously against us,' a philosophical Emperor told Fain, 'she will lose too much with the full triumph of Austria and the disaster of France. She knows well that the one is her natural enemy, and the other is her necessary support.'[35] The next day Wellington crossed the Bidasoa river out of Spain, leading the first foreign army onto French soil since Admiral Hood had vacated Toulon twenty years earlier. With Blücher and 64,000 men crossing the Elbe, and the 200,000-strong Army of Bohemia marching towards Leipzig, Napoleon left Saint-Cyr in Dresden and headed northwards with 120,000 men, hoping to chase Blücher back over the Elbe and then return to fight Schwarzenberg, while all the time posing a credible threat to Berlin.

By October 10 the three Allied armies under Schwarzenberg, Blücher and Bernadotte, totalling 325,000 men, were converging upon Leipzig, hoping to trap Napoleon's much smaller army there. 'There will inevitably be a great battle at Leipzig,' Napoleon wrote to Ney at 5 a.m. on October 13, the same day he discovered that the Bavarian army had joined the Austrians and were now threatening the Rhine.[36] Despite being greatly outnumbered (he could muster a little over 200,000 men), Napoleon decided to fight for the city which the British journalist Frederic Shoberl described the following year as 'undoubtedly the first commercial city of Germany, and the great Exchange of the Continent'.[37] He drew his men up in ranks of two rather than three, after Dr Larrey persuaded him that many of the head wounds he was seeing weren't self-inflicted, as Napoleon had suspected, but were the result of men reloading and discharging their muskets close to the heads of comrades kneeling in the ranks in front of them. 'One of the advantages of this new disposition', Napoleon said, 'will be to cause the enemy to believe that the army is one third stronger than it is in reality.'[38]

On October 14, as the Imperial Guard arrived from Düben (now Coswig), Napoleon spent the night in the house of a M. Wester in Leipzig's eastern suburb of Reudnitz. As usual the *maréchal de logis* had chalked the names of the generals who occupied each room on their doors, and a fire was immediately made up in Napoleon's room, 'as His Majesty was very fond of warmth'.[39] The Emperor then chatted to Wester's chief clerk.

NAPOLEON: 'What is your master?'
CLERK: 'He is in business, Sire.'
NAPOLEON: 'In what line?'
CLERK: 'He is a banker.'
NAPOLEON: (smiling) 'Oho! Then he is worth a plum.'

CLERK: 'Begging your Majesty's pardon, indeed he is not.'
NAPOLEON: 'Well then, perhaps he may be worth two?'

They discussed discount bills, interest rates, the clerk's wages, the present (woeful) state of business, and the owner's family. 'During the whole conversation the Emperor was in very good humour, smiled frequently, and took a great deal of snuff,' recalled Colonel von Odeleben.[40] When he left, he paid 200 francs for the pleasure of staying there, which, as one of his aides-de-camp noted, 'was certainly not the usual custom'.

The next day Schwarzenberg's 200,000 men came into contact with Murat to the south, spending the whole day in patrols and skirmishes while Blücher advanced along the Saale and White Elster rivers. Riding a cream-coloured mare that day, Napoleon distributed eagles and colours to three battalions. Drums beat as each was taken from its box and unfurled, to be given to the officers. 'In a clear solemn tone, but not very loud, which might be distinguished by the musical term *mezza voce*', a spectator recalled Napoleon saying:

> 'Soldiers of the 26th regiment of light infantry, I entrust you with the French eagle. It will be your rallying point. You swear to abandon it but with life? You swear never to suffer an insult to France. You swear to prefer death to dishonour. You swear!' He laid particular emphasis upon this last word, pronounced in a peculiar tone, and with great energy. This was the signal at which all the officers raised their swords, and all the soldiers, filled with enthusiasm, exclaimed with common consent, in a loud voice, accompanied by the ordinary acclamations: 'We swear!'

This ceremony used to be attended by band music, but no longer: 'Musicians had become scarce, since the greater part of them had been buried in the snows of Russia.'[41]

Among the half-million men who fought at Leipzig in 'The Battle of the Nations' – the largest battle in European history up to that moment – were French, Germans (on both sides), Russians, Swedes, Italians, Poles, every nationality within the Austrian Empire and even a British rocket section.[42] The battle was fought over three days, on the 16th, 18th and 19th of October 1813. Napoleon had almost the whole of the French field army under him, comprising 203,100 men, of whom only 28,000 were cavalry, and 738 guns. Those absent were Saint-Cyr's corps at Dresden (30,000 men), Rapp's besieged at Danzig (36,000), Davout's at Hamburg (40,000) and some 90,000 who were in hospital. In total by the last day of the battle the Allies had been able to bring up a total of 362,000 men and 1,456 guns, almost twice as many as the French.[43] The battlefield was vast, cut in two by the White Elster and Pleisse rivers, with open plains to the east and hills that provided artillery platforms and screened troops behind them.*

Captain Adolphe de Gauville, who was wounded at Leipzig, recalled that on the dark, gloomy and rainy morning of October 16, 'at 5 a.m. Napoleon had an armchair and a table brought to him in a field. He had a great many maps. He was giving his orders to a great number of officers and generals, who came to receive them one after the other.'[44] Napoleon calculated that he could engage 138,000 men against Schwarzenberg's force of 100,000 to the south of the city and knew he had one or at best two days to subdue him before Blücher, Bernadotte and Bennigsen arrived from the north-west, north and east respectively. (Bennigsen's advance troops – the Cossacks – arrived on the battlefield on the first day of combat, and the main body late on the 17th, ready for action the next day. Bernadotte's troops also arrived then.)

The battle began early on the 16th when the Prussians took the village of Markkleeberg from Poniatowski's Poles in bitter street fighting made worse by racial hatred. Wachau was relatively lightly held and fell quickly to Russian forces backed by a Prussian brigade, but any attempt to push beyond it was stopped by French artillery. When Napoleon arrived there sometime between noon and 1 p.m. he formed a battery of 177 guns, under whose heavy cannonade he launched a major counter-attack, forcing the Russians back onto the Leipzig Plain, where there was no cover and grapeshot cut many of them down.

The Austrian General Ignaz Gyulai threatened Napoleon's only escape route to the west – if one became necessary – so General Henri Bertrand's corps was detached to protect it, significantly weakening Napoleon's main attack. Gyulai became fixated on capturing Lindenau, near the road, and a real crisis developed in the late afternoon when the Austrians, despite strong artillery fire, stormed the burning village. Bertrand fell back and regrouped before counter-attacking at 5 p.m. He managed to clear the road completely, but Gyulai had made an important contribution by pinning down Bertrand's corps.

At 10 a.m. Klenau advanced on Liebertwolkwitz, which fell quite

---

* Today it is best viewed from the 270-foot-high platform atop the Völkerschlachtdenkmal (Monument to the Battle of the Nations).

quickly except for the church and the northern end of the village. A swift counter-attack pushed the Austrians straight back out again. General Gérard was wounded leading his largely Italian division against Kleinpösna before Mortier brought up his Young Guard divisions to secure the area. By 11 a.m. the Allies were back at their start lines, exhausted and denuded of reserves. Napoleon, surprised by their aggression, had been forced to move his own reserves in sooner than he would have liked. Friant's Old Guard took the Meusdorf sheep farm, and two divisions of the Young Guard under Oudinot and the mass of reserve cavalry concentrated behind Wachau.

As the fog lifted across the battlefield, Napoleon could assess his clear superiority. Seeing an opportunity to split the Allied line at its weakest point at Wachau, he threw Macdonald's corps in at noon to turn the Allied right flank. At about 2 p.m. he personally encouraged the 22nd Légère to storm the heights dominating Grosspösna, known as the Kolmberg, teasing them with the taunt that they were merely standing at the base under heavy fire with their arms crossed.[45] Although they took the heights, their movement was spotted by Alexander, Frederick William and Schwarzenberg, who sent in the Prussian reserves to stop them. (As earlier in the campaign, the two monarchs were now there in merely advisory and morale capacities, with the military decisions being taken by the professional soldiers.)

Out on the plain, Murat massed cavalry between Wachau and Liebertwolkwitz in dense columns to support Oudinot and Poniatowski. At 2.30 p.m. Bordessoule's cavalry led the charge in the centre, breaking through the Prince of Württemberg's infantry and getting in among the artillerymen of the Allied grand battery. Eighteen squadrons, totalling 2,500 sabres, charged the Russian Guard Cavalry Division and overthrew it, heading on towards the Allied headquarters. Yet the French infantry failed to follow up this charge, and after Bordessoule's force was slowed by marshy ground it had to retreat, and took a good deal of punishment as it did so, including from friendly fire.

Napoleon had been waiting for Marmont to arrive from the north but by 3 p.m. he decided to launch his general assault with the troops he had at hand. He pushed his artillery well forward to batter the enemy centre, launched continual cavalry charges and counter-charges, ordered infantry volleys at close range and brought the Allied line almost to breaking point, but fresh Austrian troops, some of whom waded up to their waists in the Pleisse to enter the action faster, and the sheer

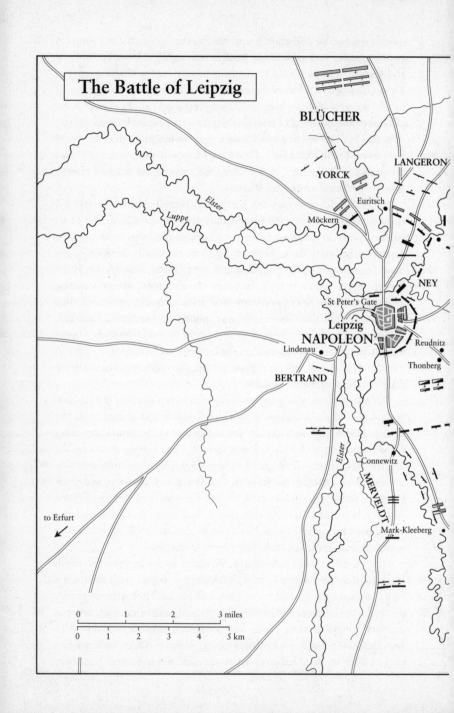

The Battle of Leipzig

BLÜCHER

LANGERON

YORCK

Euritsch

Möckern

NEY

St Peter's Gate

Leipzig
NAPOLEON

Reudnitz

Lindenau

Thonberg

BERTRAND

Elster

Luppe

Elster

Connewitz

MERVELDT

to Erfurt

Mark-Kleeberg

0	1	2	3 miles
0	1	2	3	4	5 km

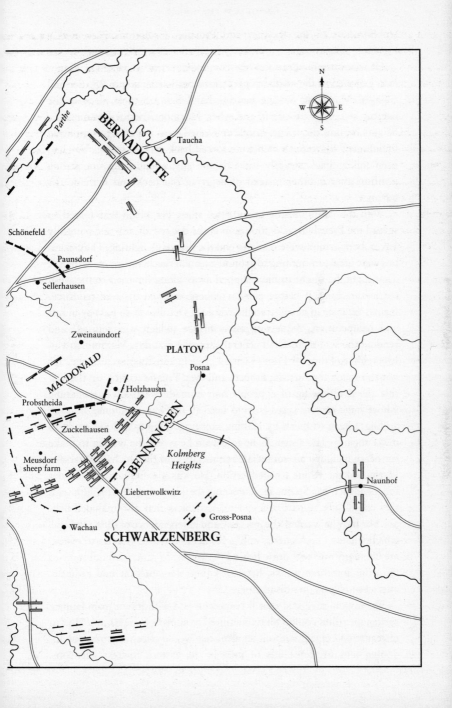

stubbornness of the Russian and Prussian formations prevented a French breakthrough.

Hearing sustained cannon-fire from the direction of Möckern, Napoleon galloped to the northern part of the battlefield, where Blücher had engaged Marmont. Savage hand-to-hand fighting took place in the narrow streets of Möckern, and when Marmont tried to get onto the heights beyond the village Yorck unleashed a cavalry charge supported by infantry. Marmont's men were forced back inside Leipzig. Ney had been falling back steadily towards the city, abandoning one strong position after another instead of delaying Blücher's and Bernadotte's advance.

With the Allies closing in on three sides, Napoleon was forced to spread the French attacks too thinly to be decisive at any one point. By 5 p.m. both armies were ready to end the first day's fighting. The casualties were great, amounting to around 25,000 French and 30,000 Allies.[46] That night, he ought to have slipped away along the road to the west, extricating himself before Schwarzenberg received massive reinforcements. Yet instead he allowed the whole of October 17 to pass by in rest and recuperation, requesting an armistice (which was refused) and sending the senior Austrian general captured that day, Maximilian von Merveldt, to Emperor Francis with a crudely anti-Russian message. 'It's not too much for Austria, France, and even Prussia to stop on the Vistula the overflowing of a people half nomad, essentially conquering, whose huge empire spreads from here all the way to China,' he said, adding 'I have to finish by making sacrifices: I know it; I am ready to make them.'[47] The sacrifices he told Fain he would be willing to make for peace included an immediate renunciation of the Duchy of Warsaw, Illyria and the Rhine Confederation. He was also willing to consider independence for Spain, Holland and the Hanseatic Towns, although that could only be part of a general settlement that also included Britain. For Italy he wanted 'the integrity and independence of the Kingdom', which sounded ambiguous, unlike his actual offer to Austria to evacuate Germany and withdraw behind the Rhine.[48] Francis did not reply to the offer for three weeks, by which time the situation had radically altered to Napoleon's disadvantage.[49]

Wellington later said that if Napoleon had withdrawn from Leipzig earlier, the Allies couldn't have ventured to approach the Rhine.[50] But to retreat from Leipzig without an armistice would effectively mean abandoning tens of thousands of men in the eastern fortress garrisons.

Napoleon feared that the Saxons and Württembergers would then fall away from him as the Bavarians already had done. So instead of retreating towards Erfurt he organized his munitions supply – the French artillery was to fire 220,000 cannonballs during the battle, three times more even than at Wagram – and concentrated his whole army in a semicircle on the north-east and southern sides of the city, while sending Bertrand and Mortier to secure the exit routes should an escape become necessary.[51] He succumbed to a heavy bout of influenza on the night of the 17th, but he had decided to fight it out. However, the arrival of Bernadotte's and Bennigsen's divisions meant that while Napoleon had been reinforced by the addition of 14,000 men of Reynier's corps since the start of the battle, Schwarzenberg had been reinforced by over 100,000 men.[52]

After riding out towards Lindenau at about 8 a.m. on October 18, Napoleon spent most of the day at the tobacco mill at Thonberg, where the Old Guard and Guard cavalry were held in reserve.* By that time, the sun was shining and the armies were ready to engage. For the renewal of the battle Schwarzenberg had organized six great converging attacks, comprising 295,000 men and 1,360 guns. He hoped to take Connewitz, Mark-Kleeberg, Probstheida, Zuckelhausen, Holzhausen, Lindenau and Taucha before crushing the French army in Leipzig itself.

When Bennigsen arrived later in the morning he captured Holzhausen and its neighbouring villages from Macdonald. To Macdonald's left were Reynier's reinforcements, who included 5,400 Saxons and 700 Württembergers, but at 9 a.m. these fresh arrivals suddenly deserted to the Allies with thirty-eight guns, leaving a yawning gap in Napoleon's line that General Jean Defrance's heavy cavalry division attempted to fill.[53] The Saxon battery actually turned around, unlimbered and began firing on the French lines. They had fought for Napoleon for seven years since deserting the Prussians after Jena, and such cool treachery was bad for French morale.

Von Bülow soon captured the village of Paunsdorf. Napoleon threw in units from the Old and Young Guard to recapture it, but the sheer weight of Prussian numbers forced even these elite units out. Probstheida, defended by Victor and Lauriston, became a veritable fortress that could not be seized at all that day despite the Tsar taking a close

---

* The mill forms the centrepiece of the magnificent diorama at the Bavarian Army Museum in Ingolstadt.

personal interest in its capture. Two Prussian brigades tried three times without success, and the 3rd Russian Infantry Division had to fall back sullenly behind its screen of light infantry. Napoleon was so concerned by the weight of these attacks that he pushed Curial's Old Guard Division up in support, but was thankful they weren't needed.

North of Leipzig a battle raged for Schönefeld between Marmont and Langeron, a French émigré general fighting in the Russian army. By bringing up all the guns of Souham's corps to add to his, Marmont managed to oppose Langeron's 180 cannon with 137 of his own. The ground between these two enormous batteries was swept clear: six French generals were killed or wounded in cannonading that carried on until nightfall, when Marmont evacuated back to his entrenchments outside Leipzig. While Langeron engaged Marmont, Blücher pushed for the suburbs of Leipzig. Ney launched two divisions in a counter-attack, contesting the village of Sellerhausen. It was in this engagement that the British fired their noisy and highly lethal Congreve rockets with powerful effect, not least on French morale. Although rockets had been known about for sixteen years, and their efficacy had been attested at Copenhagen in 1807, Napoleon hadn't developed a rocket capacity of his own.

Napoleon personally led some Old Guard and Guard cavalry over to counter-attack at Zweinaundorf at about 4.30 p.m., standing aside only at the last minute as they went into action. But the Allies fought them to a standstill and a tide of Russians and Prussians drove the French steadily backwards. 'Here, I saw the Emperor under a hail of enemy canister,' recalled Johann Röhrig, a company sergeant-major of French voltigeurs. 'His face was pale and as cold as marble. Only occasionally did an expression of rage cross his face. He saw that all was lost. We were only fighting for our withdrawal.'[54] After having to pay 2 crowns (that is, six francs, or three days' wages) for eight potatoes from some Old Guard grenadiers, Röhrig wrote of that day:

> I cannot understand that such a clever commander as the Emperor could let us starve. It would have been a very different life in that army if sufficient food had been available. And yet, no one who has not experienced it can have any idea of the enthusiasm which burst forth among the half-starved, exhausted soldiers when the Emperor was there in person. If all were demoralized and he appeared, his presence was like an electric shock. All shouted 'Vive l'Empereur!' and everyone charged blindly into the fire.[55]

Each side lost around 25,000 men in the bitter cannonades and hand-to-hand fighting that day.

On the morning of October 19, Napoleon finally decided that the army should retreat. He told Poniatowski, to whom he had awarded a marshal's baton three days earlier, 'Prince, you will defend the southern suburbs.' 'Sire, I have so few men,' replied the Pole. 'Well, you will defend yourself with what you have!' said Napoleon. 'Ah! Sire,' answered the newly minted marshal, 'we will hold on! We are all ready to die for your Majesty.'[56] Later that day, he was as good as his word. Napoleon left the city at about 10 a.m. after visiting the King of Saxony, whose battlefield commander had not defected to the Allies as so many of his men had. 'Napoleon had the appearance of composure on his countenance when he quitted Leipzig,' recalled Colonel von Odeleben, 'riding slowly through St Peter's Gate, but he was bathed in sweat, a circumstance which might proceed from bodily exertion and mental disturbance combined.'[57] The retreat was chaotic, with 'Ammunition wagons, gendarmes, artillery, cows and sheep, women, grenadiers, post-chaises, the sound, the wounded, and the dying, all crowded together, and pressed on in such confusion that it was hardly possible to hope that the French could continue their march, much less be capable of defending themselves.'[58] The confusion worsened considerably once the Allied assault on the city began at 10.30 a.m.

Pontoon bridges had not been built over the Pleisse, Luppe or White Elster rivers, so everyone had to cross by the single bridge over the Pleisse in the city, which was reached at the end of a series of narrow streets. Catastrophically, the bridge was blown up at 11.30 a.m., long before the whole army had got over it, which led to well over 20,000 men being captured unnecessarily and turned the defeat into a rout. Napoleon's 50th bulletin blamed Colonel Montfort by name for delegating the duty to a 'corporal, an ignorant fellow but ill comprehending the nature of the duty with which he was charged'.[59] People and animals were still on the bridge when the explosion shook the city, raining the body parts of humans and horses into the streets and river.[60] Some officers decided to try to swim across to avoid capture. Macdonald made it, but Poniatowski's horse, which he had ridden into the river, could not climb up the opposite bank and fell back on top of him. Both were swept away by the current.[61] The fisherman who hauled Poniatowski's corpse out of the river did well from selling his diamond-studded epaulettes, rings and snuffboxes to Polish officers who wanted to return them to his family.[62] Napoleon's red-leather briefcase for foreign news-papers, emblazoned *Gazettes Étrangères* in gold lettering, was captured, along with his carriage, and opened in the presence of Bernadotte.*

'Between a battle lost and a battle won,' Napoleon had said on the eve of the battle of Leipzig, 'the distance is immense and there stand empires.'[63] Between the dead and the wounded, Napoleon lost around 47,000 men over the three days. Some 38,000 men were captured, along with 325 guns, 900 wagons and 28 colours and standards (including 3 eagles), making it statistically easily the worst defeat of his career.[64] In his bulletin he admitted to 12,000 lost, and several hundred wagons, mainly as a result of the blown bridge. 'The disorder it has brought to the army changed the situation,' he wrote; 'the victorious French army arrives at Erfurt as a defeated army would arrive.'[65] After further deser-tions and defections, he was able to bring only 80,000 men of the Grande Armée back over the Saale out of the more than 200,000 he had had at the start of the battle. 'Typhus broke out in our disorganized ranks in a terrifying fashion,' Captain Barrès recalled. 'Thus one might say that on leaving Leipzig we were accompanied by all the plagues that can devour an army.'[66]

Napoleon conducted a fighting retreat to the Rhine, sweeping aside the Austrians at Kösen (now Bad Kösen) on the 21st, the Prussians at Freiburg (now Świedodzice, in Poland) that same day, the Russians at Hörselberg on the 27th and, in a two-day battle on the 30th and 31st, the Bavarians at Hanau. He re-crossed the Rhine at Mainz on Novem-ber 2. 'Be calm and cheerful and laugh at the alarmists,' he told his wife the next day.[67]

Napoleon still had 120,000 men besieged in the fortresses on the Elbe, Oder and Vistula, with Rapp inside Danzig (where his 40,000 effec-tives were reduced by the end to 10,000), and generals Adrien du Taillis in Torgau, Jean Lemarois in Magdeburg, Jean Lapoype in Wittenberg, Louis Grandeau in Stettin, Louis d'Albe in Küstrin and Jean de Laplane in Glogau, as well as more men in Wesel, Dresden, Erfurt, Marienburg, (now Malbork, in Poland), Modlin and Zamość. Although Davout held Hamburg and the lower Elbe, most of these eastern fortresses fell one by one in late 1813, often as the result of starvation. A few held out until the end of the 1814 campaign, but none played any useful part besides holding down local militia units in sieges. It was a sign of

---

* Today it can be seen in the excellent Armoury Museum next to the Royal Palace in Stockholm.

Napoleon's invincible optimism to have left so many men so far to the east. By 1814, most of them were prisoners-of-war.

The 1813 campaign had claimed the lives of two marshals, Bessières and Poniatowski, and no fewer than thirty-three generals. It also saw the defection of Murat, who while he was with Napoleon at Erfurt on October 24, secretly agreed to join the Allies in exchange for a guarantee that he would remain king of Naples. Yet Napoleon was not disheartened, or at least not publicly. Arriving in Paris on November 9 he (in Fain's words) 'exerted every effort to turn his remaining resources to the best account'.[68] He replaced Maret as foreign minister with Caulaincourt (after twice offering the position to the unemployed Talleyrand in order to show his conciliatory intentions), imposed an emergency levy of 300,000 new recruits, of which he got 120,000 despite the now powerful anti-conscription sentiment in the country, and seriously entertained a peace offer from the Allies, brought from Frankfurt by the Baron de Saint-Aignan, his former equerry and Caulaincourt's brother-in-law.[69] Under what were termed the Frankfurt bases of peace, France would return to her so-called 'natural frontiers' of the Ligurian Alps, the Pyrenees, the Rhine and the Ardennes – the so-called 'Bourbon frontiers' (even though the Bourbons had regularly crossed them in wars of conquest). Napoleon would have to abandon Italy, Germany, Spain and Holland, but not all of Belgium.[70] At that point, with only a few garrisons holding out in Spain and unable to defend the Rhine with anything more than bluster, Napoleon told Fain he was prepared to surrender Iberia and Germany, but he resisted giving away Italy, which in wartime 'could provide a diversion to Austria', and Holland, which 'afforded so many resources'.[71]

On November 14, the same day that the Frankfurt proposals arrived, Napoleon made a speech to Senate leaders at the Tuileries. 'All Europe was marching with us just a year ago,' he told them frankly, 'today all Europe is marching against us. The fact is that the opinion of the world is formed by France or by England . . . Posterity will say that if great and critical circumstances arose they were not too much for France or for me.'[72] The next day he instructed Caulaincourt that if the British army arrived at the Château de Marracq near Bayonne 'it be set fire to, also all the houses which belong to me, so that they may not sleep in my bed'.[73]

Although he ordered the doubling of the *droits réunis* on tobacco and postage and doubled the tax on salt in order to raise 180 million francs, he admitted to Mollien that the measures were 'a *digestif* that I was saving to the last moment of thirst'. As he was down to 30 million francs in the treasury, that moment had now arrived.[74] He ordered that all payments of pensions and salaries be suspended so that the orders made by the war administration ministry could still be honoured.

After the Allies made the Frankfurt terms public on December 1, stating that they would 'guarantee the French Empire a larger extent of territory than France ever knew under her kings', Pasquier and Lavalette informed Napoleon that their intelligence services indicated the French people wanted him to accept.[75] 'The moment of the rendezvous has arrived,' Napoleon told Savary melodramatically; 'they look at the lion as dead, who will begin taking his delayed vengeance? If France abandons me, I cannot do anything; but they'll soon regret it.'[76] The following day Caulaincourt wrote to Metternich agreeing to the 'general and summary bases'.[77] On December 10, as Wellington crossed the Nive river and Soult withdrew to the Adour, Metternich replied to say that the Allies were waiting for Britain's reply to Caulaincourt's offer. The Napoleonic Wars could have ended there and then, but the British were opposed to a peace that left France in possession of any part of the Belgian coast from which Britain could be invaded, specifically Antwerp. Castlereagh's opposition to Metternich's terms wrecked the Frankfurt peace attempt, especially once he had arrived in Europe in January 1814 and encouraged the Tsar to oppose peace of any kind with Napoleon.[78] He did not believe that a lasting peace would be possible if Napoleon remained on the throne of France.

'Brilliant victories glorified French arms during this campaign,' Napoleon told the Legislative Body on December 19, 'defections without example rendered those victories useless. Everything turned against us. Even France would be in danger were it not for the energy and unity of Frenchmen.' Only Denmark and Naples remained faithful, he said – though privately he was having doubts about Naples, telling his sister the Grand Duchess Elisa of Tuscany not to send any muskets to their sister Caroline and her husband, Murat, who were back in Italy negotiating with the Austrians once more. He told the Legislative Body that 'he would raise no objection to the re-establishment of peace', and ended defiantly: 'I have never been seduced by prosperity; adversity shall find me superior to its blows.'[79]

Napoleon's speech to the Senate was equally tough-minded. 'At the sight of the whole nation in arms, the foreigner will flee or sign peace on the bases which he himself proposed. It is no longer a question of recovering the conquests we have made.'[80] Although the Senate stayed loyal, on December 30 the Legislative Body voted by 223 to 51 in favour of a long critique of Napoleon's actions, which ended with a demand for political and civil rights. 'A barbarous and endless war swallows up periodically the youth torn from education, agriculture, commerce and the arts,' it concluded.[81] The French had allowed him his first defeat in Russia, but this second catastrophe at Leipzig, coming so soon afterwards, turned many of them against him. If he wished to remain in power, Napoleon had little alternative other than to banish the document's authors, led by Joseph Lainé, and forbid its publication. The next day he prorogued the Legislative Body.

With fewer than 80,000 men under arms, Napoleon now faced 300,000 Russians, Prussians and Austrians on the Rhine, and 100,000 Spanish, British and Portuguese coming over the Pyrenees.[82] 'The moment when the national existence is threatened is not the one to come to talk to me about constitutions and the rights of the people,' Napoleon told Savary. 'We are not going to waste our time in puerile games while the enemy is getting closer.'[83] Now that the Allies were crossing the Rhine, national unity was more important than political debate. France was about to be invaded and Napoleon was determined to fight.

28

Defiance

'When an army is inferior in number, inferior in cavalry and in artillery, it is essential to avoid a general action.'

Napoleon's Military Maxim No. 10

'It was Rome that Pompey needed to keep; there that he should have concentrated all his forces.'

Napoleon, *Caesar's Wars*

On earlier occasions when France was in danger of invasion – in 1709, 1712, 1792–3 and 1799 – her large army and great border fortresses built in the seventeenth century by the military engineer Sébastien de Vauban had protected her.[1] This time it was different. The sheer size of the Allied forces enabled them to outflank her formidable line of north-eastern forts – such as Verdun, Metz, Thionville and Mézières – and besiege them. Moreover, for this they could rely on their second-line troops, such as Landwehr, militias and the soldiers of minor German states. In 1792–3, the Austrian and Prussian armies invading France had numbered only 80,000 men, but were confronted by 220,000 Frenchmen under arms. In January 1814 Napoleon faced a total of 957,000 Allied troops with fewer than 220,000 men in the field – 60,000 of whom under Soult and 37,000 under Suchet were fighting Wellington's Anglo-Spanish-Portuguese army in the south-west of France and 50,000 under Eugène were defending Italy. Napoleon's army rarely numbered 70,000 in the coming campaign and was always dangerously weak in artillery and cavalry.[2]

Many were new conscripts, with little more than a coat and forage cap to distinguish them as soldiers. Yet they stayed with the colours; only 1 per cent of the 50,000 young conscripts who passed through the main depot at Courbevoie, in Paris, deserted during the 1814 campaign.[3] Often depicted as an ogre keen to shore up his rule by throwing children into the charnel-house of war, Napoleon in fact wanted no such thing. 'It is necessary that I get men, not children,' he wrote to Clarke on October 25, 1813. 'No one is braver than our youth, but . . . it is necessary to have men to defend France.' In June 1807 he had told Marshal Kellermann that 'Eighteen-year-old children are too young to be going to war far away.'[4]

Although Napoleon attempted to recreate the patriotism of 1793, even allowing street musicians to play the republican anthem the 'Marseillaise', which he had formerly banned, the old revolutionary cry of '*La Patrie en danger!*' no longer had its electrifying effect.[5] Still, he hoped the army and his own abilities might be enough to prevail. 'Sixty thousand and me,' he said, 'together one hundred thousand.'[6]* However, if the French had been as motivated as Napoleon had hoped, a guerrilla movement would have broken out in France when the Allies invaded, yet none arose. 'Public opinion is an invisible, mysterious, irresistible power,' Napoleon mused later. 'Nothing is more mobile, nothing more vague, nothing stronger. Capricious though it is, nevertheless it is truthful, reasonable, and right much more often than one might think.'[7]

Napoleon had entrenched the political and social advances of the Revolution largely by keeping the Bourbons out of power for fifteen years, after the ten between the Revolution and Brumaire, so a generation had passed since the fall of the Bastille and the French had grown accustomed to their newfound freedoms and institutions. But for many these benefits had been eclipsed by the price they had to pay in blood and treasure for the series of wars that six successive Legitimist coalitions had declared against Revolutionary and Napoleonic France. After twenty-two years of war the French people hankered for peace, and were willing to countenance the humiliation of Cossack campfires in the Bois de Boulogne to gain it. Napoleon soon discovered that he couldn't even rely on his prefects, only two of whom – Adrien de Lezay-Marnésia at Strasbourg and De Bry at Besançon – obeyed his order to take refuge in the departmental capital and resist the invasion. The others either

---

* Wellington fully agreed with this estimation: when asked in 1814 if he had ever been across a field of battle from Napoleon, he replied: 'No, and I am very glad I never was. I would at any time have rather heard that a reinforcement of forty thousand men had joined the French army, than that he had arrived to take command.' (Longford, *Years of the Sword* pp. 248–9)

'retired' – that is, fled to the interior at the first news of a skirmish – or, like Himbert de Flegny in the Vosges, simply surrendered. Some, such as Louis de Girardin of the Seine-Inférieure, hoisted the fleur-de-lys.[8] Several prefects managed to rediscover their Bonapartism when Napoleon returned from Elba, only to re-rediscover their royalism after Waterloo.[9] Claude de Jessaint, prefect of the Marne, managed to serve every regime without interruption or complaint from 1800 to 1838.

Napoleon was disappointed that so few Frenchmen answered the call to arms in 1814 – some 120,000 out of a nominal call-up several times that – but he hardly had the uniforms and muskets to furnish those who did arrive at the depots. The drafts of recent years had alienated the better-off peasants, his core constituency, and there had been violent anti-conscription riots. Under the Empire a total of 2,432,335 men were called up for conscription in the fifteen decrees, eighteen *sénatus-consultes* and one order of the Conseil that were issued between March 1804 and November 1813. Almost half of these came in 1813, when army recruiters ignored minimum age and height requirements.[10] (Young Guard recruits could now be 5 foot 2 inches where previously they had been required to be 5 foot 4.) Between 1800 and 1813 draft evasion had dropped from 27 per cent to 10 per cent, but by the end of 1813 it was over 30 per cent and there were major anti-draft riots in the Vaucluse and northern departments.[11] In Hazebrouck a mob of over 1,200 people nearly killed the local *sous-préfet* and four death sentences were imposed. In 1804 Napoleon had predicted that the unpopularity of conscription and the *droits réunis* would one day destroy him. As Pelet recorded, his 'anticipation came literally to pass, for the words *Plus de conscription – plus de droits réunis* furnished the motto on the flags of the Restoration in 1814'.[12] Taxes were extended from alcohol, tobacco and salt to include gold, silver, stamps and playing cards. The French paid, but resented it.[13]

After the Russian disaster Napoleon had had four months to rebuild and resupply his army before fighting resumed; now he had only six weeks. With the self-knowledge that was one of the more attractive aspects of his character, he said in early 1814: 'I am not afraid to admit that I have waged war too much. I wanted to assure for France the mastery of the world.'[14] That was not now going to happen, but he hoped that by striking hard blows using interior lines against whichever enemy force seemed to pose the greater threat to Paris, he might force acceptance of the Frankfurt bases for peace and so save his throne. At the same time he was philosophical about failure. 'What would people say if I were to die?' he asked his courtiers, and continued with a shrug before they were able to frame anything suitably oleaginous: 'They would say, "Ouf!"'[15]

A spectator at Napoleon's New Year's Day levée in the Tuileries throne room in 1814 recalled: 'His manner was calm and grave, but on his brow there was a cloud which denoted an approaching storm.'[16] He considered the peace terms Britain had demanded at the end of 1813, but rejected the idea. 'France without Ostend and Antwerp,' he told Caulaincourt on January 4,

> would not be on an equal footing with the other states of Europe. England and all the other powers recognised these limits at Frankfurt. The conquests of France within the Rhine and the Alps cannot be considered as compensation for what Austria, Russia and Prussia have acquired in Poland and Finland, and England in Asia ... I have accepted the Frankfurt proposals, but it is probable that the Allies have other ideas.[17]

He might also have added Russian gains in the Balkans and British acquisitions in the West Indies to the list. The arguments he put for continued resistance were that 'Italy is intact', that 'The depredations of the Cossacks will arm the inhabitants and double our forces' and that he had enough men under arms to fight several battles. 'Should Fortune betray me, my mind is made up,' he said with defiant resolution. 'I do not care for the throne. I shall not disgrace the nation or myself by accepting shameful conditions.' He could take the betrayals of Bavaria, Baden, Saxony and Württemberg, and those of ministers such as Fouché and Talleyrand – even of Murat and his own sister Caroline – but not that of his greatest supporter up to that point: Fortune herself. Napoleon of course knew perfectly well intellectually that Destiny and Fortune did not control his fate, but the concepts nonetheless exercised a hold on him throughout his life.

'Writing to a minister so enlightened as you are, Prince,' Napoleon began a flattering letter to Metternich on January 16 in which he asked for an armistice with Austria.[18] 'You have shown me so much personal confidence, and I myself have such great confidence in the straightforwardness of your views, and in the noble sentiments which you have always expressed.' He asked for the letter to remain secret. Of course it didn't; Metternich shared it with the other Allies, but throughout the spring of 1814 Napoleon's plenipotentiaries – principally Caulaincourt – kept up discussions with the Allies over the possibility of a peace treaty, whose terms fluctuated day by day with the fortunes of the armies. On January 21, in an attempt to win over popular opinion, the Pope was released from Fontainebleau and allowed to set off for the Vatican.

Murat's treachery was sealed on January 11 when he signed an agreement with Austria to lead 30,000 men against Eugène in Italy in return for Ancona, Romagna and the security of his throne for himself and his heirs. 'He isn't very intelligent,' Napoleon told Savary when Murat captured Rome just over a week later, 'but he'd have to be blind to imagine that he can stay there once I've gone, or when ... I've triumphed over all this.'[19] He was right; within two years Murat would be shot by a Neapolitan firing squad. 'The conduct of the King of Naples is infamous and there is no name for that of the queen', was Napoleon's response to his sister's and brother-in-law's behaviour. 'I hope to live long enough to be able to revenge myself and France for such an insult and such fearful ingratitude.'[20] By contrast, Pauline sent her brother some of her jewellery to help pay his troops. Joseph, who continued to call himself king of Spain even after Napoleon had allowed Ferdinand VII back to his country on March 24, stayed in Paris to guide the Regency Council.

'To the courage of the National Guard I entrust the Empress and the King of Rome,' Napoleon told its officers at an emotional ceremony in the Hall of the Marshals at the Tuileries on January 23. 'I depart with confidence, am going to meet the enemy, and I leave with you all that I hold most dear; the Empress and my son.'[21] The officers present cried 'Vive l'Impératrice!' and 'Vive le Roi de Rome!', and Pasquier 'saw tears running down many faces'.[22] Napoleon understood the propaganda value of his infant son, and ordered an engraving to be made of him praying, with the inscription: 'I pray to God to save my father and France.' He adored the boy, who could induce strange reflections in him; once when the infant fell and slightly hurt himself, causing a great commotion, 'the Emperor became very pensive and then said: "I've seen one cannonball take out a single line of twenty men."'[23] For all his proclaimed 'confidence' in victory, Napoleon burned his private papers on the night of the 24th, before leaving Paris for the front at six o'clock the next morning. He was never to see his wife or son again.

The Champagne region lies to the east of Paris and is crossed by the Seine, the Marne and the Aisne, river valleys that were the natural corridors for the Allied advance on the capital. The fighting there was to take place during the harshest winter in western Europe in 160 years; even the Russians were astonished at how cold it was. Hypothermia, frostbite, pneumonia, exhaustion and hunger were ever present. Typhus was again a particular concern, especially after a major outbreak at the Mainz camp. 'My troops! My troops! Do they really imagine I still have an army?' Napoleon told his prefect of police, Pasquier, at this time. 'Don't they realise that practically all the men I brought back from Germany have perished of that terrible disease which, on top of all my other disasters, proved to be the last straw? An army indeed! I shall be lucky if, three weeks from now, I manage to get together 30,000 to 40,000 men.'[24] Nine of the campaign's twelve battles were fought in an area of just 120 miles by 40 – half the size of Wales – on land that was flat and covered in snow, which was ideal country for cavalry, had he had any. Facing him were the two main Allied armies, Blücher's Army of Silesia and Schwarzenberg's Army of Bohemia, about 350,000 men. In all, the Allies fielded nearly a million troops.*

Whereas in 1812 Napoleon's army had grown so large that he had been forced to rely on his marshals taking largely independent commands, once it had contracted to 70,000 he was able to control it in the direct and personal way he had in Italy. Berthier and seven other marshals were with him – Ney, Lefebvre, Victor, Marmont, Macdonald, Oudinot and Mortier – and he was able to use them much as he had when some of them had been mere generals or divisional commanders over a decade before; each of them had only 3,000 to 5,000 troops under his command. (Of the others, Bernadotte and Murat were now fighting against him, Saint-Cyr had been captured, Jourdan, Augereau and Masséna were governing military districts, Soult and Suchet were in the south, and Davout was still holding out in Hamburg.)

Taking command of only 36,000 men and 136 guns at Vitry-le-François on January 26, Napoleon ordered Berthier to distribute 300,000 bottles of champagne and brandy to the troops there, saying, 'It's better that we should have it than the enemy.' Seeing that while Blücher had pushed well forward, Schwarzenberg had veered slightly away from him, he attacked the Army of Silesia at Brienne in the afternoon of the 29th.[25] 'I could not recognize Brienne,' Napoleon said later. 'Everything seemed changed; even distances seemed shorter.'[26] The only place he recognized was a tree under which he had read Tasso's *Jerusalem Delivered*.

---

* Whereas the Prussians and Austrians fought in half the battles each during the 1814 campaign, such was the Tsar's insistence on taking Paris (on which he was advised by Napoleon's old enemy from Corsica, Count Pozzo di Borgo) that the Russians fought in every major battle except Montereau.

Napoleon's guide during the battle was the local curate, one of his old schoolmasters, who rode Roustam's horse, which was later killed by a cannonball immediately behind Napoleon.[27] It was the surprise storming of the chateau at Brienne, during which Blücher and his staff were nearly captured, and its retention despite vigorous Russian counter-attacks, that helped give Napoleon his victory. 'As the battle did not begin until an hour before nightfall, we fought all night,' Napoleon reported to his war minister, Clarke. 'If I had had older troops I should have done better ... but with the troops I have we must consider ourselves lucky with what happened.'[28] He had come to respect his opponent and said of Blücher, 'If he was beaten, the moment afterwards he showed himself ready as ever for the fight.'[29] On Napoleon's return to his headquarters at Mézières, a Cossack band came close enough for one of them to thrust a lance at him, only to be shot dead by Gourgaud. 'It was very dark,' recalled Fain, 'and amidst the confusion of the night encampment, the parties could only recognize each other by the light of the bivouac fires.'[30] Napoleon rewarded Gourgaud with the sword he had worn at Montenotte, Lodi and Rivoli.

When he took stock of the situation after the battle he found he had lost 3,000 casualties, and Oudinot was wounded yet again. Retreating from Brienne to Bar-sur-Aube, the Prussians were joined by some of Schwarzenberg's Austrian contingents in the plain between the two towns. Napoleon couldn't refuse battle as the bridge over the Aube at Lesmont, the principal line of retreat, had been destroyed earlier in the campaign in order to stop Blücher's advance on Troyes. He had stayed a day too long, and although his force had been reinforced by Marmont's corps to number 45,000 men it was attacked across open ground by 80,000 Allies at La Rothière, 3 miles from Brienne, on February 1. The French defended the village until dark but Napoleon lost nearly 5,000 men which he could ill afford, although the Allies lost more. He also lost seventy-three guns, and was forced to retreat, sleeping in Brienne Château and ordering a retreat to Troyes over the barely rebuilt Lesmont bridge. The next day Napoleon wrote to Marie Louise telling her not to watch L'Oriflamme at the Opéra: 'So long as the territory of the Empire is overrun by enemies, you should go to no performances.'[31]

After La Rothière, believing Napoleon to be retreating to Paris, the Allies separated again, Schwarzenberg heading due west to the valleys of the Aube and Seine while Blücher marched to the Marne and Petit-Morin valleys on a parallel line, 30 miles to the north. Their armies were really too large to march together logistically, and the gap between them allowed Napoleon to operate deftly between the two forces. It was to these next four battles that Wellington was referring when he said of Napoleon's 1814 campaign, it 'has given me a greater idea of his genius than any other. Had he continued that system a little longer, it is my opinion that he would have saved Paris.'[32]

'The enemy troops behave horribly everywhere,' Napoleon wrote to Caulaincourt from a deserted Brienne. 'All the inhabitants seek refuge in the woods; no more peasants are found in the villages. The enemy eat up everything, take all the horses, cattle, clothes and all the rags of the peasants; they beat everyone, men and women, and commit rape.'[33] Of course Caulaincourt, who had been on the Russian campaign, knew perfectly well how invading armies, including the French, behaved. Was this letter written for the record? The next sentence gives a clue to its intent: 'The picture which I have just seen with my own eyes should make you understand easily how much I desire to extricate my people as soon as possible from this state of misery and suffering, which is truly terrible.'[34] Napoleon was presenting a humanitarian rationale to Caulaincourt for accepting decent terms if they were offered at the peace negotiations that had begun on February 5 at Châtillon-sur-Seine.*

The Congress of Châtillon sat until March 5. Knowing that they had the upper hand through sheer weight of numbers, the Allies dropped the proposal for France to return to her 'natural' frontiers, as they had suggested at Frankfurt, and, led by the British plenipotentiary Lord Aberdeen, demanded that France return to her 1791 frontiers instead, which didn't include any part of Belgium. At his coronation Napoleon had sworn 'to maintain the integrity of the territory of the Republic' and he meant to keep to it. 'How can you expect me to sign this treaty, and thereby violate my solemn oath!' he asked Berthier and Maret, who were urging him to end the war even on these punishing terms.

> Unexampled misfortunes have torn from me the promise of renouncing the conquests that I have myself made, but shall I renounce those that were made before me! Shall I violate the trust that was so confidently reposed in me? After the blood that has been shed, and the victories that have been gained, shall I leave France smaller than I found her? Never! Can I do so without deserving to be branded a traitor and a coward?[35]

* Excepting the Cossacks, the Allied armies were actually remarkably well disciplined in France in 1814. At the museum dedicated to Napoleon's 1814 campaign at Saint-Dizier one can see the requisition chits signed by Allied officers for cash payments to peasants and merchants for their produce.

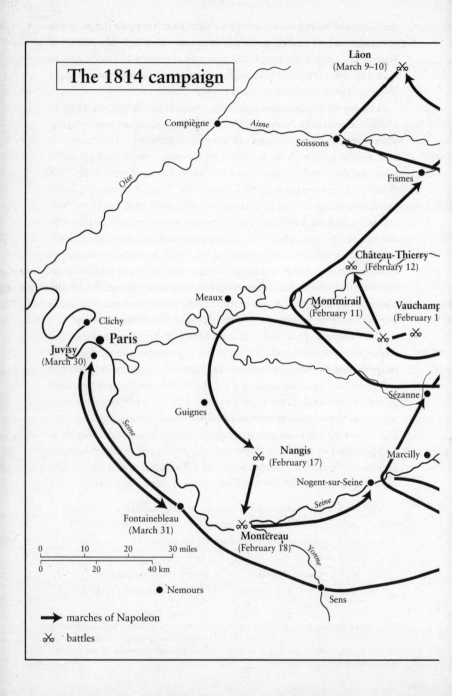

The 1814 campaign

Lâon
(March 9–10)

Compiègne

Aisne

Soissons

Oise

Fismes

Château-Thierry
(February 12)

Meaux

Montmirail
(February 11)

Vauchamp
(February 1

Clichy

Paris

Juvisy
(March 30)

Seine

Sézanne

Guignes

Marcilly

Nangis
(February 17)

Nogent-sur-Seine

Seine

Fontainebleau
(March 31)

Montereau
(February 18)

Yonne

| 0 | 10 | 20 | 30 miles |

| 0 | 20 | 40 km |

● Nemours

Sens

→ marches of Napoleon

⚔ battles

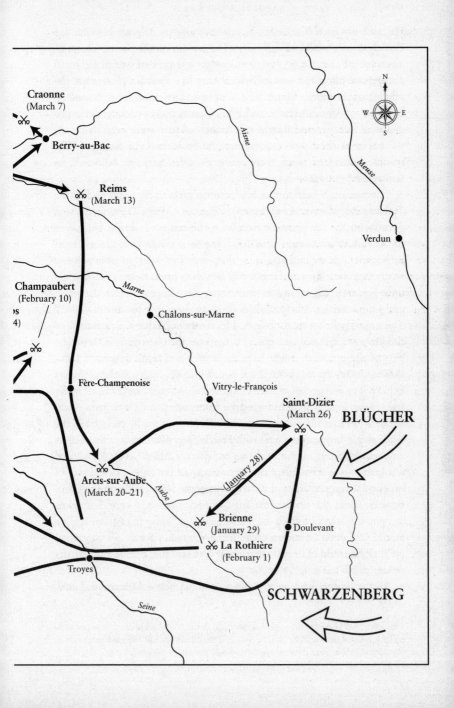

Craonne
(March 7)

Berry-au-Bac

Reims
(March 13)

Aisne

Meuse

Verdun

Champaubert
(February 10)

Marne

Châlons-sur-Marne

Fère-Champenoise

Vitry-le-François

Saint-Dizier
(March 26)

BLÜCHER

Arcis-sur-Aube
(March 20–21)

Aube

(January 28)

Brienne
(January 29)

Doulevant

Troyes

La Rothière
(February 1)

Seine

SCHWARZENBERG

He later admitted that he felt he couldn't give up Belgium because 'the French people would not allow [me] to remain on the throne except as a conqueror'. France, he said, was like 'air compressed within too small a compass, the explosion of which was like thunder'.[36] Against the advice of Berthier, Maret and Caulaincourt, therefore, Napoleon counted on Allied disunity and French patriotism – despite little evidence of either – and fought on. As his soldiers were now living off the backs of their own countrymen, he bemoaned the fact that 'The troops, instead of being their country's defenders, are becoming its scourge.'[37]

The treasury's bullion was loaded onto carts in the courtyard of the Tuileries on February 6 and secretly taken out of Paris. Denon requested permission for the Louvre's pictures to be removed, which Napoleon did not grant on grounds of morale. Napoleon tried to keep Marie Louise's spirits up, writing at 4 a.m. that day: 'I'm sorry to hear you are worrying; cheer up and be gay. My health is perfect, my affairs, while none too easy, are not in bad shape; they have improved this last week, and I hope, with the help of God, to bring them to a successful issue.'[38] The next day he wrote to Joseph, 'I fervently hope that the departure of the Empress will not take place,' otherwise 'the consternation and despair of the populace might have disastrous and tragic results.'[39] Later that same day he told him: 'Paris is not in such straits as the alarmists believe. The evil genius of Talleyrand and those who sought to drug the nation into apathy have hindered me from summoning it to arms – and see to what pass they have brought us!'[40] He had finally recognized the truth about Talleyrand – who with Fouché was planning a coup in Paris and openly discussing surrender terms with the Allies.* Napoleon could not bring himself to accept that the apathy of the nation in the face of invasion was a reflection of its loss of appetite for war. Writing to Cambacérès about the new mania for forty-hour 'misery' church services praying for salvation from the Allies, he asked, 'Have the Parisians gone mad?' To Joseph he commented, 'If these monkey tricks are continued we'll all be afraid of death. Long ago it was said that priests and doctors render death painful.'[41]

All the leaders who were planning to oust him – Talleyrand, Lainé,

---

* In 1814 men like Talleyrand and Fouché could desert Napoleon because their positions under a restoration would by now be secure; if the Bourbons had returned much earlier, regicides like them, even turncoat regicides, would have been executed.

Lanjuinais, Fouché and others – had opposed or betrayed him in the past, yet he hadn't imprisoned them, let alone executed them. In this, Napoleon resembled his hero Julius Caesar, who was assassinated by people to whom he had shown clemency and decided not to mark down for the judicial murders that Sulla had employed before him, and Octavian would afterwards.

As the political situation darkened at Châtillon, Napoleon began to think about his own death, writing to Joseph about the prospect of Paris falling. 'When it comes I will no longer exist, consequently it is not for myself that I speak,' he said on February 8. 'I repeat to you that Paris shall never be occupied during my life.'[42] Joseph replied, not very helpfully, 'If you desire peace, make it at any price. If you cannot do so, it is left to you to die with fortitude, like the last emperor of Constantinople.'[43] (Constantine XI had died in battle there in 1453 when the city was overwhelmed by the Ottomans.) Napoleon more practically replied, 'That is not the question. I am just working out a way of beating Blücher. He is advancing along the road from Montmirail. I shall beat him tomorrow.'[44] He did indeed, and then again and again in a series of high-tempo victories that, despite being very close to each other geographically and chronologically, were quite separate battles.

Posting Victor at Nogent-sur-Seine and Oudinot at Bray, Napoleon marched north to Sézanne with Ney and Mortier, and was joined on the way by Marmont. The Army of Silesia was still moving parallel to the Army of Bohemia but at a much faster pace. As it pulled too far ahead it presented not just its flank but almost its rear to Napoleon, who was poised between the two Allied armies. Spotting that the Russians had no cavalry with them and were isolated, Napoleon struck at their open flank and fell upon the centre of Blücher's over-extended army at Champaubert on February 10, destroying the best part of General Zakhar Dmitrievich Olsufiev's corps and capturing an entire brigade, for the loss of only six hundred killed, wounded and missing. He dined with Olsufiev at Champaubert's inn that evening, writing to Marie Louise, to whom he sent Olsufiev's sword, 'Have a salute fired at Les Invalides and the news published at every place of entertainment . . . I expect to reach Montmirail at midnight.'[45] The chorus of the Opéra, where Jean-Baptiste Lully's *Armide* was being performed, sang 'La Victoire est à Nous'.

On the 11th General von Sacken broke from the Trachenberg strategy and attacked Napoleon directly at Marchais on the Brie plateau overlooking the Petit-Morin valley.* Ney defended Marchais while Mortier and Friant counter-attacked the Russians at L'Épine-aux-Bois and Guyot's cavalry came around their rear, routing the Russians and Prussians. It was a classic example of Napoleon's tactic of defeating the main enemy force (under Sacken) while successfully holding off the enemy's secondary force (under the command of Yorck). Napoleon slept that night in a farmhouse at Grénaux, where, Fain recalled, 'the dead bodies having been removed, the headquarters were established'.[46] Writing to his wife at 8 p.m., Napoleon ordered a salute of sixty guns fired in Paris, claiming that he had taken 'the whole of their artillery, captured 7,000 prisoners, more than 40 guns, not a man of this routed army escaped'.[47] (He had actually captured 1,000 prisoners and 17 guns.)

The fact that many of Sacken's and Yorck's soldiers had escaped was evident the next day, when Napoleon attacked them at Château-Thierry, despite his being outnumbered two to three. Spotting that a Russian brigade was isolated on the extreme right of the Allied line, Napoleon ordered his few cavalry to ride them down, which they did, capturing a further fourteen guns.[48] Macdonald's failure to capture the bridge at Château-Thierry allowed the Allies to escape to the north side of the Marne, however. 'I've been in the saddle all day, *ma bonne* Louise,' Napoleon told the Empress from the chateau, along with another tissue of propaganda data, ending 'My health is very good.'[49] For all these victories over the Army of Silesia, nothing could make it possible for Oudinot's corps of 25,000 men and Victor's of 14,000 to hold the five bridges over the Seine and prevent Schwarzenberg's 150,000-strong Army of Bohemia from crossing.[50]

On February 14 Napoleon scored yet another victory over Blücher, at Vauchamps. Leaving Mortier at Château-Thierry at 3 a.m., he doubled back to support Marmont, whom Blücher was forcing to retreat from Étoges to Montmirail. A sudden assault of 7,000 Guard cavalry forced Blücher and Kleist to retreat to Janvilliers, where Grouchy attacked their flank and Drouot's fifty guns wrought further havoc. This secured the Marne from the Silesian army, which was beaten and dispersed, though not 'annihilated' as the official bulletin claimed.

---

* The fighting at the battle of Montmirail took place not where the memorial is today, but in and around the neighbouring village of Marchais; locally the battle is known as Marchais-Montmirail. When one visits the battlefield it is noticeable how topographically accurate Horace Vernet's splendid painting of it is, in London's National Gallery.

Napoleon could now hasten to confront the Army of Bohemia, which had forced Oudinot and Victor back from the bridges over the Seine and was driving deep into France, capturing Nemours, Fontainebleau, Moret and Nangis.* Elsewhere, in a sure sign of national demoralization, French towns and cities were starting to surrender even to small Allied units. Langres and Dijon fell without a fight, Épinal surrendered to fifty Cossacks, Mâcon to fifty hussars, Reims to a half-company, Nancy to Blücher's outriding scouts, and a single horseman took the surrender of Chaumont.[51] Napoleon's hopes for a national uprising against the invader, with guerrilla actions to rival those of Spain and Russia, were not going to be realized.

Pausing only to send 8,000 Prussian and Russian prisoners-of-war to be marched down the Parisian boulevards to substantiate his (accurate) claim of four victories in five days at Champaubert, Montmirail, Château-Thierry and Vauchamps, Napoleon left his headquarters at Montmirail at 10 a.m. on February 15 to join Victor's and Oudinot's corps at Guignes, 25 miles south-east of Paris. By the evening of the 16th he had placed his army across the main road to the capital. He found Schwarzenberg's force strung out over 50 miles and hoped to defeat it piecemeal, writing to Caulaincourt: 'I am ready to cease hostilities and to allow the enemy to return home tranquilly, if they will sign the preliminary bases of the propositions of Frankfurt.'[52] As Lord Aberdeen was still refusing to allow Napoleon to retain control over Antwerp, however, the fighting had to continue.

On February 17 Napoleon marched on Nangis, where Wittgenstein had three Russian divisions. He attacked with Kellermann on the left and General Michaud on the right, broke the Russian squares and smashed them with Drouot's guns. To secure the bridges over the Seine he then split his forces at the Nangis road junction. Victor headed for the bridge at Montereau 12 miles to the south and on the way attacked a Bavarian division at Villeneuve, but he failed to press home his advantage after a long march and many days of continual fighting. In one of his few unwarranted substitutions, Napoleon replaced him with General Étienne Gérard. He also humiliated General Guyot in front of his men, and ordered a court martial of General Alexandre Digeon when

---

* When Colonel Josef Simonyi led his Hungarian hussars into Fontainebleau Palace and emptied his pipe on Napoleon's throne, it was a conscious re-enactment of an earlier Hungarian hussar commander, Count Andreas Hadik, who in a daring raid on Berlin in 1757 had emptied his pipe on the throne of Frederick the Great (Hollins, *Hungarian Hussar* p. 44).

his battery ran out of ammunition. 'Napoleon acted with a degree of severity in which he was himself astonished,' wrote his apologist Baron Fain, 'but which he conceived to be necessary in the imperious circumstances of the moment.'[53] Military orders are naturally terse; Napoleon was often rude to his senior commanders, who were brave and conscientious soldiers, albeit of varying degrees of competence. Yet even now he could contemplate the situation with a degree of humour. 'Should fortune continue to favour us', he wrote to Eugène, 'we shall be able to preserve Italy. Perhaps the King of Naples will then change sides again.'[54]

Arriving at Montereau at the confluence of the Seine and the Yonne with the Imperial Guard at 3 p.m. on the sunny and cloudless day of February 18, Napoleon set up batteries on the Surville heights above the town, firing canister shot at full range at the Allied infantry crossing the two bridges and preventing the Württemberger engineers from demolishing them. (Looking up from the bridges the heights look like a hillock, but from the place he chose to site his guns on top of them it immediately becomes clear that they dominate the town.) The Austrians were attacked by General Louis Huguet-Chateau, whose force was beaten off, though Chateau himself was killed. Napoleon then sent in a cavalry charge led by General Pajol that crashed down the steep cobbled road, across both bridges and into the town itself.* 'I am happy with you,' he said to Pajol afterwards, as heard by Pajol's aide-de-camp, Colonel Hubert Biot. 'If all my generals had served me as you did, the enemy wouldn't be in France. Go take care of your wounds, and when you've recovered I will give you ten thousand horses to say hello to the King of Bavaria from me! ... If the day before yesterday in the morning I had been asked for four million francs to have the Montereau bridges at my disposal, I would have unhesitatingly given them.'[55] Biot afterwards joked to Pajol that in that case the Emperor might have parted with 1 million to reward him without too much difficulty.

The next day Napoleon denied to Caulaincourt that the Austrians had reached Meaux, but they had. Sacken's cannon were now distinctly audible in Paris itself, although the Russian commander pulled back on the news that Napoleon was intending to attack Blücher again.[56] That day Napoleon wrote angrily to his police minister, the usually reliable

---

* Sadly the phrase that Napoleon is supposed to have uttered that day – 'Never fear, my friends, the cannonball that will kill me has not yet been cast' – was one of a number that seem to have been invented later by a journalist writing for the *Journal Général de France*.

Savary, for permitting poems to be published in the Paris papers saying how great a soldier he was because he was constantly defeating forces thrice his number. 'You must have lost your heads in Paris to say such things when I am constantly giving out that I have 300,000 men,' wrote Napoleon, who had in fact commanded only 30,000 at Montereau; 'it is one of the first principles of war to exaggerate your forces. But how can poets, who endeavour to flatter me, and to flatter the national self-love, be made to understand this?'[57] To Montalivet, who had written of France's desire for peace, Napoleon retorted, 'You and [Savary] know no more of France than I know of China.'[58]

In a desperate attempt to split the Allies, Napoleon wrote to Emperor Francis on February 21 asking for the Frankfurt bases of peace to be re-offered 'without delay', saying that the Châtillon terms were 'the realisation of the dream of Burke, who wished France to disappear from the map of Europe. There are no Frenchmen who would not prefer death to conditions which would render them the slaves of England.' He then raised the spectre of a Protestant son of George III on the throne of Belgium.[59] As with all his earlier attempts, this had no effect.

Concerned that Augereau, whom he had made commander of the Army of the Rhône but whose heart was no longer in the fight, had still not made a significant contribution to the campaign despite having been reinforced with troops from Spain, Napoleon wrote to him in Lyons: 'If you are still the Augereau of Castiglione, keep the command; but if your sixty years weigh upon you, hand over the command to your senior general.'[60] This only had the effect of further alienating the disillusioned old warrior, who failed to march north but instead evacuated Lyons and fell back to Valence. Ney and Oudinot broached the subject of peace in a conversation with Napoleon at Nogent on the 21st, which ended in a severe reprimand and an invitation to lunch. When Wellington crossed the Adour and defeated Soult soundly at Orthez on February 27, however, the strategic situation became even more desperate.[61]

Although armistice discussions were carried on by the Comte de Flahaut at Lusigny between February 24 and 28, which Napoleon hoped might end with a return to the Frankfurt bases, he insisted that the fighting must carry on. 'I do not intend to be fettered by these negotiations,' he told Fain, as he had been during the Armistice of Pleischwitz the previous year. On March 1, 1814 the Allies signed the Treaty of Chaumont with each other, agreeing to make no separate peace with Napoleon, declaring their aim of each contributing an army of

150,000 men to oust him and end French influence over Switzerland, Italy, Belgium, Spain and the Netherlands.

As her husband's Empire was on the brink of catastrophe, Marie Louise revealed herself to be a lightweight young woman quite unsuited to the rigours of a crisis. 'I have had no news from the Emperor,' she wrote in her diary. 'He is so casual in his ways. I can see he is forgetting me.' From his replies to the trivialities in her letters about court tittle-tattle, scenes with the King of Rome's governess, matters of etiquette and so on, it seems she was either unaware of or uninterested in the earthquake taking place around her. Perhaps she was simply concentrating on the prattle of the pet parrot given her by her lady-in-waiting the Duchesse de Montebello (Lannes' widow) in order to drown out the noise of a collapsing empire and the war between her husband and her father. She and her ladies-in-waiting shredded linen to make dressings for the wounded, but what really interested her were sketching, handkerchief-embroidery, music, cards and flowers. She even asked whether she could write to Caroline Murat, to which Napoleon replied: 'My answer is *No*: she behaved improperly towards me, who of a mere nobody made a queen.'[62] On March 2 Napoleon tried to put her to some useful work organizing the donation to the military hospitals of 1,000 stretchers, straw mattresses, sheets and blankets from Fontainebleau, Compiègne, Rambouillet and other palaces. He added that he was chasing the Prussians, 'who are much exposed', and the next day he erroneously reported the wounding of 'Bulcher' (*sic*).[63]

On March 6 Victor – to whom Napoleon had given a division of the Young Guard after his unfair demotion – captured the heights above the town of Craonne, 55 miles north-east of Paris, even though the plateau was protected by three ravines and the Russians were covering the defile with sixty guns. At the battle there the next day Napoleon attempted unsuccessfully to turn both flanks but finally had to resort to a bloody frontal attack to defeat Blücher's Russian advance guard. Drouot's aggressive use of an eighty-eight-gun battery, and Ney's debouching on to the right wing, finally won Napoleon the field of battle after one of the bloodiest clashes of the campaign. The fighting took place all along the 2-mile-long plateau of the Chemin des Dames, from the Hurtebise farmhouse to the village of Cerny, between 11 a.m., when the farm was cleared, and 2.30 p.m. The very narrow front, hardly more than the width of a single field, contributed significantly to the high losses on both sides. Today's idyllic, poppy-filled meadow gives no indication of the bitterness of the resistance of the Russians, who were able to retreat unmolested so exhausted were the French. Craonne was a victory, but when news of it reached Paris the Bourse fell on the assumption that the war would now continue.[64]

The next day both sides rested and reorganized. On the 9th and 10th Napoleon attacked the main Prussian army at Lâon, the well-fortified capital of the Aisne department 85 miles north-east of Paris. (From the walls of Lâon one can see the entire battlefield laid out below, just as the Prussian and Russian officers did.) In an inversion of Austerlitz, the sun burned off the mist on the plain by 11 a.m., allowing Blücher's staff to count Napoleon's army of only 21,000 infantry and 8,000 cavalry, against 75,000 Allied infantry and 25,000 cavalry, although Napoleon had more guns. So respectful were they of his skill as a tactician, however, that they assumed there must be a ruse, and didn't counter-attack in full force, though they did engage with larger numbers.

Marmont was only 4 miles away with 9,500 men and 53 guns, but he might not have heard the battle being fought on the plain and so failed to support his Emperor. Because of his later conduct Marmont has been accused of treachery at Lâon, but a strong wind blowing from the west on that battlefield could have drowned out the noise. Yet nothing can excuse him and his staff for not posting sentries properly on the evening of the 9th, as a Prussian corps under Yorck and Kleist mounted a successful surprise night-raid on his camp which completely scattered his force. Napoleon disastrously chose to renew his attack the next day, not realizing until 3 p.m. that he was facing a vastly superior Allied force. He lost 4,000 killed and wounded, with 2,500 men and 45 guns captured.

Though his army had been reduced from 38,500 (including Marmont's troops) to fewer than 24,000 by the end of March 10, Napoleon showed extraordinary resilience and moved off immediately to attack Reims, hoping to cut through the Allied lines of communication. Yet that same day, the whole concept of lines of communication started to become moot when a letter from Talleyrand arrived at Tsar Alexander's headquarters, telling him that the siege preparations in Paris had been badly neglected by Joseph, and encouraging the Allies to march straight on to the capital.

Talleyrand's final defection was only to be expected – he had been planning for it on and off for the five years since Napoleon had called him a shit in silk stockings – but on March 11 Napoleon was given to understand that his own brother Joseph was making a more intimate betrayal by apparently attempting to seduce his wife. 'King Joseph says very tiresome things to me,' Marie Louise told the Duchesse de Montebello.[65] Writing from Soissons, Napoleon was clearly concerned. 'I have received your letter,' he told the Empress.

> Do not be too familiar with the King; keep him at a distance, never allow him to enter your private apartments, receive him ceremoniously as Cambacérès does, and when in the drawing room do not let him play the part of adviser to your behaviour and mode of life . . . When the King attempts to give you advice, which it is not his business to do, as I am not far away from you . . . be cold to him. Be very reserved in your manner to the King; no intimacy and whenever you can do so, talk to him in the presence of the Duchess and by a window.[66]

Was Joseph trying to play the role of Berville in *Clisson et Eugénie*? Napoleon suspected so, writing to the Empress the next day:

> Will it be my fate to be betrayed by the King? I would not be surprised if such were to be the case, nor would it break down my fortitude; the only thing that could shake it would be if you had any intercourse with him behind my back and if you were no longer to me what you have been. Mistrust the King; he has an evil reputation with women and an ambition which has been habitual with him in Spain . . . I say it again, keep the King away from your trust and yourself . . . All this depresses me rather; I need to be comforted by the members of my family, but as a rule I get nothing but vexation from that quarter. On your part, however, it would be both unexpected and unbearable.[67]

To Joseph himself Napoleon wrote: 'If you want to have my throne, you can have it, but I ask of you only one favour, to leave me the heart and the love of the Empress . . . If you want to perturb the Empress-Regent, wait for my death.'[68]* Was Napoleon becoming paranoid in these letters? Joseph had stopped visiting his mistresses, the Marquesa de Montehermoso and the Comtesse Saint-Jean d'Angély, and within a year Marie Louise would indeed betray Napoleon sexually, with an enemy general.[69] Marmont recorded how hubristic and divorced from reality Joseph had by now become, believing that Napoleon had removed him from his command in Spain in 1813 'because he was jeal-

---

* This letter, which was not published in the original volumes of Napoleon's correspondence in the 1850s, is in the Archives Nationales.

ous of him', and insisting that he could have ruled Spain successfully, recognized by the rest of Europe, 'without the army, without my brother'.[70] Such views, if Marmont wasn't inventing them, were of course totally delusory.

On March 16 Napoleon gave Joseph specific orders: 'Whatever happens, you must not allow the Empress and the King of Rome to fall into the enemy's hands ... Stay with my son and do not forget that I would sooner see him drowned in the Seine than captured by the enemies of France. The tale of Astyanax, captive of the Greeks, has always struck me as the saddest page of history.'[71] The infant Astyanax, son of Prince Hector of Troy, according to Euripides and Ovid, was flung off the city walls – although according to Seneca he jumped. 'Give a little kiss to my son,' Napoleon wrote less melodramatically the same day to Marie Louise. 'All you tell me about him leads me to hope that I shall find him much grown; he will soon turn three.'[72]

After taking Reims by storm on March 13, Napoleon fought at Arcis-sur-Aube on the 20th and 21st against the Austrians and Russians under Schwarzenberg, the fourth and last defensive battle of his career. He had with him only 23,000 infantry and 7,000 cavalry and he thought he was confronting the Allied rearguard, whereas in fact there were over 75,000 soldiers of the Army of Bohemia in the fields beyond the bridge over the fast-flowing, caramel-coloured river. During the 1814 campaign, Napoleon covered over 1,000 miles and slept in forty-eight different places in sixty-five days. Yet for all this movement, his three defeats – La Rothière, Lâon and Arcis – all came from staying too long in the same place, as he did at Arcis on the 21st. 'I sought a glorious death disputing foot by foot the soil of the country,' Napoleon later reminisced of the battle, where a howitzer shell disembowelled a horse he was riding but left him unscathed. 'I purposely exposed myself; the balls flew around me, my clothes were pierced, but none reached me.'[73] He later regularly mentioned Arcis as the place – along with Borodino and Waterloo – where he would have most liked to have died.

On March 21 Napoleon moved on Saint-Dizier, where he again hoped to cut the Allies' lines of communications. If Paris could only hold out for long enough he could then attack them in the rear. Yet did the Parisians have the stomach for a siege, or would they collapse as the rest of France was doing? That same day Augereau had allowed the Austrians to take Lyons without bloodshed. Napoleon nonetheless

hoped that the workers of Paris and the National Guard might barri-
cade the streets and keep the Allies out, telling Caulaincourt on the
24th, 'Only the sword can decide the present conflict. One way or the
other.'[74]

On the 23rd the Allies captured a courier with a letter from Napoleon which told Marie Louise that he was heading for the Marne 'in
order to push the enemy as far as possible from Paris and to draw closer
to my positions'. Also seized was a letter from Savary imploring Napoleon to return to Paris as the regime was crumbling and being openly
conspired against.[75] Both confirmed the Allied high command in their
plan to move on Paris. Sending his light cavalry to Bar-sur-Aube and the
Guard towards Brienne, Napoleon harried them as best he could, but
although he beat back clouds of Russian cavalry in a series of skirmishes around Saint-Dizier the next day, the main bodies of the Allied
armies were now all converging on the badly neglected defences of
Paris.[76] The capital's lack of strong fortifications was a fault Napoleon
later acknowledged fully; he had planned to put a battery of long-range
cannon on top of both the Arc de Triomphe and the Temple of Victory
at Montmartre, but neither was ready.[77]

On March 27 Macdonald brought Napoleon a copy of an enemy
Order of the Day, announcing that Marmont and Mortier had been
defeated at the battle of Fère-Champenoise on the 25th. He couldn't
believe it was true and argued that since the order was dated March
29 it must be Allied propaganda. Drouot, whom Napoleon nicknamed
'the sage of the Grande Armée' for his wise counsel, pointed out that the
printer had inserted a '6' upside-down in error. 'Quite right,' Napoleon
exclaimed on checking, 'that changes everything.'[78] He now needed to
get to Paris at all costs. That evening he gave the order to march away
from Saint-Dizier via the road to Troyes, his left flank covered by the
Seine, ready to strike towards Blücher on his right.

At a long meeting in Paris on the night of the 28th Joseph, who had
completely lost his nerve, had persuaded the Regency Council that it
was Napoleon's wish for the Empress and government to escape from
the capital and move to Blois on the Loire, using as evidence a letter that
was a month old and had since been twice superseded by different
orders. He was supported by Talleyrand (who was already drawing up
lists of ministers to serve in his post-Napoleonic provisional government), the regicide Cambacérès (who didn't want to fall into Bourbon
hands), Clarke (whom Louis XVIII soon afterwards made a peer of
France) and the Empress herself, who 'was impatient to get away'.[79]

Savary, Pasquier and the president of the Legislative Body, the Duc de Massa, thought that the Empress would get much better terms for herself and her son if she remained, and Hortense warned her that 'In leaving Paris, you lose your crown', but at 9 a.m. on March 29 the imperial convoy left the capital for Rambouillet with 1,200 men of the Old Guard, reaching Blois by April 2.[80] Cambacérès, 'accompanied by some faithful friends who would not leave him', took the seals of state to Blois in a grand mahogany box.[81]

On Wednesday, March 30, 1814, as Napoleon moved from Troyes via Sens towards Paris as fast as his soldiers could march, 30,000 Prussians, 6,500 Württembergers, 5,000 Austrians and 16,000 Russians under Schwarzenberg engaged 41,000 men under Marmont and Mortier in Montmartre and other Parisian suburbs. Despite putting out a proclamation on March 29 saying 'Let us arm to protect the city, its monuments, its wealth, our wives and children, all that is dear to us', Joseph left the city once the fighting started the next day.[82] Marmont and Mortier were hardly facing impossible odds, yet they considered the situation irretrievable and succumbed to Schwarzenberg's threats to destroy Paris. At seven o'clock the next morning, they opened talks with a view to surrendering the city.[83] Although Mortier marched his corps out of the city to the south-west, Marmont kept his corps of 11,000 men stationary over the coming days. As the enemy closed in, the elderly Marshal Sérurier, governor of Les Invalides, supervised the burning and hiding of trophies, including 1,417 captured standards and the sword and sash of Frederick the Great.

The Emperor reached Le Coeur de France, a staging post-house at Juvisy only 14 miles from Paris, sometime after 10 p.m. on March 30. General Belliard arrived there soon after to inform him of Paris's capitulation after only one day's indecisive fighting. Napoleon called Berthier over and plied Belliard with questions, saying 'Had I arrived sooner, all would have been saved.'[84] Exhausted, he sat for over a quarter of an hour with his head in his hands.[85]* He considered simply marching on to Paris regardless of the situation there, but was persuaded not to by his generals.[86] Instead he became the first French monarch to lose the capital since the English occupation of 1420–36. He sent Caulaincourt

---

* This was a characteristic pose of his when facing adversity, but also might have been the result of the headaches which, as he told his doctor, 'occasionally troubled him the greater part of his life' (BL Lowe Papers 20156 fol. 28).

to Paris to sue for peace and went to Fontainebleau, where he arrived at 6 a.m. on the 31st. An auto-da-fé of flags and eagles was conducted in the forest there (although some escaped the bonfire and can be seen in the Musée de l'Armée in Paris today).[87]

When the Allied armies entered Paris by the Saint-Denis gate on April 1, with white ribbons on their arms and green sprigs in their shakos, they were greeted by the populace with the exuberance that victorious armies always tend to receive. Lavalette was particularly disgusted by the sight of 'Women dressed as for a fete, and almost frantic with joy, waving their handkerchiefs crying: "Vive l'Empereur Alexander!"'[88] Alexander's troops bivouacked on the Champs-Élysées and Champ de Mars. There was no evidence that Parisians were willing to burn down their city sooner than cede it to their enemies, as the Russians had burned Moscow only eighteen months previously. The fickleness of the rest of the Empire might be judged from a Milanese deputation then on a visit to Paris to congratulate the man they had intended to call 'Napoleon the Great' for triumphing over all his enemies. On approaching the capital and hearing that it was being besieged they nonetheless decided to press on, and when they arrived promptly offered their congratulations to the Allies 'on the fall of the tyrant'.[89]

Fifteen years after supporting Napoleon's coup d'état at Brumaire, Talleyrand launched his own coup on March 30, 1814 and set up a provisional government in Paris that immediately began peace negotiations with the Allies.[90] Although Tsar Alexander had considered alternatives to restoring the Bourbons, including Bernadotte, the Orleanists or perhaps even a regency for the King of Rome, he and the other Allied leaders were persuaded by Talleyrand to accept Louis XVIII. Another regicide, Fouché, was brought into the provisional government, and on April 2 the Senate passed a *sénatus-consulte* deposing the Emperor and inviting 'Louis Xavier de Bourbon' to assume the throne. The provisional government also released all French soldiers from their oath of allegiance to Napoleon. When this was circulated among the troops it was noted that although the senior officers took it seriously, most of the other ranks treated it with contempt.[91] (One can be too pious about the solemnity of these oaths of loyalty, of course; Napoleon had sworn them to both Louis XVI and the Republic.)

At Fontainebleau, Napoleon considered his dwindling options. His own preference was still to march on Paris, but Maret, Savary, Caulaincourt, Berthier, Macdonald, Lefebvre, Oudinot, Ney and Moncey were uniformly opposed, though Ney never spoke to the Emperor in the bald, rude terms later ascribed to him;[92] some of them favoured joining the Empress at Blois. It was paradoxical that although the marshals hadn't forced abdication on Napoleon after he had been comprehensively beaten in Russia in 1812, nor after Leipzig in 1813, they did favour it when he was still winning victories in 1814, albeit with an army that was heavily outnumbered. They pointedly reminded him of his repeated statements only to do what was in the best interest of France.[93] Napoleon suspected that they wanted him to abdicate in order to protect and enjoy the chateaux and riches he had given them, and gave voice to this opinion in bitter moments.

Although he had asked some of them – Macdonald, Oudinot and especially Victor – to do the impossible in 1814, and had berated them when they could achieve only the extraordinary, the real explanation for their behaviour wasn't selfish, but rather that none could see how the campaign could possibly be won from the strategic position they were in, even if it were continued from the French interior. Since Napoleon's abdication was the only way the war could end, it was logical for them to call for it, albeit respectfully. However much Napoleon reviewed the Old Guard and other units, who on April 3 shouted 'Vive l'Empereur!' at the idea of marching on Paris, the marshals knew that the numbers simply no longer added up – insofar as they ever had during this campaign.[94] Macdonald stated in his memoirs that he didn't want to see the capital go the way of Moscow.[95] Ney and Macdonald had wanted Napoleon to abdicate immediately so that a regency might be salvaged from the wreckage, and Napoleon sent them and Caulaincourt to Paris to see if this was still possible. However, on April 4 Marmont marched his corps straight into the Allied camp to capitulate, along with all their arms and ammunition. This led the Tsar to demand Napoleon's unconditional abdication.[96] Alexander had taken his huge army right across Europe and nothing less would now do.

For the rest of his life, Napoleon went over the circumstances of Marmont's treachery again and again. Marmont was, he said, with slight but pardonable exaggeration, 'a man whom he had brought up from the age of sixteen'.[97] For his part, Marmont said Napoleon was 'satanically proud', as well as given to 'negligence, insouciance, laziness, capricious trust and an uncertainty as well as an unending irresolution'.[98] Napoleon was certainly proud, definitely not lazy, and if he was capriciously trusting, the Duc de Ragusa had been a prime beneficiary.

'The ungrateful wretch,' Napoleon said, 'he will be more unhappy than me.' The word *ragusard* was adopted to mean traitor, and Marmont's old company in the Guard was nicknamed 'Judas company'. Even three decades later, when he was an old man living in exile in Venice, children used to follow him about, pointing and shouting, 'There goes the man who betrayed Napoleon!'[99]

29
Elba

'I conclude my work with the year 1815, because everything which came after that belongs to ordinary history.'
Metternich, *Memoirs*

'True heroism consists of being superior to the ills of life, in whatever shape they may challenge to the combat.'
Napoleon on board HMS *Northumberland*, 1815

Once it became clear that Ney, Macdonald, Lefebvre and Oudinot had no stomach for a civil war, and the Allies had informed Caulaincourt on April 5 that they would give Napoleon the lifetime sovereignty of the Mediterranean island of Elba off Italy, the Emperor signed a provisional abdication document at Fontainebleau for Caulaincourt to use in his negotiations.[1] 'You wish for repose,' he told the marshals. 'Well then, you shall have it.'[2] The abdication was only for himself and not for his heirs, and he intended Caulaincourt to keep it secret as he would ratify it only once a treaty – covering Elba and granting financial and personal security for Napoleon and his family – was signed. Yet of course the news quickly leaked out, and the palace emptied as officers and courtiers left to make their peace with the provisional government. 'One would have thought,' said State Councillor Joseph Pelet de la Lozère of the exodus, 'that His Majesty was already in his grave.'[3] By April 7 the *Moniteur* didn't have enough space in its columns to print all the proclamations of loyalty to Louis XVIII that had been made by Jourdan, Augereau, Maison, Lagrange, Nansouty, Oudinot, Kellermann, Lefebvre, Hullin, Milhaud, Ségur, Latour-Maubourg and others.[4] Berthier was even appointed to command one of Louis XVIII's corps of Guards.[5] 'His Majesty was very sad and hardly talking,' Roustam recorded of these days.[6] After his stay at the Jelgava Palace in Latvia, where he had written to Napoleon asking for his throne back in 1800, Louis XVIII had moved to Hartwell House in Buckinghamshire, England, in 1807, from where he now prepared to move back to France in order to reclaim his throne, as soon as he received the news that Napoleon had abdicated.

Yet even denuded of an officer corps and general staff, Napoleon could still have precipitated a civil war had he wished. On April 7 rumours of his abdication prompted the 40,000-strong army at Fontainebleau to leave their billets at night and parade with arms and torches crying 'Vive l'Empereur!', 'Down with the traitors!' and 'To Paris!'[7] There were similar scenes at the barracks in Orleans, Briaire, Lyons, Douai, Thionville and Landau, and the white flag of the Bourbons was publicly burned in Clermont-Ferrand and other places. Augereau's corps was close to mutiny, and garrisons loyal to Napoleon attempted risings in Antwerp, Metz and Mainz. In Lille the troops were in open revolt for three days, actually firing on their officers as late as April 14.[8] As Charles de Gaulle was to observe: 'Those he made suffer most, the soldiers, were the very ones who were most faithful to him.'[9] Struck by these protestations of loyalty, the British foreign secretary, Lord Castlereagh, warned the secretary for war, Lord Bathurst, of 'the danger of Napoleon's remaining at Fontainebleau surrounded by troops who still, in a considerable degree, remain faithful to him'. This warning finally prompted the Allies to sign the Treaty of Fontainebleau, after five days of negotiation, on April 11, 1814.[10]

Caulaincourt and Macdonald arrived there from Paris with the treaty the next day, which now only required Napoleon's signature for its ratification. He invited them to dinner, noting the absence of Ney, who had stayed in the capital to make his peace with the Bourbons.[11] The treaty allowed Napoleon to use his imperial title and gave him Elba for life, making generous financial provisions for the whole family, although Josephine's outrageously generous alimony was cut to 1 million francs per annum. Napoleon himself was to receive 2.5 million francs per annum and Marie Louise was given the Italian duchies of Parma, Piacenza and Guastalla.[12] Napoleon wrote to her on April 13, saying: 'You are to have at least one mansion and a beautiful country ... when you tire of my Island of Elba and I begin to bore you, as I can but do when I am older and you still young.' He added: 'My health is good, my courage unimpaired, especially if you will be content with my ill-fortune and if you think you can still be happy in sharing it.'[13] He had not yet appreciated that the rationale for a Habsburg marrying a Bonaparte had been that he was Emperor of France; now that he was to be merely Emperor of Elba the desirability of the match collapsed. Getting hold of a book on the island he told Bausset, 'The air there is healthy and the inhabitants are excellent. I shall not be very badly off, and I hope that Marie Louise will not be very unhappy either.'[14] Yet only two hours before General Pierre Cambronne and a cavalry detachment arrived at Orleans on April 12 with orders from Napoleon to take her and the King of Rome the 54 miles to Fontainebleau, an Austrian delegation from Metternich took her and her retinue away to the chateau of Rambouillet, where she was told that her father would join her. At first she insisted that she could only leave with Napoleon's permission, but she was persuaded to change her mind easily enough, although she wrote to Napoleon that she was being taken against her will. It was not long before she gave up any plans she might have had to rejoin him, and went instead to Vienna. She had no intention of being not very unhappy.

For all his optimism in his letter to Marie Louise, on the night between the 12th and 13th, after dinner with Caulaincourt and Macdonald, Napoleon attempted to commit suicide.[15] He took a mixture of poisons 'the size and shape of a clove of garlic' that he had carried in a small silk bag around his neck since he was nearly captured by the Cossacks at Maloyaroslavets.[16] He did not try any other means of suicide, not least because Roustam and his chamberlain, Henri, Comte de Turenne, had removed his pistols.[17] 'My life no longer belonged to my country,' was Napoleon's own later explanation:

> the events of the last few days had again rendered me master of it – 'Why should I endure so much suffering?' I reflected, 'and who knows that my death might not place the crown on the head of my son?' France was saved. I hesitated no longer, but leaping from my bed, mixed the poison in a little water, and drank it with a sort of feeling of happiness. But time had taken away its strength; fearful pains drew forth some groans from me; they were heard, and medical assistance arrived.[18]

His valet Hubert, who slept in the adjoining room, heard him groaning, and summoned Yvan the doctor, who induced vomiting, possibly by forcing him to swallow ashes from the fireplace.[19]

Maret and Caulaincourt were also called during the night. Once it was clear that he wasn't going to die, Napoleon signed the abdication the next morning 'without further hesitation' on a plain pedestal table in the red and gold antechamber now known as the Abdication Room. 'The Allied powers having declared that the Emperor Napoleon was the only obstacle to the re-establishment of peace in Europe,' it stated, 'the Emperor Napoleon, faithful to his oath, declares that he renounces, for himself and his heirs, the thrones of France and Italy, and there is no personal sacrifice, even that of life, that he would not be ready to make in the interest of France.'[20]

When Macdonald went to the Emperor's apartments to collect the ratified treaty at 9 a.m. on April 13, Caulaincourt and Maret were still there. Macdonald found Napoleon 'seated before the fire, clothed in a simple dimity [lightweight cotton] dressing-gown, his legs bare, his feet in slippers, his head resting in his hands, and his elbows resting on his knees . . . his complexion was yellow and greenish.'[21] He merely said he had been 'very ill all night'. Napoleon was fulsome towards the loyal Macdonald, telling him: 'I did not know you well; I was prejudiced against you. I have done so much for, and loaded with favours, so many others who have abandoned and neglected me; and you, who owe me nothing, have remained faithful to me!'[22] He gave him Murad Bey's sword, they embraced, and Macdonald left to take the ratified treaty to Paris. They never saw each other again.

After the attempted suicide, Roustam fled Fontainebleau, later saying he feared that he might be mistaken for a Bourbon or Allied assassin if Napoleon succeeded in killing himself.[23]

On April 15 it was decided that generals Bertrand, Drouot and Pierre Cambronne would accompany Napoleon to Elba, with a small force of six hundred Imperial Guardsmen, the Allies having promised to protect the island from 'the Barbary Powers' – that is the North African states – under a special article of the treaty. (Barbary pirates were rife in that part of the Mediterranean.) The next day four Allied commissioners arrived at Fontainebleau to accompany him there, although only the British commissioner, Colonel Sir Neil Campbell, and the Austrian, General Franz von Koller, would actually be living on the island. Napoleon got on well with Campbell, who had been wounded at Fère-Champenoise when a Russian, mistaking him for a French officer, lanced him in the back while another sabred him across the head, even though he had called out lustily, 'Angliski polkovnik!' (English colonel). To his delight he was ordered by Castlereagh 'to attend the late chief of the French Government to the island of Elba' (a wording that indicates the uncertainty that already prevailed over Napoleon's exact status).[24]

Napoleon read the Parisian newspapers at Fontainebleau. Fain recalled that their abuse 'made but slight impression upon him, and when the hatred was carried to a point of absurdity it only forced from him a smile of pity'.[25] He told Flahaut that he was pleased not to have agreed to the Châtillon peace terms in February: 'I should have been a sadder man than I am if I had to sign a treaty taking from France one single village which was hers on the day when I swore to maintain her integrity.'[26] This refusal to renege on one iota of *la Gloire de la France* was to be a key factor in his return to power. For the present, Napoleon told his valet Constant: 'Ah well, my son, prepare your cart; we will go and plant our cabbages.'[27] The inconstant Constant had no such intention, however, and after twelve years' service he absconded on the night of April 19 with 5,000 francs in cash. (Savary had orders to hide 70,000 francs for Napoleon – a good deal more than the Banque de France's governor's annual salary.[28])

Meeting Napoleon on the 17th, Campbell, who spoke French well, wrote in his diary:

> I saw before me a short active-looking man, who was rapidly pacing the length of his apartment, like some wild animal in his cell. He was dressed in an old green uniform with gold epaulets, blue pantaloons, and red top-boots, unshaven, uncombed, with the fallen particles of snuff scattered profusely upon his upper lip and breast. Upon his becoming aware of my presence, he turned quickly towards me, and saluted me with a courteous smile, evidently endeavouring to conceal his anxiety and agitation by an assumed placidity of manner.[29]

In the quick-fire series of questions that Campbell came to know well, Napoleon asked about his wounds, military career, Russian and British decorations and, on discovering that Campbell was a Scot, the poet Ossian. They then discussed various Peninsular War sieges, as Napoleon spoke in complimentary terms about British generalship. He inquired 'anxiously' about the tragically unnecessary battle of Toulouse, which had been fought between Wellington and Soult with more than 3,000 casualties each side on April 10, and 'passed high encomiums' on Wellington, asking after 'his age, habits, etc' and observing, 'He is a man of energy. To carry on war successfully, one must possess the like quality.'[30]

'Yours is the greatest of nations,' Napoleon told Campbell. 'I esteem it more than any other. I have been your greatest enemy – frankly such; but am no longer. I have wished likewise to raise the French nation, but my plans have not succeeded. It's all destiny.' (Some of this flattery might have stemmed from his desire to sail to Elba in a British man-of-war rather than in the French corvette, *Dryade*, that he had been allocated, partly perhaps on account of pirates and partly because he may have feared assassination at the hands of a royalist captain and crew.)[31] He concluded the interview cordially with the words: 'Very well, I am at your disposal. I am your subject. I depend entirely on you.' He then gave a bow 'free from any assumption of hauteur'.[32] It is easy to see why many Britons found Napoleon a surprisingly sympathetic figure. During the negotiations over the treaty, Napoleon had instructed Caulaincourt to inquire as to whether he might come to Britain for his exile, comparing the society of Elba unfavourably with 'a single street' of London.[33]

When on April 18 it was discovered that the new minister of war, none other than the same General Dupont who had surrendered his corps at Bailén in Spain in 1808, had ordered that 'all the stores belonging to France must be removed' before Napoleon arrived on Elba, the Emperor refused to leave Fontainebleau on the grounds that the island would be left vulnerable to attack.[34] He nonetheless sent off his baggage the next day – though not his treasury of 489,000 francs, which would travel with him – and gave away books, manuscripts, swords, pistols, decorations and coins to his remaining supporters at the palace. He was understandably irritated when he heard about the Tsar's visit to Marie Louise at Rambouillet, complaining that it was 'Greek-like' for conquerors to present themselves before sorrowing wives. (Perhaps he was thinking of the family of Darius received by Alexander the Great.) He also railed against the visit the Tsar had paid to Josephine. 'Bah! He first breakfasted with Ney, and after that, visited her at Malmaison,' he said. 'What can he hope to gain from this?'[35]

When Berthier's former aide-de-camp General Charles-Tristan de Montholon visited the palace in mid-April with a (somewhat belated) plan to escape to the upper Loire, he 'found no one in those vast corridors, formerly too small for the crowd of courtiers, except the Duke of Bassano [Maret], and the aide-de-camp Colonel Victor de Bussy. The whole court, all his personal attendants . . . had forsaken their unfortunate master, and hastened towards Paris.'[36] This wasn't wholly true; still in attendance to the end were generals Bertrand, Gourgaud and Jean-Martin Petit (the commander of the Old Guard), the courtiers

Turenne and Megrigny, his private secretary Fain, his interpreter François Lelorgne d'Ideville, his aides-de-camp General Albert Fouler de
Relingue, Chevalier Jouanne, Baron de la Place and Louis Atthalin, and
two Poles, General Kossakowski and Colonel Wąsowicz. Caulaincourt
and Flahaut were absent but still loyal.[37] Montholon attached himself
to Napoleon's service, and never left it. Although loyalty and gratitude
in political adversity are rare, Napoleon still had the capacity to inspire
it, even when he had nothing to offer in return. 'When I left Fontainebleau
for Elba I had no great expectation of ever coming back to France,' he later
recalled. All that these last faithful attendants could expect was the animosity of the Bourbons.[38] Nor was the spirit of revenge confined to the
Bourbons: Count Giuseppe Prina, Napoleon's finance minister in Italy,
was dragged from the Senate in Milan and lynched over four hours by the
mob, after which tax documents were stuffed into the corpse's mouth.

One of the greatest scenes of the Napoleonic epic took place when he
left Fontainebleau for Elba at noon on Wednesday, April 20, 1814. The
huge White Horse courtyard of the palace – now known as the Cour des
Adieux – provided a magnificent backdrop, with its huge double staircase a proscenium, and the Old Guard drawn up in ranks a suitably
appreciative and lachrymose audience. (As the courier had not yet
arrived from Paris with assurances that Dupont's malicious order had
been rescinded, the commissioners were not even certain Napoleon
would actually leave, and were relieved when at 9 a.m. the grand
marshal of the palace, General Bertrand, confirmed that he would.)
Napoleon first met the Allied commissioners individually in one of the
reception rooms upstairs in the palace, speaking angrily to Koller for
over half an hour about his continued forced separation from his wife
and son. In the course of the conversation 'tears actually ran down his
cheeks'.[39] He also asked Koller whether he thought the British government would allow him to live in Britain, allowing the Austrian to make
the deserved rejoinder: 'Yes, Sire, for as you never made war in that
country, reconciliation will become the more easy.'[40] When Koller later
said that the Congress of Prague had provided a 'very favourable opportunity' for peace, Napoleon replied, 'I have been wrong, maybe, in my
plans. I have done harm in war. But it is all like a dream.'[41]

After shaking hands with the soldiers and few remaining courtiers
and 'hastily descending' the grand staircase, Napoleon ordered the two
ranks of *grognards* to form a circle around him and addressed them in
a firm voice, which nonetheless, in the recollection of the Prussian commissioner, Count Friedrich von Truchsess-Waldburg, occasionally

faltered with emotion.[42] His words recorded by Campbell and several others bear repetition at some length, both because they represent his oratory at this great crisis of his life and because they indicate the lines of argument he was to employ when he later tried to construct the historical narrative of this period:

> Officers, non-commissioned officers, and soldiers of the Old Guard, I bid you adieu! For twenty years I have found you ever brave and faithful, marching in the path of glory. All Europe was united against us. The enemy, by stealing three marches upon us, has entered Paris. I was advancing in order to drive them out. They would not have remained there three days. I thank you for the noble spirit you have evinced in that same place under these circumstances. But a portion of the army, not sharing these sentiments, abandoned me and passed over to the camp of the enemy . . . I could with the three parts of the army which remained faithful, and aided by the sympathy and efforts of the great part of the population, have fallen back upon the Loire, or upon my strongholds, and have sustained the war for several years. But a foreign and civil war would have torn the soil of our beautiful country, and at the cost of all these sacrifices and all these ravages, could we hope to vanquish united Europe, supported by the influence which the city of Paris exercised, and which a faction had succeeded in mastering? Under these circumstances I have only considered the interests of the country and the repose of France. I have made the sacrifice of all my rights, and am ready to make that of my person, for the aim of all my life has been the happiness and glory of France. As for you, soldiers, be always faithful in the path of duty and honour. Serve with fidelity your new sovereign. The sweetest occupation will henceforth be to make known to posterity all that you have done that is great . . . You are all my children. I cannot embrace you all so I will do so in the person of your general.[43]

He then kissed Petit on both cheeks, and declared, 'I will embrace these eagles, which have served us as guides in so many glorious days', whereupon he embraced one of the flags three times, for as long as half a minute, before holding up his left hand and saying: 'Farewell! Preserve me in your memories! Adieu, my children!' He then got into his carriage and was taken off at a gallop as the Guard band played a trumpet and drum salute entitled 'Pour l'Empereur'. Needless to say, officers and men wept – as did even some of the foreign officers present – while others were prostrated with grief, and all the others cried 'Vive l'Empereur!'

By nightfall the convoy of fourteen carriages with a cavalry escort had reached Briare, nearly 70 miles away, where Napoleon slept in the post-house. 'Adieu, chère Louise,' he wrote to his wife, 'love me, think of your best friend and your son.'[44] Over the next six nights, Napoleon slept at Nevers, Roanne, Lyons, Donzère, Saint-Cannat and Luc, arriving at Fréjus on the south coast at 10 a.m. on April 27. The 500-mile journey was not without danger in the traditionally pro-royalist Midi, and on different occasions Napoleon had to wear Koller's uniform, a Russian cloak and even a white Bourbon cockade in his hat to avoid recognition. At Orange his carriage had several large stones thrown through the window; at Avignon the Napoleonic eagles on the carriages were defaced and a servant was threatened with death if he didn't shout 'Vive le Roi!' (A year later, Marshal Brune was shot there by royalist assassins and his body thrown into the Rhône.) On April 23 he met Augereau near Valence. The old marshal, who had been one of Napoleon's first divisional commanders in Italy in 1796, had removed all his Napoleonic orders except for the red ribbon of the Légion d'Honneur. He now 'abused Napoleon's ambition and waste of blood for personal vanity', telling him bluntly that he ought to have died in battle.[45]

Campbell had arranged for Captain (later Admiral) Thomas Ussher to pick Napoleon up on the frigate HMS *Undaunted* at Fréjus. When he arrived there, Napoleon was met by Pauline, who proposed to share his exile. Faithless to her husbands, she nonetheless showed great fidelity to her brother in his downfall. He had wanted to leave France on the morning of the 28th but missed the tide, ate a bad langoustine at lunchtime which induced vomiting, and didn't sail until 8 p.m. He insisted upon and was given a sovereign's twenty-one-gun salute when he went aboard, despite the Royal Navy's convention not to fire salutes after sunset.[46] (The Treaty of Fontainebleau had confirmed that he was a reigning monarch and was entitled to the accompanying formalities.) In a poignant echo, he left from precisely the same jetty that he had arrived at when returning from Egypt fifteen years before.[47] Although Captain Ussher checked that his sword was loose in its scabbard in case he needed to defend his charge from the crowd, he found instead that Napoleon was cheered as he left, which Ussher found 'in the highest degree interesting'.[48] Throughout the journey, Campbell noted, 'Napoleon conducted himself with the greatest . . . cordiality towards us all . . . and the officers of his suite observed that they had never seen him more at his ease.'[49] Napoleon told Campbell that he believed that the British would force a commercial treaty on the Bourbons, who as a result 'will be driven out in six months'.[50] He asked that they land at Ajaccio, telling Ussher anecdotes of his youth, but Koller begged the captain not to consider it, possibly fearing the havoc Napoleon might wreak if he escaped into the mountains there.[51]

At 8 p.m. on May 3, *Undaunted* anchored at Elba's main harbour of Portoferraio, and Napoleon disembarked at 2 p.m. the next day. When he stepped ashore he was welcomed by the sub-prefect, local clergy and officials carrying the ceremonial keys of the island, but most importantly by cries of 'Vive l'Empereur!' and 'Vive Napoléon!' from the populace.[52] They raised the flag he had designed – white with a bee-studded red band running diagonally across it – over the fort's battery, and, in an amazing feat of memory, Napoleon recognized a sergeant in the crowd to whom he had given the cross of the Légion on the battlefield of Eylau, who promptly wept.[53] After processing to the church for a *Te Deum* he went to the town hall for a meeting with the island's principal dignitaries. He stayed in the town hall for the first few days, and then installed himself in the large and comfortable Palazzina dei Mulini overlooking Portoferraio, taking the Villa San Martino, which affords a fine view of the town from its terraces, as a summer residence.* The day after landing he inspected Portoferraio's fortifications, and the next day its iron mines, which needed to be productive as he would soon be facing a severe cash shortage.

Napoleon's financial position was not commensurate with what he considered necessary. In addition to the half a million francs he had brought from France himself, his treasurer Peyrusse delivered an extra 2.58 million and Marie Louise had sent 911,000 francs, giving a total of less than 4 million francs.[54] Although the Treaty of Fontainebleau theoretically gave him an annual income of 2.5 million francs, the Bourbons never actually remitted him a centime of it. Revenues from Elba totalled 651,995 francs in 1814 and 967,751 in 1815, yet Napoleon's civil, military and household expenses amounted to over 1.8 million francs in 1814 and nearly 1.5 million in 1815. He therefore had only enough money to cover another twenty-eight months, although with five valets there were obviously some economies he could make. To make matters worse the Bourbons would sequester the Bonaparte family's goods and properties in December.[55]

---

* San Martino is worth visiting for the superb exhibition of original caricatures of Napoleon, kept in an absurdly grandiose extension built by a distant relative in 1851.

When in 1803 Elba had been ceded to France, Napoleon had written of its 'mild and industrious population, two superb harbours and a rich mine', but now that he was its monarch he described its 20,000 acres as a '*royaume d'opérette*' (operetta kingdom).[56] Any other sovereign might have relaxed on the charming, temperate, delightful island, especially after the gruelling nature of the previous two years, but such was Napoleon's nature that he flung himself energetically into every aspect of its life – while always on the lookout for an opportunity to slip past Campbell and return to France should the political situation there favour it. During his nearly ten months on Elba he reorganized his new kingdom's defences, gave money to the poorest of its 11,400 inhabitants, installed a fountain on the roadside outside Poggio (which still produces cold, clean drinking water today), read voraciously (leaving a library of 1,100 volumes to the municipality of Portoferraio), played with his pet monkey Jénar, walked the coastline along goat-paths while humming Italian arias, grew avenues of mulberry trees (perhaps finally expelling the curse of the *pépinière*), reformed customs and excise, repaired the barracks, built a hospital, planted vineyards, paved parts of Portoferraio for the first time and irrigated land. He also organized regular rubbish collections, passed a law prohibiting children from sleeping more than five to a bed, set up a court of appeal and an inspectorate to widen roads and build bridges. While it was undeniably Lilliputian compared to his former territories, he wanted Elba to be the best-run *royaume d'opérette* in Europe.[57] His attention to the tiniest details was undimmed, even extending to the kind of bread he wanted fed to his hunting dogs.[58]

All this was achieved despite the fact that Napoleon had grown stout. Noting that he was unable to climb a rock on May 20, Campbell wrote that 'Indefatigable as he is, corpulency prevents him from walking much, and he is obliged to take the arm of some person on rough roads.'[59] This didn't seem to have the same torpor-inducing effect on Napoleon that it does on others, however. 'I have never seen a man in any situation of life with so much personal activity and restless perseverance,' Campbell noted. 'He appears to take so much pleasure in perpetual movement, and in seeing those who accompany him sink under fatigue ... After being yesterday on foot in the heat of the sun, from 5 a.m. to 3 p.m., visiting the frigates and transports ... he rode on horseback for three hours, as he told me afterwards, "to tire myself out!"'[60]

At noon on Sunday, May 29, 1814, Josephine died of pneumonia at Malmaison. She was fifty and five days earlier had gone out walking in the cold night air with Tsar Alexander after a ball there. 'She was the wife who would have gone with me to Elba,' Napoleon later said, and he decreed two days of mourning. (In 1800 George Washington had got ten.) Madame Bertrand, who told him the news, later said: 'His face did not change, he only exclaimed: "Ah! She is happy now."'[61] His last recorded letter to Josephine the previous year had ended: 'Adieu, my love: tell me that you are well. I'm informed that you are getting as fat as a Norman farmer's good wife. Napoleon.'[62] With this jocular familiarity concluded one of the supposedly great romances of history. She had been living beyond even her enormous income, but had come to terms with her new status as an ex-Empress. Napoleon superstitiously wondered whether it had been Josephine who had brought him luck, noting that his change of fortune had coincided with his divorcing her. By November he was expressing surprise to two visiting British MPs that she could possibly have died in debt, saying, 'Besides, I used to pay her dressmakers' account every year.'[63]

Madame Mère arrived from Rome to share her son's exile in early August. Campbell found her 'very pleasant and unaffected. The old lady is very handsome, of middle size, with a good figure and fresh colour.'[64] She dined and played cards with Napoleon on Sunday evenings, and when she complained, 'You're cheating, son', he would reply: 'You're rich, mother!'[65] Pauline arrived three months later, the only one of his siblings to visit. Napoleon set aside and decorated rooms for Marie Louise and the King of Rome in both his residences, either in a heart-wrenching act of optimism or as a cynical propaganda move, or possibly both. On August 10 Marie Louise wrote to him to say that, although she promised to be with him soon, she had had to return to Vienna in deference to her father's wishes.[66] On August 28, Napoleon wrote the last of his 318 surviving letters to her, from the hermitage of La Madonna di Marciano, on Monte Giove, which featured his typical statistical exactitude: 'I am here in a hermitage 3,834 feet above sea level, overlooking the Mediterranean on all sides, and in the midst of a forest of chestnut trees. Madame is staying in the village 958 feet lower down. This is a most pleasant spot ... I long to see you, and also my son.' He ended: 'Adieu, ma bonne Louise. Tout à toi. Ton Nap.'[67] But by then Marie Louise had found a *chevalier* to escort her to Vienna, the dashing one-eyed Austrian general Count Adam von Neipperg, who Napoleon had defeated in Bohemia in the 1813 campaign. Neipperg has been described as 'skilful, energetic, a thorough man of the world, an accomplished courtier, an excellent musician'.[68] In his youth he had run off with a married woman, and was himself married when he was charged with looking after Marie Louise. By September they were lovers.[69]

The hermitage of La Madonna di Marciano (which can today be reached after a 3-mile hike up the mountain) is a romantic and secluded spot with fabulous views over the island's bays and inlets, from where one can see the outlines of both Corsica and mainland Italy. On September 1, Marie Walewska arrived with Napoleon's four-year-old natural son Alexandre, and they stayed there for a couple of nights with Napoleon. She had divorced her husband in 1812, and now she had lost the Neapolitan estates that Napoleon had given her when he had broken off their affair before marrying Marie Louise. But loyalty drew her to Napoleon, however briefly. For when General Drouot warned Napoleon that island gossip had uncovered his secret – indeed a local mayor had climbed the hill to pay his formal respects to the woman everyone thought was the Empress – Marie had to leave the island.[70]

Napoleon gave the first of a series of interviews to visiting British Whig aristocrats and politicians in mid-November, when he spent four hours with George Venables-Vernon, a Whig MP, and his colleague John Fazakerley. In early December he twice met Viscount Ebrington, for a total of six and a half hours, and on Christmas Eve the future prime minister Lord John Russell. Two other Britons, John Macnamara and Frederick Douglas, the latter the son of the British minister Lord Glenbervie, met him in mid-January. All of these intelligent, well-connected and worldly interlocutors marvelled at the grasp of Napoleon's mind and his willingness to discuss any subject – including the Egyptian and Russian campaigns, his admiration for the House of Lords and his hopes for a similar aristocracy in France, his plans for securing the colonies through polygamy, the duplicity of Tsar Alexander, the 'great ability' of the Duke of Wellington, the Congress of Vienna, the mediocrity of Archduke Charles of Austria, the Italians ('lazy and effeminate'), the deaths of d'Enghien and Pichegru (neither of which he admitted was his fault), the Jaffa massacre (which he said was), King Frederick William (whom he called 'a corporal'), the relative merits of his marshals, the distinction between British pride and French vanity, and his escape from circumcision in Egypt.[71]

'They are brave fellows, those English troops of yours,' he said during one of the encounters, 'they are worth more than the others.'[72] The Britons reported that he 'talked with much cheerfulness, good humour and civility of manner' and defended his record, on one occasion pointing out that although he had not burned Moscow, the British had set fire to Washington that August.[73] Napoleon may have been trying to make a good impression in anticipation of an eventual move to London, but his intelligence and candour induced his visitors to lower their guard. 'For my own part,' he often said, 'I am no longer concerned. My day is done.' He also regularly used the expression 'I'm dead.'[74] Yet he asked lots of questions about the popularity of the Bourbons and the whereabouts of various British and French military units in southern France. He was less subtle in questioning Campbell on these subjects, to the point that the commissioner wrote to Castlereagh in October 1814 to warn him that Napoleon might be contemplating a return.[75] Yet the Royal Navy's watch was not increased beyond the lone frigate HMS *Partridge*, and Napoleon was even allowed a sixteen-gun brig, *L'Inconstant*, as the flagship of the Elban navy.

On September 15, 1814 the Great Powers convened the Congress of Vienna at the instigation of Metternich and Talleyrand, where it was hoped all the major disagreements – over the futures of Poland, Saxony, the Rhine Confederation and Murat in Naples – might be settled. After nearly a quarter of a century of war and revolution the map of Europe had to be redrawn, and each of the Powers had desiderata which needed to be accommodated with those of the others to provide the permanent peace that it was hoped would follow a general settlement.[76] The fall of Napoleon had reignited some long-standing territorial differences between the Powers, but unfortunately for him, although it stayed in formal session until June 1815, the outlines of agreement on all the major questions were in place by the time he decided to leave Elba in late February.

Precisely when Napoleon decided to try to retake his throne is unknown, but he watched closely the seemingly endless series of errors the Bourbons made after Louis XVIII's return – under Allied escort – to Paris in May 1814. Napoleon increasingly believed that the Bourbons would soon experience what he called 'a Libyan wind' – a violent sirocco desert wind that reaches hurricane speeds and was then believed to originate in the Libyan Sahara.[77] Although the king had signed a wide-ranging Charter guaranteeing civil liberties on his arrival, his government had failed to alleviate fears that they secretly wished to re-establish the Ancien Régime. Indeed, far from it. Louis' reign was officially recorded as being in its nineteenth year, as if he had ruled France ever since the death of his nephew Louis XVII in 1795 and everything that had taken place since – the Convention, Directory,

Consulate and Empire – had been merely an illegal hiatus. The Bourbons had agreed that France should go back to her 1791 borders, thereby shrinking her from 109 departments to 87.[78] There were increases in the Ancien Régime-era *droits réunis* taxes and food prices, and the Catholic Church returned to some of its pre-revolutionary power and prestige, which irritated liberals as well as republicans.[79] Official ceremonies were held at Rennes to honour the 'martyred' Chouans, and the remains of Louis XVI and Marie Antoinette were disinterred from the Madeleine cemetery and reinterred with much pomp in the Abbey of Saint-Denis. Although building work resumed at Versailles and the king appointed a 'premier *pousse-fauteuil*', whose sole job it was to push in his chair as he sat down at the table, pensions were cut, even to wounded veterans.[80] Paintings that Napoleon had brought together at the Louvre were removed from it and returned to the occupying powers.

As Napoleon had predicted, the pre-revolutionary 1786 trade agreement with Britain was reintroduced, reducing tariffs on some British goods and abolishing them on others, thus triggering a new slump for French manufacturers.[81] The British government hardly improved matters by choosing Wellington as its ambassador to France.* 'Lord Wellington's appointment must be very galling to the army,' Napoleon told Ebrington, 'as must the great attentions being shown him by the king, as if to set his own private feelings up in opposition to those of the country.'[82] Napoleon later described what he thought the Bourbons ought to have done. 'Instead of proclaiming himself Louis XVIII he should have proclaimed himself the founder of a new dynasty, and not have touched on old grievances at all. If he had done that, in all probability I should never have been induced to quit Elba.'[83]

The Bourbons' most self-defeating policies were towards the army. The tricolour, under which French soldiers had won victories across Europe for over two decades, was replaced by the white flag and fleur-de-lys, while the Légion d'Honneur was downgraded in favour of the old royal orders (one of which the *grognards* promptly nicknamed 'the bug').[84] Senior army posts were awarded to émigrés who had fought against France, and a new Household Guard superseded the Imperial Guard, while the Middle Guard, which Napoleon had instituted in 1806 and which boasted many proud battle honours, was abolished

---

* In 1818 a Bonapartist ex-soldier, Marie-André Cantillon, attempted to assassinate Wellington as his carriage entered his residence, but he and his accomplice were acquitted when the bullet he fired could not be found.

altogether.[85] Large numbers of officers were retired by the despised Dupont and 30,000 more put on half-pay, while aggressive searches continued for draft evaders.[86]* 'My first hope came when I saw in the gazettes that at the banquet at the Hôtel de Ville there were the wives of the nobility only,' Napoleon later recalled, 'and none of those of the officers of the army.'[87] In gross defiance of orders, many in the army openly celebrated Napoleon's birthday on August 15, 1814, with cannon-fire salutes and cries of 'Vive l'Empereur!' as sentries presented arms only to officers wearing the Légion d'Honneur.

Of course it was not only the Bourbons' mistakes which helped decide Napoleon to risk everything to try to regain his throne. Emperor Francis's refusal to allow his wife and son to rejoin him was another, and the fact that his expenses were running at two and a half times his income. There was also sheer ennui; he complained to Campbell of being 'shut up in this cell of a house, separated from the world, with no interesting occupation, no *savants* with me, nor any variety in my society'.[88]† Another consideration was paragraphs in the newspapers and rumours from the Congress of Vienna that the Allies were planning forcibly to remove him from Elba. Joseph de Maistre, the French ambassador to St Petersburg, had nerve-wrackingly suggested the Australian penal colony of Botany Bay as a possible destination. The exceptionally remote British island of St Helena in the mid-Atlantic had also been mentioned.[89]

On January 13, 1815, Napoleon spent two hours with John Macnamara and was delighted to hear that France was 'agitated'.[90] He admitted that he had stayed in Moscow too long and said 'I made a mistake about England in trying to conquer it.' He was adamant that his role in international affairs was over. 'History has a triumvirate of great men,' Macnamara stated, 'Alexander, Caesar, and Napoleon.' At this, Napoleon looked steadfastly at him without speaking, and Macnamara said 'he thought he saw the Emperor's eyes moisten.' It is what he had wanted people to say ever since he was a schoolboy. Eventually Napoleon replied: 'You would be right if a ball had killed me at the battle of

---

* To gauge the effect of being forced to live on half-pay, consider the naked lust for renewed war against France felt by Horatio Nelson when he was reduced to it between 1788 and 1793 (Knight, *The Pursuit of Victory* pp. 118–30).

† Nevertheless, when he did encounter such variety, as in the shape of a Norwegian gentleman, Mr Kundtzow, who was presented to him in January 1815, he could be a pedantic show-off. 'What is the population of Norway?' Napoleon asked Kundtzow, who answered, 'Two millions, Sire.' Napoleon corrected him: 'One million eight hundred thousand' (ed. North, *Napoleon on Elba* p. 171).

Moscow but my late reverses will efface all the glory of my early years.'[91] He added that Wellington was 'a brave man' but that he should not have been made ambassador. Napoleon laughed frequently during the conversation, as he did when told that the Prince Regent had welcomed his divorce from Josephine, as it had set a precedent for him to divorce the wife he hated, Caroline of Brunswick. Macnamara asked if he feared assassination. 'Not by the English; they are not assassins,' he said, but he conceded that he did have to be cautious with regard to the nearby Corsicans.[92] As he left, Macnamara told Bertrand that the Emperor 'must be a very good-humoured man and never in a passion'. Bertrand replied with a smile: 'I know him a little better than you.'[93]

By the beginning of February Campbell noted that Napoleon had 'suspended his improvements as regards roads and the finishing of his country residence', all on grounds of expense, and had also attempted to sell Portoferraio's town hall.[94] He again warned Castlereagh that 'If the payments promised to him at the time of abdication were withheld, and the want of money pressed upon him, I considered him capable of any desperate step.'[95] Tsar Alexander later lambasted Talleyrand for not paying the funds due to Napoleon: 'Why should we expect him to keep his word with us when we did not do so with him?'[96]

When Napoleon's former secretary Fleury de Chaboulon visited him in February 1815 he brought a message from Maret that France was ripe for his return. Napoleon asked about the attitude of the army. When forced to cry 'Vive le Roi!', Fleury told him, the soldiers would often add in a whisper 'de Rome'. 'And so they still love me?' Napoleon asked. 'Yes, Sire, and may I even venture to say, more than ever.' This accorded with what Napoleon was hearing from a large number of French sources and from his network of agents in France, including people like Joseph Emmery, a surgeon from Grenoble who helped plan his coming expedition and to whom he left 100,000 francs in his will. Fleury said the army blamed Marmont for the Allied victory, which prompted Napoleon to claim: 'They are right; had it not been for the infamous defection of the Duke of Ragusa, the Allies would have been lost. I was master of their rear, and of all their resources; not a man would have escaped. They would have had their [own] 29th Bulletin.'[97]

On February 16 Campbell left Elba in HMS *Partridge* 'upon a short excursion to the continent for my health'. He needed to visit either his ear doctor in Florence or his mistress, Countess Miniacci, or possibly both.[98] This gave Napoleon his chance, and the next day he ordered *L'Inconstant* to be refitted, stocked for a short voyage and painted the same colours as Royal Navy vessels.[99] On Campbell's arrival in Florence, Castlereagh's deputy at the British foreign office, Edward Cooke, told him: 'When you return to Elba, you may tell Bonaparte that he is quite forgotten in Europe: no one thinks of him now.'[100] At much the same time, Madame Mère was telling her son: 'Yes, you must go; it is your destiny to do so. You were not made to die on this desert island.'[101] Pauline, ever the most generous-hearted of his siblings, gave him a very valuable necklace that could be sold to help pay for the coming adventure. When Napoleon's valet Marchand tried to console her by saying that she would soon be reunited with her brother, she presciently corrected him, saying that she would never see him again.[102] A year later, when asked whether it was true that Drouot had tried to dissuade him from leaving Elba, Napoleon answered that it was not. In any case, he retorted curtly, 'I do not allow myself to be governed by advice.'[103] The night before Napoleon left he had been reading a life of Emperor Charles V of Austria, which he left open on the table. His elderly housekeeper kept it untouched, along with 'written papers torn into small bits' that were strewn about. When British visitors questioned her soon afterwards, she gave them 'unaffected expressions of attachment, and artless report of his uniform good humour'.[104]

Napoleon left Elba on *L'Inconstant* on the night of Sunday, February 26, 1815. Once the 300-ton, 16-gun ship had weighed anchor, the 607 Old Guard grenadiers aboard were told they were headed for France. 'Paris or death!' they cried. He took generals Bertrand, Drouot and Cambronne, M. Pons the inspector of mines, a doctor called Chevalier Fourreau, and a pharmacist, M. Gatte. They were attempting to invade a great European country with eight small vessels, the next three largest of which were only 80, 40 and 25 tons, carrying 118 Polish lancers (without their horses), fewer than 300 men of a Corsican battalion, 50 gendarmes, and around 80 civilians (including Napoleon's servants) – a total force of 1,142 men and 2 light cannon.[105] A moderate breeze carried them to France, and they narrowly missed two French frigates on the way. Napoleon spent a lot of time on deck, chatting to officers, soldiers and sailors. The commander of the lancers, Colonel Jan Jermanowski, recorded:

> Lying down, sitting, standing, and strolling around him, familiarly, they asked him unceasing questions, to which he answered unreservedly and without one sign of anger or impatience, for they were not a little

indiscreet, they required his opinions on many living characters, kings, marshals and ministers, and discussed notorious passages of his own campaigns, and even of his domestic policy.[106]

During this he spoke openly of 'his present attempt, of its difficulties, of his means, and of his hopes'.

L'Inconstant sailed into Golfe-Juan on the southern French coast on Wednesday, March 1, unloading Napoleon's force by 5 p.m. 'I have long weighed and most maturely considered the project,' Napoleon harangued his men just before they went ashore, 'the glory, the advantages we shall gain if we succeed I need not enlarge upon. If we fail, to military men, who have from their youth faced death in so many shapes, the fate which awaits us is not terrific: we know, and we despise, for we have a thousand times faced the worst which a reverse can bring.'[107] The following year he reminisced about the landing: 'Very soon a great crowd of people came around us, surprised by our appearance and astonished by our small force. Among them was a mayor, who, seeing how few we were, said to me: "We were just beginning to be quiet and happy; now you are going to stir us all up again."'[108] It was a sign of how little Napoleon was seen as a despot that people could speak to him in that way.

Knowing that Provence and the lower Rhône valley were vehemently royalist, and that for the moment he needed above all else to avoid any Bourbon armies, Napoleon resolved to take the Alpine route to the arsenal of Grenoble. His instinct was proved right when the twenty men under Captain Lamouret whom he sent off to Antibes were arrested and interned by the local garrison. He hadn't the troops to attack Toulon, and was conscious of the need to move faster than the news of his arrival, at least until he could augment his force. 'That is why I hurried on to Grenoble,' he later told his secretary General Gourgaud. 'There were troops there, muskets, and cannon; it was a centre.'[109] All he had was the capacity for speed – horses were soon bought for the lancers – and a genius for propaganda. On landing he issued two proclamations, to the French people and the army, which had been copied out on board ship by hand by as many of the men as were literate.

The army proclamation entirely blamed the 1814 defeat on the treason of Marmont and Augereau: 'Two men from our ranks have betrayed our laurels, their country, their prince, their benefactor.'[110] He turned his back on bellicosity, declaring: 'We must forget that we were masters of nations, but we must not suffer anyone meddling in our business.' In the proclamation to the people, Napoleon said that after the fall of Paris, 'My heart was torn apart, but my spirit remained resolute ... I exiled myself on a rock in the middle of the sea.'[111] It was only because Louis XVIII had sought to reintroduce feudal rights and rule through people who had for twenty-five years been 'enemies of the people' that he was acting, he claimed, despite the fact that the Bourbons had certainly not yet got around to reviving feudalism. 'Frenchmen,' he continued, 'in my exile I heard your complaints and wishes; you were claiming that government of your choice, which alone is legitimate. You were blaming me for my long sleep, you were reproaching me for sacrificing to my repose the great interests of the State.' So, 'amid all sorts of dangers, I arrived among you to regain my rights, which are yours.'[112] It was tremendous hyperbole, of course, but Napoleon knew how to appeal to soldiers who wanted to return to glory and full pay, better-off peasants who feared the return of feudal dues, millions of owners of the *biens nationaux* who wanted protection from the returning émigrés and churchmen who wanted their pre-1789 property back, workers hit by the flood of English manufactured goods and imperial civil servants who had lost their jobs to royalists.[113] The Bourbons had failed so comprehensively in less than a year that even after the defeats of 1812 and 1813 Napoleon was able to put together a fairly wide-ranging domestic coalition.

On the day he landed Napoleon bivouacked on the dunes at Cannes not far from the present-day Croisette, opposite an old chapel that is today the church of Notre-Dame. At two o'clock the next morning he joined Cambronne's advance guard, which included unmounted lancers and the two cannon. Instead of going to Aix, the Provençal capital, he took the road through Le Cannet which climbs 15 miles up to Grasse, which – since there were only five working muskets in his town – the mayor surrendered. After resting till noon, Napoleon abandoned his carriages and cannon, mounted his supplies on mules, and took the mountain road northwards. There was snow and ice on the higher parts, where some mules slipped and fell, and at points the road narrowed to single file. He walked on foot among his grenadiers, who affectionately teased him with nicknames such as '*Notre petit tondu*' (Our little cropped one) and '*Jean de l'Epée*' (Jack of the Sword).[114]

The 'Route Napoléon' was instituted by the French government in 1934 to encourage tourism, and impressive stone eagles were placed along it, of which a handful still survive today. Every town and village Napoleon went through has a sign proudly announcing the fact, and it is possible to see many of the places where he slept on what became a

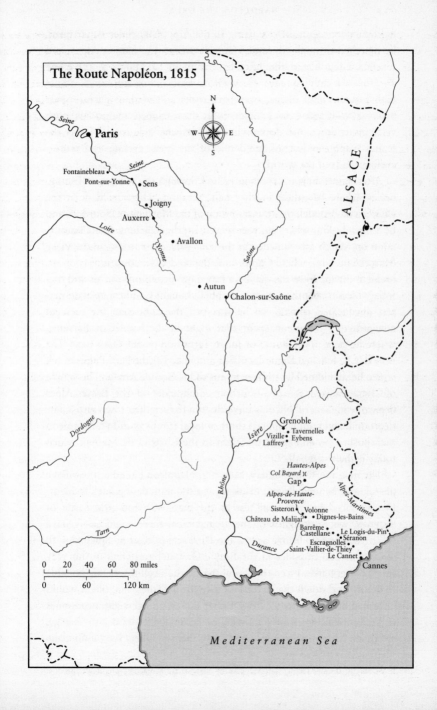

The Route Napoléon, 1815

Seine

Paris

Fontainebleau
Pont-sur-Yonne • Sens
• Joigny
Auxerre

Seine

Loire

Yonne

Saône

ALSACE

• Avallon

• Autun
• Chalon-sur-Saône

Dordogne

Isère
Vizille • Tavernelles
Laffrey • Eybens

Grenoble

Hautes-Alpes
Col Bayard)(
Gap •

Rhône

Alpes-Maritimes

Alpes-de-Haute-
Provence
Sisteron)(• Volonne
Château de Malijai • • Dignes-les-Bains
Barrême • Le Logis-du-Pin
Castellane • • Séranon
Escragnolles •
Saint-Vallier-de-Thiey
Le Cannet •
Cannes

Tarn

Durance

0   20   40   60   80 miles

0   60   120 km

Mediterranean Sea

legendary journey north. Starting in the Alpes-Maritimes department, he marched through Alpes-de-Haute-Provence and Hautes-Alpes, and reached Grenoble in the Isère by the night of March 7, travelling 190 miles in only six days. He went on foot and on horseback across high plateaux and plains, over bare rocks and verdant pasture, past Swiss-style villages, over 6,000-foot snow-capped mountains with vertiginous drops and down winding Corniche-style roads. Today the Route Napoléon is considered one of the great cycling and motor-cycling roads of the world.

After Saint-Vallier, Napoleon passed through the villages of Escrag-nolles, where he called another halt, Séranon, where he slept at the Château de Brondel, the country house of the Marquis de Gourdon, and Le Logis-du-Pin, where he was served broth. Reaching Castellane by noon on March 3 he lunched at the *sous-préfecture* (today in the Place Marcel Sauvaire), where Cambronne demanded 5,000 rations of meat, bread and wine from the mayor, a few days' provisions for his still tiny force of less than a thousand. (Campbell thought Cambronne 'a desperate, uneducated ruffian', so he was just the right man for such an adventure.[115]) Napoleon spent that night in the hamlet of Barrême, where he slept in the house of Judge Tartanson on the main road. The next day he reached Digne-les-Bains and rested at the Petit-Palais hotel, where he was joined by some veterans of his Grande Armée. The people of Digne begged the pro-Bourbon commander of the Basses-Alpes department, General Nicolas Loverdo, not to turn their town into a battleground, and finding himself short of loyal troops he didn't. Napoleon then pushed on and spent the night in the Château de Malijai, which today is the town hall.*

The next morning, Sunday, March 5, Napoleon halted at the village of Volonne, by local legend drinking at a fountain dating back to Henri IV. He faced his first real test at the massively imposing castle of Sisteron, where the guns of the great citadel there could easily have destroyed the sole bridge across the Durance. Instead he lunched with the mayor and notables in the Bras d'Or hotel and went on his way shortly afterwards. From the top of the citadel's bell-tower it is possible to see up and down the River Durance for 40 miles; Napoleon would have had nowhere else to cross. Either due to an oversight, economies or because its commander wanted an excuse not to destroy the bridge, the castle had no gunpowder, and from then on whenever Cambronne

* 'Napoleon stayed here,' says a sign at the entrance to the village, 'why don't you?'

arrived ahead of Napoleon to cajole, negotiate, bribe and, if necessary, threaten the mayors of each town, no bridge was destroyed.

Napoleon later recalled that when he reached Gap 'Some of the peasants took five-franc pieces stamped with my likeness out of their pockets, and cried, "It is he!"'[116]* 'My return dispels all your anxieties,' he wrote in a proclamation from Gap to the inhabitants of the Upper and Lower Alps, 'it ensures the conservation of all property.' In other letters he specifically played on the fears of what might happen under the Bourbons (but hadn't yet) when he stated that he opposed those 'who wish to bring back feudal rights, who wish to destroy equality between different classes, cancel sales of *biens nationaux*'.[117] He left Gap at 2 p.m. on March 6. From there the ground rises steeply, up to the Col Bayard at 3,750 feet. That night Napoleon slept in the gendarmerie in the main street of Corps.

Easily the most dramatic moment of the journey came the following day a few hundred yards south of the town of Laffrey, where Napoleon encountered a battalion of the 5th Line in a narrow area between two wooded hills on what is today called La Prairie de la Rencontre. According to Bonapartist legend, Napoleon, standing before them well within musket range, with only his far smaller number of Imperial Guardsmen protecting him, threw back his iconic grey overcoat and pointed to his breast, asking if they wanted to fire on their Emperor. In testament to the continuing power of his charisma, the troops threw down their muskets and mobbed him.[118] Napoleon had previously been informed by two officers of the pro-Bonapartist attitudes of the demi-brigade, but a single shot from a royalist officer could have brought about a very different outcome. Savary, who wasn't present, told a slightly less heroic version, in which Napoleon's conversational style and habit of question-asking saved the day.

> The Emperor approached; the battalion kept a profound silence. The officer who was in command ordered them to aim their muskets: he was obeyed; if he had ordered Fire we cannot say what would have happened. The Emperor didn't give him time: he talked to the soldiers and asked them as usual: 'Well! How are you doing in the 5th?' The soldiers answered 'Very well, Sire.' Then the Emperor said: 'I've come back to see you; do some of you want to kill me?' The soldiers shouted 'Oh! That,

---

* It wasn't an ideal guide, as that particular coin shows the right profile of a much younger Napoleon with a full head of curly hair, a strongly defined jaw and a laurel-leaf crown.

no!' Then the Emperor reviewed them as usual and thus took possession
of the 5th Regiment. The head of the battalion looked unhappy.[119]

When Napoleon himself told the story he said he had adopted a jovial,
old-comrade attitude towards the troops: 'I went forward and held out
my hand to a soldier, saying, "What, you old rascal, were you about to
fire on your Emperor?" "Look here," he answered, showing me that his
musket was not loaded.'[120] He also put the success down to having his
veterans with him: 'It was the bearskin helmets of my Guards which did
the business. They called to memory my glorious days.'[121] Whether
Napoleon had been declamatory or conversational at that tense moment,
he showed great nerve. Laffrey also represented a watershed, because
for the first time regular soldiers, rather than peasants or National
Guardsmen, had come over to his side.

After being cheered by crowds at Vizille – where Charles de La Bédoyère brought the 7th Line over to him – taking refreshment at Mère
Vigier's café in Tavernelles and having a by then well-deserved footbath
at Eybens, Napoleon entered Grenoble at 11 p.m. on March 7. There
the townspeople tore down their own city gates and presented pieces of
them to Napoleon as a souvenir of their loyalty. 'On my march from
Cannes to Grenoble I was an adventurer,' Napoleon later said; 'in Grenoble I once again became a sovereign.'[122] Rejecting an offer to stay
at the prefecture, Napoleon displayed his customary genius for public
relations by instead staying in room No. 2 of the hotel Les Trois Dau-
phins in the rue Montorge, which was run by the son of a veteran of
his Italian and Egyptian campaigns and was where he had stayed in
1791 when stationed at Valence. (Stendhal stayed in the same room in
1837, out of homage.) Any lack of comfort was made up for in Lyons
where he stayed in the archbishop's palace (today the city library), occupying the same apartments that the king's brother, the Comte d'Artois
(later King Charles X) had been forced to leave hastily that same morning. When Napoleon conducted a review of his by now sizeable force in
Lyons, he reprimanded a battalion for not manoeuvring well enough.
This, he later said, 'had a great effect; it showed he was confident of his
re-establishment'.[123] Had he adopted an imploring attitude at that key
moment, his men would have spotted it immediately. Instead, even after
his defeats and abdication, they were still willing to follow him.

The news of Napoleon's return reached Paris at noon on March 5 via
the Chappe aerial telegraph, but the government kept it secret until the
7th.[124] Ney, Macdonald and Saint-Cyr were deputed by Soult, the new

war minister, to address the problem, whereupon Ney told Louis XVIII: 'I will seize Bonaparte, I promise you, and I will bring him to you in an iron cage.'[125] Soult's order to the army stated that only traitors would join Napoleon, and 'This man is now but an adventurer. His last mad act has revealed him for what he is.'[126] And yet, for all this, the only two marshals to fight alongside Napoleon on the battlefield of Waterloo would be Ney and Soult.

On the day Napoleon left Lyons, March 13, the Allies, still in session at the Congress, issued the Vienna Declaration.

> By appearing again in France with projects of confusion and disorders, [Napoleon] has deprived himself of the protection of the law and has manifested before the world that there can be neither peace nor truce with him. The Powers consequently declare that Napoleon Bonaparte has placed himself beyond the pale of civil and social relations, and that as an enemy and disturber of the world, he has delivered himself up to public vengeance.[127]

Napoleon continued northwards, spending the following night at Chalon-sur-Saône, the 15th at Autun, the 16th at Avallon and the 17th in the prefecture at Auxerre. He was greeted by large, enthusiastic crowds and joined by further units of soldiers along the way. He sent two offi-cers in disguise to Marshal Ney, who was in command of 3,000 men at Lons-le-Saunier, telling him that if he changed sides, 'I shall receive you as I did on the morrow of the battle of the Moskowa.'[128] Ney had had every intention of fighting against Napoleon when he left Paris, but he had no wish to start a civil war, even if he could persuade his men to open fire. 'I was in the midst of storms,' he later said of his decision, 'and I lost my head.'[129] On March 14 Ney defected to Napoleon with generals Lecourbe and Bourmont (who were both very reluctant) and almost all his troops except for a few royalist officers. 'Only the Emperor Napoleon is entitled to rule over our beautiful country,' Ney told his men.[130] He later said that the Bonapartist sentiment among the men was overwhelming and he couldn't 'hold back the sea with my hands'.[131]

Napoleon met Ney on the morning of the 18th at Auxerre, but as Ney had brought along a document warning him that he needed 'to study the welfare of the French people and endeavour to repair the evils his ambition had brought upon him' it was a cold, workmanlike reunion.[132] Instead of treating him as he had 'on the morrow of the bat-tle of the Moskva', Napoleon questioned him about the morale of his troops, the state of feeling of the south-eastern departments and his experiences on the march to Dijon, to which Ney gave brief replies before being ordered to march on Paris.

On the 19th Napoleon lunched at Joigny, reached Sens by 5 p.m. and dined and slept at Pont-sur-Yonne. Then at 1 a.m. on Monday, March 20 he left for Fontainebleau, where he arrived in the White Horse courtyard eleven months to the day after leaving it. At 1.30 that morning the gouty Louis XVIII was bodily lifted into his carriage at the Tuileries – no easy task given his weight – and fled Paris. He went first to Lille, where the garrison seemed hostile, so he crossed into Belgium and then waited upon events from Ghent. With his customary veneration for anniversaries, Napoleon had wanted to enter Paris on the 20th – the King of Rome's fourth birthday – and sure enough, at nine o'clock that evening he entered the Tuileries once again as *de facto* emperor of the French.

The courtyard of the Tuileries was packed with soldiers and civilians who had come to witness his return. There are several accounts of what happened next, all agreeing on the din of excitement and the general approval that Napoleon elicited upon his arrival. Colonel Léon-Michel Routier, who had fought in Italy, Calabria and Catalonia, was walking and chatting with comrades-in-arms near the pavilion clock at the Tuileries when

> suddenly very simple carriages without any escort showed up at the wicket-gate by the river and the Emperor was announced ... The carriages enter, we all rush around them and we see Napoleon get out. Then everyone's in delirium; we jump on him in disorder, we surround him, we squeeze him, we almost suffocate him ... The memory of this unique moment in the history of the world still makes my heart pound with pleasure. Happy who, like me, was the witness of this magical arrival, the result of a road of over two hundred leagues travelled in eighteen days on French soil without spilling one drop of blood.[133]

Even General Thiébault, who until earlier that day had been in charge of the defence of southern Paris against Napoleon, felt that 'There was an instantaneous and irresistible outburst ... you would have thought the ceilings were coming down ... I seemed to have become a Frenchman once more, and nothing could equal the transports and the shouts with which I tried to show the party I was taking part in the homage rendered to him.'[134] Lavalette recalled that Napoleon walked up the staircase of the Tuileries 'slowly, with his eyes half closed, his arms extended before him, like a blind man, and expressing his joy only by a smile'.[135] Such was the press of cheering supporters that it was only with difficulty that the door to his apartment could be closed behind him. When Mollien arrived that night to offer his congratulations, he embraced him and said, 'Enough, enough, my dear, the time for compliments has passed; they let me come as they let them go.'[136]

After the dramas of the journey from Golfe-Juan, changing the regime in Paris came easily. That first night it was noticed that the fleur-de-lys covering the carpet in the palace's audience chamber could be removed, and underneath could still be seen the old Napoleonic bees. 'Immediately all the ladies set to work,' recalled a spectator of Queen Julie of Spain, Queen Hortense of Holland and their returning ladies-in-waiting, 'and in less than half an hour, to the great mirth of the company, the carpet became imperial again.'[137]

30
Waterloo

*'I sensed that Fortune was abandoning me. I no longer had in
me the feeling of ultimate success, and if one is not prepared to
take risks when the time is ripe, one ends up doing nothing.'*
Napoleon on the Waterloo campaign

*'A general-in-chief should ask himself several times in the day,
what if the enemy were to appear now to my front, or on my
right, or on my left?'*
Napoleon's Military Maxim No. 8

By the time Napoleon went to bed at three o'clock on the morning of
Tuesday, March 21, 1815, he had largely reconstituted his government.
The Vienna Declaration made it clear that the Allies would not allow
him to retain the throne, so he needed to prepare France for invasion,
but he hoped that – unlike in 1814 – ordinary Frenchmen would actively
rally to him, having now experienced the Bourbon alternative. To an
extent they did; over the next few weeks there were as many recruits as
the depots could handle. It was a wrenching moment for Frenchmen to
decide where their true loyalties lay. Of the Bonaparte family, Joseph
was received with affection by him on the 23rd – Napoleon no longer
suspected him of making a move on Marie Louise – Lucien came from
his self-imposed exile in Rome and was 'speedily admitted' into his presence and forgiven for everything, Jérôme was given the 6th Division to
command, Cardinal Fesch returned to France and Hortense became the
chatelaine of the Tuileries. Louis and Eugène stayed away, the latter at
the behest of his father-in-law, the King of Bavaria. Marie Louise
remained in Austria, fervently hoping that Napoleon, to whom she had
written for the final time on January 1, would be defeated.[1] In a letter to

a friend of April 6, the infatuated young woman mentioned the exact number of days – eighteen – since she had last seen General Neipperg, and in her last oral message to Napoleon soon afterwards she asked for a separation.[2]

The unfeigned surprise shown by senior statesmen such as Cambacérès at the news of Napoleon's return confirms that it was not the result of a widespread conspiracy, as the Bourbons suspected, but of the willpower and opportunism of one man.[3] Cambacérès reluctantly went to the justice ministry, complaining 'All I want is rest.'[4] A few – such as the adamant republican Carnot, who went to the interior ministry – joined Napoleon because they genuinely believed his assurances that he would now be acting as a constitutional monarch who respected the civil rights of Frenchmen.* Other ministers, such as Lavalette, were dyed-in-the-wool Bonapartists. Decrès went back to the naval ministry, Mollien to the treasury, Caulaincourt to the foreign ministry and Daru to war administration. Maret became secretary of state, while Boulay de la Meurthe and Regnaud de Saint-Jean d'Angély returned to their key positions in the Conseil and Molé to his old inspectorate of roads and bridges.[5] Savary took over the gendarmerie and even Fouché was allowed back into the police ministry – a sign of how indispensable he was despite his chronic untrustworthiness. Overall, Napoleon had gathered easily enough talent and experience to run an efficient administration if the military situation could somehow be squared. When he saw Rapp, who had been given a divisional command by the Bourbons, he playfully (and perhaps a little painfully) punched him in the solar plexus, saying, 'What, you rogue, you wanted to kill me?' before making him commander of the Army of the Rhine. 'In vain he sought to assume the mask of severity,' Rapp wrote in his posthumously published autobiography, but 'kind feelings always gained the ascendancy.'[6] One of the few people who wrote a letter asking for re-employment to be refused was Roustam. 'He's a coward,' Napoleon told Marchand. 'Throw that in the fire and never ask me again about it.'[7] It was understandable that he should not want as his principal bodyguard someone who had fled Fontainebleau in the night the previous year. His place was taken by Louis-Étienne Saint-Denis, who since 1811 had been dressed by Napoleon as a Mamluk and called Ali, despite his being a Frenchman born in Versailles.

---

* He kept Carnot up to the mark as he had all his earlier interior ministers. 'You will notice in the printed report', Napoleon wrote of a table outlining troop distributions in mid-May, 'that the department of the Pyrénées-Orientales has been omitted' (CN28 no. 28198).

On March 21 the *Moniteur*, which once again changed its editorial policy the moment he returned to power, printed the name NAPO-LEON in capital letters no fewer than twenty-six times in the course of four pages, telling the news of his triumphant return.[8] Napoleon rose at six o'clock that morning after only three hours' sleep, and at 1 p.m. held a grand parade in the courtyard of the Tuileries. Commandant Alexandre Coudreux described Napoleon's arrival to his son:

> The Emperor, on horseback, reviewed all the regiments and was welcomed with the enthusiasm that the presence of such a man inspired in the brave men whom for some days the last government had treated as murderers, Mamluks and brigands. For the four hours that the troops remained under arms, the cries of joy were interrupted only for the few minutes that Napoleon spent addressing the officers and non-commissioned officers gathered around him in a circle with a few of those beautiful, if vigorous phrases that belong to him alone, and that have always made us forget all our ills and defy all dangers! [Cries of 'Vive l'Empereur!' and 'Vive Napoléon!' were] repeated thousands of times, [and] must have been heard throughout the whole of Paris. In our euphoria, we all hugged each other without distinguishing between grade nor rank, and more than fifty thousand Parisians, witnessing such a fine scene, applauded these noble and generous demonstrations with all their hearts.[9]

Napoleon's work ethic remained unchanged: in the three months between his return to the Tuileries and the battle of Waterloo he wrote over nine hundred letters, the great majority of them concerned with trying to put France back onto a war footing in time for the coming hostilities. On the 23rd he ordered Bertrand to have various items brought to Paris from Elba, including a particular Corsican horse, his yellow carriage and the rest of his underwear.[10] Two days later he was already writing to his grand chamberlain, Comte Anatole de Montesquiou-Fezensac, about that year's theatre budgets.[11]

The only marshal besides Lefebvre to report for duty at the Tuileries immediately was Davout, even though he had been shamefully underused in the 1813 and 1814 campaigns, tied up in Hamburg rather than unleashed against France's enemies. After Napoleon's abdication he had been one of the few marshals who refused to take the oath of loyalty to Louis XVIII. But Napoleon now made a serious error when he appointed Davout war minister, governor of Paris and commander of the capital's

National Guard, thereby denying himself the services of his greatest marshal on the battlefields of Belgium. Some have speculated that the lack of personal rapport between the two of them might have been behind Napoleon's decision, or that Napoleon thought he needed Davout in Paris in case of a siege – but if the field campaign was not won decisively and swiftly it wouldn't matter who was in charge in Paris.[12] Napoleon did in fact understand this fully, telling Davout on May 12, 'The greatest misfortune we have to fear is that of being too weak in the north and to experience an early defeat.'[13] On the day of the battle of Waterloo, however, Davout was signing bureaucratic documents about peacetime army pay grades.[14] Years later, Napoleon regretted not putting either General Clauzel or General Lamarque in the war ministry instead.[15] At the time he inundated Davout with his customary letters, such as one on May 29 when, after an eagle-eyed review of five artillery batteries bound for Compiègne, he wrote, 'I noticed that several gun caissons didn't have their little pots of grease or all their replacement parts, as required by order.'[16]

Of the nineteen marshals on the active list (Grouchy was awarded his baton on April 15) only ten – namely Davout, Soult, Brune, Mortier, Ney, Grouchy, Saint-Cyr, Masséna, Lefebvre and Suchet – declared for Napoleon (or eleven if one counts Murat's quixotic and, as it turned out, suicidal decision to support the man whom he had been the very first to desert). But it wasn't until April 10 that Masséna in Marseilles put out a proclamation in favour of 'our chosen sovereign, the great Napoleon', and afterwards he did nothing.[17] Similarly Saint-Cyr stayed on his estate, and Lefebvre, Moncey and Mortier were too ill to be of any service. (Mortier would have commanded the Imperial Guard but for his severe sciatica.)[18] Napoleon assumed that Berthier would rejoin him, and joked that the only revenge he would take would be to oblige him to come to the Tuileries wearing the uniform of Louis XVIII's Guards. But Berthier left France for Bamberg in Bavaria, where he fell to his death from a window on June 15. Whether this was suicide, murder or an accident – there was a history of epilepsy in the family – is still unknown, but it was most probably the first.[19] We can only guess at the internal conflict and despair which may have prompted such a course in Napoleon's chief-of-staff after nearly twenty years of exceptionally close service. Berthier's absence over the coming weeks was a serious blow.

Although fourteen marshals had fought in the Austerlitz campaign, fifteen in the Jena campaign, seventeen in the Polish campaign, fifteen in the Iberian campaign, twelve in the Wagram campaign, thirteen in the Russian campaign, fourteen in the Leipzig campaign and eleven in the 1814 campaign, only three – Grouchy, Ney and Soult – were present in the Waterloo campaign. From the small pool available to him, Napoleon needed a battle-tested commander for the left wing of the Army of the North to take on Wellington and he summoned Ney, who joined the army as late as June 11. But the war-weary Ney underperformed badly throughout. On St Helena Napoleon opined that Ney 'was good for a command of ten thousand men, but beyond that he was out of his depth'.[20] His place in charge of the left wing should have been taken by Soult, whom Napoleon appointed chief-of-staff, in which job he too badly underperformed. Instead of appointing Suchet or Soult's lieutenant, General François de Monthion, chief-of-staff he wasted the former by sending him off to the Army of the Alps and kept Monthion, whom he disliked, in a junior role.

Of the other marshals, Marmont and Augereau had betrayed Napoleon in 1814; Victor stayed loyal to the Bourbons; the hitherto politically unreliable Jourdan was made a peer of France, governor of Besançon and commander of the 6th Military Division, while Macdonald and Oudinot stayed passively neutral. Oudinot, who returned to his home at Bar-le-Duc after his troops had declared for Napoleon, is credited with replying to the Emperor's offer of employment: 'I will serve no one, Sire, since I will not serve you.'[21]

In a series of proclamations from Lyons and later from the Tuileries, Napoleon swiftly undid many of the more unpopular Bourbon reforms. He cancelled changes in judicial tribunals, orders and decorations, restored the tricolour and the Imperial Guard, sequestered property owned by the Bourbons, annulled the changes to the Légion d'Honneur and restored to the regiments their old number designations that the Bourbons, with scant regard for military psychology, had replaced with royalist names. He also dissolved the legislature and convoked the electoral colleges of the Empire to meet in Paris in June at the Champ de Mars to acclaim the new constitution he was planning and 'assist at the coronation' of the Empress and the King of Rome.[22] 'Of all that individuals have done, written, or said, since the taking of Paris,' he promised, 'I shall for ever remain ignorant.'[23] He was as good as his word; it was the only sensible basis on which to attempt to restore national unity. But this did not prevent yet another rising in the Vendée, against which Napoleon was forced to deploy 25,000 troops in an Army of the Loire under Lamarque, including newly raised Young Guard units that would have been invaluable at Waterloo. Troops also had to be sent to Marseilles – which hoisted the tricolour only in mid-April – Nantes, Angers and Saumur and a number of other places in a way that had not been necessary in earlier campaigns, except 1814.[24]

Napoleon made good on his promise to abolish the hated *droits réunis* taxes on returning to power, but this reduced his ability to pay for the coming campaign.[25] Gaudin, who returned to the finance ministry, was told on April 3 that provisioning the army for the coming campaign would require an extra 100 million francs. 'I think that all the other budgets can be reduced,' Napoleon told him, 'given that ministers have allowed themselves much more than they really need.'[26] (Despite austerity measures, he still managed to find 200,000 francs in the imperial household budget for 'musicians, singers, etc.'[27]) Gaudin drew heavily on the Civil List, took 3 million francs in gold and silver from the cashier-general of Paris, raised 675,000 francs in timber taxes, borrowed 1.26 million francs from the Banque de France, sold 380,000 francs' worth of shares in the Canal du Midi, which, along with the sale of 1816 bonds and other government assets, as well as a tax on salt-mines and other industries, raised 17,434,352 francs in total.[28] It would have to be a swift and instantly victorious campaign, as France could clearly not afford a drawn out series of engagements.

In order to substantiate his claim to wish to govern France liberally, Napoleon asked the moderate Benjamin Constant to return from internal exile in the Vendée and draw up a new constitution, to be called the Acte Additionnel aux Constitutions de l'Empire. This provided for a bicameral legislature which would share powers with the Emperor on the British model, a two-stage electoral system, trial by jury, freedom of expression and even powers of impeachment of ministers. In his diary at the time, Constant described Napoleon, whom he had earlier derided in published pamphlets as akin to Genghis Khan and Attila, as 'a man who listens'.[29] Napoleon later explained that he had wanted 'to substantiate all the late innovations' in the new constitution to make it harder for anyone to restore the Bourbons.[30] Napoleon also ended all censorship (so much so that even the manifestos of enemy generals could be read in the French press), abolished the slave trade entirely, invited Madame de Staël and the American Revolutionary War hero the

Marquis de Lafayette into his new coalition (both distrusted Napoleon and refused*), and ordered that no Britons were to be detained or harassed. He also told the Conseil that he had entirely renounced all imperial ideas and that 'henceforth the happiness and the consolidation' of France 'shall be the object of all my thoughts'.[31] On April 4 he wrote to the monarchs of Europe, 'After presenting the spectacle of great campaigns to the world, from now on it will be more pleasant to know no other rivalry than that of the benefits of peace, of no other struggle than the holy conflict of the happiness of peoples.'[32]

Historians have tended to scoff at these measures and statements, yet such was the exhausted state of France in 1815, with most of the population wanting peace, that if he had remained in power Napoleon might very well have returned to the kind of pacific government of national unity that he had operated during the Consulate. But his longtime foes could not believe he would give up his imperial ambitions, and certainly could not take the risk that he would do so. Nor could they have guessed that he would be dead in six years. Instead, as one British MP not unreasonably put it, it was assumed that peace 'must always be uncertain with such a man, and . . . whilst he reigns, would require a constant armament, and hostile preparations more intolerable than war itself'.[33] On March 25 the Allies, still in congress at Vienna, formed a Seventh Coalition against him.

Napoleon took advantage of his brief return to power to restart various public works in Paris, including the elephant fountain at the Bastille, a new market place at Saint-Germain, the foreign ministry at the Quai d'Orsay and at the Louvre.[34] Talma went back to teaching acting at the Conservatory, which had been closed by the Bourbons; Denon the Louvre director, David the painter, Fontaine the architect and Corvisart the doctor returned to their old jobs in the arts and medicine; Carle Vernet's painting of Marengo was rehung at the Louvre, and some of the standards captured in the Napoleonic campaigns were put up in the Senate and Legislative Body.[35] On March 31 Napoleon visited the orphaned daughters of members of the Légion d'Honneur, whose school at Saint-Denis had had its funding cut by the Bourbons. That same day he restored the University of France to its former footing, re-appointing the Comte de Lacépède as chancellor. The Institut de France also reinstated Napoleon as a member. At a concert at the Tuileries that March to celebrate

---

* Napoleon had secured Lafayette's release after five years of Austrian captivity in 1797, but the time for gratitude was long past.

his return, the thirty-six-year-old Anne Hippolyte Boutet Salvetat, a celebrated actress known as Mademoiselle Mars, and Napoleon's old flame from the Italian campaign, Mademoiselle George, both wore the new Bonapartist emblem inspired by his springtime reappearance – a sprig of violets.

Yet none of these acts of public relations could dispel the growing belief on the part of most Frenchmen that disaster loomed. In April, conscription was extended to hitherto exempted married men. That month John Cam Hobhouse, a twenty-eight-year-old Radical writer and future British cabinet minister who was at the time living in Paris, noted: 'Napoleon is not popular, except with the actual army, and with the inhabitants of certain departments; and, perhaps even with them, his popularity is only relative.' Hobhouse was a fanatical Bonapartist, yet even he had to admit that the Saint-Germain nobles hated Napoleon, that the shopkeepers wanted peace and that although the regiments cried out 'Vive l'Empereur!' with feeling there was no echo from the populace, who made 'no noise nor any acclamations; a few low murmurs and whispers were alone heard' when the Emperor rode through the city.[36] By mid-April the conspicuous non-arrival from Vienna of Marie Louise and the King of Rome – 'the rose and the rosebud' as propagandists termed them – further alerted Parisians to the inevitability of war.[37]

At the Tuileries on April 16 Hobhouse watched Napoleon reviewing twenty-four battalions of the National Guard – which now accepted all able-bodied men between the ages of twenty and sixty. As the troops took two hours to march past, and Hobhouse was standing only ten yards away, he had ample opportunity to study his hero, who he thought looked nothing like his portraits:

> His face was of a deadly pale; his jaws overhung, but not so much as I had heard; his lips thin, but partially curled . . . His hair was of a dark dusky brown, scattered thinly over his temples: The crown of his head was bald . . . He was not fat in the upper part of his body, but projected considerably in the abdomen, so much so that his linen appeared beneath his waistcoat. He generally stood with his hands knit or folded before him . . . played with his nose; took snuff three or four times, and looked at his watch. He seemed to have a labouring in his chest, sighing or swallowing his spittle. He very seldom spoke, but when he did, smiled, in some sort, agreeably. He . . . went through the whole tedious ceremony with an air of sedate impatience.[38]

Although some soldiers stepped out of the ranks to deliver their petitions to the grenadier on guard – a hangover from the revolutionary army tradition – when others seemed scared of doing so Napoleon beckoned to have their petitions collected. One was presented by a six-year-old child dressed in a pioneer uniform, complete with false beard; he gave it to the Emperor on the end of a battle-axe, and Napoleon 'took and read [it] very complacently'.[39]

On April 22, 1815 Constant published the Acte Additionnel, which was then put to a plebiscite: 1,552,942 voted yes and 5,740 voted no, numbers which need to be treated with the same reservations as in earlier plebiscites. (People who voted both yes and no in error counted as a yes, for example; the overall turnout was only 22 per cent.[40] In the Seine-Inférieure, only 11,011 yes and 34 no votes were cast, compared with 62,218 who voted in the 1804 plebiscite.[41]) 'At no period in his life had I seen him enjoy more unruffled tranquillity,' recorded Lavalette, who reported to Napoleon daily. He put this down to the endorsement of the Acte Additionnel, which managed to blur political distinctions between liberals, moderate republicans, Jacobins and Bonapartists in what has been dubbed 'Revolutionary Bonapartism'.[42]

By late April 1815 a generally spontaneous *fédéré* militia movement was growing to hundreds of thousands of Frenchmen whose aim was to rebuild the sense of national unity France was believed to have felt at the time of the fall of the Bastille.[43] The *fédérés* held assemblies twice a week and required a signed commitment and sworn oath to confront the Bourbons with force; in much of the country they kept the royalists quiescent (at least until Waterloo, after which they were brutally suppressed).[44] Only in the fiercely anti-Bonapartist parts of France – Flanders, Artois, the Vendée and the Midi – did Revolutionary Bonapartism get nowhere. Otherwise it crossed the social classes: in Rennes the middle classes dominated the local *fédéré* organization whereas in Dijon it was made up of working men, while in Rouen it was indistinguishable from the National Guard. The *fédérés* had no effect on the war, but they were an indication of the widespread support Napoleon enjoyed in the country, and that he might have been able to stir up a guerrilla campaign after Waterloo had he chosen to do so.

On May 15 the Allies formally declared war on France. Molé saw Napoleon at the Élysée Palace, where he had moved for its secluded garden, two days later and found him 'gloomy and depressed, yet calm'. They spoke of the possible partition of the country.[45] In public Napoleon

67. Napoleon at bivouac the night between the first and second days of the battle of Wagram in July 1809. Marshal Berthier is busy at the table behind the fire; Napoleon's bodyguard, the Mamluk Roustam, is lying in the foreground.

68. (*top*) The interview between Emperor Francis of Austria (*left*), Prince Johann of Liechtenstein (*centre*) and Napoleon after the battle of Austerlitz in 1805. Five years later Francis was to become Napoleon's father-in-law.

69. Prince Clemens von Metternich, Austrian ambassador to France, foreign minister and eventually Chancellor, a subtle diplomat who timed Austria's final move against Napoleon to perfection.

70. Prince Karl von Schwarzenberg, whose careful manoeuvring of far larger forces was critical to Napoleon's defeat in 1813.

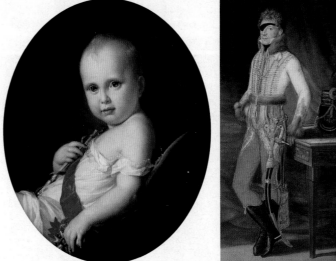

71. (*top*) The Empress Marie Louise, painted by François Gérard in the year she became Napoleon's second wife; she was eighteen and he was forty but the marriage began very successfully.

72. (*above left*) Napoleon doted on the son he had with Marie Louise, the King of Rome (later the Duke of Reichstadt). He died at the age of twenty-one of tuberculosis.

73. (*above right*) The dashing one-eyed Austrian general Adam von Neipperg, whom Napoleon defeated on the battlefield in 1813 but who became Marie Louise's lover after the Emperor's first abdication the following year.

74. (*right*) The uniforms of the Grande Armée were often magnificent, as depicted here by Carle Vernet in 1812, who helped design French flags and standards. It was dressed like this that Napoleon's troops invaded Russia.

75. (*below*) No sooner did the French capture Moscow in September 1812 than the Russians set fire to it, burning down more than two-thirds of the city.

76. (*top*) Napoleon (*centre left*) warming himself during the retreat from Moscow. 'The brilliant army that crossed the Niemen', noted Faber du Faur, the painter of this picture, 'would scarcely recognize itself now.'

77. (*above*) The crossing of the freezing Berezina on two trestle bridges in late November 1812, a miracle of deliverance for Napoleon's army.

78. (*top left*) Charles-Maurice de Talleyrand, four times foreign minister of France, was made a prince by Napoleon but plotted against him from 1807. Two years later the Emperor called him 'a shit in silk stockings'.

79. (*top right*) Joseph Fouché, the police minister, served every regime from the Jacobins to the Bourbons and managed never to be on the losing side.

80. (*above left*) Marshal Charles-Jean Bernadotte, whom Napoleon allowed to become Crown Prince of Sweden, turned on him once the Grande Armée army was fatally weakened in 1812.

81. (*above right*) Auguste de Marmont, Napoleon's oldest friend and whom he raised to the marshalate, betrayed him by surrendering Paris to the Allies in March 1814.

82. (*top*) One of the most emotional moments in the Napoleonic epic came when the Emperor bid adieu to the Old Guard at Fontainebleau Palace before going into exile on Elba in April 1814.

83. (*above*) Napoleon fleeing the battlefield of Waterloo on June 18, 1815, as depicted by the British caricaturist George Cruickshank.

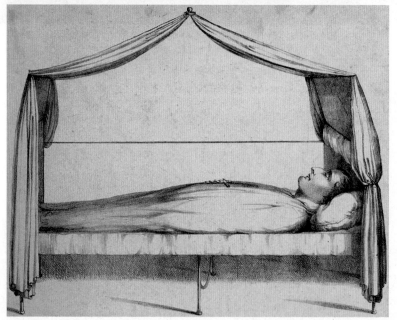

84. (*top left*) Longwood House on St Helena, where Napoleon (*in the doorway*) lived for five and a half years.

85. (*top right*) The obese, balding Napoleon on St Helena.

86. (*above*) Napoleon shortly after death on his iron campaign bed in the drawing room at Longwood, sketched by a Royal Navy captain.

maintained his customary sangfroid, however. At a review of five battalions of the Line and four of the Young Guard at the Tuileries later
that month he was pulling grenadiers' noses and playfully slapping a
colonel, after which 'the officer went away, smiling and showing his
cheek, which was red with the blow.'[46]

The Acte Additionnel was ratified at a gigantic open-air ritual called
the Champ de Mai, which confusingly took place on the Champ de
Mars, outside the École Militaire, on June 1. 'The sun, flashing on sixty
thousand bayonets,' recalled Thiébault, 'seemed to make the vast space
sparkle.'[47] During this strange mixture of religious, political and military
ceremony, loosely based on one of Charlemagne's traditions, Napoleon,
wearing a purple costume not unlike his coronation mantle, spoke to
15,000 seated Frenchmen and over 100,000 more milling in the crowd.
'As emperor, consul, soldier, I owe everything to the people,' he said. 'In
prosperity, in adversity, on the battlefield, in counsel, enthroned, in exile,
France has been the sole and constant object of my thoughts and actions.
Like the King of Athens, I sacrificed myself for my people in the hope of
seeing fulfilled the promise to preserve for France her natural integrity,
honour and rights.'[48]* He went on to explain that he had been brought
back to power by public indignation at the treatment of France and that
he had counted on a long peace because the Allies had signed treaties
with France – which they were now breaking by building up forces in
Holland, partitioning Alsace-Lorraine and preparing for war. He ended
by saying, 'My own glory, honour and happiness are indistinguishable
from those of France.' Needless to say, the speech was followed by prolonged cheering, before a massive march-past by the army, departmental
representatives and National Guard.[49] The whole court, Conseil, senior
judiciary and diplomatic and officer corps in their uniforms were present, and ladies in their diamonds. With a hundred-gun salute, drumrolls,
a vast amphitheatre, eagles emblazoned with the names of each department, gilded carriages, solemn oaths, a chanted *Te Deum*, red-coated
lancers, an altar presided over by archbishops and heralds in their finery,
it was an imposing spectacle.[50] During Mass, Napoleon looked at the
assembly through an opera glass. Hobhouse had to admit that when the
Emperor 'plumped himself down on his throne and rolled his mantle
round him he looked very ungainly and squat'.

---

* Probably a reference to King Codrus, who provoked the Dorians to kill him in *c.*1068 BC
after the Delphic Oracle prophesied that their invasion would succeed only if the King of
Athens stayed unharmed.

The newly elected chambers took their oath of allegiance to the Emperor with minimal difficulty two days later, even though the elections the previous month had resulted in a number of constitutionalists, liberals, crypto-royalists and Jacobins being elected. With the lower house immediately sidetracked into an ill-tempered debate about whether members should be allowed to read speeches from notes hidden in their hats, the legislature was unlikely to cause Napoleon much immediate cause for concern, despite the fact that his long-term opponent, the former senator the Comte Lanjuinais, had been elected its president and Lafayette was now a deputy. There was a huge firework display in the Place de la Concorde the following evening, which featured Napoleon arriving in a ship from Elba. As a spectator recorded: 'The mob cried "Vive l'Empereur and the fireworks!" and the reign of the Constitutional Monarchy began.'[51] Of course it wasn't a constitutional monarchy as in Britain, since the ministers were all appointed by Napoleon, who was his own prime minister, but neither was it the unfettered dictatorship of the pre-1814 period, and it seemed possible that it might evolve liberally.

Napoleon knew that his success or failure would ultimately be determined solely on the battlefield. On June 7 he ordered Bertrand to get his telescopes, uniforms, horses and carriages made ready 'so that I can leave two hours after having given the order', adding: 'As I will be camping often, it is important that I have my iron beds and tents.'[52] That same day he told Drouot: 'I was pained to see that the men in the two battalions that left this morning had only one pair of boots each.'[53] Two days later, on June 9, 1815, the Allies signed the Treaty of Vienna. Under Article I they reaffirmed their intention of forcing Napoleon from the throne, and under Article III they agreed that they would not lay down their arms until this was achieved.[54]

As early as March 27 Napoleon had told Davout that 'the Army of the North will be the principal army', as the closest Allied forces were in Flanders and he certainly did not intend to wait for Schwarzenberg's return to France.[55] At 4 a.m. on Monday, June 12 Napoleon left the Élysée to join the Army of the North at Avesnes, where he dined with Ney the next day. By noon on the 15th he was at Charleroi in Belgium, ready to engage the Prussian army under Blücher near Fleurus. He hoped to defeat Blücher before falling on an Anglo-Dutch-Belgian-German force under Wellington, 36 per cent of whose troops were British while 49 per cent spoke German as their first language.

Napoleon later said that 'he had relied mainly ... upon the idea, that a victory over the English army in Belgium ... would have been sufficient to have produced a change of administration in England, and have afforded him a chance of concluding an immediate general truce.'[56] Capturing Brussels, part of the French Empire until 1814, would also have been good for morale. To fight was a risk, but not so great a risk as waiting until the vast Austrian and Russian armies were ready to strike at Paris once again. Across Europe, 280,000 French soldiers faced around 800,000 Allies, although the Austrian contingent would not be in theatre for several weeks, and the Russians not for months. 'If they enter France,' Napoleon told the army from Avesnes on June 14, 'therein they will find their tomb ... For all the French who have the courage, the time has come to vanquish or perish!'[57]

The opening stages of the campaign saw him reviving the best of the strategic abilities he had shown the previous year. The French were even more scattered than the Allies at first, across an area 175 miles wide by 100 deep, but Napoleon used this fact to feint towards the west and then concentrate in the centre in classic *bataillon carré* style. The manoeuvring of the 125,000-strong Army of the North between June 6 and the 15th allowed it to cross the rivers at Marchienne, Charleroi and Châtelet without any Allied reaction of note. Wellington, who had arrived post-haste from Vienna on April 5, had been forced to string his force out along a 62-mile-wide front, trying simultaneously to guard the routes to Brussels, Antwerp and Ghent. He frustratedly acknowledged as much when he said on the evening of June 15, 'Napoleon has humbugged me, by God.'[58]

Napoleon's speed and tactical ability allowed him once again to strike at the hinge between the armies opposing him, as he had been doing for nearly twenty years. His manoeuvres were all the more impressive as half of his army was made up of raw recruits. Although veterans had been released from Spanish, Russian and Austrian prisoner-of-war camps, after the initial rush of enthusiasm only 15,000 volunteers had joined the colours, so conscription provided the balance. Morale among the troops was shaky, especially after the former Chouan leader, General Bourmont, and his staff defected to the Allies on the morning of the 15th.[59] Some of the men understandably asked why generals who had pledged oaths to the Bourbons, such as Soult, Ney, Kellermann and Bourmont, had been allowed back at all. Low morale led to poor discipline, with the Imperial Guard plundering freely in Belgium and laughing at the gendarmes sent to stop them.[60] Equipment was also wanting: the

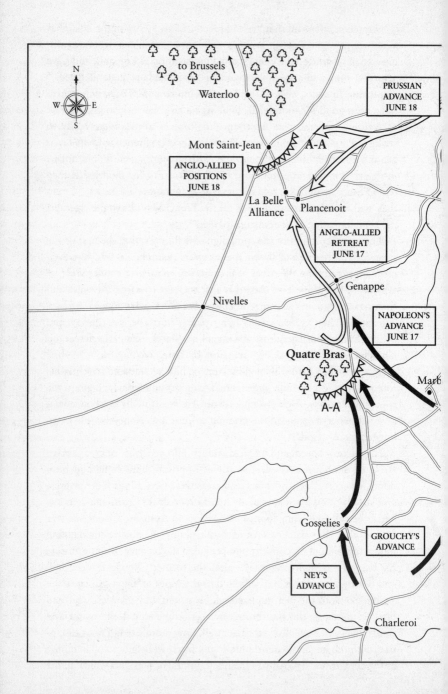

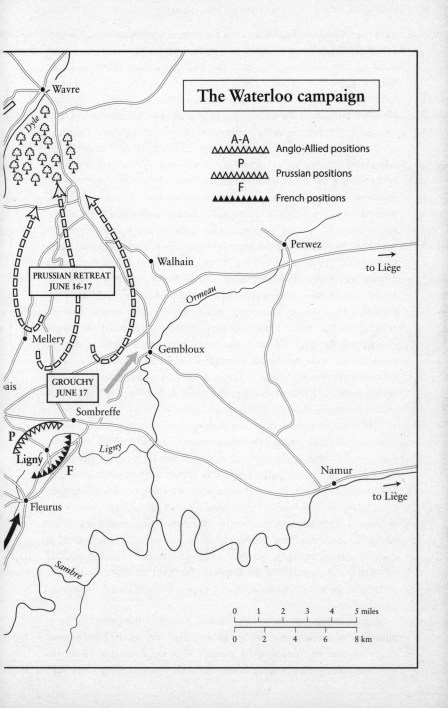

The Waterloo campaign

A-A
∧∧∧∧∧∧∧∧∧ Anglo-Allied positions
P
∧∧∧∧∧∧∧∧∧ Prussian positions
F
▲▲▲▲▲▲▲▲▲ French positions

Wavre

Dyle

Perwez

to Liège

Walhain

Ormeau

**PRUSSIAN RETREAT
JUNE 16-17**

Mellery

Gembloux

**GROUCHY
JUNE 17**

ais

Sombreffe

Ligny

Namur

to Liège

P
Ligny
F

Fleurus

Sambre

0	1	2	3	4	5 miles
0	2	4	6	8 km

14th Légère had no shakos, the 11th Cuirassiers no breastplates. ('Breast-plates aren't necessary to make war,' Napoleon blithely told Davout on June 3.) The Prussians reported that some battalions of the Imperial Guard, reconstituted on March 13 when Napoleon was in Lyons, looked more like a militia, wearing an assortment of forage caps and bicornes instead of their fearsome bearskins. The Middle Guard, disbanded by the Bourbons, had been recalled only the previous month.

On June 16, Napoleon divided his army into three. Ney took the left wing with three corps to prevent the juncture of the two enemy forces by capturing the crossroads at Quatre Bras – where the north–south Brussels–Charleroi highway crosses the vital east–west Namur–Nivelles road that was the principal lateral link between Blücher and Wellington – while Grouchy was on the right wing with his corps, and Napoleon stayed in the centre with the Imperial Guard and another corps.[61] Later that day, as Ney engaged first the Prince of Orange and then Wellington himself at Quatre Bras, Napoleon and Grouchy attacked Blücher at Ligny. 'You must go towards that steeple,' he told Gérard, 'and drive the Prussians in as far as you can. I will support you. Grouchy has my orders.'[62] While these mission-defined orders might sound somewhat casual, a general of Gérard's enormous experience knew what was expected of him. Napoleon meanwhile ordered an army corps of 20,000 men under General d'Erlon, which an order from Soult had earlier detached from Ney's command on its way to Quatre Bras, to fall on the exposed Prussian right flank at Ligny.

Had d'Erlon arrived as arranged, Napoleon's respectable victory at Ligny would have turned into a devastating rout, but instead, just as he was about to engage, he received urgent, imperative orders from Ney that he was needed at Quatre Bras, so he turned around and marched to that battlefield.[63] Before he got there and was able to make a contribution, Soult ordered him to turn round and return to Ligny, where his exhausted corps arrived too late to take part in that battle also. This confusion between Ney, Soult and d'Erlon robbed Napoleon of a decisive victory at Ligny, where Blücher lost around 17,000 casualties to Napoleon's 11,000 and the Prussians were driven from the field by nightfall.[64] Ney meanwhile lost over 4,000 men and failed to capture Quatre Bras.

'It may happen to me to lose battles,' Napoleon had told the Piedmontese envoys back in 1796, 'but no one shall ever see me lose minutes either by over-confidence or by sloth.'[65] With the Prussians seemingly retreating along their supply lines eastwards towards Liège, he could have fallen upon Wellington's force at first light on Saturday, June 17. But instead he did not rise until 8 a.m. and then wasted the next five hours reading reports from Paris, visiting the Ligny battlefield, giving directions for the care of the wounded, addressing captured Prussian officers on their country's foreign policy and talking to his own generals 'with his accustomed ease' on various political topics.[66] Only at noon did he send Grouchy off with a huge corps of 33,000 men and 96 guns to follow the Prussian army, thereby splitting his force the day before he anticipated a major battle against Wellington, rather than concentrating it.[67] 'Now then, Grouchy, follow up those Prussians,' Napoleon said, 'give them a touch of cold steel in their kidneys, but be sure to keep in communication with me by your left flank.'[68] But in sending Grouchy off, he was ignoring one of his own military maxims: 'No force should be detached on the eve of battle, because affairs may change during the night, either by the retreat of the enemy, or the arrival of large reinforcements which might enable him to resume the offensive, and render your previous dispositions disastrous.'[69]

Although visiting Ligny gave him an idea of the Prussian order of battle and of which enemy corps had been most damaged, this intelligence could never compensate for letting the Prussian army escape – which it might not have done if he had sent Grouchy off on the 16th, or very early on the 17th. Soult had sent Pajol on a reconnaissance towards Namur, where he had captured some guns and prisoners, leading Napoleon further towards the theory that most of the Prussian army was retreating in disarray on its supply lines.[70] Various comments he made that day and subsequently suggest that Napoleon thought he had so shattered the Prussians at Ligny that they could play no further significant part in the campaign. No reconnaissance was therefore sent northwards.

The Prussians had a fifteen-hour head-start on Grouchy, who didn't know in which direction they had gone. Blücher had been concussed during the battle, and his chief-of-staff, General August von Gneisenau, had ordered a retreat to the north, to stay close to Wellington's army, rather than east. This counter-intuitive move was to be described by Wellington as the most important decision of the nineteenth century. As he fought and refought the battle in his mind over the next half-decade, Napoleon blamed many factors for his defeat, but he acknowledged that either he should have given the job of staving off the Prussians to the more vigorous Vandamme or Suchet, or he should have left it to Pajol with a single division. 'I ought to have taken all the other troops with me,' he ruefully concluded.[71]

Only later on June 17 did Napoleon move off at a leisurely pace towards Quatre Bras, arriving at 1 p.m. to join Ney. By that time Wellington had learned what had happened at Ligny and was prudently retreating north himself in the pouring rain, with plenty of time to take up position on the ridge of Mont Saint-Jean. This was a few miles south of his headquarters at the village of Waterloo, in an area he had previously reconnoitred and whose myriad defensive advantages as a battlefield – only 3 miles wide with plenty of 'hidden' ground and two large stone farmhouses called Hougoumont and La Haie Sainte out in front of a ridge – he had already spotted. 'It is an approved maxim in war never to do what the enemy wishes you to do', was another of Napoleon's sayings, 'for this reason alone, because he wishes it. A field of battle, therefore, which he has previously studied and reconnoitred should be avoided.'[72] Not committing the Guard at Borodino, staying too long in Moscow and Leipzig, splitting his forces in the Leipzig and Waterloo campaigns and, finally, coming to the decisive engagement on ground which his opponent had chosen: all were the result of Napoleon not following his own military maxims.

Napoleon spent some of June 17 visiting battalions that had distinguished themselves at Ligny, and admonishing those that had not. He recognized Colonel Odoards of the 22nd Line, who used to be in his Guard, and asked him how many men he had on parade (1,830), how many they had lost the day before (220), and what was being done with abandoned Prussian muskets.[73] When Odoards told him they were being destroyed, Napoleon said they were needed by the National Guard and offered 3 francs for every one collected. Otherwise the morning of the 17th was characterized by an entirely unaccustomed torpor.

Claims were made decades after the campaign by Jérôme and Larrey that Napoleon's lethargy was the result of his suffering from haemorrhoids which incapacitated him after Ligny.[74] 'My brother, I hear that you suffer from piles,' Napoleon had written to Jérôme in May 1807. 'The simplest way to get rid of them is to apply three or four leeches. Since I used this remedy ten years ago, I haven't been tormented again.'[75] But was he in fact tormented? This might be the reason why he spent hardly any time on horseback during the battle of Waterloo – visiting the Grand Battery once at 3 p.m. and riding along the battlefront at 6 p.m. – and why he twice retired to a farmhouse at Rossomme about 1,500 yards behind the lines for short periods.[76] He swore at his page,

Gudin, for swinging him on to his saddle too violently at Le Caillou in the morning, later apologizing, saying: 'When you help a man to mount, it's best done gently.'[77] General Auguste Pétiet, who was on Soult's staff at Waterloo, recalled that

> His pot-belly was unusually pronounced for a man of forty-five. Further-more, it was noticeable during this campaign that he remained on horseback much less than in the past. When he dismounted, either to study maps or else to send messages and receive reports, members of his staff would set before him a small deal table and a rough chair made of the same wood, and on this he would remain seated for long periods at a time.[78]

A bladder infection has also been diagnosed by historians, although Napoleon's valet Marchand denied that his master suffered from one during this period, as has narcolepsy, of which there is no persuasive evidence either. 'At no point in his life did the Emperor display more energy, more authority, or greater capacity as a leader of men,' recalled one of his closest aides-de-camp, Flahaut.[79] But by 1815 Napoleon was nearly forty-six, overweight, and didn't have the raw energy of his mid-twenties. By June 18 he also had had only one proper night's sleep in six days. Flahaut's explanation for Napoleon's inaction was simply that 'After a pitched battle, and marches such as we had made on the previous day, our army could not be expected to start off again at dawn.'[80] Yet such considerations had not prevented Napoleon from fighting four battles in five days the previous year.

There is in fact no convincing evidence that any of the decisions Napoleon took on June 18 were the result of his physical state rather than his own misjudgements and the faulty intelligence he received. 'In war,' he told one of his captors the following year, 'the game is always with him who commits the fewest faults.'[81] In the Waterloo campaign that was Wellington, who had made a study of Napoleon's tactics and career, was rigorous in his deployments, and was everywhere on the battlefield. Napoleon, Soult and Ney, by contrast, fought one of the worst-commanded battles of the Napoleonic Wars. The best battlefield soldier Napoleon had fought before Waterloo had been Archduke Charles, and he was simply not prepared for a master-tactician of Wellington's calibre – one, moreover, who had never lost a battle.

When Napoleon met d'Erlon at Quatre Bras on the 17th he said either 'You have dealt a blow to the cause of France, general', or, as d'Erlon himself preferred to recall it, 'France has been lost; my dear general, put yourself at the head of the cavalry and push the English rearguard as hard as possible.'[82] That evening Napoleon seems to have come close to the fighting between the British cavalry rearguard, slowing the pursuit in the heavy rain, and the French vanguard thrusting them northwards towards the ridge of Mont Saint-Jean, though he didn't take part in a cavalry charge, as d'Erlon claimed in his memoirs.[83] He did have time to stop for the wounded Captain Elphinstone of the 7th Hussars, however, to whom he gave a drink of wine from his own hipflask and for whom he got the attention of a doctor.[84] Napoleon was perfectly capable of kindness to individual Britons while detesting their government.

At around 7 p.m., Napoleon called off the attack on the Anglo-Allied rearguard, as d'Erlon had been urging him to, and said: 'Have the troops make soup and get their arms in good order. We will see what midday brings.'[85] That night he visited the outposts, telling his men to rest well, for 'If the English army remains here tomorrow, it is mine.'[86] He chose Le Caillou farmhouse as his headquarters that night, sleeping on his camp bed on the ground floor while Soult slept on straw on the floor above. (He hadn't wanted to go the extra 3 miles back to the town of Genappes as he knew he would be receiving reports.) Corbineau, La Bédoyère, Flahaut and his other aides-de-camp spent the night riding between the various corps in the rain, recording movements and positions.

'Mamluk Ali', Napoleon's French bodyguard, recalled him lying on a bundle of straw till his room was made ready. 'When he had taken possession . . . he had his boots taken off, and we had trouble in doing it, as they had been wet all day, and after undressing he went to bed. That night he slept little, being disturbed every minute by people coming and going; one came to report, another to receive orders, etc.'[87] At least he was dry. 'Our greatcoats and trousers were caked with several pounds of mud,' Sergeant Hippolyte de Mauduit of the 1st Grenadiers à Pied recalled. 'A great many of the soldiers had lost their shoes and reached their bivouac barefoot.'[88] Never had Napoleon's obsession with shoes been more vindicated.

Napoleon later told Las Cases that he reconnoitred with Bertrand at 1 a.m. to check that Wellington's army was still there, which (despite there being no corroboration of it) he might have done. He was woken at 2 a.m. to receive a message from Grouchy, written four hours earlier, in which he reported being in contact with the Prussians near Wavre. Grouchy thought it might be the main Prussian force, whereas in fact it was only Blücher's rearguard. Napoleon didn't reply for another ten hours, despite knowing by then that Wellington was going to defend Mont Saint-Jean later that morning. It was an extraordinary error not to have brought Grouchy back to the battlefield immediately, to fall on Wellington's left flank.

'Ah! *Mon Dieu!*' Napoleon told General Gourgaud the next year, 'perhaps the rain on the seventeenth of June had more to do than is supposed with the loss of Waterloo. If I had not been so weary, I should have been on horseback all night. Events that seem very small often have very great results.'[89] He felt strongly that his thorough reconnoitring of battlefields such as Eggmühl had led to victory, but the real significance of the rain was that his artillery commander, General Drouot, suggested waiting for the ground to dry before starting the battle the next day, so that he could get his guns into place more easily and the cannonballs would bounce further when fired. It was advice Drouot was to regret for the rest of his life, for neither he nor the Emperor knew that, having eluded Grouchy, Blücher had reiterated his promise to Wellington that same morning that at least three Prussian corps would arrive on the battlefield that afternoon. Indeed, Wellington decided to fight there only on the understanding that this would happen.

Had Napoleon started his attack at sunrise, 3.48 a.m. on Sunday, June 18, instead of after 11 a.m., he would have had more than seven extra hours to break Wellington's line before Bülow's corps erupted onto his right flank.[90]* Although Napoleon ordered Ney to have the men properly fed and their equipment checked 'so that at nine o'clock precisely each of them is ready and there can be a battle', it was to be another two hours before the fighting started.[91] By then Napoleon had held a breakfast conference of senior officers in the dining room next to his bedroom at Le Caillou. When several of the generals who had fought Wellington in Spain, such as Soult, Reille and Foy, suggested that he should not rely on being able to break through the British infantry with ease, Napoleon replied, 'Because you've been beaten by Wellington you consider him to be a good general. I say that he's a bad general and that the English are bad troops. It will be a lunchtime affair!' A clearly unconvinced Soult could only say, 'I hope so!'[92] These seemingly hubris-

---

* Napoleon's decision to disband the *aérostatier* unit of military balloonists soon after becoming First Consul proved disastrous, as its use at Waterloo would have given him more than three hours' notice that the Prussian corps were on their way (ed. Chandler, *Military Maxims* pp. 19–20).

tic remarks completely contradicted his real and oft-stated views about Wellington and the British, and must be ascribed to his need to encourage his lieutenants just hours away from a major battle.

At the breakfast conference, Jérôme told Napoleon that the waiter at the King of Spain inn at Genappes where Wellington had dined on June 16 had overheard an aide-de-camp saying that the Prussians would join them in front of the Forest of Soignes, which was directly behind Mont Saint-Jean. In response to this (ultimately devastatingly accurate) information, Napoleon said, 'The Prussians and the English cannot possibly link up for another two days after such a battle as Fleurus [that is, Ligny], and given the fact that they are being pursued by a considerable body of troops.' He then added, 'The battle that is coming will save France and will be celebrated in the annals of the world. I shall have my artillery fire and my cavalry charge, so as to force the enemy to disclose his positions, and when I am quite certain which positions the English troops have taken up, I shall march straight at them with my Old Guard.'[93] Napoleon could be forgiven for not altering his entire strategy on the basis of a waiter's report of the conversation of an over-loquacious aide-de-camp, but even his own explanation of the tactics he was about to adopt betrays their total lack of sophistication. Wellington expected Napoleon to adopt a wide flanking manoeuvre of the French left – and deployed 17,500 men at Hal to guard against it – but his plan turned out to be no more imaginative than those he had employed at Eylau, Borodino or Lâon.

At 9.30 a.m. Napoleon left Le Caillou, in his orderly Jardin Ainé's recollection, 'to take up his stand half a league in advance on a hill where he could discern the movements of the British army. There he dismounted, and with his field-glass endeavoured to discover all the movements in the enemy's line.'[94] He chose a small knoll near the La Belle Alliance inn, where he spread his maps on the table while his horses stood saddled nearby.[95] 'I saw him through my glass,' recalled Foy, 'walking up and down, wearing his grey overcoat, and frequently leaning over the little table on which his map was placed.'[96] The night's rain had given way to a cloudy but dry day. Soult suggested an early attack, but Napoleon replied that they 'must wait', almost certainly to allow the Grand Battery to negotiate the mud more easily. Colonel Comte de Turenne and Monthion recalled Napoleon's tiredness in the two hours before the battle started; the Emperor 'remained a long time seated before a table . . . and . . . they frequently saw his head, overcome by sleep, sink down upon the map spread out before his heavy eyes'.[97]

Napoleon wrote to Grouchy at noon and again at 1 p.m. ordering him to rejoin him immediately. But by then it was too late.[98] (One of his messages didn't even reach Grouchy until 6 p.m.) Napoleon later claimed that he had commanded Grouchy to return earlier, but no such order has been found and Grouchy vociferously denied it.[99] A bulging file in the war ministry archives at Vincennes bears witness to the controversy between Grouchy and Gérard as to whether, without Napoleon's direct orders, Grouchy ought in any case to have marched towards the sound of the Grand Battery when it opened up in the late morning, rather than pressing on to engage the Prussian rearguard at Wavre.[100]

In the Peninsular War, Wellington had conducted several defensive battles, including Vimeiro in 1808, Talavera in 1809 and Bussaco in 1810, and was confident of holding his ground. A tough, no-nonsense Anglo-Irish aristocrat and stern, unbending Tory, he admired Napoleon as 'the first man of the day on a field of battle' but otherwise despised him as a political upstart. 'His policy was mere bullying,' Wellington said after Waterloo, 'and, military matters apart, he was a Jonathan Wild.' (Wild was a notorious criminal hanged at Tyburn in 1725.)[101] Wellington's choice of ground, with his right flank protected by Hougoumont, his left by a forest, and his centre on a lateral sunken road a few hundred yards behind the fortified La Haie Sainte, severely limited Napoleon's tactical options.* But with the Forest of Soignes behind him, Wellington took a tremendous risk in choosing this ground. If Napoleon had forced him back from the road, an orderly retreat would have been impossible.

The battle of Waterloo started around 11 a.m. with the guns of Reille's corps preparing the way for the diversionary attack on Hougoumont by Jérôme's division, followed by Foy's. The attack on the farmhouse failed, and was to draw in more and more French troops as the day progressed. For some unknown reason they did not try to smash in the farmhouse's front gates with horse artillery. Wellington reinforced it during the day and Hougoumont, like La Haie Sainte, became an invaluable breakwater that disrupted and funnelled the French advances. Jérôme fought bravely, and when his division was reduced to a mere two battalions Napoleon summoned him and said: 'My brother, I regret to have known you so late.'[102] This, Jérôme later recalled, was balm to the 'many repressed pains in his heart'.

---

* The contours of Wellington's line are almost impossible to discern today because of the Lion Mound, a 141-foot-high artificial hill that was built on top of it after the battle.

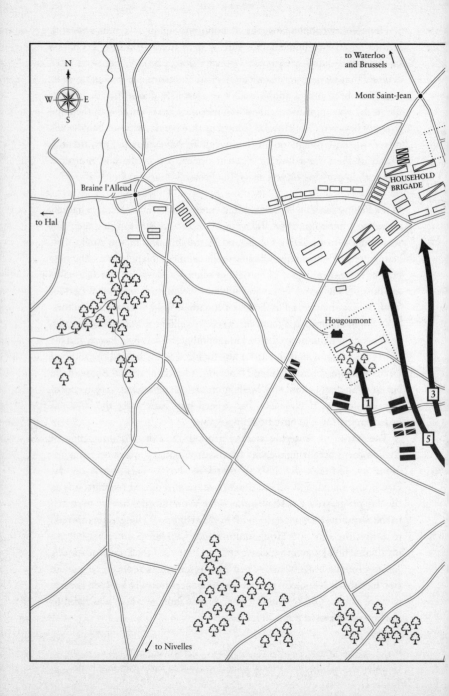

to Waterloo
and Brussels

Mont Saint-Jean

HOUSEHOLD
BRIGADE

Braine l'Alleud

to Hal

Hougoumont

1

3

5

to Nivelles

N
W E
S

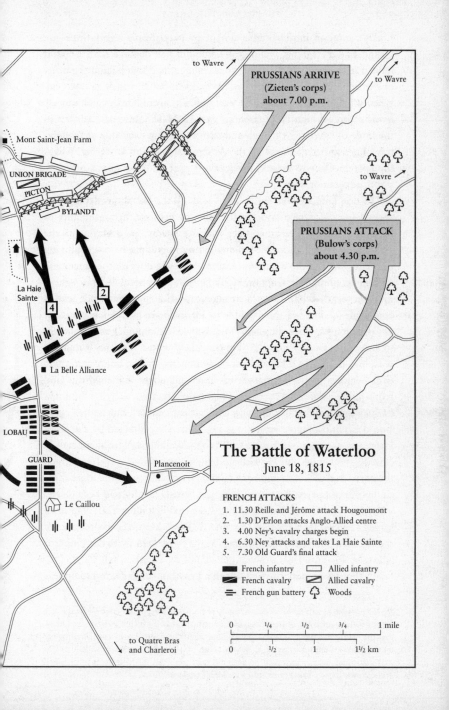

PRUSSIANS ARRIVE
(Zieten's corps)
about 7.00 p.m.

to Wavre

to Wavre

to Wavre

Mont Saint-Jean Farm

UNION BRIGADE

PICTON

BYLANDT

PRUSSIANS ATTACK
(Bulow's corps)
about 4.30 p.m.

La Haie
Sainte

[2]

[4]

■ La Belle Alliance

LOBAU

GUARD

Plancenoit

Le Caillou

The Battle of Waterloo
June 18, 1815

FRENCH ATTACKS

1. 11.30 Reille and Jérôme attack Hougoumont
2. 1.30 D'Erlon attacks Anglo-Allied centre
3. 4.00 Ney's cavalry charges begin
4. 6.30 Ney attacks and takes La Haie Sainte
5. 7.30 Old Guard's final attack

▬ French infantry	▭ Allied infantry
▰ French cavalry	▱ Allied cavalry
≡ French gun battery	♧ Woods

to Quatre Bras
and Charleroi

0	¼	½	¾	1 mile
0	½	1	1½ km	

At 1 p.m. an initial bombardment by Napoleon's eighty-three-gun Grand Battery against Wellington's line did less damage than it might have due to Wellington's orders that his men lie down behind the brow of the ridge. Napoleon unleashed his major infantry attack at 1.30 p.m. when d'Erlon's corps assaulted Wellington's centre-left through muddy fields of breast-high rye, marching past La Haie Sainte on their left in the hope of smashing through and then rolling up each side of Wellington's line, rather as they had the Austro-Russians at Austerlitz. It was the correct place to attack, the weakest part of Wellington's position, but the execution was faulty.

D'Erlon launched his entire corps with all the battalions deployed in several lines 250 men wide at the start of his assault, presumably to increase the firepower on contact with the enemy, but violating all the established French models of manoeuvring in column before deploying into line. This left the whole formation unwieldy, difficult to control and extremely vulnerable. Captain Pierre Duthilt of General de Marcognet's division recalled that it was 'a strange formation and one which was to cost us dear, since we were unable to form square as a defence against cavalry attacks, while the enemy's artillery could plough our formations to a depth of twenty ranks'.[103] No one knew whose idea this formation was, but ultimately d'Erlon must be responsible for so important a tactical decision as the formation in which his corps launched the vital front-fixing assault.* Another of Napoleon's maxims was that 'Infantry, cavalry and artillery are nothing without each other', but on this occasion d'Erlon's infantry attack was inadequately protected by the other arms, and was repulsed having failed to fix Wellington's front in place.[104] Instead the Union and Household brigades of British cavalry charged the corps and sent it fleeing back to the French lines with the loss of two eagles out of twelve. At 3 p.m., once the British cavalry had been driven away from the Grand Battery in the wake of d'Erlon's retreat, Napoleon joined General Jean-Jacques Desvaux de Saint-Maurice, commander of the Guard artillery, for a closer look at the battlefield. With the Emperor riding beside him, Desvaux was cut in half by a cannonball.[105]

At about 1.30 p.m. the first of three Prussian corps started to appear

---

* One possible reason for his decision may have been that Ney, d'Erlon and General Pierre Binet de Marcognet, one of the divisional commanders, had all fought in Spain, and knew that the British had often successfully prevented deployment into line by concentrating fire on the flanks of units attempting it. But the result of deploying his men in wide lines was that command quickly collapsed because the men were too far from their officers and non-commissioned officers (interview with John Lee, June 21, 2013).

on Napoleon's right flank. He had been warned that this might happen by a Prussian hussar who had been captured by a squadron of French chasseurs between Wavre and Plancenoit, and had been moving men off to the right flank for the better part of half an hour. He now ordered that the army be told the dark-coated bodies of men on the horizon were Grouchy's corps arriving to win the battle. As time wore on this falsehood was gradually revealed, with a corresponding drop in morale. During the afternoon Napoleon was forced to divert steadily increasing numbers to his right flank to confront the Prussians, and by 4 p.m. Bülow's 30,000 Prussians were attacking Lobau's 7,000 French infantry and cavalry between Frischermont and Plancenoit.[106] The advantage that Napoleon had enjoyed in the morning of 72,000 men and 236 guns over Wellington's 68,000 men and 136 guns was turned into a significant disadvantage once the Allies could together deploy over 100,000 men and more than 200 guns.

A series of massive cavalry charges totalling 10,000 men, the largest since Murat's charge at Eylau, was launched under Ney against Wellington's centre-right at around 4 p.m., although it is still unclear quite who – if anyone – had ordered it, since both Napoleon and Ney denied it afterwards.[107] 'There is Ney hazarding the battle which was almost won,' Napoleon told Flahaut when he saw what was happening, 'but he must be supported now, for that is our only chance.'[108] Despite thinking the charge 'premature and ill-timed', Napoleon told Flahaut to 'order all the cavalry [he] could find to assist the troops which Ney had thrown at the enemy across the ravine'.[109] (Today one can see at the Gordon Monument how deep the road was, but it is no ravine.) 'In war there are sometimes mistakes which can only be repaired by persevering in the same line of action,' Flahaut later said philosophically.[110] Unfortunately for Napoleon, this was not one of them.

Wellington's infantry now formed thirteen hollow squares (in fact they were rectangular in shape) to receive the cavalry. A horse's natural unwillingness to charge into a wall of bristling bayonets made them near-impregnable to cavalry, though Ney had broken the squares of the 42nd and 69th Foot at Quatre Bras and French cavalry had broken squares of Russians at Hof in 1807 and of Austrians at Dresden in 1813. Squares were particularly vulnerable to artillery and infantry formed in line, but this cavalry attack was unsupported by either, confirming the suspicion that it had started as an accident rather than from a deliberate order by Napoleon or Ney. Not one of the thirteen squares broke. 'It was the good discipline of the English that gained the day,'

Napoleon conceded on St Helena, after which he blamed General Guyot, who commanded the Heavy Cavalry, for charging without orders. This was unfounded as Guyot only rode in the second wave.[111]

The mystery of the battle of Waterloo is why a collection of fine and experienced French combat generals of all three arms repeatedly failed to co-ordinate their efforts, as they had done successfully on so many previous battlefields.* This was particularly true of Napoleon's favourite arm, the artillery, which consistently missed giving close support to the infantry at various important stages throughout the battle. With much of the French cavalry exhausted, its horses blown, and the Prussians arriving in force after 4.15 p.m., Napoleon would have been wise to withdraw as best he could.[112] Instead, sometime after 6 p.m., Ney succeeded in capturing La Haie Sainte and the nearby excavation area known as the Sandpit in the centre of the battlefield, and brought up a battery of horse artillery at 300 yards' range, allowing him to pound Wellington's centre with musketry and cannon, to the extent that the 27th Inniskilling Regiment of Foot, formed in square, took 90 per cent casualties. This was the crisis point of the battle, the best chance the French had of breaking through before the sheer weight of Prussian numbers crushed them. Yet when Ney sent his aide-de-camp Octave Levasseur to beg Napoleon for more troops to exploit the situation, the Emperor, his cavalry exhausted and his own headquarters now within range of Prussian artillery, refused. 'Troops?' he said sarcastically to Levasseur. 'Where would you like me to find them? Would you like me to make them?'[113] In fact at that point he had fourteen unused Guards battalions. By the time he had changed his mind half an hour later, Wellington had plugged the dangerous gaps in his centre with Brunswickers, Hanoverians and a Dutch–Belgian division.

It wasn't until around 7 p.m., once he had ridden right along the battlefront, that Napoleon sent the Middle Guard up the main road towards Brussels in a column of squares. The Imperial Guard's attack in the latter stages of Waterloo was undertaken by only about one-third of its total battlefield strength, the rest being used either to recover Plancenoit from the Prussians or to cover the retreat. Napoleon ordered Ney

---

* When Waterloo is war-gamed, France usually wins: the Napoleon player attacks early, masks Hougoumont with a maximum of one division, has the rest of Reille's corps support d'Erlon's historical attack, which uses a columnar formation and is accompanied by two divisions of Lobau's corps with the Reserve Cavalry corps in close support. Ney's cavalry charge is supported by infantry and artillery, which pulverize Wellington's squares long before the Prussians arrive.

to support it, but when the Guard was brought up, one infantry division had not been drawn out of the wood of Hougoumont, nor had a cavalry brigade been called over from the Nivelles road.[114] So the Guard ascended the slope towards Wellington's line, now well-defended once more, without a regiment of cavalry protecting its flanks and with only a few troops from Reille's corps in support. Only twelve guns took part in the attack, out of the total of ninety-six available to the Guard artillery.

The forlorn nature of this attack might be judged from the fact that the Guard took no eagles with it, although 150 bandsmen marched at its head, playing triumphant parade-ground marches.[115] Napoleon placed himself in the dead ground south-west of La Haie Sainte, at the foot of the long slope heading up towards the ridge, as the Guard marched past him cheering 'Vive l'Empereur!'[116] They started off with eight battalions, probably fewer than 4,000 men in all, escorted by some horse artillery, but dropped off three battalions along the way as a reserve. The harder ground was better for Wellington's artillery and soon, as Levasseur recalled, 'Bullets and grapeshot left the road strewn with dead and wounded.' The sheer concentration of firepower – both musketry and grapeshot – that Wellington was able to bring to bear broke the will of the Imperial Guard, and it fell back, demoralized. The cry '*La Garde recule!*' had not been heard on any battlefield since its formation as the Consular Guard in 1799. It was the signal for a general disintegration of the French army across the entire front. Although Ney was to deny having heard it when he made a speech about Waterloo in the Chamber of Peers a few days later, the cry '*Sauve qui peut!*' went up at about 8 p.m., as men threw down their muskets and tried to escape before darkness fell. When it was clear what was happening, Napoleon took an unnamed general by the arm and said: 'Come, general, the affair is over – we have lost the day – let us be off.'[117]

Two squares of the Old Guard on either side of the Charleroi–Brussels road covered the army's pell-mell retreat. General Petit commanded the square of the 1st Battalion of the 1st Grenadiers à Pied some 300 yards south of La Belle Alliance, among which Napoleon took refuge.* 'The whole army was in the most appalling disorder,' Petit recalled. 'Infantry, cavalry, artillery – everybody was fleeing in all directions.' As the square retreated steadily, the Emperor ordered Petit to

---

* This was just south of where the Victor Hugo monument is today, on the same side of the road, before the turning to Plancenoit.

sound the stirring drumroll known as the *grenadière* to rally guardsmen 'caught up in the torrent of fugitives. The enemy was close at our heels, and, fearing that he might penetrate the squares, we were obliged to fire at the men who were being pursued ... It was now almost dark.'[118]

Somewhere beyond Rossomme, Napoleon, Flahaut, Corbineau, Napoleon's orderly Jardin Aîné, some officers and the duty squadron of Chasseurs à Cheval left the square to ride down the main road. Napoleon transferred into his carriage at Le Caillou but he found the road at Genappes completely blocked by fleeing soldiers. Abandoning the carriage he mounted his horse for the flight through Quatre Bras and Charleroi.* Flahaut recalled that, as they rode off towards Charleroi, they were unable to go at much more than walking pace because of the sheer crush. 'Of personal fear there was not the slightest trace, although the state of affairs was such as to cause him the greatest uneasiness,' he wrote of Napoleon. 'He was, however, so overcome by fatigue and the exertion of the preceding days that several times he was unable to resist the sleepiness which overcame him, and if I had not been there to uphold him, he would have fallen from his horse.'[119] Getting beyond Charleroi after 5 a.m., Aîné recorded that the Emperor 'found in a little meadow on the right a small fire made by some soldiers. He stopped by it to warm himself and said to General Corbineau: "*Eh bien monsieur*, we have done a fine thing."' Even then, Napoleon was able to make a joke, however grim. Aîné remembered that Napoleon 'was at this time extremely pale and haggard and much changed. He took a small glass of wine and a morsel of bread which one of his equerries had in his pocket, and some moments later mounted, asking if the horse galloped well.'[120]

Waterloo was the second costliest single-day battle of the Napoleonic Wars after Borodino. Between 25,000 and 31,000 Frenchmen were killed or wounded, and huge numbers captured.[121] Wellington lost 17,200 men and Blücher a further 7,000. Of Napoleon's sixty-four most senior generals who served in 1815, twenty-six were killed or wounded that year. 'Incomprehensible day,' Napoleon later said of Waterloo. He admitted that 'he did not thoroughly understand the

---

* The Prussian Major von Keller captured the carriage and found in it Napoleon's hat and sword, a pair of pistols, a green velvet cap, a steel bedstead with merino mattresses, a diamond tiara, the imperial mantle, several boxes of diamonds and a large silver clock. The carriage and many of its effects were put on display in Piccadilly in London.

battle', the loss of which he blamed on 'a combination of extraordinary Fates'.[122] Yet the genuinely incomprehensible thing was quite how many unforced errors he and his senior commanders had made. With his torpor the day before the battle, his strategic error over Grouchy, his failure to co-ordinate attacks and his refusal to grasp his last, best opportunity after La Haie Sainte fell, Napoleon's performance after Ligny recalled those of his more ponderous Austrian enemies in the Italian campaigns nearly twenty years earlier. Not only did Wellington and Blücher deserve to win the battle of Waterloo: Napoleon very much deserved to lose it.

31

St Helena

'The soul wears out the body.'

Napoleon to Marie Louise

'He lived in the middle of the plains of Persia, ever missing his country.'

Napoleon on Themistocles

'All is not lost,' Napoleon wrote to Joseph the day after the battle.

> I calculate that, when I reassemble my forces, I shall have 150,000 men. The *fédérés* and National Guards (such of them as are fit to fight) will provide 100,000 men, and the regimental depots a further 50,000. Thus I shall have 300,000 men ready to bring against the enemy. I shall use carriage-horses to pull the guns; raise 100,000 men by conscription; arm them with muskets taken from royalists and from National Guards unfit for service; organize a *levée en masse* ... and overwhelm the enemy. But people must help me, not deafen me with advice ... The Austrians are slow marchers; the Prussians fear the peasantry and dare not advance too far. There is still time to retrieve the situation.[1]

Napoleon believed that if he managed to get all the forces under Grouchy (who had escaped the area with his corps intact), Rapp, Brune, Suchet and Lecourbe together, if the great border fortresses could hold out until relieved, and if he could attack the Allies' extended supply lines, he might obtain respite.[2] If nothing else, it was a tribute to his extraordinary determination and continuing energy that he so much as contemplated all this after such a rout as Waterloo. Soult drew up a general order for commanders to gather together stragglers and concentrate on Lâon, Lafère, Marle, Saint-Quentin, Bethel, Vervier, Soissons and Reims, where various unbroken units were garrisoned.[3] Jérôme and Morand meanwhile rallied parts of the army at Philippeville and Avesnes.

Napoleon knew that in order to fight on he needed the support of the chambers meeting in the Palais Bourbon, so he hastened back to Paris on horseback, and even by mail-coach, to try to beat the news of the defeat. On the journey, an innkeeper at Rocroi insisted upon being paid 300 francs in cash for the supper provided for the Emperor and his entourage, refusing a requisition chit – as sure a sign as any of Napoleon's waning authority.[4] He arrived at the Élysée at 7 a.m. on Wednesday, June 21, summoned his family and ministers, and took his first bath in several days. But although he had gone straight to Paris after Egypt and Moscow, this time his return smacked of desperation. Even John Cam Hobhouse detected 'a precipitancy that nothing can excuse' in his hero. Napoleon's swift return only emboldened his opponents, despite their having sworn solemn oaths of fidelity to him at the Champ de Mai less than three weeks before.[5]

One hundred and one cannon had been fired in Paris on June 18 to announce the victory at Ligny, which was reported to have been won over Wellington and Blücher, but the lack of any bulletins since had started to worry Parisians. Napoleon considered going to the Palais Bourbon immediately on his return, 'covered in the dust of the battlefield', as one of his supporters put it, and appealing to the legislature's sense of patriotism.[6] The hastily summoned Cambacérès, Carnot and Maret supported the idea, and his coach was made ready in the courtyard, but the majority of his ministers thought it too dangerous considering the febrile mood of the parliamentarians.* Instead, the Emperor sent a message to the chambers saying he had come back to Paris 'to consult with my ministers about measures of national salvation'.[7] He later regretted not going there in person, saying: 'I would have moved them and led them; my eloquence would have enthused them; I would have cut the heads off Lanjuinais and Lafayette and ten others . . . I have to say it: I didn't have the courage.'[8]

Nor did he have the support. The power vacuum was quickly filled by Lafayette, who appointed five members of each chamber to take on

---

* Fouché's absence from the conference was considered ominous, since he was known never to be on the losing side, and Joseph had advised that he be arrested and interned at Vincennes, but it didn't happen. Napoleon later wished he'd had him shot (ed. Latimer, *Talks* p. 195).

ministerial functions – effectively a parliamentary coup d'état.[9] Regnault de Saint-Jean d'Angély and Lucien tried to dissuade the chambers from this course but Lafayette was eloquent and persuasive in his denunciation of Napoleon. Accused of treachery by Lucien, he said: 'We have followed your brother to the sands of Africa, to the deserts of Russia: the bones of Frenchmen, scattered in every region, bear witness to our fidelity.'[10] During the day, disarmed and dejected troops started arriving in the capital, who 'reported everywhere, as they passed, that all was lost'.[11]

The bulletin Napoleon wrote on June 21 argued that Waterloo had been on the verge of being won when 'malicious malefactors' (*malveillants*) started crying out '*Sauve qui peut*', and so 'In an instant the whole army was nothing but a mass of confusion.' He ended: 'Such was the issue of the battle of Mont Saint-Jean, glorious for the French armies, and yet so fatal.'[12] It convinced few, but the use of the word fatal (*funeste*) three times left Parisians in no doubt about the catastrophe, which was now also fatal for Napoleon's chance of remaining on the throne. It is possible that Napoleon tried to poison himself again that night. Cadet de Gassicourt, the Emperor's apothecary, told General Thiébault in 1818 that he had been summoned to the Élysée on June 21 after Napoleon had swallowed poison, as he had the previous year, and then changed his mind – after which the terrified Gassicourt had managed to provoke nausea and then administer fluids.[13] Though there is no corroborating testimony, Gassicourt may well have been telling the truth.

At noon the next day, with even the most loyal of his ministers – Lavalette, Savary and Caulaincourt – arguing that it was now unavoidable, Napoleon abdicated for the second time, dictating the document 'with that rapidity of determination which was characteristic of his peculiar organisation on the field of battle'.[14] 'Frenchmen!' it began,

> In starting the war to uphold national independence, I relied on the gathering of all efforts, all wills, and the support of all national authorities; I had reason to hope for success, and I braved all the declarations of the Powers against me. Circumstances appear to have changed. I offer myself in sacrifice to the hatred of the enemies of France ... My political life is over, and I proclaim my son, under the title of Napoleon II, emperor of the French. The current ministers will form an interim government council. The interest I am passing to my son leads me to invite the Chambers

to organize, without delay, Regency by law. All must unite for public salvation and to remain an independent nation.[15]

Napoleon still hoped that he would be called upon by the legislature to lead the armies of France against the invading Allies, but if the incoming provisional government didn't require his services, he told Lavalette, he intended to live as a private citizen in the United States.[16] As America had only recently made peace with Britain after three years of war, it is perfectly possible that he would have been allowed to retire there by the US government if he had been able to get there. Lavalette records that once Napoleon had abdicated, 'he remained calm during the whole day, giving his advice on the position the army was to take, and on the manner [in which] the negotiations with the enemy were to be conducted.'[17]

The provisional government, of which Fouché became president on June 24, accepted the abdication gratefully, appointed Macdonald to command France's armies, put Lafayette in charge of the National Guard, with Oudinot as his second-in-command, and allowed Carnot to keep his old job as minister of the interior. Talleyrand became foreign minister for the fourth time.[18] When it was announced in the *Journal de l'Empire* that 'Napoleon Bonaparte' had gone to Malmaison, the change in nomenclature struck people forcibly, for if even the foremost Bonapartist paper no longer described him in imperial terms he must indeed have fallen. Yet some ultra-loyalists were still holding out: Colonel Baron Paul-Alexis de Menil of the Army of the Rhine was fighting in the Seltz Forest (in Alscace) with his 37th Line Demi-Brigade eight days after the battle of Waterloo, and some towns such as Givet, Charlemont, Longwy, Mézières, Charleville and Montmédy did not capitulate until August and September.

Shortly before he left Paris for the last time, Napoleon said farewell to an agitated and emotional Vivant Denon. Putting his hands on Denon's shoulders, he said: 'My dear friend, let's not get soppy; in a crisis like this one has to behave with *sang froid*.'[19] With his descriptions of Egypt and the Egyptian campaign, designs of bronze commemorative medals, encouragement of the Empire style in art and stewardship of the Louvre, Denon had done more than anyone else besides Napoleon himself to advance the cultural aspects of Bonapartism. He was one of the many non-soldiers of distinction who regretted Napoleon's downfall.

A man of lesser self-confidence might have had an escape route planned. Now, between his departure for Malmaison with Hortense, Bertrand

and Maret on June 25 and his surrender to the British on July 15, Napoleon did something entirely out of character: he vacillated. As the Allies and Bourbons approached Paris for a second restoration, and the Prussians sent out cavalry patrols further afield, his options started to narrow. While at Malmaison he applied to the provisional government for a passport to go to America, and asked for two frigates to take him there from Rochefort.[20] This was absurd: the Royal Navy, which was blockading the port with the seventy-four-gun HMS *Bellerophon*, would not have respected a passport issued to Napoleon by Fouché's government or anyone else.[21] On June 26 Napoleon received Marie Walewska at Malmaison, where they said goodbye.

On the 29th Napoleon was told by Fouché's emissaries, Decrès and Boulay de la Meurthe, that the government had released two frigates, the *Saale* and *Méduse*, for his use, and that since the Prussians were approaching he needed to leave Malmaison. Pausing only to visit the room in which Josephine had died, and to say goodbye to his mother and Hortense for the last time, he left the house with Bertrand and Savary at 5.30 p.m. (Ferdinand, Napoleon's premier chef, chose not to go with him as he had not been paid what he had been promised when he went to Elba.) 'If I had gone to America,' Napoleon later mused, 'we might have founded a State there.'[22] Yet on July 2, by which time he was at Niort in the Deux-Sèvres department, he was still undecided what to do and his companions were divided about whether he should join up with the army at Orleans or try to smuggle himself aboard an American merchant ship lying eight miles offshore.[23]

Instead Napoleon installed himself at the maritime prefecture of Rochefort and spent twelve days trying to work out how the *Saale*, the *Méduse* and a twenty-gun corvette and a brig could somehow get past *Bellerophon*. When Captain Philibert of the *Méduse* refused to take part in any attack, two young naval officers, Lieutenant Genty and Ensign Doret, volunteered to take Napoleon across the Atlantic in a small sailing boat, for which offence they would be scratched from the French Navy List until the fall of the Bourbons in 1830.[24]

On July 5 Joseph arrived at Rochefort and generously offered to exchange identities with his brother, since they looked alike.[25] Instead of grasping his moment, Napoleon again hesitated. When the Bourbons formally returned to power three days later he lost control over the frigates. By then Admiral Sir Henry Hotham had stationed Royal Navy vessels from Les Sables to the Gironde on the lookout for him. Napoleon also turned down several other risky possibilities, such as escaping at night in a Danish ship. By the 9th he was reviewing troops on the Île d'Aix and being cheered by the local populace, but sleeping on the *Saale* with the *Bellerophon* anchored near by.

Napoleon sent Savary and a chamberlain, the Marquis de Las Cases, to the *Bellerophon* on July 10 to negotiate the terms of his surrender with her thirty-eight-year-old captain, Frederick Maitland. He needed to avoid capture by the Bourbons – whose flag would be hoisted in Rochefort on July 12 – and the Prussians, as both would have executed him. He later said that he 'could not bring himself to submit to receive any favours from the Emperor of Austria, after knowing the manner in which he had taken part against him'.[26] Negotiations were renewed on July 14, this time conducted by Las Cases and General Charles Lallemand, commander of the Chasseurs à Cheval at Waterloo. Maitland stated that Napoleon would be well treated in England, where the weather was better than he imagined.[27] This was taken by Napoleon as meaning that he would be given asylum as a guest of the British rather than being treated as a prisoner-of-war, but that was an absurd construction to put on the casual words of a naval officer who had no power to make any formal agreement. Indeed, Maitland made it clear that he had no authority to make any promises beyond a safe passage to English waters.[28] Napoleon could even then have taken Joseph's advice and gone overland to a different port further south – there might still be alternatives in the Gironde – but instead he said goodbye to his brother on the 13th. He now preferred dignity and a measure of safety to the risk of another maritime flight such as those he had taken from Corsica, Egypt and Elba.

At around midnight on the 14th, Napoleon wrote a letter to the Prince Regent. 'Your Royal Highness,' it began, 'Exposed to the factions which divide my country and the enmity of the European Powers, I have ended my political career, and I come, like Themistocles, to seat myself at the hearth of the British people. I put myself under the protection of its laws, which I claim from your Royal Highness as the most powerful, the most constant and most generous of my enemies.'[29] For once Napoleon's classical education had failed him, for the great Athenian general Themistocles had actually joined the Persians against his native Greeks, which was not at all what Napoleon was proposing. But he was right about Britain's constancy. In 1815 alone, Britain subsidized no fewer than thirty European Powers, from the greatest – such as Prussia at £2.1 million, Russia at £2 million and Austria at £1.6 million – to Sicily at £33,333.[30] Although Austria had spent 108 months fighting against

France, Prussia 58 months and Russia 55 months, Britain was at war with her for a total of 242 months between 1793 and 1815. The Royal Navy blockaded France for two decades, and sank the French battle fleet at Trafalgar; British troops fought for six years in the Iberian peninsula between 1808 and 1814, Wellington not taking a day's leave throughout the entire period. They also landed expeditionary forces in Egypt in 1801, Calabria (where they won the battle of Maida) in 1806, Copenhagen in 1807, Walcheren (disastrously) in 1809, and Bergen-op-Zoom in Holland (also defeated) in 1814. Even when almost the whole of the rest of Europe (except Portugal and Sicily) came to terms with Napoleon after Tilsit, the British kept the flame of resistance to his hegemony alight.

Calling a meeting of advisors, Napoleon said, 'I'm not acquainted with the Prince Regent, but from all I have heard of him I cannot help placing reliance on his noble character.'[31] Here, too, his information was faulty, as the Prince Regent had one of the most ignoble characters of any British sovereign. 'There never was an individual less regretted by his fellow-creatures than this deceased king,' opined *The Times* when he died in 1830. 'What eye has wept for him? What heart has heaved one throb of unmercenary sorrow? . . . If he ever had a friend – a devoted friend in any rank of life – we protest that the name of him or her never reached us.'[32] The Prince Regent's generosity was confined to his tailors, decorators and mistresses. Napoleon had nothing he wanted and so the imperial supplicant never received a reply. He was perhaps hoping for a gentlemanly imprisonment such as Lucien's had been in Worcestershire, or perhaps on one of the country estates of the Whig aristocrats he had met on Elba.

Napoleon boarded the *Bellerophon* at 8 a.m. on Saturday, July 15, 1815 and surrendered to Captain Maitland. He decently allowed his liaison officer with the provisional government, General Beker, not to go with him, and thus to avoid any possible future accusations of having betrayed Napoleon to the British.[33] 'The deepest sadness showed on every face,' recalled his valet Marchand, 'and when the British gig arrived to take the Emperor on board, the most heartrending cries were heard' from officers and sailors alike, who shouted 'Vive l'Empereur!' across the water until he reached *Bellerophon*.[34] Some trampled on their hats in despair. As he arrived, *Bellerophon*'s marines stood to attention and sailors manned the yardarms, but Napoleon didn't receive a salute because Royal Navy regulations stated it was too early in the day for one. His first words to Maitland, on removing his hat, were: 'I come on board your ship to place myself under the protection of the laws of England.'[35] The Revolutionary and Napoleonic Wars were finally over.

Maitland gave Napoleon his own captain's cabin, and when he appeared on deck again, he showed him around the ship. Napoleon asked whether Maitland thought he had ever had a chance of escape, but the British captain assured him that a seventy-four-gun ship like the *Bellerophon* was a match for three frigates, and so the odds on escape were 'much against'.[36] As they went around, Napoleon tapped a midshipman on the head and pinched his ear good-naturedly, asking the bosun, Manning, about his duties. He 'looked quite at ease', according to another midshipman, George Home, 'and as completely at home as if he had been going on a pleasure trip on one of his own imperial yachts'.[37] He quickly won over everyone on board. One officer wrote that 'his teeth were finely set, and as white as ivory, and his mouth had a charm about it that I have never seen in any human countenance'. Maitland himself was to admit:

> It may appear surprising that a possibility could exist of a British officer being prejudiced in favour of one who had caused so many calamities to his country, but to such an extent did he possess the power of pleasing that there are few people who could have sat at the same table as him for nearly a month, as I did, without feeling a sensation of pity, allied perhaps to regret, that a man possessed of so many fascinating qualities, and who had held so high a station in life, should be reduced to the situation in which I saw him.[38]

During the journey to England, Napoleon 'showed no depression of spirits' and was treated with the formal dignities of a head of state. He let Maitland and Admiral Hotham, who went aboard soon after the surrender, see his portable library and 30-inch-wide camp bed, asked lots of questions in broken, almost unintelligible, English, and said that had Charles James Fox lived, 'it would never have come to this'.[39] At dinner on the second night he patted Maitland on the head, saying, 'If it had not been for you English, I should have been Emperor of the East; but wherever there is water to float a ship we are sure to find you in our way.'[40]

The question of how to deal with their prisoner was a tricky one for the British. The Hundred Days following his return from Elba had cost almost 100,000 men killed or wounded on all sides, and no repetition could be risked.[41] On July 20 Lord Liverpool wrote to the foreign secretary, Lord Castlereagh, who was in Vienna, to tell him how the cabinet viewed matters:

> We are all very decidedly of the opinion that it would not answer to confine him in this country. Very nice legal opinions might arise on the subject, which would be particularly embarrassing . . . He would become the object of curiosity immediately, and possibly of compassion in the course of a few months, and the circumstances of his being here, or indeed anywhere in Europe, would contribute to keep up a certain degree of ferment in France . . . St Helena is the place in the world best calculated for the confinement of such a person . . . the situation is particularly healthy. There is only one place . . . where ships can anchor, and we have the power of excluding neutral ships altogether . . . At such a place and such a distance, all intrigue would be impossible; and, being so far from the European world, he would soon be forgotten.[42]

Napoleon made some over-optimistic remarks in his career, but so did his enemies.

Napoleon saw France for the last time on July 23, casting 'many a melancholy look at the coast' but making few observations.[43] After they had anchored at Torbay on the English south coast the next day, he immediately became an irresistible 'object of curiosity' for sightseers, some of whom came down from as far as Glasgow for a glimpse of him – indeed the *Bellerophon* had to put out her boats around the ship to keep them at bay. He went out on deck and showed himself at the gangways and stern windows in order to please the public, saying that Torbay reminded him of Portoferraio. Maitland noted that Napoleon, 'whenever he observed any well-dressed women, pulled his hat off, and bowed to them'.[44]

At Plymouth on the 27th Napoleon enjoyed even greater celebrity status; three days later Maitland estimated that as many as a thousand pleasure boats had collected around the ship, averaging eight people each. Meanwhile Napoleon was 'often falling asleep on the sofa, having within these two or three years become very lethargic', a curious comment for a man who had known him for only twelve days.[45] This agreeable limbo ended at 10.30 a.m. on July 31, however, when Admiral Lord Keith and Sir Henry Bunbury, the under-secretary of state for war, arrived on *Bellerophon* to inform Napoleon – whom they addressed as 'General Bonaparte' – of his intended fate on St Helena, about which he had been forewarned by reading the British press. They told him that he could take three officers and twelve domestic staff with him, though not Savary or General Lallemand, who both would be imprisoned on Malta for, respectively, the murder of the Duc d'Enghien and betraying the Bourbons.

Napoleon replied to Keith (either with Gallic splendour or ridiculous histrionics, according to taste) by declaring that 'his blood should rather stain the planks of the *Bellerophon*' than that he should go to St Helena, and that the decision 'would throw a veil of darkness over the future history of England'.[46] He added that the climate would kill him in three months. After Keith and Bunbury had left, Napoleon told Maitand: 'It is worse than Tamerlaine's iron cage. I would prefer being delivered up to the Bourbons. Among other insults . . . they style me General; they may as well call me Archbishop.'[47] Some of the more hot-headed of his staff agreed that dying on St Helena would be 'very ignoble!' and 'Better be killed defending ourselves, or set fire to the powder magazine.' That same night General Montholon stopped Bertrand's hysterical and depressed English-born wife Fanny from drowning herself, by pulling her back through a porthole from which she was attempting to jump.[48]

Notwithstanding the despatch of another letter to the Prince Regent protesting 'I am not a prisoner, I am a guest of England', around noon on August 7 Napoleon was transferred to the eighty-gun HMS *Northumberland*, commanded by Rear-Admiral Sir George Cockburn (one of the commanders who had burned down Washington the previous year) for the 4,400-mile journey to St Helena.[49] He was accompanied by an entourage of twenty-six people willing to go to the other end of the earth with him; several more, such as his sister Pauline and Méneval, applied to go but were turned away by the British authorities. Along with General Henri Bertrand and his clearly reluctant wife and their three children, there was Montholon, his pretty wife Albine and their three-year-old son Tristan, the Marquis Emmanuel de Las Cases (who had fine secretarial skills and spoke good English, though he pretended not to) and his thirteen-year-old son, as well as General Gaspard Gourgaud, the valets Marchand and Noverraz, Napoleon's valet/bodyguard 'Mamluk Ali', his groom and coachman the brothers Achille and Joseph Archambault, a footman called Gentilini, his maître d'hôtel Francheschi Cipriani, the butler and pastry-chef Piéron, the cook Le Page, a Corsican usher-barber Santini and Rousseau the lamplighter, who doubled as a toymaker. There were also four servants of the Montholons and Bertrands.[50] When Napoleon's doctor, Louis Maingault, refused to go, the

Bellerophon's surgeon, the Irishman Barry O'Meara, took his place. All but Napoleon were stripped of their swords, and Cockburn also confiscated 4,000 gold napoleons from them, allowing them little more than pocket money with which to play cards.[51] (Nonetheless, eight members of the entourage managed to conceal money-belts hiding a total of a quarter of a million francs, which would be worth £5,000 on St Helena.[52])

On the first night on *Northumberland*, its British officers won seven or eight napoleons off the former Emperor playing *vingt-et-un* and he 'chatted in a very good-natured mood with everybody', as one recalled. 'At dinner he ate heartily, and of almost every dish, praised everything, and seemed most perfectly reconciled to his fate.'[53] Though there was no advantage to be gained, Napoleon was charming during the ten-week voyage – at least when he wasn't being 'miserably' seasick – inquiring into the state and nature of British forces in India, asserting that he had thoroughly expected Grouchy to arrive at Waterloo, declaring that Tsar Alexander was 'a more active and clever man than any of the other Sovereigns of Europe, but that he was extremely false', claiming that Spain and Portugal had privately promised not to fight against him in 1815, questioning the ship's chaplain about Anglicanism and the British consul-general of Madeira, which they sailed past on August 23, about the island's produce, its height above sea level and population. He also discussed his plans to capture the Channel Islands, predicted that Bernadotte wouldn't last in Sweden, described Desaix as 'the best general he had ever known', and denied an affair with an actress called Saint-Aubin, saying 'The prettiest women are the hardest to make love to.'[54]

Most days on the voyage Napoleon rose between 10 and 11 a.m., had a meat and wine breakfast in his bedroom, stayed there before getting dressed at 3 p.m., took a short walk on deck, played chess with Montholon (who generally contrived to lose) until dinner at 5 p.m., where Cockburn recorded he 'eats and drinks a good deal, and talks but little. He prefers meats of all kinds, highly dressed, and never touches vegetables.'[55] He then walked on deck with Cockburn for ninety minutes, played cards from 8 to 10 p.m., and went to bed. He took English lessons, complained of the heat, walked on deck in the rain, put on weight and did maths problems with Gourgaud, extracting square and cube roots. On August 15 he spoke of previous birthdays – 'Oh, how different!' – and didn't go to bed till 11.30 p.m.[56] That same day Marie Louise wrote to the Emperor Francis about her husband, saying:

I hope he will be treated with kindness and clemency and I beg you, dearest Papa, to make certain that it is so ... It is the last time I shall busy myself with his fate. I owe him a debt of gratitude for the calm unconcern [*ruhige Indifferenz*] in which he let me pass my days instead of making me unhappy.[57]

Cockburn obligingly altered their route to sail between the islands of Gomera and Palma in the Canary Islands because Napoleon wanted to see the peak at Tenerife, and as they crossed the Equator on September 23 the former Emperor ordained that a hundred napoleons be thrown over the side as an offering to Neptune. Bertrand thought it much too much, Cockburn that Neptune would be happy with five.[58] The following week he spoke about Waterloo – 'Ah! If it were only to be done over again!' – which he was to do often over the next five years.

Their destination finally came into view on Saturday, October 14. Only 85 square miles in area and 28 miles in circumference, the volcanic rock of St Helena is 1,150 miles from Angola, over 2,000 miles from Brazil and 700 miles from the nearest land at Ascension Island. It has been described as 'further away from anywhere than anywhere else in the world'.[59] From the mid-seventeenth century to 1834 this most remote, most obscure speck of the British Empire was used as a watering-station on the journey to and from India. In 1815 it had a population of 3,395 Europeans, 218 black slaves, 489 Chinese and 116 Malays.[60] The British government entered into an arrangement with the East India Company, which ran the island, by which it agreed to pay for Napoleon's imprisonment there.

Arriving at St Helena's only town, Jamestown, by sea, presents a tremendously imposing sight as 600-foot black cliffs rise up steeply and forbiddingly on either side of the small port. On October 15, leaning on Marchand's shoulder, Napoleon looked at the island through the telescope he had used at Austerlitz. 'It is not an attractive place,' he said. 'I should have done better to have stayed in Egypt.'[61] With two Royal Navy frigates patrolling the island constantly, and no vessel able to approach from any direction without being seen by the numerous signal posts on the island that communicated with each other, he must have known he was going to die there.

On October 17, as a prevailing south-easterly wind blew violently, Napoleon disembarked and was taken briefly to Longwood, the house that was being made ready for him on the Deadwood Plateau.[62] Longwood had been the lieutenant-governor's residence, but he had stayed there for only three months of the year because its elevation of 1,500 feet above sea level meant that it had – and still has – a micro-climate different from the rest of the temperate, tropical island. British officials who had lived on St Helena could legitimately call the island's climate 'perhaps the mildest and most salubrious in the world'. Wellington, who had visited in 1805 on his return from India, wrote of 'the climate apparently the most healthy I have ever lived in'.[63] But these visitors had mostly remained in or around Jamestown. Longwood, by contrast, lies in cloud for over three hundred days a year.[64] The humidity is typically 78 per cent but very often reaches 100 per cent. Everything is therefore slightly but constantly damp, even the wallpaper. The trees, bent over from the wind, all have lichen growing over them. Napoleon's playing cards had to be dried in the oven to stop them sticking together.

Longwood also had infestations of termites, rats, midges, mosquitoes and cockroaches, the last three of which it still has today (despite the fine work done by the resident honorary French consul, Michel Dancoisne-Martineau, to restore and maintain the residence). The clammy humidity throughout the September–February summer months meant that Napoleon and his entourage constantly suffered from bronchitis, catarrh and sore throats. But other than the governor's mansion less than 3 miles away, it was the only place large and secluded enough to house the former Emperor and his suite of courtiers and servants, and its prominence on the plateau made it easier to guard from the nearby Deadwood Barracks. A flag telegraph station at Longwood told the governor what Napoleon was doing, with six possibilities from 'All is well with respect to General Bonaparte' to 'General Bonaparte is missing'.[65]

In the seven weeks that it took for Longwood to be refurbished and extended, Napoleon stayed at a pretty bungalow called The Briars, closer to Jamestown, with the family of the East India Company superintendent William Balcombe, where he had one room and a pavilion in their garden.[66] This period was his happiest on St Helena, not least because he struck up an unlikely, charming and innocent friendship with the second of the Balcombes' four surviving children, Betsy, a spirited fourteen-year-old girl who spoke intelligible if ungrammatical French and to whom Napoleon behaved with avuncular indulgence. She had originally been brought up to view Napoleon, in her words, as 'a huge ogre or giant, with one large flaming eye in the centre of his forehead, and long teeth protruding from his mouth, with which he tore to pieces and devoured little girls', but she very soon came to adore him.[67] 'His smile, and the expression of his eye, could not be transmitted to canvas, and these constituted Napoleon's chief charm,' she later wrote. 'His hair was dark brown, and as fine and silky as a child's, rather too much so indeed for a man as its very softness caused it to look thin.'[68]

The friendship began when Napoleon tested Betsy on the capitals of Europe. When he asked her the capital of Russia she replied, 'Petersburg now; Moscow formerly', upon which 'He turned abruptly round, and, fixing his piercing eyes full in my face, he demanded sternly, "Who burnt it?"' She was dumbstruck, until he laughed and said: '*Oui, oui.* You know very well that it was I who burnt it!' Upon which the teenager corrected him: 'I believe, sir, the Russians burnt it to get rid of the French.'[69] Whereupon Napoleon laughed and friendship with 'Mademoiselle Betsee', 'lettle monkee', '*bambina*' and 'little scatterbrain' was born. They sang songs together, and would march around the room tunelessly humming the air 'Vive Henri Quatre'. 'I never met with anyone who bore childish liberties so well as Napoleon,' recalled Betsy. 'He seemed to enter into every sort of mirth or fun with the glee of a child, and though I have often tried his patience severely, I never knew him lose his temper or fall back upon his rank or age.'[70]

Staying with the Balcombes, Napoleon spent his time playing chess, billiards, whist (with Betsy, for sugar-plums), puss-in-the-corner (a children's game) and blindman's buff, in pistol marksmanship and relaying island social gossip. He spent many hours in hot baths, watching the clouds as they rolled towards Longwood, 'listening to the thousand crickets' after sunset and riding in his jaunting Irish carriage at breakneck speeds along the island's few but vertiginous roads. Freed of responsibility, he allowed himself a good deal of levity, almost a second childhood. When Betsy's brother Alexander called him by his British nickname 'Boney' he didn't understand the allusion, especially after Las Cases interpreted it literally. He pointed out what was by then all too obvious: 'I am not at all bony.'[71]

Napoleon told Betsy that Marie Louise was 'an amiable creature, and a very good wife', and less convincingly that 'she would have followed him to St Helena if she had been allowed'. He commended Pauline's and Mademoiselle George's beauty and that of Albine de Montholon, who Betsy said was 'renowned for her tall and graceful stature'. Albine had become pregnant on the journey to St Helena, but although the baby was christened Napoléone-Marie-Hélène she is not believed to have been Napoleon's. At some later stage, however, Albine became Napoleon's last mistress.[72] Madame Bertrand, Gourgaud and others took it for granted that this was so – Albine's bedroom was across the pantry from his – and indeed Madame Bertrand was jealous, even though she herself had rejected a pass from Napoleon.[73] Albine seems to have understood Napoleon well. 'His fire, for want of fuel, consumed himself and those around him,' she later wrote. On January 26, 1818 she gave birth to another daughter, Joséphine-Napoléone, who might well have been Napoleon's third and last illegitimate child, but who died at the Hôtel Belle-Vue in Brussels on September 30, 1819, after Albine had returned to Europe. (She went either for 'health reasons', as was claimed, or because she wanted to escape St Helena to carry on an affair with Major Basil Jackson, a Waterloo veteran and now aide to the island's governor, who left St Helena for Brussels one week after her.[74])

The existence of a ménage-à-trois (or quatre, if one includes Jackson) doesn't necessarily mean that Montholon hated Napoleon, as some modern writers have assumed. Such arrangements were not unusual among the French aristocracy, and as he had already slept with the wives of Maret and State Councillor Duchâtel, Chaptal's mistress and Pauline's reader, the Napoleonic court clearly acknowledged the concept of *droit de seigneur*. The compliant Montholon would hardly have stayed on St Helena after Albine's return to Europe, and remained a leading Bonapartist all his life – suffering seven years' imprisonment for his part in Napoleon's nephew's coup attempt of 1840 – if he had loathed him.

On December 10, 1815 Napoleon moved into Longwood, with a heavy heart. When Bertrand, who lived nearby in a cottage at Hutt's Gate, told him that his 'new palace' was ready, he replied: 'Do not call it my palace but my tomb.'[75] It comprised a billiard room (with shockingly loud green walls as the East India Company had that colour paint in abundance), a drawing room, dining room, library, staff accommodation and sleeping quarters for the Montholon family. The British government had insisted that Napoleon only have the rank of 'a general officer not in employ', who was under no circumstances to be called emperor for fear of offending the Bourbons (even though, retaining medieval claims, George III had officially included 'King of France' among his titles for the first forty-two years of his reign).[76] Britons therefore tended to call Napoleon 'Sir', 'Your Excellency' or 'General Bonaparte'. When an invitation to a ball arrived at Longwood addressed to 'General Bonaparte', Napoleon quipped: 'Send the card to the addressee; the last I heard of him was at the Pyramids and Mount Tabor.'[77]

Although Napoleon was not allowed newspapers by order of Lord Bathurst, secretary for war, on grounds of national security, news nonetheless seeped through.[78] When he heard that Joseph had successfully evaded capture and was living in Bordentown, New Jersey, he 'remained thoughtful for some time' – doubtless considering what would have happened if he had taken up the impersonation offer – before he 'then expressed satisfaction'.[79] Although he mourned the outrageous execution of General de La Bédoyère by the Bourbons on August 19, 1815, he himself reacted disgracefully to the news of their shooting Marshal Ney, telling Gourgaud: 'Ney got no more than he deserved. I regret him because he was inestimable on a field of battle, but he was too hot-headed, and too stupid to succeed in anything but a fight.'[80] Later remarks about Ney's betrayal of him at Fontainebleau in April 1814 explain his ire.[81]

Murat's execution in Calabria at the hands of the Neapolitan Bourbons initially produced a similar reaction – 'Murat has only had what he deserved' – but on further reflection he said: 'It was all my own fault. I ought to have let him stay a marshal, and never made him Grand Duke of Berg; still less King of Naples. He was off his head. He was very ambitious.'[82] In case anyone thought that hypocritical, he added, 'I rose to distinction step by step, but Murat wanted at a bound to be chief of everything.' Napoleon was impressed when he heard of the sensational escape of Lavalette from the Conciergerie prison in Paris, where he had been awaiting execution for treason, when his wife – whom Napoleon had hitherto thought of as 'a little fool' – took his place and allowed him to escape wearing her clothes.[83] (With their customary generosity, the Bourbons imprisoned her until she went insane.) Napoleon pronounced himself 'glad' when he heard of Marie Walewska's marriage in 1816 to the Bonapartist Duc d'Ornano. 'She is rich,' he said of the 10,000 francs a month that he had been giving her at one point, 'for she must have laid by considerable sums.'[84] She did not have long to enjoy them, as the following year she died of kidney failure in Liège, where the duke was in exile. Napoleon was perfectly willing to name his mistresses to Gourgaud on St Helena, when discussing his *bonnes fortunes* with women, although he insisted he had only had six or seven, whereas the true figure was at least three times that.[85]

Until April 14, 1816, although Napoleon's imprisonment was not comfortable or by any means pleasurable – for such a big man on so tiny an

island it couldn't be – it was relatively bearable. But that day a new
governor, Hudson Lowe, arrived on St Helena, to take over from the
affable Colonel Mark Wilks. At their first meeting Napoleon gave Lowe
a gold watch – which can now be seen in the National Army Museum
in London – but their relationship deteriorated swiftly. Napoleon
was already chafing at his fate, and his punctilious, unimaginative,
regulations-obsessed new jailer was a bad choice for the post. Montholon was later to admit that 'an angel from heaven could not have pleased
us as governor of St Helena', but Lowe's military career virtually guaranteed a clash.[86] In the draft of his unpublished autobiography in the
British Library, Lowe describes how he led a company during Nelson's
night attack on the Convention Redoubt in San Firenzo Bay, Corsica, in
early February 1794:

> The whole of the troops then rushed on and the party with which I was
> proceeding made its entrance at the breach, which we found absolutely
> blocked up with the bodies of the French garrison, who had been
> employed in defending it. They were all of the Regiment of La Fère ...
> They lay heaped in the breach on which we had to make our way over the
> dead and dying bodies.[87]

Since Napoleon had left the regiment a matter of months beforehand,
Lowe was trampling over his maimed and dead comrades, fighting
alongside an anti-French Corsican force he was eventually to command
himself called the Royal Corsican Rangers, despised by Napoleon as
traitors.

Lowe had also fought at Bastia and Calvi, and been quartered at the
Casa Bonaparte in Ajaccio, before serving in Portugal and Minorca and
commanding the Corsican Rangers in Egypt, where he was involved in
the French surrender in 1801, escorting the defeated French army from
Cairo to its embarkation at Rosetta, a humiliating moment of Napoleon's consulship. He had spent two years in charge of a printing press at
Capri ensuring that every success of the Allied armies in the Peninsular
War was surreptitiously pasted up in Naples and other Italian cities,
which Napoleon would not have respected as the proper work of a soldier.[88] Beyond that, Lowe knew and greatly admired Tsar Alexander
and was present at the battle of Leipzig, after which he was attached to
the staff of Blücher, whom he also revered. He was present at Napoleon's defeats at La Rothière and Lâon, and entered Paris after Marmont's
surrender. He had even put in a recommendation in early 1815 that the
ridge at Waterloo be fortified (though he was not present at the battle

itself, having a command in the force that drove Brune out of Toulon in July).[89] In his thirty-four years of service, therefore, during which he had taken no more than a total of twelve months of leave, Lowe had witnessed many of Napoleon's worst humiliations and defeats and had reversed his earliest victory. There could be no possible sympathy between the two men, and Lowe was unlikely to find any aspect of Napoleon's character attractive. 'You never commanded any men but Corsican deserters,' Napoleon sneered at him at the last of their interviews. 'You're not a general, you're only a clerk.'[90]

Napoleon's supporters made Lowe out to be ignorant, cruel and sadistic, which he wasn't, but also tactless, arrogant and small-minded, which he was. The 5th Earl of Albemarle, who had fought at Waterloo, recorded that several officers of the Corsican Rangers thought Lowe 'a man of churlish manners and an irritable and overbearing temper'.[91] Wellington was even harsher, calling Lowe 'a very bad choice; he was a man wanting in education and judgment. He was a stupid man, he knew nothing at all of the world, and like all men who knew nothing of the world, he was suspicious and jealous.'[92] Considering how well Napoleon got on with other Britons – Fox, Cornwallis, Yarmouth, Campbell, Macnamara, Ebrington, Russell, Fazakerley, Venables-Vernon, Douglas, Ussher, Maitland, O'Meara, Cockburn and the Balcombes among them, as well as many visitors on St Helena – Britain wasted an opportunity by sending such an unsympathetic martinet. Napoleon could have been drawn out and debriefed on the myriad political secrets of the European courts over the previous sixteen years, and had already told Cockburn useful naval secrets about the mining of Cherbourg harbour.

Napoleon refused to meet Lowe more than six times over four months, despite living only 3 miles from him, after which the two men fought an exceptionally petty war against each other until Napoleon's death five years later. Lowe complained about the amount of kindling Longwood burned, reprimanded William Balcombe when Betsy rode one of Napoleon's horses, refused to allow Napoleon's piano to be retuned, stopped him receiving history books, a bust of the King of Rome and ivory chess pieces with the imperial 'N' carved on them. (Napoleon was allowed no contact of any kind with his son, who was prevented from learning French and given an Austrian title, the Duke of Reichstadt, in 1818.) Lowe also refused to allow Napoleon to buy the freedom of Toby, the Balcombes' elderly Malay gardener/slave, although Lowe abolished slavery for all children born after Christmas Day

1818.[93] He even denied Napoleon's request to see Captain Murray Maxwell's boa constrictor, which could eat a goat, and banned the senior chaplain on St Helena from receiving a snuffbox from Napoleon, regarding it as the attempted bribery of an official.[94]

Lowe's most absurd moment came in May 1820, when he reported to Lord Bathurst that Montholon had spoken to the French commissioner on the island, the Marquis de Montchenu, about Longwood's success in growing vegetables, and offered him both green beans and white beans from the kitchen garden. Lowe saw this as having a deep political meaning since green was the Bonapartist colour and white the Bourbon. 'The Marquis, it appears to me,' Lowe reported to Bathurst, 'would have acted with more propriety if he had declined receiving either, or limited himself to a demand for the white alone.' This was not the only time Lowe mentioned the bean-colour issue to the (presumably completely nonplussed) secretary for war.[95] Wishing to learn English, Napoleon had a copy of children's fables sent to him, in one of which a sick lion endured with fortitude the insults of the other animals until he was finally kicked in the face by a donkey. 'I could have borne everything but this,' says the lion before expiring. 'It is me and your governor,' Napoleon told Betsy.[96]

Yet the baiting and paranoia were not all one way. Napoleon had a wall and trench built so that he could garden out of sight of Lowe's sentries; he had chairs removed so that Lowe was forced to stand during their interviews, as with a head of state; he had holes cut – indeed it is said on St Helena that he did it himself with his penknife – in the shutters of the billiards room so that he could spy on the sentry-box in his garden, even though it faces away from the house rather than towards it.[97] Calling Lowe 'the Sicilian henchman', Napoleon regularly alleged that he was an assassin sent by 'the English oligarchy' (that is, the British government), claiming that the guards around the house had orders to kill him, and that one day he would be killed by an 'accidental' bayonet thrust.[98] 'I cannot bear red,' he said during one bout of Anglophobia, 'it is the colour of England.'[99]

One major area of contention with Lowe was the governor's attempt to cut the costs of Napoleon's imprisonment, from £20,000 to £12,000 per annum (that is, from 400,000 to 240,000 francs). The rows over his expenses descended to the cost and quality of the butter served at Longwood. Lowe found it hard to understand why Napoleon needed a pastry-chef and lamp-lighter there, but for all Bertrand's protestations over the cutbacks, the household hardly went short.[100] In the last three months of 1816, for example, 3,700 bottles of wine – 830 of them claret – were delivered to Longwood.[101]*

Though Lowe couldn't have known it, Napoleon never considered trying to escape from St Helena, which is surprising considering the adventurousness of the rest of his life and the fact that until Rochefort his record for seaborne escapes – Corsica, Egypt, Elba – had been good. He did feign an escape early on, for a joke, suddenly riding up a precipice and away from his orderly officer, Captain Thomas Poppleton of the 53rd Regiment, but Cockburn failed to become alarmed and told Poppleton that he would probably find him back at Longwood, which indeed he did.[102] There was much discussion among his entourage about escaping, and several plans, including ones concocted by a Colonel Latapie and General Lallemand, who had escaped from Malta two months after being imprisoned there.[103] (Latapie was going to seize the Portuguese prison island of Fernando de Noronha, 220 miles off the Brazilian coast, incite a rebellion of the 2,000 prisoners there and sail to St Helena to free Napoleon. Napoleon himself denounced the whole idea as 'a fable they have invented to give more authority to the vexations of Sir Hudson Lowe'.[104]†) Gourgaud boasted that they often discussed how Napoleon 'might escape in a basket of soiled clothes, or in a cask of beer, or a case of sugar', but added that the Emperor had made it clear he would neither disguise himself nor make the slightest physical effort to escape, as it was too undignified.[105] Besides, Lowe's paranoia led him to station no fewer than 125 men around Longwood during the day and 72 at night.

Napoleon spent more than five and a half years on St Helena, longer than his time as First Consul, and apart from Longwood, which was destroyed by termites in the next century and had to be rebuilt, he could only leave one monument there: his memoirs. In 1802 he had said that he would 'hear the last hour strike without regret and without anxiety as to the opinion of future generations', yet his principal activity on St Helena was

---

* Napoleon received regular remittances from Lafite, his banker in Paris, and spent a total of 1,818,245 francs of his own money during his captivity, of which the destination of over 1 million francs remains a mystery (Branda, *Le prix de la gloire* p. 81). Madame Mère helped out financially with 60,000 francs per annum, but Fesch, Joseph, Lucien and Jérôme, after they had originally promised to send 100,000 francs, contributed nothing (Martineau, *Napoleon's St Helena* p. 62). Eugène reimbursed the staff 650,768 francs when they returned to Europe in 1821.

† Lowe was knighted in 1816.

an unvarnished attempt to influence that opinion.[106] That he was so successful lay both in the extraordinary nature of the tale he had to tell, and in his literary ability. 'The historian like the orator must persuade,' Napoleon told Bertrand, 'he must convince.'[107] So in June 1816 he began dictating to Las Cases (both father and son), Gourgaud, Montholon and occasionally O'Meara – sometimes for up to twelve hours a day – what was to be, when it was published two years after his death by Las Cases in four volumes under the title *Le Mémorial de Sainte-Hélène*, the greatest international bestseller of the nineteenth century.[108] Once he had finished, he dictated a 238-page book on Julius Caesar, which, as we have seen, had plenty of autobiographical overtones.

Napoleon spread maps all over the billiard table, using billiard balls to hold them open, and sought to remember the events of his sixty battles with the help of his bulletins. When asked by a visitor how he could recall the details of units that fought in each engagement, he replied: 'Madam, this is a lover's recollection of his former mistress.'[109] Yet like other statesmen engaged on this exercise, his factual recall was by no means exact. 'What a novel my life has been!' he said, and his retelling of it certainly owed as much to fiction as to fact.[110] He exaggerated achievements, underplayed defeats and pretended to a pan-Europeanism that was never his policy. (Las Cases even inserted the fraudulent document mentioned in Chapter 20.) He unsurprisingly wanted his memoirs to confound his detractors.[111] 'Many faults, no doubt, will be found in my career,' he said, 'but Arcole, Rivoli, the Pyramids, Marengo, Austerlitz, Jena, Friedland – these are granite: the teeth of envy are powerless here.'[112] He also felt the need to denigrate other great men of the past – except Julius Caesar – presumably in order to build himself up. Thus Gustavus Adolphus made few able manoeuvres, Frederick the Great 'did not understand artillery', 'Henri IV never did anything great ... St Louis was a simpleton', even Alexander the Great made 'no fine manoeuvres worthy of a great general'.[113] When, after Napoleon's death but before the *Mémorial* came out, Gourgaud published some of Napoleon's reminiscences, Marshal Grouchy believed the references to himself and Ney at Waterloo to be so garbled and incorrect that he wrote a pamphlet entitled *Doubts of the Authenticity of the Historical Memoirs Attributed to Napoleon*, stating that they could not have come from him.[114] But they had.

Napoleon's daily routine at Longwood, at least until he fell ill in 1820, was to rise at 6 a.m., take tea or coffee, wash, shave and have a full-body massage with eau-de-cologne. ('Rub harder,' he would tell his valets, 'as if you were rubbing down a donkey.')[115] He had lunch at 10 a.m., after which he dictated his memoirs and would then have a bath lasting between one hour and three (sometimes he even ate meals in the bath). He received visitors in the early evening in the drawing room, standing by the fireplace with his hat under his arm, before walking over to the Bertrands, and later returning to correct the dictated copy before dinner.[116] There he would hold senior members of his entourage entranced with his reminiscences of great people and events, but then bore them after dinner by reading aloud to them from Corneille, Voltaire, Ossian, Homer or sometimes the Bible until bedtime at 11 p.m.[117] Two of his mini-court plotted to 'lose' his copy of Voltaire's tragedy *Zaïre* if he suggested reading it one more time.[118]

In mid-June 1816 Admiral Sir Pulteney Malcolm arrived to replace Cockburn as the senior military officer on St Helena. Napoleon enjoyed his company and that of his wife, who happened to be a sister of the Captain Elphinstone he had helped the day before Waterloo. She took down their many, long and detailed conversations immediately afterwards.[119] Malcolm found him 'taller and not so fat as from his pictures he expected . . . his manner plain and agreeable'. They discussed Admiral of the Fleet Earl St Vincent's gout, Pitt's income tax – 'Almost every person complained of it, which showed that they all paid' – the 'disgrace' of slavery, Nelson's tactics at Trafalgar, how Wellington risked too much fighting at Waterloo, and the fate of the Bourbons. Discussions about d'Enghien and the Jaffa massacre showed that nothing was out of bounds.[120] In a single meeting they spoke about the Scottish aristocracy, how Wellington and Nelson chose their titles, Sheridan's play *The Rivals*, John Milton's republicanism, how much the English language had changed since Shakespeare, and whether Dryden and Addison had modernized it. Napoleon asked about Byron and contrasted Italian poetry and prose, before sitting down with Lady Malcolm to play chess. The Malcolms record Napoleon laughing a good deal, and when he saw the new ice-making machine brought to the island by its inventor, the pioneer of refrigeration Professor Leslie, he managed to break its thermometer, modestly remarking of his own clumsiness: 'That is worthy of me.'[121]

To stave off boredom Napoleon gave interviews to scores of people who visited St Helena as their ships revictualled. On June 7, 1817 he met Dr Thomas Manning, the explorer of Tibet, who was on his way to China. He wanted to know about the revenues of the Grand Lama of Lhasa and 'asked a thousand questions respecting the Chinese, their language, customs, etc'. Otherwise, life on St Helena was monotonous, enlivened occasionally by the rat infestations at Longwood. On one occasion he told Betsy he had been 'startled by observing a huge one jumping out of his hat, as he was in the act of putting it on'.[122] He would also amuse himself by imitating the famous cries of London street-vendors.

From late October 1816 – a full four and a half years before his death – Napoleon started to exhibit serious signs of ill-health. This was partly because once his relations with Lowe grew toxic he stopped riding much and became something of a hermit, but also partly because he ate few vegetables and little fruit, and because he refused to take the medicine prescribed to him, only agreeing to ever-longer hot baths. (The medicine he was prescribed included tartar emetic, mercurous chloride and a decoction of tree bark, so refusing it may not have done him much harm.) He was also afflicted by a growing depression about his fate on what he called, at different times, 'this accursed', 'frightful', 'vile' and 'miserable' rock.[123]

Barry O'Meara reported to Lowe regularly on his patient's health, and from these detailed summations, written weekly, sometimes daily, it is possible to follow his symptoms. When O'Meara fell out with Lowe in October 1817 over his diagnosis of hepatitis, which Lowe thought would be blamed on the British government for sending Napoleon somewhere inherently unhealthy, a Lowe-appointed doctor called Alexander Baxter, whom Napoleon refused to see, had to take dictation from O'Meara for his reports to the governor. This absurd situation continued until Lowe had O'Meara expelled from the island in August 1818. (Gourgaud had also by then been expelled by Lowe, for trying to communicate with Lucien Bonaparte.)

On October 20, 1816, O'Meara reported that Napoleon – whom Lowe insisted O'Meara call 'General Bonaparte' in his reports – was complaining of 'sponginess of his gums which . . . bled on a slight touch, countenance paler than usual'.[124] Thereafter Napoleon was 'in difficulty of respiration' (October 21), had 'swelling and coldness of the lower extremities' (November 10) and suffered from 'occasional attacks of nervous headaches, to which he has been subject for several years . . . slight diarrhoea' (March 5, 1817), 'some little tumefaction of the cheek and red gums' (March 28), 'swelling of the cheek . . . extremely painful' (June 30), 'severe catarrh' (July 3), 'an oedematous [swollen] appearance about the ankles ... want of rest at night, and frequent inclination to make water voided in small quantities at a time' (September 27), a dull pain 'in the right hypochondriac region and a similar sensation in the right shoulder', a rise of his pulse from 60 to 68 beats a minute, excitable bowels, a painful cheek and a pain in his side (October 9), from which O'Meara surmised: 'Should it continue or increase, there will be every reason to believe that he has experienced a bout of chronic hepatitis' (October 1).

In the autumn of 1817 O'Meara removed one of Napoleon's teeth, in the only medical operation he underwent in his life. By October 9 Napoleon had 'a dull pain in the right side further back than before, his legs are rather less swelled' and 'the sensation [of] pain in the right side still continues the same. Last night he had some symptoms of palpitations of the heart ... rather an acute pain under the scapula, and shooting down the right side, which in some degree affected the respiration ... it is probable that the pain was produced by his having sat for a considerable time out on the steps of the veranda yesterday' (October 11), 'a dull pain in the right side and want of sleep' (October 13).[125] Napoleon wasn't yet dying, but he clearly wasn't well.

By late 1817 Napoleon was suffering from depression, as well as liver problems, stomach pains and perhaps hepatitis B. 'The thoughts of the night are not gay,' he told Bertrand.[126] He nonetheless does not seem to have seriously considered committing suicide, despite having attempted it once at Fontainebleau in 1814 and possibly again at the Élysée the following year. The only indication that he might have thought about it on St Helena emerged second-hand over half a century after his death, in the 1877 memoirs of Albine de Nontholon's lover Basil Jackson, who claimed that on St Helena Gourgaud 'would ... talk strangely, even going so far as to more than insinuate that Napoleon had suggested to him self-destruction; this was on an occasion when death by means of the fumes of charcoal were talked of.'[127] (Grilled charcoal exudes carbon monoxide.) By 1818, it was true, he had written his memoirs; he was never going to see any of his family again; he complained of failing memory and libido; he was obviously ill and often in pain. He was also easily brave enough to kill himself, and his lack of religious faith meant that 'I don't have chimerical fears of Hell.'[128] 'Death is nothing but a sleep without dreams', and 'As to my body, it will become carrots or turnips. I have no dread of death. In the army I have seen many men perish who were talking to me.'[129]

'Does a man have the right to kill himself?' he had asked in his 1786 essay, 'On Suicide'. 'Yes, if his death harms no other person and if life is ill for him.'[130] He knew that Seneca, Pliny, Martial, Tacitus and Lucan all celebrated the act.[131] Yet when in 1802 a grenadier called Gobain had killed himself for love, the second such incident in a month, Napoleon sternly addressed an Order of the Day on the issue, stating that a 'soldier should know how to conquer the pain and the melancholy of his passions; that there is as much courage evinced in suffering with constancy mental pain as in remaining firm under a storm of grapeshot. That to give oneself up to chagrin without resistance and to kill oneself is to abandon the battlefield before being conquered.'[132] Although Marcus Porcius Cato's suicide was praised by his contemporaries, in his biography of Julius Caesar Napoleon asked: 'But to whom was his death useful? To Caesar. To whom did it give pleasure? To Caesar. For whom was it fatal? For Rome, for his party . . . He killed himself out of scorn, out of desperation. His death was the weakness of a great soul, the error of a Stoic, a blemish on his life.'[133] Napoleon didn't commit suicide on St Helena probably because it would give his enemies too much pleasure; as he himself put it: 'It needs more courage to suffer than to die.'[134] He told the Malcolms in June 1817,

> I have worn the imperial crown of France, the iron crown of Italy; England has now given me a greater and more glorious [one] than either of them – for it is that crown worn by the Saviour of the world – a crown of thorns. Oppression and every insult that is offered to me only adds to my glory, and it is to the persecutions of England I shall owe the brightest part of my fame.[135]

It was typically hyperbolic, unusually blasphemous and factually incorrect on many levels, but living on St Helena having once ruled most of Europe was a harsh punishment indeed (though far better than the execution that the Bourbons and Prussians had wanted for him). When there was a slight earthquake that summer, he told an aide 'that we ought to have been swallowed up, island and all. It would be so pleasant to die in company.'[136] He clutched at any future political developments that might result in his release, citing 'an insurrection in France', Lord Holland becoming prime minister, the death of Louis XVIII, and the Prince Regent's only child, Princess Charlotte, becoming queen of England, saying: 'She will bring me back to Europe.' In reality, none of these provided the least likelihood of salvation for him, especially after November 1817, when Charlotte died and was replaced as the Prince

Regent's heir by his unsympathetic younger brother, the future King William IV.[137]

In 1818 the Balcombes left the island, O'Meara was sent away and Cipriani, a Corsican with whom Napoleon used to reminisce, died. Before she left, Betsy noticed a severe deterioration in Napoleon's health after a bout of illness. 'The havoc and change it had made in his appearance was sad to look upon,' she wrote.

> His face was literally the colour of yellow wax, and his cheeks had fallen in pouches on either side of his face. His ankles were so swollen that the flesh literally hung over the sides of his shoes; he was so weak, that without resting one hand on the table near him, and the other on the shoulder of an attendant, he could not have stood.[138]

When they said goodbye for the last time, Napoleon said: 'Soon you will be sailing away towards England leaving me to die on this miserable rock. Look at those dreadful mountains – they are my prison walls.' Ever conscious of the power of gifts, he gave Betsy the handkerchief of his she was crying into, and when she asked for a lock of his hair he had Marchand cut off four, for her and other family members.[139]

The diseases that historians have ascribed to Napoleon over the years include gonorrhoea, gallstones, epilepsy, migraine, peptic ulcer, malaria, brucellosis, amoebic hepatitis, dysentery, scurvy, gout, an over-active pituitary gland, bilharzia, gas, indigestion, renal problems, hypogonadism, heart failure, cystitis, manic depression and various syndromes such as Klinefelter's, Fröhlich's and Zollinger-Ellison.[140] Almost all of these can be safely dismissed, apart from haemorrhoids, a mild case of childhood tuberculosis that had completely cleared up, bladder infection with stones, scabies, and headaches, all of which he suffered from before his time on St Helena. An extraordinarily detailed book, *Itinéraire de Napoléon au jour le jour*, first published in 1947, records where he was and what he was doing every single day of his adult life, and from which it is clear that he took remarkably few days off work from illness. Indeed he boasted as late as January 1815: 'I was never ill in my life.'[141] He caught influenza on campaign, and might indeed have been under par at Wagram, Borodino, the third day of Leipzig and possibly at Waterloo, but not to the extent that it is possible to discern any effect on his decision-making in any of those battles.

All that changed in 1818 when he began to suffer from chronic leg-swellings, more headaches, considerable nausea, low appetite,

'profuse perspiration', palpitations, pains in his right side, bad constipa-
tion and (unsurprisingly) very low spirits.[142] It was in early to
mid-1818 that the stomach cancer that was to kill him fully took hold,
although it wasn't to be properly diagnosed for over two years. In early
1818 he didn't step outside the house at all for a month. 'From the first,'
noted Walter Henry, assistant surgeon of the 66th Foot, on the staff of
the Deadwood Barracks, 'Napoleon appeared to be aware of the nature
of his malady, referring [to it as a] disease of the stomach, of which
his father died at the age of thirty-five, and with which the Princess
[Pauline] Borghese was threatened.'[143] Both Pauline and Caroline
Bonaparte were to die of cancer at forty-four and fifty-seven respectively, and Napoleon's natural son Charles Léon also died of stomach
cancer, albeit at the age of eighty-one.[144] (Had Napoleon lived to that
age, Britain would have released him when his nephew was elected
president in 1848.)

In 1809 Napoleon had told Corvisart that he wanted a lesson in
anatomy, so human body parts were brought to Malmaison for dissection in his study before lunch. Josephine noticed that he 'was paler than
usual and could not eat', and persuaded Corvisart not to continue after
lunch, for which Napoleon subsequently thanked her.[145] This was curi-
ously squeamish considering the number of eviscerated bodies that
he had seen on battlefields, but his brief lesson helped him understand
the workings of the body and ensured that now in 1818 he knew enough
to recognize that his illness was life-threatening.

Various imaginative conspiracy theories have been put forward
over the years alleging that Napoleon was poisoned with arsenic by
Montholon and/or others, based on the supposedly high arsenic content in his hair. Yet hair samples from plenty of other contemporaries
have yielded similarly high arsenic levels – such as from Josephine and
the King of Rome – and his hair had high arsenic counts at several
stages of his life before he went to St Helena. The 10.38 parts per million
of arsenic in his hair was lower, for example, than the 17 parts per
million in George III's hair.[146] It is true that Napoleon might have
benefited from a better doctor than the barely competent Francesco
Antommarchi, appointed by Madame Mère and Cardinal Fesch, who
took over in September 1819 – Napoleon refused to see any doctor
appointed by Lowe – but nothing could alter the ultimate outcome
once stomach cancer had taken hold.[147] Seven British surgeons and
Antommarchi opened his corpse at the post-mortem in the billiards
room the day after Napoleon's death, the body resting on some planks

of wood supported by trestles. In the words of the official post-mortem report:

> The internal surface of the stomach to nearly its whole length, was a mass of cancerous disease or scirrhous portions advancing to cancer, this was particularly noticed near the pylorus. The cardiac extremity for a small space near the termination of the oesophagus was the only part appearing in a healthy state, the stomach was found nearly filled with a large body of fluid resembling coffee grounds. The convex surface of the left lobe of the liver adhered to the diaphragm.[148]

The symptoms and time-course make it likely that this was not a benign stomach ulcer that became malignant, which used to happen in the days before acid-arresting medication, but a cancer from the beginning which spread until it had taken over almost the entire stomach. The autopsy showed that the cancer had spread to the lymph nodes and the tissues in contact with the stomach, but not to the liver. Adhesions in the chest cavity suggest a previous infection – early tuberculosis or bacterial pneumonia some time before – which was not related to his death. Blood-stained fluid in the pleural cavities and the pericardial cavity could have been the consequence of septic shock, which could follow a perforation of the stomach. The coffee grounds were blood that had been turned dark brown by the action of stomach acid and digestive enzymes.[149]

Cancer was diagnosed by all the doctors except Antommarchi, who was under pressure from Bertrand and Montholon to say he had suffered from gastro-hepatitis, so that 'the English oligarchy' could be blamed for choosing unhealthy Longwood for Napoleon's imprisonment.[150] The words 'and the liver was perhaps a little larger than usual', on the third page of the post-mortem report, were struck out by Lowe and didn't appear in the published version, as they implied that Napoleon suffered from hepatitis as well as from the cancer that killed him.[151] This has fixated conspiracy theorists, but was essentially irrelevant, for, as one of the doctors present, Walter Henry, wrote of the stomach:

> This organ was found most extensively disorganized: in fact it was ulcerated all over like a honeycomb. The focus of the disease was exactly the spot pointed out by Napoleon [on several occasions in his final illness] – the pylorus, or lower end where the intestines begin. At this place I put my finger into a hole made by the ulcer that had eaten through the stomach, but which was stopped by a light adhesion to the adjacent liver.[152]

He added: 'How Napoleon could have existed for any time with such an organ was wonderful, for there was not an inch of it sound.'[153]

Napoleon's fiftieth birthday was a sad affair, prompting nostalgic reminiscence. 'My heart is turned to bronze,' he said. 'I was never in love, except perhaps with Josephine a little. And I was twenty-seven years old when I first knew her. I had a sincere affection for Marie Louise.'[154] A see-saw was erected in the billiards room in January 1821 to give the Emperor some exercise, but it saw little use.[155] In February he threw some of Antommarchi's medicine out of a window, and vomited almost daily.[156] Later that month he was afflicted with 'a dry cough, vomiting, an almost unbearable burning in the intestines, general agitation, anxiety and a burning thirst'.[157] The scenes from Napoleon's final deterioration were wrenching for those around him. His complexion was likened to tallow and comparisons were made to a ghost.

On March 17, 1821 Napoleon saw the Abbé Buonavita, who had been sent by Cardinal Fesch, and gave him instructions about what should be said to Madame Mère and the family. The abbé was 'dismayed at the havoc wrought by the disease on his features and was at the same time profoundly moved by his calmness and resignation'. Napoleon tried to get into his carriage with Montholon but couldn't and 'returned shaking with a shivering chill'. Gnats swarmed around Longwood which mosquito nets failed to keep off.[158] 'Do you not think that death would be a Heaven-sent relief to me?' he asked Antommarchi in late March. 'I do not fear it, but while I shall do nothing to hasten it I shall not grasp at a straw to live.'[159]

Lowe obstinately refused to believe that Napoleon was anything more than a hypochondriac. He was persuaded of this by a British doctor, Thomas Arnott, who told him Antommarchi was lying about the fevers, and as late as April 6 said 'General Bonaparte is not affected by any serious complaint, probably more mental than any other.'[160] Arnott did admit that the heavily bearded Napoleon looked 'horrible'. (He was shaved two days later.) Others reported to Lowe that the colour of Napoleon's face was 'very pallid, cadaverous' and that his bedroom was filthy, 'but particularly the bedclothes, occasioned by General Bonaparte spitting upon them. He has got a cough and spits a good deal and never turns his head to avoid the bed linen but throws it out immediately before him.'[161] He lost between twenty-two and thirty-three pounds during the last six months of his life, although he still had over an inch of fat around his heart when he died. His sunken cheeks are nonetheless evident from the death-mask that Antommarchi made of him.

Napoleon wrote his will on April 15, 1821. 'I die in the Apostolic and Roman faith,' it began, 'in whose bosom I was born more than fifty years ago. I wish my ashes to rest by the banks of the Seine in the midst of the French nation I have loved so dearly.'[162] He divided his fortune and possessions, including many millions of francs that he didn't actually possess, between his family, servants and former generals. One bequest was for 100,000 francs to go to Cantillon, Wellington's would-be assassin, who Napoleon said 'had as much right to kill that oligarch as the latter had to send me to die on the rock of St Helena'.[163] Equally unworthy was the accusation against Lowe: 'I die before my time, murdered by the English oligarchy and its hired assassin.'[164] He stated that the 1814 and 1815 invasions of France were 'due to the treason of Marmont, Augereau, Talleyrand and Lafayette', adding, though with how much sincerity may be questioned, 'I forgive them. May the posterity of France forgive them as I have done.'

The will gave away a number of belongings that weren't his either, such as 'Frederick II's alarm clock, which I removed from Potsdam', and listed the contents of his linen cupboard, including '1 pair of braces; 4 pairs of white cashmere underpants and undershirts; 6 scarves; 6 flannel vests; 4 pairs of drawers . . . 1 little box full of my snuff . . . 1 pair of slippers, 6 girdles', and so on.[165] His 'golden toilet case for teeth, left at the dentist's' was to go to the King of Rome. Not relinquishing his penchant for organizing other people's marital lives, he gave orders for Bessières' son to marry Duroc's daughter, and for Marchand to marry the widow, sister or daughter of an officer or soldier of the Old Guard. He was unrepentant over the Duc d'Enghien, saying that 'it was necessary to the security, interest and honour of the French nation . . . In like circumstances I would do as much again.'[166] He bequeathed a pair of golden shoe buckles to Joseph, 'a little pair of golden garter buckles' to Lucien, and a golden collar clasp to Jérôme.[167] Bracelets of his hair were sent to Marie Louise, Madame Mère, each of his siblings, nephews and nieces, 'and a more substantial one for my son.' The servants did far better than Napoleon's family out of his will, excepting the King of Rome, although he did say: 'I have always been well-pleased with my most dear spouse Marie Louise; to the last I retain most tender feelings for her.' He might not have done so had he known of her liaison with

Neipperg, by whom she had two children during his lifetime, and whom she married after his death.*

'I thank my good and most excellent mother,' he wrote, 'the cardinal [Fesch], my brothers Joseph, Lucien, Jérôme, Pauline, Caroline, Julie [Joseph's wife], Hortense, Catarina [Jérôme's wife] and Eugène for their enduring concern.'[168] Caroline's inclusion in the list was particularly magnanimous considering her betrayal of him. Elisa had died in Italy the previous August. Although he wasn't in the list, Louis was also forgiven for 'the libel he published in 1820, full of false assertions and forged evidence'. (He had published a compendium of historical documents relating to his reign in Holland, which drew attention to the way he had stood up to Napoleon in defence of the Dutch.)

By April 26 Napoleon was vomiting blood and the next day a dark, coffee-coloured fluid. He asked for his draped campaign bed to be moved into the drawing room where there was better airflow, and Bertrand noted that he hardly had the strength to spit, so his vest was stained by a reddish spittle.[169] Marchand recalled that he nonetheless showed 'dignity, calm and goodness', even while complaining that the pain in his right side 'cuts me like a razor blade'.[170]

Eight codicils to Napoleon's will were drawn up before April 29, some antedated to the 27th, and on the 29th and 30th he started repeating the same sentences continuously. Although his last words before he lost the power of speech were scarcely audible ramblings – either 'France ... Army ... head of the Army' or 'France ... the head of the Army ... Josephine' – more interesting were his last lucid words.[171] In a copy of the book on Caesar that he had dictated to Marchand, his valet-cum-executor noted that between eight and nine o'clock on the evening of May 2 Napoleon dictated the words: 'I bequeath to my son my estate in Ajaccio; two houses in the environs of Salines and their gardens; all my property in the area of Ajaccio which are capable of raising 50,000 francs a year in rent.'[172] Marchand noted this down in pencil in the preface of the book and then carefully sewed it into the lining of a small red-leather box embossed with the Emperor's coat of arms, given by his descendants to the Napoleonic scholar Henry

---

* 'Although I never entertained strong sentiments of any kind for him,' Marie Louise wrote after Napoleon's death, 'I cannot forget that he is the father of my son, and far from treating me badly, as most people believe, he always showed the deepest regard for me, the only thing one can wish for from a political marriage ... I could have wished him many years of happiness and of life – so long as it would be far away from me' (Palmer, *Napoleon and Marie Louise* p. 213).

Lachouque, whose family still possess it. So, having been master of Europe and living the most adventurous life of modern times, Napoleon reverted on his deathbed to what he had been when he was trying to negotiate over the mulberry trees thirty years earlier: a Corsican landowner of the *petit noblesse* keen to maintain his family's property rights.

On May 3 Napoleon received extreme unction in private from the Abbé Ange-Paul Vignali. An only nominal Catholic in life who had made war on one pope and imprisoned another, he was received back into the bosom of the Church in death. Shortly before he died, he asked Bertrand to close his eyes afterwards, 'Because they naturally stay open', something he must have noticed, and been haunted by, from his experience of sixty battlefields.[173] During the 4th, Napoleon suffered from prolonged hiccups, and in the evening he slipped into delirium, asking the name of his son. The next day, Saturday, May 5, 1821, after a very blustery and stormy morning, the fifty-one-year-old former Emperor gave three sighs at long intervals and died at 5.49 p.m., just after the firing of the island's sunset gun.[174] What Chateaubriand called 'the mightiest breath of life that ever animated human clay' had ceased.

Napoleon was buried with full military honours in Torbett's Spring, a beautiful spot a mile from Longwood punctuated by willow trees where he had sometimes visited. He was dressed in his uniform of a colonel in the Chasseurs à Cheval. The coffin was borne along a goat-path to the grave by British grenadiers of the 66th and 20th Regiments, prompting one spectator to note 'the irony that the regimental colours under which the Emperor was being buried had the golden letters of "Talavera", "Albuera", "Vitoria" and "The Pyrenees" woven on them in strange mockery'.[175] Three salvoes of fifteen guns and three volleys of musketry were fired, creating 'a succession of fine echoes from the hills and ravines'.[176] Yet the tomb was unmarked, because even after the former Emperor's death, Lowe would not allow his gravestone to feature the imperial title 'Napoleon', while Bertrand and Montholon would not accept Lowe's wording of the non-royal 'Napoleon Bonaparte', so it was left blank.[177] (It can be seen today in the courtyard of Longwood, still without wording.) His remains were removed from the grave and taken to Paris in 1840 by Bertrand and Gourgaud and given a magnificent funeral on December 2, the anniversary of his coronation and the battle of Austerlitz. Though the day was freezing, an estimated one million Frenchmen lined the route of the cortège through Paris. Attending his interment at Les Invalides were four of his marshals: Soult, Moncey, Oudinot and Grouchy. Others who were still living but who had turned against him – Bernadotte, Marmont and Victor – did not attend.

After Napoleon's death, Louis Marchand drew up a list of the 370 books in the library at Longwood, which testifies to the Emperor's eclectic literary taste and interests. They included *Northanger Abbey*, *Paradise Lost*, Dr Johnson's *Dictionary* and *Tour of the Highlands*, various Army Lists, *Robinson Crusoe*, a history of Egypt, a biography of George III, Voltaire's *Charles XII* (which he had read in Moscow, complete with its strictures on the Russian weather), *Monarchy* by Chateaubriand, no fewer than twenty books on religion, the comic novel *Castle Rackrent*, several of Byron's works, some Shakespeare, Gibbon's *Decline and Fall of the Roman Empire*, a book on 'coquetry', *Debrett's Peerage*, eight volumes of the *Spectator*, Edmund Burke's violently anti-Jacobin *Reflections on the Revolution in France*, Adam Smith's *Wealth of Nations* (whose precepts he would have saved himself a great deal of trouble by following) and a biography of Admiral Nelson.[178]

Ancient history was well represented, of course, and the list included a very recent edition of Cornelius Nepos' *Vies des grands capitaines*, a book he had first read over forty years earlier. By the time he went to St Helena, Napoleon could be certain that it would be impossible to write a modern book entitled *Lives of the Great Captains* without including a chapter on him too. The ambition he had conceived as a schoolboy at Brienne, and from which he had never wavered, had been achieved. He had transformed the art of leadership, built an empire, handed down laws for the ages, and joined the ancients.

NAPOLEON

Conclusion
Napoleon the Great

'The greatest man of action born in Europe since Julius Caesar.'
Winston Churchill on Napoleon

'He was at one and the same time a man of great genius and great audacity.'
Napoleon on Julius Caesar

'SPIRIT SINISTER: ". . . My argument is that War makes rattling good history; but Peace is poor reading. So I back Bonaparte for the reason that he will give pleasure to posterity."'
Thomas Hardy, *The Dynasts*

What wins a ruler the soubriquet 'the Great'? Alexander, Alfred, Charles, Peter, Frederick and Catherine were all huge figures who decisively influenced the history of their times. Yet it is not difficult to think of others who were equally influential or striking, and indeed often rather better human beings (at least by modern standards), who have not been so called. Frederick Barbarossa, Henry II and Elizabeth I of England, Ferdinand and Isabella of Spain, the Holy Roman Emperor Charles V (who ruled more of Europe than anyone else between Charlemagne and Napoleon), 'the Sun King' Louis XIV, and so on.* Why does the subject of this book so deserve it?

Napoleon Bonaparte was the founder of modern France and gave his name to an age. He came to power through a military coup only six years after entering the country as a virtually penniless political refugee, and was defined for the rest of his life above all by the fact that he was an army officer. Much has been written about his Corsicanness, his origins in the *petite noblesse*, his absorption of the ideas of the

---

* Though there is a fine biography of Elizabeth I by Elizabeth Jenkins which calls her 'Elizabeth the Great'.

Enlightenment, and his inspiration by the ancient world, but the years he spent in military schooling at Brienne and the École Militaire affected him even more than any of these, and it was from the ethos of the Army that he took most of his beliefs and assumptions. The army imbued him with a strong belief in the importance of applied intelligence, hierarchy based on merit, law and order, hard work, mental toughness and physical courage, as well as a contempt for self-serving lawyers and politicians. Despite being technically a noble, the Revolution saw him accept enthusiastically its early principles of equality before the law, rational government, meritocracy and aggressive nationalism: all those ideas fitted in well with his assumptions about what would work well for the French Army. By contrast, equality of outcome, social disorder, parliamentarianism, and liberty of the press (which he saw as licence encouraging sedition) all struck him as at odds with the military ethic. Even in his own short Jacobin phase he never espoused egalitarianism. It was very much as a French army officer imbued with the military ethos that he rose, demonstrated his usefulness to the Revolution, seized power and then maintained his rule.

Any general – which Napoleon became at the age of twenty-four – must ultimately be judged by the outcome of his battles. Although his conquests ended in defeat and ignominious imprisonment, over the course of his short but packed military life Napoleon fought sixty battles and sieges and lost only seven – Acre, Aspern-Essling, Leipzig, La Rothière, Lâon, Arcis and Waterloo. Napoleon's feeling for battle, and capacity for battlefield decision-making, was extraordinary. Walking the ground of fifty-three of his sixty battlefields, I was regularly astounded by his instinctive feeling for topography, his acuity in judging distance and choosing ground, his sense of timing. 'There is a moment in combat when the slightest manoeuvre is decisive and gives superiority,' he once wrote. 'It is the drop of water that starts the overflow.'[1] He certainly never lacked confidence in his own capacity as a military leader. On St Helena, when asked why he had not taken Frederick the Great's sword when he had visited Sanssouci, he replied, 'Because I had my own.' (In fact, he did take Frederick's sword back to Les Invalides.)

Since France's defeat in the Seven Years War, not least by Frederick's sword, much important thinking had been done by her military strategists and theorists about how she could improve each of the three arms of infantry, cavalry and artillery and how they could be coordinated to far better effect. Napoleon studied deeply the works of Guibert, Gribeauval, Bourcet, Marshal de Saxe and others, and put their ideas to practical use on the battlefield. He did not invent concepts such as the *bataillon carré*, the strategy of the central position, the *ordre mixte,* the *manoeuvre sur les derrières* or even the Corps system, but he did perfect them. They allowed him to fight every kind of military engagement and turn almost any situation to his advantage. In the Italian campaign of 1796–7 alone, he continually pinned the enemy in place while turning one or other of their flanks – the right at Montenotte, the left at Rovereto, or sometimes both simultaneously as at Mondovi. He was superb at inspiring his men to attack across narrow bridges such as at Lodi and Arcole, at intuiting situations from intelligence reports as before Marengo, at pursuing a retreating enemy such as at Millesimo and Primolano. He checked an enemy offensive to his rear at Lonato and Rivoli and counterattacked successfully on both occasions. At Castiglione he trapped the enemy between two armies and took them from the rear. It takes a virtuoso to excel in every different type of tactical situation imaginable in one campaign, and Napoleon was to repeat such performances for nearly twenty years; indeed some of his best generalship was in the 1814 campaign in Champagne, when he won four separate battles in five days.

The Revolutionary armies of the *levée en masse* were not only very large by previous standards, but were fired by patriotic fervour. Once he proclaimed himself emperor he recognized that it would take something beyond mere republican virtue to create the vital *esprit de corps* necessary to inflame his troops, so with his proclamations, inspirational harangues, Orders of the Day and above all the creation of the Légion d'Honneur he appealed to the concept of soldierly honour to light what he called the 'sacred fire' of martial valour.[2] Napoleon managed to incorporate elements from both the Ancien Régime and the Revolutionary armies to create a new military culture motivated by honour, patriotism and a fierce personal devotion to himself which took his troops across the sands of Egypt, the great rivers of Europe and, ultimately disastrously, the frozen wastes of Russia.

In the five years of peace between Marengo and the Austerlitz campaign, Napoleon taught his armies manoeuvres that he was able to put to superb effect in the many campaigns thereafter. Although because of the Royal Navy he never got his opportunity to invade Britain with the Army of England stationed at Boulogne, by the time it broke camp to march eastwards after three years in continuous training it was disciplined to perfection. And unlike eighteenth-century armies, which moved in a stately manner with large baggage trains and requisitioned what they needed on campaign, the Revolutionary and later Napoleonic armies lived off the land, dispersing (within strictly controlled limits) to do so and thus – when directed by a commander of Napoleon's driving energy – able to move at an altogether different pace from their enemies. Nor did Napoleon slow himself down by besieging cities, recognizing that modern wars – his wars – would be won by lightning strokes against the main enemy in the field. His understanding of topography and mathematics allowed him to use artillery to maximum effect too, at Toulon, Jena, Wagram, Montereau and many others. He remained cool and analytical – sometimes even jocular as at Rivoli and Wagram – even when he seemed to be on the verge of defeat. What to other commanders might seem like potential disasters he took to be opportunities. When, for example, he had to fight at the end of highly extended lines of communications, as at Austerlitz and Friedland (though not at Borodino), the exposure of his strategic position seemed to inspire him to greater daring on the battlefield. Another important aspect of Napoleon's generalship was his ability to retain the initiative. Of his sixty battles, only five – the Pyramids, Marengo, Aspern-Essling, Leipzig and La Rothière – were defensive; the rest were fought offensively.

Above all, Napoleon was fast. It was a personal characteristic: we have seen how he moved from Dresden to Saint-Cloud in four days in July 1807, from Paris to Erfurt in five days in September 1808, from Valladolid to Paris in six days in January 1809. It was the same for his armies across Europe and on the battlefield: the Army of England struck its tents in Boulogne on August 29, 1805 and by October 5 was beginning to surround Mack in Ulm on the Danube. Soult's corps had covered 400 miles in twenty marching days, Davout's 370 miles without a full day's halt, and both came in without having lost a man through desertion or sickness. 'Activité, activité, vitesse!' he wrote to Masséna in April 1809, and there was no more characteristic Napoleonic command. It was only when he had too large an army personally to be able to oversee its every aspect, as in Russia in 1812, that it became lumbering and incapable of the wide encircling manoeuvres that had brought him victory in earlier years. Nor did he recognize how much his enemies had learnt from him: the deep-seated military reforms instituted by Archduke Charles in Austria, Barclay de Tolly in Russia and von Scharnhorst in Prussia were a tribute to him and his way of waging war; but they were also a danger that he failed to appreciate until it was too late. By 1812 every army in Europe had adopted his Corps system, and innovations that had given Napoleon's armies their early advantages had been copied and sometimes even improved upon.

In another vital area Napoleon suffered from an almost total lacuna: the sea. Despite having been born in a seaport, he never understood naval manoeuvres, and even after the disaster at Trafalgar he still believed that he could build an invasion fleet that would one day humiliate Britain, devoting far too much money, men and materiel to that utterly doomed enterprise. On land, however, he was a genuine military genius. Small wonder that when asked who was the greatest captain of the age, the Duke of Wellington himself replied: 'In this age, in past ages, in any age: Napoleon.'[3]

Yet even if he had not been one of the great conquerors, Napoleon would still be one of the giants of modern history, for his civil achievements equalled his military ones, and far outlasted them. Although the Terror had ended in July 1794, the Jacobins remained powerful: but from the moment he cut them and the other Vendémiaire insurrectionists down with grapeshot in the streets of Paris in October 1795 they were eclipsed as a political force. After the Terror, and the decadence and disorder of the Directory, the majority of Frenchmen wanted a conservative Republic, and they got one from a man whose ideal society looked like merely a much larger version of the Army, led politically as well as militarily by its commander-in-chief. 'We have done with the romance of the Revolution,' the First Consul told an early meeting of his Conseil d'État, 'we must now begin its history.'[4] In many respects, he was the last and greatest of the enlightened authoritarians of eighteenth-century Europe who had begun to introduce rationalism to government and improvement to the lives of their subjects. Goethe said that Napoleon was 'always enlightened by reason . . . He was in a permanent state of enlightenment'.[5] He was the Enlightenment on horseback.

In 1804 he was proclaimed 'Emperor of the French Republic', apparently a contradiction in terms, but in fact a true characterization of the nature of his rule. Napoleon consciously built upon and protected the best aspects of the French Revolution – equality before the law, rational government, meritocracy – while discarding the unsustainable revolutionary calendar of ten-day weeks, the absurd Cult of the Supreme Being, and the corruption, cronyism and hyper-inflation that characterized the dying days of the Republic. During his sixteen years in power, many of the best ideas that underpin and actuate modern democratic politics – meritocracy, equality before the law, property rights, religious toleration, secular education, sound finances, efficient administration, and so on – were rescued from the Revolutionary maelstrom and protected, codified and consolidated. Like much of the rest of Europe of the day, Napoleon's regime employed press censorship and a secret police who established a relatively efficient surveillance system. The plebiscites he held seemingly to give the French people a political voice were regularly rigged. But the approval they gave, if exaggerated, was real. Napoleon was no totalitarian dictator, and had no interest in controlling every aspect of his subjects' lives. In exercising an exceptional degree of power he was not vicious or vindictive, driven by the Corsican mores of vendetta. If he had been, men who kept betraying him such as Fouché, Murat and Talleyrand would hardly have been tolerated for as long as they were. We can count on the fingers of one hand the number of people Napoleon executed for political reasons – d'Enghien, Palm, Hofer, possibly Pichegru, effectively L'Ouverture – though this is not to excuse his massacre of Turkish prisoners at Jaffa or his responsibility for the attempted re-subjugation of Saint-Domingue, both of which surely had racial elements in their cruelty (although he was not present in the latter campaign). He did at one point re-introduce slavery in the French West Indies, but he finally abolished it throughout the French colonies in 1815.

Though France was forced back to its pre-Napoleonic frontiers by the end of 1815, most of Napoleon's refashioning of the country was sufficiently well embedded by then that it could not be reversed by the Bourbons when they returned to power. As a result, many of his civil reforms stayed in place for decades, even centuries. The Napoleonic Code forms the basis of much of European law today, while various aspects of it have been adopted by forty countries on all five inhabited continents. His bridges span the Seine and his reservoirs, canals and sewers are still in use; France's foreign ministry rests on top of part of the 2½ miles of stone quays he built along the river, and the Cour des Comptes still checks public spending accounts more than two centuries after he founded it. The *lycées* continue to provide excellent education, and the Conseil d'État still meets every Wednesday to review the proposed laws of France. The 'masses of granite' that Napoleon boasted of throwing down to anchor French society are there to this day. When Napoleon's mother was complimented on her son's achievements, she replied: *'Mais pourvu que ça dure!'*[6] They have.

In 1792, France became a crusading nation, determined to export the values and ideals of the Revolution to the rest of Europe. Europe's monarchs would have none of it, and formed the first of seven coalitions to resist the encroachments. It was these wars that Napoleon inherited and, through his military capacity, for a time took to a triumphant conclusion. In Britain, which had already had its political revolution 140 years earlier and thus enjoyed many of the benefits that the Revolution brought to France, Napoleon's threat first to invade and then economically to strangle her into submission ensured that successive governments were unsurprisingly determined to overthrow him. The ruling dynasties of Austria, Prussia and Russia were equally unsurprisingly resistant to his offers of peace on French terms. As a consequence, war was declared on him far more often than he declared it on others: by the Austrians in 1800, by the British in 1803, by the Austrians' invading his ally Bavaria in 1805, by the Prussians in 1806 and by the Austrians in 1809. The attacks on Portugal and Spain in 1807 and 1808 and Russia in 1812 were indeed initiated by Napoleon to try to enforce the Continental System – although as we have seen, the Tsar was planning an attack on him in 1812 – but the hostilities of 1813, and those of 1814 and 1815, were all declared on him. He made peace offers before all of them; indeed he made no fewer than four separate offers to Britain between the collapse of Amiens in 1803 and 1812. The Revolutionary and Napoleonic Wars cost a total of around three million military and one million civilian deaths, of whom 1.4 million were French (916,000 from the Empire period, of whom fewer than 90,000 were killed in action).[7]* Napoleon must of course take much of the responsibility for these deaths – 'If one thinks of humanity, and only of humanity,' he said, 'one should give up going to war. I don't know how war is to be conducted on the rosewater plan' – but he cannot be accused of being the only, or even the principal, warmonger of the age. France and Britain were at war for nearly half the period between the Glorious Revolution in 1688 and Waterloo in 1815, and he was only a second lieutenant when the Revolutionary Wars broke out.

'There are two ways of constructing an international order,' wrote Henry Kissinger about post-Napoleonic Europe, 'by will or by renunciation; by conquest or by legitimacy.'[8] Only the way of will and conquest was open to Napoleon, and he followed it. He boasted that he was 'of the race that founds empires', but knew perfectly well, as we repeatedly

---

* Disease accounted for more than battle in most of the armies of Europe: indeed in the Royal Navy between 1793 and 1815, where 6,663 men were killed in action and 13,621 by wrecks, fire and drowning, an extraordinary 72,102 succumbed to disease, mostly in the West Indies.

saw in Part Three, that the legitimacy of his regime depended on the maintenance of French power in Europe, on what he called his honour and the honour of France. Although by 1810 or 1812 his power was great, he knew that his conquests had not yet had sufficient time to legitimize his rule. Some distinguished historians have concluded that the Napoleonic Empire simply could not have survived because it was colonialist in nature, and one European people could not dominate another for long: yet the Turks ruled over Greece for 363 years, the Spanish ruled Holland for 158 and the Austrians ruled Northern Italy and Holland for 80. 'Chemists have a species of powder out of which they can make marble,' he said, 'but it must have time to become solid.'[9] Had he not made a few crucial military mistakes, Napoleonic Europe might well have stabilized, bordered by the Neimen at one end and the English Channel at the other, with Austria as a reluctantly allied power and Prussia a crushed client state, and Napoleon's civil reforms might then have become entrenched outside France too. But from 1810 onwards, the monarchs of Ancien Régime Europe (sinuously guided by Metternich, secretly encouraged by Talleyrand and financed by Castlereagh) strained every resource to be rid of him.* After he had gone, the Legitimist regimes reimposed a far more reactionary form of rule which was eventually overwhelmed by the nationalism to which the Revolution had given birth. Who is to say that a Europe dominated in the nineteenth century by an enlightened France would have been worse than the one that eventually transpired, in which Prussia dominated Germany and then forced itself onto the continent in ways far less benign than Napoleon?

Finally, there is the fascination of the man. The 33,000 letters now superbly presented by the Fondation Napoléon, on which this book is based, are extraordinary testimony to his protean mind. His correspondence with astronomers, chemists, mathematicians and biologists showed a respect for their work, and a capacity to engage with it, that is very rare among statesmen. 'I am always working, and I meditate a great deal,' the Emperor told Roederer in March 1809. 'If I appear always ready to answer for everything and to meet everything, it is

---

* Their decrying of Napoleonic imperialism was of course pure hypocrisy. The British were expanding across the globe, especially in Asia; within living memory Catherine the Great, Frederick the Great and Joseph II had all attempted to expand their territories in Europe. Their successors were not objecting to imperialism per se, simply to being on the losing side.

because, before entering on an undertaking, I have meditated for a long time, and have foreseen what might happen. It is not genius which reveals to me suddenly, secretly, what I have to say or do in a circumstance unexpected by other people: it is reflection, meditation.'[10] For sheer intellectual capacity and its persistent application in government, there has probably never been another ruler in history to match him.

Napoleon was able to compartmentalize his life to quite a remarkable degree, much more so even than most other great leaders. He could entirely close off one part of his mind to what was going on in the rest of it; he himself likened it to being able to open and close drawers in a cupboard.[11] On the eve of the battle of Borodino, as aides-de-camp were arriving and departing with orders to his marshals and reports from his generals, he could dictate his thoughts on the establishment of a girls' school for the orphans of members of the Légion d'Honneur, and shortly after capturing Moscow he set down the new regulations to govern the Comédie-Française. No detail about his empire was too minute for his restless, questing energy. The prefect of a department would be instructed to stop taking his young mistress to the opera; an obscure country priest would be reprimanded for giving a bad sermon on the Emperor's birthday; a corporal was warned that he was drinking too much; a demi-brigade that it could stitch the words 'Les Incomparables' in gold onto its standard. His letters and comments also show much charm, an occasional capacity for candid self-appraisal, and a fine sense of humour which allowed him to make jokes in virtually any situation, even when facing catastrophe. There are innumerable testimonies from those who know him well to the attractiveness of his personality, as well as to his unceasing energy. He could lose his temper – volcanically so on occasion – but usually with some cause. His vices included an occasional but by no means consistent ruthlessness, and, as he aged, a growing narcissism and cynicism about human nature. He was ambitious, of course, but when allied to extraordinary energy, administrative capacity, what appears to have been a near-photographic memory for people and data, a disciplined and incisive mind, and a clear idea of what France could achieve and how Europe could be ordered, we should not be surprised at that. Even Napoleon's brother Louis, whom he deposed as king of Holland, eventually came to say, 'Let us reflect upon the difficulties Napoleon had to overcome, the innumerable enemies, both external as well as internal, he had to combat, the snares of all kinds which were laid for him on every side, the continual tension of his mind, his incessant activity, the extraordinary fatigues he had to encounter, and criticism will soon be absorbed by admiration.'[12]

The most commonplace criticism of Napoleon is that in deciding to invade Russia in 1812 he was suffering from some kind of 'Napoleon Complex', a hubristic desire to rule the world, at no matter what cost to his soldiers and subjects. Yet he had no territorial aspirations in Russia, but merely wanted to force the Tsar to go back to honouring the economic blockade commitments he had made at Tilsit five years earlier. Nor was his confidence in victory so hubristic as it might seem in hindsight. He had comprehensively defeated the Russians twice before. He had no intention of fighting much beyond the border in a maximum one-month campaign. He commanded a force well over twice the size of the Russian armies in the West. He believed the Tsar would sue for peace and never anticipated the sheer level of scorched earth defence to which the Russians would go, to the extent of burning Moscow themselves. He regularly considered stopping at places like Vitebsk and Smolensk once the campaign, and the devastation of his central force through typhus, had begun. Once he was in Moscow he was well aware of the cold of the Russian winter and had left enough time to get back to quarters in Smolensk before it became intolerable. But among the thousands of military decisions that he took, the one on the night of October 25, 1812 undid him.

Napoleon was thus not some nemesis-doomed monster, a modern exemplar of ancient Greek drama or any of the dozens of historical constructions that have been thrust upon him. Rather, Napoleon's life and career stand as a rebuke to determinist analyses of history which explain events in terms of vast impersonal forces and minimize the part played by individuals. We should find this uplifting, since, as George Home, that midshipman on board HMS *Bellerophon*, put it in his memoirs, 'He showed us what one little human creature like ourselves could accomplish in a span so short.'[13]

Napoleon the Great? Yes, certainly.

Envoi

After Napoleon's defeat at Waterloo in June 1815, and the conclusion of the Congress of Vienna later that year, the Great Powers coalesced against Europeans' demands for liberal constitutions and national self-determination. Tsar Alexander I was left as the most powerful monarch in Europe, and ruled in an increasingly mystical and autocratic manner, putting down liberal revolts in Naples, Greece and Germany, until his death in 1825. Francis I of Austria relied on Metternich more and more. Having received back Austria's ancient dominions, he established the reactionary Holy Alliance but never resuscitated the Holy Roman Empire. He died in 1835 aged sixty-seven. Frederick William III of Prussia also became deeply reactionary, ignored his promises of 1813 to give Prussia a constitution, and died in 1840. Metternich remained a central figure in European diplomacy, maintaining a system of balances established by the Congress, until he was forced to escape Vienna dressed as a washerwoman in the 1848 Revolution; he died in 1859. Pius VII also turned against the Enlightenment, reinstating authoritarianism in the Papal States, which were returned to him by the Treaty of Vienna. He died in 1823. King Ferdinand VII of Spain was compelled to accept a liberal constitution in 1820, was overthrown by the Spanish people and then restored to power by the French in 1823, whom he then alienated through his lust for vengeance. He died unlamented in 1833.

Thanks in large part to the legal and political reforms undertaken by Napoleon, the Bourbons were unable to reintroduce the old ways upon their second Restoration in 1815. Louis XVIII spent his reign trying to find a middle course between his reactionary brother, the Comte d'Artois, who sought to roll back any democratic concessions, and the liberal constitutionalists, who pressed for France to follow the English model and to become a constitutional monarchy. He died in 1824, whereupon the Comte d'Artois became King Charles X. He was overthrown in the July

Revolution of 1830, which brought in the more moderate King Louis-Philippe (Charles's cousin), and died in exile in Italy in 1836. The hopes of the unreconstructed royalists died with Charles.

Much of Napoleon's family lived under papal protection in Rome after Waterloo, including his mother, who retired there with her half-brother Cardinal Fesch. At eighty-five, blind and huddled in an armchair, she dictated reminiscences to Rosa Mellini, her lady-companion. 'Everyone called me the happiest mother in the world,' she said, 'yet my life has been a succession of sorrows and torments.' She died in February 1836. Fesch died there three years later, surrounded by his fabulous art collection, much of which he donated to the cities of Ajaccio and Lyons. Louis followed his literary pursuits in Rome, but visited Holland incognito once in 1840, where he was recognized and found himself acclaimed by his former subjects. He died in Livorno in July 1846. His long-separated wife Hortense bought the Swiss chateau of Arenenberg in 1817, where she lived until her death, aged fifty-four, in October 1837. Her illegitimate son by General Flahaut would later be made Duc de Morny by Napoleon III. Eugène de Beauharnais, Duke of Leuchten-berg, lived quietly in Munich with his wife and seven children, one of whom became Empress of Brazil. He died in February 1824. Another of his daughters, Princess Josephine, married Prince Oscar, the heir to the Swedish throne and son of Bernadotte, in 1823; their son Maximilian married the daughter of Tsar Nicholas I.

Lucien was arrested after Waterloo, but allowed to retire to the Papal States, where he died, leaving eleven children from two marriages, in June 1840. Joseph stayed in Bordentown, New Jersey, using the title the Comte de Survilliers for sixteen years, and sensibly refused the crown of Mexico in 1820. For a short while he lived in Surrey, England. He defended his brother's reputation ably, and died in Florence in July 1844. In 1816 Jérôme settled into exile in Trieste and he took the name Comte de Montfort, but he always considered himself a monarch. He returned to France in 1847 and became governor of Les Invalides in 1850, and president of the Senate, dying in 1860. Caroline Murat remarried after her husband's execution and lived in Florence until her death in May 1839, with the self-invented title Countess of Lipona (an anagram of Napoli). Pauline claimed to have been about to travel to St Helena when the news of her brother's death arrived. Even though he had a mistress of ten years' standing, Camillo Borghese allowed Pauline back to his house in Florence three months before her death in June 1825. (He was involved in Bonapartist plots until his death in 1832.)

Charles-Louis-Napoléon, the youngest of King Louis of Holland's three sons, took part in the Italian Revolution of 1831, attempted to invade France at Strasbourg in 1836, visited the USA in 1837, attempted another invasion of France in 1840 and was imprisoned, but escaped in 1845. In 1848 he was elected president by 9.9 million votes, and effected a coup in 1851, becoming Emperor Napoleon III in 1852. He was overthrown after the Franco-Prussian War of 1870–71 and died in exile in 1873. Thus the imperial epic that had started in Ajaccio in 1769 fizzled out in Chislehurst, Kent, 104 years later. To the end of his life he wore the wedding ring his uncle had given his grandmother Josephine.

Marie Louise contracted a morganatic marriage with Neipperg four months after Napoleon's death. They had one legitimate child after their first two illegitimate ones before Neipperg's death in 1829. Marie Louise then married the Comte de Bombelles and died in December 1847, having ruled Parma, Piacenza and Guastalla since 1814.

Napoleon's children experienced very different fates. Napoleon II, the King of Rome and Duke of Reichstadt, was tutored by Marmont, who tried unsuccessfully to poison his mind against his father. He joined the Austrian army but died of tuberculosis at Schönbrunn on July 22, 1832, aged only twenty-one; his death mask can be seen in the Museo Napoleonica in Rome. His remains were sent to Les Invalides by Adolf Hitler in 1940 to foster friendship between Austria and the Vichy government in France. Count Alexandre Walewski was only seven when his mother Marie Walewska died, but he was given a good education by his uncle, an officer in the French army. He joined the Foreign Legion and fought in North Africa, and later became ambassador to London, where he arranged his cousin Napoleon III's visit there and also Queen Victoria's to France. He became President of the Corps Législatif and died of a heart attack at Strasbourg in 1868, aged fifty-eight. Charles Denuelle, Count Léon, Napoleon's natural son by Éléonore Denuelle de la Plaigne, grew so to resemble his biological father that passers-by stared at him in the street. He fought a duel against an orderly of Wellington's in February 1832, and attributed his survival to a button he carried given to him by Hortense. He grew into an argumentative drunken wastrel, who, though Napoleon III paid his debts and a pension, died poverty-stricken of stomach cancer in Pontoise in April 1881. His mother was widowed in the 1812 campaign. She married Count Charles-Émile-Auguste-Louis de Luxbourg in 1814, with whom she remained until his death thirty-five years later. She died in 1868.

Of Napoleon's marshals, Mortier was killed, along with eleven other people, by a bomb at a military review in 1835. It had been let off by a disgruntled Italian who hoped to assassinate King Louis-Philippe. The king wept at Mortier's funeral. Nicolas Soult, Duc de Dalmatie, went into exile in Germany until 1819, but later became a minister under the Bourbons and President of the Council and a reforming minister of war under Louis-Philippe. He represented France at Queen Victoria's coronation in 1838, when Wellington gave a dinner in his honour. He died in 1851. Bernadotte became King of Sweden in 1818 and reigned until his death in 1844; his descendant sits on the Swedish throne today. Marshal Jourdan, despite refusing to sit on the court martial that condemned Ney, became a count and member of the House of Peers in 1819. He supported the 1830 Revolution, and died three years later. Marmont, the Duc de Raguse, was briefly tutor to the King of Rome. He died in 1852, the last of the Napoleonic marshals. When his memoirs were published posthumously, a critic likened him to 'a sharpshooter who hides behind his own tombstone to pick off people who cannot reply'.

Of Napoleon's former ministers, Jean-Jacques-Régis de Cambacérès escaped to Brussels during the second Restoration, but was allowed to return to France in 1818, where he remained in very comfortable retirement until his death in 1824. Louis-Mathieu Molé became director-general of roads and bridges under the Restoration, later becoming minister of marine, then foreign minister under King Louis-Philippe and prime minister from 1836 to 1839; he died in 1855. Armand de Caulaincourt's name was placed on the proscribed list by Louis XVIII, who was persuaded to remove it by Tsar Alexander. He died in 1827. Hugues Maret, the Duc de Bassano, was made a peer by Louis-Philippe and became prime minister of France for eight days in November 1834; he died in Paris in 1839. René Savary wrote eight volumes of memoirs which he published in 1828, and briefly served as commander-in-chief of the French Army in Algeria in 1831, where he showed considerable cruelty. He died in 1833.

The group on St Helena quickly dispersed after Napoleon's death. Henri Bertrand went back to Paris and lived at Napoleon and Josephine's old house in the rue Chantereine. He died in January 1844. Count Montholon shared the captivity of Napoleon III at Ham prison from 1840 to 1846 – the same length of time, six years, as he had shared that of his uncle. He died in Paris in August 1853. Albine de Montholon had long since separated from her husband, carried on her affair with Basil Jackson in Brussels, and died in March 1848 at a ball given in her honour by her grandchildren. Emmanuel de Las Cases published *Le*

Mémorial de Sainte-Hélène in four volumes in 1823 and constantly re-issued revised editions throughout his life. He was elected a deputy of the National Assembly in 1831, and died in 1842. Louis Marchand wrote his memoirs in comfort in Auxerre. In 1822 Betsy Balcombe married Charles Abell, who subsequently deserted her. She moved to Sydney, Australia with their only child, but returned to London to teach music. On the publication of her memoir she was given land in Algiers by Napoleon III, but chose to stay in London, where she died in 1871. Francesco Antommarchi published *The Last Moments of Napoleon* in 1825 and tried to sell copies of Napoleon's death mask in 1833, but was sued over its authorship, which properly belonged to Dr Francis Burton. On his tombstone he had inscribed the words: 'An Italian doctor at the service of the Emperor and the poor'. Sir Hudson Lowe left St Helena after Napoleon's death and commanded the British troops in Ceylon (modern-day Sri Lanka) between 1825 and 1830, but was not appointed its governor. He died aged seventy-four in January 1844. Dr Vignali was murdered at his house on Corsica in June 1836.

Among Napoleon's other followers, General Charles Lefebvre-Desnouëttes was wounded in 1815, and emigrated to America. While returning to France in 1822 he was shipwrecked and drowned. Jean Rapp became a deputy of the Haut-Rhin department and later treasurer to Louis XVIII, dying in October 1821. Jacques-Louis David settled in Brussels after 1815 and returned to painting classical subjects, dying in 1825. Antoine-Jean Gros found that fewer and fewer people wanted his historical and neo-classical paintings; he died in 1835. Roustam wound up dressing in Mamluk costume for the London shows, and died in December 1845 aged sixty-five. Claude Méneval published his memoirs in 1827, was present for the return of Napoleon's body to Paris in 1840, and died in Paris in 1850. Octave Ségur, having survived being wounded and captured in Russia in 1812, returned to France after the war, but in 1818 drowned himself in the Seine on discovering his wife's infidelity.

Several of Napoleon's opponents and detractors came to sad ends. Louis de Bourrienne published vicious memoirs denigrating Napoleon in 1829 and died in a lunatic asylum at Caen in February 1834. Laure, Duchess d'Abrantès, died poverty-stricken in a wretched lodging-house in 1838, aged fifty-four. Lord Castlereagh committed suicide by cutting his own throat with a penknife on August 12, 1822. Radical poets celebrated, but Britain had lost one of her greatest foreign secretaries.

Of Napoleon's other opponents, René de Chateaubriand served in several ministerial and ambassadorial posts under the Bourbons but opposed Louis-Philippe, whom he dubbed 'the bourgeois king', until his death in 1848. His posthumous *Mémoires d'Outre-Tombe* (*Memoirs from Beyond the Grave*) castigated Napoleon severely as a tyrant, and especially blamed him for the execution of the Duc d'Enghien. Benjamin Constant was appointed to the Conseil d'État following the overthrow of the Bourbons in 1830 but died that same year. Paul Barras died at 11 p.m. on January 29, 1829. Earlier that day he had called his godson Paul Grand to his bedside and entrusted him with his memoirs, having seen the way the Bourbons had confiscated Cambacérès' papers after his death. The authorities arrived the next morning to remove his papers, but they were too late. For various personal and legal reasons the memoirs weren't published until the 1880s, and then turned out to be so bileful as to be of little historical value. Hippolyte Charles asked on his deathbed in 1837 that his letters from Josephine be burned, which all but five were. Karl von Schwarzenberg was loaded with honours and decorations, but suffered a stroke in 1817. Three years later he visited the battlefield of Leipzig for a ceremony to mark the battle's seventh anniversary, had a second stroke there and died on October 15. Sir Sidney Smith was buried at Père Lachaise in 1840, his coffin draped in the Union Jack. All three eulogies were delivered by Frenchmen. Although a member of the Légion d'Honneur, it failed to send the traditional honour guard to the man who had denied Napoleon his destiny at Acre.

Charles-Maurice de Talleyrand, Prince de Benevento, rebuked an aide for describing Napoleon's death as an 'event', saying it was merely a 'news item'. He continued to serve any regime that would have him, as foreign minister and high chamberlain to the Bourbons, and after the 1830 Revolution as ambassador to London for Louis-Philippe. He died, with the king at his bedside and the Cardinal of Paris performing extreme unction, in 1838.

When the Duke of Wellington heard the news of Napoleon's death he said to his friend Mrs Arbuthnot, 'Now I may say I am the most successful general alive.' He slept with two of Napoleon's mistresses – Giuseppina Grassini and Mademoiselle George – became an undistinguished prime minister for two years in 1828–30, and was awarded a well-deserved state funeral in 1852. When told of the splendour of Napoleon's reburial in Paris in 1840 he remarked, 'Someday or other the French would be sure to make it a matter of triumph over England,' but personally, he 'did not care a two-penny damn about that!'

Notes

1. CORSICA

Napoleon on *The Templars* is from Bausset, *Private Memoirs* p. 41   Napoleon to Caulaincourt is from Dwyer, *Napoleon* p. 45   **1**. ed. Latimer, *Talks* p. 37   **2**. Chuquet, *Jeunesse* I p. 42, Browning, *Napoleon* p. 22, Davies, *Vanished Kingdoms* p. 500   **3**. ed. Metternich, *Memoirs* I p. 277   **4**. Parker, 'Why did Napoleon' p. 142   **5**. Buhl MSS 110 Box 1 fol. 2 p. 4   **6**. ed. Wilson, *Diary* p. 46   **7**. Dwyer, *Napoleon* p. 24, Englund, *Napoleon* p. 8   **8**. Bonaparte, Joseph, *Mémoires et correspondance* X p. 25   **9**. Carrington, *Napoleon and his Parents* pp. 29–31, Englund, *Napoleon*, p. 10   **10**. Chuquet, *Jeunesse* I p. 44   **11**. Decaux, *Napoleon's Mother* p. xii   **12**. Englund, *Napoleon* p. 10   **13**. Englund, *Napoleon* p. 10   **14**. ed. Latimer, *Talks* p. 33   **15**. Markham, 'The Emperor at Work' p. 59   **16**. ed. Latimer, *Talks* p. 33   **17**. Sudhir Hazareesingh in *TLS* 12/2/2005 p. 11   **18**. Burdon, *The Life* p. 6   **19**. Williams, *A Narrative* p. 168   **20**. ed. Jones, *Intimate Account* p. 425   **21**. Chaptal, *Souvenirs* pp. 173–4   **22**. ed. Frayling, *Napoleon Wrote Fiction* p. x, Healey, *Literary Culture* p. 20 n. 37   **23**. Bonaparte, Joseph, *Mémoires et correspondance* X p. 26   **24**. Zarzeczny, *Meteors*, p. 45   **25**. Ross, 'Napoleon and Manouver Warfare' p. 1   **26**. Gillian Tindall in *TLS* 24/9/1999 p. 34, Sudhir Hazareesingh in *TLS* 20/2/2004 p. 9   **27**. Buhl MSS 110 Box 2 fol. 7 p. 11   **28**. Forrest, *Napoleon* p. 25   **29**. Markham, *Napoleon* p. 3, Rose, *Napoleon* p. 5, Dwyer, *Napoleon*, p. 25, Englund, *Napoleon* p. 15, Dwyer, 'From Corsican Nationalist' p. 136   **30**. Bourgoing, *Quelques notices* p. 1   **31**. Rapp, *Memoirs* p. 55   **32**. Coston, *Biographie* p. 20   **33**. Assier, *Napoleon I* p. 44   **34**. Kiley, *Artillery* p. 29   **35**. ed. Haythornthwaite, *Final Verdict* p. 240   **36**. Biagi, 'A Coincidence' pp. 19, 154–5   **37**. Dwyer, *Napoleon*, p. 28   **38**. Nasica, *Mémoires* p. 12   **39**. ed. Sanderson, *Bourrienne's Memoirs* p. 5   **40**. Rose, *Napoleon* I p. 11   **41**. Healey, *Literary Culture of Napoleon* p. 21   **42**. Hicks, 'The Napoleonic "Police"', Englund, *Napoleon* p. 31   **43**. ed. Gaskill, *The Reception of Ossian* p. xxvii   **44**. Levy, *Napoléon intime* p. 14, McLynn, *Napoleon* p. 21   **45**. Barral, *Histoire des Sciences* p. 7   **46**. Levy, *Napoléon intime* p. 8   **47**. ed. Sanderson, *Bourrienne's Memoirs* p. 4   **48**. Hicks, 'Late 18th Century' *passim*   **49**. Baring-Gould, *Napoleon*

p. 17, Rose, *Napoleon* I p. 12 50. ed. Sanderson, *Bourrienne's Memoirs* p. 4 51. CG1 no. 1 p. 43, June 24, 1784 52. Robb, *Parisians* p. 13 53. Forrest, *Napoleon* p. 34 54. AN AII. 1891 p. 51 55. *TLS* 30/12/1939 p. 754 56. ed. Méneval, *Memoirs* I p. 107 57. Bonaparte, Joseph, *Mémoires et correspondance* X p. 29 58. CG1 no. 5 p. 47, March 28, 1745 59. Levy, *Napoléon intime* p. 17 60. Bonaparte, *A Reply* p. 14 61. Englund, *Napoleon* p. 24 62. Boswell, *Account of Corsica* p. 77 63. CG1 no. 21 p. 65, August 29, 1788 64. NYPL MSS Coll 4854, Englund, *Napoleon* p. 25 65. Smith, *Napoleon's Regiments* p. 294 66. Chaptal, *Souvenirs* p. 184 67. Holland, *Foreign Reminiscences* pp. 211–12 68. Healey, *Literary Culture of Napoleon* Appendix A 69. ed. Castle, *Stanley Kubrick's Napoleon* p. 164 70. Levy, *Napoléon intime* p. 23 71. Rose, *Napoleon* I p. 19 72. Dwyer, 'From Corsican Nationalist' p. 134 73. Bodleian MS Curzon e1. p. 16 74. Plumptre, *A Narrative* p. 260 75. Browning, *Napoleon* p. 283, ed. Hicks, *Clisson and Eugénie* pp. 42, 63 76. Browning, *Napoleon* pp. 283–4 77. Forrest, *Napoleon* p. 24 78. Rose, *Napoleon* I p. 20, Englund, *Napoleon* p. 31 79. ed. Frayling, *Napoleon Wrote Fiction* p. 31 80. Browning, *Napoleon* pp. 285–8, ed. Hicks, *Clisson and Eugénie* pp. 42–3 81. Browning, *Napoleon* pp. 285–8 82. ed. Frayling, *Napoleon Wrote Fiction* p. 25 83. ed. Frayling, *Napoleon Wrote Fiction* pp. 36–7 84. Ibid. 85. CG1 no. 11 p. 54, April 21, 1787 86. Dwyer, *Napoleon* p. 47 87. Kiley, *Artillery of the Napoleonic Wars* p. 26 88. Kiley, *Artillery of the Napoleonic Wars* p. 29 89. ed. Johnston, *The Corsican* p. 143 90. eds. Masson and Biagi, *Napoléon inconnu* II p. 53 91. Englund, *Napoleon* p. 31 92. ed. Frayling, *Napoleon Wrote Fiction* p. 61 93. ed. Hicks, *Clisson and Eugénie* pp. 44–5 94. Chaptal, *Souvenirs* p. 308 95. CG1 no. 31 p. 78, July 22, 1789 96. CG1 no. 29 p. 76, June 12, 1789

2. REVOLUTION

Metternich on Napoleon is from ed. Metternich, *Memoirs* I p. 281 Napoleon to the Elector Frederick is from ed. North, *Napoleon on Elba* pp. 153–4 1. CG1 no. 31 p. 78, July 22, 1789 2. Pelet, *Napoleon in Council* p. 21 3. Simonetta and Arikha, *Napoleon and the Rebel* p. 10, Collins, *Napoleon and His Parliaments* p. 7 4. Rose, *Napoleon* I pp. 28–9, Forrest, *Napoleon* p. 45 5. Thrasher, *Paoli* p. 197 6. Masson and Biagi, *Napoléon inconnu* II pp. 79–83, Dwyer, 'From Corsican Nationalist' pp. 141–2 7. ed. Frayling, *Napoleon Wrote Fiction* p. 71 8. ed. Frayling, *Napoleon Wrote Fiction* p. 73 9. CG1 no. 39 p. 86, June 24, 1790 10. ed. Bingham, *Selection* I p. 11 11. ed. Bingham, *Selection* I p. 21. The pamphlet itself has not survived. 12. Bonaparte, Joseph, *Mémoires et correspondence* I p. 44 13. Pierpont Morgan Library MA 6942 14. Dwyer, 'From Corsican Nationalist' p. 147 15. Masson and Biagi, *Napoléon inconnu* II p. 128 16. Rose, *Napoleon* I p. 32 17. Dwyer, 'From Corsican Nationalist' p. 148 18. ed. Bingham, *Selection* I p. 22 19. Rose, *Napoleon* I p. 33 20. Dwyer, 'From Corsican Nationalist' p. 139 21. ed. Hicks, *Clisson and Eugénie*

p. 45   22. ed. Frayling, *Napoleon Wrote Fiction* p. ix   23. ed. Latimer, *Talks*
p. 42   24. ed. Bingham, *Selection* I p. 24   25. CG1 no. 67 p. 115, July 25,
1792   26. ed. Bingham, *Selection* I p. 24   27. Richardson, *Dictionary*
p. 469   28. ed. Bingham, *Selection* I p. 28   29. ed. Bingham, *Selection* I
p. 27   30. ed. Sanderson, *Bourrienne's Memoirs* p. 8   31. CG1 no. 65 p. 113,
June 22, 1792   32. Robb, *Parisians* p. 435   33. Orieux, *Talleyrand* p. 224
34. ed. Latimer, *Talks* pp 46–7   35. ed. Latimer, *Talks* p. 47   36. ed. Bingham,
Selection II p. 29, Thibaudeau, *Mémoires* p. 59   37. ed. Latimer, *Talks* p. 38
38. ed. Latimer, *Talks* p. 38   39. Chaptal, *Souvenirs* pp. 185–6   40. ed. Wilson,
Diary pp. 137–8   41. CG1 no. 75 p. 121, January 12, 1793   42. Pellew, *Life of
Lord Sidmouth* I p. 72   43. Sherwig, *Guineas and Gunpowder* p. 345
44. Thrasher, *Paoli* p. 255   45. CG1 no. 77 p. 122, March 2, 1793   46. Musée
National de la Maison Bonaparte   47. Dwyer, 'From Corsican Nationalist'
p. 148, ed. Latimer, *Talks* p. 38   48. Dwyer, 'From Corsican Nationalist'
p. 149   49. Paoli, *La Jeunesse de Napoléon* p. 9   50. Foladare, *Boswell's Paoli*
p. 225   51. Bodleian MS Curzon e.1. p. 23   52. ed. Frayling, *Napoleon Wrote
Fiction* p. 128, Masson and Biagi, *Napoléon inconnu* II pp. 477–97   53. Pelet,
Napoleon in Council p. 22   54. Bodleian MS Curzon e1. p. 16, ed. Wilson,
Diary p. 87   55. ed. Bingham, *Selection* I p. 32   56. ed. Latimer, *Talks* p. 43, ed.
North, *Napoleon on Elba* pp. 53–4   57. CG1 no. 111 p. 142, November 14,
1793   58. CG1 no. 95 p. 132, October 1793   59. CG1 no. 96 p. 133, October
16, 1793   60. CG1 no. 102 p. 137, October 2, 1793   61. Rose, *Napoleon* I
p. 49   62. Rose, *Napoleon* I p. 52   63. Friedman, *The Emperor's Itch* p. 33
64. ed. Latimer, *Talks* p. 43   65. Friedman, *The Emperor's Itch* pp. 22–3
66. Las Cases, *Journal* I pt 2 p. 67, O'Meara, *Napoleon at St Helena* I pp. 198–9,
229   67. CN32 p. 82   68. Williams, *A Narrative* p. 180   69. ed. Bingham,
Selection I p. 35   70. Crook, *Toulon in War and Revolution* p. 145   71. Bonaparte, *A Reply* p. 10   72. ed. North, *Napoleon on Elba* p. 152   73. Emsley,
Napoleon p. 9

3. DESIRE

Napoleon to O'Meara is from O'Meara, *Napoleon in Exile* I p. 203   Napoleon
to Bausset is from Bausset, *Private Memoirs* p. 259   1. ed. Bingham, *Selection* I
p. 36, Fraser, *Napoleon's Cursed War* p. 23   2. CG1 nos. 163, 172, 191 p. 171,
April 4, 1794, p. 174, May 7, 1794, p. 182, June 10, 1794   3. ed. Bingham, *Selection* I p. 36   4. Lavalette, *Memoirs* p. 9   5. CG1 no. 232 p. 196, August 7,
1794   6. Bonaparte, *A Reply* p. 18   7. eds. Tulard and Garros, *Itinéraire*
p. 60   8. CG1 no. 139 p. 159, January 4, 1794   9. CG1 no. 235 p. 197August
12 or 19, 1794   10. ed. Bingham, *Selection* I p. 41   11. CG1 no. 244 p. 201,
September 10, 1794   12. CG1 no. 283 p. 218, February 4, 1795   13. CG1 no.
285 p. 219, February 12, 1795   14. CG1 no. 290 p. 221, April 11, 1795
15. *Mars & Clio* Autumn 2010 p. 21   16. ed. Bingham, *Selection* I p. 44
17. Branda, *Napoléon et ses hommes* p. 9   18. Bonaparte, *A Reply* p. 19

19. CG1 no. 322 p. 248, August 10, 1795 **20.** Horne, *Age of Napoleon* p. 16 **21.** ed. Méneval, *Memoirs* I p. 104n **22.** Englund, *Napoleon* p. 76 **23.** D'Abrantès, *At the Court* p. 34 **24.** Las Cases, *Le Mémorial* I p. 401 **25.** CG1 no. 297 p. 224, May 9, 1795 **26.** CG1 no. 298 p. 224, May 22, 1795 **27.** CG1 no. 301 p. 227 June 4, 1795 **28.** CG1 no. 303 pp. 228–9, June 14, 1795 **29.** CG1 no. 321 p. 247, August 10, 1795 **30.** CG1 no. 309 p. 233, July 6, 1795 **31.** CG1 no. 310 p. 235, July 12, 1795 **32.** Bertrand, *Cahiers* II p. 218, Las Cases, *Le Mémorial* I p. 284 **33.** CG1 no. 309 p. 233, July 6, 1795 **34.** ed. Bingham, *Selection* I p. 55 **35.** CG1 no. 327 p. 252, August 20, 1795 **36.** Brown, *War, Revolution* p. 128 **37.** ed. Handel, *Leaders and Intelligence* p. 42 **38.** CG1 no. 345 p. 268, between September 15 and October 5, 1795 **39.** ed. Hicks, *Clisson and Eugénie* p. 13 **40.** ed. Hicks, *Clisson and Eugénie* p. 15 **41.** ed. Hicks, *Clisson and Eugénie* pp. 2–21 **42.** ed. Hicks, *Clisson and Eugénie* pp. 2–21 **43.** ed. Hicks, *Clisson and Eugénie* p. 67 **44.** CG1 no. 334 p. 258, September 1, 1795 **45.** Dumas, *Memoirs* II p. 40 **46.** Healey, *Literary Culture* p. 79 **47.** Bonaparte, *A Reply* p. 20 **48.** Lavalette, *Memoirs* p. 12 **49.** ed. Lecestre, *Lettres Inédites* II p. 133 **50.** CN2 no. 485 p. 15 **51.** Arnault, *Memoirs* I p. 35, Lavalette, *Memoirs* pp. 12–13 **52.** Sarrazin, *Confession* p. 13 **53.** *Annual Register* 1795 no. 37 p. 106 **54.** Gibbs, *Military Career* p. 42 **55.** D'Abrantès, *At the Court* p. 37 **56.** Christies Rare Books catalogue 27/11/2012 p. 14 **57.** Memes, *Memoirs* p. 13 **58.** Horne, *Age of Napoleon* p. 45 **59.** D'Abrantès, *At the Court* p. 237 **60.** Haig, *Napoleon and Josephine's Paris* p. 50 **61.** Haig, *Napoleon and Josephine's Paris* p. 49. **62.** Philip Mansel in *TLS* 16/1/2004 p. 23 **63.** Stuart, *Rose of Martinique* p. 277 **64.** Stuart, *Rose of Martinique* p. 206 **65.** ed. Méneval, *Memoirs* I p. 123, Bruce, *Napoleon and Josephine* p. 74 **66.** ed. Duruy, *Memoirs of Barras* II p. 72 **67.** ed. Metternich, *Memoirs* I p. 281 **68.** Thody, *French Caesarism* p. 35 **69.** Chuquet, *Jeunesse* I p. 65, Rose, *Napoleon* I p. 3 **70.** ed. Hanoteau, *Memoirs of Queen Hortense* I p. 326 n. 3 **71.** ed. Latimer, *Talks* p. 138 **72.** Bruce, *Napoleon and Josephine* p. 162 **73.** ed. Duruy, *Memoirs of Barras* II p. 79 **74.** Pratt, 'Vignettes' p. 59 **75.** Chuquet, *Jeunesse* I p. 41, Davies, *Vanished Kingdoms* p. 501 **76.** Dubroca, *Life of Bonaparte* p. 94, Poultier, *History of the War* p. 260

4. ITALY

Stendhal, *The Charterhouse of Parma* (1839) Napoleon to Chaptal is from Chaptal, *Souvenirs* p. 296 **1.** Pratt, 'Vignettes' p. 60 **2.** Boycott-Brown, *Road to Rivoli* p. 412 **3.** Chaptal, *Souvenirs* p. 204, ed. Haythornthwaite, *Final Verdict* pp. 290–92 **4.** Baldet, *La vie quotidienne* p. 33 **5.** Starke, *Letters from Italy* I p. 60 **6.** ed. Chandler, *Military Maxims* pp. 135, 205 **7.** Holland, *Foreign Reminiscences* pp. 217–19 **8.** CG1 no. 426 p. 304, March 28, 1796 **9.** ed. Hanoteau, *Napoleon in Russia* p. 367 **10.** CG1 no. 471 p. 328, April 8, 1796 **11.** ed. Haythornthwaite, *Final Verdict* pp. 290–92 **12.** ed. Bingham, *Selection* I p. 67 **13.** ed. Luvaas, *Art of War* p. 10 **14.** Gray, *Words of Napoleon*

p. xii **15.** *TLS* 12/5/1927 p. 325, Hazareesingh in *TLS* 3/2/2012 p. 4
16. AN 192AP/2, SHD GR6.YD/1 **17.** CG4 no. 8847 p. 694, April 28, 1804
18. CG1 no. 463 p. 324, April 6, 1796 **19.** ed. Chandler, *Military Maxims* p.
146 **20.** ed. Cerf, *Letters to Josephine* p. 32 **21.** ed. Cerf, *Letters to Josephine*
p. 34, CG1 nos. 464, 467 p. 325, April 6, 1796, p. 326, April 7, 1796 **22.** CG7
no. 14120 p. 111, January 19, 1807 **23.** ed. Cerf, *Letters to Josephine* p. 73,
Stuart, *Rose of Martinique* p. 206, CG3 no. 5277 p. 230, May 11, 1800, GC1 no.
1068 p. 672, November 21, 1796 **24.** ed. Cerf, *Letters to Josephine* pp. 25–6,
Pierpont Morgan Library MA 6936 and *passim* **25.** CG1 no. 463 p. 324
26. ed. Bingham, *Selection* I p. 70 **27.** ed. Bingham, *Selection* I p. 74 **28.** eds.
Dwyer and McPhee, *French Revolution and Napoleon* pp. 128–9, ed. Bingham,
Selection I p. 74 **29.** ed. Bingham, *Selection* I p. 72 **30.** ed. Bingham, *Selection*
I pp. 71–2 **31.** Foy, *History* I p. 43 **32.** ed. Chandler, *Military Maxims*
p. 111 **33.** Blaze, *Life in Napoleon's Army* pp. 42–3 **34.** Blaze, *Life in Napo-
leon's Army* p. 145 **35.** Rose, *Napoleon* I p. 88 **36.** ed. Yonge, *Man of Other
Days* II p. 112ff **37.** ed. Yonge, *Man of Other Days* II p. 122 **38.** ed. Yonge,
Man of Other Days II pp. 126–7 **39.** CG1 no. 545 p. 370, April 20, 1796 **40.**
Woolf, *Napoleon's Integration* p. 252 **41.** ed. Bingham, *Selection* I p. 76 **42.**
CG1 no. 557 p. 377, May 1, 1796 **43.** *Edinburgh Review* no. XLVI September
1814 p. 470 **44.** Plumptre, *A Narrative* III p. 352 **45.** ed. Bingham, *Selection* III
p. 55 **46.** CG1 no. 573 p. 384, May 6, 1796 **47.** CG1 no. 582 p. 389, May 9,
1796 **48.** CG1 nos. 609–11, pp. 406–7, May 18, 1796 **49.** Higgonet, *Paris*
p. 136 **50.** ed. Chandler, *Military Maxims* p. 203 **51.** Tulard, *Napoléon: les
grands moments* p. 97 **52.** Cockburn, *Buonaparte's Voyage* p. 114, Branda,
Napoléon et ses hommes p. 10 **53.** CG1 no. 589 p. 393 and CG1 no. 588 p. 392,
May 11, 1796 **54.** ed. Cerf, *Letters to Josephine* pp. 37–40 **55.** CG1 no. 595
pp. 396–7, May 13, 1796 **56.** Bruce, *Napoleon and Josephine* p. 174 **57.**
Dwyer, *Napoleon* p. 243 **58.** CG1 no. 596 p. 397, May 14, 1796 **59.** CG1 no.
597 p. 398, May 14, 1796 **60.** CG1 no. 599 p. 399, May 14, 1796 **61.** ed.
Tarbell, *Napoleon's Addresses* pp. 34–5 **62.** ed. Duruy, *Memoirs of Barras* II
p. 153 **63.** Gaffarel, *Bonaparte et les républiques italiennes* p. 5 **64.** CG1 no.
1880, p. 1107, August 6, 1797 **65.** ed. Bingham, *Selection* I pp. 82, 85 **66.**
Broers, *Napoleonic Empire in Italy* p. 31 **67.** Woolf, *Napoleon's Integration*
p. 9 **68.** Woloch, *Jacobin Legacy* p. 70 **69.** CG1 no. 627 p. 415, May 24,
1796 **70.** ed. Tarbell, *Napoleon's Addresses* pp. 36–7 **71.** ed. Tarbell, *Napoleon's Addresses* pp. 37–8 **72.** CG1 no. 639 p. 421, June 1, 1796 **73.** CG1 no.
629 p. 416, May 25, 1796 **74.** CG1 no. 629 p. 416, May 25, 1796, Chrisawn,
Emperor's Friend p. 22 **75.** ed. Haythornthwaite *Final Verdict* pp. 240–41 **76.**
Pigeard, *L'Armée* p. 182 **77.** CG1 no. 639, p. 421, June 1, 1796 **78.** CG6 no.
11392 pp. 86–7, February 4, 1806 **79.** CN6 no. 478 p. 73 **80.** CG1 no. 625,
p. 414, May 25, 1796 **81.** ed. Cerf, *Letters to Josephine* p. 43 **82.** CG1 no.
642, p. 424, June 1, 1796 **83.** ed. Fleischmann, *Memoirs* p. 51 **84.** Branda,
Napoléon et ses hommes p. 11 **85.** ed. Bingham, *Selection* I p. 95 **86.** ed. Cerf,
Letters to Josephine pp. 47–9 **87.** CG1 no. 672 p. 441, June 11, 1796
88. CG1 no. 677 p. 443, June 11, 1796, ed. Cerf, *Letters to Josephine* pp. 46–7

89. *TLS* 24/11/2006 p. 14   **90.** CG1 no. 693 p. 451, June 15, 1796   **91.** *Quarterly Review* 1833 pp. 179–84   **92.** ed. Haythornthwaite, *Final Verdict* p. 224   **93.** Summerville, *Ségur* p. 119

5. VICTORY

Napoleon to Joseph is from CN25 no. 19895 p. 218   Napoleon to Talleyrand is from CG8 no. 19233 p. 1209   **1.** Chadwick, *Popes* p. 450   **2.** Rose, *Napoleon* I p. 103   **3.** CG1 no. 845 p. 542, August 11, 1796   **4.** CG1 no. 710 p. 462, June 21, 1796   **5.** CG1 no. 711 p. 464, June 21, 1796   **6.** ed. Bingham, *Selection* I p. 96   **7.** ed. Fleischmann, *Memoirs* p. 55   **8.** ed. Fleischmann, *Memoirs* p. 56   **9.** ed. Fleischmann, Memoirs pp. 60–61   **10.** Starke, *Letters from Italy* I pp. 74–5   **11.** Knapton, *Empress Josephine* pp. 133–4, Stuart, *Rose of Martinique* p. 199   **12.** Pierpont Morgan Library MA 6938   **13.** ed. Cerf, *Letters to Josephine* p. 59   **14.** ed. Cerf, *Letters to Josephine* p. 60   **15.** Hamelin, *Douze Ans* pp. 14–15   **16.** Bibliothèque Thiers, Fonds Masson No. 223/I/81   **17.** CG1 no. 776 pp. 500–501, July 12, 1796, AN 400AP/6/p. 4   **18.** AN 400AP/6/p. 4   **19.** eds. Olsen and van Creveld, *Evolution of Operational Art* p. 32   **20.** ed. Chandler, *Military Maxims* p. 211   **21.** ed. Handel, *Leaders and Intelligence* p. 40   **22.** CG1 no. 833 p. 533, August 2, 1796   **23.** Chlapowski, *Polish Lancer* p. 60   **24.** CG1 no. 820 p. 526, July 29, 1796   **25.** ed. Bingham, *Selection* I p. 107   **26.** CG1 no. 832 p. 532, August 2, 1796   **27.** CG1 no. 826 p. 529, July 30, 1796   **28.** CG 1 no. 822 p. 527, July 30, 1796   **29.** CG1 no. 828 p. 530, July 31, 1796   **30.** ed. Latimer, *Talks* p. 261   **31.** Marbot, *Mémoires* II ch. 16   **32.** ed. Bingham, *Selection* I p. 106   **33.** Wood, 'Forgotten Sword' p. 79   **34.** CG1 no. 837 p. 538, August 7, 1796   **35.** CG1 no. 838 p. 538, August 8, 1796   **36.** CG1 no. 840 p. 540, August 9, 1796   **37.** CG1 nos. 839–40 p. 539, August 9, 796   **38.** Smith, *Data Book* p. 122   **39.** CG1 no. 961 p. 612, October 2, 1796   **40.** CG 1 no. 962 p. 614, October 2, 1796   **41.** CG1 nos. 961 and 980 p. 612, October 2, 1796, p. 620, October 8, 1796   **42.** CG1 no. 993 p. 628, October 12, 1796   **43.** CG1 no. 992 p. 628, October 12, 1796   **44.** CG1 no. 996 p. 631, October 16, 1796   **45.** Broers, *Politics of Religion* p. x   **46.** CG1 no. 1007 p. 639, October 21, 1796   **47.** CG1 no. 1008 p. 639, October 24, 1796   **48.** Paris, *Napoleon's Legion* p. 15   **49.** CG1 no. 1059 p. 664, November 13, 1796   **50.** ed. Bingham, *Selection* I p. 123   **51.** CG1 no. 1060 p. 666, November 19, 1796   **52.** CG1 no. 1086 p. 681, November 29, 1796   **53.** Rose, *Napoleon* I pp. 130–31, ed. Fleischmann, *Memoirs* p. 93   **54.** ed. Bingham, *Selection* I p. 120   **55.** CG1 no. 1084 p. 680, November 27, 1796   **56.** CG1 no. 1085 p. 681, November 28, 1796   **57.** Lavalette, *Memoirs* p. 19   **58.** CG1 no. 1093 p. 685, December 5, 1796   **59.** CG1 no. 1112 p. 696, December 8, 1796   **60.** CG1 no. 1127 p. 704, December 10, 1796   **61.** CG1 no. 1209 p. 746, December 28, 1796   **62.** CG1 no. 1274 p. 778, January 6, 1797   **63.** CG1 no. 1279 p. 782, January 7, 1797   **64.** CG1 no. 1286 p. 784, January 7, 1797   **65.** Rose, *Napoleon* I p. 136   **66.** Smith, *Data Book* p. 131, ed. Bingham, *Selection*

I p. 131   67. René, *Original Journals* p. 121   68. CG1 no. 1315 p. 802, January 22, 1797   69. ed. Fleischmann, *Memoirs* p. 91   70. ed. Bingham, *Selection* I p. 135   71. CG1 no. 1395 p. 849, February 19, 1797   72. Forrest, *Napoleon* p. 87   73. Forrest, *Napoleon* p. 86   74. Dziewanowski, 'Napoleon' p. 91, 89 Carnavalet Portraits Box 229, Bibliothèque Thiers 34/7001–7274   75. Theodore D. Buhl MSS 110 Box 1/fol. 1/pp. 18, 23, 26   76. Laskey, *A Description* p. 1   77. ed. Bingham, *Selection* I p. 142   78. Knight, *Britain Against Napoleon* p. 522   79. eds. Nafziger et al., *Imperial Bayonets* p. 165, CG1 no. 1640 p. 880   80. CG1 no. 1469 p. 885, March 22, 1797   81. CG1 no. 1476 p. 889, March 25, 1797   82. eds. Horn and Walker, *Le Précis de leadership militaire*, p. 485, Englund, *Napoleon* p. 105   83. CG7 no. 14773 p. 396, March 20, 1807   84. Bausset, *Private Memoirs* p. 67   85. Bourne, *History of Napoleon* p. 376   86. CG3 no. 5087 p. 138   87. Cottin, *Souvenirs de Roustam* p. 154   88. D'Abrantès, *At the Court* p. 117   89. ed. Summerville, *Ségur* p. 38   90. CN32 p. 68   91. ed. Haythornthwaite, *Final Verdict* p. 222   92. ed. Tarbell, *Napoleon's Addresses* p. x   93. Houssaye, *The Return of Napoleon* p. 7   94. Chaptal, *Souvenirs* p. 337

6. PEACE

Napoleon to Joseph is from ed. Bingham, *Selection* I p. 96   Napoleon to the Conseil d'État is from Johnston, *The Corsican* p. 160   1. CG1 no. 1495, p. 901, April 8, 1797   2. CG1 no. 1514 p. 914, April 16, 1797   3. CG1 no. 1514 p. 914, April 16, 1797, Dubroca, *Life of Bonaparte* p. 90   4. CG1 no. 1514 p. 916, April 16, 1797   5. CG1 no. 1497 p. 905, April 9, 1797   6. CG1 no. 1521 p. 923, April 30, 1797   7. ed. Sanderson, *Bourrienne's Memoirs* p. 55   8. CG1 no. 1516 p. 917, April 19, 1797   9. ed. Sanderson, *Bourrienne's Memoirs* p. 54   10. CG1 no. 1587 p. 962, May 27, 1797   11. ed. Bingham, *Selection* I p. 156   12. ed. Sanderson, *Bourrienne's Memoirs* p. 54   13. CG1 no. 1587 p. 962, May 27, 1797   14. ed. Sanderson, *Bourrienne's Memoirs* p. 64   15. ed. Fleischmann, *Memoirs* p. 94   16. ed. Fleischmann, *Memoirs* pp. 94–5, Markham, *Napoleon* p. 63, McLynn, *Napoleon* p. 153, Schom, *Napoleon* p. 65, ed. Bingham, *Selection* I p. 160, eds. Dwyer and Forrest, *Napoleon and His Empire* p. 1   17. Horne, *Age of Napoleon* p. 19   18. ed. Bingham, *Selection* I p. 168   19. CG1 no. 1785 p. 1058, July 15, 1797   20. Schneid, *Soldiers* p. 3   21. CG1 no. 1785 p. 1058, July 15, 1797   22. TLS 8/8/1971 p. 1208, ed. Latimer, *Talks* p. 97   23. ed. Latimer, *Talks* p. 98   24. Rose, *Napoleon* I p. 165   25. CG1 no. 1822 p. 1081, July 26, 1797   26. Rose, *Napoleon* I p. 161   27. ed. Bingham, *Selection* I p. 171   28. CG1 no. 1962 p. 1140, September 3, 1797   29. ed. Fleischmann, *Memoirs* p. 109, Brown, 'From Organic Society' p. 661, ed. Sanderson, *Bourrienne's Memoirs* p. 59, Lavalette, *Memoirs* p. 28   30. ed. Sanderson, *Bourrienne's Memoirs* p. 59   31. Hicks, 'Late 18th Century' *passim*   32. Carnot, *Reply of Carnot* p. 30   33. Lavalette, *Memoirs* p. 29   34. CG1 no. 2009 p. 1166, September 12, 1797   35. CG1 no. 2098 p. 1216, September 26, 1797

36. Dubroca, *Life of Bonaparte* p. 91 **37.** Rose, *Napoleon* I p. 169
38. ed. Méneval, *Memoirs* I p. 106 **39.** CG1 no. 2149, p. 1244, Octoebr 7, 1797 **40.** ed. Bingham, *Selection* I p. 189 **41.** ed. Sanderson, *Bourrienne's Memoirs* p. 60 **42.** CG1 no. 2170 p. 1256, October 18, 1797 **43.** Dubroca, *Life of Bonaparte* p. 90 **44.** CG1 no. 2163 p. 1253, October 17, 1797 **45.** CG1 no. 2170 p. 1257, October 18, 1797 **46.** Jenkins, *French Navy* p. 226, CG1 no. 2191 p. 1267, November 5, 1797 **47.** ed. Bingham, *Selection* I p. 192 **48.** CG1 no. 2220 pp. 1283–9, November 11, 1797 **49.** ed. Sanderson, *Bourrienne's Memoirs* p. 63 **50.** ed. Sanderson, *Bourrienne's Memoirs* p. 64 **51.** Simms, *Europe* p. 156 **52.** CG1 no. 1587, p. 963, May 27, 1797 **53.** CG1 no. 2274 p. 1313, November 30, 1797 **54.** Lavalette, *Memoirs* p. 35 **55.** ed. Bingham, *Selection* I p. 194 **56.** Espitalier, *Vers Brumaire* pp. 45–6 **57.** ed. Hanoteau, *Memoirs of Queen Hortense* I p. 32 **58.** Knapton, *Empress Josephine* p. 153 **59.** ed. North, *Napoleon on Elba* pp. 153–4, ed. Bingham, *Selection* I p. 195 **60.** Rovigo, *Mémoires* I p. 25 **61.** ed. Bingham, *Selection* I p. 200 **62.** Espitalier, *Vers Brumaire* pp. 45–7 **63.** Williams, *A Narrative* p. 5 **64.** D'Abrantès, *At the Court* p. 46, Rovigo, *Mémoires* I p. 24 **65.** ed. Sanderson, *Bourrienne's Memoirs* pp. 65–6 **66.** ed. Bingham, *Selection* I p. 195, Rose, *Napoleon* I p. 173, Lockhart, *Napoleon Buonaparte* I p. 105 **67.** ed. Sanderson, *Bourrienne's Memoirs* p. 63 **68.** CG1 no. 12280 p. 1316, November 26, 1797 **69.** Lockhart, *Napoleon Buonaparte* I pp. 105–6 **70.** Healey, *Literary Culture* p. 88, Williams, *The Life of Goethe* p. 39 **71.** ed. Hanoteau, *Memoires of Queen Hortense* I p. 33 **72.** Rovigo, *Mémoires* I p. 26 **73.** Tone, *Wolfe Tone* p. 266 **74.** ed. Sanderson, *Bourrienne's Memoirs* p. 68 **75.** CG2 no. 2315 p. 38, February 23, 1798 **76.** Holland, *Foreign Reminiscences* p. 245 **77.** ed. Sanderson, *Bourrienne's Memoirs* p. 68 **78.** Knapton, *Empress Josephine* pp. 150–53 **79.** Knapton, *Empress Josephine* p. 151 **80.** Hastier, *Le Grand Amour* p. 152 **81.** Hastier, *Le Grand Amour* pp. 152–4 **82.** Hastier, *Le Grand Amour* p. 160

7. EGYPT

The anonymous Islamic historian comes from ed. Chandler, *Military Maxims* p. 24 Napoleon to Gourgaud comes from ed. Latimer, *Talks* p. 66 **1.** Murphy, 'Napoleon's International Politics' p. 165, Volney, *Voyage* p. 235 **2.** CG1 no. 1908 p. 1118, August 16, 1797 **3.** eds. Bertaud et al., *Napoléon* p. 312 **4.** CG2 no. 2390 p. 80, April 13, 1798 **5.** Abulafia, *The Great Sea* p. 516 **6.** Rose, *Napoleon* I p. 185, ed. Handel, *Leaders and Intelligence* p. 41, ed. Hicks, *Clisson and Eugénie* p. 56 **7.** ed. Latimer, *Talks* p. 69 **8.** ed. Moreh, *Napoleon in Egypt* p. 12 **9.** CN15 no. 12924 p. 537 **10.** CN4 no. 2570 p. 128 **11.** Plumptre, *A Narrative* p. 321 **12.** Strathearn, *Napoleon in Egypt* p. 39 **13.** CG2 no. 2415 p. 94, April 19, 1798 **14.** eds. Tortel and Carlier, *Bonaparte de Toulon* p. 28 **15.** CG2 no. 2391 p. 81, April 13, 1798 **16.** Knight, *Pursuit of Victory* p. 284 **17.** ed. Frayling, *Napoleon Wrote Fiction* pp. xv–xvi **18.** Lavalette,

Memoirs p. 37   **19.** CG2 no. 2519 p. 142, June 13, 1798, Rose, *Napoleon* I
p. 184, ed. Bingham, *Selection* I p. 210, ed. North, *Napoleon on Elba* p. 76
20. CG2 no. 2547, p. 155, June 17, 1798   **21.** Anon., *Copies of Original Letters*
I pp. 239–40   **22.** ed. Bingham, *Selection* I pp. 212–13   **23.** Anon., *Copies of
Original Letters* I p. 132   **24.** ed. Bingham, *Selection* I p. 210, Rose, *Napoleon* I
p. 188, Anon., *Copies of Original Letters* I pp. 244–6, ed. Moreh, *Napoleon in
Egypt* p. 3   **25.** CG2 no. 4174 p. 820, January 28, 1799   **26.** Strathearn, *Napoleon in Egypt* p. 46, Rose *Napoleon* I p. 190   **27.** Arnault, *Memoirs* I p. 86
28. Bodleian MS Curzon e1. p. 15   **29.** Anon., *Copies of Original Letters* I
p. 134   **30.** Anon., *Copies of Original Letters* I p. 133   **31.** Jonquière,
L'Expédition II ch. 5   **32.** CG2 no. 2625 p. 193, July 24, 1798   **33.** ed. Moreh,
Napoleon in Egypt p. 8   **34.** Holland, *Foreign Reminiscences* p. 248   **35.** Bourrienne, *Memoirs* I p. 66, Stuart, *Rose of Martinique* p. 234   **36.** ed. Howard,
Letters and Documents I pp. 258–9   **37.** BL Add. MSS 23003   **38.** CG2 no.
2635, p. 199, July 25, 1798   **39.** CG3 no. 5277 p. 230, May 11, 1800   **40.** Anon.,
Copies of Original Letters II p. 111   **41.** Anon., *Copies of Original Letters* I
p. 121   **42.** Gichon, 'East Meets West' p. 106 n. 12   **43.** ed. Dufourcq, *Mémoires*
pp. 121–2   **44.** Chaptal, *Souvenirs* p. 270   **45.** Duffy, *Austerlitz* p. 137
46. Anon., *Copies of Original Letters* I p. 133   **47.** ed. Brindle, *Guns in the Desert* pp. 15–16, Anon., *Copies of Original Letters* I p. 78   **48.** ed. Bierman,
Napoleon in Egypt p. 85   **49.** ed. Latimer, *Talks* p. 209   **50.** Solé, *Conquête de
l'Égypte*, pp. 108–9   **51.** Balcombe, *To Befriend* p. 74   **52.** Bertrand, *Cahiers* I
p. 21   **53.** CN29 p. 570   **54.** ed. Kerry, *The First Napoleon* p. 99   **55.** Ebrington, *Memorandum* p. 18   **56.** ed. Kerry, *First Napoleon* p. 89   **57.** Forrest,
Napoleon p. 112   **58.** Forrest, *Napoleon* p. 108   **59.** ed. Bingham, *Selection* I
pp. 221–5   **60.** ed. Bingham, *Selection* I pp. 221–5   **61.** ed. Bingham, *Selection*
I pp. 221–5   **62.** ed. Moreh, *Napoleon in Egypt* p. 14   **63.** ed. Bierman, *Napoleon in Egypt* p. 85   **64.** ed. Ainé, *Histoire de l'expédition* pp. 13–14   **65.** ed.
Bingham, *Selection* I pp. 221–5   **66.** CG2 no. 2625 p. 193, July 24, 1798
67. ed. Latimer, *Talks* p. 64   **68.** CG2 no. 3890 p. 706, December 9, 1798, CG2
no. 2676 p. 216, July 30, 1798   **69.** CG2 no. 2870 p. 299, August 19, 1798
70. CG2 no. 2870 p. 299, August 19, 1798   **71.** CG2 no. 2857 p. 289, August
18, 1798, Smith *Data Book* p. 140   **72.** CG2 no. 2870 p. 299, August 19,
1798   **73.** Anon., *Copies of Original Letters* I p. xvi, Alison, *History of Europe* I
p. 580   **74.** Lavalette, *Memoirs* p. 43, CG2 no. 2832 p. 277   **75.** Cole, *Napoleon's Egypt* p. 123   **76.** Cole, *Napoleon's Egypt* p. 126   **77.** Byrd, 'Napoleonic
Institute' p. 4   **78.** Sudhir Hazareesingh in *TLS* 16/7/2006 p. 27   **79.** Montefiore, *Jerusalem* p. 315, CG2 no. 4280 p. 874   **80.** CG2 no. 3112 p. 399,
September 8, 1798   **81.** CG2 no. 3424 p. 523, October 11, 1798, CG2 no. 3148
p. 414, September 12, 1798   **82.** CG2 no. 3554 p. 574, October 27, 1798
83. CG2 no. 3557 p. 576, October 27, 1798   **84.** ed. Sanderson, *Bourrienne's
Memoirs* p. 80   **85.** Prat and Tonkovich, *David, Delacroix* p. 44   **86.** CG2 no.
3529, p. 564, October 23, 1798   **87.** ed. Sanderson, *Bourrienne's Memoirs*
p. 81   **88.** Lavalette, *Memoirs* p. 50, CG2 no. 3557 p. 576, October 27,
1798   **89.** CG2 no. 3656, p. 613, November 11, 1798   **90.** ed. Bingham,

Selection I p. 238 91. Strathearn, *Napoleon in Egypt* pp. 260–64 92. eds. Tulard and Garros, *Itinéraire* p. 123, Strathearn, *Napoleon in Egypt* pp. 260–64 93. Strathearn, *Napoleon in Egypt* p. 427 94. CG2 no.3740 p. 647, November 18, 1798 95. ed. Bingham, *Selection* I p. 239 96. Derogy and Carmel, *Bonaparte en Terre Sainte* p. 99 97. ed. Brindle, *Guns in the Desert* p. 35 98. ed. Brindle, *Guns in the Desert* p. 37

8. ACRE

Napoleon's Military Maxim comes from ed. Chandler, *Military Maxims* p. 83 Napoleon's *Caesar's Wars* comes from CN32 p. 44 1. CG2 no. 4235 p. 849, February 10, 1799 2. CG2 no. 4235 p. 850, February 10, 1799 3. CG2 no. 4167 p. 817, January 25, 1799 4. Derogy and Carmel, *Bonaparte en Terre Sainte*, pp. 102–4 5. CG2 no. 4235 p. 850, February 10, 1799 6. Shmuelevitz, *Napoleon and the French in Egypt* p. 19 7. CG2 no. 4265 p. 867, February 27, 1799 8. ed. Noailles, *Count Molé* p. 140 9. ed. Sanderson, *Bourrienne's Memoirs* p. 81 10. ed. Brindle, *Guns in the Desert* p. 54 11. CG2 no. 4265 p. 867, February 27, 1799 12. ed. Brindle, *Guns in the Desert* p. 60 13. ed. Brindle, *Guns in the Desert* p. 64 14. ed. Brindle, *Guns in the Desert* p. 66 15. Montefiore, *Jerusalem* p. 316, ed. Brindle, *Guns in the Desert* p. 67, ed. Weit, *Nicolas Turc* p. 53 16. ed. Jourquin, *Journal* I p. 280 17. CG2 no. 4271 p. 870, March 9, 1797 18. Berthier, *Relation des campagnes* p. 56 19. ed. Quentin, *André Peyrusse* p. 55, Jonquière, *L'Expédition* IV p. 271 20. Coxe, *The Exposé* p. 61 21. ed. Millet, *Le Chasseur Pierre Millet* p. 262 22. For the numbers debate, see CG2 no. 4271 p. 870 n. 3, Jonquière, *L'Expédition* IV pp. 270–71, Herold, *Bonaparte in Egypt* p. 306, eds. Tortel and Carlier, *Bonaparte de Toulon* p. 158, Rose, *Napoleon* I p. 201, Anon., 'The French Expedition' p. 197, ed. Brindle, *Guns in the Desert* p. 68, Plumptre, *A Narrative* p. 276, Lavalette, *Memoirs* p. 52, Berthier, *Relation des campagnes* p. 56, ed. Millet, *Le Chasseur Pierre Millet* Appendix XV p. 262, Strathearn, *Napoleon in Egypt* p. 328 23. Ebrington, *Memorandum* pp. 18–19 24. Hobhouse, *Recollections* I p. 181 25. Jonquière, *L'Expédition* IV p. 273, Rose, *Napoleon* I p. 201 26. Chandler, *Campaigns of Napoleon* p. 236, Plumptre, *A Narrative* p. 286n 27. ed. Bingham, *Selection* I p. 250 28. CG2 no. 4277, pp. 872–3, March 9, 1799 29. ed. Brindle, *Guns in the Desert* p. xix 30. ed. Jourquin, *Journal* I p. 281 31. ed. Bulos, *Bourrienne et ses erreurs* I p. 44 32. Cockburn, *Buonaparte's Voyage* p. 78 33. Cockburn, *Buonaparte's Voyage* p. 78 34. CG2 no. 4294 p. 881, March 13, 1799 35. ed. Brindle, *Guns in the Desert* p. 77 36. Lavalette, *Memoirs* p. 59 37. CG2 no. 4346 p. 911, May 10, 1799 38. Lavalette, *Memoirs* p. 58 39. Lavalette, *Memoirs* pp. 60–61 40. Lockhart, *History of Napoleon* I p. 150 41. Sparrow, *Secret Service* p. 191 42. ed. Wilson, *Diary* p. 88 43. ed. Brindle, *Guns in the Desert* p. 90, Coxe, *The Exposé passim* 44. CG2 no. 4346 p. 910, May 10, 1799 45. ed. Davis, *Original Journals* I pp. 215–16 46. ed. Latimer, *Talks* p. 246 47. CG2 no. 4362 p. 920, May 27, 1799 48. ed. Latimer, *Talks* pp. 69–70

49. Smith, *The French Expedition* p. x 50. ed. Brindle, *Guns in the Desert* p. 93 51. Strathearn, *Napoleon in Egypt* p. 6 52. ed. Iung, *Lucien Bonaparte* II ch. 14 53. Friedman, 'On the Affair' pp. 65–77 54. Rose, *Napoleon* I p. 211 55. ed. Brindle, *Guns in the Desert* p. 99 56. For the Jaffa plague debate see Lavalette, *Memoirs* p. 63, Desgenettes, *Histoire médicales* pp. 104–5, ed. Brindle, *Guns in the Desert* pp. 99–106, ed. Bulos, *Bourrienne et ses erreurs* I pp. 34–5, Cockburn, *Buonaparte's Voyage* pp. 83–5, Montefiore, *Jerusalem* p. 317, Balcombe, *To Befriend* p. 174, Ebrington, *Memorandum* p. 18, Hobhouse, *Recollections* I p. 181, ed. Lewis, *Extracts from the Journals* II p. 235, Wilson, *History* pp. 91–2 57. Balcombe, *To Befriend* pp. 175–6 58. Balcombe, *To Befriend* p. 176 59. ed. Lewis, *Extracts from the Journals* II p. 235 60. ed. Bingham, *Selection* I p. 256 61. ed. Brindle, *Guns in the Desert* p. 102 62. CG2 no. 4404 p. 940, June 19, 1799 63. ed. Bingham, *Selection* I p. 256 64. ed. Brindle, *Guns in the Desert* p. 104 65. ed. Brindle, *Guns in the Desert* p. 105 66. ed. Bingham, *Selection* I p. 254, Smith, *Data Book* p. 156, Smith, *The French Expedition* p. 9 67. CG2 no. 4479 p. 972, June 28, 1799 68. Lavalette, *Memoirs* p. 65 69. CG2 no. 4633 p. 1032, July 21, 1799 70. CG2 no. 4638 p. 1035, July 21, 1799 71. ed. Brindle, *Guns in the Desert* p. 113 72. Lavalette, *Memoirs* p. 66 73. ed. Brindle, *Guns in the Desert* p. 114 74. Smith, *Data Book* p. 161, CG2 no. 4666 p. 1048 75. CG2 no. 4758 pp. 1086–8 , August 22, 1799 76. Sauzet, *Desaix* p. 131 77. Strathearn, *Napoleon in Egypt* pp. 413–14 78. ed. North, *Napoleon on Elba* p. 30 79. ed. Cottin, *Souvenirs de Roustam* p. 75 80. CG2 no. 4757 p. 1085, August 22, 1799 81. CG2 no. 4758 p. 1086, August 22, 1799, ed. Brindle, *Guns in the Desert* pp. 120 n. 26 82. Davis, *Original Journals* I p. 263 83. Denon, *Travels in Egypt* III p. 119 84. Lavalette, *Memoirs* p. 68 85. CG3 p. 1216 86. Lavalette, *Memoirs* p. 69 87. Simonetta and Arikha, *Napoleon and the Rebel* p. 50 88. CN7 no. 15677 p. 809, Horne, *Age of Napoleon* p. 26 89. CG2 no. 4479 p. 972 n. 2, June 28, 1799 90. Ripaud, *Report passim* 91. Byrd, 'Napoleonic Institute of Egypt' p. 4

9. BRUMAIRE

Napoleon on St Helena comes from ed. Wilson, *Diary* p. 87 Napoleon on St Helena comes from Las Cases *Memoirs* I p. 529 1. Lavalette, *Memoirs* p. 71, ed. Cottin, *Souvenirs de Roustam* p. 83 2. ed. Summerville, *Exploits of Baron de Marbot* p. 7 3. ed. Summerville, *Exploits of Baron de Marbot* p. 8 4. eds. Tulard and Garros, *Itinéraire* p. 133 5. Bruce, *Napoleon and Josephine* p. 274, Mossiker, *Napoleon and Josephine* pp. 195–200, Stuart, *Rose of Martinique* pp. 248–51 6. Lavalette, *Memoirs* p. 71 7. ed. Butler, *Baron Thiébault* II p. 14, CN30 p. 305 8. ed. Butler, *Baron Thiébault* II p. 13 9. Adams, *History of the United States* I ch. 14, Dwyer, *Talleyrand* pp. 73–4 10. ed. Malmesbury, *Diaries* IV p. 257, eds. Tulard and Garros, *Itinéraire* p. 133 11. D'Abrantès, *At the Court* p. 50 12. Simonetta and Arikha, *Napoleon and the Rebel* p. 48 13. CG2 no. 4764 p. 1090, October 31, 1799   **14.** Bingham, *Selection* I p. 270   **15.** ed. Arnold, *Documentary Survey* p. 14, Lefebvre, *The Directory* p. 213   **16.** Gildea, *Children of the Revolution* p. 27   **17.** Lavalette, *Memoirs* p. 71   **18.** Roederer, *Autour de Bonaparte* p. 3   **19.** Lyons, *France Under the Directory* pp. 230–31, Carpenter, *Refugees* p. 188, Crook, *Toulon in War* p. 188, Woolf, *Napoleon's Integration* p. 254, Vandal, *L'Avènement de Bonaparte* I pp. 8ff   **20.** Bertaud, *Bonaparte prend le pouvoir* pp. 188ff   **21.** Bingham, *Selection* I p. 271   **22.** Rose, *Napoleon* I p. 218   **23.** ed. Butler, *Baron Thiébault* II p. 17   **24.** Roederer, *Autour de Bonaparte* p. 4   **25.** Simonetta and Arikha, *Napoleon and the Rebel* p. 53   **26.** Rose, *Napoleon* I p. 223   **27.** Lefebvre, *The Directory* p. 214   **28.** CN30, p. 311   **29.** ed. Latimer, *Talks* p. 73   **30.** CN30 p. 311   **31.** Sparrow, *Shadow* p. 131   **32.** Cole, *Fouché* p. 121, Forrest, *Napoleon* p. 147   **33.** ed. Plenel, *Joseph Fouché* p. ix   **34.** Zweig, *Fouché* p. 146   **35.** ed. Latimer, *Talks* p. 95n   **36.** ed. Duruy, *Memoirs of Barras* IV p. 40   **37.** ed. Butler, *Baron Thiébault* II p. 18, CN30 p. 307   **38.** CN30 p. 306   **39.** D'Abrantès, *At the Court* p. 146   **40.** Chaptal, *Souvenirs* p. 259   **41.** CG7 no. 15126 p. 562, April 6, 1807   **42.** eds. Tulard and Garros, *Itinéraire* p. 135   **43.** Rovigo, *Mémoires* I p. 234   **44.** eds. Tulard and Garros, *Itinéraire* p. 136   **45.** Lavalette, *Memoirs* p. 74, Goodspeed, *Bayonets* p. 107, Forrest, *Napoleon* p. 123   **46.** Lavalette, *Memoirs* p. 75, CN30 p. 306, Gildea, *Children of the Revolution* p. 27, Lyons, *France Under the Directory* p. 231, Crook, *Napoleon Comes to Power* p. 1   **47.** ed. Arnold, *Documentary Survey* p. 15   **48.** CN30, p. 315   **49.** McLynn, *Napoleon* p. 216   **50.** Gueniffey, *Le Dix-Huit Brumaire* p. 15   **51.** Gueniffey, *Le Dix-Huit Brumaire* p. 16   **52.** Lavalette, *Memoirs* p. 75   **53.** Crook, *Napoleon Comes to Power* p. 2   **54.** ed. Broglie, *Memoirs* p. xviii n. 1, Harris *Talleyrand* p. 113   **55.** CN30 p. 380   **56.** CN30 p. 381   **57.** Crook, *Napoleon Comes to Power* p. 2   **58.** Bigonnet, *Coup d'état* p. 23   **59.** Aulard, *Histoire politique* p. 699   **60.** Gildea, *Children of the Revolution* p. 27   **61.** Sciout, *Le Directoire* IV pp. 652–3   **62.** Lavalette, *Memoirs* p. 77   **63.** Lavalette, *Memoirs* p. 77   **64.** Berlier, *Précis de la Vie* pp. 68–9   **65.** Gildea, *Children of the Revolution* p. 27, Rose, *Napoleon* I p. 225, Lyons, *France Under the Directory* p. 232   **66.** Rose, *Napoleon* I p. 224, Roederer, *Oeuvres* III p. 302   **67.** Boissonnade, *18 Brumaire* p. 93   **68.** Rose, *Napoleon* I p. 225   **69.** Lavalette, *Memoirs* p. 71   **70.** ed. Arnold, *Documentary Survey* p. 17   **71.** ed. Haythornthwaite *Final Verdict* p. 287   **72.** Lavalette, *Memoirs* p. 76   **73.** Rovigo, *Mémoires* I p. 234   **74.** CN30 p. 319   **75.** Schlabrendorf, *Bonaparte* pp. 13–16   **76.** CG1 no. 232 p. 196, August 7, 1794   **77.** Simonetta and Arikha, *Napoleon and the Rebel* p. 5   **78.** Rovigo, *Mémoires* I p. 239   **79.** Rose, *Napoleon* I p. 225   **80.** Aulard, *Histoire politique* p. 699   **81.** Lavalette, *Memoirs* p. 77   **82.** CG2 no. 4790 p. 1103 n. 2, December 7, 1799   **83.** ed. Butler, *Baron Thiébault* II p. 21   **84.** ed. Arnold, *Documentary Survey* pp. 17–18   **85.** Crook, *Napoleon Comes to Power* p. 3, Rose, *Napoleon* I p. 226, Lyons, *France Under the Directory* p. 232   **86.** Lentz, *18-Brumaire* p. 328   **87.** Gallais, *Histoire* I p. 90   **88.** Lentz, *18-Brumaire* p. 327   **89.** Bingham, *A Selection* I p. 270   **90.** Lyons, *France Under the Directory* p. 233   **91.** Holland, *Foreign Reminiscences* p. 243

10. CONSUL

The Talleyrand quote is from Bergeron, *France Under Napoleon* p. 106 Napoleon to Fouché is from CG4 no. 9195 p. 386 1. eds. Tulard and Garros, *Itinéraire* p. 141, Forrest, *Napoleon* p. 124 2. CN30 p. 306 3. ed. Gaudin, *Mémoires* p. 45 4. ed. Gaudin, *Mémoires* p. 45 5. CN6 pp. 6–8 6. Collins, *Napoleon and His Parliaments* p. 10 7. Rudé, *Revolutionary Europe* p. 226 8. Rose, *Napoleon* I pp. 231–2 9. Boulay, *Boulay* p. 116, Rudé, *Revolutionary Europe* p. 227 10. Rose, Napoleon I p. 232 11. Brown, *Ending the Revolution* p. 301, Carpenter, *Refugees* p. 188, Lyons, *France Under the Directory* pp. 233–4 12. CG2 nos. 4766 and 4767 pp. 1091–2, November 15, 1799 13. Bourrienne, *Memoirs* I p. 315 14. Thody, *French Caesarism* p. 36 15. Roederer, *Bonaparte me disait* p. 60 16. CG3 pp. 1237–47, eds. Laven and Riall, *Napoleon's Legacy* p. 2 17. CN32 p. 84 18. ed. Arnold, *Documentary Survey* pp. 34–5, Forrest, *Napoleon* p. 170 19. France, *Constitution de la République Française* p. 16 20. Rose, Napoleon I p. 229 21. Gildea, *Children of the Revolution* p. 28 22. Ellis, *Napoleon* p. 2 23. Rose, *Napoleon* I p. 231 24. ed. Arnold, *Documentary Survey* pp. 24–33 25. Broers, *Europe under Napoleon* p. 51 26. CG2 no. 4817 p. 1115, December 25, 1799 27. Rodger, *War of the Second Coalition* p. 275 28. CG2 no. 4772 pp. 1094–5, November 24, 1799 29. Ségur, *Memoirs* p. 152 30. Emsley, *Napoleon* p. 117 31. Broers, *Napoleonic Empire in Italy* pp. 23ff 32. Mollien, *Mémoires* I p. 314 33. Hicks, 'Late 18th Century' *passim* 34. Bertaud, *La France* p. 38, Horne, *Age of Napoleon* p. 20, Markham, *Napoleon* p. 80 35. Cobban, *Modern France* II p. 13, ed. Arnold, *Documentary Survey* p. 23 36. ed. Rowe, *Collaboration and Resistance* p. 21, Forrest, *Napoleon* p. 132, Jordan, *Napoleon and the Revolution* p. 5, Gildea, *Children of the Revolution* p. 28 37. eds. Kafker and Laux, *Napoleon and His Times* p. 59 38. eds. Kafker and Laux, *Napoleon and His Times* p. 61 39. eds. Kafker and Laux, *Napoleon and His Times* p. 63 40. Lyons, *France Under the Directory* p. 234 41. CN10 no. 8922 p. 674, Emsley, *Gendarmes and the State* p. 60 42. Emsley, *Gendarmes and the State* pp. 54–7, Brown, 'From Organic Society' p. 693 43. ed. Dwyer, *Napoleon and Europe* p. 6, Forrest, *Napoleon* pp. 133, 150 44. Brown, *Ending the Revolution* p. 303 45. CG7 no. 14006 p. 60, January 11, 1807 46. Tomiche, *Napoléon Écrivain* pp. 208–12, Forrest, 'Propaganda and the Legitimation of Power' p. 428 47. Carpenter, *Refugees* p. xxiii 48. eds. Carpenter and Mansel, *The French Émigrés in Europe* p. 193, Lewis, *France* p. 234 49. McPhee, *Social History of France* p. 86 50. Brown, *Ending the Revolution* pp. 264–5 51. CG2 no. 4825 p. 1121, December 29, 1799 52. Holtman, *Napoleonic Propaganda* p. 44, Forrest, *Napoleon* p. 133 53. ed. Arnold, *Documentary Survey* pp. 37–8 54. ed. Orwicz, *Art Criticism* p. 23 n. 4 55. Montholon, *Captivity* II p. 88 56. Bertaud, *Napoleon* p. 78 57. ed. Orwicz, *Art Criticism* p. 9 58. Popkin, *The Right-Wing Press in France* pp. 170–71 59. ed. Noailles, *Count Molé* p. 190 60. Holtman, *Napoleonic Revolution* p. 165 61. Rosen, *Napoleon's Opera-Glass* p. 74 62. CG12 no. 31894 p. 1181, October 11, 1812 63. Forrest, *Napoleon* p. 137, Whitcomb

'Napoleon's Prefects' p. 1101   64. Godechot, *Les Instititions* p. 590   65. ed. Walter, *Las Cases* p. xv, eds. Laven and Riall, *Napoleon's Legacy* p. 4   66. eds. Dwyer and Forrest, *Napoleon and His Empire* p. 4, Hicks, 'The Napoleonic "Police"' p. 3   67. Woloch, *The New Regime* p. 430   68. ed. Charles, *Victor Marie du Pont* p. 37   69. Ramon, *Banque de France* p. 19, Lefebvre, *Napoleon* p. 77   70. Bruce, *Napoleon and Josephine* p. 310   71. Carnavalet Portraits 229 Bonaparte, Iᵉʳ Consul   72. ed. Lewis, *Journals and Correspondence of Miss Berry* II pp. 163–5   73. Holland, *Foreign Reminiscences* pp. 213–14   74. D'Abrantès, *At the Court* p. 74   75. D'Abrantès, *At the Court* p. 252   76. Carnavalet Portraits 229   77. Baldet, *La vie quotidienne* p. 34   78. CG3 no. 5639 p. 386, September 7, 1800   79. Roederer, *Autour de Bonaparte* p. 22   80. ed. Latimer, *Talks* p. 83   81. CG3 no. 5110 p. 148, March 16, 1800

11. MARENGO

Napoleon to the other consuls comes from CG3 no. 5330 p. 254, May 18, 1800 Napoleon's *Caesar's Wars* comes from Rose, *Napoleon* I p. 187   1. CG3 no. 4903 pp. 55–6, January 25, 1800   2. Dumas, *Memoirs* II p. 107   3. eds. Tulard and Garros, *Itinéraire* p. 153   4. ed. Summerville, *Exploits of the Baron de Marbot* p. 39   5. CG3 no. 5198 p. 189, April 25, 1800   6. CG3 no. 5310 p. 245, May 15, 1800   7. CG3 no. 5375 p. 275, May 27, 1800   8. CG3 no. 5350 p. 262, May 19, 1800   9. Uffindell, *Napoleon's Chicken Marengo* p. 28   10. CG3 no. 5341 p. 258, May 19, 1800   11. Uffindell, *Napoleon's Chicken Marengo* p. 19   12. CG3 no. 5343 p. 259, May 19, 1800   13. Uffindell, *Napoleon's Chicken Marengo* p. 31   14. ed. North, *Napoleon on Elba* p. 62   15. Uffindell, *Napoleon's Chicken Marengo* p. 31   16. CG3 no. 5366 p. 272, May 24, 1800   17. CG3 no. 5398 p. 283, June 4, 1800   18. Pierpont Morgan Library MA 6939   19. Smith, *Data Book* p. 185   20. ed. Latimer, *Talks* p. 81   21. Gachot, *Siège de Gênes passim*   22. Masson, *Napoléon et les femmes* p. 84   23. CG3 no. 5432 p. 300, June 9, 1800   24. ed. Bingham, *Selection* I pp. 307–8   25. CG2 no. 4633 p. 1032, July 21, 1799   26. CG3 no. 5434 p. 301, June 10, 1799, Smith, *Data Book* p. 186   27. CG3 no. 5295 p. 238, May 14, 1800   28. Petit, *Marengo* p. 45   29. Petit, *Marengo* p. 45   30. Wood, 'Forgotten Sword' p. 79   31. Smith, *Data Book* pp. 186–7   32. Petit, *Marengo* p. 46   33. Petit, *Marengo* p. 27   34. Rouart, *Napoléon ou la destinée* pp. 127–8   35. Petit, *Marengo* p. 26   36. Petit, *Marengo* p. 26   37. Petit, *Marengo* p. 26   38. ed. Summerville, *Exploits of Baron de Marbot* p. 50   39. Rose, *Napoleon* I p. 258, ed. Chandler, *Military Maxims* p. 156   40. Crowdy, *Incomparable* pp. 94–7   41. eds. Bertaud et al., *Napoléon* p. 184   42. Smith, *Data Book* p. 187   43. D'Abrantès, *At the Court* p. 74   44. CG3 nos. 5553 and 5743 p. 351, July 22, 1800, p. 435, November 4, 1800   45. Smith, *Data Book* p. 187   46. Innocenti, 'Souls Not Wanting' p. 78   47. Hobhouse, *Recollections* I p. 181 n. 1   48. Rovigo, *Mémoires* VIII pp. 96–7   49. CG3 no. 5435 p. 301, June 15, 1800   50. Crowdy, *Incomparable* pp. 94–7, Petit, *Marengo* p. 47   51. Johnson, *Napoleon's Cavalry* p. 28   52. Rose,

Napoleon I p. 259   53. Dumas, *Memoirs* II p. 102   54. Simms, *Europe* p. 159   55. CG3 no. 5461 p. 313, June 21, 1800   56. Hibbert, *Napoleon* p. 120

12. LAWGIVER

Napoleon to Chaptal comes from Chaptal, *Souvenirs* pp. 236–7   Napoleon on St Helena comes from Montholon, *Récit* I p. 401   1. Chaptal, *Souvenirs* pp. 236–7 2. CG1 no. 980 pp. 620–21, October 8, 1796   3. Cobban, *Modern France* II p. 30   4. ed. Crook, *Revolutionary France* p. 124   5. ed. Hanoteau, *Napoleon in Russia* p. 392   6. Woloch, *New Regime* p. 431   7. Pigeard, *L'Armée* p. 182   8. ed. Latimer, *Talks* p. 272   9. Antommarchi, *Last Days* II p. 118, ed. Latimer, *Talks* p. 270   10. Chaptal, *Souvenirs* pp. 236–7   11. Bertrand, *Cahiers* I p. 84, ed. Walter, *Las Cases* p. x, ed. Latimer, *Talks* pp. 273, 276   12. ed. Latimer, *Talks* p. 273   13. ed. Latimer, *Talks* p. 280   14. ed. Latimer, *Talks* p. 280   15. Bertrand, *Cahiers* I p. 120   16. Rudé, *Revolutionary Europe* p. 237, Roederer, *Autour de Bonaparte* p. 18   17. Roederer, *Autour de Bonaparte* p. 16   18. Gibbon, *Decline and Fall* Bk I ch. 2   19. Bertrand, *Cahiers* I p. 182 20. O'Meara, *Napoleon in Exile* II p. 139   21. Rose, *Personality of Napoleon* p. 125   22. CN21 no. 17478 p. 566   23. Roederer, *Bonaparte me disait* p. 87 24. CG3 no. 6359 p. 72   25. Anonymous, *The Concordat* p. 2   26. Cobban, *Modern France* II p. 31   27. Rose, *Napoleon* I p. 281   28. Rose, *Personality of Napoleon* p. 130   29. Tulard, *Napoleon* p. 142, Ségur, *Memoirs* p. 78, CG3 no. 6882 p. 966, May 2, 1802   30. Mansel, *Louis XVIII* p. 235, Pelet, *Napoleon in Council* p. 235   31. ed. Bingham, *Selection* II p. 4   32. Daly, *Inside Napoleonic France* p. 250   33. ed. Baldick, *Memoirs of Chateaubriand* p. 207   34. Rudé, *Revolutionary Europe* p. 232   35. Bausset, *Private Memoirs* p. 405   36. ed. Bredin, *Code Civil* p. 4, ed. Schwartz, *Code Napoleon* p. 106   37. ed. Schwartz, *Code Napoleon* p. 109 n. 44   38. ed. Schwartz, *Code Napoleon* p. 105   39. ed. Schwartz, *Code Napoleon* p. 49, eds. Laven and Riall, *Napoleon's Legacy* p. 3   40. ed. Schwartz, *Code Napoleon* p. 104   41. Rudé, *Revolutionary Europe* p. 233   42. Holtman, *Napoleonic Revolution* p. 98   43. ed. Crook, *Revolutionary France* p. 102   44. ed. Crook, *Revolutionary France* p. 102   45. Horne, *Age of Napoleon* p. 32   46. Gourgaud, *Journal* I pp. 390–91, Thody, *French Caesarism* p. 39   47. Rudé, *Revolutionary Europe* p. 236   48. Emsley, *Napoleon* p. 117   49. McPhee, *Social History of France* p. 83   50. eds. Dwyer and McPhee, *The French Revolution and Napoleon* p. 166   51. eds. Kafker and Laux, *Napoleon and His Times* p. 220   52. Rowe, 'Between Empire and Home Town' p. 643 53. ed. Crook, *Revolutionary France* p. 124   54. ed. Latimer, *Talks* p. 86 55. ed. Crook, *Revolutionary France* p. 164   56. ed. Crook, *Revolutionary France* p. 165   57. ed. Boudon, *Napoléon et les lycées* p. 382   58. ed. Lentz et al., *Quand Napoléon* p. 411, Rose, *Personality of Napoleon* p. 141, Cobban, *Modern France* II p. 34   59. ed. Lentz et al., *Quand Napoléon* p. 410   60. ed. Boudon, *Napoléon et les lycées* p. 381   61. ed. Noailles, *Count Molé* p. 63 62. ed. Arnold, *Documentary Survey* p. 260   63. ed. Noailles, *Count Molé*

p. 72   **64.** ed. Bourdon, *Napoleon au conseil d'état* p. 18   **65.** Rudé, *Revolutionary Europe* p. 231   **66.** Rose, *Personality of Napoleon* p. 136   **67.** AN 29Ap/75 p. 141   **68.** Chaptal, *Souvenirs* p. 328   **69.** Rose, *Personality of Napoleon* p. 136   **70.** Pelet, *Napoleon in Council* p. 14   **71.** Chaptal, *Souvenirs* p. 56 **72.** Lanzac, *Paris sous Napoleon* II p. 92   **73.** ed. Noailles, *Count Molé* p. 79 **74.** Pelet, *Napoleon in Council* pp. 7–8   **75.** Chaptal, *Souvenirs* p. 333   **76.** Rose, *Personality of Napoleon* p. 136   **77.** CN32 p. 84

13. PLOTS

Talleyrand on Napoleon comes from Bell, *First Total War* p. 234   Napoleon to Jourdan comes from CG3 no. 591, p. 513   **1.** CG3 no. 5476 p. 319, June 29, 1800   **2.** CG3 no. 5462 p. 314, June 22, 1800   **3.** Moorehead, *Dancing* p. 287 **4.** CG3 no. 5896 p. 505, January 9, 1801   **5.** Nester, *Art of Diplomacy* p. 121   **6.** ed. Bingham, *Selection* I p. 334   **7.** Sparrow, *Secret Service* pp. 221–2 **8.** Rapp, *Memoirs* p. 21   **9.** Thiry, *La machine infernale* p. 167, *Moniteur* 29/12/1800   **10.** Rose, *Napoleon* I p. 304, Rapp, *Memoirs* p. 21   **11.** Sparrow, *Secret Service* p. 219   **12.** Rose, *Napoleon* I p. 303   **13.** ed. Bingham, *Selection* I p. 325   **14.** Sparrow, *Secret Service* p. 217   **15.** Sparrow, *Secret Service* pp. 219–21   **16.** Sparrow, *Secret Service* p. 222   **17.** Rose, *Napoleon* I p. 304, Roederer, *Bonaparte me disait* pp. 65–70   **18.** Thibaudeau, *Bonaparte and the Consulate* p. 75   **19.** ed. Bingham, *Selection* I p. 331   **20.** Thibaudeau, *Bonaparte and the Consulate* p. 75   **21.** Bonaparte, *Confidential Correspondence* II p. 23 **22.** CG4 no. 9450 p. 978, December 17, 1804   **23.** Brown, *Ending the Revolution* p. 326, eds. Dwyer and Forrest, *Napoleon and His Empire* p. 83   **24.** Rose, *Personality of Napoleon* p. 124   **25.** Balcombe, *To Befriend* p. 177   **26.** Rovigo, *Mémoires* I p. 364   **27.** Davies, *Vanished Kingdoms* p. 510   **28.** D'Abrantès, *At the Court* p. 211   **29.** Brown, *Ending the Revolution* p. 347   **30.** ed. Bingham, *Selection* I p. 341   **31.** ed. Charles, *Victor Marie du Pont* pp. 27–8   **32.** ed. Charles, *Victor Marie du Pont* p. 28   **33.** Horne, *Age of Napoleon* p. 55   **34.** Rose, *Napoleon* I pp. 263, 310   **35.** ed. Wilson, *A Diary* p. 37   **36.** ed. Bingham, *Selection* I p. 350   **37.** ed. Haythornthwaite, *Final Verdict* p. 294   **38.** CG3 no. 6233 p. 664, April 24, 1801   **39.** *The Times* 3/10/1801   **40.** Ragsdale, *Détente* p. 105   **41.** ed. Malmesbury, *Series of Letters* II p. 11   **42.** Authority, *Preliminary Articles passim*   **43.** Rose, *Napoleon* I p. 315   **44.** ed. Sadler, *Diary* I p. 105 **45.** Barnett, *Bonaparte* p. 78   **46.** Branda, *Napoléon et ses hommes* p. 147 **47.** ed. Fleischmann, *Mémoires* p. 490, Mowat, *Diplomacy of Napoleon* p. 103 **48.** eds. Dwyer and Forrest, *Napoleon and His Empire* p. 2   **49.** Philip Mansel in *TLS* 23/11/2001 p. 18   **50.** ed. Bingham, *Selection* I p. 373   **51.** Stark, 'Society: Friend or Enemy' p. 120, James, *The Black Jacobins* p. 8, ed. Bingham, *Selection* I p. 373, Zamoyski, *Holy Madness* p. 124, ed. Nesbitt, *Toussaint L'Ouverture* p. xiii   **52.** Dubois, *Colony of Citizens* pp. 121, 214   **53.** Branda and Lentz, *Napoléon, l'esclavage* p. 49, CG3 no. 6647 p. 853, November 18, 1801 **54.** CG2 no. 4486 p. 975, June 25, 1799, Ott, *Haitian Revolution* p. 139   **55.** ed.

Bingham, *Selection* I p. 375   56. Ott, *Haitian Revolution* p. 147   57. Ott, *Haitian Revolution* p. 147   58. Ott, *Haitian Revolution* p. 146   59. James, *Black Jacobins* p. 269, Boudon, *Les habits neuf* p. 36, Dumas, *Memoirs* I p. 64, Branda and Lentz, *Napoléon, l'esclavage* p. 112, Stark, 'Society: Friend or Enemy' p. 120   60. Herold, *The Mind of Napoleon* p. 5   61. CG3 no. 6627 p. 841, October 31, 1801   62. Tulard, *Dictionnaire amoureux* p. 204   63. *Edinburgh Review* No. XIII pp. 244–6   64. Ott, *Haitian Revolution* pp. 178–9, Dubois, *Colony of Citizens* p. 403, ed. Bingham, *Selection* II p. 5   65. Ott, *Haitian Revolution* p. 159   66. Tulard, *Dictionnaire amoureux* p. 205   67. CG3 no. 7317 p. 1168, November 27, 1802   68. D'Abrantès, *At the Court* p. 224   69. eds. Ambrose and Martin, *Many Faces* pp. 241–2, Rose, *Napoleon* I p. 363   70. ed. Nesbitt, *Toussaint L'Ouverture* pp. vii–xxv   71. ed. Latimer, *Talks* p. 112   72. ed. Hanoteau, *With Napoleon in Russia* p. 305

14. AMIENS

Napoleon to Roederer comes from Roederer, *Bonaparte me disait* p. 81   Napoleon to Eugène comes from CG5 no. 10224 p. 386, June 7, 1805   1. ed. Latimer, *Talks* p. 258   2. Lentz, *Le Grand Consultat* pp. 264–8, Fraser, *Venus of Empire* p. 103   3. CG3 no. 5942 p. 528, January 19, 1801   4. ed. Tulard, *Cambacérès: lettres inédites* II pp. 19–20   5. Connelly, *Napoleon's Satellite Kingdoms* p. 2   6. ed. Chatel de Brancion, *Cambacérès* I p. 7   7. Rose, *Napoleon* I pp. 319–20   8. Villefosse and Bouissounouse, *Scourge of the Eagle passim*   9. *TLS* 4/8/1972 p. 912   10. CG3 no. 6827 p. 939, March 22, 1802   11. Buhl MSS 110 Box 1 fol. 2 p. 19   12. Grainger, *Amiens Truce* p. 211   13. Jenkins, *French Navy* p. 241   14. Burrows, *French Exile Journalism* p. 121   15. CG3 no. 6632 p. 845, November 2, 1801   16. ed. Foster, *The Two Duchesses* p. 173   17. ed. Lewis, *Extracts* II p. 186, Alger, 'British Visitors' p. 254   18. Horne, *Age of Napoleon* p. 22   19. Alger, 'British Visitors' pp. 740–41   20. BL Add. MS 51799 ff. 54–5   21. ed. North, *Napoleon on Elba* p. 49, Lockhart, *Napoleon* I pp. 264–5   22. Rose, *Napoleon* I p. 321   23. Daly, *Inside Napoleonic France* p. 251, ed. Arnold, *Documentary Survey* p. 136   24. ed. Rowe, *Collaboration and Resistance* pp. 22–5, eds. Kafker and Laux, *Napoleon and His Times* p. 65   25. Holland, *Foreign Reminiscences* p. 194   26. CG3 no. 6948 p. 998, June 19, 1802   27. CG3 no. 6366 p. 729, June 16, 1801   28. CG3 no. 6892 p. 970, May 15, 1802   29. CG3 no. 6983 p. 1014, July 3, 1802   30. Rose, *Napoleon* I p. 389   31. eds. Lewis and Lucas, *Beyond the Terror* p. 238   32. Rose, *Napoleon* I pp. 324–5   33. CG3 no. 7142 pp. 1089–90, September 5, 1802   34. Grab, 'The Geopolitical Transformation' pp. 21–22   35. CG3 no. 7174 pp. 1105–6, September 23, 1802   36. Bertrand, *Cahiers* I p. 93   37. Rose, *Napoleon* I p. 392   38. *TLS* 3/2/2012 p. 4   39. Atteridge, *Marshal Ney* pp. 71–2   40. Horne, *Age of Napoleon* p. 21   41. Cobban, *Modern France* II pp. 49–52   42. Chaptal, *Souvenirs* p. 132   43. Cobban, *Modern France* II p. 49   44. Cobban, *Modern France* II p. 51   45. Burrows, *French Exile Journalism* p. 109   46. Pelet, *Napoleon in Council* p. 308, CG3 no. 6749 pp. 899–900, February 2, 1802   47. Pelet, *Napoleon in Council* p. 308   48. Burrows, *French Exile Journalism* pp. 110–11   49. PRO FO 27/66 28 August 1802   50. Darnton, *The Devil in the Holy Water* pp. 43–5   51. CG3 no. 5490 p. 326, July 4, 1800, Englund, *Napoleon* pp. 258–9   52. Bryant, 'Graphic Warriors' p. 17   53. Champfleury, *Histoire de la caricature* IV pp. 247–397, Buhl MSS 110 Box 1 fol. 3 frontispiece   54. Ashton, *English Caricature passim*   55. Plumptre, *Narrative*, p. 245   56. Yale Center, 'Nelson and Anti-Napoleon Verse' *passim*   57. *Moniteur* of 8/8/1802, 9/10/1802, 6/11/1802, 1/1/1803, 9/1/1803, 28/2/1803, 3/3/1803   58. Burrows, *French Exile Journalism* p. 117   59. CG3 no. 6294 p. 988, June 1, 1802, CG4 no. 7503 p. 62, March 3, 1805   60. eds. Carpenter and Mansel, *French Émigrés* p. 56, Ashton, *English Caricature* I p. 174, Welschinger, *La censure* p. 86, Peltier, *Trial of John Peltier* p. xviii   61. Welschinger, *La censure* p. 143   62. CG4 no. 7425 p. 30, January 15, 1803   63. CG3, no. 7173 pp. 1104–5, September 22, 1802   64. CG3 no. 7386 p. 1199, December 28, 1802   65. Grainger, *Amiens Truce* p. 210   66. Pelet, *Napoleon in Council* p. 35   67. Thibaudeau, *Bonaparte and the Consulate* p. 119   68. Cobban, *Modern France* II p. 41   69. Aubry, *St Helena* p. 214   70. ed. Bingham, *Selection* II p. 5   71. ed. Bingham, *Selection* II p. 6   72. Wilson, *War, Society and State* p. 25   73. Mowat, *Diplomacy of Napoleon* pp. 108–9   74. CG4 no. 7515 p. 68, March 11, 1803   75. ed. Browning, *England and Napoleon* p. 116   76. Madelin, *Consulate and the Empire* p. 182   77. Rovigo, *Mémoires* II p. 457   78. ed. Browning, *England and Napoleon* p. 116   79. Alison, *History of Europe* V p. 109   80. ed. Browning, *England and Napoleon* p. ix   81. CG4 no. 7521 p. 74, March 13, 1803   82. CG4 no. 7516 p. 69, March 11, 1803   83. CG4 no. 7573 p. 100, April 14, 1803   84. CG4 no. 7629 p. 127, May 10, 1803   85. ed. Bingham, *Selection* II pp. 11–12   86. Brooks's Club Betting Book   87. Hozier, *Invasions of England* p. 312   88. ed. Malmesbury, *Diaries* IV p. 253   89. ed. Malmesbury, *Diaries* IV p. 258   90. CG4 nos. 7778, 7793 p. 193, July 3, 1803, p. 200, July 7, 1803   91. ed. Arnold, *Documentary Survey* p. 175   92. CG4 no. 7683 p. 151, May 29, 1803   93. Simms, *Europe* p. 159   94. Barbé-Marbois, *History of Louisiana* pp. 270–75   95. Rose, *Napoleon* I p. 372   96. DeConde, *This Affair of Louisiana* p. 162   97. DeConde, *This Affair of Louisiana* p. 166   98. TLS 20/2/2004 p. 10   99. Ziegler, *Sixth Great Power* p. 71, Mowat, *Diplomacy of Napoleon* p. 142 n. 1   100. DeConde, *This Affair of Louisiana* p. 173

15. CORONATION

Napoleon on the Duc d'Enghien comes from eds. Forrest and Wilson, *The Bee and the Eagle* p. 117   Napoleon to the Conseil d'État comes from ed. Haythornthwaite, *Final Verdict* p. 240   1. CG4 no. 7813 p. 209, July 11, 1803   2. CG4 no. 8217 p. 426, November 5, 1803   3. Hughes, *Forging Napoleon's Grande Armée* p. 10   4. Wheeler and Broadley, *Napoleon and the Invasion* I p. x   5. Peter Mandler in *TLS* 7/7/2006 p. 9, Pelet *Napoleon in Council* p. 39, Anon, 'Descente en Angleterre' pp. 43–4   6. Pelet, *Napoleon in Council* p. 87, Ségur,

Memoirs pp. 101–3   7. Hozier, *Invasions of England* p. 313   8. Ségur, *Memoirs* p. 124   9. SHD GR2.C/571   10. Pelet *Napoleon in Council* p. 39, ed. Bingham, *Selection* II p. 32   11. ed. Bingham, *Selection* II p. 81, Knight, *Britain Against Napoleon* p. 251   12. Desbrière, *Projets et tentatives* IV p. 3, Jenkins, *French Navy* p. 245   13. Jenkins, *French Navy* p. 240   14. CG4 no. 9025 p. 779, July 27, 1804   15. Ségur, *Memoirs* p. 128   16. CG4 no. 7847 p. 223, July 22, 1803   17. CG4 nos. 8285, 7988 p. 452, November 17, 1803, p. 317, September 1, 1803   18. CG4 no. 7914 p. 258, August 8, 1803   19. ed. Bingham, *Selection* II pp. 32–3   20. CG4 no. 8096 p. 369, October 1, 1803   21. CG4 no. 8251, p. 439, November 11, 1803   22. CG4 no. 8457 p. 557, January 3, 1804   23. CG4 no. 8313 p. 463, November 23, 1803   24. CG4 no. 8347 p. 478, November 29, 1803   25. CG3 no. 7259 p. 1145, November 2, 1802   26. CG4 no. 8253 p. 440, November 12, 1803   27. CG4 no. 8273 p. 448, November 16, 1803   28. CG4 no. 8614 p. 583, January 24, 1804   29. CG4 no. 8593 p. 575, January 13, 1804   30. ed. North, *Napoleon on Elba* p. 69   31. ed. North, *Napoleon on Elba* p. 70   32. Knight, *Britain Against Napoleon* pp. 251–61   33. ed. Lloyd, *Keith Papers* III p. 31, Pocock, *Terror Before Trafalgar* p. 106   34. Rovigo, *Mémoires* II p. 25   35. Ségur, *Memoirs* p. 100   36. Pocock, *Terror Before Trafalgar* pp. 110–11   37. Sparrow, *Shadow of the Guillotine* p. 164   38. NYPL Napoleon I folder 1   39. ed. Butler, *Baron Thiébault* II p. 106   40. Pocock, *Terror Before Trafalgar* p. 131   41. CG4 no. 8717 p. 628, 8 March, 1804   42. Pocock, *Terror Before Trafalgar* pp. 132–3, Ségur, *Memoirs* p. 99   43. Ségur, *Memoirs* p. 100   44. Pelet, *Napoleon in Council* p. 87, Ségur, *Memoirs* pp. 101–3   45. CG4 no. 8679 p. 614, February 19, 1804   46. CG4 no. 8681 p. 615, February 20, 1804   47. Pocock, *Terror Before Trafalgar* pp. 133–4   48. Ségur, *Memoirs* p. 104   49. Ségur, *Memoirs* p. 105   50. Bourrienne, *Memoirs* p. 289   51. CG4 no. 8718 p. 629, March 9, 1804   52. ed. Latimer, *Talks* p. 110, ed. North, *Napoleon on Elba* p. 146, ed. Chatel de Brancion, *Cambacérès: Mémoires* I pp. 710–11   53. Rovigo, *Mémoires* II pp. 52–3   54. Ségur, *Memoirs* p. 106   55. Rémusat, *Memoirs* I pp. 126–31, Ségur, *Memoirs* p. 117   56. Welschinger, *Le duc d'Enghien* pp. 219–39   57. Pocock, *Terror Before Trafalgar* p. 135   58. Bertaud, *Le duc d'Enghien* p. 320   59. eds. Forrest and Wilson, *The Bee and the Eagle* p. 117   60. CG4 no. 8751 p. 649, March 20, 1804   61. Las Cases, *Le Mémorial* II pp. 622, Balcombe, *To Befriend* pp. 177–8, Ségur, *Memoirs* pp. 118–19, 122   62. Ebrington, *Memorandum* p. 16, Cockburn, *Buonaparte's Voyage* p. 122   63. Cole, *The Betrayers* p. 43   64. CG4 no. 8749 p. 648, March 20, 1804   65. Ségur, *Memoirs* p. 112   66. Ségur, *Memoirs* p. 112   67. Ségur, *Memoirs* p. 121   68. Horne, *Age of Napoleon* p. 30   69. Pelet, *Napoleon in Council* p. 45   70. CG4 no. 8870 p. 704, May 13, 1804   71. Pelet, *Napoleon in Council* pp. 46–7   72. Pelet, *Napoleon in Council* p. 49   73. Ségur, *Memoirs* p. 122   74. ed. Bingham, *Selection* II p. 54   75. Ségur, *Memoirs* p. 122   76. Sparrow, *Secret Service* p. 293   77. ed. Bingham, *Selection* II p. 55   78. Cockburn, *Buonaparte's Voyage* p. 32   79. CG4 no. 9100 p. 817, August 14, 1804   80. CG5 no. 10845 p. 716, September 19, 1805   81. Pelet, *Napoleon in Council* p. 58   82. Ségur, *Memoirs* p. 124   83. Pelet, *Napoleon in Council* pp. 59–60   84. Pelet, *Napoleon in Council* p. 55, eds.

Dwyer and Forrest, *Napoleon and His Empire* p. 14 n. 7   **85.** Pelet, *Napoleon in Council* p. 66   **86.** Pelet, *Napoleon in Council* p. 71   **87.** Tissot, *Souvenirs historiques* pp. 34–5   **88.** CG4 no. 8804 p. 672, April 14, 1804   **89.** Lentz, *Napoléon et la conquête* p. 50   **90.** CG4 no. 8938 p. 738, June 14, 1804   **91.** eds. Tulard and Garros, *Itinéraire* p. 211   **92.** CG4 no. 9039 p. 785, July 30, 1804   **93.** CG5 no. 10037 p. 300, May 13, 1805   **94.** CG5 no. 9877 p. 224, April 22, 1805   **95.** Fraser, *Venus of Empire* pp. 102–3   **96.** CG4 no. 8789 p. 666, April 6, 1804   **97.** Fraser, *Venus of Empire* p. 119   **98.** ed. Latimer, *Talks* p. 236   **99.** ed. Butler, *Baron Thiébault* II p. 114   **100.** Gallaher, 'Davout and Napoleon' p. 3   **101.** Currie, *The Bâton* p. 11, ed. Chandler, *Napoleon's Marshals* p. xxxix   **102.** Jourquin, *Dictionnaire des Marechaux* pp. 54–5   **103.** ed. Chandler, *Napoleon's Marshals* p. 442   **104.** Jourquin, *Dictionnaire des Marechaux* p. 116   **105.** Jourquin, *Dictionnaire des Marechaux* p. 116   **106.** Rose, *Napoleon* I p. 24   **107.** Moreau, *Bonaparte and Moreau* p. 25   **108.** Pelet, *Napoleon in Council* p. 87   **109.** ed. Bingham, *Selection* II p. 53   **110.** Ségur, *Memoirs* p. 100   **111.** Pocock, *Terror Before Trafalgar* p. 143   **112.** ed. Bingham, *Selection* II p. 80   **113.** ed. Lentz, *Le Sacre de Napoléon* p. 105   **114.** Fraser, *The War Drama* p. 3   **115.** Fraser, *The War Drama* p. 9   **116.** MacCulloch, *History of Christianity* p. 811   **117.** Cobban, *Modern France* II p. 16   **118.** eds. Dwyer and Forrest, *Napoleon and His Empire* p. 14 n. 11   **119.** eds. Kafker and Laux, *Napoleon and His Times* p. 65   **120.** Gonneville, *Recollections* I p. 59   **121.** Paris, *Napoleon's Legion* p. 13   **122.** Hughes, *Forging Napoleon's Grande Armée* p. 3   **123.** Dumas, *Memoirs* II p. 131   **124.** Paris, *Napoleon's Legion* pp. 17–18, Thibaudeau, *Mémoires* ch. 26   **125.** Rose, *Personality of Napoleon* p. 134   **126.** D'Abrantès, *At the Court* p. 248   **127.** CG4 no. 9015 p. 775, July 21, 1804   **128.** CG4 no. 9223 p. 874, September 15, 1804   **129.** CG4 no. 9310 p. 917, October 6, 1804   **130.** CG4 nos. 9318–34 pp. 920–27, October 7, 1804   **131.** CG4, no. 8473 p. 529, December 19, 1803   **132.** CG4 no. 8924 p. 729, May 30, 1804   **133.** ed. Tulard, *Cambacérès: lettres inédites* I p. 190   **134.** ed. Bingham, *Selection* II p. 48   **135.** Rose, *Personality of Napoleon* p. 130   **136.** ed. Bingham, *Selection* III pp. 5–6   **137.** Roederer, *Bonaparte me disait* p. 112   **138.** Nester, 'Napoleon, Family Values' p. 106   **139.** Roederer, *Bonaparte me disait* p. 108   **140.** Roederer, *Bonaparte me disait* p. 113   **141.** Roederer, *Bonaparte me disait* p. 114   **142.** Roederer, *Bonaparte me disait* p. 114   **143.** CG4 nos. 9007, 9009 pp. 772–3, 17 July, 1804, p. 773, 18 July 1804   **144.** CG5 no. 10342 p. 452, June 24, 1805   **145.** ed. Castle, *Stanley Kubrick's Napoleon* p. 197   **146.** CG5 no. 9973 p. 266, May 4, 1805   **147.** Masson, *Napoleon and his Coronation* p. 225   **148.** Masson, *Napoleon and his Coronation* p. 220   **149.** Thiard, *Souvenirs* p. 5   **150.** Bausset, *Private Memoirs* p. 27   **151.** Masson, *Napoleon and his Coronation* p. 230   **152.** Knapton, *Empress Josephine* p. 151   **153.** Parker, 'Why Did Napoleon' p. 136   **154.** Masson, *Napoleon and his Coronation* p. 310   **155.** D'Abrantès, *At the Court* p. 263   **156.** Knapton, *Empress Josephine* p. 228   **157.** Brookner, *Jacques-Louis David* p. 153   **158.** Anon., *Description des cérémonies* p. 5   **159.** Prat and Tonkovich, *David, Delacroix* p. 28, Brookner, *Jacques-Louis David* p. 153   **160.** Knapton, *Empress Josephine* p. 229   **161.** Bausset, *Private Memoirs*

p. 31   **162.** Masson, *Napoleon and his Coronation* p. 230   **163.** ed. Yonge, *Marshal Bugeaud* p. 22   **164.** Sudhir Hazareesingh in *TLS* 12/2/2005 p. 11

16. AUSTERLITZ

Napoleon's quote from *Caesar's Wars* comes from CN32 p. 82   Napoleon's letter to Decrès comes from CG5 no. 10618 p. 594   **1.** ed. Haythornthwaite, *Final Verdict* pp. 215–16   **2.** ed. Butler, *Baron Thiébault* II p. 120   **3.** ed. Markham, *Imperial Glory* p. 139   **4.** Hughes, *Forging Napoleon's Grande Armée* p. 20   **5.** CG4 no. 8731 pp. 637–8, March 12, 1804   **6.** Sherwig, *Guineas and Gunpowder* pp. 345, 368   **7.** CG5 nos. 9485, 10200 p. 22, 2 January, 1805, p. 375, 3 June, 1805   **8.** ed. Bingham, *Selection* II p. 103   **9.** CG5 no. 9536 p. 50, January 30, 1805   **10.** CG5 no. 9566 p. 63, February 16, 1805   **11.** CG5 no. 10009 p. 287, May 9, 1805   **12.** CG5 no. 10163 p. 358, May 30, 1805   **13.** Balcombe, *To Befriend* pp. 184–5   **14.** Bausset, *Private Memoirs* p. 429   **15.** CG5 no. 9700 pp. 136–7, March 17, 1805   **16.** D'Abrantès, *At the Court* p. 289   **17.** Hibbert, *Napoleon* p. 296   **18.** CG5 no. 10137 p. 348, May 27, 1805   **19.** Bausset, *Private Memoirs* p. 34   **20.** Schneid, *Soldiers* p. 7   **21.** CG5 no. 10224 p. 386, June 7, 1805   **22.** Connelly, *Satellite Kingdoms* p. 2   **23.** CG5 no. 10303 p. 433, June 19, 1805   **24.** ed. Hinard, *Dictionnaire-Napoleon* p. 200   **25.** CG5 no. 10427 pp. 495–6, July 20 1805   **26.** CG5 no. 10474 p. 520, July 28, 1805   **27.** ed. North, *Napoleon on Elba* p. 155   **28.** CG5 no. 10412 pp. 489–90, July 16, 1805   **29.** CG5 no. 10493 p. 530, August 3, 1805   **30.** Bausset, *Private Memoirs* p. 45   **31.** Ségur, *Memoirs* p. 146   **32.** CG5 no. 10554 p. 561, August 13, 1805   **33.** CG5 no. 10561 pp. 565–7, August 13, 1805   **34.** Ibid.   **35.** CG5 no. 10562 p. 568, August 13, 1805   **36.** Ségur, *Memoirs* p. 146   **37.** Ségur, *Memoirs* p. 147   **38.** Muir, *Tactics and the Experience of Battle* p. 146   **39.** eds. Olsen and van Creveld, *Evolution of Operational Art* pp. 22–3   **40.** Abel, 'Jacques-Antoine-Hippolyte' p. 37, Summerville, *Napoleon's Polish Gamble* p. 28   **41.** ed. Latimer, *Talks* p. 60   **42.** CG5 no. 10661 p. 620, August 25, 1805   **43.** Ségur, *Memoirs* p. 154, Schneid, *Napoleon's Conquest of Europe* p. 93   **44.** Ségur, *Memoirs* p. 148   **45.** CG5 no. 10629 pp. 598–600, August 22, 1805   **46.** ed. Bingham, *Selection* II, p. 147   **47.** CG5 no. 10516, pp. 541–2, August 6, 1805   **48.** CG5 no. 10729 p. 659, September 1, 1805   **49.** CG5 no. 10786 p. 685, September 12, 1805   **50.** CG5 no. 10756 p. 673, September 7, 1805   **51.** eds. Kagan and Higham, *Military History of Tsarist Russia* p. 110   **52.** CG5 no. 10775 p. 680, September 10, 1805   **53.** CG5 no. 10887 p. 742, September 28, 1805   **54.** Pelet, *Napoleon in Council* pp. 282–3   **55.** Ségur, *Memoirs* p. 153   **56.** Ségur, *Memoirs* p. 154   **57.** CG5 no. 10917 pp. 757–8, October 2, 1805   **58.** Balcombe, *To Befriend* p. 75   **59.** CG5 no. 10561 pp. 565–7, August 13, 1805   **60.** CG5 no. 10960 p. 778, October 4, 1805   **61.** Ségur, *Memoirs* p. 161   **62.** ed. Markham, *Imperial Glory* p. 11   **63.** ed. Davis, *Original Journals* II p. 6   **64.** ed. Davis, *Original Journals* II p. 19   **65.** CG5 no. 10998 p. 797, October 12, 1805   **66.** Ségur, *Memoirs* p. 172   **67.** Ségur, *Memoirs* p. 173   **68.** ed. Davis, *Original Journals* II p. 10

69. Ségur, *Memoirs* p. 175   **70.** Rapp, *Memoirs* p. 34   **71.** CG5 no. 11018 p. 808, October 19, 1805   **72.** ed. Davis, *Original Journals* II p. 10   **73.** Rapp, *Memoirs* p. 37, Smith, *Data Book* p. 205   **74.** Rapp, *Memoirs* p. 38   **75.** CG5 no. 11018 p. 808, October 19, 1805   **76.** ed. Markham, *Imperial Glory* p. 20   **77.** Ségur, *Memoirs* p. 188, ed. Bingham, *Selection* II p. 159   **78.** Rovigo, *Mémoires* II p. 153   **79.** Rapp, *Memoirs* p. 38   **80.** ed. Markham, *Imperial Glory* p. 20   **81.** ed. Dwyer, *Napoleon and Europe* p. 113   **82.** ed. Latimer, *Talks* p. 236   **83.** Rodger, *Second Coalition* p. 227   **84.** CG5 no. 11067 p. 830, November 2, 1805   **85.** Ségur, *Memoirs* p. 196   **86.** ed. Davis, *Original Journals* II p. 29   **87.** ed. Davis, *Original Journals* II p. 29   **88.** Rapp, *Memoirs* pp. 59–62   **89.** Ségur, *Memoirs* p. 202   **90.** Ségur, *Memoirs* p. 205   **91.** CG5 no. 11101 p. 850, November 15, 1805   **92.** Billings, 'Napoleon' p. 79, ed. Jennings, *Croker Papers* I pp. 340–41   **93.** Ségur, *Memoirs* p. 207   **94.** Ségur, *Memoirs* p. 208   **95.** Ségur, *Memoirs* p. 208   **96.** ed. Butler, *Baron Thiébault* II p. 154   **97.** ed. Butler, *Baron Thiébault* II p. 154   **98.** Ségur, *Memoirs* p. 208   **99.** ed. Butler, *Baron Thiébault* II p. 149   **100.** CG5 no. 11148 p. 875, December 5, 1805   **101.** Rovigo, *Mémoires* II p. 196, Ségur, *Memoirs* p. 210   **102.** Rovigo, *Mémoires* II p. 198   **103.** CG5 no. 11138 p. 869, November 30, 1805   **104.** Muir, *Tactics and the Experience of Battle* p. 155   **105.** ed. Yonge, *Memoirs of Bugeaud* I p. 38   **106.** Pelet, *Napoleon in Council* p. 15 & n   **107.** ed. Summerville, *Exploits of Baron de Marbot* p. 54   **108.** ed. Bell, *Baron Lejeune* I pp. 27–8   **109.** ed. Butler, *Baron Thiébault* II p. 151   **110.** ed. Butler, *Baron Thiébault* II p. 152   **111.** ed. Butler, *Baron Thiébault* II p. 153   **112.** Ibid.   **113.** Ibid.   **114.** Haythornthwaite, *Napoleonic Cavalry* p. 119   **115.** ed. Summerville, *Exploits of Baron de Marbot* p. 56   **116.** ed. Summerville, *Exploits of Baron de Marbot* p. 57   **117.** Thiard, *Souvenirs* p. 231   **118.** ed. Summerville, *Exploits of Baron de Marbot*, p. 58, ed. Garnier, *Dictionnaire* p. 104   **119.** ed. Summerville, *Exploits of Baron de Marbot* p. 58   **120.** ed. Haythornthwaite, *Final Verdict* p. 222   **121.** Bourne, *History of Napoleon* p. 360   **122.** Smith, *Data Book* p. 217   **123.** Dumas, *Memoirs* II p. 149   **124.** CG5 no. 11144 p. 873, December 3, 1805

17. JENA

The quote about Prussia comes from Gray, *In the Words* p. 188   Napoleon to Joseph comes from CG6 no. 12758 p. 734, August 20, 1806   **1.** ed. Summerville, *Exploits of Baron de Marbot* p. 60   **2.** ed. Summerville, *Exploits of Baron de Marbot* p. 62   **3.** CG5 no. 11146 p. 873, December 4, 1805   **4.** ed. Fleischmann, *L'Épopée Impériale* p. 69   **5.** ed. Summerville, *Exploits of Baron de Marbot* p. 64   **6.** ed. Wilson, *Diary* p. 42   **7.** CG5 no. 11149 p. 876, December 5, 1805   **8.** ed. Bertrand, *Lettres de Talleyrand* pp. 209–12   **9.** ed. Butler, *Baron Thiébault* II p. 183   **10.** Horne, *Age of Napoleon* p. 57   **11.** Pelet, *Napoleon in Council* pp. 283–4   **12.** Clark, *Iron Kingdom* p. 302   **13.** CG5 no. 11186 p. 892, December 15, 1805   **14.** CG5 no. 11223 p. 910, December 25, 1805   **15.** ed. Arnold, *Documentary Survey* p. 209   **16.** Dwyer, *Talleyrand* p. 100   **17.** ed. Arnold, *Documentary Survey*

p. 213   18. Bausset, *Private Memoirs* p. 54   19. Connelly, *Satellite Kingdoms* p. 9   20. Connelly, *Satellite Kingdoms* p. 10   21. CG6 no. 12235 p. 491, June 6, 1806   22. CG5 no. 11241 p. 920, December 31, 1805   23. CG6 no. 12823 p. 768, August 31, 1806   24. CG7 no. 14927 p. 471, March 27, 1807   25. Schneid, *Conquest of Europe* p. 143   26. Schneid, *Conquest of Europe* p. 143   27. Branda, 'Did the War' p. 132   28. Branda, 'Did the War' p. 132   29. Branda, 'Did the War' pp. 135-7   30. Pelet, *Napoleon in Council* p. 275   31. Branda, 'Did the War' p. 135   32. Gates, 'The Wars of 1812' p. 45   33. ed. Noailles, *Count Molé* p. 64   34. CG6 no. 11335 p. 63, January 27, 1806   35. CG5 no. 11161 p. 880, December 12, 1805   36. CG6 no. 12223 p. 484, June 5, 1806   37. CG6 no. 12785 p. 752, August 23, 1806   38. Israel, *The Dutch Republic* pp. 1127-9   39. Israel, *The Dutch Republic* p. 1130   40. Connelly, *Satellite Kingdoms* p. 13   41. CG6 no. 13871 pp. 1284-5, December 15, 1806   42. Chaptal, *Souvenirs* p. 339   43. ed. Latimer, *Talks* p. 144   44. CG6 no. 11815 p. 289, April 1, 1806   45. CG6 no. 11833 p. 297, April 8, 1806   46. AN AF/IV/1231   47. Branda, *Le prix de la gloire* p. 57, ed. Castle, *Stanley Kubrick's Napoleon* p. 195   48. CAD P11778/16–18   49. CAD P11778   50. ed. Bingham, *Selection* II p. 255   51. CG6 no. 12748 p. 729, August 18, 1806   52. Pelet, *Napoleon in Council* p. 258   53. Pelet, *Napoleon in Council* p. 272   54. Pelet, *Napoleon in Council* p. 272   55. Pelet, *Napoleon in Council* p. 273   56. Pelet, *Napoleon in Council* p. 205   57. CG6 no. 11655 p. 213, March 12, 1806   58. Pelet, *Napoleon in Council* p. 263   59. CG6 no. 11898 pp. 325-6, April 14, 1806   60. CG6 no. 12023 p. 388, April 30, 1806   61. CG6 no. 12206 p. 475, May 31, 1806   62. ed. Arnold, *Documentary Survey* p. 226   63. Markham, 'Was Napoleon an Anti-Semite?' *passim*, eds. Kafker and Laux, *Napoleon and His Times* p. 296   64. *Moniteur* May 22, 1799   65. eds. Brenner et al., *Jewish Emancipation Reconsidered* p. 80   66. Pelet, *Napoleon in Council* p. 251   67. Benbassa, *The Jews of France* p. 88   68. Weider, 'Napoleon and the Jews' p. 3   69. Weider, 'Napoleon and the Jews' p. 2   70. Schwarzfuchs, *Napoleon, the Jews* pp. 125-30   71. Lentz, *La France et l'Europe* pp. 254-8, eds. Brenner et al., *Jewish Emancipation Reconsidered* p. 196   72. eds. Kafker and Laux, *Napoleon and His Times* p. 299   73. Mauduit, *Les derniers jours* II p. 39   74. ed. Latimer, *Talks* p. 277   75. Hazareesingh, *The Saint-Napoleon* pp. 3-4   76. Koebner, *Empire* p. 282   77. Clark, *Iron Kingdom* p. 303   78. Simms, *The Impact of Napoleon* p. 291   79. Simms, *The Impact of Napoleon* p. 292   80. Simms, *The Impact of Napoleon* p. 295   81. CG6 no. 12643 pp. 684-5, August 2, 1806   82. CG6 no. 12642 p. 684, August 2, 1806   83. ed. Metternich, *Memoirs* I p. 270   84. ed. Metternich, *Memoirs* I p. 271   85. CG6 no. 12646 p. 686, August 5, 1806   86. Clark, *Iron Kingdom* p. 301   87. ed. Summerville, *Exploits of Baron de Marbot* p. 67   88. ed. Handel, *Leaders and Intelligence* p. 42   89. CG6 no. 12897 p. 816, September 10, 1806   90. Lentz, *Napoléon et la conquête* p. 327   91. Maude, *Jena Campaign* pp. 118–19   92. Maude, *Jena Campaign* p. 121 n. 1   93. Rapp, *Memoirs* p. 73   94. Napoleonic Historical Society Newsletter (Berthier Supplement) May 2014 p. 13   95. Rapp, *Memoirs* p. 74   96. CG6 no. 13259 p. 999, October 12, 1806   97. Clark, *Iron Kingdom* p. 305   98. Hayman, 'France Against Prussia' p. 188   99. Hayman,

'France Against Prussia' p. 194   100. Clark, *Iron Kingdom* p. 306   101. Hayman, 'France Against Prussia' p. 188   102. Paret, *Cognitive Challenge of War* p. 21   103. Paret, *Cognitive Challenge of War* p. 21   104. Gallaher, *Iron Marshal*, p. 26   105. ed. Cottin, *Souvenirs de Roustam* p. 135   106. Jomini, *Summary* p. 73   107. Smith, *Data Book* pp. 225–6   108. Cook, 'Bernadotte 1806' (unpaged)   109. Rapp, *Memoirs* p. 86   110. ed. Latimer, *Talks* pp. 123–4   111. CG6 no. 13312 p. 1023, October 23, 1806, Palmer, *Bernadotte* p. 135, Cook, 'Bernadotte 1806' (unpaged)   112. CG6 no. 13267 pp. 1003–4, October 15, 1806

18. BLOCKADES

Captain Blaze quote comes from Blaze, *Life in Napoleon's Army* p. 183   Napoleon's maxim comes from ed. Chandler, *Napoleon's Military Maxims* p. 204   1. ed. Latimer, *Talks* p. 125   2. Butterfield, *Peace Tactics of Napoleon* p. 7   3. CG6 no. 12684 p. 701, August 8, 1806   4. Bausset, *Private Memoirs* p. 64   5. ed. Summerville, *Exploits of Baron de Marbot* p. 76   6. ed. Bingham, *Selection* II p. 263   7. CG6 no. 13318 p. 1028, October 23, 1806   8. CG6 no. 13915 p. 1303, December 31, 1806   9. Rovigo, *Mémoires* II pp. 287–8   10. Rapp, *Memoirs* p. 94   11. Clark, *Iron Kingdom* p. 307, ed. Markham, *Imperial Glory* p. 97, ed. Bingham, *Selection* II p. 267   12. Rapp, *Memoirs* pp. 107–8   13. Rovigo, *Mémoires* II p. 317   14. CG6 no. 13355 p. 1037, October 25, 1806   15. ed. Markham, *Imperial Glory* p. 97   16. ed. Markham, *Imperial Glory* p. 97   17. CG6 no. 13482 p. 1106, November 6, 1806   18. ed. Markham, *Imperial Glory* p. 101   19. Coignet, *Captain Coignet* p. 133   20. ed. Sage, *Private Diaries of Stendhal* p. 253   21. Branda, *Le prix de la gloire* p. 57   22. Clark, *Iron Kingdom* p. 308   23. CG6 no. 13426 p. 1076, November 3, 1806   24. CG6 no. 13413 p. 1070, November 2, 1806   25. Summerville, *Napoleon's Polish Gamble* p. 10   26. ed. North, *Napoleon on Elba* p. 49   27. ed. Arnold, *Documentary Survey* p. 230, Melvin, *Napoleon's Navigation System* p. 5 n. 6   28. Rudé, *Revolutionary Europe* p. 250   29. CG6 no. 13743 p. 1222, December 3, 1806   30. CN28 11010, 11064, 11093, 11217 and 11271   31. Melvin, *Napoleon's Navigation System* p. 14   32. Mollien, *Mémoires* II p. 444   33. *Edinburgh Review* No. 23 April, 1808 p. 228   34. *TLS* 15/2/1923 p. 99, ed. Bingham, *Selection* II p. 329 n. 1   35. *TLS* 15/2/1923 p. 99   36. Melvin, *Napoleon's Navigation System* p. 11 n. 13   37. Rapp, *Memoirs* pp. 158–61   38. CG7 no. 16785 p. 1310, November 13, 1807   39. eds. Dwyer and Forrest, *Napoleon and His Empire* p. 7   40. Knight, *Britain Against Napoleon* pp. 402–4, ed. Bingham, *Selection* III p. 113   41. Knight, *Britain Against Napoleon* p. 403   42. Gates, 'The Wars of 1812' p. 46, Knight, *Britain Against Napoleon* p. 404   43. Lentz, *Napoléon et la conquête* p. 265   44. Fain, *Manuscrit de 1812* I p. 7   45. CG8 no. 17215 p. 165, February 18, 1808   46. ed. Bingham, *Selection* III p. 45   47. Gray, *Spencer Perceval* pp. 45–6   48. *Conservative History Journal* II, Issue 1, Autumn 2012 p. 40   49. Summerville, *Napoleon's Polish*

Gamble p. 36   50. ed. Latimer, *Talks* p. 124   51. Summerville, *Napoleon's Polish Gamble* p. 38   52. CG6 no. 13719 p. 1213, December 2, 1806   53. Ibid. 54. Rapp, *Memoirs* p. 119   55. Rapp, *Memoirs* p. 120   56. Rovigo, *Mémoires* III p. 23   57. Ibid.   58. CG6 no. 13739 p. 1220, December 3, 1806   59. Summerville, *Napoleon's Polish Gamble* p. 47   60. Rapp, *Memoirs* p. 128 61. Esdaile, 'Recent Writing on Napoleon' p. 211   62. Summerville, *Napoleon's Polish Gamble* p. 136   63. Summerville, *Napoleon's Polish Gamble* p. 57 64. Summerville, *Napoleon's Polish Gamble* pp. 56–7   65. Percy, *Journal des Campagnes* p. 137   66. Summerville, *Napoleon's Polish Gamble* p. 21 67. Howard, *Napoleon's Doctors* p. 69   68. Howard, *Napoleon's Doctors* pp. 68–71   69. ed. Cottin, *Souvenirs de Roustam* p. 161   70. Cate, *War of the Two Emperors* p. 170   71. Howard, *Napoleon's Doctors* pp. 70–71   72. Howard, *Napoleon's Doctors* p. 251   73. Muir, *Tactics and the Experience of Battle* p. 9   74. Sutherland, *Marie Walewska* p. 61   75. ed. Stryjenski, *Mémoires* p. 125   76. CG7 no. 13938 p. 27, January 3, 1807   77. CG7 no. 13988 p. 52, January 8, 1807   78. Rapp, *Memoirs* p.129   79. CG7 no. 14001 p. 58, January 10, 1807   80. Arnold and Reinertsen, *Crisis in the Snows* p. 1295   81. CG7 no. 14211 p. 152, January 29, 1807   82. CG7 nos. 14134, 14139, p. 116, between January 17 and 24, 1807, p. 119, January 21 or 22, 1807   83. Branda, *Le prix de la gloire* p. 57   84. CG7 no. 16323 p. 1100, September 7, 1807   85. Summerville, *Napoleon's Polish Gamble* p. 63   86. CG7 no. 14270 p. 174, February 5, 1807   87. Blond, *La Grande Armée* p. 121   88. Smith, *Data Book* p. 241 89. Blaze, *Life in Napoleon's Army* p. 10   90. ed. Summerville, *Exploits of Baron de Marbot* p. 84   91. ed. Fleischmann, *L'Épopée Impériale* p. 123   92. Summerville, *Napoleon's Polish Gamble* p. 79   93. Muir, *Tactics and the Experience of Battle* p. 147   94. Summerville, *Napoleon's Polish Gamble* p. 87   95. Uffindell, *Napoleon's Immortals* p. 245   96. ed. Cottin, *Souvenirs de Roustam* p. 138 97. Smith, *Data Book*, p. 242   98. CG7 no. 14280 pp. 177–8, February 9, 1807   99. ed. Bingham, *Selection* II p. 294

19. TILSIT

Napoleon on Eylau comes from ed. Bingham, *Selection* II p. 292   Napoleon to Josephine comes from CG7 no. 14930 p. 472, March 27, 1807   1. CG7 no. 14277 pp. 176–7, February 9, 1807   2. Saint-Chamans, *Mémoires* p. 59   3. ed. Markham, *Imperial Glory* p. 144   4. CG7 no. 14312 p. 191, February 14, 1807   5. CG7 no. 15240 p. 608, April 13, 1807   6. SHD GR2/C 66   7. SHD GR2/C 66   8. SHD GR2/C 66   9. CG7 no. 14448 pp. 249–50, March 1, 1807   10. CG7 no. 15743 p. 837, May 27, 1807   11. CG7 no. 15224, pp. 600–601, April 12, 1807   12. CG7 no. 15947 p. 926, July 4, 1807   13. Summerville, *Napoleon's Polish Gamble* p. 118   14. Gonneville, *Recollections* I p. 50   15. Kiley, *Once There Were Titans* p. 200   16. Summerville, *Napoleon's Polish Gamble* p. 133 17. Summerville, *Napoleon's Polish Gamble* p. 134   18. Summerville, *Napoleon's Polish Gamble* p. 134   19. Wilson, *Campaigns in Poland* p. 157   20. CG7 no. 15874 p. 898, June 19, 1807   21. Smith, *Data Book* pp. 250–51   22. Woloch, *The French Veteran* p. 199   23. de la Bédoyère, *Memoirs of Napoleon* II p. 481   24. Clark, *Iron Kingdom* p. 308   25. ed. Markham, *Imperial Glory* p. 174   26. CG12 no. 31068 p. 787, July 1, 1812   27. Ibid.   28. CG7 no. 15868 p. 895, June 16, 1807   29. Clark, *Iron Kingdom* p. 308   30. Summerville, *Napoleon's Polish Gamble* p. 141   31. Clark, *Iron Kingdom* p. 314   32. Hobhouse, *Recollections* I p. 185   33. ed. Wilson, *A Diary* p. 84   34. Ebrington, *Memorandum* p. 11   35. Fox, *The Culture of Science* p. 305   36. eds. Larichev and Ostarkova, , *Paris-St Petersburg* p. 18   37. Wesling, *Napoleon* p. 3   38. ed. Latimer, *Talks* p. 124   39. ed. Arnold, *Documentary Survey* pp. 239–45, Clark, *Iron Kingdom* p. 313   40. Butterfield, *Peace Tactics passim*   41. ed. Latimer, *Talks* pp. 62–3   42. Clark, *Iron Kingdom* p. 317   43. Cockburn, *Buonaparte's Voyage* p. 91   44. ed. Cottin, *Souvenirs de Roustam* p. 151   45. ed. Latimer, *Talks* p. 125   46. ed. Latimer, *Talks* p. 125, Cockburn, *Buonaparte's Voyage* p. 87   47. Connelly, *Satellite Kingdoms* p. 15   48. CG7 no. 16812 p. 1321, November 15, 1807   49. CG7 no. 15499 p. 730, May 2, 1807   50. CG7 no. 15528 p. 743, May 4, 1807   51. CG7 no. 15982 p. 939, July 7, 1807   52. CG7 no. 15972 p. 936, July 6, 1807   53. ed. Cottin, *Souvenirs de Roustam* p. 157   54. Chaptal, *Souvenirs* p. 327   55. CG7 no. 16072 p. 987, July 29, 1807

20. IBERIA

The Duke of Wellington to Lord Castlereagh comes from ed. Wellington, 2nd Duke of, *Despatches, Correspondence and Memoranda* I p. 117   Napoleon on the Peninsular War comes from Tone, *Fatal Knot* p. 3   1. Montesquiou, *Souvenirs* p. 113   2. Blaufarb, 'The Ancien Régime Origins' p. 408   3. CN32 p. 84   4. Bergeron, *France Under Napoleon* p. 106   5. D'Abrantès, *At the Court* p. 344   6. Simms, *Europe* p. 165, Tulard, *Napoléon et la noblesse* p. 97   7. Ellis, *The Napoleonic Empire* p. 77   8. Ellis, *The Napoleonic Empire* p. 114   9. Tulard, *Napoléon et la noblesse* p. 93   10. Ellis, *The Napoleonic Empire* p. 114   11. ed. Chatel de Brancion, *Cambacérès* II p. 141   12. Rovigo, *Mémoires* III p. 236   13. CG7 no. 14909 p. 457, March 26, 1807   14. SHD GR2/C 66   15. Tulard, *Napoleon: The Myth of the Saviour* p. 185   16. Branda, *Le prix de la gloire* p. 57   17. CG7 no. 16560, p. 1208   18. Stuart, *Rose of Martinique* p. 284   19. ed. Méneval, *Memoirs* I pp. 125–6   20. ed. Park, *Napoleon in Captivity* p. 238 n. 3, Bruce, *Napoleon and Josephine* p. 305   21. Branda, *Napoléon et ses hommes* p. 208   22. Branda, *Napoléon et ses hommes* p. 29   23. Mansel, *Eagle in Splendour* p. 67   24. Sudhir Hazareesingh in *TLS* 3/2/2012 p. 4   25. Chaptal, *Souvenirs* p. 338   26. Woolf, *Napoleon's Integration* p. vii   27. Blaze, *Life in Napoleon's Army* p. 174   28. ed. Bingham, *Selection* III p. 118   29. Bausset, *Private Memoirs* p. 15   30. Markham, 'The Emperor at Work' p. 584   31. ed. Butler, *Baron Thiébault* II p. 17   32. Branda, *Napoléon et ses hommes* p. 140, ed. Butler, *Baron Thiébault* II p. 17, D'Abrantès, *At the Court* p. 156   33. Balcombe, *To Befriend* p. 51   34. Roederer, *Bonaparte me disait* pp. 85–6   35. ed.

Noailles, *Count Molé* p. 189 36. ed. Jones, *Napoleon: How He Did It* p. 184 37. ed. Méneval, *Memoirs* I p. 122 38. ed. Latimer, *Talks* p. 261 39. Méneval, *Memoirs* I p. 135 40. ed. Latimer, *Talks* p. 92 41. Chaptal, *Souvenirs* p. 354 42. ed. Méneval, *Memoirs* I p. 107 43. ed. Noailles, *Count Molé* p. 101 44. Bausset, *Private Memoirs* p. 301, Chaptal, *Souvenirs* p. 348 45. Chaptal, *Souvenirs* p. 348 46. Branda, *Napoléon et ses hommes* p. 271 47. ed. Méneval, *Memoirs* I pp. 125–6 48. ed. Méneval, *Memoirs* I pp. 121–2 49. ed. Méneval, *Memoirs* I p. 123 50. CG3 no. 5751 p. 438, November 8, 1800 51. Esdaile, *Peninsular War* p. 5 52. ed. Bingham, *Selection* I p. 349 53. CG7 no. 16336 p. 1106, September 8, 1807 54. Bausset, *Private Memoirs* p. 78 55. Esdaile, *Peninsular War* p. 7 56. Lipscombe, *Peninsular War Atlas* p. 23 57. CG7 no. 16554 p. 1204, October 17, 1807 58. ed. Woloch, *Revolution and Meanings of Freedom* p. 68 59. ed. Bingham, *Selection* II p. 352 60. ed. Bingham, *Selection* II p. 349 61. Broers, *Europe under Napoleon* p. 156 62. ed. Bingham, *Selection* II p. 349 63. CG8 no. 17350 pp. 236–7, March 9, 1808 64. ed. Woloch, *Revolution and Meanings of Freedom* p. 70 65. Rovigo, *Mémoires* III p. 251 66. ed. Woloch, *Revolution and Meanings of Freedom* p. 71 67. ed. North, *Napoleon on Elba* p. 50 68. ed. North, *Napoleon on Elba* p. 50 69. Bausset, *Private Memoirs* p. 118 70. Bausset, *Private Memoirs* p. 125 71. ed. Woloch, *Revolution and Meanings of Freedom* p. 73, Rovigo, *Mémoires* III p. 255 72. CG8 no. 17699 p. 423, April 25, 1808 73. ed. Woloch, *Revolution and Meanings of Freedom* p. 73 74. Gates, 'The Wars of 1812' p. 50 75. Gates, 'The Wars of 1812' p. 51 76. Sarrazin, *The War in Spain* p. 33 77. Esdaile, 'Recent Writing on Napoleon' p. 211, ed. Tulard, *Bibliographie critique* p. 175, Anon., 'The Unpublished Letters of Napoleon' p. 358 78. CG8 no. 17759 pp. 451–4, May 2, 1808 79. Lipscombe, *The Peninsular War Atlas* p. 23 80. Blaze, *Life in Napoleon's Army* p. 57 81. Rovigo, *Mémoires* III p. 352, Bausset, *Private Memoirs* p. 180 82. CG8 no. 17829 p. 489, May 10, 1808 83. ed. Latimer, *Talks* p. 130 84. ed. Summerville, *Exploits of Baron de Marbot* p. 283 85. CG8 no. 17699 p. 423, April 25, 1808 86. CG8 no. 17826 p. 487, May 9, 1808 87. CG8 no. 18480 p. 831, July 4, 1808 88. Tulard, *Le grand empire* p. 146 89. Rovigo, *Mémoires* III p. 358 90. ed. Woloch, *Revolution and Meanings of Freedom* pp. 75–6 91. eds. Kafker and Laux, *Napoleon and His Times* p. 220 n. 9 92. Bausset, *Private Memoirs* pp. 188–9 93. Vaughan, *Siege of Zaragoza* p. 5, Bell, *First Total War* p. 281 94. Vaughan, *Siege of Zaragoza* p. 22 95. CG8 no. 18401 p. 797, June 25, 1808, CG9 no. 18659 p. 930, July 25, 1808 96. Lipscombe, *Peninsular War Atlas* p. 52 97. ed. Latimer, *Talks* p. 257 98. Dumas, *Memoirs* II p. 186, CG8 no. 18835 p. 1036, September 6, 1808 99. CG8 no. 18685, p. 945, August 3, 1808 100. CG8 no. 18797 p. 1007, August 30, 1808 101. CG8 no. 18619 p. 909, July 19, 1808 102. CG8 no. 18707 p. 957, August 16, 1808 103. Aldington, *Wellington* p. 48 104. CG8 no. 18951 pp. 1090–91, September 18, 1808 105. CG8 no. 18869 p. 1055, September 9, 1808 106. Rovigo, *Mémoires* III p. 450 107. CG8 no. 18685 p. 945, August 3, 1808 108. Grimsted, *Foreign Ministers* p. 166 109. Grimsted, *Foreign Ministers* p. 166 110. ed. Lentz, *1810* p. 300

111. Bausset, *Private Memoirs* p. 212 112. Chevallier, *Empire Style* p. 64 113. Bausset, *Private Memoirs* p. 213 114. ed. North, *Napoleon on Elba* p. 145, Rapp, *Memoirs* p. 133 115. Dwyer, *Talleyrand* pp. 99, 116, ed. Bingham, *Selection* II p. 413 116. ed. Bingham, *Selection* II pp. 413–14 117. Bausset, *Private Memoirs* p. 212 118. eds. Larichev and Ostarkova, *Paris-St Petersburg* p. 18 119. eds. Larichev and Ostarkova, *Paris-St Petersburg* p. 18 120. *TLS* 12/5/1927 p. 325, Florange and Wunsch, *L'Entrevue* pp. 12ff, Brown, *Life of Goethe* II p. 547 n. 1 121. Florange and Wunsch, *L'Entrevue* pp. 12ff 122. Brown, *Life of Goethe* II pp. 546–7 123. Brown, *Life of Goethe* II p. 547 124. CG8 no. 19042 p. 1126, October 9, 1808 125. Brown, *Life of Goethe* II p. 547 126. Williams, *Life of Goethe* p. 39 127. Brown, *Life of Goethe* II p. 546, Florange and Wunsch, *L'Entrevue* pp. 12ff 128. Bausset, *Private Memoirs* p. 223 129. Bausset, *Private Memoirs* p. 217 130. CG8 no. 19050 p. 1130, between October 11 and 13, 1808 131. CG8 no. 19053 p. 1131, October 12, 1808 132. CG8 no. 19056 p. 1133, October 13, 1808 133. CG8 nos. 19184, 19270, p. 1186, November 4, 1808, p. 1225, November 14, 1808 134. CG8 no. 19327 pp. 1248–9, November 19, 1808 135. ed. Dwyer, *Napoleon and Europe* p. 18 136. Esdaile, 'Recent Writing on Napoleon' pp. 217–18 137. Tone, *Fatal Knot* p. 4 138. Tone, *Fatal Knot* p. 182 139. Sherwig, *Guineas and Gunpowder* pp. 367–8 140. Blaze, *Life in Napoleon's Army* pp. 58–9, Bell, *First Total War* p. 290, Gonneville, *Recollections* I p. 61 141. CG8 no. 19197 p. 1192, November 5, 1808 142. Dumas, *Memoirs* II p. 180 143. Chlapowski, *Polish Lancer* p. 45 144. Bausset, *Private Memoirs* p. 233 145. Bausset, *Private Memoirs* p. 235 146. Bausset, *Private Memoirs* p. 232 147. *The Nation*, 16/7/1896 p. 45 148. Bausset, *Private Memoirs* p. 239 149. Gonneville, *Recollections* p. 65 150. CG8 no. 19650 pp. 1388–9, December 31, 1808 151. ed. Jennings, *Croker Papers* I p. 355 152. CG8 no. 19675 p. 1402, January 2, 1809 153. Bonaparte, Napoleon, *Confidential Correspondence* II p. 4n 154. Chlapowski, *Polish Lancer* p. 72 155. Bausset, *Private Memoirs* p. 242 156. Bausset, *Private Memoirs* p. 242 157. CG8 no. 19855 p. 1497, January 15, 1809 158. Cobban, *Modern France* II p. 56, Tone, *Fatal Knot* p. 4 159. Alexander, 'French Replacement Methods' p. 192 160. Alexander, 'French Replacement Methods' p. 192 161. Lipscombe, *Peninsular War Atlas* p. 23, Alexander, 'French Replacement Methods' p. 193, Fraser, *Napoleon's Cursed War* passim 162. Lentz, *Savary* p. 188

21. WAGRAM

Napoleon's Military Maxim comes from ed. Chandler, *Military Maxims* p. 199 Napoleon to Bertrand comes from Bertrand, *Cahiers* II p. 344 1. CG8 no. 19856 p. 1498, January 15, 1809 2. CG7 no. 15264 p. 617, April 14, 1807 3. ed. Haythornthwaite, *Final Verdict* p. 244 4. ed. Butler, *Baron Thiébault* II p. 241, ed. Latimer, *Talks* p. 131, ed. Lacour-Gayet, *Chancellor Pasquier* p. 78 n. 22 5. Dumas, *Memoirs* II p. 187 6. ed. Bingham. *Selection*, III

p. 130 7. ed. Lacour-Gayet, *Chancellor Pasquier* pp. 76–80, Dwyer, *Talleyrand* p. 120, Mollien, *Mémoires* II pp. 334ff, ed. Latimer, *Talks* p. 89 8. Dwyer, *Talleyrand* p. 120, ed. Lacour-Gayet, *Chancellor Pasquier* p. 80 9. Arnold, *Crisis on the Danube* pp. 25–6 10. Rovigo, *Mémoires* IV p. 46 11. Rovigo, *Mémoires* IV p. 47 12. ed. Lentz, *1810* p. 301, Adams, *Napoleon and Russia* p. 288 13. ed. Bingham, *Selection* II p. 448 14. ed. Latimer, *Talks* p. 132 15. Chlapowski, *Polish Lancer* p. 56 16. CG9 no. 20869 p. 510, April 18, 1809 ed. Bell, *Baron Lejeune* I p. 218 17. Arnold, *Crisis on the Danube* p. 106 18. ed. Haythornthwaite, *Final Verdict* p. 233 19. Smith, *Data Book* p. 291 20. ed. Haythornthwaite, *Final Verdict* p. 233 21. ed. Latimer, *Talks* p. 143 22. Chaptal, *Souvenirs* p. 252 23. ed. Fleischmann, *L'Épopée Impériale* p. 204 24. ed. Summerville, *Exploits of Marbot* p. 126, Muir, *Tactics and the Experience of Battle* p. 152, Chlapowski, *Polish Lancer* p. 60 25. ed. Haythornthwaite, *Final Verdict* p. 223 26. CG9 no. 20975 p. 569, May 6, 1809 27. ed. Summerville, *Exploits of Marbot* p. 137 28. Blaze, *Life in Napoleon's Army* pp. 181–2 29. ed. Haythornthwaite, *Final Verdict* pp. 220–21 30. Chlapowski, *Polish Lancer* p. 64 31. Chlapowski, *Polish Lancer* p. 64 32. ed. Markham, *Imperial Glory* p. 199 33. Rothenberg, *Art of Warfare* p. 130 34. Smith, *Data Book* p. 310 35. Smith, *Data Book* p. 310 36. ed. Markham, *Imperial Glory* p. 205 37. Musée de la Préfecture de Police, Paris 38. Blond, *La Grande Armée* p. 242, ed. Summerville, *Exploits of Marbot* p. 167, Dumas, *Memoirs* II p. 196, Rovigo, *Mémoires* IV p. 125 39. Martin, *Napoleonic Friendship* p. 40 40. Martin, *Napoleonic Friendship* p. 43 41. CG9 no. 21105 p. 634, May 31, 1809 42. Rovigo, *Mémoires* IV p. 145 43. Markham, 'The Emperor at Work' p. 588 44. Rapp, *Memoirs* p. 140 45. Caulaincourt, *Mémoires* I p. 368 46. Arnold, *Crisis on the Danube* p. 122 47. Esdaile, 'Recent Writing' p. 21, Gill, *Thunder on the Danube* III p. 223 48. Dumas, *Memoirs* II p. 102, Arnold, *Napoleon Conquers Austria* p. 128 49. ed. Summerville, *Exploits of Marbot* p. 172 50. Arnold, *Napoleon Conquers Austria* pp. 135–6 51. Rothenberg, *Emperor's Last Victory* p. 181, ed. Summerville, *Exploits of Marbot* pp. 172–3 52. Arnold, *Napoleon Conquers Austria* p. 155 53. ed. Haythornthwaite, *Final Verdict* p. 223 54. Arnold, *Napoleon Conquers Austria* p. 147 55. Gill, *Thunder on the Danube* III p. 239 56. Dumas, *Memoirs* II p. 206 57. Lachouque and Brown, *Anatomy of Glory* p. 163 58. Rothenberg, *Emperor's Last Victory* p. 193 59. Blond *La Grande Armée* p. 254 60. Blaze, *Life in Napoleon's Army* p. 131 61. Rovigo, *Mémoires* IV p. 187 62. Eidahl, 'Oudinot' p. 11 63. CG9 no. 21467 p. 833, July 7, 1809 64. CG9 no. 21739 p. 975, August, 1809 65. Pelet, *Napoleon in Council* p. 96

22. ZENITH

Napoleon to Tsar Alexander comes from CG8 no. 18500 p. 840–41, July 8, 1808 Napoleon on St Helena comes from ed. Latimer, *Talks* p. 151 1. Simms, *Europe* p. 166 2. Woolf, *Napoleon's Integration* p. 10 3. Fisher, *Bonapartism*

p. 84 **4.** Fisher, *Bonapartism* p. 84 **5.** Parker, 'Why Did Napoleon Invade Russia?' pp. 142–3 **6.** ed. Dwyer, *Napoleon and Europe* p. 19 **7.** ed. Dwyer, *Napoleon and Europe* pp. 16–17 **8.** ed. Dwyer, *Napoleon and Europe* pp. 8–9, Broers, *Europe under Napoleon* pp. 88, 126–7, Hales, *Napoleon and the Pope* p. 105, Davis, *Conflict and Control* p. 23 **9.** eds. Dwyer and Forrest, *Napoleon and His Empire* p. 9, Jordan, *Napoleon and the Revolution* p. 1, ed. Dwyer, *Napoleon and Europe* p. 17 **10.** eds. Laven and Riall, *Napoleon's Legacy* p. 1 **11.** Davis, *Conflict and Control* p. 23 **12.** Woolf, 'The Construction of a European World-View' p. 95 **13.** eds. Dwyer and Forrest, *Napoleon and His Empire* p. 204 **14.** ed. Dwyer, *Napoleon and Europe* p. 11 **15.** CG7 no. 16057 p. 979, July 22, 1807 **16.** Hales, *Napoleon and the Pope* p. 120 **17.** CG9 no. 22074 p. 1179, September 14, 1809 **18.** Hales, *Napoleon and the Pope* pp. 114–19 **19.** CG9 no. 21717 p. 959, August 6, 1809 **20.** CG9 no. 21865 p. 1052, August 21, 1809 **21.** CG9 no. 21971 p. 1116, September 4, 1809 **22.** CG9 no. 21865 p. 1052, August 21, 1809 **23.** *The Nation*, 16/7/1896 p. 46, Hazareesingh, *The Saint-Napoleon* p. 4 **24.** CG9 nos. 21801–21807 pp. 1009–12, August 15 and 16, 1809 **25.** Lanfrey, *History of Napoleon the First* IV p. 218 **26.** ed. Kerry, *The First Napoleon* p. 7 **27.** ed. Kerry, *The First Napoleon* p. 7 **28.** Rovigo, *Mémoires* IV p. 217 **29.** ed. Lentz, *1810* p. 304 **30.** ed. Arnold, *Documentary Survey* pp. 290–94 **31.** ed. Caisse, *Mémoires et correspondance* VI pp. 557–79 **32.** Eyck, *Loyal Rebels* p. 191 **33.** Eyck, *Loyal Rebels* p. 194, ed. Caisse, *Mémoires et correspondance* VI p. 277 **34.** Adams, *Napoleon and Russia* p. 240 **35.** Tulard, *Napoléon: une journée* pp. 140, 172 **36.** CG7 no. 15867 p. 894, June 16, 1807 **37.** Wright, *Daughter to Napoleon* p. 213 **38.** CG7 no. 15619 p. 782, May 14, 1807 **39.** Rapp, *Memoirs* p. 142 **40.** Rapp, *Memoirs* p. 145, Rovigo, *Mémoires* IV p. 221 **41.** ed. Latimer, *Talks* p. 84 **42.** Hibbert, *Napoleon: His Wives and Women* pp. 183, 296 **43.** ed. Hanoteau, *Memoirs of Queen Hortense* I p. 289 **44.** Bausset, *Private Memoirs* p. 253 **45.** Blaufarb, 'The Ancien Régime Origins' p. 409 **46.** ed. Latimer, *Talks* p. 138 **47.** Rapp, *Memoirs* p. 152 **48.** Bausset, *Private Memoirs* p. 241 **49.** ed. Latimer, *Talks* p. 138 and n. 1 **50.** Cobban, *Modern France* II p. 57 **51.** BNF NAF 4020 pp. 9–10 **52.** Lavalette, *Memoirs* p. 99 **53.** ed. Cerf, *Letters* p. 17 **54.** Swanson, *Napoleon's Dual Courtship* pp. 6–7 **55.** Mowat, *The Diplomacy of Napoleon* p. 252 **56.** ed. Bingham, *Selection* III p. 2, Mowat, *The Diplomacy of Napoleon* p. 252 **57.** ed. Bingham, *Selection* III p. 2 **58.** ed. Lentz, *1810* p. 305 **59.** Schroeder, 'Napoleon's Foreign Policy' p. 154 **60.** Lentz, *L'Effondrement* p. 210 **61.** ed. Lentz, *1810* p. 304 **62.** CG9 no. 22761 p. 1554, December 31, 1809 **63.** ed. Lentz, *1810* p. 310 **64.** ed. Lentz, *1810* p. 311 **65.** ed. Bingham, *Selection* III p. 3, ed. Latimer, *Talks* p. 139 **66.** ed. Roncière, *Letters to Marie-Louise* p. 6 **67.** ed. Latimer, *Talks* p. 135 **68.** Lavalette, *Memoirs* p. 99 **69.** ed. Roncière, *Letters to Marie-Louise* pp. 19–20 **70.** ed. Bingham, *Selection* III p. 24 **71.** ed. Roncière, *Letters to Marie-Louise* p. 33 **72.** Chevallier, *Empire Style* p. 60 **73.** Bausset, *Private Memoirs* p. 279 **74.** Palmer, *Napoleon and Marie Louise* p. 99 **75.** ed. Metternich, *Memoirs* I p. 279 **76.** ed. Latimer, *Talks* pp. 136–7 **77.** ed. Latimer, *Talks* p. 137 **78.** Clary-et-Aldringen, *Trois mois à Paris*

pp. 70–71   79. Woloch, *French Veteran* p. 314   80. Branda, *Le prix de la gloire*,
p. 52, Philip Mansel in *TLS* 16/1/2004, p. 23   81. NYPL Napoleon I folder 3
82. Palmer, *Alexander I* p. 189   83. ed. Lacour-Gayet, *Chancellor Pasquier* p. 108
84. CG5 no. 10517 p. 543, August 6, 1805   85. Jordan, *Napoleon and the
Revolution* p. ix   86. Masson, *Napoleon and his Coronation* p. 313   87. Gildea,
Children of the Revolution p. 183   88. Stourton and Montefiore, *The British as
Art Collectors* p. 153   89. O'Brien, 'Antonio Canova's Napoleon' pp. 354–5
90. O'Brien, 'Antonio Canova's Napoleon' p. 358   91. Chevallier, *Empire Style*
p. 8   92. Wilson-Smith, *Napoleon and His Artists* p. xxix   93. Chevallier,
Empire Style passim, Wilson-Smith, *Napoleon and His Artists passim*   94. CG8
no. 18931 p. 1083, September 15, 1808   95. Horward, 'Masséna and Napoleon'
p. 84   96. Horward, *Napoleon and Iberia* p. 29   97. Chaptal, *Souvenirs* p. 304
98. Johnson, *Napoleon's Cavalry* p. 94   99. ed. Bingham, *Selection* II p. 472
100. Blaze, *Life in Napoleon's Army* p. 141   101. ed. Bingham, *Selection* III
p. 42   102. Woolf, *Ouvrard* p. 115   103. ed. Bingham, *Selection* III p. 42
104. Pelet, *Napoleon in Council* p. 96, Brice, *Riddle of Napoleon* p. 139
105. Woolf, *Ouvrard* pp. 116–18   106. Knight, *Britain Against Napoleon* p. 404 n
107. Mollien, *Mémoires* II p. 444   108. CN23 no. 18636, p. 359   109. Melvin,
Napoleon's Navigation System pp. 238–9   110. Palmer, *Alexander I* p. 195
111. Schmitt, '1812' pp. 326–7   112. ed. Roncière, *Letters to Marie-Louise*
p. 63   113. Rovigo, *Mémoires* IV p. 346   114. CN21 no. 16762 pp. 12–29
115. ed. Bingham, *Selection* III p. 50

23. RUSSIA

Tsar Alexander to Caulaincourt comes from Promyslov, 'The Grande Armée's
Retreat' p. 131 n. 34   Napoleon on St Helena comes from ed. Latimer, *Talks*
p. 210   1. Faber, *Sketches* pp. 187–8   2. Faber, *Sketches* p. 191   3. ed. Bingham, *Selection* III p. 69   4. CN21 nos. 17179 and 17187 pp. 297–302   5. Clark,
Iron Kingdom p. 353, Méneval, *Napoléon et Marie Louise* I p. 342, Palmer, *Alexander I* p. 199n   6. Cate, *Two Emperors* p. xiii   7. Lentz, *L'Effondrement* p.
202   8. Riehn, *Napoleon's Russian Campaign* p. 33   9. Riehn, *Napoleon's Russian Campaign* pp. 34–5   10. Clark, *Iron Kingdom* p. 317   11. ed. Lentz, *1810*
p. 306   12. ed. Chatel de Brancion, *Cambacérès* II p. 387   13. Thiers, *History
of France* XII p. 477   14. ed. Summerville, *Napoleon's Expedition to Russia*
p. 6, Bausset, *Private Memoirs* p. 290   15. Rudé, *Revolutionary Europe* p. 251,
Knight, *Britain Against Napoleon* ch. 13   16. Cobban, *Modern France* II
p. 52   17. Schroeder, 'Napoleon's Foreign Policy' p. 156   18. Gates, 'The Wars
of 1812' p. 48   19. Fain, *Manuscrit de 1812* I pp. 3–4   20. Fain, *Manuscrit de
1812* I p. 9   21. Knight, *Britain Against Napoleon* p. 412   22. Knight, *Britain
Against Napoleon* pp. 410–12   23. ed. Gielgud, *Prince Adam Czartoryski* II
p. 214   24. ed. Gielgud, *Prince Adam Czartoryski* II p. 216   25. ed. Gielgud,
Prince Adam Czartoryski II p. 221   26. Lieven, *Russia against Napoleon passim*   27. eds. Kagan and Higham, *Military History of Tsarist Russia* pp. 115–16,

Palmer, *Alexander I* p. 201   28. Méneval, *Napoléon et Marie Louise* I pp. 341–2   29. Palmer, *Alexander I* p. 199   30. Nafziger, *Napoleon's Invasion of Russia* p. 85   31. ed. Bingham, *Selection* III p. 84   32. Mowat, *The Diplomacy of Napoleon* p. 253   33. Palmer, *Alexander I* p. 202   34. ed. Bingham, *Selection* III p. 89   35. ed. Lentz, *1810* pp. 307–8, ed. Chatel de Brancion, *Cambacérès* II p. 391   36. ed. Lentz, *1810* p. 309   37. Bausset, *Private Memoirs* p. 290   38. Lavalette, *Memoirs* p. 102   39. Rovigo, *Mémoires* V p. 147   40. ed. Latimer, *Talks* pp. 152–3   41. Lavalette, *Memoirs* p. 102   42. Musée de la Préfecture de Police   43. ed. Cerf, *Letters to Josephine* p. 231   44. D'Abrantès, *At the Court* p. 360   45. ed. Latimer, *Talks* p. 153   46. ed. Bingham, *Selection* III p. 98   47. Esdaile, 'Recent Writing' p. 219, Lipscombe, *Peninsular War Atlas* p. 25   48. Alexander, 'French Replacement Methods' p. 196   49. ed. Bingham, *Selection* III p. 135   50. Parker, 'Why Did Napoleon Invade Russia?' p. 132   51. Whitcomb, *Napoleon's Diplomatic Service* pp. 152–8   52. Palmer, *Alexander I* p. 203   53. Palmer, *Alexander I* p. 203   54. ed. Bingham, *Selection* III p. 110   55. ed. Lacour-Gayet, *Chancellor Pasquier* p. 112   56. ed. Lacour-Gayet, *Chancellor Pasquier* p. 114   57. CN23, no. 18568 p. 302   58. Bergeron, *France Under Napoleon* pp. 102–3   59. Palmer, *Alexander I* pp. 204–5   60. Palmer, *Alexander I* p. 205   61. AN AF IV 1656   62. McLynn, *Napoleon* p. 499   63. SHD GR 4.C/73   64. Cate, *Two Emperors* p. 70   65. Palmer, *Alexander I* p. 207   66. Palmer, *Alexander I* p. 207, Arboit, '1812: Le Renseignement Russe' p. 86, ed. Lentz, *1810* p. 310, Fain, *Manuscrit de 1812* I p. 27, Bausset, *Private Memoirs* p. 289   67. ed. Chatel de Brancion, *Cambacérès* II p. 391   68. Buckland, *Metternich* p. 219   69. Palmer, *Alexander I* p. 208, Mowat, *Diplomacy of Napoleon* p. 254   70. Fain, *Manuscrit de 1812* I pp. 81–2   71. AN AF IV 1654   72. CN23 no. 18420, p. 160   73. CN23 no. 18523 p. 253   74. Fain, *Manuscrit de 1812* I pp. 16–19   75. Fain, *Manuscrit de 1812* I pp. 49–50   76. Pradt, *Histoire de l'Ambassade* p. 122   77. CG12 no. 30343 p. 429, March 30, 1812   78. Fain, *Manuscrit de 1812* I p. 32   79. Fain, *Manuscrit de 1812* I p. 310   80. Fain, *Manuscrit de 1812* I p. 311   81. CN12 no. 30225 p. 374   82. Dague, 'Henri Clarke' pp. 2–3   83. Simms, *Europe* p. 170, Fain, *Manuscrit de 1812* I pp. 57–8   84. CN23 no. 18652 p. 371   85. CG12 no. 30492 p. 517, April 25, 1812   86. ed. Lacour-Gayet, *Chancellor Pasquier* p. 119   87. ed. Lacour-Gayet, *Chancellor Pasquier* p. 118   88. ed. Metternich, *Memoirs* I p. 122   89. ed. Roncière, *Letters to Marie-Louise* p. 49   90. Cate, *Two Emperors* p. 127   91. ed. Ernouf, *Souvenirs* pp. 232–3   92. CG12 nos. 30799–30827 pp. 666–77, June 4, 1812   93. Rapp, *Memoirs* pp. 168–9   94. Fain, *Manuscrit de 1812* I pp. 88–9   95. Forrest, *Napoleon* p. 199, Evstafiev, *Resources of Russia* p. 6   96. CN23 no. 18855 p. 528   97. *TLS* 10/4/1959 p. 206, ed. Roncière, *Letters to Marie-Louise* p. 68, Soltyk, *Napoléon en 1812* pp. 8–10   98. ed. Summerville, *Napoleon's Expedition to Russia* p. 15   99. ed. Summerville, *Napoleon's Expedition to Russia* p. 15   100. Ashby, *Napoleon against Great Odds* p. 1, Weigley, *Age of Battles* p. 443, ed. Bingham, *Selection* III p. 136, Gill, *With Eagles to Glory* p. 9   101. Schroeder, 'Napoleon's Foreign Policy' p. 153   102. Gill, *With Eagles to Glory* p. 9   103. ed. Raeff, *Foot Soldier* p. xxiii   104. ed. Summerville,

Napoleon's Expedition to Russia p. 12   105. Lochet, 'Destruction of the Grande
Armée' passim, Rothenberg, Art of Warfare p. 128   106. Lochet, 'Destruction
of the Grande Armée' passim   107. Lochet, 'Destruction of the Grande Armée'
passim, Nafziger, Napoleon's Invasion of Russia p. 86   108. ed. Summerville,
Napoleon's Expedition to Russia p. 12   109. Merridale, Red Fortress p. 211

24. TRAPPED

Champagny's quote comes from Champagny, Souvenirs p. 142   Lord Montgomery's quote comes from Hansard Fifth Series House of Lords vol. ccxli col.
227   1. ed. Summerville, Napoleon's Expedition to Russia p. 17   2. ed. Roncière, Letters to Marie-Louise p. 67   3. CG12 no. 31046 p. 775, June 25, 1812
4. CG12 no. 31066 p. 786, June 30, 1812   5. Soltyk, Napoléon en 1812
pp. 35–8   6. Davies, Vanished Kingdoms p. 293   7. Zamoyski, 1812 pp. 161–3
8. CN24, no. 18962 p. 61   9. Coignet, Captain Coignet p. 201   10. ed. Brett-
James, Eyewitness Accounts p. 53   11. AN 400AP/81/pp. 22–5   12. Fain,
Manuscrit de 1812 I p. 188   13. Dumas, Memoirs II p. 232   14. AN
400AP/81/p. 30   15. CG12 no. 31077 p. 793, July 1, 1812   16. ed. Roncière,
Letters to Marie-Louise p. 75   17. CG12 no. 31068 p. 787, July 1, 1812
18. CG12 no. 31068 pp. 787–90, July 1, 1812   19. Chaptal, Souvenirs p. 302
20. Lieven, Russia against Napoleon p. 219   21. ed. Castellane, Journal I
p. 113   22. ed. Summerville, Napoleon's Expedition to Russia p. 25   23. ed.
Summerville, Napoleon's Expedition to Russia p. 26   24. Cartwright and Biddiss, Disease and History p. 91   25. ed. Hanoteau, With Napoleon in Russia
pp. 66–7   26. CG12 no. 51150 p. 829, July 8, 1812   27. ed. Brett-James, Eyewitness Accounts p. 47   28. Cartwright and Biddiss, Disease and History pp. 83ff
29. Cartwright and Biddiss, Disease and History p. 91   30. CG12 no. 31201
p. 858, July 12, 1812   31. Rose, Napoleon's Campaign in Russia pp. 101–2
32. Rose, Napoleon's Campaign in Russia p. 182   33. Cobb, Police and the
People p. 111 n. 1   34. Prinzing, Epidemics Resulting from Wars p. 106
35. Kerckhove, Histoire des maladies p. 405   36. Kerckhove, Histoire des mala-
dies pp. 406–7   37. Gourgaud, Napoleon and the Grand Army p. 12   38. ed.
Castellane, Journal I p. 113   39. CG12 no. 31184 p. 847, July 10, 1812   40. ed.
Brett-James, Eyewitness Accounts p. 51   41. ed. Brett-James, Eyewitness
Accounts p. 53   42. Austin, 1812 p. 160   43. Saint-Denis, Napoleon from the
Tuileries p. 66   44. Rossetti, 'Journal' pp. 217–19   45. CG12 no. 31261 p. 889,
July 19, 1812   46. Rossetti, 'Journal' pp. 217–19   47. ed. Hanoteau, With
Napoleon in Russia p. 634   48. ed. Markham, Imperial Glory p. 262, Smith,
Data Book p. 382   49. CG12 no. 31335 p. 926, July 26, 1812   50. CG12 nos.
31291, 31337 p. 904, July 22, 1812, p. 927, July 26, 1812   51. ed. Summerville,
Napoleon's Expedition to Russia p. 34   52. ed. Summerville, Napoleon's Exped-
ition to Russia p. 35   53. Labaume, The Crime of 1812 p. 80   54. ed.
Summerville, Napoleon's Expedition to Russia p. 36   55. CG12 no. 31396
p. 952, August 2, 1812   56. ed. Summerville, Napoleon's Expedition to Russia

p. 38   57. Nicolson, *Napoleon: 1812* p. 99   58. ed. Roncière, *Letters to Marie-Louise* p. 86   59. ed. Summerville, *Napoleon's Expedition to Russia* p. 40   60. CG12 no. 31435 p. 971, August 7, 1812   61. ed. Summerville, *Napoleon's Expedition to Russia* p. 44   62. ed. Summerville, *Napoleon's Expedition to Russia* p. 45   63. ed. Summerville, *Napoleon's Expedition to Russia* pp. 41–4   64. Fain, *Manuscrit de 1812* I pp. 321–4   65. ed. Castellane, *Journal* I p. 112   66. ed. Summerville, *Napoleon's Expedition to Russia* p. 50, ed. Haythornthwaite, *Final Verdict* p. 223   67. ed. Summerville, *Napoleon's Expedition to Russia* p. 284 n. 5   68. ed. Summerville, *Napoleon's Expedition to Russia* p. 67   69. ed. Latimer, *Talks* p. 159   70. Rossetti, 'Journal' pp. 232–3   71. Rapp, *Memoirs* p. 193   72. ed. Summerville, *Napoleon's Expedition to Russia* pp. 61–2   73. ed. Summerville, *Napoleon's Expedition to Russia* p. 61   74. Lochet, 'The Destruction of the Grande Armée' *passim*   75. ed. Summerville, *Napoleon's Expedition to Russia* p. 68   76. ed. Summerville, *Napoleon's Expedition to Russia* p. 265   77. CG12 no. 31608 pp. 1046–7, August 26, 1812   78. ed. Kerry, *The First Napoleon* p. 20   79. Girod de l'Ain, *Dix ans* pp. 252–4   80. CG12 no. 31610 p. 1047, August 26, 1812   81. Wesling, *Napoleon* p. 154   82. CG12 no. 31659 p. 1071, September 2, 1812   83. CG12 no. 31666 p. 1075, September 3, 1812   84. CG12 no. 31671 pp. 1076–7, September 3, 1812   85. Cartwright and Biddiss, *Disease and History* p. 94   86. Fain, *Manuscrit de 1812* II p. 8   87. Castelot, *La Campagne* p. 143.   88. Bausset, *Private Memoirs* p. 315, Weigley, *Age of Battles* p. 449, Cartwright and Biddiss, *Disease and History* p. 94, Forrest, *Napoleon* p. 308   89. ed. Summerville, *Napoleon's Expedition to Russia* p. 82, TLS 10/4/1959 p. 206, Brett-James, *Eyewitness Accounts* p. 131   90. ed. Bell, *Baron Lejeune* II pp. 216–18   91. Rapp, *Memoirs* p. 201, ed. Bell, *Baron Lejeune* II pp. 205–6, Fain, *Manuscrit de 1812* II p. 11   92. CN24 no. 19182 p. 207   93. Rapp, *Memoirs* p. 202   94. Rapp, *Memoirs* p. 203   95. Fain, *Manuscrit de 1812* II p. 19   96. ed. Summerville, *Napoleon's Expedition to Russia* p. 75   97. ed. Summerville, *Napoleon's Expedition to Russia* p. 82   98. Fain, *Manuscrit de 1812* II p. 41   99. ed. Summerville, *Napoleon's Expedition to Russia* p. 73   100. Headley, *Imperial Guard* p. 127   101. Headley, *Imperial Guard* p. 127   102. Bausset, *Private Memoirs* p. 320   103. Rapp, *Memoirs* p. 208   104. ed. Summerville, *Napoleon's Expedition to Russia* pp. 82, 84   105. ed. Summerville, *Napoleon's Expedition to Russia* p. 73   106. Smith, *Data Book* pp. 389–90   107. CG12 no. 31678 p. 1080, September 8, 1812   108. Bausset, *Private Memoirs* p. 319   109. ed. Latimer, *Talks* p. 158   110. Dumas, *Memoirs* II p. 440   111. Fain, *Manuscrit de 1812* II p. 45   112. Pawly, *Red Lancers* pp. 37–8   113. ed. North, *With Napoleon's Guard* p. 61   114. ed. Summerville, *Napoleon's Expedition to Russia* p. 70

25. RETREAT

Napoleon's military maxim comes from ed. Chandler, *Napoleon's Military Maxims* p. 57   1. Bausset, *Private Memoirs* p. 319   2. ed. Summerville, *Napoleon's Expedition to Russia* p. 86   3. CG12 no. 31708 p. 1091, September 10, 1812

4. Palmer, *Napoleon in Russia* p. 132   5. ed. Brett-James, *Eyewitness Accounts* p. 144, Merridale, *Red Fortress* p. 211   6. Vaskin, 'Three Mistakes of Napoleon' p. 1, Soltyk, *Napoléon en 1812* pp. 26–70   7. ed. Summerville, *Napoleon's Expedition to Russia* p. 90   8. ed. Brett-James, *Eyewitness Accounts* p. 172   9. ed. Summerville, *Napoleon's Expedition to Russia* p. 90, Olivier, *Burning of Moscow* p. 43   10. Merridale, *Red Fortress* p. 212   11. ed. Summerville, *Napoleon's Expedition to Russia* p. 90   12. Merridale, *Red Fortress* p. 211   13. Olivier, *Burning of Moscow* p. 189, Rostopchine, *L'Incendie de Moscou* p. 103   14. Rapp, *Memoirs* p. 210, ed. Kerry, *The First Napoleon* p. 24, Merridale, *Red Fortress* p. 216   15. Cockburn, *Buonaparte's Voyage* p. 18   16. Merridale, *Red Fortress* p. 216   17. ed. Summerville, *Napoleon's Expedition to Russia* p. 96   18. ed. Summerville, *Napoleon's Expedition to Russia* p. 94   19. ed. Summerville, *Napoleon's Expedition to Russia* p. 97   20. Merridale, *Red Fortress* p. 211   21. ed. Fleischmann, *L'Épopée Impériale* p. 266   22. Peyrusse, *Mémorial et Archives* p. 97   23. Merridale, *Red Fortress* p. 211   24. Ebrington, *Memorandum* p. 12   25. Ebrington, *Memorandum* p. 12   26. Merridale, *Red Fortress* p. 211   27. SHD GR C2/167   28. Fain, *Manuscrit de 1812* II pp. 93–94   29. Fain, *Manuscrit de 1812* II p. 95   30. Fain, *Manuscrit de 1812* II p. 96   31. Fain, *Manuscrit de 1812* II p. 97   32. ed. Summerville, *Napoleon's Expedition to Russia* p. 100   33. ed. Latimer, *Talks* p. 158   34. eds. Kagan and Higham, *Military History of Tsarist Russia* p. 118   35. Fain, *Manuscrit de 1812* II p. 99   36. CG12 no. 31731 p. 1101, September 18, 1812   37. CG12 no. 31736 p. 1103, September 20, 1812   38. ed. Bingham, *Selection* III p. 176   39. ed. North, *With Napoleon's Guard* p. 37   40. SHD GR C2/524, Austin, *1812* pp. 156–7   41. ed. Castellane, *Journal* I p. 161   42. Bausset, *Private Memoirs* pp. 330–31   43. Rapp, *Memoirs* p. 210   44. Merridale, *Red Fortress* p. 215   45. Lieven, *Russia against Napoleon* pp. 89, 134–5   46. CG12 no. 31411 p. 959, August 5, 1812   47. ed. Bingham, *Selection* III p. 199   48. ed. Summerville, *Napoleon's Expedition to Russia* p. 109   49. CG12 no. 31862 pp. 1160–61, October 6, 1812   50. CG12 no. 31863 p. 1161, October 6, 1812   51. Fain, *Manuscrit de 1812* II p. 55   52. Fain, *Manuscrit de 1812* II pp. 151–2   53. Fain, *Manuscrit de 1812* II p. 152   54. Bausset, *Private Memoirs* p. 336   55. ed. Roncière, *Letters to Marie-Louise* p. 115   56. Adlerfeld, *King Charles XII* III p. 96n   57. Fain, *Manuscrit de 1812* II p. 152   58. Labaume, *Crime of 1812* p. 168   59. Smith, *Data Book* p. 395, ed. Summerville, *Napoleon's Expedition to Russia* p. 123, Rothenberg, *Art of Warfare* p. 130   60. ed. Castellane, *Journal* I p. 171   61. CG12 nos. 31938, 31941 pp. 1201–3, October 18, 1812   62. Merridale, *Red Fortress* p. 215   63. CG12 no. 31958 p. 1211, October 21, 1812   64. Austin, *1812* p. 184   65. Labaume, *Crime of 1812* p. 183   66. ed. Summerville, *Napoleon's Expedition to Russia* pp. 132–5, Bausset, *Private Memoirs* p. 33, Fain, *Manuscrit de 1812* II p. 250   67. ed. Hanoteau, *With Napoleon in Russia* p. 298   68. Fain, *Manuscrit de 1812* II p. 253   69. CG12 no. 32019 p. 1240, November 6, 1812   70. ed. Summerville, *Napoleon's Expedition to Russia* pp. 136–8   71. ed. Summerville, *Napoleon's Expedition to Russia* pp. 136–8   72. ed. Summerville, *Napoleon's Expedition to Russia* p. 138   73. CG12 no.

31971 p. 1219, October 26, 1812 74. ed. Latimer, *Talks* p. 159 75. Labaume, *Crime of 1812* p. 185 76. Labaume, *Crime of 1812* p. 186 77. Labaume, *Crime of 1812* p. 189 78. Labaume, *Crime of 1812* p. 193 79. Labaume, *Crime of 1812* p. 195 80. Labaume, *Crime of 1812* p. 218 81. Wilson, *Narrative of Events* pp. 225–60 82. Labaume, *Crime of 1812* p. 163 83. Labaume, *Crime of 1812* p. 206 84. Bell, *First Total War* p. 261 85. *The Nation*, 16/7/1896 p. 45 86. ed. Tulard, *Cambacérès: lettres inédites* p. 14 87. Emsley, *Gendarmes and the State* p. 62, Rovigo, *Mémoires* VI pp. 4, 53, Lavalette, *Memoirs* pp. 105–9, Lentz, *La conspiration du Général Malet* p. 271n, Cobban, *Modern France* II p. 60, ed. Lacour-Gayet, *Chancellor Pasquier* pp. 120–21, eds. Dwyer and McPhee, *The French Revolution and Napoleon* p. 188 88. Dague, 'Henri Clarke' p. 10 n. 25 89. ed. Noailles, *Count Molé* p. 129 90. Lavalette, *Memoirs* p. 109 91. Fain, *Manuscrit de 1812* II p. 285 92. Guérard, *Reflections* p. 91 93. ed. Brett-James, *Eyewitness Accounts* pp. 233–9 94. Langeron, *Mémoires de Langeron* p. 93 95. Wilson, *Narrative of Events* pp. 255–60 96. eds. Hennet and Martin, *Lettres interceptées* p. 319 97. CG12 no. 32026 p. 1242 98. Labaume, *Crime of 1812* p. 224 99. Rose, *Napoleon's Campaign in Russia* p. 105 100. Smith, *Data Book* p. 404 101. ed. Bingham, *Selection* III p. 184 102. Bausset, *Private Memoirs* p. 349 103. ed. Brett-James, *Eyewitness Accounts* p. 207 104. Bausset, *Private Memoirs* p. 350 105. Langeron, *Mémoires de Langeron* p. 89 106. ed. Cisterne, *Journal de marche* pp. 140–45 107. Mikaberidze, *The Battle of the Berezina passim* 108. Rossetti, 'Journal du Général Rossetti' p. 33 109. CG12 no. 32071 p. 1270, November 24, 1812 110. Saint-Cyr, *Mémoires* III pp. 230–31 111. ed. Cisterne, *Journal de marche* pp. 140–45 112. Rossetti, 'Journal du Général Rossetti' p. 37 113. Fain, *Manuscrit de 1812* II p. 329 114. ed. Cisterne, *Journal de marche* pp. 140–45 115. ed. Cisterne, *Journal de marche* pp. 140–45 116. ed. Cisterne, *Journal de marche* pp. 140–45 117. ed. Brett-James, *Eyewitness Accounts* p. 256 118. ed. Brett-James, *Eyewitness Accounts* pp. 256–7 119. Rossetti, 'Journal du Général Rossetti' p. 39 120. Rossetti, 'Journal du Général Rossetti' p. 38 121. ed. Brett-James, *Eyewitness Accounts* p. 258 122. ed. Brett-James, *Eyewitness Accounts* p. 246 123. ed. Raeff, *Napoleonic Foot Soldier* p. 81 124. Kiley, *Once There Were Titans* p. 196 125. CG12 no. 32079 p. 1276, November 27, 1812 126. ed. Brett-James, *Eyewitness Accounts* p. 260 127. Langeron, *Mémoires de Langeron* p. 218 128. ed. Brett-James, *Eyewitness Accounts* p. 262 129. CG12 no. 32084 p. 1278, November 29, 1812 130. ed. Markham, *Imperial Glory* pp. 310–13 131. Clark, *Iron Kingdom* p. 356 132. Namier, *Vanished Supremacies* pp. 1–3 133. ed. Noailles, *Count Molé* p. 164 134. Clark, *Iron Kingdom* pp. 358–90 135. CN24 no. 19490, p. 430 136. ed. Hanoteau, *With Napoleon in Russia* I p. 203 137. Cartwright and Biddiss, *Disease and History* p. 98 138. Schneid, 'The Dynamics of Defeat' pp. 7–8 139. Labaume, *Crime of 1812* p. 205 140. *The Nation* 16/7/1896 p. 46 141. Rapp, *Memoirs* p. 250 142. ed. Bingham, *Selection* III p. 195 143. Fain, *Manuscrit de 1813* I p. 8 144. Rapp, *Memoirs* p. 24 145. SHD GR21.YC/679 146. SHD GR21.YC/36 147. Kiley, *Once*

There Were Titans p. 293 n. 3   **148.** ed. Raeff, *Napoleonic Foot Soldier* p. xxvi   **149.** Schneid, 'The Dynamics of Defeat' p. 12   **150.** Eidahl, 'Marshal Oudinot' p. 14, Labaume, *Crime of 1812* p. 233   **151.** ed. Brett-James, *Eyewitness Accounts* p. 282

26. RESILIENCE

Molé to Napoleon comes from ed. Noailles, *Count Molé* p. 193   Metternich on Napoleon comes from ed. Metternich, *Memoirs* I p. 283   **1.** Saint-Cyr, *Mémoires* IV p. 2   **2.** ed. Noailles, *Count Molé* p. 138   **3.** ed. Hanoteau, *Memoirs of Queen Hortense* II p. 51   **4.** Bowden, *Napoleon's Grande Armée* pp. 27–8, CN25 no. 19689 p. 51   **5.** ed. Noailles, *Count Molé* p. 147, Lamy, 'La cavalerie française' p. 40   **6.** Schroeder, 'Napoleon's Foreign Policy' p. 152   **7.** ed. Butler, *Baron Thiébault* II p. 373   **8.** Blaze, *Life in Napoleon's Army* p. 3   **9.** ed. Chandler, *Napoleon's Marshals* pp. 30–32   **10.** CN24 no. 19388 p. 341   **11.** ed. Bingham, *Selection* III p. 209   **12.** Evstafiev, *Memorable Predictions* p. 71   **13.** Fain, *Manuscrit de 1813* I p. 8   **14.** CN24 no. 19462 p. 402   **15.** CN24 no. 19424 p. 368   **16.** CN24 no. 19402 p. 354   **17.** Fain, *Manuscrit de 1813* I pp. 193–5   **18.** Bausset, *Private Memoirs* p. 373   **19.** ed. Noailles, *Count Molé* p. 168   **20.** ed. Noailles, *Count Molé* p. 156   **21.** CN25 no. 19910 p. 232   **22.** ed. Noailles, *Count Molé* p. 161   **23.** ed. Noailles, *Count Molé* p. 161   **24.** ed. Noailles, *Count Molé* p. 162   **25.** ed. Noailles, *Count Molé* p. 163   **26.** ed. Noailles, *Count Molé* p. 172   **27.** Fain, *Manuscrit de 1813* I pp. 77, 219–23   **28.** CN24 no. 19581 p. 520   **29.** Schmidt, 'Idea and Slogan' pp. 610–13   **30.** McPhee, *Social History* p. 87, Woloch, *New Regime* pp. 152–3   **31.** CN24 no. 19608 p. 539   **32.** CN24 no. 19457 p. 397   **33.** CN24 no. 19625 p. 556   **34.** Simms, *Struggle for Mastery* pp. 75–82   **35.** Simms, *Europe* p. 173   **36.** Leggiere, *Napoleon and Berlin passim*   **37.** CN27 no. 21231 pp. 150–51   **38.** CN25 no. 19664 p. 30   **39.** CN25 no. 19688 pp. 46–51   **40.** CN25 no. 19706 pp. 70–72   **41.** CN25 no. 19659 p. 25   **42.** CN25 no. 19632 p. 5   **43.** CN25 no. 19640 p. 9   **44.** ed. Noailles, *Count Molé* p. 193   **45.** ed. Noailles, *Count Molé* p. 194   **46.** ed. Noailles, *Count Molé* p. 195   **47.** Ashby, *Napoleon against Great Odds* p. 15   **48.** ed. Roncière, *Letters to Marie-Louise* p. 140   **49.** CN25 no. 19647 p. 15   **50.** CN25 no. 19914 pp. 235–6   **51.** Johnson, *Napoleon's Cavalry* p. 22   **52.** CN25 no. 19941 p. 253   **53.** CN25 no. 19977 p. 276   **54.** Bausset, *Private Memoirs* p. 375   **55.** Wood, 'Forgotten Sword' p. 81   **56.** Fain, *Manuscrit de 1813* I p. 349   **57.** Brett-James, *Europe Against Napoleon* p. 23   **58.** CN25 no. 19951 pp. 258–62   **59.** Brett-James, *Europe Against Napoleon* p. 24   **60.** ed. Roncière, *Letters to Marie-Louise* p. 149   **61.** CN25 no. 19963 pp. 268–9   **62.** ed. Markham, *Imperial Glory* pp. 33–7   **63.** CN25 no. 19899 pp. 222–3   **64.** ed. Roncière, *Letters to Marie-Louise* p. 152, Fain, *Manuscrit de 1813* I pp. 374–7   **65.** CN25 no. 19994 p. 285   **66.** ed. Roncière, *Letters to Marie-Louise* p. 154   **67.** ed. Bingham, *Selection* III p. 240   **68.** CN25 no. 20017 pp. 299–300   **69.** ed. Roncière,

Letters to Marie-Louise p. 157 70. CN25 no. 20029 and 20030 pp. 307–8
71. Rovigo, *Mémoires* VI p. 102 72. ed. Roncière, *Letters to Marie-Louise*
p. 158 73. CN25 no. 20042 pp. 321–2 74. Ebrington, *Memorandum* pp.
18–19 75. ed. Roncière, *Letters to Marie-Louise* p. 160 76. CN25 no. 20096
p. 368 77. CN25 no. 20070 pp. 346–7 78. Clark, *Iron Kingdom* p. 365
79. CN25 no. 20140 pp. 393–7 80. CN25 no. 20070 p. 347 81. Fain, *Manuscrit de 1813* I p. 449 82. ed. Bingham, *Selection* III p. 250 83. Fain, *Manuscrit de 1813* II pp. 26–31 84. Fain, *Manuscrit de 1813* II pp. 26–31 85. Fain,
Manuscrit de 1813 II pp. 26–31 86. CN25 no. 20119 p. 382 87. Bausset,
Private Memoirs p. 383 88. ed. Roncière, *Letters to Marie-Louise* p. 169
89. Price, 'Napoleon and Metternich in 1813' pp. 482–503 90. Price, 'Napoleon
and Metternich in 1813' p. 503, CN25 no. 20175 pp. 423–6, Fain, *Manuscrit de
1813* II pp. 36–42, Ashby, *Napoleon against Great Odds* p. 15, ed. Metternich,
Memoirs I p. 413 n. 67 and II pp. 538–40 91. Price, 'Napoleon and Metternich
in 1813' p. 501 92. CN25 no. 20175 pp. 423–6 93. Price, 'Napoleon and
Metternich in 1813' pp. 494, 503 94. ed. Metternich, *Memoirs* I pp. 185–8
95. ed. Metternich, *Memoirs* I p. 190 96. CN25 no. 20175 pp. 423–6 97. ed.
Roncière, *Letters to Marie-Louise* p. 169 98. ed. Roncière, *Letters to Marie-Louise* p. 171 99. ed. Latimer, *Talks* p. 143 100. ed. Roncière, *Letters
to Marie-Louise* pp. 171–2 101. Sked, *Radetsky* p. 41 102. Fain, *Manuscrit
de 1813* II pp. 79–80 103. CN26 no. 20327 pp. 2–3 104. Fain, *Manuscrit de
1813* II p. 93

27. LEIPZIG

Le Moniteur statement comes from CN10 no. 8237 p. 116 Military Maxim No.
25 comes from ed. Chandler, *Military Maxims* p. 145 1. ed. Walter, *Las Cases*
p. xv 2. Odeleben, *Circumstantial Narrative* II p. 189 3. Lamy, 'La cavalerie
française' pp. 42–3 4. Menzl, *Germany* IV p. 1585 5. CN26 no. 20375 pp.
48–9 6. CN26 no. 20360 pp. 34–6 7. Chandler, *Campaigns of Napoleon*
pp. 900–902 8. Gallaher, 'Political Considerations and Strategy' p. 68 n. 2
9. Gallaher, 'Political Considerations and Strategy' p. 68 10. CN26 nos. 20381
and 20390 pp. 71–2, 80–82 11. ed. Roncière, *Letters to Marie-Louise*
p. 184 12. ed. Roncière, *Letters to Marie-Louise* p. 186 13. Eidahl, 'Marshal
Oudinot' p. 15 14. ed. Roncière, *Letters to Marie-Louise* p. 186 15. CN26 no.
20445 pp. 118–19 16. ed. Bingham, *Selection* III p. 262 17. Karlen, *Napoleon's
Glands* p. 11 18. ed. Chandler, *Military Maxims* p. 165 19. *TLS* 12/5/1927
p. 325 20. Smith, *Data Book* pp. 443–5 21. ed. Latimer, *Talks* p. 254 and
n. 1 22. ed. Bingham, *Selection* III p. 266 23. ed. Roncière, *Letters to Marie-Louise* p. 190 24. ed. Roncière, *Letters to Marie-Louise* pp. 190–91 25. ed.
Roncière, *Letters to Marie-Louise* p. 191 26. CN26 no. 20482 p. 147 27. ed.
Bingham, *Selection* III p. 267 28. Clark, *Iron Kingdom* p. 367, Nafziger, *Napoleon
at Leipzig* p. 70 29. Chandler, *On the Napoleonic Wars* p. 112 30. Smith, *Data
Book* pp. 446–7 31. eds. Tulard and Garros, *Itinéraire* p. 423, Fain, *Manuscrit*

de 1813 II p. 312   32. eds. Tulard and Garros, *Itineraire* p. 423, Fain, *Manuscrit de 1813* II p. 312   33. CN26 no. 20546 p. 190   34. ed. Butler, *Baron Thiébault* II p. 381   35. Fain, *Manuscrit de 1813* II pp. 351–2   36. ed. Bingham, *Selection* III p. 277   37. Shoberl, *Narrative* p. vii   38. CN26 no. 20791–3 pp. 349–52   39. Odeleben, *Circumstantial Narrative* II p. 312   40. Odeleben, *Circumstantial Narrative* II pp. 315–16   41. Odeleben, *Circumstantial Narrative* I p. 187, CN26 no. 20809 pp. 361–2   42. Clark, *Iron Kingdom* p. 367   43. Smith, *Data Book* pp. 461–70, Lamy, 'La cavalerie française' p. 43   44. ed. Fleischmann, *L'Épopée Imperiale* p. 323   45. Nafziger, *Napoleon at Leipzig* p. 113   46. ed. Pope, *Cassell Dictionary* p. 299   47. Fain, *Manuscrit de 1813* II pp. 410–11   48. Fain, *Manuscrit de 1813* II p. 412   49. eds. Tulard and Garros, *Itinéraire* p. 426   50. Brett-James, *Europe Against Napoleon* p. 164   51. Bruyere-Ostells, *Leipzig* p. 177   52. Nafziger, *Napoleon at Leipzig* p. 189   53. eds. Nafziger et al., *Poles and Saxons* pp. 244–5   54. Smith, *1813 Leipzig* p. 188   55. Smith, *1813 Leipzig* p. 189   56. Fain, *Manuscrit de 1813* II p. 432   57. Odeleben, *Circumstantial Narrative* II p. 42n   58. Odeleben, *Circumstantial Narrative* II p. 43   59. ed. Davis, *Original Journals* p. 400, CN26 no. 20830 p. 378   60. Clark, *Iron Kingdom* p. 371   61. ed. Brindle, *With Napoleon's Guns* p. 187n   62. Odeleben, *Circumstantial Narrative* II p. 45n   63. ed. Haythornthwaite, *Final Verdict* p. 300   64. Ashby, *Napoleon against Great Odds* p. 17   65. CN26 no. 20830 pp. 374–9   66. ed. Roncière, *Letters to Marie-Louise* p. 200   67. ed. Barrès, *Memoirs* p. 193   68. Fain, *Memoirs of the Invasion* p. 1   69. ed. Lacour-Gayet, *Chancellor Pasquier* p. 139   70. Koebner, *Empire* p. 284, Fain, *Memoirs of the Invasion* p. 6   71. Fain, *Memoirs of the Invasion* p. 8   72. CN26 no. 20886 p. 424   73. CN26 no. 20895 p. 429   74. CN26 no. 20902 pp. 434–5   75. ed. Lacour-Gayet, *Chancellor Pasquier* p. 139 n. 10   76. Rovigo, *Mémoires* VI p. 239   77. Fain, *Memoirs of the Invasion* p. 11   78. Watson, *Reign of George III* p. 560   79. ed. Bingham, *Selection* III p. 286, Fain, *Memoirs of the Invasion* p. 12   80. ed. Bingham, *Selection* III p. 286   81. Cobban, *Modern France* II p. 62   82. Ashby, *Napoleon against Great Odds* p. 1   83. Rovigo, *Mémoires* VI p. 262

28. DEFIANCE

Napoleon's maxim comes from ed. Chandler, *Military Maxims* p. 114   Napoleon on Pompey comes from CN32 p. 47   1. Crouzet, 'The Second Hundred Years War' p. 441   2. Ashby, *Napoleon against Great Odds* p. 183   3. Elting, *Swords* p. 329   4. CG7 no. 15830 p. 875, June 4, 1807   5. Ashby, *Napoleon against Great Odds* p. 4   6. Dziewanowski, 'Napoleon' p. 91   7. Las Cases, *Memorial* I p. 232   8. Richardson, *French Prefectoral Corps* pp. 44–6, Cobban, *Modern France* II p. 25   9. Daly, *Inside Napoleonic France* p. 255   10. Pigeard, *La Conscription* pp. 269–70   11. Price, 'Napoleon and Metternich' p. 500   12. Pelet, *Napoleon in Council* p. 261   13. Pelet, *Napoleon in Council* p. 267   14. Markham, *Awakening of Europe* p. 174   15. Guérard, *Reflections* p. 94   16. D'Abrantès,

At the Court p. 21　17. ed. Bingham, *Selection* III p. 293　18. ed. Bingham, *Selection* III p. 298　19. Rovigo, *Mémoires* VI p. 289　20. ed. Bingham, *Selection* III p. 313　21. Fain, *Memoirs of the Invasion* p. 48　22. ed. Lacour-Gayet, *Chancellor Pasquier* p. 145, Rovigo, *Mémoires* VI p. 301　23. Boigne, *Mémoires* pp. 280–81　24. ed. Lacour-Gayet, *Chancellor Pasquier* p. 138　25. ed. Bingham, *Selection* III p. 301　26. ed. Latimer, *Talks* p. 39　27. Fain, *Memoirs of the Invasion* pp. 77–80　28. ed. Bingham, *Selection* III p. 301　29. ed. North, *Napoleon on Elba*, p. 63　30. Fain, *Memoirs of the Invasion* p. 79, ed. Fleischmann, *L'Épopée Impériale* pp. 346–7　31. ed. Roncière, *Letters to Marie-Louise* p. 206　32. Stanhope, *Notes of Conversations* p. 6　33. ed. Bingham, *Selection* III p. 302　34. ed. Bingham, *Selection* III p. 302　35. Fain, *Memoirs of the Invasion* p. 94　36. ed. Gallatin, *Diary of James Gallatin* p. 53　37. ed. Bingham, *Selection* III p. 320　38. ed. Roncière, *Letters to Marie-Louise* p. 207　39. ed. Roncière, *Letters to Marie-Louise* p. 209　40. ed. Roncière, *Letters to Marie-Louise* p. 209　41. ed. Bingham, *Selection* III p. 302　42. ed. Bingham, *Selection* III p. 306　43. ed. Roncière, *Letters to Marie-Louise* p. 212　44. ed. Roncière, *Letters to Marie-Louise* p. 213, Fain, *Memoirs of the Invasion* p. 97　45. ed. Roncière, *Letters to Marie-Louise* p. 214　46. Fain, *Memoirs of the Invasion* p. 102　47. ed. Roncière, *Letters to Marie-Louise* p. 215　48. Smith, *Data Book* p. 496　49. ed. Roncière, *Letters to Marie-Louise* pp. 216–17　50. Innocenti, 'Souls Not Wanting' p. 56　51. Cobban, *Modern France* II p. 62, ed. Roncière, *Letters to Marie-Louise* p. 204　52. ed. Bingham, *Selection* III p. 315　53. Fain, *Memoirs of the Invasion* p. 116　54. ed. Bingham, *Selection* III p. 317　55. ed. Fleischmann, *L'Épopée Impériale* p. 358　56. ed. Bingham, *Selection* III p. 317　57. ed. Bingham, *Selection* III p. 316　58. ed. Bingham, *Selection* III p. 325　59. ed. Bingham, *Selection* III pp. 322–3　60. ed. Bingham, *Selection* III p. 321　61. Lentz, *L'Effondrement* p. 570　62. ed. Roncière, *Letters to Marie-Louise* p. 233　63. ed. Roncière, *Letters to Marie-Louise* p. 234　64. Foch, 'La Battaille de Laon' p. 11　65. ed. Roncière, *Letters to Marie-Louise* pp. 236–7　66. ed. Roncière, *Letters to Marie-Louise* p. 237　67. ed. Roncière, *Letters to Marie-Louise* p. 238　68. AN 440 AP 12　69. Ross, *Reluctant King* p. 228　70. Marmont, *Memoirs* p. 69　71. ed. Roncière, *Letters to Marie-Louise* p. 241　72. ed. Roncière, *Letters to Marie-Louise* p. 241　73. Bausset, *Private Memoirs* p. 425, ed. North, *Napoleon on Elba* p. 27, McLynn, *Napoleon* p. 584, Anon., 'More about Napoleon' p. 228　74. ed. Roncière, *Letters to Marie-Louise* p. 245, ed. North, *Napoleon on Elba* p. 64　75. Chardigny, *L'Homme Napoléon* pp. 154–5　76. Ashby, *Napoleon against Great Odds* p. 272　77. ed. Latimer, *Talks* pp. 87–8　78. ed. Roncière, *Letters to Marie-Louise* p. 245　79. ed. Lacour-Gayet, *Chancellor Pasquier* p. 146, Bausset, *Private Memoirs* pp. 398–402　80. ed. Roncière, *Letters to Marie-Louise* p. 249　81. Bausset, *Private Memoirs* p. 405　82. ed. Roncière, *Letters to Marie-Louise* p. 249　83. Lavalette, *Memoirs* p. 121, Mikaberidze, 'Russian Eagles over the Seine' pp. 155–6　84. eds. Tulard and Garros, *Itinéraire* p. 444　85. Lavalette, *Memoirs* p. 122　86. ed. Gallatin, *Diary of James Gallatin* p. 53, Hobhouse, *Substance of Some Letters*

p. 226   87. INV AA 1751–1758, 1761   88. Lavalette, *Memoirs* p. 123, Mika-beridze, 'Russian Eagles over the Seine' p. 158   89. Bourrienne, *Memoirs* IV p. 230   90. Waresquiel, *Talleyrand* p. 125   91. Lentz, *L'Effondrement* p. 568   92. Lentz, *L'Effondrement* p. 569   93. Innocenti, 'Souls Not Wanting' p. 51   94. Houssaye, *Campaign of 1814* p. 502   95. ed. Rousset, *Recollections of Marshal Macdonald* II pp. 246–7   96. Lentz, *L'Effondrement* p. 572   97. Hobhouse, *Recollections* I p. 183, ed. North, *Napoleon on Elba* p. 65   98. Cronin, *Napoleon* p. 554, Raguse, *Mémoires* VI p. 274   99. Houssaye, *Campaign of 1814* p. 499

29. ELBA

Metternich on 1815 comes from ed. Metternich, *Memoirs* III pp. 338–9   Napoleon on board HMS *Northumberland* comes from Warden, *Letters Written on Board HMS Northumberland* p. 58   1. Lentz, *L'Effondrement* p. 570, ed. Cisterne, *Journal de marche* p. 250, ed. Park, *Napoleon in Captivity* p. 36   2. Houssaye, *The Campaign of 1814* p. 507, Lentz, *L'Effondrement* p. 573, Fain *Memoirs of the Invasion* p. 212   3. Houssaye, *The Campaign of 1814* p. 507   4. Houssaye, *The Campaign of 1814* p. 508   5. SHD GR6.YD/1   6. ed. Cottin, *Souvenirs de Roustam* p. 191   7. Houssaye, *The Campaign of 1814* p. 508   8. Houssaye, *Campaign of 1814* p. 511   9. Kauffmann, *Black Room at Longwood*, p. xvii   10. ed. North, *Napoleon on Elba* p. 32 n. 31   11. ed. Rousset, *Recollections of Marshal Macdonald* II p. 197   12. ed. North, *Napoleon on Elba* p. 17   13. ed. Roncière, *Letters to Marie-Louise* p. 258   14. Bausset, *Private Memoirs* p. 423   15. Fain, *Memoirs of the Invasion* p. 258; Philip Dwyer dates it to April 7 in eds. Dwyer and McPhee, *The French Revolution and Napoleon* p. 191; Wairy says April 11 in ed. Jones, *Napoleon: An Intimate Account* p. 420   16. Saint-Denis, *Napoleon from the Tuileries to St Helena* p. 66   17. ed. Cottin, *Souvenirs de Roustam* pp. 196–7, ed. Roncière, *Letters to Marie-Louise* p. 262   18. Montholon, *History of the Captivity* III p. 135, Fain, *Memoirs of the Invasion* p. 259   19. ed. Roncière, *Letters to Marie-Louise* p. 263   20. Lentz, *L'Effondrement* p. 574, Fain, *Memoirs of the Invasion* p. 259   21. ed. Rousset, *Recollections of Marshal Macdonald* II p. 199   22. ed. Rousset, *Recollections of Marshal Macdonald* II p. 199   23. ed. Cottin, *Souvenirs de Roustam* p. 198   24. ed. North, *Napoleon on Elba* p. 14   25. Fain, *Memoirs of the Invasion* p. 264   26. Kerry, *First Napoleon* pp. 71–2   27. ed. Jones, *Napoleon: An Intimate Account* p. 420   28. ed. North, *Napoleon on Elba* p. 30   29. ed. North, *Napoleon on Elba* p. 18   30. ed. North, *Napoleon on Elba* p. 19   31. ed. North, *Napoleon on Elba* pp. 37–8, 46   32. ed. North, *Napoleon on Elba* p. 20   33. ed. North, *Napoleon on Elba* p. 27   34. ed. North, *Napoleon on Elba* p. 25   35. ed. North, *Napoleon on Elba* p. 27   36. Montholon, *History of the Captivity* I p. 1   37. Wolff, *Island Empire* pp. 158–9   38. ed. Latimer, *Talks* p. 167   39. ed. North, *Napoleon on Elba* pp. 31–2   40. ed. North, *Napoleon on Elba* p. 32

41. ed. North, *Napoleon on Elba* p. 33 **42.** Wolff, *Island Empire* p. 159, Fain, *Memoirs of the Invasion* p. 267 **43.** ed. North, *Napoleon on Elba* pp. 34–5, Wolff, *Island Empire* pp. 159–60, Rovigo, *Mémoires* VII pp. 212–13, AN 400AP/5 **44.** ed. Roncière, *Letters to Marie-Louise* p. 269 **45.** ed. North, *Napoleon on Elba* p. 39 **46.** ed. North, *Napoleon on Elba* p. 47 **47.** BNF NAF 20071 p. 2 **48.** ed. Rose, *Napoleon's Last Voyages* p. 32 **49.** ed. North, *Napoleon on Elba* p. 47 **50.** ed. Rose, *Napoleon's Last Voyages* p. 36 **51.** ed. Rose, *Napoleon's Last Voyages* p. 46 **52.** ed. Rose, *Napoleon's Last Voyages* p. 51 **53.** ed. Rose, *Napoleon's Last Voyages* p. 52 **54.** Branda, *Le prix de la gloire* p. 62 **55.** Branda, *Le prix de la gloire* p. 64, ed. Rose, *Napoleon's Last Voyages* p. 52 **56.** ed. Bingham, *Selection* II p. 4, ed. North, *Napoleon on Elba* p. 31 **57.** ed. Rose, *Napoleon's Last Voyages* p. 52, ed. North, *Napoleon on Elba* p. 62, Wolff, *Island Empire* pp. 8–9, Houssaye, *The Return of Napoleon* p. 4 **58.** ed. Tarbell, *Napoleon's Addresses* p. xvii **59.** ed. North, *Napoleon on Elba* p. 74 **60.** ed. North, *Napoleon on Elba* p. 81 **61.** ed. Latimer, *Talks* p. 138 n. 2 and p. 56 **62.** ed. Cerf, *Letters to Josephine* p. 234 **63.** ed. Kerry, *First Napoleon* p. 99 **64.** ed. North, *Napoleon on Elba* p. 105 **65.** Christophe, *Napoleon on Elba* p. 138 **66.** ed. Roncière, *Letters to Marie-Louise* p. 277 **67.** ed. Roncière, *Letters to Marie-Louise* p. 277, ed. Palmstierna, *Dearest Louise* pp. 222–3 **68.** Saint-Amand, *Marie-Louise and the Decadence of Empire* p. 2 **69.** ed. Palmstierna, *Dearest Louise* p. 223 **70.** Pocock, *Stopping Napoleon* pp. 211–12, Sutherland, *Marie Walewska* pp. 218ff **71.** Kissinger, *A World Restored passim* **72.** ed. Kerry, *First Napoleon* p. 82, Ebrington, *Memorandum* p. 27 **73.** ed. Kerry, *First Napoleon* p. 95 **74.** ed. Kerry, *First Napoleon* p. 105 **75.** ed. Kerry, *First Napoleon* p. 95, ed. Gallatin, *Diary of James Gallatin* p. 54 **76.** ed. North, *Napoleon on Elba* p. 140 **77.** ed. Kerry, *First Napoleon* p. 95 **78.** ed. Rowe, *Collaboration and Resistance* p. 22 **79.** Forrest, *Napoleon* p. 280. Some priests even refused the sacrament to purchasers of *biens nationaux*. Alexander, *Bonapartism and Revolutionary Tradition* p. 3 **80.** Hobhouse, *Substance of Some Letters* pp. 28–42, CN28 no. 21714 p. 30 **81.** Daly, *Inside Napoleonic France* p. 256, McPhee, *Social History* p. 88 **82.** Ebrington, 'Conversation' *passim* **83.** Bodleian MS Curzon e.1. p. 18 **84.** Fleischmann, *En Écoutant Parler* p. 31 **85.** Alexander, *Bonapartism and Revolutionary Tradition* p. 4 **86.** Cobban, *Modern France* II p. 65 **87.** ed. Latimer, *Talks* p. 167 **88.** ed. North, *Napoleon on Elba* pp. 14, 159 **89.** ed. North, *Napoleon on Elba* pp. 140 n. 75, 165, Holland, *Foreign Reminiscences* p. 196 **90.** Hobhouse, *Recollections* I pp. 178–83 **91.** Hobhouse, *Recollections* I p. 183 **92.** Hobhouse, *Recollections* I p. 187 **93.** Hobhouse, *Recollections* I p. 188 **94.** ed. North, *Napoleon on Elba* p. 166 **95.** ed. North, *Napoleon on Elba* p. 177 **96.** ed. North, *Napoleon on Elba* p. 177 n. 86 **97.** Fleury de Chaboulon, *Memoirs* I pp. 55–6 **98.** ed. North, *Napoleon on Elba* p. 172, Pocock, *Stopping Napoleon* p. 216 **99.** Kircheisen, *Napoleon* p. 685 **100.** ed. North, *Napoleon on Elba* p. 172 **101.** ed. Hanoteau, *Queen Hortense* II p. 213 **102.** Fraser, *Venus of Empire* p. 216 **103.** ed. Latimer, *Talks* p. 225 **104.** Hobhouse, *Substance of Some Letters* p. 66 n. 2 **105.** ed. North, *Napoleon on Elba* pp. 188–9, Mudford,

An Historical Account p. 56   106. Hobhouse, *Substance of Some Letters* p. 55   107. Hobhouse, *Substance of Some Letters* p. 55   108. ed. Latimer, *Talks* p. 172   109. ed. Latimer, *Talks* p. 178   110. CN28 no. 21682 p. 3   111. CN28 no. 21681 p. 1   112. eds. Dwyer and McPhee, *The French Revolution and Napoleon* pp. 195–6   113. Jarrett, *Congress of Vienna* p. 158   114. Hobhouse, *Substance of Some Letters* p. 57   115. ed. North, *Napoleon on Elba* p. 179   116. ed. Latimer, *Talks* p. 17   117. CN28 no. 21684–6 pp. 6–7   118. Cockburn, *Buonaparte's Voyage* pp. 41–2, Hobhouse, *Substance of Some Letters* p. 58   119. Rovigo, *Mémoires* VII pp. 351–2   120. ed. Latimer, *Talks* p. 55   121. ed. Latimer, *Talks* p. 183   122. ed. Latimer, *Talks* p. 175   123. ed. Wilson, *Diary of St Helena* p. 90   124. Houssaye, *The Return of Napoleon* p. 66, Reiset, *Souvenirs* III p. 75   125. Waresquiel, *Les cent jours* p. 241   126. Houssaye, *The Return of Napoleon* p. 67, BNF Micr D71/86, *Le Moniteur* 9/3/1815   127. Thornton, *Napoleon after Waterloo* p. 54   128. Atteridge, *Marshal Ney* p. 170   129. Atteridge, *Marshal Ney* p. 170   130. Houssaye, *Return of Napoleon* p. 110   131. Houssaye, *Return of Napoleon* p. 108   132. Atteridge, *Marshal Ney* p. 172   133. ed. Fleischmann, *L'Épopée Impériale* pp. 390–91, ed. Routier, *Récits d'un soldat* pp. 175–6   134. ed. Butler, *Baron Thiébault* II pp. 418–19   135. Lavalette, *Memoirs* p. 154   136. Villemain, *Souvenirs* II p. 48   137. Lavalette, *Memoirs* p. 150

30. WATERLOO

Napoleon on Waterloo comes from Field, *Waterloo* p. 22   Napoleon's Maxim comes from ed. Chandler, *Military Maxims* p. 109   1. Rapp, *Memoirs* p. 13   2. ed. Roncière, *Letters to Marie-Louise* p. 281   3. AN 286 AP3 dossier 32   4. ed. Noailles, *Count Molé* p. 213   5. BNF Micr D.71/86 *Le Moniteur* 21/3/1815   6. Rapp, *Memoirs* p. 4   7. ed. Cottin, *Souvenirs de Roustam*, p. xxxv   8. BNF Micr D.71/86   9. ed. Schlumberger, *Lettres* p. 245   10. CN28 no. 21696 p. 20   11. CN28 no. 21711 p. 29   12. Gallaher, 'Davout and Napoleon' p. 7   13. CN28 no. 21896 p. 177   14. SHD GR16/C21 and SHD GR 15.C/39   15. ed. Latimer, *Talks* p. 187   16. CN28 no 21987 p. 241   17. Marshall-Cornwall, *Marshal Masséna* p. 259   18. Jourquin, *Dictionnaire des Marechaux* pp. 70–71   19. SHD GR6.YD/1, ed. Butler, *Baron Thiébault* II p. 420, Macirone, *Interesting Facts* pp. 146–8   20. Chandler, *On the Napoleonic Wars* p. 112   21. ed. Stiegler, *Récits de guerre* p. 307   22. Hobhouse, *Substance of Some Letters* pp. 116–17   23. Hobhouse, *Substance of Some Letters* p. 118   24. CN28 nos. 21813, 21948 pp. 102, 214   25. Mudford, *An Historical Account* p. 193   26. CN28 no. 21761 p. 66   27. CN28 no. 21876 p. 162   28. Branda, *Le prix de la gloire* p. 73   29. Charvet, *Literary History* p. 57   30. Cockburn, *Buonaparte's Voyage* p. 72   31. Beslay, *Souvenirs* p. 50, Hobhouse, *Substance of Some Letters* pp. 88, 122–4, McPhee, *Social History* p. 88, CN28 nos. 21743 and 21753 pp. 51, 60   32. CN28 no. 21769 p. 76   33. Hobhouse, *Substance of Some Letters* p. 160   34. Hobhouse, *Substance of*

Some Letters p. 126   35. CN28 no. 21713 p. 29   36. Hobhouse, *Substance of Some Letters* p. 87   37. ed. Palmstierna, *Dearest Louise* p. 226   38. Hobhouse, *Substance of Some Letters* p. 18   39. Hobhouse, *Substance of Some Letters* p. 18   40. Bluche, *Le plébiscite* p. 36 n. 109, ed. Fontana, *Benjamin Constant* pp. 11–13, eds. Dwyer and McPhee, *The French Revolution and Napoleon* p. 199   41. Daly, *Inside Napoleonic France* p. 257, ed. Rowe, *Collaboration and Resistance* p. 29   42. Lavalette, *Memoirs* p. 150   43. Emsley, *Napoleon* p. 116, Daly, *Inside Napoleonic France* p. 258   44. Alexander, *Bonapartism and Revolutionary Tradition* p. 284   45. ed. Noailles, *Count Molé* p. 225   46. Hobhouse, *Substance of Some Letters* p. 189   47. ed. Butler, *Baron Thiébault* II p. 420   48. BNF Micr D.71/86, CN28 no. 21997 p. 246   49. *Le Moniteur* 2/6/1815   50. Hobhouse, *Substance of Some Letters* pp. 190–94, Williams, *A Narrative* p. 160   51. Williams, *A Narrative* p. 166   52. CN28 no. 22030 p. 265   53. CN28 no. 22030 p. 265   54. Thornton, *Napoleon after Waterloo* p. 56   55. CN28 no. 21733 p. 44   56. Cockburn, *Buonaparte's Voyage* pp. 45–6   57. CN28 no. 22052 p. 281   58. Davies, *Wellington's Wars* p. 226   59. CN28 no. 21999 p. 249   60. Houssaye, *1815* III p. 48   61. Chandler, *Campaigns of Napoleon* p. 1040   62. Muir, *Tactics and the Experience of Battle* p. 147   63. Hayman, *Soult* p. 227   64. Field, *Waterloo* p. 29   65. Rose, *Napoleon* I p. 88   66. Gardner, *Quatre Bras* p. 127   67. Macbride, *With Napoleon at Waterloo* p. 182   68. ed. Kerry, *First Napoleon* p. 117   69. Field, *Waterloo* p. 31   70. ed. Latimer, *Talks* p. 189   71. ed. Chandler, *Military Maxims* p. 150   72. ed. Chandler, *Military Maxims* p. 128   73. Fantin des Odoards, *Journal* p. 431   74. Albermarle, *Fifty Years* II p. 21, *Quarterly Review* July 1875 p. 225, Forrest, *Napoleon* p. 308   75. CG7 no. 15797 p. 862   76. Adkin, *Waterloo Companion* p. 79   77. Albermarle, *Fifty Years* II p. 23   78. Pétiet, *Souvenirs Militaires* pp. 195–6   79. ed. Kerry, *First Napoleon* p. 125   80. ed. Kerry, *First Napoleon* p. 120   81. Forsyth, *History of the Captivity* I p. 140   82. Germain, *Drouët d'Erlon* pp. 175–6, Field, *Waterloo* p. 32, D'Erlon, *Vie militaire* p. 96   83. D'Erlon, *Vie militaire*, pp. 96–7   84. Balcombe, *To Befriend* p. 117   85. D'Erlon, *Vie militaire* pp. 96–7, ed. Maricourt, *Général Noguès* p. 270   86. Field, *Waterloo* p. 33, Macbride, *With Napoleon at Waterloo* p. 183   87. Saint-Denis, *Napoleon from the Tuileries to St Helena* p. 113   88. Mauduit, *Les derniers jours* II p. 231   89. ed. Latimer, *Talks* p. 143   90. Gardner, *Quatre Bras* p. 37 n. 18   91. SHD GR15/C5/18 June 1815   92. Hayman, *Soult* p. 228, Houssaye *1815* III pp. 244ff   93. ed. Girod de l'Ain, *Vie militaire* pp. 278–9   94. Macbride, *With Napoleon at Waterloo* p. 183   95. Gardner, *Quatre Bras* p. 222   96. Adkin, *Waterloo Companion* p. 79   97. Gardner, *Quatre Bras* p. 236 n. 148, Albermarle, *Fifty Years* p. 21, *Quarterly Review* July 1875 p. 225   98. SHD GR15/C5/18 June 1815, Houssaye, *1815* III pp. 191–2, Hayman, *Soult* p. 230   99. Field, *Waterloo* p. 43   100. SHD GR15/C5/18 June 1815   101. ed. Jennings, *Croker Papers* I p. 340   102. Bonaparte, Jérôme, *Mémoires et Correspondance* VII p. 95, Boudon, *Le roi Jérôme* p. 442   103. ed. Lévi, *Mémoires du Capitaine Duthilt* pp. 391ff   104. ed. Chandler, *Military Maxims* p. 187   105. Linck, *Napoleon's Generals* p. 62   106. Davies, *Wellington's*

Wars p. 239   107. Roberts, *Waterloo* pp. 126–8   108. ed. Kerry, *First Napoleon* p. 126   109. ed. Kerry, *First Napoleon* pp. 126, 129   110. ed. Kerry, *First Napoleon* p. 129   111. ed. Latimer, *Talks* p. 189   112. D'Erlon, *Vie militaire* pp. 96–8   113. ed. Brett-James, *Hundred Days* p. 139   114. Ropes, *Campaign of Waterloo* p. 337   115. Levasseur, *Souvenirs Militaires* pp. 303–4   116. Fuller, *Decisive Battles* p. 204   117. Williams, *A Narrative* p. 184   118. Smith, 'General Petit's Account'   119. ed. Kerry, *First Napoleon* p. 131   120. Macbride, *With Napoleon at Waterloo* pp. 184–5   121. Smith, *Data Book*, p. 539   122. ed. Latimer, *Talks* p. 187, Lancesseur, *L'Enigme de Waterloo* p. 146

31. ST HELENA

Napoleon to Marie Louise comes from ed. Roncière, *Letters to Marie-Louise* p. 60   Napoleon on Themistocles comes from ed. Frayling, *Napoleon Wrote Fiction* p. 37   1. ed. Lecestre, *Lettres inédites* II pp. 357–8   2. ed. Haythornthwaite, *Final Verdict* p. 191   3. SHD GR17.C/193   4. ed. Latimer, *Talks* p. 2   5. Hobhouse, *Substance of Some Letters* p. 240   6. Montholon, *History of the Captivity* I p. 4   7. CN28 no. 22062 p. 299   8. Villepin, *Les cent jours* p. 450   9. Williams, *A Narrative* pp. 189–91   10. Hobhouse, *Substance of Some Letters* p. 244, Unger, *Lafayette* p. 345   11. Cockburn, *Buonaparte's Voyage* p. 25   12. CN28 no. 22061 p. 293, *Le Moniteur* 21/6/1815, BNF Micr D.71/86   13. ed. Calmettes, *Général Thiébault* V pp. 373–4   14. Montholon, *History of the Captivity* I p. 7   15. CN28 no. 22063 p. 299, BNF Micr D.71/86, *Le Moniteur* 23/6/1815   16. ed. Latimer, *Talks* p. 3, Lavalette, *Memoirs* p. 172   17. Lavalette, *Memoirs* p. 171   18. BNF Micr D.71/86, *Le Moniteur* 24/6/1815   19. ed. Jennings, *Croker Papers* I p. 62   20. Rovigo, *Mémoires* VIII pp. 175–6   21. ed. Jennings, *Croker Papers* I p. 328   22. ed. Latimer, *Talks* p. 264   23. ed. Jennings, *Croker Papers* I p. 68   24. ed. Latimer, *Talks* p. 12 n. 2   25. Markham, 'Napoleon's Last Hours' p. 39   26. Cockburn, *Buonaparte's Voyage* p. 48   27. Markham, 'Napoleon's Last Hours' p. 42   28. Maitland, *Surrender of Napoleon* pp. 175–6, Bodleian MS Curzon d.2 *passim*   29. CN28 no. 22066 p. 301   30. Sherwig, *Guineas and Gunpowder* pp. 345, 368   31. Rovigo, *Mémoires* IV p. 161   32. *The Times* 15 July 1830   33. Smith, *Data Book* pp. 535–60   34. Markham, 'Napoleon's Last Hours' p. 47   35. ed. Jones, *In Napoleon's Shadow* pp. 285–6   36. Markham, 'Napoleon's Last Hours' p. 48, Home, *Memoirs of an Aristocrat* p. 212   37. Maitland, *Surrender of Napoleon* p. 77   38. Home, *Memoirs of an Aristocrat* p. 227   39. Markham, 'The Emperor at Work' p. 587   40. Maitland, *Surrender of Napoleon* p. 85   41. Maitland, *Surrender of Napoleon* p. 98   42. ed. Londonderry, *Memoirs and Correspondence* X p. 415   43. Maitland, *Surrender of Napoleon* p. 107   44. Maitland, *Surrender of Napoleon* p. 118   45. Maitland, *Surrender of Napoleon* p. 137   46. ed. Latimer, *Talks* p. 25, Maitland, *Surrender of Napoleon* p. 130   47. Maitland, *Surrender of Napoleon* p. 141   48. Maitland, *Surrender of Napoleon* p. 154   49. Maitland, *Surrender of Napoleon* p. 173   50. Cockburn, *Buonaparte's*

Voyage pp. 15–16, ed. Kemble, *St Helena* pp. 7–8, Balcombe, *To Befriend* pp. 12, 80, Martineau, *Napoleon's St Helena* p. 40   51. Maitland, *Surrender of Napoleon* p. 189, Cockburn, *Buonaparte's Voyage* p. 15   52. Martineau, *Napoleon's St Helena* p. 51   53. Cockburn, *Buonaparte's Voyage* pp. 17–18   54. Cockburn, *Buonaparte's Voyage passim*, Latimer, *Talks* pp. 29–31   55. Cockburn, *Buonaparte's Voyage* p. 60   56. ed. Latimer, *Talks* p. 29, Cockburn, *Buonaparte's Voyage* p. 40   57. Palmer, *Napoleon and Marie Louise* p. 201   58. ed. Latimer, *Talks* p. 31   59. Martineau, *Napoleon's St Helena* p. 1, ed. Latimer, *Talks* p. 33   60. Blackburn, *The Emperor's Last Island* p. 5   61. Tulard, *Dictionnaire amoureux* p. 505   62. Martineau, *Napoleon's St Helena* p. 11   63. ed. Wilson, *Diary of St Helena* p. 13   64. Interview with Michel Dancoisne-Martineau at Longwood 4/5/2013   65. Martineau, *Napoleon's St Helena* p. 37   66. Tyrwhitt MSS Osborn fc112 no. 22   67. Balcombe, *To Befriend* pp. 34, 135   68. Balcombe, *To Befriend* pp. 42–3   69. Balcombe, *To Befriend* pp. 43–4   70. Balcombe, *To Befriend* p. 55   71. Balcombe, *To Befriend* p. 56   72. Balcombe, *To Befriend* pp. 83–5, 166   73. Bodleian MS Curzon e1. p. 12, ed. Kemble, *St Helena* p. 2, Giles, *Napoleon Bonaparte* p. 111   74. Montholon, *Journal secret* p. 8   75. Vernon, *Early Recollections* p. 168   76. Rosebery, *Last Phase* p. 62   77. Martineau, *Napoleon's St Helena* p. 22   78. Brunyee, *Napoleon's Britons* p. 81   79. ed. Latimer, *Talks* p. 142   80. ed. Latimer, *Talks* p. 191   81. ed. Park, *Napoleon in Captivity* p. 36   82. ed. Latimer, *Talks* p. 221   83. ed. Latimer, *Talks* p. 145   84. ed. Latimer, *Talks* p. 259   85. ed. Latimer, *Talks* p. 245   86. Forsyth, *History of the Captivity* I p. 137   87. BL Add. MS 56088 fols. 89–90   88. BL Add. MS 56088 fols. 97ff   89. BL Add. MS 56088 fol. 101   90. Martineau, *Napoleon's St Helena* pp. 55–6   91. Albermarle, *Fifty Years* II p. 103   92. Rosebery, *Last Phase* p. 68   93. Martineau, *Napoleon's St Helena* p. 17, BL Add. MS 80775 fol. 143, 20202 fol. 42, Balcombe, *To Befriend* p. 115   94. BL Lowe Papers 20202 fol. 20   95. Unwin, *Terrible Exile* pp. 184–5, Forsyth, *History of the Captivity* III pp. 224–5   96. Balcombe, *To Befriend* p. 188   97. ed. Haythornthwaite, *Final Verdict* p. 199   98. ed. Walter, *Las Cases* p. viii   99. ed. Latimer, *Talks* pp. 240–42   100. Branda, *Le prix de la gloire* p. 77   101. Forrest, *Napoleon* p. 304   102. Balcombe, *To Befriend* pp. 67–9   103. ed. Park, *Napoleon in Captivity* pp. 149, 153–5   104. ed. Park, *Napoleon in Captivity* p. 161   105. ed. Park, *Napoleon in Captivity* pp. 166–7   106. ed. Arnold, *Documentary Survey* p. 138   107. Bertrand, *Cahiers* II p. 344   108. Tulard, *Napoleon: The Myth of the Saviour* p. 346, ed. Woloch, *Revolution and the Meanings of Freedom* p. 36   109. ed. Haythornthwaite, *Final Verdict* p. 286   110. Rouart, *Napoléon ou la destinée* p. 9   111. ed. Latimer, *Talks* p. 208   112. ed. Haythornthwaite, *Final Verdict* p. 301   113. ed. Latimer, *Talks* pp. 207, 210, 218   114. Grouchy, *Doubts of the Authenticity* pp. 3–4   115. Martineau, *Napoleon's St Helena* p. 39   116. ed. Haythornthwaite, *Final Verdict* p. 197   117. Martineau, *Napoleon's St Helena* p. 49   118. Healey, *Literary Culture* p. 82   119. ed. Wilson, *Diary of St Helena* p. 7   120. ed. Wilson, *Diary of St Helena* pp. 29, 31–2, Bodleian MS Curzon e.1.

p. 17, O'Meara, *Napoleon in Exile* I pp. 284–6   **121.** ed. Wilson, *Diary of St Helena* p. 50   **122.** Balcombe, *To Befriend* p. 163   **123.** Balcombe, *To Befriend* p. 182, ed. Wilson, *Diary of St Helena* p. 103   **124.** BL Lowe Papers 20156 fol. 2   **125.** BL Lowe Papers 20156 *passim*   **126.** Bertrand, *Cahiers* I p. 118, AN 390/AP/32   **127.** Jackson, *Notes and Reminiscences* p. 153   **128.** Forrest, *Napoleon* p. 309, ed. Latimer, *Talks* pp. 258–60   **129.** ed. Latimer, *Talks* p. 276, Constant, *Memoirs of Constant* I p. 162   **130.** CN31 p. 579, Browning, *Napoleon* pp. 283–4   **131.** Griffin, 'Philosophy, Cato and Roman Suicide' p. 1   **132.** ed. Bingham, *Selection* I p. 392   **133.** CN32 p. 70   **134.** ed. Latimer, *Talks* p. 245   **135.** ed. Wilson, *Diary of St Helena* p. 152   **136.** ed. Latimer, *Talks* p. 265   **137.** ed. Latimer, *Talks* pp. 201–3   **138.** Balcombe, *To Befriend* p. 154   **139.** Balcombe, *To Befriend* p. 182   **140.** Richardson, *The Apocalypse of Napoleon* p. 223, Weider and Hapgood, *Murder of Napoleon* pp. 175–6, ed. Jones, *Napoleon: An Intimate Account* p. 425, Forrest, *Napoleon* p. 310   **141.** Hobhouse, *Recollections* I p. 185   **142.** BL Lowe Papers 20156 fols. 30ff   **143.** Henry, *Trifles from My Portfolio* II p. 5   **144.** Bruce, *Napoleon and Josephine* p. 500, Fraser, *Venus of Empire*, p. 250, Hibbert, *Napoleon: His Wives and Women* p. 331   **145.** ed. Noailles, *Count Molé* p. 124   **146.** Richardson, *The Apocalypse of Napoleon* p. 229   **147.** Bodleian MS Curzon e1. pp. 2–3   **148.** Bodleian MS Curzon c.2. pp.1–2   **149.** My thanks for Drs Guy O'Keeffe and Michael Crumplin   **150.** Richardson, *Napoleon's Death* p. 166, Henry, *Trifles from My Portfolio* II p. 10   **151.** NYPL Napoleon I folder 3   **152.** Henry, *Trifles from My Portfolio* II p. 10   **153.** Henry, *Trifles from My Portfolio* II p. 10   **154.** ed. Latimer, *Talks* p. 139   **155.** eds. Chevallier et al., *Sainte-Hélène* p. 70   **156.** Henry, *Trifles from My Portfolio* II p. 5, Masson, *Napoleon at St Helena* p. 246   **157.** Masson, *Napoleon at St Helena* p. 247   **158.** Masson, *Napoleon at St Helena* p. 248   **159.** Masson, *Napoleon at St Helena* p. 248   **160.** BL Lowe Papers 20157 fol. 3 Arnott   **161.** BL Lowe Papers 20157 fol. 3   **162.** AN 400AP/5   **163.** ed. Jonge, *Napoleon's Last Will* p. 78   **164.** ed. Jonge, *Napoleon's Last Will* p. 36   **165.** ed. Jonge, *Napoleon's Last Will* p. 46   **166.** ed. Jonge, *Napoleon's Last Will* p. 36   **167.** ed. Jonge, *Napoleon's Last Will* p. 46   **168.** ed. Jonge, *Napoleon's Last Will* p. 36   **169.** Richardson, *Napoleon's Death* p. 163   **170.** ed. Marchand, *Précis des Guerres de César* p. 3   **171.** ed. Marchand, *Précis des Guerres de César* p. 15, Richardson, *Napoleon's Death* pp. 163–4, Antommarchi, *Last Days of Napoleon* II p. 152   **172.** ed. Marchand, *Précis des Guerres de César* p. 14   **173.** Albermarle, *Fifty Years* II p. 105   **174.** Henry, *Trifles from My Portfolio* II p. 7, Richardson, *Napoleon's Death* p. 164, Antommarchi, *Last Days of Napoleon* II p. 105   **175.** Henry, *Trifles from My Portfolio* II p. 11   **176.** Henry, *Trifles from My Portfolio* II p. 11   **177.** Balcombe, *To Befriend* p. 116   **178.** BNF NAF 25548

CONCLUSION: NAPOLEON THE GREAT

Churchill on Napoleon is from *A History of the English-Speaking Peoples* III, ix, ch. 3   Napoleon on Julius Caesar is from CN32 p. 63   1. CN32 p. 82   2. Hughes, *Forging Napoleon's Grande Armée passim*   3. Longford, *Pillar of State* p. 413   4. Rose, *Napoleon* I p. 266   5. Horne, *Age of Napoleon* p. 52   6. Sudhir Hazareesingh, *TLS*, February 12, 2005   7. Gates, *Napoleonic Wars* p. 272   8. Kissinger, *A World Restored* p. 172   9. Kerry, *The First Napoleon* p. 93   10. Lt-Col Pierron, 'Les Methodes de Guerre Actuelles' (Paris 1878), *RUSI Journal* vol. 23, no 99 1879   11. *Quarterly Review* 1833 pp. 179–84   12. Bonaparte, *Reply to Sir Walter Scott* p. 39   13. Home, *Memoirs of an Aristocrat* p. 223

Bibliography

BOOKS

The bibliography of works on Napoleon is notoriously immense. More books have been published with his name in the title than there have been days since his death. The complete list of books consulted for this work can be found on www.andrew-roberts.net, but for reasons of space only those I have quoted are in this bibliography. All books were published in London or Paris unless otherwise stated.

The *Correspondance Générale*, published by the Fondation Napoléon since 2004, will comprise all the 33,000 letters signed by Napoleon. It is a publishing undertaking as monumental as it is invaluable, a landmark in Napoleonic scholarship. These are the volumes cited in the Notes as 'CG' with the volume number following:

I ed. Lentz, Thierry, *Les Apprentissages 1784–1797* 2004
II ed. Lentz, Thierry, *La Campagne d'Égypte et l'Avènement 1798–1799* 2005
III ed. Lentz, Thierry, *Pacifications 1800–1802* 2006
IV ed. Houdecek, François, *Ruptures et fondation 1803–1804* 2006
V eds. Kerautret, Michel and Madec, Gabriel, *Boulogne, Trafalgar, Austerlitz 1805* 2008
VI ed. Kerautret, Michel, *Vers le Grand Empire 1806* 2009
VII eds. Kerautret, Michel and Madec, Gabriel, *Tilsit, l'Apogée de l'Empire 1807* 2010
VIII ed. Madec, Gabriel, *Expansions méridonales et résistances 1808–Janvier 1809* 2011
IX ed. Gueniffey, Patrice, *Wagram Février 1809–Février 1810* 2013
XII ed. Lentz, Thierry, *La Campagne de Russie 1812* 2012

The edition of Napoleon's letters, published in 32 volumes in 1858 and edited by Henri Plon, *Correspondance de Napoléon Ier*, is cited as 'CN'.

Adams, Henry, *History of the United States during the Administrations of Jefferson and Madison* 1967

Adams, Michael, *Napoleon and Russia* 2006

Adkin, Mark, *The Waterloo Companion* 2001

Adlerfeld, Gustavus, *The Military History of King Charles VII of Sweden* 3 vols. 1740

ed. Ainé, Desgranges, *Histoire de l'expédition des français en Égypte* 1839

Albermarle, Earl of, *Fifty Years of My Life* 2 vols. 1876

Albion, Robert Greenhalgh, *Forests and Sea Power* 1927

Aldington, Richard, *Wellington* 1946

Alexander, Robert S., *Bonapartism and Revolutionary Tradition in France* 1991
Napoleon 2001

Alison, Sir Archibald, *The History of Europe from the Commencement of the French Revolution to the Restoration of the Bourbons* vol. 1 1843

Allison, Charles W., *Ney* (Charlotte, NC) 1946

eds. Ambrose, Douglas and Martin, Robert W. T., *The Many Faces of Alexander Hamilton* (New York) 2006

Anonymous, *Copies of Original Letters from the Army of General Bonaparte in Egypt, Intercepted by the Fleet under the Command of Admiral Lord Nelson* 3 vols. 1798, 1799 and 1800
The Concordat Between His Holiness Pope Pius VII and Bonaparte Chief Consul to the French Republic (Dublin) 1802
A Short View of the Causes Which Led to and Justified the War with France 1803
The Atrocities of the Corsican Daemon, or, a Glance at Buonaparte 1803
Description des cérémonies et des fêtes qui ont eu lieu pour le couronnement de leurs majestés 1807
An Exact and Impartial Account of the Most Important Events Which have Occurred in Aranjuez, Madrid and Bayonne 1808
Relation de la bataille de Mont St Jean par un Temoin Occulaire 1815
Napoleon's Appeal to the British Nation on His Treatment at St Helena 1817
A Review of Warden's Letters from St Helena Containing Remarks on Bonaparte's Massacres at Jaffa and El Arish (Boston) 1817
The Battle of Waterloo (New York) 1819
Memoirs of the Public and Private Life of Napoleon Bonaparte 1827
Life of Napoleon Bonaparte (Philadelphia) 1845

Antommarchi, Francesco, *The Last Days of Napoleon* 2 vols. 1826

ed. Appleton, D., *The Confidential Correspondence of Napoleon Bonaparte With His Brother Joseph* 2 vols. 1855

Arnault, A. V., *Memoirs of the Public and Private Life of Napoleon Bonaparte* 2 vols. (Boston) 1833

ed. Arnold, Eric, *A Documentary Survey of Napoleonic France* (Maryland) 1994

Arnold, James, *Crisis on the Danube* 1990

Arnold, James R. and Reinertsen, Ralph R., *Crisis in the Snows* 2007

Ashby, Ralph, *Napoleon against Great Odds* 2010

Ashton, John, *English Caricature and Satire on Napoleon I* 2 vols. 1884

Assier, Alexandre, *Napoléon I à l'École Royale Militaire de Brienne* 1874

Atteridge, A. H., *Marshal Ney* 2005

Aubry, Octave, *St Helena* 1936

Aulard, François, *Histoire politique de la Révolution française* 1901

Austin, Paul Britten, *1812* 2000

Authority, *Preliminary Articles of Peace between His Britannick Majesty and the French Republick* 1801

Babbage, Charles, *Reflections on the Decline of Science in England* 1830

Balcombe, Betsy, *To Befriend an Emperor* 2005

Baldet, M., *La vie quotidienne dans les armées de Napoléon* 1964

ed. Baldick, Robert, *The Memoirs of Chateaubriand* 1961

Barbé-Marbois, François, *History of Louisiana* 1829

Baring-Gould, S., *The Life of Napoleon Bonaparte* 1897

Barnett, Correlli, *Bonaparte* 1978

Barral, Georges, *Histoire des sciences sous Napoleon Bonaparte* 1889

ed. Barrès, Maurice, *Memoirs of a French Napoleonic Officer: Jean-Baptiste Barrès* 1988

Bausset-Roquefort, Baron Louis François de, *Private Memoirs of the Court of Napoleon* (Philadelphia) 1828

Bell, David A., *The First Total War* 2007

ed. Bell, Nancy, *Memoirs of Baron Lejeune* 2 vols. 1897

Benbassa, Esther, *The Jews of France* (Princeton) 1999

Bergeron, Louis, *France Under Napoleon* (Princeton) 1981

Berlier, Théophile, *Précis de la vie politique de Théophile Berlier* 1838

Bertaud, Jean-Paul, *Bonaparte prend le pouvoir* 1987

    La France de Napoléon 1987

    Le duc d'Enghien 2001

    Quand les enfants parlaient de gloire 2006

Berthier, Louis-Alexandre, *The French Expedition into Syria* 1799

    Relation des campagnes du Général Bonaparte en Égypte et en Syrie 1801

Bertrand, Henri-Gratien, *Cahiers de Sainte-Hélène* 3 vols. 1951

    Napoleon at St Helena 1952

ed. Bertrand, Pierre, *Lettres de Talleyrand à Napoléon* 1889

Beslay, Charles, *Mes souvenirs* 1873

ed. Bierman, Irene A., *Napoleon in Egypt* 2003

Bigonnet, M., *Coup d'état du dix-huit Brumaire* 1819

ed. Bingham, D. A., *A Selection from the Letters and Despatches of the First Napoleon* 3 vols. 1884

Blackburn, Julia, *The Emperor's Last Island* 1991

Blaufarb, Rafe, *The French Army 1750–1820* 2002

Blaze, Captain Elzéar, *Life in Napoleon's Army* 1995

Blond, Georges, *La Grande Armée* 2005

Bluche, Frédéric, *Le plébiscite des cent jours* (Geneva) 1974

eds. Bogle, James and Uffindell, Andrew, *A Waterloo Hero* 2013

Boigne, Countess de, *Les mémoires de la Comtesse de Boigne* 1999

Boissonnade, Euloge, *18 Brumaire An VII* 1999

Bonaparte, Caroline, *Memoirs* (New York) 1910

Bonaparte, Jérôme, *Mémoires et correspondance du Roi Jérome et de la Reine Catherine* vol. VII 1866

Bonaparte, Joseph, *Mémoires et correspondance politique et militaire du Roi Joseph* 10 vols. 1855

Bonaparte, Louis, *A Reply to Sir Walter Scott's History of Napoleon* (Philadelphia) 1829

Bonaparte, Lucien, *Memoirs of Lucien Bonaparte, Prince of Canino* 2009

Bonaparte, Napoleon, *The Confidential Correspondence of Napoleon Bonaparte with his Brother Joseph* 2 vols. 1855

Supplément à la correspondance de Napoléon Ier 1887

Boswell, James, *An Account of Corsica* 1769

Boudon, Jacques-Olivier, *Le roi Jérôme* 2008

Les habits neuf de Napoléon 2009

ed. Boudon, Jacques-Olivier, *Napoléon et les lycées* 2004

Boulay de la Meurthe, Count F. J., *Boulay de la Meurthe* 1868

Bourgogne, Adrien, *Memoirs of Sergeant Bourgogne* 1929

Bourgoing, Chevalier, *Quelques notices sur les premières années du Buonaparte* 1797

Bourne, George, *The History of Napoleon Bonaparte* (Baltimore) 1806

Bourrienne, Louis-Antoine Fauvelet de, *Memoirs of Napoleon Bonaparte* 1836

Bowden, Scott, *Napoleon's Grande Armée of 1813* 1990

Bowle, John, *Napoleon* 1973

Boycott-Brown, Martin, *The Road to Rivoli* 2001

Branda, Pierre, *Le prix de la gloire* 2007

Napoléon et ses hommes 2012

Branda, Pierre and Lentz, Thierry, *Napoléon, l'esclavage et les colonies* 2006

Bredin, Jean-Denis, *Code civil des Français bicentenaire de 1804 à 2004* 2004

eds. Brenner, Michael, Caron, Vicki and Kaufmann, Uri R., *Jewish Emancipation Reconsidered* 2003

Brett-James, Antony, *Europe Against Napoleon* 1970

ed. Brett-James, Antony, *The Hundred Days* 1964

Eyewitness Accounts of Napoleon's Defeat in Russia (New York) 1966

Brice, Raoul, *The Riddle of Napoleon* 1937

ed. Brindle, Rosemary, *Captain Joseph-Marie Moiret* 2001

Guns in the Desert 2002

With Napoleon's Guns 2005

Campaigning for Napoleon: Maurice de Tascher 1806–1813 2006

Broers, Michael, *Europe under Napoleon 1799–1815* 1996

Napoleonic Imperialism and the Savoyard Monarchy 1997

The Politics of Religion in Italy 2002

The Napoleonic Empire in Italy 1796–1814 2005

Napoleon's Other War 2010

ed. Broglie, Duc de, *Memoirs of the Prince de Talleyrand* 1891

Brookner, Anita, *Jacques-Louis David* 1980

Brown, Howard G., *War, Revolution and the Bureaucratic State* 1995
 Ending the French Revolution 2006

Brown, Peter Hume, *Life of Goethe* 2 vols. 1920

Browning, Oscar, *Napoleon, the First Phase* 1895

ed. Browning, Oscar, *England and Napoleon in 1803, the Despatches of Lord Whitworth* 1887

Bruce, Evangeline, *Napoleon and Josephine* 1995

Brunyee, Paul F., *Napoleon's Britons and the St Helena Decision* 2009

Bruyere-Ostells, Walter, *Leipzig* 2013

Buckland, C. S. B., *Metternich and the British Government from 1809 to 1813* 1932

ed. Bulos, A., *Bourrienne et ses erreurs voluntaires et involuntaires* 2 vols. 1830

Burdon, William, *The Life and Character of Bonaparte* 1804

Burrows, Simon, *French Exile Journalism and European Politics 1792–1814* 2000

ed. Butler, A. J., *The Memoirs of Baron Thiébault*, 1896

Butterfield, Herbert, *The Peace Tactics of Napoleon 1806–1808* 1929

ed. Caisse, A. du, *Mémoires et correspondance politique et militaire du Prince Eugène* 10 vols. 1858–60

ed. Calmettes, Fernand, *Mémoires du Général Thiébault* vol. V 1895

Campbell, Neil, *Napoleon at Fontainebleau and Elba* 1869

Carnot, Lazare, *Reply of L. N. M. Carnot* 1799
 Mémoires historiques et militaires sur Carnot 1824

Carpenter, Kirsty, *Refugees of the French Revolution: Émigrés in London 1789–1802* 1999

eds. Carpenter, Kirsty and Mansel, Philip, *The French Émigrés in Europe and the Struggle Against the Revolution 1789–1814* 1999

Cartwright, Frederick and Biddiss, Michael, *Disease and History* 1972

ed. Castellane, Boniface de, *Journal du Maréchal de Castellane* vol. 1 1896

Castelot, André, *La Campagne de Russie* 1991

ed. Castle, Alison, *Stanley Kubrick's Napoleon* 2009

Cate, Curtis, *The War of the Two Emperors* (New York) 1985

ed. Cerf, Leon, *Letters of Napoleon to Josephine* 1931

Chadwick, Owen, *The Popes and the European Revolution* 1981

Champagny, J.-B. Nompère de, *Souvenirs* 1846

Champfleury Jules, *Histoire de la caricature* 4 vols. 1885

Chandler, David, *Campaigns of Napoleon* 1965
 Napoleon 1973
 Dictionary of the Napoleonic Wars (New York) 1993
 On the Napoleonic Wars 1994
 Jena 1806 2005

ed. Chandler, David, *The Military Maxims of Napoleon* 1987
 Napoleon's Marshals 1987

Chaptal, Jean-Antoine, *Mes souvenirs de Napoléon* 1893

Chardigny, Louis, *Les maréchaux de Napoléon* 1977
     L'Homme Napoléon 1986
ed. Charles, David W., *Victor Marie du Pont* 1961
Charvet, P. E., *A Literary History of France* vol. IV 1967
Chateaubriand, F. A. de, *Of Buonaparte and the Bourbons* 1814
ed. Chatel de Brancion, Laurence, *Cambacérès: mémoires inédits* 2 vols. 1999
Chevallier, Bernard, *Empire Style* 2008
eds. Chevallier, Bernard, Dancoisne-Martineau, Michel and Lentz, Thierry,
     Sainte-Hélène, Île de Mémoire 2005
Chlapowski, Dezydery, *Memoirs of a Polish Lancer* 2002
Chrisawn, Margaret, *The Emperor's Friend* 2001
Christophe, Robert, *Napoleon on Elba*, 1964
Chuquet, Arthur, *La jeunesse de Napoléon* 3 vols. 1897–99
ed. Cisterne, Raoul de, *Journal de marche du Grenadier Pils* 1895
Clark, Christopher, *Iron Kingdom* 2006
Clary-et-Aldringen, Prince Charles de, *Trois mois à Paris lors du marriage de
     l'Empereur Napoléon I et de L'Archduchesse Marie-Louise* 1914
Cobb, Richard, *The Police and the People* 1970
Cobban, Alfred, *A History of Modern France* vol. II 1961
Cockburn, Sir George, *Buonaparte's Voyage to Saint Helena* (Boston) 1833
Coignet, Jean-Roch, *Captain Coignet* 2007
Cole, Hubert, *Fouché* 1971
     The Betrayers 1972
Cole, Juan, *Napoleon's Egypt* (New York) 2007
Collins, Irene, *The Government and the Newspaper Press in France 1814–1881*
     1959
     Napoleon and His Parliaments 1979
Connelly, Owen, *Napoleon's Satellite Kingdoms* (New York) 1965
     Blundering to Glory 1993
Constant, Louis, *Memoirs of Constant* 4 vols. 1896
Coston, F. G. de, *Biographie des premières années de Napoléon Bonaparte* 1840
ed. Cottin, Paul, *Souvenirs de Roustam* 1911
Coxe, Peter, *The Exposé* 1809
Croker, John Wilson, *An Answer to O'Meara's Napoleon in Exile* 1823
Cronin, Vincent, *Napoleon* 1971
Crook, Malcolm, *Toulon in War and Revolution* 1991
     Napoleon Comes to Power 1998
ed. Crook, Malcolm, *Revolutionary France 1788–1880* 2002
Crowdy, T. E., *Incomparable: Napoleon's 9th Light Infantry Regiment* 2012
Currie, Laurence, *The Bâton in the Knapsack* 1934
D'Abrantès, Duchess, *Memoirs of Napoleon, his Court and his Family* 2 vols.
     1857
     At the Court of Napoleon 1991
Daly, Gavin, *Inside Napoleonic France* 2001
Darnton, Robert, *The Devil in the Holy Water* 2010

Davies, Huw, *Wellington's Wars* 2011

Davies, Norman, *Vanished Kingdoms* 2011

ed. Davis, J., *Original Journals of the Eighteen Campaign of Napoleon Bonaparte* 2 vols. 1817

Davis, J. A., *Conflict and Control* 1988

Decaux, Alain, *Napoleon's Mother* 1962

DeConde, Alexander, *This Affair of Louisiana* 1976

Denon, Vivant, *Travels in Upper and Lower Egypt* 3 vols. 1803

D'Erlon, Le Maréchal Drouet, Comte, *Vie militaire* 1844

Derogy, Jacques and Carmel, Hesi, *Bonaparte en Terre sainte* 1992

Desbrière, Édouard, *Projets et tentatives de débarquement aux îles Britanniques* 5 vols. 1900–1902

Desgenettes, René-Nicolas, *Histoire médicales de l'Armée d'Orient* 1802

Dubois, Laurent, *A Colony of Citizens* (Chapel Hill, NC) 2004

Dubroca, Louis Jean, *Life of Bonaparte, First Consul of France* 1802

Duffy, Christopher, *Austerlitz* 1977

ed. Dufourcq, Albert, *Mémoires du Général Baron Desvernois* 1898

Dumas, Lt-Gen. Comte Mathieu, *Memoirs of his own Time* 2 vols. 1839

ed. Duruy, George, *Memoirs of Barras* 4 vols. (New York) 1895

Dwyer, Philip, *Talleyrand* 2002

  Napoleon: The Path to Power 2008

ed. Dwyer, Philip, *Napoleon and Europe* 2003

eds. Dwyer, Philip and Forrest, Alan, *Napoleon and His Empire* 2007

eds. Dwyer, Philip and McPhee, Peter, *The French Revolution and Napoleon* 2002

Ebrington, Lord, *Memorandum of Two Conversations between the Emperor Napoleon and Viscount Ebrington* 1823

Ellis, Geoffrey, *Napoleon's Continental Blockade* 1981

  Napoleon 1997

  The Napoleonic Empire 2003

Elting, John, *Swords around a Throne* 1986

Emsley, Clive, *The Longman Companion to Napoleonic Europe* 1993

  Gendarmes and the State in Nineteenth-Century Europe 1999

  Napoleon: Conquest, Reform and Reorganisation 2003

Englund, Steven, *Napoleon* 2004

ed. Ernouf, Baron, *Souvenirs d'un officier polonais* 1877

Esdaile, Charles, *The Wars of Napoleon* 1995

  The Peninsular War 2002

  Fighting Napoleon (New Haven, CT) 2004

Espitalier, Albert, *Vers Brumaire* 1914

Etruria, Maria Louisa, Queen of, *Memoirs of the Queen of Etruria* 1823

Evstafiev, Alexis, *The Resources of Russia, in the Event of a War with France* 1812

Eyck, F. G., *Loyal Rebels* (Maryland) 1986

Faber, Theodor von, *Sketches of the Internal State of France* 1811

Fain, Agathon-Jean-François, Baron, *Manuscrit de mil huit cent treize* 2 vols. 1824
   Manuscrit de mil huit cent douze 2 vols. 1827
   Memoirs of the Invasion of France by the Allied Armies in 1814 1834
   Mémoires 2001
Fantin des Odoards, Louis-Florimond, *Journal de Général Fantin des Odoards 1800–1830* 1895
Field, Andrew, *Waterloo* 2012
Fisher, H. A. L., *Studies in Napoleonic Statesmanship* 1903
   Bonapartism 1961
ed. Fleischmann, General, *Memoirs of the Count Miot de Melito* 1881
Fleischmann, Théo, *Histoire de la ferme du Caillou* 1954
   Napoléon en bivouac 1957
   En écoutant parler les grognards de Napoléon 1962
   Napoléon et la musique 1965
ed. Fleischmann, Théo, *L'Épopée Impériale* 1964
Fleury de Chaboulon, Baron, *Memoirs of the Private Life, Return and Reign of Napoleon in 1815* 2 vols. 1820
Florange, Charles and Wunsch, A., *L'Entrevue de Napoleon et de Goethe* 1932
Foladare, Joseph, *Boswell's Paoli* 1979
ed. Fontana, Biancamaria, *Benjamin Constant: Political Writings* 1988
Fontanes, Louis, Marquis de, *Parallèle entre César, Cromwell, Monck et Bonaparte* 1800
Foord, Edward, *Napoleon's Russian Campaign* 1914
Forrest, Alan, *Conscripts and Deserters* 1989
   Napoleon's Men 2002
   Napoleon 2011
eds. Forrest, Alan and Jones, Peter, *Reshaping France* 1991
eds. Forrest, Alan, Hagemann, Karen and Rendall, Jane, *Soldiers, Citizens and Civilians: Experiences and Perceptions of the Revolutionary and Napoleonic Wars 1790–1820* 2009
eds. Forrest, Alan and Wilson, Peter H., *The Bee and the Eagle* 2008
Forsyth, William, *History of the Captivity of Napoleon at St Helena* 3 vols. 1853
ed. Foster, Vere, *The Two Duchesses* 1898
Fox, Robert, *The Culture of Science in France 1700–1900* 1992
Foy, General, *Discours du Général Foy* vol. I 1826
   History of the War in the Peninsula under Napoleon 2 vols. 1829
France, *Constitution de la République Française* 1800
Fraser, Edward, *The War Drama of the Eagles* 1912
Fraser, Flora, *Venus of Empire* 2009
Fraser, Ronald, *Napoleon's Cursed War* (New York) 2008
ed. Frayling, Christopher, *Napoleon Wrote Fiction* 1972
Freedman, Lawrence, *Strategy* 2013
French Government, *Code civil des français* 1805
Friedman, Dr Reuben, *The Emperor's Itch* (New York) 1940
Fuller, J. F. C., *The Decisive Battles of the Western World* 1970

Gachot, J. Édouard, *Siège de Gênes* 1908

Gaffarel, Paul, *Bonaparte et les républiques italiennes* 1895

Gallaher, John G., *The Iron Marshal* 2000

Gallais, M., *Histoire du Dix-Huit Brumaire* 4 vols. 1814–17

ed. Gallatin, Count, *The Diary of James Gallatin* 1914

Gardner, Dorsey, *Quatre Bras, Ligny and Waterloo* 1882

ed. Garnier, Jacques, *Dictionnaire Perrin des guerres et des batailles de l'histoire de France* 2004

eds. Garnier, Jacques and Tulard, Jean, *Nouvelle bibliographie critique des mémoires sur l'époque napoléonienne* 1991

ed. Gaskill, Howard, *The Reception of Ossian in Europe* 2006

Gates, David, *The Napoleonic Wars 1803–1815* 1997

ed. Gaudin, Martin, *Mémoires, souvenirs, opinions et écrits du Duc de Gaëte* 1826

Germain, Pierre, *Drouët d'Erlon* 1985

Geyl, Pieter, *Napoleon: For and Against* 1949

Gibbs, Montgomery B., *The Military Career of Napoleon the Great* (Chicago) 1895

ed. Gielgud, Adam, *Memoirs of Prince Adam Czartoryski* 2 vols. 1888

Gildea, Robert, *Children of the Revolution: The French 1799–1914* 2008

Gill, John H., *With Eagles to Glory* 1992

　　Thunder on the Danube 3 vols. 2008–2010

Gillevoison, C. A. G. Duchesne de, *Le Maréchal Moncey* 1902

Gilmour, David, *The Pursuit of Italy* 2011

Girod de l'Ain, Général, *Dix ans de mes souvenirs militaires* 2000

ed. Girod de l'Ain, Maurice, *Vie militaire du Général Foy* 1900

Giubelli, Antonio, *Napoleon on the Island of Elba* 2008

Godechot, Jacques, *Les instititions de la France sous la Révolution et l'Empire* 1985

Gonneville, Aymar-Olivier de, *Recollections of Colonel de Gonneville* 2 vols. 2009

Goodspeed, D. J., *Bayonets at St-Cloud* 1965

Gourgaud, General Baron Gaspard, *The Campaign of 1815* 1818

　　Napoleon and the Grand Army in Russia 1825

　　Journal de Sainte-Hélène 2 vols. 1944–47

ed. Gourgaud, General Gaspard, *Memoirs of the History of France During the Reign of Napoleon dictated by the Emperor at St Helena* 2 vols. 1823

Grainger, John D., *The Amiens Truce* 2004

ed. Gray, Daniel Savage, *In the Words of Napoleon* (Troy, AL) 1977

Gray, Denis, *Spencer Perceval* 1963

Grimsted, Patricia Kennedy, *The Foreign Ministers of Alexander I* (Oakland, CA) 1969

Grouchy, Count de, *Doubts of the Authenticity of the Historical Memoirs Attributed to Napoleon* (Philadelphia) 1820

Grouchy, Marquis de, *Mémoires de Maréchal de Grouchy* 5 vols. 1873

Gueniffey, Patrice, *Le Dix-Huit Brumaire* 2008

Guérard, Albert Léon, *Reflections on the Napoleonic Legend* 1924

Haig, Diana, *Walks Through Napoleon and Josephine's Paris* 2003

Hales, E. E. Y., *Napoleon and the Pope* 1961

Hamelin, Antoine, *Douze ans de ma vie* 1926

ed. Handel, Michael, *Leaders and Intelligence* 1989

ed. Hanoteau, Jean, *The Memoirs of Queen Hortense* 2 vols. (New York) 1927
    With Napoleon in Russia 2 vols. 1935

Harris, Robin, *Talleyrand* 2007

Hastier, Louis, *Le grand amour de Joséphine* 1955

Hayman, Peter, *Soult: Napoleon's Maligned Marshal* 1990

ed. Haythornthwaite, Philip, *The Napoleonic Source Book* 1990
    Napoleon: The Final Verdict 1996
    Napoleonic Cavalry 2001
    Napoleonic Infantry 2001

Hazareesingh, Sudhir, *The Saint-Napoleon* (Cambridge, MA) 2004

Headley, J. T., *The Imperial Guard of Napoleon* 1851

Healey, F. G., *The Literary Culture of Napoleon* 1959

eds. Hennet, Léon and Martin, le Commandant, *Lettres interceptées par les Russes* 1913

Henry, Walter, *Trifles from My Portfolio* 2 vols. (Quebec) 1839

Herold, C., *The Mind of Napoleon* (New York) 1955
    Bonaparte in Egypt 1962
    The Age of Napoleon 1963

Hibbert, Christopher, *Napoleon: His Wives and Women* (New York) 2002

ed. Hicks, Peter, *Clisson and Eugénie* 2009
    Lieutenant Woodberry 2013

Higonnet, Patrice, *Paris* 2002

Hobhouse, John Cam (Baron Broughton), *The Substance of Some Letters Written by an Englishman Resident at Paris* 2 vols. 1816
    Recollections of a Long Life 6 vols. 1909

Holland, Lord, *Foreign Reminiscences* 1850

Hollins, David, *Hungarian Hussar 1756–1815* 2003

Holtman, Robert B., *Napoleonic Propaganda* (Louisiana) 1950
    The Napoleonic Revolution (Philadelphia) 1967

Home, George, *Memoirs of an Aristocrat, and Reminiscences of the Emperor Napoleon* 1837

eds. Horn, Colonel Bernd and Walker, Robert W., *Le Précis de leadership militaire* (Ontario) 2008

Horne, Alistair, *Napoleon, Master of Europe 1805–1807* 1979
    How Far from Austerlitz? 1996
    The Age of Napoleon 2004

Horward, Donald D., *Napoleon and Iberia* 1994

Houssaye, Henry, *Napoleon and the Campaign of 1814* 1914
    Le dernier jour de Napoléon à la Malmaison 1914
    1815 3 vols. 1917
    The Return of Napoleon 1934

ed. Howard, J. E., *Letters and Documents of Napoleon* vol. I 1961

Howard, Martin, *Napoleon's Doctors* 2006

Hozier, Captain H. M., *The Invasions of England* vol. II 1876

Hughes, Michael, *Forging Napoleon's Grande Armée* 2012

Israel, Jonathan I., *The Dutch Republic* 1995

ed. Iung, Theodore, *Lucien Bonaparte et ses mémoires* 3 vols. 1882

Jackson, Basil, *Notes and Reminiscences of a Staff Officer* 1903

James, C. L. R., *The Black Jacobins* 1938

Jarrett, Mark, *The Congress of Vienna and its Legacy* 2013

Jefferson, Thomas, *Memoirs, Correspondence and Private Papers* 4 vols. 1829

Jenkins, E. H., *A History of the French Navy* 1973

ed. Jennings, Louis J., *The Croker Papers*, 3 vols. 1885

ed. Jimack, Peter, *A History of the Two Indies* 2006

Johnson, David, *Napoleon's Cavalry and its Leaders* (New York) 1978

Johnson, Paul, *Napoleon* 2003

ed. Johnston, R. M., *The Corsican* (New York) 1930

    In the Words of Napoleon 2002

eds. Jomard, E. F., et al., *Description de l'Égypte* 21 vols. 1809–23

Jomini, General Baron A. H. de, *The Political and Military History of the Campaign of Waterloo* 1853

    Summary of the Art of War 1854

    Life of Napoleon 4 vols. (New York) 1864

ed. Jones, Proctor Patterson, *Napoleon* 1992

    Napoleon, How He Did It 1998

    In Napoleon's Shadow (San Francisco) 1998

ed. Jonge, Alex de, *Napoleon's Last Will and Testament* 1977

Jonquière, Clément de la, *L'Expédition d'Égypte 1798–1801* 4 vols. 1908

Jordan, David P., *Napoleon and the Revolution* 2012

Jourdan, Annie, *Napoléon* 1998

Jourquin, Jacques, *Dictionnaire des maréchaux du Premier Empire* 1999

ed. Jourquin, Jacques, *Journal de Capitaine François* 2 vols. 1984

eds. Kafker, Frank and Laux, James, *Napoleon and His Times* (Florida) 1989

eds. Kagan, Frederick W and Higham, Robin, *The Military History of Tsarist Russia* 2002

Karlen, Arno, *Napoleon's Glands* 1984

Kauffmann, Jean-Paul, *The Black Room at Longwood* 1997

Kemble, James, *Napoleon Immortal* 1959

ed. Kemble, James, *St Helena During Napoleon's Exile* 1969

Kerckhove, J. L. R. de, *Histoire des maladies observées à la Grande Armée en 1812* 1836

ed. Kerry, the Earl of, *The First Napoleon* 1925

Kiley, Kevin, *Artillery of the Napoleonic Wars* 2004

    Once There Were Titans: Napoleon's Generals and Their Battles 2007

Kircheisen, Friedrich, *Napoleon* 1931

Kissinger, Henry, *A World Restored* 1957

Knapton, Ernest John, *Empress Josephine* (Cambridge, MA) 1963

Knight, Roger, *The Pursuit of Victory* 2006
    Britain Against Napoleon 2013
Koebner, Richard, *Empire* 1961
Kolli, Baron de, *Memoirs of the Baron de Kolli* 1823
Labaume, Eugène, *The Crime of 1812 and its Retribution* (New York) 1912
La Bédoyère, Charles de, *Memoirs of the Public and Private Life of Napoleon Bonaparte* 2 vols. 1835
Lachouque, Henry and Brown, Anne S. K., *The Anatomy of Glory* 1978
Lacour-Gayet, G., *Talleyrand 1754–1838* 1933
ed. Lacour-Gayet, Robert, *Mémoires du Comte Beugnot* 1959
    The Memoirs of Chancellor Pasquier 1967
Lancesseur, Pierre de, *L'Enigme de Waterloo* 2012
Langeron, L. A.-A., Comte de, *Mémoires de Langeron* 1902
Lanzac de Laborie, Léon de, *Paris sous Napoleon* vol. II 1905
ed. Lanzac de Laborie, Léon de, *Mémorial de J. de Norvins* 3 vols. 1896
eds. Larichev, E. and Ostarkova, I., *Paris-St Petersburg 1800–1830* (Moscow) 2003
Las Cases, Comte Emmanuel de, *Memoirs of Emanuel Augustus Dieudonné Count de Las Casas* 1818
    Le Mémorial de Sainte-Hélène 4 vols. 1823
    Mémorial de Saint-Hélène: Journal of the Private Life and Conversations of the Emperor Napoleon at St Helena 4 vols. 1823
    The Life, Exile, and Conversations of the Emperor Napoleon 4 vols. 1835
Laskey, Captain J. C., *A Description of the Series of Medals Struck at the National Medal Mint by Order of Napoleon Bonaparte* 1818
ed. Latimer, Elizabeth, *Talks of Napoleon at St-Helena* 1903
Lavalette, Count Marie, *The Memoirs of Count Lavalette* (Philadelphia) 1832
eds. Laven, David and Riall, Lucy, *Napoleon's Legacy* 2000
ed. Lecestre, Léon, *Lettres inédites de Napoléon Ier* 2 vols. 1897
Lefebvre, Georges, *Napoleon 1799–1807* 2 vols. 1935
    The Directory 1964
Leggiere, Michael, *Napoleon and Berlin* 2002
Lentz, Thierry, *Roederer* 1989
    Le 18-Brumaire 1997
    Dictionnaire des ministres de Napoléon 1999
    Le Grand Consultat 1799–1804 1999
    Savary 2001
    Napoléon et la conquête de l'Europe 1804–1810 2002
    L'Effondrement du système napoléonien 1810–1814 2004
    La France et l'Europe de Napoléon 1804–1814 2007
    La conspiration du Général Malet 2012
    Napoléon diplomate 2012
ed. Lentz, Thierry, *Le Sacre de Napoléon* 2003
    1810: Le tournant de l'Empire 2010
Lentz, Thierry and Imhoff, Denis, *La Moselle et Napoléon* 1986

Lentz, Thierry and Macé, Jacques, *La mort de Napoléon* 2009

eds. Lentz, Thierry et al., *Quand Napoléon inventait la France* 2008

Levasseur, Octave, *Souvenirs militaires* 1914

Levy, Arthur, *Napoléon intime* 1893

Lewis, Gwynne, *France 1715–1804* 2004

eds. Lewis, Gwynne and Lucas, Colin, *Beyond the Terror* 1983

ed. Lewis, Theresa, *Extracts from the Journals and Correspondence of Miss Berry* vols. II and III 1866

Lieven, Dominic, *Russia against Napoleon* 2009

Linck, Tony, *Napoleon's Generals: The Waterloo Campaign* 1993

Lipscombe, Nick, *The Peninsular War Atlas* 2010

ed. Lloyd, Charles, *The Keith Papers* 3 vols. 1955

Lockhart, J. G., *The History of Napoleon Buonaparte* 2 vols. 1831

ed. Londonderry, 2nd Marquess of, *Memoirs and Correspondence of Viscount Castlereagh* 12 vols. 1848–53

Longford, Elizabeth, *Wellington: Years of the Sword* 1971
Wellington: Pillar of State 1972

Lullin de Châteauvieux, Jacob Frédéric, *Manuscript Transmitted from St Helena by an Unknown Channel* 1817

ed. Luvaas, Jay, *Napoleon on the Art of War* 1999

Lyons, Martyn, *France Under the Directory* 1975
Napoleon Bonaparte and the Legacy of the French Revolution 1994

Macbride, Mackenzie, *With Napoleon at Waterloo* (Philadelphia) 1911

MacCulloch, Diarmaid, *A History of Christianity* 2009

Macirone, Francis, *Interesting Facts Relating to the Fall and Death of Joachim Murat* 1817

McLynn, Frank, *Napoleon* 1997

McPhee, Peter, *A Social History of France* 2004

Madelin, Louis, *The Consulate and the Empire* 1934

ed. Madelin, Louis, *Lettres inédites de Napoléon Ier à Marie-Louise* 1935

Maitland, Sir Frederick Lewis, *The Surrender of Napoleon* 1904

ed. Malmesbury, 3rd Earl of, *Diaries and Correspondence of James Harris, 1st Earl of Malmesbury* vol. IV 1844
A Series of Letters of the First Earl of Malmesbury vol. II 1870

Mansel, Philip, *Louis XVIII* 1981
The Eagle in Splendour 1987
The Court of France 1789–1830 1988
Prince of Europe 2003

Marbot, Baron de, *Mémoires du Général Baron de Marbot* 3 vols. 1891

ed. Marchand, Louis, *Précis des Guerres de César, par Napoléon* 1836

ed. Maricourt, Baron André, *Mémoires du Général Noguès* 1922

Markham, David, *Napoleon's Road to Glory* 2003

ed. Markham, David, *Imperial Glory* 2003

Markham, Felix, *Napoleon and the Awakening of Europe* 1954
Napoleon 1963

Marshall-Cornwall, James, *Marshal Massena* 1965

Martin, Andy, *Napoleon the Novelist* 2001

Martin, Brian, *Napoleonic Friendship* 2011

Martineau, Gilbert, *Napoleon's St Helena* 1968
   Napoleon Surrenders 1971

Masséna, André, *Mémoires* 1848

Masson, Frédéric, *Napoleon at Home* 2 vols. 1894
   Napoléon et les femmes 1894
   Napoléon dans sa jeunesse 1907
   Napoleon and his Coronation 1911
   The Private Diaries of the Empress Marie-Louise 1922
   Napoleon at St Helena 1949

eds. Masson, Frédéric and Biagi, Guido, *Napoléon inconnu* 2 vols. 1

Maude, F. N., *The Jena Campaign* 2007
   The Leipzig Campaign 2007

Mauduit, Hippolyte de, *Les derniers jours de la Grande Armée* 2 vols. 1847–48

Melvin, Frank Edgar, *Napoleon's Navigation System* (New York) 1919

Memes, John, *Memoirs of the Empress Josephine* (New York) 1832

Méneval, Baron Claude-François, *Napoléon et Marie-Louise* 3 vols. 1843–45

ed. Méneval, Baron Napoleon, *Memoirs to Serve for the History of Napoleon I from 1802 to 1815* 3 vols. 1894

Menzl, Wolfgang, *Germany from the Earliest Period* vol. IV 1898

Merridale, Catherine, *Red Fortress* 2013

ed. Metternich, Prince Richard, *Memoirs of Prince Metternich 1773–1815* vols. I and II 1880

Mikaberidze, Alexander, *The Battle of Borodino* 2007
   The Battle of the Berezina 2010

ed. Millet, Stanislaw, *Le Chasseur Pierre Millet* 1903

Mollien, Comte, *Mémoires d'un ministre du trésor public* 3 vols. 1898

Montefiore, Simon Sebag, *Jerusalem* 2011

Montesquiou, Anatole de, *Souvenirs sur la Révolution, l'Empire, la Restauration et le Règne de Louis-Philippe* 1961

Montesquiou-Fezensac, Raymond de, *The Russian Campaign 1812* 1970

Montholon, Albine de, *Journal secret d'Albine de Montholon* 2002

Montholon, General Count Charles-Tristan de, *History of the Captivity of Napoleon at St Helena* 3 vols. 1846

Moorehead, Caroline, *Dancing to the Precipice* 2009

Moreau, Jean, *Bonaparte and Moreau* (Philadelphia) 1806

ed. Moreh, Schmuel, *Napoleon in Egypt* 1993

Mossiker, Frances, *Napoleon and Josephine* 1964

Mowat, Robert, *The Diplomacy of Napoleon* 1924

Mudford, William, *An Historical Account of the Battle of Waterloo* 1817

Muir, Rory, *Britain and the Defeat of Napoleon* 1996
   Tactics and the Experience of Battle in the Age of Napoleon 1998

Nafziger, George, *Napoleon's Invasion of Russia* (Novato, CA) 1988
   Napoleon at Dresden 1994
   Imperial Bayonets 1996
   Napoleon at Leipzig 1997
Nafziger, George, Wesolowski, Mariusz T. and Devoe, Tom, *The Poles and Saxons during the Napoleonic Wars* (Chicago) 1991
Namier, Sir Lewis, *Vanished Supremacies* 1970
Nasica, Abbé T., *Mémoires sur l'enfance et la jeunesse de Napoléon* 1852
Nepos, Cornelius, *Vies des Grands Capitaines* 1818
ed. Nesbitt, Nick, *Toussaint L'Ouverture* 2008
Nester, Wiliam R., *Napoleon and the Art of Diplomacy* 2011
Nicolson, Nigel, *Napoleon* 1985
ed. Noailles, Marquis de, *The Life and Memoirs of Count Molé* vol. I 1923
ed. North, Jonathan, *With Napoleon in Russia* 2001
   Napoleon on Elba 2004
   With Napoleon's Guard in Russia 2013
Odeleben, Baron Ernst von, *A Circumstantial Narrative of the Campaign in Saxony in 1813* 1820
Olivier, Daria, *The Burning of Moscow* 1966
eds. Olsen, John and van Creveld, Martin, *The Evolution of Operational Art from Napoleon to the Present* 2011
O'Meara, Barry, *Napoleon in Exile, or, a Voice from St Helena* 2 vols. 1820
Orieux, Jean, *Talleyrand* (New York) 1974
ed. Orwicz, Michael R., *Art Criticism and its Institutions in Nineteenth-Century France* 1994
Ott, Thomas, *The Haitian Revolution 1789–1804* (Knoxville, TN) 1973
Palmer, Alan, *Alexander I* 1974
   An Encyclopaedia of Napoleon's Europe 1984
   Bernadotte 1990
   Napoleon and Marie Louise 2001
   Napoleon in Russia 2003
ed. Palmstierna, C.-F., *My Dearest Louise* 1955
Paoli, François, *La Jeunesse de Napoléon* 2005
Paret, Peter, *The Cognitive Challenge of War* 2009
Paris, William Francklyn, *Napoleon's Legion* 1927
ed. Park, Julian, *Napoleon in Captivity* 1827
Pawly, Ronald, *Napoleon's Red Lancers* 2003
Pelet de la Lozère, Baron Joseph, *Napoleon in Council* 1837
Pellapra, Emilie de, *A Daughter of Napoleon* (New York) 1922
Peltier, John, *The Trial of John Peltier, Esq, for a Libel Against Napoleon Buonaparté* 1803
Percy, Pierre-François, *Journal des campagnes du Baron Percy* 1986
Pétiet, Général Baron Auguste, *Souvenirs militaires de l'histoire contemporaine* 1844

Petit, Joseph, *Marengo* 1801

Peyrusse, Guillame, *Mémorial et archives de M. le Baron Peyrusse* (Carcassonne) 1869

Pigeard, Alain, *L'Armée de Napoléon 1800–1815* 2000
  La conscription au temps de Napoléon 2003
  Napoléon amoureux 2007

ed. Plenel, Edwy, *Joseph Fouché, ministre de la police* 1993

Plumptre, Anne, *A Narrative of a Three Years' Residence in France 1802–1805* 3 vols. 1810

Pocock, Tom, *The Terror Before Trafalgar* 2002
  Stopping Napoleon 2004

Pontécoulant, Philippe-Gustave, *Napoleon à Waterloo* 2004

ed. Pope, Stephen, *The Cassell Dictionary of the Napoleonic Wars* 1999

Popkin, Jeremy, *The Right-Wing Press in France 1792–1800* (Chapel Hill, NC) 1980

Poultier, François, *A Sketch of the History of the War in Europe* (New York) 1798

Pradt, Abbé de, *Histoire de l'ambassade dans le Grand Duché de Varsovie* 1815

Prat, Louis-Antoine and Tonkovich, Jennifer, *David, Delacroix and Revolutionary France* 2011

Price, Munro, *The Perilous Crown* 2007

Prinzing, Friedrich, *Epidemics Resulting from Wars* 1916

ed. Quentin, Roger, *André Peyrusse* 2010

ed. Raeff, Marc, *The Diary of a Napoleonic Foot Soldier* 1991

Ragsdale, Hugh, *Détente in the Napoleonic Era* 1980

Raguse, Duc de, *Mémoires du Maréchal Marmont* 9 vols. 1857

Ramon, G., *Histoire de la Banque de France* 1929

Rapp, General Count, *Memoirs of General Count Rapp* 1823

Reiset, Le Vicomte de, *Souvenirs du Lieutenant Général Vicomte de Reiset 1814–1836* vol. III 1899

ed. Rémusat, Paul de, *Memoirs of Madame de Rémusat* 3 vols. 1880
  A Selection of the Letters of Madame de Rémusat 1881

ed. René, François, *Original Journals of the Eighteen Campaigns of Napoleon Bonaparte* 2 vols. 1817

Reynier, General Jean, *Mémoires du Comte Reynier* 1827

Ribbe, Claude, *Le crime de Napoléon* 2005

Richardson, Hubert N. B., *A Dictionary of Napoleon and His Times* 1920

Richardson, Nicholas, *The French Prefectoral Corps 1814–1830* 1966

Richardson, Robert, *The Apocalypse of Napoleon* 2009

Riehn, Richard, *Napoleon's Russian Campaign* (New York) 1991

Ripaud, Citizen, *Report of the Commission of Arts* 1800

Robb, Graham, *Parisians* 2010

Roberts, Andrew, *Waterloo* 2011

Rodger, A. B., *The War of the Second Coalition 1798–1801* 1964

Rodger, N. A. M., *Command of the Ocean* 2006

Roederer, Pierre-Louis, *Autour de Bonaparte* 1909
    Bonaparte me disait 1942

ed. Roncière, Charles de la, *The Letters of Napoleon to Marie-Louise* 1935

Ropes, John, *The Campaign of Waterloo* (New York) 1892

Rose, John Holland, *The Life of Napoleon* 2 vols. 1903
    The Personality of Napoleon 1912

ed. Rose, J. H., *Napoleon's Last Voyages* 1906

Rosebery, Lord, *Napoleon: The Last Phase* 1900

Rosen, Lew, *Napoleon's Opera-Glass* 1897

Ross, Michael, *The Reluctant King* 1976

Rostopchine, Fyodor, *L'Incendie de Moscou* 2000

Rothenberg, Gunther E., *The Art of Warfare in the Age of Napoleon* 1977
    The Napoleonic Wars 1999
    The Emperor's Last Victory 2005

Rouart, Jean-Marie, *Napoléon ou la destinée* 2012

ed. Rousset, Camille, *Recollections of Marshal Macdonald* 2 vols. 1892

ed. Routier, Colonel Léon, *Récits d'un soldat de la République et de l'Empire* 2004

Rovigo, Duc de, *Mémoires du duc de Rovigo* 8 vols. 1828

ed. Rowe, Michael, *Collaboration and Resistance in Napoleonic Europe* 2003

Rudé, George, *Revolutionary Europe* 1964

ed. Sadler, Thomas, *Diary, Reminiscences and Correspondence of Henry Crabb Robinson* 3 vols. 1869

ed. Sage, Robert, *The Private Diaries of Stendhal* (New York) 1954

Saint-Amand, Imbert de, *Marie Louise and the Decadence of the Empire* (New York) 1902
    Marie Louise, the Island of Elba, and the Hundred Days (New York) 1902

eds. St-Cère, Jacques and Schlitter, H., *Napoléon à Sainte-Hélène* n.d.

Saint-Chamans, Gén. Comte Alfred de, *Mémoires du Général Comte de Saint-Chamans* 1896

Saint-Cyr, Laurent Gouvion, *Mémoires pour servir à l'histoire militaire* 4 vols. 1831

Saint-Denis, Louis Étienne (Known as Ali), *Napoleon from the Tuileries to St Helena* 1922
    Souvenirs du Mameluck Ali 1926

Saint-Hilaire, Émile de, *Napoléon au Conseil-d'État* 1843

eds. Saint-Pierre, Louis and Saint-Pierre, Antoinette, *Mémoires du Maréchal Soult* 1955

ed. Sanderson, Edgar, *Bourrienne's Memoirs of Napoleon Bonaparte* 1900

Sarrazin, General, *Confession of General Buonaparté to the Abbé Maury* 1811
    History of the War in Spain and Portugal 1815

Sauzet, Armand, *Desaix, le sultan juste* 1954

Savary, Anne-Jean-Marie, *Memoirs Relative to the Duke D'Enghien* 1823

Savatier, René, *L'Art de faire les lois* 1927

Schlabrendorf, Graf Gustav von, *Bonaparte and the French People* 1804
    Napoleon and the French People Under his Empire 1806

ed. Schlumberger, Gustave, *Lettres du commandant Coudreux* 1908

Schneid, Frederick C., *Soldiers of Napoleon's Kingdom of Italy* 1995
  Napoleon's Italian Campaigns 1805–1815 2002
  Napoleon's Conquest of Europe (New Haven, CT) 2005

Schom, Alan, *Napoleon Bonaparte* 1997

Schroeder, Paul, *The Transformation of European Politics 1763–1848* 1994

Schur, Nathan, *Napoleon in the Holy Land* 1999

ed. Schwartz, Bernard, *The Code Napoleon and the Common-Law World* (New York) 1956

Schwarzfuchs, Simon, *Napoleon, the Jews and the Sanhedrin* (Philadelphia) 1979

Sciout, Ludovic, *Le Directoire* vol. 4 1895

Ségur, General Count Philippe de, *Memoirs of an Aide-de-Camp of Napoleon 1800–1812* 2005

Ségur, Paul de, *Napoléon et la Grande Armée en 1812* 1824

Shepherd, Rev. William, *Paris in 1802 and 1814* 1814

Sherwig, John M., *Guineas and Gunpowder* (Cambridge, MA) 1969

Shmuelevitz, Aryeh, *Napoleon and the French in Egypt and the Holy Land* (Istanbul) 2010

Shoberl, Frederic, *Narrative of the Most Remarkable Events which Occurred in and near Leipzig* 1814

Simms, Brendan, *The Impact of Napoleon* 1997
  The Struggle for Mastery in Germany 1779–1850 1998
  Europe: The Struggle for Supremacy 2013

Simonetta, Marcello and Arikha, Noga, *Napoleon and the Rebel* 2011

Six, Georges, *Dictionnaire biographique des généraux et amiraux français de la Révolution et de l'Empire 1792–1814* 2 vols. 1934

Sked, Alan, *Radetzky* 2011

Smith, Digby, *The Greenhill Napoleonic Wars Data Book* 1998
  Napoleon's Regiments 2000
  1813 Leipzig 2001
  The Decline and Fall of Napoleon's Empire 2005
  'Charge!' 2007

Smith, Sir William Sidney, *The French Expedition into Syria* 1799

Solé, Robert, *La conquête de l'Égypte* 2006

Soltyk, Roman, *Napoléon en 1812* 1838

ed. Soult, fils, *Mémoires du Maréchal-Général Soult* 3 vols. 1854

Sparrow, Elizabeth, *Secret Service* 1999
  Shadow of the Guillotine 2013

Staël, Madame Germaine de, *An Appeal to the Nations of Europe against the Continental System* 1813
  Dix années d'exil 2 vols. 2000

Stanhope, 5th Earl, *Notes of Conversations with the Duke of Wellington 1831–1851* 1888

Starke, Mariana, *Letters from Italy Between the Years 1792 and 1798* 2 vols. 1800

Stendhal (Henri Beyle), *The Red and the Black* 2004
  The Charterhouse of Parma 2006
ed. Stiegler, Gaston, *Récits de guerre et de foyer* 1894
eds. Stoker, Donald, Schneid, Frederick and Blanton, Harold, *Conscription in the Napoleonic Era* 2009
Stourton, James and Montefiore, Charles Sebag, *The British as Art Collectors* 2012
Strathearn, Paul, *Napoleon in Egypt* 2007
ed. Stryjenski, Casimir, *Mémoires de la Comtesse Potocka* 1897
Stuart, Andrea, *Rose of Martinique* 2003
Suchet, Marshal Louis Gabriel, *Memoirs of the War in Spain* 2 vols. 1829
Summerville, Christopher, *Napoleon's Polish Gamble* 2005
ed. Summerville, Christopher, *Napoleon's Expedition to Russia* 2003
ed. Summerville, C. J., *The Exploits of Baron de Marbot* 2000
Sutherland, Christine, *Marie Walewska* 1979
Swanson, William C., *Napoleon's Dual Courtship* (privately published) 1923
ed. Tarbell, Ida M., *Napoleon's Addresses* (Boston) 1897
Thiard, A. M. T., *Souvenirs diplomatiques et militaires* 1900
Thibaudeau, Antoine, *Bonaparte and the Consulate* 1908
  Mémoires sur la Consultat 1799 à 1804 1913
Thiers, Louis Adolphe, *History of the Consulate and the Empire of France under Napoleon* vol. XII 1893
Thiry, Jean, *La machine infernale* 1952
Thody, Philip, *French Caesarism from Napoleon to Charles de Gaulle* 1989
Thornton, Michael, *Napoleon after Waterloo* (Stanford, CA) 1968
Thrasher, Peter, *Pasquale Paoli* 1970
Thuillier, Guy, *Regards sur la haute administration de France* 1979
Tissot, P. F., *Souvenirs historiques sur la vie et la mort de F. Talma* 1826
  Histoires de Napoléon 2 vols. 1833
Tolstoy, Leo, *War and Peace* 1869
Tomiche, Nada, *Napoléon écrivain* 1952
Tone, John L., *The Fatal Knot* 1994
Tone, Theodore Wolfe, *The Life of Theodore Wolfe Tone* 1828
ed. Tortel, Christian, *Avec Bonaparte en Égypte et en Syrie* 1976
eds. Tortel, Christian and Carlier, Patricia, *Bonaparte de Toulon au Caire* 1996
Tranié, Jean, *Napoléon et son entourage* 2001
Tranié, Jean and Camigniani, J.-C., *Napoléon Bonaparte, la première campagne d'Italie 1796–97* 1990
Troyat, Henri, *Alexander of Russia* 1982
Tulard, Jean, *L'Anti-Napoléon* 1965
  Napoléon et la noblesse d'Empire 1979
  Le grand empire 1982
  Napoleon: The Myth of the Saviour 1984
  Napoléon: une journée particulière 1994
  Murat 1999

Les vingt jours 1–20 March 1815 2001

Napoléon: les grands moments d'un destin 2006

Dictionnaire amoureux de Napoléon 2012

ed. Tulard, Jean, *Proclamations, orders du jour, bulletins de la Grande Armée* 1964

Bibliographie critique des mémoires sur le Consultat et l'Empire 1971

Cambacérès, lettres inédites à Napoléon 2 vols. 1973

Dictionnaire Napoléon 1989

La Berline de Napoléon 2012

eds. Tulard, Jean and Garros, Louis, *Itinéraire de Napoléon au jour de jour* 1992

Turnbull, Patrick, *Napoleon's Second Empress* 1971

Uffindell, Andrew, *The Eagle's Last Triumph* 1994

Napoleon's Immortals 2007

Napoleon's Chicken Marengo 2011

Underwood, Thomas Richard, *A Narrative of Memorable Events in Paris in the year 1814* 1828

Unger, Harlow, *Layfayette* 2002

Unwin, Brian, *Terrible Exile* 2010

Vandal, Albert, *Napoléon et Alexandre I* 3 vols. 1893

L'Avènement de Bonaparte 2 vols. 1907

Van-Ess, Willem Lodewyk, *The Life of Napoleon Buonaparte* 4 vols. (Philadelphia) 1809

Vaughan, C. R., *Narrative of the Siege of Zaragoza* 1809

Vernon, B. J., *Early Recollections of Jamaica to Which are Added Trifles from St Helena* 1848

Villefosse, Louis de and Bouissounouse, Janine, *The Scourge of the Eagle* 1972

Villemain, Abel-François, *Souvenirs contemporains d'histoire et de littérature* 2 vols. 1854

Villepin, Dominique de, *Les cent jours* 2001

Volney, Constantin de, *Voyage en Égypte et en Syrie* 1787

Vossler, Lieutenant H. A., *With Napoleon in Russia 1812* 1998

Wairy, Constant, *Mémoires de Constant* 1831

ed. Walter, Gérard, *Le Comte de Las Cases* 2 vols. 1956

Warden, William, *Letters Written on Board HMS* Northumberland *and at St Helena* 1817

Waresquiel, Emmanuel de, *Talleyrand* 2011

Watson, Stephen, *The Reign of George III* 1960

Weider, Ben and Forshufvud, Sten, *Assassination at St Helena Revisited* (New York) 1995

Weider, Ben and Hapgood, David, *The Murder of Napoleon* 1982

Weigley, Russell, F., *The Age of Battles* (Bloomington, IN) 1991

ed. Weit, Gaston, *Nicolas Turc, chronique d'Égypte 1798–1804* (Cairo) 1950

Weller, Jac, *Wellington in India* 1972

ed. Wellington, 2nd Duke of, *Despatches, Correspondence and Memoranda of Field Marshal Arthur, Duke of Wellington, K.G.* 15 vols. 1858–72

Welschinger, Henri, *La censure sous le premier empire* 1882
  Le duc d'Enghien 1888

Wesling, Molly, *Napoleon in Russian Cultural Mythology* (New York) 2001

Wheeler, H. B. F. and Broadley, A. B., *Napoleon and the Invasion of England* 2 vols. 1907

Whitcomb, Edward A., *Napoleon's Diplomatic Service* (Durham, NC) 1979

Williams, Helen Maria, *A Narrative of the Events Which Have Taken Place in France* 1815

Williams, John R., *The Life of Goethe* 1998

Williams, Kate, *Josephine* 2013

ed. Wilson, Sir Arnold, *A Diary of St Helena, the Journal of Lady Malcolm* 1929

Wilson, Peter H., *War, Society and State in Württemberg 1677–1793* 1995

Wilson, Sir Robert, *History of the British Expedition to Egypt* 1802
  Brief Remarks on the Character and Composition of the Russian Army in the Years 1806 and 1807 1810
  Campaigns in Poland in the Years 1806 and 1807 1810
  Narrative of Events during the Invasion of Russia by Napoleon Bonaparte 1860

Wilson-Smith, Timothy, *Napoleon and His Artists* 1996
  Napoleon: Man of War, Man of Peace 2002

Winograd, Lee, *Strategical Considerations Concerning the Battle of Acre during Napoleon's Holy Land Campaign* (Tel Aviv) 1973

Wolff, Sir Henry Drummond, *The Island Empire* 1855

Woloch, Isser, *Jacobin Legacy* (Princeton, NJ) 1970
  The French Veteran from the Revolution to the Restoration 1979
  The New Regime: Transformations of the French Civic Order 1789–1820s 1994
  Napoleon and His Collaborators 2001

ed. Woloch, Isser, *Revolution and the Meanings of Freedom in the Nineteenth Century* (Stanford, CA) 1996

Woolf, Otto, *Ouvrard: Speculator of Genius* 1962

Woolf, Stuart, *Napoleon's Integration of Europe* 1991

Wright, Constance, *Daughter to Napoleon* (New York) 1961

ed. Wright, O. W., *History of Charles XII by M. de Voltaire* 1887

Yevstafiev, Aleksey Grigoryevich, *The Resources of Russia in the Event of a War with France* 1813

ed. Yonge, Charlotte M., *A Man of Other Days* 2 vols. 1877
  Memoirs of Marshal Bugeaud vol. I 1884

Zamoyski, Adam, *Holy Madness* 1999
  1812: Napoleon's Fatal March on Moscow 2005

Zarzeczny, Matthew, *Meteors that Enlighten the Earth* 2013

Ziegler, Philip, *The Sixth Great Power* 1988

Zweig, Stefan, *Joseph Fouché* 1930

ARTICLES, ESSAYS AND UNPUBLISHED THESES

Abel, Jonathan, 'Jacques-Antoine-Hippolyte, Comte de Guibert's Military Reforms' *Napoleonic Scholarship* vol. 1 no. 3 May 2010

Abramova, Inna, 'Les médailles relatives à la guerre de 1812 et à Napoléon du Musée de Vitebsk' *Études Napoléoniennes* nos. 31–34 1994

Alexander, Don W., 'French Replacement Methods during the Peninsular War' *Military Affairs* vol. 44 issue 4 December 1980

Alger, J. G., 'Napoleon in Egypt' *Westminster Review* vol. 150 no. 4 1898
'British Visitors to Paris 1802–1803' *English Historical Review* vol. 14 October 1899

Allégret, Marc, 'Autour de la rédaction du Code Civil' *Revue du Souvenir Napoléonien* no. 495 April–June 2013

Anonymous, 'Bonaparte's Campaign in Russia' *Edinburgh Review* no. 24 February 1815
'Mémoires pour servir à l'histoire des expéditions en Égypte et en Syrie par J. Miot' *Quarterly Review* no. 25 April 1815
'Letters from France' *Edinburgh Review* no. 51 February 1816
'Descente en Angleterre' *Notes and Queries* 21 July 1855
'Marshal Marmont's *Memoirs*' *Edinburgh Review* no. 106 July 1857
'The Napoleon Correspondence' *Edinburgh Review* no. 258 Oct 1867
'More about Napoleon' *Quarterly Review* vol. 139 July 1875
'The Unpublished Letters of Napoleon' *Quarterly Review* vol. 187 1898
'The French Expedition to Egypt in 1798' *Edinburgh Review* no. 208 July 1908

Arboit, Gérard, '1812: Le reseignement Russe face à Napoléon' *Revue de l'Institut Napoléon* no. 204 2012

Arnold, James R., 'A Reappraisal of Column versus Line in the Peninsular War' April 2004 *Napoleon Series* website

Beaucour, Fernand, 'Les besoins en voitures pour le chauffage de l'armée au Camp de Boulogne en Janvier 1804' *Études Napoléoniennes* nos. 31–34 1994

Beerbuehl, Margrit Schulte, 'Crossing the Channel: Nathan Mayer Rothschild and his Trade with the Continent during the Early Years of the Blockades 1803–1808' *The Rothschild Archive Review of the Year* 2007/8

Bertaud, Jean-Paul, 'Napoleon's Officers' *Past and Present* no. 111 1986

Biagi, Guido, 'A Coincidence in Napoleon's Life' *Century Magazine* November 1894

Billings, Mark, 'Napoleon: A Dealer of Hope' *Napoleonic Scholarship* vol. 1 no. 3 May 2010

Blaufarb, Rafe, 'The Ancien Régime Origins of Napoleonic Social Reconstruction' *French History* vol. 14 no. 4 2000

Boisson, Daniel, 'Maréchaux et généraux français tués et blessés en 1812' *Les Amis du Patrimonie Napoléonien* no. 35 July 2012

Brack, General de, 'Waterloo' *La Revue de France* vol. 4 July 1932

Branda, Pierre, 'Did the War Pay for the War? An Assessment of Napoleon's Attempts to Make his Campaigns Self-Financing' *Napoleonic Scholarship* vol. 1 no. 4 November 2011

Brier, Bob and Wood, Mary Mendenhall, 'Napoleon in Egypt: The Battle of Chobrakit' *Napoleonic Scholarship* vol. 1 no. 2 December 1998

Broers, Michael, 'The Napoleonic Police and Their Legacy' *History Today* May 1999
  'Cultural Imperialism in a European Context?' *Past and Present* no. 170 2001
  'Napoleon, Charlemagne and Lotharingia: Acculturation and the Boundaries of Napoleonic Europe' *Historical Journal* vol. 44 2001

Brown, Howard G., 'From Organic Society to Security State: The War on Brigandage in France 1797–1802' *Journal of Modern History* vol. 69 1997

Bryant, Mark, 'Graphic Warriors: War Cartoonists 1792–1945' *The London Library Magazine* Winter 2011

Burrows, Simon, 'Culture and Misperception: The Law and the Press in the Outbreak of War in 1803' *International History Review* vol. 18 1996

Byrd, Melanie, 'The Napoleonic Institute of Egypt' *Napoleonic Scholarship* vol. 1 no. 2 December 1998

Chandler, David, 'Napoleon and Death' *Napoleonic Scholarship* vol. 1 no. 1 April 1997

Chaplin, Dr T. H. Arnold, 'Napoleon's Funeral: A Lost Record' *Times Literary Supplement* 30 September 1915

Choffat, Thierry, 'La Bérézina: victoire française' *Centre d'Études et de Recherches sur le Bonapartisme* no. 48 Spring 2013

Cook, John, 'Bernadotte 1806: Is There a Case for the Defence?' *Napoleon Series* website

Crook, Malcolm, 'Time for a Hero? Reappraising Napoleon on the Bicentenary of his Rise to Power' *History* vol. 87 issue 288 October 2002

Crouzet, François, 'The Second Hundred Years War' *French History* vol. 10 1997

Dague, Everett, 'Henri Clarke, Minister of War, and the Malet Conspiracy' *Napoleonic Scholarship* vol. 1 no. 2 December 1998

Davies, Huw J., 'Diplomats as Spymasters: A Case Study of the Peninsular War 1809–1813' *Journal of Military History* vol. 76 no. 1 January 2012

Davies, Peter, 'Who Killed Napoleon Bonaparte?' *The Waterloo Journal* vol. 32 no. 3 Winter 2010

Desclaux, Dr, 'A propos de la "Gale" de Napoléon' *Journal des Patriciens* April 1932

'Détenu', 'The Journal of a Detenu: An Eye-witness of the Events in Paris' *London Magazine* September 1825

Dhombres, Nicole, 'Napoléon et les scientifiques Part I: 1779–1798' *La Revue du Souvenir Napoléonien* no. 350 1985

Dufraisse, Roger, 'Napoleon et l'Empereur' *Études Napoléoniennes* nos. 31–34 1994

Dunne, John, 'Napoleon's Mayoral Problem' *Modern & Contemporary French History* vol. 8 2000

Dupâquier, J., 'Problèmes démographiques de la France Napoléonienne' *Revue d'Histoire Moderne et Contemporaine* vol. 17 1970

Dusoulier, Louis, 'En vendant La Louisiane' *Les Annales de l'Empire: les Compagnons de l'Empire* no. 4 2003

Dutcher, George Matthew, 'Napoleon and the Napoleonic Period' *The Journal of Modern History* vol. 4 no. 3 September 1932

Dwyer, Philip G., 'From Corsican Nationalist to French Revolutionary: Problems of Identity in the Writings of the Young Napoleon 1785–1793' *French History* vol. 16 2002

'Napoleon Bonaparte as Hero and Saviour' *French History* vol. 18 2004

'"It Still Makes Me Shudder": Memories of Massacres and Atrocities During the Revolutionary and Napoleonic Wars' *War in History* vol. 16 no. 4 2009

Dziewanowski, Lieutenant M. K., 'Napoleon: Legend and Propaganda' *Military Affairs* vol. 9 issue 1 January 1945

Ebrington, Lord, 'A Conversation with Napoleon at Elba' *Macmillan's Magazine* December 1894

Eidahl, Kyle, 'Marshal Nicolas Charles Oudinot' *Napoleonic Scholarship* vol. 1 no. 1 April 1997

Ela, Alfred, 'Napoleon's Wounds' *The Boston Medical and Surgical Journal* vol. 174 nos. 22 and 24 June 1916

Epstein, James, 'Politics of Colonial Sensation: The Trial of Thomas Picton and the Cause of Louisa Calderon' *American Historical Review* June 2007

Esdaile, Charles, 'Spanish Guerrillas: Heroes or Villains?' *History Today* no. 38 April 1988

'Recent Writing on Napoleon and His Wars' *The Journal of Military History* vol. 73 issue 1 January 2009

Feinberg, Herb, 'North to Palestine: Napoleon Marches Against the Turks' *Napoleonic Scholarship* vol. 1 no. 2 December 1998

Field, Andrew, 'The Famous Words: The Capture of Cambronne at Waterloo' *Waterloo Journal* vol. 35 no. 1 Spring 2013

Fitzsimmons, Michael P., 'The Debate on Guilds under Napoleon' *Proceedings of the Western Society for French History* vol. 36 2008

Foch, Marshal, 'La battaille de Laon' *Revue de France* May 1921

Forrest, Alan, 'Propaganda and the Legitimation of Power in Napoleonic France' *French History* vol. 18 2004

Friedman, Elias, 'On the Affair of the Murder of the French Soldiers in the Carmelite Monastery during Napoleon's Campaign' *Ariel Journal on the Land of Israel* no. 37 March 1985 (in Hebrew)

Gallaher, John, 'Political Considerations and Strategy: The Dresden Phase of the Leipzig Campaign' *Military Affairs* vol. 49 issue 2 April 1985

'Davout and Napoleon' *Napoleonic Scholarship* vol. 1 no. 1 April 1997

Gates, David, 'The Wars of 1812: A French Perspective' *Mars & Clio* no. 34 Summer 2012

George, Christopher T., 'The Eroica Riddle: Did Napoleon Remain Beethoven's "Hero"?' *Napoleonic Scholarship* vol. 1 no. 2 December 1998

Gichon, Mordechai, 'Jaffa, 1799' *Napoleonic Scholarship* vol. 1 no. 2 December 1998

    'East Meets West: The Clash Between French and Oriental Society during Napoleon's Campaign in Egypt' *Napoleonic Scholarship* vol. 1 no. 3 May 2010

Gill, Conrad, 'The Relations Between England and France in 1802' *English Historical Review* vol. 24 1909

Glover, Richard, 'The French Fleet 1807–1814' *Journal of Modern History* vol. 39 no. 3 September 1967

Grab, Alexander, 'Army, State and Society: Conscription and Desertion in Napoleonic Italy 1802–1814' *Journal of Modern History* vol. 47 1995

    'State Power, Brigandage and Rural Resistance in Napoleonic Italy' *European History Quarterly* vol. 25 1995

    'The Geopolitical Transformation of the Italian Peninsula Under Napoleon' *Napoleonic Scholarship* vol. 1 no. 3 May 2010

Griffin, Miriam, 'Philosophy, Cato and Roman Suicide' *Greece & Rome* vol. 33 no. 1 April 1986

Groutso, Igor, 'Le sort des aigles napoléoniennes pendant le campagne de 1812' *Études Napoléoniennes* nos. 31–34 1994

Hartley, Janet, 'Napoleon in Russia: Saviour or Anti-Christ?' *History Today* vol. 41 no. 1 1991

Harvey, A. D., 'European Attitudes to Britain during the French Revolutionary and Napoleonic Era' *History* vol. 63 1978

Hayman, Neil M., 'France Against Prussia: The Jena Campaign of 1806' *Military Affairs* vol. 30 issue 4 Winter 1966

Hazareesingh, Sudhir, 'Memory and Political Imagination: The Legend of Napoleon Revisited' *French History* vol. 18 2004

    'God of War' *Times Literary Supplement* 3 February 2012

Hicks, Peter, 'The Napoleonic "Police" or "Security" State in Context' in *Napoleonica. La Revue* nos. 2–10 2009

    'Late 18th Century and very early 19th Century British writings on Napoleon: Myth and History' *Fondation Napoléon* website

Hochel, Marian, 'Dominique-Vivant Denon: Napoleon's Chief Arts Adviser' *Napoleonic Scholarship* vol. 1 no. 4 November 2011

Hollins, Dave, 'The Hidden Hand: Espionage and Napoleon' *Osprey Military Journal* vol. 2 no. 2 25 March 2000

Holmes-Wilson, Captain C., 'Nelson and Napoleon: A Criticism of Sea Power' *Minutes of Proceedings of the Royal Artillery Institution* vol. 30 1903–4

Horward, Donald D., 'Masséna and Napoleon: Abandonment in Portugal' *Military Affairs* vol. 37 issue 3 October 1973

    'Napoleon in Review: A Bibliographical Essay' *Military Affairs* vol. 43 issue 3 October 1979

Innocenti, Claudio, 'Souls Not Wanting: The Marshalate's Betrayal of Napoleon' *Napoleonic Scholarship* vol. 1 no. 3 May 2010

Jourdan, Annie, 'Napoleon and History' *French History* vol. 10 1996

'The Grand Paris of Napoleon: From a Dream of Magnificence to a Dream of Utility' *Napoleonic Scholarship* vol. 1 no. 4 November 2011

Keene, Edward, 'The Treaty-making Revolution of the Nineteenth Century' *International History Review* vol. 34 no. 3 September 2012

Lamy, Gautier, 'La cavalerie française de 1813' *La Revue Napoléon* no. 9 June 2013

Lewin, Peter K., Hancock, Ronald G.V. and Voynovich, Paul, 'Napoleon Bonaparte: No Evidence of Arsenic Poisoning' *Nature* vol. 299 14 October 1982

Lochet, Jean, 'The Destruction of the Grande Armée and its Cavalry in Russia 1812' www.magweb.com

Lugli, Alessandro et al., 'Napoleon Bonaparte's Gastric Cancer: A Clinico-pathologic Approach to Staging, Pathogenesis, and Etiology' *Nature Clinical Practice Gastroenterology and Hepatology* vol. 4 no. 1 2007

Maamar, Sayah, 'Propos critiques sur l'Université Impériale vers 1810' *Études Napoléoniennes* nos. 31–34 1994

McErlean, J. M. P., 'Governor Raffles' Fifteen Minutes with Napoleon' *The Waterloo Journal* vol. 27 no. 1 Spring 2005

Markham, Felix, 'The Emperor at Work' *History Today* September 1963

Markham, J. David, 'Napoleon's Last Hours in France' *Napoleonic Scholarship* vol. 1 no. 3 May 2010

'Was Napoleon an Anti-Semite? Napoleon, the Jews and Religious Freedom' Speech to the Symposium on the Bicentenary of the Sanhedrin, Tel Aviv, Israel 31 May 2007

Mikaberidze, Alexander, '"The Russian Eagles over the Seine": Russian Occupation of Paris in 1814' *Napoleonic Scholarship* vol. 1 no. 4 November 2011

Murphy, Orville T., 'Napoleon's International Politics: How Much Did He Owe to the Past?' *Journal of Military History* vol. 54 April 1990

Nester, William, 'Napoleon, Family Values and the Fate of Europe' *Napoleonic Scholarship* vol. 1 no. 4 November 2011

Norris, A. H. and Bremner, R. W., 'The Lines of Torres Vedras' *The British Historical Society of Portugal* 1986

O'Brien, David, 'Antonio Canova's Napoleon as Mars the Peacemaker and the Limits of Imperial Portraiture' *French History* vol. 18 no. 4 2004

Ocampo, Emilio, 'Rescuing Napoleon from St Helena' *Napoleonic Scholarship* vol. 1 no. 4 November 2011

Packwood, Allen, 'A Tale of Two Statesmen: Churchill and Napoleon' *Finest Hour* no. 157 Winter 2012–13

Parker, Harold T., 'Why Did Napoleon Invade Russia?' *Journal of Military History* vol. 54 April 1990

Paz, Ignacio, '1808, the Point of Implosion for the Napoleonic Empire' *Napoleonic Series* website

Pierron, Lt.-Col., 'Les methodes de guerre actuelles' (Paris 1878) *Royal United Services Institute Journal* vol. 23 no. 99 1879

Pratt, Fletcher, 'Vignettes of Napoleon in Italy 1796' *Journal of American Military History* vol. 2 issue 2 Summer 1938

Price, Munro, 'Napoleon and Metternich in 1813' *French History* vol. 26 no. 4 December 2012

Promyslov, Nikolay, 'The Grande Armée's Retreat as Seen from the Intercepted Soldiers' Correspondence' *Napoleonic Scholarship* vol. 1 no. 4 November 2011

Reid, Loren, 'The Last Speech of William Pitt' *Quarterly Journal of Speech* vol. 49 issue 2 1963

Riaud, Xavier, 'Napoleon and His Teeth' *Napoleonic Scholarship* vol. 1 no. 3 May 2010

Rose, J. Holland, 'A Document Relating to the Continental System' *English Historical Review* no. 69 1903

Ross, Steven, 'Napoleon and Manouver Warfare' 28th Harmon Memorial Lecture in Military History, United States Air Force Academy, Colorado 1985

Rossetti, Marie-Joseph, 'Journal du Général Rossetti' *La Revue de France* vol. 5 March 1933

Rowe, Michael, 'Between Empire and Home Town: Napoleonic Rule on the Rhine 1799–1814' *The Historical Journal* vol. 42 1999

Sainsbury, J., 'Thirty Facsimiles of the Different Signatures of the Emperor Napoleon and a Sketch of the Events Connecting Them' 1836

Schmidt, H. D., 'The Idea and Slogan of "Perfidious Albion"' *Journal of the History of Ideas* no. 14 1953

Schmitt, Hans, '1812: Stein, Alexander I and the Crusade against Napoleon' *Journal of Modern History* vol. 31 March 1959

Schneid, Frederick C., 'The Dynamics of Defeat: French Army Leadership, December 1812–March 1813' *Journal of Military History* vol. 63 issue 1 January 1999

Schroeder, Paul W., 'Napoleon's Foreign Policy: A Criminal Enterprise' *Journal of Military History* vol. 54 April 1990

Sibalis, Michael, 'Conspiracy on St Helena? (Mis)remembering Napoleon's Exile' *French History and Civilization* vol. 4 2011

Siegfried, Susan L., 'The Politicisation of Art Criticism in the Post-Revolutionary Press' in ed. Orwicz, Michael R., *Art Criticism and Its Institutions in Nineteenth Century France* 1994

Smith, G. C. Moore, 'General Petit's Account of the Waterloo Campaign' *English Historical Review* vol. 18 no. 70 1903

Sparrow, Elizabeth, 'The Alien Office 1792–1806' *Historical Journal* vol. 33 no. 2 1990

Stark, Nicholas, 'Society: Friend or Enemy of the Blacks' *Napoleonic Scholarship* vol. 1 no. 4 November 2011

Uffindell, Andrew, 'Napoleon Fights for Paris' *Military Illustrated* no. 251 April 2009

Vaskin, Alexander, 'Three Mistakes of Napoleon' *Nezavisimaya Gazeta* 30 August 2012

Weider, Ben, 'The Assassination of Napoleon' *Napoleonic Scholarship* vol. 1 no. 1 April 1997

'Napoleon and the Jews' *Napoleonic Scholarship* vol. 1 no. 2 December 1998

Weigall, Arthur, 'Napoleon's "Great Adventure"' *Blackwood's Magazine* no. 191 April 1912

Whitcomb, E. A., 'Napoleon's Prefects' *American Historical Review* no. 79 1974

Woloch, Isaac, 'Napoleonic Conscription: State Power and Civil Society' *Past and Present* no. 111 1986

Wood, William J., 'Forgotten Sword' *Military Affairs* October 1970

Woolf, Stuart, 'French Civilisation and Ethnicity in the Napoleonic Empire' *Past and Present* no. 124 1989

'The Construction of a European World-View in the Revolutionary–Napoleonic Period' *Past and Present* no. 137 1992

Yale Center, 'Nelson and Anti-Napoleon Verse' Yale University pamphlet [n.d.]

Yarrow, Dr H., 'The Death of Napoleon on St Helena' *Journal of the Association of the Friends of Waterloo Committee* December 1982

SOME NAPOLEONIC WEBSITES

Fondation Napoléon www.napoleon.org
Musée de l'Armée www.invalides.org
Napoleonic Alliance www.napoleonic–alliance.com
Napoleonic Guide www.napoleonguide.com
Napoleon Internet Guide www.napoleonbonaparte.nl
Napoleonic Literature www.napoleonic-literature.com
Napoleonic Series www.napoleonseries.org
Le Souvenir Napoléonien http://www.souvenirnapoleonien.org
War Times Journal www.wtj.com

ARCHIVES

Prince Peter Bagration, Russian State Military Historical Archive, Moscow
Antoine-Alexandre Barbier, Bibliothèque National de France, Paris
Hortense de Beauharnais, Archives Nationales, Paris
Marshal Alexandre Berthier, Bibliothèque National de France, Paris, and Service Historique de la Défense, Vincennes
General Henri Bertrand, Bibliothèque National de France, Paris
Sir Charles Blagden, Beinecke Library, Yale
Caroline Bonaparte, Archives Nationales, Paris
Elisa Bonaparte, Archives Nationales, Paris
Jérome Bonaparte, Archives Nationales, Paris

Joseph Bonaparte, Archives Nationales, Paris, and Service Historique de la Défense, Vincennes

Josephine Bonaparte, Archives Nationales, Paris

Letizia Bonaparte (Madame Mère), Archives Nationales, Paris

Louis Bonaparte, Archives Nationales, Paris

Lucien Bonaparte, Archives Nationales, Paris

Emperor Napoleon I, Archives Nationales, Paris

Pauline Bonaparte, Archives Nationales, Paris

Theodore D. Buhl, Sterling Memorial Library, Yale

Cabinet du Ministre de l'Intérieur, Archives Nationales, Paris

Jean-Jacques Cambacérès, Archives Nationales, Paris

Vicomte de Charrier-Moissard, Bibliothèque National de France, Paris

Thomas Cholmondeley (Lord Delamore), Beinecke Library, Yale

Conseil d'Administration de la Justice, Archives Nationales, Paris

Conseils d'Administration de la Légion d'Honneur, Archives Nationales, Paris

Conseils d'Administration de la Maison de l'Empereur, Archives Nationales, Paris, and Bibliothèque National de France, Paris

Conseil d'Administration des Relations Extérieurs, Archives Nationales, Paris

Conseil d'État, Archives Nationales, Paris

Lord Curzon, Bodleian Library, Oxford

Comte Pierre-Antoine Daru, Service Historique de la Défense, Vincennes

Louis-Nicolas Davout, Service Historique de la Défense, Vincennes

Sir William Fellowes, Beinecke Library, Yale

French Foreign Ministry, Centre des Archives Diplomatiques, La Courneuve

Sir William Gell, Beinecke Library, Yale

Sir John Harper, Beinecke Library, Yale

Keith Hearl, Rhodes House Library, Oxford

General Lazare Hoche, Archives Nationales, Paris

Marshal François-Christophe Kellermann, Archives Nationales, Paris

General Jean-Baptiste Kléber, Archives Nationales, Paris

Stanley Kubrick, London College of Communication, London

La Grande Armée, Service Historiques de la Défense, Vincennes

Jean Lannes, Service Historiques de la Défense, Vincennes

General Bernard Lauriston, Archives Nationales, Paris

Sir Hudson Lowe, British Library, London

Susan Marie Mackenzie, Beinecke Library, Yale

Hugues Maret, Service Historique de la Défense, Vincennes

Marshal Joachim Murat, Service Historique de la Défense, Vincennes

Comte Louis de Narbonne, Archives Nationales, Paris

François de Neufchâteau, Archives Nationales, Paris

Frederick Sheldon Parker, Sterling Memorial Library, Yale

Louis-Marie de la Revellière-Lépeaux, Beinecke Library, Yale

Count Pierre-Louis Roederer, Archives Nationales, Paris

Fyodr Rostopchin, Russian State Military Historical Archive, Moscow

Marshal Gouvion Saint-Cyr, Archives Nationales, Paris

General Barthélemy Schérer, Archives Nationales, Paris
Marshal Nicolas Soult, Archives Nationales, Paris
Adolphe Thiers, Bibliothèque Thiers, Paris
Sir Thomas Tyrwhitt, Beinecke Library, Yale
Marshal Claude Victor-Perrin, Archives Nationales, Paris
Jane Waldie Watts, Beinecke Library, Yale
War Ministry, Service Historique de la Défense, Vincennes
Sir Nathaniel Wraxall, Beinecke Library, Yale

Index

ALLEN LANE
an imprint of
PENGUIN BOOKS

Recently Published

James Rebanks, *The Shepherd's Life: A Tale of the Lake District*

David Brooks, *The Road to Character*

Joseph Stiglitz, *The Great Divide*

Ken Robinson and Lou Aronica, *Creative Schools: Revolutionizing Education from the Ground Up*

Clotaire Rapaille and Andrés Roemer, *Move UP: Why Some Cultures Advances While Others Don't*

Jonathan Keates, *William III and Mary II: Partners in Revolution*

David Womersley, *James II: The Last Catholic King*

Richard Barber, *Henry II: A Prince Among Princes*

Jane Ridley, *Victoria: Queen, Matriarch, Empress*

John Gray, *The Soul of the Marionette: A Short Enquiry into Human Freedom*

Emily Wilson, *Seneca: A Life*

Michael Barber, *How to Run a Government: So That Citizens Benefit and Taxpayers Don't Go Crazy*

Dana Thomas, *Gods and Kings: The Rise and Fall of Alexander McQueen and John Galliano*

Steven Weinberg, *To Explain the World: The Discovery of Modern Science*

Jennifer Jacquet, *Is Shame Necessary?: New Uses for an Old Tool*

Eugene Rogan, *The Fall of the Ottomans: The Great War in the Middle East, 1914-1920*

Norman Doidge, *The Brain's Way of Healing: Stories of Remarkable Recoveries and Discoveries*

John Hooper, *The Italians*

Sven Beckert, *Empire of Cotton: A New History of Global Capitalism*

Mark Kishlansky, *Charles I: An Abbreviated Life*

Philip Ziegler, *George VI: The Dutiful King*

David Cannadine, *George V: The Unexpected King*

Stephen Alford, *Edward VI: The Last Boy King*

John Guy, *Henry VIII: The Quest for Fame*

Robert Tombs, *The English and their History: The First Thirteen Centuries*

Neil MacGregor, *Germany: The Memories of a Nation*

Uwe Tellkamp, *The Tower: A Novel*

Roberto Calasso, *Ardor*

Slavoj Žižek, *Trouble in Paradise: Communism After the End of History*

Francis Pryor, *Home: A Time Traveller's Tales from Britain's Prehistory*

R. F. Foster, *Vivid Faces: The Revolutionary Generation in Ireland, 1890-1923*

Andrew Roberts, *Napoleon the Great*

Shami Chakrabarti, *On Liberty*

Bessel van der Kolk, *The Body Keeps the Score: Mind, Brain and Body in the Transformation of Trauma*

Brendan Simms, *The Longest Afternoon: The 400 Men Who Decided the Battle of Waterloo*

Naomi Klein, *This Changes Everything: Capitalism vs the Climate*

Owen Jones, *The Establishment: And How They Get Away with It*

Caleb Scharf, *The Copernicus Complex: Our Cosmic Significance in a Universe of Planets and Probabilities*

Martin Wolf, *The Shifts and the Shocks: What We've Learned - and Have Still to Learn - from the Financial Crisis*

Steven Pinker, *The Sense of Style: The Thinking Person's Guide to Writing in the 21st Century*

Vincent Deary, *How We Are: Book One of the How to Live Trilogy*

Henry Kissinger, *World Order*

Alexander Watson, *Ring of Steel: Germany and Austria-Hungary at War, 1914-1918*

Richard Vinen, *National Service: Conscription in Britain, 1945-1963*

Paul Dolan, *Happiness by Design: Finding Pleasure and Purpose in Everyday Life*

Mark Greengrass, *Christendom Destroyed: Europe 1517-1650*

Hugh Thomas, *World Without End: The Global Empire of Philip II*

Richard Layard and David M. Clark, *Thrive: The Power of Evidence-Based Psychological Therapies*

Uwe Tellkamp, *The Tower: A Novel*

Zelda la Grange, *Good Morning, Mr Mandela*